Pillsbury

COMPLETE
COOK
BOOK

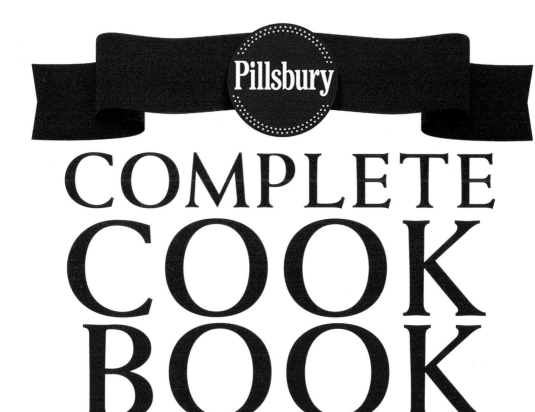

COMPLETE COOK BOOK

Recipes from America's Most-Trusted Kitchens

By The Pillsbury Company

Clarkson Potter/Publishers
New York

Credits

THE PILLSBURY COMPANY
Publisher: Sally Peters
Associate Publisher: Diane B. Anderson
Senior Editors: Maureen Rosener, Jackie Sheehan
Senior Food Editor: Andrea Bidwell, C.C.P.
Managing Editor: Karen Goodsell
Recipe Editors: Nancy A. Lilleberg,
Grace R. Wells
Copy Editor: Dawn Carlson
Contributing Editor: Ginger Hope
Contributing Writers: Mary Caldwell,
Catherine Hanley
Photography: Graham Brown Photography,
Tad Ware Photography
The Studio Central
Food Stylists: Sue Brosious, Sue Brue,
JoAnn Cherry, Sue Finley,
Sharon Harding, Cindy Ojczyk,
Lisa Golden Schroeder, Barb Standal
Recipe System Coordinator: Renee Schimel
Recipe Typists: Michelle Baringer, Jackie Ranney
Nutrition Information: Margaret Reinhardt,
M.P.H., LN, Gayle M. Smith

PILLSBURY PUBLICATIONS
Publisher: Sally Peters
Publication Managers: Diane B. Anderson,
William Monn
Senior Editors: Jackie Sheehan, Maureen Rosener
Senior Food Editor: Andrea Bidwell, C.C.P.
Circulation Manager: Karen Goodsell
Circulation Coordinator: Rebecca Bogema
Publication Secretary: Jackie Ranney
Recipe System: Renee Schimel, Mary Prokott,
Amanda Bloomgren

CLARKSON POTTER/PUBLISHERS
THE CROWN PUBLISHING GROUP
President and Publisher: Chip Gibson
Vice President–Editorial Director: Lauren Shakely
Senior Editor: Katie Workman
Editorial Assistant: Julia Coblentz
Designer: Lauren Monchik
Executive Managing Editor: Amy Boorstein
Associate Managing Editor: Mark McCauslin
Senior Production Editor: Liana Faughnan
Senior Production Manager: Jane Searle
Publicist: Wendy Schuman

Frontispiece: Roast Turkey (page 80)

Library of Congress Cataloging-in-Publication Data
Pillsbury complete cookbook: recipes from America's most-trusted kitchens/by the Pillsbury Company.
1. Cookery.   I. Pillsbury Company.
TX714 .P549 2000
641.5—dc21   99-046945
ISBN 0-609-60284-5
10   9   8   7   6   5   4   3   2   1
First Edition

CONTENTS

™

INTRODUCTION

The world of cooking is an ever-changing one. As the publisher of Pillsbury *Classic*® *Cookbooks*, the leading cookbook magazine and a full array of hardcover cookbooks, we are keenly aware of the latest preferences in food and cooking. The Pillsbury publications staff is in continual dialogue with our readers through surveys, reader correspondence, our Web site and ongoing research on food trends so that our publications keep pace with your interests and needs. Today's recipes are shorter, quicker and leaner, and the pantry of 2000 and beyond includes couscous, pesto and other "new" choices. We've listened to your requests for a blend of recipes that include familiar favorites, contemporary flavors and recipes that update traditional dishes with a simple "twist."

To ensure your success in the kitchen, every recipe has been tested many times in the Pillsbury kitchens. You'll also find nutrition information for every recipe including dietary exchanges so you can make food choices that meet your needs.

In order to provide you with the most complete up-to-date source of recipes and food information, we have included the following helpful features:

Each recipe includes:
Preparation time
Number of servings
Easy-to-follow directions
Nutrition information including dietary exchanges
High-altitude adjustments, when appropriate

Beautiful food photographs give you an accurate picture of completed recipes and offer easy serving ideas.

Step-by-step photographs lead you through important cooking techniques.

Cook's Notes and Tips offer ingredient information, substitutions, alternative cooking techniques, make-ahead directions, serving ideas and more.

Detailed ingredient and cooking charts help you find important cooking information at a glance.

Low-fat and 20-minute flags in the recipe index provided on each chapter divider help you quickly locate these recipes within the chapter.

Canning & Cooking Basics, a special chapter at the end of the book, provides a wealth of useful cooking information to help new cooks get started while giving experienced cooks the depth of information that only an all-purpose cookbook can provide.

A complete Cookbook Glossary helps you become more familiar with food and cooking terms.

The convenient ring-bound format keeps pages open and flat while in use, and the loose-leaf style makes it easy to add additional recipes and notes to your book.

It's a pleasure to share Pillsbury's finest with you and we hope you will enjoy it today and for years to come.

For more cooking tips and recipes, visit us on our Web site at www.pillsbury.com.

MENU IDEAS

There are hundreds of recipes in this book you can put together to create menus for all of your meal occasions. We've put together a sample of menus for breakfasts, lunches, dinners and entertaining you can use when you need to plan a menu quickly or to spark your imagination and creativity as you plan meals for your family and for special get-togethers. Page numbers are listed for the recipes included in this book.

Southwestern Brunch for 12
Garden Fresh Salsa, page 13
Tortilla chips
Black Bean and Corn Enchilada Egg Bake, page 252
Sliced chorizo or other pork sausage
Margarita Fruit Salad, page 262
   or
Sliced fresh fruit
Sunrise Mimosas, page 27

Hearty Breakfast for 4
Four-Grain Pancakes or Waffles, page 64
Pancake syrup
Glazed Apples and Canadian Bacon, page 142
   or
Scrambled Eggs, page 244
Sliced cantaloupe
Orange juice and coffee

Family Lunch for 4
Powerful Peanut Butter Sandwiches, page 238
   or
Cheese and Veggie Wraps, page 240
Mom's Chicken Noodle Soup, page 69
Sliced apples and/or pears
Chocolate Chip Cookies, page 408
   or
Homemade Chewy Granola Bars, page 430
Milk

Dinner on the Deck for 4
Grilled Steak with Charred Sweet Onions, page 104
Savory Butter Roasted Corn, page 297
Mixed Potato Salad, page 268
   or
Deli potato salad
French Bread Braids, page 48
   or
Crusty French rolls
Fresh Blueberry Pie, page 392
Iced tea with lemon

Roast Chicken Dinner for 6
Lemon-Herb Roasted Chicken, page 162
   or
Roast Chicken, page 178
Chicken Gravy, page 182
Perfect Mashed Potatoes, page 304
Buttered broccoli or baby carrots
Streusel-Topped Peach Pie, page 394
Ice water and coffee

Chili Supper for 6
Classic Guacamole, page 13
Tortilla chips
Smoky Hot Beef Chili, page 80
   or
Chunky Chicken Chili, page 79
Corn Muffins, page 36
Carrot and celery sticks
Triple Chocolate Pudding, page 349
Milk

Home-Style Pork Chop Dinner for 4
Braised Pork Chops with Cream Gravy, page 140
Baked Potatoes, page 302
Baking Powder Biscuits, page 32
Buttered peas
Chocolate Zucchini Cake, page 360

Asian Stir-Fry for 4

Pepper Steak, page 115
Hot cooked rice or Chinese noodles
Chopped green salad
    with
Asian Dressing, page 286
Egg rolls
Orange sherbet and fortune cookies
Hot tea with lemon

Vegetarian Italian Feast for 6

Spinach Lasagna, page 227
    or
Linguini with Roasted Vegetables, page 224
Crisp green salad
    with
Italian Dressing, page 288
Cantaloupe and honeydew wedges
Italian Breadsticks, page 60
Double Chocolate-Orange Biscotti, page 422
Cappuccino or coffee

Burger Bash for 4

Hamburgers
Low-Fat French Fries, page 304
    or
Dressed-Up Deli Coleslaw, page 259
Boston Baked Beans, page 320
Selection of sliced pickles and olives
Assorted canned juices and soft drinks

Catch-of-the-Day Supper for 6

Light Spinach Dip, page 15
    with
Cut-up fresh vegetables
Broiled Snapper with Cilantro Sauce, page 204
    or
Baked Stuffed Fish, page 191
Wild Rice and Mushrooms, page 317
Lemon-Buttered Asparagus, page 292
    or
Dill Baby Carrots, page 295
Bakery dinner rolls
Vanilla Custard Ice Cream, page 348
    with
Brandied Cherry Sauce, page 355

Picnic for 8

Deviled Eggs, page 3
Cashew-Curry-Chicken Salad, page 275
    or
Ham and Macaroni Picnic Salad, page 274
Selection of sliced cheeses
Rustic Italian Bread, page 51
S'More Snack Cake, page 370
    or
Whole Wheat Zucchini Bars, page 428
Assorted bottled water and juices

APPETIZERS
& BEVERAGES

APPETIZERS & BEVERAGES

 ot or cold, simple or fancy, appetizers welcome guests and get the party off to a congenial start. This guide will help you plan and serve a fine opening course, whether the occasion calls for an elaborate assortment, a single, memorable specialty or an informal finger-food feast.

You'll also find tips on party beverages, from the basics of perfect coffee and tea to a selection of festive punches, both with and without alcohol.

Planning Appetizers

If a full meal will follow, choose light, small nibblers that will stimulate but not satisfy the appetite. A single special appetizer can serve as a first course for a formal dinner.

When an appetizer buffet is the main food event, include heartier selections and a wider array of tidbits, spreads and dips. For six to eight people, plan on four to six different appetizers.

Because appetizers are essentially samplers, variety is key. Each selection should offer a new flavor, texture and color. Avoid duplicating the dinner menu, too. For example, if the main course includes a cheese sauce or cheese filling, an appetizer of fresh vegetables or seafood might be a better choice than a round of baked Brie cheese.

Even if you love traditional sour cream dips and high-fat morsels such as pepperoni, it's a courtesy to also offer plenty of other foods for people watching their fat or cholesterol intake.

For cocktail parties and other stand-up gatherings, serve appetizers that are easy to eat without a utensil. Small canapés and other bite-sized tidbits are great choices. For a buffet, if guests will be balancing plates on their laps, choose foods that are already in bite-sized pieces or can be easily cut with a fork.

Choose appetizers that will remain attractive until the last person is served, or have fresh trays ready to replace those that begin to look depleted. Don't add dip to a bowl that's been standing at room temperature; set out a new bowl instead.

Make-Ahead Tips

To reduce the time you spend in the kitchen away from your guests, plan only one or two items that must be prepared at the last minute. Some dips and marinated dishes actually improve if made one or two days ahead. Many others can be at least partially prepared in advance. However, the final assembly of some recipes should happen shortly before serving time to avoid sogginess, dryness or staleness.

Microwave heating works well for many appetizers. Serve hot appetizers promptly after cooking or reheating, or keep them at an ideal temperature with electric trays, chafing dishes, slow cookers or fondue pots.

If possible, decorate the party area and set out nonperishables the night before or early in the day of the event.

Freezing Appetizers

Many recipes can be made in advance and frozen. Do not freeze appetizers made with hard-cooked eggs, mayonnaise, gelatin or fresh vegetables.

- ✦ For best appearance, place individual appetizers on a tray in a single layer. Freeze them until firm, then transfer them to an airtight container or resealable plastic bag.
- ✦ If you need to stack them, place waxed paper or plastic wrap between layers. Separate the layers before thawing.
- ✦ Allow enough time for frozen foods to thaw in the refrigerator to avoid danger of spoilage.
- ✦ Use frozen appetizers within three months. Do not refreeze them after thawing.

Big Batches

If you are preparing large quantities of an appetizer, set up an assembly line rather than making them one at a time. For small canapés, for example, set out all the bread squares on a large tray, butter them all, then arrange the topping on each.

Cranberry-Glazed Appetizer Meatballs

PREP TIME: 40 MINUTES (READY IN 1 HOUR
10 MINUTES) ◆ YIELD: 60 MEATBALLS; 30 SERVINGS

MEATBALLS
1½ lb. ground beef
½ cup finely chopped onion
½ cup unseasoned dry bread crumbs
½ teaspoon salt
⅛ teaspoon pepper
2 eggs, slightly beaten

SAUCE
1 (12-oz.) bottle (1½ cups) chili sauce
1 (8-oz.) can (about 1 cup) jellied cranberry
sauce

1. Heat oven to 375°F. In large bowl, combine all meatball ingredients; blend well. Shape into 1-inch balls; place in ungreased 15 × 10 × 1-inch baking pan.
2. Bake at 375°F. for 25 to 30 minutes or until meatballs are browned and no longer pink in center.
3. Meanwhile, in large saucepan, combine sauce ingredients; blend well. Bring to a boil over medium heat. Reduce heat to low; simmer 5 minutes, stirring occasionally.
4. Add meatballs to sauce; stir to coat. Cook over medium heat for 5 minutes or until thoroughly heated, stirring occasionally.

NUTRITION PER SERVING: Serving Size: ¹⁄₃₀ of Recipe ◆ Calories: 80 ◆ Calories from Fat: 35 ◆ **GRAMS AND % DAILY VALUE:** Total Fat: 4 g 6% ◆ Saturated Fat: 1 g 5% ◆ Cholesterol: 30 mg 10% ◆ Sodium: 220 mg 9% ◆ Total Carbohydrate: 7 g 2% ◆ Dietary Fiber: 0 g 0% ◆ Sugars: 5 g ◆ Protein: 5 g ◆ Vitamin A: 4% ◆ Vitamin C: 2% ◆ Calcium: 0% ◆ Iron: 4% ◆ **DIETARY EXCHANGES:** ½ Fruit, ½ Lean Meat, ½ Fat OR ½ Carbohydrate, ½ Lean Meat, ½ Fat

Deviled Eggs

PREP TIME: 40 MINUTES ◆ YIELD: 12 DEVILED EGGS

12 eggs
1 teaspoon dry mustard or 2 teaspoons
prepared mustard
Dash pepper
⅓ cup mayonnaise, salad dressing or sour cream
1 tablespoon vinegar
1 teaspoon Worcestershire sauce
Paprika or chopped fresh parsley

1. Place eggs in large saucepan; cover eggs with cold water. Bring to a boil. Reduce heat; simmer about 15 minutes. Immediately drain; run cold water over eggs to stop cooking.

2. Peel eggs; halve lengthwise. Remove yolks; place in small bowl. Mash yolks with fork.
3. Add all remaining ingredients except paprika; mix until fluffy. Spoon or pipe mixture into egg white halves. Sprinkle with paprika.

NUTRITION INFORMATION PER SERVING: Serving Size: 1 Deviled Egg ◆ Calories: 120 ◆ Calories from Fat: 90 ◆ **% DAILY VALUE:** Total Fat: 10 g 15% ◆ Saturated Fat: 2 g 10% ◆ Cholesterol: 215 mg 72% ◆ Sodium: 100 mg 4% ◆ Total Carbohydrate: 1 g 1% ◆ Dietary Fiber: 0 g 0% ◆ Sugars: 1 g ◆ Protein: 6 g ◆ Vitamin A: 8% ◆ Vitamin C: 0% ◆ Calcium: 2% ◆ Iron: 4% ◆ **DIETARY EXCHANGES:** 1 Medium-Fat Meat, 1 Fat

Maple-Apple Party Riblets

PREP TIME: 25 MINUTES (READY IN 1 HOUR
25 MINUTES) ◆ YIELD: 8 SERVINGS

2 lb. pork back ribs, cut across bones to
form riblets
½ cup real maple syrup
¼ cup apple jelly
1 tablespoon soy sauce
¼ cup chopped fresh chives
½ teaspoon dry mustard

1. Heat oven to 450°F. Line 15 × 10 × 1-inch baking pan with foil. Cut ribs into individual riblets. Place, meaty side down, in foil-lined pan; cover with foil. Bake at 450°F. for 30 minutes.
2. Meanwhile, in small saucepan, combine syrup, jelly, soy sauce, chives and dry mustard; mix well. Cook over low heat for 8 to 10 minutes or until hot and well blended, stirring occasionally. Remove from heat.
3. Reduce oven temperature to 350°F. Remove ribs from oven. Uncover; drain liquid from ribs. Turn ribs meaty side up; brush with syrup mixture.
4. Bake, uncovered, at 350°F. for 30 minutes. Brush with syrup mixture; bake an additional 10 to 15 minutes or until ribs are tender and glazed.

NUTRITION INFORMATION PER SERVING: Serving Size: ⅛ of Recipe ◆ Calories: 280 ◆ Calories from Fat: 140 ◆ **% DAILY VALUE:** Total Fat: 16 g 25% ◆ Saturated Fat: 6 g 30% ◆ Cholesterol: 65 mg 22% ◆ Sodium: 190 mg 8% ◆ Total Carbohydrate: 20 g 7% ◆ Dietary Fiber: 0 g 0% ◆ Sugars: 17 g ◆ Protein: 14 g ◆ Vitamin A: 0% ◆ Vitamin C: 0% ◆ Calcium: 4% ◆ Iron: 6% ◆ **DIETARY EXCHANGES:** 1½ Fruit, 2 High-Fat Meat OR 1½ Carbohydrate, 2 High-Fat Meat

Shrimp Cocktail

Shrimp Cocktail

PREP TIME: 5 MINUTES ✦ YIELD: 16 SERVINGS

COCKTAIL SAUCE
- ½ cup ketchup
- ½ cup chili sauce
- 2 to 3 teaspoons prepared horseradish
- 1 teaspoon Worcestershire sauce

SHRIMP
- 14 oz. (about 64) shelled deveined cooked shrimp

1. In small bowl, combine all cocktail sauce ingredients; mix well. Cover; refrigerate until serving time to blend flavors.
2. Arrange shrimp on serving tray. Cover; refrigerate until serving time. Serve shrimp with sauce.

NUTRITION INFORMATION PER SERVING: Serving Size: ¹⁄₁₆ of Recipe ✦ Calories: 50 ✦ Calories from Fat: 10 ✦ **% DAILY VALUE:** Total Fat: 1 g 2% ✦ Saturated Fat: 0 g 0% ✦ Cholesterol: 50 mg 17% ✦ Sodium: 270 mg 11% ✦ Total Carbohydrate: 4 g 1% ✦ Dietary Fiber: 0 g 0% ✦ Sugars: 2 g ✦ Protein: 6 g ✦ Vitamin A: 4% ✦ Vitamin C: 6% ✦ Calcium: 0% ✦ Iron: 4% ✦ **DIETARY EXCHANGES:** ½ Fruit, 1 Very Lean Meat OR ½ Carbohydrate, 1 Very Lean Meat

Shrimp Balls

PREP TIME: 1 HOUR ✦ YIELD: 24 APPETIZERS

- Oil for deep frying
- 1 lb. shelled deveined uncooked shrimp
- 1 (8-oz.) can sliced water chestnuts, drained
- 4 teaspoons cornstarch
- 2 tablespoons chopped green onions
- 1 tablespoon dry sherry
- ¾ teaspoon grated gingerroot
- ½ teaspoon salt
- 1 egg, beaten

1. In deep fryer, heavy saucepan or wok, heat 2 to 3 inches of oil to 375°F.

2. Meanwhile, in food processor bowl with metal blade, combine shrimp, water chestnuts, cornstarch, onions, sherry, gingerroot and salt; process until finely chopped. Add egg; process until combined.
3. Drop shrimp mixture by teaspoonfuls into hot oil (375°F.). Fry 3 to 4 minutes or until shrimp turn pink and balls are deep golden brown. Drain on paper towels. Serve warm with a variety of dipping sauces.

NUTRITION INFORMATION PER SERVING: Serving Size: 1 Appetizer ✦ Calories: 45 ✦ Calories from Fat: 25 ✦ **% DAILY VALUE:** Total Fat: 3 g 5% ✦ Saturated Fat: 0 g 0% ✦ Cholesterol: 35 mg 12% ✦ Sodium: 85 mg 4% ✦ Total Carbohydrate: 2 g 1% ✦ Dietary Fiber: 0 g 0% ✦ Sugars: 0 g ✦ Protein: 3 g ✦ Vitamin A: 0% ✦ Vitamin C: 0% ✦ Calcium: 0% ✦ Iron: 2% ✦ **DIETARY EXCHANGES:** ½ Very Lean Meat, ½ Fat

Cream Cheese Puffs

PREP TIME: 40 MINUTES ✦ YIELD: 14 APPETIZERS

- Oil for deep frying
- 14 wonton skins
- ½ cup soft cream cheese with chives and onions (from 8-oz. container) or plain soft cream cheese

1. In deep fryer, heavy saucepan or wok, heat 2 to 3 inches of oil to 375°F.
2. Meanwhile, place 1 wonton skin on work surface with 1 corner facing you. Cover remaining skins with damp paper towel to prevent drying out. Lightly brush edges of wonton skin with water. Place 2 teaspoons

Cream Cheese Puffs, Shrimp Balls

cream cheese just below center of wonton skin. Fold corner farthest from you down over filling to form a triangle; press edges to seal well. Bring 2 outer points of triangle together; press to seal well, using small amount of water if necessary. Repeat with remaining wonton skins and cream cheese. Cover cream cheese puffs with plastic wrap; set aside.

3. Fry cream cheese puffs, a few at a time, in hot oil (375°F.) for 1 to 3 minutes or until golden brown, turning once. Drain on paper towels. Serve warm with a variety of dipping sauces.

NUTRITION INFORMATION PER SERVING: Serving Size: 1 Appetizer ◆ Calories: 90 ◆ Calories from Fat: 60 ◆ **% DAILY VALUE:** Total Fat: 7 g 11% ◆ Saturated Fat: 2 g 10% ◆ Cholesterol: 10 mg 3% ◆ Sodium: 70 mg 3% ◆ Total Carbohydrate: 5 g 2% ◆ Dietary Fiber: 0 g 0% ◆ Sugars: 0 g ◆ Protein: 1 g ◆ Vitamin A: 2% ◆ Vitamin C: 0% ◆ Calcium: 0% ◆ Iron: 2% ◆ **DIETARY EXCHANGES:** ½ Starch, 1 Fat OR ½ Carbohydrate, 1 Fat

Stuffed Party Mushrooms

PREP TIME: 20 MINUTES (READY IN 45 MINUTES) ◆ YIELD: 10 SERVINGS

    1 lb. medium-sized fresh whole mushrooms
    ¼ cup grated Parmesan cheese
    ¼ cup unseasoned dry bread crumbs
    ¼ cup finely chopped onion
    ½ teaspoon dried oregano leaves
    ¼ teaspoon salt
    ⅛ teaspoon pepper
    1 garlic clove, minced

1. Heat oven to 350°F. Brush or wipe mushrooms with damp cloth. Remove stems from mushrooms; set caps aside. Finely chop mushroom stems.

2. In medium bowl, combine chopped stems and all remaining ingredients; mix well. Press mixture firmly into mushroom caps, mounding on top. Place in ungreased 13 × 9-inch pan.*

3. Bake at 350°F. for 18 to 23 minutes or until thoroughly heated. Serve warm.

TIP: * At this point, stuffed mushrooms can be covered and refrigerated for up to 4 hours. Bake as directed above.

NUTRITION INFORMATION PER SERVING: Serving Size: ¹⁄₁₀ of Recipe ◆ Calories: 30 ◆ Calories from Fat: 10 ◆ **% DAILY VALUE:** Total Fat: 1 g 2% ◆ Saturated Fat: 0 g 0% ◆ Cholesterol: 0 mg 0% ◆ Sodium: 95 mg 4% ◆ Total Carbohydrate: 3 g 1% ◆ Dietary Fiber: 1 g 2% ◆ Sugars: 1 g ◆ Protein: 2 g ◆ Vitamin A: 0% ◆ Vitamin C: 0% ◆ Calcium: 4% ◆ Iron: 4% ◆ **DIETARY EXCHANGES:** 1 Vegetable

Mini Swiss Quiches

PREP TIME: 25 MINUTES (READY IN 1 HOUR 10 MINUTES) ◆ YIELD: 24 APPETIZERS

    1 (15-oz.) pkg. refrigerated pie crusts
    6 oz. (1½ cups) shredded Swiss cheese
    2 tablespoons sliced green onions
    1 tablespoon chopped pimientos
    2 eggs
    ½ cup milk
    ¼ teaspoon salt
      Dash nutmeg

1. Allow both pie crust pouches to stand at room temperature for 15 to 20 minutes. Heat oven to 375°F. Spray 24 miniature muffin cups with nonstick cooking spray.

2. Unfold 1 pie crust; press out fold lines. Place crust on work surface. With floured 2½-inch round cookie cutter, cut 12 rounds. Repeat with remaining pie crust.

3. Press 1 round of dough in bottom and up sides of each sprayed muffin cup. Place 1 tablespoon cheese in each cup. Top each with a few onion slices and pimiento pieces.

4. In 2-cup measuring cup, combine eggs, milk, salt and nutmeg; beat well with fork. Pour mixture into crusts, filling to within ¼ inch of top.

5. Bake at 375°F. for 25 to 30 minutes or until golden brown. Cool slightly; lift quiches from cups with tip of knife. Serve warm.

NUTRITION INFORMATION PER SERVING: Serving Size: 1 Appetizer ◆ Calories: 80 ◆ Calories from Fat: 45 ◆ **% DAILY VALUE:** Total Fat: 5 g 8% ◆ Saturated Fat: 3 g 15% ◆ Cholesterol: 25 mg 8% ◆ Sodium: 90 mg 4% ◆ Total Carbohydrate: 6 g 2% ◆ Dietary Fiber: 0 g 0% ◆ Sugars: 1 g ◆ Protein: 3 g ◆ Vitamin A: 2% ◆ Vitamin C: 0% ◆ Calcium: 8% ◆ Iron: 0% ◆ **DIETARY EXCHANGES:** ½ Starch, 1 Fat OR ½ Carbohydrate, 1 Fat

Mini Swiss Quiches

Roasted Chicken Nachos

PREP TIME: 25 MINUTES ◆ YIELD: 8 SERVINGS

  8 oz. tortilla chips
  ¾ cup chunky style salsa
  1 (15-oz.) can black beans, drained, rinsed
  3 frozen charbroiled mesquite chicken breast
      patties, thawed, chopped
  1 tomato, chopped
  8 oz. (2 cups) finely shredded Mexican natural
      cheese blend

1. Heat oven to 400°F. Line 15 × 10 × 1-inch baking pan with foil. Spread half of tortilla chips evenly in foil-lined pan.
2. In medium bowl, combine salsa and beans; mix well. Spoon half of bean mixture over chips. Top with half each of chicken, tomato and cheese. Repeat layers.
3. Bake at 400°F. for 12 to 14 minutes or until cheese is melted. Serve immediately.

NUTRITION INFORMATION PER SERVING: Serving Size: ⅛ of Recipe ◆ Calories: 360 ◆ Calories from Fat: 170 ◆ % DAILY VALUE: Total Fat: 19 g 29% ◆ Saturated Fat: 8 g 40% ◆ Cholesterol: 40 mg 13% ◆ Sodium: 780 mg 33% ◆ Total Carbohydrate: 29 g 10% ◆ Dietary Fiber: 4 g 16% ◆ Sugars: 2 g ◆ Protein: 18 g ◆ Vitamin A: 10% ◆ Vitamin C: 4% ◆ Calcium: 25% ◆ Iron: 8% ◆ DIETARY EXCHANGES: 2 Starch, 1½ Medium-Fat Meat, 2 Fat OR 2 Carbohydrate, 1½ Medium-Fat Meat, 2 Fat

Beef Canapés with Caper Mayonnaise

PREP TIME: 30 MINUTES ◆ YIELD: 24 APPETIZERS

  24 slices baguette or small French bread
      (¼ to ½ inch thick)
  2 tablespoons olive oil
  ½ cup mayonnaise
  ¼ cup grated Parmesan cheese
  2 tablespoons chopped fresh chives
  2 to 4 tablespoons drained capers
  ¼ teaspoon garlic powder
  ½ lb. thinly sliced cooked roast beef, cut
      into 24 pieces
  2 Italian plum tomatoes, cut into 24 thin slices
      Chopped fresh chives, if desired

1. Heat oven to 350°F. Place bread slices on ungreased cookie sheet; brush lightly with oil. Bake at 350°F. for 8 to 10 minutes or until crisp. Cool 5 minutes or until completely cooled.
2. Meanwhile, in small bowl, combine mayonnaise, cheese, 2 tablespoons chives, capers and garlic powder; mix well. Spread mayonnaise mixture on bread slices. Top with roast beef and tomato slice. Sprinkle with chives.

NUTRITION INFORMATION PER SERVING: Serving Size: 1 Appetizer ◆ Calories: 90 ◆ Calories from Fat: 50 ◆ % DAILY VALUE: Total Fat: 6 g 9% ◆ Saturated Fat: 1 g 5% ◆ Cholesterol: 10 mg 3% ◆ Sodium: 230 mg 10% ◆ Total Carbohydrate: 6 g 2% ◆ Dietary Fiber: 0 g 0% ◆ Sugars: 1 g ◆ Protein: 3 g ◆ Vitamin A: 0% ◆ Vitamin C: 0% ◆ Calcium: 2% ◆ Iron: 2% ◆ DIETARY EXCHANGES: ½ Starch, 1 Fat OR ½ Carbohydrate, 1 Fat

Cucumber-Dill Stuffed Cherry Tomatoes

PREP TIME: 30 MINUTES (READY IN 2 HOURS 30 MINUTES) ◆ YIELD: 24 APPETIZERS

TOMATOES
  24 cherry tomatoes

FILLING
  1 (3-oz.) pkg. cream cheese, softened
  2 tablespoons mayonnaise or salad dressing
  ¼ cup finely chopped seeded cucumber
  1 tablespoon finely chopped green onions
  2 teaspoons chopped fresh dill or ¼ teaspoon
      dried dill weed

1. Remove stems from tomatoes. Cut thin slice off bottom of each tomato. With small spoon or melon baller, carefully hollow out tomato, leaving ⅛-inch shell. Invert tomato shells on paper towels to drain.*
2. In small bowl, combine cream cheese and mayonnaise; blend well. Stir in cucumber, onions and dill; mix well.
3. Fill tomato shells with cream cheese mixture.** Refrigerate at least 2 hours before serving to blend flavors.

TIPS: * At this point, tomatoes can be covered and refrigerated for up to 24 hours.
** For easy filling, place cream cheese mixture in plastic squeeze bottle. Cut off ¾ of bottle tip with scissors. Squeeze cream cheese mixture into tomato shells.

NUTRITION INFORMATION PER SERVING: Serving Size: 1 Appetizer ◆ Calories: 20 ◆ Calories from Fat: 20 ◆ % DAILY VALUE: Total Fat: 2 g 3% ◆ Saturated Fat: 1 g 5% ◆ Cholesterol: 5 mg 2% ◆ Sodium: 15 mg 1% ◆ Total Carbohydrate: 0 g 0% ◆ Dietary Fiber: 0 g 0% ◆ Sugars: 0 g ◆ Protein: 0 g ◆ Vitamin A: 0% ◆ Vitamin C: 0% ◆ Calcium: 0% ◆ Iron: 0% ◆ DIETARY EXCHANGES: ½ Fat

Chicken Liver Pâté

PREP TIME: 15 MINUTES (READY IN 1 HOUR 35 MINUTES)
♦ YIELD: 2 CUPS

  1 lb. chicken livers
  1½ cups water
  ⅓ cup margarine or butter
  1 medium apple, peeled, chopped
  1 medium onion, chopped
  1 garlic clove, minced
  Dash dried thyme leaves
  Dash dried marjoram leaves
  ⅓ cup dry sherry
  ¼ teaspoon salt
  Dash pepper

1. In medium saucepan, simmer chicken livers in water for 2 to 3 minutes. Drain, reserving ¾ cup liquid.
2. Melt margarine in medium skillet. Add livers; cook until brown. Add apple, onion, garlic, thyme, marjoram, sherry and reserved liquid; mix well. Simmer 15 to 20 minutes or until liquid is absorbed, stirring occasionally.
3. In blender container or food processor bowl with metal blade, process mixture until pureed. Stir in salt and pepper. Spoon into serving bowl. Cover; refrigerate at least 1 hour before serving to blend flavors. Serve with Melba toast rounds or crackers.

NUTRITION INFORMATION PER SERVING: Serving Size: 1 Tablespoon ♦ Calories: 30 ♦ Calories from Fat: 20 ♦ **% DAILY VALUE:** Total Fat: 2 g 3% ♦ Saturated Fat: 1 g 5% ♦ Cholesterol: 55 mg 18% ♦ Sodium: 55 mg 2% ♦ Total Carbohydrate: 1 g 1% ♦ Dietary Fiber: 0 g 0% ♦ Sugars: 1 g ♦ Protein: 2 g ♦ Vitamin A: 30% ♦ Vitamin C: 2% ♦ Calcium: 0% ♦ Iron: 4% ♦ **DIETARY EXCHANGES:** ½ Lean Meat

Bacon-Wrapped Rumaki

PREP TIME: 20 MINUTES (READY IN 50 MINUTES)
♦ YIELD: 24 APPETIZERS

  1 (8-oz.) can whole water chestnuts, drained, cut into 24 equal pieces if necessary
  ¼ cup soy sauce
  1 tablespoon sugar
  8 slices bacon, cut into thirds

1. In small bowl, combine water chestnut pieces, soy sauce and sugar; mix well. Let stand at room temperature for 30 minutes to marinate.
2. Drain water chestnuts; discard marinade. Wrap 1 piece of bacon around each water chestnut; secure with toothpick. Place on broiler pan or on rack in shallow baking pan.
3. Broil 4 to 6 inches from heat for 4 to 7 minutes on each side or until bacon is crisp.

NUTRITION INFORMATION PER SERVING: Serving Size: 1 Appetizer ♦ Calories: 20 ♦ Calories from Fat: 10 ♦ **% DAILY VALUE:** Total Fat: 1 g 2% ♦ Saturated Fat: 0 g 0% ♦ Cholesterol: 0 mg 0% ♦ Sodium: 75 mg 3% ♦ Total Carbohydrate: 2 g 1% ♦ Dietary Fiber: 0 g 0% ♦ Sugars: 0 g ♦ Protein: 1 g ♦ Vitamin A: 0% ♦ Vitamin C: 0% ♦ Calcium: 0% ♦ Iron: 0% ♦ **DIETARY EXCHANGES:** ½ Fat

VARIATIONS

Chicken Liver Rumaki: Cut ½ lb. chicken livers into 24 equal pieces. In small bowl, combine chicken livers, ½ cup purchased French salad dressing and ¼ teaspoon garlic salt. Let stand at room temperature for 15 minutes to marinate. Drain chicken livers; discard marinade. Wrap with bacon; broil as directed in recipe.

Olive Rumaki: Use 24 pimiento-stuffed green olives for the water chestnuts. Prepare, marinate and broil as directed in recipe.

Pineapple Rumaki: In small bowl, combine 24 fresh, canned or frozen pineapple chunks, well drained, and ⅓ cup purchased French salad dressing. Let stand at room temperature for 15 minutes to marinate. Drain pineapple; discard marinade. Wrap with bacon; broil as directed in recipe.

Scallop Rumaki: Use ½ lb. fresh or frozen scallops, thawed, cut into 24 equal pieces for the water chestnuts. Prepare, marinate and broil as directed in recipe.

Smoked Oyster Rumaki: Use two 3.75-oz. cans (about 24) smoked oysters, drained, for the water chestnuts. Prepare, marinate and broil as directed in recipe.

Spicy Honey Chicken Drumettes

PREP TIME: 10 MINUTES (READY IN 2 HOURS 10 MINUTES) ◆ YIELD: 12 DRUMETTES

  ¼ cup honey
  ¼ cup soy sauce
  ¼ cup chili sauce
  ¼ teaspoon ginger
  ¼ teaspoon dry mustard
  ½ teaspoon hot pepper sauce
  12 chicken drumettes

1. In 12 × 8-inch (2-quart) baking dish, combine honey, soy sauce, chili sauce, ginger, dry mustard and hot pepper sauce; mix well. Add drumettes; turn to coat. Cover; refrigerate 1 hour to marinate.
2. Heat oven to 375°F. Uncover dish. Bake chicken in marinade at 375°F. for 45 to 60 minutes or until chicken is fork-tender and no longer pink next to bone, brushing with marinade occasionally.

NUTRITION INFORMATION PER SERVING: Serving Size: 1 Drumette ◆ Calories: 50 ◆ Calories from Fat: 25 ◆ **% DAILY VALUE:** Total Fat: 3 g 5% ◆ Saturated Fat: 1 g 5% ◆ Cholesterol: 15 mg 5% ◆ Sodium: 120 mg 5% ◆ Total Carbohydrate: 2 g 1% ◆ Dietary Fiber: 0 g 0% ◆ Sugars: 2 g ◆ Protein: 4 g ◆ Vitamin A: 0% ◆ Vitamin C: 0% ◆ Calcium: 0% ◆ Iron: 0% ◆ **DIETARY EXCHANGES:** ½ High-Fat Meat

Easy Pesto Pinwheels

PREP TIME: 30 MINUTES ◆ YIELD: 16 APPETIZERS

  1 (8-oz.) can refrigerated crescent dinner rolls
  ⅓ cup purchased pesto
  ¼ cup chopped roasted red bell peppers
    (from 7.25-oz. jar)

1. Heat oven to 350°F. Unroll dough into 2 long rectangles. Firmly press perforations to seal. Spread rectangles with pesto to within ¼ inch of edges. Sprinkle with roasted peppers.
2. Starting at shortest side, roll up each rectangle; pinch edges to seal. Cut each roll into 8 slices. Place, cut side down, on ungreased cookie sheet.
3. Bake at 350°F. for 13 to 17 minutes or until golden brown. Immediately remove from cookie sheet. Serve warm.

NUTRITION INFORMATION PER SERVING: Serving Size: 1 Appetizer ◆ Calories: 60 ◆ Calories from Fat: 35 ◆ **% DAILY VALUE:** Total Fat: 4 g 6% ◆ Saturated Fat: 1 g 5% ◆ Cholesterol: 0 mg 0% ◆ Sodium: 125 mg 5% ◆ Total Carbohydrate: 6 g 2% ◆ Dietary Fiber: 0 g 0% ◆ Sugars: 1 g ◆ Protein: 1 g ◆ Vitamin A: 0% ◆ Vitamin C: 4% ◆ Calcium: 0% ◆ Iron: 0% ◆ **DIETARY EXCHANGES:** ½ Starch, ½ Fat OR ½ Carbohydrate, ½ Fat

Shrimp and Pineapple Kabobs

PREP TIME: 25 MINUTES ◆ YIELD: 12 KABOBS

  2 medium green bell peppers, cut
    into 24 (1-inch) pieces
  24 (1 to 1½-inch) chunks fresh pineapple
  12 uncooked medium shrimp, shelled, deveined
  ½ cup purchased sweet-and-sour sauce
  ½ teaspoon dry mustard
  2 teaspoons chopped fresh chives
    or 1 teaspoon freeze-dried chopped
    chives

1. On each of twelve 4 to 6-inch wooden skewers, thread 1 pepper piece, 1 pineapple chunk, 1 shrimp, 1 pineapple chunk and 1 pepper piece. Place kabobs on broiler pan.
2. In small bowl, combine remaining ingredients; mix well. Brush kabobs with sweet and sour mixture.
3. Broil 4 to 6 inches from heat for 3 minutes. Turn kabobs; brush with remaining mixture. Broil an additional 2 to 4 minutes or until shrimp turn pink.

NUTRITION INFORMATION PER SERVING: Serving Size: 1 Kabob ◆ Calories: 40 ◆ Calories from Fat: 0 ◆ **% DAILY VALUE:** Total Fat: 0 g 0% ◆ Saturated Fat: 0 g 0% ◆ Cholesterol: 10 mg 3% ◆ Sodium: 75 mg 3% ◆ Total Carbohydrate: 9 g 3% ◆ Dietary Fiber: 1 g 3% ◆ Sugars: 6 g ◆ Protein: 1 g ◆ Vitamin A: 2% ◆ Vitamin C: 20% ◆ Calcium: 0% ◆ Iron: 2% ◆ **DIETARY EXCHANGES:** ½ Fruit OR ½ Carbohydrate

Clockwise from top left: Easy Pesto Pinwheels, Shrimp and Pineapple Kabobs, Spicy Honey Chicken Drumettes

Top to bottom: Spicy Cajun Dip (page 18), Fiesta Quesadillas

Turkey Club Tortilla Roll-Ups

PREP TIME: 50 MINUTES ♦ YIELD: 48 APPETIZERS

  6 (7 or 8-inch) flour tortillas
  ½ cup mayonnaise or salad dressing
  4 oz. cream cheese, softened
  ½ cup chopped drained pepperoncini
  2 tablespoons chopped fresh cilantro
  4 slices bacon, crisply cooked, crumbled
  ½ cup chopped tomato
  ½ lb. thinly sliced cooked turkey
  6 leaves leaf lettuce

1. Warm tortillas as directed on package.
2. Meanwhile, in small bowl, combine mayonnaise and cream cheese; mix until smooth. Stir in pepperoncini, cilantro and bacon.
3. Spread about 2 tablespoons mayonnaise mixture on each warm tortilla. Top each with 1 rounded tablespoon tomato, ⅙ of turkey and 1 lettuce leaf. Roll up each tortilla tightly. Cut each roll into 8 pieces; secure each piece with cocktail toothpick. Serve immediately, or cover tightly and refrigerate until serving time.

NUTRITION INFORMATION PER SERVING: Serving Size: 1 Appetizer ♦ Calories: 45 ♦ Calories from Fat: 25 ♦ **% DAILY VALUE:** Total Fat: 3 g 5% ♦ Saturated Fat: 1 g 5% ♦ Cholesterol: 10 mg 3% ♦ Sodium: 75 mg 3% ♦ Total Carbohydrate: 3 g 1% ♦ Dietary Fiber: 0 g 0% ♦ Sugars: 0 g ♦ Protein: 2 g ♦ Vitamin A: 0% ♦ Vitamin C: 0% ♦ Calcium: 0% ♦ Iron: 0% ♦ **DIETARY EXCHANGES:** 1 Fat

Fiesta Quesadillas

PREP TIME: 25 MINUTES ♦ YIELD: 32 APPETIZERS

  1 (10-oz.) can diced tomatoes with green chiles, drained
  1 (7-oz.) can vacuum-packed whole kernel corn, drained
  1 tablespoon chopped fresh cilantro
16 (6-inch) flour tortillas
  1 cup fat-free refried beans (from 16-oz. can)
  8 oz. (2 cups) shredded Mexican natural cheese blend

1. In medium bowl, combine tomatoes, corn and cilantro; mix well.
2. Spread each of 8 tortillas with 2 tablespoons refried beans. Top each of remaining 8 tortillas with ¼ cup cheese and scant 2 tablespoons corn mixture; spread evenly. Cover each with 1 bean-covered tortilla, bean side down.
3. In large nonstick skillet over medium heat, heat 1 quesadilla for 1 to 2 minutes on each side or until cheese is melted and tortilla is toasted.* Remove quesadilla from skillet; repeat with remaining quesadillas.**
4. To serve, cut each quesadilla into 4 wedges. If desired, serve with nonfat sour cream and salsa.

> **TIPS:** * A large griddle heated to 400°F. can be used to heat 3 or 4 quesadillas at a time.
> ** At this point, quesadillas can be wrapped in foil and placed in a warm oven until serving time.

NUTRITION INFORMATION PER SERVING: Serving Size: 1 Appetizer ♦ Calories: 80 ♦ Calories from Fat: 25 ♦ **% DAILY VALUE:** Total Fat: 3 g 5% ♦ Saturated Fat: 2 g 10% ♦ Cholesterol: 5 mg 2% ♦ Sodium: 190 mg 8% ♦ Total Carbohydrate: 9 g 3% ♦ Dietary Fiber: 1 g 4% ♦ Sugars: 1 g ♦ Protein: 3 g ♦ Vitamin A: 2% ♦ Vitamin C: 0% ♦ Calcium: 6% ♦ Iron: 2% ♦ **DIETARY EXCHANGES:** ½ Starch, ½ Fat OR ½ Carbohydrate, ½ Fat

Turkey Club Tortilla Roll-Ups

Party Sandwiches

Start with 1-lb. loaves of unsliced sandwich bread—rye, white, pumpernickel, whole wheat or another favorite.

If possible, ask the bakery to machine-slice the bread lengthwise into ½-inch slices. To do it yourself, freeze the bread for 30 minutes, trim the crust and use a long-bladed, serrated knife to make the lengthwise ½-inch slices.

To prevent sogginess, spread the bread with softened butter or margarine before topping with the sandwich spread. Use 1 or more spreads on the same sandwich. (See Salad Spreads on this page and page 11.) Mix and match the garnish to accent the color and flavor of the spread.

Many sandwiches can be prepared a day ahead. Wrap them in plastic wrap and refrigerate until serving time. Do not freeze.

Ribbon Sandwiches

Use 2 lengthwise slices of dark bread and 2 lengthwise slices of white bread. Spread 2 dark slices and 1 white slice with softened margarine or butter. Top buttered slices with ½ to 1 cup spread. Stack slices with spread, alternating dark slices with white. Top with remaining white bread slice. If necessary, trim edges to make them even. Wrap in plastic wrap and refrigerate 2 to 3 hours. To serve, cut each loaf crosswise into ½-inch slices; cut each slice in half.

Pinwheel Sandwiches

Slightly flatten 1 lengthwise slice of bread with a rolling pin. Spread with softened margarine or butter. Top with ½ to 1 cup of the desired spread. Beginning at the short end, roll up the bread tightly in jelly-roll fashion. If desired, frost roll with softened cream cheese and roll in chopped nuts. Refrigerate 2 to 3 hours before slicing. To serve, cut roll crosswise into ½-inch slices.

Open-Faced Sandwiches

Cut bread slices into squares, triangles or cookie-cutter shapes. Top with your choice of spreads; garnish as desired.

Frosted Sandwich Loaf

Use 5 lengthwise slices of bread. Spread 4 slices with softened margarine or butter. Top with ½ to 1 cup of the desired spread.

Stack slices with spread; top with remaining slice. In small bowl, beat two 8-oz. packages of cream cheese with ½ cup half-and-half until soft enough to spread. Frost loaf. Refrigerate 2 to 3 hours. Garnish as desired. To serve, cut crosswise into ½-inch slices.

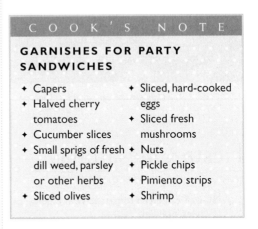

COOK'S NOTE

GARNISHES FOR PARTY SANDWICHES

- Capers
- Halved cherry tomatoes
- Cucumber slices
- Small sprigs of fresh dill weed, parsley or other herbs
- Sliced olives
- Sliced, hard-cooked eggs
- Sliced fresh mushrooms
- Nuts
- Pickle chips
- Pimiento strips
- Shrimp

Chicken Salad Spread

YIELD: 1 CUP

> ¾ cup finely chopped cooked chicken
> ⅓ cup finely chopped celery
> 2 tablespoons chopped pimientos
> 2 tablespoons mayonnaise or salad dressing
> Salt and pepper

In small bowl, combine all ingredients; mix well. Refrigerate.

NUTRITION INFORMATION PER SERVING: Serving Size: 1 Tablespoon • Calories: 25 • Calories from Fat: 20 • **% DAILY VALUE:** Total Fat: 2 g 3% • Saturated Fat: 0 g 0% • Cholesterol: 5 mg 2% • Sodium: 35 mg 1% • Total Carbohydrate: 0 g 0% • Dietary Fiber: 0 g 0% • Sugars: 0 g • Protein: 2 g • Vitamin A: 0% • Vitamin C: 2% • Calcium: 0% • Iron: 0% • **DIETARY EXCHANGES:** ½ Fat

Egg Salad Spread

YIELD: 1 CUP

> 4 eggs
> 1 teaspoon chopped pimientos
> ½ teaspoon chopped chives
> ⅛ teaspoon salt
> 3 tablespoons mayonnaise or salad dressing
> Dash pepper

1. Place eggs in medium saucepan; cover with water. Bring to a boil. Reduce heat; simmer about 15 minutes. Immediately drain; run cold water over eggs to stop cooking. Peel eggs; chop.

2. In small bowl, combine eggs and all remaining ingredients; mix well. Refrigerate.

NUTRITION INFORMATION PER SERVING: Serving Size: 1 Tablespoon ◆ Calories: 35 ◆ Calories from Fat: 25 ◆ **% DAILY VALUE:** Total Fat: 3 g 5% ◆ Saturated Fat: 1 g 5% ◆ Cholesterol: 55 mg 18% ◆ Sodium: 45 mg 2% ◆ Total Carbohydrate: 0 g 0% ◆ Dietary Fiber: 0 g 0% ◆ Sugars: 0 g ◆ Protein: 2 g ◆ Vitamin A: 0% ◆ Vitamin C: 0% ◆ Calcium: 0% ◆ Iron: 0% ◆ **DIETARY EXCHANGES:** ½ Medium-Fat Meat

Seafood Salad Spread

YIELD: 1 CUP

1 (6-oz.) can crabmeat, tuna or shrimp, drained, flaked
2 tablespoons chopped dill pickle
2 tablespoons mayonnaise or salad dressing
½ teaspoon lemon juice

In small bowl, combine all ingredients; mix well. Refrigerate.

NUTRITION INFORMATION PER SERVING: Serving Size: 1 Tablespoon ◆ Calories: 15 ◆ Calories from Fat: 10 ◆ **% DAILY VALUE:** Total Fat: 1 g 2% ◆ Saturated Fat: 0 g 0% ◆ Cholesterol: 10 mg 3% ◆ Sodium: 55 mg 2% ◆ Total Carbohydrate: 0 g 0% ◆ Dietary Fiber: 0 g 0% ◆ Sugars: 0 g ◆ Protein: 2 g ◆ Vitamin A: 0% ◆ Vitamin C: 0% ◆ Calcium: 0% ◆ Iron: 0% ◆ **DIETARY EXCHANGES:** Free

Ham Salad Spread

YIELD: 1 CUP

8 oz. (1 cup) ground cooked ham
1 to 2 tablespoons pickle relish
1 tablespoon minced onion
2 tablespoons mayonnaise or salad dressing

In small bowl, combine all ingredients; mix well. Refrigerate.

NUTRITION INFORMATION PER SERVING: Serving Size: 1 Tablespoon ◆ Calories: 35 ◆ Calories from Fat: 20 ◆ **% DAILY VALUE:** Total Fat: 2 g 3% ◆ Saturated Fat: 0 g 0% ◆ Cholesterol: 10 mg 3% ◆ Sodium: 230 mg 10% ◆ Total Carbohydrate: 1 g 1% ◆ Dietary Fiber: 0 g 0% ◆ Sugars: 1 g ◆ Protein: 3 g ◆ Vitamin A: 0% ◆ Vitamin C: 0% ◆ Calcium: 0% ◆ Iron: 0% ◆ **DIETARY EXCHANGES:** ½ Medium-Fat Meat

Sun-Dried Tomato and Cheese Pizza

PREP TIME: 30 MINUTES ◆ YIELD: 35 APPETIZERS

1 (10-oz.) can refrigerated pizza crust
½ cup oil-packed sun-dried tomatoes, drained, coarsely chopped
½ cup sliced pitted kalamata or ripe olives
6 oz. (1½ cups) shredded Cheddar cheese

2 oz. (½ cup) shredded fresh Parmesan cheese
½ cup sliced green onions

1. Heat oven to 425°F. Grease 15 × 10 × 1-inch baking pan. Unroll dough; place in greased pan. Starting at center, press out with hands. Bake at 425°F. for 8 to 10 minutes or until light golden brown.
2. Sprinkle partially baked crust with all remaining ingredients. Bake an additional 3 to 5 minutes or until cheese is melted.
3. To serve, cut into small squares.

NUTRITION INFORMATION PER SERVING: Serving Size: 1 Appetizer ◆ Calories: 60 ◆ Calories from Fat: 25 ◆ **% DAILY VALUE:** Total Fat: 3 g 5% ◆ Saturated Fat: 1 g 5% ◆ Cholesterol: 5 mg 2% ◆ Sodium: 150 mg 6% ◆ Total Carbohydrate: 5 g 2% ◆ Dietary Fiber: 0 g 0% ◆ Sugars: 1 g ◆ Protein: 3 g ◆ Vitamin A: 0% ◆ Vitamin C: 2% ◆ Calcium: 6% ◆ Iron: 0% ◆ **DIETARY EXCHANGES:** ½ Starch, ½ Fat OR ½ Carbohydrate, ½ Fat

Mediterranean Salsa with Crostini

PREP TIME: 20 MINUTES (READY IN 40 MINUTES)
◆ YIELD: 4 CUPS SALSA; 32 SERVINGS

CROSTINI
32 (¼-inch-thick) slices French bread
Nonstick cooking spray

SALSA
6 Italian plum tomatoes, finely chopped
1 cup finely chopped fresh mushrooms
2 tablespoons sliced green onions
1 (4¼-oz.) can chopped ripe olives, drained
1 (6-oz.) jar marinated artichoke hearts, drained, finely chopped
1 tablespoon chopped fresh parsley
2 teaspoons dried basil leaves
¼ teaspoon salt
1 tablespoon balsamic or red wine vinegar

1. Heat oven to 325°F. Line cookie sheet with foil. Place bread slices on foil-lined cookie sheet; spray lightly with nonstick cooking spray. Bake at 325°F. for 6 to 9 minutes or until crisp. Place crostini on wire rack; cool completely.
2. Meanwhile, in decorative bowl, combine all salsa ingredients; toss gently to mix. Let stand at room temperature for 20 minutes to blend flavors or refrigerate until serving time. Serve salsa with crostini.

NUTRITION INFORMATION PER SERVING: Serving Size: ⅟₃₂ of Recipe ◆ Calories: 30 ◆ Calories from Fat: 10 ◆ **% DAILY VALUE:** Total Fat: 1 g 2% ◆ Saturated Fat: 0 g 0% ◆ Cholesterol: 0 mg 0% ◆ Sodium: 90 mg 4% ◆ Total Carbohydrate: 4 g 1% ◆ Dietary Fiber: 0 g 0% ◆ Sugars: 1 g ◆ Protein: 1 g ◆ Vitamin A: 0% ◆ Vitamin C: 4% ◆ Calcium: 0% ◆ Iron: 2% ◆ **DIETARY EXCHANGES:** 1 Vegetable

Bean and Corn Salsa

PREP TIME: 10 MINUTES ✦ YIELD: 4 CUPS

- 1 (15-oz.) can black beans, drained, rinsed
- 1 (11-oz.) can vacuum-packed whole kernel corn, drained
- 1 cup chopped tomatoes or 1 (14.5-oz.) can diced tomatoes, drained
- ½ cup chopped green onions
- 2 tablespoons chopped fresh cilantro
- ½ cup purchased Italian salad dressing
- 2 serrano chiles, seeded, chopped, if desired

In large bowl, combine all ingredients; mix well. Serve immediately, or cover and refrigerate until serving time. Serve with tortilla chips or over grilled meat.

NUTRITION INFORMATION PER SERVING: Serving Size: ¼ Cup ◆ Calories: 70 ◆ Calories from Fat: 35 ◆ **% DAILY VALUE:** Total Fat: 4 g 6% ◆ Saturated Fat: 1 g 5% ◆ Cholesterol: 0 mg 0% ◆ Sodium: 135 mg 6% ◆ Total Carbohydrate: 7 g 2% ◆ Dietary Fiber: 1 g 4% ◆ Sugars: 2 g ◆ Protein: 2 g ◆ Vitamin A: 4% ◆ Vitamin C: 30% ◆ Calcium: 0% ◆ Iron: 2% ◆ **DIETARY EXCHANGES:** ½ Starch, ½ Fat OR ½ Carbohydrate, ½ Fat

Pineapple Salsa

PREP TIME: 10 MINUTES ✦ YIELD: 1 CUP

- 1 cup finely chopped fresh pineapple or 1 (8-oz.) can crushed pineapple, drained
- 2 tablespoons orange marmalade
- 1 tablespoon chopped fresh cilantro
- 2 teaspoons chopped fresh jalapeño chile
- 2 teaspoons diced pimientos
- 1½ teaspoons lime juice
- ¼ teaspoon salt

In medium bowl, combine all ingredients; mix well. Serve immediately, or cover and refrigerate until serving time. Serve with chips or cooked shrimp.

NUTRITION INFORMATION PER SERVING: Serving Size: 2 Tablespoons ◆ Calories: 25 ◆ Calories from Fat: 0 ◆ **% DAILY VALUE:** Total Fat: 0 g 0% ◆ Saturated Fat: 0 g 0% ◆ Cholesterol: 0 mg 0% ◆ Sodium: 70 mg 3% ◆ Total Carbohydrate: 6 g 2% ◆ Dietary Fiber: 0 g 0% ◆ Sugars: 4 g ◆ Protein: 0 g ◆ Vitamin A: 0% ◆ Vitamin C: 15% ◆ Calcium: 0% ◆ Iron: 0% ◆ **DIETARY EXCHANGES:** ½ Fruit OR ½ Carbohydrate

Clockwise from top left: Garden Fresh Salsa (page 13), Bean and Corn Salsa, Pineapple Salsa

Garden Fresh Salsa

PREP TIME: 10 MINUTES ◆ YIELD: 2 CUPS

    2 large tomatoes, seeded, coarsely chopped
    1 to 2 serrano chiles, seeded, chopped
    1/3 cup chopped green onions
    2 tablespoons chopped fresh cilantro
    2 tablespoons fresh lime juice
    1/4 teaspoon salt

In medium bowl, combine all ingredients; mix well. Serve immediately, or cover and refrigerate until serving time. Salsa can be stored in refrigerator for up to 1 week. Serve with tortilla chips or over grilled meat.

NUTRITION INFORMATION PER SERVING: Serving Size: 1/4 Cup ◆ Calories: 20 ◆ Calories from Fat: 0 ◆ **% DAILY VALUE:** Total Fat: 0 g 0% ◆ Saturated Fat: 0 g 0% ◆ Cholesterol: 0 mg 0% ◆ Sodium: 75 mg 3% ◆ Total Carbohydrate: 4 g 1% ◆ Dietary Fiber: 1 g 3% ◆ Sugars: 2 g ◆ Protein: 1 g ◆ Vitamin A: 8% ◆ Vitamin C: 70% ◆ Calcium: 0% ◆ Iron: 2% ◆ **DIETARY EXCHANGES:** 1 Vegetable

Green Chile Cheesecake Spread

PREP TIME: 15 MINUTES (READY IN 1 HOUR 50 MINUTES) ◆ YIELD: 4 CUPS

    1/4 cup unseasoned dry bread crumbs
    1/2 cup sour cream
    2 (8-oz.) pkg. cream cheese, softened
    1 (5-oz.) jar pasteurized process cheese spread
    1 (1 1/4-oz) pkg. taco seasoning mix
    2 eggs
    1 (4.5-oz.) can chopped green chiles
    1 (2-oz.) jar diced pimientos, drained

1. Heat oven to 350°F. Grease bottom and 1 inch up sides of 10-inch springform pan. Sprinkle bread crumbs in bottom of greased pan. Tilt pan to coat with crumbs 1 inch up sides. Shake pan to evenly distribute crumbs across bottom.
2. In large bowl, combine sour cream, cream cheese, cheese spread, taco seasoning mix and eggs; beat until smooth. Fold in chiles and pimientos until well blended. Spoon into greased crumb-lined pan; spread evenly.
3. Bake at 350°F. for 30 to 35 minutes or until center is set. Cool about 1 hour or until completely cooled.
4. To serve, remove sides of pan. Place cheesecake on serving plate. Serve with tortilla chips for dipping or crackers for spreading. Store in refrigerator.

NUTRITION INFORMATION PER SERVING: Serving Size: 1 Tablespoon ◆ Calories: 35 ◆ Calories from Fat: 25 ◆ **% DAILY VALUE:** Total Fat: 3 g 5% ◆ Saturated Fat: 2 g 10% ◆ Cholesterol: 15 mg 5% ◆ Sodium: 115 mg 5% ◆ Total Carbohydrate: 1 g 1% ◆ Dietary Fiber: 0 g 0% ◆ Sugars: 0 g ◆ Protein: 1 g ◆ Vitamin A: 4% ◆ Vitamin C: 2% ◆ Calcium: 2% ◆ Iron: 0% ◆ **DIETARY EXCHANGES:** 1/2 Fat

Classic Guacamole

PREP TIME: 15 MINUTES (READY IN 45 MINUTES) ◆ YIELD: 3 CUPS

    2 large ripe avocados, peeled, pitted and mashed
    1/4 cup finely chopped onion
    2 tablespoons lemon juice
    2 to 5 drops hot pepper sauce, if desired
    1/4 to 1/2 teaspoon garlic powder
    1/4 teaspoon salt
      Dash pepper
    1 medium tomato, chopped
    2 tablespoons finely chopped green chiles or 1 small chile, chopped

1. In blender container or food processor bowl with metal blade, combine all ingredients except tomato and green chiles; cover and blend until smooth. Place in medium bowl.
2. Stir in tomato and green chiles. Cover; refrigerate at least 30 minutes before serving to blend flavors. Serve with tortilla or corn chips.

> **TIP:** To serve guacamole in avocado shells, cut unpeeled avocados in half lengthwise. Remove pits; scoop fruit from shells with spoon. Prepare recipe as directed above. Fill shells with dip; refrigerate at least 30 minutes before serving.

NUTRITION INFORMATION PER SERVING: Serving Size: 1/4 Cup ◆ Calories: 60 ◆ Calories from Fat: 45 ◆ **% DAILY VALUE:** Total Fat: 5 g 8% ◆ Saturated Fat: 1 g 5% ◆ Cholesterol: 0 mg 0% ◆ Sodium: 50 mg 2% ◆ Total Carbohydrate: 4 g 1% ◆ Dietary Fiber: 2 g 8% ◆ Sugars: 1 g ◆ Protein: 1 g ◆ Vitamin A: 6% ◆ Vitamin C: 15% ◆ Calcium: 0% ◆ Iron: 2% ◆ **DIETARY EXCHANGES:** 1 Vegetable, 1 Fat

VARIATIONS

Bacon Guacamole: Stir in 2 slices crisply cooked bacon, crumbled, with the tomato and green chiles.

Creamy Guacamole: Add 1/4 cup mayonnaise or sour cream.

Tomato and Basil Bruschetta

PREP TIME: 15 MINUTES ◆ YIELD: 2 SERVINGS

    4 (½-inch-thick) slices coarse-textured bread
        (about 4 x 3 inches)
    1 garlic clove, peeled, cut in half
    8 teaspoons extra-virgin olive oil
    ¼ teaspoon salt
    ⅛ teaspoon coarsely ground black pepper
    1 small tomato, cut into 8 thin slices
    1 tablespoon chopped fresh basil

1. Grill, broil or toast bread slices on both sides until light golden brown. While hot, rub cut side of garlic over 1 side of each bread slice.
2. Drizzle 1 teaspoon oil over garlic-rubbed side of each bread slice; sprinkle with salt and pepper. Top each with tomato slices; sprinkle with basil. Drizzle remaining oil over tomato slices. Serve immediately.

NUTRITION INFORMATION PER SERVING: Serving Size: ½ of Recipe ◆ Calories: 310 ◆ Calories from Fat: 180 ◆ **% DAILY VALUE:** Total Fat: 20 g 31% ◆ Saturated Fat: 3 g 15% ◆ Cholesterol: 0 mg 0% ◆ Sodium: 580 mg 24% ◆ Total Carbohydrate: 28 g 9% ◆ Dietary Fiber: 2 g 8% ◆ Sugars: 3 g ◆ Protein: 5 g ◆ Vitamin A: 4% ◆ Vitamin C: 8% ◆ Calcium: 4% ◆ Iron: 8% ◆ **DIETARY EXCHANGES:** 2 Starch, 3½ Fat OR 2 Carbohydrate, 3½ Fat

Gruyère Chicken Triangles

PREP TIME: 1 HOUR 30 MINUTES (READY IN 1 HOUR 50 MINUTES) ◆ YIELD: 60 APPETIZERS

    1 cup finely chopped cooked chicken
    1 cup chopped cooked broccoli
    4 oz. (1 cup) shredded Gruyère cheese
    ¼ cup chopped roasted red bell peppers
        (from 7.25-oz. jar)
    ½ teaspoon dried fines herbes
    20 (17 x 12-inch) sheets frozen phyllo (filo)
        pastry, thawed
        Nonstick cooking spray
        Paprika

1. Heat oven to 375°F. In medium bowl, combine chicken, broccoli, cheese, roasted peppers and fines herbes; mix well.
2. Unroll phyllo sheets; cover with plastic wrap or cloth towel to prevent drying out. Place 1 phyllo sheet on work surface; spray with nonstick cooking spray. Top with second phyllo sheet; spray again. With sharp knife, cut phyllo into six 12-inch-long strips.

3. For each appetizer, place 1 rounded teaspoon chicken mixture at end of 1 strip. Fold 1 corner of strip diagonally over filling. Continue folding to end of strip into a triangular bundle, as if folding a flag (see diagram). Place on ungreased cookie sheet. Repeat with remaining phyllo sheet. Sprinkle bundles with paprika.

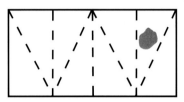

4. Bake at 375°F. for 15 to 20 minutes or until golden brown. Serve warm.

NUTRITION INFORMATION PER SERVING: Serving Size: 1 Appetizer ◆ Calories: 50 ◆ Calories from Fat: 25 ◆ **% DAILY VALUE:** Total Fat: 3 g 5% ◆ Saturated Fat: 1 g 5% ◆ Cholesterol: 4 mg 1% ◆ Sodium: 40 mg 2% ◆ Total Carbohydrate: 4 g 1% ◆ Dietary Fiber: 0 g 0% ◆ Sugars: 0 g ◆ Protein: 2 g ◆ Vitamin A: 2% ◆ Vitamin C: 4% ◆ Calcium: 2% ◆ Iron: 0% ◆ **DIETARY EXCHANGES:** ½ Starch, ½ Fat OR ⅓ Carbohydrate, ½ Fat

Easy Vegetable Pizza

PREP TIME: 20 MINUTES (READY IN 1 HOUR 55 MINUTES) ◆ YIELD: 60 APPETIZERS

    2 (8-oz.) cans refrigerated crescent dinner
        rolls
    1 (8-oz.) pkg. cream cheese, softened
    ½ cup sour cream
    1 teaspoon dried dill weed
    ⅛ teaspoon garlic powder
    20 small fresh broccoli florets
    20 cucumber or zucchini slices
    10 cherry tomatoes, halved
    2 tablespoons tiny fresh parsley sprigs, if desired

1. Heat oven to 375°F. Unroll dough into 4 long rectangles. Place crosswise in ungreased 15 × 10 × 1-inch baking pan; press over bottom and 1 inch up sides to form crust. Firmly press perforations to seal.
2. Bake at 375°F. for 13 to 17 minutes or until golden brown. Cool 15 minutes or until completely cooled.
3. In small bowl, combine cream cheese, sour cream, dill and garlic powder; blend until smooth. Spread evenly over cooled crust. Cover; refrigerate 1 to 2 hours.
4. Just before serving, cut into 1½-inch squares. Top each square with broccoli floret, cucumber slice or tomato half. Garnish each with parsley.

NUTRITION INFORMATION PER SERVING: Serving Size: 1 Appetizer ◆ Calories: 45 ◆ Calories from Fat: 25 ◆ **% DAILY VALUE:** Total Fat: 3 g 5% ◆ Saturated Fat: 1 g 5% ◆ Cholesterol: 5 mg 2% ◆ Sodium: 70 mg 3% ◆ Total Carbohydrate: 3 g 1% ◆ Dietary Fiber: 0 g 0% ◆ Sugars: 1 g ◆ Protein: 1 g ◆ Vitamin A: 4% ◆ Vitamin C: 4% ◆ Calcium: 0% ◆ Iron: 0% ◆ **DIETARY EXCHANGES:** ½ Vegetable, ½ Fat

Dilly Dip

PREP TIME: 10 MINUTES (READY IN 2 HOURS 10 MINUTES) ◆ YIELD: 2 CUPS

1½ cups sour cream
⅔ cup mayonnaise
2 tablespoons instant minced onion
2 tablespoons dried parsley flakes
2 tablespoons dried dill weed
1 teaspoon celery salt or seasoned salt

In medium bowl, combine all ingredients; mix well. Cover; refrigerate at least 2 hours before serving to blend flavors. Serve with cut-up fresh vegetables.

NUTRITION INFORMATION PER SERVING: Serving Size: 1 Tablespoon ◆ Calories: 60 ◆ Calories from Fat: 50 ◆ **% DAILY VALUE:** Total Fat: 6 g 9% ◆ Saturated Fat: 2 g 10% ◆ Cholesterol: 10 mg 3% ◆ Sodium: 90 mg 4% ◆ Total Carbohydrate: 1 g 1% ◆ Dietary Fiber: 0 g 0% ◆ Sugars: 1 g ◆ Protein: 0 g ◆ Vitamin A: 2% ◆ Vitamin C: 0% ◆ Calcium: 0% ◆ Iron: 0% ◆ **DIETARY EXCHANGES:** 1½ Fat

Light Spinach Dip

PREP TIME: 10 MINUTES (READY IN 2 HOURS 10 MINUTES) ◆ YIELD: 3⅔ CUPS

½ cup skim milk
½ cup fat-free mayonnaise or salad dressing
1 (8-oz.) container light sour cream
3 cups frozen cut leaf spinach, thawed, squeezed to drain
¼ cup chopped green onions
1 teaspoon seasoned salt
½ teaspoon dried dill weed
1 (8-oz.) can water chestnuts, drained, chopped

1. In medium bowl, combine milk and mayonnaise; beat with wire whisk until smooth. Stir in sour cream; blend well.
2. Add all remaining ingredients; mix well. Cover; refrigerate at least 2 hours before serving to blend flavors. Serve with cut-up fresh vegetables.

NUTRITION INFORMATION PER SERVING: Serving Size: 1 Tablespoon ◆ Calories: 10 ◆ Calories from Fat: 0 ◆ **% DAILY VALUE:** Total Fat: 0 g 0% ◆ Saturated Fat: 0 g 0% ◆ Cholesterol: 0 mg 0% ◆ Sodium: 50 mg 2% ◆ Total Carbohydrate: 2 g 1% ◆ Dietary Fiber: 0 g 0% ◆ Sugars: 1 g ◆ Protein: 0 g ◆ Vitamin A: 4% ◆ Vitamin C: 0% ◆ Calcium: 0% ◆ Iron: 0% ◆ **DIETARY EXCHANGES:** Free

VEGETABLE DIPPER QUANTITIES

VEGETABLE	YIELD
2 lb. broccoli or cauliflower	About 30 (1¼-inch) florets
1 lb. carrots	About 60 (3 × ½-inch) sticks
1¾ lb. celery	About 100 (4 × ½-inch) sticks
1 pint cherry tomatoes	About 25 tomatoes
1½ lb. cucumber or 1 lb. zucchini	About 50 (¼-inch) slices

COOK'S NOTE

FRESH VEGETABLE DIPPERS

The classic vegetable platter is sometimes called crudités (CRUDE-ee-tays), which is simply French for "raw foods." Select a contrast of colors, allowing at least four pieces per person. Cut up the vegetables, then keep them in ice water. Drain just before serving.

You can arrange the dippers in a basket lined first with plastic wrap, then lettuce leaves, or on a platter lined with lettuce leaves or bordered with parsley or curly cabbage.

◆ Raw or slightly steamed asparagus spears
◆ Raw or slightly steamed broccoli florets
◆ Carrot sticks
◆ Raw or slightly steamed cauliflower florets
◆ Celery sticks
◆ Cherry tomatoes
◆ Cucumber slices or sticks
◆ Green beans or wax beans
◆ Green onions
◆ Green, red or yellow bell pepper strips
◆ Jicama sticks
◆ Kohlrabi wedges
◆ Mushrooms
◆ Pea pods
◆ Radishes
◆ Zucchini or summer squash slices or sticks

Lemon Yogurt Fruit Dip

Lemon Yogurt Fruit Dip

PREP TIME: 5 MINUTES (READY IN 1 HOUR 5 MINUTES)
✦ YIELD: 1¾ CUPS

  1 (8-oz.) container lemon yogurt
  1 (8-oz.) container sour cream
  1 teaspoon ginger
  1 tablespoon honey
  ½ teaspoon grated lemon peel
  ½ teaspoon lemon juice

1. In small bowl, combine all ingredients; blend well. Cover; refrigerate 1 to 2 hours before serving to blend flavors.
2. Serve dip with assorted fresh fruit such as whole strawberries, pineapple chunks, seedless grapes, melon wedges and apple, pear or banana slices.

NUTRITION INFORMATION PER SERVING: Serving Size: 1 Tablespoon ✦ Calories: 30 ✦ Calories from Fat: 20 ✦ % DAILY VALUE: Total Fat: 2 g 3% ✦ Saturated Fat: 1 g 5% ✦ Cholesterol: 4 mg 1% ✦ Sodium: 10 mg 0% ✦ Total Carbohydrate: 2 g 1% ✦ Dietary Fiber: 0 g 0% ✦ Sugars: 1 g ✦ Protein: 1 g ✦ Vitamin A: 0% ✦ Vitamin C: 0% ✦ Calcium: 2% ✦ Iron: 0% ✦ DIETARY EXCHANGES: ½ Fat

Chili Potato Dippers with Cheddar Jalapeño Dip

PREP TIME: 15 MINUTES (READY IN 40 MINUTES)
✦ YIELD: 1¼ CUPS DIP; 8 SERVINGS

DIPPERS
  4 medium russet potatoes
  2 tablespoons olive or vegetable oil
  1 teaspoon chili powder
  ½ teaspoon garlic powder

CHEDDAR JALAPEÑO DIP
  ⅓ cup sour cream
  ⅓ cup mayonnaise or salad dressing
  ¼ cup finely chopped tomato
  1 oz. (¼ cup) finely shredded extra-sharp Cheddar cheese
  1 to 2 jalapeño chiles, seeded, finely chopped
  2 tablespoons sliced green onions

1. Heat oven to 450°F. Line 15 × 10 × 1-inch baking pan with foil; spray foil with nonstick cooking spray.
2. Cut potatoes into thin wedges. In large bowl, combine potatoes, oil, chili powder and garlic powder; toss to coat. Place in sprayed foil-lined pan.
3. Bake at 450°F. for 20 to 30 minutes or until tender and golden brown, turning once.
4. Meanwhile, in medium bowl, combine all dip ingredients except onions; mix well. Sprinkle with green onions.

NUTRITION INFORMATION PER SERVING: Serving Size: ⅛ of Recipe ✦ Calories: 210 ✦ Calories from Fat: 130 ✦ % DAILY VALUE: Total Fat: 14 g 22% ✦ Saturated Fat: 4 g 20% ✦ Cholesterol: 15 mg 5% ✦ Sodium: 90 mg 4% ✦ Total Carbohydrate: 17 g 6% ✦ Dietary Fiber: 2 g 8% ✦ Sugars: 2 g ✦ Protein: 3 g ✦ Vitamin A: 6% ✦ Vitamin C: 20% ✦ Calcium: 4% ✦ Iron: 6% ✦ DIETARY EXCHANGES: 1 Starch, 3 Fat OR 1 Carbohydrate, 3 Fat

Chili Potato Dippers with Cheddar Jalapeño Dip

3. Stir in cheese until melted. Add spinach; mix well. Cook until thoroughly heated. Serve with slices of baguette-style French bread or cut-up fresh vegetables.

NUTRITION INFORMATION PER SERVING: Serving Size: 1 Tablespoon ◆ Calories: 15 ◆ Calories from Fat: 10 ◆ % DAILY VALUE: Total Fat: 0 g 0% ◆ Saturated Fat: 0 g 0% ◆ Cholesterol: 2 mg 1% ◆ Sodium: 70 mg 3% ◆ Total Carbohydrate: 1 g 1% ◆ Dietary Fiber: 0 g 0% ◆ Sugars: 1 g ◆ Protein: 1 g ◆ Vitamin A: 6% ◆ Vitamin C: 2% ◆ Calcium: 4% ◆ Iron: 0% ◆ DIETARY EXCHANGES: ½ Fat

COOK'S NOTE

HANDLING JALAPEÑOS

Jalapeños and other hot chiles can bite you before you bite them. Capsaicin, the substance that makes chiles hot, can irritate your skin and especially your eyes. Cover your hands with plastic bags or thin rubber gloves, or wash your hands well and scrub under your nails after handling hot chiles; otherwise, an inadvertent rub of the eye could cause a three-alarm mishap.

Hot Spinach Jalapeño Cheese Dip

Hot Spinach Jalapeño Cheese Dip

PREP TIME: 30 MINUTES ◆ YIELD: 4 CUPS

1½ cups skim milk
2 tablespoons all-purpose flour
½ cup finely chopped onion
¼ teaspoon pepper
1 teaspoon Worcestershire sauce
1 (8-oz.) pkg. Mexican pasteurized process cheese spread with jalapeño chiles, cut into ½-inch pieces
2 (9-oz.) pkg. frozen spinach in a pouch, thawed, squeezed to drain

1. Place 1¼ cups of the milk in large non-stick saucepan; place over medium-high heat. In small bowl, combine remaining ¼ cup milk and flour; blend with wire whisk until smooth. Add to milk in saucepan; cook about 5 minutes, stirring constantly, until thickened.

2. Add onion, pepper and Worcestershire sauce; mix well. Bring just to a boil. Reduce heat; simmer 10 minutes or until onion is tender, stirring occasionally.

Layered Ranchero Dip

PREP TIME: 20 MINUTES ✦ YIELD: 11 CUPS

2 (10.5-oz.) cans jalapeño-flavored bean dip
1 (8-oz.) container sour cream
⅔ cup mayonnaise or salad dressing
1 (1¼-oz.) pkg. taco seasoning mix
1 to 2 (4.5-oz.) cans chopped green chiles, drained
4 ripe medium avocados
2 tablespoons lemon or lime juice
¼ teaspoon garlic powder
8 oz. (2 cups) shredded Cheddar cheese
2 cups sliced green onions
2 cups chopped tomatoes
1 (6-oz.) can pitted ripe olives, chopped

1. On large round serving platter, spread bean dip in thin layer. In small bowl, combine sour cream, mayonnaise and taco seasoning mix; blend well. Spread over bean dip. Sprinkle with chiles.
2. Peel and pit avocados; place in small bowl. Mash avocados. Add lemon juice and garlic powder; mix well. Spread over chiles.
3. Sprinkle with cheese, onions, tomatoes and olives. Serve with tortilla chips.

NUTRITION INFORMATION PER SERVING: Serving Size: ¼ Cup ◆ Calories: 110 ◆ Calories from Fat: 80 ◆ **% DAILY VALUE:** Total Fat: 9 g 14% ◆ Saturated Fat: 3 g 15% ◆ Cholesterol: 10 mg 3% ◆ Sodium: 230 mg 10% ◆ Total Carbohydrate: 5 g 2% ◆ Dietary Fiber: 2 g 8% ◆ Sugars: 1 g ◆ Protein: 3 g ◆ Vitamin A: 8% ◆ Vitamin C: 6% ◆ Calcium: 8% ◆ Iron: 6% ◆ **DIETARY EXCHANGES:** ½ Starch, 1½ Fat OR ½ Carbohydrate, 1½ Fat

Spicy Cajun Dip

PREP TIME: 20 MINUTES ✦ YIELD: 2 CUPS

½ cup dry-pack sun-dried tomatoes
1 (8-oz.) pkg. ⅓-less-fat cream cheese (Neufchâtel), softened
½ cup nonfat plain yogurt
¼ cup chili sauce
¼ cup chopped green bell pepper
¼ cup chopped green onions
1 garlic clove, minced
½ teaspoon celery seed
⅛ teaspoon ground red pepper (cayenne)

1. In small bowl, pour 1 cup boiling water over tomatoes. Let stand at room temperature for 5 to 10 minutes. Drain and chop tomatoes.
2. Meanwhile, in another small bowl, combine cream cheese, yogurt and chili sauce; mix well. Add tomatoes and all remaining ingredients; mix well. Refrigerate until serving time.
3. Just before serving, stir dip. Serve with cut-up fresh vegetables or garlic-flavored bagel crisps.

NUTRITION INFORMATION PER SERVING: Serving Size: 2 Tablespoons ◆ Calories: 45 ◆ Calories from Fat: 25 ◆ **% DAILY VALUE:** Total Fat: 3 g 5% ◆ Saturated Fat: 2 g 10% ◆ Cholesterol: 10 mg 3% ◆ Sodium: 150 mg 6% ◆ Total Carbohydrate: 3 g 1% ◆ Dietary Fiber: 0 g 0% ◆ Sugars: 2 g ◆ Protein: 2 g ◆ Vitamin A: 6% ◆ Vitamin C: 4% ◆ Calcium: 2% ◆ Iron: 0% ◆ **DIETARY EXCHANGES:** ½ Vegetable, ½ Fat

Roasted Vegetables with Spicy Aïoli Dip

PREP TIME: 20 MINUTES (READY IN 40 MINUTES)
◆ YIELD: ¾ CUP DIP; 8 SERVINGS

AÏOLI DIP
- ½ cup mayonnaise
- ¼ cup sour cream
- 2 tablespoons taco sauce
- 2 teaspoons chopped garlic in water (from 4.5-oz. jar)

VEGETABLES
- 1 medium red bell pepper, cut into 1½-inch squares
- 1 medium red onion, cut into wedges
- 1 medium yellow summer squash, cut into 1½-inch slices
- 12 fresh whole mushrooms
- ¼ lb. fresh whole green beans, trimmed
- 1 tablespoon olive or vegetable oil

1. In small bowl, combine all dip ingredients; mix well. Refrigerate at least 30 minutes to blend flavors.
2. Meanwhile, heat oven to 450°F. In large bowl, combine all vegetables with oil; toss to coat evenly. Arrange vegetables in ungreased 15 × 10 × 1-inch baking pan.
3. Bake at 450°F. for 15 to 20 minutes or until crisp-tender. Serve warm vegetables with dip.

NUTRITION INFORMATION PER SERVING: Serving Size: ⅛ of Recipe ◆ Calories: 160 ◆ Calories from Fat: 130 ◆ % DAILY VALUE: Total Fat: 14 g 22% ◆ Saturated Fat: 3 g 15% ◆ Cholesterol: 10 mg 3% ◆ Sodium: 110 mg 5% ◆ Total Carbohydrate: 7 g 2% ◆ Dietary Fiber: 2 g 8% ◆ Sugars: 4 g ◆ Protein: 2 g ◆ Vitamin A: 15% ◆ Vitamin C: 35% ◆ Calcium: 4% ◆ Iron: 4% ◆ DIETARY EXCHANGES: 1 Vegetable, 3 Fat

Warm Roasted Pepper and Artichoke Spread

PREP TIME: 15 MINUTES (READY IN 40 MINUTES)
◆ YIELD: 3¼ CUPS

- 1 cup grated Parmesan cheese
- ½ cup fat-free mayonnaise or salad dressing
- 1 (8-oz.) pkg. cream cheese, softened
- 1 small garlic clove
- 1 (14-oz.) can artichoke hearts, drained, finely chopped
- ⅓ cup finely chopped roasted red bell peppers (from 7.25-oz. jar)

1. Heat oven to 350°F. In food processor bowl with metal blade, combine Parmesan cheese, mayonnaise, cream cheese and garlic; process until smooth.
2. Place mixture in large bowl. Add artichoke hearts and roasted peppers; mix well. Spread in ungreased 9-inch quiche dish or glass pie pan.
3. Bake at 350°F. for 20 to 25 minutes or until thoroughly heated. Serve warm with crackers, cut-up fresh vegetables or cocktail bread slices.

NUTRITION INFORMATION PER SERVING: Serving Size: 1 Tablespoon ◆ Calories: 25 ◆ Calories from Fat: 20 ◆ % DAILY VALUE: Total Fat: 2 g 3% ◆ Saturated Fat: 1 g 5% ◆ Cholesterol: 5 mg 2% ◆ Sodium: 85 mg 4% ◆ Total Carbohydrate: 1 g 1% ◆ Dietary Fiber: 0 g 0% ◆ Sugars: 0 g ◆ Protein: 1 g ◆ Vitamin A: 2% ◆ Vitamin C: 2% ◆ Calcium: 4% ◆ Iron: 0% ◆ DIETARY EXCHANGES: ½ Vegetable, ½ Fat

Baked Crabmeat Spread

PREP TIME: 20 MINUTES (READY IN 35 MINUTES)
◆ YIELD: 1½ CUPS

- 2 tablespoons margarine or butter
- ½ cup chopped red bell pepper
- 2 tablespoons sliced green onions
- 1 garlic clove, minced
- 2 tablespoons all-purpose flour
- ¼ teaspoon white pepper
- 1 cup milk
- ¼ cup grated Parmesan cheese
- ½ cup frozen or canned cooked crabmeat
- 1 oz. (¼ cup) shredded Cheddar cheese

1. Heat oven to 350°F. Grease 9-inch pie pan. Melt margarine in skillet over medium heat. Add bell pepper, onions and garlic; cook and stir 2 to 3 minutes or until vegetables are tender. Stir in flour and pepper; cook 1 minute.
2. Gradually add milk; cook until mixture boils, stirring constantly. Stir in Parmesan cheese. Remove from heat; fold in crabmeat. Pour into greased pan. Sprinkle with Cheddar cheese.
3. Bake at 350°F. for 10 to 15 minutes or until thoroughly heated and cheese is melted. Serve with Melba toast rounds.

NUTRITION INFORMATION PER SERVING: Serving Size: 2 Tablespoons ◆ Calories: 60 ◆ Calories from Fat: 35 ◆ % DAILY VALUE: Total Fat: 4 g 6% ◆ Saturated Fat: 2 g 10% ◆ Cholesterol: 10 mg 3% ◆ Sodium: 160 mg 7% ◆ Total Carbohydrate: 3 g 1% ◆ Dietary Fiber: 0 g 0% ◆ Sugars: 1 g ◆ Protein: 4 g ◆ Vitamin A: 8% ◆ Vitamin C: 10% ◆ Calcium: 8% ◆ Iron: 0% ◆ DIETARY EXCHANGES: ½ Lean Meat, ½ Fat

Crescent-Wrapped Brie

Crescent-Wrapped Brie

PREP TIME: 20 MINUTES (READY IN 1 HOUR)
✦ YIELD: 12 SERVINGS

1 (8-oz.) can refrigerated crescent dinner rolls
1 (8-oz.) round natural Brie cheese
1 egg, beaten

1. Heat oven to 350°F. Unroll dough. Separate dough crosswise into 2 sections. Pat dough and firmly press perforations to seal, forming 2 squares. Place 1 square on ungreased cookie sheet. Place cheese on center of dough.

2. With small cookie or canapé cutter, cut 1 shape from each corner of remaining square; set cutouts aside.

3. Place remaining square on top of cheese round. Press dough evenly around cheese; fold bottom edges over top edges. Gently stretch dough evenly around cheese; press to seal completely. Brush with beaten egg. Top with cutouts; brush with additional beaten egg.

4. Bake at 350°F. for 20 to 24 minutes or until golden brown. Cool 15 minutes before serving.

NUTRITION INFORMATION PER SERVING: Serving Size: ¹⁄₁₂ of Recipe ♦ Calories: 130 ♦ Calories from Fat: 80 ♦ **% DAILY VALUE:** Total Fat: 9 g 14% ♦ Saturated Fat: 4 g 20% ♦ Cholesterol: 35 mg 12% ♦ Sodium: 270 mg 11% ♦ Total Carbohydrate: 7 g 2% ♦ Dietary Fiber: 0 g 0% ♦ Sugars: 1 g ♦ Protein: 6 g ♦ Vitamin A: 4% ♦ Vitamin C: 0% ♦ Calcium: 4% ♦ Iron: 4% ♦ **DIETARY EXCHANGES:** ½ Starch, ½ High-Fat Meat, 1 Fat OR ½ Carbohydrate, ½ High-Fat Meat, 1 Fat

Baked Brie with Mango

PREP TIME: 10 MINUTES (READY IN 25 MINUTES)
✦ YIELD: 8 SERVINGS

1 (8-oz.) round Brie cheese (do not remove rind)
2 tablespoons raspberry preserves
¼ cup diced peeled mango
1 tablespoon brown sugar

1. Heat oven to 400°F. Place Brie cheese in small, shallow baking dish or 8-inch pie pan. Spread raspberry preserves over cheese; top with mango. Sprinkle with brown sugar.

2. Bake at 400°F. for 10 to 12 minutes or until sides of cheese are softened. Serve with crackers.

NUTRITION INFORMATION PER SERVING: Serving Size: ⅛ of Recipe ♦ Calories: 120 ♦ Calories from Fat: 70 ♦ **% DAILY VALUE:** Total Fat: 8 g 12% ♦ Saturated Fat: 5 g 25% ♦ Cholesterol: 30 mg 10% ♦ Sodium: 180 mg 8% ♦ Total Carbohydrate: 6 g 2% ♦ Dietary Fiber: 0 g 0% ♦ Sugars: 5 g ♦ Protein: 6 g ♦ Vitamin A: 8% ♦ Vitamin C: 2% ♦ Calcium: 6% ♦ Iron: 0% ♦ **DIETARY EXCHANGES:** ½ Fruit, 1 High-Fat Meat OR ½ Carbohydrate, 1 High-Fat Meat

Apple Cheese Ball (page 21)

Salmon and Cream Cheese Pâté

Salmon and Cream Cheese Pâté

PREP TIME: 25 MINUTES (READY IN 1 HOUR 25 MINUTES)
✦ YIELD: 1¾ CUPS

  1 (14½-oz.) can red salmon, drained, skin and
      bones removed, flaked
  1 (8-oz.) container soft cream cheese with
      chives and onions
  2 teaspoons lemon juice
 ¼ cup finely chopped red bell pepper
 ½ teaspoon dried dill weed

1. Line small bowl or decorative mold(s) with plastic wrap or cheesecloth. In medium bowl, combine all ingredients; mix well. Spoon into lined bowl; press gently. Cover; refrigerate 1 to 2 hours before serving to blend flavors.

2. To serve, unmold pâté onto serving plate; remove plastic wrap. Garnish as desired. Serve with mini bagel chips, crackers or cocktail bread slices.

NUTRITION INFORMATION PER SERVING: Serving Size: 1 Table-spoon ◆ Calories: 50 ◆ Calories from Fat: 35 ◆ **% DAILY VALUE:** Total Fat: 4 g 6% ◆ Saturated Fat: 2 g 10% ◆ Cholesterol: 15 mg 5% ◆ Sodium: 105 mg 4% ◆ Total Carbohydrate: 0 g 0% ◆ Dietary Fiber: 0 g 0% ◆ Sugars: 0 g ◆ Protein: 4 g ◆ Vitamin A: 4% ◆ Vitamin C: 2% ◆ Calcium: 4% ◆ Iron: 0% ◆ **DIETARY EXCHANGES:** ½ High-Fat Meat

Apple Cheese Ball

PREP TIME: 15 MINUTES (READY IN 1 HOUR 15 MINUTES)
✦ YIELD: 1¾ CUPS

  1 (8-oz.) pkg. cream cheese, softened
  4 oz. (1 cup) shredded Cheddar cheese
 ¼ teaspoon cinnamon
 ¾ cup finely chopped dried apples
 ⅓ cup finely chopped nuts
  1 bay leaf
  1 cinnamon stick, halved

1. In large bowl, combine cream cheese, Cheddar cheese and cinnamon; beat until well blended. Stir in apples.

2. Shape mixture into ball; roll in nuts. Insert bay leaf and cinnamon stick on top of ball to resemble stem and leaf of apple. Refrigerate at least 1 hour or until firm. Serve with crackers. Store in refrigerator up to 2 weeks.

NUTRITION INFORMATION PER SERVING: Serving Size: 1 Table-spoon ◆ Calories: 60 ◆ Calories from Fat: 45 ◆ **% DAILY VALUE:** Total Fat: 5 g 8% ◆ Saturated Fat: 3 g 15% ◆ Cholesterol: 15 mg 5% ◆ Sodium: 50 mg 2% ◆ Total Carbohydrate: 2 g 1% ◆ Dietary Fiber: 0 g 0% ◆ Sugars: 1 g ◆ Protein: 2 g ◆ Vitamin A: 4% ◆ Vitamin C: 0% ◆ Calcium: 4% ◆ Iron: 0% ◆ **DIETARY EXCHANGES:** 1 Fat

Party Snack Mix

PREP TIME: 10 MINUTES (READY IN 40 MINUTES)
✦ YIELD: 12 CUPS

  4 cups bite-sized crispy corn squares cereal
  2 cups bite-sized crispy wheat squares cereal
  2 cups pretzel sticks
  2 cups Spanish peanuts or mixed nuts
 ½ cup butter, melted
  1 tablespoon Worcestershire sauce
 ⅛ teaspoon hot pepper sauce
  1 teaspoon salt
 ¼ teaspoon garlic powder

1. Heat oven to 325°F. In large bowl, combine cereals, pretzel sticks and peanuts.

2. In small bowl, combine butter, Worcestershire sauce, hot pepper sauce, salt and garlic powder; mix well. Pour seasoning mixture over cereal mixture; toss to coat. Spread in ungreased 15 × 10 × 1-inch baking pan.

3. Bake at 325°F. for 25 to 30 minutes or until lightly toasted, stirring occasionally.

NUTRITION INFORMATION PER SERVING: Serving Size: ½ Cup ◆ Calories: 180 ◆ Calories from Fat: 90 ◆ **% DAILY VALUE:** Total Fat: 10 g 15% ◆ Saturated Fat: 2 g 10% ◆ Cholesterol: 0 mg 0% ◆ Sodium: 410 mg 17% ◆ Total Carbohydrate: 17 g 6% ◆ Dietary Fiber: 2 g 8% ◆ Sugars: 1 g ◆ Protein: 5 g ◆ Vitamin A: 4% ◆ Vitamin C: 8% ◆ Calcium: 0% ◆ Iron: 20% ◆ **DIETARY EXCHANGES:** 1 Starch, 2 Fat OR 1 Carbohydrate, 2 Fat

GUIDE TO WINE SELECTION

Here is a simple guide to different wines from around the world. As you go down the list, the wines become drier and stronger in taste. Mild-tasting wines are typically fruitier, smooth and mellow. Strong tastes are typically drier (not sweet) with more acidity, bitterness and, at the end of the red wines, tannic or astringent (the mouth-drying sensation).

WINE TYPE	DISTINCTIVE REGIONS OF PRODUCTION
Sparkling Wines and Champagnes	
Sweet	
Asti Spumanti or Spumante	Italy and sometimes U.S.
Moscato d'Asti	Italy
Demi-Sec Sparkling Wines and Champagnes	U.S. and France
Extra-Dry Sparkling Wines and Champagnes	U.S. and France
Inexpensive Sparkling Wines	International
Dry	
Blanc de Noirs Sparkling Wines and Champagnes	U.S. and France
Brut Sparkling Wines and Champagnes	International
White and Rosé Table Wines	
Sweet	
White Zinfandel and other Blush Wines (sweet to almost dry)	U.S.
Rosé (sweet)	International
Riesling (sweet to almost dry)	U.S., Germany
Gewürztraminer (sweet to almost dry)	U.S., Germany
Chenin Blanc (sweet to almost dry)	U.S., France (Vouvray)
Dry, light to medium intensity	
Rosé (dry)	U.S., France (Tavel Rosé, Rosé d'Anjou)
Riesling (dry)	U.S., France (Alsace), Germany (labeled "trocken")
Gewürztraminer (dry)	U.S., France (Alsace), Germany
Pinot Blanc	U.S., France (Alsace and Burgundy), Germany
Pinot Grigio	Italy
Dry, medium to full intensity	
Pinot Gris or Pinot Grigio	U.S., France (Alsace), Italy
Viognier	U.S., France (Condrieu)
Semillon (medium intensity, often oak-aged)	U.S., Australia, France (white Bordeaux)
Sauvignon/Fumé Blanc and Meritage (a wide range of styles, from light to medium intensity, often oak-aged)	U.S., France (Sancerre, Pouilly Fumé, white Bordeaux), South America, South Africa
Chardonnay (dry, light to full intensity, typically less fruit and oak flavors than U.S. or Australian versions)	France (White Burgundy: Chablis, Puligny or Chassagne Montrachet, Pouilly-Fuissé, Mâcon), South America, Italy, South Africa
Chardonnay (slightly sweet, very fruity, usually oak-aged)	U.S., Australia

WINE TYPE	DISTINCTIVE REGIONS OF PRODUCTION
Chardonnay (dry, medium to full intensity with lots of fruit and oak flavors)	U.S., Australia

Red Table Wines
Dry, light to medium intensity

Gamay, Gamay Beaujolais (mild and fruity to medium intensity with mild tannins)	U.S., France (Beaujolais)
Dolcetto (mild and fruity to medium intensity with mild tannins)	U.S., Italy
Pinot Noir (light to full intensity, fruity with mild to moderate tannins)	U.S., France (red Burgundy), Australia, Germany
Tempranillo (light to full intensity, fruity with mild to moderate tannins)	Spain
Sangiovese (light to full intensity, fruity with mild to moderate tannins)	U.S., Italy (Chianti—light to medium intensity; Brunello di Montalcino—full intensity and tannic)

Dry, medium to full intensity

Zinfandel (a full range of styles, from light to full intensity, fruity with mild to moderate tannins to strong tannins)	U.S.
Syrah, Shiraz and Petite Syrah	U.S., France (Rhône), Australia
Nebbiolo (medium to full intensity, moderate to strong tannins)	U.S., Italy (Barolo, Barbaresco)
Merlot (light to full intensity, mild to moderate tannins)	U.S., France (Bordeaux: St. Emilion, Pomerol, Médoc), Australia, Italy, South America
Meritage (medium to full intensity, moderate to strong tannins)	U.S.
Cabernet Sauvignon (medium to full intensity, moderate to strong tannins)	U.S., France (Bordeaux: Médoc), Australia, Italy, South America

Dessert Wines
Very sweet and intense

Riesling and Gewürztraminer	U.S., Germany (Beerenauslese, Trockenbeerenauslese, Eiswein), France (Alsace), Austria, Canada
Semillon, Sauvignon Blanc	U.S., France (Sauternes, Barsac, Monbaziallac) Australia

Fortified Wines

Sherry (sweet to dry as indicated)	U.S.
Sherry (sweet: oloroso; medium: amontillado; to very dry: fino)	Spain
Madeira (sweet: Malmsey; medium: Bual; to dry: Sercial)	Madeira
Marsala (both sweet and dry versions)	Italy
Port (full range from dry to sweet, mild to strong tannins)	Portugal
Port (sweet, full intensity, medium to strong tannins)	U.S., Australia

Party Beverages

Whether you keep things simple with two or three choices, or stock a full-service bar, drinks are an important part of the menu. If you serve alcoholic beverages, be sure to offer ample alcohol-free alternatives such as fruit juice, soft drinks and ice water. If you're offering coffee and tea, include decaffeinated versions, especially in the evening.

Tropical Fruit Rum Slush

PREP TIME: 20 MINUTES (READY IN 8 HOURS 40 MINUTES) ◆ YIELD: 24 (1-CUP) SERVINGS

    2 cups sugar
    3 cups water
    3 ripe bananas, mashed
    1 (12-oz.) can frozen tropical fruit drink
        concentrate, thawed
    3 cups pineapple juice
    ¼ cup lemon juice
    1 (1-liter) bottle rum
    3 (1-liter) bottles lemon-lime flavored
        carbonated beverage, chilled

1. In large saucepan, combine sugar and water; mix well. Bring to a boil. Boil 5 minutes. Cool.
2. In large nonmetal container, combine bananas, fruit drink concentrate, pineapple juice, lemon juice, rum and sugar mixture; mix well. Freeze at least 8 hours or overnight.
3. Twenty to 30 minutes before serving, remove frozen mixture from freezer; let stand at room temperature.

COOK'S NOTE

WARMING A PUNCH BOWL

Before filling a punch bowl with a hot beverage, "temper" the bowl by filling it with hot tap water. Let it stand for about 10 minutes. Drain when you are ready to transfer the hot punch to the warm bowl.

Tempering serves two purposes: it minimizes the risk of stress cracks from a hot liquid hitting cold glass, and it keeps the punch warm a bit longer.

You can temper teapots, coffee pots and mugs in the same way.

---

4. For each serving, spoon ½ cup slush mixture into glass. Add ½ cup carbonated beverage; stir gently. Serve immediately.

NUTRITION INFORMATION PER SERVING: Serving Size: 1 Cup ◆ Calories: 280 ◆ Calories from Fat: 0 ◆ % DAILY VALUE: Total Fat: 0 g 0% ◆ Saturated Fat: 0 g 0% ◆ Cholesterol: 0 mg 0% ◆ Sodium: 25 mg 1% ◆ Total Carbohydrate: 46 g 15% ◆ Dietary Fiber: 0 g 0% ◆ Sugars: 42 g ◆ Protein: 0 g ◆ Vitamin A: 0% ◆ Vitamin C: 30% ◆ Calcium: 0% ◆ Iron: 2% ◆ DIETARY EXCHANGES: 3 Fruit, 2 Fat OR 3 Carbohydrate, 2 Fat

Party Punch

PREP TIME: 10 MINUTES ◆ YIELD: 15 (½-CUP) SERVINGS

    1 (6-oz.) can frozen lemonade concentrate,
        thawed
    1 (6-oz.) can frozen orange juice concentrate,
        thawed
    2 cups white Catawba grape juice, chilled
    1 (1-liter) bottle (4¼ cups) lemon-lime
        flavored carbonated beverage, chilled
        Ice ring or ice mold, if desired

PUNCH FOR A BUNCH

NUMBER OF PEOPLE	BEFORE DINNER (FIGURING 2 TO 3 SERVINGS IN A 4-OZ. GLASS)	PARTY (FIGURING 4 TO 5 SERVINGS IN A 4-OZ GLASS, ASSUMING PUNCH IS THE MAIN BEVERAGE)
4	1 to 1½ quarts	2 to 2½ quarts
6	1½ to 2 quarts	3 to 4 quarts
8	2 to 3 quarts	1 to 1½ gallons
12	1 to 1½ gallons	1½ to 2 gallons
20	1½ to 2 gallons	2½ to 3 gallons
50	3 to 4½ gallons	6 to 7½ gallons

1. Just before serving, in punch bowl, combine lemonade and orange juice concentrates; blend well.

2. Add grape juice and carbonated beverage; stir gently. Place ice ring in bowl.

NUTRITION INFORMATION PER SERVING: Serving Size: ½ Cup • Calories: 100 • Calories from Fat: 0 • % DAILY VALUE: Total Fat: 0 g 0% • Saturated Fat: 0 g 0% • Cholesterol: 0 mg 0% • Sodium: 10 mg 0% • Total Carbohydrate: 25 g 8% • Dietary Fiber: 0 g 0% • Sugars: 23 g • Protein: 1 g • Vitamin A: 0% • Vitamin C: 35% • Calcium: 0% • Iron: 0% • DIETARY EXCHANGES: 1½ Fruit OR 1½ Carbohydrate

Cranberry-Raspberry Wine Coolers

PREP TIME: 20 MINUTES (READY IN 3 HOURS 50 MINUTES) ♦ YIELD: 12 (½-CUP) SERVINGS

  1 (10-oz.) pkg. frozen raspberries in syrup, thawed
  2 cups raspberry-cranberry juice drink blend, chilled
  3 cups white zinfandel wine, chilled
1½ cups lemon-lime flavored carbonated beverage, chilled
  12 fresh orange or star fruit slices

1. In medium bowl, combine raspberries and ½ cup of the raspberry-cranberry drink;

Cranberry-Raspberry Wine Coolers

MAKING AN ICE RING

Here's how to make a pretty ice ring for the punch bowl: Arrange fruit pieces in the bottom of a ring-shaped cake pan or decorative gelatin mold. Choose a combination of pineapple chunks, peach slices, mandarin orange segments, maraschino cherries and fresh or frozen berries. Add enough water (distilled water makes for a more clear ice ring) or fruit juice to partially cover the fruit and hold it in place. Freeze. Add more of the same liquid to fill the mold; freeze until firm. To loosen the ice ring, dip the mold briefly in hot water. Remove the ice ring and float it, fruit side up, in the punch bowl.

mix well. Spoon into 12 sections of ice cube tray. Freeze 3½ hours or until firm.

2. To serve, place 1 ice cube in each of 12 wine glasses. In large pitcher, combine remaining raspberry-cranberry drink, wine and carbonated beverage; stir gently. Pour into glasses. Garnish with orange slices.

NUTRITION INFORMATION PER SERVING: Serving Size: ½ Cup • Calories: 110 • Calories from Fat: 0 • % DAILY VALUE: Total Fat: 0 g 0% • Saturated Fat: 0 g 0% • Cholesterol: 0 mg 0% • Sodium: 5 mg 0% • Total Carbohydrate: 18 g 6% • Dietary Fiber: 1 g 4% • Sugars: 16 g • Protein: 0 g • Vitamin A: 0% • Vitamin C: 45% • Calcium: 0% • Iron: 2% • DIETARY EXCHANGES: 1 Fruit, 1 Fat OR 1 Carbohydrate, 1 Fat

Ultimate Chocolate Malt

PREP TIME: 5 MINUTES ♦ YIELD: 4 (1-CUP) SERVINGS

½ cup milk or chocolate milk
¼ cup chocolate-flavored syrup
¼ cup chocolate malted milk powder
  1 quart (4 cups) chocolate ice cream, softened

1. In blender container, combine milk, syrup and malted milk powder; cover and blend about 10 seconds.

2. Add ice cream; cover and blend until smooth. Pour into glasses. Serve immediately.

NUTRITION INFORMATION PER SERVING: Serving Size: 1 Cup • Calories: 370 • Calories from Fat: 140 • % DAILY VALUE: Total Fat: 16 g 25% • Saturated Fat: 10 g 50% • Cholesterol: 60 mg 20% • Sodium: 160 mg 7% • Total Carbohydrate: 50 g 17% • Dietary Fiber: 0 g 0% • Sugars: 38 g • Protein: 6 g • Vitamin A: 10% • Vitamin C: 2% • Calcium: 20% • Iron: 4% • DIETARY EXCHANGES: 2 Starch, 1½ Fruit, 3 Fat OR 3½ Carbohydrate, 3 Fat

Tips for Perfect Coffee

Start with clean equipment. Coffee gets its flavor from essential oils in the beans. These oils, however, can cause a stale flavor if they build up. Scrub all coffee equipment, especially metal pots and parts, in hot, soapy water after each use.

Use fresh coffee. Store whole beans and ground coffee in an airtight container in the refrigerator or freezer. Unopened cans of vacuum-packed coffee and jars of instant coffee will keep one year at room temperature in a cool, dry place. Once opened, coffee stays fresh for two to three weeks in a cool place, eight weeks in the refrigerator and six months in the freezer.

Use high-quality or gold filters for the best flavor. Poor-quality filters can add an "off" flavor.

Serve coffee immediately after brewing. Use an insulated carafe or jug rather than keeping the pot on a warmer.

BASIC COFFEE RECIPE

SERVINGS (¾ CUP EACH)	GROUND COFFEE	WATER
6	¼ to ½ cup	4½ cups
12	¾ to 1¼ cups (about ¼ lb.)	9 cups
25	2 to 2½ cups (about ½ lb.)	5 quarts
50	4 to 4½ cups (about 1 lb.)	10 quarts

Note: Plan for 1⅓ to 2 (¾-cup) servings per person. Serve with cream or milk and sugar.

Types of Tea

BLACK, GREEN AND OOLONG TEA

Tea varieties fall into three categories: black, green and oolong.

- ◆ Black teas have a rich aroma and amber color when brewed. Varieties include Ceylon, Darjeeling, English breakfast, Earl Grey (flavored with oil from the rind of bergamot, a citrus fruit) and Lapsang souchong. Varieties of black tea flavored with spices are increasingly available.
- ◆ Green teas, gaining popularity because of their reputed health benefits, have a slightly bitter flavor and pale green color when brewed.
- ◆ Oolong tea is a cross between black and green tea. Popular varieties include jasmine and Formosa oolong.

CHAI

In many languages around the world, *chai* simply means "tea." In Japanese culture, the centuries-old chai ceremony is as much about social ritual as it is about drinking hot tea.

In America, tea and beverage purveyors are beginning to stock "chai mixtures." These mixtures blend tea and spices, which are typically steeped in a mixture of hot milk and/or boiling water, then strained and sweetened to taste. Caffeine-free herbal versions are available, too.

HERBAL "TEAS"

True herbal teas are not made with tea leaves at all, but with a blend of herbs, spices and other aromatic ingredients. Many require longer steeping to fully develop the flavor. Herbal teas are usually caffeine-free, but some are mixed with regular tea leaves. Some also contain sugar.

Not every herbal tea is a good choice for people wishing to avoid caffeine. Pregnant or nursing women, in particular, should consult their physician about the ingredients in herbal teas.

Tips for Better Tea

Many tea purists insist on china pots and cups. Buy tea in small batches. Store it in a cool place in a tightly sealed container.

Tea bags tend to contain more powder than good-quality loose tea. Loose tea needs a little longer to brew, but the flavor is superior.

Start with cold, fresh water. The flavor of the water affects tea more than coffee, so you may wish to use bottled or filtered water if your tap water is heavily flavored.

Prewarm the teapot by filling it with hot tap water; empty it just before adding the dry tea and boiling water.

Use two or three tea bags or two to three teaspoons of loose tea per pot, depending on the size of the pot and how strong you like your tea. Put the tea in the pot and add water.

Remove the kettle from the heat just as the water comes to a full rolling boil. Pour immediately over the tea.

Let the tea steep until it reaches the desired strength; remove tea bags before serving. Do not squeeze the tea bags into the pot; squeezing releases tannin, which can make the brew bitter.

Keep the tea warm with a British-style cozy (an insulated or quilted fabric cover) or improvise by covering the pot with one or two kitchen towels.

Fruit Sangria

PREP TIME: 10 MINUTES ♦ YIELD: 10 (½-CUP) SERVINGS

2 cups dry red wine, chilled
2 cups orange juice
2 tablespoons lime juice
¼ cup sugar
1 cup club soda, chilled

1. In large nonmetal container or bowl, combine wine, orange juice, lime juice and sugar; stir until sugar is dissolved.
2. Just before serving, slowly add club soda, stirring gently to blend. Serve over ice.

NUTRITION INFORMATION PER SERVING: Serving Size: ½ Cup ♦ Calories: 70 ♦ Calories from Fat: 0 ♦ % DAILY VALUE: Total Fat: 0 g 0% ♦ Saturated Fat: 0 g 0% ♦ Cholesterol: 0 mg 0% ♦ Sodium: 10 mg 0% ♦ Total Carbohydrate: 11 g 4% ♦ Dietary Fiber: 0 g 0% ♦ Sugars: 11 g ♦ Protein: 0 g ♦ Vitamin A: 0% ♦ Vitamin C: 35% ♦ Calcium: 0% ♦ Iron: 0% ♦ DIETARY EXCHANGES: 1 Fruit OR 1 Carbohydrate

Strawberry Yogurt Smoothies

PREP TIME: 10 MINUTES ♦ YIELD: 4 (¾-CUP) SERVINGS

2 cups sliced fresh strawberries
1 medium peach or nectarine, pitted, cut into quarters
½ cup powdered sugar
½ cup nonfat vanilla yogurt
½ cup skim milk
¼ teaspoon cinnamon, if desired
2 teaspoons vanilla

In blender or food processor, combine all ingredients; blend until smooth. If necessary, add additional powdered sugar for desired sweetness. Serve immediately, or cover and refrigerate up to 24 hours. Blend before serving.

NUTRITION INFORMATION PER SERVING: Serving Size: ¾ Cup ♦ Calories: 130 ♦ Calories from Fat: 0 ♦ % DAILY VALUE: Total Fat: 0 g 0% ♦ Saturated Fat: 0 g 0% ♦ Cholesterol: 0 mg 0% ♦ Sodium: 35 mg 1% ♦ Total Carbohydrate: 29 g 10% ♦ Dietary Fiber: 2 g 8% ♦ Sugars: 26 g ♦ Protein: 3 g ♦ Vitamin A: 4% ♦ Vitamin C: 80% ♦ Calcium: 10% ♦ Iron: 2% ♦ DIETARY EXCHANGES: 1 Starch, 1 Fruit OR 2 Carbohydrate

Old-Fashioned Lemonade

PREP TIME: 25 MINUTES ♦ YIELD: 4 (1-CUP) SERVINGS

4 lemons
¾ cup sugar
4 cups cold water

1. Cut lemons into very thin slices; remove seeds. Place slices in large nonmetal bowl; sprinkle with sugar. Let stand 10 minutes.
2. Press lemons with back of spoon to extract juice. Add water, stirring and pressing lemons to extract juice. Remove lemon slices. Serve over ice. If desired, garnish with additional lemon slices.

NUTRITION INFORMATION PER SERVING: Serving Size: 1 Cup ♦ Calories: 170 ♦ Calories from Fat: 0 ♦ % DAILY VALUE: Total Fat: 0 g 0% ♦ Saturated Fat: 0 g 0% ♦ Cholesterol: 0 mg 0% ♦ Sodium: 0 mg 0% ♦ Total Carbohydrate: 43 g 14% ♦ Dietary Fiber: 2 g 8% ♦ Sugars: 39 g ♦ Protein: 1 g ♦ Vitamin A: 0% ♦ Vitamin C: 50% ♦ Calcium: 0% ♦ Iron: 2% ♦ DIETARY EXCHANGES: 3 Fruit OR 3 Carbohydrate

Sunrise Mimosas

PREP TIME: 10 MINUTES ♦ YIELD: 12 (¾-CUP) SERVINGS

1 (10-oz.) pkg. frozen strawberries in syrup, thawed, undrained
3 cups 100% tangerine juice (made from frozen concentrate)
2 (750 ml.) bottles champagne
6 strawberries with stems, halved, if desired

1. In blender container, puree strawberries.
2. In nonmetal pitcher, combine strawberry puree, tangerine juice and champagne; mix gently. Serve over ice in stemmed goblets. Garnish each goblet with strawberry half.

NUTRITION INFORMATION PER SERVING: Serving Size: ¾ Cup ♦ Calories: 140 ♦ Calories from Fat: 0 ♦ % DAILY VALUE: Total Fat: 0 g 0% ♦ Saturated Fat: 0 g 0% ♦ Cholesterol: 0 mg 0% ♦ Sodium: 0 mg 0% ♦ Total Carbohydrate: 16 g 5% ♦ Dietary Fiber: 1 g 2% ♦ Sugars: 12 g ♦ Protein: 0 g ♦ Vitamin A: 8% ♦ Vitamin C: 50% ♦ Calcium: 0% ♦ Iron: 0% ♦ DIETARY EXCHANGES: 1 Fruit, 1½ Fat OR 1 Carbohydrate, 1½ Fat

Rich and Creamy Eggnog

PREP TIME: 10 MINUTES (READY IN 1 HOUR 10 MINUTES) ◆ YIELD: 10 (½-CUP) SERVINGS

　4 cups milk
　1 (3.4-oz.) pkg. instant vanilla pudding and pie filling mix
　1 (8-oz.) carton (1 cup) refrigerated or frozen fat-free egg product, thawed
　1 teaspoon vanilla
　1 teaspoon rum extract or ¼ cup light rum
　¼ teaspoon salt
　¼ teaspoon nutmeg
　　Whipped cream, if desired
　　Nutmeg, if desired

1. In large bowl, combine 2 cups of the milk and pudding mix; beat 1 minute or until smooth.
2. Add remaining 2 cups milk, egg product, vanilla, rum extract, salt and ¼ teaspoon nutmeg; beat well. Cover; refrigerate at least 1 hour before serving. Serve topped with whipped cream and a sprinkle of nutmeg.

NUTRITION INFORMATION PER SERVING: Serving Size: ½ Cup ◆ Calories: 130 ◆ Calories from Fat: 45 ◆ **% DAILY VALUE:** Total Fat: 5 g 8% ◆ Saturated Fat: 3 g 15% ◆ Cholesterol: 20 mg 7% ◆ Sodium: 280 mg 12% ◆ Total Carbohydrate: 16 g 5% ◆ Dietary Fiber: 0 g 0% ◆ Sugars: 14 g ◆ Protein: 6 g ◆ Vitamin A: 8% ◆ Vitamin C: 0% ◆ Calcium: 15% ◆ Iron: 2% ◆ **DIETARY EXCHANGES:** ½ Starch, ½ Low-Fat Milk, ½ Fat OR 1 Carbohydrate, ½ Fat

Rich and Creamy Eggnog

Hot Cocoa

PREP TIME: 10 MINUTES ◆ YIELD: 4 (1-CUP) SERVINGS

　⅓ cup sugar
　3 tablespoons unsweetened cocoa
　　Dash salt
　½ cup hot water
　3 cups milk
　¼ cup miniature marshmallows, if desired

1. In medium saucepan, combine sugar, cocoa, salt and water; mix well. Bring to a boil. Reduce heat to low; simmer 2 minutes, stirring occasionally.
2. Add milk; cook until thoroughly heated. DO NOT BOIL.
3. Just before serving, beat until frothy with wire whisk. Top each serving with marshmallows.

NUTRITION INFORMATION PER SERVING: Serving Size: 1 Cup ◆ Calories: 180 ◆ Calories from Fat: 35 ◆ **% DAILY VALUE:** Total Fat: 4 g 6% ◆ Saturated Fat: 3 g 15% ◆ Cholesterol: 15 mg 5% ◆ Sodium: 125 mg 5% ◆ Total Carbohydrate: 30 g 10% ◆ Dietary Fiber: 1 g 4% ◆ Sugars: 27 g ◆ Protein: 7 g ◆ Vitamin A: 8% ◆ Vitamin C: 2% ◆ Calcium: 25% ◆ Iron: 4% ◆ **DIETARY EXCHANGES:** 1 Fruit, 1 Low-Fat Milk OR 2 Carbohydrate

New England Mulled Cider

PREP TIME: 10 MINUTES (READY IN 40 MINUTES) ◆ YIELD: 8 (1-CUP) SERVINGS

　2 quarts (8 cups) apple cider
　¼ cup firmly packed brown sugar
　½ teaspoon cardamom
　½ teaspoon nutmeg
　2 cinnamon sticks
　　Peel from 1 orange

1. In large saucepan, combine all ingredients; mix well. Bring to a boil. Reduce heat; simmer 30 minutes.
2. Remove cinnamon sticks and orange peel. Keep warm in hot pot or coffee pot.

NUTRITION INFORMATION PER SERVING: Serving Size: 1 Cup ◆ Calories: 140 ◆ Calories from Fat: 0 ◆ **% DAILY VALUE:** Total Fat: 0 g 0% ◆ Saturated Fat: 0 g 0% ◆ Cholesterol: 0 mg 0% ◆ Sodium: 10 mg 0% ◆ Total Carbohydrate: 36 g 12% ◆ Dietary Fiber: 0 g 0% ◆ Sugars: 31 g ◆ Protein: 0 g ◆ Vitamin A: 0% ◆ Vitamin C: 2% ◆ Calcium: 2% ◆ Iron: 6% ◆ **DIETARY EXCHANGES:** 2½ Fruit OR 2½ Carbohydrate

BREADS, SOUPS
& STEWS

BREADS, SOUPS & STEWS

ragrant breads and flavorful soups and stews offer homestyle comfort for any occasion. In this chapter, you'll find a bread for every meal, mood and menu, plus soups and stews as elegant as vichyssoise and as simple as chicken soup.

Muffin Tips

Like other quick breads, muffins do best with a light touch. Mix muffin batter gently, stir only enough to moisten the dry ingredients—to keep the muffins tender and to avoid the "peaked" shape.

Most muffins, especially reduced-fat versions, are best served warm from the oven. Reheating briefly in the oven or microwave can revive flavor and texture.

Lightly spray paper muffin cups with nonstick cooking spray to prevent muffins from sticking to the paper.

COOK'S NOTE

HOW TO PREPARE MUFFINS

For tender, moist muffins, combine the dry ingredients and additions such as blueberries by stirring them together in a large bowl. Push the flour mixture up the sides of the bowl to make a well. Combine the liquid ingredients and pour them all at once into the well.

Stir to moisten dry ingredients, counting 12 to 15 strokes. Batter will remain lumpy.

Muffin cups can be lightly greased or lined with paper baking cups. Fill each cup ²/₃ full with batter for pebbly-topped, rounded muffins.

Muffins

PREP TIME: 10 MINUTES (READY IN 40 MINUTES)
◆ YIELD: 12 MUFFINS

  2 cups all-purpose flour
  ½ cup sugar
  3 teaspoons baking powder
  ½ teaspoon salt
  ¾ cup milk
  ⅓ cup oil
  1 egg

1. Heat oven to 400°F. Grease bottoms only of 12 muffin cups or line with paper baking cups. In medium bowl, combine flour, sugar, baking powder and salt; mix well.

2. In small bowl, combine milk, oil and egg; beat well. Add to flour mixture all at once; stir just until dry ingredients are moistened. (Batter will be lumpy.) Divide batter evenly into greased muffin cups.

3. Bake at 400°F. for 20 to 25 minutes or until toothpick inserted in center comes out clean. Cool 1 minute; remove from pan. Serve warm.

HIGH ALTITUDE (above 3500 feet)**:** No change.

NUTRITION INFORMATION PER SERVING: Serving Size: 1 Muffin ◆ Calories: 180 ◆ Calories from Fat: 60 ◆ **% DAILY VALUE:** Total Fat: 7 g 11% ◆ Saturated Fat: 1 g 5% ◆ Cholesterol: 20 mg 7% ◆ Sodium: 220 mg 9% ◆ Total Carbohydrate: 25 g 8% ◆ Dietary Fiber: 1 g 2% ◆ Sugars: 9 g ◆ Protein: 3 g ◆ Vitamin A: 0% ◆ Vitamin C: 0% ◆ Calcium: 10% ◆ Iron: 6% ◆ **DIETARY EXCHANGES:** 1 Starch, ½ Fruit, 1½ Fat OR 1½ Carbohydrate, 1½ Fat

VARIATIONS

Apple Muffins: Decrease sugar to ¼ cup; add 1 teaspoon cinnamon to flour. Stir 1 cup finely chopped, peeled apple into dry ingredients. Substitute apple juice for milk. Bake at 400°F. for 18 to 22 minutes.
Blueberry Muffins: Stir 1 cup fresh or frozen blueberries (do not thaw) and 1 teaspoon grated lemon or orange peel into dry ingredients.
Chocolate Chip Muffins: Add ¾ cup miniature chocolate chips with flour. Before baking, sprinkle batter in cups with

a combination of 3 tablespoons sugar and 2 tablespoons brown sugar.

Jam Muffins: Place ½ teaspoon any flavor jam on each muffin before baking; press into batter. If desired, sprinkle with finely chopped nuts.

Lemon Muffins: Add 1 tablespoon grated lemon peel with flour.

Orange Muffins: Add 1 tablespoon grated orange peel with flour; substitute orange juice for milk.

Streusel-Topped Muffins: In small bowl, combine ¼ cup firmly packed brown sugar, 1 tablespoon margarine or butter, softened, ½ teaspoon cinnamon and ¼ cup chopped nuts or flaked coconut; stir with fork until crumbly. Sprinkle over muffins before baking.

Sugar-Coated Muffins: After baking, brush tops of hot muffins with 2 tablespoons melted margarine or butter; dip in mixture of ¼ cup sugar and ½ teaspoon cinnamon.

Whole Wheat Muffins: Use 1 cup all-purpose flour and 1 cup whole wheat flour.

Basic Corn Muffins

PREP TIME: 10 MINUTES (READY IN 35 MINUTES)
♦ YIELD: 12 MUFFINS

1½ cups all-purpose flour
½ cup cornmeal
2 tablespoons sugar
3 teaspoons baking powder
¼ teaspoon salt
1 (7-oz.) can vacuum-packed whole kernel corn, well drained
1 cup milk
3 tablespoons oil
1 egg

1. Heat oven to 400°F. Line 12 muffin cups with paper baking cups. In medium bowl, combine flour, cornmeal, sugar, baking powder and salt; mix well. Stir in corn.

2. In small bowl, combine milk, oil and egg; blend well. Add to flour mixture; stir just until dry ingredients are moistened. Divide batter evenly into paper-lined muffin cups.

3. Bake at 400°F. for 18 to 23 minutes or until golden brown. Cool 1 minute; remove from pan. Serve warm.

HIGH ALTITUDE *(above 3500 feet)*: No change.

NUTRITION INFORMATION PER SERVING: Serving Size: 1 Muffin ♦ Calories: 150 ♦ Calories from Fat: 45 ♦ **% DAILY VALUE:** Total Fat: 5 g 8% ♦ Saturated Fat: 1 g 5% ♦ Cholesterol: 20 mg 7% ♦ Sodium: 210 mg 9% ♦ Total Carbohydrate: 21 g 7% ♦ Dietary Fiber: 1 g 4% ♦ Sugars: 4 g ♦ Protein: 4 g ♦ Vitamin A: 2% ♦ Vitamin C: 0% ♦ Calcium: 10% ♦ Iron: 6% ♦ **DIETARY EXCHANGES:** 1½ Starch, 1 Fat OR 1½ Carbohydrate, 1 Fat

Bran Muffins

PREP TIME: 30 MINUTES ♦ YIELD: 30 MUFFINS

2 cups shreds of whole bran cereal
2½ cups buttermilk
½ cup oil
2 eggs
2½ cups all-purpose flour
1½ cups sugar
1¼ teaspoons baking soda
1 teaspoon baking powder
½ teaspoon salt
¾ cup raisins, if desired

1. In large bowl, combine cereal and buttermilk; mix well. Let stand 5 minutes until cereal is softened. Add oil and eggs; blend well.

2. Add all remaining ingredients; mix well. Batter can be baked immediately or stored in tightly covered container in refrigerator for up to 2 weeks.

3. When ready to bake, heat oven to 400°F. Grease desired number of muffin cups or line with paper baking cups. Stir batter; fill greased muffin cups ¾ full.

4. Bake at 400°F. for 18 to 20 minutes or until toothpick inserted in center comes out clean. Immediately remove from pan. Serve warm.

HIGH ALTITUDE *(above 3500 feet)*: Increase flour to 2¾ cups; decrease sugar to 1¼ cups. Bake as directed above.

NUTRITION INFORMATION PER SERVING: Serving Size: 1 Muffin ♦ Calories: 150 ♦ Calories from Fat: 35 ♦ **% DAILY VALUE:** Total Fat: 4 g 6% ♦ Saturated Fat: 1 g 5% ♦ Cholesterol: 15 mg 5% ♦ Sodium: 140 mg 6% ♦ Total Carbohydrate: 26 g 9% ♦ Dietary Fiber: 2 g 8% ♦ Sugars: 14 g ♦ Protein: 3 g ♦ Vitamin A: 4% ♦ Vitamin C: 4% ♦ Calcium: 6% ♦ Iron: 8% ♦ **DIETARY EXCHANGES:** 1 Starch, ½ Fruit, ½ Fat OR 1½ Carbohydrate, ½ Fat

Banana-Chocolate Chip Muffins

PREP TIME: 15 MINUTES (READY IN 45 MINUTES)
◆ YIELD: 18 MUFFINS

½ cup margarine or butter, softened
½ cup firmly packed brown sugar
1½ cups (3 large) mashed ripe bananas
¼ cup milk
1 teaspoon vanilla
2 eggs
2 cups all-purpose flour
1 teaspoon baking powder
1 teaspoon baking soda
¼ teaspoon salt
½ cup miniature chocolate chips
½ cup chopped walnuts

1. Heat oven to 375°F. Grease bottoms only of 18 muffin cups or line with paper baking cups. In large bowl, combine margarine and brown sugar; beat until fluffy. Add bananas, milk, vanilla and eggs; blend well.
2. Add flour, baking powder, baking soda and salt; stir just until dry ingredients are moistened. Stir in chocolate chips and walnuts. Fill greased muffin cups ⅔ full.
3. Bake at 375°F. for 20 to 25 minutes or until toothpick inserted in center comes out clean. Cool 3 minutes; remove from pan. Serve warm.

HIGH ALTITUDE (*above 3500 feet*): Decrease baking soda to ½ teaspoon. Bake at 400°F. for 20 to 25 minutes.

NUTRITION INFORMATION PER SERVING: Serving Size: 1 Muffin ◆ Calories: 190 ◆ Calories from Fat: 80 ◆ **% DAILY VALUE:** Total Fat: 9 g 14% ◆ Saturated Fat: 2 g 10% ◆ Cholesterol: 25 mg 8% ◆ Sodium: 200 mg 8% ◆ Total Carbohydrate: 23 g 8% ◆ Dietary Fiber: 1 g 4% ◆ Sugars: 11 g ◆ Protein: 3 g ◆ Vitamin A: 6% ◆ Vitamin C: 0% ◆ Calcium: 4% ◆ Iron: 6% ◆ **DIETARY EXCHANGES:** 1 Starch, ½ Fruit, 1½ Fat OR 1½ Carbohydrate, 1½ Fat

Almond Streusel Mini-Muffins

PREP TIME: 30 MINUTES ◆ YIELD: 36 MINI-MUFFINS

TOPPING
¼ cup sugar
¼ cup finely chopped blanched almonds
2 tablespoons all-purpose flour
2 tablespoons margarine or butter

MUFFINS
2 cups all-purpose flour
½ cup sugar

3 teaspoons baking powder
¼ teaspoon nutmeg
⅛ teaspoon salt
1 egg
¾ cup milk
⅓ cup oil
½ teaspoon almond extract

1. Heat oven to 400°F. Spray 36 miniature muffin cups with nonstick cooking spray. In small bowl, combine all topping ingredients; mix well. Set aside.
2. In medium bowl, combine 2 cups flour, ½ cup sugar, baking powder, nutmeg and salt; mix well. In another small bowl, beat egg slightly. Add milk, oil and almond extract; beat well. Add all at once to flour mixture; stir just until dry ingredients are moistened. Divide batter evenly into sprayed muffin cups. Sprinkle topping evenly over batter in cups.*
3. Bake at 400°F. for 10 to 15 minutes or until toothpick inserted in center comes out clean. Immediately remove from pan. Serve warm or cool.

> **TIP:** * If necessary to bake muffins in batches, batter can be held at room temperature for 30 minutes.

HIGH ALTITUDE (*above 3500 feet*): Decrease baking powder to 2 teaspoons. Bake as directed above.

NUTRITION INFORMATION PER SERVING: Serving Size: 1 Mini-Muffin ◆ Calories: 70 ◆ Calories from Fat: 25 ◆ **% DAILY VALUE:** Total Fat: 3 g 5% ◆ Saturated Fat: 1 g 5% ◆ Cholesterol: 5 mg 2% ◆ Sodium: 60 mg 3% ◆ Total Carbohydrate: 10 g 3% ◆ Dietary Fiber: 0 g 0% ◆ Sugars: 5 g ◆ Protein: 1 g ◆ Vitamin A: 0% ◆ Vitamin C: 0% ◆ Calcium: 4% ◆ Iron: 2% ◆ **DIETARY EXCHANGES:** ½ Starch, ½ Fat OR ½ Carbohydrate, ½ Fat

Baking Powder Biscuits

PREP TIME: 30 MINUTES ◆ YIELD: 14 BISCUITS

2 cups all-purpose flour
3 teaspoons baking powder
½ teaspoon salt
½ cup shortening
¾ to 1 cup milk

1. Heat oven to 450°F. In large bowl, combine flour, baking powder and salt; mix well. With pastry blender or fork, cut in shortening until mixture resembles coarse crumbs. Stirring with fork, add enough milk until mixture leaves sides of bowl and forms a soft, moist dough.

Baking Powder Biscuits (page 32)

2. On floured surface, toss dough lightly until no longer sticky. Roll or press dough to ½-inch thickness. Cut with floured 2-inch round cutter. Place on ungreased cookie sheet.

3. Bake at 450°F. for 8 to 12 minutes or until light golden brown. Serve warm.

1. FOOD PROCESSOR DIRECTIONS: In food processor bowl with metal blade, combine flour, baking powder and salt; process with 5 on/off pulses to mix. Add shortening to flour mixture; process until mixture resembles coarse crumbs. Add ½ to ⅔ cup milk; process with on/off pulses *just* until ball starts to form.

2. On lightly floured surface, roll or press dough to ½-inch thickness. Cut with floured 2-inch round cutter. Continue as directed above.

HIGH ALTITUDE (*above 3500 feet*): No change.

NUTRITION INFORMATION PER SERVING: Serving Size: 1 Biscuit ♦ Calories: 140 ♦ Calories from Fat: 70 ♦ **% DAILY VALUE:** Total Fat: 8 g 12% ♦ Saturated Fat: 2 g 10% ♦ Cholesterol: 0 mg 0% ♦ Sodium: 190 mg 8% ♦ Total Carbohydrate: 15 g 5% ♦ Dietary Fiber: 0 g 0% ♦ Sugars: 1 g ♦ Protein: 2 g ♦ Vitamin A: 0% ♦ Vitamin C: 0% ♦ Calcium: 8% ♦ Iron: 6% ♦ **DIETARY EXCHANGES:** 1 Starch, 1½ Fat OR 1 Carbohydrate, 1½ Fat

VARIATIONS

Buttermilk Biscuits: Add ¼ teaspoon baking soda to flour. Substitute buttermilk for milk.

Cheese Biscuits: Add 4 oz. (1 cup) shredded Cheddar cheese to flour-shortening mixture. Bake on *greased* cookie sheet.

Drop Biscuits: Increase milk to 1¼ cups. Drop dough by spoonfuls onto *greased* cookie sheets.

Soft-Sided Biscuits: Place biscuits in 9-inch round or square pan or on cookie sheet with sides touching. Bake at 450°F. for 12 to 14 minutes.

Southern-Style Biscuits: Decrease shortening to ¼ cup.

Thin-Crispy Biscuits: Roll dough to ¼-inch thickness. Cut biscuits with floured 3-inch round cutter.

Sour Cream Drop Biscuits

PREP TIME: 25 MINUTES ♦ YIELD: 12 BISCUITS

  2 cups all-purpose flour
  1 tablespoon sugar
  3 teaspoons baking powder
  ½ teaspoon salt
  ¼ cup shortening
  ⅔ cup milk
  ⅔ cup sour cream

1. Heat oven to 450°F. Grease cookie sheet. In medium bowl, combine flour, sugar, baking powder and salt; mix well. With pastry blender or fork, cut in shortening until mixture is crumbly.

2. In small bowl, combine milk and sour cream; blend well. Add all at once to flour mixture; stir just until dry ingredients are moistened. Drop dough by tablespoonfuls onto greased cookie sheet.

3. Bake at 450°F. for 10 to 12 minutes or until golden brown. Serve warm.

HIGH ALTITUDE (*above 3500 feet*): No change.

NUTRITION INFORMATION PER SERVING: Serving Size: 1 Biscuit ♦ Calories: 150 ♦ Calories from Fat: 60 ♦ **% DAILY VALUE:** Total Fat: 7 g 11% ♦ Saturated Fat: 3 g 15% ♦ Cholesterol: 5 mg 2% ♦ Sodium: 230 mg 10% ♦ Total Carbohydrate: 18 g 6% ♦ Dietary Fiber: 1 g 2% ♦ Sugars: 3 g ♦ Protein: 3 g ♦ Vitamin A: 2% ♦ Vitamin C: 0% ♦ Calcium: 10% ♦ Iron: 6% ♦ **DIETARY EXCHANGES:** 1 Starch, 1½ Fat OR 1 Carbohydrate, 1½ Fat

C O O K ' S   N O T E

HOW TO PREPARE BAKING POWDER BISCUITS

Using a fork or pastry blender, cut shortening into flour until it's the consistency of coarse meal. Add milk; stir with a fork until the mixture leaves the sides of the bowl and forms a soft, moist dough.

  Roll out dough until ½ inch thick; cut with a 2-inch floured cutter.

BISCUIT TIPS

Treat your biscuits gently; overhandling can toughen the dough. The amount of liquid you need varies slightly depending on the moisture content of the flour, which in turn depends on environment and weather. Add the liquid a little at a time, gently stirring all the while with a fork. When the mixture no longer sticks to the sides of the bowl and forms a soft dough, you have added enough liquid.

Turn the dough onto a floured work surface and knead gently about 10 times, or just enough to smooth the dough slightly and remove any stickiness.

Cut the dough with a sharp knife or biscuit cutter dipped in flour; the traditional drinking-glass method can squash the sides and prevent proper rising.

Scottish Scones

PREP TIME: 15 MINUTES (READY IN 45 MINUTES) ◆ YIELD: 8 SCONES

SCONES

1½ cups all-purpose flour
¾ cup rolled oats
¼ cup firmly packed brown sugar
2 teaspoons baking powder
½ teaspoon salt
½ teaspoon cinnamon
½ cup margarine or butter
½ cup milk

TOPPING

1 tablespoon margarine or butter, melted
1 tablespoon sugar
¼ teaspoon cinnamon

1. Heat oven to 375°F. Lightly grease cookie sheet. In medium bowl, combine flour, oats, brown sugar, baking powder, salt and ½ teaspoon cinnamon; mix well. With pastry blender or fork, cut in ½ cup margarine until mixture is crumbly. Add milk all at once; stir just until dry ingredients are moistened.
2. On floured surface, gently knead dough 5 or 6 times. Place on greased cookie sheet; press into 6-inch round, about 1 inch thick. Brush top with melted margarine.
3. In small bowl, combine sugar and ¼ tea-

spoon cinnamon; mix well. Sprinkle over top. Cut into 8 wedges; separate slightly.
4. Bake at 375°F. for 20 to 30 minutes or until golden brown. Cut into wedges. Serve warm.

HIGH ALTITUDE *(above 3500 feet)*: No change.

NUTRITION INFORMATION PER SERVING: Serving Size: 1 Scone ◆ Calories: 270 ◆ Calories from Fat: 130 ◆ **% DAILY VALUE:** Total Fat: 14 g 22% ◆ Saturated Fat: 3 g 15% ◆ Cholesterol: 0 mg 0% ◆ Sodium: 420 mg 18% ◆ Total Carbohydrate: 33 g 11% ◆ Dietary Fiber: 2 g 8% ◆ Sugars: 10 g ◆ Protein: 4 g ◆ Vitamin A: 10% ◆ Vitamin C: 0% ◆ Calcium: 10% ◆ Iron: 10% ◆ **DIETARY EXCHANGES:** 1½ Starch, ½ Fruit, 2½ Fat OR 2 Carbohydrate, 2½ Fat

Banana Bread

PREP TIME: 15 MINUTES (READY IN 2 HOURS 20 MINUTES) ◆ YIELD: 1 (16-SLICE) LOAF

¾ cup sugar
½ cup margarine or butter, softened
2 eggs
1 cup (2 medium) mashed ripe bananas
⅓ cup milk
1 teaspoon vanilla
2 cups all-purpose flour
½ cup chopped nuts, if desired
1 teaspoon baking soda
½ teaspoon salt

1. Heat oven to 350°F. Grease bottom only of 9×5 or 8×4-inch loaf pan. In large bowl, combine sugar and margarine; beat until light and fluffy. Add eggs; beat well. Add bananas, milk and vanilla; blend well.
2. In small bowl, combine flour, nuts, baking soda and salt; mix well. Add to banana mixture; stir just until dry ingredients are moistened. Pour into greased pan.
3. Bake at 350°F. for 50 to 60 minutes or until toothpick inserted in center comes out clean. Cool 5 minutes; remove from pan. Cool 1 hour or until completely cooled. Wrap tightly and store in refrigerator.

HIGH ALTITUDE *(above 3500 feet)*: Increase flour to 2 cups plus 1 tablespoon. Bake at 375°F. for 45 to 55 minutes.

NUTRITION INFORMATION PER SERVING: Serving Size: 1 Slice ◆ Calories: 190 ◆ Calories from Fat: 80 ◆ **% DAILY VALUE:** Total Fat: 9 g 14% ◆ Saturated Fat: 2 g 10% ◆ Cholesterol: 25 mg 8% ◆ Sodium: 220 mg 9% ◆ Total Carbohydrate: 25 g 8% ◆ Dietary Fiber: 1 g 3% ◆ Sugars: 11 g ◆ Protein: 3 g ◆ Vitamin A: 6% ◆ Vitamin C: 0% ◆ Calcium: 0% ◆ Iron: 6% ◆ **DIETARY EXCHANGES:** 1 Starch, ½ Fruit, 1½ Fat OR 1½ Carbohydrate, 1½ Fat

VARIATION

Applesauce Bread: Substitute 1 cup applesauce for mashed bananas and add ¾ teaspoon cinnamon with flour.

Apple Cinnamon Cream Cheese Swirl Loaf

PREP TIME: 15 MINUTES (READY IN 2 HOURS 45 MINUTES) ✦ YIELD: 1 (16-SLICE) LOAF

FILLING
  2 (3-oz.) pkg. cream cheese, softened
  ¼ cup sugar
  1 egg

BREAD
  1 (15.6-oz.) pkg. apple cinnamon or cranberry quick bread mix
  ¾ cup water
  2 tablespoons oil
  1 egg

1. Heat oven to 350°F. Generously grease bottom only of 8×4 or 9×5-inch loaf pan. In small bowl, combine all filling ingredients; beat at medium speed until smooth, about 1 minute. Set aside.
2. In large bowl, combine all bread ingredients; stir 50 to 75 strokes with spoon until mix is moistened. Pour half of batter into greased pan; pour filling over batter, spreading to cover. Pour remaining batter over filling. To marble, pull knife through batter in wide curves; turn pan and repeat.
3. Bake at 350°F. for 65 to 75 minutes or until toothpick inserted in center comes out clean. Cool 15 minutes; remove from pan. Cool 1 hour or until completely cooled before slicing. Wrap tightly and store in refrigerator.

HIGH ALTITUDE (*above 3500 feet*)**:** Add 2 table-spoons flour to dry bread mix. Bake at 375°F. for 55 to 65 minutes.

NUTRITION INFORMATION PER SERVING: Serving Size: 1 Slice ✦ Calories: 180 ✦ Calories from Fat: 60 ✦ **% DAILY VALUE:** Total Fat: 7 g 11% ✦ Saturated Fat: 3 g 15% ✦ Cholesterol: 40 mg 13% ✦ Sodium: 160 mg 7% ✦ Total Carbohydrate: 27 g 9% ✦ Dietary Fiber: 1 g 3% ✦ Sugars: 16 g ✦ Protein: 3 g ✦ Vitamin A: 4% ✦ Vitamin C: 0% ✦ Calcium: 2% ✦ Iron: 6% ✦ **DIETARY EXCHANGES:** 1 Starch, 1 Fruit, 1 Fat OR 2 Carbohydrate, 1 Fat

Nut Bread

PREP TIME: 15 MINUTES (READY IN 2 HOURS 35 MINUTES) ✦ YIELD: 1 (16-SLICE) LOAF

  ¾ cup sugar
  ½ cup margarine or butter, softened
  1 cup buttermilk
  2 eggs
  2 cups all-purpose flour
  1 cup chopped nuts
  ½ teaspoon baking powder
  ½ teaspoon baking soda
  ½ teaspoon salt

1. Heat oven to 350°F. Grease bottom only of 9×5 or 8×4-inch loaf pan. In large bowl, combine sugar and margarine; beat until light and fluffy. Add buttermilk and eggs; blend well.
2. In small bowl, combine all remaining ingredients; mix well. Add to buttermilk mixture; stir just until dry ingredients are moistened. Pour into greased pan.
3. Bake at 350°F. for 55 to 65 minutes or until toothpick inserted in center comes out clean. Cool 15 minutes; remove from pan. Cool 1 hour or until completely cooled. Wrap tightly and store in refrigerator.

HIGH ALTITUDE (*above 3500 feet*)**:** Increase flour to 2 cups plus 1 tablespoon. Bake at 375°F. for 50 to 60 minutes.

NUTRITION INFORMATION PER SERVING: Serving Size: 1 Slice ✦ Calories: 210 ✦ Calories from Fat: 100 ✦ **% DAILY VALUE:** Total Fat: 11 g 17% ✦ Saturated Fat: 2 g 10% ✦ Cholesterol: 25 mg 8% ✦ Sodium: 210 mg 9% ✦ Total Carbohydrate: 24 g 8% ✦ Dietary Fiber: 1 g 3% ✦ Sugars: 10 g ✦ Protein: 4 g ✦ Vitamin A: 6% ✦ Vitamin C: 0% ✦ Calcium: 4% ✦ Iron: 6% ✦ **DIETARY EXCHANGES:** 1½ Starch, 2 Fat OR 1½ Carbohydrate, 2 Fat

VARIATIONS

Date Bread: Substitute brown sugar for sugar; decrease nuts to ½ cup. Stir in 1 cup chopped dates and 1 teaspoon grated orange peel after flour addition.

Streusel Bread: For filling, combine ½ cup firmly packed brown sugar, ½ cup chopped walnuts, 1 teaspoon cinnamon and 1 table-spoon margarine or butter, melted; mix well. For batter, substitute brown sugar for sugar; decrease nuts to ½ cup. Spread half of batter in greased and floured 9×5-inch loaf pan. Spoon filling down center of batter; spread to within ½ inch of sides. Carefully spoon remaining batter over filling, spreading gently to cover. Bake at 350°F. for 50 to 55 minutes.

Classic Cornbread

PREP TIME: 10 MINUTES (READY IN 35 MINUTES)
◆ YIELD: 9 SERVINGS

  1 cup all-purpose flour
  1 cup cornmeal
  2 tablespoons sugar
  3 teaspoons baking powder
  ½ teaspoon salt
  1 cup milk
  ¼ cup oil or melted shortening
  1 egg, slightly beaten

1. Heat oven to 425°F. Grease 8 or 9-inch square pan. In medium bowl, combine flour, cornmeal, sugar, baking powder and salt; mix well. Stir in all remaining ingredients just until smooth. Pour batter into greased pan.
2. Bake at 425°F. for 18 to 22 minutes or until toothpick inserted in center comes out clean. Cut into squares. Serve warm.

HIGH ALTITUDE (*above 3500 feet*): Decrease baking powder to 2 teaspoons. Bake as directed above.

NUTRITION INFORMATION PER SERVING: Serving Size: ⅑ of Recipe ◆ Calories: 190 ◆ Calories from Fat: 70 ◆ **% DAILY VALUE:** Total Fat: 8 g 12% ◆ Saturated Fat: 1 g 5% ◆ Cholesterol: 25 mg 8% ◆ Sodium: 310 mg 13% ◆ Total Carbohydrate: 26 g 9% ◆ Dietary Fiber: 1 g 4% ◆ Sugars: 5 g ◆ Protein: 4 g ◆ Vitamin A: 4% ◆ Vitamin C: 0% ◆ Calcium: 15% ◆ Iron: 8% ◆ **DIETARY EXCHANGES:** 1½ Starch, 1½ Fat OR 1½ Carbohydrate, 1½ Fat

VARIATIONS

Bacon Cornbread: Cook 4 to 5 slices bacon until crisp; drain on paper towel. Substitute bacon drippings for oil. Sprinkle batter with crumbled bacon before baking.
Corn Muffins: Spoon batter into greased muffin cups. Bake 15 to 20 minutes. Immediately remove from muffin cups.
YIELD: 12 MUFFINS
Corn Sticks: Spoon batter into well-greased, hot corn stick pan, filling ⅔ full. Bake 12 to 15 minutes. Immediately remove from pan. YIELD: 18 CORN STICKS
Cornbread Ring: Spoon batter into greased 1½-quart (6-cup) ring mold. Bake 15 to 20 minutes. Immediately remove from mold.
Mexican Cornbread: Prepare batter using 2 eggs, slightly beaten. Stir in 2 oz. (½ cup) shredded Cheddar cheese, ¼ cup chopped green chiles and ¼ cup finely chopped onion. Bake 20 to 25 minutes.

Brown Bread

PREP TIME: 20 MINUTES (READY IN 2 HOURS 20 MINUTES) ◆ YIELD: 2 (16-SLICE) LOAVES

  2 cups raisins
    Boiling water
  ½ cup firmly packed brown sugar
  ¼ cup margarine or butter, softened
  1 cup cornmeal
  ½ cup molasses
  2 cups buttermilk
  1 egg
  3 cups all-purpose flour
  2 teaspoons baking soda

1. Heat oven to 350°F. Grease and flour bottoms only of two 1-quart casseroles or two 8 × 4-inch loaf pans. In small bowl, cover raisins with boiling water; let stand 5 minutes. Drain.
2. In large bowl, combine brown sugar and margarine; beat until light and fluffy. Add cornmeal, molasses, buttermilk and egg; blend well. Stir in flour and baking soda until well mixed. Fold in raisins. Pour batter into greased and floured casseroles.

Brown Bread

3. Bake at 350°F. for 40 to 50 minutes or until toothpick inserted in center comes out clean. Cool 10 minutes; remove from casseroles. Cool 1 hour or until completely cooled. Wrap tightly and store in refrigerator.

HIGH ALTITUDE (*above 3500 feet*)**:** No change.

NUTRITION INFORMATION PER SERVING: Serving Size: 1 Slice ◆ Calories: 140 ◆ Calories from Fat: 20 ◆ **% DAILY VALUE:** Total Fat: 2 g 3% ◆ Saturated Fat: 0 g 0% ◆ Cholesterol: 5 mg 2% ◆ Sodium: 120 mg 5% ◆ Total Carbohydrate: 27 g 9% ◆ Dietary Fiber: 1 g 4% ◆ Sugars: 13 g ◆ Protein: 3 g ◆ Vitamin A: 0% ◆ Vitamin C: 0% ◆ Calcium: 4% ◆ Iron: 6% ◆ **DIETARY EXCHANGES:** 1 Starch, 1 Fruit OR 2 Carbohydrate

Spoon Bread

PREP TIME: 25 MINUTES (READY IN I HOUR 15 MINUTES)
◆ YIELD: 8 (½-CUP) SERVINGS

    2 cups water
    I cup white cornmeal
    I teaspoon seasoned salt
    I cup buttermilk
    2 tablespoons margarine or butter, melted
    2 teaspoons baking powder
    3 eggs, separated

1. Heat oven to 375°F. Grease 2-quart casserole. In medium saucepan, bring water to a boil. Slowly stir in cornmeal and salt. Reduce heat to medium; cook about 5 minutes or until very thick, stirring constantly. Remove from heat; stir in buttermilk. Cool 5 minutes.
2. Gradually beat in 2 tablespoons margarine, baking powder and egg yolks. In small bowl, beat egg whites until stiff but not dry. Fold into cornmeal mixture. Pour batter into greased casserole.
3. Bake at 375°F. for 40 to 50 minutes or until golden brown and knife inserted near center comes out clean. Serve immediately with margarine, if desired.

NUTRITION INFORMATION PER SERVING: Serving Size: ½ Cup ◆ Calories: 130 ◆ Calories from Fat: 50 ◆ **% DAILY VALUE:** Total Fat: 6 g 9% ◆ Saturated Fat: 1 g 5% ◆ Cholesterol: 80 mg 27% ◆ Sodium: 410 mg 17% ◆ Total Carbohydrate: 14 g 5% ◆ Dietary Fiber: 1 g 4% ◆ Sugars: 2 g ◆ Protein: 5 g ◆ Vitamin A: 6% ◆ Vitamin C: 0% ◆ Calcium: 10% ◆ Iron: 6% ◆ **DIETARY EXCHANGES:** 1 Starch, 1 Fat OR 1 Carbohydrate, 1 Fat

---

C O O K ' S   N O T E

QUICK LOAF TIPS

The loaf commonly develops a lengthwise crack during baking. This "split crust" is perfectly normal.

To avoid crumbling, cool the loaf completely before slicing. Often you'll get the best slices a day after baking.

Quick Cheese and Pepper Bread

PREP TIME: 15 MINUTES (READY IN I HOUR 15 MINUTES)
◆ YIELD: I (16-SLICE) LOAF

    2 cups all-purpose flour
    4 oz. (I cup) shredded sharp or medium
        Cheddar cheese
    I tablespoon sugar
    ½ teaspoon baking powder
    ½ teaspoon baking soda
    ½ teaspoon salt
    ½ teaspoon coarse ground black pepper
    I cup buttermilk
    ⅓ cup margarine or butter, melted
    2 eggs

1. Heat oven to 350°F. Grease bottom only of 9×5 or 8×4-inch loaf pan. In medium bowl, combine flour, cheese, sugar, baking powder, baking soda, salt and pepper; mix well.
2. In small bowl, combine buttermilk, margarine and eggs; blend well. Add to flour mixture; stir just until dry ingredients are moistened. Pour into greased pan.
3. Bake at 350°F. for 35 to 45 minutes or until toothpick inserted in center comes out clean. Cool 15 minutes; remove from pan. Serve warm or cool completely on wire rack. Wrap tightly and store in refrigerator.

HIGH ALTITUDE (*above 3500 feet*)**:** No change.

NUTRITION INFORMATION PER SERVING: Serving Size: 1 Slice ◆ Calories: 140 ◆ Calories from Fat: 60 ◆ **% DAILY VALUE:** Total Fat: 7 g 11% ◆ Saturated Fat: 2 g 10% ◆ Cholesterol: 35 mg 12% ◆ Sodium: 230 mg 10% ◆ Total Carbohydrate: 14 g 5% ◆ Dietary Fiber: 0 g 0% ◆ Sugars: 2 g ◆ Protein: 5 g ◆ Vitamin A: 6% ◆ Vitamin C: 0% ◆ Calcium: 8% ◆ Iron: 6% ◆ **DIETARY EXCHANGES:** 1 Starch, 1 Fat OR 1 Carbohydrate, 1 Fat

Whole Wheat Soda Bread

PREP TIME: 15 MINUTES (READY IN 1 HOUR)
✦ YIELD: 1 (12-SLICE) LOAF

2 cups whole wheat flour
1 teaspoon baking soda
½ teaspoon salt
1 cup buttermilk
2 tablespoons honey
1 egg, well beaten

1. Heat oven to 375°F. Grease cookie sheet. In large bowl, combine flour, baking soda and salt; mix well.
2. In small bowl, combine buttermilk, honey and egg; blend well. Add to flour mixture; stir gently just until dry ingredients are moistened. (Dough will be sticky.) Shape dough into flat 7-inch round loaf on greased cookie sheet.
3. Bake at 375°F. for 25 to 30 minutes or until golden brown. Immediately remove from cookie sheet; cool on wire rack for 15 minutes. Serve warm or cool.

HIGH ALTITUDE (*above 3500 feet*): No change.

NUTRITION INFORMATION PER SERVING: Serving Size: 1 Slice ✦ Calories: 100 ✦ Calories from Fat: 10 ✦ **% DAILY VALUE:** Total Fat: 1 g 2% ✦ Saturated Fat: 0 g 0% ✦ Cholesterol: 20 mg 7% ✦ Sodium: 220 mg 9% ✦ Total Carbohydrate: 18 g 6% ✦ Dietary Fiber: 2 g 8% ✦ Sugars: 4 g ✦ Protein: 4 g ✦ Vitamin A: 0% ✦ Vitamin C: 0% ✦ Calcium: 4% ✦ Iron: 4% ✦ **DIETARY EXCHANGES:** 1 Starch OR 1 Carbohydrate

Peach Kuchen

PREP TIME: 15 MINUTES (READY IN 1 HOUR)
✦ YIELD: 8 SERVINGS

½ cup margarine or butter, softened
¼ cup sugar
1 teaspoon vanilla
1 egg
1 cup all-purpose flour
½ teaspoon baking powder
¼ teaspoon salt
1 (29-oz.) can sliced peaches, well drained
3 tablespoons sugar
½ to 1 teaspoon cinnamon

1. Heat oven to 350°F. Grease 9-inch springform pan. In medium bowl, combine margarine and ¼ cup sugar; beat until light and fluffy. Add vanilla and egg; beat well. Add flour, baking powder and salt; blend well.
2. Spread dough over bottom and 1 inch up sides of greased pan. Arrange peach slices in spoke fashion over dough.
3. In small bowl, combine 3 tablespoons sugar and cinnamon; mix well. Sprinkle over peaches and edges of dough.
4. Bake at 350°F. for 30 to 35 minutes or until edges are golden brown. Cool 10 minutes; remove sides of pan. Serve warm or cool.

HIGH ALTITUDE (*above 3500 feet*): No change.

NUTRITION INFORMATION PER SERVING: Serving Size: ⅛ of Recipe ✦ Calories: 240 ✦ Calories from Fat: 110 ✦ **% DAILY VALUE:** Total Fat: 12 g 18% ✦ Saturated Fat: 2 g 10% ✦ Cholesterol: 25 mg 8% ✦ Sodium: 240 mg 10% ✦ Total Carbohydrate: 30 g 10% ✦ Dietary Fiber: 2 g 8% ✦ Sugars: 16 g ✦ Protein: 3 g ✦ Vitamin A: 20% ✦ Vitamin C: 4% ✦ Calcium: 4% ✦ Iron: 8% ✦ **DIETARY EXCHANGES:** 1 Starch, 1 Fruit, 2 Fat OR 2 Carbohydrate, 2 Fat

VARIATION

Pear-Cardamom Kuchen: Add 1 teaspoon cardamom with flour. Substitute 1 (29-oz.) can pear halves, well drained and sliced, for peaches. In topping, add ½ teaspoon cardamom and decrease cinnamon to ⅛ teaspoon.

Cinnamon Coffee Cake

PREP TIME: 20 MINUTES (READY IN 1 HOUR)
✦ YIELD: 9 SERVINGS

COFFEE CAKE
1¾ cups all-purpose flour
¾ cup sugar
2 teaspoons baking powder
¼ teaspoon baking soda
¼ teaspoon salt
¼ teaspoon nutmeg
¾ cup buttermilk
⅓ cup margarine or butter, melted
1 teaspoon vanilla
2 eggs, beaten

TOPPING
¼ cup margarine or butter, melted
3 tablespoons sugar
½ teaspoon cinnamon

1. Heat oven to 350°F. Grease bottom only of 9-inch square pan. In large bowl, combine all coffee cake ingredients; stir just until dry ingredients are moistened. Spread batter in greased pan.
2. Bake at 350°F. for 30 to 40 minutes or until toothpick inserted in center comes out clean.

3. Generously pierce hot cake with fork. Brush or drizzle ¼ cup melted margarine over hot cake. In small bowl, combine 3 tablespoons sugar and cinnamon; mix well. Sprinkle over hot cake. Serve warm.

HIGH ALTITUDE (*above 3500 feet*)**:** Increase flour to 1¾ cups plus 2 tablespoons. Bake as directed above.

NUTRITION INFORMATION PER SERVING: Serving Size: ⅙ of Recipe ◆ Calories: 300 ◆ Calories from Fat: 120 ◆ **% DAILY VALUE:** Total Fat: 13 g 20% ◆ Saturated Fat: 3 g 15% ◆ Cholesterol: 50 mg 17% ◆ Sodium: 380 mg 16% ◆ Total Carbohydrate: 41 g 14% ◆ Dietary Fiber: 1 g 3% ◆ Sugars: 22 g ◆ Protein: 5 g ◆ Vitamin A: 10% ◆ Vitamin C: 0% ◆ Calcium: 10% ◆ Iron: 8% ◆ **DIETARY EXCHANGES:** 1½ Starch, 1 Fruit, 2½ Fat OR 2½ Carbohydrate, 2½ Fat

Caramel Biscuit Ring-a-Round

PREP TIME: 15 MINUTES (READY IN 50 MINUTES)
◆ YIELD: 10 SERVINGS

¾ cup firmly packed brown sugar
½ cup chopped nuts
⅓ cup margarine or butter
2 tablespoons water
2 (7-oz.) cans refrigerated biscuits

1. Heat oven to 400°F. Generously grease 12-cup Bundt® pan. In small saucepan, combine brown sugar, nuts, margarine and water; heat until margarine melts, stirring occasionally.
2. Separate dough into 20 biscuits. Cut each biscuit into quarters; place in large bowl. Pour brown sugar mixture over biscuits; toss lightly to coat evenly. Spoon coated biscuit pieces into greased pan.
3. Bake at 400°F. for 20 to 30 minutes or until golden brown. Cool in pan 3 minutes; invert onto serving plate. Serve warm.

NUTRITION INFORMATION PER SERVING: Serving Size: ¹⁄₁₀ of Recipe ◆ Calories: 260 ◆ Calories from Fat: 100 ◆ **% DAILY VALUE:** Total Fat: 11 g 17% ◆ Saturated Fat: 2 g 10% ◆ Cholesterol: 0 mg 0% ◆ Sodium: 460 mg 19% ◆ Total Carbohydrate: 36 g 12% ◆ Dietary Fiber: 1 g 3% ◆ Sugars: 18 g ◆ Protein: 4 g ◆ Vitamin A: 6% ◆ Vitamin C: 0% ◆ Calcium: 4% ◆ Iron: 8% ◆ **DIETARY EXCHANGES:** 1½ Starch, 1 Fruit, 2 Fat OR 2½ Carbohydrate, 2 Fat

Blueberry-Poppy Seed Brunch Cake

PREP TIME: 30 MINUTES (READY IN 1 HOUR 35 MINUTES)
◆ YIELD: 8 SERVINGS

CAKE
⅔ cup sugar
½ cup margarine or butter, softened
2 teaspoons grated lemon peel
1 egg
1½ cups all-purpose flour
2 tablespoons poppy seed
½ teaspoon baking soda
¼ teaspoon salt
½ cup sour cream

FILLING
2 cups fresh or frozen blueberries, thawed, drained on paper towels
⅓ cup sugar
2 teaspoons all-purpose flour
¼ teaspoon nutmeg

GLAZE
⅓ cup powdered sugar
1 to 2 teaspoons milk

1. Heat oven to 350°F. Grease and flour bottom and sides of 9 or 10-inch springform pan. In large bowl, combine ⅔ cup sugar and margarine; beat until light and fluffy. Add lemon peel and egg; beat 2 minutes at medium speed.
2. In medium bowl, combine 1½ cups flour, poppy seed, baking soda and salt; mix well. Add to margarine mixture alternately with sour cream, beating until well combined. Spread batter over bottom and 1 inch up sides of greased and floured pan, making sure batter on sides is ¼ inch thick.
3. In another medium bowl, combine all filling ingredients; mix well. Spoon over batter.
4. Bake at 350°F. for 45 to 55 minutes or until crust is golden brown. Cool 10 minutes; remove sides of pan.
5. In small bowl, blend powdered sugar and enough milk for desired drizzling consistency. Drizzle over warm cake. Serve warm or cool.

HIGH ALTITUDE (*above 3500 feet*)**:** Increase flour in cake to 1¾ cups. Bake as directed above.

NUTRITION INFORMATION PER SERVING: Serving Size: ⅛ of Recipe ◆ Calories: 390 ◆ Calories from Fat: 150 ◆ **% DAILY VALUE:** Total Fat: 17 g 26% ◆ Saturated Fat: 4 g 20% ◆ Cholesterol: 35 mg 12% ◆ Sodium: 300 mg 13% ◆ Total Carbohydrate: 55 g 18% ◆ Dietary Fiber: 2 g 8% ◆ Sugars: 34 g ◆ Protein: 5 g ◆ Vitamin A: 15% ◆ Vitamin C: 6% ◆ Calcium: 6% ◆ Iron: 8% ◆ **DIETARY EXCHANGES:** 1½ Starch, 2 Fruit, 3½ Fat OR 3½ Carbohydrate, 3½ Fat

Country Apple Coffee Cake

Country Apple Coffee Cake

PREP TIME: 20 MINUTES (READY IN 1 HOUR 10 MINUTES)
✦ YIELD: 8 SERVINGS

COFFEE CAKE
  2 tablespoons margarine or butter, softened
1½ cups chopped peeled apples
  1 (12-oz.) can refrigerated flaky biscuits
  ⅓ cup firmly packed brown sugar
  ¼ teaspoon cinnamon
  ⅓ cup light corn syrup
1½ teaspoons whiskey, if desired
  1 egg
  ½ cup pecan halves or pieces

GLAZE
  ⅓ cup powdered sugar
  ¼ teaspoon vanilla
  1 to 2 teaspoons milk

1. Heat oven to 350°F. Using 1 tablespoon of the margarine, generously grease 9-inch round cake pan or 8-inch square pan. Spread 1 cup of the apples in greased pan.
2. Separate dough into 10 biscuits; cut each into quarters. Arrange biscuit pieces, points up, over apples. Top with remaining ½ cup apples.
3. In small bowl, combine remaining 1 tablespoon margarine, brown sugar, cinnamon, corn syrup, whiskey and egg; beat 2 to 3 minutes or until sugar is partially dissolved. Stir in pecans. Spoon over biscuit pieces and apples.
4. Bake at 350°F. for 35 to 45 minutes or until deep golden brown. Cool 5 minutes. If desired, remove from pan.
5. In small bowl, blend all glaze ingredients, adding enough milk for desired drizzling consistency. Drizzle over warm cake. Serve warm or cool. Store in refrigerator.

NUTRITION INFORMATION PER SERVING: Serving Size: ⅛ of Recipe ✦ Calories: 330 ✦ Calories from Fat: 130 ✦ **% DAILY VALUE:** Total Fat: 14 g 22% ✦ Saturated Fat: 2 g 10% ✦ Cholesterol: 25 mg 8% ✦ Sodium: 510 mg 21% ✦ Total Carbohydrate: 47 g 16% ✦ Dietary Fiber: 2 g 8% ✦ Sugars: 24 g ✦ Protein: 4 g ✦ Vitamin A: 4% ✦ Vitamin C: 0% ✦ Calcium: 2% ✦ Iron: 8% ✦ **DIETARY EXCHANGES:** 1½ Starch, 1½ Fruit, 2½ Fat OR 3 Carbohydrate, 2½ Fat

Perfect Popovers

PREP TIME: 10 MINUTES (READY IN 1 HOUR)
✦ YIELD: 10 POPOVERS

  3 eggs, room temperature
1¼ cups milk, room temperature
1¼ cups all-purpose flour
  ¼ teaspoon salt

1. Heat oven to 450°F. Generously grease 10 popover cups or 6-oz. custard cups.* In small bowl, beat eggs with eggbeater or wire whisk until lemon colored and foamy. Add milk; blend well.

2. Add flour and salt; beat with eggbeater just until batter is smooth and foamy on top. Pour batter into greased cups, filling about ⅔ full.

3. Bake at 450°F. for 15 minutes. (DO NOT OPEN OVEN.) Reduce oven temperature to 350°F.; bake an additional 25 to 35 minutes or until high, hollow and deep golden brown. Remove from oven; insert sharp knife into each popover to allow steam to escape. Remove from cups. Serve warm.

> **TIP:** * Greased standard muffin pans can be substituted for the popover cups. Fill alternating greased cups with batter to prevent sides of popovers from touching.

HIGH ALTITUDE (*above 3500 feet*)**:** Increase flour to 1¼ cups plus 2 tablespoons. Bake at 450°F. for 15 minutes. Reduce oven temperature to 350°F.; bake an additional 20 to 30 minutes.

NUTRITION INFORMATION PER SERVING: Serving Size: 1 Popover ♦ Calories: 90 ♦ Calories from Fat: 20 ♦ **% DAILY VALUE:** Total Fat: 2 g 3% ♦ Saturated Fat: 1 g 5% ♦ Cholesterol: 65 mg 22% ♦ Sodium: 90 mg 4% ♦ Total Carbohydrate: 14 g 5% ♦ Dietary Fiber: 0 g 0% ♦ Sugars: 2 g ♦ Protein: 5 g ♦ Vitamin A: 4% ♦ Vitamin C: 0% ♦ Calcium: 4% ♦ Iron: 6% ♦ **DIETARY EXCHANGES:** 1 Starch, ½ Fat OR 1 Carbohydrate, ½ Fat

VARIATION

Dill-Parmesan Popovers: Add 2 tablespoons grated Parmesan cheese and 1 teaspoon dried dill weed with flour.

Perfect Popovers (page 40)

Fluffy Dumplings

PREP TIME: 25 MINUTES ✦ YIELD: 12 DUMPLINGS

1½ cups all-purpose flour
  2 teaspoons baking powder
 ½ teaspoon salt
 ⅔ cup milk
  2 tablespoons oil
  1 egg, slightly beaten

1. In medium bowl, combine flour, baking powder and salt; mix well. Add milk, oil and egg; stir just until dry ingredients are moistened.

2. Drop dough by rounded tablespoonfuls onto boiling soup or stew mixture. Reduce heat; cover tightly and cook 13 to 16 minutes or until dumplings are fluffy and no longer doughy on bottom.

HIGH ALTITUDE (*above 3500 feet*)**:** No change.

NUTRITION INFORMATION PER SERVING: Serving Size: 1 Dumpling ♦ Calories: 90 ♦ Calories from Fat: 25 ♦ **% DAILY VALUE:** Total Fat: 3 g 5% ♦ Saturated Fat: 1 g 5% ♦ Cholesterol: 20 mg 7% ♦ Sodium: 180 mg 8% ♦ Total Carbohydrate: 13 g 4% ♦ Dietary Fiber: 0 g 0% ♦ Sugars: 1 g ♦ Protein: 3 g ♦ Vitamin A: 0% ♦ Vitamin C: 0% ♦ Calcium: 6% ♦ Iron: 4% ♦ **DIETARY EXCHANGES:** 1 Starch, ½ Fat OR 1 Carbohydrate, ½ Fat

VARIATIONS

Chive-Basil Dumplings: Add 1 tablespoon chopped fresh chives and ½ teaspoon dried basil leaves, crushed, to flour.
Parsley-Sage Dumplings: Add 1 tablespoon chopped fresh parsley and ½ teaspoon dried sage leaves, finely crushed, to flour.

Delicious White Bread

PREP TIME: 35 MINUTES (READY IN 4 HOURS)
◆ YIELD: 2 (18-SLICE) LOAVES

    5 to 6 cups all-purpose flour
    3 tablespoons sugar
    2 teaspoons salt
    2 pkg. active dry yeast
    2 cups water
    ¼ cup oil or shortening
    1 tablespoon margarine or butter, melted

1. In large bowl, combine 2 cups flour, sugar, salt and yeast; mix well. In small saucepan, heat water and oil until very warm (120 to 130°F.). Add warm liquid to flour mixture; blend at low speed until moistened. Beat 3 minutes at medium speed. By hand, stir in an additional 2½ to 3 cups flour until dough pulls cleanly away from sides of bowl.
2. On floured surface, knead in ½ to 1 cup flour until dough is smooth and elastic, about 5 minutes. Place dough in greased bowl; cover loosely with greased plastic wrap and cloth towel. Let rise in warm place (80 to 85°F.) until light and doubled in size, 45 to 60 minutes.
3. Grease two 8×4 or 9×5-inch loaf pans. Punch down dough several times to remove all air bubbles. Divide dough in half; shape into loaves. Place in greased pans. Cover; let rise in warm place until dough fills pans and tops of loaves are about 1 inch above pan edges, 30 to 35 minutes.
4. Heat oven to 375°F. Uncover dough. Bake 40 to 50 minutes or until loaves sound hollow when lightly tapped. Immediately remove from pans; place on wire racks. Brush with melted margarine. Cool 1 hour or until completely cooled.

HIGH ALTITUDE (*above 3500 feet*): No change.

NUTRITION INFORMATION PER SERVING: Serving Size: 1 Slice ◆ Calories: 90 ◆ Calories from Fat: 20 ◆ **% DAILY VALUE:** Total Fat: 2 g 3% ◆ Saturated Fat: 0 g 0% ◆ Cholesterol: 0 mg 0% ◆ Sodium: 125 mg 5% ◆ Total Carbohydrate: 17 g 6% ◆ Dietary Fiber: 1 g 3% ◆ Sugars: 1 g ◆ Protein: 2 g ◆ Vitamin A: 0% ◆ Vitamin C: 0% ◆ Calcium: 0% ◆ Iron: 6% ◆ **DIETARY EXCHANGES:** 1 Starch OR 1 Carbohydrate

VARIATIONS

Breadsticks: After first rise time, punch down dough. Divide dough in half. Cut each half into 32 pieces; shape each into 8-inch-long breadstick. Place on greased cookie sheets. Brush with beaten egg white; sprinkle with sesame seed. Cover; let rise in warm place about 30 minutes or until doubled in size. Bake at 400°F. for about 14 minutes. YIELD: 64 BREADSTICKS

Butter-Topped Mini-Loaves: After first rise time, punch down dough. Divide dough into 12 equal pieces. Shape each piece into a 7-inch oblong loaf; taper ends. Place loaves 3 inches apart on greased cookie sheets. Cover; let rise in warm place until doubled in size, about 45 minutes. Make ¼-inch-deep slit down center of each loaf. Drizzle each with 1 teaspoon melted butter. If desired, sprinkle with sesame seed or poppy seed. Bake at 375°F. for 20 to 25 minutes or until loaves sound hollow when lightly tapped.
YIELD: 12 MINI-LOAVES

Cinnamon Swirl Bread: After first rise time, punch down dough. Divide dough in half. Shape each half into 14×7-inch rectangle. Brush with melted margarine or butter. Sprinkle each with mixture of ¼ cup sugar and 1 teaspoon cinnamon. Starting with 7-inch side, roll up. Seal edges; place seam side down in greased loaf pans. Let rise and bake as directed above.

Hamburger Buns: After first rise time, punch down dough. Divide dough in half; shape each half into eight 2-inch balls. If desired, flatten slightly. Place on greased cookie sheets. Cover; let rise in warm place about 30 minutes. Bake at 400°F. for about 15 minutes. YIELD: 16 BUNS

Raisin Bread: Add ½ teaspoon cinnamon with the salt and stir in 1 cup raisins after beating step. Continue as directed above.

C O O K ' S   N O T E

YEAST TIP

Yeast is a living organism: If the liquid is too hot, the yeast will be killed; too cold, and the yeast will remain dormant and not raise the dough.

YEAST BREADS

Yeast breads differ from quick breads not only in the leavening but also in the mixing technique. While most quick breads need gentle mixing, yeast breads require firm, decisive handling to develop their characteristic texture.

Yeast breads fall into two main categories: batter breads and kneaded breads. Batter breads are quicker to prepare, since they require no kneading. Their texture after baking is generally coarser than that of kneaded breads.

Kneading is hands-on work that can be very satisfying for the baker. It also can be done in a mixer or food processor fitted with a dough hook, or in a bread machine.

Kneaded breads gain their texture from gluten, a protein in flour that stretches as the dough rises. Bread flour has more gluten than all-purpose flour or cake flour, producing bread with higher volume and more even texture. In most yeast breads, unless otherwise specified, you can use either all-purpose or bread flour (but not cake flour). Bread machine recipes, on the other hand, work best with bread flour.

YEAST: THE PROOF IS IN THE BUBBLES

Before using yeast, check the expiration date on the package. If in doubt, you can check the yeast: Dissolve the yeast, along with up to a tablespoon of the recipe's sugar (but no salt) in ½ cup of the recipe's liquid that has been heated to lukewarm, 90 to 100°F. (A drop of the liquid on the inside of your wrist should feel neither very warm nor very cool but about the same temperature as your skin.) Let the mixture stand at room temperature for about 10 minutes; if the mixture is foamy, the yeast is still active and you can proceed with the recipe.

Speedy Whole Wheat Bread

PREP TIME: 30 MINUTES (READY IN 2 HOURS 35 MINUTES) ◆ YIELD: 2 (16-SLICE) LOAVES

2½ to 3 cups all-purpose flour
3 tablespoons sesame seed, toasted
2 teaspoons salt
3 pkg. active dry yeast
2¼ cups water
¼ cup honey
3 tablespoons margarine or butter
3 cups whole wheat flour
1 egg white, beaten
Sesame seed, toasted

1. In large bowl, combine 2 cups all-purpose flour, 3 tablespoons sesame seed, salt and yeast; mix well. In small saucepan, heat water, honey and margarine until very warm (120 to 130°F.). Add warm liquid to flour mixture; blend at low speed until moistened. Beat 3 minutes at medium speed. By hand, stir in whole wheat flour and an additional ¼ to ½ cup all-purpose flour until dough pulls cleanly away from sides of bowl.
2. On floured surface, knead in ¼ to ½ cup all-purpose flour until dough is smooth and elastic, 5 to 8 minutes. Place dough in greased bowl; cover loosely with greased plastic wrap and cloth towel. Place bowl in pan of warm water (about 95°F.); let rise 15 minutes.
3. Grease large cookie sheet or 15×10×1-inch baking pan. Punch down dough several times to remove all air bubbles. Divide dough in half; shape into round balls. Place 3 inches apart on greased cookie sheet.
4. With sharp knife, make three ⅛-inch-deep slashes on top of each loaf. Carefully brush loaves with egg white; sprinkle with sesame seed. Cover; let rise in warm place until light and doubled in size, about 15 minutes.
5. Heat oven to 375°F. Uncover dough. Bake 25 to 35 minutes or until loaves sound hollow when lightly tapped. Immediately remove from cookie sheet; cool on wire racks for 1 hour or until completely cooled.

HIGH ALTITUDE (above 3500 feet): No change.

NUTRITION INFORMATION PER SERVING: Serving Size: 1 Slice ◆ Calories: 110 ◆ Calories from Fat: 20 ◆ % DAILY VALUE: Total Fat: 2 g 3% ◆ Saturated Fat: 0 g 0% ◆ Cholesterol: 0 mg 0% ◆ Sodium: 150 mg 6% ◆ Total Carbohydrate: 20 g 7% ◆ Dietary Fiber: 2 g 8% ◆ Sugars: 3 g ◆ Protein: 3 g ◆ Vitamin A: 0% ◆ Vitamin C: 0% ◆ Calcium: 0% ◆ Iron: 6% ◆ DIETARY EXCHANGES: 1½ Starch OR 1½ Carbohydrate

HOW TO PREPARE YEAST BREADS

To knead, sprinkle work surface lightly with flour. With floured hands, form dough into a ball; sprinkle lightly with flour by kneading. Fold edges of dough toward center. Push dough down and away with heels of both hands. Give

dough a quarter turn. Repeat folding, pushing and turning until dough is smooth and elastic and small blisters appear on the surface. Knead as long as recipe directions specify. During kneading, continue to add flour in small amounts until the dough is no

longer sticky and can be easily handled. Bread is dry and heavy if not sufficiently kneaded. A range of flour is given to accommodate various flour conditions. Flour can gain or lose moisture depending on weather conditions and how it is stored.

Place dough in a lightly greased bowl large enough for it to double in size. Turn dough to coat with grease. Cover the bowl with plastic wrap and a cloth towel to prevent drying. When the dough is doubled in size, an indentation will remain in the dough when poked lightly with 2 fingers. If the indentation fills up rapidly let the dough rise a little longer.

Each recipe gives specific directions for shaping the dough. Whatever the shape, roll out dough on a lightly floured surface.

Cracked Wheat Raisin Bread

PREP TIME: 40 MINUTES (READY IN 3 HOURS 55 MINUTES) ◆ YIELD: 2 (20-SLICE) LOAVES

1½ cups uncooked cracked wheat
1 cup raisins
½ cup firmly packed brown sugar
2 teaspoons salt
3 tablespoons margarine or butter
2 cups boiling water
2 pkg. active dry yeast
⅔ cup warm water
5 to 6 cups all-purpose flour
1 egg, beaten

1. In large bowl, combine cracked wheat, raisins, brown sugar, salt, margarine and 2 cups boiling water; mix well. Let cool to 105 to 115°F.
2. In small bowl, dissolve yeast in warm water (105 to 115°F.). Add dissolved yeast and 2 cups flour to cracked wheat mixture; blend at low speed until moistened. Beat 2 minutes at medium speed. By hand, stir in an additional 2½ to 3 cups flour until dough pulls cleanly away from sides of bowl.
3. On floured surface, knead in remaining ½ to 1 cup flour until dough is smooth and elastic, about 10 minutes. Place dough in greased bowl; cover loosely with greased plastic wrap and cloth towel. Let rise in warm place (80 to 85°F.) until light and doubled in size, 45 to 60 minutes.
4. Grease large cookie sheet. Punch down dough several times to remove all air bub-

Top to bottom: Microwave Apple Butter (page 454), Cracked Wheat Raisin Bread

bles. Divide dough in half; shape each into a ball. Place on greased cookie sheet. Cover; let rise in warm place until light and doubled in size, 45 to 60 minutes.

5. Heat oven to 350°F. Uncover dough. With sharp knife, slash a ½-inch-deep lattice design on top of each loaf. Brush with beaten egg. Bake at 350°F. for 35 to 45 minutes or until loaves sound hollow when lightly tapped. Immediately remove from cookie sheet; cool on wire racks for 1 hour or until completely cooled.

HIGH ALTITUDE (*above 3500 feet*)**:** No change.

NUTRITION INFORMATION PER SERVING: Serving Size: 1 Slice ◆ Calories: 120 ◆ Calories from Fat: 10 ◆ % DAILY VALUE: Total Fat: 1 g 2% ◆ Saturated Fat: 0 g 0% ◆ Cholesterol: 5 mg 2% ◆ Sodium: 120 mg 5% ◆ Total Carbohydrate: 24 g 8% ◆ Dietary Fiber: 2 g 8% ◆ Sugars: 5 g ◆ Protein: 3 g ◆ Vitamin A: 0% ◆ Vitamin C: 0% ◆ Calcium: 0% ◆ Iron: 6% ◆ DIETARY EXCHANGES: 1 Starch, ½ Fruit OR 1½ Carbohydrate

Whole Wheat Raisin Loaf

PREP TIME: 30 MINUTES (READY IN 4 HOURS)
◆ YIELD: 2 (16-SLICE) LOAVES

    2 to 3 cups all-purpose flour
    ½ cup sugar
    3 teaspoons salt
    1 teaspoon cinnamon
    ½ teaspoon nutmeg
    2 pkg. active dry yeast
    2 cups milk
    ¾ cup water
    ¼ cup oil
    4 cups whole wheat flour
    1 cup rolled oats
    1 cup raisins
    1 tablespoon margarine or butter, melted
    1 teaspoon sugar, if desired

1. In large bowl, combine 1½ cups all-purpose flour, ½ cup sugar, salt, cinnamon, nutmeg and yeast; mix well. In medium saucepan, heat milk, water and oil until very warm (120 to 130°F.). Add warm liquid to flour mixture; blend at low speed until moistened. Beat 3 minutes at medium speed. By hand, stir in whole wheat flour, rolled oats, raisins and an additional ¼ to ¾ cup all-purpose flour until dough pulls cleanly away from sides of bowl.

2. On floured surface, knead in remaining ¼ to ¾ cup all-purpose flour until dough is smooth and elastic, about 5 minutes. Place

dough in greased bowl; cover loosely with greased plastic wrap and cloth towel. Let rise in warm place (80 to 85°F.) until light and doubled in size, 20 to 30 minutes.

3. Grease two 9×5 or 8×4-inch loaf pans. Punch down dough several times to remove all air bubbles. Divide dough in half; shape into loaves. Place in greased pans. Cover; let rise in warm place until light and doubled in size, 30 to 45 minutes.

4. Heat oven to 375°F. Uncover dough. Bake 40 to 50 minutes or until deep golden brown and loaves sound hollow when lightly tapped. If loaves become too brown, cover loosely with foil during last 10 minutes of baking. Immediately remove from pans; cool on wire racks for 1½ hours or until completely cooled. Brush tops of loaves with margarine; sprinkle with 1 teaspoon sugar.

HIGH ALTITUDE (*above 3500 feet*)**:** No change.

NUTRITION INFORMATION PER SERVING: Serving Size: 1 Slice ◆ Calories: 160 ◆ Calories from Fat: 25 ◆ % DAILY VALUE: Total Fat: 3 g 5% ◆ Saturated Fat: 1 g 5% ◆ Cholesterol: 0 mg 0% ◆ Sodium: 210 mg 9% ◆ Total Carbohydrate: 29 g 10% ◆ Dietary Fiber: 3 g 12% ◆ Sugars: 7 g ◆ Protein: 5 g ◆ Vitamin A: 0% ◆ Vitamin C: 0% ◆ Calcium: 4% ◆ Iron: 8% ◆ DIETARY EXCHANGES: 2 Starch OR 2 Carbohydrate

COOK'S NOTE

THE UPPER CRUST

The crust is often the most coveted part of homemade bread. Try these techniques for yeast breads:

◆ Crisp crust: Brush loaf gently before baking with water. Cool loaf completely before wrapping.

◆ Shiny crust: Brush loaf gently before baking with 1 beaten egg combined with 1 tablespoon water. If desired, sprinkle with sesame seed, poppy seed or coarse salt.

◆ Soft, tender crust: Brush loaf gently before or after baking with milk or melted butter.

◆ Glaze for a sweeter loaf, such as Cracked Wheat Raisin Bread (page 44): Brush the warm baked loaf with melted jelly or a mixture of powdered sugar and milk.

Rye Bread

PREP TIME: 35 MINUTES (READY IN 3 HOURS 50 MINUTES) ✦ YIELD: 2 (22-SLICE) LOAVES

    2 pkg. active dry yeast
    1 cup warm water
    1 cup warm milk
    ½ cup molasses
    ¼ cup shortening, melted
    2 teaspoons salt
    3 to 3½ cups all-purpose flour
    3 cups medium rye flour
    1 tablespoon water
    1 egg yolk

1. In small bowl, dissolve yeast in warm water (105 to 115°F.). In large bowl, combine warm milk (105 to 115°F.), molasses, shortening and salt; blend well. Add dissolved yeast. Add 2 cups all-purpose flour; blend at low speed until moistened. Beat 3 minutes at medium speed. By hand, stir in 3 cups rye flour and an additional ¾ to 1 cup all-purpose flour until dough pulls cleanly away from sides of bowl.
2. On floured surface, knead in ¼ to ½ cup all-purpose flour until dough is smooth and elastic, about 5 minutes. Place dough in greased bowl; cover loosely with greased plastic wrap and cloth towel. Let rise in warm place (80 to 85°F.) until light and doubled in size, 45 to 60 minutes.
3. Grease 2 cookie sheets. Punch down dough several times to remove all air bubbles. Divide dough in half; shape into balls. Shape dough into two 12-inch oblong loaves; round ends. Place on greased cookie sheets. With sharp knife, make four ¼-inch-deep diagonal slashes on top of each loaf. Cover; let rise in warm place until doubled in size, 20 to 30 minutes.
4. Heat oven to 350°F. Uncover dough. In small bowl, combine water and egg yolk; beat well. Brush over loaves. Bake at 350°F. for 35 to 45 minutes or until loaves sound hollow when lightly tapped. Immediately remove from cookie sheets; cool on wire racks for 1 hour or until completely cooled.

HIGH ALTITUDE (*above 3500 feet*): Decrease first rise time by 15 to 30 minutes. Decrease second rise time by 10 minutes. Bake as directed above.

NUTRITION INFORMATION PER SERVING: Serving Size: 1 Slice ✦ Calories: 90 ✦ Calories from Fat: 20 ✦ % **DAILY VALUE:** Total Fat: 2 g 3% ✦ Saturated Fat: 0 g 0% ✦ Cholesterol: 5 mg 2% ✦ Sodium: 100 mg 4% ✦ Total Carbohydrate: 16 g 5% ✦ Dietary Fiber: 1 g 4% ✦ Sugars: 3 g ✦ Protein: 2 g ✦ Vitamin A: 0% ✦ Vitamin C: 0% ✦ Calcium: 0% ✦ Iron: 4% ✦ **DIETARY EXCHANGES:** 1 Starch OR 1 Carbohydrate

Two-Tone Rye Twist Loaves

PREP TIME: 45 MINUTES (READY IN 4 HOURS 15 MINUTES) ✦ YIELD: 2 (12-SLICE) LOAVES

    3½ to 4 cups all-purpose flour
    2½ cups medium rye flour
    1 tablespoon salt
    1 tablespoon grated orange peel
    2 pkg. active dry yeast
    2 cups milk
    ¼ cup molasses
    ¼ cup margarine or butter
    2 teaspoons unsweetened cocoa
    1 to 2 teaspoons anise seed
    1 teaspoon instant coffee granules or crystals

1. In large bowl, combine 2½ cups all-purpose flour and the rye flour; mix well. Set aside.
2. In another large bowl, combine 2 cups of the flour mixture, salt, orange peel and yeast; mix well. In medium saucepan, heat milk, molasses and margarine until very warm (120 to 130°F.). Add warm liquid to flour-yeast mixture; blend at low speed until moistened. Beat 3 minutes at medium speed. Pour half of batter into another bowl; set aside.
3. To remaining batter, stir in cocoa, anise seed, instant coffee and 1 to 1½ cups flour mixture to form a stiff dough. On floured surface, knead in ½ to 1 cup flour mixture until dough is smooth and elastic, about 5 minutes.
4. To reserved batter, stir in remaining flour mixture and ½ to ¾ cup of the remaining all-purpose flour to make a stiff dough. On floured surface, knead in ½ to ¾ cup additional all-purpose flour until dough is smooth and elastic, about 5 minutes. Place doughs in separate greased bowls; cover loosely with greased plastic wrap and cloth towels. Let rise in warm place (80 to 85°F.) until light and doubled in size, about 1 hour.
5. Grease 2 cookie sheets. Punch down doughs several times to remove all air bub-

IF DOUGH FAILS TO RISE

Heavy, sluggish dough that doesn't rise may be due to expired yeast, excessive salt, lack of sugar or dough that is too hot or too cold. Of these problems, only the last one can be rectified, by warming the dough just enough to encourage rising. If too much salt or a too-hot liquid has killed the yeast, it's best to start over.

bles. Divide each dough in half. Roll each part into 14-inch rope. For each loaf, twist 1 dark and 1 light rope together, pinching ends to seal. Place on greased cookie sheets. Cover; let rise until doubled in size, about 1 hour.

6. Heat oven to 350°F. Uncover dough. Bake 25 to 30 minutes or until loaves sound hollow when lightly tapped. Immediately remove from cookie sheets; cool on wire racks for 1 hour or until completely cooled.

HIGH ALTITUDE (*above 3500 feet*)**:** No change.

NUTRITION INFORMATION PER SERVING: Serving Size: 1 Slice ◆ Calories: 160 ◆ Calories from Fat: 25 ◆ **% DAILY VALUE:** Total Fat: 3 g 5% ◆ Saturated Fat: 1 g 5% ◆ Cholesterol: 0 mg 0% ◆ Sodium: 300 mg 13% ◆ Total Carbohydrate: 28 g 9% ◆ Dietary Fiber: 2 g 8% ◆ Sugars: 4 g ◆ Protein: 4 g ◆ Vitamin A: 2% ◆ Vitamin C: 0% ◆ Calcium: 4% ◆ Iron: 8% ◆ **DIETARY EXCHANGES:** 2 Starch OR 2 Carbohydrate

Sourdough Bread

PREP TIME: 45 MINUTES (READY IN 5 DAYS 13 HOURS 10 MINUTES) ◆ YIELD: 3 (16-SLICE) LOAVES

STARTER
 1 pkg. active dry yeast
 2 cups warm water
3½ cups all-purpose flour
 1 tablespoon sugar or honey

BREAD
 1 cup starter
5½ to 6 cups all-purpose flour
 ¼ cup sugar
 1 tablespoon salt
1⅔ cups warm water
 ⅓ cup oil

1. In large nonmetal bowl, dissolve yeast in 2 cups warm water (105 to 115°F.); let stand 5 minutes. Add 3½ cups flour and 1 tablespoon sugar; blend well. Cover loosely with plastic wrap and cloth towel. Let stand in warm place (80 to 85°F.) for 5 days, stirring at least once each day. When starter is ready for use, it is bubbly and may have a yellow liquid layer on top. Stir well before using.*

2. Place 1 cup starter in large bowl.** Add 2 cups flour, ¼ cup sugar, salt, 1⅔ cups warm water (105 to 115°F.) and oil; blend well. Stir in 2½ to 2¾ cups flour until dough pulls cleanly away from sides of bowl.

3. On floured surface, knead in remaining 1 to 1¼ cups flour until dough is smooth and elastic, about 5 minutes. Place dough in greased bowl; cover loosely with plastic wrap and cloth towel. Let rise in warm place for at least 8 hours or overnight.

4. Grease 3 cookie sheets or 9-inch round cake pans.*** Uncover dough. Punch down dough several times to remove air bubbles. Divide dough into 3 equal parts. Work dough with hands to remove all air bubbles. Shape into round loaves. Place on greased cookie sheets. Cover; let rise in warm place until doubled in size, 2 to 3 hours.

5. Heat oven to 400°F. Uncover dough. With sharp knife, make three ¼-inch-deep slashes on top of each loaf. Bake at 400°F. for 20 to 25 minutes or until loaves sound hollow when lightly tapped. Immediately remove from cookie sheets; cool on wire racks for 1 hour or until completely cooled.

TIPS: * If starter will not be used immediately, cover and refrigerate until ready to use. Return to room temperature before using.
** If desired, starter can be replenished for future use. After removing 1 cup starter, add to remaining starter 1 cup flour, ⅔ cup warm water (105 to 115°F.) and 1 teaspoon sugar or honey; blend well. Cover loosely with plastic wrap and cloth towel. Let stand in warm place (80 to 85°F.) for 10 to 12 hours or overnight. The starter will become bubbly and rise. Stir, cover and store in refrigerator. Repeat this process each time the starter is used. If starter is used once a week it will remain active. If not used, stir in 1 teaspoon sugar or honey weekly.
*** Three 8x4-inch loaf pans can be used. Bake at 400°F. for 25 to 30 minutes.

HIGH ALTITUDE (*above 3500 feet*)**:** No change.

NUTRITION INFORMATION PER SERVING: Serving Size: 1 Slice ◆ Calories: 90 ◆ Calories from Fat: 20 ◆ **% DAILY VALUE:** Total Fat: 2 g 3% ◆ Saturated Fat: 0 g 0% ◆ Cholesterol: 0 mg 0% ◆ Sodium: 135 mg 6% ◆ Total Carbohydrate: 17 g 6% ◆ Dietary Fiber: 1 g 2% ◆ Sugars: 2 g ◆ Protein: 2 g ◆ Vitamin A: 0% ◆ Vitamin C: 0% ◆ Calcium: 0% ◆ Iron: 6% ◆ **DIETARY EXCHANGES:** 1 Starch OR 1 Carbohydrate

French Bread Braids

French Bread Braids

PREP TIME: 40 MINUTES (READY IN 3 HOURS
40 MINUTES) ◆ YIELD: 2 (18-SLICE) LOAVES

4¾ to 5¾ cups all-purpose flour
1 tablespoon sugar
3 teaspoons salt
2 pkg. active dry yeast
2 cups water
2 tablespoons shortening
1 tablespoon water
1 egg white

1. In large bowl, combine 3 cups flour, sugar, salt and yeast; mix well. In small saucepan, heat 2 cups water and shortening until very warm (120 to 130°F.). Add warm liquid to flour mixture; blend at low speed until moistened. Beat 3 minutes at medium speed. By hand, stir in an additional 1½ to 2¼ cups flour to form a stiff dough.
2. On floured surface, knead in ¼ to ½ cup flour until dough is smooth and elastic, about 8 minutes. Place dough in greased bowl; cover loosely with greased plastic wrap and cloth towel. Let rise in warm place (80 to 85°F.) until light and doubled in size, 45 to 60 minutes.
3. Grease large cookie sheet. Punch down dough several times to remove all air bubbles. Divide dough in half; divide each half into 3 equal parts. Roll each part into 14-inch rope. Braid 3 ropes together; seal ends. Place on greased cookie sheet. Repeat with other half of dough.

4. In small bowl, combine 1 tablespoon water and egg white; beat slightly. Carefully brush over loaves. Cover; let rise in warm place until light and doubled in size, 20 to 30 minutes.
5. Heat oven to 375°F. Uncover dough; brush loaves again with egg white mixture. Bake at 375°F. for 25 to 30 minutes or until golden brown. Immediately remove from cookie sheet; cool on wire racks for 1 hour or until completely cooled.

HIGH ALTITUDE *(above 3500 feet)*: No change.

NUTRITION INFORMATION PER SERVING: Serving Size: 1 Slice ◆ Calories: 80 ◆ Calories from Fat: 10 ◆ **% DAILY VALUE:** Total Fat: 1 g 2% ◆ Saturated Fat: 0 g 0% ◆ Cholesterol: 0 mg 0% ◆ Sodium: 180 mg 8% ◆ Total Carbohydrate: 16 g 5% ◆ Dietary Fiber: 1 g 2% ◆ Sugars: 1 g ◆ Protein: 2 g ◆ Vitamin A: 0% ◆ Vitamin C: 0% ◆ Calcium: 0% ◆ Iron: 6% ◆ **DIETARY EXCHANGES:** 1 Starch OR 1 Carbohydrate

C O O K ' S   N O T E

KEEP RISING DOUGH COVERED

To prevent yeast dough from drying out during rising, cover the dough. Spray a length of plastic wrap with nonstick cooking spray. Press the sprayed side of the plastic directly onto the surface of the dough.

COOK'S NOTE

HOW TO BRAID YEAST BREAD DOUGH

On a lightly floured surface, divide the dough into 3 equal parts. Roll each part into a rope the length called for in the recipe. Place the ropes lengthwise on a greased cookie sheet.

From the center, braid the ropes loosely to each end. To seal the ends, pinch them together and tuck them under the loaf. Let the bread rise and bake as directed in the recipe.

Onion Lover's Twist

PREP TIME: 40 MINUTES (READY IN 3 HOURS 45 MINUTES) ✦ YIELD: 2 (16-SLICE) LOAVES

BREAD
3½ to 4½ cups all-purpose flour
¼ cup sugar
1½ teaspoons salt
1 pkg. active dry yeast
¾ cup water
½ cup milk
¼ cup margarine or butter
1 egg

FILLING
¼ cup margarine or butter, melted
1 cup finely chopped onions
1 tablespoon grated Parmesan cheese
1 tablespoon sesame or poppy seed
½ to 1 teaspoon garlic salt
1 teaspoon paprika

1. In large bowl, combine 2 cups flour, sugar, salt and yeast; mix well. In small saucepan, heat water, milk and ¼ cup margarine until very warm (120 to 130°F.). Add warm liquid and egg to flour mixture; blend at low speed until moistened. Beat 3 minutes at medium speed.

2. By hand, stir in remaining 1½ to 2½ cups flour to form a soft dough. Cover loosely with greased plastic wrap and cloth towel. Let rise in warm place (80 to 85°F.) until light and doubled in size, 45 to 60 minutes.

3. Grease large cookie sheet. Combine all filling ingredients. Set aside.

4. Stir down dough to remove air bubbles. On floured surface, toss dough until no longer sticky. Roll dough into 18×12-inch rectangle. Cut to make two 12×9-inch rectangles; cut each into three 9×4-inch strips.

5. Spread 2 tablespoons onion mixture over each strip to within ½ inch of edges. Bring long edges of each strip together over filling; pinch edges and ends to seal.

6. On greased cookie sheet, braid 3 rolls together; pinch ends to seal. Repeat with remaining 3 rolls for second loaf. Cover; let rise in warm place until light and doubled in size, 25 to 30 minutes.

7. Heat oven to 350°F. Uncover dough. Bake 27 to 35 minutes or until golden brown and loaves sound hollow when lightly tapped. Immediately remove from cookie sheet; cool on wire racks for 1 hour or until completely cooled.

HIGH ALTITUDE (above 3500 feet)**:** No change.

NUTRITION INFORMATION PER SERVING: Serving Size: 1 Slice ✦ Calories: 130 ✦ Calories from Fat: 50 ✦ **% DAILY VALUE:** Total Fat: 6 g 9% ✦ Saturated Fat: 1 g 5% ✦ Cholesterol: 5 mg 2% ✦ Sodium: 230 mg 10% ✦ Total Carbohydrate: 16 g 5% ✦ Dietary Fiber: 1 g 3% ✦ Sugars: 2 g ✦ Protein: 3 g ✦ Vitamin A: 6% ✦ Vitamin C: 0% ✦ Calcium: 0% ✦ Iron: 6% ✦ **DIETARY EXCHANGES:** 1 Starch, 1 Fat OR 1 Carbohydrate, 1 Fat

Left to right: Onion Lover's Twist and Whole Wheat Raisin Loaf (page 45)

Seed-Crusted Challah

PREP TIME: 40 MINUTES (READY IN 2 HOURS 55 MINUTES) ◆ YIELD: 1 (14-SLICE) LOAF

BREAD
1¾ to 2¼ cups all-purpose flour
  2 tablespoons brown sugar
  1 teaspoon salt
  1 pkg. fast-acting yeast
  1 cup water
  2 tablespoons margarine or butter
  1 egg
 ⅔ cup whole wheat flour
  1 tablespoon water
  1 egg yolk

SEED MIXTURE
  1 teaspoon poppy seed
  1 teaspoon sesame seed
 ½ teaspoon fennel seed
 ½ teaspoon caraway seed
 ⅛ teaspoon celery, cumin or dill seed

1. In large bowl, combine 1½ cups all-purpose flour, brown sugar, salt and yeast; mix well. In small saucepan, heat 1 cup water and margarine until very warm (120 to 130°F.). Add warm liquid and egg to flour mixture; blend at low speed until moistened. Beat 3 minutes at medium speed.

2. By hand, stir in whole wheat flour and an additional ¼ to ¾ cup all-purpose flour until dough pulls cleanly away from sides of bowl. Cover loosely with greased plastic wrap and cloth towel. Let rest 10 minutes.

3. Grease cookie sheet. On floured surface, knead dough about 25 times until smooth. Divide dough into 3 equal parts. Roll each part into 12-inch rope. Braid 3 ropes together; seal ends. Place on greased cookie sheet. Cover; let rise in warm place (80 to 85°F.) until light and doubled in size, 30 to 40 minutes.

4. Heat oven to 375°F. In small bowl, combine 1 tablespoon water and egg yolk; beat well. In another small bowl, combine all seed mixture ingredients; mix well. Brush braid with egg yolk mixture; sprinkle with seed mixture.

5. Bake at 375°F. for 20 to 25 minutes or until loaf sounds hollow when lightly tapped. Immediately remove from cookie sheet; cool on wire rack for 1 hour or until completely cooled.

HIGH ALTITUDE *(above 3500 feet)*: No change.

NUTRITION INFORMATION PER SERVING: Serving Size: 1 Slice ◆ Calories: 130 ◆ Calories from Fat: 25 ◆ **% DAILY VALUE:** Total Fat: 3 g 5% ◆ Saturated Fat: 1 g 5% ◆ Cholesterol: 30 mg 10% ◆ Sodium: 180 mg 8% ◆ Total Carbohydrate: 22 g 7% ◆ Dietary Fiber: 1 g 4% ◆ Sugars: 2 g ◆ Protein: 4 g ◆ Vitamin A: 2% ◆ Vitamin C: 0% ◆ Calcium: 0% ◆ Iron: 8% ◆ **DIETARY EXCHANGES:** 1½ Starch OR 1½ Carbohydrate

Herb Focaccia

PREP TIME: 25 MINUTES (READY IN 1 HOUR 35 MINUTES) ◆ YIELD: 1 (16-SLICE) LOAF

3½ cups all-purpose flour
  1 teaspoon sugar
  1 teaspoon salt
  1 pkg. fast-acting yeast
  1 cup water
  2 tablespoons oil
  1 egg
  3 to 4 tablespoons olive oil
  1 teaspoon dried rosemary or basil leaves, crushed

1. Grease cookie sheet. In large bowl, combine 1 cup flour, sugar, salt and yeast; mix well. In small saucepan, heat water and oil until very warm (120 to 130°F.). Add warm liquid and egg to flour mixture; blend at low speed until moistened. Beat 2 minutes at medium speed. By hand, stir in an additional 1¾ cups flour until dough pulls cleanly away from sides of bowl.

2. On floured surface, knead in ¾ cup flour until dough is smooth and elastic, about 5 minutes. Cover with large bowl; let rest 5 minutes.

3. Place dough on greased cookie sheet.* Roll or press to 12-inch round. Cover loosely with greased plastic wrap and cloth towel. Let rise in warm place (80 to 85°F.) until light and doubled in size, about 30 minutes.

4. Heat oven to 400°F. Uncover dough. With fingers or handle of wooden spoon, poke holes in dough at 1-inch intervals. Drizzle 3 to 4 tablespoons olive oil over top of dough. Sprinkle evenly with rosemary.

5. Bake at 400°F. for 17 to 27 minutes or until golden brown. Immediately remove from cookie sheet; cool on wire rack for 10 minutes. Serve warm or cool.

TIPS: * For two smaller loaves, grease 2 cookie sheets. Divide dough in half. Roll or press each half into an 8-inch round. Continue as directed above. Bake 10 to 20 minutes.

Baked focaccia can be wrapped and frozen for up to 3 months.

HIGH ALTITUDE (*above 3500 feet*): No change.

NUTRITION INFORMATION PER SERVING: Serving Size: 1 Slice ◆ Calories: 150 ◆ Calories from Fat: 50 ◆ **% DAILY VALUE:** Total Fat: 6 g 9% ◆ Saturated Fat: 1 g 5% ◆ Cholesterol: 15 mg 5% ◆ Sodium: 140 mg 6% ◆ Total Carbohydrate: 21 g 7% ◆ Dietary Fiber: 1 g 3% ◆ Sugars: 1 g ◆ Protein: 3 g ◆ Vitamin A: 0% ◆ Vitamin C: 0% ◆ Calcium: 0% ◆ Iron: 8% ◆ **DIETARY EXCHANGES:** 1 Starch, ½ Fruit, 1 Fat OR 1½ Carbohydrate, 1 Fat

COOK'S NOTE

HOW TO SHAPE FOCACCIA

Using greased or floured hands or rolling pin, roll or press kneaded dough into a 12-inch round on a greased cookie sheet. Press or roll from the center of the dough to the outside. Let rise as directed in the recipe.

With your fingers or the handle of a wooden spoon, poke indentations in the dough at 1-inch intervals. The indentations allow the olive oil and herb topping to penetrate the dough. Sprinkle herbs evenly over the dough.

Rustic Italian Bread

PREP TIME: 10 MINUTES (READY IN 2 HOURS 30 MINUTES) ◆ YIELD: 1 (12-SLICE) LOAF

    1 cup water heated to 120 to 130°F.
    2 tablespoons olive oil
    3 cups all-purpose flour
    2 teaspoons sugar
    ½ teaspoon salt
    1 pkg. active dry yeast
      Cornmeal
    1 egg white, beaten

1. BREAD MACHINE DIRECTIONS: Place all ingredients except cornmeal and egg white in bread machine pan according to manufacturer's directions. Process on dough setting.

2. Sprinkle ungreased cookie sheet with cornmeal. At end of dough cycle, remove dough from machine; place on lightly floured surface. Punch down dough several times to remove all air bubbles. (If dough is sticky, knead in additional flour before shaping.) Shape dough into baguette-shaped loaf about 12 inches long. Place on cornmeal-coated cookie sheet. Cover loosely with greased plastic wrap and cloth towel. Let rise in warm place (80 to 85°F.) until light and doubled in size, 20 to 25 minutes.

3. Heat oven to 375°F. Uncover dough. With sharp knife, make 1 deep lengthwise slash on top of loaf. Brush loaf with egg white. Bake at 375°F. for 25 to 35 minutes or until loaf sounds hollow when lightly tapped. Immediately remove from cookie sheet; cool on wire rack for 1 hour or until completely cooled.

1. CONVENTIONAL DIRECTIONS: In large bowl, combine flour, sugar, salt and yeast; mix well. Add warm water and oil; mix well. Turn dough out onto lightly floured surface. Knead dough 5 minutes or until smooth. Place dough in greased bowl; cover with greased plastic wrap and cloth towel. Let rise in warm place (80 to 85°F.) until light and doubled in size, 30 to 40 minutes.

2. Sprinkle ungreased cookie sheet with cornmeal. Punch down dough several times to remove all air bubbles. Shape dough into baguette-shaped loaf about 12 inches long. Place on cornmeal-coated cookie sheet. Cover loosely with greased plastic wrap and cloth towel. Let rise in warm place (80 to 85°F.) until light and doubled in size, 25 to 30 minutes. Continue as directed above.

HIGH ALTITUDE (*above 3500 feet*)**:** No change.

NUTRITION INFORMATION PER SERVING: Serving Size: 1 Slice ◆ Calories: 140 ◆ Calories from Fat: 25 ◆ **% DAILY VALUE:** Total Fat: 3 g 5% ◆ Saturated Fat: 0 g 0% ◆ Cholesterol: 0 mg 0% ◆ Sodium: 95 mg 4% ◆ Total Carbohydrate: 25 g 8% ◆ Dietary Fiber: 1 g 4% ◆ Sugars: 1 g ◆ Protein: 4 g ◆ Vitamin A: 0% ◆ Vitamin C: 0% ◆ Calcium: 0% ◆ Iron: 8% ◆ **DIETARY EXCHANGES:** 1½ Starch, ½ Fat OR 1½ Carbohydrate, ½ Fat

Old-Fashioned Batter Bread

PREP TIME: 25 MINUTES (READY IN 2 HOURS
55 MINUTES) ◆ YIELD: 1 (16-SLICE) LOAF

    2 to 2½ cups all-purpose flour
    ¾ cup rolled oats
    1 teaspoon salt
    1 pkg. active dry yeast
    1 cup water
    ¼ cup light molasses
    ¼ cup margarine or butter
    1 egg

1. In large bowl, combine 1 cup flour, oats, salt and yeast; mix well.
2. In small saucepan, heat water, molasses and margarine until very warm (120 to 130°F.). Add warm liquid and egg to flour mixture; blend at low speed until moistened. Beat 3 minutes at medium speed.
3. By hand, stir in remaining 1 to 1½ cups flour to form a stiff batter. Cover loosely with greased plastic wrap and cloth towel. Let rise in warm place (80 to 85°F.) until light and almost doubled in size, 25 to 30 minutes.
4. Grease 1½-quart casserole or 8 × 4-inch loaf pan. Stir down batter to remove all air bubbles. Turn batter into greased casserole. Cover; let rise in warm place until dough reaches top of casserole, 15 to 20 minutes.

Old-Fashioned Batter Bread

5. Heat oven to 375°F. Uncover dough. Bake 35 to 40 minutes or until loaf sounds hollow when lightly tapped. Immediately remove from casserole; cool on wire rack for 1 hour or until completely cooled.

HIGH ALTITUDE (above 3500 feet)**:** No change.

NUTRITION INFORMATION PER SERVING: Serving Size: 1 Slice ◆ Calories: 130 ◆ Calories from Fat: 35 ◆ **% DAILY VALUE:** Total Fat: 4 g 6% ◆ Saturated Fat: 1 g 5% ◆ Cholesterol: 15 mg 5% ◆ Sodium: 170 mg 7% ◆ Total Carbohydrate: 21 g 7% ◆ Dietary Fiber: 1 g 4% ◆ Sugars: 3 g ◆ Protein: 3 g ◆ Vitamin A: 4% ◆ Vitamin C: 0% ◆ Calcium: 0% ◆ Iron: 8% ◆ **DIETARY EXCHANGES:** 1 Starch, ½ Fruit, ½ Fat OR 1½ Carbohydrate, ½ Fat

---

COOK'S NOTE

WHERE DOUGH LIKES TO REST

Yeast dough likes a warm, cozy, draft-free place while it's stretching and rising to double its size. One easy way to control the environment: Bring a pan of water to a boil and place the pan on the bottom rack of an unheated oven. Cover the dough with lightly greased plastic wrap and place it on the top oven rack. Shut the oven door. If the oven is otherwise occupied, place a baking rack over a pan of hot water and set the bowl of dough on top of the rack, covered with lightly greased plastic wrap and a towel.

Dilly Casserole Bread

PREP TIME: 20 MINUTES (READY IN 3 HOURS)
◆ YIELD: 1 (18-SLICE) LOAF

    2 to 2⅔ cups all-purpose flour
    2 tablespoons sugar
    2 to 3 teaspoons instant minced onion
    2 teaspoons dill seed
    1 teaspoon salt
    ¼ teaspoon baking soda
    1 pkg. active dry yeast
    ¼ cup water
    1 tablespoon margarine or butter
    1 cup small-curd creamed cottage cheese
    1 egg
    2 teaspoons margarine or butter, melted
    ¼ teaspoon coarse salt, if desired

1. In large bowl, combine 1 cup flour, sugar, onion, dill seed, 1 teaspoon salt, baking soda and yeast; mix well.
2. In small saucepan, heat water, 1 tablespoon margarine and cottage cheese until very warm (120 to 130°F.). Add warm liquid and egg to flour mixture; blend at low speed

until moistened. Beat 3 minutes at medium speed.

3. By hand, stir in remaining 1 to 1⅔ cups flour to form a stiff batter. Cover loosely with greased plastic wrap and cloth towel. Let rise in warm place (80 to 85°F.) until light and doubled in size, 45 to 60 minutes.

4. Generously grease 1½ or 2-quart casserole. Stir down batter to remove all air bubbles. Turn batter into greased casserole. Cover; let rise in warm place until light and doubled in size, 30 to 45 minutes.

5. Heat oven to 350°F. Uncover dough. Bake 30 to 40 minutes or until loaf is deep golden brown and sounds hollow when lightly tapped. If necessary, cover with foil to prevent overbrowning. Remove from casserole; place on wire rack. Brush loaf with melted margarine; sprinkle with coarse salt. Cool 15 minutes. Serve warm or cool.

1. FOOD PROCESSOR DIRECTIONS: In small bowl, dissolve yeast in ¼ cup *warm* water (105 to 115°F.). In food processor bowl with metal blade, combine 2 cups flour, sugar, onion, dill seed, 1 teaspoon salt, baking soda and 1 tablespoon margarine; process 5 seconds. Add cottage cheese and egg; process about 10 seconds or until blended.

2. With machine running, pour yeast mixture through feed tube. Continue processing until blended, about 20 seconds or until mixture pulls away from sides of bowl and forms a ball. (If dough does not form a ball, add additional flour, 1 tablespoon at a time.)

3. Carefully scrape dough from blade and bowl; place in greased bowl. Cover; let rise. Continue as directed above.

Dilly Casserole Bread (page 52)

HIGH ALTITUDE *(above 3500 feet)*: Bake at 375°F. for 35 to 40 minutes.

NUTRITION INFORMATION PER SERVING: Serving Size: 1 Slice ◆ Calories: 100 ◆ Calories from Fat: 20 ◆ **% DAILY VALUE:** Total Fat: 2 g 3% ◆ Saturated Fat: 1 g 5% ◆ Cholesterol: 15 mg 5% ◆ Sodium: 230 mg 10% ◆ Total Carbohydrate: 16 g 5% ◆ Dietary Fiber: 1 g 3% ◆ Sugars: 2 g ◆ Protein: 4 g ◆ Vitamin A: 0% ◆ Vitamin C: 0% ◆ Calcium: 0% ◆ Iron: 6% ◆ **DIETARY EXCHANGES:** 1 Starch, ½ Fat OR 1 Carbohydrate, ½ Fat

Buttered Bread Crumbs

PREP TIME: 5 MINUTES ✦ YIELD: ½ CUP

  2 to 3 tablespoons butter
½ cup unseasoned dry bread crumbs
⅛ teaspoon salt

In small saucepan, melt butter. Add bread crumbs and salt; mix well.

NUTRITION INFORMATION PER SERVING: Serving Size: 1 Tablespoon ◆ Calories: 70 ◆ Calories from Fat: 45 ◆ **% DAILY VALUE:** Total Fat: 5 g 8% ◆ Saturated Fat: 3 g 15% ◆ Cholesterol: 10 mg 3% ◆ Sodium: 135 mg 6% ◆ Total Carbohydrate: 5 g 2% ◆ Dietary Fiber: 0 g 0% ◆ Sugars: 0 g ◆ Protein: 1 g ◆ Vitamin A: 4% ◆ Vitamin C: 0% ◆ Calcium: 0% ◆ Iron: 2% ◆ **DIETARY EXCHANGES:** ½ Starch, 1 Fat OR ½ Carbohydrate, 1 Fat

Buttered Croutons

PREP TIME: 10 MINUTES (READY IN 45 MINUTES) ✦ YIELD: 4 CUPS

10 slices bread
½ cup butter, melted

1. Heat oven to 300°F. Trim crusts from bread; cut slices into ½-inch cubes. Spread cubes in ungreased 15 × 10 × 1-inch baking pan. Drizzle butter over cubes; toss to coat.

2. Bake at 300°F. for 30 to 35 minutes or until dry, crisp and golden brown, stirring occasionally. Store covered in refrigerator.

NUTRITION INFORMATION PER SERVING: Serving Size: ¼ Cup ◆ Calories: 80 ◆ Calories from Fat: 50 ◆ **% DAILY VALUE:** Total Fat: 6 g 9% ◆ Saturated Fat: 4 g 20% ◆ Cholesterol: 15 mg 5% ◆ Sodium: 110 mg 5% ◆ Total Carbohydrate: 5 g 2% ◆ Dietary Fiber: 0 g 0% ◆ Sugars: 0 g ◆ Protein: 1 g ◆ Vitamin A: 4% ◆ Vitamin C: 0% ◆ Calcium: 0% ◆ Iron: 0% ◆ **DIETARY EXCHANGES:** ½ Starch, 1 Fat OR ½ Carbohydrate, 1 Fat

VARIATIONS

Garlic Croutons: Add 2 garlic cloves, minced, or ¼ teaspoon garlic powder to butter.

Herb Croutons: Add 2 teaspoons dried basil leaves, finely crushed, to butter.

Carrot-Onion-Dill Bread

	SMALL LOAF (8 slices)	LARGE LOAF (12 slices)
Water, room temperature	¾ cup	1¼ cups
Shredded carrots	⅓ cup	½ cup
Bread flour	2 cups	3 cups
Instant nonfat dry milk	1 tablespoon	2 tablespoons
Sugar	1 teaspoon	2 teaspoons
Salt	1 teaspoon	1¼ teaspoons
Margarine or butter, room temperature	1 tablespoon	2 tablespoons
Dried dill weed	⅛ teaspoon	¼ teaspoon
Dried minced onion	1 tablespoon	1½ tablespoons
Active dry yeast	1¼ teaspoons	2 teaspoons

1. If bread machine typically uses 2 cups flour, use small loaf recipe. If machine uses 3 cups flour, use large loaf recipe.
2. Follow manufacturer's directions for loading ingredients into machine. Measure ingredients carefully.
3. Select regular, rapid or delayed-time bake cycle and follow manufacturer's directions for starting machine.

HIGH ALTITUDE (*above 3500 feet*)**:** For small loaf, increase water by 1 to 2 tablespoons and decrease yeast by ¼ to ½ teaspoon. For large loaf, increase water by 1½ to 3 tablespoons and decrease yeast by ¼ to ¾ teaspoon. Continue as directed above.

NUTRITION INFORMATION PER SERVING: Serving Size: 1 Slice ◆ Calories: 150 ◆ Calories from Fat: 20 ◆ **% DAILY VALUE:** Total Fat: 2 g 3% ◆ Saturated Fat: 0 g 0% ◆ Cholesterol: 0 mg 0% ◆ Sodium: 290 mg 12% ◆ Total Carbohydrate: 27 g 9% ◆ Dietary Fiber: 1 g 4% ◆ Sugars: 2 g ◆ Protein: 5 g ◆ Vitamin A: 25% ◆ Vitamin C: 0% ◆ Calcium: 0% ◆ Iron: 10% ◆ **DIETARY EXCHANGES:** 1½ Starch, ½ Fat OR 1½ Carbohydrate, ½ Fat

---

COOK'S NOTE

BREAD MACHINE TIPS

+ Use bread flour, not all-purpose flour.
+ Measure ingredients precisely. The machine cannot adjust to slight variations the way an experienced baker can.
+ Bread machine recipes usually call for yeast by the teaspoonful rather than by the packet.
+ Jarred yeast is handier and easier to measure than envelopes of yeast, and if you use a bread machine regularly you probably will go through a jar of yeast before it expires.
+ Remove the baked loaf from the pan promptly to avoid sogginess.
+ Some machines cannot handle whole-grain flours or heavy doughs; others can.

Light Grain Bread

	SMALL LOAF (8 slices)	LARGE LOAF (12 slices)
Water, room temperature	¾ cup	1¼ cups
Bread flour	2 cups	3 cups
Instant nonfat dry milk	1 tablespoon	1½ tablespoons
Molasses	1 tablespoon	1½ tablespoons
Honey	1 tablespoon	1½ tablespoons
Salt	¾ teaspoon	1¼ teaspoons
Margarine or butter, room temperature	1 tablespoon	2 tablespoons
Wheat germ	3 tablespoons	¼ cup
Shelled sunflower seeds	2 tablespoons	3 tablespoons
Active dry yeast	1½ teaspoons	2½ teaspoons

1. If bread machine typically uses 2 cups flour, use small loaf recipe. If machine uses 3 cups flour, use large loaf recipe.
2. Follow manufacturer's directions for loading ingredients into machine. Measure ingredients carefully.

3. Select regular, rapid or delayed-time bake cycle and follow manufacturer's directions for starting machine.

HIGH ALTITUDE *(above 3500 feet)*: For small loaf, increase liquid by 1 to 2 tablespoons and decrease yeast by ¼ to ½ teaspoon. For large loaf, increase liquid by 1½ to 3 tablespoons and decrease yeast by ¼ to ¾ teaspoon. Continue as directed above.

NUTRITION INFORMATION PER SERVING: Serving Size: 1 Slice ♦ Calories:180 ♦ Calories from Fat: 25 ♦ % DAILY VALUE: Total Fat: 3 g 5% ♦ Saturated Fat: 1 g 5% ♦ Cholesterol: 0 mg 0% ♦ Sodium: 220 mg 9% ♦ Total Carbohydrate: 31 g 10% ♦ Dietary Fiber: 2 g 8% ♦ Sugars: 5 g ♦ Protein: 6 g ♦ Vitamin A: 0% ♦ Vitamin C: 0% ♦ Calcium: 2% ♦ Iron: 10% ♦ DIETARY EXCHANGES: 2 Starch, ½ Fat OR 2 Carbohydrate, ½ Fat

BREAD MACHINE TROUBLESHOOTING
If your bread isn't turning out as expected, the following suggestions may help.

PROBLEM	SOLUTION
Center of loaf is underbaked.	Reduce wet ingredients by a tablespoon at a time; increase kneading time for whole wheat or other coarse flour.
Loaf over-rises and then falls.	Decrease sugar or yeast or liquid, or increase salt slightly.
Texture is too coarse or full of holes.	Decrease liquid or yeast, or increase salt slightly.
Loaf is too heavy.	Increase yeast or sugar slightly; if using whole wheat or another coarse flour, substitute some bread flour.

Spiced Apple Bread

	SMALL LOAF (8 slices)	LARGE LOAF (12 slices)
Unsweetened apple juice, room temperature	½ cup	¾ cup
Natural applesauce, room temperature	¼ cup	½ cup
Margarine or butter, room temperature	1 tablespoon	2 tablespoons
Bread flour	1⅔ cups	2½ cups
Rolled oats	⅓ cup	¾ cup
Sugar	4 teaspoons	¼ cup
Salt	½ teaspoon	1 teaspoon
Cinnamon	¾ teaspoon	1 teaspoon
Ginger	⅛ teaspoon	¼ teaspoon
Active dry yeast	1¼ teaspoons	2½ teaspoons

1. If bread machine typically uses 2 cups flour, use small loaf recipe. If machine uses 3 cups flour, use large loaf recipe.
2. Follow manufacturer's directions for loading ingredients into machine. Measure ingredients carefully.
3. Select regular, rapid or delayed-time bake cycle and follow manufacturer's directions for starting machine.

HIGH ALTITUDE *(above 3500 feet)*: For small loaf, increase apple juice by 1 to 2 tablespoons and decrease yeast by ¼ to ½ teaspoon. For large loaf, increase apple juice by 1½ to 3 tablespoons and decrease yeast by ¼ to ¾ teaspoon. Continue as directed above.

NUTRITION INFORMATION PER SERVING: Serving Size: 1 Slice ♦ Calories:180 ♦ Calories from Fat: 25 ♦ % DAILY VALUE: Total Fat: 3 g 5% ♦ Saturated Fat: 0 g 0% ♦ Cholesterol: 0 mg 0% ♦ Sodium: 200 mg 8% ♦ Total Carbohydrate: 32 g 11% ♦ Dietary Fiber: 2 g 8% ♦ Sugars: 7 g ♦ Protein: 5 g ♦ Vitamin A: 0% ♦ Vitamin C: 0% ♦ Calcium: 0% ♦ Iron: 10% ♦ DIETARY EXCHANGES: 2 Starch, ½ Fat OR 2 Carbohydrate, ½ Fat

Basic Dinner Rolls

PREP TIME: 35 MINUTES (READY IN 2 HOURS
40 MINUTES) ◆ YIELD: 32 ROLLS

5¾ to 6¾ cups all-purpose flour
¼ cup sugar
2 teaspoons salt
2 pkg. active dry yeast
1 cup water
1 cup milk
½ cup margarine or butter
1 egg
Melted margarine or butter, if desired

Basic Dinner Rolls

1. In large bowl, combine 2 cups flour, sugar, salt and yeast; mix well. In small

---

C O O K ' S   N O T E

HOW TO SHAPE DINNER ROLLS

Pan Rolls: Lightly grease 13×9-inch pan. Using half of dough, divide into 16 equal pieces. Shape each into a ball, pulling edges under to make a smooth top. Place balls, smooth side up, in greased pan.
Cover; let rise in warm place until light and doubled in size, 20 to 30 minutes.
YIELD: 16 ROLLS

Bowknot Rolls: Lightly grease cookie sheets. Using half of dough, divide dough into 16 equal pieces. On lightly floured surface, roll each piece into a 9-inch rope. Tie each into a loose knot.
Place 2 to 3 inches apart on greased cookie sheets. After rising, bake 12 to 15 minutes or until golden brown.
YIELD: 16 ROLLS

Cloverleaf Rolls: Lightly grease 12 muffin cups. Using half of dough, divide dough into 12 equal pieces; divide each into thirds. Shape each into a ball, pulling edges under to make a smooth top.
Place 3 balls, smooth side up, in each greased muffin cup. After rising, bake 14 to

18 minutes or until golden brown.
YIELD: 12 ROLLS

Crescent Rolls: Lightly grease cookie sheets. Using half of dough, divide dough in half again; shape each half into a ball. On lightly floured surface, roll each ball into a 12-inch round. Spread each with 1 tablespoon softened
margarine or butter. Cut each round into 12 wedges. Beginning at wide end of wedge, roll toward point. Place, point side down, 2 to 3 inches apart on greased cookie sheets. Curve ends to form a crescent shape. After rising, bake 12 to 15 minutes or until golden brown.
YIELD: 24 ROLLS

Crown Rolls: Lightly grease 12 muffin cups. Using half of dough, divide dough into 12 equal pieces. Shape each into a ball, pulling edges under to make a smooth top. Place 1 ball, smooth side up, in each greased muffin cup.
Using kitchen scissors dipped in flour, cut balls of dough into quarters almost to bottom. After rising, bake 14 to 18 minutes or until golden brown.
YIELD: 12 ROLLS

saucepan, heat water, milk and ½ cup margarine until very warm (120 to 130°F.). Add warm liquid and egg to flour mixture; blend at low speed until moistened. Beat 3 minutes at medium speed. By hand, stir in an additional 2½ to 3 cups flour until dough pulls cleanly away from sides of bowl.

2. On floured surface, knead in 1¼ to 1¾ cups flour until dough is smooth and elastic, 8 to 10 minutes. Place dough in greased bowl; cover loosely with greased plastic wrap and cloth towel. Let rise in warm place (80 to 85°F.) until light and doubled in size, 45 to 60 minutes.

3. Punch down dough several times to remove all air bubbles. Divide dough in half. Shape each half as directed in "How to Shape Dinner Rolls," page 56.

4. Heat oven to 400°F. Uncover dough. Bake 16 to 20 minutes or until golden brown. Immediately remove rolls from pans; cool on wire racks for 15 minutes. Brush with melted margarine. Serve warm or cool.

HIGH ALTITUDE (*above 3500 feet*)**:** No change.

NUTRITION INFORMATION PER SERVING: Serving Size: 1 Roll • Calories: 140 • Calories from Fat: 35 • % DAILY VALUE: Total Fat: 4 g 6% • Saturated Fat: 1 g 5% • Cholesterol: 5 mg 2% • Sodium: 180 mg 8% • Total Carbohydrate: 22 g 7% • Dietary Fiber: 1 g 3% • Sugars: 2 g • Protein: 3 g • Vitamin A: 4% • Vitamin C: 0% • Calcium: 0% • Iron: 8% • DIETARY EXCHANGES: 1½ Starch, ½ Fat OR 1½ Carbohydrate, ½ Fat

Basic Sweet Roll Dough

PREP TIME: 25 MINUTES (READY IN 1 HOUR 25 MINUTES)

 6 to 7 cups all-purpose flour
½ cup sugar
 2 teaspoons salt
 2 pkg. active dry yeast
 1 cup water
 1 cup milk
½ cup margarine or butter
 1 egg

1. In large bowl, combine 2 cups flour, sugar, salt and yeast; mix well. In small saucepan, heat water, milk and margarine until very warm (120 to 130°F.). Add warm liquid and egg to flour mixture; blend at low speed until moistened. Beat 3 minutes at medium speed. By hand, stir in an additional 3 cups flour until dough pulls cleanly away from sides of bowl.

2. On floured surface, knead in 1 to 2 cups flour until dough is smooth and elastic, 8 to 10 minutes. Place dough in greased bowl; cover loosely with greased plastic wrap and cloth towel. Let rise in warm place (80 to 85°F.) until light and doubled in size, 45 to 60 minutes.

3. Punch down dough several times to remove all air bubbles. Divide dough in half. Shape as directed in the following 3 recipes.

HIGH ALTITUDE (*above 3500 feet*)**:** No change.

Caramel-Nut Sweet Rolls

PREP TIME: 20 MINUTES (READY IN 1 HOUR 40 MINUTES) • YIELD: 20 ROLLS

TOPPING
½ cup firmly packed brown sugar
½ cup margarine or butter, softened
 2 tablespoons light corn syrup
¼ cup chopped nuts

ROLLS
½ recipe Basic Sweet Roll Dough (this page)
 2 tablespoons margarine or butter, softened
¼ cup sugar
 1 teaspoon cinnamon

1. Generously grease 13×9-inch pan. In small bowl, combine brown sugar, ½ cup margarine and corn syrup; blend well. Drop mixture by spoonfuls into greased pan; spread evenly. Sprinkle with nuts.

2. On lightly floured surface, roll dough to 20×12-inch rectangle. Spread with 2 tablespoons margarine. In small bowl, combine sugar and cinnamon; mix well. Sprinkle over dough. Starting with 20-inch side, roll up jelly-roll fashion; pinch edges firmly to seal seams. Cut into twenty 1-inch slices; place cut side down in prepared pan.

3. Cover; let rise in warm place (80 to 85°F.) until light and doubled in size, 35 to 45 minutes.

4. Heat oven to 375°F. Uncover dough. Bake 25 to 30 minutes or until deep golden brown. Cool in pan 1 minute; invert onto wire rack. Serve warm.

NUTRITION INFORMATION PER SERVING: Serving Size: 1 Roll • Calories: 210 • Calories from Fat: 80 • % DAILY VALUE: Total Fat: 9 g 14% • Saturated Fat: 2 g 10% • Cholesterol: 5 mg 2% • Sodium: 210 mg 9% • Total Carbohydrate: 30 g 10% • Dietary Fiber: 1 g 3% • Sugars: 12 g • Protein: 3 g • Vitamin A: 8% • Vitamin C: 0% • Calcium: 2% • Iron: 8% • DIETARY EXCHANGES: 1 Starch, 1 Fruit, 1½ Fat OR 2 Carbohydrate, 1½ Fat

Cinnamon Sweet Rolls

PREP TIME: 25 MINUTES (READY IN 1 HOUR 50 MINUTES)
✦ YIELD: 20 ROLLS

ROLLS
½ recipe Basic Sweet Roll Dough (page 57)

FILLING
¼ cup margarine or butter, softened
½ cup sugar
2 teaspoons cinnamon

ICING
¾ cup powdered sugar
1 tablespoon margarine or butter, softened
¼ teaspoon vanilla
1 to 2 tablespoons milk

1. Generously grease 13×9-inch pan. On lightly floured surface, roll out dough to 20×12-inch rectangle. Spread with ¼ cup margarine.
2. In small bowl, combine sugar and cinnamon; mix well. Sprinkle over dough. Starting with 20-inch side, roll up jelly-roll fashion; pinch edges firmly to seal seams. Cut into twenty 1-inch slices; place cut side down in greased pan.
3. Cover; let rise in warm place (80 to 85°F.) until light and doubled in size, 35 to 45 minutes.
4. Heat oven to 375°F. Uncover dough. Bake 25 to 30 minutes or until golden brown. Immediately remove from pan; place on wire rack.
5. In small bowl, blend all icing ingredients, adding enough milk for desired drizzling consistency. Drizzle over warm rolls. Serve warm.

NUTRITION INFORMATION PER SERVING: Serving Size: 1 Roll ✦ Calories: 180 ✦ Calories from Fat: 50 ✦ % DAILY VALUE: Total Fat: 6 g 9% ✦ Saturated Fat: 1 g 5% ✦ Cholesterol: 5 mg 2% ✦ Sodium: 170 mg 7% ✦ Total Carbohydrate: 29 g 10% ✦ Dietary Fiber: 1 g 3% ✦ Sugars: 13 g ✦ Protein: 3 g ✦ Vitamin A: 5% ✦ Vitamin C: 0% ✦ Calcium: 0% ✦ Iron: 6% ✦ DIETARY EXCHANGES: 1 Starch, 1 Fruit, 1 Fat OR 2 Carbohydrate, 1 Fat

---

COOK'S NOTE

OVERNIGHT METHOD

After letting the dough rise once, refrigerate it overnight, covered with greased plastic wrap. In the morning, punch down the dough and let it rise again, then bake.

Refrigerated Coffee Cake Dough

PREP TIME: 20 MINUTES

3¾ to 4 cups all-purpose flour
¼ cup sugar
1 teaspoon salt
2 pkg. active dry yeast
1 cup milk
¼ cup water
½ cup margarine or butter
2 eggs

1. In large bowl, combine 1½ cups flour, sugar, salt and yeast; mix well.
2. In small saucepan, heat milk, water and margarine until very warm (120 to 130°F.). Add warm liquid and eggs to flour mixture; blend at low speed until moistened. Beat 3 minutes at medium speed.
3. By hand, stir in 2¼ to 2½ cups flour to make a stiff dough. Cover tightly; refrigerate overnight. Shape as directed in the following 3 recipes.

HIGH ALTITUDE (*above 3500 feet*): No change.

Fresh Apple Coffee Cake

PREP TIME: 20 MINUTES (READY IN 1 HOUR 45 MINUTES)
✦ YIELD: 15 SERVINGS

COFFEE CAKE
1 recipe Refrigerated Coffee Cake Dough (above)
4 cups sliced peeled apples
¾ cup sugar
3 tablespoons all-purpose flour
½ teaspoon cinnamon
2 tablespoons margarine or butter

GLAZE
½ cup powdered sugar
3 to 4 teaspoons milk

1. Generously grease 13×9-inch pan. Press dough in greased pan. Arrange apple slices in rows on top of dough.
2. In small bowl, combine sugar, flour and cinnamon; mix well. With pastry blender or fork, cut in margarine until mixture is crumbly. Sprinkle evenly over apples. Cover loosely with plastic wrap and cloth towel.

Let rise in warm place (80 to 85°F.) until light and doubled in size, 40 to 45 minutes.

3. Heat oven to 375°F. Uncover dough. Bake 30 to 40 minutes or until edges are golden brown and apples are tender.

4. In small bowl, blend powdered sugar and enough milk for desired drizzling consistency. Drizzle over warm coffee cake. Serve warm.

NUTRITION INFORMATION PER SERVING: Serving Size: 1/15 of Recipe ◆ Calories: 310 ◆ Calories from Fat: 80 ◆ **% DAILY VALUE:** Total Fat: 9 g 14% ◆ Saturated Fat: 2 g 10% ◆ Cholesterol: 30 mg 10% ◆ Sodium: 250 mg 10% ◆ Total Carbohydrate: 51 g 17% ◆ Dietary Fiber: 2 g 8% ◆ Sugars: 22 g ◆ Protein: 6 g ◆ Vitamin A: 8% ◆ Vitamin C: 0% ◆ Calcium: 4% ◆ Iron: 10% ◆ **DIETARY EXCHANGES:** 2 Starch, 1 Fruit, 1½ Fat OR 3 Carbohydrate, 1½ Fat

Streusel Coffee Cake

PREP TIME: 10 MINUTES (READY IN 1 HOUR 25 MINUTES)
◆ YIELD: 15 SERVINGS

  1 recipe Refrigerated Coffee Cake Dough
    (page 58)
  ½ cup all-purpose flour
  ⅓ cup firmly packed brown sugar
  1 teaspoon cinnamon
  ¼ cup margarine or butter
  ½ cup chopped nuts

1. Grease 13×9-inch pan. Press dough in greased pan. Cover loosely with plastic wrap and cloth towel. Let rise in warm place (80 to 85°F.) until light and doubled in size, 45 to 60 minutes.

2. In small bowl, combine flour, brown sugar and cinnamon; mix well. With pastry blender or fork, cut in margarine until mixture is crumbly. Stir in nuts.

3. Heat oven to 375°F. Uncover dough. Sprinkle brown sugar mixture over dough. Bake at 375°F. for 20 to 25 minutes or until golden brown. Serve warm.

NUTRITION INFORMATION PER SERVING: Serving Size: 1/15 of Recipe ◆ Calories: 300 ◆ Calories from Fat: 120 ◆ **% DAILY VALUE:** Total Fat: 13 g 20% ◆ Saturated Fat: 2 g 10% ◆ Cholesterol: 30 mg 10% ◆ Sodium: 270 mg 11% ◆ Total Carbohydrate: 40 g 13% ◆ Dietary Fiber: 2 g 8% ◆ Sugars: 10 g ◆ Protein: 6 g ◆ Vitamin A: 10% ◆ Vitamin C: 0% ◆ Calcium: 4% ◆ Iron: 15% ◆ **DIETARY EXCHANGES:** 2 Starch, ½ Fruit, 2½ Fat OR 2½ Carbohydrate, 2½ Fat

Pineapple Nut Coffee Cake

PREP TIME: 25 MINUTES (READY IN 2 HOURS)
◆ YIELD: 2 (12-SLICE) COFFEE CAKES

COFFEE CAKE
  ¼ cup sugar
  1 tablespoon cornstarch
  1 (8-oz.) can crushed pineapple in
    unsweetened juice, undrained
  2 tablespoons margarine or butter
  ½ cup chopped nuts
  ½ cup raisins, if desired
  1 recipe Refrigerated Coffee Cake Dough
    (page 58)

TOPPING
  ¼ cup sugar
  2 tablespoons all-purpose flour
  1 tablespoon margarine or butter, softened

1. In small saucepan, combine ¼ cup sugar, cornstarch and pineapple with juice; blend well. Cook over medium heat for about 3 minutes or until thickened, stirring constantly. Remove from heat; stir in 2 tablespoons margarine, nuts and raisins. Cool 30 minutes.

2. Grease 2 cookie sheets. Turn dough out onto lightly floured surface; divide in half. Roll half of dough into 12×6-inch rectangle; place on greased cookie sheet. Spread half of pineapple mixture lengthwise down center ⅓ of rectangle. Cut 1-inch-wide strips on each side of rectangle just to edge of pineapple mixture.

3. To give braided appearance, fold strips of dough at an angle across pineapple mixture, alternating from side to side. Repeat with second half of dough. Cover loosely with greased plastic wrap and cloth towel. Let rise in warm place (80 to 85°F.) until light and doubled in size, 30 to 40 minutes.

4. Heat oven to 375°F. In small bowl, combine all topping ingredients; blend well. Uncover dough. Sprinkle half of topping on each coffee cake.

5. Bake at 375°F. for 20 to 25 minutes or until golden brown. Serve warm.

NUTRITION INFORMATION PER SERVING: Serving Size: 1 Slice ◆ Calories: 200 ◆ Calories from Fat: 70 ◆ **% DAILY VALUE:** Total Fat: 8 g 12% ◆ Saturated Fat: 1 g 5% ◆ Cholesterol: 20 mg 7% ◆ Sodium: 160 mg 7% ◆ Total Carbohydrate: 29 g 10% ◆ Dietary Fiber: 1 g 4% ◆ Sugars: 11 g ◆ Protein: 4 g ◆ Vitamin A: 6% ◆ Vitamin C: 0% ◆ Calcium: 2% ◆ Iron: 8% ◆ **DIETARY EXCHANGES:** 1 Starch, 1 Fruit, 1½ Fat OR 2 Carbohydrate, 1½ Fat

Italian Breadsticks

PREP TIME: 30 MINUTES (READY IN 2 HOURS)
✦ YIELD: 24 BREADSTICKS

1 pkg. active dry yeast
⅔ cup warm water
2 to 2¼ cups all-purpose flour
1½ teaspoons sugar
1 teaspoon garlic salt
¼ cup shortening
1 tablespoon water
1 egg white
Sesame or poppy seed

1. In large bowl, dissolve yeast in ⅔ cup warm water (105 to 115°F.). Add 1 cup flour, sugar, garlic salt and shortening; blend at low speed until moistened. Beat 3 minutes at medium speed. By hand, stir in an additional 1 to 1¼ cups flour to form a soft dough.

2. Place dough in greased bowl; cover loosely with greased plastic wrap and cloth towel. Let rise in warm place (80 to 85°F.) until light and doubled in size, 30 to 40 minutes.

Left to right: Herb Focaccia (page 50), Italian Breadsticks

3. Grease 15×10×1-inch baking pan. On lightly floured surface, knead dough about 10 times or until no longer sticky. Roll into 15×10-inch rectangle; place in greased pan. Starting with 10-inch side, cut dough into 12 strips. Cut strips in half crosswise forming 24 sticks.

4. In small bowl, combine 1 tablespoon water and egg white; beat slightly. Brush over sticks. Sprinkle with sesame seed. Cover; let rise in warm place, 15 to 20 minutes.

5. Heat oven to 375°F. Uncover dough. Bake 18 to 22 minutes or until golden brown. Immediately remove from pan; cool on wire rack for 5 minutes. Serve warm.

> **TIP:** For softer breadsticks, dough can be baked in greased 13×9-inch pan. Cut into 20 breadsticks.

HIGH ALTITUDE *(above 3500 feet)*: No change.

NUTRITION INFORMATION PER SERVING: Serving Size: 1 Breadstick ✦ Calories: 70 ✦ Calories from Fat: 25 ✦ **% DAILY VALUE:** Total Fat: 3 g 5% ✦ Saturated Fat: 1 g 5% ✦ Cholesterol: 0 mg 0% ✦ Sodium: 80 mg 3% ✦ Total Carbohydrate: 9 g 3% ✦ Dietary Fiber: 0 g 0% ✦ Sugars: 0 g ✦ Protein: 2 g ✦ Vitamin A: 0% ✦ Vitamin C: 0% ✦ Calcium: 0% ✦ Iron: 4% ✦ **DIETARY EXCHANGES:** ½ Starch, ½ Fat OR ½ Carbohydrate, ½ Fat

Soft Pretzels

PREP TIME: 45 MINUTES (READY IN 2 HOURS)
✦ YIELD: 12 PRETZELS

3 to 3½ cups all-purpose flour
1 tablespoon sugar
1 teaspoon salt
1 pkg. active dry yeast
1 cup water
1 tablespoon shortening
6 cups water
¼ cup baking soda
1 tablespoon water
1 egg white
Coarse salt or sesame seed

1. In large bowl, combine 1 cup flour, sugar, salt and yeast; mix well. In small saucepan, heat 1 cup water and shortening until very warm (120 to 130°F.). Add warm liquid to flour mixture; blend at low speed until moistened. Beat 3 minutes at medium speed. Stir in an additional 1½ to 1¾ cups flour until dough pulls cleanly away from sides of bowl.

2. On floured surface, knead in ½ to ¾ cup flour until dough is smooth and elastic, about 5 minutes. Place dough in greased bowl; cover loosely with greased plastic

wrap and cloth towel. Let rise in warm place (80 to 85°F.) until doubled in size, 45 to 60 minutes.

3. Grease cookie sheets. Punch down dough several times to remove all air bubbles. Shape dough into ball. Divide dough into 12 pieces. Roll each into 16-inch rope; form each rope into pretzel shape. Place on greased cookie sheets. Cover; let rise in warm place until light, 15 to 20 minutes.

4. Heat oven to 400°F. In large nonaluminum saucepan, combine 6 cups water and baking soda; mix well. Bring to a boil. Drop pretzels, one at a time, into water that is just boiling; cook 5 seconds on each side. Remove pretzels from water with slotted spoon; place on greased cookie sheet. In small bowl, combine 1 tablespoon water and egg white; beat well. Brush over pretzels. Sprinkle with coarse salt.

5. Bake at 400°F. for 8 to 10 minutes or until golden brown. Immediately remove from cookie sheets; cool on wire racks for 5 minutes. Serve warm.

HIGH ALTITUDE (*above 3500 feet*): No change.

NUTRITION INFORMATION PER SERVING: Serving Size: 1 Pretzel • Calories: 140 • Calories from Fat: 10 • % DAILY VALUE: Total Fat: 1 g 2% • Saturated Fat: 0 g 0% • Cholesterol: 0 mg 0% • Sodium: 850 mg 35% • Total Carbohydrate: 29 g 10% • Dietary Fiber: 1 g 4% • Sugars: 2 g • Protein: 4 g • Vitamin A: 0% • Vitamin C: 0% • Calcium: 0% • Iron: 10% • DIETARY EXCHANGES: 1½ Starch, ½ Fruit OR 2 Carbohydrate

Basic Pizza Crust

PREP TIME: 20 MINUTES (READY IN 1 HOUR 25 MINUTES)
♦ YIELD: 2 CRUSTS; 8 SERVINGS EACH

    2¼ to 2¾ cups all-purpose flour
    1 teaspoon sugar
    1 teaspoon salt
    1 pkg. fast-acting yeast
    1 cup water
    2 tablespoons olive or vegetable oil

1. In large bowl, combine 1½ cups flour, sugar, salt and yeast; mix well. In small saucepan, heat water until very warm (120 to 130°F.). Add warm water and oil to flour mixture; blend at low speed until well moistened. Beat 2 minutes at medium speed. By hand, stir in an additional ½ to ¾ cup flour until dough pulls cleanly away from sides of bowl.

2. On floured surface, knead in ¼ to ½ cup flour until dough is smooth and elastic, 3 to 5 minutes. Place dough in greased bowl;

cover loosely with greased plastic wrap and cloth towel. Let rise in warm place (80 to 85°F.) until doubled in size, 30 minutes.

3. Place oven rack at lowest position; heat oven to 425°F. Grease two 12-inch pizza pans. Punch down dough several times to remove all air bubbles. Divide dough in half; press in greased pizza pans.

4. Bake at 425°F. on lowest oven rack for 15 minutes. Top as desired with favorite pizza toppings. Bake an additional 15 to 20 minutes or until crust is golden brown and toppings are thoroughly heated.

1. FOOD PROCESSOR DIRECTIONS: In food processor bowl with metal blade, combine 2¼ cups flour, sugar, salt and yeast; process 5 seconds.

2. In small saucepan, heat water until very warm (120 to 130°F.). With machine running, pour water and oil through feed tube; continue processing until dough forms a ball. (If dough does not form a ball, add an additional ½ cup flour, 1 tablespoon at a time.) Process an additional 40 to 60 seconds.

3. Carefully scrape dough from blade and bowl; place in greased bowl. Cover; let rise. Continue as directed above.

> **TIP:** To freeze 1 pizza crust, prepare as directed above. Grease 12-inch pizza pan. Press half of dough in greased pan. Bake at 425°F. for 15 minutes. Cool. Place in moisture-proof freezer bag. Freeze for up to 2 months. Thaw before using and top with favorite pizza toppings. Bake at 425°F. on lowest oven rack for 18 to 22 minutes or until crust is golden brown and toppings are thoroughly heated.

HIGH ALTITUDE (*above 3500 feet*): No change.

NUTRITION INFORMATION PER SERVING: Serving Size: 1⁄16 of Recipe • Calories: 90 • Calories from Fat: 20 • % DAILY VALUE: Total Fat: 2 g 3% • Saturated Fat: 0 g 0% • Cholesterol: 0 mg 0% • Sodium: 135 mg 6% • Total Carbohydrate: 17 g 6% • Dietary Fiber: 1 g 3% • Sugars: 1 g • Protein: 2 g • Vitamin A: 0% • Vitamin C: 0% • Calcium: 0% • Iron: 6% • DIETARY EXCHANGES: 1 Starch OR 1 Carbohydrate

Cake Doughnuts

PREP TIME: 40 MINUTES ✦ YIELD: 30 DOUGHNUTS

    4 cups all-purpose flour
    1 cup sugar
    3 teaspoons baking powder
    1 teaspoon baking soda
    1 teaspoon salt
    ½ teaspoon nutmeg
    1 cup buttermilk
    ¼ cup margarine or butter, melted
    1 teaspoon vanilla
    2 eggs, slightly beaten
      Oil for deep frying

1. In large bowl, combine flour, sugar, baking powder, baking soda, salt and nutmeg; mix well. Add all remaining ingredients except oil for frying; stir *just* until dry ingredients are moistened. If desired, refrigerate dough for easier handling.
2. Fill large saucepan or electric skillet ⅔ full with oil. Heat to 375°F.
3. On well-floured surface, knead dough 1 to 2 minutes or until no longer sticky. Roll half of dough at a time to ½-inch thickness. Cut with floured doughnut cutter.
4. With pancake turner, slip doughnuts and holes into hot oil (375°F.). Fry doughnuts and holes 1 to 1½ minutes on each side or until deep golden brown. Drain on paper towels. If desired, roll doughnuts and holes in powdered or granulated sugar, cinnamon-sugar mixture or drizzle with glaze.

HIGH ALTITUDE *(above 3500 feet)*: No change.

NUTRITION INFORMATION PER SERVING: Serving Size: 1 Doughnut ✦ Calories: 130 ✦ Calories from Fat: 45 ✦ **% DAILY VALUE:** Total Fat: 5 g 8% ✦ Saturated Fat: 1 g 5% ✦ Cholesterol: 15 mg 5% ✦ Sodium: 190 mg 8% ✦ Total Carbohydrate: 20 g 7% ✦ Dietary Fiber: 0 g 0% ✦ Sugars: 7 g ✦ Protein: 2 g ✦ Vitamin A: 0% ✦ Vitamin C: 0% ✦ Calcium: 4% ✦ Iron: 4% ✦ **DIETARY EXCHANGES:** ½ Starch, 1 Fruit, 1 Fat OR 1½ Carbohydrate, 1 Fat

VARIATIONS

Chocolate Doughnuts: Increase sugar to 1¼ cups and omit nutmeg. Add 1 oz. melted unsweetened chocolate or 1 envelope premelted unsweetened chocolate with eggs.

Orange Doughnuts: Omit nutmeg and add 2 tablespoons grated orange peel. Decrease buttermilk to ½ cup; add ½ cup orange juice.

Basic Crepes

PREP TIME: 30 MINUTES ✦ YIELD: 20 CREPES

    4 eggs
    1⅓ cups milk
    2 tablespoons margarine or butter, melted,
        or oil
    1 cup all-purpose flour
    ½ teaspoon salt, if desired

1. In medium bowl, beat eggs slightly. Add all remaining ingredients; beat until smooth.
2. Heat crepe pan, or 7 or 8-inch skillet over medium-high heat (375°F.) until hot. Grease pan lightly with oil.
3. Pour scant ¼ cup batter into hot pan, immediately tilting pan until batter covers bottom. Cook until edges start to dry and center is set. If desired, turn to brown other side.* Fill with desired filling.

> **TIP:** * At this point, crepes can be wrapped in foil and refrigerated for up to 3 days or frozen for up to 3 months. To thaw, place package of crepes in 300°F. oven for 10 to 15 minutes.

NUTRITION INFORMATION PER SERVING: Serving Size: 1 Crepe ✦ Calories: 60 ✦ Calories from Fat: 25 ✦ **% DAILY VALUE:** Total Fat: 3 g 5% ✦ Saturated Fat: 1 g 5% ✦ Cholesterol: 45 mg 15% ✦ Sodium: 90 mg 4% ✦ Total Carbohydrate: 6 g 2% ✦ Dietary Fiber: 0 g 0% ✦ Sugars: 1 g ✦ Protein: 2 g ✦ Vitamin A: 2% ✦ Vitamin C: 0% ✦ Calcium: 2% ✦ Iron: 2% ✦ **DIETARY EXCHANGES:** ½ Starch, ½ Fat OR ½ Carbohydrate, ½ Fat

Easy Crepes

PREP TIME: 30 MINUTES ✦ YIELD: 12 CREPES

    1 cup buttermilk complete pancake and waffle
        mix
    1 cup water
    2 eggs

1. In small bowl, combine all ingredients; beat with eggbeater or wire whisk until batter is smooth.
2. Heat crepe pan, or 7 or 8-inch skillet over medium-high heat (375°F.) until hot. Grease pan lightly with oil.
3. Pour scant ¼ cup batter into hot pan, immediately tilting pan until batter covers bottom. Cook until edges start to dry and center is set. If desired, turn to brown other side.* Fill with desired fillings.

> **TIP:** * At this point, crepes can be wrapped in foil and refrigerated for up to 3 days or frozen for up to 3 months. To thaw, place package of crepes in 300°F. oven for 10 to 15 minutes.

NUTRITION INFORMATION PER SERVING: Serving Size: 1 Crepe ♦ Calories: 45 ♦ Calories from Fat: 10 ♦ % DAILY VALUE: Total Fat: 1 g 2% ♦ Saturated Fat: 0 g 0% ♦ Cholesterol: 35 mg 12% ♦ Sodium: 160 mg 7% ♦ Total Carbohydrate: 7 g 2% ♦ Dietary Fiber: 0 g 0% ♦ Sugars: 1 g ♦ Protein: 2 g ♦ Vitamin A: 0% ♦ Vitamin C: 0% ♦ Calcium: 4% ♦ Iron: 4% ♦ DIETARY EXCHANGES: ½ Starch OR ½ Carbohydrate

VARIATION

Easy Dessert Crepes: Add 2 tablespoons sugar with pancake and waffle mix.

Pancakes

PREP TIME: 20 MINUTES
♦ YIELD: 16 (4-INCH) PANCAKES; 8 SERVINGS

  2 eggs
  2 cups buttermilk*
  ¼ cup oil
  1¾ cups all-purpose flour**
  2 tablespoons sugar
  2 teaspoons baking powder
  1 teaspoon baking soda
  ½ teaspoon salt

1. Heat griddle or large skillet over medium-high heat (375°F.) until hot. In large bowl, beat eggs. Stir in buttermilk and oil. Add all remaining ingredients; stir just until large lumps disappear. (For thicker pancakes, thicken batter with additional flour; for thinner pancakes, thin batter with additional buttermilk.)
2. Lightly grease heated griddle. A few drops of water sprinkled on griddle will sizzle and bounce when heat is just right. For each pancake, pour about ¼ cup batter onto hot griddle. Cook about 2 minutes or until edges look cooked and bubbles begin to break on surface. Turn pancakes; cook until golden brown.

TIPS: *To prepare pancakes using regular milk, decrease milk to 1¾ cups, increase baking powder to 4 teaspoons and omit baking soda. ** Self-rising flour can be substituted for all-purpose. Omit baking powder; decrease baking soda to ½ teaspoon and salt to ¼ teaspoon.

NUTRITION INFORMATION PER SERVING: Serving Size: ⅛ of Recipe ♦ Calories: 210 ♦ Calories from Fat: 80 ♦ % DAILY VALUE: Total Fat: 9 g 14% ♦ Saturated Fat: 2 g 10% ♦ Cholesterol: 55 mg 18% ♦ Sodium: 490 mg 20% ♦ Total Carbohydrate: 27 g 9% ♦ Dietary Fiber: 1 g 3% ♦ Sugars: 6 g ♦ Protein: 6 g ♦ Vitamin C: 0% ♦ Calcium: 15% ♦ Iron: 8% ♦ DIETARY EXCHANGES: 2 Starch, 1 Fat OR 2 Carbohydrate, 1 Fat

VARIATIONS

Apple Pancakes: Add ½ cup shredded peeled apple and ½ teaspoon cinnamon.

Blueberry Pancakes: Add 1 cup fresh or frozen blueberries, thawed and well drained.
Cheese Pancakes: Add ½ cup shredded cheese.
Nut Pancakes: Add ½ cup chopped nuts.
Whole Wheat Pancakes: Use 1 cup all-purpose flour and ¾ cup whole wheat flour.

Peaches 'n Cream Oven-Puffed Pancake

PREP TIME: 15 MINUTES (READY IN 35 MINUTES)
♦ YIELD: 4 SERVINGS

PANCAKE
  ½ cup all-purpose flour
  2 tablespoons sugar
  ¼ teaspoon salt
  ½ cup milk
  2 eggs, beaten
  1 tablespoon margarine or butter
  1 (16-oz.) can sliced peaches in extra light syrup, drained, reserving 3 tablespoons liquid
  2 tablespoons chopped pecans
  ⅛ teaspoon cinnamon

CREAM SAUCE
  ¼ cup sour cream
  2 tablespoons powdered sugar
  3 tablespoons reserved peach liquid
  ⅛ teaspoon almond extract

1. Heat oven to 425°F. In medium bowl, combine flour, sugar, salt, milk and eggs; beat with wire whisk or eggbeater until smooth.
2. Place margarine in 9-inch pie pan; melt in 425°F. oven for 2 to 4 minutes or just until margarine sizzles. Remove pan from oven; tilt to coat bottom with melted margarine. Immediately pour batter into hot pan. Top with peach slices, pecans and cinnamon.
3. Bake at 425°F. for 16 to 20 minutes or until puffed and golden brown.
4. Meanwhile, in small bowl, combine all cream sauce ingredients; mix well. Cut pancake into wedges. Serve immediately with cream sauce.

HIGH ALTITUDE (above 3500 feet)**:** No change.

NUTRITION INFORMATION PER SERVING: Serving Size: ¼ of Recipe ♦ Calories: 260 ♦ Calories from Fat: 110 ♦ % DAILY VALUE: Total Fat: 12 g 18% ♦ Saturated Fat: 4 g 20% ♦ Cholesterol: 115 mg 38% ♦ Sodium: 230 mg 10% ♦ Total Carbohydrate: 32 g 11% ♦ Dietary Fiber: 2 g 8% ♦ Sugars: 18 g ♦ Protein: 7 g ♦ Vitamin A: 20% ♦ Vitamin C: 4% ♦ Calcium: 8% ♦ Iron: 8% ♦ DIETARY EXCHANGES: 2 Starch, 2 Fat OR 2 Carbohydrate, 2 Fat

Four-Grain Pancakes

PREP TIME: 40 MINUTES
✦ YIELD: 16 (4-INCH) PANCAKES; 4 SERVINGS

¾ cup whole wheat flour
½ cup all-purpose flour
½ cup cornmeal
⅓ cup quick-cooking rolled oats
2 teaspoons baking powder
1 teaspoon baking soda
½ teaspoon salt
2 cups buttermilk
⅓ cup margarine or butter, melted
3 tablespoons maple-flavored syrup
2 eggs, beaten

1. In large bowl, combine all ingredients; stir until large lumps disappear. (Batter will be thick. For thinner pancakes, thin batter with a small amount of water.)
2. Heat griddle or large skillet over medium-high heat (375°F.) until hot. Lightly grease griddle with oil. For each pancake, pour about ¼ cup batter onto hot griddle. Cook 2½ to 3 minutes or until edges look cooked and bubbles begin to break on surface. Turn pancakes; cook 2 to 2½ minutes or until golden brown. If desired, serve with additional syrup.

NUTRITION INFORMATION PER SERVING: Serving Size: ¼ of Recipe ✦ Calories: 480 ✦ Calories from Fat: 180 ✦ **% DAILY VALUE:** Total Fat: 20 g 31% ✦ Saturated Fat: 5 g 25% ✦ Cholesterol: 110 mg 37% ✦ Sodium: 1190 mg 50% ✦ Total Carbohydrate: 61 g 20% ✦ Dietary Fiber: 5 g 20% ✦ Sugars: 12 g ✦ Protein: 14 g ✦ Vitamin A: 20% ✦ Vitamin C: 0% ✦ Calcium: 30% ✦ Iron: 15% ✦ **DIETARY EXCHANGES:** 4 Starch, ½ Medium-Fat Meat, 3 Fat OR 4 Carbohydrate, ½ Medium-Fat Meat, 3 Fat

VARIATION

Four-Grain Waffles: Heat waffle iron. Spread batter evenly in hot waffle iron. Bake 2 to 3 minutes or until steaming stops and waffle is golden brown. Repeat with remaining batter. If desired, serve with additional syrup. YIELD: 8 (5-INCH) WAFFLES; 4 SERVINGS

Four-Grain Pancakes

C O O K ' S N O T E

PANCAKE TIPS

Mix batter gently for tender pancakes. Before cooking the first pancake, heat the ungreased griddle or skillet to 375 to 400°F. (medium-high). When the griddle has reached the right temperature, a drop of water flicked onto the surface will dance around before evaporating.

Grease the griddle lightly. This is usually only necessary for the first batch of pancakes.

Turn pancakes only once, when the top starts to bubble and the edges are dry.

Thick batter makes thick, puffy pancakes. If you prefer thinner pancakes, add more liquid to the batter.

Waffles

PREP TIME: 20 MINUTES ◆ YIELD: 4 WAFFLES

2 eggs, separated
2 cups buttermilk*
2 cups all-purpose flour
2 teaspoons baking powder
1 teaspoon baking soda
½ teaspoon salt
½ cup margarine or butter, melted, or oil

1. Heat waffle iron. Place egg yolks in large bowl, whites in small bowl. To yolks, add buttermilk; beat well. Add flour, baking powder, baking soda and salt; beat until smooth. Stir in melted margarine.
2. Beat egg whites until soft peaks form. Fold whites into batter.
3. Spread batter evenly in hot waffle iron. Bake until steaming stops and waffle is golden brown. Repeat with remaining waffle batter.

TIP: *To prepare waffles using regular milk, decrease milk to 1¾ cups, increase baking powder to 4 teaspoons and omit baking soda.

HIGH ALTITUDE (*above 3500 feet*): No change.

NUTRITION INFORMATION PER SERVING: Serving Size: 1 Waffle ◆ Calories: 520 ◆ Calories from Fat: 240 ◆ % DAILY VALUE: Total Fat: 27 g 42% ◆ Saturated Fat: 6 g 30% ◆ Cholesterol: 110 mg 37% ◆ Sodium: 1250 mg 52% ◆ Total Carbohydrate: 55 g 18% ◆ Dietary Fiber: 2 g 8% ◆ Sugars: 6 g ◆ Protein: 14 g ◆ Vitamin A: 25% ◆ Vitamin C: 0% ◆ Calcium: 30% ◆ Iron: 20% ◆ DIETARY EXCHANGES: 4 Starch, 4½ Fat OR 4 Carbohydrate, 4½ Fat

VARIATIONS

Apple Waffles: Add 1 shredded peeled apple and ½ teaspoon cinnamon to batter.
Banana Waffles: Brush waffle iron with oil before heating. Place banana slices on batter before closing lid of waffle iron.
Blueberry Waffles: Add 1 cup fresh or frozen drained blueberries to batter.
Nut Waffles: Add ⅓ to ½ cup chopped nuts with flour.
Whole Wheat Waffles: Use 1½ cups all-purpose flour and ½ cup whole wheat flour.

Pancake and Waffle Toppings

Store these toppings in the refrigerator.

Brown Sugar Syrup: In medium saucepan, combine 1 cup firmly packed brown sugar and 1 cup water; mix well. Bring to a boil, stirring constantly. Boil 5 minutes. Remove from heat; stir in 1 tablespoon butter and ½ teaspoon maple flavor.
YIELD: 1 CUP

Currant-Butter Syrup: In small saucepan, combine 2 tablespoons butter and 1 (10-oz.) jar currant jelly. Cook over low heat until melted, stirring constantly.
YIELD: 1 CUP

Easy Blueberry Topping: In small saucepan, combine 1 (21-oz.) can blueberry pie filling and ¼ cup butter. Cook over low heat until butter is melted, stirring frequently.
YIELD: 2 CUPS

Honey 'n Maple Syrup: In small saucepan, combine 1 cup maple-flavored syrup and 2 tablespoons honey; mix well. Cook until thoroughly heated.
YIELD: 1 CUP

Orange Syrup: In small saucepan, combine ½ cup sugar, ¼ cup frozen orange juice concentrate and ¼ cup butter; mix well. Cook over low heat until sugar is dissolved, stirring constantly.
YIELD: ¾ CUP

Spiced Maple Syrup: In medium saucepan, melt ½ cup butter. Stir in 1 cup maple-flavored syrup, ½ teaspoon cinnamon, ⅛ teaspoon nutmeg and ⅛ teaspoon allspice. Bring to a boil. Cook over low heat for 5 minutes, stirring occasionally. Stir well before serving; serve immediately.
YIELD: 1½ CUPS

Strawberry Topping: In small saucepan, heat 1 (10-oz.) jar strawberry preserves or jam over low heat until melted, stirring occasionally.
YIELD: 1 CUP

SOUPS & STEWS

Beef Broth

PREP TIME: 30 MINUTES (READY IN 7 HOURS 30 MINUTES) ✦ YIELD: 7 CUPS

    2 lb. meaty beef bones, such as shank, cracked into 3-inch pieces, or short ribs
    2 lb. cracked beef soup bones or knuckle bones
    1 cup cut-up carrot
    2 stalks celery with leaves, cut into 2-inch pieces
    2 small onions, quartered
    10 cups water
    1 (8-oz.) can whole tomatoes, undrained, cut up
 1½ teaspoons salt
    ½ teaspoon dried thyme leaves
    5 peppercorns
    2 fresh parsley sprigs
    1 garlic clove, crushed
    1 bay leaf
    ¾ teaspoon salt

1. Heat oven to 450°F. Place all bones in large roasting pan. Bake at 450°F. for 30 minutes.
2. Add carrot, celery and onions. Bake an additional 45 to 60 minutes or until bones are very deep brown but not charred, turning bones and vegetables occasionally.
3. Transfer ingredients from roasting pan to

8-quart stockpot or two 5-quart Dutch ovens. Discard fat in roasting pan. Add 2 cups of the water to roasting pan; heat and scrape to loosen any browned meat drippings. Pour hot liquid and remaining 8 cups water over bones and vegetables in stockpot. Bring to a boil. Reduce heat; partially cover and simmer 30 minutes.
4. Skim and discard residue that rises to surface. Add all remaining ingredients except ¾ teaspoon salt; partially cover and simmer an additional 5 hours.
5. Remove bones from broth. Cool slightly. Remove meat from bones; refrigerate or freeze for a later use.
6. Strain broth; stir in ¾ teaspoon salt. Cool uncovered in refrigerator. Skim fat from broth; discard. Cover; store in refrigerator up to 3 days or freeze up to 6 months.

NUTRITION INFORMATION: Not possible to calculate because of recipe variables.

Vegetable Beef Soup with Barley

PREP TIME: 1 HOUR (READY IN 7 HOURS) ✦ YIELD: 12 (1⅓-CUP) SERVINGS

    2 to 3 lb. cracked beef soup bones or knuckle bones
 1½ lb. boneless beef chuck roast, cut into ½-inch cubes
    1 cup chopped onions
    2 garlic cloves, crushed
   14 cups water
    3 carrots, sliced
    3 stalks celery, sliced
    4 potatoes, unpeeled, cubed (about 4 cups)
    2 medium parsnips, peeled, cubed (about 2 cups)
 1⅓ cups frozen cut green beans
    ¾ cup uncooked barley
    2 teaspoons salt
    1 teaspoon pepper
    1 bay leaf
    1 tablespoon Worcestershire sauce
    1 small head cabbage, cut into 1½-inch pieces

1. Heat oven to 450°F. Place all bones in large roasting pan. Bake at 450°F. for 1 to 1½ hours or until bones are very deep brown but not charred, turning bones occasionally.
2. In large stockpot, combine bones, cubed beef, onions and garlic. Discard fat in roasting pan. Add 2 cups of the water to roasting

pan; heat and scrape to loosen any browned meat drippings. Pour hot liquid and remaining water over bones and beef in stockpot. Bring to a boil. Reduce heat to medium; simmer 2 to 4 hours or until meat is tender. Skim and discard residue that rises to surface.

3. Remove bones from broth. Cool slightly. Remove meat from bones. Add meat to broth. Cool broth uncovered in refrigerator.

4. Skim fat from broth; discard. Stir in all remaining ingredients except cabbage. Bring to a boil. Reduce heat to medium; cover and cook 15 to 20 minutes or until vegetables are crisp-tender. Add cabbage; cover and cook until cabbage is tender. Remove bay leaf.

NUTRITION INFORMATION PER SERVING: Serving Size: 1¼ Cups ◆ Calories: 240 ◆ Calories from Fat: 50 ◆ **% DAILY VALUE:** Total Fat: 6 g 9% ◆ Saturated Fat: 2 g 10% ◆ Cholesterol: 40 mg 13% ◆ Sodium: 430 mg 18% ◆ Total Carbohydrate: 30 g 10% ◆ Dietary Fiber: 7 g 28% ◆ Sugars: 6 g ◆ Protein: 17 g ◆ Vitamin A: 110% ◆ Vitamin C: 40% ◆ Calcium: 6% ◆ Iron: 20% ◆ **DIETARY EXCHANGES:** 1½ Starch, 1 Vegetable, 1½ Lean Meat OR 1½ Carbohydrate, 1 Vegetable, 1½ Lean Meat

New England Clam Chowder

PREP TIME: 40 MINUTES ◆ YIELD: 4 (1¼-CUP) SERVINGS

    3 slices bacon, cut into small pieces
    1 cup diced peeled potatoes
    ½ cup chopped celery
    ¼ cup chopped onion
    ¼ teaspoon salt
    ⅛ teaspoon dried thyme leaves, crushed
    ⅛ teaspoon pepper
    2 (6½-oz.) cans minced clams, drained, reserving liquid
    ¼ cup all-purpose flour
    3 cups milk

1. Cook bacon in large saucepan over medium heat until crisp. Remove bacon from saucepan; drain on paper towels. Set aside.

2. Add potatoes, celery, onion, salt, thyme, pepper and reserved clam liquid to bacon drippings. Bring to a boil. Reduce heat to low; cover and simmer 10 minutes or until vegetables are crisp-tender.

3. In 1-quart jar with tight-fitting lid, combine flour and milk; shake until smooth. Gradually stir into vegetable mixture. Cook over medium heat 15 minutes or until thickened, stirring frequently. Stir in clams. Heat gently, stirring frequently. DO NOT BOIL. Sprinkle bacon over each serving.

NUTRITION INFORMATION PER SERVING: Serving Size: 1¼ Cups ◆ Calories: 310 ◆ Calories from Fat: 130 ◆ **% DAILY VALUE:** Total Fat: 14 g 22% ◆ Saturated Fat: 6 g 30% ◆ Cholesterol: 55 mg 18% ◆ Sodium: 470 mg 20% ◆ Total Carbohydrate: 25 g 8% ◆ Dietary Fiber: 1 g 4% ◆ Sugars: 10 g ◆ Protein: 20 g ◆ Vitamin A: 15% ◆ Vitamin C: 25% ◆ Calcium: 30% ◆ Iron: 70% ◆ **DIETARY EXCHANGES:** 1½ Starch, 2 Very Lean Meat, 2½ Fat OR 1½ Carbohydrate, 2 Very Lean Meat, 2½ Fat

Manhattan Clam Chowder

PREP TIME: 25 MINUTES (READY IN 1 HOUR) ◆ YIELD: 6 (1½-CUP) SERVINGS

    5 slices bacon, cut into small pieces
    1 cup chopped onions
    1 cup chopped celery
    ¼ cup finely chopped green bell pepper
    3 cups water
    2 cups diced peeled potatoes
    1 cup diced carrots
    1 tablespoon chopped fresh parsley
    1 teaspoon salt
    ¼ teaspoon dried thyme leaves, crushed
    ⅛ teaspoon pepper
    3 (6½-oz.) cans minced clams, drained, reserving liquid
    1 (16-oz.) can tomatoes, undrained, cut up
    1 bay leaf

1. Cook bacon in large saucepan over medium heat until crisp. Remove bacon from saucepan; drain on paper towels. Set aside. Reserve 2 tablespoons drippings in saucepan.

2. Add onions, celery and bell pepper to drippings; cook and stir until tender. Add water, potatoes, carrots, parsley, salt, thyme, pepper, reserved clam liquid, tomatoes and bay leaf. Bring to a boil. Reduce heat to low; cover and simmer 25 to 35 minutes or until vegetables are tender.

3. Remove bay leaf. Stir in clams. Cook until thoroughly heated, stirring frequently. DO NOT BOIL. Sprinkle bacon over each serving.

NUTRITION INFORMATION PER SERVING: Serving Size: 1½ Cups ◆ Calories: 220 ◆ Calories from Fat: 70 ◆ **% DAILY VALUE:** Total Fat: 8 g 12% ◆ Saturated Fat: 3 g 15% ◆ Cholesterol: 40 mg 13% ◆ Sodium: 730 mg 30% ◆ Total Carbohydrate: 21 g 7% ◆ Dietary Fiber: 3 g 12% ◆ Sugars: 5 g ◆ Protein: 15 g ◆ Vitamin A: 130% ◆ Vitamin C: 45% ◆ Calcium: 10% ◆ Iron: 70% ◆ **DIETARY EXCHANGES:** 1 Starch, 1 Vegetable, 1½ Very Lean Meat, 1½ Fat OR 1 Carbohydrate, 1 Vegetable, 1½ Very Lean Meat, 1½ Fat

Chicken Broth

PREP TIME: 30 MINUTES (READY IN 5 HOURS)
◆ YIELD: 8 CUPS

    2 lb. chicken backs, necks and/or wings
    2 quarts (8 cups) water
    2 small onions, quartered
    1 cup coarsely chopped celery with leaves
    ½ cup sliced carrots
    2 teaspoons chopped fresh parsley
    1 teaspoon salt
    ¼ teaspoon pepper
    1 bay leaf
    ½ teaspoon salt

1. In Dutch oven, combine chicken and water. Bring to a boil. Skim and discard residue that rises to surface. Reduce heat; partially cover and simmer 30 minutes.
2. Add all remaining ingredients except ½ teaspoon salt; partially cover and simmer an additional 4 hours.
3. Remove bones from broth. Cool slightly. Remove meat from bones; refrigerate or freeze for a later use.
4. Strain broth; stir in ½ teaspoon salt. Cool uncovered in refrigerator. Skim fat from broth; discard. Cover; store in refrigerator up to 3 days or freeze up to 6 months.

NUTRITION INFORMATION: Not possible to calculate because of recipe variables.

COOK'S NOTE

BROTH SUBSTITUTIONS

When a recipe calls for chicken or beef broth, you can use homemade stock or a purchased product. Purchased products are almost always saltier than homemade, so taste the soup or stew before adding any salt.

◆ One 14½-ounce can of ready-to-serve beef or chicken broth equals 1¾ cups broth.
◆ One 10½-ounce can of condensed beef broth (or 10½-ounce can of condensed chicken broth) diluted with 1 soup can of water equals 2⅔ cups broth.
◆ One beef or chicken-flavor bouillon cube or 1 teaspoon of beef or chicken-flavor instant bouillon dissolved in 1 cup water equals 1 cup broth.
◆ 1 teaspoon beef or chicken base diluted with 1 cup water equals 1 cup broth.

Chicken Wild Rice Soup

PREP TIME: 15 MINUTES (READY IN 1 HOUR)
◆ YIELD: 6 (1½-CUP) SERVINGS

    8 slices bacon
    2 cups water
    3 (10½-oz.) cans condensed chicken broth
    ½ cup uncooked wild rice*
    ½ cup finely chopped green onions
    ½ cup margarine or butter
    ¾ cup all-purpose flour
    ½ teaspoon salt
    ¼ teaspoon poultry seasoning
    ⅛ teaspoon pepper
    2 cups half-and-half
  1½ cups cubed cooked chicken
    1 tablespoon diced pimientos
    2 to 3 tablespoons dry sherry, if desired

1. Cook bacon in large skillet over medium heat until crisp. Remove from skillet; drain on paper towels. Crumble.
2. In Dutch oven or large saucepan, combine water and broth. Add wild rice and onions. Bring to a boil. Reduce heat to low; cover and simmer 45 to 55 minutes or until rice is tender.
3. Melt margarine in medium saucepan over medium heat. Stir in flour, salt, poultry seasoning and pepper. Cook 1 minute or until smooth and bubbly, stirring constantly. Gradually stir in half-and-half; cook until slightly thickened, stirring constantly.
4. Slowly add flour mixture to rice mixture, stirring constantly. Add bacon, chicken, pimientos and sherry. Cook over low heat until thoroughly heated, stirring frequently. DO NOT BOIL.

TIP: * Uncooked regular long-grain white rice can be substituted for the wild rice; reduce simmering time to 20 to 30 minutes or until rice is tender.

NUTRITION INFORMATION PER SERVING: Serving Size: 1½ Cups ◆ Calories: 520 ◆ Calories from Fat: 300 ◆ % DAILY VALUE: Total Fat: 33 g 51% ◆ Saturated Fat: 11 g 55% ◆ Cholesterol: 70 mg 23% ◆ Sodium: 1490 mg 62% ◆ Total Carbohydrate: 28 g 9% ◆ Dietary Fiber: 2 g 8% ◆ Sugars: 5 g ◆ Protein: 26 g ◆ Vitamin A: 25% ◆ Vitamin C: 4% ◆ Calcium: 10% ◆ Iron: 15% ◆ DIETARY EXCHANGES: 2 Starch, 3 Lean Meat, 4½ Fat OR 2 Carbohydrate, 3 Lean Meat, 4½ Fat

Mom's Chicken Noodle Soup

PREP TIME: 15 MINUTES (READY IN 50 MINUTES)
✦ YIELD: 5 (1½-CUP) SERVINGS

1½ cups cubed cooked chicken
1 cup sliced carrots
½ cup chopped celery
½ cup chopped onion
1 parsnip, peeled, cubed (¾ cup)
2 teaspoons chopped fresh parsley
1 teaspoon chopped fresh dill
4 (14½-oz.) cans ready-to-serve chicken broth
3½ oz. (2 cups) uncooked wide egg noodles

1. In Dutch oven or large saucepan, combine all ingredients except noodles; mix well. Cook over medium heat 20 minutes or until vegetables are tender, stirring occasionally.
2. Add egg noodles; cook 15 minutes or until of desired doneness.

NUTRITION INFORMATION PER SERVING: Serving Size: 1½ Cups ✦ Calories: 230 ✦ Calories from Fat: 50 ✦ **% DAILY VALUE:** Total Fat: 6 g 9% ✦ Saturated Fat: 2 g 10% ✦ Cholesterol: 55 mg 18% ✦ Sodium: 1110 mg 46% ✦ Total Carbohydrate: 23 g 8% ✦ Dietary Fiber: 3 g 12% ✦ Sugars: 4 g ✦ Protein: 22 g ✦ Vitamin A: 140% ✦ Vitamin C: 10% ✦ Calcium: 4% ✦ Iron: 15% ✦ **DIETARY EXCHANGES:** 1½ Starch, 2½ Very Lean Meat, ½ Fat OR 1½ Carbohydrate, 2½ Very Lean Meat, ½ Fat

Mom's Chicken Noodle Soup

Italian Chicken Orzo Soup

Italian Chicken Orzo Soup

PREP TIME: 10 MINUTES (READY IN 45 MINUTES)
✦ YIELD: 5 (1½-CUP) SERVINGS

1 tablespoon oil
½ cup chopped onion
1 cup sliced carrot
1½ cups cubed cooked chicken
7 oz. (1 cup) uncooked orzo or rosamarina (rice-shaped pasta)
½ teaspoon dried Italian seasoning
3 (14½-oz.) cans ready-to-serve chicken broth
1½ cups milk
2 tablespoons all-purpose flour
1 cup frozen cut green beans, thawed

1. Heat oil in Dutch oven over medium-high heat until hot. Add onion and carrot; cook and stir 3 to 5 minutes or until onion is tender, stirring occasionally.
2. Add chicken, orzo, Italian seasoning and broth; mix well. Bring to a boil. Reduce heat to low; simmer 15 minutes or until orzo is tender, stirring occasionally.
3. In small bowl, combine milk and flour; beat with wire whisk until smooth. Add flour mixture and green beans to soup; blend well. Simmer 10 minutes or until soup is thickened, stirring occasionally.

NUTRITION INFORMATION PER SERVING: Serving Size: 1½ Cups ✦ Calories: 350 ✦ Calories from Fat: 80 ✦ **% DAILY VALUE:** Total Fat: 9 g 14% ✦ Saturated Fat: 3 g 15% ✦ Cholesterol: 45 mg 15% ✦ Sodium: 870 mg 36% ✦ Total Carbohydrate: 42 g 14% ✦ Dietary Fiber: 3 g 12% ✦ Sugars: 8 g ✦ Protein: 26 g ✦ Vitamin A: 140% ✦ Vitamin C: 6% ✦ Calcium: 15% ✦ Iron: 15% ✦ **DIETARY EXCHANGES:** 2½ Starch, 1 Vegetable, 2½ Lean Meat OR 2½ Carbohydrate, 1 Vegetable, 2½ Lean Meat

Easy Bean Soup

PREP TIME: 30 MINUTES (READY IN 3 HOURS
30 MINUTES) ◆ YIELD: 9 (1½-CUP) SERVINGS

- 1 (16-oz.) pkg. dried navy beans, sorted, rinsed
- 2 quarts (8 cups) water
- 1 (1½-lb.) ham shank
- 1 cup chopped onions
- ¼ cup chopped fresh parsley
- 1 teaspoon salt
- 1 teaspoon dried basil leaves
- ½ teaspoon pepper
- ½ teaspoon nutmeg
- ½ teaspoon dried oregano leaves
- 2 garlic cloves, minced
- 1 bay leaf
- 2 cups thinly sliced carrots
- 1 cup chopped celery
- ½ cup mashed potato flakes

1. In Dutch oven, combine beans and about 6 cups water. Bring to a boil. Reduce heat to low; simmer uncovered for 2 minutes. Remove from heat. Cover; let stand 1 hour. Drain and discard water.

2. Add 2 quarts (8 cups) water, ham shank, onions, parsley, salt, basil, pepper, nutmeg, oregano, garlic and bay leaf to beans. Bring to a boil. Reduce heat; cover and simmer 1½ hours or until beans are tender.

3. Remove from heat. Remove ham shank from soup. Cool slightly. Remove meat from bone; cut into bite-sized pieces. Return meat to soup. Add carrots, celery and potato flakes; mix well. Return to heat; cover and simmer an additional 20 to 30 minutes or until carrots and celery are crisp-tender. Remove bay leaf.

NUTRITION INFORMATION PER SERVING: Serving Size: 1½ Cups ◆ Calories: 310 ◆ Calories from Fat: 90 ◆ **% DAILY VALUE:** Total Fat: 10 g 15% ◆ Saturated Fat: 4 g 20% ◆ Cholesterol: 20 mg 7% ◆ Sodium: 630 mg 26% ◆ Total Carbohydrate: 39 g 13% ◆ Dietary Fiber: 9 g 36% ◆ Sugars: 6 g ◆ Protein: 16 g ◆ Vitamin A: 160% ◆ Vitamin C: 10% ◆ Calcium: 10% ◆ Iron: 20% ◆ **DIETARY EXCHANGES:** 2½ Starch, 1 Lean Meat, 1 Fat OR 2½ Carbohydrate, 1 Lean Meat, 1 Fat

---

COOK'S NOTE

SOUP FOR STARTERS

Soup makes a nice first course, whetting the appetite and complementing the main dish to follow. A good appetizer soup will contrast—but not clash—in flavor, texture, color and perhaps temperature from other menu items. Allow ¾ to 1 cup per serving.

Black Bean and Ham Soup

PREP TIME: 15 MINUTES (READY IN 2 HOURS
45 MINUTES) ◆ YIELD: 6 (1½-CUP) SERVINGS

- 8 oz. (1¼ cups) dried black beans, sorted, rinsed
- 5½ oz. cooked ham, cubed (1 cup)
- ½ cup chopped onion
- ½ cup thin green bell pepper strips
- 1 (15-oz.) can chunky tomato sauce with onions, celery and green bell peppers
- 1 (10¾-oz.) can condensed tomato soup
- 3 cups water
- 1 teaspoon cumin
- 3 teaspoons chili powder

1. Place beans in Dutch oven; add water until about 1 inch above beans. Bring to a boil. Boil 2 minutes. Remove from heat; cover and let stand 1 hour.

2. Drain and discard water. Add all remaining ingredients to beans; mix well. Bring to a boil. Reduce heat to low; simmer 1½ to 2 hours or until beans are tender, stirring occasionally.

NUTRITION INFORMATION PER SERVING: Serving Size: 1½ Cups ◆ Calories: 240 ◆ Calories from Fat: 25 ◆ **% DAILY VALUE:** Total Fat: 3 g 5% ◆ Saturated Fat: 1 g 5% ◆ Cholesterol: 10 mg 3% ◆ Sodium: 1050 mg 44% ◆ Total Carbohydrate: 39 g 13% ◆ Dietary Fiber: 8 g 32% ◆ Sugars: 9 g ◆ Protein: 15 g ◆ Vitamin A: 25% ◆ Vitamin C: 50% ◆ Calcium: 8% ◆ Iron: 20% ◆ **DIETARY EXCHANGES:** 2 Starch, 2 Vegetable, 1 Very Lean Meat OR 2 Carbohydrate, 2 Vegetable, 1 Very Lean Meat

Beer Cheese Soup

PREP TIME: 40 MINUTES ◆ YIELD: 7 (1-CUP) SERVINGS

- ¼ cup margarine or butter
- 1 cup chopped onions
- ½ cup chopped celery
- ½ cup chopped carrot
- ¼ cup chopped fresh parsley
- 2 garlic cloves, crushed
- ¼ cup all-purpose flour
- 3 teaspoons dry mustard
- ⅛ teaspoon pepper
- 2 cups half-and-half or milk
- 1 cup chicken broth
- 12 oz. (2½ cups) cubed American cheese
- 1 (12-oz.) can beer
- 2 cups popped popcorn

1. Melt margarine in large saucepan or Dutch oven over medium heat. Stir in onions, celery, carrot, parsley and garlic. Cook 5 to 6 minutes or until vegetables are crisp-tender.

2. Stir in flour, dry mustard and pepper; mix well. Cook 1 minute, stirring constantly. Gradually add half-and-half and chicken broth; mix well. Cook 10 to 15 minutes or until soup is thickened and thoroughly heated, stirring occasionally.

3. Add cheese and beer; cook 5 to 8 minutes or until cheese is melted, stirring frequently. DO NOT BOIL. Sprinkle individual servings with popcorn.

NUTRITION INFORMATION PER SERVING: Serving Size: 1 Cup • Calories: 410 • Calories from Fat: 280 • % DAILY VALUE: Total Fat: 31 g 48% • Saturated Fat: 16 g 80% • Cholesterol: 70 mg 23% • Sodium: 950 mg 40% • Total Carbohydrate: 15 g 5% • Dietary Fiber: 1 g 4% • Sugars: 6 g • Protein: 15 g • Vitamin A: 80% • Vitamin C: 8% • Calcium: 40% • Iron: 6% • DIETARY EXCHANGES: 1 Starch, 1½ High-Fat Meat, 4 Fat OR 1 Carbohydrate, 1½ High-Fat Meat, 4 Fat

Cheddar Cheese Soup

PREP TIME: 35 MINUTES ✦ YIELD: 6 (1-CUP) SERVINGS

½ cup finely chopped onion
¼ cup finely chopped carrot
¼ cup finely chopped celery
3 cups vegetable or chicken broth
1 tablespoon cornstarch
2 tablespoons water
4 oz. (1 cup) diced sharp Cheddar cheese
1 (10¾-oz.) can condensed cream of
    potato soup
1 (8-oz.) jar pasteurized process cheese
    spread

1. In large saucepan, combine onion, carrot, celery and broth. Bring to a boil. Reduce heat to low; cover and simmer 10 minutes or until vegetables are tender.*

2. In small bowl, combine cornstarch and water; mix well. Stir into broth mixture. Bring to a boil. Reduce heat to low. Add Cheddar cheese, potato soup and cheese spread. With wire whisk, stir until cheese is melted and mixture is well combined. DO NOT BOIL.

TIP: * If desired, broth mixture can be pureed in blender or food processor until smooth.

NUTRITION INFORMATION PER SERVING: Serving Size: 1 Cup • Calories: 240 • Calories from Fat: 140 • % DAILY VALUE: Total Fat: 16 g 25% • Saturated Fat: 10 g 50% • Cholesterol: 45 mg 15% • Sodium: 1580 mg 66% • Total Carbohydrate: 13 g 4% • Dietary Fiber: 1 g 3% • Sugars: 7 g • Protein: 12 g • Vitamin A: 45% • Vitamin C: 0% • Calcium: 35% • Iron: 4% • DIETARY EXCHANGES: 1 Starch, 1½ High-Fat Meat, ½ Fat OR 1 Carbohydrate, 1½ High-Fat Meat, ½ Fat

COOK'S NOTE

MAKING SOUP IN AN ELECTRIC SLOW COOKER

Most stove-top soup recipes can easily be made in an electric slow cooker, too. Be sure to use a slow cooker (which has heating coils around the sides of the pot), not a food warmer, which heats only the bottom. For ease in cleaning, we recommend a slow cooker with a removable liner.

Read the manufacturer's instructions for specific advice on converting recipes for your slow cooker. Some general tips:

✦ For food safety reasons, recipes in the slow cooker need to reach a safe cooking temperature (140°F.) within three hours. For that reason, do not assemble ingredients ahead of time. Refrigerate them, or use frozen ingredients. Thaw meat in the refrigerator or microwave, not at room temperature.

✦ To ensure proper cooking, cut the meat and vegetables into uniformly sized pieces.

✦ Most slow-cooker soups and stews take at least 7 hours, and probably closer to 8 or 10 hours if they contain meat.

✦ Fill the slow cooker only half to three-quarters full. Slow-cooker recipes require less liquid than stove-top versions; check the manufacturer's instructions.

✦ Add dairy products such as milk, whipping cream, sour cream or cheese during the last 5 to 6 minutes of cooking time to prevent them from curdling.

✦ Colors fade over long cooking times, so use colorful garnishes. Some vegetables, such as green onions, retain more flavor and better texture if added toward the end of cooking time. For more intense fresh herb flavor and color, add some fresh herbs at the beginning of cooking time and more just before serving.

✦ For the best texture, quick cooking ingredients such as frozen vegetables, pasta and instant rice should be added during the last 15 to 30 minutes of cooking.

Golden Split Pea Soup

PREP TIME: 25 MINUTES (READY IN 1 HOUR 25 MINUTES)
✦ YIELD: 7 (1-CUP) SERVINGS

- 1 (16-oz.) pkg. dried yellow split peas, sorted, rinsed
- 7 cups water
- 1 cup sliced carrots
- ½ cup chopped onion
- ½ cup chopped celery
- 1 tablespoon chicken-flavor instant bouillon
- 1 teaspoon salt
- ½ teaspoon hot pepper sauce
- 1 cup chopped cooked ham, if desired

1. In Dutch oven or large saucepan, combine all ingredients except ham. Bring to a boil over medium-high heat. Reduce heat to low; simmer 45 to 60 minutes or until peas and vegetables are very tender.

2. In blender container or food processor bowl with metal blade, blend half of soup until smooth. Return to Dutch oven; stir in ham. Cook over medium-low heat until thoroughly heated, stirring frequently.

NUTRITION INFORMATION PER SERVING: Serving Size: 1 Cup ✦ Calories: 270 ✦ Calories from Fat: 20 ✦ **% DAILY VALUE:** Total Fat: 2 g 3% ✦ Saturated Fat: 1 g 5% ✦ Cholesterol: 10 mg 3% ✦ Sodium: 1030 mg 43% ✦ Total Carbohydrate: 43 g 14% ✦ Dietary Fiber: 16 g 64% ✦ Sugars: 4 g ✦ Protein: 20 g ✦ Vitamin A: 100% ✦ Vitamin C: 4% ✦ Calcium: 4% ✦ Iron: 15% ✦ **DIETARY EXCHANGES:** 2½ Starch, 1 Vegetable, 1½ Very Lean Meat OR 2½ Carbohydrate, 1 Vegetable, 1½ Very Lean Meat

Vegetable-Split Pea Soup

Golden Split Pea Soup

Vegetable-Split Pea Soup

PREP TIME: 15 MINUTES (READY IN 3 HOURS)
✦ YIELD: 7 (1½-CUP) SERVINGS

- 2 cups dried green split peas, sorted, rinsed
- 5 cups water
- 2 (11.5-oz.) cans (3 cups) tomato juice
- 3 garlic cloves, minced
- 1 teaspoon salt
- ½ teaspoon pepper
- 2 cups coarsely chopped cabbage
- 1 cup chopped carrots
- 1 cup chopped peeled turnip or potato
- ⅓ cup grated or shredded Parmesan cheese, if desired

1. In Dutch oven or stockpot, combine split peas and 12 cups (3 quarts) water. Bring to a boil. Boil 2 minutes. Remove from heat; cover and let stand 1 hour.

2. Drain and discard liquid from peas; return peas to Dutch oven. Add 5 cups water, tomato juice, garlic, salt and pepper. Bring to a boil. Reduce heat; cover and simmer 1 hour or until peas are tender.

3. Add cabbage, carrots and turnip; simmer 20 to 30 minutes or until vegetables are tender.

4. To serve, ladle soup into bowls; top with cheese.

NUTRITION INFORMATION PER SERVING: Serving Size: 1½ Cups ✦ Calories: 250 ✦ Calories from Fat: 20 ✦ **% DAILY VALUE:** Total Fat: 2 g 3% ✦ Saturated Fat: 1 g 5% ✦ Cholesterol: 4 mg 1% ✦ Sodium: 760 mg 32% ✦ Total Carbohydrate: 42 g 14% ✦ Dietary Fiber: 16 g 64% ✦ Sugars: 7 g ✦ Protein: 17 g ✦ Vitamin A: 110% ✦ Vitamin C: 35% ✦ Calcium: 15% ✦ Iron: 20% ✦ **DIETARY EXCHANGES:** 2½ Starch, 1 Vegetable, 1 Very Lean Meat OR 2½ Carbohydrate, 1 Vegetable, 1 Very Lean Meat

650 mg 27% ♦ Total Carbohydrate: 63 g 21% ♦ Dietary Fiber: 16 g 64% ♦ Sugars: 12 g ♦ Protein: 23 g ♦ Vitamin A: 120% ♦ Vitamin C: 15% ♦ Calcium: 25% ♦ Iron: 30% ♦ **DIETARY EXCHANGES:** 4 Starch, ½ Vegetable, 1½ Very Lean Meat OR 4 Carbohydrate, ½ Vegetable, 1½ Very Lean Meat

Top to bottom: Hearty Bean Soup with Noodles, Black Bean and Ham Soup (page 70)

Hearty Bean Soup with Noodles

PREP TIME: 15 MINUTES (READY IN 3 HOURS 45 MINUTES) ♦ YIELD: 6 (1½-CUP) SERVINGS

  1 (16-oz.) pkg. dried navy beans, sorted, rinsed
  2 quarts (8 cups) water
  1 (½-lb.) meaty ham bone
  1 cup chopped onions
  1 cup julienne-cut (2 x ⅛ x ⅛-inch) carrots
  ½ cup sliced celery
  1 teaspoon salt
  ¼ teaspoon pepper
2½ oz. (1½ cups) uncooked wide egg noodles
  2 cups milk
  2 teaspoons white vinegar

1. Place beans in Dutch oven or large saucepan; add water until about 1 inch above beans. Bring to a boil. Boil 2 minutes. Remove from heat; cover and let stand 1 hour.
2. Drain liquid from beans; return beans to saucepan. Add 2 quarts (8 cups) water, ham bone and ½ cup of the onions. Cover; simmer 1½ to 2 hours or until beans are tender, stirring occasionally.
3. Skim off fat. Remove ham bone; cool. Cut meat from bone; add meat to bean mixture. Add remaining ½ cup onions, carrots, celery, salt and pepper; mix well. Simmer 1 hour, stirring occasionally.
4. Add noodles; cook over low heat for 15 minutes or until noodles are tender. Stir in milk and vinegar; cook 4 to 5 minutes or until thoroughly heated.

NUTRITION INFORMATION PER SERVING: Serving Size: 1½ Cups ♦ Calories: 380 ♦ Calories from Fat: 35 ♦ **% DAILY VALUE:** Total Fat: 4 g 6% ♦ Saturated Fat: 2 g 10% ♦ Cholesterol: 25 mg 8% ♦ Sodium:

Vegetarian Navy Bean Soup

PREP TIME: 30 MINUTES (READY IN 10 HOURS 30 MINUTES) ♦ YIELD: 8 (1-CUP) SERVINGS

  1 (16-oz.) pkg. dried navy beans, sorted, rinsed
  2 quarts (8 cups) water
  1 cup finely chopped carrots
  1 cup finely chopped celery, including leaves
  ½ cup finely chopped onion
  1 cup vegetable juice cocktail
  1 tablespoon chicken-flavor instant bouillon
  ⅛ teaspoon crushed red pepper flakes

1. In large saucepan or Dutch oven, combine beans and water. Bring to a boil. Boil 30 minutes. Remove from heat; let stand 1½ hours or until beans are tender.
2. In 3½ to 4-quart slow cooker, combine beans with water and all remaining ingredients; mix well. Cover and cook on low setting for 6 to 8 hours or until beans and vegetables are very tender.
3. If desired, in blender container or food processor bowl with metal blade, puree part or all of soup until smooth.

NUTRITION INFORMATION PER SERVING: Serving Size: 1 Cup ♦ Calories: 210 ♦ Calories from Fat: 10 ♦ **% DAILY VALUE:** Total Fat: 1 g 2% ♦ Saturated Fat: 0 g 0% ♦ Cholesterol: 0 mg 0% ♦ Sodium: 470 mg 20% ♦ Total Carbohydrate: 39 g 13% ♦ Dietary Fiber: 9 g 36% ♦ Sugars: 6 g ♦ Protein: 12 g ♦ Vitamin A: 90% ♦ Vitamin C: 15% ♦ Calcium: 10% ♦ Iron: 20% ♦ **DIETARY EXCHANGES:** 2½ Starch, ½ Very Lean Meat OR 2½ Carbohydrate, ½ Very Lean Meat

Vegetarian Navy Bean Soup

Tuscan-Style Minestrone

PREP TIME: 25 MINUTES ◆ YIELD: 4 (1⅔-CUP) SERVINGS

  1 tablespoon olive oil
  2 cups cubed zucchini
  ½ cup finely chopped onion
  ½ cup grated carrot
  2 garlic cloves, minced
  2 cups thinly sliced savoy cabbage
  1 (28-oz.) can crushed tomatoes, undrained
  1 (15-oz.) can cannellini beans, drained
  1 cup chicken broth
  1 teaspoon dried rosemary leaves, crushed
  2 teaspoons sugar
  ¼ to ½ teaspoon salt

1. Heat oil in large saucepan or Dutch oven over medium heat until hot. Add zucchini, onion, carrot and garlic; cook and stir 3 minutes or until onion is tender.
2. Add cabbage; cook and stir 2 minutes or until cabbage is tender.
3. Stir in all remaining ingredients. Bring to a boil. Reduce heat to low; cover and simmer 10 minutes to blend flavors.

NUTRITION INFORMATION PER SERVING: Serving Size: 1⅔ Cups ◆ Calories: 220 ◆ Calories from Fat: 35 ◆ **% DAILY VALUE:** Total Fat: 4 g 6% ◆ Saturated Fat: 1 g 5% ◆ Cholesterol: 0 mg 0% ◆ Sodium: 910 mg 38% ◆ Total Carbohydrate: 36 g 12% ◆ Dietary Fiber: 10 g 40% ◆ Sugars: 13 g ◆ Protein: 11 g ◆ Vitamin A: 110% ◆ Vitamin C: 45% ◆ Calcium: 15% ◆ Iron: 25% ◆ **DIETARY EXCHANGES:** 2 Starch, 1 Vegetable, ½ Very Lean Meat, ½ Fat OR 2 Carbohydrate, 1 Vegetable, ½ Very Lean Meat, ½ Fat

Mushroom Cream Soup

PREP TIME: 25 MINUTES ◆ YIELD: 4 (¾-CUP) SERVINGS

  ¼ cup margarine or butter
  1 (8-oz.) pkg. (3 cups) sliced fresh
      mushrooms*
  ¼ cup finely chopped onion
  ¼ cup finely chopped celery
  3 tablespoons all-purpose flour
  ½ teaspoon dried basil leaves, finely crushed
  ¼ teaspoon salt
  ⅛ teaspoon pepper
  1½ cups chicken broth
  1½ cups milk

1. Melt margarine in large saucepan over medium meat. Add mushrooms, onion and celery; cook and stir until tender.

2. Stir in flour, basil, salt and pepper. Cook 1 minute or until smooth and bubbly, stirring constantly. Gradually add chicken broth and milk. Cook until slightly thickened, stirring constantly. DO NOT BOIL.

TIP: * One 4.5-oz. jar sliced mushrooms can be substituted for fresh mushrooms. Reserve the mushroom liquid for part of the chicken broth.

NUTRITION INFORMATION PER SERVING: Serving Size: ¾ Cup ◆ Calories: 210 ◆ Calories from Fat: 130 ◆ **% DAILY VALUE:** Total Fat: 14 g 22% ◆ Saturated Fat: 3 g 15% ◆ Cholesterol: 5 mg 2% ◆ Sodium: 610 mg 25% ◆ Total Carbohydrate: 13 g 4% ◆ Dietary Fiber: 1 g 4% ◆ Sugars: 6 g ◆ Protein: 7 g ◆ Vitamin A: 15% ◆ Vitamin C: 4% ◆ Calcium: 15% ◆ Iron: 6% ◆ **DIETARY EXCHANGES:** 1 Starch, ½ Very Lean Meat, 2½ Fat OR 1 Carbohydrate, ½ Very Lean Meat, 2½ Fat

Cream of Broccoli Soup

PREP TIME: 30 MINUTES ◆ YIELD: 6 (1-CUP) SERVINGS

  1 (1-lb.) pkg. frozen cut broccoli
  ¼ cup margarine or butter
  ¼ cup all-purpose flour
  1 tablespoon instant minced onion
  1 tablespoon chicken-flavor instant bouillon
  ½ teaspoon salt
  ½ teaspoon dry mustard
  ¼ to ½ teaspoon dried dill weed
      Dash pepper
  2 cups milk
  3 cups water
      Sour cream, if desired

1. Cook broccoli as directed on package. Drain.
2. Melt margarine in large saucepan over medium heat. Stir in flour, instant minced onion, bouillon, salt, dry mustard, dill and pepper. Gradually add milk, stirring constantly. Stir in broccoli and water. Cook until slightly thickened, stirring occasionally. Remove from heat.
3. In food processor bowl with metal blade or blender container, puree half of mixture at a time until smooth. Return mixture to saucepan. Cook until thoroughly heated. Top each serving with sour cream.

NUTRITION INFORMATION PER SERVING: Serving Size: 1 Cup ◆ Calories: 230 ◆ Calories from Fat: 140 ◆ **% DAILY VALUE:** Total Fat: 16 g 25% ◆ Saturated Fat: 6 g 30% ◆ Cholesterol: 20 mg 7% ◆ Sodium: 830 mg 35% ◆ Total Carbohydrate: 14 g 5% ◆ Dietary Fiber: 3 g 12% ◆ Sugars: 7 g ◆ Protein: 7 g ◆ Vitamin A: 45% ◆ Vitamin C: 50% ◆ Calcium: 20% ◆ Iron: 6% ◆ **DIETARY EXCHANGES:** 1 Starch, ½ Very Lean Meat, 3 Fat OR 1 Carbohydrate, ½ Very Lean Meat, 3 Fat

Home-Style Cream of Tomato Soup

PREP TIME: 25 MINUTES ✦ YIELD: 5 (1⅓-CUP) SERVINGS

2 tablespoons margarine or butter
¼ cup chopped onion
½ cup mashed potato flakes
2 (16-oz.) cans stewed tomatoes, cut up
    if desired
3 cups milk
¼ teaspoon salt
⅛ to ¼ teaspoon pepper

1. Melt margarine in large saucepan over medium heat. Add onion; cook 1 to 2 minutes until crisp-tender.
2. Add all remaining ingredients; cook 8 to 10 minutes or until thoroughly heated and flavors are blended, stirring frequently.

NUTRITION INFORMATION PER SERVING: Serving Size: 1⅓ Cups ✦ Calories: 250 ✦ Calories from Fat: 70 ✦ % DAILY VALUE: Total Fat: 8 g 12% ✦ Saturated Fat: 3 g 15% ✦ Cholesterol: 10 mg 3% ✦ Sodium: 660 mg 28% ✦ Total Carbohydrate: 36 g 12% ✦ Dietary Fiber: 3 g 12% ✦ Sugars: 13 g ✦ Protein: 8 g ✦ Vitamin A: 30% ✦ Vitamin C: 45% ✦ Calcium: 25% ✦ Iron: 10% ✦ DIETARY EXCHANGES: 2 Starch, 1 Vegetable, 1½ Fat OR 2 Carbohydrate, 1 Vegetable, 1½ Fat

Vichyssoise

PREP TIME: 20 MINUTES (READY IN 1 HOUR 40 MINUTES) ✦ YIELD: 5 SERVINGS

2 tablespoons butter
3 medium leeks, sliced
3 medium potatoes, peeled, sliced
4 cups chicken broth
2 cups half-and-half
½ teaspoon salt, if desired
    Chopped chives

1. Melt butter in large saucepan over medium heat. Add leeks; cook and stir until tender. Add potatoes and broth. Cover; simmer 15 to 20 minutes or until potatoes are tender.
2. In blender container or food processor bowl with metal blade, process mixture until smooth and creamy. Stir in half-and-half and salt. Refrigerate 1 hour or until cold.
3. To serve, ladle into bowls; sprinkle with chives.

NUTRITION INFORMATION PER SERVING: Serving Size: ⅕ of Recipe ✦ Calories: 310 ✦ Calories from Fat: 150 ✦ % DAILY VALUE: Total Fat: 17 g 26% ✦ Saturated Fat: 10 g 50% ✦ Cholesterol: 50 mg 17% ✦ Sodium: 940 mg 39% ✦ Total Carbohydrate: 30 g 10% ✦ Dietary Fiber: 3 g 12% ✦ Sugars: 8 g ✦ Protein: 9 g ✦ Vitamin C: 20% ✦ Calcium: 15% ✦ Iron: 15% ✦ DIETARY EXCHANGES: 1½ Starch, 1½ Vegetable, 3½ Fat OR 1½ Carbohydrate, 1½ Vegetable, 3½ Fat

Spicy Gazpacho

PREP TIME: 15 MINUTES ✦ YIELD: 7 (1-CUP) SERVINGS

2 medium tomatoes, chopped
1 small cucumber, chopped
1 small onion, chopped
½ green bell pepper, chopped
1 garlic clove, minced
1 tablespoon wine vinegar or lemon juice
1 to 2 dashes hot pepper sauce
1 (24-oz.) can (3 cups) spicy hot vegetable
    juice cocktail or tomato juice, chilled

1. In large bowl, combine all ingredients; mix well.
2. Cover; refrigerate until serving time.

NUTRITION INFORMATION PER SERVING: Serving Size: 1 Cup ✦ Calories: 35 ✦ Calories from Fat: 0 ✦ % DAILY VALUE: Total Fat: 0 g 0% ✦ Saturated Fat: 0 g 0% ✦ Cholesterol: 0 mg 0% ✦ Sodium: 280 mg 12% ✦ Total Carbohydrate: 8 g 3% ✦ Dietary Fiber: 2 g 8% ✦ Sugars: 5 g ✦ Protein: 1 g ✦ Vitamin A: 30% ✦ Vitamin C: 70% ✦ Calcium: 0% ✦ Iron: 4% ✦ DIETARY EXCHANGES: 1½ Vegetable

Sausage Tortellini Soup

PREP TIME: 35 MINUTES ✦ YIELD: 6 (1½-CUP) SERVINGS

½ lb. bulk turkey Italian sausage
½ cup chopped onion
1 cup sliced carrots
1 (28-oz.) can tomato puree
1 (14½-oz.) can ready-to-serve chicken broth
2 cups water
1 teaspoon dried basil leaves
1 (9-oz.) pkg. refrigerated cheese-filled
    tortellini
3 cups frozen cut broccoli

1. In Dutch oven, combine sausage and onion; cook over medium heat 8 minutes or until sausage is no longer pink. Drain.
2. Add carrots; cook and stir 1 minute. Add tomato puree, broth, water and basil. Bring to a boil. Add tortellini; return to a boil. Add broccoli. Cook 6 to 8 minutes or until tortellini is tender.

NUTRITION INFORMATION PER SERVING: Serving Size: 1½ Cups ✦ Calories: 280 ✦ Calories from Fat: 60 ✦ % DAILY VALUE: Total Fat: 7 g 11% ✦ Saturated Fat: 3 g 15% ✦ Cholesterol: 45 mg 15% ✦ Sodium: 650 mg 27% ✦ Total Carbohydrate: 37 g 12% ✦ Dietary Fiber: 5 g 20% ✦ Sugars: 10 g ✦ Protein: 17 g ✦ Vitamin A: 150% ✦ Vitamin C: 45% ✦ Calcium: 8% ✦ Iron: 20% ✦ DIETARY EXCHANGES: 2 Starch, 1½ Vegetable, 1 Medium-Fat Meat OR 2 Carbohydrate, 1½ Vegetable, 1 Medium-Fat Meat

Baked Potato Soup

Baked Potato Soup

PREP TIME: 45 MINUTES ✦ YIELD: 7 (1½-CUP) SERVINGS

    4 large baking potatoes
    4 slices bacon
    6 cups milk
    ½ cup all-purpose flour
    4 green onions, sliced
    5 oz. (1¼ cups) shredded sharp
        Cheddar cheese
    ¾ teaspoon salt
    ¼ teaspoon pepper
    1 (8-oz.) container sour cream

1. Pierce potatoes with fork; place on microwave-safe paper towel or roasting rack in microwave. Microwave on HIGH for 15 to 20 minutes or until tender, turning once halfway through cooking. Cool slightly.

2. Meanwhile, cook bacon in Dutch oven over medium heat until crisp. Remove from skillet; drain on paper towels. Crumble; set aside.

3. In same Dutch oven, combine milk and flour; blend well. Cook over medium heat for about 15 minutes or until bubbly and thickened, stirring frequently.

4. Cut cooked potatoes in half. Scoop out cooked potato from skins; place in medium bowl. Discard skins. Mash potatoes well.

5. Add potatoes, bacon, 2 tablespoons of the onions, 1 cup of the cheese, salt and pepper to milk mixture. Cook and stir until cheese is melted. Add sour cream; cook and stir until soup is thoroughly heated.

6. To serve, ladle soup into bowls; sprinkle with remaining onions and ¼ cup cheese.

NUTRITION INFORMATION PER SERVING: Serving Size: 1½ Cups ✦ Calories: 400 ✦ Calories from Fat: 180 ✦ **% DAILY VALUE:** Total Fat: 20 g 31% ✦ Saturated Fat: 12 g 60% ✦ Cholesterol: 55 mg 18% ✦ Sodium: 540 mg 23% ✦ Total Carbohydrate: 38 g 13% ✦ Dietary Fiber: 2 g 8% ✦ Sugars: 13 g ✦ Protein: 17 g ✦ Vitamin A: 20% ✦ Vitamin C: 20% ✦ Calcium: 45% ✦ Iron: 6% ✦ **DIETARY EXCHANGES:** 2½ Starch, 1½ High-Fat Meat, 1 Fat OR 2½ Carbohydrate, 1½ High-Fat Meat, 1 Fat

French Onion Soup Gratinée

PREP TIME: 25 MINUTES (READY IN 50 MINUTES)
✦ YIELD: 6 (1-CUP) SERVINGS

    3 tablespoons margarine or butter
    4 cups thinly sliced onions
    5 cups beef broth
    1 beef-flavor bouillon cube or 1 teaspoon
        beef-flavor instant bouillon
    1 teaspoon Worcestershire sauce
        Dash pepper
    4 oz. (1 cup) shredded Swiss cheese
    ¼ cup grated Parmesan cheese
    6 slices French bread, toasted

1. Melt margarine in Dutch oven or large saucepan over low heat. Add onions; cook 15 minutes or until golden brown and tender, stirring occasionally.

2. Add broth, bouillon cube, Worcestershire sauce and pepper. Bring to a boil. Reduce heat to low; cover and simmer 20 to 25 minutes.

3. Meanwhile, in medium bowl, combine Swiss and Parmesan cheeses.

4. To serve, place 6 ovenproof soup bowls on cookie sheet. Ladle soup into bowls. Top each with slice of toasted bread; sprinkle each with about 2 tablespoons cheese mixture.

5. Broil 4 to 6 inches from heat for 1 to 3 minutes or until cheese is bubbly.

NUTRITION INFORMATION PER SERVING: Serving Size: 1 Cup ✦ Calories: 250 ✦ Calories from Fat: 120 ✦ **% DAILY VALUE:** Total Fat: 13 g 20% ✦ Saturated Fat: 6 g 30% ✦ Cholesterol: 20 mg 7% ✦ Sodium: 1150 mg 48% ✦ Total Carbohydrate: 21 g 7% ✦ Dietary Fiber: 2 g 8% ✦ Sugars: 5 g ✦ Protein: 13 g ✦ Vitamin A: 8% ✦ Vitamin C: 6% ✦ Calcium: 30% ✦ Iron: 6% ✦ **DIETARY EXCHANGES:** 1 Starch, 1 Vegetable, 1 High-Fat Meat, 1 Fat OR 1 Carbohydrate, 1 Vegetable, 1 High-Fat Meat, 1 Fat

French Onion Soup Gratinée

Easy Corn Chowder

smooth. Add flour mixture to chowder; cook and stir until bubbly and thickened.

NUTRITION INFORMATION PER SERVING: Serving Size: 1 Cup ◆ Calories: 260 ◆ Calories from Fat: 70 ◆ **% DAILY VALUE:** Total Fat: 8 g 12% ◆ Saturated Fat: 3 g 15% ◆ Cholesterol: 10 mg 3% ◆ Sodium: 1080 mg 45% ◆ Total Carbohydrate: 39 g 13% ◆ Dietary Fiber: 3 g 12% ◆ Sugars: 15 g ◆ Protein: 9 g ◆ Vitamin A: 10% ◆ Vitamin C: 10% ◆ Calcium: 20% ◆ Iron: 4% ◆ **DIETARY EXCHANGES:** 2½ Starch, 1½ Fat OR 2½ Carbohydrate, 1½ Fat

Easy Corn Chowder

PREP TIME: 30 MINUTES ◆ YIELD: 3 (1-CUP) SERVINGS

  1 (11-oz.) can vacuum-packed whole kernel corn, undrained
½ cup chopped onion
½ cup cubed peeled potatoes
⅓ cup water
  2 teaspoons chicken-flavor instant bouillon
1¾ cups milk
  1 tablespoon margarine or butter
  2 tablespoons all-purpose flour

1. In large saucepan, combine corn, onion, potatoes, water and bouillon. Bring to a boil. Reduce heat to low; cover and simmer 10 minutes or until potatoes are tender, stirring occasionally.
2. Stir in 1½ cups of the milk and margarine. In small bowl, combine remaining ¼ cup milk and flour; beat with wire whisk until

> ### COOK'S NOTE
>
> ### BROTH AND CONSOMMÉ
>
> *Broth* or *stock* is the thin liquid remaining after simmering and straining ingredients such as vegetables, meat or poultry. It's easy to make your own, as long as you have time to wait for the slow simmering to bring out all the flavor. Homemade broth, often the base for sauces, soups and gravies, can be refrigerated for several days or frozen. Freeze in ice cube trays or in plastic containers (allow 1½ inches of headroom for expansion).
>
> *Consommé* is broth made from beef, veal or poultry that has been clarified (the liquid is no longer cloudy and no sediment remains).

Minute Minestrone

PREP TIME: 30 MINUTES ◆ YIELD: 5 (1½-CUP) SERVINGS

  2 tablespoons margarine or butter
¼ cup chopped onion
  1 medium zucchini, sliced
  1 (10-oz.) pkg. frozen baby lima beans in a pouch with butter sauce
  2 (10½-oz.) cans condensed beef broth
  1 (14.5 or 16-oz.) can whole tomatoes, undrained, cut up
  1 cup water
  2 oz. uncooked vermicelli, broken into pieces (½ cup)
  1 tablespoon grated Parmesan cheese
¼ teaspoon dried basil leaves
¼ teaspoon pepper
⅛ teaspoon garlic salt
    Dash ground red pepper (cayenne)

1. Melt margarine in large saucepan over medium heat. Add onion and zucchini; cook and stir until vegetables are crisp-tender.
2. Remove frozen lima beans from pouch; add to cooked vegetables. Stir in all remaining ingredients. Simmer about 15 minutes or until vermicelli is tender, stirring occasionally.

NUTRITION INFORMATION PER SERVING: Serving Size: 1½ Cups ◆ Calories: 220 ◆ Calories from Fat: 60 ◆ **% DAILY VALUE:** Total Fat: 7 g 11% ◆ Saturated Fat: 2 g 10% ◆ Cholesterol: 3 mg 1% ◆ Sodium: 1040 mg 43% ◆ Total Carbohydrate: 26 g 9% ◆ Dietary Fiber: 5 g 20% ◆ Sugars: 4 g ◆ Protein: 12 g ◆ Vitamin A: 20% ◆ Vitamin C: 20% ◆ Calcium: 8% ◆ Iron: 15% ◆ **DIETARY EXCHANGES:** 1½ Starch, 1 Vegetable, 1 Very Lean Meat, 1 Fat OR 1½ Carbohydrate, 1 Vegetable, 1 Very Lean Meat, 1 Fat

Minute Minestrone

Hot Borscht

PREP TIME: 15 MINUTES (READY IN 1 HOUR)
♦ YIELD: 10 (1-CUP) SERVINGS

  1 tablespoon oil
  1 cup chopped onions
  1 garlic clove, minced
  4 cups purchased coleslaw blend
      (from 16-oz. pkg.)
  2 (16-oz.) cans diced beets, drained
  2 (14½-oz.) cans ready-to-serve beef broth
  1 (14.5-oz.) can diced peeled tomatoes,
      undrained
  ⅓ cup red wine vinegar
  2 cups water
  ½ cup sour cream
  ¼ cup chopped fresh dill

1. Heat oil in Dutch oven or stockpot over medium heat until hot. Add onions and garlic; cook and stir 2 minutes or until tender. Add coleslaw blend; cook over low heat 1 to 2 minutes or until cabbage wilts, stirring occasionally.

2. Add all remaining ingredients except sour cream and dill. Bring to a boil. Reduce heat to low; partially cover and simmer 45 minutes. Top each serving with sour cream and fresh dill.

NUTRITION INFORMATION PER SERVING: Serving Size: 1 Cup ♦ Calories: 90 ♦ Calories from Fat: 35 ♦ **% DAILY VALUE:** Total Fat: 4 g 6% ♦ Saturated Fat: 2 g 10% ♦ Cholesterol: 5 mg 2% ♦ Sodium: 460 mg 19% ♦ Total Carbohydrate: 10 g 3% ♦ Dietary Fiber: 2 g 8% ♦ Sugars: 7 g ♦ Protein: 3 g ♦ Vitamin A: 25% ♦ Vitamin C: 20% ♦ Calcium: 6% ♦ Iron: 10% ♦ **DIETARY EXCHANGES:** 2 Vegetable, 1 Fat

Chili Verde

PREP TIME: 15 MINUTES (READY IN 40 MINUTES)
♦ YIELD: 6 (1½-CUP) SERVINGS

CHILI
  1 tablespoon olive or vegetable oil
  1 lb. boneless pork loin chops, cubed
  2 onions, chopped
  3 garlic cloves, minced
  2 Anaheim chiles, seeded, chopped
  1 green bell pepper, chopped
  2 (15-oz.) cans spicy chili beans, undrained
  1 (28-oz.) can crushed tomatoes, undrained
  2 teaspoons cumin
  2 teaspoons chili powder

TOPPING
  2 oz. queso fresco or feta cheese,
      crumbled (½ cup)
  ¼ cup chopped fresh cilantro

1. Heat oil in large saucepan or Dutch oven over medium-high heat until hot. Add pork; cook and stir 3 to 4 minutes or until lightly browned. Add onions and garlic; cook and stir 1 to 2 minutes.

2. Stir in all remaining chili ingredients. Bring to a boil. Reduce heat to medium-low; cook 15 to 20 minutes or until pork is tender, stirring occasionally. Top each serving with cheese and cilantro.

NUTRITION INFORMATION PER SERVING: Serving Size: 1½ Cups ♦ Calories: 360 ♦ Calories from Fat: 100 ♦ **% DAILY VALUE:** Total Fat: 11 g 17% ♦ Saturated Fat: 4 g 20% ♦ Cholesterol: 55 mg 18% ♦ Sodium: 900 mg 38% ♦ Total Carbohydrate: 38 g 13% ♦ Dietary Fiber: 10 g 40% ♦ Sugars: 9 g ♦ Protein: 27 g ♦ Vitamin A: 30% ♦ Vitamin C: 60% ♦ Calcium: 15% ♦ Iron: 30% ♦ **DIETARY EXCHANGES:** 2½ Starch, 3 Lean Meat OR 2½ Carbohydrate, 3 Lean Meat

Chili con Carne

PREP TIME: 30 MINUTES (READY IN 2 HOURS)
♦ YIELD: 6 (1¼-CUP) SERVINGS

  1 lb. ground beef
  ½ cup chopped onion
  ¾ cup water
  ½ cup chopped green bell pepper
  3 teaspoons chili powder
  ¼ teaspoon pepper
  ¼ teaspoon hot pepper sauce
  1 to 2 garlic cloves, minced
  1 (28-oz.) can whole tomatoes, undrained,
      cut up
  1 (10¾-oz.) can condensed tomato soup
  1 (6-oz.) can tomato paste
  1 (4.5-oz.) can diced green chiles, drained
  1 (15.5 or 15-oz.) can red kidney or pinto
      beans, drained, rinsed

1. In medium skillet, combine ground beef and onion. Cook over medium heat for 8 to 10 minutes or until beef is thoroughly cooked.

2. In large saucepan, combine ground beef mixture and all remaining ingredients except kidney beans. Bring to a boil. Reduce heat; cover and simmer 1½ to 2 hours, stirring occasionally.

3. Stir in kidney beans; simmer until thoroughly heated.

NUTRITION INFORMATION PER SERVING: Serving Size: 1¼ Cups ♦ Calories: 310 ♦ Calories from Fat: 110 ♦ **% DAILY VALUE:** Total Fat: 12 g 18% ♦ Saturated Fat: 5 g 25% ♦ Cholesterol: 45 mg 15% ♦ Sodium: 920 mg 38% ♦ Total Carbohydrate: 31 g 10% ♦ Dietary Fiber: 7 g 28% ♦ Sugars: 8 g ♦ Protein: 19 g ♦ Vitamin A: 45% ♦ Vitamin C: 80% ♦ Calcium: 10% ♦ Iron: 25% ♦ **DIETARY EXCHANGES:** 2 Starch, 2 Medium-Fat Meat OR 2 Carbohydrate, 2 Medium-Fat Meat

White Chicken Chili

PREP TIME: 30 MINUTES ◆ YIELD: 9 (1-CUP) SERVINGS

1 tablespoon oil
1 cup chopped onions
2 garlic cloves, minced
1 lb. boneless skinless chicken breasts, cut into bite-sized pieces
3 (14½-oz.) cans ready-to-serve chicken broth
2 (15-oz.) cans cannellini beans, drained
2 (4.5-oz.) cans chopped green chiles, drained
1 teaspoon dried oregano leaves
½ teaspoon cumin
Dash ground red pepper (cayenne), if desired
6 oz. (1½ cups) shredded Monterey Jack cheese
Chopped fresh cilantro, if desired

1. Heat oil in large saucepan or Dutch oven over medium-high heat until hot. Add onions, garlic and chicken; cook and stir until chicken is no longer pink.
2. Stir in all remaining ingredients except cheese and cilantro. Bring to a boil. Reduce heat to low; simmer 10 to 15 minutes to blend flavors, stirring occasionally.
3. To serve, ladle chili into soup bowls. Top each serving with cheese and cilantro.

NUTRITION INFORMATION PER SERVING: Serving Size: 1 Cup ◆ Calories: 250 ◆ Calories from Fat: 90 ◆ % DAILY VALUE: Total Fat: 10 g 15% ◆ Saturated Fat: 4 g 20% ◆ Cholesterol: 45 mg 15% ◆ Sodium: 670 mg 28% ◆ Total Carbohydrate: 17 g 6% ◆ Dietary Fiber: 4 g 16% ◆ Sugars: 3 g ◆ Protein: 23 g ◆ Vitamin A: 8% ◆ Vitamin C: 60% ◆ Calcium: 20% ◆ Iron: 10% ◆ DIETARY EXCHANGES: 1 Starch, 3 Very Lean Meat, 1½ Fat OR 1 Carbohydrate, 3 Very Lean Meat, 1½ Fat

Sausage and Black Bean Chili

PREP TIME: 30 MINUTES (READY IN 1 HOUR 15 MINUTES) ◆ YIELD: 6 SERVINGS

⅔ cup uncooked regular long-grain white rice
1⅓ cups water
1 lb. bulk chorizo or Italian sausage
1 cup chopped onions
2 garlic cloves, crushed
2 jalapeño chiles, seeded, chopped
2 (15-oz.) cans black beans, drained, rinsed
1 (28-oz.) can Italian plum tomatoes, undrained, cut up
1 cup beer or tomato juice
1 tablespoon chopped fresh cilantro
1 teaspoon cumin
4 oz. (1 cup) shredded Cheddar cheese

1. Cook rice in water as directed on package.
2. Meanwhile, in large saucepan or Dutch oven, combine sausage, onions, garlic and chiles. Cook 8 to 10 minutes or until sausage is well browned. Drain. Stir in all remaining ingredients except rice and cheese. Cook over medium heat 30 to 45 minutes or until slightly thickened.
3. To serve, ladle chili over cooked rice in individual serving bowls; sprinkle with cheese.

NUTRITION INFORMATION PER SERVING: Serving Size: ⅙ of Recipe ◆ Calories: 580 ◆ Calories from Fat: 260 ◆ % DAILY VALUE: Total Fat: 29 g 45% ◆ Saturated Fat: 12 g 60% ◆ Cholesterol: 70 mg 23% ◆ Sodium: 1010 mg 42% ◆ Total Carbohydrate: 49 g 16% ◆ Dietary Fiber: 10 g 40% ◆ Sugars: 7 g ◆ Protein: 29 g ◆ Vitamin A: 20% ◆ Vitamin C: 35% ◆ Calcium: 20% ◆ Iron: 25% ◆ DIETARY EXCHANGES: 3 Starch, 1 Vegetable, 2½ High-Fat Meat, 1½ Fat OR 3 Carbohydrate, 1 Vegetable, 2½ High-Fat Meat, 1½ Fat

Chunky Chicken Chili

PREP TIME: 45 MINUTES ◆ YIELD: 6 (1½-CUP) SERVINGS

4 boneless skinless chicken breast halves, cut into bite-sized pieces
1 cup chopped onions
½ cup chopped celery
½ cup chopped carrot
2 garlic cloves, minced
1 cup salsa
1 (28-oz.) can whole tomatoes, undrained, cut up
1 (8-oz.) can tomato sauce
3 teaspoons chili powder
½ teaspoon cumin
1 (15-oz.) can garbanzo beans, drained
1 green bell pepper, chopped

1. Spray large nonstick saucepan with non-stick cooking spray. Heat over medium-high heat until hot. Add chicken, onions, celery, carrot and garlic; cook and stir until chicken is no longer pink.
2. Stir in salsa, tomatoes, tomato sauce, chili powder and cumin. Bring to a boil. Reduce heat to low; cover and simmer 30 minutes, stirring occasionally. Stir in garbanzo beans and bell pepper; simmer until thoroughly heated.

NUTRITION INFORMATION PER SERVING: Serving Size: 1½ Cups ◆ Calories: 240 ◆ Calories from Fat: 35 ◆ % DAILY VALUE: Total Fat: 4 g 6% ◆ Saturated Fat: 1 g 5% ◆ Cholesterol: 45 mg 15% ◆ Sodium: 900 mg 38% ◆ Total Carbohydrate: 27 g 9% ◆ Dietary Fiber: 7 g 28% ◆ Sugars: 8 g ◆ Protein: 23 g ◆ Vitamin A: 90% ◆ Vitamin C: 45% ◆ Calcium: 10% ◆ Iron: 15% ◆ DIETARY EXCHANGES: 1½ Starch, 1 Vegetable, 2½ Very Lean Meat OR 1½ Carbohydrate, 1 Vegetable, 2½ Very Lean Meat

Zesty Black and White Bean Chili

Zesty Black and White Bean Chili

PREP TIME: 35 MINUTES ✦ YIELD: 5 (1⅓-CUP) SERVINGS

  1 cup chopped onions
  1 garlic clove, minced
  ¼ cup all-purpose flour
  1 to 2 teaspoons chili powder
  ½ teaspoon cumin
1½ cups milk
  2 (9-oz.) pkg. frozen shoepeg white corn
    in a pouch
  1 (15.5-oz.) can great northern beans,
    drained, rinsed
  1 (15-oz.) can black beans, drained, rinsed
  1 (14½-oz.) can ready-to-serve chicken broth
  1 (4.5-oz.) can chopped green chiles,
    undrained
  2 tablespoons chopped fresh cilantro
  2 tablespoons finely chopped red bell pepper

1. Spray Dutch oven or large saucepan with nonstick cooking spray. Heat over medium-high heat until hot. Add onions and garlic; cook until onions are tender.
2. Stir in flour, chili powder and cumin. Gradually stir in milk. Add all remaining ingredients except cilantro and bell pepper; stir to combine.
3. Bring to a boil, stirring constantly. Reduce heat to low; simmer 15 minutes or until thickened, stirring occasionally. Stir in cilantro. If desired, add salt and pepper to taste.
4. To serve, ladle chili into serving bowls; sprinkle with bell pepper.

NUTRITION INFORMATION PER SERVING: Serving Size: 1⅓ Cups ✦ Calories: 320 ✦ Calories from Fat: 35 ✦ % DAILY VALUE: Total Fat: 4 g 6% ✦ Saturated Fat: 1 g 5% ✦ Cholesterol: 5 mg 2% ✦ Sodium: 750 mg 31% ✦ Total Carbohydrate: 56 g 19% ✦ Dietary Fiber: 12 g 48% ✦ Sugars: 10 g ✦ Protein: 16 g ✦ Vitamin A: 15% ✦ Vitamin C: 20% ✦ Calcium: 25% ✦ Iron: 20% ✦ DIETARY EXCHANGES: 3½ Starch, 1 Very Lean Meat OR 3½ Carbohydrate, 1 Very Lean Meat

Smoky Hot Beef Chili

PREP TIME: 20 MINUTES (READY IN 1 HOUR 15 MINUTES)
✦ YIELD: 6 (1¼-CUP) SERVINGS

CHILI
  1 tablespoon oil
  ¾ lb. beef sirloin, cut into 1-inch pieces
  1 cup chopped onions
  1 medium green bell pepper, seeded, chopped
  2 garlic cloves, crushed
  2 (28-oz.) cans Italian plum tomatoes,
    undrained, cut up
  2 to 3 chipotle chiles, cut up
  1 teaspoon salt
  1 teaspoon Liquid Smoke
  ½ teaspoon pepper

TOPPING
  1 avocado, peeled, pitted and chopped
  1 teaspoon lime juice
  ½ cup sour cream

1. Heat oil in large saucepan or Dutch oven over medium-high heat until hot. Add beef; cook 8 to 10 minutes or until beef is well browned. Stir in onions, bell pepper and garlic. Cook 4 to 5 minutes or until vegetables are crisp-tender.

Smoky Hot Beef Chili

2. Stir in all remaining chili ingredients. Bring mixture just to a boil. Reduce heat to low; simmer 45 to 55 minutes or until slightly thickened, stirring occasionally.

3. In small bowl, combine avocado and lime juice. To serve chili, ladle chili into bowls; top with sour cream and chopped avocado.

NUTRITION INFORMATION PER SERVING: Serving Size: 1¼ Cups ◆ Calories: 260 ◆ Calories from Fat: 130 ◆ **% DAILY VALUE:** Total Fat: 14 g 22% ◆ Saturated Fat: 5 g 25% ◆ Cholesterol: 40 mg 13% ◆ Sodium: 780 mg 33% ◆ Total Carbohydrate: 19 g 6% ◆ Dietary Fiber: 5 g 20% ◆ Sugars: 9 g ◆ Protein: 15 g ◆ Vitamin A: 40% ◆ Vitamin C: 80% ◆ Calcium: 10% ◆ Iron: 20% ◆ **DIETARY EXCHANGES:** ½ Starch, 2 Vegetable, 1½ Lean Meat, 2 Fat OR ½ Carbohydrate, 2 Vegetable, 1½ Lean Meat, 2 Fat

Brunswick Stew

PREP TIME: 40 MINUTES ◆ YIELD: 6 SERVINGS

    2 tablespoons margarine or butter
    ½ cup chopped onion
    1 medium green bell pepper, chopped
    2 cups chicken broth
    2 cups cubed cooked chicken
    1 (14.5 or 16-oz.) can whole tomatoes, undrained, cut up
    1 (15.5-oz.) can butter beans, drained
    1 (7-oz.) can vacuum-packed whole kernel corn
    ¼ teaspoon salt
    ⅛ teaspoon pepper
    ⅛ to ¼ teaspoon crushed red pepper flakes
    ½ cup sliced fresh or frozen okra
    ⅓ cup water
    3 tablespoons all-purpose flour

1. Melt margarine in large saucepan over medium-high heat. Add onion and bell pepper; cook and stir until crisp-tender. Stir in broth, chicken, tomatoes, beans, corn, salt, pepper and crushed red pepper. Bring to a boil. Reduce heat to low; simmer 15 minutes.

2. Add okra; simmer an additional 5 minutes or until okra is tender.

3. In small bowl, combine water and flour; blend until smooth. Stir into chicken mixture. Cook over medium heat until mixture boils and thickens, stirring constantly.

NUTRITION INFORMATION PER SERVING: Serving Size: ⅙ of Recipe ◆ Calories: 240 ◆ Calories from Fat: 70 ◆ **% DAILY VALUE:** Total Fat: 8 g 12% ◆ Saturated Fat: 2 g 10% ◆ Cholesterol: 40 mg 13% ◆ Sodium: 770 mg 32% ◆ Total Carbohydrate: 23 g 8% ◆ Dietary Fiber: 5 g 20% ◆ Sugars: 5 g ◆ Protein: 20 g ◆ Vitamin A: 15% ◆ Vitamin C: 30% ◆ Calcium: 6% ◆ Iron: 10% ◆ **DIETARY EXCHANGES:** 1 Starch, 1 Vegetable, 2 Very Lean Meat, ½ Fat OR 1 Carbohydrate, 1 Vegetable, 2 Very Lean Meat, ½ Fat

Tuscan Bean Stew

PREP TIME: 25 MINUTES ◆ YIELD: 4 (1½-CUP) SERVINGS

    1 tablespoon olive oil
    2 teaspoons ground sage
    3 garlic cloves, minced
    1 (33.5-oz.) can peeled plum tomatoes with basil, undrained, cut up
    1 (15.5 or 15-oz.) can kidney beans
    1 (15-oz.) can black beans, drained, rinsed
    1 (15-oz.) can garbanzo beans, drained, rinsed
    ⅓ cup dry red wine
    1 tablespoon sugar
    ¼ teaspoon salt
    ¼ teaspoon pepper

1. Heat oil in Dutch oven or 3-quart saucepan over medium heat until hot. Add sage and garlic; cook and stir 2 to 3 minutes or until garlic is tender.

2. Stir in all remaining ingredients. Bring to a boil. Reduce heat to low; simmer 15 to 20 minutes or until slightly thickened, stirring occasionally.

NUTRITION INFORMATION PER SERVING: Serving Size: 1½ Cups ◆ Calories: 370 ◆ Calories from Fat: 50 ◆ **% DAILY VALUE:** Total Fat: 6 g 9% ◆ Saturated Fat: 1 g 5% ◆ Cholesterol: 0 mg 0% ◆ Sodium: 980 mg 41% ◆ Total Carbohydrate: 59 g 20% ◆ Dietary Fiber: 16 g 64% ◆ Sugars: 10 g ◆ Protein: 18 g ◆ Vitamin A: 30% ◆ Vitamin C: 40% ◆ Calcium: 20% ◆ Iron: 25% ◆ **DIETARY EXCHANGES:** 4 Starch, 1 Very Lean Meat, ½ Fat OR 4 Carbohydrate, 1 Very Lean Meat, ½ Fat

Tuscan Bean Stew

Oven Beef Stew

PREP TIME: 20 MINUTES (READY IN 5 HOURS
20 MINUTES) ✦ YIELD: 8 (1½-CUP) SERVINGS

　2 lb. beef stew meat, cut into 1½-inch cubes
　1 (14.5 or 16-oz.) can whole tomatoes,
　　　undrained, cut up
　1 (10½-oz.) can condensed beef broth
　1 (8-oz.) can sliced water chestnuts, undrained
　1 (4.5-oz.) jar whole mushrooms, undrained
　1 cup red wine or water
　2 cups cubed peeled parsnips or potatoes
　1 cup chopped onions
　1 cup chopped celery
　6 carrots, cut into 1-inch pieces
　½ cup all-purpose flour
　1 tablespoon Worcestershire sauce
　1 teaspoon sugar
　1 teaspoon salt
　1 teaspoon dried marjoram leaves
　¼ teaspoon garlic powder
　¼ teaspoon pepper

1. Heat oven to 250°F. In ovenproof Dutch oven, combine all ingredients; mix well. Cover.

COOK'S NOTE

STORING SOUP AND STEW

✦ Refrigerate leftovers immediately for quick
　and thorough cooling and to prevent
　spoilage.
✦ Soup can be refrigerated in a tightly
　covered container for up to three days.
✦ For longer storage, freeze soup in
　tightly sealed, labeled containers. (Allow
　1½ inches of headroom for expansion.)
　Use within four months for best flavor.
✦ Single-portion containers work well for
　busy households where family members
　cannot always dine together.
✦ Soup or stew made with beans, vegetables
　or meat retain flavor and texture well
　when frozen and reheated. Recipes featur-
　ing eggs, seafood, and dairy products such
　as cheese, milk and cream are not recom-
　mended for freezing.
✦ If you plan to freeze the soup, omit any
　flour or egg thickener and add it instead
　when you reheat the soup.
✦ Thaw frozen soup or stew in the refriger-
　ator, in the microwave or on the stove
　top. Do not thaw it at room temperature.

2. Bake at 250°F. for 5 hours or until beef is tender.

NUTRITION INFORMATION PER SERVING: Serving Size: 1½ Cups ✦ Calories: 320 ✦ Calories from Fat: 60 ✦ % DAILY VALUE: Total Fat: 7 g 11% ✦ Saturated Fat: 2 g 10% ✦ Cholesterol: 75 mg 25% ✦ Sodium: 740 mg 31% ✦ Total Carbohydrate: 29 g 10% ✦ Dietary Fiber: 6 g 24% ✦ Sugars: 9 g ✦ Protein: 30 g ✦ Vitamin A: 310% ✦ Vitamin C: 25% ✦ Calcium: 6% ✦ Iron: 25% ✦ DIETARY EXCHANGES: 2 Starch, 3½ Lean Meat OR 2 Carbohydrate, 3½ Lean Meat

Veal Marengo

PREP TIME: 40 MINUTES ✦ YIELD: 6 SERVINGS

　1 tablespoon margarine or butter
　1 lb. lean veal steak, cut into thin strips
　1 cup sliced fresh mushrooms
　1 large onion, thinly sliced
　1 garlic clove, minced
　1 teaspoon dried thyme leaves
　⅛ teaspoon pepper
　3 medium tomatoes, peeled and cut into
　　　wedges or 1 (14.5 or 16-oz.) can whole
　　　tomatoes, drained and cut into wedges
　½ cup dry white wine or beef broth
　12 oz. (6¾ cups) uncooked wide egg noodles
　1 tablespoon all-purpose flour
　　　Chopped fresh parsley, if desired

1. Melt margarine in large skillet over medium-high heat. Add veal; cook and stir until no longer pink. Remove veal from pan; cover to keep warm.
2. To drippings in skillet, add mushrooms, onion, garlic, thyme and pepper. Cook over medium-high heat until onion is tender. Stir in tomatoes and wine. Simmer 15 minutes to blend flavors, stirring occasionally.
3. Meanwhile, cook noodles to desired doneness as directed on package. Drain; rinse with hot water. Toss veal with flour; add to tomato mixture. Cook and stir until thickened. Serve over hot cooked noodles; sprinkle with parsley.

NUTRITION INFORMATION PER SERVING: Serving Size: ⅙ of Recipe ✦ Calories: 350 ✦ Calories from Fat: 60 ✦ % DAILY VALUE: Total Fat: 7 g 11% ✦ Saturated Fat: 2 g 10% ✦ Cholesterol: 95 mg 32% ✦ Sodium: 80 mg 3% ✦ Total Carbohydrate: 48 g 16% ✦ Dietary Fiber: 3 g 12% ✦ Sugars: 5 g ✦ Protein: 20 g ✦ Vitamin A: 10% ✦ Vitamin C: 20% ✦ Calcium: 4% ✦ Iron: 20% ✦ DIETARY EXCHANGES: 3 Starch, ½ Vegetable, 1½ Very Lean Meat, 1 Fat OR 3 Carbohydrate, ½ Vegetable, 1½ Very Lean Meat, 1 Fat

Baked Burgundy Beef Stew

PREP TIME: 15 MINUTES (READY IN 2 HOURS 15 MINUTES) ◆ YIELD: 5 (1½-CUP) SERVINGS

  2 lb. beef top round steak, cut
       into 1-inch cubes
  ¼ cup all-purpose flour
  1 tablespoon oil
  ½ cup sliced celery
  1 cup frozen small whole onions
  2 cups fresh baby carrots
  1 (14½-oz.) can ready-to-serve beef broth
  1 (14½-oz.) can pasta-style chunky tomatoes,
       undrained
  1 cup dry red wine
  ½ teaspoon salt
  ½ teaspoon dried thyme leaves
  ½ teaspoon dry mustard
  2 tablespoons water
  1 tablespoon all-purpose flour

1. Heat oven to 325°F. In large bowl, combine beef and ¼ cup flour; toss to coat evenly. Heat oil in ovenproof Dutch oven over medium-high heat until hot. Add beef; cook and stir until browned. Add all remaining ingredients except water and 1 tablespoon flour; mix well. Cover.

2. Bake at 325°F. for 1½ hours or until beef is fork-tender.

3. In small bowl, combine water and 1 tablespoon flour; beat with wire whisk until smooth. Add to stew; stir gently to mix. Bake an additional 30 minutes or until thickened.

NUTRITION INFORMATION PER SERVING: Serving Size: 1½ Cups ◆ Calories: 390 ◆ Calories from Fat: 110 ◆ % DAILY VALUE: Total Fat: 12 g 18% ◆ Saturated Fat: 4 g 20% ◆ Cholesterol: 95 mg 32% ◆ Sodium: 770 mg 32% ◆ Total Carbohydrate: 22 g 7% ◆ Dietary Fiber: 3 g 12% ◆ Sugars: 7 g ◆ Protein: 40 g ◆ Vitamin A: 260% ◆ Vitamin C: 20% ◆ Calcium: 8% ◆ Iron: 30% ◆ DIETARY EXCHANGES: 1 Starch, 1 Vegetable, 5 Lean Meat OR 1 Carbohydrate, 1 Vegetable, 5 Lean Meat

Old-Fashioned Lamb Stew

PREP TIME: 30 MINUTES (READY IN 2 HOURS 45 MINUTES) ◆ YIELD: 5 (1½-CUP) SERVINGS

  2 lb. boneless lamb, cut into 1-inch cubes
  ½ teaspoon sugar
  1 tablespoon oil
  ⅓ cup all-purpose flour
  2 tablespoons chopped fresh parsley
  1 teaspoon salt
  ¼ teaspoon dried thyme leaves
  ¼ teaspoon pepper
  1 garlic clove, minced
  2 cups water
  1 cup dry red wine or water
  1 teaspoon Worcestershire sauce
  1 bay leaf
  6 to 8 carrots, cut into 1-inch pieces
  4 stalks celery, cut into 1-inch pieces
  4 small onions, quartered
  2 to 3 medium potatoes, unpeeled,
       cut into pieces

1. Sprinkle lamb cubes with sugar. Heat oil in Dutch oven over medium heat until hot. Add lamb; cook and stir until browned.

2. Stir in flour, parsley, salt, thyme, pepper and garlic. Cook 1 minute, stirring constantly.

3. Gradually stir in water, wine and Worcestershire sauce. Add bay leaf. Bring to a boil. Reduce heat to low; cover and simmer 1½ hours or until lamb is tender, stirring occasionally.

4. Stir in carrots, celery, onions and potatoes. Cover; simmer an additional 30 to 45 minutes or until vegetables are tender. Remove bay leaf.

NUTRITION INFORMATION PER SERVING: Serving Size: 1½ Cups ◆ Calories: 480 ◆ Calories from Fat: 120 ◆ % DAILY VALUE: Total Fat: 13 g 20% ◆ Saturated Fat: 4 g 20% ◆ Cholesterol: 120 mg 40% ◆ Sodium: 590 mg 25% ◆ Total Carbohydrate: 42 g 14% ◆ Dietary Fiber: 7 g 28% ◆ Sugars: 11 g ◆ Protein: 41 g ◆ Vitamin A: 650% ◆ Vitamin C: 30% ◆ Calcium: 8% ◆ Iron: 30% ◆ DIETARY EXCHANGES: 2½ Starch, 1 Vegetable, 4½ Lean Meat OR 2½ Carbohydrate, 1 Vegetable, 4½ Lean Meat

Oven Chicken Stew

PREP TIME: 30 MINUTES (READY IN 2 HOURS)
◆ YIELD: 6 (1⅓-CUP) SERVINGS

    1 teaspoon salt
    ½ teaspoon poultry seasoning
    ½ teaspoon paprika
    ¼ teaspoon pepper
    3 to 3½ lb. cut-up frying chicken
    2 tablespoons oil
    2 tablespoons tomato paste
    1 cup chicken broth
    3 medium carrots, cut in half crosswise,
        quartered lengthwise
    1 (16-oz.) pkg. frozen small whole onions
    1 (6-oz.) jar whole mushrooms, drained
    1¾ cups frozen sweet peas, thawed
    3 tablespoons cornstarch
    ¼ cup water

1. Heat oven to 350°F. In small bowl, combine salt, poultry seasoning, paprika and pepper; mix well. Rub onto chicken pieces. Heat oil in Dutch oven over medium-high heat until hot. Add chicken; cook until browned on both sides.
2. Remove chicken from Dutch oven; drain and discard drippings. Add tomato paste to Dutch oven; stir in chicken broth. Bring to a boil. Return chicken to Dutch oven. Stir in carrots, onions and mushrooms; cover.
3. Bake at 350°F. for 1½ hours or until chicken is fork-tender and juices run clear.
4. Stir in peas. Place on burner over medium-high heat. In small bowl, combine cornstarch and water; blend until smooth. Stir into chicken mixture; cook until mixture thickens and boils, stirring frequently.

Oven Chicken Stew

Festive Oyster Stew

NUTRITION INFORMATION PER SERVING: Serving Size: 1⅓ Cups ◆ Calories: 400 ◆ Calories from Fat: 170 ◆ **% DAILY VALUE:** Total Fat: 19 g 29% ◆ Saturated Fat: 5 g 25% ◆ Cholesterol: 90 mg 30% ◆ Sodium: 820 mg 34% ◆ Total Carbohydrate: 24 g 8% ◆ Dietary Fiber: 6 g 24% ◆ Sugars: 10 g ◆ Protein: 34 g ◆ Vitamin A: 320% ◆ Vitamin C: 20% ◆ Calcium: 8% ◆ Iron: 15% ◆ **DIETARY EXCHANGES:** 1½ Starch, 1 Vegetable, 4 Lean Meat, 1 Fat OR 1½ Carbohydrate, 1 Vegetable, 4 Lean Meat, 1 Fat

Festive Oyster Stew

PREP TIME: 30 MINUTES ◆ YIELD: 8 (1½-CUP) SERVINGS

    2 (8-oz.) cans whole oysters, drained,
        reserving liquid
    ¼ cup margarine or butter
    1 red bell pepper, chopped
    ¾ cup chopped onions
    ½ cup all-purpose flour
    1 teaspoon salt
    ¼ teaspoon white pepper
    1 quart (4 cups) half-and-half
    1 quart (4 cups) milk
    2 cups frozen Southern-style hash-brown
        potatoes
    ½ teaspoon hot pepper sauce
    1 cup chopped fresh spinach

1. Cut oysters in half; set aside.
2. Melt margarine in Dutch oven or large saucepan over medium heat. Add bell pepper and onions; cook and stir until tender. Stir in flour, salt and pepper. Cook 1 minute, stirring constantly.
3. Gradually stir in half-and-half, milk and reserved oyster liquid. Add potatoes and hot pepper sauce; mix well. Cook over medium heat until stew is slightly thickened and potatoes are tender, stirring frequently.
4. Stir in oysters and spinach. Cook over medium heat until thoroughly heated, stirring frequently.

NUTRITION INFORMATION PER SERVING: Serving Size: 1½ Cups ◆ Calories: 380 ◆ Calories from Fat: 220 ◆ **% DAILY VALUE:** Total Fat: 24 g 37% ◆ Saturated Fat: 12 g 60% ◆ Cholesterol: 85 mg 28% ◆ Sodium: 520 mg 22% ◆ Total Carbohydrate: 26 g 9% ◆ Dietary Fiber: 1 g 4% ◆ Sugars: 13 g ◆ Protein: 14 g ◆ Vitamin A: 45% ◆ Vitamin C: 35% ◆ Calcium: 30% ◆ Iron: 25% ◆ **DIETARY EXCHANGES:** 1½ Starch, 1½ Lean Meat, 4 Fat OR 1½ Carbohydrate, 1½ Lean Meat, 4 Fat

Bouillabaisse

PREP TIME: 15 MINUTES (READY IN 45 MINUTES)
✦ YIELD: 12 SERVINGS

    2 tablespoons olive or vegetable oil
    1 medium onion, chopped
    2 garlic cloves, minced
    ¼ cup chopped fresh parsley
    1½ teaspoons salt
    ¼ teaspoon saffron, crushed, or curry powder
    ¼ teaspoon pepper
    1 bay leaf
    1 quart (4 cups) water
    1 teaspoon lemon juice
    1 lb. fish fillets, cut into 2-inch pieces
    1 (12-oz.) pkg. (3 cups) frozen uncooked
       shrimp
    1 (6-oz.) pkg. (¾ cup) frozen uncooked
       crabmeat or lobster meat
    1 pint (2 cups) fresh oysters or clams,
       undrained
    1 (8-oz.) can tomato sauce

1. Heat oil in Dutch oven or large saucepan over medium-high heat until hot. Add onion and garlic; cook and stir 2 to 3 minutes or until crisp-tender.
2. Add all remaining ingredients; mix well. Bring to a boil. Reduce heat to low; cover and simmer 20 to 30 minutes or until shrimp turn pink, stirring occasionally. Remove bay leaf. Serve in large soup bowls.

Southern-Style Shrimp Gumbo

NUTRITION INFORMATION PER SERVING: Serving Size: 1/12 of Recipe ✦ Calories: 140 ✦ Calories from Fat: 45 ✦ % DAILY VALUE: Total Fat: 5 g 8% ✦ Saturated Fat: 1 g 5% ✦ Cholesterol: 90 mg 30% ✦ Sodium: 690 mg 29% ✦ Total Carbohydrate: 5 g 2% ✦ Dietary Fiber: 0 g 0% ✦ Sugars: 1 g ✦ Protein: 19 g ✦ Vitamin A: 8% ✦ Vitamin C: 10% ✦ Calcium: 6% ✦ Iron: 25% ✦ DIETARY EXCHANGES: ½ Starch, 2½ Very Lean Meat, ½ Fat OR ½ Carbohydrate, 2½ Very Lean Meat, ½ Fat

Southern-Style Shrimp Gumbo

PREP TIME: 10 MINUTES (READY IN 45 MINUTES)
✦ YIELD: 8 SERVINGS

    2 cups uncooked regular long-grain white rice
    4 cups water
    2 tablespoons margarine or butter
    ½ cup chopped onion
    1 green bell pepper, cut into strips
    2 garlic cloves, minced
    2 tablespoons all-purpose flour
    1 (14½-oz.) can ready-to-serve chicken broth
    ¼ teaspoon salt
    ¼ teaspoon pepper
    ½ teaspoon hot pepper sauce
    1 (28-oz.) can crushed tomatoes, undrained
    1 (10-oz.) pkg. frozen cut okra, thawed
    1 lb. shelled deveined uncooked shrimp
    1 tablespoon chopped fresh parsley

1. Cook rice in water as directed on package.
2. Meanwhile, melt margarine in Dutch oven over medium heat. Add onion, bell pepper and garlic; cook until tender.
3. Sprinkle onion mixture with flour; stir to coat. Add broth, salt, pepper and hot pepper sauce; mix well. Bring to a boil. Stir in tomatoes and okra. Simmer 10 minutes, stirring occasionally.
4. Stir in shrimp. Simmer an additional 5 to 6 minutes or until shrimp turn pink. Stir in parsley.
5. To serve, spoon ¾ cup rice into each of 8 individual soup bowls; spoon gumbo over rice.

NUTRITION INFORMATION PER SERVING: Serving Size: 1/8 of Recipe ✦ Calories: 270 ✦ Calories from Fat: 35 ✦ % DAILY VALUE: Total Fat: 4 g 6% ✦ Saturated Fat: 1 g 5% ✦ Cholesterol: 80 mg 27% ✦ Sodium: 520 mg 22% ✦ Total Carbohydrate: 43 g 14% ✦ Dietary Fiber: 3 g 12% ✦ Sugars: 5 g ✦ Protein: 15 g ✦ Vitamin A: 20% ✦ Vitamin C: 30% ✦ Calcium: 10% ✦ Iron: 25% ✦ DIETARY EXCHANGES: 3 Starch, 1 Very Lean Meat OR 3 Carbohydrate, 1 Very Lean Meat

Cioppino

PREP TIME: 1 HOUR ◆ YIELD: 6 (1½-CUP) SERVINGS

    1 tablespoon oil
 1½ cups chopped onions
    6 garlic cloves, minced
    1 cup chopped fresh parsley
    1 (28-oz.) can whole tomatoes, undrained,
        cut up
    1 (14.5-oz.) can stewed tomatoes, undrained,
        cut up
    1 (8-oz.) can no-salt-added tomato sauce
  ¾ cup dry white wine or fish broth
    2 teaspoons dried basil leaves
  ¼ teaspoon pepper
  12 small clams in the shell, washed
    1 lb. fresh halibut or cod, cut into 1½-inch
        pieces
    1 lb. fresh medium shrimp, shelled, deveined
    6 oz. fresh chunk crabmeat

1. Heat oil in 5-quart Dutch oven over medium-high heat until hot. Add onions, garlic and parsley; cook and stir 3 to 5 minutes or until onions are crisp-tender, stirring occasionally.
2. Add tomatoes, stewed tomatoes, tomato sauce, wine, basil and pepper. Bring to a boil. Reduce heat to low; simmer 10 minutes, stirring occasionally.
3. Return to a boil. Add clams and halibut. Cover; cook over medium heat 4 to 6 minutes or until clam shells open and fish flakes easily with fork. Add shrimp; cover and cook until shrimp turn pink.
4. Add crabmeat. Simmer, uncovered, 5 minutes or until thoroughly heated. If desired, serve with thick slices of French bread to dip into broth.

NUTRITION INFORMATION PER SERVING: Serving Size: 1½ Cups ◆ Calories: 290 ◆ Calories from Fat: 50 ◆ % DAILY VALUE: Total Fat: 6 g 9% ◆ Saturated Fat: 1 g 5% ◆ Cholesterol: 130 mg 43% ◆ Sodium: 750 mg 31% ◆ Total Carbohydrate: 18 g 6% ◆ Dietary Fiber: 3 g 12% ◆ Sugars: 8 g ◆ Protein: 36 g ◆ Vitamin A: 40% ◆ Vitamin C: 60% ◆ Calcium: 15% ◆ Iron: 40% ◆ DIETARY EXCHANGES: 1 Starch, 1 Vegetable, 4½ Very Lean Meat, ½ Fat OR 1 Carbohydrate, 1 Vegetable, 4½ Very Lean Meat, ½ Fat

Beans, Corn and Zucchini Stew

PREP TIME: 20 MINUTES (READY IN 40 MINUTES) ◆ YIELD: 4 (1½-CUP) SERVINGS

    1 tablespoon oil
  ½ cup uncooked regular long-grain white rice
    1 medium onion, cut into thin wedges
    1 garlic clove, minced
    2 (14½-oz.) cans ready-to-serve vegetable
        or chicken broth
    1 medium zucchini, diced (2 cups)
    2 cups frozen whole kernel corn
    1 (15.5 or 15-oz.) can pinto or light red kidney
        beans, drained, rinsed
  ½ teaspoon dried basil leaves
  ¼ teaspoon dried oregano leaves
  ¼ teaspoon cumin
  ⅛ teaspoon pepper

1. Heat oil in large saucepan or Dutch oven over medium-high heat until hot. Add rice, onion and garlic; cook and stir 2 to 3 minutes or until onion is crisp-tender.
2. Stir in all remaining ingredients. Bring to a boil. Reduce heat to medium-low; cover and cook 15 to 20 minutes or until rice is tender and broth is slightly thickened.

NUTRITION INFORMATION PER SERVING: Serving Size: 1½ Cups ◆ Calories: 300 ◆ Calories from Fat: 50 ◆ % DAILY VALUE: Total Fat: 6 g 9% ◆ Saturated Fat: 1 g 5% ◆ Cholesterol: 0 mg 0% ◆ Sodium: 1070 mg 45% ◆ Total Carbohydrate: 53 g 18% ◆ Dietary Fiber: 7 g 28% ◆ Sugars: 9 g ◆ Protein: 9 g ◆ Vitamin A: 10% ◆ Vitamin C: 10% ◆ Calcium: 8% ◆ Iron: 15% ◆ DIETARY EXCHANGES: 3½ Starch, 1 Fat OR 3½ Carbohydrate, 1 Fat

Chunky Lentil Stew

PREP TIME: 20 MINUTES (READY IN 1 HOUR) ◆ YIELD: 6 (1-CUP) SERVINGS

    3 cups water
    1 (14.5 or 16-oz.) can whole tomatoes,
        undrained, cut up
    1 cup uncooked lentils
    1 cup shredded cabbage
  ½ cup chopped carrot
  ½ cup chopped celery
  ½ cup chopped onion
  ½ cup mashed potato flakes
    6 oz. (1 cup) chopped smoked kielbasa sausage
    2 teaspoons chicken-flavor instant bouillon
        or 2 chicken-flavor bouillon cubes
    1 teaspoon dried marjoram leaves
    1 bay leaf

1. In large saucepan, combine all ingredients. Bring to a boil.

2. Reduce heat to low; cover and simmer 35 to 40 minutes or until lentils are tender. Remove bay leaf.

NUTRITION INFORMATION PER SERVING: Serving Size: 1 Cup ✦ Calories: 250 ✦ Calories from Fat: 70 ✦ % DAILY VALUE: Total Fat: 8 g 12% ✦ Saturated Fat: 3 g 15% ✦ Cholesterol: 20 mg 7% ✦ Sodium: 770 mg 32% ✦ Total Carbohydrate: 30 g 10% ✦ Dietary Fiber: 12 g 48% ✦ Sugars: 5 g ✦ Protein: 15 g ✦ Vitamin A: 70% ✦ Vitamin C: 20% ✦ Calcium: 8% ✦ Iron: 25% ✦ DIETARY EXCHANGES: 1½ Starch, 1 Vegetable, 1 High-Fat Meat OR 1½ Carbohydrate, 1 Vegetable, 1 High-Fat Meat

Coq au Vin

PREP TIME: 20 MINUTES (READY IN 1 HOUR 10 MINUTES)
✦ YIELD: 6 SERVINGS

```
  8  slices bacon, cut into ½-inch pieces
  3  to 3½ lb. cut-up frying chicken, skin removed
     if desired
1½  cups frozen small whole onions
  1  (4.5-oz.) jar whole mushrooms, drained
  2  tablespoons chopped fresh parsley
 ½  teaspoon dried thyme leaves
  2  garlic cloves, minced
 ¼  cup all-purpose flour
1½  cups dry red wine
  1  to 2 teaspoons chopped fresh parsley,
     if desired
```

1. Heat oven to 400°F. Cook bacon in large skillet or Dutch oven over medium heat until crisp. Remove bacon from skillet; drain on paper towels. Reserve drippings in skillet. Add chicken to drippings; cook until browned on all sides. Drain. Place chicken in ungreased 2½ to 3-quart casserole; sprinkle with bacon.

2. In same skillet, combine onions, mushrooms, 2 tablespoons parsley, thyme and garlic. Cook over medium heat until thoroughly heated, stirring occasionally.

3. Stir in flour; gradually stir in wine. Cook until mixture boils and thickens, stirring constantly. Pour over chicken and bacon in casserole; cover tightly.

4. Bake at 400°F. for 40 to 50 minutes or until chicken is fork-tender and juices run clear. Sprinkle with parsley.

NUTRITION INFORMATION PER SERVING: Serving Size: ⅙ of Recipe ✦ Calories: 290 ✦ Calories from Fat: 100 ✦ % DAILY VALUE: Total Fat: 11 g 17% ✦ Saturated Fat: 3 g 15% ✦ Cholesterol: 85 mg 28% ✦ Sodium: 310 mg 13% ✦ Total Carbohydrate: 10 g 3% ✦ Dietary Fiber: 1 g 4% ✦ Sugars: 3 g ✦ Protein: 29 g ✦ Vitamin A: 4% ✦ Vitamin C: 8% ✦ Calcium: 4% ✦ Iron: 10% ✦ DIETARY EXCHANGES: ½ Starch, 1 Vegetable, 4 Lean Meat OR ½ Carbohydrate, 1 Vegetable, 4 Lean Meat

Pork Stew

PREP TIME: 20 MINUTES (READY IN 1 HOUR)
✦ YIELD: 6 (1⅓-CUP) SERVINGS

```
  1  tablespoon oil
1½  lb. boneless pork loin, cut into ¾-inch cubes
  1  (14½-oz.) can ready-to-serve chicken broth
  1  cup water
  1  medium onion, cut into 8 wedges
 ½  teaspoon salt
 ½  teaspoon dried marjoram leaves
 ⅛  teaspoon pepper
 10  to 12 small red potatoes, quartered
1½  cups sliced carrots
  1  cup frozen sweet peas
 ½  cup half-and-half
 ¼  cup all-purpose flour
```

1. Heat oil in 4-quart saucepan or Dutch oven over medium-high heat until hot. Add pork cubes; cook 3 to 5 minutes or until browned, stirring occasionally. Add broth, water, onion, salt, marjoram and pepper. Bring to a boil. Reduce heat to low; cover and simmer 20 minutes.

2. Add potatoes, carrots and peas. Return to a boil. Reduce heat to low; cover and simmer an additional 15 to 20 minutes or until vegetables are tender.

3. In small bowl, combine half-and-half and flour; blend until smooth. Gradually stir into pork mixture. Cook and stir over medium-high heat until mixture is bubbly and thickened.

NUTRITION INFORMATION PER SERVING: Serving Size: 1⅓ Cups ✦ Calories: 350 ✦ Calories from Fat: 120 ✦ % DAILY VALUE: Total Fat: 13 g 20% ✦ Saturated Fat: 5 g 25% ✦ Cholesterol: 70 mg 23% ✦ Sodium: 500 mg 21% ✦ Total Carbohydrate: 31 g 10% ✦ Dietary Fiber: 4 g 16% ✦ Sugars: 5 g ✦ Protein: 28 g ✦ Vitamin A: 180% ✦ Vitamin C: 25% ✦ Calcium: 6% ✦ Iron: 10% ✦ DIETARY EXCHANGES: 2 Starch, 3 Lean Meat, ½ Fat OR 2 Carbohydrate, 3 Lean Meat, ½ Fat

Hearty Meatball Stew

PREP TIME: 30 MINUTES (READY IN 1 HOUR)
✦ YIELD: 5 SERVINGS

1 lb. ground turkey
1 egg
¼ cup chopped onion
½ teaspoon garlic salt
¼ teaspoon pepper
1 tablespoon oil
1 beef-flavor bouillon cube or 1 teaspoon beef-flavor instant bouillon
1½ cups boiling water
1 (10¾-oz.) can condensed golden mushroom soup
4 carrots, cut into ½-inch pieces
3 stalks celery, cut into ½-inch pieces
1 medium onion, sliced
1 (11-oz.) can vacuum-packed whole kernel corn

1. In medium bowl, combine ground turkey, egg, onion, garlic salt and pepper; mix well. Shape into 1½-inch meatballs.
2. Heat oil in Dutch oven over medium-high heat until hot. Add meatballs; cook until browned.
3. In small bowl, dissolve bouillon in boiling water. Add bouillon mixture and all remaining ingredients to meatballs; stir gently. Cover; bring to a boil. Reduce heat to low; simmer 25 to 30 minutes or until vegetables are tender.

NUTRITION INFORMATION PER SERVING: Serving Size: ⅕ of Recipe • Calories: 360 • Calories from Fat: 160 • % DAILY VALUE: Total Fat: 18 g 28% • Saturated Fat: 4 g 20% • Cholesterol: 110 mg 37% • Sodium: 1040 mg 43% • Total Carbohydrate: 26 g 9% • Dietary Fiber: 4 g 16% • Sugars: 8 g • Protein: 23 g • Vitamin A: 330% • Vitamin C: 15% • Calcium: 8% • Iron: 15% • DIETARY EXCHANGES: 1½ Starch, 2½ Lean Meat, 2 Fat OR 1½ Carbohydrate, 2½ Lean Meat, 2 Fat

Rich Oven Veal Stew

PREP TIME: 30 MINUTES (READY IN 2 HOURS)
✦ YIELD: 6 (1⅓-CUP) SERVINGS

½ cup all-purpose flour
½ teaspoon salt
½ teaspoon nutmeg
¼ teaspoon white pepper
2 lb. lean boneless veal, cubed
¼ cup margarine or butter
1 tablespoon oil
2 cups dry white wine or beef broth
8 small new red potatoes
3 carrots, cut into ½-inch slices
2 medium onions, quartered
½ lb. large fresh mushrooms, quartered
½ cup sour cream
Salt

1. Heat oven to 350°F. In 1-gallon resealable food storage plastic bag, combine flour, ½ teaspoon salt, nutmeg and white pepper; shake to mix. Add veal cubes; shake to coat.
2. Melt margarine with oil in Dutch oven over medium-high heat. Add veal; cook and stir until browned. Stir in wine, potatoes, carrots, onions and mushrooms. Bring to a boil. Remove from heat; cover.
3. Bake at 350°F. for 1½ hours or until veal and vegetables are tender. Add sour cream; mix well. Season to taste with salt.

NUTRITION INFORMATION PER SERVING: Serving Size: 1⅓ Cups • Calories: 560 • Calories from Fat: 160 • % DAILY VALUE: Total Fat: 18 g 28% • Saturated Fat: 6 g 30% • Cholesterol: 135 mg 45% • Sodium: 480 mg 20% • Total Carbohydrate: 49 g 16% • Dietary Fiber: 5 g 20% • Sugars: 7 g • Protein: 37 g • Vitamin A: 210% • Vitamin C: 25% • Calcium: 10% • Iron: 25% • DIETARY EXCHANGES: 3 Starch, 1 Vegetable, 3½ Lean Meat, 2 Fat OR 3 Carbohydrate, 1 Vegetable, 3½ Lean Meat, 2 Fat

COOK'S NOTE

HOW TO THICKEN STEWS

Check the recipe for the ratio of flour or cornstarch to water. Add the water to a jar with a tight-fitting lid. Add the flour or cornstarch and shake until completely mixed and smooth.

Add the mixture to the stew gradually, stirring constantly until the stew comes to a boil and thickens.

BEEF
& VEAL

BEEF & VEAL

W hile food fads come and go, beef has carved out an unshakable place on the American table. Taking to heart the message of moderation, many people are finding that by eating meat a little less routinely, they savor every bite of that fragrant roast or tender veal cutlet. The facts and tips in this chapter will help you make the mouthwatering most of every beef and veal dish you serve.

Shopping for Quality

Meat that is prepackaged should be tightly wrapped and dated to indicate freshness. Avoid torn packages, meat that smells "off" or looks slimy, or packages with ice crystals that may indicate thawing and refreezing.

Buying cuts of beef: The meat should be deep red with a fine-grained, firm texture. Fat should look creamy white in color. The most expensive cuts are typically marbled with a visible network of white flecks and streaks of fat throughout. Marbling gives the meat flavor, tenderness and juiciness.

Buying ground beef: Ground beef with higher fat content is a lighter shade of red. In general, the higher the fat content, the lower the price. Since most of the fat melts away during cooking, the price savings is not as great as it may seem. When preparing higher-fat ground beef, it's best to drain the fat.

Storing Meat

Fresh meat is highly perishable. Store it in the coldest part of the refrigerator (usually the bottom shelf), double-wrapped in plastic or set it in a pan to catch any drips. Use or freeze fresh ground beef within a day, other raw meats within two days. If meat becomes dark gray, slimy or smells "off," discard it.

Store cooked meat, tightly wrapped, in the refrigerator for up to four or five days, or in the freezer for up to three months. After three months the meat is still safe, but its flavor and texture suffer.

Handling Meat

Raw meat may harbor bacteria that are invisible and odorless, so always handle it separately from foods that will be served uncooked. Thoroughly wash cutting boards, knives and other utensils in hot soapy water after using them for raw meat.

Meat should be kept cold or hot. Do not partially cook beef or veal and finish cooking later; the in-between temperature may promote the growth of harmful bacteria. This goes for microwave defrosting, too. Since microwave ovens do not defrost meats evenly, some spots may get too hot while others remain partially frozen. Plan to cook microwave-thawed meats immediately rather than thawing in the morning and cooking at suppertime, for instance.

If meats will be transported, keep hot meats hot (above 140°F.) and cold meats chilled (below 40°F.). Refrigerate leftovers as soon as possible after a meal to prevent spoilage.

Basic Cooking Techniques

Cooking methods for beef and veal fall into two main categories: dry heat (such as roasting or grilling) and moist heat (such as stewing or braising).

In general, tender meats with a higher fat content (such as steaks and standing rib roasts) are delicious cooked with dry heat. The surface becomes nicely browned while the inside remains juicy and tender.

Stewing and other moist-heat techniques are especially good for less-tender cuts of meat. The long, slow cooking breaks down tough fibers, turning inexpensive cuts such as stew beef or pot roast into amazingly tender and flavorful dishes.

DRY HEAT METHODS
ROASTING
- Preheat oven to 325°F.
- Place meat, fat side up, on a rack in a shallow roasting pan. Season as desired. A generous sprinkling of salt and black pepper is traditional, simple and delicious. Do not add liquid or cover the pan. Roast until the internal temperature reaches the level desired for doneness.

BROILING

+ Place meat on a rack in a broiler pan.
+ Set the pan two to five inches from the heat. The thicker the cut, the farther the meat should be placed from the heat.
+ Give your full attention to the broiler throughout cooking. Broiled meats cook fast and can become overcooked almost instantly.
+ Broil one side until browned.
+ Turn the meat over. Season the cooked side; cook until other side is browned and the interior reaches desired doneness.

PAN-FRYING

+ Preheat a skillet over medium heat.
+ For lean meats, add enough vegetable oil, margarine, butter or nonstick cooking spray to cover the bottom of the pan. The fat keeps food from sticking and adds flavor. However, fatty meats such as ground beef can be added directly to a dry, preheated skillet.
+ Heat the oil or sprayed pan before adding the meat. Don't cover the pan during cooking.
+ Turn the meat occasionally to brown both sides and cook it thoroughly.

GRILLING

+ Preheat a gas grill or start coals 30 to 40 minutes in advance. Start cooking when coals are evenly coated with gray ash.
+ Carefully rub a little oil on the grill rack to prevent sticking.

+ Place meat directly over the coals. When the first side is browned, flip the meat and continue cooking until the second side is browned and the inside is done to your liking.

Cook roasts and other thick cuts by indirect heat. Arrange the coals on one half of the grill. Set the meat on the grill rack so it is not directly over the coals. Cover the grill during cooking.

MOIST HEAT METHODS

BRAISING

+ In a heavy pan, brown the meat in a small amount of oil or nonstick cooking spray. Pour off the fat.
+ Season as desired. Add a small amount of liquid to the pan and cover the pan tightly.
+ Simmer on the stove top or in the oven until the meat is fork-tender.

STEWING

+ In a Dutch oven or heavy pan, brown the meat in a small amount of fat or nonstick cooking spray. Do not crowd the pan, or the meat will steam rather than brown.
+ Cover the meat completely with a liquid such as water, beer, wine, juice or broth. Cover the pan.
+ Bring to a boil, reduce heat to a simmer and cook 2 to 4 hours until the meat is tender.

TIMETABLE FOR ROASTING BEEF

ROAST	WEIGHT (POUNDS)	THERMOMETER READING	COOKING TIME (MINUTES PER POUND)
RIB, BONE-IN *Roast at 325°F.*	4 to 6	145°F. (Medium-Rare) 160°F. (Medium) 170°F. (Well)	23 to 25 27 to 30 32 to 34
RIB, ROLLED OR BONELESS *Roast at 325°F.*	4 to 6	145°F. (Medium-Rare) 160°F. (Medium) 170°F. (Well)	28 to 33 32 to 38 37 to 42
EYE ROUND *Roast at 325°F.*	2 to 3	145°F. (Medium-Rare)	20 to 25
ROUND OR RUMP *Roast at 325°F.*	2½ to 4	145°F. (Medium-Rare) 160°F. (Medium) 170°F. (Well)	30 to 35 35 to 40 40 to 45
TENDERLOIN *Roast at 425°F.*	4 to 6	145°F. (Medium-Rare) 160°F. (Medium) 170°F. (Well)	45 to 60 minutes total

Source: National Cattlemen's Beef Association

Beef

• RETAIL CUTS •
WHERE THEY COME FROM
HOW TO COOK THEM

ROUND
SIRLOIN
SHORT LOIN
RIB
CHUCK

FLANK
SHORT PLATE
BRISKET
FORE SHANK

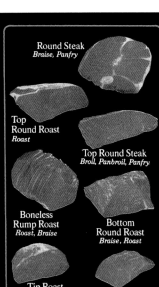

Round Steak
Braise, Panfry

Top Round Roast
Roast

Top Round Steak
Broil, Panbroil, Panfry

Boneless Rump Roast
Roast, Braise

Bottom Round Roast
Braise, Roast

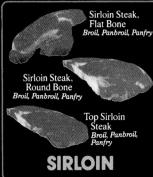

Tip Roast, Cap Off
Roast, Braise

Eye Round Roast
Braise, Roast

Tip Steak
Broil, Panbroil, Panfry

ROUND

Sirloin Steak, Flat Bone
Broil, Panbroil, Panfry

Sirloin Steak, Round Bone
Broil, Panbroil, Panfry

Top Sirloin Steak
Broil, Panbroil, Panfry

SIRLOIN

Shank Cross Cut
Braise, Cook in Liquid

Brisket, Whole
Braise, Cook in Liquid

Corned Brisket, Point Half
Braise, Cook in Liquid

Brisket, Flat Half
Braise

FORE SHANK & BRISKET

Chuck Eye Roast
Braise, Roast

Boneless Top Blade Steak
Braise, Panfry

Arm Pot Roast
Braise

Boneless Shoulder Pot Roast
Braise

Cross Rib Pot Roast
Braise

Mock Tender
Braise

Blade Roast
Braise

Under Blade Pot Roast
Braise, Roast

7-Bone Pot Roast
Braise

Short Ribs
Braise, Cook in Liquid

Flanken-Style Ribs
Braise, Cook in Liquid

CHUCK

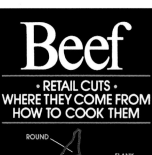

T-Bone Steak
Broil, Panbroil, Panfry

Boneless Top Loin Steak
Broil, Panbroil, Panfry

Tenderloin Roast
Roast, Broil

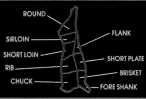

Porterhouse Steak
Broil, Panbroil, Panfry

Tenderloin Steak
Broil, Panbroil, Panfry

SHORT LOIN

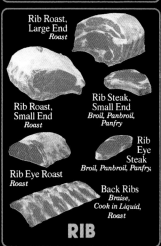

Rib Roast, Large End
Roast

Rib Roast, Small End
Roast

Rib Steak, Small End
Broil, Panbroil, Panfry

Rib Eye Roast
Roast

Rib Eye Steak
Broil, Panbroil, Panfry

Back Ribs
Braise, Cook in Liquid, Roast

RIB

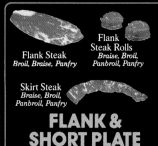

Flank Steak
Broil, Braise, Panfry

Flank Steak Rolls
Braise, Broil, Panbroil, Panfry

Skirt Steak
Braise, Broil, Panbroil, Panfry

FLANK & SHORT PLATE

Ground Beef
Broil, Panfry, Panbroil Roast (Bake)

Cubed Steak
Panfry, Braise

Beef for Stew
Braise, Cook in Liquid

Cubes for Kabobs
Broil, Braise

OTHER CUTS

Standing Rib Roast

Standing Rib Roast

PREP TIME: 25 MINUTES (READY IN 4 HOURS 25 MINUTES) ✦ YIELD: 10 SERVINGS

1 (4½ to 5-lb.) standing beef rib roast

1. Heat oven to 325°F. Place roast, fat side up, on rack in shallow roasting pan. Insert meat thermometer so bulb reaches center of thickest part of meat, but does not rest in fat or on bone.
2. Bake at 325°F. for 2¼ to 3¼ hours or until meat thermometer registers desired temperature of 140°F. for rare, 160°F. for medium or 170°F. for well done.
3. For ease in carving, let roast stand covered 10 to 15 minutes. To carve roast, slice from outside toward rib bone and then cut along bone to remove slice of meat. If desired, season to taste with salt and pepper.

NUTRITION INFORMATION PER SERVING: Serving Size: ¹/₁₀ of Recipe ✦ Calories: 230 ✦ Calories from Fat: 120 ✦ **% DAILY VALUE:** Total Fat: 13 g 20% ✦ Saturated Fat: 5 g 25% ✦ Cholesterol: 80 mg 27% ✦ Sodium: 75 mg 3% ✦ Total Carbohydrate: 0 g 0% ✦ Dietary Fiber: 0 g 0% ✦ Sugars: 0 g ✦ Protein: 28 g ✦ Vitamin A: 0% ✦ Vitamin C: 0% ✦ Calcium: 0% ✦ Iron: 15% ✦ **DIETARY EXCHANGES:** 4 Lean Meat

COOK'S NOTE

REST THE ROAST

Letting the roasted meat stand out on the counter for about 15 minutes before slicing it improves the roast. The oven's heat has forced the juices inward during cooking. As the meat rests, the juices redistribute more evenly throughout the meat.

COOK'S NOTE

CARVING A RIB ROAST

To slice the roast, make several slices (½ inch to 1 inch thick) from outside of the roast toward the rib bone. Cut along the inner side of the rib bone to loosen each slice.

At the meat market, you can ask the butcher to cut between the bone and the meat,

and then tie it back together. This way, you can still roast the meat with the bone but slicing the meat is easier.

Yorkshire Pudding

PREP TIME: 35 MINUTES ✦ YIELD: 8 SERVINGS

¼ cup roast beef drippings*
2 eggs
1 cup all-purpose flour
½ teaspoon salt
1 cup milk

1. Heat oven to 425°F. Pour beef drippings into 9-inch square pan; tilt pan to coat bottom and sides. Place pan in oven to heat about 2 minutes.
2. In small bowl, beat eggs slightly. Add flour, salt and milk; beat just until blended. DO NOT OVERBEAT. Pour batter into hot pan.
3. Bake at 425°F. for 15 minutes. Reduce oven temperature to 350°F.; bake an additional 10 to 15 minutes or until puffed and golden brown. Serve immediately.

TIP: * One-fourth cup shortening, melted, can be substituted for roast beef drippings.

NUTRITION INFORMATION PER SERVING: Serving Size: ⅛ of Recipe ✦ Calories: 110 ✦ Calories from Fat: 35 ✦ **% DAILY VALUE:** Total Fat: 4 g 6% ✦ Saturated Fat: 2 g 10% ✦ Cholesterol: 60 mg 20% ✦ Sodium: 180 mg 8% ✦ Total Carbohydrate: 14 g 5% ✦ Dietary Fiber: 0 g 0% ✦ Sugars: 2 g ✦ Protein: 5 g ✦ Vitamin A: 2% ✦ Vitamin C: 0% ✦ Calcium: 4% ✦ Iron: 6% ✦ **DIETARY EXCHANGES:** 1 Starch, ½ Fat OR 1 Carbohydrate, ½ Fat

Beef Roast

1. Allow ⅓ to ½ lb. per serving for bone-in roast and ¼ to ⅓ lb. per serving for boneless roast. Heat oven to 325°F. Place roast, fat side up, on rack in shallow roasting pan. If desired, sprinkle with salt and pepper. Insert meat thermometer so bulb reaches center of thickest part of meat, but does not rest in fat or on bone. Do not add water or cover.
2. Bake at 325°F. to desired degree of doneness using "Timetable for Roasting Beef," page 91.
3. After removing roast from pan, skim off fat from meat juices. Add ⅓ to ½ cup water to meat juices. Cook over medium-high heat, stirring and scraping bottom of pan until mixture begins to boil. If desired, strain. Season to taste with salt and pepper. Serve with roast.

NUTRITION INFORMATION PER SERVING: Serving Size: 4 oz. Cooked Beef ◆ Calories: 250 ◆ Calories from Fat: 130 ◆ **% DAILY VALUE:** Total Fat: 14 g 22% ◆ Saturated Fat: 6 g 30% ◆ Cholesterol: 90 mg 30% ◆ Sodium: 80 mg 3% ◆ Total Carbohydrate: 0 g 0% ◆ Dietary Fiber: 0 g 0% ◆ Sugars: 0 g ◆ Protein: 31 g ◆ Vitamin A: 0% ◆ Vitamin C: 0% ◆ Calcium: 0% ◆ Iron: 20% ◆ **DIETARY EXCHANGES:** 4½ Lean Meat

Brown Sauce

PREP TIME: 15 MINUTES ◆ YIELD: 2 CUPS

    2 tablespoons margarine or butter
    2 tablespoons all-purpose flour
    ¾ teaspoon salt
    ⅛ teaspoon pepper
    2 beef-flavor bouillon cubes or 2 teaspoons
        beef-flavor instant bouillon*
    2 cups water*

1. Melt margarine in small saucepan over medium heat. Add flour; cook until golden brown, stirring constantly.
2. Add all remaining ingredients. Cook until mixture boils and thickens, stirring constantly.

TIP: * One 10½-oz. can condensed beef broth with enough water added to make 2 cups liquid can be substituted for bouillon cubes and water. If desired, use ½ cup red wine or dry sherry for part of the water.

NUTRITION INFORMATION PER SERVING: Serving Size: 1 Tablespoon ◆ Calories: 10 ◆ Calories from Fat: 10 ◆ **% DAILY VALUE:** Total Fat: 1 g 2% ◆ Saturated Fat: 0 g 0% ◆ Cholesterol: 0 mg 0% ◆ Sodium: 220 mg 5% ◆ Total Carbohydrate: 0 g 0% ◆ Dietary Fiber: 0 g 0% ◆ Sugars: 0 g ◆ Protein: 0 g ◆ Vitamin A: 0% ◆ Vitamin C: 0% ◆ Calcium: 0% ◆ Iron: 0% ◆ **DIETARY EXCHANGES:** Free

VARIATIONS
Bordelaise Sauce: Add 2 tablespoons minced green onions, 1 minced garlic clove, 1 finely chopped carrot, 1 small bay leaf and 4 peppercorns to margarine before adding flour; cook and stir over medium heat until tender. Continue as directed above. Strain to remove vegetables and spices before serving. If desired, stir in ½ teaspoon dried parsley flakes and dash dried thyme leaves. Serve warm.
Madeira Sauce: Substitute ½ cup Madeira wine for ½ cup of the water.
Mushroom Sauce: After mixture comes to a boil, stir in one 4.5-oz. jar whole or sliced mushrooms, drained. Cook until thoroughly heated.

Pan Gravy

PREP TIME: 15 MINUTES ◆ YIELD: 2 CUPS

    3 tablespoons all-purpose flour*
    3 tablespoons meat or poultry drippings*
    2 cups water or broth
    ¼ teaspoon salt
    ⅛ teaspoon pepper

1. In skillet or roasting pan, add flour to drippings; blend well. Cook over low heat until smooth and browned, stirring constantly.
2. Add water; cook until mixture boils and thickens, stirring constantly. Stir in salt and pepper.

TIP: * Flour and drippings can be decreased to 2 tablespoons each for thin gravy or increased to 4 tablespoons each for thick gravy.

NUTRITION INFORMATION PER SERVING: Serving Size: 1 Tablespoon ◆ Calories: 20 ◆ Calories from Fat: 20 ◆ **% DAILY VALUE:** Total Fat: 2 g 3% ◆ Saturated Fat: 1 g 5% ◆ Cholesterol: 2 mg 1% ◆ Sodium: 35 mg 1% ◆ Total Carbohydrate: 0 g 0% ◆ Dietary Fiber: 0 g 0% ◆ Sugars: 0 g ◆ Protein: 0 g ◆ Vitamin A: 0% ◆ Vitamin C: 0% ◆ Calcium: 0% ◆ Iron: 0% ◆ **DIETARY EXCHANGES:** ½ Fat

COOK'S NOTE

GRAVY TIP

Measure the amount of drippings called for in the recipe and return to the skillet or roasting pan; heat. In a jar with a lid, combine the flour and liquid called for in the recipe; shake until smooth. Gradually stir into the hot drippings. Cook and stir until gravy thickens and boils.

Marinated Rolled Rib Roast

PREP TIME: 30 MINUTES (READY IN 10 HOURS 40 MINUTES) ◆ YIELD: 10 SERVINGS

MARINADE
¼ cup wine vinegar
¼ cup oil
3 tablespoons chopped fresh parsley
1 teaspoon seasoned salt
1 teaspoon dried thyme leaves
½ teaspoon pepper
1 tablespoon soy sauce
2 garlic cloves, minced

ROAST
1 (3 to 4-lb.) rolled beef rib roast

1. In 13×9-inch (3-quart) baking dish or large resealable food storage plastic bag, combine all marinade ingredients; mix well. Add roast; turn to coat. Cover dish or seal bag; refrigerate 8 to 12 hours, turning several times.

2. Heat oven to 350°F. Drain roast, reserving marinade. Place roast on rack in shallow roasting pan. Insert meat thermometer so bulb reaches center of thickest part of meat, but does not rest in fat or on bone.

3. Bake at 350°F. for 1½ to 2 hours or until meat thermometer registers desired temperature of 145°F. for medium-rare or 160°F. for medium doneness, basting with marinade every 20 to 30 minutes.

4. Remove roast from oven. Cover with tent of foil; let stand 10 to 15 minutes before slicing. Discard any remaining marinade.

NUTRITION INFORMATION PER SERVING: Serving Size: ¹/₁₀ of Recipe ◆ Calories: 200 ◆ Calories from Fat: 110 ◆ **% DAILY VALUE:** Total Fat: 12 g 18% ◆ Saturated Fat: 4 g 20% ◆ Cholesterol: 65 mg 22% ◆ Sodium: 125 mg 5% ◆ Total Carbohydrate: 0 g 0% ◆ Dietary Fiber: 0 g 0% ◆ Sugars: 0 g ◆ Protein: 23 g ◆ Vitamin A: 0% ◆ Vitamin C: 0% ◆ Calcium: 0% ◆ Iron: 15% ◆ **DIETARY EXCHANGES:** 3½ Lean Meat

Braised Brisket of Beef

PREP TIME: 20 MINUTES (READY IN 11 HOURS 30 MINUTES) ◆ YIELD: 12 SERVINGS

1 (3-lb.) beef brisket (not corned-style)
1½ cups white wine vinegar
¼ cup firmly packed brown sugar
1 teaspoon dried basil leaves
½ teaspoon salt
1 (12-oz.) bottle chili sauce
2 medium onions, thinly sliced

1. Place brisket in resealable food storage plastic bag or 3-quart casserole, cutting meat in half if necessary to fit. In medium bowl, combine vinegar, brown sugar, basil, salt and chili sauce; blend well. Pour over brisket; turn to coat. Seal bag or cover dish. Refrigerate 8 hours or overnight, turning once.

2. Heat oven to 325°F. Place brisket and marinade in Dutch oven or 3-quart casserole. Place onions over top; cover. Bake at 325°F. for 2 hours, basting twice with marinade.

3. Remove cover; bake an additional 1 hour or until beef is tender, basting frequently. Let stand 10 minutes.

4. To serve, thinly slice across grain of beef; arrange on serving platter. With slotted spoon, place onions over beef. Discard cooking liquid.

NUTRITION INFORMATION PER SERVING: Serving Size: ¹/₁₂ of Recipe ◆ Calories: 200 ◆ Calories from Fat: 70 ◆ **% DAILY VALUE:** Total Fat: 8 g 12% ◆ Saturated Fat: 3 g 15% ◆ Cholesterol: 55 mg 18% ◆ Sodium: 510 mg 21% ◆ Total Carbohydrate: 15 g 5% ◆ Dietary Fiber: 1 g 2% ◆ Sugars: 10 g ◆ Protein: 18 g ◆ Vitamin A: 8% ◆ Vitamin C: 6% ◆ Calcium: 0% ◆ Iron: 10% ◆ **DIETARY EXCHANGES:** 1 Fruit, 2½ Lean Meat OR 1 Carbohydrate, 2½ Lean Meat

---

COOK'S NOTE

CHECKING FOR DONENESS

Professional chefs may press a roast with their fingers to determine if the meat is rare, medium or well done, but home cooks need a less subjective, more reliable method—namely, a meat thermometer. See the "Timetable for Roasting Beef" on page 91 for thermometer readings and cooking times.

A conventional meat thermometer stays in the meat throughout cooking. Some people think this lets too much juice escape. An inexpensive instant-read thermometer is an easy alternative. A little before you think the roast is nearly done, insert the instant-read thermometer's probe three inches into the center of the meat; make sure the tip doesn't rest on fat or bone. After 30 seconds, the thermometer renders an accurate temperature. Remove the thermometer; it should not remain in the oven. Remove the roast from the oven when it reaches about 5°F. below the temperature you want; the roast continues to cook as it rests on the counter.

Beefeater's Pepper-Crusted Roast

Beefeater's Pepper-Crusted Roast

PREP TIME: 10 MINUTES (READY IN 2 HOURS 20 MINUTES) ✦ YIELD: 6 SERVINGS

    1 tablespoon butter, melted
    1 tablespoon Worcestershire sauce
    1 (4-lb.) beef rib roast
    3 tablespoons crushed multicolored
        peppercorns
    1 tablespoon chopped fresh thyme
        or 1 teaspoon dried thyme leaves

1. Heat oven to 350°F. In small bowl, combine butter and Worcestershire sauce; mix well. Place roast in ungreased shallow roasting pan. Brush butter mixture over roast. Press peppercorns into top of roast; sprinkle with thyme. Insert meat thermometer so bulb reaches center of thickest part of meat, but does not rest in fat or on bone.

C O O K ' S   N O T E

SLICING A ROAST

More expensive cuts such as prime rib and filet mignon are tender enough to be cut into thick (½ to 1-inch-thick) slices. More economical cuts, such as a rump roast, are full-flavored but less tender. Cutting perpendicular to the grain of the meat gives more tender slices. If you're not sure, cut a sample slice and examine it. If you see long, stringy fibers of meat, it's cut *with* the grain and will be tougher to chew.

---

2. Bake uncovered at 350°F. for 1½ to 2 hours or until meat thermometer registers 145°F. for medium-rare or 160°F. for medium doneness.

3. Remove roast from oven. Cover with tent of foil. Let stand 10 to 15 minutes before carving.

NUTRITION INFORMATION PER SERVING: Serving Size: ⅙ of Recipe ♦ Calories: 340 ♦ Calories from Fat: 170 ♦ **% DAILY VALUE:** Total Fat: 19 g 29% ♦ Saturated Fat: 8 g 40% ♦ Cholesterol: 115 mg 38% ♦ Sodium: 150 mg 6% ♦ Total Carbohydrate: 3 g 1% ♦ Dietary Fiber: 1 g 4% ♦ Sugars: 0 g ♦ Protein: 38 g ♦ Vitamin A: 0% ♦ Vitamin C: 0% ♦ Calcium: 4% ♦ Iron: 30% ♦ **DIETARY EXCHANGES:** 5½ Lean Meat, ½ Fat

Hoedown BBQ Chuck Roast

PREP TIME: 15 MINUTES (READY IN 7 HOURS 30 MINUTES) ✦ YIELD: 8 SERVINGS

ROAST
    1 (4-lb.) beef chuck blade roast (2 inches
        thick)

MARINADE
    ½ cup soy sauce
    ½ cup ketchup
    ¼ cup sugar
    ¼ cup red wine vinegar
    1 to 2 garlic cloves, minced,
        or ½ to 1 teaspoon garlic powder
    ⅛ teaspoon pepper

1. GRILL DIRECTIONS: Trim fat from roast. In 12 × 8-inch (2-quart) baking dish or resealable food storage plastic bag, combine all marinade ingredients; blend well. Add roast; turn to coat. Cover dish or seal bag; refrigerate 6 hours or overnight, turning once or twice.

2. Heat grill. When ready to grill, remove roast from marinade; reserve and refrigerate marinade. Place roast on gas grill over medium-low heat or on charcoal grill 4 to 6 inches from medium coals; cover grill.* Cook 50 to 75 minutes or until of desired doneness, turning once and basting with reserved marinade during last 15 minutes of cooking. Discard any remaining marinade.

TIPS: * If cooking on grill without cover, a tent of foil can be used to cover roast.

To bake roast in oven, place in shallow baking pan; bake at 325°F. for 1¼ to 1½ hours, turning once and basting with reserved marinade during last 15 minutes of baking.

NUTRITION INFORMATION PER SERVING: Serving Size: ⅛ of Recipe ✦ Calories: 240 ✦ Calories from Fat: 110 ✦ % DAILY VALUE: Total Fat: 12 g 18% ✦ Saturated Fat: 5 g 25% ✦ Cholesterol: 95 mg 32% ✦ Sodium: 370 mg 15% ✦ Total Carbohydrate: 3 g 1% ✦ Dietary Fiber: 0 g 0% ✦ Sugars: 2 g ✦ Protein: 29 g ✦ Vitamin A: 0% ✦ Vitamin C: 0% ✦ Calcium: 0% ✦ Iron: 20% ✦ DIETARY EXCHANGES: 4 Lean Meat

New England Boiled Dinner

PREP TIME: 15 MINUTES (READY IN 4 HOURS 15 MINUTES) ✦ YIELD: 8 SERVINGS

    1 (3-lb.) corned beef*
       Water
    1 teaspoon peppercorns or ¼ teaspoon
       pepper
    6 whole cloves
    1 bay leaf
    6 potatoes, peeled and quartered
    6 carrots, halved lengthwise
    1 medium head cabbage, cut into 6 wedges

1. Place corned beef in large saucepan or Dutch oven; cover with water. Add peppercorns, cloves and bay leaf. Bring to a boil. Reduce heat to low; cover and simmer 3 to 3½ hours or until tender.
2. Add potatoes and carrots. Cover; simmer 15 minutes. Add cabbage; cook 15 minutes or until vegetables are tender. Remove bay leaf.
3. To serve, cut corned beef into pieces. Serve with cooking liquid and vegetables.

TIP: * If corned beef is packaged with spice packet, omit peppercorns, cloves and bay leaf.

NUTRITION INFORMATION PER SERVING: Serving Size: ⅛ of Recipe ✦ Calories: 440 ✦ Calories from Fat: 210 ✦ % DAILY VALUE: Total Fat: 23 g 35% ✦ Saturated Fat: 8 g 40% ✦ Cholesterol: 120 mg 40% ✦ Sodium: 1400 mg 58% ✦ Total Carbohydrate: 31 g 10% ✦ Dietary Fiber: 6 g 24% ✦ Sugars: 8 g ✦ Protein: 26 g ✦ Vitamin A: 310% ✦ Vitamin C: 60% ✦ Calcium: 8% ✦ Iron: 20% ✦ DIETARY EXCHANGES: 1½ Starch, 2 Vegetable, 2½ Medium-Fat Meat, 2 Fat OR 1½ Carbohydrate, 2 Vegetable, 2½ Medium-Fat Meat, 2 Fat

Pot Roast and Gravy

Pot Roast and Gravy

PREP TIME: 20 MINUTES (READY IN 2 HOURS 20 MINUTES) ✦ YIELD: 6 SERVINGS

    2 tablespoons oil
    1 (3 to 4-lb.) beef chuck, blade or 7-bone
       roast
   ½ teaspoon pepper
    4 medium onions, quartered
    4 celery stalks, cut into pieces
    1 bay leaf
    2 beef-flavor bouillon cubes or 2 teaspoons
       beef-flavor instant bouillon
 1½ cups boiling water
    6 medium potatoes, halved
    6 medium carrots, cut into pieces
   ¼ cup cold water
    3 tablespoons all-purpose flour
       Salt to taste

1. Heat oven to 325°F. In 5-quart Dutch oven or roasting pan, heat oil over medium-high heat. Add roast; cook 5 minutes on each side or until browned. Drain and discard drippings, if desired. Sprinkle pepper on both sides of roast.
2. Add 1 of the onions, 1 of the celery stalks and bay leaf to roast. Dissolve bouillon cubes in boiling water; reserve ¾ cup. Pour remaining ¾ cup of bouillon around roast. Bring to a boil. Cover; bake at 325°F. for 1 hour.
3. Add remaining vegetables; cover and bake an additional 1 to 1¼ hours or until roast and vegetables are tender.
4. To prepare gravy, place roast and vegetables on warm platter; cover loosely to keep warm. Measure drippings from Dutch oven. Skim off fat. Add reserved ¾ cup bouillon to drippings to make 3 cups; return to Dutch oven.
5. In small jar with tight-fitting lid, combine cold water and flour; shake well to blend. Gradually stir into drippings. Cook over medium heat until mixture boils and thickens, stirring constantly. Add salt to taste. Serve with roast and vegetables.

NUTRITION INFORMATION PER SERVING: Serving Size: ⅙ of Recipe ✦ Calories: 510 ✦ Calories from Fat: 130 ✦ % DAILY VALUE: Total Fat: 14 g 22% ✦ Saturated Fat: 4 g 20% ✦ Cholesterol: 130 mg 43% ✦ Sodium: 440 mg 18% ✦ Total Carbohydrate: 49 g 16% ✦ Dietary Fiber: 7 g 28% ✦ Sugars: 10 g ✦ Protein: 48 g ✦ Vitamin A: 410% ✦ Vitamin C: 35% ✦ Calcium: 8% ✦ Iron: 40% ✦ DIETARY EXCHANGES: 2½ Starch, 2 Vegetable, 5 Lean Meat OR 2½ Carbohydrate, 2 Vegetable, 5 Lean Meat

Roasted Beef Tenderloin

PREP TIME: 15 MINUTES (READY IN 1 HOUR 15 MINUTES)
✦ YIELD: 12 SERVINGS

1 (4½ to 5-lb.) beef tenderloin roast

1. Heat oven to 425°F. Remove excess surface fat and connective tissue from roast; if desired, sprinkle with salt and pepper. Place roast on rack in shallow roasting pan. Turn thin ends under; if desired, brush with oil or melted margarine. Insert meat thermometer so bulb reaches center of thickest part of meat. Do not add water or cover.
2. Bake at 425°F. for 45 to 55 minutes or until meat thermometer registers 140°F. To serve, cut into slices across grain of meat.

NUTRITION INFORMATION PER SERVING: Serving Size: ¹⁄₁₂ of Recipe ✦ Calories: 220 ✦ Calories from Fat: 110 ✦ **% DAILY VALUE:** Total Fat: 12 g 18% ✦ Saturated Fat: 5 g 25% ✦ Cholesterol: 85 mg 28% ✦ Sodium: 65 mg 3% ✦ Total Carbohydrate: 0 g 0% ✦ Dietary Fiber: 0 g 0% ✦ Sugars: 0 g ✦ Protein: 29 g ✦ Vitamin A: 0% ✦ Vitamin C: 0% ✦ Calcium: 0% ✦ Iron: 20% ✦ **DIETARY EXCHANGES:** 4 Lean Meat

Grilled Steak

1. Steaks for grilling should be at least ¾ inch thick. Allow ½ to ¾ lb. per serving of steak with bones or ⅓ to ½ lb. per serving of boneless steak. For less tender cuts such as chuck and top round steak, use high-quality beef or marinate beef to tenderize before grilling. Trim excess fat from steaks so drippings will not catch fire. Without cutting into meat, slash fat edge at 1-inch intervals to prevent curling.
2. If using charcoal grill, coals are ready when your hand can be held about 4 to 5 inches from coals for 4 to 5 seconds. Spread coals apart to lower temperature; move coals together for more heat.
3. Place steaks on gas grill over medium heat or on charcoal grill 4 to 6 inches from medium coals.
4. Grill to desired doneness, turning once, using "Timetable for Grilling Steak," page 107. If desired, sprinkle with salt and pepper.

NUTRITION INFORMATION PER SERVING: Serving Size: 4 oz. Cooked Beef ✦ Calories: 210 ✦ Calories from Fat: 70 ✦ **% DAILY VALUE:** Total Fat: 8 g 12% ✦ Saturated Fat: 3 g 15% ✦ Cholesterol: 100 mg 33% ✦ Sodium: 75 mg 3% ✦ Total Carbohydrate: 0 g 0% ✦ Dietary Fiber: 0 g 0% ✦ Sugars: 0 g ✦ Protein: 34 g ✦ Vitamin A: 0% ✦ Vitamin C: 0% ✦ Calcium: 0% ✦ Iron: 20% ✦ **DIETARY EXCHANGES:** 4 Lean Meat

Broiled Steak

1. Allow ½ to ¾ lb. per serving of steak with bones or ⅓ to ½ lb. per serving of boneless steak. Use tender cuts of beef such as sirloin for broiling. Trim excess fat from steaks so drippings will not catch fire. Without cutting into meat, slash fat edge at 1-inch intervals to prevent curling.
2. Place steak on broiler pan. Place or adjust broiler pan so top of 1-inch-thick steak is 4 inches from heat and 2-inch-thick steak is 6 inches from heat.
3. Broil to desired doneness, turning once, using "Timetable for Broiling Steak," page 99. If desired, sprinkle with salt and pepper.

NUTRITION INFORMATION PER SERVING: Serving Size: 4 oz. Cooked Beef ✦ Calories: 210 ✦ Calories from Fat: 70 ✦ **% DAILY VALUE:** Total Fat: 8 g 12% ✦ Saturated Fat: 3 g 15% ✦ Cholesterol: 100 mg 33% ✦ Sodium: 75 mg 3% ✦ Total Carbohydrate: 0 g 0% ✦ Dietary Fiber: 0 g 0% ✦ Sugars: 0 g ✦ Protein: 34 g ✦ Vitamin A: 0% ✦ Vitamin C: 0% ✦ Calcium: 0% ✦ Iron: 20% ✦ **DIETARY EXCHANGES:** 4 Lean Meat

Bearnaise Sauce

PREP TIME: 20 MINUTES ✦ YIELD: 1 CUP

½ cup margarine or butter
1 tablespoon finely chopped onion
1 teaspoon dried tarragon leaves
½ teaspoon dried chervil leaves
¼ teaspoon salt
Dash pepper
¼ cup hot water
4 egg yolks
2 tablespoons white wine
4 teaspoons lemon juice

1. In small saucepan or top of double boiler, combine margarine, onion, tarragon, chervil, salt, pepper and hot water. Cook over low heat or over hot, but not boiling, water until margarine is melted, stirring frequently.
2. In small bowl, beat egg yolks slightly. Blend small amount of margarine mixture into beaten egg yolks; add to margarine mixture in saucepan. Cook, beating mixture with eggbeater or wire whisk, for 6 to 8 minutes or until thick and smooth. Add wine and lemon juice; blend well. Serve immediately.

NUTRITION INFORMATION PER SERVING: Serving Size: 1 Tablespoon ✦ Calories: 70 ✦ Calories from Fat: 60 ✦ **% DAILY VALUE:** Total Fat: 7 g 11% ✦ Saturated Fat: 1 g 5% ✦ Cholesterol: 55 mg 18% ✦ Sodium: 100 mg 4% ✦ Total Carbohydrate: 0 g 0% ✦ Dietary Fiber: 0 g 0% ✦ Sugars: 0 g ✦ Protein: 1 g ✦ Vitamin A: 6% ✦ Vitamin C: 0% ✦ Calcium: 0% ✦ Iron: 0% ✦ **DIETARY EXCHANGES:** 1½ Fat

TIMETABLE FOR BROILING STEAK

STEAK	THICKNESS	TOTAL COOKING TIME (MEDIUM-RARE TO MEDIUM)
RIB-EYE	¾ inch	8 to 10 minutes
	1 inch	14 to 18 minutes
	1½ inches	21 to 27 minutes
RIB, SMALL END	¾ inch	9 to 12 minutes
	1 inch	13 to 17 minutes
	1½ inches	24 to 31 minutes
PORTERHOUSE/T-BONE	¾ inch	10 to 13 minutes
	1 inch	15 to 20 minutes
	1½ inches	27 to 32 minutes
TOP LOIN *(New York Strip)*	¾ inch	9 to 11 minutes
	1 inch	13 to 17 minutes
TENDERLOIN *(Filet Mignon)*	1 inch	13 to 16 minutes
	1½ inches	18 to 22 minutes
TOP SIRLOIN	1 inch	16 to 21 minutes
	1½ inches	26 to 31 minutes
TOP ROUND	1 inch	17 to 18 minutes
	1½ inches	27 to 29 minutes
CHUCK SHOULDER	¾ inch	10 to 13 minutes
	1 inch	16 to 21 minutes

Source: National Cattlemen's Beef Association

Sweet and Zesty Barbecue Sauce

PREP TIME: 10 MINUTES ✦ YIELD: 2¼ CUPS

  1 (12-oz.) bottle chili sauce
  1 (12-oz.) jar orange marmalade
  2 tablespoons red wine vinegar
  1 tablespoon Worcestershire sauce
  1 teaspoon prepared mustard
  ¼ teaspoon garlic powder

In medium bowl, combine all ingredients; blend well. Brush on meat during last 15 minutes of grilling time.

NUTRITION INFORMATION PER SERVING: Serving Size: 1 Tablespoon ◆ Calories: 35 ◆ Calories from Fat: 0 ◆ **% DAILY VALUE:** Total Fat: 0 g 0% ◆ Saturated Fat: 0 g 0% ◆ Cholesterol: 0 mg 0% ◆ Sodium: 135 mg 6% ◆ Total Carbohydrate: 9 g 3% ◆ Dietary Fiber: 0 g 0% ◆ Sugars: 6 g ◆ Protein: 0 g ◆ Vitamin A: 2% ◆ Vitamin C: 2% ◆ Calcium: 0% ◆ Iron: 0% ◆ **DIETARY EXCHANGES:** ½ Fruit OR ½ Carbohydrate

Soy Sauce Marinade

PREP TIME: 10 MINUTES ✦ YIELD: 1¼ CUPS (ENOUGH FOR 4 SERVINGS OF MEAT)

  ¾ cup oil
  ¼ cup soy sauce
  3 tablespoons honey or sugar
  2 tablespoons vinegar or lemon juice
  ½ teaspoon ginger
  1 green onion, chopped
  1 garlic clove, minced

1. In small bowl, combine all ingredients; mix well. Pour mixture over 1 to 2 lb. of steak. Cover; refrigerate at least 2 hours to marinate.
2. Grill or broil as desired, spooning or brushing marinade over steaks halfway through cooking. Discard any remaining marinade.

NUTRITION INFORMATION: Not possible to calculate because of recipe variables.

Pan-Broiled Steak Smothered in Mushrooms

PREP TIME: 30 MINUTES ◆ YIELD: 4 SERVINGS

    1 tablespoon olive or vegetable oil
    4 (4-oz.) beef tenderloin steaks
    ¼ teaspoon salt
    ¼ teaspoon coarse ground black pepper
    1 tablespoon butter
    2 large shallots, minced
    1 (8-oz.) pkg. (3 cups) sliced fresh mushrooms
    ¼ cup red wine
    ¼ cup beef broth

1. Heat oil in large skillet over medium-high heat until hot. Add steaks; sprinkle with salt and pepper. Cook steaks until of desired doneness, turning once. Remove steaks from skillet; cover to keep warm.
2. Add butter and shallots to skillet; cook and stir until shallots are tender. Add mushrooms and wine; cook 3 to 5 minutes, stirring occasionally. Add broth; cook until thoroughly heated. Serve over steaks.

NUTRITION INFORMATION PER SERVING: Serving Size: ¼ of Recipe ◆ Calories: 230 ◆ Calories from Fat: 130 ◆ **% DAILY VALUE:** Total Fat: 14 g 22% ◆ Saturated Fat: 5 g 25% ◆ Cholesterol: 60 mg 20% ◆ Sodium: 250 mg 10% ◆ Total Carbohydrate: 4 g 1% ◆ Dietary Fiber: 1 g 4% ◆ Sugars: 1 g ◆ Protein: 19 g ◆ Vitamin A: 4% ◆ Vitamin C: 4% ◆ Calcium: 0% ◆ Iron: 20% ◆ **DIETARY EXCHANGES:** 1 Vegetable, 2 Medium-Fat Meat, 1 Fat

Broiled Mongolian-Style Steak

PREP TIME: 20 MINUTES (READY IN 8 HOURS 20 MINUTES) ◆ YIELD: 4 SERVINGS

    2 tablespoons water
    2 tablespoons hoisin sauce
    1 tablespoon ketchup
    1 teaspoon cornstarch
    1 teaspoon rice vinegar
    ½ teaspoon beef-flavor instant bouillon
    ¼ teaspoon Worcestershire sauce
    ⅛ teaspoon pepper
    ¾ lb. beef flank or boneless top sirloin steak

1. To prepare marinade, in small bowl, combine all ingredients except steak; blend well. Set aside.
2. Score top of steak diagonally in a crisscross pattern about ⅛ inch deep. Place steak in resealable food storage plastic bag. Pour

Pan-Broiled Steak Smothered in Mushrooms

marinade over steak; seal bag. Turn bag to coat steak. Refrigerate 8 hours or overnight, turning bag occasionally.
3. Place steak on broiler pan. Discard marinade. Broil 4 to 6 inches from heat for 10 to 15 minutes or until steak is of desired doneness, turning once.

NUTRITION INFORMATION PER SERVING: Serving Size: ¼ of Recipe ◆ Calories: 110 ◆ Calories from Fat: 50 ◆ **% DAILY VALUE:** Total Fat: 6 g 9% ◆ Saturated Fat: 3 g 15% ◆ Cholesterol: 35 mg 12% ◆ Sodium: 110 mg 5% ◆ Total Carbohydrate: 2 g 1% ◆ Dietary Fiber: 0 g 0% ◆ Sugars: 1 g ◆ Protein: 13 g ◆ Vitamin A: 0% ◆ Vitamin C: 0% ◆ Calcium: 0% ◆ Iron: 10% ◆ **DIETARY EXCHANGES:** 2 Lean Meat

Steak Neapolitan

PREP TIME: 20 MINUTES ◆ YIELD: 4 SERVINGS

    1 teaspoon oil
    2 tablespoons lemon juice
    4 (4-oz.) beef tenderloin steaks (about 1 inch thick)
    1 cup finely chopped onions
    1 cup dry Marsala wine
    2 tablespoons chopped fresh Italian parsley

1. Heat oil in large skillet over medium-high heat until hot. Add lemon juice and steaks; cook about 5 minutes on each side or until of desired doneness. Remove steaks from skillet; cover to keep warm.
2. Add onions and wine to juice mixture in skillet; cook and stir 4 minutes or until wine is reduced to about ½ cup.
3. To serve, spoon onion mixture over steaks; sprinkle with parsley.

NUTRITION INFORMATION PER SERVING: Serving Size: ¼ of Recipe ◆ Calories: 160 ◆ Calories from Fat: 70 ◆ **% DAILY VALUE:** Total Fat: 8 g 12% ◆ Saturated Fat: 3 g 15% ◆ Cholesterol: 50 mg 17% ◆ Sodium: 390 mg 16% ◆ Total Carbohydrate: 5 g 2% ◆ Dietary Fiber: 0 g 0% ◆ Sugars: 5 g ◆ Protein: 18 g ◆ Vitamin A: 0% ◆ Vitamin C: 6% ◆ Calcium: 0% ◆ Iron: 15% ◆ **DIETARY EXCHANGES:** 1 Vegetable, 2½ Lean Meat

Pepper Steaks with Blackberry Glaze

PREP TIME: 25 MINUTES ◆ YIELD: 4 SERVINGS

GLAZE
1/2 cup blackberry jam
1/4 cup red wine vinegar

STEAKS
3 teaspoons coarse ground black pepper
4 (4-oz.) boneless beef strip steaks
1/2 cup fresh or frozen blackberries, thawed

1. GRILL DIRECTIONS: Heat grill. In small saucepan, combine jam and vinegar. Cook over medium heat until jam is melted, stirring constantly. Remove from heat.
2. Rub pepper on both sides of each steak. When ready to grill, place steaks on gas grill over medium heat or on charcoal grill 4 to 6 inches from medium-high coals. Cook 8 to 12 minutes or until of desired doneness, turning once.
3. To serve, spread steaks with glaze; top with berries.

> **TIP:** To broil steaks, place on broiler pan; broil 4 to 6 inches from heat using times above as a guide, turning once.

NUTRITION INFORMATION PER SERVING: Serving Size: 1/4 of Recipe ◆ Calories: 250 ◆ Calories from Fat: 35 ◆ **% DAILY VALUE:** Total Fat: 4 g 6% ◆ Saturated Fat: 1 g 5% ◆ Cholesterol: 60 mg 20% ◆ Sodium: 45 mg 2% ◆ Total Carbohydrate: 30 g 10% ◆ Dietary Fiber: 2 g 8% ◆ Sugars: 21 g ◆ Protein: 24 g ◆ Vitamin A: 0% ◆ Vitamin C: 8% ◆ Calcium: 2% ◆ Iron: 15% ◆ **DIETARY EXCHANGES:** 2 Fruit, 3 1/2 Very Lean Meat OR 2 Carbohydrate, 3 1/2 Very Lean Meat

Pepper Steaks with Blackberry Glaze

Beef with Chili Rub and Sour Cream

Beef with Chili Rub and Sour Cream

PREP TIME: 25 MINUTES ◆ YIELD: 4 SERVINGS

2 tablespoons chili powder
3 teaspoons dried oregano leaves
1 teaspoon cumin
1/2 teaspoon salt
1/2 teaspoon pepper
1/4 teaspoon onion powder
1/4 teaspoon ground red pepper (cayenne)
1 lb. boneless beef top sirloin steak
   (1/2 to 3/4 inch thick)
1/4 cup sour cream

1. GRILL DIRECTIONS: Heat grill. In small bowl, combine all ingredients except beef and sour cream; mix well. Brush both sides of beef with water. Sprinkle seasoning mixture over both sides; with fingers, rub into beef.
2. When ready to grill, place beef on gas grill over medium-high heat or on charcoal grill 4 to 6 inches from medium-high coals; cover grill. Cook 9 to 12 minutes or until beef is of desired doneness, turning once. Let stand 5 minutes before serving.
3. To serve, cut beef diagonally into thin slices. Top each serving with 1 tablespoon sour cream.

> **TIP:** To broil steak, place on broiler pan; broil 4 to 6 inches from heat using times above as a guide, turning once.

NUTRITION INFORMATION PER SERVING: Serving Size: 1/4 of Recipe ◆ Calories: 190 ◆ Calories from Fat: 80 ◆ **% DAILY VALUE:** Total Fat: 9 g 14% ◆ Saturated Fat: 4 g 20% ◆ Cholesterol: 65 mg 22% ◆ Sodium: 360 mg 15% ◆ Total Carbohydrate: 4 g 1% ◆ Dietary Fiber: 2 g 8% ◆ Sugars: 1 g ◆ Protein: 22 g ◆ Vitamin A: 30% ◆ Vitamin C: 4% ◆ Calcium: 6% ◆ Iron: 20% ◆ **DIETARY EXCHANGES:** 1 Vegetable, 3 Lean Meat

COOK'S NOTE

MARINATE FOR FLAVOR AND TENDERNESS

Marinades serve a dual purpose, infusing meat with wonderful flavor and tenderizing it at the same time. Marinades usually include an acidic ingredient that tenderizes, such as vinegar, wine, juice or tomatoes; a salty flavor such as salt or soy sauce; and sweet, spicy or aromatic ingredients such as freshly grated gingerroot, hot pepper flakes, garlic, onion and herbs.

To marinate meat, put all ingredients into a glass or ceramic bowl or in a resealable plastic bag. After adding the meat to the marinade, store it in the refrigerator for at least 30 minutes before cooking.

For most cooking methods, it's best to drain off the marinade before cooking. In any case, to avoid potential illness, never serve a marinade that has held raw meat unless you boil it first for 5 minutes.

Marinated Steaks

PREP TIME: 30 MINUTES (READY IN 6 HOURS 30 MINUTES) ◆ YIELD: 4 SERVINGS

MARINADE
- 1/4 cup dry red wine
- 1 tablespoon soy sauce
- 1/2 teaspoon dried thyme leaves
- 1/2 teaspoon hot pepper sauce
- 1/4 teaspoon pepper
- 1/8 teaspoon salt
- 1 bay leaf
- 1 garlic clove, minced, or 1/2 teaspoon chopped garlic in water (from 4.5-oz. jar)

STEAKS
- 4 (4-oz.) boneless beef eye of round steaks (3/4 inch thick)

1. GRILL DIRECTIONS: In 12 × 8-inch (2-quart) baking dish or resealable food storage plastic bag, combine all marinade ingredients; mix well. Add steaks; turn to coat. Cover dish or seal bag. Refrigerate at least 6 hours or overnight to marinate, turning once.

2. Heat grill. When ready to grill, drain steaks, reserving marinade. Remove and discard bay leaf. Place steaks on gas grill over medium heat or on charcoal grill 4 to 6 inches from medium coals. Cook 10 to 15 minutes or until of desired doneness, turning once and brushing frequently with reserved marinade. Discard any remaining marinade.

> **TIP:** To broil steaks, place on broiler pan; broil 4 to 6 inches from heat using times above as a guide, turning once and brushing with marinade as directed.

NUTRITION INFORMATION PER SERVING: Serving Size: 1/4 of Recipe ◆ Calories: 120 ◆ Calories from Fat: 35 ◆ **% DAILY VALUE:** Total Fat: 4 g 6% ◆ Saturated Fat: 1 g 5% ◆ Cholesterol: 50 mg 17% ◆ Sodium: 125 mg 5% ◆ Total Carbohydrate: 0 g 0% ◆ Dietary Fiber: 0 g 0% ◆ Sugars: 0 g ◆ Protein: 21 g ◆ Vitamin A: 0% ◆ Vitamin C: 0% ◆ Calcium: 0% ◆ Iron: 8% ◆ **DIETARY EXCHANGES:** 3 Lean Meat

Chili-Basil Grilled Flank Steak

PREP TIME: 25 MINUTES (READY IN 8 HOURS 25 MINUTES) ◆ YIELD: 4 SERVINGS

- 1 lb. beef flank steak
- 1/2 cup white wine vinegar
- 1/2 cup chili sauce
- 2 tablespoons brown sugar
- 1 teaspoon dried basil leaves
- 1/4 teaspoon salt

1. GRILL DIRECTIONS: Score steak on both sides diagonally in a crisscross pattern about 1/4 inch deep. Place steak in 12 × 8-inch (2-quart) baking dish or resealable food storage plastic bag. In small bowl, combine remaining ingredients; blend well. Pour over steak; turn to coat. Cover dish or seal bag. Refrigerate 8 hours or overnight, turning once.

2. Heat grill. When ready to grill, place steak on gas grill over medium-high heat or on charcoal grill 4 to 6 inches from medium-high coals. Discard marinade. Cook 10 to 15 minutes or until of desired doneness, turning once.

3. To serve, slice steak diagonally into thin slices.

> **TIP:** To broil steak, place on broiler pan; broil 4 to 6 inches from heat using times above as a guide, turning once.

NUTRITION INFORMATION PER SERVING: Serving Size: 1/4 of Recipe ◆ Calories: 160 ◆ Calories from Fat: 70 ◆ **% DAILY VALUE:** Total Fat: 8 g 12% ◆ Saturated Fat: 3 g 15% ◆ Cholesterol: 45 mg 15% ◆ Sodium: 190 mg 8% ◆ Total Carbohydrate: 4 g 1% ◆ Dietary Fiber: 0 g 0% ◆ Sugars: 3 g ◆ Protein: 17 g ◆ Vitamin A: 2% ◆ Vitamin C: 0% ◆ Calcium: 0% ◆ Iron: 15% ◆ **DIETARY EXCHANGES:** 1/2 Fruit, 2 1/2 Lean Meat OR 1/2 Carbohydrate, 2 1/2 Lean Meat

FIVE POPULAR STEAKS

TYPE OF STEAK	SOURCE	QUALITIES	BEST COOKING TECHNIQUES
RIB-EYE	Rib section	Very tender, moist and boneless	Grilling, broiling, pan-frying
PORTERHOUSE	Short loin behind the ribs, with meat from both the tenderloin and top loin	One of the best-tasting and most expensive steaks. Contains a T-shaped bone but more tenderloin meat than the T-bone steak	Grilling, broiling, pan-frying
T-BONE	Center of the short loin, just behind the ribs	Very tender and flavorful, with a distinctive T-shaped bone	Grilling, broiling, pan-frying
SIRLOIN	Lower torso and hip	Tender	Grilling, broiling, pan-frying
TOP ROUND	Back of the leg	Least tender of the five, but marinating helps	Marinating, then grilling or broiling; also good stewed or braised

Source: National Cattlemen's Beef Association

Grilled Blue Cheese Steak

PREP TIME: 30 MINUTES ◆ YIELD: 6 SERVINGS

4 oz. blue cheese, crumbled (1 cup)
1 tablespoon mayonnaise or salad dressing
1 teaspoon white wine Worcestershire sauce
    or Worcestershire sauce
2 garlic cloves, minced
1 (1½-lb.) boneless beef sirloin steak
    (1½ inches thick)

1. GRILL DIRECTIONS: Heat grill. In small bowl, combine cheese, mayonnaise, Worcestershire sauce and garlic; blend well.
2. When ready to grill, place steak on gas grill over medium-high heat or on charcoal grill 4 to 6 inches from medium-high coals. Cook 15 to 20 minutes or until of desired doneness, turning once.
3. Remove steak from grill. Spoon cheese mixture over steak. Let stand 1 to 2 minutes or until cheese is slightly melted. Cut steak into pieces to serve.

TIP: To broil steak, place on broiler pan; broil 4 to 6 inches from heat using times above as a guide, turning once. Continue as directed.

NUTRITION INFORMATION PER SERVING: Serving Size: ⅙ of Recipe ◆ Calories: 210 ◆ Calories from Fat: 110 ◆ **% DAILY VALUE:** Total Fat: 12 g 18% ◆ Saturated Fat: 6 g 30% ◆ Cholesterol: 75 mg 25% ◆ Sodium: 330 mg 14% ◆ Total Carbohydrate: 1 g 1% ◆ Dietary Fiber: 0 g 0% ◆ Sugars: 1 g ◆ Protein: 24 g ◆ Vitamin A: 2% ◆ Vitamin C: 0% ◆ Calcium: 10% ◆ Iron: 15% ◆ **DIETARY EXCHANGES:** 3½ Lean Meat, ½ Fat

C O O K ' S   N O T E

RARE STEAK OR ROAST IS OKAY

While pink-centered burgers are a hazard, a rare steak will likely be all right. Why? A solid cut of meat, such as a steak or roast, is essentially sterile on the inside. Grinding and mixing beef, on the other hand, can contaminate the whole batch with surface bacteria.

Check relatively thin cuts of beef, such as steak, by cutting into the center with a steak knife. The meat can be pink, if you like rare or medium, but it should not look translucent or raw in the middle. For roasts, check the temperature with a meat thermometer.

4. If necessary, allow butter to stand at room temperature for about 15 minutes to soften. To serve, cut steak into 4 serving pieces; place on serving plates. Cut butter into 4 slices; place on center of hot steaks. Serve immediately.

TIP: To broil steaks, place on broiler pan; broil 4 to 6 inches from heat using times above as a guide, turning once.

NUTRITION INFORMATION PER SERVING: Serving Size: ¼ of Recipe ♦ Calories: 310 ♦ Calories from Fat: 230 ♦ % DAILY VALUE: Total Fat: 25 g 38% ♦ Saturated Fat: 14 g 70% ♦ Cholesterol: 115 mg 38% ♦ Sodium: 410 mg 17% ♦ Total Carbohydrate: 0 g 0% ♦ Dietary Fiber: 0 g 0% ♦ Sugars: 0 g ♦ Protein: 21 g ♦ Vitamin A: 15% ♦ Vitamin C: 0% ♦ Calcium: 0% ♦ Iron: 15% ♦ DIETARY EXCHANGES: 3 Lean Meat, 3 Fat

Blackened Sirloin with Southwestern Butter

Blackened Sirloin with Southwestern Butter

PREP TIME: 30 MINUTES (READY IN 2 HOURS)
♦ YIELD: 4 SERVINGS

SOUTHWESTERN BUTTER
  6 tablespoons butter, slightly softened
  ¼ teaspoon cumin
  ¼ teaspoon dried oregano leaves
  ¼ teaspoon chili powder
  ⅛ teaspoon dried thyme leaves
  ⅛ teaspoon pepper
    Dash ground red pepper (cayenne)

STEAK
  1 lb. boneless beef sirloin steak
    (1 to 1½ inches thick)
  1 tablespoon butter, melted
  2 teaspoons blackened steak seasoning

1. GRILL DIRECTIONS: In small bowl, combine all butter ingredients; blend well. Place butter on piece of plastic wrap. Shape into 4-inch log. Refrigerate 1 hour or until firm.

2. Meanwhile, brush each side of steak with 1 tablespoon melted butter; rub each side of steak with 1 teaspoon blackened steak seasoning. Let stand at room temperature for 30 minutes.

3. Heat grill. When ready to grill, place steak on gas grill over medium heat or on charcoal grill 4 to 6 inches from medium coals. Cook 8 to 20 minutes or until of desired doneness, turning once.

Grilled Steak with Charred Sweet Onions

PREP TIME: 25 MINUTES (READY IN 40 MINUTES)
♦ YIELD: 4 SERVINGS

STEAK
  2 tablespoons Worcestershire sauce
  1 tablespoon olive or vegetable oil
  1 teaspoon dried thyme leaves
  1 teaspoon dried rosemary leaves
  1 large garlic clove, minced
  1 lb. boneless beef sirloin steak
    (¾ inch thick)

Grilled Steak with Charred Sweet Onions

ONIONS

2 sweet onions, cut into ½-inch-thick slices
I tablespoon olive or vegetable oil
½ teaspoon paprika

1. GRILL DIRECTIONS: In small bowl, combine all steak ingredients except steak; mix well. Place steak in shallow glass dish or resealable food storage plastic bag. Pour oil mixture over steak; turn steak to coat. Cover dish or seal bag. Let stand at room temperature for 15 to 30 minutes to marinate.

2. Meanwhile, heat grill. Brush onions lightly with 1 tablespoon oil; sprinkle with paprika.

3. When ready to grill, if desired, sprinkle steak with salt and pepper. (Steak can be cut into 4 servings before grilling, if desired.) Place steak and onions on gas grill over medium heat or on charcoal grill 4 to 6 inches from medium coals. Cook 10 to 15 minutes or until steak is of desired doneness and onions are tender, turning once.

> **TIP:** To broil steak and onions, place on broiler pan; broil 4 to 6 inches from heat using times above as a guide, turning once.

NUTRITION INFORMATION PER SERVING: Serving Size: ¼ of Recipe ✦ Calories: 190 ✦ Calories from Fat: 80 ✦ **% DAILY VALUE:** Total Fat: 9 g 14% ✦ Saturated Fat: 2 g 10% ✦ Cholesterol: 60 mg 20% ✦ Sodium: 65 mg 3% ✦ Total Carbohydrate: 5 g 2% ✦ Dietary Fiber: 1 g 4% ✦ Sugars: 3 g ✦ Protein: 21 g ✦ Vitamin A: 4% ✦ Vitamin C: 4% ✦ Calcium: 2% ✦ Iron: 15% ✦ **DIETARY EXCHANGES:** 1 Vegetable, 3 Lean Meat

Porterhouse Steaks with Grilled Vegetables

Porterhouse Steaks with Grilled Vegetables

PREP TIME: 35 MINUTES ✦ YIELD: 4 SERVINGS

VEGETABLES

8 oz. assorted fresh wild mushrooms or mushrooms, cut in half
I red bell pepper, cut into strips
I yellow bell pepper, cut into strips
I poblano chile, seeded, cut into strips
3 tablespoons butter, melted
2 garlic cloves, minced

STEAK

2 tablespoons olive oil
½ teaspoon coarsely ground assorted peppercorns or black peppercorns
¼ teaspoon salt
4 (6 to 8-oz.) beef porterhouse steaks (¾ inch thick)

1. GRILL DIRECTIONS: Heat grill. Place mushrooms, bell peppers and chile in disposable foil pan or in center of 18 × 12-inch sheet of heavy-duty foil. In small bowl, combine butter and garlic; mix well. Pour butter mixture over vegetables. Cover pan with foil or seal packet securely using double-fold seals.

2. In small bowl, combine oil, peppercorns and salt; mix well. Brush each steak with oil mixture.

3. When ready to grill, place steaks and vegetables on gas grill over medium-high heat or on charcoal grill 4 to 6 inches from medium-high coals. Cook 10 to 20 minutes or until steaks are of desired doneness and bell peppers are crisp-tender, turning steaks once. Serve vegetables with steaks.

> **TIP:** To broil steaks, place on broiler pan; broil 4 to 6 inches from heat using times above as a guide, turning once. Cook vegetables in skillet over medium-high heat for 6 to 8 minutes, stirring occasionally.

NUTRITION INFORMATION PER SERVING: Serving Size: ¼ of Recipe ✦ Calories: 390 ✦ Calories from Fat: 250 ✦ **% DAILY VALUE:** Total Fat: 28 g 43% ✦ Saturated Fat: 10 g 50% ✦ Cholesterol: 95 mg 32% ✦ Sodium: 300 mg 13% ✦ Total Carbohydrate: 6 g 2% ✦ Dietary Fiber: 2 g 8% ✦ Sugars: 3 g ✦ Protein: 29 g ✦ Vitamin A: 30% ✦ Vitamin C: 100% ✦ Calcium: 2% ✦ Iron: 25% ✦ **DIETARY EXCHANGES:** 1 Vegetable, 4 Lean Meat, 3 Fat

Family Favorite Grilled Steak

PREP TIME: 30 MINUTES (READY IN 24 HOURS 30 MINUTES) ◆ YIELD: 6 SERVINGS

  1 cup ketchup
  ¼ cup cider vinegar
  1 tablespoon prepared horseradish
  2 tablespoons prepared mustard
  ½ teaspoon Liquid Smoke, if desired
  ¼ teaspoon coarse ground black pepper
  1½ lb. boneless beef top round steak (¾ inch thick)

1. GRILL DIRECTIONS: In 12 × 8-inch (2-quart) baking dish or resealable food storage plastic bag, combine all ingredients except steak; blend well. Add steak; turn to coat. Cover dish or seal bag. Refrigerate at least 24 hours, turning occasionally.
2. Heat grill. When ready to grill, remove steak from marinade; reserve marinade. Place steak on gas grill over medium-high heat or on charcoal grill 4 to 6 inches from medium-high coals. Cook 10 to 20 minutes or until of desired doneness, brushing steak with marinade and turning once or twice.
3. In small saucepan over medium-high heat, heat remaining marinade until mixture comes to a boil, stirring occasionally. Serve marinade with steak.

> **TIP:** To broil steak, place on broiler pan; broil 4 to 6 inches from heat using times above as a guide, turning and brushing with marinade as directed.

NUTRITION INFORMATION PER SERVING: Serving Size: ⅙ of Recipe ◆ Calories: 190 ◆ Calories from Fat: 45 ◆ **% DAILY VALUE:** Total Fat: 5 g 8% ◆ Saturated Fat: 2 g 10% ◆ Cholesterol: 60 mg 20% ◆ Sodium: 570 mg 24% ◆ Total Carbohydrate: 12 g 4% ◆ Dietary Fiber: 1 g 2% ◆ Sugars: 4 g ◆ Protein: 24 g ◆ Vitamin A: 8% ◆ Vitamin C: 8% ◆ Calcium: 0% ◆ Iron: 15% ◆ **DIETARY EXCHANGES:** 1 Starch, 3 Very Lean Meat, ½ Fat OR 1 Carbohydrate, 3 Very Lean Meat, ½ Fat

---

COOK'S NOTE

GRILLING STEAK

Grilling steak, like other types of grilling, is as much art as science, and the times on page 107 and in the recipes are approximate. Timing may vary due to the type of grill, the type and amount of charcoal you use, the thickness of the meat and other variables.

Grilled T-Bone Steaks with Red Hot Sauce

PREP TIME: 25 MINUTES ◆ YIELD: 4 SERVINGS

STEAK
  2 tablespoons olive oil
  2 garlic cloves, minced
  4 (6 to 8-oz.) beef T-bone steaks (½ inch thick)

SAUCE
  ½ cup mayonnaise or salad dressing
  ¼ cup chopped onion
  2 tablespoons chili puree with garlic*

1. GRILL DIRECTIONS: Heat grill. In small bowl, combine oil and garlic; mix well. Brush steaks with garlic mixture.
2. When ready to grill, place steaks on gas grill over medium-high heat or on charcoal grill 4 to 6 inches from medium-high coals. Cook 10 to 20 minutes or until of desired doneness, turning once.
3. Meanwhile, in small microwave-safe bowl, combine all sauce ingredients; mix well. Microwave on HIGH for 30 to 40 seconds or until warm, stirring once halfway through cooking. Serve with steaks.

> **TIPS:** * Chili puree with garlic can be found in the Asian section of most supermarkets or in Asian food stores.
>   To broil steaks, place on broiler pan; broil 4 to 6 inches from heat using times above as a guide, turning once.

NUTRITION INFORMATION PER SERVING: Serving Size: ¼ of Recipe ◆ Calories: 430 ◆ Calories from Fat: 310 ◆ **% DAILY VALUE:** Total Fat: 34 g 52% ◆ Saturated Fat: 7 g 35% ◆ Cholesterol: 75 mg 25% ◆ Sodium: 560 mg 23% ◆ Total Carbohydrate: 3 g 1% ◆ Dietary Fiber: 0 g 0% ◆ Sugars: 1 g ◆ Protein: 27 g ◆ Vitamin A: 6% ◆ Vitamin C: 0% ◆ Calcium: 0% ◆ Iron: 20% ◆ **DIETARY EXCHANGES:** 4 Lean Meat, 4½ Fat

Beef Fondue

PREP TIME: 20 MINUTES ◆ YIELD: 4 SERVINGS

  4 lettuce leaves
  2 lb. boneless beef sirloin steak or tenderloin, cut into 1-inch cubes
  Oil for deep frying

1. Line 4 individual dishes with lettuce leaves. Arrange beef cubes over lettuce.
2. Place fondue pot base in center of table. Heat oil in fondue pot over medium heat to about 375°F. or until it browns a cube of

TIMETABLE FOR GRILLING STEAK

STEAK	THICKNESS	TOTAL GRILLING TIME (MEDIUM RARE TO MEDIUM)
RIB-EYE	¾ inch	6 to 8 minutes
	1 inch	9 to 14 minutes
	1½ inches	17 to 27 minutes
RIB, SMALL END	¾ inch	9 to 12 minutes
	1 inch	13 to 17 minutes
	1½ inches	24 to 31 minutes
PORTERHOUSE/T-BONE	¾ inch	10 to 12 minutes
	1 inch	14 to 16 minutes
	1½ inches	20 to 24 minutes
TOP LOIN *(New York Strip)*	¾ inch	10 to 12 minutes
	1 inch	15 to 18 minutes
TENDERLOIN *(Filet Mignon)*	1 inch	13 to 15 minutes
	1½ inches	14 to 16 minutes
TOP SIRLOIN	1 inch	17 to 21 minutes
	1½ inches	22 to 26 minutes
TOP ROUND	1 inch	16 to 18 minutes
	1½ inches	25 to 30 minutes
CHUCK SHOULDER	¾ inch	14 to 17 minutes
	1 inch	16 to 22 minutes

Source: National Cattlemen's Beef Association

bread quickly. Place fondue pot over base. (If using electric pot, use base to heat oil.)

3. With fondue fork, spear beef. Cook in hot oil until of desired doneness. Place on plate; eat with dinner fork, dipping beef into desired sauces.

NUTRITION INFORMATION PER SERVING: Serving Size: ¼ of Recipe ◆ Calories: 470 ◆ Calories from Fat: 310 ◆ **% DAILY VALUE:** Total Fat: 34 g 52% ◆ Saturated Fat: 7 g 35% ◆ Cholesterol: 120 mg 40% ◆ Sodium: 90 mg 4% ◆ Total Carbohydrate: 0 g 0% ◆ Dietary Fiber: 0 g 0% ◆ Sugars: 0 g ◆ Protein: 41 g ◆ Vitamin A: 0% ◆ Vitamin C: 0% ◆ Calcium: 0% ◆ Iron: 25% ◆ **DIETARY EXCHANGES:** 6 Lean Meat, 3 Fat

Sour Cream Horseradish Sauce

PREP TIME: 5 MINUTES ◆ YIELD: ⅔ CUP

½ cup sour cream
2 tablespoons prepared horseradish
2 teaspoons lemon juice
Dash paprika

In small bowl, combine all ingredients except paprika; blend well. Sprinkle with paprika.

NUTRITION INFORMATION PER SERVING: Serving Size: 1 Tablespoon ◆ Calories: 25 ◆ Calories from Fat: 25 ◆ **% DAILY VALUE:** Total Fat: 3 g 5% ◆ Saturated Fat: 2 g 10% ◆ Cholesterol: 4 mg 1% ◆ Sodium: 15 mg 1% ◆ Total Carbohydrate: 0 g 0% ◆ Dietary Fiber: 0 g 0% ◆ Sugars: 0 g ◆ Protein: 0 g ◆ Vitamin A: 0% ◆ Vitamin C: 0% ◆ Calcium: 0% ◆ Iron: 0% ◆ **DIETARY EXCHANGES:** ½ Fat

Asian Sauce

PREP TIME: 5 MINUTES ◆ YIELD: 1 CUP

¾ cup hoisin sauce
2 tablespoons finely chopped green onions
2 tablespoons soy sauce

In small bowl, combine all ingredients; blend well.

NUTRITION INFORMATION PER SERVING: Serving Size: 1 Tablespoon ◆ Calories: 30 ◆ Calories from Fat: 0 ◆ **% DAILY VALUE:** Total Fat: 0 g 0% ◆ Saturated Fat: 0 g 0% ◆ Cholesterol: 0 mg 0% ◆ Sodium: 360 mg 15% ◆ Total Carbohydrate: 7 g 2% ◆ Dietary Fiber: 0 g 0% ◆ Sugars: 6 g ◆ Protein: 1 g ◆ Vitamin A: 0% ◆ Vitamin C: 0% ◆ Calcium: 0% ◆ Iron: 0% ◆ **DIETARY EXCHANGES:** ½ Starch OR ½ Carbohydrate

Southwest Steak Kabobs

PREP TIME: 30 MINUTES ✦ YIELD: 4 KABOBS

- ¼ cup margarine or butter, melted
- ¼ cup chopped fresh cilantro
- ½ teaspoon cumin
- ¼ teaspoon garlic salt
- ½ teaspoon hot pepper sauce
- 2 ears fresh sweet corn, husked, each cut into 4 pieces
- 8 pickled sweet red cherry peppers
- 1 lb. boneless beef sirloin steak, cut into 1-inch cubes

1. GRILL DIRECTIONS: Heat grill. In small bowl, combine margarine, cilantro, cumin, garlic salt and hot pepper sauce; mix well. Alternately thread corn, peppers and beef cubes onto four 12 to 14-inch metal skewers.
2. When ready to grill, place kabobs on gas grill over medium heat or on charcoal grill 4 to 6 inches from medium coals. Cook 7 to 8 minutes or until corn is tender and beef is of desired doneness, turning once and brushing frequently with margarine mixture.

> **TIP:** To broil kabobs, place on broiler pan; broil 4 to 6 inches from heat using times above as a guide, turning and brushing with margarine mixture as directed.

NUTRITION INFORMATION PER SERVING: Serving Size: 1 Kabob ◆ Calories: 230 ◆ Calories from Fat: 80 ◆ **% DAILY VALUE:** Total Fat: 9 g 14% ◆ Saturated Fat: 2 g 10% ◆ Cholesterol: 60 mg 20% ◆ Sodium: 340 mg 14% ◆ Total Carbohydrate: 13 g 4% ◆ Dietary Fiber: 2 g 8% ◆ Sugars: 2 g ◆ Protein: 23 g ◆ Vitamin A: 10% ◆ Vitamin C: 15% ◆ Calcium: 0% ◆ Iron: 15% ◆ **DIETARY EXCHANGES:** 1 Starch, 3 Lean Meat OR 1 Carbohydrate, 3 Lean Meat

Parsley-Potato Topped Oven Swiss Steak

Parsley-Potato Topped Oven Swiss Steak

PREP TIME: 20 MINUTES (READY IN 2 HOURS 55 MINUTES) ✦ YIELD: 6 SERVINGS

SWISS STEAK
- 1 lb. boneless beef round steak (½ inch thick), cut into 6 pieces
- 2 carrots, sliced (1 cup)
- 1 large onion, halved, thinly sliced
- 1 (12-oz.) jar home-style beef gravy
- 1 (14.5-oz.) can diced tomatoes, undrained
- ¼ teaspoon dried thyme leaves
- ⅛ teaspoon pepper

TOPPING
- 1½ cups water
- 3 tablespoons margarine or butter
- 2¼ cups mashed potato flakes
- ¾ cup milk
- 3 tablespoons finely chopped fresh parsley
- ¼ teaspoon salt
- ¼ teaspoon dried thyme leaves
- 1 egg, beaten
  Paprika

1. Heat oven to 325°F. Arrange beef in ungreased 12 × 8-inch (2-quart) baking dish. Top with carrots and onion.
2. In medium bowl, combine gravy, tomatoes, ¼ teaspoon thyme and pepper; mix well. Spoon over beef and vegetables. Cover with foil. Bake at 325°F. for 2 hours.
3. In medium saucepan, bring water and margarine to a boil. Remove from heat. Stir in potato flakes, milk, parsley, salt and ¼ teaspoon thyme. Add egg; mix well.
4. Uncover baking dish; spoon or pipe potato mixture over hot steak mixture. Sprinkle with paprika. Bake uncovered an additional 30 to 35 minutes or until potatoes are set and light golden brown.

NUTRITION INFORMATION PER SERVING: Serving Size: ⅙ of Recipe ◆ Calories: 350 ◆ Calories from Fat: 120 ◆ **% DAILY VALUE:** Total Fat: 13 g 20% ◆ Saturated Fat: 4 g 20% ◆ Cholesterol: 80 mg 27% ◆ Sodium: 700 mg 29% ◆ Total Carbohydrate: 34 g 11% ◆ Dietary Fiber: 4 g 16% ◆ Sugars: 6 g ◆ Protein: 23 g ◆ Vitamin A: 150% ◆ Vitamin C: 20% ◆ Calcium: 10% ◆ Iron: 20% ◆ **DIETARY EXCHANGES:** 2 Starch, 1 Vegetable, 2 Lean Meat, 1 Fat OR 2 Carbohydrate, 1 Vegetable, 2 Lean Meat, 1 Fat

Beefy Turnovers

Beefy Turnovers

PREP TIME: 30 MINUTES (READY IN 2 HOURS 5 MINUTES)
✦ YIELD: 8 TURNOVERS

DOUGH
   3 cups all-purpose flour
   4 teaspoons baking powder
   ⅛ teaspoon salt
   ⅔ cup light ricotta cheese
   ⅓ to ½ cup skim milk
   3 tablespoons oil
   2 egg whites

FILLING
   1 lb. boneless beef top round steak, diced
   1 medium russet or Idaho baking potato,
      peeled, finely chopped (1 cup)
   ½ cup chopped onion
   ½ cup chopped carrot
   1 teaspoon salt
   ¼ teaspoon ground thyme
   ¼ teaspoon pepper
   1 egg, beaten

1. In medium bowl, combine flour, baking powder and ⅛ teaspoon salt; mix well. In small bowl, combine ricotta cheese and all remaining dough ingredients; blend well. Add all at once to flour mixture; stir just until dry ingredients are moistened. (Mixture will be dry and crumbly.) Gently press mixture into ball; wrap in plastic wrap. Refrigerate at least 1 hour or until dough is thoroughly chilled.

2. Meanwhile, in large bowl, combine all filling ingredients except egg; mix well. Refrigerate until ready to prepare turnovers.

3. Heat oven to 400°F. Spray 2 cookie sheets with nonstick cooking spray.

4. Divide chilled dough into 8 equal pieces.

Roll each piece into 7½-inch round. Place scant ½ cup filling in center of each round. Fold dough over filling to form semicircles; press edges firmly with fork to seal. Place on sprayed cookie sheets. Brush with beaten egg. Cut ½-inch slit in top of each turnover.

5. Bake at 400°F. for 25 to 35 minutes or until crust is golden brown and beef is no longer pink, switching cookie sheets on oven racks halfway through baking to ensure even browning.

HIGH ALTITUDE *(over 3500 feet)*: No change.

NUTRITION INFORMATION PER SERVING: Serving Size: 1 Turnover ✦ Calories: 350 ✦ Calories from Fat: 90 ✦ **% DAILY VALUE:** Total Fat: 10 g 15% ✦ Saturated Fat: 3 g 15% ✦ Cholesterol: 60 mg 20% ✦ Sodium: 620 mg 26% ✦ Total Carbohydrate: 43 g 14% ✦ Dietary Fiber: 2 g 8% ✦ Sugars: 3 g ✦ Protein: 21 g ✦ Vitamin A: 45% ✦ Vitamin C: 4% ✦ Calcium: 25% ✦ Iron: 20% ✦ **DIETARY EXCHANGES:** 3 Starch, 1½ Lean Meat, ½ Fat OR 3 Carbohydrate, 1½ Lean Meat, ½ Fat

Country Short Ribs

PREP TIME: 30 MINUTES (READY IN 3 HOURS)
✦ YIELD: 6 SERVINGS

   3½ to 4 lb. beef short ribs
   1 (10½-oz.) can condensed beef broth
   ½ cup dry red wine
   1 teaspoon Worcestershire sauce
   ¼ teaspoon dried marjoram leaves
   ¼ teaspoon garlic powder
   ⅛ teaspoon pepper
   3 tablespoons cold water
   2 tablespoons all-purpose flour

1. Heat oven to 325°F. Place short ribs in ungreased 13×9-inch (3-quart) baking dish. In small bowl, combine broth, wine, Worcestershire sauce, marjoram, garlic powder and pepper. Pour over ribs in baking dish; cover.

2. Bake at 325°F. for 2 to 2½ hours or until ribs are tender.

3. To prepare gravy, place ribs on platter; cover loosely to keep warm. In small jar with tight-fitting lid, combine cold water and flour; shake well to blend. In medium saucepan over medium-high heat, bring pan drippings to a boil. Skim off fat. Gradually add flour mixture, stirring constantly until mixture thickens and boils. Serve gravy with ribs.

NUTRITION INFORMATION PER SERVING: Serving Size: ⅙ of Recipe ✦ Calories: 270 ✦ Calories from Fat: 140 ✦ **% DAILY VALUE:** Total Fat: 15 g 23% ✦ Saturated Fat: 6 g 30% ✦ Cholesterol: 75 mg 25% ✦ Sodium: 320 mg 13% ✦ Total Carbohydrate: 2 g 1% ✦ Dietary Fiber: 0 g 0% ✦ Sugars: 0 g ✦ Protein: 28 g ✦ Vitamin A: 0% ✦ Vitamin C: 0% ✦ Calcium: 0% ✦ Iron: 15% ✦ **DIETARY EXCHANGES:** 4 Lean Meat, 1 Fat

Baked Chimichangas with Shredded Beef

PREP TIME: 30 MINUTES (READY IN 2 HOURS 55 MINUTES) ✦ YIELD: 8 CHIMICHANGAS

SHREDDED BEEF
1 (1½-lb.) beef chuck roast
½ cup chopped onion
1 to 2 teaspoons crushed red pepper flakes
1 teaspoon coarse ground black pepper
6 cups water

CHIMICHANGAS
8 (9 or 10-inch) flour tortillas
1 (16-oz.) can refried beans
½ cup chopped onion
2 medium tomatoes, seeded, chopped
3 tablespoons margarine or butter, melted
½ cup salsa
½ cup sour cream
½ cup purchased guacamole

1. In large saucepan, combine all shredded beef ingredients. Cover; cook over medium-high heat until mixture comes to a boil. Reduce heat to medium; cook 1 to 1½ hours or until beef is fork-tender, stirring occasionally and adding water if necessary.
2. Remove beef from water.* Cool 15 minutes or until easy to handle. To shred beef, with 2 forks, pull beef apart along the grain of the beef.**
3. Heat oven to 350°F. Spread ¼ cup refried beans onto center of each tortilla. Top each with ½ cup shredded beef, 1 tablespoon onion and 2 tablespoons tomato. Fold sides of tortillas toward center; fold ends up. Place, seam side down, on ungreased cookie sheet. Brush each filled tortilla with melted margarine.
4. Bake at 350°F. for 30 to 40 minutes or until golden brown and thoroughly heated. Serve with salsa, sour cream and guacamole.

> **TIPS:** * Cooking liquid can be refrigerated to use as broth in soups or stews. Remove fat from broth before using.
> ** At this point, beef can be refrigerated for 1 day or wrapped and frozen for up to 1 month.

NUTRITION INFORMATION PER SERVING: Serving Size: 1 Chimichanga ◆ Calories: 430 ◆ Calories from Fat: 150 ◆ **% DAILY VALUE:** Total Fat: 17 g 26% ◆ Saturated Fat: 6 g 30% ◆ Cholesterol: 50 mg 17% ◆ Sodium: 740 mg 31% ◆ Total Carbohydrate: 46 g 15% ◆ Dietary Fiber: 6 g 24% ◆ Sugars: 5 g ◆ Protein: 22 g ◆ Vitamin A: 10% ◆ Vitamin C: 10% ◆ Calcium: 10% ◆ Iron: 25% ◆ **DIETARY EXCHANGES:** 3 Starch, 2 Medium-Fat Meat, 1 Fat OR 3 Carbohydrate, 2 Medium-Fat Meat, 1 Fat

Scandinavian Meatballs

PREP TIME: 25 MINUTES (READY IN 1 HOUR 15 MINUTES) ✦ YIELD: 12 SERVINGS

MEATBALLS
1½ lb. ground beef
¾ lb. ground pork
⅓ cup unseasoned dry bread crumbs
½ teaspoon salt
½ teaspoon onion powder
¼ teaspoon sugar
¼ teaspoon ginger
¼ teaspoon nutmeg
⅛ teaspoon pepper
⅓ cup milk
2 eggs

SAUCE
⅓ cup margarine or butter
⅓ cup all-purpose flour
2 tablespoons beef-flavor instant bouillon
⅛ teaspoon nutmeg
⅛ teaspoon pepper
4 cups milk

1. Heat oven to 350°F. In large bowl, combine all meatball ingredients; mix well. Shape into 48 meatballs about 1 inch in diameter. Place meatballs in ungreased 15×10×1-inch baking pan.
2. Bake at 350°F. for 55 to 60 minutes or until meatballs are well browned. Drain.
3. Meanwhile, melt margarine in large saucepan over low heat. Stir in flour, bouillon, ⅛ teaspoon nutmeg and ⅛ teaspoon pepper. Cook 1 minute until smooth and bubbly, stirring constantly. Gradually stir in 4 cups milk. Cook over medium heat until slightly thickened and bubbly, stirring constantly. Remove from heat. Add meatballs to sauce.

NUTRITION INFORMATION PER SERVING: Serving Size: 1/12 of Recipe ◆ Calories: 300 ◆ Calories from Fat: 180 ◆ **% DAILY VALUE:** Total Fat: 20 g 31% ◆ Saturated Fat: 7 g 35% ◆ Cholesterol: 95 mg 32% ◆ Sodium: 530 mg 22% ◆ Total Carbohydrate: 10 g 3% ◆ Dietary Fiber: 0 g 0% ◆ Sugars: 5 g ◆ Protein: 19 g ◆ Vitamin A: 10% ◆ Vitamin C: 0% ◆ Calcium: 15% ◆ Iron: 10% ◆ **DIETARY EXCHANGES:** ½ Starch, 2½ Medium-Fat Meat, 1½ Fat OR ½ Carbohydrate, 2½ Medium-Fat Meat, 1½ Fat

Italian Classic Lasagna

PREP TIME: 30 MINUTES (READY IN 2 HOURS 10 MINUTES) ♦ YIELD: 8 SERVINGS

NOODLES
6 uncooked lasagna noodles

MEAT SAUCE
1 lb. ground beef
½ lb. bulk Italian sausage
¾ cup chopped onions
1 (28-oz.) can Italian plum tomatoes, undrained, cut up
1 (6-oz.) can tomato paste
1 teaspoon dried basil leaves
½ teaspoon dried oregano leaves
½ teaspoon sugar
¼ teaspoon garlic powder
¼ teaspoon salt

CHEESE MIXTURE
1 (15-oz.) container ricotta cheese
1 cup cottage cheese
2 eggs, beaten
½ cup grated Parmesan cheese
¼ cup chopped fresh parsley
16 oz. (4 cups) shredded mozzarella cheese

1. Cook lasagna noodles to desired doneness as directed on package. Drain; place in cold water.
2. Meanwhile, in large saucepan or Dutch oven, combine ground beef, sausage and onions; cook over medium heat for 8 to 10 minutes or until beef and sausage are thoroughly cooked, stirring frequently. Drain. Add all remaining meat sauce ingredients; mix well. Bring to a boil. Reduce heat to low; simmer 30 to 45 minutes or until very thick, stirring occasionally.
3. In medium bowl, combine all cheese mixture ingredients except mozzarella cheese; blend well.
4. Heat oven to 350°F. Spread about ½ cup meat sauce over bottom of ungreased 13 × 9-inch (3-quart) baking dish. Top with 3 noodles, half of the ricotta cheese mixture, half of the remaining meat sauce and half of the mozzarella cheese. Repeat layers, ending with mozzarella cheese.
5. Bake at 350°F. for 35 to 45 minutes or until bubbly. Cover; let stand 10 to 15 minutes before serving.

NUTRITION INFORMATION PER SERVING: Serving Size: ⅛ of Recipe ♦ Calories: 590 ♦ Calories from Fat: 290 ♦ % DAILY VALUE: Total Fat: 32 g 49% ♦ Saturated Fat: 16 g 80% ♦ Cholesterol: 160 mg 53% ♦ Sodium: 1220 mg 51% ♦ Total Carbohydrate: 28 g 9% ♦ Dietary Fiber: 3 g 12% ♦ Sugars: 6 g ♦ Protein: 47 g ♦ Vitamin A: 40% ♦ Vitamin C: 30% ♦ Calcium: 70% ♦ Iron: 20% ♦ DIETARY EXCHANGES: 1½ Starch, 1 Vegetable, 6 Medium-Fat Meat OR 1½ Carbohydrate, 1 Vegetable, 6 Medium-Fat Meat

Traditional Meat Loaf

PREP TIME: 15 MINUTES (READY IN 1 HOUR 35 MINUTES) ♦ YIELD: 6 SERVINGS

1 teaspoon beef-flavor instant bouillon
¼ cup hot water
1½ lb. ground beef
¾ cup cracker crumbs or unseasoned dry bread crumbs
½ cup chopped onion
2 teaspoons dried basil leaves
½ teaspoon garlic powder
¼ teaspoon pepper
⅓ cup ketchup
⅛ teaspoon hot pepper sauce
1 egg, slightly beaten

1. Heat oven to 350°F. In large bowl, dissolve beef bouillon in hot water. Add all remaining ingredients; mix well. Spoon mixture into ungreased 8 × 4-inch loaf pan or shape mixture into 8 × 4-inch loaf in ungreased 12 × 8-inch (2-quart) baking dish. Insert meat thermometer so bulb reaches center of meat loaf.
2. Bake at 350°F. for 1¼ hours or until beef is thoroughly cooked in center and meat thermometer reaches 160°F. Let stand 5 minutes before slicing.

NUTRITION INFORMATION PER SERVING: Serving Size: ⅙ of Recipe ♦ Calories: 290 ♦ Calories from Fat: 160 ♦ % DAILY VALUE: Total Fat: 18 g 28% ♦ Saturated Fat: 7 g 35% ♦ Cholesterol: 105 mg 35% ♦ Sodium: 500 mg 21% ♦ Total Carbohydrate: 12 g 4% ♦ Dietary Fiber: 1 g 3% ♦ Sugars: 2 g ♦ Protein: 21 g ♦ Vitamin A: 4% ♦ Vitamin C: 4% ♦ Calcium: 4% ♦ Iron: 15% ♦ DIETARY EXCHANGES: 1 Starch, 3 Medium-Fat Meat OR 1 Carbohydrate, 3 Medium-Fat Meat

Lazy-Day Overnight Lasagna

NUTRITION INFORMATION PER SERVING: Serving Size: 1/12 of Recipe ◆ Calories: 350 ◆ Calories from Fat: 150 ◆ **% DAILY VALUE:** Total Fat: 17 g 26% ◆ Saturated Fat: 9 g 45% ◆ Cholesterol: 75 mg 25% ◆ Sodium: 580 mg 24% ◆ Total Carbohydrate: 23 g 8% ◆ Dietary Fiber: 2 g 8% ◆ Sugars: 1 g ◆ Protein: 25 g ◆ Vitamin A: 15% ◆ Vitamin C: 6% ◆ Calcium: 40% ◆ Iron: 10% ◆ **DIETARY EXCHANGES:** 1½ Starch, 3 Medium-Fat Meat OR 1½ Carbohydrate, 3 Medium-Fat Meat

Beef Stroganoff with Parsley Noodles

PREP TIME: 40 MINUTES ◆ YIELD: 6 SERVINGS

  8 oz. (4 cups) uncooked medium egg noodles
  1 teaspoon dried parsley flakes
  3 tablespoons margarine or butter
  1 (8-oz.) pkg. fresh whole mushrooms, sliced
  ½ cup chopped onion
  1 garlic clove, minced
  1 lb. boneless beef sirloin steak, cut into 1-inch strips
  1 (10½-oz.) can condensed beef consommé
  2 tablespoons ketchup
  ½ teaspoon salt, if desired
  3 tablespoons all-purpose flour
  1 cup sour cream

1. Cook noodles to desired doneness as directed on package. Drain. Add parsley and 1 tablespoon of the margarine; toss to combine. Cover to keep warm.

2. Meanwhile, in large nonstick skillet over medium heat, melt 1 tablespoon of the remaining margarine. Add mushrooms, onion and garlic; cook 2 to 3 minutes or until tender. Remove mushroom mixture; set aside.

3. In same skillet, melt remaining 1 tablespoon margarine. Add beef; cook and stir until browned. Reserve ⅓ cup of the beef consommé. Add remaining consommé, ketchup, salt and mushroom mixture to skillet; mix well.

4. In small jar with tight-fitting lid, combine reserved consommé and flour; shake well to blend. Gradually add to beef mixture, stirring constantly. Cook and stir until thickened. Stir in sour cream; cook until thoroughly heated. DO NOT BOIL. Serve over parsley noodles.

NUTRITION INFORMATION PER SERVING: Serving Size: ⅙ of Recipe ◆ Calories: 420 ◆ Calories from Fat: 170 ◆ **% DAILY VALUE:** Total Fat: 19 g 29% ◆ Saturated Fat: 8 g 40% ◆ Cholesterol: 95 mg 32% ◆ Sodium: 630 mg 26% ◆ Total Carbohydrate: 37 g 12% ◆ Dietary Fiber: 2 g 8% ◆ Sugars: 5 g ◆ Protein: 24 g ◆ Vitamin A: 15% ◆ Vitamin C: 4% ◆ Calcium: 8% ◆ Iron: 25% ◆ **DIETARY EXCHANGES:** 2½ Starch, 2½ Lean Meat, 2 Fat OR 2½ Carbohydrate, 2½ Lean Meat, 2 Fat

Lazy-Day Overnight Lasagna

PREP TIME: 20 MINUTES (READY IN 13 HOURS 35 MINUTES) ◆ YIELD: 12 SERVINGS

  1 lb. ground beef or mild Italian sausage
  1 (28-oz.) jar spaghetti sauce
  1 cup water
  1 (15-oz.) container ricotta cheese
  2 tablespoons chopped fresh chives
  ½ teaspoon dried oregano leaves
  1 egg
  8 oz. uncooked lasagna noodles
  1 (16-oz.) pkg. sliced mozzarella cheese
  2 tablespoons grated Parmesan cheese

1. In large skillet, cook ground beef over medium heat for 8 to 10 minutes or until thoroughly cooked, stirring frequently. Drain well. Add spaghetti sauce and water; blend well.

2. In medium bowl, combine ricotta cheese, chives, oregano and egg; mix well.

3. In ungreased 13×9-inch (3-quart) baking dish or lasagna pan, spread 1½ cups of the meat sauce. Top with half each of noodles, ricotta cheese mixture and mozzarella cheese. Repeat with 1½ cups meat sauce and remaining noodles, ricotta cheese mixture and mozzarella cheese. Top with remaining meat sauce. Sprinkle with Parmesan cheese. Cover; refrigerate 12 hours or overnight.

4. Heat oven to 350°F. Uncover baking dish; bake 50 to 60 minutes or until noodles are tender and casserole is bubbly. Cover; let stand 15 minutes before serving.

Beef Stroganoff with Parsley Noodles (page 112)

Quick Hungarian Goulash

PREP TIME: 30 MINUTES ✦ YIELD: 4 (1¼-CUP) SERVINGS

    1   tablespoon oil
    1   lb. boneless beef sirloin steak, cut into thin
           strips
    1   medium onion, coarsely chopped
    1   medium green bell pepper, coarsely chopped
 1½   cups water
    1   (14.5 or 16-oz.) can diced tomatoes,
           undrained
    1   (8-oz.) can tomato sauce
    1   teaspoon sugar
    3   teaspoons paprika
   ½   teaspoon salt
   ½   teaspoon caraway seed
   ¼   teaspoon pepper
    4   oz. (1½ cups) uncooked rotini (spiral pasta)

1. Heat oil in 12-inch skillet or Dutch oven over medium-high heat until hot. Add beef strips; cook and stir 3 to 5 minutes or until browned.
2. Add all remaining ingredients except rotini; mix well. Bring to a boil. Add rotini. Reduce heat to medium; cook uncovered 10 to 15 minutes or until rotini is tender, stirring occasionally.

NUTRITION INFORMATION PER SERVING: Serving Size: 1¼ Cups ✦ Calories: 330 ✦ Calories from Fat: 80 ✦ **% DAILY VALUE:** Total Fat: 9 g 14% ✦ Saturated Fat: 2 g 10% ✦ Cholesterol: 60 mg 20% ✦ Sodium: 830 mg 35% ✦ Total Carbohydrate: 36 g 12% ✦ Dietary Fiber: 4 g 16% ✦ Sugars: 8 g ✦ Protein: 27 g ✦ Vitamin A: 45% ✦ Vitamin C: 50% ✦ Calcium: 6% ✦ Iron: 30% ✦ **DIETARY EXCHANGES:** 2 Starch, 1 Vegetable, 2½ Lean Meat OR 2 Carbohydrate, 1 Vegetable, 2½ Lean Meat

Swiss Steak

PREP TIME: 15 MINUTES (READY IN 1 HOUR 45 MINUTES)
✦ YIELD: 6 SERVINGS

   ¼   cup all-purpose flour
    1   teaspoon salt
   ¼   teaspoon pepper
    2   to 2½ lb. beef round steak (½ to ¾ inch
           thick), cut into serving-sized pieces
    1   to 2 tablespoons oil
    1   large onion, sliced
    1   (8-oz.) can whole tomatoes, undrained, cut
           up*
    1   (8-oz.) can tomato sauce*

1. In small bowl, combine flour, salt and pepper; mix well. Coat beef with flour mixture, using all of mixture.
2. Heat oil in large skillet over medium-high heat until hot. Add beef; cook until browned.
3. Add all remaining ingredients. Bring to a boil. Reduce heat to low; cover and simmer 1¼ to 1½ hours or until beef is tender. If desired, serve with hot cooked potatoes or noodles.

TIPS: * One 10¾-oz. can condensed tomato soup and ½ cup water can be substituted for tomatoes and tomato sauce.
   Mushrooms, peas or green beans can be added to recipe. Add mushrooms with onion; add peas and green beans during last 10 to 15 minutes of cooking.

NUTRITION INFORMATION PER SERVING: Serving Size: ⅙ of Recipe ✦ Calories: 110 ✦ Calories from Fat: 45 ✦ **% DAILY VALUE:** Total Fat: 5 g 8% ✦ Saturated Fat: 1 g 5% ✦ Cholesterol: 0 mg 0% ✦ Sodium: 740 mg 31% ✦ Total Carbohydrate: 14 g 5% ✦ Dietary Fiber: 2 g 8% ✦ Sugars: 5 g ✦ Protein: 2 g ✦ Vitamin A: 15% ✦ Vitamin C: 15% ✦ Calcium: 4% ✦ Iron: 6% ✦ **DIETARY EXCHANGES:** 1 Starch, 4½ Lean Meat OR 1 Carbohydrate, 4½ Lean Meat

Swiss Steak

Paprika Beef

PREP TIME: 35 MINUTES ✦ YIELD: 4 SERVINGS

    8 oz. (5 cups) uncooked wide egg noodles
    1 tablespoon olive or vegetable oil
    1 lb. boneless beef sirloin steak, cut into thin
        bite-sized strips
    1 (8-oz.) pkg. (3 cups) sliced fresh mushrooms
    1 large onion, sliced
    2 garlic cloves, minced
    3 teaspoons paprika
    1 (8-oz.) can tomato sauce
    ¼ cup sour cream
    1 teaspoon all-purpose flour
    2 tablespoons chopped fresh parsley

1. Cook noodles to desired doneness as directed on package. Drain; cover to keep warm.

2. Meanwhile, heat oil in large skillet over medium-high heat until hot. If desired, sprinkle beef strips with salt and pepper. Add half of beef to skillet; cook and stir 3 to 4 minutes or until browned. Remove beef; set aside. Repeat with remaining beef strips; remove from skillet.

3. Add mushrooms, onion and garlic to skillet; cook and stir over medium heat for 2 to 3 minutes or until vegetables are tender. Return beef to skillet. Add paprika; mix well. Cook 1 minute. Stir in tomato sauce.

4. In small bowl, combine sour cream and flour. Add to beef mixture; cook 1 minute or until thoroughly heated. If mixture becomes too thick, stir in 1 to 2 tablespoons water.

5. Add parsley to cooked noodles; toss well. Serve beef mixture over noodles.

NUTRITION INFORMATION PER SERVING: Serving Size: ¼ of Recipe ✦ Calories: 470 ✦ Calories from Fat: 130 ✦ **% DAILY VALUE:** Total Fat: 14 g 22% ✦ Saturated Fat: 5 g 25% ✦ Cholesterol: 120 mg 40% ✦ Sodium: 410 mg 17% ✦ Total Carbohydrate: 54 g 18% ✦ Dietary Fiber: 4 g 16% ✦ Sugars: 8 g ✦ Protein: 32 g ✦ Vitamin A: 35% ✦ Vitamin C: 20% ✦ Calcium: 8% ✦ Iron: 35% ✦ **DIETARY EXCHANGES:** 3 Starch, 2 Vegetable, 2½ Lean Meat, 1 Fat OR 3 Carbohydrate, 2 Vegetable, 2½ Lean Meat, 1 Fat

Stuffed Green Peppers

PREP TIME: 35 MINUTES (READY IN 1 HOUR 15 MINUTES) ✦ YIELD: 4 SERVINGS

    ⅓ cup uncooked regular long-grain white rice
    ⅔ cup water
    4 large green bell peppers
    1 lb. ground beef
    ¼ cup chopped celery
    2 tablespoons chopped onion
    ½ teaspoon salt
        Dash pepper
    ¼ cup ketchup
    1 medium tomato, chopped
    1 (8-oz.) can tomato sauce
    1 teaspoon sugar
    ¼ teaspoon dried basil leaves
    1 oz. (¼ cup) shredded Cheddar cheese

1. Cook rice in water as directed on package.

2. Meanwhile, heat oven to 350°F. Cut tops from bell peppers; remove membrane and seeds. In large saucepan, bring enough water to cover peppers to a boil. Add peppers; cook over medium heat for 5 minutes. Drain; set peppers aside.

3. In large skillet, combine ground beef, celery and onion; cook 8 to 10 minutes or until beef is thoroughly cooked, stirring frequently. Drain.

4. Add cooked rice, salt, pepper, ketchup and tomato; mix well. Spoon mixture into peppers. Place peppers in ungreased shallow baking pan.

5. In small bowl, combine tomato sauce, sugar and basil; mix well. Spoon half of sauce over peppers.

6. Bake at 350°F. for 30 to 40 minutes or until peppers are tender, spooning remaining sauce over peppers and sprinkling with cheese during last 5 minutes of baking.

NUTRITION INFORMATION PER SERVING: Serving Size: ¼ of Recipe ✦ Calories: 380 ✦ Calories from Fat: 170 ✦ **% DAILY VALUE:** Total Fat: 19 g 29% ✦ Saturated Fat: 8 g 40% ✦ Cholesterol: 75 mg 25% ✦ Sodium: 910 mg 38% ✦ Total Carbohydrate: 29 g 10% ✦ Dietary Fiber: 4 g 16% ✦ Sugars: 9 g ✦ Protein: 23 g ✦ Vitamin A: 35% ✦ Vitamin C: 130% ✦ Calcium: 10% ✦ Iron: 20% ✦ **DIETARY EXCHANGES:** 1½ Starch, 1 Vegetable, 2½ Medium-Fat Meat, 1 Fat OR 1½ Carbohydrate, 1 Vegetable, 2½ Medium-Fat Meat, 1 Fat

VARIATION

Stuffed Cabbage Leaves: Heat oven to 350°F. In large saucepan, cook 12 large cabbage leaves in boiling water for 5 minutes. Drain; set aside. Prepare beef mixture as directed above, adding *1 egg* with rice. Divide mixture onto cabbage leaves. Fold edges of each leaf in; roll filling inside. Secure with toothpicks. Place rolls in ungreased 13×9-inch (2-quart) baking dish. In small bowl, combine tomato sauce, sugar and basil; mix well. Spoon over cabbage rolls. Cover with foil. Bake at 350°F. for 40 to 50 minutes or until thoroughly heated. Remove foil; sprinkle with *4 oz. (1 cup)* shredded Cheddar cheese. Return to oven; bake until cheese is melted.   YIELD: 6 SERVINGS

Pepper Steak

PREP TIME: 30 MINUTES ◆ YIELD: 4 SERVINGS

  2 cups uncooked instant rice, if desired
  2 cups water
  1 cup beef broth
  ¼ cup hoisin sauce
  1 tablespoon cornstarch
  ¼ to ½ teaspoon coarse ground black pepper
  3 tablespoons ketchup
  1 tablespoon rice vinegar
  ½ teaspoon Worcestershire sauce
  1 tablespoon oil
  1 lb. beef flank or boneless top sirloin steak, thinly sliced
  1 medium onion, cut into 8 pieces
  1 medium green bell pepper, cut into strips
  1 medium red bell pepper, cut into strips
  1 medium yellow bell pepper, cut into strips

1. Cook rice in water as directed on package.
2. Meanwhile, in small bowl, combine broth, hoisin sauce, cornstarch, pepper, ketchup, vinegar and Worcestershire sauce; blend well. Set aside.
3. Heat oil in large skillet or wok over medium-high heat until hot. Add beef and onion; cook and stir 2 to 3 minutes or until beef is no longer pink. Add bell peppers and cornstarch mixture; cook and stir 2 to 3 minutes or until vegetables are crisp-tender and sauce is bubbly and thickened. Serve over rice.

NUTRITION INFORMATION PER SERVING: Serving Size: ¼ of Recipe ◆ Calories: 480 ◆ Calories from Fat: 120 ◆ **% DAILY VALUE:** Total Fat: 13 g 20% ◆ Saturated Fat: 4 g 20% ◆ Cholesterol: 45 mg 15% ◆ Sodium: 690 mg 29% ◆ Total Carbohydrate: 66 g 22% ◆ Dietary Fiber: 3 g 12% ◆ Sugars: 13 g ◆ Protein: 24 g ◆ Vitamin A: 35% ◆ Vitamin C: 140% ◆ Calcium: 4% ◆ Iron: 30% ◆ **DIETARY EXCHANGES:** 3 Starch, 1 Fruit, 1 Vegetable, 2 Medium-Fat Meat OR 4 Carbohydrate, 1 Vegetable, 2 Medium-Fat Meat

Parmesan Chicken-Fried Steak

PREP TIME: 30 MINUTES ◆ YIELD: 4 SERVINGS

STEAK
  ⅓ cup all-purpose flour
  ½ teaspoon salt
  ½ teaspoon garlic powder
  ¼ teaspoon pepper
  ⅓ cup milk
  ⅓ cup unseasoned dry bread crumbs
  ⅓ cup grated Parmesan cheese
  ½ teaspoon dried oregano leaves
  1 lb. boneless beef round steak (½ inch thick), cut into 4 pieces
  3 tablespoons oil

GRAVY
  1 tablespoon butter
  1 tablespoon all-purpose flour
  1 cup half-and-half or milk
  ¼ teaspoon salt
  ¼ teaspoon coarse ground black pepper

1. In shallow dish, combine ⅓ cup flour, ½ teaspoon salt, garlic powder and ¼ teaspoon pepper; mix well. Place milk in second shallow dish. In third shallow dish, combine bread crumbs, cheese and oregano; mix well.
2. Place 1 steak piece between 2 pieces of plastic wrap or waxed paper. Working from center, pound steak pieces with flat side of meat mallet or rolling pin until about ¼ inch thick; remove wrap. Repeat with remaining steak pieces. Dip each in flour mixture to coat. Dip in milk; dip in bread crumb mixture to coat.
3. Heat oil in large skillet over medium heat until hot. Add steak; cook 10 to 15 minutes or until tender, turning once. Remove steak from skillet; cover to keep warm.
4. To make gravy, melt butter in same skillet. With wire whisk, stir in 1 tablespoon flour; cook until light brown. Add all remaining gravy ingredients; cook and stir over medium heat until bubbly and thickened. Serve gravy over steak.

NUTRITION INFORMATION PER SERVING: Serving Size: ¼ of Recipe ◆ Calories: 450 ◆ Calories from Fat: 250 ◆ **% DAILY VALUE:** Total Fat: 28 g 43% ◆ Saturated Fat: 11 g 55% ◆ Cholesterol: 95 mg 32% ◆ Sodium: 700 mg 29% ◆ Total Carbohydrate: 20 g 7% ◆ Dietary Fiber: 1 g 3% ◆ Sugars: 4 g ◆ Protein: 30 g ◆ Vitamin A: 10% ◆ Vitamin C: 0% ◆ Calcium: 20% ◆ Iron: 20% ◆ **DIETARY EXCHANGES:** 1½ Starch, 3½ Lean Meat, 3 Fat OR 1½ Carbohydrate, 3½ Lean Meat, 3 Fat

Pepper Corned Beef Hash

Pepper Corned Beef Hash

PREP TIME: 30 MINUTES ◆ YIELD: 4 (1-CUP) SERVINGS

    1 tablespoon oil
    2 cups cubed cooked corned beef*
    2 cups frozen hash-brown potatoes
    ½ cup chopped green bell pepper
    ½ cup chopped red bell pepper
    ½ cup chopped onion
    ¼ teaspoon pepper

1. Heat oil in large nonstick skillet over medium heat until hot. Add all remaining ingredients; mix well.
2. Cook 10 to 15 minutes or until bell peppers are tender and mixture is thoroughly heated, stirring occasionally.

TIP: * One 12-oz. can corned beef, cubed, can be substituted for the corned beef.

NUTRITION INFORMATION PER SERVING: Serving Size: 1 Cup ◆ Calories: 300 ◆ Calories from Fat: 150 ◆ **% DAILY VALUE:** Total Fat: 17 g 26% ◆ Saturated Fat: 5 g 25% ◆ Cholesterol: 70 mg 23% ◆ Sodium: 820 mg 34% ◆ Total Carbohydrate: 22 g 7% ◆ Dietary Fiber: 2 g 8% ◆ Sugars: 2 g ◆ Protein: 15 g ◆ Vitamin A: 15% ◆ Vitamin C: 50% ◆ Calcium: 2% ◆ Iron: 15% ◆ **DIETARY EXCHANGES:** 1 Starch, 2 Medium-Fat Meat, 1½ Fat OR 1 Carbohydrate, 2 Medium-Fat Meat, 1½ Fat

Mom's Skillet Goulash

PREP TIME: 35 MINUTES ◆ YIELD: 6 (1⅓-CUP) SERVINGS

     8 oz. (2½ cups) uncooked rotini (spiral pasta)
     1 lb. ground beef
    1½ cups chopped celery
     1 cup chopped onions
     2 (14.5 or 16-oz.) cans whole tomatoes,
        undrained, cut up
     1 (10¾-oz.) can condensed tomato soup
     1 teaspoon dried basil leaves
     ½ teaspoon salt
     ¼ teaspoon pepper

1. Cook rotini to desired doneness as directed on package. Drain.
2. Meanwhile, in large saucepan or Dutch oven, combine ground beef, celery and onions. Cook over medium heat for 8 to 10 minutes or until beef is thoroughly cooked, stirring frequently. Drain.
3. Add cooked rotini and all remaining ingredients; mix well. Cook 10 to 15 minutes or until thoroughly heated, stirring occasionally.

NUTRITION INFORMATION PER SERVING: Serving Size: 1⅓ Cups ◆ Calories: 370 ◆ Calories from Fat: 110 ◆ **% DAILY VALUE:** Total Fat: 12 g 18% ◆ Saturated Fat: 4 g 20% ◆ Cholesterol: 45 mg 15% ◆ Sodium: 750 mg 31% ◆ Total Carbohydrate: 45 g 15% ◆ Dietary Fiber: 4 g 16% ◆ Sugars: 9 g ◆ Protein: 20 g ◆ Vitamin A: 25% ◆ Vitamin C: 60% ◆ Calcium: 8% ◆ Iron: 25% ◆ **DIETARY EXCHANGES:** 2½ Starch, 1 Vegetable, 1½ Medium-Fat Meat, ½ Fat OR 2½ Carbohydrate, 1 Vegetable, 1½ Medium-Fat Meat, ½ Fat

Classic Beef Fajitas

PREP TIME: 25 MINUTES (READY IN 2 HOURS 25 MINUTES) ◆ YIELD: 4 FAJITAS

MARINADE
    2 tablespoons lime juice
    2 tablespoons honey
    1 tablespoon oil
    2 teaspoons chili powder
    2 garlic cloves, minced

FAJITAS
    ¾ lb. boneless beef top round steak,
        cut into thin strips
    1 onion, thinly sliced
    1 red or green bell pepper, cut into strips
    4 (8-inch) flour tortillas, heated
    ⅓ cup purchased guacamole
    ⅓ cup salsa

1. In medium glass bowl, combine all marinade ingredients; blend well. Add beef strips; stir to coat. Cover; refrigerate 2 to 3 hours to marinate, stirring occasionally.
2. Spray large nonstick skillet with nonstick cooking spray. Heat over medium-high heat until hot. Add beef and marinade; cook and stir 2 minutes. Add onion and bell pepper; cook and stir 2 to 3 minutes or until vegetables are crisp-tender and beef is no longer pink. Drain.
3. To serve, spoon ¼ of guacamole onto center of each tortilla. Top each with ¼ of beef mixture and salsa. Fold bottom edge of tortilla over filling toward center; fold sides in toward center, leaving top open.

NUTRITION INFORMATION PER SERVING: Serving Size: 1 Fajita ♦ Calories: 340 ♦ Calories from Fat: 100 ♦ % DAILY VALUE: Total Fat: 11 g 17% ♦ Saturated Fat: 3 g 15% ♦ Cholesterol: 40 mg 13% ♦ Sodium: 520 mg 22% ♦ Total Carbohydrate: 38 g 13% ♦ Dietary Fiber: 3 g 12% ♦ Sugars: 13 g ♦ Protein: 21 g ♦ Vitamin A: 30% ♦ Vitamin C: 45% ♦ Calcium: 6% ♦ Iron: 15% ♦ DIETARY EXCHANGES: 1½ Starch, 1 Fruit, 2½ Lean Meat, ½ Fat OR 2½ Carbohydrate, 2½ Lean Meat, ½ Fat

Italian Spaghetti with Meat Sauce

PREP TIME: 40 MINUTES ♦ YIELD: 8 SERVINGS

    1 (16-oz.) pkg. uncooked spaghetti
    1 lb. extra-lean ground beef
    1 cup chopped onions
    1 cup sliced fresh mushrooms
    ½ cup chopped green bell pepper
    2 garlic cloves, minced
    2 (6-oz.) cans tomato paste
    1 (15-oz.) can tomato sauce
    2 cups water
    3 teaspoons dried parsley flakes
    3 teaspoons dried Italian seasoning
 1½ teaspoons dried basil leaves
    ½ teaspoon sugar
    ½ teaspoon pepper
    ¾ teaspoon Worcestershire sauce
    ¼ cup grated Parmesan cheese, if desired

1. Cook spaghetti to desired doneness as directed on package. Drain; cover to keep warm.
2. Meanwhile, spray large skillet with nonstick cooking spray. Heat over medium heat until hot. Add ground beef, onions, mushrooms, bell pepper and garlic; cook 8 to

Classic Beef Fajitas (page 116)

10 minutes or until beef is thoroughly cooked, stirring frequently. Drain well.
3. Stir in tomato paste and tomato sauce; mix well. Gradually stir in water. Stir in parsley, Italian seasoning, basil, sugar, pepper and Worcestershire sauce. Bring to a boil. Reduce heat to low; cover and simmer 15 minutes, stirring occasionally.
4. Serve sauce over spaghetti; sprinkle with Parmesan cheese.

NUTRITION INFORMATION PER SERVING: Serving Size: ⅛ of Recipe ♦ Calories: 400 ♦ Calories from Fat: 80 ♦ % DAILY VALUE: Total Fat: 9 g 14% ♦ Saturated Fat: 3 g 15% ♦ Cholesterol: 40 mg 13% ♦ Sodium: 760 mg 32% ♦ Total Carbohydrate: 58 g 19% ♦ Dietary Fiber: 5 g 20% ♦ Sugars: 6 g ♦ Protein: 22 g ♦ Vitamin A: 35% ♦ Vitamin C: 40% ♦ Calcium: 10% ♦ Iron: 25% ♦ DIETARY EXCHANGES: 3 Starch, 2 Vegetable, 1½ Lean Meat, ½ Fat OR 3 Carbohydrate, 2 Vegetable, 1½ Lean Meat, ½ Fat

Main Dish Spanish Rice

PREP TIME: 20 MINUTES (READY IN 1 HOUR) ♦ YIELD: 5 (1-CUP) SERVINGS

    1 lb. ground beef
    6 slices bacon, cut into small pieces
    1 medium onion, thinly sliced
    ¼ cup chopped green bell pepper
    ¾ cup uncooked regular long-grain white rice
    ¼ cup ketchup
    1 (14.5 to 16-oz.) can whole tomatoes, undrained, cut up
    1 (8-oz.) can tomato sauce
    ½ teaspoon salt
    ⅛ teaspoon pepper
    2 drops hot pepper sauce

1. In large skillet, cook ground beef over medium heat for 8 to 10 minutes or until thoroughly cooked, stirring frequently. Drain well. Remove beef from skillet; set aside.
2. In same skillet, cook bacon until crisp. Remove bacon; drain on paper towel, reserving 2 tablespoons drippings in skillet.
3. Add onion and bell pepper to reserved drippings in skillet; cook and stir until crisp-tender. Add cooked ground beef, bacon and all remaining ingredients; mix well. Bring to a boil. Reduce heat to low; cover and simmer 30 to 40 minutes or until rice is tender.

NUTRITION INFORMATION PER SERVING: Serving Size: 1 Cup ♦ Calories: 380 ♦ Calories from Fat: 150 ♦ % DAILY VALUE: Total Fat: 17 g 26% ♦ Saturated Fat: 6 g 30% ♦ Cholesterol: 60 mg 20% ♦ Sodium: 940 mg 39% ♦ Total Carbohydrate: 35 g 12% ♦ Dietary Fiber: 3 g 12% ♦ Sugars: 6 g ♦ Protein: 21 g ♦ Vitamin A: 26% ♦ Vitamin C: 30% ♦ Calcium: 6% ♦ Iron: 20% ♦ DIETARY EXCHANGES: 2 Starch, 1 Vegetable, 2 Medium-Fat Meat, 1 Fat OR 2 Carbohydrate, 1 Vegetable, 2 Medium-Fat Meat, 1 Fat

Tater Nugget Hot Dish

PREP TIME: 20 MINUTES (READY IN 1 HOUR 10 MINUTES)
◆ YIELD: 6 (1¼-CUP) SERVINGS

 1 lb. ground beef
 ¾ cup chopped onions
 ½ cup chopped celery
 1 (10¾-oz.) can condensed cream of
    mushroom soup
 1 (10¾-oz.) can condensed cream of chicken
    soup
 ⅛ teaspoon garlic powder
 ⅛ teaspoon pepper
 1 cup frozen cut green beans, thawed
 1 (16-oz.) pkg. frozen potato nuggets

1. Heat oven to 375°F. In large saucepan, brown ground beef, onions and celery until beef is thoroughly cooked. Drain well.
2. Stir in soups, garlic powder, pepper and green beans. Spoon into ungreased 2-quart casserole. Top with potato nuggets.
3. Bake at 375°F. for 40 to 50 minutes or until casserole is bubbly and potato nuggets are golden brown.

NUTRITION INFORMATION PER SERVING: Serving Size: 1¼ Cups ◆ Calories: 430 ◆ Calories from Fat: 230 ◆ % DAILY VALUE: Total Fat: 25 g 38% ◆ Saturated Fat: 10 g 50% ◆ Cholesterol: 50 mg 17% ◆ Sodium: 1370 mg 57% ◆ Total Carbohydrate: 34 g 11% ◆ Dietary Fiber: 4 g 16% ◆ Sugars: 4 g ◆ Protein: 17 g ◆ Vitamin A: 6% ◆ Vitamin C: 10% ◆ Calcium: 6% ◆ Iron: 15% ◆ DIETARY EXCHANGES: 2 Starch, 1½ Medium-Fat Meat, 3½ Fat OR 2 Carbohydrate, 1½ Medium-Fat Meat, 3½ Fat

---

COOK'S NOTE

WELL DONE IS DONE WELL

Undercooked ground beef can cause food poisoning. Cook hamburgers and meatballs until no trace of pink remains. Ground beef has so much exposed surface area that it is more prone to bacterial contamination than whole cuts of meat. Cooking it thoroughly kills the bacteria.

Beef and Bean Burritos

PREP TIME: 25 MINUTES ◆ YIELD: 10 BURRITOS

 1 lb. ground beef
 1 medium onion, chopped
 1 cup refried beans (from 16-oz. can)
 ¼ cup taco sauce
 1½ teaspoons chili powder
 ½ teaspoon salt
 ¼ teaspoon pepper
 10 (7 or 8-inch) flour tortillas, heated
 1 cup shredded lettuce
 4 oz. (1 cup) shredded Cheddar cheese
 1 tomato, chopped
 ½ cup salsa, if desired

1. In large skillet, combine ground beef and onion; cook over medium heat for 8 to 10 minutes or until beef is thoroughly cooked, stirring frequently. Drain.
2. Stir in beans, taco sauce, chili powder, salt and pepper; mix well. Reduce heat to low; simmer 5 minutes.
3. Spoon about ¼ cup beef mixture onto center of each tortilla. Top each with lettuce, cheese and tomato. Fold bottom ⅓ of each tortilla over filling; fold sides in toward center, leaving top open. Serve with salsa.

NUTRITION INFORMATION PER SERVING: Serving Size: 1 Burrito ◆ Calories: 290 ◆ Calories from Fat: 120 ◆ % DAILY VALUE: Total Fat: 13 g 20% ◆ Saturated Fat: 5 g 25% ◆ Cholesterol: 40 mg 13% ◆ Sodium: 580 mg 24% ◆ Total Carbohydrate: 27 g 9% ◆ Dietary Fiber: 3 g 12% ◆ Sugars: 3 g ◆ Protein: 15 g ◆ Vitamin A: 8% ◆ Vitamin C: 8% ◆ Calcium: 15% ◆ Iron: 15% ◆ DIETARY EXCHANGES: 2 Starch, 1½ Medium-Fat Meat, ½ Fat OR 2 Carbohydrate, 1½ Medium-Fat Meat, ½ Fat

Basic Meatballs

PREP TIME: 30 MINUTES ◆ YIELD: 16 MEATBALLS

 1 lb. ground beef
 ¼ cup unseasoned dry bread or cracker
    crumbs
 ½ teaspoon salt
 ⅛ teaspoon pepper
 1 small onion, chopped
 1 egg
 1 tablespoon oil

1. In medium bowl, combine all ingredients except oil; mix well. Shape into 1½ to 2-inch meatballs.
2. Heat oil in large skillet over medium-high heat until hot. Add meatballs; cook

10 to 12 minutes or until thoroughly cooked, turning occasionally. Drain.

> **TIP:** To bake meatballs in oven, arrange in ungreased 15 x 10 x 1-inch baking pan; bake at 400°F. for 15 minutes or until thoroughly cooked.

NUTRITION INFORMATION PER SERVING: Serving Size: 4 Meatballs • Calories: 300 • Calories from Fat: 190 • **% DAILY VALUE:** Total Fat: 21 g 32% • Saturated Fat: 7 g 35% • Cholesterol: 120 mg 40% • Sodium: 400 mg 17% • Total Carbohydrate: 6 g 2% • Dietary Fiber: 0 g 0% • Sugars: 1 g • Protein: 21 g • Vitamin A: 0% • Vitamin C: 0% • Calcium: 4% • Iron: 15% • **DIETARY EXCHANGES:** ½ Starch, 3 Medium-Fat Meat, 1 Fat OR ½ Carbohydrate, 3 Medium-Fat Meat, 1 Fat

VARIATIONS

Cocktail Meatballs: Shape into 1-inch meatballs; continue as directed above.
YIELD: 24 MEATBALLS

Speedy Swedish Meatballs: In large skillet, combine cooked meatballs with one 10¾-oz. can condensed cream of mushroom or chicken soup, ¼ cup water or milk and ⅛ teaspoon nutmeg or allspice. Cover; simmer 15 minutes, stirring occasionally. YIELD: 4 SERVINGS

Liver, Bacon and Onions

PREP TIME: 25 MINUTES ♦ YIELD: 4 SERVINGS

　1　lb. beef liver
　¼　cup all-purpose flour
　½　teaspoon salt
　⅛　teaspoon pepper
　4　slices bacon
　2　medium onions, sliced

1. Cut liver into serving-sized pieces. In shallow bowl, combine flour, salt and pepper; mix well. Coat liver with flour mixture.
2. In large skillet, cook bacon over medium heat until crisp. Remove bacon; drain on paper towel, reserving drippings in skillet.
3. Add liver and onions to skillet; cook 2 to 3 minutes on each side or until thoroughly cooked. Serve topped with crisp bacon.

NUTRITION INFORMATION PER SERVING: Serving Size: ¼ of Recipe • Calories: 220 • Calories from Fat: 60 • **% DAILY VALUE:** Total Fat: 7 g 11% • Saturated Fat: 3 g 15% • Cholesterol: 330 mg 110% • Sodium: 430 mg 18% • Total Carbohydrate: 14 g 5% • Dietary Fiber: 1 g 4% • Sugars: 3 g • Protein: 24 g • Vitamin A: 600% • Vitamin C: 25% • Calcium: 0% • Iron: 35% • **DIETARY EXCHANGES:** ½ Starch, 1 Vegetable, 3 Lean Meat OR ½ Carbohydrate, 1 Vegetable, 3 Lean Meat

French Dip Sandwiches

PREP TIME: 15 MINUTES ♦ YIELD: 6 SANDWICHES

1½　lb. sliced cooked roast beef
1½　cups water
　2　beef-flavored bouillon cubes
　　　or ½ cup beef pan drippings
　1　teaspoon instant minced onion
　½　teaspoon soy sauce
12　slices crusty French bread or 6 sandwich buns, split

1. In medium saucepan, combine beef, water and bouillon. Cook over medium heat until thoroughly heated, stirring occasionally. Add onion and soy sauce. Cook 2 to 3 minutes.
2. Serve between slices of crusty French bread or in sandwich buns. Individual portions of bouillon mixture (au jus) can be served for dipping sandwiches.

NUTRITION INFORMATION PER SERVING: Serving Size: 1 Sandwich • Calories: 270 • Calories from Fat: 60 • **% DAILY VALUE:** Total Fat: 7 g 11% • Saturated Fat: 2 g 10% • Cholesterol: 65 mg 22% • Sodium: 660 mg 28% • Total Carbohydrate: 26 g 9% • Dietary Fiber: 2 g 8% • Sugars: 2 g • Protein: 25 g • Vitamin A: 0% • Vitamin C: 0% • Calcium: 4% • Iron: 20% • **DIETARY EXCHANGES:** 1½ Starch, 3 Lean Meat OR 1½ Carbohydrate, 3 Lean Meat

---

COOK'S NOTE

LIGHTEN UP

If you love beef but are cutting back on dietary fat, here are a few tips:

♦ Choose leaner cuts, and use low-fat techniques such as marinating or moist cooking methods to improve tenderness and flavor.

♦ Trim away visible fat before cooking.

♦ Savor a smaller portion. Instead of serving a slab of meat to each person, use 3 to 4 ounces per serving and include several side dishes in the menu.

♦ Choose a recipe that mingles a small amount of meat with other hearty ingredients, such as pasta, rice or vegetables, so the meal will be satisfying with less meat.

Tangy Barbecued Beef Sandwiches

Philly Beef Steak Sandwiches

PREP TIME: 20 MINUTES ✦ YIELD: 4 SANDWICHES

½ lb. boneless beef sirloin steak, cut into thin
    strips
1 large onion, halved lengthwise, sliced
    (1½ cups)
1 green, red or yellow bell pepper, cut into
    bite-sized strips
2 tablespoons lite soy sauce
1½ teaspoons Worcestershire sauce
¼ teaspoon cornstarch
2 oz. (½ cup) shredded sharp Cheddar cheese
4 hoagie buns, split, heated*

1. Spray large nonstick skillet with nonstick cooking spray. Heat over medium-high heat until hot. Add beef and onion; cook 3 to 4 minutes or until beef is browned, stirring occasionally.
2. Add bell pepper; cook 1 to 2 minutes or until crisp-tender. In small bowl, combine soy sauce, Worcestershire sauce and corn-starch; blend well. Stir into mixture in skillet; cook until thickened.
3. Sprinkle cheese evenly onto bottom halves of buns. Top each with beef mixture and top halves of buns.

> **TIP:** *To heat buns, wrap in foil. Heat at 400°F. for 5 to 8 minutes or until hot.

NUTRITION INFORMATION PER SERVING: Serving Size: 1 Sandwich ✦ Calories: 430 ✦ Calories from Fat: 110 ✦ **% DAILY VALUE:** Total Fat: 12 g 18% ✦ Saturated Fat: 5 g 25% ✦ Cholesterol: 45 mg 15% ✦ Sodium: 1060 mg 44% ✦ Total Carbohydrate: 57 g 19% ✦ Dietary Fiber: 4 g 16% ✦ Sugars: 5 g ✦ Protein: 24 g ✦ Vitamin A: 6% ✦ Vitamin C: 25% ✦ Calcium: 20% ✦ Iron: 25% ✦ **DIETARY EXCHANGES:** 3½ Starch, 1 Vegetable, 1½ Medium-Fat Meat, ½ Fat OR 3½ Carbohydrate, 1 Vegetable, 1½ Medium-Fat Meat, ½ Fat

Tangy Barbecued Beef Sandwiches

PREP TIME: 15 MINUTES (READY IN 6 HOURS 15 MINUTES) ✦ YIELD: 22 SANDWICHES

1 (3½ to 4-lb.) boneless beef chuck roast,
    cut crosswise into ¼-inch slices*
1 cup chopped onions
4 garlic cloves, minced
½ cup firmly packed brown sugar
2 teaspoons dry mustard
1 teaspoon chili powder
1 teaspoon paprika
⅓ cup vinegar
⅓ cup Worcestershire sauce
3 tablespoons lemon juice
1¾ cups ketchup
22 sandwich buns, split

1. In 3½ to 4-quart slow cooker, combine all ingredients except buns; mix well.
2. Cover; cook on low setting for 5 to 6 hours or until beef is tender, stirring occasionally. Serve in buns.

> **TIPS:** *To make slicing beef easier, freeze 20 to 30 minutes or until firm, but not frozen.
>   To cook beef mixture on stove top, combine all ingredients in Dutch oven. Bring to a boil. Reduce heat; simmer 2½ to 3 hours.

NUTRITION INFORMATION PER SERVING: Serving Size: 1 Sandwich ✦ Calories: 270 ✦ Calories from Fat: 50 ✦ **% DAILY VALUE:** Total Fat: 6 g 9% ✦ Saturated Fat: 2 g 10% ✦ Cholesterol: 45 mg 15% ✦ Sodium: 570 mg 24% ✦ Total Carbohydrate: 34 g 11% ✦ Dietary Fiber: 2 g 8% ✦ Sugars: 13 g ✦ Protein: 19 g ✦ Vitamin A: 6% ✦ Vitamin C: 6% ✦ Calcium: 8% ✦ Iron: 20% ✦ **DIETARY EXCHANGES:** 2 Starch, 2 Lean Meat OR 2 Carbohydrate, 2 Lean Meat

COOK'S NOTE

FREEZING MEAT

Beef and veal freeze well. For easiest defrosting, freeze single portions individually, such as burgers and small steaks. Wrap them in plastic wrap, then put them into a resealable plastic freezer bag for extra protection and to prevent stray burgers from getting lost at the back of the freezer. Label and date each package.

Sloppy Joes

PREP TIME: 40 MINUTES ✦ YIELD: 6 SANDWICHES

    1 lb. lean ground beef
 1/2 cup chopped green bell pepper or celery
 1/2 cup chopped onion
    1 tablespoon brown sugar
    1 teaspoon dry mustard
 1/4 teaspoon salt
 1/8 teaspoon pepper
 1/2 cup ketchup
    1 tablespoon vinegar
    1 tablespoon Worcestershire sauce
    1 (8-oz.) can tomato sauce
    6 sandwich buns, split

1. In large skillet, combine ground beef, bell pepper and onion; cook over medium heat for 8 to 10 minutes or until beef is thoroughly cooked, stirring frequently. Drain well.

2. Add all remaining ingredients except buns; mix well. Cover; simmer 15 to 20 minutes, stirring occasionally. Serve in buns.

NUTRITION INFORMATION PER SERVING: Serving Size: 1 Sandwich ✦ Calories: 320 ✦ Calories from Fat: 110 ✦ % DAILY VALUE: Total Fat: 12 g 18% ✦ Saturated Fat: 4 g 20% ✦ Cholesterol: 45 mg 15% ✦ Sodium: 900 mg 38% ✦ Total Carbohydrate: 35 g 12% ✦ Dietary Fiber: 2 g 8% ✦ Sugars: 12 g ✦ Protein: 18 g ✦ Vitamin A: 15% ✦ Vitamin C: 20% ✦ Calcium: 8% ✦ Iron: 15% ✦ DIETARY EXCHANGES: 1½ Starch, 1 Fruit, 2 Medium-Fat Meat OR 2½ Carbohydrate, 2 Medium-Fat Meat

Grilled Italian Steak and Vegetable Sandwiches

Grilled Italian Steak and Vegetable Sandwiches

PREP TIME: 30 MINUTES (READY IN 8 HOURS 30 MINUTES) ✦ YIELD: 6 SANDWICHES

 1/2 cup red wine vinegar
 1/2 cup oil
    3 garlic cloves, minced
    2 tablespoons chopped fresh parsley
        or 2 teaspoons dried parsley flakes
    2 tablespoons chopped fresh oregano
        or 2 teaspoons dried oregano leaves
    2 tablespoons chopped fresh basil
        or 2 teaspoons dried basil leaves
 1/2 teaspoon coarse ground black pepper
    1 (3/4-lb.) boneless beef sirloin steak
    1 onion, cut into thick wedges
    1 small eggplant (about 8 oz.), cut
        into 1/8-inch-thick slices
    1 red bell pepper, seeded, cut
        into 1/2-inch-thick rings
    6 hoagie buns, split
    6 green leaf lettuce leaves

1. GRILL DIRECTIONS: In large glass bowl or resealable food storage plastic bag, combine vinegar, oil, garlic, parsley, oregano, basil and pepper; mix well. Add steak, onion, eggplant and bell pepper; toss gently to combine. Cover; refrigerate 8 hours or overnight to marinate.

2. Heat grill. Drain off and discard marinade. Arrange vegetables in grill basket.* When ready to grill, place steak and grill basket on gas grill over medium heat or on charcoal grill 4 to 6 inches from medium coals. Cook 8 to 12 minutes or until steak is of desired doneness and vegetables are crisp-tender, turning once.

3. Meanwhile, place buns, cut side down, on grill. Cook 1 to 2 minutes or until lightly toasted. To serve, cut steak into very thin slices. Layer lettuce, steak and vegetables in toasted buns.

TIP: * Grill baskets can be found with the grilling accessories at your local department or discount store.

NUTRITION INFORMATION PER SERVING: Serving Size: 1 Sandwich ✦ Calories: 400 ✦ Calories from Fat: 90 ✦ % DAILY VALUE: Total Fat: 10 g 15% ✦ Saturated Fat: 2 g 10% ✦ Cholesterol: 30 mg 10% ✦ Sodium: 630 mg 26% ✦ Total Carbohydrate: 57 g 19% ✦ Dietary Fiber: 5 g 20% ✦ Sugars: 7 g ✦ Protein: 20 g ✦ Vitamin A: 20% ✦ Vitamin C: 30% ✦ Calcium: 10% ✦ Iron: 20% ✦ DIETARY EXCHANGES: 3½ Starch, 1 Vegetable, 1 Lean Meat, 1 Fat OR 3½ Carbohydrate, 1 Vegetable, 1 Lean Meat, 1 Fat

Veal Scaloppine with Marsala Sauce

PREP TIME: 20 MINUTES ✦ YIELD: 6 SERVINGS

  6 veal cutlets (about 1½ lb.)
  2 tablespoons all-purpose flour
  2 tablespoons unseasoned dry bread crumbs
  ¼ teaspoon salt
  2 teaspoons oil
  ½ cup sweet Marsala wine
  2 tablespoons chopped fresh parsley

1. Place 1 veal cutlet between 2 pieces of plastic wrap or waxed paper. Working from center, gently pound cutlet with flat side of meat mallet or rolling pin until about ¼ inch thick; remove wrap. Repeat with remaining cutlets.
2. In pie pan or shallow dish, combine flour, bread crumbs and salt; mix well. Lightly coat cutlets with flour mixture.
3. Heat oil in large skillet over medium-high heat until hot. Add cutlets; cook about 1 minute on each side or until browned. Remove from skillet; cover to keep warm.
4. Add wine to skillet; bring to a boil. Cook 1 to 2 minutes or until wine is slightly reduced. Serve wine sauce over veal; sprinkle with parsley.

NUTRITION INFORMATION PER SERVING: Serving Size: ⅙ of Recipe ✦ Calories: 170 ✦ Calories from Fat: 45 ✦ % DAILY VALUE: Total Fat: 5 g 8% ✦ Saturated Fat: 2 g 10% ✦ Cholesterol: 95 mg 32% ✦ Sodium: 270 mg 11% ✦ Total Carbohydrate: 5 g 2% ✦ Dietary Fiber: 0 g 0% ✦ Sugars: 1 g ✦ Protein: 26 g ✦ Vitamin A: 0% ✦ Vitamin C: 0% ✦ Calcium: 0% ✦ Iron: 6% ✦ DIETARY EXCHANGES: 3 Lean Meat

Veal Roast

1. Allow ⅓ to ½ lb. per serving for bone-in roast and ¼ to ⅓ per serving for boneless roast. Heat oven to 325°F. Place roast, fat side up, in shallow roasting pan. If desired, sprinkle with salt and pepper. Insert meat thermometer so bulb reaches center of thickest part of meat, but does not rest in fat or on bone. Do not add water or cover.
2. Bake at 325°F. using "Timetable for Roasting Veal," below. Roast can be basted occasionally with additional margarine or pan drippings to add moistness.

NUTRITION INFORMATION PER SERVING: Serving Size: 4 oz. Cooked Veal ✦ Calories: 210 ✦ Calories from Fat: 60 ✦ % DAILY VALUE: Total Fat: 7 g 11% ✦ Saturated Fat: 2 g 10% ✦ Cholesterol: 135 mg 45% ✦ Sodium: 100 mg 4% ✦ Total Carbohydrate: 0 g 0% ✦ Dietary Fiber: 0 g 0% ✦ Sugars: 0 g ✦ Protein: 36 g ✦ Vitamin A: 0% ✦ Vitamin C: 0% ✦ Calcium: 2% ✦ Iron: 8% ✦ DIETARY EXCHANGES: 5 Very Lean Meat, ½ Fat

Breaded Veal Cutlets

PREP TIME: 10 MINUTES (READY IN 30 MINUTES) ✦ YIELD: 2 SERVINGS

  1 egg
  ⅓ cup unseasoned dry bread crumbs
  2 (3-oz.) veal cutlets
  1 tablespoon oil
  1 (8-oz.) can tomato sauce
  ½ teaspoon dried Italian seasoning
  2 oz. (½ cup) shredded mozzarella cheese

1. Beat egg slightly in shallow bowl. Place bread crumbs in another shallow dish. Dip each cutlet in egg; coat with bread crumbs.
2. Heat oil in medium nonstick skillet over

TIMETABLE FOR ROASTING VEAL

ROAST	WEIGHT (POUNDS)	THERMOMETER READING	COOKING TIME (MINUTES PER POUND)
RIB *Roast at 325°F.*	4 to 5	160°F. (Medium) 170°F. (Well)	25 to 27 29 to 31
LOIN *Roast at 325°F.*	3 to 4	160°F. (Medium) 170°F. (Well)	34 to 36 38 to 40
RUMP OR SHOULDER, BONELESS *Roast at 325°F.*	3 to 4	160°F. (Medium) 170°F. (Well)	31 to 35 38 to 40

Source: National Cattlemen's Beef Association

medium-high heat until hot. Add cutlets; cook on both sides until browned.

3. Reduce heat; stir in tomato sauce and Italian seasoning. Cover; simmer 12 to 17 minutes or until cutlets are tender. Sprinkle with cheese; cover and cook 1 to 2 minutes or until cheese is melted.

NUTRITION INFORMATION PER SERVING: Serving Size: ½ of Recipe ♦ Calories: 390 ♦ Calories from Fat: 160 ♦ % DAILY VALUE: Total Fat: 18 g 28% ♦ Saturated Fat: 6 g 30% ♦ Cholesterol: 200 mg 67% ♦ Sodium: 1050 mg 44% ♦ Total Carbohydrate: 22 g 7% ♦ Dietary Fiber: 2 g 8% ♦ Sugars: 5 g ♦ Protein: 36 g ♦ Vitamin A: 30% ♦ Vitamin C: 20% ♦ Calcium: 25% ♦ Iron: 20% ♦ DIETARY EXCHANGES: 1½ Starch, 4½ Lean Meat, ½ Fat OR 1½ Carbohydrate, 4½ Lean Meat, ½ Fat

German Wiener Schnitzel

PREP TIME: 30 MINUTES ♦ YIELD: 6 SERVINGS

  6 veal cutlets (⅜ inch thick)
  2 tablespoons all-purpose flour
  ½ teaspoon salt
  ¼ teaspoon pepper
  2 eggs, slightly beaten
  1 tablespoon milk
  1 to 1½ cups unseasoned dry bread crumbs
  6 tablespoons oil

1. Place 1 veal cutlet between 2 pieces of plastic wrap or waxed paper. Working from center, gently pound cutlet with flat side of meat mallet or rolling pin until about ⅛ inch thick; remove wrap. Repeat with remaining cutlets.

2. In small bowl, combine flour, salt and pepper; mix well. In another small bowl, combine egg and milk; blend well. Coat each cutlet with seasoned flour; dip in egg mixture. Coat with crumbs.*

3. In large skillet, heat 3 tablespoons of the oil over medium-high heat until hot. Cook 3 cutlets at a time for 5 to 7 minutes or until golden brown on both sides. Repeat with remaining 3 tablespoons oil and remaining 3 cutlets. Serve immediately.

TIP: *To make ahead, prepare to this point. Cover; refrigerate up to 3 hours before cooking.

NUTRITION INFORMATION PER SERVING: Serving Size: ⅙ of Recipe ♦ Calories: 390 ♦ Calories from Fat: 180 ♦ % DAILY VALUE: Total Fat: 20 g 31% ♦ Saturated Fat: 4 g 20% ♦ Cholesterol: 165 mg 55% ♦ Sodium: 480 mg 20% ♦ Total Carbohydrate: 22 g 7% ♦ Dietary Fiber: 1 g 3% ♦ Sugars: 2 g ♦ Protein: 31 g ♦ Vitamin A: 2% ♦ Vitamin C: 0% ♦ Calcium: 8% ♦ Iron: 15% ♦ DIETARY EXCHANGES: 1½ Starch, 4 Very Lean Meat, 3 Fat OR 1½ Carbohydrate, 4 Very Lean Meat, 3 Fat

Veal Parmigiana with Vermicelli

PREP TIME: 30 MINUTES (READY IN 1 HOUR) ♦ YIELD: 6 SERVINGS

PARMIGIANA
  6 veal cutlets (¼ inch thick)
  ½ cup grated Parmesan cheese
  ¼ cup unseasoned dry bread crumbs
  ½ teaspoon dried oregano leaves
  ¼ teaspoon pepper
  ¼ cup all-purpose flour
  2 eggs, slightly beaten
  2 to 3 tablespoons oil
  1 (2.5-oz.) jar sliced mushrooms, drained
  1 (28-oz.) jar spaghetti sauce

VERMICELLI
  8 oz. uncooked vermicelli or spaghetti
  1 to 2 tablespoons butter
  ¼ cup grated Parmesan cheese, if desired
  4 oz. (1 cup) shredded mozzarella cheese

1. Place 1 veal cutlet between 2 pieces of plastic wrap or waxed paper. Working from center, gently pound cutlet with flat side of meat mallet or rolling pin until about ⅛ inch thick; remove wrap. Repeat with remaining cutlets.

2. Heat oven to 350°F. In pie pan or shallow dish, combine ½ cup Parmesan cheese, bread crumbs, oregano and pepper; mix well. Coat each cutlet with flour; dip in eggs. Coat with Parmesan cheese mixture.

3. Heat oil in large skillet over medium-high heat until hot. Add cutlets; cook 6 to 7 minutes or until golden brown on both sides. Remove from skillet. Arrange cutlets in ungreased 13×9-inch (3-quart) baking dish; sprinkle with mushrooms. Spoon spaghetti sauce over mushrooms. Bake at 350°F. for 25 to 30 minutes or until bubbly.

4. Meanwhile, cook vermicelli to desired doneness as directed on package. Drain; toss with butter and ¼ cup Parmesan cheese. Cover to keep warm.

5. Remove baking dish from oven; sprinkle veal with mozzarella cheese. Serve veal over vermicelli.

NUTRITION INFORMATION PER SERVING: Serving Size: ⅙ of Recipe ♦ Calories: 610 ♦ Calories from Fat: 230 ♦ % DAILY VALUE: Total Fat: 26 g 40% ♦ Saturated Fat: 10 g 50% ♦ Cholesterol: 195 mg 65% ♦ Sodium: 1030 mg 43% ♦ Total Carbohydrate: 48 g 16% ♦ Dietary Fiber: 4 g 16% ♦ Sugars: 2 g ♦ Protein: 46 g ♦ Vitamin A: 20% ♦ Vitamin C: 10% ♦ Calcium: 46% ♦ Iron: 25% ♦ DIETARY EXCHANGES: 3 Starch, 5 Medium-Fat Meat OR 3 Carbohydrate, 5 Medium-Fat Meat

Veal

• RETAIL CUTS •
WHERE THEY COME FROM
HOW TO COOK THEM

Rib Roast
Roast

Boneless Rib Roast
Roast

Crown Roast
Roast

Boneless Rib Chop
Braise, Panfry, Broil

Rib Chop
Braise, Panfry, Broil

Short Ribs
Braise, Cook in Liquid

RIB

Blade Roast
Braise, Roast

Arm Roast
Braise, Roast

Blade Steak
Braise, Panfry

Arm Steak
Braise, Panfry

Boneless Shoulder Arm Roast
Braise, Roast

Boneless Shoulder Eye Roast
Braise, Roast

SHOULDER

LEG (ROUND)
SIRLOIN
LOIN
RIB
SHOULDER
FORESHANK & BREAST

Boneless Rump Roast
Braise, Roast

Round Steak
Braise, Panfry

Top Round Steak
Braise, Panfry

Leg Cutlet
Braise, Panfry, Broil

LEG (ROUND)

Breast
Braise, Roast

Boneless Breast Roast
Braise, Roast

Cross Cut Shank
Braise, Cook in Liquid

Riblet
Braise, Cook in Liquid

Shank
Braise, Cook in Liquid

FORESHANK & BREAST

Loin Roast
Roast

Boneless Loin Roast
Roast

Loin Chop
Braise, Panfry, Broil

Kidney Chop
Braise, Panfry

Top Loin Chop
Braise, Panfry, Broil

Butterfly Chop
Braise, Panfry, Broil

LOIN

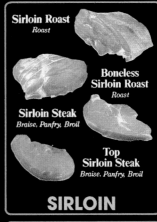

Sirloin Roast
Roast

Boneless Sirloin Roast
Roast

Sirloin Steak
Braise, Panfry, Broil

Top Sirloin Steak
Braise, Panfry, Broil

SIRLOIN

Veal for Stew
Braise, Cook in Liquid

Ground Veal
Panfry, Broil

Cubes for Kabobs
Braise

Cubed Steak
Braise, Panfry

OTHER CUTS

PORK
& LAMB

PORK & LAMB

T ender lamb chops glazed with spiced apricots . . . chili-hot Chinese barbecued spareribs . . . hearty pork loin roast with baby carrots. . . . There are so many tantalizing ways to serve pork and lamb beyond the classic pork chops with applesauce and lamb with mint jelly. Today's pork and lamb are leaner than those of decades past, and updated cooking techniques keep the meat juicy and tender. This chapter contains more than seventy recipes for pork and lamb, including traditional American favorites as well as innovative dishes inspired by international cuisines.

Buying Pork

Choose pork that looks light pink to rose in color with firm, fine-grained texture. Any fat should be firm and white in color and bone should be pinkish.

C O O K ' S   N O T E

TIPS FOR ROASTING PORK OR LAMB

+ Preheat the oven.
+ Set a rack in the roasting pan to allow airflow around the entire roast to promote browning. If your roasting pan has no rack, you can use a wire cake rack—or simply set the meat directly on the bottom of the pan, perhaps on a bed of sliced onions or herb sprigs.
+ Place meat in the pan, fat side up. As the fat melts during roasting, it naturally bastes the meat, keeping it moist.
+ Check the internal temperature with a meat thermometer to ensure meat is safely cooked. (For internal temperatures, see "Timetable for Roasting Fresh Pork" on page 130, "Timetable for Roasting Smoked Pork" on page 147 and "Timetable for Roasting Lamb" on page 151.)
+ Let the cooked meat stand for about 15 minutes, loosely covered with foil to retain warmth, before carving. This lets the juices redistribute throughout the meat and makes carving easier.

Pork Roast

1. Allow ⅓ to ½ lb. per serving for bone-in roast and ¼ to ⅓ lb. per serving for boneless roast. Heat oven to 325°F. Place roast, fat side up, on rack in shallow roasting pan. If desired, sprinkle with salt and pepper. Insert meat thermometer so bulb reaches center of thickest part of meat, but does not rest in fat or on bone. Do not add water or cover.
2. Bake at 325°F. until meat thermometer registers 165°F. using "Timetable for Roasting Fresh Pork," page 130.

NUTRITION INFORMATION PER SERVING: Serving Size: 4 oz. Cooked Pork ✦ Calories: 230 ✦ Calories from Fat: 100 ✦ **% DAILY VALUE:** Total Fat: 11 g 17% ✦ Saturated Fat: 4 g 20% ✦ Cholesterol: 90 mg 30% ✦ Sodium: 65 mg 3% ✦ Total Carbohydrate: 0 g 0% ✦ Dietary Fiber: 0 g 0% ✦ Sugars: 0 g ✦ Protein: 32 g ✦ Vitamin A: 0% ✦ Vitamin C: 0% ✦ Calcium: 2% ✦ Iron: 6% ✦ **DIETARY EXCHANGES:** 4 Lean Meat

C O O K ' S   N O T E

CARVING A PORK LOIN ROAST

Remove backbone by cutting close along the bone. Place roast with bone side up facing the carver. Make slices by cutting close along each side of the rib bone. One slice will contain the rib bone; the next will be boneless.

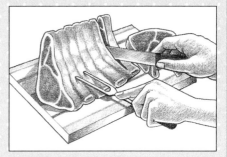

Wine Marinade for Pork Roast

PREP TIME: 10 MINUTES ♦ YIELD: 1 CUP
(ENOUGH FOR 4 SERVINGS OF MEAT)

    2 tablespoons chopped fresh parsley
    ½ teaspoon salt
    ¼ teaspoon pepper
    2 garlic cloves, sliced
    1 cup dry white wine

1. In small bowl, combine all ingredients; mix well. Place 4 to 6-lb. pork roast in resealable food storage plastic bag or nonmetal container. Pour mixture over pork. Seal bag or cover bowl.
2. Refrigerate at least 2 hours or overnight to marinate, stirring once or twice.

NUTRITION INFORMATION: Not possible to calculate because of recipe variables.

Caribbean Jerk Marinade

PREP TIME: 10 MINUTES ♦ YIELD: ⅓ CUP
(ENOUGH FOR 4 SERVINGS OF MEAT)

    3 jalapeño chiles, stems and seeds removed
    2 tablespoons chopped green onions
    3 teaspoons allspice
    ½ teaspoon cinnamon
    ½ teaspoon nutmeg
    ¼ teaspoon salt
    2 tablespoons water
    1 tablespoon honey
    4 teaspoons fresh lime juice
    1 teaspoon steak sauce

1. In blender container, combine all ingredients; blend until smooth. Pour mixture over pork cutlets, tenderloin, chops or cubes for kabobs. Let stand at room temperature for 15 minutes to marinate.
2. Bake, grill or broil pork as desired, spooning or brushing marinade over pork halfway through cooking. Discard any remaining marinade.

NUTRITION INFORMATION: Not possible to calculate because of recipe variables.

Citrus-Ginger Marinade

PREP TIME: 5 MINUTES ♦ YIELD: 1 CUP
(ENOUGH FOR 4 SERVINGS OF MEAT)

    ⅔ cup frozen pineapple-orange juice
        concentrate, thawed
    2 tablespoons hoisin sauce
    1 tablespoon dark brown sugar
    1 tablespoon grated gingerroot
    ¼ teaspoon crushed red pepper flakes

1. In small bowl, combine all ingredients; mix well. Pour mixture over pork cutlets, tenderloin, chops or cubes for kabobs. Let stand at room temperature for 15 minutes to marinate.
2. Bake, grill or broil pork as desired, spooning or brushing marinade over pork halfway through cooking. Discard any remaining marinade.

NUTRITION INFORMATION: Not possible to calculate because of recipe variables.

Autumn Pork Roast Dinner

PREP TIME: 15 MINUTES (READY IN 8 HOURS 15 MINUTES) ♦ YIELD: 6 SERVINGS

    1 (1¾ to 2-lb.) boneless rolled pork loin roast
    ¼ teaspoon salt
    ⅛ teaspoon pepper
    3 large sweet potatoes, peeled, thinly sliced
    1 medium onion, sliced, separated into rings
    ¾ teaspoon dried thyme leaves
    1 quart (4 cups) apple juice

1. Sprinkle pork roast with salt and pepper; place in 3½ or 4-quart slow cooker. Place sliced sweet potatoes around and on top of roast. Top with onion; sprinkle with thyme. Pour apple juice over onion.
2. Cover; cook on low setting for at least 8 hours or until pork is no longer pink in center and sweet potatoes are tender.

NUTRITION INFORMATION PER SERVING: Serving Size: ⅙ of Recipe ♦ Calories: 380 ♦ Calories from Fat: 100 ♦ **% DAILY VALUE:** Total Fat: 11 g 17% ♦ Saturated Fat: 4 g 20% ♦ Cholesterol: 90 mg 30% ♦ Sodium: 170 mg 7% ♦ Total Carbohydrate: 37 g 12% ♦ Dietary Fiber: 2 g 8% ♦ Sugars: 21 g ♦ Protein: 34 g ♦ Vitamin A: 260% ♦ Vitamin C: 20% ♦ Calcium: 6% ♦ Iron: 15% ♦ **DIETARY EXCHANGES:** 1½ Starch, ½ Fruit, 4 Lean Meat OR 2 Carbohydrate, 4 Lean Meat

Fennel-Garlic Pork Roast

Crown Roast of Pork

PREP TIME: 15 MINUTES (READY IN 3 HOURS
45 MINUTES) ◆ YIELD: 8 SERVINGS

  1 (7-lb.) pork crown roast, backbone removed
1½ teaspoons salt
 ¼ teaspoon pepper

1. Heat oven to 325°F. Place roast in roasting pan, rib bones up. Sprinkle with salt and pepper. Wrap tips of bones in foil to prevent excess browning. Insert meat thermometer so bulb reaches center of thickest part of meat, but does not rest in fat or on bone. Do not add water or cover.
2. Bake on lowest oven rack at 325°F. for 3 to 3½ hours or until meat thermometer registers 160°F. To serve, remove foil and cover bone ends with paper frills or spiced crab apples. Serve with stuffing, if desired.

NUTRITION INFORMATION PER SERVING: Serving Size: ⅛ of Recipe
◆ Calories: 420 ◆ Calories from Fat: 180 ◆ % DAILY VALUE: Total Fat:
20 g 31% ◆ Saturated Fat: 7 g 35% ◆ Cholesterol: 170 mg 57% ◆
Sodium: 520 mg 22% ◆ Total Carbohydrate: 0 g 0% ◆ Dietary
Fiber: 0 g 0% ◆ Sugars: 0 g ◆ Protein: 61 g ◆ Vitamin A: 0% ◆ Vitamin C: 0% ◆ Calcium: 4% ◆ Iron: 15% ◆ DIETARY EXCHANGES:
8 Lean Meat

Fennel-Garlic
Pork Roast

PREP TIME: 10 MINUTES (READY IN 1 HOUR 15 MINUTES)
◆ YIELD: 8 SERVINGS

  1 (2½-lb.) boneless rolled pork loin roast
  1 tablespoon fennel seeds
  1 tablespoon chopped fresh thyme
    or 1 teaspoon dried thyme leaves
½ teaspoon salt
½ teaspoon coarse ground black pepper
  2 tablespoons olive oil
  3 garlic cloves, minced

1. Heat oven to 375°F. Place roast in shallow baking pan. In small bowl, combine all remaining ingredients; blend well. Spread mixture over pork. Insert meat thermometer so bulb reaches center of thickest part of pork.
2. Bake at 375°F. for 40 to 50 minutes or until pork is no longer pink in center and meat thermometer registers 160°F.
3. Remove pork from oven. Cover with tent of foil. Let stand 10 to 15 minutes before carving.

NUTRITION INFORMATION PER SERVING: Serving Size: ⅛ of Recipe
◆ Calories: 240 ◆ Calories from Fat: 120 ◆ % DAILY VALUE: Total Fat:
13 g 20% ◆ Saturated Fat: 4 g 20% ◆ Cholesterol: 85 mg 28% ◆
Sodium: 200 mg 8% ◆ Total Carbohydrate: 1 g 1% ◆ Dietary Fiber:
0 g 0% ◆ Sugars: 0 g ◆ Protein: 29 g ◆ Vitamin A: 0% ◆ Vitamin C:
0% ◆ Calcium: 4% ◆ Iron: 8% ◆ DIETARY EXCHANGES: 4 Lean Meat

Honey-Mustard
Pork Tenderloin

PREP TIME: 15 MINUTES (READY IN 50 MINUTES)
◆ YIELD: 4 SERVINGS

  1 tablespoon honey
  1 tablespoon Dijon mustard
  2 teaspoons olive or vegetable oil
  2 garlic cloves, minced
½ teaspoon dried oregano leaves
  1 (¾-lb.) pork tenderloin

1. Heat oven to 425°F. Line 15 × 10 × 1-inch baking pan with foil.
2. In small bowl, combine honey, mustard, oil, garlic and oregano; mix well. Brush pork tenderloin with mixture; place on foil-lined pan.
3. Bake at 425°F. for 25 to 30 minutes or until pork is no longer pink in center. Let stand 5 minutes. Cut diagonally into slices.

NUTRITION INFORMATION PER SERVING: Serving Size: ¼ of Recipe
◆ Calories: 150 ◆ Calories from Fat: 50 ◆ % DAILY VALUE: Total Fat:
6 g 9% ◆ Saturated Fat: 1 g 5% ◆ Cholesterol: 50 mg 17% ◆ Sodium:
130 mg 5% ◆ Total Carbohydrate: 5 g 2% ◆ Dietary Fiber: 0 g 0% ◆
Sugars: 4 g ◆ Protein: 18 g ◆ Vitamin A: 0% ◆ Vitamin C: 0% ◆ Calcium: 0% ◆ Iron: 6% ◆ DIETARY EXCHANGES: ½ Fruit, 2 Lean Meat
OR ½ Carbohydrate, 2 Lean Meat

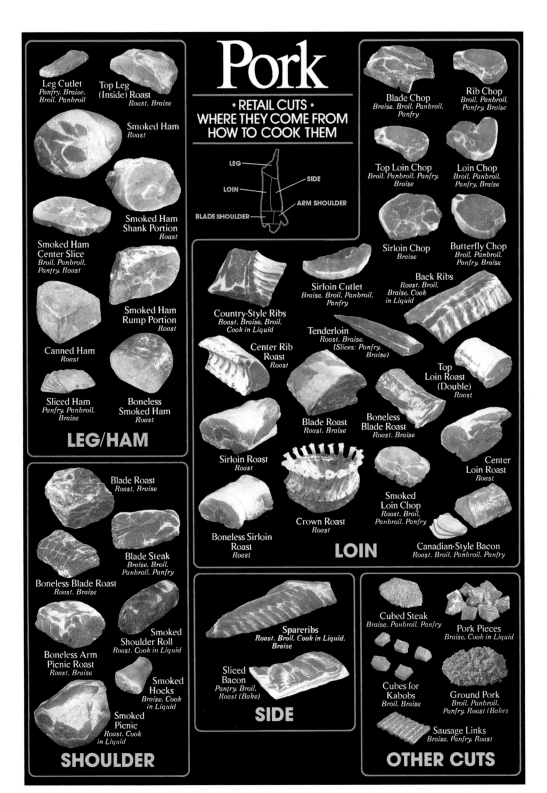

Pork

• RETAIL CUTS •
WHERE THEY COME FROM
HOW TO COOK THEM

LEG
SIDE
LOIN
ARM SHOULDER
BLADE SHOULDER

LEG/HAM

Leg Cutlet
*Panfry, Braise,
Broil, Panbroil*

Top Leg
(Inside) Roast
Roast, Braise

Smoked Ham
Roast

Smoked Ham
Shank Portion
Roast

Smoked Ham
Center Slice
*Broil, Panbroil,
Panfry, Roast*

Smoked Ham
Rump Portion
Roast

Canned Ham
Roast

Sliced Ham
*Panfry, Panbroil,
Braise*

Boneless
Smoked Ham
Roast

SHOULDER

Blade Roast
Roast, Braise

Blade Steak
*Braise, Broil,
Panbroil, Panfry*

Boneless Blade Roast
Roast, Braise

Boneless Arm
Picnic Roast
Roast, Braise

Smoked
Shoulder Roll
Roast, Cook in Liquid

Smoked
Hocks
*Braise, Cook
in Liquid*

Smoked
Picnic
*Roast, Cook
in Liquid*

LOIN

Blade Chop
*Braise, Broil, Panbroil,
Panfry*

Rib Chop
*Broil, Panbroil,
Panfry, Braise*

Top Loin Chop
*Broil, Panbroil, Panfry,
Braise*

Loin Chop
*Broil, Panbroil,
Panfry, Braise*

Sirloin Chop
Braise

Butterfly Chop
*Broil, Panbroil,
Panfry, Braise*

Sirloin Cutlet
*Braise, Broil, Panbroil,
Panfry*

Back Ribs
*Roast, Broil,
Braise, Cook
in Liquid*

Country-Style Ribs
*Roast, Braise, Broil,
Cook in Liquid*

Tenderloin
*Roast, Braise,
(Slices: Panfry,
Braise)*

Center Rib
Roast
Roast

Top
Loin Roast
(Double)
Roast

Blade Roast
Roast, Braise

Boneless
Blade Roast
Roast, Braise

Sirloin Roast
Roast

Center
Loin Roast
Roast

Smoked
Loin Chop
*Roast, Broil,
Panbroil, Panfry*

Crown Roast
Roast

Boneless Sirloin
Roast
Roast

Canadian-Style Bacon
Roast, Broil, Panbroil, Panfry

SIDE

Spareribs
*Roast, Broil, Cook in Liquid,
Braise*

Sliced
Bacon
*Panfry, Broil,
Roast (Bake)*

OTHER CUTS

Cubed Steak
Braise, Panbroil, Panfry

Pork Pieces
Braise, Cook in Liquid

Cubes for
Kabobs
Broil, Braise

Ground Pork
*Broil, Panbroil,
Panfry, Roast (Bake)*

Sausage Links
Braise, Panfry, Roast

Roast Pork with Garlic Pepper Crust

PREP TIME: 15 MINUTES (READY IN 1 HOUR)
♦ YIELD: 4 SERVINGS

    4 to 6 garlic cloves, minced
    1 tablespoon chopped fresh parsley
        or 1 teaspoon dried parsley flakes
    1 teaspoon coarse ground black pepper
    ½ teaspoon dried thyme leaves
    1 tablespoon lime or lemon juice
    1 teaspoon olive oil
    2 (½-lb.) pork tenderloins

1. Heat oven to 450°F. Line shallow roasting pan with foil; spray foil with nonstick cooking spray. In small bowl, combine garlic, parsley, pepper and thyme. In small cup, combine lime juice and oil.
2. Brush pork tenderloins with lime juice mixture, coating well. Rub garlic-pepper mixture over top and sides of tenderloins, pressing lightly. Place in sprayed foil-lined pan, garlic-pepper side up.
3. Bake at 450°F. for 25 to 35 minutes or until pork is no longer pink in center. Let stand 5 to 10 minutes before cutting diagonally into ½-inch slices.

NUTRITION INFORMATION PER SERVING: Serving Size: ¼ of Recipe
♦ Calories: 150 ♦ Calories from Fat: 45 ♦ % DAILY VALUE: Total Fat: 5 g 8% ♦ Saturated Fat: 2 g 10% ♦ Cholesterol: 65 mg 22% ♦ Sodium: 50 mg 2% ♦ Total Carbohydrate: 2 g 1% ♦ Dietary Fiber: 0 g 0% ♦ Sugars: 0 g ♦ Protein: 24 g ♦ Vitamin A: 0% ♦ Vitamin C: 4% ♦ Calcium: 2% ♦ Iron: 10% ♦ DIETARY EXCHANGES: 3 Lean Meat

Mu Shu Pork

PREP TIME: 30 MINUTES (READY IN 1 HOUR)
♦ YIELD: 4 SERVINGS

    ½ lb. boneless pork loin chops, cut
        into 1 x ⅛ x ⅛-inch strips
    1 tablespoon dry sherry
    1 teaspoon sugar
    1 teaspoon soy sauce
    ⅓ cup water
    1 tablespoon cornstarch
    ½ teaspoon chicken-flavor instant bouillon
    1 tablespoon margarine or butter
    3 eggs, beaten
    1 cup thinly sliced Chinese (napa) cabbage
    ½ cup fresh bean sprouts
    ½ cup chopped fresh mushrooms

TIMETABLE FOR ROASTING FRESH PORK

ROAST	WEIGHT (POUNDS)	THERMOMETER READING	COOKING TIME (MINUTES PER POUND)
LOIN, BONELESS *Roast at 350°F.*	2 to 5	160°F. (Medium) 170°F. (Well)	20 to 30
LOIN, BONE-IN *Roast at 325°F.*	2 to 4	160°F. (Medium) 170°F. (Well)	20 to 25
CROWN *Roast at 325°F.*	6 to 10	160°F. (Medium) 170°F. (Well)	20 to 25
TENDERLOIN *Roast at 425°F.*	1 to 1½	160°F. (Medium) 170°F. (Well)	20 to 30 minutes total
FRESH HAM LEG, BONE-IN *Roast at 350°F.*	12 to 16	160°F. (Medium) 170°F. (Well)	22 to 26
FRESH HAM LEG, BONELESS *Roast at 350°F.*	5 to 8	160°F. (Medium) 170°F. (Well)	35 to 40
RIB, BONELESS *Roast at 350°F.*	2 to 4	160°F. (Medium) 170°F. (Well)	20 to 25

Source: USDA and National Pork Producers Council.

2 green onions, halved lengthwise, cut
   into 1-inch pieces
8 teaspoons hoisin sauce
8 (7-inch) flour tortillas

1. In medium bowl, combine pork strips, sherry, sugar and soy sauce; mix well. Refrigerate at least 30 minutes or up to 6 hours.
2. In small bowl, combine water, cornstarch and bouillon; blend well. Set aside.
3. Melt margarine in large skillet or wok over medium-high heat. Add eggs; cook 2 to 3 minutes or until firm, turning once. Remove eggs from skillet; cut into thin strips.
4. Add pork mixture to skillet; cook and stir 2 to 3 minutes or until no longer pink. Add cabbage, bean sprouts and mushrooms; cook and stir 1 minute or until crisp-tender. Add cornstarch mixture to skillet; cook and stir until thickened and bubbly. Add eggs and onions to skillet; stir gently to combine. Remove from heat.
5. Spread 1 teaspoon hoisin sauce on each tortilla. Top each with about ½ cup pork mixture; roll up. Serve immediately.

NUTRITION INFORMATION PER SERVING: Serving Size: ¼ of Recipe ♦ Calories: 440 ♦ Calories from Fat: 140 ♦ **% DAILY VALUE:** Total Fat: 16 g 25% ♦ Saturated Fat: 4 g 20% ♦ Cholesterol: 195 mg 65% ♦ Sodium: 890 mg 37% ♦ Total Carbohydrate: 51 g 17% ♦ Dietary Fiber: 3 g 12% ♦ Sugars: 9 g ♦ Protein: 24 g ♦ Vitamin A: 20% ♦ Vitamin C: 15% ♦ Calcium: 15% ♦ Iron: 25% ♦ **DIETARY EXCHANGES:** 3 Starch, 1 Vegetable, 2 Lean Meat, 1½ Fat OR 3 Carbohydrate, 1 Vegetable, 2 Lean Meat, 1½ Fat

Golden Pork Chow Mein

PREP TIME: 30 MINUTES ♦ YIELD: 6 SERVINGS

   1 tablespoon oil
1½ lb. lean pork steak, bones removed, cut
      into ¼-inch slices
   1 cup sliced carrots
   ½ cup diagonally sliced celery
   1 cup water
   2 tablespoons soy sauce
   2 teaspoons sugar
   1 teaspoon beef-flavor instant bouillon
   ½ teaspoon garlic powder
   ½ teaspoon grated gingerroot
      or ⅛ teaspoon ground ginger
   8 to 9 oz. (4 cups) fresh bean sprouts
   ½ cup diagonally sliced green onions
   1 (2-oz.) jar sliced pimientos, drained
   ¼ cup cold water
   2 tablespoons cornstarch
      Chow mein noodles

COOK'S NOTE

TIPS FOR STIR-FRYING PORK OR LAMB

These quick stove-top techniques can be the starting point for many different meals, combining the meat with vegetables and grains or pasta.

♦ Trim off and discard all visible fat. Cut meat into uniform pieces for even cooking. Freezing the meat for 30 minutes or so will firm it just enough to make slicing easier. Cut against the grain for more tender meat.
♦ Heat the skillet or wok before adding the meat.
♦ Nonstick cooking spray is best applied before heating the pan. If you're using regular cooking oil, heat the pan, then add a little oil. If you're using a wok, drizzle the oil around the inside top edge of the pan and let it drip into the center.
♦ Cook meat in batches, if necessary, to avoid crowding the pan. If the chunks of meat are crowded, they will steam instead of truly being stir-fried, and won't have an appealing browned exterior.

1. Heat oil in large skillet or wok over medium-high heat until hot. Add pork; cook and stir until browned. Remove pork from skillet; cover to keep warm.
2. To liquid in skillet, add carrots, celery, 1 cup water, soy sauce, sugar, bouillon, garlic powder and gingerroot; mix well. Reduce heat to medium-low. Cover; simmer 4 to 5 minutes or until vegetables are crisp-tender. Stir in cooked pork, bean sprouts, onions and pimientos; cook until thoroughly heated.
3. In small bowl, combine ¼ cup water and cornstarch; blend until smooth. Gradually stir into mixture in skillet. Cook and stir over medium-high heat until sauce is bubbly and thickened. Serve over chow mein noodles.

NUTRITION INFORMATION PER SERVING: Serving Size: ⅙ of Recipe ♦ Calories: 310 ♦ Calories from Fat: 140 ♦ **% DAILY VALUE:** Total Fat: 15 g 23% ♦ Saturated Fat: 3 g 15% ♦ Cholesterol: 50 mg 17% ♦ Sodium: 650 mg 27% ♦ Total Carbohydrate: 23 g 8% ♦ Dietary Fiber: 3 g 12% ♦ Sugars: 4 g ♦ Protein: 21 g ♦ Vitamin A: 60% ♦ Vitamin C: 25% ♦ Calcium: 4% ♦ Iron: 15% ♦ **DIETARY EXCHANGES:** 1 Starch, 1 Vegetable, 2 Lean Meat, 2 Fat OR 1 Carbohydrate, 1 Vegetable, 2 Lean Meat, 2 Fat

Pork Roast and Vegetables with Brown Gravy

Pork Roast and Vegetables with Brown Gravy

PREP TIME: 15 MINUTES (READY IN 2 HOURS 25 MINUTES) ✦ YIELD: 8 SERVINGS

1 (2½-lb.) boneless pork loin roast
1 small onion, thinly sliced
2 teaspoons dried parsley flakes
½ teaspoon dried marjoram leaves
½ teaspoon dried rosemary leaves
¼ teaspoon crushed red pepper flakes
1 (14½-oz.) can ready-to-serve beef broth
⅛ teaspoon pepper
1 bay leaf
1 lb. fresh baby carrots
8 small red potatoes, unpeeled, quartered
1 tablespoon water
4 teaspoons cornstarch

1. Heat oven to 325°F. With sharp knife, make 6 horizontal cuts down center of roast, each 2 inches long and 2 inches deep. Stuff each cut with slices of onion; reserve any remaining onion. Place roast in ovenproof Dutch oven.

2. In small bowl, combine parsley, marjoram, rosemary and crushed red pepper flakes; sprinkle evenly over top of roast. Insert meat thermometer into thickest part of roast without touching fat. Pour broth around roast.

3. Place reserved onion slices, pepper and bay leaf in broth in Dutch oven. Arrange carrots and potatoes around roast; cover. Bake at 325°F. for 1¾ to 2 hours or until meat thermometer registers 160°F.

4. Remove roast from Dutch oven; place on serving platter. With slotted spoon, remove vegetables and arrange around roast; cover to keep warm.

5. Bring pan juices in Dutch oven to a boil. Boil 10 to 12 minutes or until reduced to half. Remove and discard bay leaf.

6. In small bowl, combine water and cornstarch; blend until smooth. Add to pan juices; cook and stir until mixture is bubbly and thickened. (If desired, gravy can be strained.) Serve gravy with roast and vegetables.

NUTRITION INFORMATION PER SERVING: Serving Size: ⅛ of Recipe ✦ Calories: 290 ✦ Calories from Fat: 45 ✦ **% DAILY VALUE:** Total Fat: 5 g 8% ✦ Saturated Fat: 2 g 10% ✦ Cholesterol: 80 mg 27% ✦ Sodium: 250 mg 10% ✦ Total Carbohydrate: 29 g 10% ✦ Dietary Fiber: 4 g 16% ✦ Sugars: 5 g ✦ Protein: 33 g ✦ Vitamin A: 320% ✦ Vitamin C: 20% ✦ Calcium: 4% ✦ Iron: 20% ✦ **DIETARY EXCHANGES:** 1½ Starch, 1 Vegetable, 3 Lean Meat OR 1½ Carbohydrate, 1 Vegetable, 3 Lean Meat

Rosemary Roasted Pork Tenderloin

PREP TIME: 15 MINUTES (READY IN 50 MINUTES) ✦ YIELD: 3 SERVINGS

5 teaspoons olive or vegetable oil
1 (¾-lb.) pork tenderloin
1 tablespoon chopped fresh rosemary
    or 1 teaspoon dried rosemary leaves
1 large garlic clove, minced
⅛ teaspoon salt
¼ teaspoon coarse ground black pepper

1. Heat oven to 425°F. Heat 2 teaspoons of the oil in large skillet over medium-high heat until hot. Add pork tenderloin; cook until golden brown on all sides.

2. Place pork tenderloin in ungreased shallow baking pan. In small cup, combine re-

Rosemary Roasted Pork Tenderloin

maining 3 teaspoons oil, rosemary and garlic; mix well. Brush rosemary mixture over pork tenderloin. Sprinkle with salt and pepper.

3. Bake at 425°F. for 18 to 25 minutes or until pork is no longer pink in center. Let stand 10 minutes before cutting into slices.

NUTRITION INFORMATION PER SERVING: Serving Size: ⅓ of Recipe ♦ Calories: 210 ♦ Calories from Fat: 110 ♦ % DAILY VALUE: Total Fat: 12 g 18% ♦ Saturated Fat: 2 g 10% ♦ Cholesterol: 65 mg 22% ♦ Sodium: 135 mg 6% ♦ Total Carbohydrate: 1 g 1% ♦ Dietary Fiber: 1 g 2% ♦ Sugars: 0 g ♦ Protein: 24 g ♦ Vitamin A: 0% ♦ Vitamin C: 0% ♦ Calcium: 2% ♦ Iron: 10% ♦ DIETARY EXCHANGES: 3½ Lean Meat, ½ Fat

Lime-Marinated Pork with Citrus Salsa

PREP TIME: 1 HOUR ♦ YIELD: 6 SERVINGS

SALSA
½ cup chopped fresh orange sections
½ cup chopped green bell pepper
¼ cup sliced red onion
1 medium tomato, seeded, chopped
½ red jalapeño chile, finely chopped
1 tablespoon chopped fresh mint
1 teaspoon grated lime peel

PORK
2 tablespoons lime juice
2 teaspoons olive or vegetable oil
4 garlic cloves, minced
½ teaspoon salt
¼ teaspoon coarse ground black pepper
2 (¾-lb.) pork tenderloins

1. GRILL DIRECTIONS: In medium bowl, combine all salsa ingredients; mix well. Let stand at room temperature for 1 hour to blend flavors.

2. Meanwhile, heat grill. In small bowl, combine lime juice, oil, garlic, salt and pepper; mix well. Brush oil mixture over pork tenderloins, coating all sides.

3. When ready to grill, place pork on gas grill over medium heat or on charcoal grill 4 to 6 inches from medium coals. Cook 20 to 30 minutes or until pork is no longer pink in center, turning occasionally. Serve with salsa.

TIP: To broil pork tenderloins, place on broiler pan; broil 4 to 6 inches from heat using times above as a guide, turning occasionally.

NUTRITION INFORMATION PER SERVING: Serving Size: ⅙ of Recipe ♦ Calories: 170 ♦ Calories from Fat: 50 ♦ % DAILY VALUE: Total Fat: 6 g 9% ♦ Saturated Fat: 2 g 10% ♦ Cholesterol: 65 mg 22% ♦ Sodium: 230 mg 10% ♦ Total Carbohydrate: 5 g 2% ♦ Dietary Fiber: 1 g 4% ♦ Sugars: 3 g ♦ Protein: 24 g ♦ Vitamin A: 10% ♦ Vitamin C: 35% ♦ Calcium: 2% ♦ Iron: 8% ♦ DIETARY EXCHANGES: 1 Vegetable, 3 Lean Meat

Caribbean Pork Tenderloins

Caribbean Pork Tenderloins

PREP TIME: 55 MINUTES ♦ YIELD: 6 SERVINGS

1 teaspoon garlic powder
1 teaspoon dried thyme leaves
1 teaspoon allspice
1 teaspoon nutmeg
½ teaspoon salt
½ teaspoon mace
½ teaspoon cloves
¼ teaspoon coarse ground black pepper
2 (¾-lb.) pork tenderloins

1. GRILL DIRECTIONS: Heat grill. In small bowl, combine all ingredients except pork tenderloins; mix well. Rub mixture over pork, coating well.

2. When ready to grill, place pork on gas grill over medium-high heat or on charcoal grill 4 to 6 inches from medium-high coals. Cook 20 to 30 minutes or until pork is no longer pink in center, turning pork occasionally. To serve, cut pork into slices.

TIP: To bake pork tenderloins in oven, place in ungreased shallow baking pan; bake at 350°F. for 40 to 50 minutes.

NUTRITION INFORMATION PER SERVING: Serving Size: ⅙ of Recipe ♦ Calories: 140 ♦ Calories from Fat: 35 ♦ % DAILY VALUE: Total Fat: 4 g 6% ♦ Saturated Fat: 2 g 10% ♦ Cholesterol: 65 mg 22% ♦ Sodium: 230 mg 10% ♦ Total Carbohydrate: 1 g 1% ♦ Dietary Fiber: 0 g 0% ♦ Sugars: 0 g ♦ Protein: 24 g ♦ Vitamin A: 0% ♦ Vitamin C: 0% ♦ Calcium: 0% ♦ Iron: 10% ♦ DIETARY EXCHANGES: 3 Lean Meat

Chinese Barbecued Ribs

PREP TIME: 1 HOUR 30 MINUTES ✦ YIELD: 6 SERVINGS

½ cup oyster sauce
¼ cup hoisin sauce
¼ cup honey
3 tablespoons lite soy sauce
1 to 2 teaspoons chili paste, if desired
⅓ cup finely chopped green onions
3½ to 4 lb. pork spareribs, cut into 6-inch
    sections

1. GRILL DIRECTIONS: Heat grill. In small bowl, combine all ingredients except spareribs; mix well. Set aside.
2. When ready to grill, place spareribs on gas grill over medium heat or on charcoal grill 6 to 8 inches from medium coals. Brush with sauce. Cover; cook 1 to 1¼ hours or until meat is tender and starts to pull away from bone, brushing frequently with additional sauce.
3. To serve, cut ribs apart carefully with knife and arrange on platter. Bring any remaining sauce to a boil. Serve sauce with ribs.

> TIP: To bake ribs in oven, place on wire rack in foil-lined 15 x 10 x 1-inch baking pan; bake at 350°F. for 1 to 1½ hours, brushing frequently with sauce.

NUTRITION INFORMATION PER SERVING: Serving Size: ⅙ of Recipe ✦ Calories: 570 ✦ Calories from Fat: 320 ✦ **% DAILY VALUE:** Total Fat: 36 g 55% ✦ Saturated Fat: 13 g 65% ✦ Cholesterol: 145 mg 48% ✦ Sodium: 1650 mg 69% ✦ Total Carbohydrate: 26 g 9% ✦ Dietary Fiber: 0 g 0% ✦ Sugars: 23 g ✦ Protein: 36 g ✦ Vitamin A: 0% ✦ Vitamin C: 0% ✦ Calcium: 8% ✦ Iron: 20 ✦ **DIETARY EXCHANGES:** 1 Starch, ½ Fruit, 4½ High-Fat Meat OR 1½ Carbohydrate, 4½ High-Fat Meat

Spareribs on the Grill

PREP TIME: 1 HOUR ✦ YIELD: 6 SERVINGS

4 to 5 lb. pork spareribs, cut into sections
1 recipe Deluxe Barbecue Sauce, at right,
    or Sweet and Zesty Barbecue Sauce,
    page 99

1. GRILL DIRECTIONS: Heat grill. Arrange ribs in 12 x 8-inch (2-quart) microwave-safe baking dish. (Ribs will be in 2 layers.) Cover with microwave-safe waxed paper. Microwave on HIGH for 20 minutes, rearranging and turning ribs once during cooking.

2. When ready to grill, place ribs on gas grill over medium heat or on charcoal grill 4 to 6 inches from medium-high coals. Brush with sauce. Cook 10 minutes. Reduce heat to medium-low.* Cook an additional 10 to 20 minutes or until browned, turning frequently and basting with sauce.

> TIPS: *To reduce heat for charcoal grill, spread coals farther apart using oven mitt and long-handled tongs.
> To precook ribs in oven, place on rack in 13 x 9-inch pan, or on broiler pan; bake at 350°F. for 1 hour.

NUTRITION INFORMATION PER SERVING: Serving Size: ⅙ of Recipe ✦ Calories: 720 ✦ Calories from Fat: 410 ✦ **% DAILY VALUE:** Total Fat: 45 g 69% ✦ Saturated Fat: 17 g 85% ✦ Cholesterol: 180 mg 60% ✦ Sodium: 1640 mg 68% ✦ Total Carbohydrate: 33 g 11% ✦ Dietary Fiber: 1 g 4% ✦ Sugars: 22 g ✦ Protein: 45 g ✦ Vitamin A: 20% ✦ Vitamin C: 20% ✦ Calcium: 10% ✦ Iron: 20% ✦ **DIETARY EXCHANGES:** 1 Starch, 1 Fruit, 6 High-Fat Meat OR 2 Carbohydrate, 6 High-Fat Meat

Deluxe Barbecue Sauce

PREP TIME: 25 MINUTES ✦ YIELD: 3 CUPS

1 cup ketchup
1 cup chili sauce
½ cup finely chopped onion
¼ cup firmly packed brown sugar
1 teaspoon celery seed
1 teaspoon salt
¼ teaspoon instant minced garlic
2 tablespoons Worcestershire sauce
2 tablespoons lemon juice
1 teaspoon prepared mustard

In medium saucepan, combine all ingredients. Bring to a boil, stirring until well blended. Reduce heat to low; simmer 15 minutes, stirring occasionally.

NUTRITION INFORMATION PER SERVING: Serving Size: 1 Tablespoon ✦ Calories: 15 ✦ Calories from Fat: 0 ✦ **% DAILY VALUE:** Total Fat: 0 g 0% ✦ Saturated Fat: 0 g 0% ✦ Cholesterol: 0 mg 0% ✦ Sodium: 190 mg 8% ✦ Total Carbohydrate: 4 g 1% ✦ Dietary Fiber: 0 g 0% ✦ Sugars: 3 g ✦ Protein: 0 g ✦ Vitamin A: 2% ✦ Vitamin C: 2% ✦ Calcium: 0% ✦ Iron: 0% ✦ **DIETARY EXCHANGES:** Free

Honey-Mustard Rib Glaze

PREP TIME: 10 MINUTES ✦ YIELD: 1¼ CUPS

½ cup honey
½ cup vinegar
⅓ cup Dijon mustard
¼ cup chopped onion
1 garlic clove, minced
1 teaspoon celery salt
½ teaspoon paprika

In medium saucepan, combine all ingredients. Bring to a boil, stirring until well blended. Use as a glaze for grilled meats.

NUTRITION INFORMATION PER SERVING: Serving Size: 1 Tablespoon ✦ Calories: 30 ✦ Calories from Fat: 0 ✦ **% DAILY VALUE:** Total Fat: 0 g 0% ✦ Saturated Fat: 0 g 0% ✦ Cholesterol: 0 mg 0% ✦ Sodium: 130 mg 5% ✦ Total Carbohydrate: 8 g 3% ✦ Dietary Fiber: 0 g 0% ✦ Sugars: 7 g ✦ Protein: 0 g ✦ Vitamin A: 0% ✦ Vitamin C: 0% ✦ Calcium: 0% ✦ Iron: 0% ✦ **DIETARY EXCHANGES:** ½ Fruit OR ½ Carbohydrate

Baked Ribs and Sauerkraut

PREP TIME: 20 MINUTES (READY IN 2 HOURS 40 MINUTES) ✦ YIELD: 6 SERVINGS

3 lb. pork spareribs or country-style ribs
½ teaspoon salt
¼ teaspoon pepper
1 (32-oz.) jar sauerkraut, undrained
¼ cup water
2 tablespoons brown sugar
2 tart apples, peeled, chopped
1 small onion, chopped

1. Heat oven to 450°F. Cut ribs into serving-sized pieces. Place in ungreased 13×9-inch pan; sprinkle with salt and pepper. Bake at 450°F. for 20 minutes.
2. Reduce oven temperature to 350°F. Remove ribs from pan; drain meat drippings from pan. In same pan, combine sauerkraut and remaining ingredients; spread evenly over bottom. Arrange ribs on top of sauerkraut mixture.
3. Bake at 350°F. for 1½ to 2 hours or until ribs are tender, stirring occasionally.

NUTRITION INFORMATION PER SERVING: Serving Size: ⅙ of Recipe ✦ Calories: 430 ✦ Calories from Fat: 240 ✦ **% DAILY VALUE:** Total Fat: 27 g 42% ✦ Saturated Fat: 10 g 50% ✦ Cholesterol: 105 mg 35% ✦ Sodium: 1260 mg 53% ✦ Total Carbohydrate: 19 g 6% ✦ Dietary Fiber: 5 g 20% ✦ Sugars: 12 g ✦ Protein: 27 g ✦ Vitamin A: 0% ✦ Vitamin C: 30% ✦ Calcium: 10% ✦ Iron: 25% ✦ **DIETARY EXCHANGES:** 1 Fruit, 1 Vegetable, 3½ High-Fat Meat OR 1 Carbohydrate, 1 Vegetable, 3½ High-Fat Meat

Southern-Style Barbecued Ribs

PREP TIME: 30 MINUTES (READY IN 1 HOUR) ✦ YIELD: 4 SERVINGS

SAUCE
½ cup chopped onions
¼ cup cider vinegar
¼ cup lemon juice
2 tablespoons margarine or butter
1 tablespoon sugar
½ to 1 teaspoon coarse ground black pepper
½ teaspoon salt
¼ teaspoon dry mustard
1½ teaspoons Worcestershire sauce
½ teaspoon Liquid Smoke, if desired

RIBS
1 lb. boneless pork country-style ribs
1 quart (4 cups) water
1 cup vinegar
1 teaspoon crushed red pepper flakes

1. GRILL DIRECTIONS: In medium saucepan, combine all sauce ingredients; bring to a boil over medium heat. Boil 10 to 12 minutes or until slightly thickened, stirring occasionally.
2. Meanwhile, place ribs in large saucepan; add water, 1 cup vinegar and red pepper flakes. Bring to a boil over medium-high heat. Reduce heat; cover and simmer 30 minutes. Drain.*
3. Heat grill. When ready to grill, brush ribs with sauce. Place on gas grill over medium heat or on charcoal grill 4 to 6 inches from medium coals. Cook 10 to 20 minutes or until ribs are browned and tender, turning and brushing with sauce once. Heat remaining sauce to a boil and serve with ribs.

TIPS: *At this point, ribs and sauce can be refrigerated for up to 24 hours.
To broil ribs, place on broiler pan; broil 4 to 6 inches from heat using times above as a guide, turning and brushing with sauce once.

NUTRITION INFORMATION PER SERVING: Serving Size: ¼ of Recipe ✦ Calories: 380 ✦ Calories from Fat: 250 ✦ **% DAILY VALUE:** Total Fat: 28 g 43% ✦ Saturated Fat: 9 g 45% ✦ Cholesterol: 80 mg 27% ✦ Sodium: 400 mg 17% ✦ Total Carbohydrate: 11 g 4% ✦ Dietary Fiber: 1 g 3% ✦ Sugars: 4 g ✦ Protein: 20 g ✦ Vitamin A: 10% ✦ Vitamin C: 6% ✦ Calcium: 4% ✦ Iron: 6% ✦ **DIETARY EXCHANGES:** ½ Starch, 2½ High-Fat Meat, 1½ Fat OR ½ Carbohydrate, 2½ High-Fat Meat, 1½ Fat

Chinese Sweet-and-Sour Pork

PREP TIME: 40 MINUTES ◆ YIELD: 4 SERVINGS

1⅓ cups uncooked regular long-grain white rice
2⅔ cups water
¼ cup cornstarch
2 tablespoons all-purpose flour
1 teaspoon sugar
¼ teaspoon baking soda
3 tablespoons water
1 egg, beaten
½ lb. boneless pork loin chops, cut
    into 2 x ½ x ¼-inch pieces
    Oil for frying
3 tablespoons brown sugar
2 tablespoons cornstarch
½ teaspoon chicken-flavor instant bouillon
½ cup water
3 tablespoons rice vinegar
2 tablespoons ketchup
2 teaspoons soy sauce
1 (20-oz.) can pineapple chunks in
    unsweetened juice, drained,
    reserving 3 tablespoons liquid
1 garlic clove, minced
1 green bell pepper, cut into ¾-inch pieces

1. Cook rice in 2⅔ cups water as directed on package.
2. Meanwhile, in medium bowl, combine ¼ cup cornstarch, flour, sugar, baking soda, 3 tablespoons water and egg; mix well. Add pork; stir until well blended.
3. In deep fryer, heavy saucepan or wok, heat 2 to 3 inches of oil to 375°F. Fry bat-

Chinese Sweet-and-Sour Pork

tered pork pieces, ¼ of total amount at a time, for 2 to 3 minutes or until golden brown and no longer pink in center, turning once. Drain on paper towels. Reserve 1 tablespoon oil from deep fryer.
4. In small saucepan, combine brown sugar, 2 tablespoons cornstarch, bouillon, ½ cup water, vinegar, ketchup, soy sauce and reserved 3 tablespoons pineapple liquid; blend well. Cook over medium-high heat until bubbly and thickened, stirring constantly. Keep warm.
5. Heat reserved 1 tablespoon oil in large skillet or wok until hot. Add garlic and bell pepper; cook and stir 2 to 3 minutes or until pepper is crisp-tender. Stir in pineapple chunks, pork and sauce. Cook until thoroughly heated. Serve immediately over rice.

NUTRITION INFORMATION PER SERVING: Serving Size: ¼ of Recipe ◆ Calories: 640 ◆ Calories from Fat: 220 ◆ % DAILY VALUE: Total Fat: 24 g 37% ◆ Saturated Fat: 4 g 20% ◆ Cholesterol: 85 mg 28% ◆ Sodium: 510 mg 21% ◆ Total Carbohydrate: 86 g 29% ◆ Dietary Fiber: 2 g 8% ◆ Sugars: 25 g ◆ Protein: 19 g ◆ Vitamin A: 6% ◆ Vitamin C: 35% ◆ Calcium: 6% ◆ Iron: 20% ◆ DIETARY EXCHANGES: 2½ Starch, 3 Fruit, 1½ Medium-Fat Meat, 3 Fat OR 5½ Carbohydrate, 1½ Medium-Fat Meat, 3 Fat

Pork Cutlets with Southwestern Sauce

PREP TIME: 40 MINUTES ◆ YIELD: 4 SERVINGS

1 cup uncooked regular long-grain white rice
2 cups water
1 lb. pork cutlets
1 tablespoon oil
1 (14.5 or 16-oz.) can whole tomatoes,
    undrained, cut up
1 (8-oz.) can tomato sauce
1 (4.5-oz.) can chopped green chiles
½ teaspoon salt
¼ teaspoon onion powder
¼ teaspoon cumin
¼ cup raisins
1 (1-lb.) pkg. frozen mixed vegetables

1. Cook rice in water as directed on package.
2. Meanwhile, if necessary, cut pork into 4 serving-sized pieces. Heat oil in large skillet over medium-high heat until hot. Add pork; cook until lightly browned on both sides.
3. Reduce heat to medium. Stir in tomatoes, tomato sauce, chiles, salt, onion powder and cumin; cook 5 minutes.

Pork Cutlets with Southwestern Sauce (page 136)

4. Add raisins and frozen vegetables. Bring to a boil. Reduce heat to low; cover and simmer 15 to 20 minutes or until vegetables and pork are tender, stirring occasionally. Serve over rice.

NUTRITION INFORMATION PER SERVING: Serving Size: ¼ of Recipe ◆ Calories: 580 ◆ Calories from Fat: 140 ◆ **% DAILY VALUE:** Total Fat: 16 g 25% ◆ Saturated Fat: 5 g 25% ◆ Cholesterol: 80 mg 27% ◆ Sodium: 1370 mg 57% ◆ Total Carbohydrate: 76 g 25% ◆ Dietary Fiber: 7 g 28% ◆ Sugars: 13 g ◆ Protein: 32 g ◆ Vitamin A: 80% ◆ Vitamin C: 45% ◆ Calcium: 10% ◆ Iron: 30% ◆ **DIETARY EXCHANGES:** 4 Starch, 3 Vegetable, 2½ Medium-Fat Meat OR 4 Carbohydrate, 3 Vegetable, 2½ Medium-Fat Meat

Maple-Mustard Country-Style Ribs

PREP TIME: 10 MINUTES (READY IN 8 HOURS 10 MINUTES) ◆ YIELD: 4 SERVINGS

1 large onion, cut into ¼-inch slices, separated into rings
⅓ cup maple-flavored syrup
¼ cup spicy brown mustard or country-style Dijon mustard
2½ to 3 lb. pork country-style ribs, trimmed of fat, cut into 3-inch pieces

1. Place onion rings in 3½ or 4-quart slow cooker. In small bowl, combine syrup and mustard; mix well. Spread evenly on ribs. Place coated ribs over onion.
2. Cover; cook on low setting for at least 8 hours or until ribs are tender.

NUTRITION INFORMATION PER SERVING: Serving Size: ¼ of Recipe ◆ Calories: 680 ◆ Calories from Fat: 420 ◆ **% DAILY VALUE:** Total Fat: 47 g 72% ◆ Saturated Fat: 18 g 90% ◆ Cholesterol: 165 mg 55% ◆ Sodium: 370 mg 15% ◆ Total Carbohydrate: 21 g 7% ◆ Dietary Fiber: 1 g 4% ◆ Sugars: 12 g ◆ Protein: 43 g ◆ Vitamin A: 0% ◆ Vitamin C: 4% ◆ Calcium: 6% ◆ Iron: 10% ◆ **DIETARY EXCHANGES:** 1½ Fruit, 6 High-Fat Meat OR 1½ Carbohydrate, 6 High-Fat Meat

Savory Grilled Pork Chops with Fruit Salsa

PREP TIME: 25 MINUTES (READY IN 2 HOURS 25 MINUTES) ◆ YIELD: 6 SERVINGS

PORK CHOPS
1 (8-oz.) can pineapple tidbits in unsweetened juice
⅓ cup lite soy sauce
2 garlic cloves, minced
6 (4-oz.) center-cut pork chops

SALSA
Reserved pineapple tidbits
½ cup chopped fresh strawberries
1 medium nectarine, chopped
2 tablespoons sliced green onions
2 tablespoons finely chopped cilantro
1 tablespoon sugar
1 tablespoon vinegar
1 tablespoon lite soy sauce

1. GRILL DIRECTIONS: Drain pineapple, reserving liquid; set pineapple aside. In ungreased 13×9-inch (3-quart) baking dish, combine reserved pineapple liquid, ⅓ cup soy sauce and garlic; blend well. Add pork chops; turn to coat. Cover; refrigerate 2 to 3 hours to marinate, turning occasionally.
2. Meanwhile, in medium bowl, combine pineapple tidbits and all remaining salsa ingredients; mix well. Cover; refrigerate while pork chops are marinating.
3. Heat grill. When ready to grill, remove pork chops from marinade; discard marinade. Place pork chops on gas grill over medium-high heat or on charcoal grill 4 to 6 inches from medium-high coals. Cook 10 to 14 minutes or until no longer pink in center, turning once. Serve salsa with pork chops.

TIP: To broil pork chops, place on broiler pan; broil 4 to 6 inches from heat using times above as a guide, turning once.

NUTRITION INFORMATION PER SERVING: Serving Size: ⅙ of Recipe ◆ Calories: 170 ◆ Calories from Fat: 45 ◆ **% DAILY VALUE:** Total Fat: 5 g 8% ◆ Saturated Fat: 2 g 10% ◆ Cholesterol: 45 mg 15% ◆ Sodium: 290 mg 12% ◆ Total Carbohydrate: 13 g 4% ◆ Dietary Fiber: 1 g 4% ◆ Sugars: 10 g ◆ Protein: 17 g ◆ Vitamin A: 4% ◆ Vitamin C: 15% ◆ Calcium: 2% ◆ Iron: 6% ◆ **DIETARY EXCHANGES:** 1 Fruit, 2 Lean Meat OR 1 Carbohydrate, 2 Lean Meat

Grilled Stuffed Pork Chops

PREP TIME: 30 MINUTES ◆ YIELD: 4 SERVINGS

STUFFING

  1 teaspoon dried marjoram leaves
  1 teaspoon freeze-dried chopped chives
  1 teaspoon dried basil leaves
  2 cups herb-seasoned stuffing mix
  1/3 cup finely chopped onion
  1/2 cup hot water
  1/4 cup margarine or butter, melted

PORK CHOPS

  4 pork loin chops (1 inch thick)

1. GRILL DIRECTIONS: Heat grill. In medium bowl, combine marjoram, chives and basil; mix well. Reserve 2 teaspoons herb mixture; set aside. To remaining herb mixture, add stuffing mix, onion, water and margarine; mix well.

2. Cut deep horizontal pocket in one side of each pork chop. Stuff each chop with about 1/2 cup stuffing mixture; press firmly. Sprinkle reserved herb mixture on both sides of each chop.

3. When ready to grill, place chops on gas grill over medium-high heat or on charcoal grill 4 to 6 inches from medium-high coals. Cook 15 to 20 minutes or until pork is no longer pink in center, turning once.

> **TIP:** To broil pork chops, place on broiler pan; broil 4 to 6 inches from heat using times above as a guide, turning once.

NUTRITION INFORMATION PER SERVING: Serving Size: 1/4 of Recipe ◆ Calories: 460 ◆ Calories from Fat: 220 ◆ **% DAILY VALUE:** Total Fat: 24 g 37% ◆ Saturated Fat: 6 g 30% ◆ Cholesterol: 100 mg 33% ◆ Sodium: 600 mg 25% ◆ Total Carbohydrate: 23 g 8% ◆ Dietary Fiber: 2 g 8% ◆ Sugars: 2 g ◆ Protein: 38 g ◆ Vitamin A: 10% ◆ Vitamin C: 2% ◆ Calcium: 6% ◆ Iron: 15% ◆ **DIETARY EXCHANGES:** 1 1/2 Starch, 4 1/2 Lean Meat, 2 Fat OR 1 1/2 Carbohydrate, 4 1/2 Lean Meat, 2 Fat

COOK'S NOTE

TIPS FOR GRILLING CHOPS

Place 1-inch-thick chops 4 to 6 inches from moderately hot coals. Cook 20 to 30 minutes or until tender and thoroughly cooked, turning once. Brush on any sauce or glaze in the last 10 minutes or so of cooking time to avoid burning it.

COOK'S NOTE

TIPS FOR BROILING CHOPS

Broiling is an easy, quick way to cook pork or lamb chops. The hot flame or broiler element sears the exterior, browning the surface while keeping the interior juicy.

◆ The thicker the chops, the farther they should be from the flame to avoid flare-ups from sizzling fat and to allow time for the interior to cook without scorching the surface. For 1-inch-thick chops, set the broiler pan so the meat is about 4 inches from the heat. For 2-inch-thick chops, the meat should be about 6 inches from the heat.

◆ Turn the meat only once, when the first side is nicely browned.

◆ Watch carefully! Broiling can quickly go from nicely done to overdone.

Pork Loin Chops with Fresh Tomato Relish

PREP TIME: 20 MINUTES ◆ YIELD: 4 SERVINGS

PORK CHOPS

  4 (3-oz.) boneless pork loin chops
  1/4 teaspoon salt
  Dash pepper

RELISH

  2 tablespoons apple jelly
  2 teaspoons rice vinegar
  1 teaspoon tomato paste
  1/4 teaspoon salt
  1/8 teaspoon dried thyme leaves
  1 medium tomato, diced
  1/4 cup diced zucchini
  1 teaspoon chopped fresh parsley

1. Spray broiler pan with nonstick cooking spray. Sprinkle pork chops with 1/4 teaspoon salt and dash pepper; place on sprayed pan. Broil 4 to 6 inches from heat for 8 to 12 minutes or until pork is no longer pink in center, turning once.

2. Meanwhile, in small saucepan or microwave-safe bowl, combine jelly, vinegar, tomato paste, ¼ teaspoon salt and thyme; mix well. Heat over medium heat or microwave on HIGH for 30 to 40 seconds until jelly melts, stirring occasionally.

3. In small bowl, combine tomato, zucchini and parsley. Pour hot jelly mixture over tomato mixture; mix well. Serve relish with pork chops.

NUTRITION INFORMATION PER SERVING: Serving Size: ¼ of Recipe • Calories: 140 • Calories from Fat: 45 • **% DAILY VALUE:** Total Fat: 5 g 8% • Saturated Fat: 2 g 10% • Cholesterol: 35 mg 12% • Sodium: 310 mg 13% • Total Carbohydrate: 9 g 3% • Dietary Fiber: 1 g 3% • Sugars: 6 g • Protein: 14 g • Vitamin A: 6% • Vitamin C: 10% • Calcium: 0% • Iron: 4% • **DIETARY EXCHANGES:** ½ Fruit, 2 Lean Meat OR ½ Carbohydrate, 2 Lean Meat

Breaded Pork Chops

PREP TIME: 20 MINUTES ✦ YIELD: 4 SERVINGS

2 tablespoons all-purpose flour
½ teaspoon salt
½ teaspoon paprika
⅛ teaspoon pepper
1 egg, slightly beaten
1 to 2 teaspoons Worcestershire sauce
½ cup unseasoned dry bread crumbs
4 boneless pork loin chops
2 tablespoons oil

1. In small bowl, combine flour, salt, paprika and pepper; mix well. In another small bowl, combine egg and Worcestershire sauce. Coat pork chops with seasoned flour; dip in egg mixture and coat with crumbs.

2. In large skillet, heat oil over medium-high heat until hot. Add chops; cook until browned on both sides. Reduce heat to medium; cook 5 to 7 minutes or until pork is no longer pink in center.

NUTRITION INFORMATION PER SERVING: Serving Size: ¼ of Recipe • Calories: 310 • Calories from Fat: 150 • **% DAILY VALUE:** Total Fat: 17 g 26% • Saturated Fat: 4 g 20% • Cholesterol: 120 mg 40% • Sodium: 470 mg 20% • Total Carbohydrate: 13 g 4% • Dietary Fiber: 1 g 2% • Sugars: 1 g • Protein: 27 g • Vitamin A: 4% • Vitamin C: 0% • Calcium: 6% • Iron: 10% • **DIETARY EXCHANGES:** 1 Starch, 3½ Lean Meat, 1 Fat OR 1 Carbohydrate, 3½ Lean Meat, 1 Fat

VARIATIONS

Cheese-Topped Pork Chops: Decrease bread crumbs to ¼ cup. Mix crumbs with ¼ cup grated Parmesan cheese. When chops are thoroughly cooked, top each with slice of mozzarella cheese and tomato slice. Cover; heat until tomato is hot and cheese begins to melt.

Oven-Baked Breaded Pork Chops: Prepare as directed above. Place in ungreased shallow baking pan. Bake at 425°F. for 30 to 35 minutes or until no longer pink in center.

Stuffed Apple-Glazed Pork Chops

PREP TIME: 30 MINUTES (READY IN 1 HOUR 35 MINUTES) ✦ YIELD: 4 SERVINGS

PORK CHOPS
4 pork loin chops (1 inch thick)

STUFFING
2 slices raisin bread, toasted, cut into cubes (about 1 cup)
½ cup chopped apple
½ cup chopped pecans
½ teaspoon salt
¼ teaspoon grated orange peel
⅛ teaspoon cinnamon
Dash pepper
3 tablespoons orange juice

GLAZE
2 tablespoons sugar
1 tablespoon cornstarch
1 cup apple juice
2 tablespoons margarine or butter

1. Heat oven to 350°F. Cut deep horizontal pocket in each pork chop.

2. In medium bowl, combine all stuffing ingredients; mix well. Stuff each chop with ¼ of stuffing mixture; place chops in ungreased 13×9-inch pan. Bake at 350°F. for 30 minutes.

3. Meanwhile, in small saucepan, combine sugar and cornstarch; mix well. Stir in apple juice. Cook over medium-low heat until mixture boils and thickens, stirring frequently. Remove from heat; stir in margarine.

4. Remove pork chops from oven. Pour glaze evenly over chops. Return to oven; bake an additional 30 to 35 minutes or until pork chops are no longer pink in center.

NUTRITION INFORMATION PER SERVING: Serving Size: ¼ of Recipe • Calories: 440 • Calories from Fat: 220 • **% DAILY VALUE:** Total Fat: 24 g 37% • Saturated Fat: 5 g 25% • Cholesterol: 65 mg 22% • Sodium: 440 mg 18% • Total Carbohydrate: 29 g 10% • Dietary Fiber: 3 g 12% • Sugars: 19 g • Protein: 26 g • Vitamin A: 6% • Vitamin C: 10% • Calcium: 4% • Iron: 10% • **DIETARY EXCHANGES:** ½ Starch, 1½ Fruit, 3½ Medium-Fat Meat, 1 Fat OR 2 Carbohydrate, 3½ Medium-Fat Meat, 1 Fat

Braised Pork Chops with Cream Gravy

Braised Pork Chops with Cream Gravy

PREP TIME: 15 MINUTES (READY IN 55 MINUTES)
✦ YIELD: 4 SERVINGS

4 pork loin chops (½ inch thick)
½ cup water
2 teaspoons dried parsley flakes
¼ teaspoon salt
¼ teaspoon onion powder
¼ teaspoon dried thyme leaves
¼ teaspoon Worcestershire sauce
⅓ cup milk
2 tablespoons all-purpose flour

1. In large skillet over medium-high heat, brown pork chops on both sides. Add water, parsley flakes, salt, onion powder, thyme and Worcestershire sauce. Cover; simmer 20 to 30 minutes or until pork chops are tender.
2. Remove pork chops from skillet; keep warm. In small bowl, combine milk and flour; blend until smooth. Gradually stir into hot mixture in skillet. Cook until mixture boils and thickens, stirring constantly. Serve gravy with pork chops.

NUTRITION INFORMATION PER SERVING: Serving Size: ¼ of Recipe ✦ Calories: 180 ✦ Calories from Fat: 70 ✦ **% DAILY VALUE:** Total Fat: 8 g 12% ✦ Saturated Fat: 3 g 15% ✦ Cholesterol: 65 mg 22% ✦ Sodium: 190 mg 8% ✦ Total Carbohydrate: 4 g 1% ✦ Dietary Fiber: 0 g 0% ✦ Sugars: 1 g ✦ Protein: 24 g ✦ Vitamin A: 0% ✦ Vitamin C: 0% ✦ Calcium: 4% ✦ Iron: 6% ✦ **DIETARY EXCHANGES:** 3½ Lean Meat

Pork Chop Dinner with Bacon and Cider Gravy

PREP TIME: 30 MINUTES ✦ YIELD: 4 SERVINGS

4 oz. (2½ cups) uncooked extra-wide egg noodles
2 cups frozen cut green beans
3 slices bacon, cut into small pieces
4 (4-oz.) boneless pork loin chops
¼ cup chopped onion
1 cup apple cider or juice
1 teaspoon honey mustard
¼ teaspoon salt
¼ teaspoon dried thyme leaves
⅛ teaspoon pepper
1 tablespoon water
1 tablespoon cornstarch

1. Cook noodles to desired doneness as directed on package, adding green beans during last 4 minutes of cooking time. Drain; cover to keep warm.
2. Meanwhile, in large skillet, cook bacon over medium heat until brown and crisp. With slotted spoon, remove bacon from skillet; drain on paper towels. Drain and discard all drippings from skillet.
3. Place pork chops in skillet near center. Sprinkle onion around pork chops. Cook 3 to 5 minutes or until pork chops are golden brown, turning once. In small bowl, combine cider, mustard, salt, thyme and pepper; mix well. Pour over chops. Reduce heat to low; cover and cook 10 to 15 minutes or until pork is no longer pink in center.
4. Arrange noodles and green beans on serving platter. Place pork chops on top of noodle mixture; cover to keep warm.
5. In small bowl, combine water and cornstarch; blend until smooth. Add to juices in skillet; mix well. Cook and stir over medium-low heat until bubbly and thickened; boil 1 minute. (If desired, gravy can be strained.)
6. To serve, pour gravy over pork chops and noodles. Sprinkle with bacon.

NUTRITION INFORMATION PER SERVING: Serving Size: ¼ of Recipe ✦ Calories: 340 ✦ Calories from Fat: 90 ✦ **% DAILY VALUE:** Total Fat: 10 g 15% ✦ Saturated Fat: 3 g 15% ✦ Cholesterol: 85 mg 28% ✦ Sodium: 300 mg 13% ✦ Total Carbohydrate: 34 g 11% ✦ Dietary Fiber: 2 g 8% ✦ Sugars: 9 g ✦ Protein: 28 g ✦ Vitamin A: 4% ✦ Vitamin C: 6% ✦ Calcium: 4% ✦ Iron: 15% ✦ **DIETARY EXCHANGES:** 1½ Starch, ½ Fruit, 1 Vegetable, 3 Lean Meat OR 2 Carbohydrate, 1 Vegetable, 3 Lean Meat

Maple-Glazed Pork Chops

Maple-Glazed Pork Chops

PREP TIME: 35 MINUTES ✦ YIELD: 4 SERVINGS

PORK CHOPS
  4 pork chops (¾ inch thick)
  ¼ teaspoon salt
  ¼ teaspoon coarse ground black pepper

MAPLE GLAZE
  ¾ cup pure maple syrup or maple-flavored
    syrup
  2 tablespoons brown sugar
  2 tablespoons ketchup
  2 tablespoons prepared mustard
  1 tablespoon Worcestershire sauce

1. GRILL DIRECTIONS: Heat grill. Rub both sides of pork chops with salt and pepper. In small saucepan, combine all glaze ingredients; mix well. Bring to a boil, stirring constantly. Set aside.
2. When ready to grill, place pork chops on gas grill over medium heat or on charcoal grill 4 to 6 inches from medium coals. Cook 15 minutes, turning once.
3. Brush pork chops with glaze. Cook an additional 10 minutes or until no longer pink, turning once and brushing frequently with glaze. Bring any remaining glaze to a boil; serve with pork chops.

TIP: To broil pork chops, place on broiler pan; broil 4 to 6 inches from heat using times above as a guide, turning once and brushing frequently with glaze.

NUTRITION INFORMATION PER SERVING: Serving Size: ¼ of Recipe ✦ Calories: 370 ✦ Calories from Fat: 70 ✦ **% DAILY VALUE:** Total Fat: 8 g 12% ✦ Saturated Fat: 4 g 20% ✦ Cholesterol: 50 mg 17% ✦ Sodium: 430 mg 18% ✦ Total Carbohydrate: 54 g 18% ✦ Dietary Fiber: 0 g 0% ✦ Sugars: 36 g ✦ Protein: 20 g ✦ Vitamin A: 0% ✦ Vitamin C: 0% ✦ Calcium: 2% ✦ Iron: 6% ✦ **DIETARY EXCHANGES:** 3½ Fruit, 3 Lean Meat

Spice-Rubbed Pork Chops

PREP TIME: 15 MINUTES (READY IN 45 MINUTES) ✦ YIELD: 4 SERVINGS

  1 tablespoon brown sugar
  1½ teaspoons chili powder
  ¼ teaspoon salt
  ¼ teaspoon cumin
  ¼ teaspoon pepper
  ⅛ teaspoon allspice
  4 pork loin chops (¾ inch thick)

1. GRILL DIRECTIONS: In small bowl, combine all ingredients except pork chops; mix well. Rub pork chops on both sides with spice mixture. Let stand at room temperature for 30 minutes.
2. Meanwhile, heat grill. When ready to grill, place pork chops on gas grill over medium heat or on charcoal grill 4 to 6 inches from medium coals. Cook 8 to 10 minutes or until pork is no longer pink in center, turning once.

TIP: To broil pork chops, place on broiler pan; broil 4 to 6 inches from heat using times above as a guide, turning once.

NUTRITION INFORMATION PER SERVING: Serving Size: ¼ of Recipe ✦ Calories: 180 ✦ Calories from Fat: 70 ✦ **% DAILY VALUE:** Total Fat: 8 g 12% ✦ Saturated Fat: 3 g 15% ✦ Cholesterol: 65 mg 22% ✦ Sodium: 190 mg 8% ✦ Total Carbohydrate: 4 g 1% ✦ Dietary Fiber: 0 g 0% ✦ Sugars: 3 g ✦ Protein: 23 g ✦ Vitamin A: 6% ✦ Vitamin C: 0% ✦ Calcium: 2% ✦ Iron: 6% ✦ **DIETARY EXCHANGES:** 3 Lean Meat

Spice-Rubbed Pork Chops

Country Breaded Pork Chops

PREP TIME: 10 MINUTES (READY IN 35 MINUTES)
◆ YIELD: 4 SERVINGS

 1/2 cup corn flake crumbs
  1 tablespoon Dijon mustard
  2 teaspoons orange juice
 1/4 teaspoon dried thyme leaves
  4 (4-oz.) pork loin chops

1. Heat oven to 425°F. Line cookie sheet with foil; spray foil lightly with nonstick cooking spray.
2. Place crumbs in shallow dish. In small bowl, combine mustard, orange juice and thyme; mix well. Brush 1 side of each pork chop with mustard mixture. Place 1 chop, mustard side down, in crumbs; brush remaining side of chop with mustard mixture. Turn chop to coat both sides well with crumbs. Place on sprayed foil-lined cookie sheet. Repeat with remaining chops.
3. Bake at 425°F. for 20 to 25 minutes or until pork chops are tender and no longer pink in center.

NUTRITION INFORMATION PER SERVING: Serving Size: 1/4 of Recipe ◆ Calories: 170 ◆ Calories from Fat: 50 ◆ **% DAILY VALUE:** Total Fat: 6 g 9% ◆ Saturated Fat: 2 g 10% ◆ Cholesterol: 50 mg 17% ◆ Sodium: 240 mg 10% ◆ Total Carbohydrate: 10 g 3% ◆ Dietary Fiber: 0 g 0% ◆ Sugars: 1 g ◆ Protein: 18 g ◆ Vitamin A: 6% ◆ Vitamin C: 8% ◆ Calcium: 0% ◆ Iron: 25% ◆ **DIETARY EXCHANGES:** 1/2 Starch, 2 1/2 Lean Meat OR 1/2 Carbohydrate, 2 1/2 Lean Meat

Beer and Bratwurst

PREP TIME: 10 MINUTES (READY IN 30 MINUTES)
◆ YIELD: 4 SERVINGS

  1 lb. (about 4) uncooked bratwurst
  1 (12-oz.) can beer
  1 medium onion, sliced
 10 black peppercorns

1. GRILL DIRECTIONS: Heat grill. In large saucepan, combine all ingredients. Bring just to a boil over medium-high heat. Reduce heat to low; cover and simmer 10 minutes. Remove bratwurst and, if necessary, continue simmering onions until tender.
2. Immediately place bratwurst on gas grill over medium heat or on charcoal grill 4 to 6 inches from medium coals. Cook 6 to 10 minutes or until browned, turning once. To serve, drain onions and serve with bratwurst.

> **TIP:** To broil bratwurst, place on broiler pan; broil 4 to 6 inches from heat using times above as a guide, turning once.

NUTRITION INFORMATION PER SERVING: Serving Size: 1/4 of Recipe ◆ Calories: 300 ◆ Calories from Fat: 200 ◆ **% DAILY VALUE:** Total Fat: 22 g 34% ◆ Saturated Fat: 8 g 40% ◆ Cholesterol: 50 mg 17% ◆ Sodium: 480 mg 20% ◆ Total Carbohydrate: 7 g 2% ◆ Dietary Fiber: 1 g 3% ◆ Sugars: 2 g ◆ Protein: 13 g ◆ Vitamin A: 0% ◆ Vitamin C: 4% ◆ Calcium: 4% ◆ Iron: 6% ◆ **DIETARY EXCHANGES:** 1 Vegetable, 2 High-Fat Meat, 1 1/2 Fat

Glazed Apples and Canadian Bacon

PREP TIME: 25 MINUTES ◆ YIELD: 8 SERVINGS

 1/2 cup firmly packed brown sugar
 1/8 teaspoon pepper
  1 tablespoon lemon juice
  2 large red and/or green cooking apples, cored, each cut into 16 wedges
  1 lb. sliced Canadian bacon

1. In large skillet, combine brown sugar, pepper and lemon juice; mix well. Cook and stir over medium heat until brown sugar is melted. Add apples; cook 5 to 6 minutes or until tender, stirring occasionally. With slotted spoon, place apples on serving platter.
2. Add Canadian bacon to same skillet; cook 1 to 2 minutes or until hot, turning once. Arrange on platter with apples. Spoon any remaining liquid in skillet over apples and Canadian bacon.

NUTRITION INFORMATION PER SERVING: Serving Size: 1/8 of Recipe ◆ Calories: 180 ◆ Calories from Fat: 35 ◆ **% DAILY VALUE:** Total Fat: 4 g 6% ◆ Saturated Fat: 1 g 5% ◆ Cholesterol: 30 mg 10% ◆ Sodium: 810 mg 34% ◆ Total Carbohydrate: 23 g 8% ◆ Dietary Fiber: 1 g 4% ◆ Sugars: 21 g ◆ Protein: 12 g ◆ Vitamin A: 0% ◆ Vitamin C: 4% ◆ Calcium: 2% ◆ Iron: 4% ◆ **DIETARY EXCHANGES:** 1 1/2 Fruit, 1 1/2 Lean Meat OR 1 1/2 Carbohydrate, 1 1/2 Lean Meat

COOK'S NOTE

NO MORE OVERCOOKED PORK

In the past, conventional wisdom was to cook pork extra long in order to kill dangerous trichina contamination that might be in the meat. Good news: trichina has not been a problem in the United States for decades. Cooking pork to an internal temperature of 160° F. is high enough for safety yet low enough that the meat remains moist.

Pasta Carbonara

PREP TIME: 20 MINUTES ✦ YIELD: 6 (1½-CUP) SERVINGS

    1 (16-oz.) pkg. uncooked linguine
    2 teaspoons margarine or butter
    1¼ cups finely chopped Canadian bacon
    1 cup finely chopped onions
    1 garlic clove, minced
    ¾ cup skim milk
    ½ cup refrigerated or frozen fat-free egg
        product, thawed
    ½ teaspoon cracked black pepper
    ¼ cup grated Parmesan cheese

1. Cook linguine to desired doneness as directed on package. Drain; cover to keep warm.

2. Meanwhile, in Dutch oven or large saucepan, melt margarine over medium heat. Add bacon, onions and garlic; cook and stir 4 minutes or until onions are tender.

3. Add cooked linguine, milk, egg product and pepper to bacon mixture; toss gently to mix. Cook 1 minute or until thoroughly heated. Remove from heat; toss gently. Sprinkle with cheese.

NUTRITION INFORMATION PER SERVING: Serving Size: 1½ Cups ✦ Calories: 390 ✦ Calories from Fat: 50 ✦ % DAILY VALUE: Total Fat: 6 g 9% ✦ Saturated Fat: 2 g 10% ✦ Cholesterol: 20 mg 7% ✦ Sodium: 550 mg 23% ✦ Total Carbohydrate: 62 g 21% ✦ Dietary Fiber: 2 g 8% ✦ Sugars: 6 g ✦ Protein: 21 g ✦ Vitamin A: 4% ✦ Vitamin C: 2% ✦ Calcium: 15% ✦ Iron: 20% ✦ DIETARY EXCHANGES: 4 Starch, 1½ Lean Meat OR 4 Carbohydrate, 1½ Lean Meat

Fusilli with Fiery Tomato Sauce and Sausage

PREP TIME: 25 MINUTES ✦ YIELD: 4 (1½-CUP) SERVINGS

    8 oz. (3 cups) uncooked fusilli (curly spaghetti)
        or rotini (spiral pasta)
    1 tablespoon olive or vegetable oil
    ¾ lb. smoked sausage, cut into ¼-inch slices
    2 garlic cloves, minced
    1 (28-oz.) can crushed tomatoes, undrained
    2 tablespoons capers, if desired
    1 teaspoon chili powder
    ½ to 1 teaspoon crushed red pepper flakes

1. Cook fusilli to desired doneness as directed on package. Drain.

2. Meanwhile, heat oil in large saucepan over medium-high heat until hot. Add sausage; cook 2 to 3 minutes or until browned. Add garlic; cook 1 minute.

3. Stir in tomatoes, capers, chili powder and red pepper flakes. Reduce heat; simmer 10 minutes or until hot and slightly thickened, stirring occasionally.

4. Add cooked fusilli; toss gently to mix.

NUTRITION INFORMATION PER SERVING: Serving Size: 1½ Cups ✦ Calories: 590 ✦ Calories from Fat: 270 ✦ % DAILY VALUE: Total Fat: 30 g 46% ✦ Saturated Fat: 10 g 50% ✦ Cholesterol: 60 mg 20% ✦ Sodium: 1210 mg 50% ✦ Total Carbohydrate: 58 g 19% ✦ Dietary Fiber: 5 g 20% ✦ Sugars: 9 g ✦ Protein: 22 g ✦ Vitamin A: 30% ✦ Vitamin C: 25% ✦ Calcium: 8% ✦ Iron: 35% ✦ DIETARY EXCHANGES: 3½ Starch, 1 Vegetable, 1½ High-Fat Meat, 3 Fat OR 3½ Carbohydrate, 1 Vegetable, 1½ High-Fat Meat, 3 Fat

Twenty-Minute Cassoulet

PREP TIME: 20 MINUTES ✦ YIELD: 8 (1-CUP) SERVINGS

    1 lb. smoked kielbasa sausage or turkey
        sausage, cut in half lengthwise, sliced
    1 cup sliced celery
    ½ cup chopped onion
    2 garlic cloves, minced
    ½ teaspoon dried thyme leaves
    ½ teaspoon dried rosemary leaves, crushed
    2 (15.5-oz.) cans great northern beans,
        drained, rinsed
    1 (15.5 or 15-oz.) can light red kidney beans,
        drained, rinsed
    1 (14.5-oz.) can diced tomatoes, undrained
    1 teaspoon brown sugar
    ¼ cup sliced green onions

1. In nonstick Dutch oven or large saucepan, brown sausage over medium heat, stirring frequently. With slotted spoon, remove sausage; set aside.

2. Reserve ½ teaspoon drippings in Dutch oven. Add celery, onion, garlic, thyme and rosemary; cook and stir 5 minutes or until vegetables are crisp-tender.

3. Add cooked sausage and remaining ingredients except green onions. Bring to a boil. Reduce heat to low; cover and simmer 10 minutes or until thoroughly heated. Top each serving with sliced green onions.

NUTRITION INFORMATION PER SERVING: Serving Size: 1 Cup ✦ Calories: 320 ✦ Calories from Fat: 140 ✦ % DAILY VALUE: Total Fat: 16 g 25% ✦ Saturated Fat: 6 g 30% ✦ Cholesterol: 40 mg 13% ✦ Sodium: 920 mg 38% ✦ Total Carbohydrate: 27 g 9% ✦ Dietary Fiber: 8 g 32% ✦ Sugars: 4 g ✦ Protein: 16 g ✦ Vitamin A: 8% ✦ Vitamin C: 10% ✦ Calcium: 15% ✦ Iron: 20% ✦ DIETARY EXCHANGES: 2 Starch, 1½ High-Fat Meat, ½ Fat OR 2 Carbohydrate, 1½ High-Fat Meat, ½ Fat

Spinach and Sausage Phyllo Bake

PREP TIME: 45 MINUTES (READY IN 1 HOUR 50 MINUTES)
✦ YIELD: 8 SERVINGS

1 lb. bulk pork or Italian sausage
½ cup thinly sliced purchased roasted red bell peppers (from 7.25-oz. jar)
1 (2¼-oz.) can sliced ripe olives, drained
4 oz. (1 cup) shredded mozzarella cheese
5 eggs, beaten
4 oz. (1 cup) shredded Cheddar cheese
1 cup ricotta cheese
1 (9-oz.) pkg. frozen spinach in a pouch, thawed, drained
16 (17 x 12-inch) sheets frozen phyllo (filo) pastry, thawed
½ cup butter, melted

1. Heat oven to 350°F. In large skillet over medium heat, brown sausage; drain. Cool slightly. Stir in roasted peppers, olives, mozzarella cheese and eggs; mix well.
2. In medium bowl, combine Cheddar cheese, ricotta cheese and spinach; mix well.
3. Unroll phyllo pastry; cover with plastic wrap or towel. Place 1 sheet of phyllo in ungreased 13 x 9-inch (3-quart) baking dish, folding to fit. Brush lightly with melted butter. Continue layering and brushing with butter using 3 additional sheets of phyllo.
4. Spoon half of sausage mixture over phyllo. Layer and brush with butter 4 more phyllo sheets. Top with spinach mixture. Layer and brush with butter 4 more phyllo sheets. Top with remaining sausage mixture. Layer and brush with butter 4 more phyllo sheets. Score top of phyllo in diamond shapes.

Spinach and Sausage Phyllo Bake

5. Bake at 350°F. for 50 to 60 minutes or until puffed and golden brown. Let stand 5 minutes before serving.

NUTRITION INFORMATION PER SERVING: Serving Size: ⅛ of Recipe ✦ Calories: 550 ✦ Calories from Fat: 340 ✦ **% DAILY VALUE:** Total Fat: 38 g 58% ✦ Saturated Fat: 18 g 90% ✦ Cholesterol: 230 mg 77% ✦ Sodium: 1070 mg 45% ✦ Total Carbohydrate: 25 g 8% ✦ Dietary Fiber: 2 g 8% ✦ Sugars: 2 g ✦ Protein: 27 g ✦ Vitamin A: 50% ✦ Vitamin C: 25% ✦ Calcium: 35% ✦ Iron: 20% ✦ **DIETARY EXCHANGES:** 1½ Starch, 1 Vegetable, 3 High-Fat Meat, 2 Fat OR 1½ Carbohydrate, 1 Vegetable, 3 High-Fat Meat, 2 Fat

Chunky Skillet Sausage Stew

Chunky Skillet Sausage Stew

PREP TIME: 35 MINUTES ✦ YIELD: 6 SERVINGS

1 lb. smoked sausage, cut into 1½ to 2-inch chunks
6 small new red potatoes, unpeeled, quartered
1 small onion, cut into 8 wedges
1 (14.5-oz.) can stewed tomatoes, undrained
⅛ teaspoon pepper
½ medium head cabbage, cut into 6 wedges

1. In large skillet, combine all ingredients except cabbage; mix well. Arrange cabbage wedges over top.
2. Bring to a boil. Reduce heat to medium-low; cover and cook 15 to 20 minutes or until vegetables are tender. Spoon sauce from skillet over cabbage wedges before serving.

NUTRITION INFORMATION PER SERVING: Serving Size: ⅙ of Recipe ✦ Calories: 390 ✦ Calories from Fat: 210 ✦ **% DAILY VALUE:** Total Fat: 23 g 35% ✦ Saturated Fat: 8 g 40% ✦ Cholesterol: 55 mg 18% ✦ Sodium: 890 mg 37% ✦ Total Carbohydrate: 32 g 11% ✦ Dietary Fiber: 5 g 20% ✦ Sugars: 6 g ✦ Protein: 14 g ✦ Vitamin A: 10% ✦ Vitamin C: 50% ✦ Calcium: 8% ✦ Iron: 20% ✦ **DIETARY EXCHANGES:** 1½ Starch, 2 Vegetable, 1 High-Fat Meat, 3 Fat OR 1½ Carbohydrate, 2 Vegetable, 1 High-Fat Meat, 3 Fat

Baked Ham with Orange-Mustard Glaze

Very Berry Picnic Ham

PREP TIME: 30 MINUTES (READY IN 3 HOURS 40 MINUTES) ◆ YIELD: 12 SERVINGS

HAM

  1 (7 to 8-lb.) fully cooked smoked picnic shoulder ham
1½ teaspoons whole cloves
  ¼ cup seedless raspberry jam, heated
  ½ teaspoon lemon juice

SAUCE

  ½ cup chopped fresh or frozen cranberries
  2 tablespoons sugar
  2 tablespoons orange juice
  ¼ teaspoon allspice
  ½ cup seedless raspberry jam

1. Heat oven to 325°F. Trim fat on ham to ¼ inch; discard excess fat. Using knife, score top of ham in diamond pattern; insert whole cloves. Place ham, scored side up, in shallow roasting pan. Insert meat thermometer so bulb reaches center of thickest part of meat, but does not rest in fat or on bone.
2. Bake at 325°F. for 2¾ to 3 hours or until thermometer reaches 140°F.
3. In small bowl, combine ¼ cup jam and lemon juice; brush over baked ham. Bake an additional 10 minutes.
4. Meanwhile, in small saucepan, combine cranberries, sugar, orange juice and allspice; mix well. Bring to a boil over medium heat. Boil 1 minute or until cranberries are tender, stirring occasionally. Stir in ½ cup jam. Serve ham slices with sauce.

NUTRITION INFORMATION PER SERVING: Serving Size: ¹⁄₁₂ of Recipe ◆ Calories: 340 ◆ Calories from Fat: 110 ◆ % DAILY VALUE: Total Fat: 12 g 18% ◆ Saturated Fat: 4 g 20% ◆ Cholesterol: 85 mg 28% ◆ Sodium: 2130 mg 89% ◆ Total Carbohydrate: 16 g 5% ◆ Dietary Fiber: 0 g 0% ◆ Sugars: 12 g ◆ Protein: 43 g ◆ Vitamin A: 0% ◆ Vitamin C: 4% ◆ Calcium: 2% ◆ Iron: 10% ◆ DIETARY EXCHANGES: 1 Fruit, 6 Very Lean Meat, 1½ Fat OR 1 Carbohydrate, 6 Very Lean Meat, 1½ Fat

Very Berry Picnic Ham

Baked Ham with Orange-Mustard Glaze

PREP TIME: 20 MINUTES (READY IN 3 HOURS) ◆ YIELD: 16 SERVINGS

  1 (6 to 8-lb.) fully cooked bone-in ham half
  1 cup water
  1 cup dry sherry or orange juice
  ⅔ cup orange marmalade
  ⅓ cup stone-ground mustard
  3 teaspoons dry mustard

1. Heat oven to 325°F. Place ham, fat side up, in disposable foil roasting pan on cookie sheet or on rack in shallow roasting pan. Pour water into pan. Bake at 325°F. for 1 hour.
2. Remove ham from oven. Add sherry to roasting pan. If necessary, trim fat from ham. Score ham diagonally at 1-inch intervals, cutting about ¼ inch deep; score in opposite direction to form diamond shapes. Insert meat thermometer so bulb reaches center of thickest part of ham, but does not rest in fat or on bone.
3. In small bowl, combine marmalade and mustards; mix well. Brush half of marmalade mixture over ham; baste with pan juices. Return to oven; bake 1 to 1½ hours or until meat thermometer registers 140°F., basting frequently with pan juices and brushing with remaining marmalade mixture.
4. Let ham stand in roasting pan for 15 minutes before slicing, basting frequently with pan juices.

NUTRITION INFORMATION PER SERVING: Serving Size: ¹⁄₁₆ of Recipe ◆ Calories: 200 ◆ Calories from Fat: 60 ◆ % DAILY VALUE: Total Fat: 7 g 11% ◆ Saturated Fat: 2 g 10% ◆ Cholesterol: 70 mg 23% ◆ Sodium: 1770 mg 74% ◆ Total Carbohydrate: 3 g 1% ◆ Dietary Fiber: 0 g 0% ◆ Sugars: 2 g ◆ Protein: 32 g ◆ Vitamin A: 0% ◆ Vitamin C: 0% ◆ Calcium: 0% ◆ Iron: 6% ◆ DIETARY EXCHANGES: 4 Lean Meat

Baked Ham

1. Allow ⅓ to ½ lb. per serving for bone-in ham and ¼ to ⅓ lb. per serving for boneless ham. Heat oven to 325°F. Place ham, fat side up, on rack in shallow roasting pan. Insert meat thermometer so bulb reaches center of thickest part of ham, but does not rest in fat or on bone.

2. Bake at 325°F. until meat thermometer registers 140°F., using "Timetable for Roasting Smoked Pork," page 147.

3. To glaze baked ham, pour drippings from pan; discard drippings. If necessary, trim fat, leaving only a thin layer on ham. Score ham by cutting diamond shapes about ¼ inch deep through fat. If desired, insert 1 whole clove in each diamond. Spoon desired glaze (pages 146 to 147) over ham. Return to oven; bake an additional 15 to 20 minutes.

NUTRITION INFORMATION PER SERVING: Serving Size: 4 oz. Cooked Ham ⋄ Calories: 150 ⋄ Calories from Fat: 50 ⋄ **% DAILY VALUE:** Total Fat: 6 g 9% ⋄ Saturated Fat: 2 g 10% ⋄ Cholesterol: 55 mg 18% ⋄ Sodium: 1610 mg 67% ⋄ Total Carbohydrate: 1 g 1% ⋄ Dietary Fiber: 0 g 0% ⋄ Sugars: 0 g ⋄ Protein: 22 g ⋄ Vitamin A: 0% ⋄ Vitamin C: 0% ⋄ Calcium: 0% ⋄ Iron: 4% ⋄ **DIETARY EXCHANGES:** 4 Lean Meat

---

COOK'S NOTE

CARVING A WHOLE HAM OR LEG OF LAMB

Place meat fat side up; remove a few slices from thin side, forming a base on which to set meat.

Turn the meat onto the base.

Cut slices down to the leg bone.

To release slices, run the knife horizontally along the bone. For additional servings, turn the meat over to its original position and slice in a similar manner.

Brown Sugar Glaze for Ham

PREP TIME: 5 MINUTES ✦ YIELD: I CUP

> 1 cup firmly packed brown sugar
> 2 tablespoons all-purpose flour
> ½ teaspoon dry mustard
> ⅛ teaspoon dry sherry, vinegar or water

In small bowl, combine all ingredients; mix well. Brush glaze on ham during last 15 to 30 minutes of baking.

NUTRITION INFORMATION PER SERVING: Serving Size: 1 Tablespoon ⋄ Calories: 60 ⋄ Calories from Fat: 0 ⋄ **% DAILY VALUE:** Total Fat: 0 g 0% ⋄ Saturated Fat: 0 g 0% ⋄ Cholesterol: 0 mg 0% ⋄ Sodium: 5 mg 0% ⋄ Total Carbohydrate: 14 g 5% ⋄ Dietary Fiber: 0 g 0% ⋄ Sugars: 13 g ⋄ Protein: 0 g ⋄ Vitamin A: 0% ⋄ Vitamin C: 0% ⋄ Calcium: 0% ⋄ Iron: 0% ⋄ **DIETARY EXCHANGES:** 1 Fruit OR 1 Carbohydrate

Spicy Raisin Sauce

PREP TIME: 10 MINUTES ✦ YIELD: I CUP

> ½ cup firmly packed brown sugar
> 1 tablespoon cornstarch
> ¼ teaspoon cinnamon
> ¼ cup raisins
> 1 tablespoon margarine or butter
> 1 cup water
> 2 tablespoons lemon juice

In small saucepan, combine brown sugar, cornstarch and cinnamon; blend well. Add all remaining ingredients; stir to combine. Bring mixture to a boil over medium-high heat, stirring occasionally. Boil and stir 1 minute. Reduce heat; simmer 8 to 10 minutes to blend flavors.

NUTRITION INFORMATION PER SERVING: Serving Size: 1 Tablespoon ⋄ Calories: 45 ⋄ Calories from Fat: 10 ⋄ **% DAILY VALUE:** Total Fat: 1 g 2% ⋄ Saturated Fat: 0 g 0% ⋄ Cholesterol: 0 mg 0% ⋄ Sodium: 10 mg 0% ⋄ Total Carbohydrate: 9 g 3% ⋄ Dietary Fiber: 0 g 0% ⋄ Sugars: 8 g ⋄ Protein: 0 g ⋄ Vitamin A: 0% ⋄ Vitamin C: 0% ⋄ Calcium: 0% ⋄ Iron: 0% ⋄ **DIETARY EXCHANGES:** ½ Fruit OR ½ Carbohydrate

Creamy Mustard Sauce

PREP TIME: 10 MINUTES (READY IN 2 HOURS 10 MINUTES) ✦ YIELD: I CUP

> 1 cup sour cream
> 2 tablespoons prepared mustard
> 2 tablespoons apple cider
> 1 teaspoon prepared horseradish

In small bowl, combine all ingredients. Cover; refrigerate 2 to 24 hours to blend flavors.

NUTRITION INFORMATION PER SERVING: Serving Size: 1 Tablespoon ⋄ Calories: 30 ⋄ Calories from Fat: 25 ⋄ **% DAILY VALUE:** Total Fat: 3 g 5% ⋄ Saturated Fat: 2 g 10% ⋄ Cholesterol: 5 mg 2% ⋄ Sodium: 30 mg 1% ⋄ Total Carbohydrate: 1 g 1% ⋄ Dietary Fiber: 0 g 0% ⋄ Sugars: 1 g ⋄ Protein: 0 g ⋄ Vitamin A: 2% ⋄ Vitamin C: 0% ⋄ Calcium: 0% ⋄ Iron: 0% ⋄ **DIETARY EXCHANGES:** ½ Fat

TIMETABLE FOR ROASTING SMOKED PORK

SMOKED HAM CUT	WEIGHT (POUNDS)	THERMOMETER READING	COOKING TIME (MINUTES PER POUND)
HAM—COOK BEFORE EATING		165°F.	
Whole (boneless)	8 to 12		17 to 21
Whole (bone-in)	14 to 16		18 to 20
Half (bone-in)	7 to 8		22 to 25
Portion (boneless)	3 to 5		35 to 40
Roast at 325°F.			
HAM—FULLY COOKED		130 to 140°F.	
Whole (boneless)	8 to 12		15 to 18
Whole (bone-in)	14 to 16		15 to 18
Half (boneless)	4 to 6		18 to 25
Half (bone-in)	7 to 8		18 to 25
Portion (bone-in)	3 to 4		27 to 33
Roast at 325°F.			
ARM PICNIC SHOULDER			
Cook before eating	5 to 8	165°F.	30 to 35
Fully cooked	5 to 8	140°F.	25 to 30
Roast at 325°F.			

Source: USDA and National Pork Producers Council

Cranberry-Glazed Ham Loaf

PREP TIME: 30 MINUTES (READY IN 2 HOURS)
♦ YIELD: 2 LOAVES; 5 SERVINGS EACH

LOAF
    2 lb. ground ham
    ¾ lb. extra-lean ground beef
    1 cup soft bread crumbs
    1 cup cranberry juice cocktail
    2 eggs, slightly beaten

GLAZE
    ½ cup cranberry juice cocktail
    ⅓ cup firmly packed brown sugar
    ½ teaspoon dry mustard

1. Heat oven to 350°F. In large bowl, combine all loaf ingredients; mix well. Shape into 2 loaves. Place side by side in ungreased 9-inch square pan. Bake at 350°F. for 1 hour. Drain.
2. Meanwhile, in small saucepan, combine all glaze ingredients. Bring to a boil. Reduce heat to low; simmer 1 minute or until brown sugar is dissolved, stirring constantly.
3. Brush ham loaves with part of glaze. Bake an additional 25 to 30 minutes or until meat is firm, basting frequently. Let stand 5 minutes before serving.

NUTRITION INFORMATION PER SERVING: Serving Size: ¹⁄₁₀ of Recipe ♦ Calories: 260 ♦ Calories from Fat: 90 ♦ **% DAILY VALUE:** Total Fat: 10 g 15% ♦ Saturated Fat: 3 g 15% ♦ Cholesterol: 105 mg 35% ♦ Sodium: 1360 mg 57% ♦ Total Carbohydrate: 16 g 5% ♦ Dietary Fiber: 0 g 0% ♦ Sugars: 13 g ♦ Protein: 26 g ♦ Vitamin A: 0% ♦ Vitamin C: 15% ♦ Calcium: 2% ♦ Iron: 10% ♦ **DIETARY EXCHANGES:** 1 Fruit, 3½ Lean Meat OR 1 Carbohydrate, 3½ Lean Meat

Pineapple Glaze for Ham

PREP TIME: 5 MINUTES ♦ YIELD: 1½ CUPS

    1 cup firmly packed brown sugar
    ¾ cup drained crushed pineapple

In small bowl, combine ingredients; mix well. Brush glaze on ham during last 15 to 30 minutes of baking.

NUTRITION INFORMATION PER SERVING: Serving Size: 1 Tablespoon ♦ Calories: 40 ♦ Calories from Fat: 0 ♦ **% DAILY VALUE:** Total Fat: 0 g 0% ♦ Saturated Fat: 0 g 0% ♦ Cholesterol: 0 mg 0% ♦ Sodium: 0 mg 0% ♦ Total Carbohydrate: 10 g 3% ♦ Dietary Fiber: 0 g 0% ♦ Sugars: 10 g ♦ Protein: 0 g ♦ Vitamin A: 0% ♦ Vitamin C: 0% ♦ Calcium: 0% ♦ Iron: 0% ♦ **DIETARY EXCHANGES:** ½ Fruit OR ½ Carbohydrate

Au Gratin Potatoes and Ham

PREP TIME: 15 MINUTES (READY IN 9 HOURS
15 MINUTES) ✦ YIELD: 7 (1-CUP) SERVINGS

    6 cups sliced peeled potatoes (6 medium)
    1 medium onion, coarsely chopped
1½ cups cubed cooked ham
    4 oz. (1 cup) shredded American cheese
    1 (10¾-oz.) can condensed cream of
        mushroom soup
    ½ cup milk
    ¼ to ½ teaspoon dried thyme leaves

1. In 3½ or 4-quart slow cooker, layer half each of the potatoes, onion, ham and cheese; repeat layers. In small bowl, combine soup, milk and thyme; pour over top.
2. Cover; cook on high setting for 1 hour. Reduce heat to low setting; cook for 6 to 8 hours or until potatoes are tender.

NUTRITION INFORMATION PER SERVING: Serving Size: 1 Cup ◆ Calories: 370 ◆ Calories from Fat: 90 ◆ **% DAILY VALUE:** Total Fat: 10 g 15% ◆ Saturated Fat: 5 g 25% ◆ Cholesterol: 30 mg 10% ◆ Sodium: 990 mg 41% ◆ Total Carbohydrate: 54 g 18% ◆ Dietary Fiber: 9 g 36% ◆ Sugars: 4 g ◆ Protein: 15 g ◆ Vitamin A: 4% ◆ Vitamin C: 20% ◆ Calcium: 15% ◆ Iron: 45% ◆ **DIETARY EXCHANGES:** 3½ Starch, 1 Lean Meat, 1 Fat OR 3½ Carbohydrate, 1 Lean Meat, 1 Fat

Grilled Ham Slice with Pineapple Salsa

PREP TIME: 30 MINUTES ✦ YIELD: 6 SERVINGS

PINEAPPLE SALSA
    1 (8-oz.) can crushed pineapple, drained
    2 tablespoons orange marmalade
    1 tablespoon chopped fresh cilantro
    2 teaspoons chopped fresh jalapeño chile
    2 teaspoons lime juice
    ¼ teaspoon salt

HAM
    1 (1½-lb.) fully cooked center-cut ham slice
        (¾ to 1 inch thick)

1. GRILL DIRECTIONS: Heat grill. In small bowl, combine all salsa ingredients; mix well.
2. When ready to grill, place ham on gas grill over medium heat or on charcoal grill 4 to 6 inches from medium coals. Cook 10 to 20 minutes or until thoroughly heated, turning 2 or 3 times. Serve with pineapple salsa.

TIP: To broil ham, place on broiler pan; broil 4 to 6 inches from heat using times above as a guide, turning 2 or 3 times.

NUTRITION INFORMATION PER SERVING: Serving Size: ⅙ of Recipe ◆ Calories: 140 ◆ Calories from Fat: 35 ◆ **% DAILY VALUE:** Total Fat: 4 g 6% ◆ Saturated Fat: 1 g 5% ◆ Cholesterol: 40 mg 13% ◆ Sodium: 1310 mg 55% ◆ Total Carbohydrate: 9 g 3% ◆ Dietary Fiber: 0 g 0% ◆ Sugars: 6 g ◆ Protein: 17 g ◆ Vitamin A: 0% ◆ Vitamin C: 6% ◆ Calcium: 0% ◆ Iron: 4% ◆ **DIETARY EXCHANGES:** ½ Fruit, 2 Lean Meat OR ½ Carbohydrate, 2 Lean Meat

Hot Ham and Swiss on Rye

PREP TIME: 10 MINUTES (READY IN 30 MINUTES)
✦ YIELD: 8 SANDWICHES

    ½ cup margarine or butter, softened
    ¼ cup horseradish mustard
    ¼ cup chopped onion
    4 teaspoons poppy seed
    8 rye sandwich buns, split
    8 thin slices boiled ham
    8 slices (3½ x 3½-inch) Swiss cheese

1. Heat oven to 350°F. In small bowl, combine margarine, mustard, onion and poppy seed. Spread mixture on cut surfaces of buns. Fill each bun with 1 slice ham and 1 slice cheese.
2. Wrap each sandwich in foil; place on ungreased cookie sheet. Bake at 350°F. for 15 to 20 minutes or until thoroughly heated.

NUTRITION INFORMATION PER SERVING: Serving Size: 1 Sandwich ◆ Calories: 380 ◆ Calories from Fat: 210 ◆ **% DAILY VALUE:** Total Fat: 23 g 35% ◆ Saturated Fat: 8 g 40% ◆ Cholesterol: 40 mg 13% ◆ Sodium: 980 mg 41% ◆ Total Carbohydrate: 24 g 8% ◆ Dietary Fiber: 3 g 12% ◆ Sugars: 2 g ◆ Protein: 18 g ◆ Vitamin A: 15% ◆ Vitamin C: 0% ◆ Calcium: 35% ◆ Iron: 10% ◆ **DIETARY EXCHANGES:** 1½ Starch, 2 Medium-Fat Meat, 2½ Fat OR 1½ Carbohydrate, 2 Medium-Fat Meat, 2½ Fat

Grilled Ham Slice with Pineapple Salsa

Shredded Pork Tacos

PREP TIME: 15 MINUTES (READY IN 2 HOURS)
✦ YIELD: 12 TACOS

SHREDDED PORK

1½ lb. boneless pork
  1 cup chopped onions
  1 (14.5 or 16-oz.) can whole tomatoes,
      undrained, cut up
  2 to 3 jalapeño chiles, seeded, chopped
  1 to 2 ancho chiles, cut into pieces
  ½ teaspoon salt
  ¼ teaspoon pepper
    Water

TACOS

  12 crisp corn taco shells
  1 cup shredded lettuce
  4 oz. (1 cup) shredded Cheddar cheese
  ½ cup chopped seeded tomato
  ½ cup sour cream
  1 avocado, peeled, chopped

1. In large saucepan, combine all shredded pork ingredients with enough water to cover pork. Cover; cook over medium-high heat until mixture comes to a boil, stirring occasionally. Reduce heat to medium; cook 1 to 1½ hours or until pork is fork-tender, stirring occasionally and adding water if needed.

2. Remove pork from liquid; reserve liquid. Strain cooked vegetables from cooking liquid; reserve vegetables and liquid. Cool pork for 15 minutes or until easy to handle. To shred pork, using 2 forks, pull pork apart along the grain of the meat.

3. In medium saucepan, combine shredded pork, all of the reserved cooked vegetables and 2 tablespoons of the reserved cooking liquid; mix well.* Cook over medium heat for 4 to 5 minutes or until thoroughly heated, stirring occasionally.

4. To assemble tacos, layer lettuce, cheese, warm shredded pork, tomato, sour cream and avocado into taco shells.

> **TIP:** * At this point, pork can be refrigerated for up to 24 hours or wrapped and frozen for up to 1 month.

NUTRITION INFORMATION PER SERVING: Serving Size: 1 Taco ✦ Calories: 260 ✦ Calories from Fat: 140 ✦ **% DAILY VALUE:** Total Fat: 15 g 23% ✦ Saturated Fat: 6 g 30% ✦ Cholesterol: 50 mg 17% ✦ Sodium: 290 mg 12% ✦ Total Carbohydrate: 15 g 5% ✦ Dietary Fiber: 3 g 12% ✦ Sugars: 3 g ✦ Protein: 17 g ✦ Vitamin A: 45% ✦ Vitamin C: 20% ✦ Calcium: 15% ✦ Iron: 8% ✦ **DIETARY EXCHANGES:** 1 Starch, 2 Medium-Fat Meat, ½ Fat OR 1 Carbohydrate, 2 Medium-Fat Meat, ½ Fat

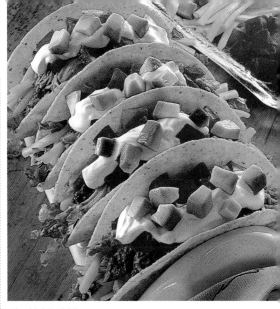

Shredded Pork Tacos

Peppered Pork Pitas with Garlic Sauce

PREP TIME: 20 MINUTES ✦ YIELD: 8 SANDWICHES

GARLIC SAUCE

  ⅓ cup mayonnaise or salad dressing
  2 tablespoons milk
  2 garlic cloves, minced

PORK PITAS

  1 lb. boneless pork loin chops, cut into thin
      strips
  1 tablespoon olive or vegetable oil
  1 teaspoon coarse ground black pepper
  1 (7.25-oz.) jar roasted red bell peppers,
      drained, sliced
  4 (6-inch) pita (pocket) breads, halved

1. In small bowl, combine mayonnaise, milk and garlic; mix well. Set aside.

2. In medium bowl, combine pork, oil and pepper; mix well. Heat large skillet over medium-high heat until hot. Add pork mixture; cook 3 to 4 minutes or until pork is lightly browned and no longer pink, stirring occasionally. Stir in roasted peppers; heat until warm.

3. Lightly brush insides of pita bread halves with garlic sauce. Fill each with pork mixture. If desired, drizzle remaining garlic sauce over top.

NUTRITION INFORMATION PER SERVING: Serving Size: 2 Sandwiches ✦ Calories: 520 ✦ Calories from Fat: 240 ✦ **% DAILY VALUE:** Total Fat: 27 g 42% ✦ Saturated Fat: 6 g 30% ✦ Cholesterol: 80 mg 27% ✦ Sodium: 480 mg 20% ✦ Total Carbohydrate: 38 g 13% ✦ Dietary Fiber: 2 g 8% ✦ Sugars: 2 g ✦ Protein: 31 g ✦ Vitamin A: 30% ✦ Vitamin C: 80% ✦ Calcium: 8% ✦ Iron: 15% ✦ **DIETARY EXCHANGES:** 2 Starch, 1½ Vegetable, 3 Lean Meat, 3½ Fat OR 2 Carbohydrate, 1½ Vegetable, 3 Lean Meat, 3½ Fat

Slow-Cooked Barbecued Pork on Buns

PREP TIME: 20 MINUTES (READY IN 8 HOURS 20 MINUTES) ◆ YIELD: 18 SANDWICHES

1 (3-lb.) boneless pork roast, cut into thin strips
¾ cup chopped onions
¼ cup cornstarch
¼ cup firmly packed brown sugar
2 teaspoons dry mustard
½ teaspoon salt
¼ teaspoon garlic powder
¼ teaspoon ground red pepper (cayenne)
1½ cups ketchup
2 tablespoons Worcestershire sauce
18 sandwich buns, split

1. In 3½ or 4-quart slow cooker, combine all ingredients except buns; mix well.
2. Cover; cook on low setting for 6 to 8 hours or until pork is tender. Spoon about ⅓ cup pork mixture into each sandwich bun.

> **TIP:** To bake pork mixture in oven, combine all ingredients except buns in ungreased 13 x 9-inch (3-quart) baking dish; cover. Bake at 325°F. for 1½ hours.

NUTRITION INFORMATION PER SERVING: Serving Size: 1 Sandwich ◆ Calories: 270 ◆ Calories from Fat: 60 ◆ % DAILY VALUE: Total Fat: 7 g 11% ◆ Saturated Fat: 2 g 10% ◆ Cholesterol: 40 mg 13% ◆ Sodium: 580 mg 24% ◆ Total Carbohydrate: 33 g 11% ◆ Dietary Fiber: 2 g 8% ◆ Sugars: 10 g ◆ Protein: 18 g ◆ Vitamin A: 4% ◆ Vitamin C: 4% ◆ Calcium: 8% ◆ Iron: 10% ◆ DIETARY EXCHANGES: 2 Starch, 1½ Medium-Fat Meat OR 2 Carbohydrate, 1½ Medium-Fat Meat

COOK'S NOTE

BUYING LAMB

Look for lamb that is pink to light red in color; a darker red color probably indicates older meat. Any fat should look firm and white. The parchmentlike covering on a leg of lamb (called the "fell") is usually left on to help retain juices during roasting the leg whole, but can be trimmed from steaks or chops before cooking.

COOK'S NOTE

GLAZES FOR LAMB ROASTS

A simple glaze brushed onto the meat promotes browning and adds flavor. Some easy choices:

Zesty Garlic Glaze

Combine 1 tablespoon paprika, ½ teaspoon dried basil leaves, 3 minced garlic cloves, ⅓ cup water, ⅓ cup dry sherry, 2 tablespoons oil and 2 tablespoons soy sauce. Brush lamb with glaze every 30 minutes during roasting.

Jelly Glaze

Melt ¾ cup mint or apricot preserves over low heat. Brush glaze on lamb during last hour of roasting.

Herbed Jelly Glaze

Melt ¾ cup currant jelly and stir in 1 tablespoon melted butter, 1 tablespoon cider vinegar and 1 tablespoon chopped fresh tarragon or 1 teaspoon dried tarragon leaves. Brush glaze on lamb during last hour of roasting.

Plum-Good Glaze

In blender container, combine a drained 16-oz. can (2 cups) pitted purple plums plus ¼ cup liquid from the can, 2 tablespoons lemon juice, 1 tablespoon soy sauce, 1 teaspoon dried basil leaves and 1 teaspoon Worcestershire sauce. Blend at medium speed until smooth. Brush lamb with glaze every 30 minutes during roasting.

Sweet-n-Spicy Glaze

Combine ¼ cup firmly packed brown sugar, 1½ teaspoons salt, ½ teaspoon dry mustard, ½ teaspoon chili powder, ¼ teaspoon ginger, ¼ teaspoon cloves, 1 minced garlic clove and 1 tablespoon lemon juice. Brush glaze on lamb during the last hour of roasting.

Lamb Roast

1. Allow ⅓ to ½ lb. per serving for bone-in roast and ¼ to ⅓ lb. per serving for boneless roast. Heat oven to 325°F. Place roast, fat side up, on rack in shallow roasting pan. If desired, sprinkle with salt and pepper unless using glaze with salt or soy sauce added. Insert meat thermometer so bulb reaches

TIMETABLE FOR ROASTING LAMB

ROAST	WEIGHT (POUNDS)	THERMOMETER READING	COOKING TIME (MINUTES PER POUND)
LEG, BONE-IN *Roast at 325°F.*	5 to 7	145°F. (Medium-Rare) 160°F. (Medium) 170°F. (Well)	20 to 25 25 to 30 30 to 35
LEG, BONE-IN *Roast at 325°F.*	7 to 9	145°F. (Medium-Rare) 160°F. (Medium) 170°F. (Well)	15 to 20 20 to 25 25 to 30
LEG, BONELESS *Roast at 325°F.*	4 to 7	145°F. (Medium-Rare) 160°F. (Medium) 170°F. (Well)	25 to 30 30 to 35 35 to 40
LEG HALF, SHANK OR SIRLOIN OR SHOULDER *Roast at 325°F.*	3 to 4	145°F. (Medium-Rare) 160°F. (Medium) 170°F. (Well)	30 to 35 35 to 40 40 to 45

Source: National Livestock and Meat Board

center of thickest part of meat, but does not rest in fat or on bone.

2. Bake at 325°F. to desired degree of doneness using "Timetable for Roasting Lamb," above. Let stand 15 minutes before carving.

NUTRITION INFORMATION PER SERVING: Serving Size: 4 oz. Cooked Lamb • Calories: 220 • Calories from Fat: 90 • % DAILY VALUE: Total Fat: 10 g 15% • Saturated Fat: 4 g 20% • Cholesterol: 105 mg 35% • Sodium: 80 mg 3% • Total Carbohydrate: 0 g 0% • Dietary Fiber: 0 g 0% • Sugars: 0 g • Protein: 32 g • Vitamin A: 0% • Vitamin C: 0% • Calcium: 0% • Iron: 15% • DIETARY EXCHANGES: 4 Lean Meat

Butterflied Leg of Lamb with Rosemary and Thyme

PREP TIME: 10 MINUTES (READY IN 1 HOUR 5 MINUTES) ◆ YIELD: 8 SERVINGS

1 (2¼-lb.) boneless sirloin half leg of lamb
2 tablespoons chopped fresh rosemary
   or 2 teaspoons dried rosemary leaves
1 tablespoon chopped fresh thyme
   or 1 teaspoon dried thyme leaves
3 large garlic cloves, minced
½ teaspoon coarse ground black pepper
¼ teaspoon salt
1½ teaspoons olive oil

1. Heat oven to 450°F. Place rack in shallow roasting pan; spray with nonstick cooking spray. Remove netting or string from leg of lamb; unroll. For ease in turning, place 2 wooden or metal skewers horizontally through lamb to hold lamb together.

2. In small bowl, combine all remaining ingredients; mix well. Spread mixture over both sides of lamb; place on sprayed rack in pan. Insert meat thermometer so bulb reaches center of thickest part of lamb.

3. Bake at 450°F. for 40 to 45 minutes, turning once, or until meat thermometer registers desired temperature of 140°F. for rare or 160°F. for medium doneness.

4. Remove lamb from oven; cover loosely with foil. Let stand 10 minutes before carving. To serve, remove skewers from lamb; slice diagonally into ½-inch-thick slices.

NUTRITION INFORMATION PER SERVING: Serving Size: ⅛ of Recipe • Calories: 150 • Calories from Fat: 60 • % DAILY VALUE: Total Fat: 7 g 11% • Saturated Fat: 2 g 10% • Cholesterol: 70 mg 23% • Sodium: 120 mg 5% • Total Carbohydrate: 1 g 1% • Dietary Fiber: 0 g 0% • Sugars: 0 g • Protein: 22 g • Vitamin A: 0% • Vitamin C: 0% • Calcium: 0% • Iron: 10% • DIETARY EXCHANGES: 3 Lean Meat

Lamb

• RETAIL CUTS •
WHERE THEY COME FROM
HOW TO COOK THEM

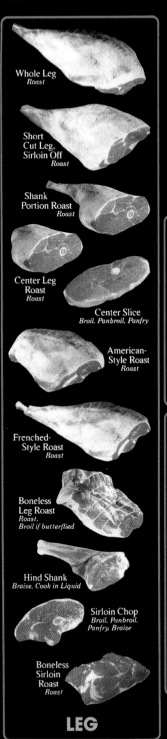

Whole Leg
Roast

Short Cut Leg, Sirloin Off
Roast

Shank Portion Roast
Roast

Center Leg Roast
Roast

Center Slice
Broil, Panbroil, Panfry

American-Style Roast
Roast

Frenched-Style Roast
Roast

Boneless Leg Roast
Roast, Broil if butterflied

Hind Shank
Braise, Cook in Liquid

Sirloin Chop
Broil, Panbroil, Panfry, Braise

Boneless Sirloin Roast
Roast

LEG

LEG

LOIN

RIB

SHOULDER

FORESHANK & BREAST

Loin Roast
Roast

Loin Chop
Broil, Panbroil, Panfry

Double Loin Chop
Broil, Panbroil, Panfry

LOIN

Shank
Braise, Cook in Liquid

Spareribs
Braise, Broil, Roast

Boneless Rolled Breast
Roast, Braise

Riblets
Braise, Cook in Liquid, Broil

FORESHANK & BREAST

Rib Roast
Roast

Rib Chop
Broil, Panbroil, Panfry, Roast

Frenched Rib Chop
Broil, Panbroil, Panfry

Crown Roast
Roast

RIB

Square-Cut Shoulder, Whole
Roast, Braise

Pre-Sliced Shoulder
Roast, Braise

Boneless Shoulder Roast
Roast, Braise

Neck Slice
Braise, Cook in Liquid

Blade Chop
Braise, Broil, Panbroil, Panfry

Arm Chop
Braise, Broil, Panbroil, Panfry

SHOULDER

Lamb for Stew
Braise, Cook in Liquid

Cubes for Kabobs
Broil, Braise

Ground Lamb
Broil, Panbroil, Roast (Bake)

OTHER CUTS

Petite Rack of Lamb

PREP TIME: 30 MINUTES (READY IN I HOUR)
◆ YIELD: 2 SERVINGS

LAMB

  I (6-rib) rack of lamb (about ¾ lb.)
  I tablespoon chopped fresh parsley
  ½ teaspoon dried rosemary leaves
  ¼ teaspoon salt
  ¼ teaspoon dry mustard
  ¼ teaspoon pepper
  I tablespoon margarine or butter, softened
  I small garlic clove, minced

SAUCE, IF DESIRED

  ¼ cup beef broth
  ¼ cup dry white wine*
  I tablespoon water
  I to 2 teaspoons cornstarch

1. Heat oven to 450°F. Place lamb in shallow roasting pan with rib bones pointing down. In small bowl, combine parsley, rosemary, salt, dry mustard, pepper, margarine and garlic; mix well. Rub mixture on lamb. Insert meat thermometer so bulb reaches center of thickest part of meat, but does not rest in fat or on bone.
2. Bake at 450°F. for about 30 minutes or until meat thermometer registers desired temperature of 140°F. for rare or 160°F. for medium doneness. Place lamb on platter; keep warm.
3. To prepare sauce, drain fat from meat drippings. Add broth to pan; stir to loosen brown particles. Strain into small saucepan; add wine. In small bowl, combine water and cornstarch; blend well. Stir into wine mixture. Bring to a boil, stirring constantly until clear and thickened. Serve sauce with lamb.

Apricot-Glazed Lamb Chops

TIP: * One-fourth cup additional beef broth can be substituted for the dry white wine.

NUTRITION INFORMATION PER SERVING: Serving Size: ½ of Recipe ◆ Calories: 230 ◆ Calories from Fat: 130 ◆ **% DAILY VALUE:** Total Fat: 14 g 22% ◆ Saturated Fat: 4 g 20% ◆ Cholesterol: 50 mg 17% ◆ Sodium: 480 mg 20% ◆ Total Carbohydrate: 4 g 1% ◆ Dietary Fiber: 0 g 0% ◆ Sugars: 0 g ◆ Protein: 16 g ◆ Vitamin A: 8% ◆ Vitamin C: 4% ◆ Calcium: 2% ◆ Iron: 8% ◆ **DIETARY EXCHANGES:** 2½ Medium-Fat Meat, 1 Fat

Apricot-Glazed Lamb Chops

PREP TIME: 30 MINUTES (READY IN I HOUR)
◆ YIELD: 4 SERVINGS

  I (16-oz.) can apricot halves, drained, reserving liquid
  ¼ cup oil
  2 tablespoons vinegar
  ¼ teaspoon salt
  4 lamb chops (I inch thick)
  2 tablespoons brown sugar
  2 teaspoons cornstarch
    Dash allspice
  2 tablespoons orange juice

1. In shallow baking dish, combine ½ cup of the reserved apricot liquid, oil, vinegar and salt. (Reserve remaining apricot liquid for sauce.) Place lamb chops in apricot mixture, turning to coat all sides. Refrigerate 30 minutes.
2. Remove chops from marinade, reserving marinade. Place lamb chops on broiler pan. Broil 4 to 6 inches from heat for 9 to 11 minutes or until browned and of desired doneness, turning chops and basting occasionally with reserved marinade.
3. Meanwhile, reserve 8 apricot halves for garnish. In blender container or food processor bowl with metal blade, combine remaining apricots and reserved apricot liquid, brown sugar, cornstarch, allspice and orange juice. Blend or process 1 minute or until smooth; pour into small saucepan. Cook and stir over medium heat until thickened.
4. To serve, arrange lamb chops on serving platter; garnish with reserved apricot halves. Serve with warm apricot sauce.

NUTRITION INFORMATION PER SERVING: Serving Size: ¼ of Recipe ◆ Calories: 330 ◆ Calories from Fat: 160 ◆ **% DAILY VALUE:** Total Fat: 18 g 28% ◆ Saturated Fat: 3 g 15% ◆ Cholesterol: 40 mg 13% ◆ Sodium: 170 mg 7% ◆ Total Carbohydrate: 28 g 9% ◆ Dietary Fiber: 2 g 8% ◆ Sugars: 23 g ◆ Protein: 13 g ◆ Vitamin A: 30% ◆ Vitamin C: 8% ◆ Calcium: 2% ◆ Iron: 10% ◆ **DIETARY EXCHANGES:** 2 Fruit, 2 Lean Meat, 2 Fat OR 2 Carbohydrate, 2 Lean Meat, 2 Fat

Broiled Lamb Chops

1. Place lamb rib, loin or shoulder chops on broiler pan. Place or adjust broiler pan so tops of 1-inch-thick chops are 4 inches from heat and 2-inch-thick chops are 6 inches from heat.

2. Broil 1-inch-thick chops 10 to 12 minutes; 2-inch-thick chops 20 to 22 minutes, turning once during cooking. Sprinkle with salt and pepper* unless using glaze or marinade containing salt or soy sauce.

> **TIP:** * Other seasonings for lamb chops include a dash of garlic salt, paprika or curry powder added with salt and pepper.

NUTRITION INFORMATION PER SERVING: Serving Size: 4 oz. Cooked Lamb ◆ Calories: 260 ◆ Calories from Fat: 140 ◆ **% DAILY VALUE:** Total Fat: 15 g 23% ◆ Saturated Fat: 5 g 25% ◆ Cholesterol: 100 mg 33% ◆ Sodium: 90 mg 4% ◆ Total Carbohydrate: 0 g 0% ◆ Dietary Fiber: 0 g 0% ◆ Sugars: 0 g ◆ Protein: 30 g ◆ Vitamin A: 0% ◆ Vitamin C: 0% ◆ Calcium: 2% ◆ Iron: 10% ◆ **DIETARY EXCHANGES:** 4 Lean Meat

Jelly Glaze for Lamb

PREP TIME: 5 MINUTES ◆ YIELD: ¾ CUP

¾ cup mint, currant or apricot jelly

Melt jelly in small saucepan over low heat. Brush on lamb during last hour of baking.

NUTRITION INFORMATION PER SERVING: Serving Size: 1 Tablespoon ◆ Calories: 50 ◆ Calories from Fat: 0 ◆ **% DAILY VALUE:** Total Fat: 0 g 0% ◆ Saturated Fat: 0 g 0% ◆ Cholesterol: 0 mg 0% ◆ Sodium: 10 mg 0% ◆ Total Carbohydrate: 13 g 4% ◆ Dietary Fiber: 0 g 0% ◆ Sugars: 10 g ◆ Protein: 0 g ◆ Vitamin A: 0% ◆ Vitamin C: 2% ◆ Calcium: 0% ◆ Iron: 0% ◆ **DIETARY EXCHANGES:** 1 Fruit OR 1 Carbohydrate

Broiled Lamb Chops with Mint Sauce

PREP TIME: 20 MINUTES ◆ YIELD: 4 SERVINGS

MINT SAUCE
⅓ cup apple jelly
2 tablespoons vinegar
2 tablespoons water
2 teaspoons dried mint flakes
¼ teaspoon salt

LAMB
4 lamb chops (1 inch thick)

1. In small saucepan, combine all sauce ingredients. Bring to a boil. Reduce heat to low; simmer 5 minutes.

2. Meanwhile, place lamb chops on broiler pan; brush with sauce. Broil 4 to 6 inches from heat for 9 to 11 minutes or until browned and of desired doneness, turning chops and brushing with sauce once during cooking. Bring remaining sauce to a boil. Serve sauce with lamb chops.

NUTRITION INFORMATION PER SERVING: Serving Size: ¼ of Recipe ◆ Calories: 170 ◆ Calories from Fat: 45 ◆ **% DAILY VALUE:** Total Fat: 5 g 8% ◆ Saturated Fat: 2 g 10% ◆ Cholesterol: 40 mg 13% ◆ Sodium: 170 mg 7% ◆ Total Carbohydrate: 18 g 6% ◆ Dietary Fiber: 0 g 0% ◆ Sugars: 12 g ◆ Protein: 12 g ◆ Vitamin A: 0% ◆ Vitamin C: 0% ◆ Calcium: 0% ◆ Iron: 8% ◆ **DIETARY EXCHANGES:** 1 Fruit, 2 Lean Meat OR 1 Carbohydrate, 2 Lean Meat

Lamb Kabobs with Couscous

PREP TIME: 30 MINUTES (READY IN 45 MINUTES) ◆ YIELD: 4 SERVINGS

KABOBS
1 lb. boneless lean leg of lamb, cut into 1½-inch pieces
2 tablespoons fresh lemon juice
½ teaspoon dried oregano leaves
½ teaspoon cumin
⅛ teaspoon salt
⅛ teaspoon pepper
2 large garlic cloves, minced
1 green or red bell pepper, cut into 1½-inch pieces

COUSCOUS
1 (14.5-oz.) can ready-to-serve fat-free chicken broth with ⅓ less sodium
1 carrot, grated
1 cup uncooked couscous

1. In medium bowl, combine lamb, lemon juice, oregano, cumin, salt, pepper and garlic; toss to coat. Cover; let stand 15 minutes at room temperature to marinate.

2. Thread lamb and bell pepper pieces onto four 10 to 12-inch metal skewers. Discard marinade. Broil 4 to 6 inches from heat for 6 to 10 minutes, turning once, or until lamb is of desired doneness.

3. Meanwhile, in medium saucepan, combine broth and carrot. Bring to a boil. Remove from heat; add couscous. Let stand 5 to 8 minutes or until liquid is absorbed. Serve kabobs with couscous.

NUTRITION INFORMATION PER SERVING: Serving Size: ¼ of Recipe ◆ Calories: 330 ◆ Calories from Fat: 50 ◆ **% DAILY VALUE:** Total Fat: 6 g 9% ◆ Saturated Fat: 2 g 10% ◆ Cholesterol: 65 mg 22% ◆ Sodium: 370 mg 15% ◆ Total Carbohydrate: 40 g 13% ◆ Dietary Fiber: 3 g 12% ◆ Sugars: 3 g ◆ Protein: 28 g ◆ Vitamin A: 100% ◆ Vitamin C: 25% ◆ Calcium: 4% ◆ Iron: 15% ◆ **DIETARY EXCHANGES:** 2½ Starch, 2½ Lean Meat OR 2½ Carbohydrate, 2½ Lean Meat

Red Wine and Oregano Marinade

PREP TIME: 10 MINUTES ✦ YIELD: ¼ CUP
(ENOUGH FOR 4 SERVINGS OF MEAT)

¼ cup finely chopped onion
¼ cup finely chopped fresh oregano
    or 2 teaspoons dried oregano leaves
6 garlic cloves, minced
¼ teaspoon pepper
¼ cup dry red wine
3 tablespoons soy sauce
1 tablespoon olive oil
1 tablespoon red wine vinegar

In blender container, combine all ingredients; blend well. Pour mixture over lamb chops or cubes for kabobs. Let stand at room temperature for 15 minutes to marinate.

NUTRITION INFORMATION: Not possible to calculate because of recipe variables.

Lamb Patties

PREP TIME: 30 MINUTES ✦ YIELD: 4 SERVINGS

1 lb. ground lamb
2 tablespoons chopped onion
½ teaspoon salt
⅛ teaspoon pepper

1. In medium bowl, combine all ingredients; mix well. Shape into 4 patties.
2. Broil on broiler pan or grill 3 to 4 inches from heat for 6 to 8 minutes on each side or until no longer pink in center.

NUTRITION INFORMATION PER SERVING: Serving Size: ¼ of Recipe ✦ Calories: 210 ✦ Calories from Fat: 140 ✦ % DAILY VALUE: Total Fat: 15 g 23% ✦ Saturated Fat: 6 g 30% ✦ Cholesterol: 75 mg 25% ✦ Sodium: 330 mg 14% ✦ Total Carbohydrate: 0 g 0% ✦ Dietary Fiber: 0 g 0% ✦ Sugars: 0 g ✦ Protein: 19 g ✦ Vitamin A: 0% ✦ Vitamin C: 0% ✦ Calcium: 0% ✦ Iron: 8% ✦ DIETARY EXCHANGES: 3 Medium-Fat Meat

Lamb Pita Burgers

PREP TIME: 40 MINUTES ✦ YIELD: 6 SANDWICHES

BURGERS
1 lb. ground lamb
½ cup finely crushed cracker crumbs
½ teaspoon salt
½ teaspoon ground coriander
¼ cup water
1 garlic clove, crushed
1 egg
3 (6-inch) pita (pocket) breads

TOPPING
½ cup chopped seeded tomato
½ cup chopped seeded cucumber
½ cup sliced green onions
1 tablespoon chopped fresh basil
    or 1 teaspoon dried basil leaves
1 teaspoon chopped fresh oregano
    or ½ teaspoon dried oregano leaves
1 teaspoon chopped fresh mint
    or ½ teaspoon dried mint leaves
⅛ teaspoon pepper
1 garlic clove, minced
½ cup plain yogurt

1. GRILL DIRECTIONS: Heat grill. In large bowl, combine all burger ingredients except pita breads; mix well. Shape mixture into 6 patties, about 3½ inches in diameter. In medium bowl, combine all topping ingredients.
2. When ready to grill, place patties on gas grill over medium-high heat or on charcoal grill 4 to 6 inches from medium-high coals. Cook 10 to 15 minutes or until no longer pink in center, turning once.
3. Meanwhile, wrap pita breads in 18×12-inch piece of foil; place on grill to warm during last 5 minutes of cooking. Cut pita breads in half; place 1 cooked patty in each half. Spoon salad topping into pita breads with patties.

TIP: To broil patties, place on broiler pan; broil 4 to 6 inches from heat using times above as a guide, turning once.

NUTRITION INFORMATION PER SERVING: Serving Size: 1 Sandwich ✦ Calories: 290 ✦ Calories from Fat: 120 ✦ % DAILY VALUE: Total Fat: 13 g 20% ✦ Saturated Fat: 5 g 25% ✦ Cholesterol: 85 mg 28% ✦ Sodium: 490 mg 20% ✦ Total Carbohydrate: 25 g 8% ✦ Dietary Fiber: 1 g 4% ✦ Sugars: 2 g ✦ Protein: 19 g ✦ Vitamin A: 6% ✦ Vitamin C: 10% ✦ Calcium: 10% ✦ Iron: 15% ✦ DIETARY EXCHANGES: 1½ Starch, 2 Medium-Fat Meat, ½ Fat OR 1½ Carbohydrate, 2 Medium-Fat Meat, ½ Fat

Lamb and Asparagus Stir-Fry

PREP TIME: 30 MINUTES ◆ YIELD: 6 SERVINGS

13½ oz. (6 cups) uncooked medium
    egg noodles
½ cup vegetable broth
2 teaspoons cornstarch
¾ teaspoon dried rosemary leaves, crushed
¼ teaspoon salt
¼ teaspoon coarse ground black pepper
2 teaspoons olive oil
1 lb. boneless lean lamb sirloin or
    round steak, cut into thin strips
1 large onion, halved, thinly sliced
1 lb. fresh asparagus spears, cut diagonally
    into 1-inch pieces
1 small red bell pepper, cut
    into 2 x ¼ x ¼-inch strips

1. Cook noodles to desired doneness as directed on package. Drain; cover to keep warm.
2. Meanwhile, in small bowl or jar with tight-fitting lid, combine broth, cornstarch, rosemary, salt and pepper; blend or shake well. Set aside.
3. Heat oil in large nonstick skillet or wok over medium-high heat until hot. Add lamb; cook and stir 3 minutes. Add onion and asparagus; cook and stir an additional 3 min-

Lamb and Asparagus Stir-Fry

utes or until onion is tender and lamb is no longer pink. Add bell pepper; cook and stir 1 minute. Add broth mixture; cook and stir until thickened. Serve lamb mixture over noodles.

NUTRITION INFORMATION PER SERVING: Serving Size: ⅙ of Recipe ◆ Calories: 380 ◆ Calories from Fat: 70 ◆ % DAILY VALUE: Total Fat: 8 g 12% ◆ Saturated Fat: 2 g 10% ◆ Cholesterol: 100 mg 33% ◆ Sodium: 220 mg 9% ◆ Total Carbohydrate: 53 g 18% ◆ Dietary Fiber: 4 g 16% ◆ Sugars: 6 g ◆ Protein: 23 g ◆ Vitamin A: 20% ◆ Vitamin C: 30% ◆ Calcium: 4% ◆ Iron: 25% ◆ DIETARY EXCHANGES: 3 Starch, 1 Vegetable, 1½ Lean Meat, ½ Fat OR 3 Carbohydrate, 1 Vegetable, 1½ Lean Meat, ½ Fat

Lamb Simmered with Tomatoes and Onion

PREP TIME: 15 MINUTES (READY IN 35 MINUTES) ◆ YIELD: 4 SERVINGS

2 teaspoons olive oil
4 (4-oz.) lamb shoulder chops
¼ teaspoon salt
⅛ teaspoon pepper
1 medium onion, sliced
1 garlic clove, minced
½ teaspoon cumin
½ teaspoon paprika
½ cup dry red wine
1 (14.5-oz.) can diced tomatoes, drained

1. Heat oil in medium nonstick skillet over medium-high heat until hot. Sprinkle lamb chops with salt and pepper; place in skillet. Cook 2 to 3 minutes on each side or until lightly browned. Remove lamb from skillet; cover to keep warm.
2. Add onion to skillet. Reduce heat to medium; cover and cook 3 minutes or until onion begins to brown, stirring occasionally.
3. Add garlic, cumin and paprika; cook and stir an additional 1 minute.
4. Add wine and tomatoes; return chops to skillet. Bring to a boil. Reduce heat to low; simmer, uncovered, 20 minutes or until lamb is of desired doneness. If desired, serve with cooked potatoes, pasta or rice.

NUTRITION INFORMATION PER SERVING: Serving Size: ¼ of Recipe ◆ Calories: 270 ◆ Calories from Fat: 120 ◆ % DAILY VALUE: Total Fat: 13 g 20% ◆ Saturated Fat: 4 g 20% ◆ Cholesterol: 85 mg 28% ◆ Sodium: 270 mg 11% ◆ Total Carbohydrate: 8 g 3% ◆ Dietary Fiber: 2 g 8% ◆ Sugars: 4 g ◆ Protein: 26 g ◆ Vitamin A: 15% ◆ Vitamin C: 20% ◆ Calcium: 6% ◆ Iron: 15% ◆ DIETARY EXCHANGES: 1½ Vegetable, 3½ Lean Meat, ½ Fat

POULTRY

POULTRY

Poultry may well be the cornerstone of American entrées, from the classic Thanksgiving turkey to Southern fried chicken. Poultry's relatively low fat content, convenient packaging and ease of preparation appeal to today's health-conscious, time-crunched cooks. Its mild flavor and versatility lend it to techniques as simple as roasting with salt and pepper or as intriguing as Teriyaki Grilled Chicken Kabobs.

Shopping for Quality

Fresh poultry: Fresh, uncooked chicken should be firm and moist but not slimy. A chicken's skin color reveals not its quality or flavor but its diet. Turkey skin, on the other hand, should be white, but the skin is often hidden under an opaque wrapper. All poultry should smell fresh and be free of skin tears and bruises.

Frozen poultry: The poultry should be solid to the touch. Avoid packages with torn wrappers, ice crystals or freezer burn. Freezer burn affects both the texture and flavor of the meat; it is indicated by a dry surface, which may have gray or white spots.

HOW MUCH TO BUY

TYPE OF POULTRY	PER SERVING, UNCOOKED
Bone-in chicken	½ pound
Whole turkey	1 pound
Duck or goose	14 ounces
Cornish game hen	1 bird
Boneless pieces	4 to 6 ounces

Handling Poultry Safely

Poultry must stay cold. At the grocery store, add it to the cart toward the end of shopping. Take it right home and refrigerate it, in a bag or on a plate to catch any drips.

Raw poultry may contain salmonella or other potentially harmful bacteria. Thorough cooking destroys these bacteria. In the meantime, keep raw poultry from touching other foods as well as utensils, work surfaces and dishes that will be used to touch other foods.

Use hot, soapy water to wash all surfaces that come into contact with raw poultry.

Cook poultry thoroughly. Refrigerate leftovers promptly.

Storing Poultry

Plan to cook or freeze fresh poultry within a day of purchase, regardless of the date on the wrapper. If you will use it within a day, refrigerate it until the last possible moment. If you freeze it, wrap each piece in plastic wrap. For extra protection, combine all the wrapped pieces in a plastic resealable freezer bag.

Use frozen whole birds within a year, frozen pieces within nine months, ground poultry within three months. Storing it longer is not dangerous, but the color, flavor and texture of the meat will deteriorate. Freeze giblets separately. If you wish, freeze necks, giblets and backs together to save for soup stock.

Most frozen cooked chicken will taste best within four months.

Thawing Poultry

Never thaw poultry at room temperature.

✦ Refrigerator method: If you have the luxury of time and foresight, place frozen poultry in the refrigerator to thaw. Large frozen turkeys require three or four days. A whole chicken will thaw in one or two days; parts may be ready within several hours.

✦ Cold water method: Submerge the frozen bird, still wrapped, in a large bowl of cold water. Change the water every half hour to keep it cold. This keeps the surface temperature low enough to discourage bacteria growth.

✦ Microwave method: Thawing whole birds in the microwave is not advisable, because the outside will begin to cook while the inside is still rock-hard. To thaw pieces, follow manufacturer's directions. Cook immediately after defrosting.

Do not refreeze poultry that has been thawed.

Basic Cooking Techniques

These time-tested methods are the foundation of every great chicken recipe. The techniques also stand on their own as simple, reliable ways to serve chicken.

BAKING

Heat the oven to 325° or 350°F. Rinse chicken pieces and pat them dry. In a baking dish, arrange pieces of chicken in a single layer skin side up. Sprinkle pieces with salt, pepper and other seasonings as desired. Baking takes about an hour at 350°F., slightly less at 375°F. If you have a convection oven, turn on the fan to cook chicken faster and yield a nicely browned exterior.

BRAISING

Brown the poultry pieces in a pan on the stove top, then cook them, tightly covered, over low heat in a small amount of simmering liquid (water, wine, beer, juice, broth) until the meat is fork-tender, at least an hour.

BROILING

Preheat the broiler. Rinse chicken pieces and pat them dry. Sprinkle with salt, pepper and other seasonings as desired. Place the chicken, skin side down, on the broiler pan and broil until browned. Turn the chicken over and broil until the skin is nicely browned and the meat is thoroughly cooked. Approximately 5 to 6 minutes per side for boneless, skinless chicken and 10 to 15 minutes per side for bone-in chicken.

POACHING

In a covered pan, simmer chicken pieces in a flavorful liquid such as chicken broth, wine or water flavored with seasonings and aromatic vegetables such as onion and garlic. When poaching, the liquid should cover the meat. Simmer about 15 minutes per pound. This is a great way to cook chicken, especially the breast, without adding fat.

MICROWAVING

Cooking in the microwave is better for small or medium amounts of chicken. Roasting a whole bird is better done in a conventional oven. Cooking times vary according to the amount of meat and how it's cut up. To test doneness, use a meat thermometer or pierce the skin of the thickest piece of meat and watch the juices that emerge. If the juices run clear, the meat is done. If there is any pink in the liquid, continue cooking.

ROASTING

See "Timetable for Roasting Poultry," page 163.

PANFRYING

This panfrying method can be used for any chicken parts but is best for cut-up or boneless meat. The meat is browned in a small amount of fat on the stove top, developing a lovely browned exterior. Heat the pan and the oil, then add the meat, taking care not to crowd the pan. Cook the first side until it's browned and the edges start to look white. Flip the meat and continue to cook until the second side is browned and the chicken is white and opaque throughout.

STIR-FRYING

Cut skinless, boneless chicken into small pieces of uniform size. Heat a wok or large skillet over high heat, then add a "girdle" of oil inside the wok—pour a small amount of oil in a circle around the top inside edge and let the oil drip down to coat the wok. Peanut or corn oil works best; olive oil tends to smoke and burn over high heat. Add the chopped meat a little at a time to the center of the wok. As the meat begins to cook, move it up the side of the pan and add more chicken to the center. Stir-fry until the meat is browned outside and thoroughly cooked.

Fried Chicken

PREP TIME: 50 MINUTES ♦ YIELD: 5 SERVINGS

⅓ cup all-purpose flour
1 teaspoon salt
¼ teaspoon pepper
¼ to ½ teaspoon poultry seasoning
3 to 3½ lb. cut-up frying chicken
1 cup oil or shortening

1. In resealable food storage plastic bag, combine flour, salt, pepper and poultry seasoning. Add chicken, a few pieces at a time; shake to coat.
2. Heat oil in large skillet over medium heat until hot. Add chicken; cook until browned on all sides.* Reduce heat to low; cover and cook 30 minutes or until chicken is fork-tender and juices run clear. Remove cover during last 10 minutes of cooking to crisp chicken.

> **TIP:** *After browning, chicken can be placed in ungreased shallow baking pan and baked uncovered at 350°F. for about 45 minutes.

NUTRITION INFORMATION PER SERVING: Serving Size: ⅕ of Recipe ♦ Calories: 500 ♦ Calories from Fat: 330 ♦ **% DAILY VALUE:** Total Fat: 37 g 57% ♦ Saturated Fat: 7 g 35% ♦ Cholesterol: 110 mg 37% ♦ Sodium: 530 mg 22% ♦ Total Carbohydrate: 7 g 2% ♦ Dietary Fiber: 0 g 0% ♦ Sugars: 0 g ♦ Protein: 35 g ♦ Vitamin A: 4% ♦ Vitamin C: 0% ♦ Calcium: 2% ♦ Iron: 10% ♦ **DIETARY EXCHANGES:** ½ Starch, 5 Lean Meat, 4 Fat OR ½ Carbohydrate, 5 Lean Meat, 4 Fat

---

COOK'S NOTE

CHICKEN NUTRITION

No matter which chicken part you prefer, keep the profile as healthy as possible by: trimming visible fat before cooking, choosing low-fat cooking techniques, removing skin before eating (cooking it with or without the skin makes no difference so long as you don't eat the skin) and controlling the portion size.

Crisp Oven-Fried Chicken

PREP TIME: 15 MINUTES (READY IN 1 HOUR 15 MINUTES) ♦ YIELD: 4 SERVINGS

1½ cups mashed potato flakes
1 teaspoon seasoned salt
½ teaspoon paprika
¼ teaspoon garlic powder
¼ teaspoon pepper
¼ cup margarine or butter, melted
1 tablespoon water
1 egg
3 to 3½ lb. cut-up frying chicken

1. Heat oven to 400°F. In large bowl, combine potato flakes, seasoned salt, paprika, garlic powder and pepper. Add margarine; mix well. In medium bowl, beat water with egg.
2. Dip chicken pieces in egg mixture; coat all sides with potato flake mixture. Place chicken, skin side up, in ungreased 13 × 9-inch pan.
3. Bake at 400°F. for 55 to 60 minutes or until chicken is fork-tender and juices run clear.

NUTRITION INFORMATION PER SERVING: Serving Size: ¼ of Recipe ♦ Calories: 580 ♦ Calories from Fat: 310 ♦ **% DAILY VALUE:** Total Fat: 34 g 52% ♦ Saturated Fat: 9 g 45% ♦ Cholesterol: 190 mg 63% ♦ Sodium: 710 mg 30% ♦ Total Carbohydrate: 22 g 7% ♦ Dietary Fiber: 2 g 8% ♦ Sugars: 1 g ♦ Protein: 46 g ♦ Vitamin A: 20% ♦ Vitamin C: 0% ♦ Calcium: 4% ♦ Iron: 15% ♦ **DIETARY EXCHANGES:** 1½ Starch, 6 Medium-Fat Meat, ½ Fat OR 1½ Carbohydrate, 6 Medium-Fat Meat, ½ Fat

Crisp Oven-Fried Chicken

Garlic Roasted Chicken

PREP TIME: 10 MINUTES (READY IN 1 HOUR 5 MINUTES)
✦ YIELD: 4 SERVINGS

    3 to 3½ lb. cut-up frying chicken, skin removed
    3 tablespoons margarine or butter, melted
    1 tablespoon dried parsley flakes
    2 tablespoons soy sauce
    1 teaspoon cornstarch
    ½ teaspoon grated gingerroot
    4 to 6 garlic cloves, minced

1. Heat oven to 350°F. Arrange chicken pieces in ungreased 12 × 8-inch (2-quart) baking dish. In small bowl, combine all remaining ingredients; blend well. Brush chicken with soy mixture.
2. Bake at 350°F. for 45 to 55 minutes or until chicken is fork-tender and juices run clear, basting with drippings halfway through cooking.

NUTRITION INFORMATION PER SERVING: Serving Size: ¼ of Recipe ✦ Calories: 330 ✦ Calories from Fat: 160 ✦ **% DAILY VALUE:** Total Fat: 18 g 28% ✦ Saturated Fat: 4 g 20% ✦ Cholesterol: 115 mg 38% ✦ Sodium: 730 mg 30% ✦ Total Carbohydrate: 3 g 1% ✦ Dietary Fiber: 0 g 0% ✦ Sugars: 0 g ✦ Protein: 38 g ✦ Vitamin A: 10% ✦ Vitamin C: 2% ✦ Calcium: 4% ✦ Iron: 10% ✦ **DIETARY EXCHANGES:** 5½ Lean Meat, ½ Fat

Herbed Butter-Basted Chicken

PREP TIME: 1 HOUR 10 MINUTES ✦ YIELD: 4 SERVINGS

    ¼ cup butter, melted
    ½ teaspoon dried thyme leaves
    ½ teaspoon dried sage leaves
    ¼ teaspoon dried rosemary leaves, crushed
    ⅛ teaspoon garlic powder
    3 to 3½ lb. cut-up or quartered frying chicken, skin removed if desired

1. GRILL DIRECTIONS: Heat grill. In small bowl, combine all ingredients except chicken; mix well.
2. When ready to grill, place chicken, skin side down, on gas grill over low heat or on charcoal grill 4 to 6 inches from medium coals. Cook 45 to 60 minutes or until chicken is fork-tender and juices run clear, turning once and brushing frequently with butter mixture. Discard any remaining butter mixture.

TIP: To bake chicken in oven, place in ungreased 13×9-inch (3-quart) baking dish. Bake at 350°F. for 45 to 60 minutes. Transfer to broiler pan; broil 4 to 6 inches from heat for 2 to 4 minutes, brushing twice with butter mixture.

NUTRITION INFORMATION PER SERVING: Serving Size: ¼ of Recipe ✦ Calories: 390 ✦ Calories from Fat: 220 ✦ **% DAILY VALUE:** Total Fat: 24 g 37% ✦ Saturated Fat: 8 g 40% ✦ Cholesterol: 145 mg 48% ✦ Sodium: 160 mg 7% ✦ Total Carbohydrate: 0 g 0% ✦ Dietary Fiber: 0 g 0% ✦ Sugars: 0 g ✦ Protein: 43 g ✦ Vitamin A: 8% ✦ Vitamin C: 0% ✦ Calcium: 2% ✦ Iron: 10% ✦ **DIETARY EXCHANGES:** 6 Lean Meat, 1½ Fat

Spicy Barbecued Chicken

PREP TIME: 20 MINUTES (READY IN 1 HOUR)
✦ YIELD: 4 SERVINGS

    2½ to 3 lb. quartered frying chicken
    ½ cup chopped onion
    1 garlic clove, minced
    1 (8-oz.) can tomato sauce
    3 tablespoons brown sugar
    2 teaspoons chili powder
    ⅓ cup vinegar
    2 to 3 drops hot pepper sauce
    1 tomato, peeled, seeded and chopped

1. Heat oven to 350°F. Place chicken in large saucepan or Dutch oven. Add water to cover. Bring to a boil. Reduce heat to low; cover and simmer 10 minutes. Drain.
2. Meanwhile, in small saucepan, combine all remaining ingredients; mix well. Bring to a boil. Reduce heat to low; simmer 5 minutes.
3. Arrange chicken in ungreased 13 × 9-inch pan. Brush chicken with ½ cup sauce. Bake at 350°F. for 30 to 40 minutes or until chicken is fork-tender and juices run clear, basting occasionally with sauce. Bring any remaining sauce to a boil; serve with chicken.

NUTRITION INFORMATION PER SERVING: Serving Size: ¼ of Recipe ✦ Calories: 400 ✦ Calories from Fat: 170 ✦ **% DAILY VALUE:** Total Fat: 19 g 29% ✦ Saturated Fat: 5 g 25% ✦ Cholesterol: 115 mg 38% ✦ Sodium: 470 mg 20% ✦ Total Carbohydrate: 19 g 6% ✦ Dietary Fiber: 2 g 8% ✦ Sugars: 14 g ✦ Protein: 38 g ✦ Vitamin A: 30% ✦ Vitamin C: 20% ✦ Calcium: 4% ✦ Iron: 15% ✦ **DIETARY EXCHANGES:** 1 Starch, 1 Vegetable, 4½ Lean Meat, 1 Fat OR 1 Carbohydrate, 1 Vegetable, 4½ Lean Meat, 1 Fat

Pan-Roasted Chicken with Summer Vegetables

PREP TIME: 30 MINUTES (READY IN 1 HOUR)
◆ YIELD: 4 SERVINGS

1/4 cup all-purpose flour
1/4 teaspoon salt
1/4 teaspoon coarse ground black pepper
3 to 3 1/2 lb. cut-up frying chicken
2 tablespoons olive or vegetable oil
1 large onion, sliced
2 garlic cloves, minced
2 medium tomatoes, coarsely chopped
1 red bell pepper, cut into large pieces
1 small zucchini, sliced
1 small yellow summer squash, sliced
1 tablespoon chopped fresh basil

1. In resealable plastic bag, combine flour, salt and pepper; shake to mix. Add chicken pieces to bag in batches; shake to coat.
2. Heat oil in large skillet or Dutch oven over medium-high heat until hot. Add chicken; cook until golden brown on all sides.
3. Remove chicken from skillet. Add onion and garlic to skillet; cook over medium heat until tender. Add tomatoes. Return chicken to skillet; cover and cook over medium-low heat for 30 minutes.
4. Add bell pepper, zucchini and summer squash; cover and cook an additional 5 to 10 minutes or until chicken is fork-tender, juices run clear and vegetables are crisp-tender.
5. Remove chicken from skillet; place on serving platter. Add basil to skillet; mix well. Serve vegetables over chicken.

NUTRITION INFORMATION PER SERVING: Serving Size: 1/4 of Recipe ◆ Calories: 520 ◆ Calories from Fat: 260 ◆ **% DAILY VALUE:** Total Fat: 29 g 45% ◆ Saturated Fat: 7 g 35% ◆ Cholesterol: 135 mg 45% ◆ Sodium: 270 mg 11% ◆ Total Carbohydrate: 19 g 6% ◆ Dietary Fiber: 4 g 16% ◆ Sugars: 7 g ◆ Protein: 46 g ◆ Vitamin A: 40% ◆ Vitamin C: 70% ◆ Calcium: 6% ◆ Iron: 20% ◆ **DIETARY EXCHANGES:** 1 Starch, 1 Vegetable, 6 Lean Meat, 2 Fat OR 1 Carbohydrate, 1 Vegetable, 6 Lean Meat, 2 Fat

Lemon-Herb Roasted Chicken

PREP TIME: 15 MINUTES (READY IN 2 HOURS 25 MINUTES) ◆ YIELD: 6 SERVINGS

1 (6-lb.) whole roasting chicken
1 lemon, thinly sliced
1 tablespoon chopped fresh Italian parsley
    or 1 teaspoon dried parsley flakes
1 tablespoon chopped fresh sage
    or 1 teaspoon dried sage leaves
1 tablespoon chopped fresh thyme
    or 1 teaspoon dried thyme leaves
2 large garlic cloves, sliced
2 tablespoons butter, softened
1/4 teaspoon salt
1/4 teaspoon coarse ground black pepper

1. Heat oven to 425°F. Remove and discard neck and giblets from chicken. Rinse chicken with cold water; pat dry. Loosen skin covering chicken breast meat by slipping fingers down from top between skin and breast meat, gently making a pocket. Place 4 lemon slices and 1 teaspoon of the parsley in pocket. Place remaining lemon slices, remaining parsley, sage and thyme in cavity of chicken.
2. Rub garlic over outside of chicken; place garlic in cavity. Loosely tie legs together. Place chicken in shallow roasting pan. Rub outside of chicken with butter; sprinkle with salt and pepper. Insert meat thermometer so bulb reaches center of thickest part of thigh, but does not rest on bone. Do not cover or add water.
3. Bake at 425°F. for 1 1/2 to 2 hours or until chicken is fork-tender, juices run clear and meat thermometer registers 180 to 185°F. Baste chicken with pan juices every 30 minutes. If necessary, cover chicken with tent of foil halfway through cooking time to prevent excessive browning. Let stand 5 to 10 minutes before carving. Remove and discard lemons from inside of chicken.

NUTRITION INFORMATION PER SERVING: Serving Size: 1/6 of Recipe ◆ Calories: 450 ◆ Calories from Fat: 250 ◆ **% DAILY VALUE:** Total Fat: 28 g 43% ◆ Saturated Fat: 9 g 45% ◆ Cholesterol: 165 mg 55% ◆ Sodium: 270 mg 11% ◆ Total Carbohydrate: 1 g 1% ◆ Dietary Fiber: 0 g 0% ◆ Sugars: 0 g ◆ Protein: 49 g ◆ Vitamin A: 10% ◆ Vitamin C: 8% ◆ Calcium: 4% ◆ Iron: 15% ◆ **DIETARY EXCHANGES:** 7 Lean Meat, 1 1/2 Fat

TIMETABLE FOR ROASTING POULTRY

POULTRY	WEIGHT (POUNDS)	THERMOMETER READING	TOTAL ROASTING TIME (HOURS) STUFFED	TOTAL ROASTING TIME (HOURS) UNSTUFFED
WHOLE BROILER/ FRYER CHICKEN *Roast at 350°F.*	3 to 4	180° to 185°F. (poultry) 165°F. (stuffing)	1½ to 2	1¼ to 1½
WHOLE ROASTING CHICKEN *Roast at 350°F.*	5 to 7	180° to 185°F. (poultry) 165°F. (stuffing)	2¼ to 2¾	2 to 2¼
WHOLE CAPON *Roast at 350°F.*	4 to 8	180° to 185°F. (poultry) 165°F. (stuffing)	2¼ to 3½	2 to 3
WHOLE TURKEY *Roast at 325°F.*	8 to 12 12 to 14 14 to 18 18 to 20 20 to 24	180° to 185°F. (poultry) 165° (stuffing)	3 to 3½ 3½ to 4 4 to 4½ 4¼ to 4¾4¾ to 5¼	2¾ to 3 3 to 3¾ 3¾ to 4¼ 4¼ to 4½ 4½ to 5
WHOLE TURKEY BREAST *Roast at 325°F.*	4 to 6 6 to 8	180° to 185°F. (poultry) 165°F. (stuffing)	3 to 3½ 2 to 2½	1½ to 2¼ 2¼ to 3¼
WHOLE CORNISH GAME HEN *Roast at 350°F.*	1 to 1½	180° to 185°F. (poultry) 165°F. (stuffing)	1 to 1½	50 to 60 minutes total
WHOLE DOMESTIC DUCK *Roast at 375°F.*	3 to 5	180° to 185°F. (poultry) 165°F. (stuffing)	1¼ to 2	1 to 1½
WHOLE WILD DUCK *Roast at 350°F.*	3 to 5	180° to 185°F. (poultry) 165°F. (stuffing)	1¼ to 2	1 to 1½
WHOLE GOOSE *Roast at 325°F.*	4 to 8 8 to 14	180° to 185°F. (poultry) 165°F. (stuffing)	1¾ to 3¾ 3 to 6¼	1½ to 3¼ (20 to 25 min./lb.) 2¾ to 5¾ (20 to 25 min./lb.)

Source: U.S. Department of Agriculture

Roasted Chicken and Vegetables Provençal

Roasted Chicken and Vegetables Provençal

PREP TIME: 30 MINUTES (READY IN 1 HOUR 35 MINUTES)
✦ YIELD: 4 SERVINGS

  8 small new red potatoes, quartered
  1 small yellow summer squash, cut into 1-inch
    pieces
  1 small zucchini, cut into 1-inch pieces
  1 red bell pepper, cut into 1-inch pieces
  1 medium red onion, cut into eighths
  1 (8-oz.) pkg. fresh whole mushrooms
  ¼ cup olive oil
  2 teaspoons dried basil leaves
  2 teaspoons dried thyme leaves
  ½ teaspoon salt
  ½ teaspoon coarse ground black pepper
  3 garlic cloves, minced
  3 to 3½ lb. cut-up frying chicken, skin removed

1. Heat oven to 375°F. In ungreased 13×9-inch (3-quart) baking dish, combine potatoes, summer squash, zucchini, bell pepper, onion and mushrooms.

2. In small bowl, combine oil, basil, thyme, salt, pepper and garlic; mix well. Brush half of oil mixture on vegetables. Place chicken pieces, meaty side up, over vegetables. Brush chicken with remaining oil mixture.

3. Bake at 375°F. for 45 minutes. Baste with pan juices; bake an additional 15 to 20 minutes or until chicken is fork-tender, juices run clear and vegetables are tender. Baste with pan juices before serving.

Braised Chicken Paprikash

PREP TIME: 1 HOUR ✦ YIELD: 6 SERVINGS

  3 tablespoons all-purpose flour
  3 to 3½ lb. cut-up frying chicken, skin removed
  4 tablespoons margarine or butter
  1 (12-oz.) jar home-style chicken gravy
  ½ cup finely chopped onion
  ½ cup thinly sliced red or green bell pepper
  3 teaspoons paprika
  8 oz. (4 cups) uncooked wide egg noodles
  ½ cup soft bread crumbs
  ½ cup sour cream
  ⅛ teaspoon pepper

1. Place flour in resealable food storage plastic bag. Add chicken, a few pieces at a time; shake to coat. Melt 3 tablespoons of the margarine in large skillet over medium-high heat. Add chicken; cook 4 to 5 minutes on each side or until light golden brown.

2. In small bowl, combine gravy, onion, bell pepper and paprika; pour over chicken. Cover; cook over low heat for 40 to 45 minutes or until chicken is fork-tender and juices run clear, stirring occasionally. Skim fat from surface and discard.

3. Meanwhile, cook noodles to desired doneness as directed on package. Drain; cover to keep warm.

4. In small saucepan, melt remaining 1 tablespoon margarine over medium heat. Add bread crumbs; cook and stir until light golden brown. Set aside.

5. Stir sour cream and pepper into chicken with gravy. Cook over low heat until thoroughly heated, stirring constantly. DO NOT BOIL. Serve chicken over noodles; top with gravy. Sprinkle with bread crumbs.

Sage and Rosemary Roast Chicken

PREP TIME: 15 MINUTES (READY IN 1 HOUR 45 MINUTES)
✦ YIELD: 4 SERVINGS

    3 to 3½ lb. cut-up or quartered frying chicken
    4 medium baking potatoes, unpeeled, quartered
    1 bunch (about 8) green onions, trimmed, cut into 2-inch pieces
    ½ teaspoon dried sage leaves
    ½ teaspoon dried rosemary leaves, crushed
    ¼ teaspoon salt
    ¼ teaspoon coarse ground black pepper

1. Heat oven to 375°F. Arrange chicken, potatoes and onions in ungreased 13 × 9-inch (3-quart) baking dish. Sprinkle with sage, rosemary, salt and pepper.

2. Bake at 375°F. for 1¼ to 1½ hours or until chicken is fork-tender, juices run clear and potatoes are tender.

NUTRITION INFORMATION PER SERVING: Serving Size: ¼ of Recipe ◆ Calories: 590 ◆ Calories from Fat: 190 ◆ **% DAILY VALUE:** Total Fat: 21 g 32% ◆ Saturated Fat: 6 g 30% ◆ Cholesterol: 135 mg 45% ◆ Sodium: 280 mg 12% ◆ Total Carbohydrate: 53 g 18% ◆ Dietary Fiber: 6 g 24% ◆ Sugars: 3 g ◆ Protein: 48 g ◆ Vitamin A: 8% ◆ Vitamin C: 35% ◆ Calcium: 6% ◆ Iron: 30% ◆ **DIETARY EXCHANGES:** 3½ Starch, 5½ Lean Meat, ½ Fat OR 3½ Carbohydrate, 5½ Lean Meat, ½ Fat

Chicken Cacciatore

PREP TIME: 1 HOUR ✦ YIELD: 6 SERVINGS

    ¼ cup all-purpose flour
    3 to 3½ lb. cut-up frying chicken, skin removed
    2 tablespoons oil
    1 (14.5 or 16-oz.) can whole tomatoes, undrained, cut up
    1 medium onion, sliced
    1 medium green bell pepper, sliced
    1 teaspoon dried Italian seasoning
    ½ teaspoon sugar
    ½ teaspoon salt
    ⅛ teaspoon pepper

1. Place flour in resealable food storage plastic bag. Add chicken, a few pieces at a time; shake to coat.

2. Heat oil in large skillet over medium-high heat until hot. Add chicken; brown well on all sides. Drain and discard oil from skillet.

3. Add all remaining ingredients to skillet. Bring to a boil. Reduce heat to low; cover and simmer 30 to 40 minutes or until chicken is fork-tender and juices run clear, stirring occasionally. If desired, serve over hot cooked pasta.

NUTRITION INFORMATION PER SERVING: Serving Size: ⅙ of Recipe ◆ Calories: 240 ◆ Calories from Fat: 100 ◆ **% DAILY VALUE:** Total Fat: 11 g 17% ◆ Saturated Fat: 2 g 10% ◆ Cholesterol: 75 mg 25% ◆ Sodium: 370 mg 15% ◆ Total Carbohydrate: 10 g 3% ◆ Dietary Fiber: 2 g 8% ◆ Sugars: 3 g ◆ Protein: 26 g ◆ Vitamin A: 10% ◆ Vitamin C: 25% ◆ Calcium: 4% ◆ Iron: 10% ◆ **DIETARY EXCHANGES:** 2 Vegetable, 3 Lean Meat, ½ Fat

Poached Chicken Breasts

PREP TIME: 20 MINUTES (READY IN 1 HOUR)
✦ YIELD: 3 CUPS CUT-UP COOKED CHICKEN;
4 CUPS BROTH

    4 boneless skinless chicken breast halves
    1 stalk celery, sliced
    1 medium carrot, sliced
    1 small onion, quartered
    1 teaspoon chopped fresh parsley
    ¼ teaspoon salt
    ⅛ teaspoon dried thyme leaves
    ⅛ teaspoon pepper
    1 bay leaf
    1 garlic clove, sliced

1. Place chicken breast halves in large saucepan. Add cold water to cover. Bring to a boil. Reduce heat to low; partially cover and simmer 10 minutes. Skim foam from surface and discard.

2. Add all remaining ingredients; simmer an additional 30 to 40 minutes or until chicken is fork-tender.

3. Remove chicken from broth; cool 15 minutes. Strain broth. Cool broth uncovered in refrigerator. Cut up chicken as desired. Store chicken and cooled broth tightly covered in refrigerator or freezer.

NUTRITION INFORMATION PER SERVING: Serving Size: ½ Cup Cooked Chicken ◆ Calories: 130 ◆ Calories from Fat: 45 ◆ **% DAILY VALUE:** Total Fat: 5 g 8% ◆ Saturated Fat: 1 g 5% ◆ Cholesterol: 60 mg 20% ◆ Sodium: 60 mg 3% ◆ Total Carbohydrate: 0 g 0% ◆ Dietary Fiber: 0 g 0% ◆ Sugars: 0 g ◆ Protein: 20 g ◆ Vitamin A: 0% ◆ Vitamin C: 0% ◆ Calcium: 0% ◆ Iron: 4% ◆ **DIETARY EXCHANGES:** 2½ Lean Meat

Herb Cheese-Stuffed Chicken Breasts

PREP TIME: 10 MINUTES (READY IN 45 MINUTES)
◆ YIELD: 4 SERVINGS

  4 boneless skinless chicken breast halves
  2 oz. feta cheese, crumbled (¼ cup)
¼ cup chopped fresh parsley
  2 teaspoons chopped fresh oregano
      or ¼ teaspoon dried oregano leaves
  2 tablespoons olive or vegetable oil
  2 (14.5-oz.) cans Italian-style diced tomatoes,
      undrained
¼ cup sliced ripe olives
  4 teaspoons cornstarch

1. Heat oven to 350°F. Using sharp knife, cut 3-inch slit in meaty side of each chicken breast half to form pocket.
2. In small bowl, combine feta cheese, parsley, oregano and oil; mix well. Gently spoon ¼ of mixture into each pocket. Place chicken in ungreased 13×9-inch (3-quart) baking dish.
3. In medium bowl, combine tomatoes, olives and cornstarch; mix well. Pour over chicken.
4. Bake at 350°F. for 35 to 40 minutes or until chicken is fork-tender and juices run clear.

NUTRITION INFORMATION PER SERVING: Serving Size: ¼ of Recipe ◆ Calories: 320 ◆ Calories from Fat: 130 ◆ **% DAILY VALUE:** Total Fat: 14 g 22% ◆ Saturated Fat: 4 g 20% ◆ Cholesterol: 85 mg 28% ◆ Sodium: 750 mg 31% ◆ Total Carbohydrate: 18 g 6% ◆ Dietary Fiber: 3 g ◆ Sugars: 5 g ◆ Protein: 31 g ◆ Vitamin A: 30% ◆ Vitamin C: 35% ◆ Calcium: 15% ◆ Iron: 15% ◆ **DIETARY EXCHANGES:** ½ Starch, 2 Vegetable, 4 Very Lean Meat, 2 Fat OR ½ Carbohydrate, 2 Vegetable, 4 Very Lean Meat, 2 Fat

Oven Chicken Cordon Bleu

PREP TIME: 20 MINUTES (READY IN 50 MINUTES)
◆ YIELD: 4 SERVINGS

  4 boneless skinless chicken breast halves
  2 teaspoons Dijon mustard
  4 teaspoons chopped fresh chives
  4 very thin slices cooked ham
      (about ¾ oz. each)
  4 very thin slices Swiss cheese
      (about ¾ oz. each)
  1 egg white
  1 tablespoon water
⅓ cup corn flake crumbs
¼ teaspoon paprika

1. Heat oven to 375°F. Spray 8-inch square (2-quart) baking dish with nonstick cooking spray. Place 1 chicken breast half, boned side up, between 2 pieces of plastic wrap or waxed paper. Working from center, gently pound chicken with flat side of meat mallet or rolling pin until about ¼ inch thick; remove wrap. Repeat with remaining chicken breast halves.
2. Spread each chicken breast half with ½ teaspoon mustard; sprinkle each with 1 teaspoon chives. Cut ham and cheese slices to fit chicken. Top each chicken breast half with ham and cheese slice. Roll up, tucking ends inside.
3. In shallow bowl, combine egg white and water; beat slightly. Place corn flake crumbs in shallow dish. Coat chicken rolls with egg white mixture; roll in crumbs. Place in sprayed baking dish; sprinkle with paprika.
4. Bake at 375°F. for 25 to 30 minutes or until chicken is fork-tender and juices run clear.

NUTRITION INFORMATION PER SERVING: Serving Size: ¼ of Recipe ◆ Calories: 270 ◆ Calories from Fat: 90 ◆ **% DAILY VALUE:** Total Fat: 10 g 15% ◆ Saturated Fat: 5 g 25% ◆ Cholesterol: 105 mg 35% ◆ Sodium: 580 mg 24% ◆ Total Carbohydrate: 7 g 2% ◆ Dietary Fiber: 0 g 0% ◆ Sugars: 1 g ◆ Protein: 38 g ◆ Vitamin A: 10% ◆ Vitamin C: 4% ◆ Calcium: 20% ◆ Iron: 20% ◆ **DIETARY EXCHANGES:** ½ Starch, 5 Very Lean Meat, 1 Fat OR ½ Carbohydrate, 5 Very Lean Meat, 1 Fat

Baked Chicken Kiev

PREP TIME: 35 MINUTES (READY IN 1 HOUR 10 MINUTES)
◆ YIELD: 4 SERVINGS

¼ cup butter, softened
  2 tablespoons chopped fresh parsley
  1 tablespoon chopped green onions
  1 teaspoon chopped fresh rosemary
      or ½ teaspoon dried rosemary leaves
¼ teaspoon salt
      Dash pepper
  2 garlic cloves, minced
  4 boneless skinless chicken breast halves
¼ cup all-purpose flour
¼ cup unseasoned dry bread crumbs
  1 egg
      Paprika
      Nonstick cooking spray

1. In small bowl, combine butter, parsley, onions, rosemary, salt, pepper and garlic; mix well. Shape mixture into 3-inch log; refrigerate until firm.
2. Heat oven to 350°F. Place 1 chicken breast half, boned side up, between 2 pieces of plastic wrap or waxed paper. Working

from center, gently pound chicken with flat side of meat mallet or rolling pin until about ⅛ to ¼ inch thick; remove wrap. Repeat with remaining chicken breast halves.

3. Cut butter log crosswise into 4 equal pieces. Place 1 piece of butter on each chicken breast half. Fold in sides; roll up jelly-roll fashion, pressing ends to seal. If necessary, secure with toothpicks.

4. Place flour and bread crumbs in separate shallow bowls. Place egg in another shallow bowl; beat well. Coat chicken with flour; dip in beaten egg. Roll chicken in bread crumbs; place in ungreased 8-inch square (2-quart) baking dish. Sprinkle with paprika. Spray chicken rolls with nonstick cooking spray.

5. Bake at 350°F. for 30 to 35 minutes or until chicken is fork-tender and juices run clear.

NUTRITION INFORMATION PER SERVING: Serving Size: ¼ of Recipe • Calories: 330 • Calories from Fat: 160 • % DAILY VALUE: Total Fat: 18 g 28% • Saturated Fat: 9 g 45% • Cholesterol: 155 mg 52% • Sodium: 380 mg 16% • Total Carbohydrate: 12 g 4% • Dietary Fiber: 1 g 3% • Sugars: 1 g • Protein: 30 g • Vitamin A: 15% • Vitamin C: 4% • Calcium: 4% • Iron: 10% • DIETARY EXCHANGES: 1 Starch, 4 Very Lean Meat, 2½ Fat OR 1 Carbohydrate, 4 Very Lean Meat, 2½ Fat

Easy Chicken Parmigiana

PREP TIME: 30 MINUTES ✦ YIELD: 4 SERVINGS

  6 oz. (2 cups) uncooked penne (medium
     pasta tubes)
¼ cup grated Parmesan cheese
¼ cup unseasoned dry bread crumbs
  4 boneless skinless chicken breast halves
  1 tablespoon oil
  1 (14.5-oz.) can Italian-style diced tomatoes,
     undrained
  1 small zucchini, cut into thin 1½-inch-long
     strips
  2 tablespoons chopped ripe olives

1. Cook penne to desired doneness as directed on package. Drain; cover to keep warm.

2. Meanwhile, in shallow bowl, combine cheese and bread crumbs; mix well. Coat chicken breast halves with cheese mixture. Heat oil in large skillet over medium-high heat until hot. Add chicken; cook 3 to 5 minutes on each side or until browned.

3. Stir in tomatoes and zucchini. Bring to a boil. Reduce heat to low; cover and simmer 12 to 15 minutes or until chicken is fork-

tender and juices run clear, stirring and turning chicken occasionally. Serve chicken mixture with penne. Sprinkle with olives.

NUTRITION INFORMATION PER SERVING: Serving Size: ¼ of Recipe • Calories: 430 • Calories from Fat: 110 • % DAILY VALUE: Total Fat: 12 g 18% • Saturated Fat: 3 g 15% • Cholesterol: 80 mg 27% • Sodium: 800 mg 33% • Total Carbohydrate: 43 g 14% • Dietary Fiber: 3 g 12% • Sugars: 7 g • Protein: 37 g • Vitamin A: 10% • Vitamin C: 10% • Calcium: 15% • Iron: 20% • DIETARY EXCHANGES: 2 Starch, 2 Vegetable, 4 Very Lean Meat, 1½ Fat OR 2 Carbohydrate, 2 Vegetable, 4 Very Lean Meat, 1½ Fat

Grilled Caribbean Chicken

PREP TIME: 30 MINUTES ✦ YIELD: 4 SERVINGS

  1 teaspoon allspice
½ teaspoon dried thyme leaves
½ teaspoon paprika
¼ teaspoon hot pepper sauce
  2 teaspoons olive or vegetable oil
  2 teaspoons lime juice
  4 boneless skinless chicken breast halves

1. GRILL DIRECTIONS: Heat grill. In small bowl, combine all ingredients except chicken; mix well. Rub mixture on chicken breast halves. Let stand at room temperature for 15 minutes to marinate.

2. When ready to grill, place chicken on gas grill over medium heat or on charcoal grill 4 to 6 inches from medium coals. Cook 8 to 10 minutes or until chicken is fork-tender and juices run clear, turning once.

TIP: To broil chicken, place on sprayed broiler pan; boil 4 to 6 inches from heat using times above as a guide, turning once.

NUTRITION INFORMATION PER SERVING: Serving Size: ¼ of Recipe • Calories: 160 • Calories from Fat: 45 • % DAILY VALUE: Total Fat: 5 g 8% • Saturated Fat: 1 g 5% • Cholesterol: 75 mg 25% • Sodium: 65 mg 3% • Total Carbohydrate: 1 g 1% • Dietary Fiber: 0 g 0% • Sugars: 0 g • Protein: 27 g • Vitamin A: 4% • Vitamin C: 0% • Calcium: 2% • Iron: 6% • DIETARY EXCHANGES: 4 Very Lean Meat, ½ Fat

COOK'S NOTE

TESTING FOR DONENESS

Chicken pieces: Cut into the meat with a small, sharp knife. The meat should still look moist, but any visible juices should be clear, not pink. The meat should not look pink, except for dark meat nearest the bone.

Piccata Chicken

Piccata Chicken

PREP TIME: 30 MINUTES ✦ YIELD: 4 SERVINGS

    4 boneless skinless chicken breast halves
 1/4 cup all-purpose flour
 1/4 teaspoon salt
 1/4 teaspoon white pepper
    2 tablespoons oil
 1/2 cup chicken broth
    2 teaspoons Worcestershire sauce
 1/4 teaspoon dried marjoram leaves
    2 tablespoons fresh lemon juice
 1/4 cup chopped fresh parsley

1. Place 1 chicken breast half, boned side up, between 2 pieces of plastic wrap or waxed paper. Working from center, gently pound chicken with flat side of meat mallet or rolling pin until about 1/4 inch thick; remove wrap. Repeat with remaining chicken breast halves.

2. In shallow bowl, combine flour, salt and pepper. Coat chicken breast halves with flour mixture.

3. Heat oil in large skillet over medium-high heat until hot. Add chicken; cook 3 to 5 minutes on each side or until golden brown, fork-tender and juices run clear. Remove chicken from skillet; cover to keep warm.

4. Add broth, Worcestershire sauce and marjoram to skillet; cook and stir 1 to 2 minutes. Stir in lemon juice and parsley. Serve over chicken.

NUTRITION INFORMATION PER SERVING: Serving Size: 1/4 of Recipe ♦ Calories: 230 ♦ Calories from Fat: 90 ♦ % DAILY VALUE: Total Fat: 10 g 15% ♦ Saturated Fat: 2 g 10% ♦ Cholesterol: 75 mg 25% ♦ Sodium: 320 mg 13% ♦ Total Carbohydrate: 7 g 2% ♦ Dietary Fiber: 0 g 0% ♦ Sugars: 0 g ♦ Protein: 28 g ♦ Vitamin A: 4% ♦ Vitamin C: 10% ♦ Calcium: 2% ♦ Iron: 8% ♦ DIETARY EXCHANGES: 1/2 Starch, 4 Very Lean Meat, 1 Fat OR 1/2 Carbohydrate, 4 Very Lean Meat, 1 Fat

Chicken Marengo

PREP TIME: 30 MINUTES ✦ YIELD: 4 SERVINGS

    1 tablespoon olive or vegetable oil
    4 bone-in chicken breast halves, skin removed
    1 tablespoon all-purpose flour
 1/2 teaspoon dried basil leaves
 1/4 teaspoon garlic powder
 1/8 teaspoon pepper
 1/2 cup dry white wine or chicken broth
    2 tablespoons tomato paste
    2 (14.5 or 16-oz.) cans regular or Italian whole
       tomatoes, well drained, cut up
 1/2 cup coarsely chopped green bell pepper
    1 medium onion, cut into 8 thin wedges
 1/4 cup halved or sliced ripe olives

1. Heat oil in large nonstick skillet over medium-high heat until hot. Add chicken breast halves; cook until browned on all sides.

2. Meanwhile, in medium bowl, combine flour, basil, garlic powder, pepper, wine and tomato paste; blend until smooth. Stir in tomatoes.

3. Move chicken to side of skillet; add tomato mixture. Place chicken, meaty side up, in tomato mixture. Bring to a boil. Reduce heat to medium-low; cover and cook 10 minutes, stirring occasionally.

4. Turn chicken; stir in bell pepper and onion. Cover; cook an additional 8 to 10 minutes or until chicken is fork-tender

Chicken Marengo

and juices run clear, stirring occasionally. Stir in olives.

NUTRITION INFORMATION PER SERVING: Serving Size: ¼ of Recipe • Calories: 270 • Calories from Fat: 60 • **% DAILY VALUE:** Total Fat: 7 g 11% • Saturated Fat: 1 g 5% • Cholesterol: 75 mg 25% • Sodium: 230 mg 10% • Total Carbohydrate: 17 g 6% • Dietary Fiber: 3 g 12% • Sugars: 7 g • Protein: 30 g • Vitamin A: 15% • Vitamin C: 60% • Calcium: 10% • Iron: 15% • **DIETARY EXCHANGES:** 4 Vegetable, 3 Very Lean Meat, 1½ Fat

---

C O O K ' S   N O T E

CONVENIENT CUTS

Look for these shortcut forms of poultry in the supermarket:

Meat Department
+ Boneless skinless chicken breast halves
+ Preseasoned chicken breast halves
+ Boneless chicken strips
+ Uncooked chicken patties

Frozen Food Section
+ Cubed, cooked chicken
+ Boneless chicken breast halves
+ Preseasoned chicken strips
+ Turkey breast tenderloins

Canned Food Section
+ Water-packed canned chicken or turkey

Deli Department
+ Whole roasted chicken
+ Sliced cooked chicken or turkey

Lemon Chicken

PREP TIME: 30 MINUTES ✦ YIELD: 4 SERVINGS

CHICKEN
   ¾ cup finely crushed corn flakes cereal
   ½ teaspoon ginger
   ⅛ teaspoon pepper
   I egg white
   I teaspoon water
   I teaspoon soy sauce
   4 boneless skinless chicken breast halves

SAUCE
   ½ cup chicken broth
   I tablespoon cornstarch
   ⅓ cup honey
   3 tablespoons fresh lemon juice
   I teaspoon ketchup
   ⅛ teaspoon garlic powder
   I teaspoon grated lemon peel
   2 green onions, cut into ½-inch pieces, including tops

1. Line cookie sheet with foil; place in oven. Heat oven to 450°F. In pie pan, combine crushed cereal, ginger and pepper; mix well. In small bowl, beat egg white, water and soy sauce until frothy. Brush both sides of chicken with egg-white mixture. Place in pie pan; spoon cereal mixture over chicken to coat evenly.

2. Remove hot foil-lined cookie sheet from oven; arrange coated chicken on sheet. Bake at 450°F. for 15 to 20 minutes or until chicken is fork-tender and juices run clear.

3. Meanwhile, in medium saucepan, combine broth and cornstarch; blend until smooth. Add honey, lemon juice, ketchup and garlic powder; mix well. Bring to a boil over medium-high heat, stirring constantly. Remove from heat; stir in lemon peel.

4. To serve, cut each chicken breast half crosswise into 6 or 7 pieces; arrange on 4 individual plates. Spoon sauce over chicken; sprinkle with onions.

NUTRITION INFORMATION PER SERVING: Serving Size: ¼ of Recipe • Calories: 310 • Calories from Fat: 25 • **% DAILY VALUE:** Total Fat: 3 g 5% • Saturated Fat: 1 g 5% • Cholesterol: 75 mg 25% • Sodium: 450 mg 19% • Total Carbohydrate: 41 g 14% • Dietary Fiber: 1 g 4% • Sugars: 24 g • Protein: 30 g • Vitamin A: 10% • Vitamin C: 15% • Calcium: 2% • Iron: 35% • **DIETARY EXCHANGES:** 1 Starch, 1½ Fruit, 4 Very Lean Meat OR 2½ Carbohydrate, 4 Very Lean Meat

Lemon Chicken

Chicken and Black Bean Burritos

PREP TIME: 30 MINUTES ✦ YIELD: 6 BURRITOS

1 tablespoon oil
3 boneless skinless chicken breast halves,
    cut into thin strips
1 (15-oz.) can black beans, drained, rinsed
3 tablespoons water
½ teaspoon cumin
1 garlic clove, minced

2 to 3 drops hot pepper sauce
6 (8 to 10-inch) flour tortillas
6 lettuce leaves
1 small tomato, seeded, chopped
¼ cup sliced green onions
2 tablespoons chopped fresh cilantro

1. Heat oven to 350°F. Heat oil in large skillet over medium-high heat until hot. Add chicken; cook and stir 5 minutes or until chicken is no longer pink. Remove from skillet; cover to keep warm.

2. In same skillet, combine beans, water, cumin, garlic and hot pepper sauce; mix well. Cook over medium-high heat until thoroughly heated, stirring occasionally and mashing beans slightly.

3. Meanwhile, wrap tortillas in foil. Bake at 350°F. for 10 minutes or until warm.

4. Place 1 lettuce leaf on each warm tortilla; spoon about 2 tablespoons bean mixture down center of each. Top each with ⅓ cup cooked chicken; sprinkle with tomato, onions and cilantro. Fold in sides of each tortilla over filling, overlapping to form triangle.

NUTRITION INFORMATION PER SERVING: Serving Size: 1 Burrito ✦ Calories: 330 ✦ Calories from Fat: 70 ✦ **% DAILY VALUE:** Total Fat: 8 g 12% ✦ Saturated Fat: 2 g 10% ✦ Cholesterol: 35 mg 12% ✦ Sodium: 440 mg 18% ✦ Total Carbohydrate: 42 g 14% ✦ Dietary Fiber: 5 g 20% ✦ Sugars: 1 g ✦ Protein: 22 g ✦ Vitamin A: 2% ✦ Vitamin C: 4% ✦ Calcium: 10% ✦ Iron: 20% ✦ **DIETARY EXCHANGES:** 3 Starch, 2 Very Lean Meat, ½ Fat OR 3 Carbohydrate, 2 Very Lean Meat, ½ Fat

---

COOK'S NOTE

HOW TO BONE A CHICKEN BREAST

Remove the skin. Lay the breast bone side up. Using a sharp knife, cut through the cartilage at the V of the neck.

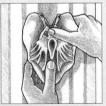

To remove the keel bone (dark spoon-shaped bone), bend the breast back until the keel bone breaks through the membrane. Run your finger under the edge of the keel bone; pull partially away from the breast and pull down to remove the white cartilage.

To remove the rib bones, insert the knife point under the long first rib on one side of the breast. Resting the knife

against the bones, gradually scrape the meat away from the bones. Cut the rib away. Cut through the shoulder joint and run the point of the knife under the joint. Remove the shoulder joint. Repeat with the other side of the breast; run the point of the knife close to the bone. Remove the wishbone. Cut the breast in half, if desired.

Chicken Almond Ding

PREP TIME: 25 MINUTES ✦ YIELD: 4 SERVINGS

1⅓ cups uncooked regular long-grain white rice
2⅔ cups water
1 cup chicken broth
2 tablespoons cornstarch
2 tablespoons soy sauce
1 tablespoon rice vinegar
1 teaspoon sugar
¼ teaspoon salt, if desired
1 tablespoon oil
2 garlic cloves, minced
½ cup slivered almonds
4 boneless skinless chicken breast halves,
    cut into ½-inch pieces
1 medium red bell pepper, cut
    into ¾-inch pieces
1 cup fresh pea pods, trimmed, cut diagonally
    in half
1 (8-oz.) can sliced water chestnuts, drained
2 cups chopped Chinese (napa) cabbage

1. Cook rice in water as directed on package.

2. Meanwhile, in small bowl, combine broth, cornstarch, soy sauce, vinegar, sugar and salt; mix well. Set aside.

3. Heat oil in large skillet or wok over medium-high heat until hot. Add garlic, almonds and chicken; cook and stir 3 to 4 minutes or until chicken is no longer pink and almonds are golden brown.

4. Add bell pepper; cook and stir 2 to 3 minutes. Add pea pods and water chestnuts; cook and stir 3 to 4 minutes or until vegetables are crisp-tender. Add cabbage and cornstarch mixture; cook and stir until sauce is bubbly and thickened. Serve over rice.

NUTRITION INFORMATION PER SERVING: Serving Size: ¼ of Recipe • Calories: 560 • Calories from Fat: 140 • **% DAILY VALUE:** Total Fat: 15 g 23% • Saturated Fat: 2 g 10% • Cholesterol: 75 mg 25% • Sodium: 940 mg 39% • Total Carbohydrate: 67 g 22% • Dietary Fiber: 5 g 20% • Sugars: 7 g • Protein: 38 g • Vitamin A: 45% • Vitamin C: 90% • Calcium: 15% • Iron: 25% • **DIETARY EXCHANGES:** 4 Starch, 1 Vegetable, 3½ Lean Meat, ½ Fat OR 4 Carbohydrate, 1 Vegetable, 3½ Lean Meat, ½ Fat

Subgum Chicken Stir-Fry

PREP TIME: 20 MINUTES ✦ YIELD: 4 SERVINGS

  2 cups uncooked instant white rice
  2 cups water
  1 cup chicken broth
  2 tablespoons cornstarch
  3 tablespoons oyster sauce
  2 teaspoons soy sauce
  1 tablespoon oil
  ¼ cup chopped onion
  1 garlic clove, minced
  4 boneless skinless chicken breast halves,
      cut into 1-inch pieces
  1 cup thinly sliced bok choy
  1 cup fresh bean sprouts
  1 green bell pepper, cut into ¼-inch strips
  1 (8-oz.) can sliced bamboo shoots, drained

1. Cook rice in water as directed on package.

2. Meanwhile, in small bowl, combine broth, cornstarch, oyster sauce and soy sauce; mix well. Set aside.

3. Heat oil in large skillet or wok over medium-high heat until hot. Add onion, garlic and chicken; cook and stir 3 to 4 minutes or until chicken is no longer pink.

4. Add bok choy, bean sprouts, bell pepper and bamboo shoots; cook and stir 3 to 4 minutes or until vegetables are crisp-tender. Gradually add cornstarch mixture; cook until bubbly and thickened, stirring constantly. Serve over rice.

NUTRITION INFORMATION PER SERVING: Serving Size: ¼ of Recipe • Calories: 440 • Calories from Fat: 70 • **% DAILY VALUE:** Total Fat: 8 g 12% • Saturated Fat: 2 g 10% • Cholesterol: 75 mg 25% • Sodium: 1000 mg 42% • Total Carbohydrate: 58 g 19% • Dietary Fiber: 3 g 12% • Sugars: 5 g • Protein: 34 g • Vitamin A: 4% • Vitamin C: 30% • Calcium: 6% • Iron: 25% • **DIETARY EXCHANGES:** 3 Starch, 2 Vegetable, 3 Very Lean Meat, 1 Fat OR 3 Carbohydrate, 2 Vegetable, 3 Very Lean Meat, 1 Fat

Colorful Chicken Fried Rice

PREP TIME: 25 MINUTES ✦ YIELD: 6 (1-CUP) SERVINGS

  ⅔ cup uncooked regular long-grain white rice
1⅓ cups water
  ¼ cup ketchup
  2 tablespoons soy sauce
  1 teaspoon ginger
  ½ teaspoon salt
  ⅛ teaspoon pepper
  4 boneless skinless chicken breast halves,
      cut into thin bite-sized pieces
  1 tablespoon oil or margarine
  2 garlic cloves, minced
  2 cups frozen mixed vegetables, thawed
  ¼ cup finely chopped onion
  1 (8-oz.) can pineapple chunks, drained

1. Cook rice in water as directed on package.

2. Meanwhile, in medium bowl, combine ketchup, soy sauce, ginger, salt and pepper; blend well. Add chicken; stir to coat. Set aside.

3. Heat oil in large skillet over medium heat. Add garlic; cook and stir until light golden brown. Add chicken mixture; cook and stir 3 to 5 minutes or until chicken is no longer pink.

4. Add mixed vegetables, onion and pineapple; cook and stir 3 to 4 minutes or until vegetables are crisp-tender. Add rice; cook and stir 1 to 2 minutes or until rice is thoroughly heated.

NUTRITION INFORMATION PER SERVING: Serving Size: 1 Cup • Calories: 240 • Calories from Fat: 45 • **% DAILY VALUE:** Total Fat: 5 g 8% • Saturated Fat: 1 g 5% • Cholesterol: 50 mg 17% • Sodium: 700 mg 29% • Total Carbohydrate: 27 g 9% • Dietary Fiber: 2 g 8% • Sugars: 5 g • Protein: 21 g • Vitamin A: 15% • Vitamin C: 10% • Calcium: 4% • Iron: 10% • **DIETARY EXCHANGES:** 1 Starch, 1 Fruit, 2½ Very Lean Meat, ½ Fat OR 2 Carbohydrate, 2½ Very Lean Meat, ½ Fat

Chicken and Fluffy Dumplings

PREP TIME: 25 MINUTES (READY IN 2 HOURS 10 MINUTES) ◆ YIELD: 4 SERVINGS

CHICKEN
2½ to 3 lb. cut-up frying chicken
  4 to 4½ cups water
  2 stalks celery with leaves, cut into 1-inch pieces
  ½ cup sliced carrot
  2 sprigs fresh parsley, if desired
  1 bay leaf
  1 teaspoon salt
  ¼ teaspoon pepper

DUMPLINGS
  ¾ cup all-purpose flour
  1 teaspoon chopped fresh parsley
  1 teaspoon baking powder
  ¼ teaspoon salt
    Dash nutmeg, if desired
  ⅓ cup milk
  1 tablespoon oil or melted shortening
  1 egg, slightly beaten

GRAVY
  ½ cup water
  ¼ cup all-purpose flour
  ¼ teaspoon salt
  ⅛ teaspoon pepper

1. In 4-quart Dutch oven, combine all chicken ingredients. Bring to a boil. Cover; simmer 1 to 1½ hours or until chicken is fork-tender and juices run clear. Skim off fat.
2. In medium bowl, combine ¾ cup flour, chopped parsley, baking powder, ¼ teaspoon salt and nutmeg; mix well. Add all remaining dumpling ingredients; stir just until dry ingredients are moistened.
3. Bring broth and chicken in Dutch oven to a boil. Drop dough by tablespoonfuls onto boiling broth and hot chicken. Cover tightly. Reduce heat to low; *do not lift cover.* Simmer 12 to 15 minutes or until dumplings are fluffy and dry.
4. To prepare gravy, arrange dumplings and chicken on serving platter; cover to keep warm. Strain 1⅔ cups broth into medium saucepan. In small bowl, combine ½ cup water and ¼ cup flour; blend until smooth. Bring broth to a boil. Gradually stir in flour mixture; cook and stir until thickened. Stir in ¼ teaspoon salt and ⅛ teaspoon pepper. Pour over chicken and dumplings.

NUTRITION INFORMATION PER SERVING: Serving Size: ¼ of Recipe ◆ Calories: 500 ◆ Calories from Fat: 220 ◆ **% DAILY VALUE:** Total Fat: 24 g 37% ◆ Saturated Fat: 6 g 30% ◆ Cholesterol: 170 mg 57% ◆ Sodium: 1080 mg 45% ◆ Total Carbohydrate: 28 g 9% ◆ Dietary Fiber: 2 g 8% ◆ Sugars: 3 g ◆ Protein: 42 g ◆ Vitamin A: 90% ◆ Vitamin C: 4% ◆ Calcium: 15% ◆ Iron: 20% ◆ **DIETARY EXCHANGES:** 2 Starch, 5 Lean Meat, 1½ Fat OR 2 Carbohydrate, 5 Lean Meat, 1½ Fat

Teriyaki Grilled Chicken Kabobs

PREP TIME: 30 MINUTES (READY IN 2 HOURS 30 MINUTES) ◆ YIELD: 4 KABOBS

MARINADE
  2 tablespoons brown sugar
  3 tablespoons soy sauce
  2 tablespoons dry sherry
  1 tablespoon oil
  ¼ teaspoon ginger
  ⅛ teaspoon garlic powder

KABOBS
  8 boneless skinless chicken thighs
  1 large red bell pepper, cut into 8 pieces
  1 medium zucchini, cut into 8 pieces
  8 (1 to 2-inch) chunks fresh pineapple or 8 canned pineapple chunks

1. GRILL DIRECTIONS: In 12×8-inch (2-quart) baking dish or resealable food storage plastic bag, combine all marinade ingredients; mix well. Cut chicken thighs in half; add to marinade. Cover dish or seal bag. Refrigerate at least 2 hours to marinate, turning chicken once.
2. Heat grill. Remove chicken from marinade; reserve marinade. Alternately thread chicken, bell pepper, zucchini and pineapple onto four 12-inch metal skewers.
3. When ready to grill, place kabobs on gas grill over medium heat or on charcoal grill 4 to 6 inches from medium-high coals. Cook 15 to 20 minutes or until chicken is no longer pink, turning often and brushing frequently with reserved marinade. Discard any remaining marinade.

TIP: To broil kabobs, place on broiler pan; broil 4 to 6 inches from heat using times above as a guide, turning often and brushing frequently with reserved marinade.

NUTRITION INFORMATION PER SERVING: Serving Size: 1 Kabob ◆ Calories: 280 ◆ Calories from Fat: 120 ◆ **% DAILY VALUE:** Total Fat: 13 g 20% ◆ Saturated Fat: 3 g 15% ◆ Cholesterol: 100 mg 33% ◆ Sodium: 300 mg 13% ◆ Total Carbohydrate: 12 g 4% ◆ Dietary Fiber: 2 g 8% ◆ Sugars: 8 g ◆ Protein: 29 g ◆ Vitamin A: 35% ◆ Vitamin C: 70% ◆ Calcium: 4% ◆ Iron: 10% ◆ **DIETARY EXCHANGES:** ½ Fruit, 1 Vegetable, 4 Lean Meat OR ½ Carbohydrate, 1 Vegetable, 4 Lean Meat

Teriyaki Grilled Chicken Kabobs (page 172)

Chicken à la King

PREP TIME: 20 MINUTES ✦ YIELD: 6 SERVINGS

½ cup margarine or butter
1 (4-oz.) can mushroom pieces and stems,
    drained, reserving liquid
⅔ cup chopped green bell pepper
½ cup all-purpose flour
¼ to ½ teaspoon pepper
1 tablespoon chicken-flavor instant bouillon
1½ cups milk
1¼ cups water
2½ cups cubed cooked chicken
1 (2-oz.) jar chopped pimientos, drained
6 puff pastry shells, baked

1. Melt margarine in large skillet over medium heat. Add mushrooms and bell pepper; cook and stir until bell pepper is crisp-tender.
2. Stir in flour and pepper. Cook over low heat until mixture is smooth and bubbly, stirring constantly. Stir in bouillon, milk, water and reserved mushroom liquid. Bring to a boil, stirring constantly. Boil 1 minute, stirring constantly.
3. Stir in chicken and pimientos. Cook until thoroughly heated, stirring occasionally. Serve over puff pastry shells.

NUTRITION INFORMATION PER SERVING: Serving Size: ⅙ of Recipe ✦ Calories: 570 ✦ Calories from Fat: 330 ✦ **% DAILY VALUE:** Total Fat: 37 g 57% ✦ Saturated Fat: 7 g 35% ✦ Cholesterol: 55 mg 18% ✦ Sodium: 980 mg 41% ✦ Total Carbohydrate: 33 g 11% ✦ Dietary Fiber: 2 g 8% ✦ Sugars: 4 g ✦ Protein: 25 g ✦ Vitamin A: 30% ✦ Vitamin C: 40% ✦ Calcium: 10% ✦ Iron: 15% ✦ **DIETARY EXCHANGES:** 2 Starch, 2½ Lean Meat, 6 Fat OR 2 Carbohydrate, 2½ Lean Meat, 6 Fat

Double-Dipped Chicken Nuggets

PREP TIME: 10 MINUTES (READY IN 30 MINUTES)
✦ YIELD: 6 SERVINGS

¼ cup all-purpose flour
½ teaspoon seasoned salt
1 cup finely crushed corn flakes cereal
4 boneless skinless chicken breast halves, cut
    into 1-inch pieces
¼ cup margarine or butter, melted

1. Heat oven to 400°F. In plastic bag, combine flour and seasoned salt; shake to mix. Place crushed cereal in another plastic bag.
2. Add chicken pieces to flour mixture in bag; shake to coat. Dip floured pieces in margarine; coat with crushed cereal. Place in ungreased 15×10×1-inch baking pan.
3. Bake at 400°F. for 15 to 20 minutes or until chicken is no longer pink.

NUTRITION INFORMATION PER SERVING: Serving Size: ⅙ of Recipe ✦ Calories: 230 ✦ Calories from Fat: 90 ✦ **% DAILY VALUE:** Total Fat: 10 g 15% ✦ Saturated Fat: 2 g 10% ✦ Cholesterol: 50 mg 17% ✦ Sodium: 410 mg 17% ✦ Total Carbohydrate: 16 g 5% ✦ Dietary Fiber: 1 g 2% ✦ Sugars: 1 g ✦ Protein: 19 g ✦ Vitamin A: 15% ✦ Vitamin C: 8% ✦ Calcium: 0% ✦ Iron: 30% ✦ **DIETARY EXCHANGES:** 1 Starch, 2 Lean Meat, 1 Fat OR 1 Carbohydrate, 2 Lean Meat, 1 Fat

Double-Dipped Chicken Nuggets

Chicken Paprikash Pot Pie

PREP TIME: 35 MINUTES (READY IN 1 HOUR 20 MINUTES)
◆ YIELD: 6 SERVINGS

    1 (15-oz.) pkg. refrigerated pie crusts or Pastry
        for Two-Crust Pie, page 385
    4 slices bacon, cut into 1/2-inch pieces
    3/4 lb. boneless skinless chicken breast halves,
        cut into 1/2-inch pieces
    1 cup coarsely chopped onions
    1 cup coarsely chopped red or green bell
        pepper
    1 cup sliced carrots
    1 cup frozen sweet peas
    1/2 cup sour cream
    1 (12-oz.) jar home-style chicken gravy
    3 tablespoons cornstarch
    3 teaspoons paprika

1. Heat oven to 425°F. Prepare pie crusts for *two-crust pie* using 9-inch pie pan.
2. In large skillet over medium heat, cook bacon until crisp. Reserve 1 tablespoon drippings with bacon in skillet.
3. Add chicken to skillet; cook and stir until no longer pink. Add onions, bell pepper and carrots; cook and stir until vegetables are tender. Stir in peas.
4. In small bowl, combine all remaining ingredients; mix well. Stir into chicken mixture in skillet. Spoon into crust-lined pan. Top with second crust and flute edges; cut slits or small designs in several places on top of crust.
5. Bake at 425°F. for 30 to 35 minutes or until crust is golden brown. Cover edge of crust with strips of foil after 10 to 15 minutes of baking to prevent excessive browning. Let stand 10 minutes before serving.

NUTRITION INFORMATION PER SERVING: Serving Size: 1/6 of Recipe ◆ Calories: 550 ◆ Calories from Fat: 270 ◆ **% DAILY VALUE:** Total Fat: 30 g 46% ◆ Saturated Fat: 12 g 60% ◆ Cholesterol: 65 mg 22% ◆ Sodium: 750 mg 31% ◆ Total Carbohydrate: 52 g 17% ◆ Dietary Fiber: 3 g 12% ◆ Sugars: 7 g ◆ Protein: 19 g ◆ Vitamin A: 160% ◆ Vitamin C: 45% ◆ Calcium: 8% ◆ Iron: 10% ◆ **DIETARY EXCHANGES:** 3 Starch, 1 Vegetable, 1 Very Lean Meat, 5 1/2 Fat OR 3 Carbohydrate, 1 Vegetable, 1 Very Lean Meat, 5 1/2 Fat

Chicken Tetrazzini Casserole

PREP TIME: 20 MINUTES (READY IN 55 MINUTES)
◆ YIELD: 10 SERVINGS

    7 oz. uncooked spaghetti
    1/4 cup margarine or butter
    1 (8-oz.) pkg. (3 cups) sliced fresh mushrooms
    3 tablespoons all-purpose flour
    2 cups chicken broth
    3/4 cup half-and-half
    3 tablespoons dry sherry, if desired
    1 tablespoon chopped fresh parsley
    1/2 teaspoon salt
    1/8 teaspoon nutmeg
        Dash pepper
    3 cups cubed cooked chicken
    3/4 cup grated Parmesan cheese
    1 to 2 teaspoons chopped fresh parsley,
        if desired

1. Heat oven to 350°F. Cook spaghetti to desired doneness as directed on package. Drain; cover to keep warm.
2. Meanwhile, melt margarine in Dutch oven or large saucepan over medium heat. Add mushrooms; cook until tender, stirring occasionally.
3. Stir in flour; cook 1 minute or until smooth and bubbly, stirring constantly. Gradually stir in chicken broth. Cook and stir over medium heat until slightly thickened and bubbly. Remove from heat.
4. Add half-and-half, sherry, 1 tablespoon parsley, salt, nutmeg and pepper; mix well. Add chicken and cooked spaghetti; toss to combine. Spoon into ungreased 13×9-inch (3-quart) baking dish. Sprinkle with cheese.
5. Bake at 350°F. for 30 to 35 minutes or until thoroughly heated. Just before serving, sprinkle with parsley.

NUTRITION INFORMATION PER SERVING: Serving Size: 1/10 of Recipe ◆ Calories: 280 ◆ Calories from Fat: 120 ◆ **% DAILY VALUE:** Total Fat: 13 g 20% ◆ Saturated Fat: 5 g 25% ◆ Cholesterol: 50 mg 17% ◆ Sodium: 450 mg 19% ◆ Total Carbohydrate: 20 g 7% ◆ Dietary Fiber: 1 g 3% ◆ Sugars: 2 g ◆ Protein: 20 g ◆ Vitamin A: 8% ◆ Vitamin C: 2% ◆ Calcium: 15% ◆ Iron: 10% ◆ **DIETARY EXCHANGES:** 1 1/2 Starch, 2 Lean Meat, 1 Fat OR 1 1/2 Carbohydrate, 2 Lean Meat, 1 Fat

Quick Chicken Divan

PREP TIME: 15 MINUTES (READY IN 50 MINUTES)
♦ YIELD: 6 SERVINGS

1 (1-lb.) pkg. frozen cut broccoli
2 cups cubed cooked chicken
1 (10¾-oz.) can condensed cream of chicken soup
½ cup mayonnaise or salad dressing
1 teaspoon lemon juice
2 oz. (½ cup) shredded Cheddar cheese
½ cup soft bread crumbs
2 tablespoons margarine or butter, melted

1. Heat oven to 350°F. Grease 12 × 8-inch (2-quart) baking dish. Cook broccoli as directed on package; drain.
2. Arrange broccoli in greased baking dish. Layer chicken over broccoli. In small bowl, combine soup, mayonnaise and lemon juice; mix well. Spread over chicken; sprinkle with cheese.
3. In small bowl, combine bread crumbs and margarine; sprinkle over top. Bake at 350°F. for 30 to 35 minutes or until thoroughly heated.

NUTRITION INFORMATION PER SERVING: Serving Size: ⅙ of Recipe ♦ Calories: 370 ♦ Calories from Fat: 250 ♦ % DAILY VALUE: Total Fat: 28 g 43% ♦ Saturated Fat: 7 g 35% ♦ Cholesterol: 65 mg 22% ♦ Sodium: 680 mg 28% ♦ Total Carbohydrate: 10 g 3% ♦ Dietary Fiber: 2 g 8% ♦ Sugars: 2 g ♦ Protein: 20 g ♦ Vitamin A: 35% ♦ Vitamin C: 60% ♦ Calcium: 15% ♦ Iron: 10% ♦ DIETARY EXCHANGES: ½ Starch, 1 Vegetable, 2½ Lean Meat, 4 Fat OR ⅓ Carbohydrate, 1 Vegetable, 2½ Lean Meat, 4 Fat

Chicken, Artichoke and Rice Casserole

PREP TIME: 1 HOUR (READY IN 2 HOURS)
♦ YIELD: 12 SERVINGS

½ cup uncooked regular long-grain white rice
1 cup water
½ cup uncooked wild rice
1¼ cups water
1 tablespoon margarine or butter
2 cups julienne-cut (2 x ¼ x ¼-inch) carrots
½ cup chopped green bell pepper
⅓ cup chopped green onions
2 (10¾-oz.) cans condensed cream of chicken soup
½ cup milk
¼ cup dry sherry
2½ cups cubed cooked chicken
2 slices bacon, crisply cooked, crumbled

8 oz. (2 cups) shredded mozzarella cheese
1 to 2 (14-oz.) cans artichoke hearts, drained, quartered
¼ cup grated Parmesan cheese
2 teaspoons dried parsley flakes

1. Cook white rice in 1 cup water and wild rice in 1¼ cups water as directed on packages.
2. Meanwhile, heat oven to 350°F. Grease 13 × 9-inch (3-quart) baking dish. Melt margarine in large skillet over medium-high heat. Add carrots, bell pepper and onions; cook and stir until crisp-tender. Stir in soup, milk, sherry, chicken, bacon and mozzarella cheese; blend well. Remove from heat.
3. Combine white and wild rice; spread evenly over bottom of greased baking dish. Arrange artichokes over rice. Spoon chicken mixture evenly over artichokes.* Sprinkle with Parmesan cheese and parsley flakes; cover tightly with foil.
4. Bake at 350°F. for 40 minutes. Uncover; bake an additional 15 to 20 minutes or until casserole is thoroughly heated.

> TIP: * Recipe can be prepared to this point, covered and refrigerated up to 24 hours. Sprinkle casserole with Parmesan cheese and parsley flakes; cover tightly with foil. Bake at 350°F. for 1 hour. Uncover; bake an additional 15 to 20 minutes or until casserole is thoroughly heated.

NUTRITION INFORMATION PER SERVING: Serving Size: 1/12 of Recipe ♦ Calories: 280 ♦ Calories from Fat: 100 ♦ % DAILY VALUE: Total Fat: 11 g 17% ♦ Saturated Fat: 4 g 20% ♦ Cholesterol: 45 mg 15% ♦ Sodium: 650 mg 27% ♦ Total Carbohydrate: 23 g 8% ♦ Dietary Fiber: 4 g 16% ♦ Sugars: 3 g ♦ Protein: 20 g ♦ Vitamin A: 130% ♦ Vitamin C: 15% ♦ Calcium: 25% ♦ Iron: 10% ♦ DIETARY EXCHANGES: 1½ Starch, 2 Lean Meat, 1 Fat OR 1½ Carbohydrate, 2 Lean Meat, 1 Fat

COOK'S NOTE

QUICK CUBED CHICKEN

If you don't have leftover cooked chicken when a recipe calls for cubed, cooked chicken, place four boneless skinless chicken breast halves (1½ to 2 pounds) in a 2-quart microwave-safe dish; cover. Microwave on HIGH for 8 to 10 minutes or until chicken is fork-tender and no longer pink in center. Halfway through cooking, rearrange and turn the chicken pieces. Cool; cut into cubes. Yields 2½ to 3 cups.

water chestnuts; cook and stir until mixture is bubbly and slightly thickened. Remove from heat. Pour into sprayed casserole.

4. Bake at 350°F. for 30 minutes. Stir in almonds; cover and bake an additional 30 to 45 minutes or until rice is tender and liquid is absorbed.

NUTRITION INFORMATION PER SERVING: Serving Size: 1¼ Cups ♦ Calories: 330 ♦ Calories from Fat: 80 ♦ **% DAILY VALUE:** Total Fat: 9 g 14% ♦ Saturated Fat: 1 g 5% ♦ Cholesterol: 50 mg 17% ♦ Sodium: 890 mg 37% ♦ Total Carbohydrate: 34 g 11% ♦ Dietary Fiber: 4 g 16% ♦ Sugars: 3 g ♦ Protein: 28 g ♦ Vitamin A: 0% ♦ Vitamin C: 2% ♦ Calcium: 4% ♦ Iron: 15% ♦ **DIETARY EXCHANGES:** 2 Starch, 1 Vegetable, 2½ Very Lean Meat, 1 Fat OR 2 Carbohydrate, 1 Vegetable, 2½ Very Lean Meat, 1 Fat

Chicken Wild Rice Amandine

Chicken Wild Rice Amandine

PREP TIME: 35 MINUTES (READY IN 1 HOUR 50 MINUTES)
♦ YIELD: 8 (1¼-CUP) SERVINGS

1½ cups uncooked wild rice
1 tablespoon oil
1½ lb. boneless skinless chicken breast halves, cubed
¼ cup chopped onion
1 (8-oz.) pkg. (3 cups) sliced fresh mushrooms
2 (14½-oz.) cans ready-to-serve chicken broth
¼ cup soy sauce
¼ teaspoon hot pepper sauce
¼ cup all-purpose flour
1 (8-oz.) can sliced water chestnuts, drained
½ cup slivered almonds

1. Heat oven to 350°F. Spray 3-quart casserole with nonstick cooking spray. Rinse wild rice; place in large saucepan. Add enough water to cover. Bring to a boil over high heat. Reduce heat; cover and simmer 10 minutes.

2. Meanwhile, heat oil in Dutch oven over medium-high heat until hot. Add chicken; cook and stir 6 to 8 minutes or until lightly browned. Add onion and mushrooms; cook and stir 5 to 6 minutes or until onion and mushrooms are tender. Drain wild rice. Add to mixture in Dutch oven.

3. In large bowl, combine broth, soy sauce, hot pepper sauce and flour; blend well. Stir into chicken mixture in Dutch oven. Add

Sour Cream Chicken Enchiladas

PREP TIME: 30 MINUTES (READY IN 55 MINUTES)
♦ YIELD: 8 SERVINGS

2 tablespoons margarine or butter, melted
½ cup chopped onion
1 garlic clove, minced
½ cup sliced ripe olives, drained
1 (10¾-oz.) can condensed cream of chicken soup
1 (8-oz.) container sour cream
1 (4.5-oz.) can chopped green chiles, drained
1½ cups cubed cooked chicken
6 oz. (1½ cups) shredded Cheddar cheese
¼ cup milk
10 corn tortillas, heated

1. Heat oven to 350°F. To make sauce, melt margarine in medium saucepan over medium heat. Add onion and garlic; cook and stir until onion is tender. Add ¼ cup of the olives, soup, ½ cup of the sour cream and green chiles; mix well. Reserve ¾ cup sauce; set aside. Stir chicken and ½ cup of the cheese into remaining sauce.

2. In small bowl, combine reserved ¾ cup sauce with remaining sour cream and milk; blend well. Spread ½ cup sauce over bottom of ungreased 13×9-inch (3-quart) baking dish.

3. Place about ¼ cup chicken mixture down center of each warm tortilla; roll up. Place, seam side down, over sauce in baking dish. Spoon remaining sauce over top of filled tortillas, covering completely.

4. Bake at 350°F. for 20 to 25 minutes or until thoroughly heated. To serve, sprinkle with remaining 1 cup cheese and ¼ cup olives. Let stand 5 minutes before serving.

NUTRITION INFORMATION PER SERVING: Serving Size: ⅛ of Recipe • Calories: 350 • Calories from Fat: 200 • % DAILY VALUE: Total Fat: 22 g 34% • Saturated Fat: 10 g 50% • Cholesterol: 65 mg 22% • Sodium: 630 mg 26% • Total Carbohydrate: 22 g 7% • Dietary Fiber: 2 g 8% • Sugars: 3 g • Protein: 17 g • Vitamin A: 20% • Vitamin C: 35% • Calcium: 30% • Iron: 8% • DIETARY EXCHANGES: 1½ Starch, 2 Lean Meat, 3 Fat OR 1½ Carbohydrate, 2 Lean Meat, 3 Fat

Party Chicken Fajitas

PREP TIME: 25 MINUTES ✦ YIELD: 16 FAJITAS

 1 tablespoon oil
2½ lb. boneless skinless chicken breasts,
    cut into ½-inch strips
 1 large onion, sliced
 1 large red bell pepper, sliced
 1 teaspoon chili powder
 ¼ cup lime juice
16 (8 to 10-inch) flour tortillas
 2 cups shredded lettuce
 1 large tomato, chopped
 1 cup salsa
 1 cup guacamole

1. Heat oil in large skillet over medium-high heat until hot. Add chicken, onion and bell pepper; cook and stir 8 to 10 minutes or until chicken is no longer pink. Stir in chili powder and lime juice.

2. Spoon about ½ cup chicken mixture down center of each tortilla. Top each with lettuce, tomato, salsa and guacamole; roll up.

NUTRITION INFORMATION PER SERVING: Serving Size: 1 Fajita • Calories: 240 • Calories from Fat: 60 • % DAILY VALUE: Total Fat: 7 g 11% • Saturated Fat: 2 g 10% • Cholesterol: 40 mg 13% • Sodium: 430 mg 18% • Total Carbohydrate: 24 g 8% • Dietary Fiber: 2 g 8% • Sugars: 3 g • Protein: 19 g • Vitamin A: 10% • Vitamin C: 20% • Calcium: 6% • Iron: 10% • DIETARY EXCHANGES: 1½ Starch, 1 Vegetable, 2 Very Lean Meat, ½ Fat OR 1½ Carbohydrate, 1 Vegetable, 2 Very Lean Meat, ½ Fat

Mexican-Style Chicken Wraps

PREP TIME: 20 MINUTES ✦ YIELD: 6 SERVINGS

 1 tablespoon oil
 3 boneless skinless chicken breast halves,
    cut into thin bite-sized strips
 1 (15.25-oz.) can whole kernel sweet corn,
    drained
 1 cup chunky-style salsa
 6 (8 to 10-inch) flour tortillas
 3 oz. (¾ cup) shredded Cheddar cheese
    Sour cream

1. Heat oil in large skillet over medium-high heat until hot. Add chicken; cook and stir 5 to 6 minutes or until no longer pink.

2. Stir in corn and salsa. Reduce heat to medium; cook 4 to 6 minutes or until thoroughly heated.

3. Meanwhile, warm tortillas as directed on package. Spoon chicken mixture down center of each tortilla; sprinkle with cheese. Roll up. Serve with sour cream and, if desired, additional salsa.

NUTRITION INFORMATION PER SERVING: Serving Size: ⅙ of Recipe • Calories: 410 • Calories from Fat: 140 • % DAILY VALUE: Total Fat: 16 g 25% • Saturated Fat: 7 g 35% • Cholesterol: 60 mg 20% • Sodium: 800 mg 33% • Total Carbohydrate: 43 g 14% • Dietary Fiber: 3 g 12% • Sugars: 4 g • Protein: 23 g • Vitamin A: 10% • Vitamin C: 4% • Calcium: 20% • Iron: 15% • DIETARY EXCHANGES: 3 Starch, 2 Very Lean Meat, 2½ Fat OR 3 Carbohydrate, 2 Very Lean Meat, 2½ Fat

VARIATION

Grilled Quesadillas: Prepare chicken mixture as directed above. Spread hot chicken mixture on each tortilla. Sprinkle each with cheese; fold in half. Place on grill over medium heat; cook 30 to 60 seconds, turning once. To serve, cut each quesadilla into 3 wedges. Serve with sour cream and, if desired, additional salsa.

COOK'S NOTE

NONSTICK TRICKS

With a nonstick skillet and nonstick cooking spray, you can get the appealing color and flavor of panfried chicken without all the oil. For best results, spray the skillet before heating.

Nonstick cooking spray is real cooking oil, mixed with small amounts of propellants in an aerosol can. The spray disperses oil in a far thinner layer than would be possible with regular oil or butter. A one-second spray contains about .6 grams of fat. You can make your own nonstick cooking spray at home, with a refillable canister sold at kitchen and houseware stores.

An inexpensive nonstick pan can give years of service if it is carefully maintained:

✦ Use only plastic or wooden utensils—not metal, which can mar the finish.
✦ Wash gently with hot soapy water and a sponge or plastic scrubber.
✦ Do not store other pans or dishes directly on the nonstick surface. If you must stack pans, protect the nonstick surface with a kitchen towel or paper towels.

Slow-Cooked Turkey Dinner

PREP TIME: 15 MINUTES (READY IN 7 HOURS 45 MINUTES) ◆ YIELD: 4 SERVINGS

    6 small red potatoes (about 2½ inches in
        diameter), unpeeled, quartered
    2 cups sliced carrots
 1½ lb. turkey thighs, skin removed
    ¼ cup all-purpose flour
    2 tablespoons dry onion soup mix
    ⅓ cup chicken broth or water
    1 (10¾-oz.) can condensed cream of
        mushroom soup

1. Place potatoes and carrots in 3½ or 4-quart slow cooker. Place turkey thighs over vegetables.
2. In medium bowl, blend all remaining ingredients. Pour over turkey. Cover; cook on high setting for 30 minutes.
3. Reduce setting to low; cook at least 7 hours or until turkey is fork-tender, juices run clear and vegetables are tender.

NUTRITION INFORMATION PER SERVING: Serving Size: ¼ of Recipe ◆ Calories: 450 ◆ Calories from Fat: 110 ◆ % DAILY VALUE: Total Fat: 12 g 18% ◆ Saturated Fat: 4 g 20% ◆ Cholesterol: 65 mg 22% ◆ Sodium: 1360 mg 57% ◆ Total Carbohydrate: 57 g 19% ◆ Dietary Fiber: 6 g 24% ◆ Sugars: 9 g ◆ Protein: 28 g ◆ Vitamin A: 340% ◆ Vitamin C: 30% ◆ Calcium: 8% ◆ Iron: 25% ◆ DIETARY EXCHANGES: 3½ Starch, 1 Vegetable, 2 Lean Meat, 1 Fat OR 3½ Carbohydrate, 1 Vegetable, 2 Lean Meat, 1 Fat

Bacon Cheddar Chicken Fillet Melts

PREP TIME: 30 MINUTES ◆ YIELD: 4 SANDWICHES

    4 boneless skinless chicken breast halves
    8 slices bacon
    1 small red onion, sliced
    4 slices pumpernickel bread, toasted
    4 teaspoons steak sauce
    4 oz. (1 cup) shredded Cheddar cheese

1. Place 1 chicken breast half, boned side up, between 2 pieces of plastic wrap or waxed paper. Working from center, gently pound chicken with flat side of meat mallet or rolling pin until about ¼ inch thick; remove wrap. Repeat with remaining chicken breast halves.
2. In large skillet over medium heat, cook bacon until crisp. Remove bacon from skillet; drain on paper towels. Reserve 1 tablespoon drippings in skillet.

3. Add onion to drippings; cook and stir 2 to 4 minutes or until tender. Remove onion from skillet. Add chicken to skillet; cook 6 to 8 minutes on each side or until chicken is fork-tender and juices run clear.
4. Place toasted bread slices on ungreased cookie sheet; spread each slice with 1 teaspoon steak sauce. Top each with chicken, bacon slices, onion and cheese. Broil 4 to 6 inches from heat for 1 to 2 minutes or until cheese is melted.

NUTRITION INFORMATION PER SERVING: Serving Size: 1 Sandwich ◆ Calories: 440 ◆ Calories from Fat: 210 ◆ % DAILY VALUE: Total Fat: 23 g 35% ◆ Saturated Fat: 11 g 55% ◆ Cholesterol: 115 mg 38% ◆ Sodium: 740 mg 31% ◆ Total Carbohydrate: 18 g 6% ◆ Dietary Fiber: 2 g 8% ◆ Sugars: 3 g ◆ Protein: 40 g ◆ Vitamin A: 6% ◆ Vitamin C: 0% ◆ Calcium: 25% ◆ Iron: 10% ◆ DIETARY EXCHANGES: 1 Starch, 5 Very Lean Meat, 4 Fat OR 1 Carbohydrate, 5 Very Lean Meat, 4 Fat

Roast Chicken

PREP TIME: 30 MINUTES (READY IN 1 HOUR 35 MINUTES) ◆ YIELD: 4 SERVINGS

    1 (3 to 3½-lb.) whole frying chicken
    2 tablespoons margarine or butter, melted
    2 tablespoons white wine Worcestershire
        sauce

1. Heat oven to 375°F. Remove and discard neck and giblets from chicken. Rinse chicken with cold water; pat dry. Using string, tie legs and tail together. Close neck cavity by bringing loose skin over opening and holding in place with metal skewer. Twist wing tips under back.
2. Place chicken, breast side up, on rack in shallow roasting pan. In small bowl, combine margarine and Worcestershire sauce; brush chicken with half of mixture. Insert meat thermometer so bulb reaches center of thickest part of thigh, but does not rest on bone. Do not cover or add water.
3. Bake at 375°F. for 55 to 65 minutes or until chicken is fork-tender, juices run clear and meat thermometer registers 180 to 185°F. Brush with remaining margarine mixture halfway through baking. Untie chicken legs about 10 minutes before end of baking time. Let stand 5 to 10 minutes before carving.

NUTRITION INFORMATION PER SERVING: Serving Size: ¼ of Recipe ◆ Calories: 250 ◆ Calories from Fat: 100 ◆ % DAILY VALUE: Total Fat: 11 g 17% ◆ Saturated Fat: 3 g 15% ◆ Cholesterol: 115 mg 38% ◆ Sodium: 150 mg 6% ◆ Total Carbohydrate: 0 g 0% ◆ Dietary Fiber: 0 g 0% ◆ Sugars: 0 g ◆ Protein: 37 g ◆ Vitamin A: 2% ◆ Vitamin C: 0% ◆ Calcium: 0% ◆ Iron: 8% ◆ DIETARY EXCHANGES: 5 Lean Meat

HOW TO ROAST AND CARVE POULTRY

1. Preheat oven to 325°F.
2. Remove giblets and neck from the body cavity.
3. Rinse the bird inside and out with cold water. Drain; pat dry with paper towels.

4. To stuff the bird: Place it breast side down and lightly fill the neck cavity with a small amount of stuffing. Pull the neck skin over the cavity; fasten skin to the back with a skewer. Turn the bird over; loosely fill the large interior cavity with stuffing.

5. Tuck the drumsticks under the band of skin; bend the wing tips under the back. Tie the ends of the drumsticks together with clean kitchen twine.

6. Place the bird breast side up on a rack in a shallow roasting pan. Rub the surface with oil or softened butter or margarine.

For store-bought ducks and geese: Prick the skin in several places before roasting to allow excess fat to escape. Do not rub skin with oil, butter or margarine. During roasting, skim off excess fat.

7. Insert a meat thermometer into the inside thigh muscle of the bird so that the tip does not touch the bone, unless you use an instant-read thermometer, which doesn't remain in the bird during cooking.

8. Cover bird loosely with tented foil; smaller birds should not be covered.

9. Roast in preheated 325°F. oven. See "Timetable for Roasting Poultry," page 163.

10. During the last half of roasting time, the bird may be basted with pan drippings or sauce. Uncover a turkey during the last 30 minutes of cooking time to brown the skin. Other birds can be covered toward the end of roasting to prevent overbrowning.

11. Begin checking for doneness after about an hour for whole broiler/fryer chickens of about 3 pounds. Begin checking larger birds during the last hour of cooking time. The bird is done when the internal temperature reaches 180 to 185°F. If the bird is stuffed, the center of the stuffing must reach 165°F. If no thermometer is available, pierce the skin between the leg and the thigh; the bird is done when juices run clear, when legs move up and down easily and skin has shrunk back from the tips of the drumstick.

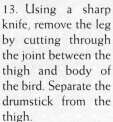

12. For easier carving and to set the juices, allow the bird to stand, loosely covered with foil to hold in warmth, for about 15 minutes.

13. Using a sharp knife, remove the leg by cutting through the joint between the thigh and body of the bird. Separate the drumstick from the thigh.

14. Make a deep horizontal cut to the bone into the breast meat just above the wing.

15. Beginning near the front of the breast, cut thin slices down to the horizontal cut. Repeat with the other side of the bird.

Roast Turkey

◆ YIELD: 12 TO 18 SERVINGS

1 (12 to 18-lb.) whole turkey
½ teaspoon salt
  Wild Rice and Sausage Dressing, page 181,
    or Bread Stuffing for Poultry, page 182
⅓ cup margarine or butter, melted

1. Heat oven to 325°F. Remove and discard neck and giblets from turkey. Rinse turkey with cold water; pat dry. Sprinkle cavity of turkey with salt.
2. Spoon dressing loosely into neck and body cavities of turkey. Turn wings back and tuck tips over shoulder joints. Refasten drumsticks with metal piece or tuck under skin at tail. Fasten neck skin to back with skewers.
3. Place turkey, breast side up, in roasting pan. Insert meat thermometer so bulb reaches center of thickest part of thigh, but does not rest on bone. Spoon margarine over turkey. Do not add water or cover.
4. Bake at 325°F. until turkey is fork-tender, juices run clear and meat thermometer registers 180 to 185°F. using "Timetable for Roasting Poultry," page 163. If necessary,

Roast Turkey

cover turkey breast with tent of foil during last 1½ to 2 hours of baking to prevent excessive browning.
5. Let stand 15 to 20 minutes before carving. Remove skewers. Remove stuffing; place in serving bowl.

NUTRITION INFORMATION PER SERVING: Serving Size: ⅟₁₈ of Recipe ◆ Calories: 640 ◆ Calories from Fat: 280 ◆ **% DAILY VALUE:** Total Fat: 31 g 48% ◆ Saturated Fat: 9 g 45% ◆ Cholesterol: 205 mg 68% ◆ Sodium: 710 mg 30% ◆ Total Carbohydrate: 18 g 6% ◆ Dietary Fiber: 1 g 4% ◆ Sugars: 1 g ◆ Protein: 72 g ◆ Vitamin A: 4% ◆ Vitamin C: 0% ◆ Calcium: 8% ◆ Iron: 30% ◆ **DIETARY EXCHANGES:** 1 Starch, 10 Lean Meat OR 1 Carbohydrate, 10 Lean Meat

Herb-Roasted Turkey Breast

PREP TIME: 30 MINUTES (READY IN 2 HOURS 45 MINUTES) ◆ YIELD: 16 SERVINGS

½ teaspoon dried rosemary leaves, crushed
½ teaspoon dried sage leaves
½ teaspoon dried thyme leaves
½ teaspoon dried marjoram leaves
1 (5 to 6-lb.) whole turkey breast
1 medium onion, peeled, quartered
1 garlic clove, peeled

1. Heat oven to 325°F. In small bowl, combine rosemary, sage, thyme and marjoram. Loosen skin covering turkey breast and pull away, leaving attached at neck. If necessary, use sharp knife to loosen connecting membrane. Rub herb mixture evenly over turkey breast meat. Replace skin over breast, tucking under bottom of breast.
2. Place turkey breast, skin side up, on rack in roasting pan. Place onion and garlic inside neck opening. Insert meat thermometer so bulb reaches center of thickest part of breast meat, but does not rest on bone. Do not cover or add water.
3. Bake at 325°F. for 1¾ to 2¼ hours or until turkey is fork-tender, juices run clear and meat thermometer registers 165 to 170°F. Let stand 10 to 15 minutes before carving. Remove and discard onion and garlic from neck opening.

NUTRITION INFORMATION PER SERVING: Serving Size: ⅟₁₆ of Recipe ◆ Calories: 170 ◆ Calories from Fat: 35 ◆ **% DAILY VALUE:** Total Fat: 4 g 6% ◆ Saturated Fat: 1 g 5% ◆ Cholesterol: 105 mg 35% ◆ Sodium: 60 mg 3% ◆ Total Carbohydrate: 1 g 1% ◆ Dietary Fiber: 0 g 0% ◆ Sugars: 0 g ◆ Protein: 34 g ◆ Vitamin A: 0% ◆ Vitamin C: 0% ◆ Calcium: 2% ◆ Iron: 10% ◆ **DIETARY EXCHANGES:** 5 Very Lean Meat

Turkey on the Gas Grill

PREP TIME: 20 MINUTES (READY IN 4 HOURS)
✦ YIELD: 14 SERVINGS

1 (10 to 12-lb.) whole turkey
1 teaspoon seasoned salt
¼ teaspoon pepper
3 to 4 tablespoons oil or melted margarine

1. GRILL DIRECTIONS: Prepare gas grill for cooking with indirect heat. For dual burner grill, heat only one side. Place drip pan on rock on unheated side; add ½ inch of water to pan. Heat grill on high for 5 minutes.
2. Meanwhile, remove and discard neck and giblets from turkey. Rinse turkey with cold water; pat dry. Sprinkle cavity of turkey with seasoned salt and pepper. Fasten neck skin to back with skewers. Turn wings back and tuck tips under shoulder joints. Refasten drumsticks with metal piece or tuck them under band of skin at tail. Rub outside surface of turkey with oil. Insert meat thermometer so bulb reaches center of thickest part of thigh, but does not rest on bone.

Turkey on the Gas Grill

3. When ready to grill, place turkey, breast side up, on grill rack directly over drip pan. *Reduce heat to medium;* cover. Cook turkey 15 to 18 minutes per pound until fork-tender, juices run clear and meat thermometer registers 180 to 185°F. (about 2½ to 3½ hours). Avoid opening cover until ready to check thermometer. (There is no need to baste or turn turkey.) Let stand 15 to 20 minutes before carving.

NUTRITION INFORMATION PER SERVING: Serving Size: 1/14 of Recipe ✦ Calories: 450 ✦ Calories from Fat: 220 ✦ % DAILY VALUE: Total Fat: 24 g 37% ✦ Saturated Fat: 6 g 30% ✦ Cholesterol: 170 mg 57% ✦ Sodium: 250 mg 10% ✦ Total Carbohydrate: 0 g 0% ✦ Dietary Fiber: 0 g 0% ✦ Sugars: 0 g ✦ Protein: 58 g ✦ Vitamin A: 0% ✦ Vitamin C: 0% ✦ Calcium: 6% ✦ Iron: 20% ✦ DIETARY EXCHANGES: 8 Lean Meat

Wild Rice and Sausage Dressing

PREP TIME: 10 MINUTES (READY IN 1 HOUR 5 MINUTES)
✦ YIELD: 16 (¾-CUP) SERVINGS

5 cups water
2 teaspoons chicken-flavor instant bouillon
  or 2 chicken-flavor bouillon cubes
1½ teaspoons salt
¾ cup uncooked wild rice
1½ cups uncooked regular long-grain white rice
1 lb. bulk pork sausage
1½ cups chopped celery
¾ cup chopped onions

1. In large saucepan, combine water, bouillon and salt; bring to a boil. Add wild rice. Reduce heat to low; cover and simmer 20 minutes.
2. Add long-grain rice. Cover; simmer an additional 25 minutes or until rice is tender and liquid is absorbed.
3. Meanwhile, in large skillet, combine sausage, celery and onions; cook until browned. Drain.
4. Stir in rice mixture. Serve as a side dish or use to stuff turkey or Cornish game hens.

TIP: If desired, dressing can be baked in greased, covered casserole at 325°F. for 35 to 50 minutes or until thoroughly heated.

NUTRITION INFORMATION PER SERVING: Serving Size: ¾ Cup ✦ Calories: 150 ✦ Calories from Fat: 45 ✦ % DAILY VALUE: Total Fat: 5 g 8% ✦ Saturated Fat: 2 g 10% ✦ Cholesterol: 10 mg 3% ✦ Sodium: 510 mg 21% ✦ Total Carbohydrate: 21 g 7% ✦ Dietary Fiber: 1 g 4% ✦ Sugars: 1 g ✦ Protein: 5 g ✦ Vitamin A: 0% ✦ Vitamin C: 0% ✦ Calcium: 0% ✦ Iron: 6% ✦ DIETARY EXCHANGES: 1 Starch, 1 Vegetable, 1 Fat OR 1 Carbohydrate, 1 Vegetable, 1 Fat

Bread Stuffing for Poultry

PREP TIME: 20 MINUTES ◆ YIELD: 9 CUPS
(ENOUGH TO STUFF 18-LB. TURKEY)

½ cup margarine or butter
1 medium onion, chopped
2 stalks celery, chopped
8 cups unseasoned dry bread cubes*
2 tablespoons finely chopped fresh parsley, if desired
2 teaspoons poultry seasoning, sage or savory
1 teaspoon salt
¼ teaspoon pepper
½ cup chicken broth or water

1. Melt margarine in large skillet over medium heat. Add onion and celery; cook until tender, stirring occasionally.
2. In large bowl, combine bread cubes, parsley, poultry seasoning, salt and pepper; mix well. Add broth and onion mixture; stir gently until moisture is absorbed. (Stuffing will become more moist during cooking because it absorbs juices from bird.)

TIPS: * Day-old soft bread cubes can be substituted for dry bread cubes. Decrease broth to ¼ cup.
Allow about ½ cup stuffing per pound of poultry. If necessary, recipe can be halved, or bake any remaining stuffing in covered greased casserole at 325°F. for 35 to 50 minutes or until thoroughly heated.

NUTRITION INFORMATION PER SERVING: Serving Size: ½ Cup ◆ Calories: 100 ◆ Calories from Fat: 50 ◆ % DAILY VALUE: Total Fat: 6 g 9% ◆ Saturated Fat: 1 g 5% ◆ Cholesterol: 0 mg 0% ◆ Sodium: 290 mg 12% ◆ Total Carbohydrate: 9 g 3% ◆ Dietary Fiber: 1 g 2% ◆ Sugars: 1 g ◆ Protein: 2 g ◆ Vitamin A: 6% ◆ Vitamin C: 0% ◆ Calcium: 2% ◆ Iron: 4% ◆ DIETARY EXCHANGES: ½ Starch, 1 Fat OR ½ Carbohydrate, 1 Fat

VARIATIONS

Chestnut Stuffing: Add 1 to 1½ cups chopped, shelled, roasted chestnuts to stuffing. To roast chestnuts, cut X-shaped slit on one side of shell. Place on ungreased cookie sheet. Bake at 400°F. for 15 to 20 minutes, stirring occasionally. Cool slightly; remove shells.
Cornbread Stuffing: Substitute crumbled, baked cornbread for part or all of bread cubes. Decrease poultry seasoning to 1 teaspoon. Cornbread stuffing is also good with the sausage variation.
Oyster Stuffing: Add ½ to 1 pint fresh chopped cooked oysters to stuffing. To

cook oysters, simmer with oyster liquid for about 5 minutes or until oysters are set; drain.
Sausage Stuffing: Add ½ lb. cooked pork sausage to stuffing. To cook sausage, place in small skillet, cook and stir until browned; drain. Reserve drippings. Add sausage to bread cube mixture. Decrease poultry seasoning to 1 teaspoon and salt to ¼ teaspoon. Drippings can be substituted for part of margarine used to cook onion and celery.
Water Chestnut Stuffing: Add ½ to 1 cup chopped water chestnuts to stuffing.

COOK'S NOTE

STUFFING TIPS

Allow ½ cup stuffing per pound of poultry. Stuff the bird immediately before roasting, never in advance. Spoon the stuffing lightly into the bird's cavity; it will expand during roasting. Stuffing must reach an internal temperature of 165°F. to be safe.

Bake any remaining stuffing in a greased, covered casserole at 325°F. for 35 to 50 minutes or until thoroughly heated. (In fact, some cooks prefer to make all the stuffing this way, basting it with a little of the juices that run into the roasting pan for great flavor.)

After roasting, remove the stuffing at once and transfer it to a serving dish. Otherwise, the meat and the stuffing cool at different rates, which can create ideal conditions for growth of harmful bacteria.

Chicken or Turkey Gravy

PREP TIME: 15 MINUTES ◆ YIELD: 2½ CUPS

2 cups hot milk*
¼ cup poultry drippings
¼ cup cold milk
¼ cup all-purpose flour*
Salt and pepper

1. In medium skillet or roasting pan, add hot milk to drippings. In small bowl, combine cold milk and flour; mix until smooth.

2. Add flour mixture to hot liquid in skillet. Cook until mixture boils and thickens, stirring constantly. Add salt and pepper to taste.

> **TIP:** * For thinner gravy, increase milk. To thicken, add flour dissolved in cold water. Heat to boiling, stirring constantly.

NUTRITION INFORMATION PER SERVING: Serving Size: ¼ Cup ◆ Calories: 80 ◆ Calories from Fat: 50 ◆ **% DAILY VALUE:** Total Fat: 6 g 9% ◆ Saturated Fat: 2 g 10% ◆ Cholesterol: 10 mg 3% ◆ Sodium: 55 mg 2% ◆ Total Carbohydrate: 5 g 2% ◆ Dietary Fiber: 0 g 0% ◆ Sugars: 3 g ◆ Protein: 2 g ◆ Vitamin A: 2% ◆ Vitamin C: 0% ◆ Calcium: 6% ◆ Iron: 0% ◆ **DIETARY EXCHANGES:** ½ Starch, 1 Fat OR ½ Carbohydrate, 1 Fat

Giblet Gravy

PREP TIME: 15 MINUTES (READY IN 2 HOURS 15 MINUTES) ◆ YIELD: 2 CUPS

  Turkey or chicken giblets
2 stalks celery, sliced
1 medium onion, sliced
1 teaspoon salt
¼ teaspoon pepper
  Milk or water
3 tablespoons poultry drippings*
3 tablespoons all-purpose flour*

1. In medium saucepan, combine giblets and enough water to cover. Add celery, onion, salt and pepper. Bring to a boil. Reduce heat to low; simmer 1 to 2 hours or until giblets are tender.
2. Drain giblet mixture, reserving 2 cups giblet broth. (If necessary, add more milk or water to giblet broth to make 2 cups.) Set giblets aside; discard celery and onion.
3. Remove turkey or chicken from roasting pan. Remove 3 tablespoons drippings; place in same saucepan. Stir in flour. Cook over low heat until smooth and browned, stirring constantly.
4. Gradually add 2 cups giblet broth; cook until mixture boils and thickens, stirring constantly. Chop giblets and add to gravy, if desired. If desired, add salt and pepper to taste.

> **TIP:** * Flour and drippings can be decreased to 2 tablespoons each for thinner gravy, or increased to 4 tablespoons each for thicker gravy.

NUTRITION INFORMATION PER SERVING: Serving Size: ¼ Cup ◆ Calories: 100 ◆ Calories from Fat: 50 ◆ **% DAILY VALUE:** Total Fat: 6 g 9% ◆ Saturated Fat: 2 g 10% ◆ Cholesterol: 90 mg 30% ◆ Sodium: 290 mg 12% ◆ Total Carbohydrate: 4 g 1% ◆ Dietary Fiber: 0 g 0% ◆ Sugars: 2 g ◆ Protein: 7 g ◆ Vitamin A: 25% ◆ Vitamin C: 0% ◆ Calcium: 4% ◆ Iron: 8% ◆ **DIETARY EXCHANGES:** ½ Starch, ½ Very Lean Meat, 1 Fat OR ½ Carbohydrate, ½ Very Lean Meat, 1 Fat

Cornish Hens with Apple-Raisin Stuffing

PREP TIME: 30 MINUTES (READY IN 1 HOUR 45 MINUTES) ◆ YIELD: 8 SERVINGS

STUFFING
3 tablespoons margarine or butter
½ cup chopped green onions
1 red baking apple, unpeeled, chopped
4 cups unseasoned dry bread cubes
½ cup raisins
¼ teaspoon salt
¼ teaspoon allspice
¼ cup apple juice

CORNISH HENS
4 (24-oz.) Cornish game hens
¼ teaspoon salt
⅛ teaspoon pepper
¼ cup apple jelly
2 tablespoons margarine or butter

1. Heat oven to 350°F. Melt 3 tablespoons margarine in large skillet over medium-high heat. Add onions and apple; cook and stir until tender. Stir in remaining stuffing ingredients.
2. Remove and discard neck and giblets from game hens. Split each game hen in half. Rinse game hens with cold water; pat dry. Sprinkle with salt and pepper.
3. Spread stuffing in ungreased 15×10× 1-inch baking pan. Place game hens, skin side up, over stuffing.
4. In small saucepan over low heat, melt jelly with 2 tablespoons margarine. Brush over game hens.
5. Bake at 350°F. for 1 to 1¼ hours or until game hens are fork-tender and juices run clear.

NUTRITION INFORMATION PER SERVING: Serving Size: ⅛ of Recipe ◆ Calories: 400 ◆ Calories from Fat: 140 ◆ **% DAILY VALUE:** Total Fat: 16 g 25% ◆ Saturated Fat: 4 g 20% ◆ Cholesterol: 100 mg 33% ◆ Sodium: 430 mg 18% ◆ Total Carbohydrate: 29 g 10% ◆ Dietary Fiber: 2 g 8% ◆ Sugars: 15 g ◆ Protein: 34 g ◆ Vitamin A: 8% ◆ Vitamin C: 4% ◆ Calcium: 6% ◆ Iron: 15% ◆ **DIETARY EXCHANGES:** 1 Starch, 1 Fruit, 4½ Lean Meat, ½ Fat OR 2 Carbohydrate, 4½ Meat, ½ Fat

Grilled Turkey Drumsticks

PREP TIME: 45 MINUTES (READY IN 1 HOUR 5 MINUTES)
✦ YIELD: 4 SERVINGS

    4 turkey drumsticks (about 2 lb.)
    6 cups water
1½ cups beer
    1 medium onion, sliced
    ¾ cup chili sauce
    1 teaspoon dry mustard

1. GRILL DIRECTIONS: In Dutch oven or large saucepan, combine turkey drumsticks, water, 1¼ cups of the beer and onion. Bring to a boil. Reduce heat; cover and simmer 30 minutes. Drain; discard liquid.
2. Meanwhile, heat grill. In small bowl, combine remaining ¼ cup beer, chili sauce and dry mustard; mix well. Set aside.
3. When ready to grill, place drumsticks on gas grill over medium heat or on charcoal grill 4 to 6 inches from medium-high coals; brush with sauce. Cover grill; cook 20 to 30 minutes or until turkey is fork-tender and juices run clear, turning and brushing frequently with sauce. Bring any remaining sauce to a boil; serve with turkey drumsticks.

> **TIP:** To broil drumsticks, place on foil-lined broiler pan; broil 4 to 6 inches from heat using times above as a guide, turning and brushing frequently with sauce.

Grilled Turkey Drumsticks

Grilled Turkey Tenderloins

NUTRITION INFORMATION PER SERVING: Serving Size: ¼ of Recipe ✦ Calories: 260 ✦ Calories from Fat: 60 ✦ **% DAILY VALUE:** Total Fat: 7 g 11% ✦ Saturated Fat: 2 g 10% ✦ Cholesterol: 85 mg 28% ✦ Sodium: 780 mg 33% ✦ Total Carbohydrate: 13 g 4% ✦ Dietary Fiber: 0 g 0% ✦ Sugars: 9 g ✦ Protein: 35 g ✦ Vitamin A: 15% ✦ Vitamin C: 10% ✦ Calcium: 4% ✦ Iron: 20% ✦ **DIETARY EXCHANGES:** 1 Fruit, 5 Very Lean Meat, ½ Fat OR 1 Carbohydrate, 5 Very Lean Meat, ½ Fat

Grilled Turkey Tenderloins

PREP TIME: 45 MINUTES (READY IN 4 HOURS 45 MINUTES) ✦ YIELD: 4 SERVINGS

    ¼ cup oil
    ¼ cup soy sauce
    ¼ teaspoon dried basil leaves
    ¼ teaspoon dried marjoram leaves
    ¼ teaspoon dried thyme leaves
    1 lb. fresh turkey tenderloins

1. GRILL DIRECTIONS: In 8-inch square (2-quart) glass baking dish or resealable food storage plastic bag, combine all ingredients except turkey; mix well. Add turkey; turn to coat. Cover dish or seal bag. Refrigerate 2 to 4 hours to marinate, turning occasionally.
2. Heat grill. When ready to grill, remove turkey from marinade; reserve marinade. Place turkey on gas grill over low heat or on charcoal grill 4 to 6 inches from medium coals. Cook 20 to 30 minutes or until turkey is fork-tender and juices run clear, turning once and brushing frequently with reserved marinade. Discard any remaining marinade.

> **TIP:** To broil turkey, place on oiled broiler pan; broil 4 to 6 inches from heat using times above as a guide, turning once and brushing frequently with reserved marinade.

NUTRITION INFORMATION PER SERVING: Serving Size: ¼ of Recipe ✦ Calories: 140 ✦ Calories from Fat: 35 ✦ **% DAILY VALUE:** Total Fat: 4 g 6% ✦ Saturated Fat: 1 g 5% ✦ Cholesterol: 75 mg 25% ✦ Sodium: 300 mg 13% ✦ Total Carbohydrate: 0 g 0% ✦ Dietary Fiber: 0 g 0% ✦ Sugars: 0 g ✦ Protein: 27 g ✦ Vitamin A: 0% ✦ Vitamin C: 0% ✦ Calcium: 0% ✦ Iron: 8% ✦ **DIETARY EXCHANGES:** 4 Very Lean Meat

Turkey Slice Sauté with Vegetables

PREP TIME: 35 MINUTES ✦ YIELD: 5 SERVINGS

½ lb. fresh whole green beans
    or 2 cups frozen cut green beans
1½ to 2 cups sliced carrots
 1 cup sliced celery
 2 tablespoons margarine or butter
 1 to 1¼ lb. fresh turkey breast slices
 1 cup sliced fresh mushrooms
¼ cup sliced green onions or 2 tablespoons
    finely chopped shallots
¼ cup dry white wine
 2 tablespoons lemon juice
½ teaspoon salt
¼ teaspoon pepper

1. Place green beans, carrots and celery in steamer basket over boiling water. Reduce heat; cover and steam 10 minutes or until vegetables are crisp-tender. Cover to keep warm.
2. Meanwhile, melt margarine in large skillet over medium heat. Add turkey breast slices; cook 2 to 3 minutes, turning once. Add mushrooms, onions, wine and lemon juice. Reduce heat; cover and simmer 2 to 3 minutes or until turkey is no longer pink. Sprinkle with salt and pepper.
3. Arrange steamed vegetables and turkey slices on warm serving platter. Spoon mushroom mixture over turkey.

NUTRITION INFORMATION PER SERVING: Serving Size: ⅕ of Recipe ✦ Calories: 210 ✦ Calories from Fat: 45 ✦ **% DAILY VALUE:** Total Fat: 5 g 8% ✦ Saturated Fat: 1 g 5% ✦ Cholesterol: 75 mg 25% ✦ Sodium: 360 mg 15% ✦ Total Carbohydrate: 10 g 3% ✦ Dietary Fiber: 4 g 16% ✦ Sugars: 5 g ✦ Protein: 29 g ✦ Vitamin A: 280% ✦ Vitamin C: 20% ✦ Calcium: 6% ✦ Iron: 15% ✦ **DIETARY EXCHANGES:** 2 Vegetable, 3½ Very Lean Meat, ½ Fat

Turkey Slice Sauté with Vegetables

Honey-Mustard Chicken Sandwiches

Honey-Mustard Chicken Sandwiches

PREP TIME: 35 MINUTES ✦ YIELD: 4 SANDWICHES

⅓ cup honey
 1 tablespoon sliced green onions
½ teaspoon dried tarragon leaves, if desired
 3 tablespoons Dijon mustard
 4 boneless skinless chicken breast halves
 4 lettuce leaves
 4 slices tomato
 1 avocado, peeled, pitted and sliced
 4 kaiser rolls, split

1. GRILL DIRECTIONS: Heat grill. In small saucepan, combine honey, onions, tarragon and mustard; blend well. Bring to a boil. Reduce heat to low; simmer about 5 minutes or until slightly thickened.
2. When ready to grill, place chicken on gas grill over medium heat or on charcoal grill 4 to 6 inches from medium coals. Cook 15 to 18 minutes or until chicken is fork-tender and juices run clear, turning once and brushing occasionally with mustard mixture.
3. Layer lettuce leaf, chicken breast half, tomato slice and avocado slices in each kaiser roll.

> **TIP:** To broil chicken, place on broiler pan; broil 4 to 6 inches from heat using times above as a guide, turning once and brushing occasionally with mustard mixture.

NUTRITION INFORMATION PER SERVING: Serving Size: 1 Sandwich ✦ Calories: 410 ✦ Calories from Fat: 120 ✦ **% DAILY VALUE:** Total Fat: 13 g 20% ✦ Saturated Fat: 2 g 10% ✦ Cholesterol: 75 mg 25% ✦ Sodium: 450 mg 19% ✦ Total Carbohydrate: 40 g 13% ✦ Dietary Fiber: 4 g 16% ✦ Sugars: 8 g ✦ Protein: 34 g ✦ Vitamin A: 8% ✦ Vitamin C: 8% ✦ Calcium: 8% ✦ Iron: 20% ✦ **DIETARY EXCHANGES:** 2 Starch, ½ Fruit, 4 Very Lean Meat, 2 Fat OR 2½ Carbohydrate, 4 Very Lean Meat, 2 Fat

Greek Marinated Turkey Slices

PREP TIME: 30 MINUTES ◆ YIELD: 4 SERVINGS

    2 tablespoons lemon juice
    1 tablespoon olive or vegetable oil
    2 garlic cloves, minced
    ½ teaspoon dried oregano leaves
    ¼ teaspoon salt
    ⅛ teaspoon pepper
    4 (3-oz.) fresh turkey breast slices

1. In shallow glass dish, combine all ingredients except turkey; mix well. Add turkey breast slices; turn to coat. Refrigerate 15 minutes to marinate.
2. Spray broiler pan with nonstick cooking spray. Remove turkey from marinade; place on sprayed pan. Discard marinade.
3. Broil 4 to 6 inches from heat for 6 to 8 minutes or until turkey is fork-tender and juices run clear, turning once.

NUTRITION INFORMATION PER SERVING: Serving Size: ¼ of Recipe ◆ Calories: 90 ◆ Calories from Fat: 10 ◆ % DAILY VALUE: Total Fat: 1 g 2% ◆ Saturated Fat: 0 g 0% ◆ Cholesterol: 55 mg 18% ◆ Sodium: 70 mg 3% ◆ Total Carbohydrate: 0 g 0% ◆ Dietary Fiber: 0 g 0% ◆ Sugars: 0 g ◆ Protein: 20 g ◆ Vitamin A: 0% ◆ Vitamin C: 0% ◆ Calcium: 0% ◆ Iron: 6% ◆ DIETARY EXCHANGES: 3 Very Lean Meat

Turkey Saltimbocca

PREP TIME: 20 MINUTES (READY IN 1 HOUR 30 MINUTES) ◆ YIELD: 6 SERVINGS

    1 cup herb-seasoned stuffing mix (not cubes)
    1½ lb. fresh turkey breast slices
    6 thin slices cooked ham
    6 fresh sage leaves, chopped, or 3 teaspoons dried sage leaves
    6 tablespoons shredded mozzarella cheese
    1 medium tomato, seeded, chopped

1. Heat oven to 375°F. Line 15 × 10 × 1-inch baking pan with foil; spray with nonstick cooking spray. Place stuffing mix in small shallow bowl.
2. Place 1 turkey breast slice between 2 pieces of plastic wrap or waxed paper. Working from center, gently pound turkey with flat side of meat mallet or rolling pin until about ¼ inch thick; remove wrap. Repeat with remaining turkey breast slices.
3. Place 1 ham slice and 1 chopped sage leaf on each turkey slice. Top each with 1 tablespoon cheese and about 1 tablespoon chopped tomato; roll up tightly, jelly-roll

fashion. Secure each roll with toothpick. Coat turkey rolls with stuffing mix. Place, seam side down, in sprayed pan. Cover pan with foil.
4. Bake at 375°F. for 30 minutes. Uncover; bake an additional 20 to 30 minutes or until turkey is no longer pink.

NUTRITION INFORMATION PER SERVING: Serving Size: ⅙ of Recipe ◆ Calories: 200 ◆ Calories from Fat: 25 ◆ % DAILY VALUE: Total Fat: 3 g 5% ◆ Saturated Fat: 1 g 5% ◆ Cholesterol: 90 mg 30% ◆ Sodium: 520 mg 22% ◆ Total Carbohydrate: 9 g 3% ◆ Dietary Fiber: 1 g 4% ◆ Sugars: 1 g ◆ Protein: 34 g ◆ Vitamin A: 4% ◆ Vitamin C: 4% ◆ Calcium: 8% ◆ Iron: 10% ◆ DIETARY EXCHANGES: ½ Starch, 4½ Very Lean Meat OR ½ Carbohydrate, 4½ Very Lean Meat

Roast Goose with Chestnut-Prune Stuffing

PREP TIME: 30 MINUTES (READY IN 3 HOURS 40 MINUTES) ◆ YIELD: 8 SERVINGS

GOOSE
    1 (8 to 9-lb.) whole goose
    1 teaspoon salt

STUFFING
    ¼ cup chopped onion
    ¼ cup chopped celery
    1 cup chopped pitted prunes
    1 (10-oz.) can peeled chestnuts, drained, quartered
    3 cups cornbread stuffing mix
    1 teaspoon salt
    1 teaspoon allspice
    ¼ teaspoon pepper
    1½ cups apple cider or juice

1. Heat oven to 450°F. Remove and discard neck, giblets and excess fat from inside of goose. Rinse goose with cold water; pat dry. Sprinkle cavity of goose with 1 teaspoon salt.
2. Spray large nonstick skillet with nonstick cooking spray. Heat over medium-high heat until hot. Add onion and celery; cook 3 to 4 minutes or until tender, stirring occasionally.
3. Stir in prunes and chestnuts; cook 2 to 3 minutes or until thoroughly heated, stirring occasionally. Remove from heat. Add stuffing mix, 1 teaspoon salt, allspice and pepper; mix lightly. Add apple cider; mix just until moistened.
4. Spoon stuffing loosely into cavity of goose; close cavity with metal skewers or sew shut with string. Tuck wing tips under; secure legs with string. Place goose, breast

side up, on rack in shallow roasting pan. Pour enough boiling water into pan to just reach rack. Prick skin generously with meat fork. Do not cover.

5. Bake at 450°F. for 15 to 20 minutes or until goose begins to brown.

6. Reduce oven temperature to 350°F. Insert meat thermometer so bulb reaches center of thickest part of thigh, but does not rest on bone. Bake 1¾ to 2 hours or until meat thermometer registers 180 to 185°F., basting every 20 to 30 minutes with pan juices. Remove excess fat as it accumulates in pan. Tent loosely with foil if goose becomes too brown.

7. Let stand 20 minutes before carving. Remove skewers and/or string from goose. Remove stuffing; place in serving bowl.

NUTRITION INFORMATION PER SERVING: Serving Size: ⅛ of Recipe (without skin) • Calories: 700 • Calories from Fat: 250 • **% DAILY VALUE:** Total Fat: 28 g 43% • Saturated Fat: 10 g 50% • Cholesterol: 205 mg 68% • Sodium: 970 mg 40% • Total Carbohydrate: 47 g 16% • Dietary Fiber: 5 g 20% • Sugars: 15 g • Protein: 65 g • Vitamin A: 10% • Vitamin C: 15% • Calcium: 6% • Iron: 45% • **DIETARY EXCHANGES:** 2 Starch, 1 Fruit, 8½ Lean Meat, ½ Fat OR 3 Carbohydrate, 8½ Lean Meat, ½ Fat

Duckling a l'Orange

PREP TIME: 30 MINUTES (READY IN 3 HOURS 30 MINUTES) ✦ YIELD: 6 SERVINGS

DUCKLING

 1 (4½ to 5-lb.) whole duckling
 1 teaspoon salt
 2 oranges, unpeeled, quartered
 3 peppercorns or ⅛ teaspoon pepper
 1 garlic clove, minced
 3 to 4 tablespoons orange marmalade

SAUCE

 2 tablespoons sugar
 1 tablespoon cornstarch
 1 tablespoon grated orange peel
 ⅔ cup orange juice
 3 tablespoons pan drippings
 2 tablespoons orange-flavored liqueur

1. Heat oven to 400°F. Remove and discard neck and giblets from duckling. Rinse duckling with cold water; pat dry. Sprinkle cavity of duckling with salt. Place oranges, peppercorns and garlic in cavity. Close body openings by bringing loose skin over openings and securing with metal skewers. Tie wings to body.

2. Place duckling, breast side up, on rack in shallow roasting pan. Insert meat thermometer so bulb reaches center of thickest part of breast meat, but does not rest on bone. Do not cover or add water. Bake at 400°F. for 15 minutes.

3. Reduce oven temperature to 325°F. Bake 3 hours or until duckling is fork-tender and meat thermometer registers 180 to 185°F., basting occasionally with pan juices. During last 15 minutes of baking, spread with orange marmalade. Let stand 5 to 10 minutes before carving.

4. In small saucepan, combine sugar, cornstarch and orange peel. Stir in orange juice and 3 tablespoons drippings from roasting pan. Bring to a boil, stirring occasionally. Stir in liqueur. Remove and discard oranges, peppercorns and garlic from inside of duckling. Serve duckling with orange sauce.

NUTRITION INFORMATION PER SERVING: Serving Size: ⅙ of Recipe • Calories: 380 • Calories from Fat: 180 • **% DAILY VALUE:** Total Fat: 20 g 31% • Saturated Fat: 7 g 35% • Cholesterol: 110 mg 37% • Sodium: 440 mg 18% • Total Carbohydrate: 19 g 6% • Dietary Fiber: 0 g 0% • Sugars: 15 g • Protein: 28 g • Vitamin A: 2% • Vitamin C: 15% • Calcium: 2% • Iron: 20% • **DIETARY EXCHANGES:** 1½ Fruit, 4 Medium-Fat Meat OR 1½ Carbohydrate, 4 Medium-Fat Meat

Spicy Rub

PREP TIME: 10 MINUTES ✦ YIELD: 4 SERVINGS

 1 tablespoon oil
 ½ teaspoon onion powder
 ⅛ teaspoon salt
 ¼ teaspoon allspice
 ¼ teaspoon ground thyme
 ⅛ teaspoon ground red pepper (cayenne)
   Dash cinnamon

1. In small bowl, combine all ingredients; mix well.

2. Rub mixture evenly on both sides of desired chicken pieces. Grill or broil as desired.

NUTRITION INFORMATION PER SERVING: Serving Size: ¼ of Recipe • Calories: 25 • Calories from Fat: 25 • **% DAILY VALUE:** Total Fat: 3 g 5% • Saturated: 0 g 0% • Cholesterol: 0 mg 0% • Sodium: 65 mg 3% • Total Carbohydrate: 0 g 0% • Dietary Fiber: 0 g 0% • Sugars: 0 g • Protein: 0 g • Vitamin A: 0% • Vitamin C: 0% • Calcium: 0% • Iron: 0% • **DIETARY EXCHANGES:** ½ Fat

Thyme and Rosemary Herb Rub

PREP TIME: 10 MINUTES ◆ YIELD: 4 SERVINGS

    2 tablespoons chopped fresh thyme
        or 2 teaspoons dried thyme leaves
    2 tablespoons chopped fresh rosemary
        or 2 teaspoons dried rosemary leaves,
        crushed
    1 tablespoon olive or vegetable oil
    2 teaspoons paprika
    1 teaspoon salt
    1 teaspoon coarse ground black pepper

1. In small bowl, combine all ingredients; mix well.
2. Rub mixture evenly on both sides of desired chicken pieces. Grill or broil as desired.

NUTRITION INFORMATION PER SERVING: Serving Size: ¼ of Recipe ◆ Calories: 40 ◆ Calories from Fat: 35 ◆ **% DAILY VALUE:** Total Fat: 4 g 6% ◆ Saturated Fat: 1 g 5% ◆ Cholesterol: 0 mg 0% ◆ Sodium: 530 mg 22% ◆ Total Carbohydrate: 1 g 1% ◆ Dietary Fiber: 1 g 3% ◆ Sugars: 0 g ◆ Protein: 0 g ◆ Vitamin A: 15% ◆ Vitamin C: 0% ◆ Calcium: 0% ◆ Iron: 4% ◆ **DIETARY EXCHANGES:** 1 Fat

Southern Barbecue Basting Sauce

PREP TIME: 15 MINUTES ◆ YIELD: 1½ CUPS

    ¾ cup ketchup
    ¼ cup finely chopped onion
    ¼ cup water
    ¼ cup margarine or butter
    2 tablespoons vinegar
    1 tablespoon Worcestershire sauce
    1 teaspoon lemon-pepper seasoning
    1 teaspoon dry mustard
    ¼ teaspoon ground red pepper (cayenne)
        Few drops hot pepper sauce

1. In small saucepan, combine all ingredients; mix well. Cook over low heat for 10 minutes, stirring occasionally.
2. Brush over poultry frequently during baking or grilling. If desired, bring any remaining sauce to a boil; serve with poultry.

NUTRITION INFORMATION PER SERVING: Serving Size: ¼ Cup ◆ Calories: 110 ◆ Calories from Fat: 70 ◆ **% DAILY VALUE:** Total Fat: 8 g 12% ◆ Saturated Fat: 1 g 5% ◆ Cholesterol: 0 mg 0% ◆ Sodium: 530 mg 22% ◆ Total Carbohydrate: 9 g 3% ◆ Dietary Fiber: 1 g 2% ◆ Sugars: 4 g ◆ Protein: 1 g ◆ Vitamin A: 15% ◆ Vitamin C: 6% ◆ Calcium: 0% ◆ Iron: 0% ◆ **DIETARY EXCHANGES:** ½ Fruit, 1½ Fat OR ½ Carbohydrate, 1½ Fat

VARIATION

Sweet and Spicy Basting Sauce: Substitute one 10-oz. jar peach preserves for ketchup.

Curry-Peach Glaze

PREP TIME: 10 MINUTES ◆ YIELD: ¼ CUP

    ½ cup peach preserves
    ¼ cup margarine or butter
    1 teaspoon curry powder

1. In small saucepan, combine all ingredients; mix well. Cook over medium heat until melted and smooth, stirring constantly.
2. Brush over poultry frequently during baking or grilling. If desired, heat any remaining sauce to a boil; serve with poultry.

NUTRITION INFORMATION PER SERVING: Serving Size: 1 Tablespoon ◆ Calories: 70 ◆ Calories from Fat: 35 ◆ **% DAILY VALUE:** Total Fat: 4 g 6% ◆ Saturated Fat: 1 g 5% ◆ Cholesterol: 0 mg 0% ◆ Sodium: 50 mg 2% ◆ Total Carbohydrate: 9 g 3% ◆ Dietary Fiber: 0 g 0% ◆ Sugars: 6 g ◆ Protein: 0 g ◆ Vitamin A: 4% ◆ Vitamin C: 0% ◆ Calcium: 0% ◆ Iron: 0% ◆ **DIETARY EXCHANGES:** ½ Fruit, 1 Fat OR ½ Carbohydrate, 1 Fat

VARIATIONS

Honey-Lemon Glaze: Substitute ¼ cup honey for the preserves and 1 tablespoon lemon juice for the curry powder.
Honey-Pineapple Glaze: Substitute ¼ cup pineapple syrup or juice and ¼ cup honey for the preserves and ½ teaspoon mace or nutmeg for the curry powder.
Soy-Butter Glaze: Substitute ⅓ cup soy sauce and ¼ cup light or dark corn syrup for the preserves and ⅛ teaspoon garlic powder for the curry powder.

Herb-Lemon Basting Sauce

PREP TIME: 10 MINUTES ◆ YIELD: ½ CUP

    ⅓ cup lemon juice
    ¼ cup oil
    1 teaspoon dried rosemary leaves, crushed
    ½ teaspoon dried thyme leaves
    ¼ teaspoon garlic powder
        Dash pepper
        Dash paprika

1. In small bowl, combine all ingredients; mix well.
2. Brush over poultry frequently during baking or grilling. If desired, bring any remaining sauce to a boil; serve with poultry.

NUTRITION INFORMATION PER SERVING: Serving Size: 1 Tablespoon ◆ Calories: 70 ◆ Calories from Fat: 60 ◆ **% DAILY VALUE:** Total Fat: 7 g 11% ◆ Saturated Fat: 1 g 5% ◆ Cholesterol: 0 mg 0% ◆ Sodium: 0 mg 0% ◆ Total Carbohydrate: 1 g 1% ◆ Dietary Fiber: 0 g 0% ◆ Sugars: 0 g ◆ Protein: 0 g ◆ Vitamin A: 0% ◆ Vitamin C: 4% ◆ Calcium: 0% ◆ Iron: 0% ◆ **DIETARY EXCHANGES:** 1½ Fat

FISH
& SHELLFISH

FISH & SHELLFISH

I f you have cooked fish and shellfish, you may already appreciate them as a practical and delicious choice for quick-and-easy weeknight meals and leisurely company dinners. New research about the health benefits has led many people to make fish and shellfish a more frequent part of their diet. This is far from a recipe for monotony; the broad-based category comprises both freshwater and saltwater varieties of fish, shellfish and crustaceans such as crabs and lobster.

Storing Fish and Shellfish

As soon as you buy the fish, go straight home and place it in the coldest part of the refrigerator. It's best used the same day it's purchased. If you will not cook the fish within 24 hours, wrap it securely in foil, freezer paper or plastic freezer wrap. Put it into a resealable plastic bag for extra protection and label it with the contents and date. Shellfish purchased frozen can be stored in the original wrapping.

Properly wrapped, lean fish keeps for up to six months at 0°F. or lower. (Check the temperature of your freezer with a freezer thermometer—some home freezers don't go this low.) Fish with high fat content is better if used within three months.

Cooked shellfish, securely wrapped, can be refrigerated for two or three days.

Safety First

Fresh fish and shellfish are highly perishable and should be used, if at all possible, the same day as purchased. Follow the same commonsense procedures that you would for raw meats: With hot, soapy water, thoroughly wash all utensils, dishes and work surfaces that have come into contact with raw fish and shellfish. To avoid cross-contamination, do not let raw fish or shell-fish touch foods that will be served raw or the dishes and utensils that will be used to prepare them.

Thawing Fish and Shellfish

Frozen fish and shellfish can be poached or baked without thawing first. The cooking time will be slightly longer. Frozen, breaded fish should always be cooked from the frozen state.

Never thaw fish or shellfish at room temperature, which can make conditions right for harmful bacteria growth. Do not refreeze thawed, raw fish.

Thaw fish and shellfish in one of three ways: in the refrigerator overnight, in a bowl of cold water or in the microwave oven.

To defrost in the microwave, follow manufacturer's directions or use the lowest defrost setting (no more than 30 percent power). A pound of fillets defrosts in about five or six minutes. The fish may still feel cool to the touch; be sure it does not start cooking.

Cook fish and shellfish immediately after thawing it.

Baked Whole Fish

PREP TIME: 10 MINUTES (READY IN 55 MINUTES)
♦ YIELD: 6 SERVINGS

    1 (2 to 3-lb.) dressed whole fish
    ½ teaspoon salt
    2 tablespoons margarine or butter, melted

1. Heat oven to 350°F. Grease shallow roasting pan. Sprinkle inside of fish with salt. Place in greased pan; brush with about 1 tablespoon of the margarine.
2. Bake at 350°F. for 40 to 45 minutes or until fish flakes easily with fork, basting occasionally with remaining 1 tablespoon melted margarine.

NUTRITION INFORMATION PER SERVING: Serving Size: ⅙ of Recipe ♦ Calories: 230 • Calories from Fat: 90 ♦ % DAILY VALUE: Total Fat: 10 g 15% • Saturated Fat: 3 g 15% • Cholesterol: 110 mg 37% ♦ Sodium: 280 mg 12% • Total Carbohydrate: 0 g 0% ♦ Dietary Fiber: 0 g 0% • Sugars: 0 g • Protein: 36 g • Vitamin A: 2% • Vitamin C: 4% • Calcium: 15% • Iron: 4% • DIETARY EXCHANGES: 5 Very Lean Meat, 1 Fat

Baked Stuffed Fish

PREP TIME: 20 MINUTES (READY IN 1 HOUR 5 MINUTES)
◆ YIELD: 6 SERVINGS

STUFFING
 ¼ cup margarine or butter
 ¼ cup chopped celery
 2 tablespoons chopped onion
 2 cups soft bread cubes
 ¼ teaspoon salt
 ¼ teaspoon dried thyme leaves
 ⅛ teaspoon pepper

FISH
 1 (2 to 3-lb.) dressed whole fish*
 ½ teaspoon salt
 2 tablespoons margarine or butter, melted

1. Heat oven to 400°F. Grease shallow roasting pan. Melt ¼ cup margarine in medium skillet over medium heat. Add celery and onion; cook and stir until tender. Stir in all remaining stuffing ingredients.

2. Sprinkle inside of fish with ½ teaspoon salt. Fill opening with stuffing. Secure edges of fish together with skewers or toothpicks. Place in greased pan; brush with melted margarine.

3. Bake at 400°F. for 45 minutes or until fish flakes easily with fork, basting occasionally with margarine. Remove skewers before serving. To serve, cut into sections by slicing through backbone.

> **TIP:** * Smaller fish can also be stuffed. Allow ½ cup stuffing per 12 to 16-oz. fish.

NUTRITION INFORMATION PER SERVING: Serving Size: ⅙ of Recipe ◆ Calories: 340 ◆ Calories from Fat: 160 ◆ **% DAILY VALUE:** Total Fat: 18 g 28% ◆ Saturated Fat: 4 g 20% ◆ Cholesterol: 110 mg 37% ◆ Sodium: 520 mg 22% ◆ Total Carbohydrate: 7 g 2% ◆ Dietary Fiber: 0 g 0% ◆ Sugars: 1 g ◆ Protein: 37 g ◆ Vitamin A: 10% ◆ Vitamin C: 4% ◆ Calcium: 15% ◆ Iron: 6% ◆ **DIETARY EXCHANGES:** ½ Starch, 5 Very Lean Meat, 3 Fat OR ½ Carbohydrate, 5 Very Lean Meat, 3 Fat

VARIATIONS

Baked Crab-Stuffed Fish: Add ½ cup cooked crabmeat with bread cubes.
Baked Dill-Stuffed Fish: Add ¼ cup chopped dill pickle or ¼ teaspoon dried dill weed with bread cubes.
Baked Lemon-Stuffed Fish: Add 2 teaspoons grated lemon peel and 2 tablespoons lemon juice with bread cubes.
Baked Mushroom-Stuffed Fish: Cook ½ cup sliced fresh mushrooms with celery and onion.
Baked Shrimp-Stuffed Fish: Add ½ cup cooked shrimp with bread cubes.

HOW MUCH TO BUY

Larger fish have proportionately more meat per pound due to less waste. If you are serving plentiful side dishes, smaller servings will probably suffice.

TYPE OF FISH	PER SERVING, UNCOOKED
Whole or drawn fish	1 pound
Dressed or pan-dressed fish	½ pound
Steaks or fillets	⅓ to ½ pound

COOK'S NOTE

HOW TO CARVE A WHOLE FISH

With a sharp knife held parallel to the work surface, loosen the top fillet by running the blade along the length of the fish just above the backbone.

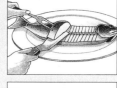

 Cut the loosened fillet into serving-sized portions and lift off each portion with a spatula. Remove any large, obvious bones from each serving.

 When the top layer has been completely served, lift off and discard the backbone and attached ribs.

 Cut the remaining fillet into serving-sized portions.

COOK'S NOTE

SHOPPING FOR QUALITY

◆ Fresh fish should have a fresh, mild smell, not a strong "fishy" odor.
◆ The flesh should look firm and elastic; the skin should be shiny but not slimy.
◆ Eyes should look bright, clear and bulging, without a filmy or sunken appearance.

Poached Fish

PREP TIME: 30 MINUTES ◆ YIELD: 4 SERVINGS

    1 tablespoon salt
    4 peppercorns
    2 stalks celery, cut into pieces
    2 carrots, cut into pieces
    2 slices lemon
    2 bay leaves
    1 medium onion, sliced
    1 quart (4 cups) water*
    2 lb. dressed whole fish or fish fillets

1. In large skillet, combine all ingredients except fish. Bring to a boil. Reduce heat to low; simmer 5 minutes to blend flavors.
2. Add fish; cover and simmer 20 minutes or until fish flakes easily with fork. If liquid does not cover fish, turn fish over after 10 minutes for even cooking. With slotted spoon, remove fish from liquid; place on serving platter.

TIP: * If desired, use ½ cup dry white wine for part of liquid.

NUTRITION INFORMATION PER SERVING: Serving Size: ¼ of Recipe ◆ Calories: 250 ◆ Calories from Fat: 90 ◆ **% DAILY VALUE:** Total Fat: 10 g 15% ◆ Saturated Fat: 3 g 15% ◆ Cholesterol: 125 mg 42% ◆ Sodium: 100 mg 4% ◆ Total Carbohydrate: 0 g 0% ◆ Dietary Fiber: 0 g 0% ◆ Sugars: 0 g ◆ Protein: 41 g ◆ Vitamin A: 0% ◆ Vitamin C: 4% ◆ Calcium: 15% ◆ Iron: 4% ◆ **DIETARY EXCHANGES:** 6 Very Lean Meat, 1 Fat

Panfried Fish

PREP TIME: 20 MINUTES ◆ YIELD: 4 SERVINGS

    1 egg, slightly beaten
    ¼ cup milk
    ½ cup all-purpose flour or cornmeal
    1 lb. fish fillets
    ¼ cup oil or shortening

1. In shallow dish, combine egg and milk; blend well. Place flour in another shallow dish. Dip fish in egg mixture; coat with flour.
2. Heat oil in large skillet over medium-high heat. Add fish; cook 5 to 7 minutes or until golden brown and fish flakes easily with fork, turning once during cooking. If desired, season with salt and pepper to taste.

NUTRITION INFORMATION PER SERVING: Serving Size: ¼ of Recipe ◆ Calories: 290 ◆ Calories from Fat: 140 ◆ **% DAILY VALUE:** Total Fat: 16 g 25% ◆ Saturated Fat: 2 g 10% ◆ Cholesterol: 105 mg 35% ◆ Sodium: 95 mg 4% ◆ Total Carbohydrate: 13 g 4% ◆ Dietary Fiber: 0 g 0% ◆ Sugars: 1 g ◆ Protein: 24 g ◆ Vitamin A: 4% ◆ Vitamin C: 0% ◆ Calcium: 4% ◆ Iron: 8% ◆ **DIETARY EXCHANGES:** 1 Starch, 3 Medium-Fat Meat OR 1 Carbohydrate, 3 Medium-Fat Meat

Batter-Fried Fish

PREP TIME: 25 MINUTES ◆ YIELD: 4 SERVINGS

    1 lb. fish fillets, cut into serving-sized pieces
      Oil for frying
    ½ cup milk
    1 egg
    ½ cup all-purpose flour
    ½ teaspoon salt
      Dash hot pepper sauce

1. Heat 1 to 1½ inches oil in Dutch oven, large saucepan or deep fryer to 375°F. In medium bowl, combine milk and egg; beat well. Add flour, salt and hot pepper sauce; beat until smooth. Dip fish in batter; allow excess to drain off.
2. With slotted spoon, add fish to hot oil; fry at 375°F. for 3 to 4 minutes or until fish is golden brown and flakes easily with fork, turning once. Drain on paper towels. If desired, serve with Tartar Sauce, below.

NUTRITION INFORMATION PER SERVING: Serving Size: ¼ of Recipe ◆ Calories: 300 ◆ Calories from Fat: 140 ◆ **% DAILY VALUE:** Total Fat: 16 g 25% ◆ Saturated Fat: 3 g 15% ◆ Cholesterol: 105 mg 35% ◆ Sodium: 370 mg 15% ◆ Total Carbohydrate: 14 g 5% ◆ Dietary Fiber: 0 g 0% ◆ Sugars: 2 g ◆ Protein: 24 g ◆ Vitamin A: 4% ◆ Vitamin C: 0% ◆ Calcium: 6% ◆ Iron: 8% ◆ **DIETARY EXCHANGES:** 1 Starch, 3 Medium-Fat Meat OR 1 Carbohydrate, 3 Medium-Fat Meat

Tartar Sauce

PREP TIME: 20 MINUTES ◆ YIELD: 1½ CUPS

    1 cup mayonnaise or salad dressing
    ¼ cup finely chopped dill pickle or pickle relish
    2 tablespoons finely chopped fresh parsley
    1 tablespoon lemon juice
    1 tablespoon chopped pimientos
    ½ teaspoon finely chopped onion
    ¼ teaspoon Worcestershire sauce

In small bowl, combine all ingredients; mix well. Cover; refrigerate 15 minutes or until chilled.

NUTRITION INFORMATION PER SERVING: Serving Size: 1 Tablespoon ◆ Calories: 60 ◆ Calories from Fat: 60 ◆ **% DAILY VALUE:** Total Fat: 7 g 11% ◆ Saturated Fat: 1 g 5% ◆ Cholesterol: 5 mg 2% ◆ Sodium: 75 mg 3% ◆ Total Carbohydrate: 0 g 0% ◆ Dietary Fiber: 0 g 0% ◆ Sugars: 0 g ◆ Protein: 0 g ◆ Vitamin A: 0% ◆ Vitamin C: 2% ◆ Calcium: 0% ◆ Iron: 0% ◆ **DIETARY EXCHANGES:** 1½ Fat

Broiled Fish Fillets

PREP TIME: 20 MINUTES ✦ YIELD: 6 SERVINGS

2 lb. fish fillets (¼ to ½ inch thick),* cut
　　into serving-sized pieces
¼ cup margarine or butter, melted

1. Arrange fish fillets, skin side up, on
broiler pan. Brush both sides of fish with
margarine.
2. Broil 4 to 6 inches from heat for 5 to
8 minutes or until fish flakes easily with fork,
turning once and basting with margarine. If
desired, season with salt and pepper to taste.

> **TIP:** * To broil fish steaks that are ½ to 1 inch
> thick, broil 10 to 12 minutes.

NUTRITION INFORMATION PER SERVING: Serving Size: ⅙ of Recipe
✦ Calories: 140 ✦ Calories from Fat: 25 ✦ **% DAILY VALUE:** Total Fat:
3 g 5% ✦ Saturated Fat: 1 g 5% ✦ Cholesterol: 65 mg 22% ✦ Sodium:
115 mg 5% ✦ Total Carbohydrate: 0 g 0% ✦ Dietary Fiber: 0 g 0% ✦
Sugars: 0 g ✦ Protein: 27 g ✦ Vitamin A: 2% ✦ Vitamin C: 0% ✦ Calcium: 0% ✦ Iron: 4% ✦ **DIETARY EXCHANGES:** 4 Very Lean Meat

Oven-Fried Fish

PREP TIME: 20 MINUTES (READY IN 40 MINUTES)
✦ YIELD: 4 SERVINGS

3 tablespoons margarine or butter
¼ cup all-purpose flour
½ teaspoon onion salt
1 egg, slightly beaten
1 tablespoon water
1 tablespoon lemon juice
½ to ¾ cup crushed corn flakes, crackers or
　　bread crumbs
1 lb. fish fillets (½ inch thick)

1. Heat oven to 350°F. Melt margarine in
13×9-inch (3-quart) glass baking dish in
oven. In shallow pan, combine flour and
onion salt.
2. In medium bowl, combine egg, water and
lemon juice. Place corn flakes in another
medium bowl. Coat fish fillets with flour
mixture; dip in egg mixture. Coat with corn
flakes. Place fish in baking dish; turn to coat
with melted margarine.
3. Bake at 350°F. for 15 to 20 minutes or
until fish flakes easily with fork.

NUTRITION INFORMATION PER SERVING: Serving Size: ¼ of Recipe
✦ Calories: 280 ✦ Calories from Fat: 100 ✦ **% DAILY VALUE:** Total Fat:
11 g 17% ✦ Saturated Fat: 2 g 10% ✦ Cholesterol: 100 mg 33% ✦
Sodium: 800 mg 33% ✦ Total Carbohydrate: 20 g 7% ✦ Dietary
Fiber: 1 g 3% ✦ Sugars: 1 g ✦ Protein: 24 g ✦ Vitamin A: 20% ✦
Vitamin C: 10% ✦ Calcium: 2% ✦ Iron: 35% ✦ **DIETARY
EXCHANGES:** 1½ Starch, 3 Lean Meat OR 1½ Carbohydrate, 3 Lean
Meat

Grilled Walleye with Pecan Butter

Grilled Walleye with Pecan Butter

PREP TIME: 25 MINUTES ✦ YIELD: 4 SERVINGS

¼ cup butter, softened
2 teaspoons chopped fresh chives
2 teaspoons orange juice
½ cup chopped pecans, toasted
4 (6-oz.) walleye fillets
¼ teaspoon salt
　Dash coarse ground black pepper

1. GRILL DIRECTIONS: Heat grill. Cut
two 12-inch-square pieces of heavy-duty
foil. With tip of sharp knife, cut 2-inch slits
every 2 inches across foil. Spray foil with
nonstick cooking spray.
2. In small bowl, combine butter, chives,
orange juice and ¼ cup of the pecans; mix
well.
3. When ready to grill, place foil pieces on
gas grill over medium heat or on charcoal
grill 4 to 6 inches from medium coals. Sprinkle walleye fillets with salt and pepper. Place
fillets on foil; cook 8 to 12 minutes or until
fish flakes easily with fork, turning once.
During last minute of cooking time, top fillets with pecan butter. Remove fillets from
heat; place on serving platter. Sprinkle with
remaining ¼ cup pecans.

> **TIP:** To broil walleye, place on broiler pan; broil
> 4 to 6 inches from heat using times above as a
> guide, turning once.

NUTRITION INFORMATION PER SERVING: Serving Size: ¼ of Recipe
✦ Calories: 360 ✦ Calories from Fat: 210 ✦ **% DAILY VALUE:** Total Fat:
23 g 35% ✦ Saturated Fat: 8 g 40% ✦ Cholesterol: 175 mg 58% ✦
Sodium: 340 mg 14% ✦ Total Carbohydrate: 4 g 1% ✦ Dietary
Fiber: 1 g 4% ✦ Sugars: 1 g ✦ Protein: 34 g ✦ Vitamin A: 10% ✦
Vitamin C: 0% ✦ Calcium: 20% ✦ Iron: 15% ✦ **DIETARY
EXCHANGES:** 5 Very Lean Meat, 4 Fat

FISH VARIETIES

SOFT TEXTURED FISH	FLAKY TEXTURED FISH	FIRM TEXTURED FISH
Mild flavor: Flounder, sea trout, sole, skate	**Mild flavor:** Black sea bass, butterfish, cod, haddock, mullet, orange roughy, perch, pollock, pompano, porgy, red snapper, rockfish, shad, tilefish, trout, walleye, whitefish, whiting (hake)	**Mild flavor:** Carp, catfish, dolphin fish (mahi-mahi), grouper, halibut, salmon, shark, striped bass, swordfish, tilapia
Stronger flavor: Bluefish, herring	**Stronger flavor:** Mackerel, salmon, sardine, smelt	**Stronger flavor:** Monkfish, tuna
Best cooking methods: Bake, microwave, panfry, steam	**Best cooking methods:** Bake, broil, grill, microwave, panfry, poach, steam	**Best cooking methods:** Bake, broil, grill, microwave, steam, stir-fry
The delicate flesh needs gentle handling or it may fall apart.	The flesh separates into large flakes when fully cooked.	The flesh is firm and resembles meat.

Salmon à la King

PREP TIME: 25 MINUTES ◆ YIELD: 4 SERVINGS

    1 (11-oz.) can refrigerated soft breadsticks
 ¼ cup margarine or butter
 ½ cup coarsely chopped green bell pepper
 ½ cup sliced celery
    3 tablespoons all-purpose flour
 ¼ teaspoon salt
 1½ cups milk
    1 (14¾-oz.) can salmon, drained, flaked
    1 (2-oz.) jar chopped pimientos, drained
       Fresh dill, if desired

1. Heat oven to 350°F. Separate breadsticks. Stack 3 breadsticks together; stretch to a 10-inch rope. Twist rope; shape into ring, pinching ends to seal. Place on ungreased cookie sheet. Repeat with remaining breadsticks. Bake at 350°F. for 18 to 22 minutes or until golden brown.
2. Meanwhile, melt margarine in large skillet over medium-high heat. Add bell pepper and celery; cook and stir 1 minute. Stir in flour and salt; cook until mixture is smooth and bubbly. Gradually add milk. Cook until mixture boils and thickens, stirring constantly.
3. Gently fold in salmon and pimientos; cook until thoroughly heated. Serve over baked breadstick rings. Garnish with fresh dill.

NUTRITION INFORMATION PER SERVING: Serving Size: ¼ of Recipe ◆ Calories: 530 ◆ Calories from Fat: 220 ◆ **% DAILY VALUE:** Total Fat: 24 g 37% ◆ Saturated Fat: 6 g 30% ◆ Cholesterol: 45 mg 15% ◆ Sodium: 1350 mg 56% ◆ Total Carbohydrate: 48 g 16% ◆ Dietary Fiber: 2 g 8% ◆ Sugars: 10 g ◆ Protein: 28 g ◆ Vitamin A: 30% ◆ Vitamin C: 40% ◆ Calcium: 15% ◆ Iron: 20% ◆ **DIETARY EXCHANGES:** 3 Starch, 3 Lean Meat, 3 Fat OR 3 Carbohydrate, 3 Lean Meat, 3 Fat

Salmon Burgers with Lemon-Dill Sauce

PREP TIME: 25 MINUTES ◆ YIELD: 4 SANDWICHES

SAUCE
 ½ cup mayonnaise or salad dressing
 ¼ cup chopped green onions
    1 tablespoon chopped fresh dill or 1 teaspoon dried dill weed
    2 teaspoons chopped fresh chives
 ¼ teaspoon grated lemon peel
    1 teaspoon lemon juice

BURGERS
    1 (7½-oz.) can salmon, drained, flaked
 ½ cup shredded zucchini
    2 tablespoons unseasoned dry bread crumbs
    2 tablespoons chopped green onions
 ½ teaspoon salt
 ¼ teaspoon pepper
    1 egg, beaten
    4 lettuce leaves
    4 sourdough English muffins, split, toasted

1. In small bowl, combine all sauce ingredients; mix well. Cover; refrigerate 1 hour.

2. Meanwhile, in medium bowl, combine salmon, zucchini, bread crumbs, 2 tablespoons green onions, salt, pepper and egg; mix well. Shape mixture into four 3 to 4-inch patties.

3. Spray large nonstick skillet with nonstick cooking spray. Add patties; cook over medium-high heat for 5 to 8 minutes or until firm and golden brown, turning once.

4. To serve, layer lettuce, burgers and sauce on bottom halves of English muffins. Cover with top halves of muffins.

> **TIP:** To broil burgers, place on oiled broiler pan; broil 4 to 6 inches from heat using times above as a guide, turning once.

NUTRITION INFORMATION PER SERVING: Serving Size: 1 Sandwich ◆ Calories: 440 ◆ Calories from Fat: 250 ◆ **% DAILY VALUE:** Total Fat: 28 g 43% ◆ Saturated Fat: 5 g 25% ◆ Cholesterol: 90 mg 30% ◆ Sodium: 970 mg 40% ◆ Total Carbohydrate: 31 g 10% ◆ Dietary Fiber: 2 g 8% ◆ Sugars: 9 g ◆ Protein: 16 g ◆ Vitamin A: 10% ◆ Vitamin C: 8% ◆ Calcium: 25% ◆ Iron: 15% ◆ **DIETARY EXCHANGES:** 2 Starch, 1½ Lean Meat, 4½ Fat OR 2 Carbohydrate, 1½ Lean Meat, 4½ Fat

Salmon Loaf

PREP TIME: 15 MINUTES (READY IN 1 HOUR 15 MINUTES)
◆ YIELD: 6 SERVINGS

1 (14¾-oz.) can salmon, drained and flaked, reserving liquid
2 eggs, beaten
2 cups soft bread cubes or ⅓ cup unseasoned dry bread crumbs
2 tablespoons finely chopped fresh parsley
¼ teaspoon salt
⅛ teaspoon pepper
1 small onion, chopped
2 tablespoons lemon juice

1. Heat oven to 350°F. Generously grease 8 × 4-inch loaf pan or 8-inch square pan. In large bowl, combine salmon, reserved liquid and all remaining ingredients; mix well. Press in greased loaf pan or form into loaf shape in greased square pan.

2. Bake at 350°F. for 50 to 60 minutes or until loaf is golden brown and knife inserted in center comes out clean. Let stand 5 minutes. Loosen edges and remove from pan. To serve, cut into slices.

> **TIP:** To make ahead, prepare, cover and refrigerate up to 24 hours. Bake as directed above.

NUTRITION INFORMATION PER SERVING: Serving Size: ⅙ of Recipe ◆ Calories: 140 ◆ Calories from Fat: 50 ◆ **% DAILY VALUE:** Total Fat: 6 g 9% ◆ Saturated Fat: 2 g 10% ◆ Cholesterol: 95 mg 32% ◆ Sodium: 490 mg 20% ◆ Total Carbohydrate: 7 g 2% ◆ Dietary Fiber: 1 g 2% ◆ Sugars: 1 g ◆ Protein: 15 g ◆ Vitamin A: 6% ◆ Vitamin C: 4% ◆ Calcium: 2% ◆ Iron: 8% ◆ **DIETARY EXCHANGES:** ½ Starch, 2 Lean Meat OR ½ Carbohydrate, 2 Lean Meat

C O O K ' S N O T E

FISH AND SHELLFISH NUTRITION

Although the precise nutritive value of fish and shellfish varies according to variety and origin, not to mention cooking method, all are good choices for lighter eating. Fish is an excellent source of easily digestible protein and is rich in vitamins and minerals, especially B vitamins, potassium and iodine. Shellfish abound in calcium, phosphorus and magnesium. Researchers have linked consumption of the omega-3 fatty acids found in fish to reduced risk of heart disease and cancer.

Fat content varies by species and even by season, but all fish and shellfish are relatively low in calories. Even high-fat fish contain less fat than most meats, and most of the fat is unsaturated. However, a rich sauce or a dip in melted butter negates the lean profile.

C O O K ' S N O T E

BUYING CANNED SALMON

For salads and entrées in which appearance is important, purchase chinook or sockeye salmon. They are a little bit more expensive than chum or pink varieties, but they break easily into attractive chunks. For loaves and patties in which ingredients are mashed and blended together, the less expensive varieties work fine.

Dill-Marinated Salmon Steaks

PREP TIME: 20 MINUTES (READY IN 2 HOURS
20 MINUTES) ✦ YIELD: 4 SERVINGS

    2 tablespoons lemon juice
    1 tablespoon oil
    1 teaspoon dried dill weed
    ¼ teaspoon salt
    ⅛ teaspoon pepper
    4 (4 to 6-oz.) salmon steaks (1 inch thick)

1. GRILL DIRECTIONS: In small bowl, combine all ingredients except salmon steaks; mix well. Place salmon in shallow nonmetal container or resealable food storage plastic bag. Add lemon juice mixture; turn to coat both sides. Cover; refrigerate at least 2 hours to marinate.
2. Heat grill. Cut four 18×12-inch pieces of heavy-duty foil. Remove salmon from marinade; place 1 steak on each piece of foil. Wrap each packet securely using double-fold seals, allowing room for heat expansion.
3. When ready to grill, place packets, seam side down, on gas grill over medium-high heat or on charcoal grill 4 to 6 inches from medium-high coals. Cook 10 to 15 minutes or until fish flakes easily with fork, turning once. Open packets carefully to allow hot steam to escape.

> **TIP:** To bake salmon, place in 13 x 19-inch (3-quart) baking dish; cover with foil. Bake at 400°F. for 15 to 20 minutes.

Dill-Marinated Salmon Steaks

NUTRITION INFORMATION PER SERVING: Serving Size: ¼ of Recipe ✦ Calories: 310 ✦ Calories from Fat: 150 ✦ **% DAILY VALUE:** Total Fat: 17 g 26% ✦ Saturated Fat: 3 g 15% ✦ Cholesterol: 125 mg 42% ✦ Sodium: 130 mg 5% ✦ Total Carbohydrate: 0 g 0% ✦ Dietary Fiber: 0 g 0% ✦ Sugars: 0 g ✦ Protein: 40 g ✦ Vitamin A: 6% ✦ Vitamin C: 0% ✦ Calcium: 0% ✦ Iron: 4% ✦ **DIETARY EXCHANGES:** 5½ Lean Meat

Lemon-Poached Salmon

PREP TIME: 20 MINUTES ✦ YIELD: 4 SERVINGS

    3 cups water
    2 tablespoons sliced green onions
    ½ lemon, sliced
    ⅛ teaspoon salt
      Dash pepper
    4 (4-oz.) salmon steaks

1. In large skillet, combine all ingredients except salmon. Bring to a boil. Reduce heat to low; simmer 5 minutes to blend flavors.
2. Add salmon; cover and simmer 6 to 9 minutes or until salmon flakes easily with fork. With slotted spoon, remove salmon from liquid; place on serving platter. If desired, garnish with dill and additional lemon slices.

NUTRITION INFORMATION PER SERVING: Serving Size: ¼ of Recipe ✦ Calories: 200 ✦ Calories from Fat: 100 ✦ **% DAILY VALUE:** Total Fat: 11 g 17% ✦ Saturated Fat: 2 g 10% ✦ Cholesterol: 85 mg 28% ✦ Sodium: 65 mg 3% ✦ Total Carbohydrate: 0 g 0% ✦ Dietary Fiber: 0 g 0% ✦ Sugars: 0 g ✦ Protein: 26 g ✦ Vitamin A: 4% ✦ Vitamin C: 0% ✦ Calcium: 0% ✦ Iron: 2% ✦ **DIETARY EXCHANGES:** 3½ Lean Meat

COOK'S NOTE

FISH STEAKS VS. FISH FILLETS

Fish steaks are cross-section slices, usually with a piece of backbone, cut ¾ inch to 1½ inches thick from larger dressed fish. The edible portion is about 85 percent of weight.

Fillets are the sides of fish cut away from the backbone. They are often boneless and skinless. The edible  portion is about 100 percent of the weight.

Fettuccine with Pesto Cream and Salmon

Fettuccine with Pesto Cream and Salmon

PREP TIME: 30 MINUTES ✦ YIELD: 4 (1½-CUP) SERVINGS

    8 oz. uncooked fettuccine
    2 teaspoons olive or vegetable oil
    1 teaspoon grated lemon peel
    1 garlic clove, minced
    ¼ teaspoon salt
      Dash pepper
    2 (6-oz.) salmon fillets
    1 cup whipping cream
    ½ cup purchased pesto
    1 oz. (¼ cup) shredded fresh Parmesan cheese
      Freshly ground black pepper, if desired

1. Cook fettuccine to desired doneness as directed on package. Drain; cover to keep warm.

2. Meanwhile, in small bowl, combine oil, lemon peel, garlic, salt and dash pepper; mix well. Spray broiler pan with nonstick cooking spray. Place salmon, skin side down, on sprayed pan. Brush top of salmon with oil mixture.

3. Broil 3 to 4 inches from heat for 10 minutes or until fish flakes easily with fork.

4. Remove skin from broiled salmon; discard skin. Break salmon into bite-sized pieces.

5. In large saucepan, bring cream just to a boil over medium heat. Add cooked fettuccine; toss to coat. Gently fold salmon and pesto into fettuccine. Sprinkle each serving with cheese and freshly ground pepper.

NUTRITION INFORMATION PER SERVING: Serving Size: 1½ Cups ✦ Calories: 700 ✦ Calories from Fat: 390 ✦ % DAILY VALUE: Total Fat: 43 g 66% ✦ Saturated Fat: 18 g 90% ✦ Cholesterol: 205 mg 68% ✦ Sodium: 560 mg 23% ✦ Total Carbohydrate: 44 g 15% ✦ Dietary Fiber: 2 g 8% ✦ Sugars: 4 g ✦ Protein: 33 g ✦ Vitamin A: 25% ✦ Vitamin C: 0% ✦ Calcium: 20% ✦ Iron: 20% ✦ DIETARY EXCHANGES: 3 Starch, 3½ Lean Meat, 6 Fat OR 3 Carbohydrate, 3½ Lean Meat, 6 Fat

Grilled Salmon with Herbed Tartar Sauce

PREP TIME: 20 MINUTES ✦ YIELD: 4 SERVINGS

SAUCE
    ½ cup mayonnaise
    2 tablespoons chopped fresh herbs (basil, dill weed, chives and/or parsley)
    ¼ teaspoon Worcestershire sauce

SALMON
    2 tablespoons olive or vegetable oil
    1 tablespoon lemon juice
    4 (6-oz.) salmon fillets
    ⅛ teaspoon salt
    ⅛ teaspoon pepper

1. GRILL DIRECTIONS: Heat grill. In blender container or food processor bowl with metal blade, combine all sauce ingredients; blend at high speed until well mixed, stopping often to scrape down sides. Place in serving bowl; refrigerate.

2. In small bowl, combine oil and lemon juice; mix well.

3. When ready to grill, brush salmon fillets with lemon mixture; sprinkle with salt and pepper. Carefully oil grill rack. Place salmon on gas grill over medium heat or on charcoal grill 4 to 6 inches from medium coals. Cook 8 to 12 minutes or until fish flakes easily with fork, turning once. Serve with sauce.

TIP: To broil salmon, place on broiler pan; broil 4 to 6 inches from heat using times above as a guide, turning once.

NUTRITION INFORMATION PER SERVING: Serving Size: ¼ of Recipe ✦ Calories: 520 ✦ Calories from Fat: 360 ✦ % DAILY VALUE: Total Fat: 40 g 62% ✦ Saturated Fat: 6 g 30% ✦ Cholesterol: 140 mg 47% ✦ Sodium: 330 mg 14% ✦ Total Carbohydrate: 1 g 1% ✦ Dietary Fiber: 0 g 0% ✦ Sugars: 1 g ✦ Protein: 40 g ✦ Vitamin A: 10% ✦ Vitamin C: 2% ✦ Calcium: 0% ✦ Iron: 6% ✦ DIETARY EXCHANGES: 5½ Lean Meat, 6 Fat

Grilled Salmon with Herbed Tartar Sauce

Veracruz-Style Red Snapper

PREP TIME: 45 MINUTES ◆ YIELD: 6 SERVINGS

SAUCE
  2 tablespoons margarine or butter
  1 cup coarsely chopped onions
  2 garlic cloves, minced, or 1 teaspoon
     chopped garlic in water (from 4.5-oz. jar)
  1 (14.5 or 16-oz.) can whole tomatoes,
     undrained, cut up
  ½ cup sliced pimiento-stuffed green olives
  2 to 4 tablespoons chopped green chiles
  1 tablespoon capers, if desired
  1 tablespoon lemon juice

SNAPPER
  1½ lb. red snapper steaks (1 inch thick)*
  2 to 4 tablespoons margarine or butter,
     melted
  1 tablespoon lemon juice
     Dash paprika
  2 tablespoons chopped fresh parsley or
     coriander, if desired

1. GRILL DIRECTIONS: Melt 2 table-spoons margarine in medium saucepan over medium-high heat. Add onions and garlic; cook and stir until tender. Add all remaining sauce ingredients; blend well. Bring to a boil. Reduce heat to low; simmer 30 to 45 minutes or until sauce thickens, stirring occasionally.
2. Meanwhile, heat grill. When ready to grill, carefully oil grill rack. Place snapper steaks on gas grill over medium heat or on charcoal grill 4 to 6 inches from medium coals. Brush steaks with 2 tablespoons of the melted margarine. Cook 10 to 15 minutes or until fish flakes easily with fork, turning once and brushing occasionally with remaining margarine.
3. To serve, arrange fish on serving platter; drizzle with 1 tablespoon lemon juice and sprinkle with paprika. Spoon warm sauce over fish and sprinkle with chopped parsley.

TIPS: * Red snapper fillets, halibut steaks or fillets, or swordfish steaks or fillets can be sub-stituted for red snapper steaks.
   To broil snapper, place on oiled broiler pan; broil 4 to 6 inches from heat using times above as a guide, turning once and brushing occasion-ally with remaining margarine.

NUTRITION INFORMATION PER SERVING: Serving Size: ⅙ of Recipe ◆ Calories: 280 ◆ Calories from Fat: 140 ◆ % DAILY VALUE: Total Fat: 15 g 23% ◆ Saturated Fat: 3 g 15% ◆ Cholesterol: 45 mg 15% ◆ Sodium: 620 mg 26% ◆ Total Carbohydrate: 7 g 2% ◆ Dietary Fiber: 2 g 8% ◆ Sugars: 3 g ◆ Protein: 28 g ◆ Vitamin A: 25% ◆ Vitamin C: 40% ◆ Calcium: 8% ◆ Iron: 6% ◆ DIETARY EXCHANGES: 1½ Vegetable, 3½ Very Lean Meat, 2½ Fat

Orange Roughy with Dill Butter

PREP TIME: 20 MINUTES (READY IN 40 MINUTES)
◆ YIELD: 4 SERVINGS

  3 tablespoons butter
  4 (4 to 6-oz.) orange roughy fillets
  ½ teaspoon dried dill weed
     Dash salt
     Dash pepper
  1½ teaspoons butter
  2 tablespoons unseasoned dry bread crumbs

1. Heat oven to 350°F. Melt 3 tablespoons butter in 12 × 8-inch (2-quart) baking dish in oven.
2. Place orange roughy in dish; turn to coat with butter. Sprinkle with dill, salt and pepper.
3. Bake at 350°F. for 15 to 20 minutes or until fish flakes easily with fork.
4. Meanwhile, melt 1½ teaspoons butter in small skillet or saucepan over medium heat. Add bread crumbs; cook until crumbs are light golden brown, stirring constantly. Sprinkle over fish during last 3 minutes of baking time.

NUTRITION INFORMATION PER SERVING: Serving Size: ¼ of Recipe ◆ Calories: 190 ◆ Calories from Fat: 100 ◆ % DAILY VALUE: Total Fat: 11 g 17% ◆ Saturated Fat: 6 g 30% ◆ Cholesterol: 55 mg 18% ◆ Sodium: 250 mg 10% ◆ Total Carbohydrate: 2 g 1% ◆ Dietary Fiber: 0 g 0% ◆ Sugars: 0 g ◆ Protein: 21 g ◆ Vitamin A: 10% ◆ Vitamin C: 0% ◆ Calcium: 6% ◆ Iron: 2% ◆ DIETARY EXCHANGES: 3 Very Lean Meat, 2 Fat

Panfried Trout with Caper Sauce

PREP TIME: 20 MINUTES ◆ YIELD: 4 SERVINGS

  1 tablespoon lemon juice
  1 teaspoon dried dill weed
  ¼ teaspoon pepper
  4 (8-oz.) dressed whole trout
     Salt
  ⅓ cup all-purpose flour
  4 tablespoons margarine or butter

SAUCE
  1 tablespoon all-purpose flour
  ¼ teaspoon salt
  1 cup milk
  2 tablespoons capers, drained
  1 tablespoon lemon juice
  2 teaspoons dried parsley flakes

1. In small bowl, combine 1 tablespoon lemon juice, dill and pepper. Sprinkle inside of each trout with salt and the lemon mixture. Place ⅓ cup flour in shallow dish. Add trout; turn to coat.

2. Melt 2 tablespoons of the margarine in large skillet over medium heat. Add 2 trout; cook about 10 minutes or until fish is lightly browned and flakes easily with fork at thickest portion, turning once. Place fish on platter; cover to keep warm. Repeat with remaining 2 tablespoons margarine and fish.

3. Stir 1 tablespoon flour and 1/4 teaspoon salt into pan drippings until smooth and bubbly. Gradually add milk; cook until mixture boils and thickens, stirring constantly. Stir in capers, 1 tablespoon lemon juice and parsley. Serve over fish.

NUTRITION INFORMATION PER SERVING: Serving Size: ¼ of Recipe ◆ Calories: 440 ◆ Calories from Fat: 210 ◆ **% DAILY VALUE:** Total Fat: 23 g 35% ◆ Saturated Fat: 6 g 30% ◆ Cholesterol: 125 mg 42% ◆ Sodium: 620 mg 26% ◆ Total Carbohydrate: 13 g 4% ◆ Dietary Fiber: 0 g 0% ◆ Sugars: 3 g ◆ Protein: 44 g ◆ Vitamin A: 15% ◆ Vitamin C: 8% ◆ Calcium: 25% ◆ Iron: 8% ◆ **DIETARY EXCHANGES:** 1 Starch, 6 Very Lean Meat, 3½ Fat OR 1 Carbohydrate, 6 Very Lean Meat, 3½ Fat

Flounder en Papillote

PREP TIME: 25 MINUTES ◆ YIELD: 4 SERVINGS

    2 tablespoons margarine or butter
    ½ cup chopped red bell pepper
    ¼ cup sliced green onions
    1 (4.5-oz.) jar sliced mushrooms, drained
    2 tablespoons all-purpose flour
    ¼ teaspoon salt
    ⅛ teaspoon white pepper
    ⅓ cup milk
    2 tablespoons white wine or sherry
      Parchment paper or foil
    1 lb. flounder, sole or orange roughy fillets

1. Heat oven to 425°F. Melt margarine in medium saucepan over medium heat. Add bell pepper, onions and mushrooms; cook and stir 2 minutes. Stir in flour, salt and pepper; cook until mixture is bubbly. Gradually add milk and wine. Cook until mixture boils and thickens, stirring constantly. Remove from heat.

2. Cut four 10 × 12-inch heart-shaped pieces from parchment paper. Divide flounder into 4 equal portions; place each portion on left half of a heart-shaped parchment. Spoon sauce over flounder. Bring right side of parchment over flounder to meet left side of

parchment; seal open edges securely with double-fold seals. Place on ungreased cookie sheet.

3. Bake at 425°F. for 10 to 12 minutes or until paper begins to turn golden brown. To serve, cut X-shaped slit in top of parchment; carefully tear back to expose flounder.

NUTRITION INFORMATION PER SERVING: Serving Size: ¼ of Recipe ◆ Calories: 200 ◆ Calories from Fat: 70 ◆ **% DAILY VALUE:** Total Fat: 8 g 12% ◆ Saturated Fat: 2 g 10% ◆ Cholesterol: 60 mg 20% ◆ Sodium: 440 mg 18% ◆ Total Carbohydrate: 7 g 2% ◆ Dietary Fiber: 1 g 4% ◆ Sugars: 3 g ◆ Protein: 23 g ◆ Vitamin A: 20% ◆ Vitamin C: 30% ◆ Calcium: 6% ◆ Iron: 6% ◆ **DIETARY EXCHANGES:** 1½ Vegetable, 3 Very Lean Meat, 1 Fat

COOK'S NOTE

BUYING CANNED TUNA

Canned tuna comes in several forms: fancy or solid-pack, chunk-style or flaked. When appearance is important, buy fancy or solid-pack. Chunk-style and flaked tuna are good for casseroles and sandwich fillings. Canned tuna is available packed in water or vegetable oil; it may also be available in low-salt or no-salt form.

Creamed Tuna on Toast

PREP TIME: 15 MINUTES ◆ YIELD: 6 SERVINGS

    ½ cup milk
    1 (10¾-oz.) can condensed cream of celery
      soup
    ½ teaspoon instant minced onion
    1 (15-oz.) can sweet peas, drained
    1 (6-oz.) can water-packed tuna, drained, flaked
    1 tablespoon chopped pimientos
    6 to 8 slices bread, toasted, buttered if desired

1. In medium saucepan, combine milk, soup and onion; cook over medium heat until smooth, stirring frequently.

2. Stir in peas, tuna and pimientos; cook until thoroughly heated, stirring occasionally. Serve over toast.

NUTRITION INFORMATION PER SERVING: Serving Size: ⅙ of Recipe ◆ Calories: 240 ◆ Calories from Fat: 80 ◆ **% DAILY VALUE:** Total Fat: 9 g 14% ◆ Saturated Fat: 4 g 20% ◆ Cholesterol: 30 mg 10% ◆ Sodium: 830 mg 35% ◆ Total Carbohydrate: 27 g 9% ◆ Dietary Fiber: 3 g 12% ◆ Sugars: 4 g ◆ Protein: 12 g ◆ Vitamin A: 15% ◆ Vitamin C: 10% ◆ Calcium: 10% ◆ Iron: 10% ◆ **DIETARY EXCHANGES:** 2 Starch, 1 Very Lean Meat, 1 Fat OR 2 Carbohydrate, 1 Very Lean Meat, 1 Fat

Tarragon Grilled Fish and Vegetables

Tarragon Grilled Fish and Vegetables

PREP TIME: 35 MINUTES ◆ YIELD: 4 SERVINGS

- 2 tablespoons olive or vegetable oil
- 2 carrots, cut into julienne strips (1½ x ¼ x ¼ inch)
- 1 zucchini, cut into julienne strips (1½ x ¼ x ¼ inch)
- 1 small red bell pepper, cut into thin strips
- ½ cup sliced red onion
- 4 (6-oz.) orange roughy fillets
- 4 teaspoons chopped fresh tarragon or 1½ teaspoons dried tarragon leaves
- 2 tablespoons margarine or butter, chilled

1. GRILL DIRECTIONS: Heat grill. Heat oil in medium skillet over medium-high heat until hot. Add carrots, zucchini, bell pepper and onion; cook and stir 2 to 3 minutes or until vegetables are crisp-tender.

2. Cut four 18 × 12-inch pieces of heavy-duty foil. Place 1 orange roughy fillet on each; sprinkle with salt and pepper, if desired. Top each fillet with ¼ of vegetable mixture, tarragon and margarine. Wrap each packet securely using double-fold seals, allowing room for heat expansion.

3. When ready to grill, place packets, seam side up, on gas grill over medium heat or on charcoal grill 4 to 6 inches from medium coals. Cook 12 to 18 minutes or until fish flakes easily with fork, rearranging packets several times during cooking. Open packets carefully to allow hot steam to escape.

TIP: To bake packets in oven, place on 15 x 10 x 1-inch baking pan. Bake at 400°F. for 15 to 20 minutes.

COOK'S NOTE

GRILLING FISH

Almost any fish can be grilled, as long as you grease the grill and the fish itself to prevent sticking. Thick steaks or fillets of firm-textured fish, such as salmon or swordfish, can be placed directly on the grill. Swordfish, tuna and other "meaty" fish also work well in kabobs. For more delicate fish, such as bluefish, butterfish or whitefish, use a well-greased grill basket or a piece of greased heavy-duty foil. You can improvise a grill basket by sandwiching the fish between two ordinary cake racks and wiring them together.

Fish Creole

PREP TIME: 35 MINUTES ◆ YIELD: 4 SERVINGS

- 1 lb. fish fillets
- 1 tablespoon margarine or butter
- ⅓ cup chopped onion
- ¼ cup chopped celery
- 2 tablespoons finely chopped green bell pepper
- 2 to 3 teaspoons sugar
- ¼ teaspoon dried oregano leaves
- ⅛ teaspoon pepper
- 1 (8-oz.) can stewed tomatoes, undrained, cut up

Fish Creole

1. Heat oven to 350°F. Arrange fish fillets in ungreased 12 × 8-inch (2-quart) or 8-inch square baking dish.
2. Melt margarine in medium skillet over medium-high heat. Add onion, celery and bell pepper; cook and stir until tender. Stir in all remaining ingredients. Spoon mixture over fish.
3. Bake at 350°F. for 15 to 20 minutes or until fish flakes easily with fork.

NUTRITION INFORMATION PER SERVING: Serving Size: ¼ of Recipe ◆ Calories: 160 ◆ Calories from Fat: 35 ◆ % DAILY VALUE: Total Fat: 4 g 6% ◆ Saturated Fat: 1 g 5% ◆ Cholesterol: 50 mg 17% ◆ Sodium: 230 mg 10% ◆ Total Carbohydrate: 9 g 3% ◆ Dietary Fiber: 1 g 4% ◆ Sugars: 5 g ◆ Protein: 21 g ◆ Vitamin A: 10% ◆ Vitamin C: 15% ◆ Calcium: 4% ◆ Iron: 6% ◆ DIETARY EXCHANGES: 2 Vegetable, 2½ Very Lean Meat, ½ Fat

Fresh Tuna with Gremolata

PREP TIME: 20 MINUTES ◆ YIELD: 4 SERVINGS

¼ cup finely chopped fresh parsley
2 tablespoons grated lemon peel
1 teaspoon olive oil
1 garlic clove, minced
4 (4-oz.) tuna steaks (1 inch thick)
¼ teaspoon salt

1. In small bowl, combine parsley, lemon peel, oil and garlic; mix well. Set aside.
2. Line broiler pan with foil; spray with nonstick cooking spray. Place tuna steaks on foil-lined pan; sprinkle with salt.
3. Broil 4 to 6 inches from heat for 4 to 5 minutes on each side or until fish flakes easily with fork, topping with parsley mixture during last 1 minute of broiling time.

NUTRITION INFORMATION PER SERVING: Serving Size: ¼ of Recipe ◆ Calories: 170 ◆ Calories from Fat: 60 ◆ % DAILY VALUE: Total Fat: 7 g 11% ◆ Saturated Fat: 2 g 10% ◆ Cholesterol: 45 mg 15% ◆ Sodium: 180 mg 8% ◆ Total Carbohydrate: 1 g 1% ◆ Dietary Fiber: 0 g 0% ◆ Sugars: 0 g ◆ Protein: 27 g ◆ Vitamin A: 50% ◆ Vitamin C: 10% ◆ Calcium: 0% ◆ Iron: 8% ◆ DIETARY EXCHANGES: 4 Very Lean Meat, 1 Fat

Tuna Casserole

PREP TIME: 20 MINUTES (READY IN 55 MINUTES) ◆ YIELD: 6 (1¼-CUP) SERVINGS

1 (7-oz.) pkg. (1½ cups) uncooked elbow macaroni
1 cup milk
4 oz. (1 cup) shredded Cheddar cheese
1 (10¾-oz.) can condensed cream of mushroom soup

1 (6-oz.) can tuna, drained, flaked
1 (4-oz.) can mushroom pieces and stems, drained
2 tablespoons chopped pimientos, if desired
2 teaspoons instant minced onion
½ teaspoon dry mustard
½ cup crushed potato chips

1. Heat oven to 350°F. Grease 2-quart casserole. Cook macaroni in large saucepan or Dutch oven to desired doneness as directed on package. Drain; return to saucepan.
2. Add all remaining ingredients except potato chips to cooked macaroni; stir to combine. Pour mixture into greased casserole; sprinkle with potato chips.
3. Bake at 350°F. for 25 to 35 minutes or until thoroughly heated.

NUTRITION INFORMATION PER SERVING: Serving Size: 1¼ Cups ◆ Calories: 330 ◆ Calories from Fat: 120 ◆ % DAILY VALUE: Total Fat: 13 g 20% ◆ Saturated Fat: 6 g 30% ◆ Cholesterol: 30 mg 10% ◆ Sodium: 660 mg 28% ◆ Total Carbohydrate: 35 g 12% ◆ Dietary Fiber: 2 g 8% ◆ Sugars: 5 g ◆ Protein: 18 g ◆ Vitamin A: 10% ◆ Vitamin C: 20% ◆ Calcium: 20% ◆ Iron: 10% ◆ DIETARY EXCHANGES: 2½ Starch, 1½ Very Lean Meat, 2 Fat OR 2½ Carbohydrate, 1½ Very Lean Meat, 2 Fat

Tuna Salad Buns

PREP TIME: 25 MINUTES ◆ YIELD: 6 SANDWICHES

4 oz. (1 cup) cubed or shredded American or Cheddar cheese
¼ cup sliced pimiento-stuffed green olives
2 tablespoons chopped onion
2 tablespoons chopped green bell pepper
2 tablespoons pickle relish, drained
⅓ cup mayonnaise or salad dressing
1 (6-oz.) can water-packed tuna, drained, flaked
6 sandwich buns, split

1. Heat oven to 350°F. In medium bowl, combine all ingredients except sandwich buns; mix well. Fill buns with mixture.* Wrap each in foil. Place on ungreased cookie sheet.
2. Bake at 350°F. for 15 minutes or until cheese melts.

TIP: * For open-faced sandwiches, spread filling on bun halves or toasted bread. Broil 3 to 5 minutes or until cheese melts.

NUTRITION INFORMATION PER SERVING: Serving Size: 1 Sandwich ◆ Calories: 330 ◆ Calories from Fat: 170 ◆ % DAILY VALUE: Total Fat: 19 g 29% ◆ Saturated Fat: 6 g 30% ◆ Cholesterol: 35 mg 12% ◆ Sodium: 840 mg 35% ◆ Total Carbohydrate: 25 g 8% ◆ Dietary Fiber: 1 g 4% ◆ Sugars: 7 g ◆ Protein: 15 g ◆ Vitamin A: 6% ◆ Vitamin C: 2% ◆ Calcium: 20% ◆ Iron: 10% ◆ DIETARY EXCHANGES: 1½ Starch, 1½ Very Lean Meat, 3½ Fat OR 1½ Carbohydrate, 1½ Very Lean Meat, 3½ Fat

FISH IN THE MICROWAVE

Microwave cooking is a good method for fish, particularly lean fish, because it preserves the delicate flavor and natural moistness. It takes only about three minutes per pound on HIGH. For even cooking, arrange fish fillets like the spokes of a wheel, with the thicker portions of the fillets at the outer rim of the baking dish. You can tuck part of the thin end under the fillet for more even thickness. Cover the fish to keep it moist, using microwave-safe plastic wrap or a covered casserole. If your microwave oven has no automatic carousel, turn the dish halfway through cooking.

Check for doneness after the minimum suggested cooking time. If necessary, continue to cook, checking every 30 to 60 seconds. To avoid overcooking, stop when the outer flesh is opaque but the center is still translucent. Let fish stand, covered, a few minutes to finish cooking.

Creamy Parsley Sauce

PREP TIME: 20 MINUTES ♦ YIELD: ⅓ CUP

¼ cup mayonnaise or salad dressing
1 tablespoon chopped fresh parsley
¼ teaspoon salt
Dash garlic powder
2 tablespoons sour cream
1½ teaspoons lemon juice

In small bowl, combine all ingredients; mix well. Cover; refrigerate 15 minutes or until chilled.

NUTRITION INFORMATION PER SERVING: Serving Size: 1 Tablespoon ♦ Calories: 90 ♦ Calories from Fat: 90 ♦ % DAILY VALUE: Total Fat: 10 g 15% ♦ Saturated Fat: 2 g 10% ♦ Cholesterol: 10 mg 3% ♦ Sodium: 170 mg 7% ♦ Total Carbohydrate: 1 g 1% ♦ Dietary Fiber: 0 g 0% ♦ Sugars: 1 g ♦ Protein: 0 g ♦ Vitamin A: 2% ♦ Vitamin C: 2% ♦ Calcium: 0% ♦ Iron: 0% ♦ DIETARY EXCHANGES: 2 Fat

Grilled Whitefish with Dill Tartar Sauce

PREP TIME: 15 MINUTES ♦ YIELD: 4 SERVINGS

SAUCE
⅓ cup mayonnaise or salad dressing
1 tablespoon sweet pickle relish
1 tablespoon chopped fresh dill or 1 teaspoon dried dill weed

FISH
¼ cup butter, melted
1 teaspoon lemon juice
4 (4-oz.) whitefish, haddock or orange roughy fillets

1. GRILL DIRECTIONS: Heat grill. In small bowl, combine all sauce ingredients; mix well. Set aside. In separate small bowl, combine butter and lemon juice; blend well.
2. When ready to grill, carefully oil grill rack. Place whitefish on gas grill over medium heat or on charcoal grill 4 to 6 inches from medium coals. Brush with butter mixture. Cook 6 to 9 minutes or until fish flakes easily with fork, turning once and brushing occasionally with butter mixture. Serve with sauce.

TIP: To broil whitefish, place on broiler pan; broil 4 to 6 inches from heat using times above as a guide, turning once and brushing occasionally with butter mixture.

NUTRITION INFORMATION PER SERVING: Serving Size: ¼ of Recipe ♦ Calories: 390 ♦ Calories from Fat: 300 ♦ % DAILY VALUE: Total Fat: 33 g 51% ♦ Saturated Fat: 10 g 50% ♦ Cholesterol: 110 mg 37% ♦ Sodium: 310 mg 13% ♦ Total Carbohydrate: 2 g 1% ♦ Dietary Fiber: 0 g 0% ♦ Sugars: 2 g ♦ Protein: 22 g ♦ Vitamin A: 15% ♦ Vitamin C: 0% ♦ Calcium: 4% ♦ Iron: 4% ♦ DIETARY EXCHANGES: 3 Very Lean Meat, 6 Fat

Savory Marinated Fish

PREP TIME: 20 MINUTES ♦ YIELD: 6 SERVINGS

1½ lb. fish fillets
½ cup dry white wine or apple juice
¼ cup lemon juice
1 garlic clove, minced
½ teaspoon dried savory or thyme leaves
Lemon, if desired

1. Arrange fish fillets in single layer in ungreased 12 × 8-inch (2-quart) baking dish. In small bowl, combine wine, lemon juice, garlic and savory; pour over fish. Cover with plastic wrap; refrigerate 1 to 4 hours to marinate, turning occasionally.

2. Remove fish from marinade. Arrange, skin side down, on broiler pan. Broil 4 to 6 inches from heat for 4 to 8 minutes or until fish flakes easily with fork, brushing occasionally with marinade. Discard any remaining marinade. Garnish with lemon.

NUTRITION INFORMATION PER SERVING: Serving Size: 1/6 of Recipe • Calories: 110 • Calories from Fat: 10 • % DAILY VALUE: Total Fat: 4 g 2% • Saturated Fat: 0 g 0% • Cholesterol: 50 mg 17% • Sodium: 70 mg 3% • Total Carbohydrate: 2 g 1% • Dietary Fiber: 0 g 0% • Sugars: 1 g • Protein: 20 g • Vitamin A: 0% • Vitamin C: 10% • Calcium: 0% • Iron: 4% • DIETARY EXCHANGES: 3 Very Lean Meat

VARIATIONS

Italian Marinated Fish: Substitute 1 cup purchased Italian salad dressing, 1 tablespoon lemon juice and 1/2 teaspoon salt for the wine, lemon juice, garlic and savory.

Wine Marinated Fish: Reduce wine to 1/4 cup. Substitute 1/4 cup oil, 1 thinly sliced lemon and 1 tablespoon minced fresh parsley for the lemon juice, garlic and savory.

Italian Barbecued Swordfish Steaks with Tomato Relish

PREP TIME: 30 MINUTES ✦ YIELD: 4 SERVINGS

FISH
1/2 cup purchased fat-free Italian salad dressing
1 teaspoon paprika
1/4 teaspoon coarse ground black pepper
4 (4 to 6-oz.) swordfish steaks (1 inch thick)

RELISH
1 large tomato, seeded, chopped
1 (2 1/4-oz.) can sliced ripe olives, drained
1 to 2 tablespoons chopped fresh basil or parsley

1. GRILL DIRECTIONS: In small bowl, combine dressing, paprika and pepper; mix well. Place swordfish steaks in resealable food storage plastic bag. Pour dressing mixture over fish; seal bag. Turn bag to coat both sides of fish. Refrigerate 15 minutes to marinate.

2. Meanwhile, heat grill. In medium bowl, combine tomato, olives and basil; mix well.

3. When ready to grill, carefully oil grill rack. Remove fish from marinade; reserve marinade. Place fish on gas grill over medium heat or on charcoal grill 4 to 6 inches from medium-high coals. Cook 10 to 13 minutes or until fish flakes easily with fork, turning once and brushing occasionally with marinade. Discard any remaining marinade. Serve relish with fish.

TIP: To broil swordfish, place on sprayed broiler pan; broil 4 to 6 inches from heat using times above as a guide, turning once and brushing occasionally with reserved marinade.

NUTRITION INFORMATION PER SERVING: Serving Size: 1/4 of Recipe • Calories: 220 • Calories from Fat: 70 • % DAILY VALUE: Total Fat: 8 g 12% • Saturated Fat: 2 g 10% • Cholesterol: 60 mg 20% • Sodium: 570 mg 24% • Total Carbohydrate: 6 g 2% • Dietary Fiber: 1 g 4% • Sugars: 3 g • Protein: 31 g • Vitamin A: 20% • Vitamin C: 15% • Calcium: 2% • Iron: 10% • DIETARY EXCHANGES: 1/2 Starch, 4 Very Lean Meat, 1 Fat OR 1/2 Carbohydrate, 4 Very Lean Meat, 1 Fat

Catfish Cakes

PREP TIME: 25 MINUTES ✦ YIELD: 5 SERVINGS

1 lb. catfish fillets
3/4 cup cornmeal
1 teaspoon baking powder
1/4 cup chopped green onions
1/4 cup finely chopped red or green bell pepper
1 teaspoon dried Creole seasoning
1/4 cup buttermilk
1 egg
2 to 3 tablespoons oil

1. Poach catfish following directions in Poached Fish, page 192.

2. Place catfish in large bowl; break into small pieces with fork. Add cornmeal, baking powder, onions, bell pepper and Creole seasoning; mix well. In small bowl, combine buttermilk and egg; mix well. Add to catfish mixture; mix well.

3. Heat 1 tablespoon of the oil on griddle or in large skillet over medium-high heat. Drop catfish mixture by rounded tablespoonfuls onto hot griddle; flatten to form patty. Cook 2 to 4 minutes or until lightly browned, turning once during cooking. Add remaining 1 to 2 tablespoons oil as needed during cooking.

NUTRITION INFORMATION PER SERVING: Serving Size: 1/5 of Recipe • Calories: 300 • Calories from Fat: 120 • % DAILY VALUE: Total Fat: 13 g 20% • Saturated Fat: 2 g 10% • Cholesterol: 85 mg 28% • Sodium: 360 mg 15% • Total Carbohydrate: 25 g 8% • Dietary Fiber: 2 g 8% • Sugars: 2 g • Protein: 20 g • Vitamin A: 15% • Vitamin C: 10% • Calcium: 8% • Iron: 8% • DIETARY EXCHANGES: 1 1/2 Starch, 2 Medium-Fat Meat, 1/2 Fat OR 1 1/2 Carbohydrate, 2 Medium-Fat Meat, 1/2 Fat

Broiled Snapper with Cilantro Sauce

PREP TIME: 25 MINUTES ◆ YIELD: 6 SERVINGS

SAUCE
- ½ cup sour cream
- ¼ cup chopped fresh cilantro
- ¼ cup mayonnaise or salad dressing
- 2 tablespoons chopped fresh parsley
- 1 teaspoon chopped shallots

SNAPPER
- 2 tablespoons margarine or butter, melted
- 1 tablespoon chopped fresh parsley
- 1 tablespoon lemon juice
- 4 (6 to 8-oz.) red snapper fillets (¾ to 1 inch thick)

1. In blender container, combine all sauce ingredients; blend on high speed until well mixed. Set aside.

2. In small bowl, combine margarine, 1 tablespoon parsley and lemon juice; mix well. Brush margarine mixture over snapper fillets. If desired, sprinkle fillets with salt and pepper. Place fillets, skin side down, on broiler pan.

3. Broil 4 to 6 inches from heat for 8 to 10 minutes or until fish flakes easily with fork. Serve sauce with fillets.

NUTRITION INFORMATION PER SERVING: Serving Size: ⅙ of Recipe ◆ Calories: 290 ◆ Calories from Fat: 150 ◆ **% DAILY VALUE:** Total Fat: 17 g 26% ◆ Saturated Fat: 5 g 25% ◆ Cholesterol: 70 mg 23% ◆ Sodium: 210 mg 9% ◆ Total Carbohydrate: 2 g 1% ◆ Dietary Fiber: 0 g 0% ◆ Sugars: 1 g ◆ Protein: 32 g ◆ Vitamin A: 15% ◆ Vitamin C: 6% ◆ Calcium: 8% ◆ Iron: 2% ◆ **DIETARY EXCHANGES:** 4½ Very Lean Meat, 3 Fat

Broiled Snapper with Cilantro Sauce

Fish Fillets with California Salsa

Fish Fillets with California Salsa

PREP TIME: 20 MINUTES ◆ YIELD: 4 SERVINGS

SALSA
- 1½ cups chopped tomato
- 1 cup chopped peeled ripe avocado
- ¼ cup sliced green onions
- 2 tablespoons chopped fresh cilantro
- ½ teaspoon salt
- 2 jalapeño chiles, chopped

FISH
- 2 tablespoons oil
- 2 tablespoons lime juice
- 1 lb. orange roughy fillets

1. GRILL DIRECTIONS: Heat grill. Cut two 12-inch-square pieces of heavy-duty foil; pierce several holes in foil. In medium bowl, combine all salsa ingredients; mix well. Set aside.

2. In small bowl, combine oil and lime juice; mix well.

3. When ready to grill, place foil pieces on gas grill over medium heat or on charcoal grill 4 to 6 inches from medium coals. Brush fish fillets with oil mixture; place on foil pieces. Cook 6 to 7 minutes or until fish flakes easily with fork, turning once. Serve salsa over grilled fish.

TIP: To broil fish, place directly on broiler pan; broil 4 to 6 inches from heat using times above as a guide, turning once.

NUTRITION INFORMATION PER SERVING: Serving Size: ¼ of Recipe ♦ Calories: 230 ♦ Calories from Fat: 130 ♦ **% DAILY VALUE:** Total Fat: 14 g 22% ♦ Saturated Fat: 2 g 10% ♦ Cholesterol: 25 mg 8% ♦ Sodium: 350 mg 15% ♦ Total Carbohydrate: 8 g 3% ♦ Dietary Fiber: 3 g 12% ♦ Sugars: 3 g ♦ Protein: 18 g ♦ Vitamin A: 15% ♦ Vitamin C: 40% ♦ Calcium: 4% ♦ Iron: 6% ♦ **DIETARY EXCHANGES:** 2 Vegetable, 2 Very Lean Meat, 2½ Fat

Steamed Clams

PREP TIME: 30 MINUTES ♦ YIELD: 4 SERVINGS

> 4 lb. soft-shell clams (about 24)
> 2 teaspoons salt
> ¼ cup butter, melted, or Clarified Butter, page 215

1. Wash clams thoroughly under cold running water. Place in large bowl; cover with cold water and salt. Let stand 15 minutes. Drain.
2. In large saucepan, bring ½ inch water to a boil. Add clams. Cover tightly; steam over medium heat for 5 to 10 minutes or until shells open.
3. Remove any sand from cooking broth by straining through several layers of cheesecloth. Serve clams with cups of cooking broth and melted butter.

NUTRITION INFORMATION PER SERVING: Serving Size: ¼ of Recipe ♦ Calories: 220 ♦ Calories from Fat: 120 ♦ **% DAILY VALUE:** Total Fat: 13 g 20% ♦ Saturated Fat: 7 g 35% ♦ Cholesterol: 90 mg 30% ♦ Sodium: 210 mg 9% ♦ Total Carbohydrate: 4 g 1% ♦ Dietary Fiber: 0 g 0% ♦ Sugars: 0 g ♦ Protein: 22 g ♦ Vitamin A: 20% ♦ Vitamin C: 20% ♦ Calcium: 8% ♦ Iron: 130% ♦ **DIETARY EXCHANGES:** 3 Very Lean Meat, 2½ Fat

Clam Sauce with Linguine

PREP TIME: 25 MINUTES ♦ YIELD: 3 SERVINGS

> 6 oz. uncooked linguine
> 2 tablespoons olive or vegetable oil
> ¼ cup finely chopped onion
> 1 garlic clove, minced
> 2 tablespoons chopped fresh parsley
> ½ teaspoon dried oregano leaves
> ½ teaspoon dried basil leaves
> ⅛ teaspoon pepper
> ¼ cup dry white wine
> 1 (6½-oz.) can minced clams, drained, reserving liquid
> 2 tablespoons grated Parmesan cheese, if desired

1. Cook linguine to desired doneness as directed on package. Drain; cover to keep warm.
2. Meanwhile, heat oil in medium skillet over medium-high heat. Add onion and garlic; cook 1 to 2 minutes or until onion is tender, stirring constantly. Stir in parsley, oregano, basil, pepper, wine and reserved clam liquid. Cook 5 minutes, stirring constantly.
3. Add clams; cook until thoroughly heated. Serve sauce over cooked linguine. Sprinkle each serving with Parmesan cheese.

NUTRITION INFORMATION PER SERVING: Serving Size: ⅓ of Recipe ♦ Calories: 370 ♦ Calories from Fat: 110 ♦ **% DAILY VALUE:** Total Fat: 12 g 18% ♦ Saturated Fat: 2 g 10% ♦ Cholesterol: 25 mg 8% ♦ Sodium: 190 mg 8% ♦ Total Carbohydrate: 46 g 15% ♦ Dietary Fiber: 2 g 8% ♦ Sugars: 3 g ♦ Protein: 17 g ♦ Vitamin A: 8% ♦ Vitamin C: 15% ♦ Calcium: 10% ♦ Iron: 60% ♦ **DIETARY EXCHANGES:** 3 Starch, 1 Very Lean Meat, 2 Fat OR 3 Carbohydrate, 1 Very Lean Meat, 2 Fat

Clam Sauce with Linguine

COOK'S NOTE

HOW TO PEEL SHRIMP

 To peel or shell shrimp, remove legs first. Using your fingers, open shell lengthwise down the belly of the shrimp. Starting at the head end, pull the shell away from the body. The tail can either be left intact or removed by gently pulling it off.

HOW TO DEVEIN SHRIMP

To devein, use a sharp knife to make  a shallow cut down the back of the shrimp. Use the tip of the knife to pull out the dark vein running down the back. Thoroughly rinse under cold running water.

Deveining is optional. The black vein that usually runs along the outer curve is not harmful and has no flavor, but some people find it unappetizing.

Batter-Fried Shrimp or Scallops

PREP TIME: 25 MINUTES ◆ YIELD: 4 SERVINGS

    1 lb. shelled deveined uncooked medium
        shrimp or scallops
    Oil for frying
    ½ cup milk
    1 egg
    ½ cup all-purpose flour
    ½ teaspoon salt
    Dash hot pepper sauce

1. Heat 1 to 1½ inches oil in Dutch oven, large saucepan or deep fryer to 375°F. In medium bowl, combine milk and egg; beat well. Add flour, salt and hot pepper sauce; beat until smooth. Dip shrimp in batter, allow excess to drain off.
2. With slotted spoon, add shrimp to hot oil; fry at 375°F. for 3 to 4 minutes or until golden brown. Drain on paper towels.

NUTRITION INFORMATION PER SERVING: Serving Size: ¼ of Recipe ◆ Calories: 290 ◆ Calories from Fat: 150 ◆ **% DAILY VALUE:** Total Fat: 17 g 26% ◆ Saturated Fat: 3 g 15% ◆ Cholesterol: 215 mg 72% ◆ Sodium: 480 mg 20% ◆ Total Carbohydrate: 14 g 5% ◆ Dietary Fiber: 0 g 0% ◆ Sugars: 2 g ◆ Protein: 21 g ◆ Vitamin A: 6% ◆ Vitamin C: 2% ◆ Calcium: 8% ◆ Iron: 20% ◆ **DIETARY EXCHANGES:** 1 Starch, 2½ Medium-Fat Meat, ½ Fat OR 1 Carbohydrate, 2½ Medium-Fat Meat, ½ Fat

VARIATION

Batter-Fried Butterflied Shrimp: Remove shell except for tail portion. With sharp knife, cut almost all the way through shrimp lengthwise to form butterfly shape; keep tail intact and remove black vein. Dip in batter; fry as directed.

Zesty Seafood Cocktail Sauce

PREP TIME: 20 MINUTES ◆ YIELD: ¾ CUP

    ½ cup chili sauce
    2 tablespoons lemon juice
    1 teaspoon prepared horseradish
    ½ teaspoon celery seed
    ½ teaspoon Worcestershire sauce

In small bowl, combine all ingredients; mix well. Cover; refrigerate 15 minutes or until chilled.

NUTRITION INFORMATION PER SERVING: Serving Size: 1 Tablespoon ◆ Calories: 10 ◆ Calories from Fat: 0 ◆ **% DAILY VALUE:** Total Fat: 0 g 0% ◆ Saturated Fat: 0 g 0% ◆ Cholesterol: 0 mg 0% ◆ Sodium: 160 mg 7% ◆ Total Carbohydrate: 3 g 1% ◆ Dietary Fiber: 0 g 0% ◆ Sugars: 2 g ◆ Protein: 0 g ◆ Vitamin A: 4% ◆ Vitamin C: 4% ◆ Calcium: 0% ◆ Iron: 0% ◆ **DIETARY EXCHANGES:** Free

COOK'S NOTE

GRILLING SHRIMP AND SCALLOPS

Grilling enhances the briny sweetness of shrimp and scallops. Thaw frozen fish and shellfish before grilling; shrimp can be peeled or left in the shell. Grease the grill rack first. Jumbo shrimp and sea scallops can be set directly on the grill, but it is much easier to use a grill basket or thread them onto a skewer. Grill the shellfish about 4 to 6 inches from medium-high coals, turning once and basting occasionally with melted butter, salad dressing or a marinade. Grill for 15 to 20 minutes or until the meat is white and opaque inside.

SHELLFISH COOKING METHODS

SHELLFISH	SUGGESTED COOKING METHODS
Crab	Steam, boil
Hard-shell clams (cockles, littleneck, cherrystones)	Steam, stir-fry
Lobster	Steam, boil, broil, grill
Mussels	Steam, poach
Oysters	Stew, roast, broil
Scallops	Poach, bake, broil, stir-fry, panfry, grill
Shrimp	Boil, broil, grill, stir-fry
Soft-shell clams (steamers)	Steam

COOK'S NOTE

SCALLOPS

Types

There are two basic types: sea scallops, which measure about 2 inches in diameter, and bay scallops, usually about ½ inch in diameter. Bay scallops may be sweeter and more tender. The two types can be used interchangeably in recipes as long as you adjust the cooking time for size or cut large sea scallops into smaller pieces for bay scallop recipes.

Shopping for Quality

Fresh scallops should have a slightly sweet smell and a creamy pink to tan color. They should be moist and shiny with a little liquid around them and no dried-out or discolored patches.

How Much to Buy

Allow 3 to 4 oz. (uncooked) per serving.

Preparation

If sea scallops have a tough tendon on the side, remove it before cooking.

Boiled Shrimp

PREP TIME: 20 MINUTES ✦ YIELD: 4 SERVINGS

> ½ teaspoon salt
> 1 lb. fresh uncooked medium or large shrimp

1. In large saucepan, bring to a boil enough water to cover shrimp; add salt. Add shrimp; immediately reduce heat to medium.
2. Cook 3 to 5 minutes or until shrimp turn pink. DO NOT BOIL. Shrimp will become tough if overcooked. Plunge into cold water to stop cooking. Drain.
3. Peel and devein shrimp. Serve warm or chilled.

NUTRITION INFORMATION PER SERVING: Serving Size: ¼ of Recipe ✦ Calories: 80 ✦ Calories from Fat: 10 ✦ **% DAILY VALUE:** Total Fat: 1 g 2% ✦ Saturated Fat: 0 g 0% ✦ Cholesterol: 160 mg 53% ✦ Sodium: 190 mg 8% ✦ Total Carbohydrate: 0 g 0% ✦ Dietary Fiber: 0 g 0% ✦ Sugars: 0 g ✦ Protein: 17 g ✦ Vitamin A: 4% ✦ Vitamin C: 2% ✦ Calcium: 4% ✦ Iron: 15% ✦ **DIETARY EXCHANGES:** 2 Very Lean Meat

Mediterranean Shrimp and Bow Ties

PREP TIME: 25 MINUTES ✦ YIELD: 4 (1½-CUP) SERVINGS

> 6 oz. (3 cups) uncooked bow tie pasta (farfalle)
> 1 tablespoon olive or vegetable oil
> 1 lb. shelled deveined uncooked medium or large shrimp
> ½ cup green onion pieces (½ inch)
> 2 garlic cloves, minced
> ½ teaspoon dried oregano leaves
> ¼ teaspoon salt
> 2 tablespoons lemon juice
> ½ cup sliced kalamata or ripe olives

1. Cook pasta to desired doneness as directed on package. Drain; cover to keep warm.
2. Meanwhile, heat oil in large skillet over medium-high heat until hot. Add shrimp, onions and garlic; cook and stir 3 to 5 minutes or until shrimp turn pink. Remove from heat.
3. Add pasta to skillet with all remaining ingredients. Cook 1 to 2 minutes or until thoroughly heated.

NUTRITION INFORMATION PER SERVING: Serving Size: 1½ Cups ✦ Calories: 320 ✦ Calories from Fat: 90 ✦ **% DAILY VALUE:** Total Fat: 10 g 15% ✦ Saturated Fat: 1 g 5% ✦ Cholesterol: 160 mg 53% ✦ Sodium: 600 mg 25% ✦ Total Carbohydrate: 35 g 12% ✦ Dietary Fiber: 1 g 4% ✦ Sugars: 2 g ✦ Protein: 23 g ✦ Vitamin A: 4% ✦ Vitamin C: 6% ✦ Calcium: 6% ✦ Iron: 25% ✦ **DIETARY EXCHANGES:** 2 Starch, 1 Vegetable, 2 Very Lean Meat, 1½ Fat OR 2 Carbohydrate, 1 Vegetable, 2 Very Lean Meat, 1½ Fat

Shrimp Creole

PREP TIME: 20 MINUTES (READY IN 1 HOUR 10 MINUTES)
◆ YIELD: 6 SERVINGS

　1 cup uncooked regular long-grain white rice
　2 cups water
　¼ cup oil
　1 medium green bell pepper, cut into thin
　　　strips
　2 medium onions, thinly sliced
　½ cup chopped celery
　1 garlic clove, minced
　1 (14.5 or 16-oz.) can whole tomatoes,
　　　undrained, cut up
　¼ cup chili sauce
　1 teaspoon lemon juice
　¼ to ½ teaspoon hot pepper sauce
　½ cup slivered almonds
　¼ cup raisins
　¼ cup chopped fresh parsley
　¼ teaspoon salt
　¼ teaspoon pepper
　¼ teaspoon dried thyme leaves
　¼ teaspoon curry powder
　1 bay leaf
　1 lb. shelled deveined cooked medium
　　　shrimp

1. Cook rice in water as directed on package.
2. Meanwhile, heat oil in large skillet over medium-high heat until hot. Add bell pepper, onions, celery and garlic; cook and stir until crisp-tender.
3. Add all remaining ingredients except shrimp. Reduce heat to low; cover and simmer 40 to 50 minutes or until flavors are blended, stirring occasionally.
4. Add shrimp. Simmer an additional 10 minutes or until thoroughly heated. Remove bay leaf. Serve over rice.

NUTRITION INFORMATION PER SERVING: Serving Size: ⅙ of Recipe ◆ Calories: 380 ◆ Calories from Fat: 140 ◆ % DAILY VALUE: Total Fat: 15 g 23% ◆ Saturated Fat: 2 g 10% ◆ Cholesterol: 150 mg 50% ◆ Sodium: 540 mg 23% ◆ Total Carbohydrate: 40 g 13% ◆ Dietary Fiber: 4 g 16% ◆ Sugars: 10 g ◆ Protein: 22 g ◆ Vitamin A: 20% ◆ Vitamin C: 40% ◆ Calcium: 10% ◆ Iron: 25% ◆ DIETARY EXCHANGES: 1½ Starch, ½ Fruit, 2 Vegetable, 2 Very Lean Meat, 2½ Fat OR 2 Carbohydrate, 2 Vegetable, 2 Very Lean Meat, 2½ Fat

Kung Pao Shrimp

PREP TIME: 20 MINUTES ◆ YIELD: 4 SERVINGS

　3 tablespoons hoisin sauce
　1 tablespoon dry sherry
　1 teaspoon sugar
　½ to 1 teaspoon chili paste
　1 egg white
　1 tablespoon cornstarch
　¾ lb. shelled deveined uncooked medium
　　　shrimp
　1 tablespoon oil
　½ teaspoon grated gingerroot
　1 garlic clove, minced
　¼ cup dry-roasted peanuts

1. In small bowl, combine hoisin sauce, sherry, sugar and chili paste; mix well. Set aside.
2. In medium bowl, combine egg white and cornstarch; beat well. Add shrimp; mix well to coat. Set aside.
3. Heat oil in large skillet or wok over medium-high heat until hot. Add shrimp mixture, ginger and garlic; cook and stir 2 to 3 minutes or until shrimp turn pink. Add sauce mixture; cook and stir 1 to 2 minutes or until shrimp are well coated. Stir in peanuts.

NUTRITION INFORMATION PER SERVING: Serving Size: ¼ of Recipe ◆ Calories: 190 ◆ Calories from Fat: 80 ◆ % DAILY VALUE: Total Fat: 9 g 14% ◆ Saturated Fat: 1 g 5% ◆ Cholesterol: 120 mg 40% ◆ Sodium: 530 mg 22% ◆ Total Carbohydrate: 12 g 4% ◆ Dietary Fiber: 1 g 4% ◆ Sugars: 8 g ◆ Protein: 16 g ◆ Vitamin A: 4% ◆ Vitamin C: 2% ◆ Calcium: 4% ◆ Iron: 15% ◆ DIETARY EXCHANGES: 1 Starch, 2 Lean Meat OR 1 Carbohydrate, 2 Lean Meat

Kung Pao Shrimp

COOK'S NOTE

COOKING SHRIMP

Bring to a boil enough water to cover the shrimp. Add the shrimp and reduce heat to a simmer. As soon as the shells start to turn pink, approximately 3 to 5 minutes, depending on size, start to test for doneness by removing one from the pot and cutting into the center. As soon as the center is white instead of grayish and translucent, drain the pot. Overcooking makes shrimp rubbery.

Shrimp Scampi

Shrimp Scampi

PREP TIME: 20 MINUTES ◆ YIELD: 4 SERVINGS

- 8 oz. uncooked fettuccine
- 2 tablespoons margarine or butter
- 1 tablespoon olive or vegetable oil
- 4 garlic cloves, minced
- 1 lb. shelled deveined uncooked medium shrimp
- ¼ cup chopped fresh parsley
- 2 teaspoons grated lemon peel
- ¼ teaspoon salt
- ¼ teaspoon pepper
- ⅓ cup dry white wine or chicken broth

1. Cook fettuccine to desired doneness as directed on package. Drain; cover to keep warm.

2. Meanwhile, melt margarine with oil in medium skillet over medium heat. Add garlic; cook and stir 1 minute. Add shrimp; cook and stir 1 minute.

3. Add all remaining ingredients; cook and stir 1 to 2 minutes or until shrimp turn pink. Serve shrimp mixture over fettuccine.

NUTRITION INFORMATION PER SERVING: Serving Size: ¼ of Recipe ◆ Calories: 390 ◆ Calories from Fat: 110 ◆ % DAILY VALUE: Total Fat: 12 g 18% ◆ Saturated Fat: 2 g 10% ◆ Cholesterol: 215 mg 72% ◆ Sodium: 400 mg 17% ◆ Total Carbohydrate: 42 g 14% ◆ Dietary Fiber: 2 g 8% ◆ Sugars: 2 g ◆ Protein: 26 g ◆ Vitamin A: 15% ◆ Vitamin C: 10% ◆ Calcium: 6% ◆ Iron: 30% ◆ DIETARY EXCHANGES: 3 Starch, 2½ Very Lean Meat, 1½ Fat OR 3 Carbohydrate, 2½ Very Lean Meat, 1½ Fat

---

COOK'S NOTE

SHRIMP

Purchasing

You can buy shrimp either raw or cooked. Most of the shrimp sold in the United States is flash-frozen on the fishing boat. It may be sold frozen or the market may thaw it before displaying it at the fish counter. Occasionally you may find shrimp that has not been previously frozen.

Shrimp is sold by the pound and described by the "count," which means the approximate number of individual shrimp in a pound. The higher the count, the smaller the shrimp. The smallest can be significantly less expensive and although the texture and flavor remain the same, peeling them takes longer.

Canned "salad" shrimp has been cooked and peeled. Often very small shrimp are used. The texture is softer than that of fresh or frozen shrimp.

Two pounds raw shrimp will yield about 1 pound peeled, cooked shrimp.

Shopping for Quality

Uncooked shrimp should smell of the sea with no hint of ammonia and have a firm-looking flesh. The shells will be translucent and may look grayish, possibly tinged with green or pink.

Cooked shrimp (shelled or unshelled) should look pink.

Packages of frozen shrimp should be tightly sealed, solid, and free from ice crystals.

Preparation

Shrimp may be peeled before cooking, especially if they will be served hot. Peeling after cooking is easier and suitable if shrimp will be served cold.

Scalloped Oysters

PREP TIME: 15 MINUTES (READY IN 40 MINUTES)
♦ YIELD: 4 SERVINGS

¼ cup margarine or butter
2 cups soft bread crumbs
¼ cup grated Parmesan cheese
¼ teaspoon salt
  Dash mace, if desired
1 pint (2 cups) fresh oysters, drained*
¼ cup dry sherry or dry white wine**

1. Heat oven to 375°F. Melt margarine in 8 or 9-inch square pan in oven. Stir in bread crumbs, Parmesan cheese, salt and mace. Remove and reserve about half of crumbs; arrange remaining crumbs evenly in pan.
2. Place oysters over crumbs; pour sherry over oysters. Sprinkle with reserved crumbs.
3. Bake at 375°F. for 20 to 25 minutes or until light golden brown.

TIPS: * Two 8-oz. cans oysters, drained, can be substituted for fresh oysters. Omit salt.
** Oysters packed in light cream can be substituted for the fresh oysters and sherry.

NUTRITION INFORMATION PER SERVING: Serving Size: ¼ of Recipe ♦ Calories: 310 ♦ Calories from Fat: 160 ♦ % DAILY VALUE: Total Fat: 18 g 28% ♦ Saturated Fat: 5 g 25% ♦ Cholesterol: 100 mg 33% ♦ Sodium: 960 mg 40% ♦ Total Carbohydrate: 19 g 6% ♦ Dietary Fiber: 1 g 2% ♦ Sugars: 2 g ♦ Protein: 17 g ♦ Vitamin A: 15% ♦ Vitamin C: 6% ♦ Calcium: 20% ♦ Iron: 60% ♦ DIETARY EXCHANGES: 1½ Starch, 2 Lean Meat, 2 Fat OR 1½ Carbohydrate, 2 Lean Meat, 2 Fat

Fried Oysters

PREP TIME: 25 MINUTES ♦ YIELD: 4 SERVINGS

⅓ cup all-purpose flour
1 teaspoon salt
⅛ teaspoon pepper
1 egg
1 tablespoon water
⅔ cup cracker crumbs or unseasoned dry
  bread crumbs
¼ cup oil or butter
1 pint (2 cups) fresh oysters, drained

1. In shallow dish, combine flour, salt and pepper. In another shallow dish, combine egg and water; beat well. Place crumbs in medium bowl.
2. Heat oil in medium skillet over medium-high heat until hot. Coat oysters with flour mixture; dip in egg mixture. Coat with crumbs. Add oysters to pan; cook 8 to 10 minutes or until golden brown, turning

once. If desired, serve with lemon wedges or Tartar Sauce, page 192.

TIP: Oysters can be cooked in deep fryer at 375°F. for 2 to 3 minutes.

NUTRITION INFORMATION PER SERVING: Serving Size: ¼ of Recipe ♦ Calories: 350 ♦ Calories from Fat: 200 ♦ % DAILY VALUE: Total Fat: 22 g 34% ♦ Saturated Fat: 4 g 20% ♦ Cholesterol: 145 mg 48% ♦ Sodium: 1020 mg 43% ♦ Total Carbohydrate: 22 g 7% ♦ Dietary Fiber: 0 g 0% ♦ Sugars: 0 g ♦ Protein: 16 g ♦ Vitamin A: 4% ♦ Vitamin C: 6% ♦ Calcium: 10% ♦ Iron: 70% ♦ DIETARY EXCHANGES: 1½ Starch, 1½ Lean Meat, 3½ Fat OR 1½ Carbohydrate, 1½ Lean Meat, 3½ Fat

VARIATIONS

Fried Clams: Substitute fresh clams, shells removed, for oysters.
Fried Frog Legs: Substitute 3 lb. frog legs for oysters. Cook about 10 minutes on each side or until golden brown. If legs are large, add a little water. Cover; simmer 10 minutes. Remove cover; continue frying until crisp.

Mussels in Wine Sauce

PREP TIME: 30 MINUTES (READY IN 40 MINUTES)
♦ YIELD: 4 SERVINGS

4 lb. fresh mussels
1 teaspoon oil
2 garlic cloves, minced
2 cups dry white wine
1 teaspoon dried thyme leaves
1 teaspoon cracked black pepper
2 lemons, cut into wedges

1. Place mussels in large bowl; cover with cold water. Let stand 20 minutes. Remove beards from mussels; scrub well under cold running water. Discard any mussels that do not close.
2. Heat oil in large saucepan over medium heat until hot. Add garlic; cook about 1 minute. Stir in wine, thyme and pepper. Bring to a boil. Add cleaned mussels. Cover; cook about 5 minutes or until mussels are open. Discard any mussels that do not open. Serve mussels with lemon wedges.

NUTRITION INFORMATION PER SERVING: Serving Size: ¼ of Recipe ♦ Calories: 130 ♦ Calories from Fat: 25 ♦ % DAILY VALUE: Total Fat: 3 g 5% ♦ Saturated Fat: 1 g 5% ♦ Cholesterol: 35 mg 12% ♦ Sodium: 550 mg 23% ♦ Total Carbohydrate: 10 g 3% ♦ Dietary Fiber: 1 g 3% ♦ Sugars: 3 g ♦ Protein: 16 g ♦ Vitamin A: 4% ♦ Vitamin C: 30% ♦ Calcium: 4% ♦ Iron: 30% ♦ DIETARY EXCHANGES: ½ Fruit, 2½ Very Lean Meat OR ½ Carbohydrate, 2½ Very Lean Meat

Crescent Tuna Melt

PREP TIME: 30 MINUTES (READY IN 55 MINUTES)
◆ YIELD: 8 SERVINGS

2 eggs
1/3 cup mayonnaise or salad dressing
2 tablespoons chopped dill pickle
1 tablespoon prepared mustard
1 tablespoon instant minced onion
    or 1/4 cup chopped onion
1 (9-oz.) can water-packed tuna, drained, flaked
1 (8-oz.) can refrigerated crescent dinner rolls
6 oz. (1 1/2 cups) shredded Cheddar or Swiss
    cheese
1 tablespoon sesame seed, toasted if desired

1. Place eggs in medium saucepan; cover with cold water. Bring to a boil. Reduce heat; simmer about 15 minutes. Immediately drain; run cold water over eggs to stop cooking. Peel eggs and chop.
2. Meanwhile, heat oven to 375°F. In medium bowl, combine mayonnaise, dill pickle, mustard and onion; mix well. Stir in tuna and eggs.
3. Separate dough into 2 long rectangles. Place on ungreased cookie sheet with long sides overlapping 1/2 inch; firmly press perforations and edges to seal. Cover with waxed paper. Press or roll to form 14×9-inch rectangle; remove waxed paper.
4. Spoon tuna mixture in 3-inch strip lengthwise down center of dough to within 1/4 inch of each end. Sprinkle 3/4 cup of the cheese over filling. Make cuts 1 inch apart on longest sides of rectangle just to edge of filling. To give braided appearance, fold strips of dough at an angle halfway across filling with edges of strips just slightly overlapping, alternating from side to side.
5. Bake at 375°F. for 17 to 24 minutes or until deep golden brown. Remove from oven; sprinkle with remaining 3/4 cup cheese and sesame seed. Bake an additional 2 to 3 minutes or until cheese is melted. Cool 5 minutes before serving.

NUTRITION INFORMATION PER SERVING: Serving Size: 1/8 of Recipe ◆ Calories: 310 ◆ Calories from Fat: 200 ◆ % DAILY VALUE: Total Fat: 22 g 34% ◆ Saturated Fat: 8 g 40% ◆ Cholesterol: 90 mg 30% ◆ Sodium: 560 mg 23% ◆ Total Carbohydrate: 12 g 4% ◆ Dietary Fiber: 1 g 2% ◆ Sugars: 3 g ◆ Protein: 16 g ◆ Vitamin A: 8% ◆ Vitamin C: 0% ◆ Calcium: 15% ◆ Iron: 8% ◆ DIETARY EXCHANGES: 1 Starch, 2 Lean Meat, 3 Fat OR 1 Carbohydrate, 2 Lean Meat, 3 Fat

Crabmeat and Avocado Wraps

PREP TIME: 15 MINUTES ◆ YIELD: 4 SERVINGS

4 (10-inch) flour tortillas
2/3 cup purchased Alfredo sauce
2 (6-oz.) cans crabmeat, well drained, flaked
1 ripe avocado, pitted, peeled and cubed
2 cups shredded lettuce
1/4 cup sliced green onions

1. Heat tortillas as directed on package.
2. Meanwhile, in medium saucepan, combine Alfredo sauce and crabmeat; cook over medium heat just until thoroughly heated, stirring occasionally. Fold in avocado.
3. Spoon half of mixture across center of each tortilla; top with lettuce and onions. Fold sides over filling. Fold bottom up over filling and continue rolling to enclose filling.

NUTRITION INFORMATION PER SERVING: Serving Size: 1/4 of Recipe ◆ Calories: 470 ◆ Calories from Fat: 230 ◆ % DAILY VALUE: Total Fat: 25 g 38% ◆ Saturated Fat: 9 g 45% ◆ Cholesterol: 85 mg 28% ◆ Sodium: 660 mg 28% ◆ Total Carbohydrate: 38 g 13% ◆ Dietary Fiber: 5 g 20% ◆ Sugars: 3 g ◆ Protein: 22 g ◆ Vitamin A: 8% ◆ Vitamin C: 10% ◆ Calcium: 20% ◆ Iron: 15% ◆ DIETARY EXCHANGES: 2 1/2 Starch, 2 Very Lean Meat, 4 1/2 Fat OR 2 1/2 Carbohydrate, 2 Very Lean Meat, 4 1/2 Fat

Cajun-Spiced Grouper Sandwiches

PREP TIME: 20 MINUTES ◆ YIELD: 4 SANDWICHES

4 (4-oz.) grouper or cod fillets
2 teaspoons dried Cajun seasoning
4 onion sandwich buns, split, toasted
1/4 cup tartar sauce
4 tomato slices
4 lettuce leaves

1. Spray medium skillet with nonstick cooking spray. Heat over medium-high heat until hot. Pat fillets dry with paper towel; sprinkle both sides with Cajun seasoning. Cook 10 to 14 minutes or until fish flakes easily with fork, turning once.
2. To assemble sandwiches, spread sandwich bun halves with tartar sauce. Fill each with tomato slice, lettuce leaf and cooked fillet.

NUTRITION INFORMATION PER SERVING: Serving Size: 1 Sandwich ◆ Calories: 340 ◆ Calories from Fat: 110 ◆ % DAILY VALUE: Total Fat: 12 g 18% ◆ Saturated Fat: 2 g 10% ◆ Cholesterol: 55 mg 18% ◆ Sodium: 850 mg 35% ◆ Total Carbohydrate: 31 g 10% ◆ Dietary Fiber: 2 g 8% ◆ Sugars: 2 g ◆ Protein: 26 g ◆ Vitamin A: 4% ◆ Vitamin C: 4% ◆ Calcium: 8% ◆ Iron: 15% ◆ DIETARY EXCHANGES: 2 Starch, 3 Very Lean Meat, 1 1/2 Fat OR 2 Carbohydrate, 3 Very Lean Meat, 1 1/2 Fat

Coquilles St. Jacques

PREP TIME: 40 MINUTES ◆ YIELD: 4 SERVINGS

¼ cup margarine or butter
¼ cup chopped celery
1½ cups sliced fresh mushrooms
2 medium green onions, sliced,
    or 2 tablespoons chopped onion
2 tablespoons all-purpose flour
2 tablespoons chopped green bell pepper
¼ teaspoon salt
⅛ teaspoon pepper
½ bay leaf
½ cup dry white wine
1 lb. scallops
¼ cup whipping cream or evaporated milk
1 egg yolk
1 tablespoon chopped pimientos
2 tablespoons margarine or butter, melted
3 tablespoons unseasoned dry bread crumbs
3 tablespoons grated Parmesan cheese

1. Lightly grease 4 individual baking dishes, shells or 1½-quart shallow casserole. Melt ¼ cup margarine in large saucepan over medium heat. Add celery, mushrooms and onions; cook and stir until tender. Stir in flour, bell pepper, salt, pepper, bay leaf and wine; mix well. Add scallops. Cook until mixture boils and thickens, stirring occasionally.
2. Reduce heat to low; cover and simmer 5 minutes or until scallops are opaque. (Cook 10 to 15 minutes if scallops are frozen.)
3. In small bowl, combine whipping cream and egg yolk; beat well. Gradually stir into scallops. Stir in pimientos. Cook and stir just until mixture begins to bubble. Remove bay leaf.
4. Spoon mixture into greased baking dishes. Place on ungreased cookie sheet. Combine 2 tablespoons melted margarine, bread crumbs and Parmesan cheese. Sprinkle over each serving. Broil 2 to 3 inches from heat until thoroughly heated and crumbs are golden brown.

> **TIP:** To make ahead, prepare, cover and refrigerate for up to 12 hours before broiling. Remove cover and broil as directed above.

NUTRITION INFORMATION PER SERVING: Serving Size: ¼ of Recipe ◆ Calories: 440 ◆ Calories from Fat: 260 ◆ **% DAILY VALUE:** Total Fat: 29 g 45% ◆ Saturated Fat: 9 g 45% ◆ Cholesterol: 120 mg 40% ◆ Sodium: 790 mg 33% ◆ Total Carbohydrate: 13 g 4% ◆ Dietary Fiber: 1 g 4% ◆ Sugars: 2 g ◆ Protein: 27 g ◆ Vitamin A: 25% ◆ Vitamin C: 15% ◆ Calcium: 25% ◆ Iron: 10% ◆ **DIETARY EXCHANGES:** 1 Starch, 3½ Very Lean Meat, 5 Fat OR 1 Carbohydrate, 3½ Very Lean Meat, 5 Fat

Linguine with Seafood Sauce

PREP TIME: 20 MINUTES ◆ YIELD: 8 SERVINGS

12 oz. uncooked linguine
4 tablespoons margarine or butter
4 green onions, sliced
1 garlic clove, minced
1 (12-oz.) pkg. frozen shelled deveined uncooked medium shrimp, thawed, drained
1 (6½-oz.) can minced clams, undrained
1 cup chicken broth
½ cup dry white wine
2 tablespoons lemon juice
¼ cup chopped fresh parsley
1 teaspoon dried basil leaves
1 teaspoon dried oregano leaves
¼ teaspoon pepper
2 tablespoons cornstarch
2 tablespoons cold water
¼ cup sour cream

Linguine with Seafood Sauce

COOK'S NOTE

COOKING SCALLOPS

The most important thing with scallops is to avoid overcooking. The delicate meat can quickly go from delectably tender to disappointingly rubbery. Remove scallops from the heat as soon as the center is creamy white and opaque; serve at once.

1. Cook linguine to desired doneness as directed on package. Drain; cover to keep warm.

2. Meanwhile, melt 2 tablespoons of the margarine in large skillet over medium heat. Add onions and garlic; cook and stir until onions are tender. Stir in shrimp, clams, broth, wine, lemon juice, parsley, basil, oregano and pepper. Bring to a boil. Reduce heat to low; simmer 5 minutes.

3. In small bowl, combine cornstarch and water; blend well. Gradually stir into seafood mixture. Cook until mixture boils and thickens, stirring constantly.

4. In large bowl, combine linguine, sour cream and remaining 2 tablespoons margarine; toss to coat. Serve seafood sauce over linguine.

NUTRITION INFORMATION PER SERVING: Serving Size: ⅛ of Recipe ◆ Calories: 290 ◆ Calories from Fat: 90 ◆ **% DAILY VALUE:** Total Fat: 10 g 15% ◆ Saturated Fat: 3 g 15% ◆ Cholesterol: 105 mg 35% ◆ Sodium: 380 mg 16% ◆ Total Carbohydrate: 35 g 12% ◆ Dietary Fiber: 2 g 8% ◆ Sugars: 3 g ◆ Protein: 14 g ◆ Vitamin A: 10% ◆ Vitamin C: 8% ◆ Calcium: 6% ◆ Iron: 20% ◆ **DIETARY EXCHANGES:** 2½ Starch, 1 Very Lean Meat, 1½ Fat OR 2½ Carbohydrate, 1 Very Lean Meat, 1½ Fat

Boiled Crab

PREP TIME: 30 MINUTES ◆ YIELD: 2 SERVINGS*

1 (1 to 2-lb.) Dungeness crab
2 teaspoons salt
¼ cup butter, melted, or Clarified Butter, page 215

1. In large stockpot or kettle, bring to a boil enough water to cover crab; add salt. If crab is alive, pick up from the rear, holding the last 1 or 2 legs on either side. Plunge crab into boiling water. Return to a boil. Reduce heat to medium; cover and cook 15 minutes.

2. Remove crab from water; plunge into cold water to stop cooking. Crack claws and legs using claw cracker or nutcracker. With fork, remove meat. Serve with melted butter.

TIP: * For 4 servings, use 2 crabs and ½ cup butter. Do not increase salt.

NUTRITION INFORMATION PER SERVING: Serving Size: ½ of Recipe ◆ Calories: 310 ◆ Calories from Fat: 220 ◆ **% DAILY VALUE:** Total Fat: 24 g 37% ◆ Saturated Fat: 14 g 70% ◆ Cholesterol: 140 mg 47% ◆ Sodium: 620 mg 26% ◆ Total Carbohydrate: 1 g 1% ◆ Dietary Fiber: 0 g 0% ◆ Sugars: 0 g ◆ Protein: 23 g ◆ Vitamin A: 20% ◆ Vitamin C: 4% ◆ Calcium: 6% ◆ Iron: 2% ◆ **DIETARY EXCHANGES:** 3½ Very Lean Meat, 4 Fat

COOK'S NOTE

CRAB

Types

Varieties of crab differ by region. Dungeness crab is from the Pacific coast, king crab and snow crab are found in the North Pacific, blue crab comes from the Atlantic and Gulf coasts and stone crab from Florida. Soft-shell crabs are not a different variety but are blue crabs that have shed their hard shells and can be eaten without removing the meat from the shell.

Alaska king crab is usually sold as frozen, cooked crab legs. Cooked crabmeat (out of the shell) is available frozen or canned, and occasionally fresh. Lump meat, the most costly, is choice meat from the body of the crab. Flaked meat consists of small pieces from the body. Claw meat is darker than the meat from the body.

Shopping for Quality

Fresh, uncooked crabs should be sold alive, displayed in a tank of salt water. They should look active, not sluggish. Cooked whole crabs, available fresh and frozen, should have bright red shells and a mild aroma.

How Much to Buy

Allow ⅓ to ½ pound per serving. Four pounds of crab in the shell yields 1 pound of cooked crabmeat. One 6-ounce package of frozen crabmeat or one 6½-ounce can of cooked flaked crabmeat is equivalent to 1 cup of cooked lump crabmeat.

Maryland Deviled Crab

PREP TIME: 20 MINUTES (READY IN 40 MINUTES)
◆ YIELD: 4 SERVINGS

    3 tablespoons margarine or butter
    2 tablespoons chopped onion
    2 tablespoons chopped green bell pepper
    2 tablespoons all-purpose flour
    ¾ cup milk
    8 oz. cooked crabmeat, drained, flaked (2 cups)
    1 tablespoon chopped fresh parsley
    ½ teaspoon dry mustard
    2 teaspoons lemon juice
    ½ teaspoon Worcestershire sauce
    ½ teaspoon hot pepper sauce
    1 egg, slightly beaten
    ½ cup soft bread crumbs
    2 tablespoons margarine or butter, melted

1. Heat oven to 400°F. Lightly grease 1-quart casserole or 4 individual baking dishes or shells. Melt 3 tablespoons margarine in medium saucepan over medium heat. Add onion and bell pepper; cook and stir until tender. Stir in flour. Gradually add milk. Cook until mixture boils and thickens, stirring constantly.

2. Add all remaining ingredients except bread crumbs and 2 tablespoons margarine; mix well. Spoon into greased casserole. In small bowl, combine bread crumbs and 2 tablespoons margarine. Sprinkle evenly over crab mixture.

3. Bake at 400°F. for 15 to 20 minutes or until thoroughly heated.

NUTRITION INFORMATION PER SERVING: Serving Size: ¼ of Recipe ◆ Calories: 260 ◆ Calories from Fat: 160 ◆ % DAILY VALUE: Total Fat: 18 g 28% ◆ Saturated Fat: 4 g 20% ◆ Cholesterol: 85 mg 28% ◆ Sodium: 860 mg 36% ◆ Total Carbohydrate: 9 g 3% ◆ Dietary Fiber: 0 g 0% ◆ Sugars: 3 g ◆ Protein: 15 g ◆ Vitamin A: 20% ◆ Vitamin C: 10% ◆ Calcium: 10% ◆ Iron: 6% ◆ DIETARY EXCHANGES: ½ Starch, 2 Very Lean Meat, 3½ Fat OR ½ Carbohydrate, 2 Very Lean Meat, 3½ Fat

Delaware Crab Cakes

PREP TIME: 20 MINUTES ◆ YIELD: 16 CRAB CAKES

    ½ cup unseasoned dry bread crumbs
    ¼ cup chopped green onions
    ¼ cup nonfat plain yogurt
    1 tablespoon chopped fresh dill
    1 teaspoon dry mustard
    ¼ to ½ teaspoon pepper
    1 tablespoon lemon juice
    1 egg, beaten
    1 (8-oz.) pkg. frozen imitation crabmeat
        (surimi), thawed, finely chopped,
        or 1 (6-oz.) can crabmeat, drained, flaked
    1 teaspoon oil

1. In large bowl, combine all ingredients except oil; mix well. Shape mixture into 16 patties, about ½ inch thick.

2. Heat oil in large nonstick skillet over medium heat until hot. Add patties; cook 6 to 8 minutes or until golden brown, turning after 3 minutes. If desired, serve with Zesty Seafood Cocktail Sauce, page 206.

NUTRITION INFORMATION PER SERVING: Serving Size: 1 Crab Cake ◆ Calories: 35 ◆ Calories from Fat: 10 ◆ % DAILY VALUE: Total Fat: 1 g 2% ◆ Saturated Fat: 0 g 0% ◆ Cholesterol: 15 mg 5% ◆ Sodium: 160 mg 7% ◆ Total Carbohydrate: 4 g 1% ◆ Dietary Fiber: 0 g 0% ◆ Sugars: 2 g ◆ Protein: 3 g ◆ Vitamin A: 0% ◆ Vitamin C: 0% ◆ Calcium: 0% ◆ Iron: 2% ◆ DIETARY EXCHANGES: ½ Starch OR ½ Carbohydrate

---

COOK'S NOTE

HOW TO EAT HARD-SHELL CRAB

To remove meat from a cooked hard-shell crab, first twist off the legs and claws close to the body. Break each claw and leg with a nutcracker; remove the meat with a cocktail fork or nut pick.

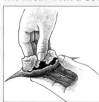

Holding the crab in both hands, insert your thumb under the shell by the apron hinge. Pull the body away from the shell.

With a spoon, remove the meat and roe from the shell. Discard the stomach bag located between the eyes. Discard the shell.

Broiled Lobster Tails

PREP TIME: 30 MINUTES ✦ YIELD: 2 SERVINGS

2 (8-oz.) lobster tails
¼ cup butter, melted
½ teaspoon salt
¼ teaspoon paprika
   Clarified Butter (this page)

1. Prepare fresh lobster for broiling by cutting along underside of tail with shears; clip off fins along edges. Peel back soft undershell and discard. To prevent curling, bend tail back to crack shell or insert skewer between meat and shell. Lay cut side up on broiler pan.

2. In small bowl, combine melted butter, salt and paprika; brush over lobster.

3. Broil 4 to 6 inches from heat for 10 to 15 minutes or until lobster meat is firm. Serve with Clarified Butter.

> **TIP:** If desired, frozen lobster tail can be simmered, covered, in salted boiling water for about 15 minutes. Prepare as directed for broiling. Broil for 2 to 3 minutes.

NUTRITION INFORMATION PER SERVING: Serving Size: ½ of Recipe ✦ Calories: 130 ✦ Calories from Fat: 35 ✦ **% DAILY VALUE:** Total Fat: 4 g 6% ✦ Saturated Fat: 2 g 10% ✦ Cholesterol: 85 mg 28% ✦ Sodium: 490 mg 20% ✦ Total Carbohydrate: 1 g 1% ✦ Dietary Fiber: 0 g 0% ✦ Sugars: 0 g ✦ Protein: 22 g ✦ Vitamin A: 6% ✦ Vitamin C: 0% ✦ Calcium: 6% ✦ Iron: 2% ✦ **DIETARY EXCHANGES:** 3 Very Lean Meat, ½ Fat

VARIATION

Broiled Butterflied Lobster Tails: Cut lobster lengthwise through center of hard top shell with shears, then cut through meat with sharp knife without cutting through soft undershell. Spread open. Cook as directed above.

COOK'S NOTE

HOW MUCH TO BUY

Allow one whole 1 to 2-pound lobster or ½-pound lobster tail per serving. One ½-pound tail or a 1-pound whole lobster will yield 4 to 5 ounces, or 1 cup, of cooked lobster meat.

Cooked lobster meat does not need to be reheated before serving, only thawed if frozen.

COOK'S NOTE

HOW TO EAT LOBSTER

Place lobster on its back. With sharp kitchen scissors, cut lengthwise down the body to the tail. Do not cut through the back of the shell.

Twist off the head from the tail. With kitchen shears, cut away membrane to expose the meat.

Remove the sack near the back of the head and the dark vein, which runs through the tail. The green tomalley (liver) and the coral roe (only in females) are edible.

Twist off the large claws from the body of the lobster. Using a nutcracker, crack the claws and remove the meat.

Clarified Butter

PREP TIME: 10 MINUTES

In small saucepan over low heat, slowly melt desired amount of butter. Remove from heat; let stand 2 to 3 minutes or until clear part can be spooned off into serving dish. Discard milky portion. Serve warm.

NUTRITION INFORMATION PER SERVING: Serving Size: 1 Tablespoon ✦ Calories: 110 ✦ Calories from Fat: 110 ✦ **% DAILY VALUE:** Total Fat: 12 g 18% ✦ Saturated Fat: 7 g 35% ✦ Cholesterol: 30 mg 10% ✦ Sodium: 115 mg 5% ✦ Total Carbohydrate: 0 g 0% ✦ Dietary Fiber: 0 g 0% ✦ Sugars: 0 g ✦ Protein: 0 g ✦ Vitamin A: 8% ✦ Vitamin C: 0% ✦ Calcium: 0% ✦ Iron: 0% ✦ **DIETARY EXCHANGES:** 2½ Fat

VARIATION

Clarified Lemon Butter: Add 1 tablespoon lemon juice to ¼ cup clarified butter.

Boiled Lobster

PREP TIME: 30 MINUTES ✦ YIELD: 2 SERVINGS*

    2 teaspoons salt
    2 (1-lb.) live lobsters
 1/4 cup butter, melted, or Clarified Butter,
        page 215

1. In large stockpot or kettle, bring to a boil enough water to cover lobsters; add salt. With long tongs, pick up lobster just behind eyes. Plunge live lobsters, headfirst, into boiling water. Return to a boil. Reduce heat to medium; cover and cook 7 minutes or until lobsters turn bright red.
2. Remove lobsters from water; plunge into cold water to stop cooking. Drain; turn on back. With sharp knife or kitchen scissors, cut lobster in half lengthwise. Remove sac near head and dark vein that runs along underside of tail. Crack claws and legs using claw cracker or nutcracker. With fork, remove meat. Serve with melted butter.

TIP: * For 4 servings, use 4 lobsters and 1/2 cup butter. Do not increase salt.

NUTRITION INFORMATION PER SERVING: Serving Size: 1/2 of Recipe ✦ Calories: 320 ✦ Calories from Fat: 220 ✦ % DAILY VALUE: Total Fat: 24 g 37% ✦ Saturated Fat: 14 g 70% ✦ Cholesterol: 145 mg 48% ✦ Sodium: 680 mg 28% ✦ Total Carbohydrate: 2 g 1% ✦ Dietary Fiber: 0 g 0% ✦ Sugars: 0 g ✦ Protein: 24 g ✦ Vitamin A: 20% ✦ Vitamin C: 0% ✦ Calcium: 8% ✦ Iron: 2% ✦ DIETARY EXCHANGES: 3 1/2 Very Lean Meat, 4 1/2 Fat

Lobster Newburg

PREP TIME: 25 MINUTES ✦ YIELD: 4 SERVINGS

 1 1/2 cups half-and-half
  1/4 cup dry sherry or dry white wine
    2 egg yolks, slightly beaten
  1/4 cup margarine or butter
 4 1/2 teaspoons all-purpose flour
  1/2 teaspoon salt
        Dash paprika
    1 lb. cooked lobster meat, cut into
        chunks (2 cups)*
        Toast points or patty shells

1. In small bowl, combine half-and-half, sherry and egg yolks; set aside. Melt margarine in medium saucepan over medium heat. Stir in flour, salt and paprika; cook 1 minute or until mixture is smooth and bubbly, stirring constantly.
2. Reduce heat to low. Gradually add half-and-half mixture. Cook until thickened, stirring constantly. Stir in lobster; cook until thoroughly heated. Serve over toast points.

TIP: * Two 8-oz. cans lobster, drained, can be substituted for the cooked lobster.

NUTRITION INFORMATION PER SERVING: Serving Size: 1/4 of Recipe ✦ Calories: 410 ✦ Calories from Fat: 210 ✦ % DAILY VALUE: Total Fat: 23 g 35% ✦ Saturated Fat: 9 g 45% ✦ Cholesterol: 115 mg 38% ✦ Sodium: 1100 mg 46% ✦ Total Carbohydrate: 21 g 7% ✦ Dietary Fiber: 1 g 3% ✦ Sugars: 6 g ✦ Protein: 29 g ✦ Vitamin A: 20% ✦ Vitamin C: 0% ✦ Calcium: 20% ✦ Iron: 8% ✦ DIETARY EXCHANGES: 1 1/2 Starch, 3 1/2 Very Lean Meat, 4 Fat OR 1 1/2 Carbohydrate, 3 1/2 Very Lean Meat, 4 Fat

VARIATIONS
Crab Newburg: Substitute cooked crabmeat for lobster.
Shrimp Newburg: Substitute cooked shrimp for lobster.

Lobster Thermidor

PREP TIME: 20 MINUTES ✦ YIELD: 4 SERVINGS

    1 (10 3/4-oz.) can condensed cream of shrimp
        or mushroom soup
  1/4 teaspoon dry mustard
        Dash ground red pepper (cayenne)
  1/4 cup milk
    8 oz. cooked lobster meat, cut into
        chunks (1 cup)*
    1 (4.5-oz.) jar sliced mushrooms, drained
        Grated Parmesan cheese
        Paprika

1. Lightly grease 4 individual baking dishes or shells. In medium saucepan, heat soup over low heat, stirring occasionally. Stir in mustard, ground red pepper, milk, lobster and mushrooms. Cook over low heat until thoroughly heated, stirring occasionally.
2. Spoon into greased baking dishes. Place on ungreased cookie sheet. Sprinkle with Parmesan cheese and paprika.
3. Broil 3 to 4 inches from heat for 2 to 3 minutes or until hot and bubbly.

TIP: * One 8-oz. can lobster, drained, can be substituted for the cooked lobster.

NUTRITION INFORMATION PER SERVING: Serving Size: 1/4 of Recipe ✦ Calories: 140 ✦ Calories from Fat: 45 ✦ % DAILY VALUE: Total Fat: 5 g 8% ✦ Saturated Fat: 3 g 15% ✦ Cholesterol: 55 mg 18% ✦ Sodium: 1000 mg 42% ✦ Total Carbohydrate: 8 g 3% ✦ Dietary Fiber: 1 g 4% ✦ Sugars: 1 g ✦ Protein: 16 g ✦ Vitamin A: 6% ✦ Vitamin C: 0% ✦ Calcium: 10% ✦ Iron: 4% ✦ DIETARY EXCHANGES: 1/2 Starch, 2 Very Lean Meat, 1/2 Fat OR 1/2 Carbohydrate, 2 Very Lean Meat, 1/2 Fat

VEGETARIAN COOKING

VEGETARIAN COOKING

A meal without meat is not a radical concept. Think of macaroni and cheese, vegetable soup and omelets. Now the rising interest in vegetarianism has inspired fresh new ideas. In many restaurants, meatless entrées are among the most irresistible and imaginative on the menu. Likewise, some of the best new recipes for home cooks are in this growing repertoire.

Low-fat vegetarian diets are linked with lower rates of disease and can also help reverse coronary artery disease. Even if you are not interested in becoming a full-fledged vegetarian, occasional meatless meals can yield health benefits.

Vegetarian Definitions
Although some people use the term loosely, calling themselves vegetarian even if they eat seafood and even poultry, the terms have precise meanings:

+ *Lacto-ovo* vegetarians eat dairy products (lacto) and eggs (ovo).
+ *Lacto* vegetarians eat dairy products but no eggs.
+ *Vegan* vegetarians follow a plant-based diet exclusively and consume no animal products whatsoever, not even milk or eggs.

Becoming a Vegetarian (Even Part-Time)
If you're considering vegetarianism, or just increasing the number of meatless meals you eat every week, keep in mind that "vegetarian" is not a synonym for "low-fat." Many delicious meatless entrées are as high in fat as (and sometimes even higher than) the meat courses they replace.

Protein intake should not be a major worry. Most adult women need about 50 grams of protein per day (pregnant women need more—consult your physician). Men usually need about 63 grams. These amounts are readily attained from a varied vegetarian diet. However, since no single vegetable contains all the essential protein components, it is important to eat a varied selection of beans, grains and other vegetables. The notion that it was necessary to eat "complementary proteins" together at the same meal has been discounted; the protein "puzzle pieces" can fit together over the course of the day.

Vegans need dietary supplements or fortified foods to ensure adequate intake of vitamin B_{12}, vitamin D and possibly of iron. Legumes and dried fruits are among the plant foods richest in iron, but the body cannot absorb iron as easily from plant foods as from animal foods. Take the iron along with foods or drinks rich in vitamin C to maximize your ability to absorb the iron.

Three servings daily of low-fat dairy products provide enough calcium. Calcium-fortified tofu, some soy beverages and dark green, leafy vegetables all contain some calcium, although in lesser amounts or in a form less readily absorbed by the body. Vegans may need a calcium supplement.

Choose low- or reduced-fat versions of dairy products, including skim milk, nonfat yogurt and sour cream, and low-fat cheese.

Emphasize recipes with little or no added fat and concentrate on low-fat or nonfat cooking techniques, such as steaming, microwaving, broiling, baking or stewing instead of frying.

Choose hearty foods with lots of texture and flavor: potatoes, beans and pasta, for example. Intensify the flavors with fresh herbs, hot peppers and seasoning blends.

Vegetarian Food Pyramid
If you follow a vegetarian eating plan, you can use the "Vegetarian Food Pyramid" on page 219. Following the pyramid as a daily food guide ensures adequate intakes of all the nutrients needed for good health. The suggested daily servings are provided next to each food group and the "Serving Size" table on page 219 helps define serving size.

Vegetarian Food Pyramid

VEGETABLE FATS AND
OILS, SWEETS AND SALT
Eat Sparingly

LOW-FAT OR NONFAT, MILK,
YOGURT, FRESH CHEESE, AND
FORTIFIED ALTERNATIVE GROUP
2–3 servings
Eat Moderately

LEGUME, NUT, SEED AND MEAT
ALTERNATIVE GROUP
2–3 servings
Eat Moderately

VEGETABLE GROUP
3–5 servings
Eat Generously

FRUIT GROUP
2–4 servings
Eat Generously

WHOLE GRAIN BREAD,
CEREAL, PASTA AND
RICE GROUP
6–11 servings
Eat Liberally

© The Health Connection 1994. Call 1-800-548-8700 to order copies of the pyramid.

SERVING SIZES

FATS, OILS AND SWEETS—USE SPARINGLY

Milk, Yogurt and Cheese Group
2–3 SERVINGS DAILY*

1 cup milk
1 cup yogurt
1½ oz. natural cheese

**Vegetarians who choose not to use milk, yogurt or cheese:
Use food sources rich in calcium such as soy milk fortified
with calcium, vitamin D and vitamin B₁₂.*

Bread, Cereal, Rice and Pasta Group
6–11 SERVINGS DAILY

1 slice bread
½ bagel
1 oz. ready-to-eat cereal
½ cup cooked cereal
½ cup cooked rice, pasta and other grains

Legumes, Nuts, Seeds, Eggs and Meat Alternative Group
2–3 SERVINGS DAILY

1 cup soy milk
½ cup cooked dry beans or peas
1 egg or 2 eggs
2 tablespoons nuts or seeds
¼ cup tofu or tempeh
2 tablespoons peanut butter

Fruit Group
2–4 SERVINGS DAILY

¾ cup juice
¼ cup dried fruit
½ cup chopped, raw fruit
½ cup canned fruit
1 medium-sized piece of fruit, such as
banana, apple or orange

Vegetable Group
3–5 SERVINGS DAILY

½ cup cooked or chopped raw vegetables
1 cup raw leafy vegetables

Colorful Vegetable Stroganoff

Colorful Vegetable Stroganoff

PREP TIME: 40 MINUTES ✦ YIELD: 9 (1-CUP) SERVINGS

 12 oz. uncooked linguine
  2 cups fresh broccoli florets
  2 cups sliced carrots
 ⅓ cup sliced ripe olives
  1 cup cottage cheese
 ¾ cup sour cream
 ½ cup grated Parmesan cheese
  3 tablespoons margarine or butter
  1 medium onion, chopped
  1 garlic clove, minced
  1 (4.5-oz.) jar sliced mushrooms, drained
  2 tablespoons all-purpose flour
 ½ teaspoon salt
 ¼ teaspoon pepper
  2 cups milk

1. Cook linguine to desired doneness as directed on package, adding broccoli and carrots during last 5 minutes of cooking time. Drain; return to saucepan. Stir in olives.
2. Meanwhile, in small bowl, combine cottage cheese, sour cream and ¼ cup of the Parmesan cheese; mix well. Set aside.
3. Melt margarine in 3-quart saucepan. Add onion, garlic and mushrooms; cook over medium heat 2 to 3 minutes or until onion is tender. Stir in flour, salt and pepper; cook until mixture is smooth and bubbly. Gradually add milk; cook until mixture is thickened and bubbly, stirring constantly.
4. Stir about 1 cup hot sauce into cottage cheese mixture; stir cottage cheese mixture into sauce. Cook until thoroughly heated. Do not boil. Pour cottage cheese mixture over linguine and vegetables; toss to mix.

Place on serving platter; sprinkle with remaining ¼ cup Parmesan cheese.

NUTRITION INFORMATION PER SERVING: Serving Size: 1 Cup ✦ Calories: 340 ✦ Calories from Fat: 130 ✦ **% DAILY VALUE:** Total Fat: 14 g 22% ✦ Saturated Fat: 6 g 30% ✦ Cholesterol: 55 mg 18% ✦ Sodium: 520 mg 22% ✦ Total Carbohydrate: 39 g 13% ✦ Dietary Fiber: 3 g 12% ✦ Sugars: 8 g ✦ Protein: 15 g ✦ Vitamin A: 170% ✦ Vitamin C: 25% ✦ Calcium: 20% ✦ Iron: 15% ✦ **DIETARY EXCHANGES:** 2½ Starch, 1 Lean Meat, 2 Fat OR 2½ Carbohydrate, 1 Lean Meat, 2 Fat

Fresh Tomato Basil Sauce over Pasta

PREP TIME: 25 MINUTES ✦ YIELD: 4 SERVINGS

  8 oz. any variety pasta
  2 tablespoons olive or vegetable oil
  2 garlic cloves, minced
  2 lb. Italian plum tomatoes (about 14), coarsely chopped
 ¼ cup chopped fresh basil or 1 tablespoon dried basil leaves
 ½ teaspoon salt
 ⅛ teaspoon pepper

1. Cook pasta to desired doneness as directed on package. Drain; cover to keep warm.
2. Meanwhile, heat oil in large saucepan over medium-high heat until hot. Add garlic; cook 1 minute. Stir in tomatoes, basil, salt and pepper. Bring to a boil. Cook over medium heat for 10 to 15 minutes or until tomatoes are tender and sauce begins to thicken.
3. Serve sauce over pasta. If a smoother sauce is desired, process half of sauce at a time in food processor or blender until smooth.

NUTRITION INFORMATION PER SERVING: Serving Size: ¼ of Recipe ✦ Calories: 320 ✦ Calories from Fat: 70 ✦ **% DAILY VALUE:** Total Fat: 8 g 12% ✦ Saturated Fat: 1 g 5% ✦ Cholesterol: 0 mg 0% ✦ Sodium: 290 mg 12% ✦ Total Carbohydrate: 54 g 18% ✦ Dietary Fiber: 4 g 16% ✦ Sugars: 7 g ✦ Protein: 9 g ✦ Vitamin A: 30% ✦ Vitamin C: 50% ✦ Calcium: 2% ✦ Iron: 20% ✦ **DIETARY EXCHANGES:** 3 Starch, 1 Vegetable, 1½ Fat OR 3 Carbohydrate, 1 Vegetable, 1½ Fat

Fresh Tomato Basil Sauce over Pasta

Linguine with Red Pepper Pesto

PREP TIME: 40 MINUTES ✦ YIELD: 4 (1-CUP) SERVINGS

1 red bell pepper, halved, seeded
⅓ cup firmly packed fresh basil leaves
¼ cup chopped pecans, toasted*
4 garlic cloves
⅓ cup olive oil
⅓ cup grated Parmesan cheese
¼ teaspoon salt
¼ teaspoon pepper
8 oz. uncooked linguine
2 tablespoons milk
2 tablespoons hot water
2 tablespoons grated Parmesan cheese

1. Place bell pepper halves, cut side down, on broiler pan. Broil 4 to 6 inches from heat for 8 to 10 minutes or until skins are charred. Place pepper halves in brown paper bag for 10 minutes. Peel peppers and discard skin.
2. To make pesto, in food processor bowl with metal blade or blender container, combine bell pepper halves, basil, pecans, garlic and oil; process until smooth. Transfer mixture to small bowl. Add ⅓ cup cheese, salt and pepper; mix well.
3. Meanwhile, in large saucepan, cook linguine to desired doneness as directed on package. Drain; leave in strainer. Place pesto in same saucepan.
4. Add milk and hot water; cook and stir over medium heat 1 minute or until thoroughly heated. Add linguine; toss gently to coat. Spoon mixture onto serving platter; sprinkle with 2 tablespoons cheese. If desired, garnish with chopped fresh basil or parsley. Serve immediately.

> **TIP:** * To toast pecans, spread on cookie sheet; bake at 350°F. for 5 to 10 minutes or until golden brown, stirring occasionally. Or, spread in thin layer in microwave-safe pie pan. Microwave on HIGH for 4 to 7 minutes or until golden brown, stirring frequently.

NUTRITION INFORMATION PER SERVING: Serving Size: 1 Cup ✦ Calories: 480 ✦ Calories from Fat: 240 ✦ **% DAILY VALUE:** Total Fat: 27 g 42% ✦ Saturated Fat: 5 g 25% ✦ Cholesterol: 10 mg 3% ✦ Sodium: 360 mg 15% ✦ Total Carbohydrate: 47 g 16% ✦ Dietary Fiber: 3 g 12% ✦ Sugars: 4 g ✦ Protein: 13 g ✦ Vitamin A: 25% ✦ Vitamin C: 45% ✦ Calcium: 20% ✦ Iron: 15% ✦ **DIETARY EXCHANGES:** 3 Starch, ½ Lean Meat, 5 Fat OR 3 Carbohydrate, ½ Lean Meat, 5 Fat

Penne Provençal

PREP TIME: 30 MINUTES ✦ YIELD: 6 (1⅓-CUP) SERVINGS

8 oz. (2 cups) uncooked penne (tube-shaped pasta)
3 cups diced peeled eggplant
2 (14.5-oz.) cans diced tomatoes, undrained
1 (15-oz.) can navy beans, drained, rinsed
3 garlic cloves, minced
2 teaspoons sugar
2 tablespoons chopped fresh Italian parsley

1. Cook penne to desired doneness as directed on package. Drain; cover to keep warm.
2. Meanwhile, in Dutch oven or large saucepan, combine eggplant, tomatoes, beans, garlic and sugar; mix well. Bring to a boil over medium-high heat. Reduce heat to low; simmer 10 to 15 minutes or until eggplant is tender. If desired, add coarse ground black pepper to taste.
3. Add penne to eggplant mixture; toss gently to mix. Sprinkle with parsley.

NUTRITION INFORMATION PER SERVING: Serving Size: 1⅓ Cups ✦ Calories: 270 ✦ Calories from Fat: 10 ✦ **% DAILY VALUE:** Total Fat: 1 g 2% ✦ Saturated Fat: 0 g 0% ✦ Cholesterol: 0 mg 0% ✦ Sodium: 370 mg 15% ✦ Total Carbohydrate: 53 g 18% ✦ Dietary Fiber: 7 g 28% ✦ Sugars: 9 g ✦ Protein: 12 g ✦ Vitamin A: 20% ✦ Vitamin C: 25% ✦ Calcium: 8% ✦ Iron: 20% ✦ **DIETARY EXCHANGES:** 3 Starch, 1 Vegetable OR 3 Carbohydrate, 1 Vegetable

Penne Provençal

Fettuccine Alfredo

PREP TIME: 25 MINUTES ✦ YIELD: 6 SERVINGS

12 oz. uncooked fettuccine
¾ cup butter
1 cup whipping cream
¼ teaspoon white pepper
1¼ cups grated Parmesan cheese
2 teaspoons chopped fresh parsley, if desired
¼ teaspoon nutmeg, if desired

1. Cook fettuccine to desired doneness as directed on package. Drain; cover to keep warm.
2. Meanwhile, melt butter in 6-quart Dutch oven over low heat. Stir in cream and pepper. Cook about 5 minutes or until mixture thickens slightly, stirring frequently.
3. Stir in Parmesan cheese; cook over low heat just until cheese is melted, stirring constantly. Immediately stir in cooked fettuccine; toss to coat with sauce. Stir in parsley and nutmeg. If sauce begins to separate, stir in a little more cream and cook over low heat until smooth.

NUTRITION INFORMATION PER SERVING: Serving Size: ⅙ of Recipe ✦ Calories: 650 ✦ Calories from Fat: 410 ✦ % DAILY VALUE: Total Fat: 46 g 71% ✦ Saturated Fat: 28 g 140% ✦ Cholesterol: 185 mg 62% ✦ Sodium: 650 mg 27% ✦ Total Carbohydrate: 42 g 14% ✦ Dietary Fiber: 2 g 8% ✦ Sugars: 3 g ✦ Protein: 18 g ✦ Vitamin A: 35% ✦ Vitamin C: 0% ✦ Calcium: 35% ✦ Iron: 15% ✦ DIETARY EXCHANGES: 3 Starch, 1 High-Fat Meat, 7 Fat OR 3 Carbohydrate, 1 High-Fat Meat, 7 Fat

Low-Fat Alfredo Sauce over Fettuccine

PREP TIME: 25 MINUTES ✦ YIELD: 5 (1½-CUP) SERVINGS

12 oz. uncooked fettuccine
2 teaspoons margarine or butter
1 teaspoon olive oil
3 large garlic cloves, minced
¼ cup finely chopped red bell pepper
¼ cup sliced green onions
¼ cup chopped fresh parsley or 3 teaspoons dried parsley flakes
1 tablespoon all-purpose flour
1 (12-oz.) can lite evaporated skimmed milk
½ teaspoon dried basil leaves
¼ teaspoon dried oregano leaves
¼ cup grated Parmesan cheese

1. Cook fettuccine to desired doneness as directed on package. Drain.
2. Meanwhile, melt margarine with oil in large nonstick skillet or Dutch oven over medium-high heat. Add garlic; cook 1 minute. Add bell pepper, onions, parsley and flour; cook and stir 1 minute. Gradually stir in milk; blend well. Bring to a boil, stirring constantly. Cook 3 to 5 minutes or until sauce boils and thickens, stirring frequently.
3. Remove skillet from heat; stir in basil and oregano. Add cooked fettuccine; toss gently to coat. Sprinkle with cheese.

NUTRITION INFORMATION PER SERVING: Serving Size: 1½ Cups ✦ Calories: 310 ✦ Calories from Fat: 50 ✦ % DAILY VALUE: Total Fat: 6 g 9% ✦ Saturated Fat: 2 g 10% ✦ Cholesterol: 60 mg 20% ✦ Sodium: 180 mg 8% ✦ Total Carbohydrate: 50 g 17% ✦ Dietary Fiber: 2 g 8% ✦ Sugars: 10 g ✦ Protein: 15 g ✦ Vitamin A: 15% ✦ Vitamin C: 15% ✦ Calcium: 25% ✦ Iron: 15% ✦ DIETARY EXCHANGES: 3½ Starch, ½ Medium-Fat Meat OR 3½ Carbohydrate, ½ Medium-Fat Meat

Spicy Corn and Zucchini with Ramen Noodles

PREP TIME: 20 MINUTES ✦ YIELD: 3 (1⅓-CUP) SERVINGS

NOODLES
1 (3-oz.) pkg. any flavor ramen noodle soup mix

SAUCE
1 teaspoon sugar
1 teaspoon cornstarch
¼ to ½ teaspoon crushed red pepper flakes
¼ cup water
2 tablespoons soy sauce

STIR-FRY
1 tablespoon oil
2 medium zucchini, cut into ¼-inch-thick slices (2 cups)
1 medium onion, cut into thin wedges
1 garlic clove, minced
1 (14-oz.) can baby corn nuggets, drained, rinsed

1. In medium saucepan, bring 2 cups water to a boil. Add noodles from soup mix; boil 2 to 3 minutes or until noodles are tender. Drain; cover to keep warm. (Discard seasoning packet or reserve for another use.)
2. Meanwhile, in small bowl, combine all sauce ingredients; mix well. Set aside.
3. Heat oil in large nonstick skillet over

medium-high heat until hot. Add zucchini, onion and garlic; cook and stir 2 minutes. Reduce heat to medium-low; stir in corn and sauce mixture. Cook 2 to 4 minutes or until vegetables are crisp-tender and mixture is bubbly and thickened, stirring frequently. Stir in cooked noodles.

NUTRITION INFORMATION PER SERVING: Serving Size: 1⅓ Cups ◆ Calories: 180 ◆ Calories from Fat: 70 ◆ **% DAILY VALUE:** Total Fat: 8 g 12% ◆ Saturated Fat: 2 g 10% ◆ Cholesterol: 0 mg 0% ◆ Sodium: 710 mg 40% ◆ Total Carbohydrate: 21 g 7% ◆ Dietary Fiber: 4 g 16% ◆ Sugars: 6 g ◆ Protein: 5 g ◆ Vitamin A: 10% ◆ Vitamin C: 15% ◆ Calcium: 6% ◆ Iron: 10% ◆ **DIETARY EXCHANGES:** 1½ Starch, 1½ Fat OR 1½ Carbohydrate, 1½ Fat

New Potato, Pasta and Vegetable Stir-Fry

PREP TIME: 30 MINUTES ◆ YIELD: 4 (1¾-CUP) SERVINGS

  8 oz. (3 cups) uncooked bow tie pasta (farfalle)
  2 tablespoons olive or vegetable oil
  1 medium onion, cut into 8 wedges
  4 new red potatoes, unpeeled, sliced
  8 oz. fresh asparagus spears, trimmed, cut into 2-inch pieces
  1 medium red or yellow bell pepper, cut into strips
  2 tablespoons chopped fresh oregano
  ½ teaspoon salt
  ⅛ teaspoon pepper
  4 oz. (1 cup) shredded Swiss cheese

1. Cook pasta to desired doneness as directed on package. Drain.

2. Meanwhile, heat oil in large skillet over medium-high heat until hot. Add onion; cook and stir 2 minutes. Add potatoes; cover and cook 5 to 6 minutes or until partially cooked, stirring occasionally.

3. Stir in asparagus, bell pepper, oregano, salt and pepper. Reduce heat to medium-low; cover and cook 5 to 8 minutes or until vegetables are tender, stirring occasionally.

4. Stir in cooked pasta; cook until thoroughly heated. Remove from heat. Sprinkle with cheese. Cover; let stand until cheese is melted.

NUTRITION INFORMATION PER SERVING: Serving Size: 1¾ Cups ◆ Calories: 510 ◆ Calories from Fat: 140 ◆ **% DAILY VALUE:** Total Fat: 16 g 25% ◆ Saturated Fat: 6 g 30% ◆ Cholesterol: 25 mg 8% ◆ Sodium: 350 mg 15% ◆ Total Carbohydrate: 72 g 24% ◆ Dietary Fiber: 6 g 24% ◆ Sugars: 7 g ◆ Protein: 19 g ◆ Vitamin C: 70% ◆ Calcium: 30% ◆ Iron: 25% ◆ **DIETARY EXCHANGES:** 4½ Starch, 1 Vegetable, ½ High-Fat Meat, 2 Fat OR 4½ Carbohydrate, 1 Vegetable, ½ High-Fat Meat, 2 Fat

Five-Spice Mushroom and Broccoli Stir-Fry

PREP TIME: 35 MINUTES ◆ YIELD: 4 SERVINGS

  1 (7-oz.) pkg. uncooked vermicelli
  ½ cup orange juice
  1 tablespoon cornstarch
  ¾ teaspoon Chinese five-spice powder
  ⅛ to ¼ teaspoon crushed red pepper flakes
  2 tablespoons soy sauce
  2 teaspoons honey or sugar
  8 large mushrooms (12 oz.), cut into ¼-inch-thick slices
  1 cup fresh baby carrots, quartered lengthwise
  1 medium onion, cut into thin wedges
  1 garlic clove, minced
  3 cups small broccoli florets (about 6 oz.)

1. Cook vermicelli to desired doneness as directed on package. Drain; cover to keep warm.

2. Meanwhile, in small bowl, combine orange juice, cornstarch, five-spice powder, red pepper flakes, soy sauce and honey; blend well. Set aside.

3. Spray large nonstick skillet with nonstick cooking spray. Heat over medium-high heat until hot. Add mushrooms, carrots, onion and garlic; cook and stir 4 minutes.

4. Add broccoli; cover and cook 2 to 4 minutes or until vegetables are crisp-tender, stirring occasionally. Add orange juice mixture; cook and stir 2 to 3 minutes or until bubbly and thickened. Serve over cooked vermicelli.

NUTRITION INFORMATION PER SERVING: Serving Size: ¼ of Recipe ◆ Calories: 300 ◆ Calories from Fat: 20 ◆ **% DAILY VALUE:** Total Fat: 2 g 3% ◆ Saturated Fat: 0 g 0% ◆ Cholesterol: 0 mg 0% ◆ Sodium: 550 mg 23% ◆ Total Carbohydrate: 59 g 20% ◆ Dietary Fiber: 6 g 24% ◆ Sugars: 13 g ◆ Protein: 11 g ◆ Vitamin A: 180% ◆ Vitamin C: 90% ◆ Calcium: 6% ◆ Iron: 25% ◆ **DIETARY EXCHANGES:** 3½ Starch, 1 Vegetable OR 3½ Carbohydrate, 1 Vegetable

Ravioli with Salsa-Black Bean Sauce

PREP TIME: 15 MINUTES ✦ YIELD: 3 (1⅓-CUP) SERVINGS

1 (9-oz.) pkg. refrigerated cheese-filled ravioli
1 (14.5-oz.) can salsa-style tomatoes,
    undrained
1 (15-oz.) can black beans, drained
2 teaspoons chili powder
½ teaspoon cumin
2 tablespoons chopped fresh cilantro

1. In large saucepan, cook ravioli to desired doneness as directed on package. Drain in colander; cover to keep warm.
2. In same saucepan, combine tomatoes, beans, chili powder and cumin; mix well. Cook over medium heat for 5 minutes or until thoroughly heated, stirring occasionally.
3. Carefully stir in cooked ravioli. Spoon onto serving platter; sprinkle with cilantro.

NUTRITION INFORMATION PER SERVING: Serving Size: 1⅓ Cups ✦ Calories: 450 ✦ Calories from Fat: 100 ✦ **% DAILY VALUE:** Total Fat: 11 g 17% ✦ Saturated Fat: 5 g 25% ✦ Cholesterol: 75 mg 25% ✦ Sodium: 930 mg 39% ✦ Total Carbohydrate: 64 g 21% ✦ Dietary Fiber: 10 g 40% ✦ Sugars: 6 g ✦ Protein: 23 g ✦ Vitamin A: 35% ✦ Vitamin C: 25% ✦ Calcium: 30% ✦ Iron: 25% ✦ **DIETARY EXCHANGES:** 4 Starch, 1 Vegetable, 1 Very Lean Meat, 1½ Fat OR 4 Carbohydrate, 1 Vegetable, 1 Very Lean Meat, 1½ Fat

Ravioli with Salsa-Black Bean Sauce

Linguine with Roasted Vegetables

PREP TIME: 35 MINUTES ✦ YIELD: 6 (1⅓-CUP) SERVINGS

6 oz. uncooked linguine
4 tomatoes, coarsely chopped
1 eggplant, unpeeled, cubed
1 red bell pepper, cut into 1-inch pieces
1 zucchini, sliced
4 garlic cloves, minced
3 tablespoons olive or vegetable oil
1 teaspoon dried basil leaves
½ teaspoon salt
⅛ teaspoon pepper
2 oz. (½ cup) shredded fresh Parmesan cheese

1. Cook linguine to desired doneness as directed on package. Drain; cover to keep warm.
2. Meanwhile, heat oven to 450°F. Spray 15 × 10 × 1-inch baking pan with nonstick cooking spray. In large bowl, combine tomatoes, eggplant, bell pepper, zucchini and garlic. Toss with 2 tablespoons of the oil, basil, salt and pepper. Place vegetables on sprayed pan.
3. Bake at 450°F. for 12 to 15 minutes or until vegetables are tender and lightly browned.
4. Place cooked linguine in serving bowl. Add remaining 1 tablespoon oil and roasted vegetables; toss gently to mix. Sprinkle with cheese.

NUTRITION INFORMATION PER SERVING: Serving Size: 1⅓ Cups ✦ Calories: 240 ✦ Calories from Fat: 90 ✦ **% DAILY VALUE:** Total Fat: 10 g 15% ✦ Saturated Fat: 3 g 15% ✦ Cholesterol: 5 mg 2% ✦ Sodium: 340 mg 14% ✦ Total Carbohydrate: 29 g 10% ✦ Dietary Fiber: 3 g 12% ✦ Sugars: 5 g ✦ Protein: 9 g ✦ Vitamin A: 30% ✦ Vitamin C: 50% ✦ Calcium: 15% ✦ Iron: 10% ✦ **DIETARY EXCHANGES:** 1½ Starch, 1 Vegetable, ½ Lean Meat, 1½ Fat OR 1½ Carbohydrate, 1 Vegetable, ½ Lean Meat, 1½ Fat

Linguine with Roasted Vegetables

Chunky Marinara Sauce

PREP TIME: 20 MINUTES (READY IN 40 MINUTES)
◆ YIELD: 4 (⅔-CUP) SERVINGS

2 teaspoons olive or vegetable oil
¼ cup chopped green bell pepper
¼ cup chopped onion
1 garlic clove, minced
1 (14.5-oz.) can diced tomatoes, undrained
1 (8-oz.) can tomato sauce
1 teaspoon sugar
½ teaspoon dried oregano leaves
¼ teaspoon salt

1. Heat oil in medium saucepan over medium-high heat until hot. Add bell pepper, onion and garlic; cook 2 to 4 minutes or until vegetables are crisp-tender, stirring frequently.
2. Add all remaining ingredients; mix well. Bring to a boil. Reduce heat to low; simmer 15 to 20 minutes or until flavors are blended, stirring frequently. Serve over hot cooked pasta.

NUTRITION INFORMATION PER SERVING: Serving Size: ⅔ Cup ◆ Calories: 80 ◆ Calories from Fat: 25 ◆ **% DAILY VALUE:** Total Fat: 3 g 5% ◆ Saturated Fat: 0 g 0% ◆ Cholesterol: 0 mg 0% ◆ Sodium: 630 mg 26% ◆ Total Carbohydrate: 11 g 4% ◆ Dietary Fiber: 2 g 8% ◆ Sugars: 6 g ◆ Protein: 2 g ◆ Vitamin A: 25% ◆ Vitamin C: 35% ◆ Calcium: 4% ◆ Iron: 6% ◆ **DIETARY EXCHANGES:** 2 Vegetable, ½ Fat

Veggie Kabobs with Cumin-Scented Couscous

PREP TIME: 35 MINUTES ◆ YIELD: 4 SERVINGS

COUSCOUS
1½ cups water
1 teaspoon vegetable-flavor instant bouillon
1 teaspoon cumin
⅛ teaspoon pepper
¼ cup chopped fresh parsley
1 (15-oz.) can garbanzo beans, drained, rinsed
1 cup uncooked couscous

KABOBS
8 fresh whole mushrooms
2 medium zucchini, cut into 1-inch-thick slices
1 medium red bell pepper, cut into 1½-inch pieces
½ small red onion, cut into 8 wedges

2 tablespoons olive or vegetable oil
1 tablespoon white wine vinegar
¼ teaspoon garlic salt

1. In medium saucepan, combine all couscous ingredients except couscous. Bring to a boil. Remove from heat; stir in couscous. Cover; let stand while broiling kabobs.
2. Meanwhile, spray broiler pan with nonstick cooking spray. Thread mushrooms, zucchini, bell pepper and onion onto four 12-inch metal skewers. Place on sprayed pan.
3. In small bowl, combine oil, vinegar and garlic salt; mix well. Brush over kabobs.
4. Broil 4 to 6 inches from heat for 10 to 12 minutes or until vegetables are crisp-tender, turning once halfway through cooking. Fluff couscous with fork; serve with kabobs.

NUTRITION INFORMATION PER SERVING: Serving Size: ¼ of Recipe ◆ Calories: 370 ◆ Calories from Fat: 80 ◆ **% DAILY VALUE:** Total Fat: 9 g 14% ◆ Saturated Fat: 1 g 5% ◆ Cholesterol: 0 mg 0% ◆ Sodium: 610 mg 25% ◆ Total Carbohydrate: 58 g 19% ◆ Dietary Fiber: 9 g 36% ◆ Sugars: 5 g ◆ Protein: 13 g ◆ Vitamin A: 30% ◆ Vitamin C: 60% ◆ Calcium: 8% ◆ Iron: 15% ◆ **DIETARY EXCHANGES:** 3½ Starch, 1 Vegetable, 1½ Fat OR 3½ Carbohydrate, 1 Vegetable, 1½ Fat

Pesto

PREP TIME: 15 MINUTES ◆ YIELD: 2 CUPS

4 garlic cloves
4 cups lightly packed fresh basil leaves, rinsed, patted dry
1 cup olive oil
½ cup pine nuts or blanched almonds
1 teaspoon salt
6 oz. (1½ cups) grated fresh Parmesan cheese

1. In food processor bowl with metal blade, process garlic until finely chopped. Add all remaining ingredients except cheese. Process until smooth and well blended. Stir in cheese.
2. Use immediately or store in jar with tight-fitting lid. Refrigerate up to 1 week or freeze for longer storage. Serve over hot cooked pasta or as an ingredient in appetizers or soups.

NUTRITION INFORMATION PER SERVING: Serving Size: 1 Tablespoon ◆ Calories: 100 ◆ Calories from Fat: 80 ◆ **% DAILY VALUE:** Total Fat: 9 g 14% ◆ Saturated Fat: 2 g 10% ◆ Cholesterol: 4 mg 1% ◆ Sodium: 150 mg 6% ◆ Total Carbohydrate: 1 g 1% ◆ Dietary Fiber: 0 g 0% ◆ Sugars: 0 g ◆ Protein: 3 g ◆ Vitamin A: 4% ◆ Vitamin C: 0% ◆ Calcium: 8% ◆ Iron: 2% ◆ **DIETARY EXCHANGES:** 2 Fat

Vegetable-Filled Manicotti

PREP TIME: 30 MINUTES (READY IN 1 HOUR 25 MINUTES)
♦ YIELD: 6 SERVINGS

1 (26-oz.) jar spaghetti sauce
1 cup water
1 (15-oz.) container light ricotta cheese
¼ cup grated Parmesan cheese
¾ cup shredded carrot
½ cup finely chopped red bell pepper
1 teaspoon cracked black pepper
1 egg
12 uncooked manicotti

1. Heat oven to 350°F. In medium bowl, combine spaghetti sauce and water; mix well. Spread 1 cup of sauce mixture in bottom of ungreased 13×9-inch (3-quart) baking dish.
2. In large bowl, combine ricotta cheese, Parmesan cheese, carrot, bell pepper, pepper and egg; blend well. Stuff cheese mixture evenly into uncooked manicotti; arrange over sauce in baking dish. Top with remaining sauce mixture. Cover tightly with foil.
3. Bake at 350°F. for 45 to 55 minutes or until manicotti are tender and sauce is bubbly.

NUTRITION INFORMATION PER SERVING: Serving Size: ⅙ of Recipe ♦ Calories: 330 ♦ Calories from Fat: 100 ♦ **% DAILY VALUE:** Total Fat: 11 g 17% ♦ Saturated Fat: 5 g 25% ♦ Cholesterol: 60 mg 20% ♦ Sodium: 690 mg 29% ♦ Total Carbohydrate: 40 g 13% ♦ Dietary Fiber: 3 g 12% ♦ Sugars: 4 g ♦ Protein: 17 g ♦ Vitamin A: 100% ♦ Vitamin C: 30% ♦ Calcium: 30% ♦ Iron: 15% ♦ **DIETARY EXCHANGES:** 1½ Starch, 1 Fruit, 2 Medium-Fat Meat OR 2½ Carbohydrate, 2 Medium-Fat Meat

Spinach and Tofu Manicotti

PREP TIME: 30 MINUTES (READY IN 1 HOUR 10 MINUTES)
♦ YIELD: 4 SERVINGS

8 uncooked manicotti
2 cups spaghetti sauce
1 (8-oz.) pkg. fat-free cream cheese
1 teaspoon dried basil leaves
⅛ teaspoon garlic powder
2 cups frozen cut leaf spinach, thawed, well drained
¼ cup grated Parmesan cheese
1 (12.3-oz.) pkg. firm tofu, drained
2 oz. (½ cup) shredded mozzarella cheese

1. Cook manicotti to desired doneness as directed on package. Drain; cover to keep warm.

2. Meanwhile, heat oven to 350°F. Spread 1 cup of the spaghetti sauce in bottom of ungreased 12×8-inch (2-quart) baking dish.
3. In large bowl, combine cream cheese, basil and garlic powder; mix well. Add spinach, Parmesan cheese and tofu; mix with fork until texture resembles cottage cheese.
4. Stuff tofu mixture into each cooked manicotti; arrange in baking dish over sauce. Top with remaining 1 cup sauce. Cover tightly with foil.
5. Bake at 350°F. for 25 to 35 minutes or until thoroughly heated. Remove foil; sprinkle with mozzarella cheese. Let stand 5 minutes before serving.

NUTRITION INFORMATION PER SERVING: Serving Size: ¼ of Recipe ♦ Calories: 400 ♦ Calories from Fat: 100 ♦ **% DAILY VALUE:** Total Fat: 11 g 17% ♦ Saturated Fat: 4 g 20% ♦ Cholesterol: 20 mg 7% ♦ Sodium: 1100 mg 46% ♦ Total Carbohydrate: 45 g 15% ♦ Dietary Fiber: 5 g 20% ♦ Sugars: 5 g ♦ Protein: 30 g ♦ Vitamin A: 70% ♦ Vitamin C: 20% ♦ Calcium: 70% ♦ Iron: 25% ♦ **DIETARY EXCHANGES:** 3 Starch, 3 Lean Meat OR 3 Carbohydrate, 3 Lean Meat

Spinach Gnocchi

PREP TIME: 40 MINUTES (READY IN 1 HOUR)
♦ YIELD: 3 SERVINGS

½ cup all-purpose flour
1 (9-oz.) pkg. frozen spinach in a pouch, thawed, squeezed to drain
1 cup mashed potatoes
¾ cup soft bread crumbs
1 egg
¼ cup grated Parmesan cheese
⅛ teaspoon white pepper
⅛ teaspoon nutmeg
1½ cups spaghetti sauce

1. In large bowl, combine flour and all ingredients except spaghetti sauce. Mix until mixture forms a smooth dough. Divide dough into quarters. Form each quarter into log ¾ inch thick and 12 inches long. Cut each log into 1-inch pieces. If necessary, roll pieces lightly in additional flour to keep from sticking.
2. Heat oven to 325°F. Grease 12×8-inch (2-quart) baking dish. In large saucepan, bring 4 cups water to a boil. Reduce heat to low; drop dough pieces, a few at a time, into simmering water. Cook 4 minutes. Remove gnocchi with slotted spoon; place in greased baking dish. Repeat with remaining dough pieces.
3. Bake at 325°F. for 20 to 25 minutes or until thoroughly heated.

4. Meanwhile, heat spaghetti sauce. Serve sauce over gnocchi.

NUTRITION INFORMATION PER SERVING: Serving Size: ⅓ of Recipe ✦ Calories: 400 ✦ Calories from Fat: 80 ✦ **% DAILY VALUE:** Total Fat: 9 g 14% ✦ Saturated Fat: 3 g 15% ✦ Cholesterol: 75 mg 25% ✦ Sodium: 1110 mg 46% ✦ Total Carbohydrate: 63 g 21% ✦ Dietary Fiber: 6 g 24% ✦ Sugars: 3 g ✦ Protein: 17 g ✦ Vitamin A: 70% ✦ Vitamin C: 45% ✦ Calcium: 30% ✦ Iron: 25% ✦ **DIETARY EXCHANGES:** 4 Starch, 1 Vegetable, ½ Lean Meat, 1 Fat OR 4 Carbohydrate, 1 Vegetable, ½ Lean Meat, 1 Fat

Grown-Up Mac and Cheese

PREP TIME: 30 MINUTES ✦ YIELD: 4 (1½-CUP) SERVINGS

  8 oz. (2½ cups) uncooked mostaccioli or penne (tube-shaped pasta)
  2 tablespoons margarine or butter
  2 tablespoons all-purpose flour
  ¼ teaspoon salt
  ⅛ teaspoon white pepper
    Dash nutmeg
1¼ cups half-and-half
  2 oz. (½ cup) shredded fontina cheese
  2 oz. (½ cup) shredded Swiss cheese
  2 oz. (½ cup) shredded fresh Parmesan cheese
  2 tablespoons dry white wine
  2 Italian plum tomatoes, thinly sliced
  1 teaspoon olive or vegetable oil
  2 tablespoons sliced green onions

1. Heat oven to 350°F. Spray 1½-quart casserole with nonstick cooking spray. Cook mostaccioli to desired doneness as directed on package. Drain.
2. Meanwhile, melt margarine in large saucepan over medium heat. Stir in flour, salt, pepper and nutmeg; cook and stir until bubbly. Gradually add half-and-half, stirring constantly. Cook until mixture boils and thickens, stirring frequently. Remove from heat. Stir in fontina, Swiss and Parmesan cheeses until melted. (Cheeses will be stringy.) Stir in wine.
3. Add mostaccioli to cheese sauce; stir gently to coat. Pour into sprayed dish. Arrange sliced tomatoes around outside edge of dish. Brush tomatoes with oil; sprinkle with onions.
4. Bake at 350°F. for 20 to 25 minutes or until edges are bubbly and mixture is thoroughly heated.

NUTRITION INFORMATION PER SERVING: Serving Size: 1½ Cups ✦ Calories: 570 ✦ Calories from Fat: 260 ✦ **% DAILY VALUE:** Total Fat: 29 g 45% ✦ Saturated Fat: 15 g 75% ✦ Cholesterol: 70 mg 23% ✦ Sodium: 650 mg 27% ✦ Total Carbohydrate: 51 g 17% ✦ Dietary Fiber: 2 g 8% ✦ Sugars: 6 g ✦ Protein: 24 g ✦ Vitamin A: 20% ✦ Vitamin C: 6% ✦ Calcium: 50% ✦ Iron: 15% ✦ **DIETARY EXCHANGES:** 3½ Starch, 2 High-Fat Meat, 2 Fat OR 3½ Carbohydrate, 2 High-Fat Meat, 2 Fat

Spinach Lasagna

PREP TIME: 40 MINUTES (READY IN 1 HOUR 20 MINUTES) ✦ YIELD: 6 SERVINGS

  9 uncooked lasagna noodles
2½ cups milk
  ¼ cup all-purpose flour
  1 teaspoon garlic salt
  2 (9-oz.) pkg. frozen spinach in a pouch, thawed, squeezed to drain
  1 cup cottage cheese
  6 oz. (1½ cups) shredded mozzarella cheese
  ¼ cup grated Parmesan cheese

1. Cook lasagna noodles to desired doneness as directed on package. Drain; rinse with hot water.
2. Meanwhile, heat oven to 350°F. In medium saucepan, combine milk, flour and garlic salt; blend well. Cook over medium heat, stirring constantly, until mixture boils and thickens. Reserve ½ cup sauce for top layer of lasagna; stir spinach into remaining sauce.
3. In medium bowl, combine cottage cheese and mozzarella. Spread ½ cup spinach sauce in bottom of ungreased 13 × 9-inch (3-quart) baking dish. Top with 3 lasagna noodles, half of cheese mixture and half of remaining spinach sauce; repeat layers. Top with last 3 noodles and reserved ½ cup sauce. Sprinkle with Parmesan cheese.
4. Bake at 350°F. for 30 to 40 minutes. Let stand 5 to 10 minutes before serving. If desired, garnish individual servings with fresh basil and tomato wedges.

NUTRITION INFORMATION PER SERVING: Serving Size: ⅙ of Recipe ✦ Calories: 340 ✦ Calories from Fat: 90 ✦ **% DAILY VALUE:** Total Fat: 10 g 15% ✦ Saturated Fat: 6 g 30% ✦ Cholesterol: 30 mg 10% ✦ Sodium: 940 mg 39% ✦ Total Carbohydrate: 37 g 12% ✦ Dietary Fiber: 2 g 8% ✦ Sugars: 8 g ✦ Protein: 25 g ✦ Vitamin A: 70% ✦ Vitamin C: 20% ✦ Calcium: 50% ✦ Iron: 15% ✦ **DIETARY EXCHANGES:** 2 Starch, 1 Vegetable, 2½ Lean Meat, ½ Fat OR 2 Carbohydrate, 1 Vegetable, 2½ Lean Meat, ½ Fat

Creamy Mushroom Lasagna with Fresh Tomatoes

PREP TIME: I HOUR (READY IN I HOUR 25 MINUTES)
◆ YIELD: 8 SERVINGS

LASAGNA
    I oz. (I cup) dried porcini mushrooms
    8 uncooked lasagna noodles
    I (15-oz.) container light ricotta cheese
    2 eggs
    ½ cup grated Parmesan cheese
    2 tablespoons chopped fresh parsley
        or 2 teaspoons dried parsley flakes
    ½ teaspoon salt
    ⅛ teaspoon pepper
    2 teaspoons olive or vegetable oil
    5 oz. (1⅔ cups) sliced cremini or white
        mushrooms
    I large garlic clove, minced
    2 tablespoons dry sherry
    ¼ cup whipping cream
    8 oz. (2 cups) shredded provolone cheese

TOMATOES
    2 teaspoons olive or vegetable oil
    2 tablespoons finely chopped shallots
    I garlic clove, minced
    2 tablespoons chopped fresh basil
        or 2 teaspoons dried basil leaves
    6 large Italian plum tomatoes,
        chopped (2 cups)

1. Rehydrate porcini mushrooms as directed on package. Drain mushrooms; coarsely chop. Set aside.
2. Meanwhile, cook lasagna noodles to desired doneness as directed on package. Drain; place in cold water.
3. Heat oven to 350°F. Spray 13×9-inch (3-quart) baking dish with nonstick cooking spray. In large bowl, combine ricotta cheese, eggs, Parmesan cheese, parsley, salt and pepper; mix well. Set aside.
4. Heat 2 teaspoons oil in large skillet over medium heat until hot. Add rehydrated porcini mushrooms, cremini mushrooms and minced large garlic clove; cook and stir 2 to 3 minutes or until mushrooms are tender. Add sherry; cook until most of the liquid has evaporated. Stir in cream; bring to a boil. Remove skillet from heat.
5. To assemble lasagna, drain lasagna noodles; arrange 4 noodles in bottom of sprayed dish. Spoon and spread half of cheese mixture over noodles. Evenly spoon half of mushroom mixture over cheese. Sprinkle with 1 cup of the provolone cheese. Repeat layers. Cover with foil.
6. Bake at 350°F. for 20 to 30 minutes or until filling is set and edges are bubbly.
7. While lasagna is baking, prepare tomatoes. In same large skillet, heat 2 teaspoons oil over medium heat until hot. Add shallots and 1 minced garlic clove; cook and stir until tender. Stir in basil and tomatoes; cook just until thoroughly heated. Spoon tomatoes over individual servings of lasagna.

NUTRITION INFORMATION PER SERVING: Serving Size: ⅛ of Recipe ◆ Calories: 380 ◆ Calories from Fat: 190 ◆ **% DAILY VALUE:** Total Fat: 21 g 32% ◆ Saturated Fat: 11 g 55% ◆ Cholesterol: 105 mg 35% ◆ Sodium: 590 mg 25% ◆ Total Carbohydrate: 26 g 9% ◆ Dietary Fiber: 2 g 8% ◆ Sugars: 4 g ◆ Protein: 22 g ◆ Vitamin A: 20% ◆ Vitamin C: 15% ◆ Calcium: 45% ◆ Iron: 10% ◆ **DIETARY EXCHANGES:** 1½ Starch, 1 Vegetable, 2 High-Fat Meat, 1 Fat OR 1½ Carbohydrate, 1 Vegetable, 2 High-Fat Meat, 1 Fat

Potatoes Curry

PREP TIME: 40 MINUTES ◆ YIELD: 4 (1½-CUP) SERVINGS

    4 cups coarsely chopped cauliflower
    ¾ lb. small red potatoes (about 8), cut
        into ¾-inch pieces (2 to 2½ cups)
    I cup frozen sweet peas, thawed
    2 medium tomatoes, chopped
    I (15-oz.) can garbanzo beans, drained, rinsed
    3 teaspoons curry powder
    ¼ teaspoon salt
    2 teaspoons olive oil
    ½ cup water

1. GRILL DIRECTIONS: Heat grill. In large bowl, combine cauliflower, potatoes, peas, tomatoes and garbanzo beans. Add curry powder and salt; mix well. Add oil; toss to coat.
2. Cut four 12-inch squares of heavy-duty foil or double thicknesses of regular foil. Divide vegetable mixture evenly onto foil squares. Sprinkle each with 2 tablespoons water. Wrap each packet securely using double-fold seals, allowing room for heat expansion.
3. When ready to grill, place packets on gas grill over medium heat or on charcoal grill 4 to 6 inches from medium coals. Cook 15 to 20 minutes or until potatoes are tender.

TIP: To bake packets, place on ungreased cookie sheet. Bake at 450°F. for 20 to 30 minutes.

NUTRITION INFORMATION PER SERVING: Serving Size: 1½ Cups ✦ Calories: 290 ✦ Calories from Fat: 45 ✦ **% DAILY VALUE:** Total Fat: 5 g 8% ✦ Saturated Fat: 1 g 5% ✦ Cholesterol: 0 mg 0% ✦ Sodium: 380 mg 16% ✦ Total Carbohydrate: 50 g 17% ✦ Dietary Fiber: 12 g 48% ✦ Sugars: 6 g ✦ Protein: 11 g ✦ Vitamin A: 10% ✦ Vitamin C: 90% ✦ Calcium: 8% ✦ Iron: 20% ✦ **DIETARY EXCHANGES:** 3 Starch, 1 Vegetable, ½ Fat OR 3 Carbohydrate, 1 Vegetable, ½ Fat

Eggs Foo Yong

PREP TIME: 30 MINUTES ✦ YIELD: 5 SERVINGS

EGGS
- 6 eggs
- ½ cup finely chopped onion
- 2 tablespoons chopped green bell pepper
- ½ teaspoon salt
  Dash pepper
- 1 (16-oz.) can bean sprouts, drained, rinsed
- 2 tablespoons oil

SAUCE
- 1 tablespoon cornstarch
- 2 teaspoons sugar
- 1 vegetable or chicken-flavor instant bouillon
  Dash ginger
- 1 cup water
- 2 tablespoons soy sauce

1. Heat oven to 300°F. In large bowl, beat eggs well. Add onion, bell pepper, salt, pepper and bean sprouts; mix well.
2. Heat oil in large skillet over medium heat. Drop egg mixture by tablespoonfuls into skillet. Cook until golden brown on both sides. Drain on paper towels. If necessary, add more oil to skillet. Place egg patties on ovenproof dish; keep warm in 300°F. oven while preparing sauce.
3. In small saucepan, combine all sauce ingredients; blend well. Cook until mixture boils and thickens, stirring constantly. Serve egg patties with sauce.

Potatoes Curry (page 228)

NUTRITION INFORMATION PER SERVING: Serving Size: ⅓ of Recipe ✦ Calories: 170 ✦ Calories from Fat: 110 ✦ **% DAILY VALUE:** Total Fat: 12 g 18% ✦ Saturated Fat: 3 g 15% ✦ Cholesterol: 255 mg 85% ✦ Sodium: 1030 mg 43% ✦ Total Carbohydrate: 7 g 2% ✦ Dietary Fiber: 1 g 3% ✦ Sugars: 4 g ✦ Protein: 9 g ✦ Vitamin A: 8% ✦ Vitamin C: 4% ✦ Calcium: 4% ✦ Iron: 8% ✦ **DIETARY EXCHANGES:** ½ Starch, 1 Medium-Fat Meat, 1 Fat OR ½ Carbohydrate, 1 Medium-Fat Meat, 1 Fat

Polenta Wedges with Spaghetti Sauce

PREP TIME: 40 MINUTES ✦ YIELD: 6 SERVINGS

POLENTA
- 1 cup yellow cornmeal
- 1 cup water
- 1 (14½-oz.) can ready-to-serve vegetable or chicken broth
- ⅓ cup grated Parmesan cheese
- ¼ cup chopped fresh parsley
- 1 (2-oz.) jar diced pimientos, drained

SAUCE
- ¾ cup spaghetti sauce
- 2 teaspoons olive oil

1. Line cookie sheet with foil. In medium nonstick saucepan, combine cornmeal and water; beat with wire whisk until well blended. Add broth; bring to a boil over medium-high heat. Cook 10 to 15 minutes, stirring constantly with wire whisk, until mixture is very thick and begins to pull away from sides of pan while stirring.
2. Remove from heat. Reserve 1 tablespoon of the Parmesan cheese for topping; stir remaining Parmesan cheese, parsley and pimientos into cornmeal mixture. Spread evenly in ungreased 9-inch round cake pan. Cover; refrigerate 10 minutes or until set.
3. Meanwhile, heat spaghetti sauce in small saucepan; cover to keep warm.
4. Turn polenta out onto foil-lined cookie sheet, tapping bottom of pan to release. Cut into 6 wedges; separate slightly. Brush tops with oil; sprinkle with reserved tablespoon of Parmesan cheese.
5. Broil 4 to 6 inches from heat for 3 to 5 minutes or until thoroughly heated. To serve, spoon spaghetti sauce over polenta wedges.

NUTRITION INFORMATION PER SERVING: Serving Size: ⅙ of Recipe ✦ Calories: 150 ✦ Calories from Fat: 45 ✦ **% DAILY VALUE:** Total Fat: 5 g 8% ✦ Saturated Fat: 1 g 5% ✦ Cholesterol: 4 mg 1% ✦ Sodium: 540 mg 23% ✦ Total Carbohydrate: 20 g 7% ✦ Dietary Fiber: 2 g 8% ✦ Sugars: 2 g ✦ Protein: 5 g ✦ Vitamin A: 15% ✦ Vitamin C: 15% ✦ Calcium: 8% ✦ Iron: 8% ✦ **DIETARY EXCHANGES:** 1½ Starch, ½ Fat OR 1½ Carbohydrate, ½ Fat

Mediterranean Pasta Torte

PREP TIME: 30 MINUTES (READY IN 1 HOUR 25 MINUTES)
◆ YIELD: 6 SERVINGS

12 oz. (3 cups) uncooked ziti (long tubular pasta)
2½ cups cubed (½-inch) peeled eggplant (8 oz.)
1 medium onion, chopped
1 (15-oz.) can chunky tomato sauce with onions, celery and green bell peppers, undrained
½ teaspoon cinnamon
½ teaspoon dried oregano leaves, crushed
2 cups milk
2 tablespoons all-purpose flour
¼ teaspoon salt
⅛ teaspoon pepper
2 eggs
½ cup grated Parmesan cheese
3 tablespoons unseasoned dry bread crumbs
2 teaspoons margarine or butter, melted

1. Heat oven to 350°F. Spray 12 × 8-inch (2-quart) baking dish and 14 × 12-inch sheet of foil with nonstick cooking spray. Set aside. In Dutch oven or large saucepan, cook ziti to desired doneness as directed on package. Drain; return to Dutch oven. Cover to keep warm.

2. Meanwhile, in medium saucepan, combine eggplant, onion, tomato sauce, cinnamon and oregano; mix well. Bring to a boil. Reduce heat to low; simmer 10 to 15 minutes or until onion and eggplant are crisp-tender, stirring frequently.

3. In another medium saucepan, combine ½ cup of the milk, flour, salt and pepper; mix with wire whisk until smooth. Stir in remaining 1½ cups milk. Cook over medium heat until mixture boils and thickens, stirring constantly. Boil and stir 1 minute. Remove from heat.

4. In medium bowl, beat eggs; gradually add half of the hot milk mixture to beaten eggs, stirring constantly. Stir egg mixture back into mixture in saucepan. Add cheese; mix well. Add to cooked ziti; toss gently to coat evenly. Place half of ziti mixture in sprayed dish. Spoon tomato sauce over ziti. Top with remaining ziti mixture. Cover tightly with sprayed foil.

5. Bake at 350°F. for 35 to 45 minutes or until casserole is bubbly.

6. In small bowl, combine bread crumbs and melted margarine; mix well. Sprinkle over top; bake uncovered for an additional 5 minutes. Let stand 5 minutes before serving.

NUTRITION INFORMATION PER SERVING: Serving Size: ⅙ of Recipe ◆ Calories: 390 ◆ Calories from Fat: 80 ◆ % DAILY VALUE: Total Fat: 9 g 14% ◆ Saturated Fat: 4 g 20% ◆ Cholesterol: 85 mg 28% ◆ Sodium: 740 mg 31% ◆ Total Carbohydrate: 61 g 20% ◆ Dietary Fiber: 4 g 16% ◆ Sugars: 11 g ◆ Protein: 17 g ◆ Vitamin A: 20% ◆ Vitamin C: 15% ◆ Calcium: 25% ◆ Iron: 20% ◆ DIETARY EXCHANGES: 3½ Starch, 1½ Vegetable, ½ Lean Meat, 1 Fat OR 3½ Carbohydrate, 1½ Vegetable, ½ Lean Meat, 1 Fat

Thai Tofu and Vegetables in Peanut Sauce

PREP TIME: 30 MINUTES ◆ YIELD: 4 SERVINGS

1 (6-oz.) pkg. uncooked rice sticks (rice noodles)
1 (10-oz.) pkg. firm or extra-firm tofu, cut into ¾-inch cubes (1½ cups)
1 tablespoon peanut oil
½ (3.5-oz.) pkg. peanut sauce mix
1 cup coconut milk
2 cups shredded Chinese (napa) cabbage
2 cups shredded spinach
1 cup cut (1-inch) green onions
1 cup fresh bean sprouts
¼ cup coarsely chopped dry-roasted peanuts

1. Cook rice sticks as directed on package.

2. Meanwhile, gently press tofu between layers of paper towels to remove excess moisture.

3. Heat oil in large nonstick skillet or wok over medium heat until hot. Add tofu; cook and gently stir 4 to 5 minutes or until lightly browned. Remove from skillet; cover to keep warm.

4. Drain rice sticks; cover to keep warm.

5. In same skillet, combine sauce mix and coconut milk; mix well. Bring to a boil, stirring constantly. Reduce heat to low; simmer 4 minutes, stirring occasionally. Add cabbage, spinach, onions, bean sprouts and tofu; cook and stir until thoroughly heated. Serve over cooked rice sticks; sprinkle with peanuts.

NUTRITION INFORMATION PER SERVING: Serving Size: ¼ of Recipe ◆ Calories: 550 ◆ Calories from Fat: 240 ◆ % DAILY VALUE: Total Fat: 27 g 42% ◆ Saturated Fat: 14 g 70% ◆ Cholesterol: 0 mg 0% ◆ Sodium: 550 mg 23% ◆ Total Carbohydrate: 61 g 20% ◆ Dietary Fiber: 6 g 24% ◆ Sugars: 15 g ◆ Protein: 16 g ◆ Vitamin A: 60% ◆ Vitamin C: 35% ◆ Calcium: 20% ◆ Iron: 35% ◆ DIETARY EXCHANGES: 2 Starch, 1½ Fruit, 1½ Vegetable, 1 Medium-Fat Meat, 4 Fat OR 3½ Carbohydrate, 1½ Vegetable, 1 Medium-Fat Meat, 4 Fat

TOFU

Tofu, made of soybean curd that is pressed into a block, is high in protein and low in fat, making it a good choice for rounding out vegetarian meals. It has a very mild flavor of its own, and can easily carry the flavor of hot peppers, garlic and other ingredients.

Varieties of tofu include *firm*, which holds its shape for use in soups and stir-fries; *soft*, which works well for blended dishes; and *silken*, which is smooth and delicate, somewhat like custard.

Tofu comes packed in water. After you open the package, change the water every other day. Tofu is highly perishable and should be refrigerated for no more than a week. It can be frozen for up to 3 months. Freezing will change the texture, making it slightly chewier. Discard tofu if it develops a sour or "off" odor.

Easy ways to use tofu include:

+ Mash with cottage cheese, chopped celery, chopped onion and herbs to make a sandwich spread.
+ Boost protein content and thickness of a milk shake.
+ Cut into tiny cubes or strips as a garnish for soup or tossed salad.
+ Add to the blender when pureeing soup.
+ Mash with potatoes.
+ Add to a vegetable stir-fry.

Jerked Tofu and Vegetable Packets

PREP TIME: 30 MINUTES ◆ YIELD: 4 SERVINGS

1 (10-oz.) pkg. firm or extra-firm tofu, well drained, cut into 8 cubes
1 cup fresh or canned pineapple chunks
1 medium zucchini, cut into ½-inch-thick slices
1 small yellow summer squash, cut into ½-inch-thick slices
1 red bell pepper, cut into 16 pieces
¼ cup purchased jerk seasoning sauce

1. GRILL DIRECTIONS: Heat grill. Cut four 18 × 12-inch pieces of heavy-duty foil; spray with nonstick cooking spray. In medium bowl, combine all ingredients except seasoning sauce. Drizzle with sauce; toss gently to coat.
2. Divide mixture evenly onto sprayed foil pieces. Wrap each packet securely with double-fold seals, allowing room for heat expansion.
3. When ready to grill, place packets on gas grill over medium heat or on charcoal grill 4 to 6 inches from medium coals. Cook 15 to 20 minutes or until vegetables are tender, turning packets over once.

> **TIP:** To bake packets, place on cookie sheet; bake at 450°F. for 15 to 20 minutes or until vegetables are tender, turning packets over once.

NUTRITION INFORMATION PER SERVING: Serving Size: ¼ of Recipe ◆ Calories: 120 ◆ Calories from Fat: 35 ◆ **% DAILY VALUE:** Total Fat: 4 g 6% ◆ Saturated Fat: 1 g 5% ◆ Cholesterol: 0 mg 0% ◆ Sodium: 250 mg 10% ◆ Total Carbohydrate: 15 g 5% ◆ Dietary Fiber: 3 g 12% ◆ Sugars: 9 g ◆ Protein: 6 g ◆ Vitamin A: 25% ◆ Vitamin C: 70% ◆ Calcium: 10% ◆ Iron: 8% ◆ **DIETARY EXCHANGES:** ½ Fruit, 2 Vegetable, ½ Medium-Fat Meat OR ½ Carbohydrate, 2 Vegetable, ½ Medium-Fat Meat

Tofu Piccata

PREP TIME: 25 MINUTES ◆ YIELD: 8 SERVINGS

⅓ cup all-purpose flour
1 teaspoon garlic salt
1 teaspoon lemon-pepper seasoning
1 teaspoon paprika
1 lb. firm tofu
2 tablespoons oil
¼ cup water
1 teaspoon grated lemon peel
3 tablespoons lemon juice

1. In small shallow bowl, combine flour, garlic salt, lemon-pepper seasoning and paprika; mix well.
2. Cut tofu into 8 slices. If necessary, dip slices in water to moisten. Dip each slice in flour mixture, turning to coat both sides.
3. Heat oil in large nonstick skillet over medium-high heat until hot. Add tofu slices; cook 2 to 4 minutes on each side or until golden brown.
4. Add water, lemon peel and lemon juice to skillet. Reduce heat to low; simmer 5 minutes or until thoroughly heated.

NUTRITION INFORMATION PER SERVING: Serving Size: ⅛ of Recipe ◆ Calories: 100 ◆ Calories from Fat: 50 ◆ **% DAILY VALUE:** Total Fat: 6 g 9% ◆ Saturated Fat: 1 g 5% ◆ Cholesterol: 0 mg 0% ◆ Sodium: 280 mg 12% ◆ Total Carbohydrate: 6 g 2% ◆ Dietary Fiber: 0 g 0% ◆ Sugars: 1 g ◆ Protein: 5 g ◆ Vitamin A: 4% ◆ Vitamin C: 4% ◆ Calcium: 10% ◆ Iron: 6% ◆ **DIETARY EXCHANGES:** ½ Starch, ½ Medium-Fat Meat, ½ Fat OR ½ Carbohydrate, ½ Medium-Fat Meat, ½ Fat

Vegetarian Fajitas

Vegetarian Fajitas

PREP TIME: 15 MINUTES ✦ YIELD: 8 FAJITAS

2 tablespoons oil
1 green bell pepper, sliced
1 yellow bell pepper, sliced
1 medium onion, sliced
1 (11-oz.) can vacuum-packed whole kernel
    corn, drained
1 large tomato, chopped
¼ teaspoon salt
⅛ teaspoon pepper
8 (8-inch) flour tortillas, heated
    Guacamole, sour cream and/or salsa, if
    desired

1. Heat oil in large skillet or wok over medium-high heat until hot. Add bell peppers and onion; cook and stir 2 to 3 minutes or until vegetables are crisp-tender. Add corn, tomato, salt and pepper; cook until thoroughly heated.
2. To serve, place ½ cup vegetable mixture in center of each warm tortilla. Top with desired toppings; roll up.

NUTRITION INFORMATION PER SERVING: Serving Size: 1 Fajita ✦ Calories: 260 ✦ Calories from Fat: 100 ✦ **% DAILY VALUE:** Total Fat: 11 g 17% ✦ Saturated Fat: 4 g 20% ✦ Cholesterol: 5 mg 2% ✦ Sodium: 540 mg 23% ✦ Total Carbohydrate: 34 g 11% ✦ Dietary Fiber: 3 g 12% ✦ Sugars: 6 g ✦ Protein: 6 g ✦ Vitamin A: 8% ✦ Vitamin C: 40% ✦ Calcium: 8% ✦ Iron: 8% ✦ **DIETARY EXCHANGES:** 2 Starch, ½ Vegetable, 2 Fat OR 2 Carbohydrate, ½ Vegetable, 2 Fat

Black Bean Enchiladas

PREP TIME: 20 MINUTES (READY IN 40 MINUTES)
✦ YIELD: 8 ENCHILADAS

2 (10-oz.) cans enchilada sauce
1 tablespoon olive or vegetable oil
1 onion, sliced, separated into rings
1 small red bell pepper, sliced
3 garlic cloves, minced
1 (15-oz.) can black beans, drained, rinsed
8 (6-inch) soft corn tortillas, heated
8 oz. (2 cups) shredded colby-Monterey Jack
    cheese blend

1. Heat oven to 425°F. Spoon ⅔ cup of the enchilada sauce in bottom of ungreased 12 × 8-inch (2-quart) baking dish.
2. Heat oil in medium skillet over medium-high heat until hot. Add onion, bell pepper and garlic; cook and stir 2 to 3 minutes or until onion is tender.
3. In medium bowl, combine onion mixture and beans; mix well. Spoon about 2 tablespoons bean mixture down center of each tortilla. Top each with 2 tablespoons cheese; roll up. Place, seam side down, over enchilada sauce in baking dish.
4. Spoon remaining enchilada sauce over filled enchiladas. Sprinkle with remaining 1 cup cheese.
5. Bake at 425°F. for 15 to 20 minutes or until thoroughly heated.

NUTRITION INFORMATION PER SERVING: Serving Size: 1 Enchilada ✦ Calories: 270 ✦ Calories from Fat: 120 ✦ **% DAILY VALUE:** Total Fat: 13 g 20% ✦ Saturated Fat: 6 g 30% ✦ Cholesterol: 25 mg 8% ✦ Sodium: 570 mg 24% ✦ Total Carbohydrate: 25 g 8% ✦ Dietary Fiber: 4 g 16% ✦ Sugars: 3 g ✦ Protein: 12 g ✦ Vitamin A: 15% ✦ Vitamin C: 15% ✦ Calcium: 25% ✦ Iron: 8% ✦ **DIETARY EXCHANGES:** 1½ Starch, 1 Vegetable, 1 Very Lean Meat, 2 Fat OR 1½ Carbohydrate, 1 Vegetable, 1 Very Lean Meat, 2 Fat

Black Bean Enchiladas

Lentil Rice Loaf

Coconut Curried Vegetables with Rice

PREP TIME: 30 MINUTES ✦ YIELD: 4 SERVINGS

  1 cup uncooked regular long-grain white rice
  2 cups water
  2 tablespoons all-purpose flour
1½ teaspoons curry powder
  ½ teaspoon salt
  ⅛ teaspoon pepper
  1 (14-oz.) can light coconut milk
  1 teaspoon lime juice
  1 (1-lb.) pkg. frozen broccoli, carrots and
     cauliflower
  1 cup frozen sweet peas

1. Cook rice in water as directed on package.
2. Meanwhile, in small bowl, combine flour, curry powder, salt, pepper and ¼ cup of the coconut milk; beat with wire whisk until smooth. Stir in remaining coconut milk and lime juice. Set aside.
3. In large saucepan, combine frozen vegetables, peas and ½ cup water. Bring to a boil. Reduce heat to low; cover and simmer 6 to 8 minutes or until vegetables are crisp-tender. Drain; set aside.
4. Pour coconut milk mixture into same saucepan. Bring to a boil, stirring constantly. Boil and stir 1 minute. Stir in vegetables. Cook over medium heat until thoroughly heated, stirring frequently. Serve over rice.

NUTRITION INFORMATION PER SERVING: Serving Size: ¼ of Recipe ◆ Calories: 310 ◆ Calories from Fat: 50 ◆ **% DAILY VALUE:** Total Fat: 6 g 9% ◆ Saturated Fat: 5 g 25% ◆ Cholesterol: 0 mg 0% ◆ Sodium: 420 mg 18% ◆ Total Carbohydrate: 55 g 18% ◆ Dietary Fiber: 5 g 20% ◆ Sugars: 9 g ◆ Protein: 8 g ◆ Vitamin A: 60% ◆ Vitamin C: 35% ◆ Calcium: 6% ◆ Iron: 35% ◆ **DIETARY EXCHANGES:** 1½ Starch, 1½ Fruit, 2 Vegetable, 1 Fat OR 3 Carbohydrate, 2 Vegetable, 1 Fat

Coconut Curried Vegetables with Rice

Lentil Rice Loaf

PREP TIME: 45 MINUTES (READY IN 2 HOURS)
✦ YIELD: 6 SERVINGS

  3 cups water
  ¾ cup uncooked lentils, sorted, rinsed
  1 cup uncooked regular long-grain white rice
  ½ cup finely chopped onion
  ½ teaspoon salt
  1 (14-oz.) jar spaghetti sauce
  ½ cup unseasoned dry bread crumbs
  ½ cup shredded carrot
  ⅛ teaspoon coarse ground black pepper
  1 egg, slightly beaten

1. In medium saucepan, combine water and lentils. Bring to a boil. Reduce heat; cover and simmer 5 minutes. Add rice, onion and salt; mix well. Cover; simmer an additional 15 to 18 minutes or until liquid is absorbed and lentils and rice are tender. Remove from heat; cool 10 minutes.
2. Heat oven to 350°F. Grease 8×4-inch loaf (1½-quart) glass baking dish. (Do not use metal pan.) Add ¼ cup of the spaghetti sauce and remaining ingredients to lentil mixture; mix well, mashing mixture slightly while mixing. Press mixture firmly in greased dish.
3. Bake at 350°F. for 40 to 45 minutes or until top is golden brown and loaf is firm. Remove from oven; cool 10 minutes. Loosen edges with knife, if necessary; invert loaf onto serving platter.
4. In small saucepan, heat remaining spaghetti sauce for 3 to 4 minutes or until hot. To serve, slice loaf; place on individual serving plates. Spoon warm sauce over each slice.

NUTRITION INFORMATION PER SERVING: Serving Size: ⅙ of Recipe ◆ Calories: 290 ◆ Calories from Fat: 25 ◆ **% DAILY VALUE:** Total Fat: 3 g 5% ◆ Saturated Fat: 1 g 5% ◆ Cholesterol: 35 mg 12% ◆ Sodium: 540 mg 23% ◆ Total Carbohydrate: 52 g 17% ◆ Dietary Fiber: 10 g 40% ◆ Sugars: 3 g ◆ Protein: 13 g ◆ Vitamin A: 60% ◆ Vitamin C: 10% ◆ Calcium: 6% ◆ Iron: 25% ◆ **DIETARY EXCHANGES:** 3 Starch, 2 Vegetable OR 3 Carbohydrate, 2 Vegetable

Vegetable and Bean Polenta Pie

PREP TIME: 35 MINUTES (READY IN 1 HOUR 15 MINUTES)
✦ YIELD: 6 SERVINGS

POLENTA
1½ cups yellow cornmeal
2½ cups chicken broth
  2 tablespoons margarine or butter
  1 egg, slightly beaten
  ¼ cup grated Parmesan cheese

FILLING
  1 tablespoon olive or vegetable oil
  1 cup coarsely chopped onions
  1 cup coarsely chopped green bell pepper
  1 small zucchini, cut into ½-inch cubes
  1 (15.5 or 15-oz.) can dark red kidney beans, drained
  1 (14.5-oz.) can diced tomatoes with garlic, oregano and basil, undrained
  1 (6-oz.) can tomato paste
  4 oz. (1 cup) shredded mozzarella cheese

1. Heat oven to 375°F. Grease 9 or 10-inch deep-dish glass pie pan. In medium saucepan, combine cornmeal and broth. Cook over medium heat until mixture begins to boil, stirring constantly. Continue to boil 2 to 3 minutes or until mixture is thickened. Remove from heat; stir in margarine, egg and Parmesan cheese. Set aside.
2. Heat oil in large skillet over medium-high heat until hot. Add onions and bell pepper; cook and stir until tender. Stir in zucchini, beans, tomatoes and tomato paste. Bring to a boil. Reduce heat to medium-low; cook 5 minutes.
3. Spread cornmeal mixture in bottom and up sides of greased pie pan. Spoon vegetable mixture over top. Sprinkle with mozzarella cheese.
4. Bake at 375°F. for 30 to 35 minutes or until set. Let stand 5 minutes before serving.

NUTRITION INFORMATION PER SERVING: Serving Size: ⅙ of Recipe ✦ Calories: 390 ✦ Calories from Fat: 130 ✦ % DAILY VALUE: Total Fat: 14 g 22% ✦ Saturated Fat: 5 g 25% ✦ Cholesterol: 50 mg 17% ✦ Sodium: 1030 mg 43% ✦ Total Carbohydrate: 48 g 16% ✦ Dietary Fiber: 8 g 32% ✦ Sugars: 6 g ✦ Protein: 18 g ✦ Vitamin A: 35% ✦ Vitamin C: 45% ✦ Calcium: 30% ✦ Iron: 20% ✦ DIETARY EXCHANGES: 3 Starch, 1 Vegetable, 1 Medium-Fat Meat, 1 Fat OR 3 Carbohydrate, 1 Vegetable, 1 Medium-Fat Meat, 1 Fat

Quesadillas

PREP TIME: 15 MINUTES ✦ YIELD: 4 QUESADILLAS

  8 (9 or 10-inch) flour tortillas
  8 oz. (2 cups) shredded Cheddar or Monterey Jack cheese
  ½ cup salsa
  ½ cup sliced ripe olives, if desired
  1 medium avocado, sliced, if desired

1. Heat oven to 350°F. Place 4 tortillas on ungreased large cookie sheet. Top each with cheese, salsa, olives and avocado. Top each with second tortilla.
2. Bake at 350°F. for 5 minutes or until cheese is melted.

NUTRITION INFORMATION PER SERVING: Serving Size: 1 Quesadilla ✦ Calories: 700 ✦ Calories from Fat: 320 ✦ % DAILY VALUE: Total Fat: 36 g 55% ✦ Saturated Fat: 15 g 75% ✦ Cholesterol: 60 mg 20% ✦ Sodium: 1260 mg 53% ✦ Total Carbohydrate: 69 g 23% ✦ Dietary Fiber: 7 g 28% ✦ Sugars: 4 g ✦ Protein: 25 g ✦ Vitamin A: 20% ✦ Vitamin C: 4% ✦ Calcium: 60% ✦ Iron: 30% ✦ DIETARY EXCHANGES: 4 Starch, ½ Fruit, 2 High-Fat Meat, 3½ Fat OR 4½ Carbohydrate, 2 High-Fat Meat, 3½ Fat

Garden Vegetable Quesadillas

PREP TIME: 40 MINUTES ✦ YIELD: 4 QUESADILLAS

  1 tablespoon olive or vegetable oil
  1 cup thinly sliced fresh mushrooms
  1 medium onion, cut into thin wedges
  1 red bell pepper, cut into thin strips
  2 garlic cloves, minced
  ¼ teaspoon salt
  ¼ teaspoon pepper
  4 cups fresh spinach leaves, cut into strips
  1 tablespoon chopped fresh cilantro
  4 (10-inch) flour tortillas
  4 oz. (1 cup) shredded mozzarella cheese
  ½ cup chunky-style salsa

1. Heat oil in 12-inch skillet over medium-high heat until hot. Add mushrooms, onion, bell pepper, garlic, salt and pepper; cook and stir 3 minutes. Reduce heat to low; add spinach leaves. Cook an additional 1 to 2 minutes or until spinach is wilted. Remove from heat; stir in cilantro.
2. Place ¼ of vegetable mixture on half of each tortilla; sprinkle each with ¼ cup cheese. Fold remaining halves of tortillas over filling. Place tortillas on ungreased cookie sheet.

3. Broil 6 to 8 inches from heat for 2 minutes. Turn quesadillas over; broil an additional 1 to 2 minutes or until quesadillas are golden brown and cheese is melted. Serve with salsa.

NUTRITION INFORMATION PER SERVING: Serving Size: 1 Quesadilla ◆ Calories: 280 ◆ Calories from Fat: 100 ◆ **% DAILY VALUE:** Total Fat: 11 g 17% ◆ Saturated Fat: 4 g 20% ◆ Cholesterol: 15 mg 5% ◆ Sodium: 660 mg 28% ◆ Total Carbohydrate: 31 g 10% ◆ Dietary Fiber: 4 g 16% ◆ Sugars: 4 g ◆ Protein: 14 g ◆ Vitamin A: 100% ◆ Vitamin C: 70% ◆ Calcium: 30% ◆ Iron: 20% ◆ **DIETARY EXCHANGES:** 1½ Starch, 1½ Vegetable, 1 Medium-Fat Meat, 1 Fat OR 1½ Carbohydrate, 1½ Vegetable, 1 Medium-Fat Meat, 1 Fat

Spinach Potato Loaf

PREP TIME: 20 MINUTES (READY IN 1 HOUR 10 MINUTES)
◆ YIELD: 6 SERVINGS

LOAF
3 eggs
4 cups frozen hash-brown potatoes, thawed
2 cups frozen cut leaf spinach, thawed, squeezed to drain
1 cup Italian style bread crumbs
½ cup chopped onion
1 (4.5-oz.) can mushroom pieces and stems, drained, chopped
½ teaspoon salt
¼ teaspoon coarse ground black pepper
⅛ teaspoon nutmeg
SAUCE
1 (10¾-oz.) can condensed cream of mushroom soup with roasted garlic and herbs
⅓ cup milk

1. Heat oven to 350°F. Spray 8 × 4-inch loaf pan with nonstick cooking spray. In large bowl, beat eggs. Add all remaining loaf ingredients; mix well. Press mixture firmly in sprayed pan.
2. Bake at 350°F. for 45 to 50 minutes or until top is golden brown and loaf is firm. Remove loaf from oven; cool 5 minutes.
3. Meanwhile, in small saucepan, combine soup and milk; mix well. Cook over medium heat until hot, stirring frequently.
4. To serve, loosen edges of loaf with knife, if necessary; invert onto serving platter. Cut loaf into slices. Serve sauce over slices.

NUTRITION INFORMATION PER SERVING: Serving Size: ⅙ of Recipe ◆ Calories: 320 ◆ Calories from Fat: 80 ◆ **% DAILY VALUE:** Total Fat: 9 g 14% ◆ Saturated Fat: 2 g 10% ◆ Cholesterol: 110 mg 37% ◆ Sodium: 980 mg 41% ◆ Total Carbohydrate: 47 g 16% ◆ Dietary Fiber: 5 g 20% ◆ Sugars: 4 g ◆ Protein: 12 g ◆ Vitamin A: 30% ◆ Vitamin C: 20% ◆ Calcium: 15% ◆ Iron: 20% ◆ **DIETARY EXCHANGES:** 3 Starch, 1 Vegetable, 1½ Fat OR 3 Carbohydrate, 1 Vegetable, 1½ Fat

Vegetarian Fried Rice

PREP TIME: 45 MINUTES ◆ YIELD: 3 (1⅓-CUP) SERVINGS

1½ cups uncooked instant brown rice
1½ cups water
½ cup sliced fresh mushrooms
½ cup shredded carrot
¼ cup sliced green onions
¼ cup chopped green bell pepper
¼ teaspoon ginger
1 garlic clove, minced
2 tablespoons lite soy sauce
2 eggs, beaten
⅛ teaspoon pepper
¾ cup frozen sweet peas, thawed

1. Cook rice in water as directed on package.
2. Meanwhile, spray large nonstick skillet or wok with nonstick cooking spray. Heat over medium heat until hot. Add mushrooms, carrot, onions, bell pepper, ginger and garlic; cook and stir 1 minute.
3. Reduce heat to low. Stir in cooked rice and soy sauce; cook 5 minutes, stirring occasionally.
4. Push rice mixture to side of skillet; add eggs and pepper to other side. Cook over low heat for 3 to 4 minutes, stirring constantly until eggs are cooked.
5. Add peas to rice and egg mixture; stir gently to combine. Cook until thoroughly heated. If desired, serve with additional soy sauce.

NUTRITION INFORMATION PER SERVING: Serving Size: 1⅓ Cups ◆ Calories: 270 ◆ Calories from Fat: 45 ◆ **% DAILY VALUE:** Total Fat: 5 g 8% ◆ Saturated Fat: 1 g 5% ◆ Cholesterol: 140 mg 47% ◆ Sodium: 540 mg 23% ◆ Total Carbohydrate: 44 g 15% ◆ Dietary Fiber: 5 g 20% ◆ Sugars: 3 g ◆ Protein: 11 g ◆ Vitamin A: 120% ◆ Vitamin C: 20% ◆ Calcium: 4% ◆ Iron: 10% ◆ **DIETARY EXCHANGES:** 2½ Starch, 1 Vegetable, 1 Fat OR 2½ Carbohydrate, 1 Vegetable, 1 Fat

Mexican Rice and Veggie Skillet

PREP TIME: 30 MINUTES ◆ YIELD: 4 (1½-CUP) SERVINGS

1 (15.5 or 15-oz.) can kidney beans, drained, rinsed
1 (14.5-oz.) can stewed tomatoes, undrained
1 (10-oz.) can mild enchilada sauce
1 cup water
2 cups frozen mixed vegetables
1½ cups uncooked instant brown rice

1. In large nonstick skillet, combine all ingredients except rice; mix well. Bring to a boil. Stir in rice. Reduce heat to low; cover and simmer 18 to 20 minutes or until liquid is absorbed and rice is tender, stirring occasionally.
2. Remove skillet from heat. Fluff mixture with fork. If desired, add salt and pepper to taste.

NUTRITION INFORMATION PER SERVING: Serving Size: 1½ Cups ◆ Calories: 300 ◆ Calories from Fat: 25 ◆ % DAILY VALUE: Total Fat: 3 g 5% ◆ Saturated Fat: 0 g 0% ◆ Cholesterol: 0 mg 0% ◆ Sodium: 640 mg 27% ◆ Total Carbohydrate: 58 g 19% ◆ Dietary Fiber: 8 g 32% ◆ Sugars: 5 g ◆ Protein: 11 g ◆ Vitamin A: 35% ◆ Vitamin C: 20% ◆ Calcium: 10% ◆ Iron: 15% ◆ DIETARY EXCHANGES: 2½ Starch, 1 Fruit, 1 Vegetable, ½ Fat OR 3½ Carbohydrate, 1 Vegetable, ½ Fat

Asparagus Risotto

PREP TIME: 55 MINUTES ◆ YIELD: 4 (1¼-CUP) SERVINGS

3½ cups vegetable or chicken broth
3½ cups water
1 tablespoon margarine or butter
½ cup chopped onion
¼ cup shredded carrot
¼ lb. fresh asparagus, cut into 1-inch pieces, reserving tips
1 garlic clove, minced
¼ cup dry white wine
1 (12-oz.) pkg. (1⅔ cups) uncooked short-grain Arborio rice
2 oz. (½ cup) shredded fresh Parmesan cheese

1. In large saucepan, combine broth and water. Bring to a boil. Reduce heat; simmer while preparing risotto.
2. Meanwhile, melt margarine in large skillet over medium-high heat. Add onion, carrot and asparagus stems; cook and stir 1 to 2 minutes or until onion and carrot are tender. Stir in garlic and wine; cook 1 minute or until wine boils.

Asparagus Risotto

3. Add rice and 1 cup of the simmering liquid. Cook until liquid is absorbed into rice, stirring frequently. Continue to add liquid 1 cup at a time, cooking until liquid is absorbed, stirring frequently.
4. When 4 cups liquid have been absorbed, stir in asparagus tips. Test rice for doneness. Continue adding ½ cup liquid at a time until rice is tender but still firm and creamy. (Process takes 15 to 20 minutes.)
5. Remove skillet from heat. Stir in cheese. Serve immediately.

NUTRITION INFORMATION PER SERVING: Serving Size: 1¼ Cups ◆ Calories: 420 ◆ Calories from Fat: 70 ◆ % DAILY VALUE: Total Fat: 8 g 12% ◆ Saturated Fat: 3 g 15% ◆ Cholesterol: 10 mg 3% ◆ Sodium: 1200 mg 50% ◆ Total Carbohydrate: 74 g 25% ◆ Dietary Fiber: 3 g 12% ◆ Sugars: 5 g ◆ Protein: 11 g ◆ Vitamin A: 50% ◆ Vitamin C: 4% ◆ Calcium: 15% ◆ Iron: 25% ◆ DIETARY EXCHANGES: 5 Starch, 1 Fat OR 5 Carbohydrate, 1 Fat

COOK'S NOTE

ASPARAGUS

Buy asparagus spears that look firm, not shriveled; the ends should be moist. The thickness of the spear is a matter of personal preference and market availability. To prepare asparagus, snap off the base of the spear where it breaks naturally. Remove the triangular leaves if they are harboring grit. You can peel the lower portion of thick stems if they seem tough. To serve as a side dish, steam or boil the spears until they are fork-tender.

Asparagus Stir-Fry

PREP TIME: 25 MINUTES ✦ YIELD: 4 SERVINGS

- 2 cups uncooked instant rice
- 2 cups water
- 1 teaspoon olive oil
- 3 carrots, sliced (about 1 cup)
- 1 small onion, cut into 8 wedges
- 1 lb. fresh asparagus, cut into 1-inch pieces
- 1 (8-oz.) pkg. fresh whole mushrooms, quartered
- ⅓ cup water
- 1 teaspoon grated lemon peel
- ¼ teaspoon dried thyme leaves
- ¼ teaspoon pepper

1. Cook rice in water as directed on package.

2. Meanwhile, heat oil in 12-inch nonstick skillet over medium-high heat until hot. Add carrots and onion; cook and stir 2 minutes. Add asparagus and mushrooms; cook and stir 4 minutes or just until asparagus is crisp-tender.

2. Stir in water, lemon peel, thyme and pepper. Cover; cook over medium heat for 2 to 3 minutes or until vegetables are crisp-tender. Serve over rice.

NUTRITION INFORMATION PER SERVING: Serving Size: ¼ of Recipe ✦ Calories: 250 ✦ Calories from Fat: 20 ✦ **% DAILY VALUE:** Total Fat: 2 g 3% ✦ Saturated Fat: 0 g 0% ✦ Cholesterol: 0 mg 0% ✦ Sodium: 30 mg 1% ✦ Total Carbohydrate: 49 g 16% ✦ Dietary Fiber: 6 g 24% ✦ Sugars: 7 g ✦ Protein: 8 g ✦ Vitamin A: 320% ✦ Vitamin C: 25% ✦ Calcium: 6% ✦ Iron: 15% ✦ **DIETARY EXCHANGES:** 2½ Starch, 2 Vegetable OR 2½ Carbohydrate, 2 Vegetable

Asparagus Stir-Fry

Cheesy Rice Casserole

Cheesy Rice Casserole

PREP TIME: 30 MINUTES (READY IN 1 HOUR 30 MINUTES) ✦ YIELD: 4 (1¾-CUP) SERVINGS

- 1 tablespoon oil
- ¼ cup chopped onion
- ¼ cup chopped green bell pepper
- 1 garlic clove, minced
- 1 cup uncooked regular long-grain white rice
- 2 cups water
- 1¼ cups milk
- 3 eggs
- 1 tablespoon all-purpose flour
- 1 teaspoon salt
- 2 cups frozen mixed vegetables
- 8 oz. (2 cups) shredded Italian blend cheese

1. Heat oven to 350°F. Spray 2-quart casserole with nonstick cooking spray.

2. Heat oil in large saucepan over medium heat until hot. Add onion, bell pepper and garlic; cook 2 to 3 minutes or until vegetables are tender, stirring occasionally.

3. Add rice and water; mix well. Bring to a boil. Reduce heat to low; cover and simmer 15 minutes or until rice is tender and liquid is absorbed.

4. Meanwhile, in medium bowl, combine milk, eggs, flour and salt; beat well. Add egg mixture, frozen vegetables and 1½ cups of the cheese to cooked rice; mix well. Spoon mixture into sprayed casserole. Sprinkle with remaining ½ cup cheese.

5. Bake at 350°F. for 55 to 60 minutes or until casserole is golden brown and knife inserted near center comes out clean.

NUTRITION INFORMATION PER SERVING: Serving Size: 1¾ Cups ✦ Calories: 540 ✦ Calories from Fat: 220 ✦ **% DAILY VALUE:** Total Fat: 24 g 37% ✦ Saturated Fat: 12 g 60% ✦ Cholesterol: 205 mg 68% ✦ Sodium: 1210 mg 50% ✦ Total Carbohydrate: 53 g 18% ✦ Dietary Fiber: 3 g 12% ✦ Sugars: 8 g ✦ Protein: 27 g ✦ Vitamin A: 40% ✦ Vitamin C: 10% ✦ Calcium: 60% ✦ Iron: 20% ✦ **DIETARY EXCHANGES:** 3½ Starch, 2½ High-Fat Meat, ½ Fat OR 3½ Carbohydrate, 2½ High-Fat Meat, ½ Fat

Portobello Muffuletta Sandwiches

PREP TIME: 15 MINUTES ◆ YIELD: 4 SANDWICHES

OLIVE SALAD
1/2 cup chopped celery
6 tablespoons chopped pimiento-stuffed olives
2 tablespoons reduced-calorie mayonnaise or
    salad dressing

SANDWICHES
12 oz. portobello mushrooms, cut
    into 1/2-inch-thick slices
2 teaspoons olive or vegetable oil
1/4 teaspoon garlic powder
4 (6-inch) French rolls, halved lengthwise
4 (3/4-oz.) slices provolone or mozzarella
    cheese
1 medium tomato, thinly sliced

1. In small bowl, combine all olive salad ingredients; mix well. Set aside.
2. Spray broiler pan with nonstick cooking spray. Place mushroom slices on sprayed pan. In small bowl, combine oil and garlic powder; mix well. Brush half of oil mixture on mushrooms.
3. Broil 4 to 6 inches from heat for 5 to 6 minutes or until tender, turning and brushing with remaining oil mixture once halfway through cooking. Remove mushrooms from pan.
4. Place rolls, cut side up, on broiler pan. Broil 4 to 6 inches from heat for 30 to 60 seconds or until golden brown.
5. Place cheese on bottom halves of rolls. Top with mushrooms, olive salad and tomato slices. Cover with top halves of rolls.

NUTRITION INFORMATION PER SERVING: Serving Size: 1 Sandwich ◆ Calories: 450 ◆ Calories from Fat: 150 ◆ % DAILY VALUE: Total Fat: 17 g 26% ◆ Saturated Fat: 6 g 30% ◆ Cholesterol: 15 mg 5% ◆ Sodium: 1170 mg 49% ◆ Total Carbohydrate: 57 g 19% ◆ Dietary Fiber: 5 g 20% ◆ Sugars: 4 g ◆ Protein: 16 g ◆ Vitamin A: 8% ◆ Vitamin C: 10% ◆ Calcium: 25% ◆ Iron: 25% ◆ DIETARY EXCHANGES: 3½ Starch, 1 Vegetable, ½ High-Fat Meat, 2 Fat OR 3½ Carbohydrate, 1 Vegetable, ½ High-Fat Meat, 2 Fat

Hummus Sandwiches

PREP TIME: 20 MINUTES ◆ YIELD: 4 SANDWICHES

1 (15-oz.) can garbanzo beans, drained, rinsed
1/4 cup sesame seed
1/8 teaspoon ground red pepper (cayenne)
2 tablespoons lemon juice
2 tablespoons water
3 garlic cloves, minced
8 slices pumpernickel bread
1 large tomato, sliced
1 cup alfalfa sprouts

1. In food processor bowl with metal blade, combine garbanzo beans, sesame seed, ground red pepper, lemon juice, water and garlic; process until smooth. Cover; refrigerate at least 10 minutes to blend flavors.
2. To make sandwiches, generously spread 4 bread slices with bean mixture. Top with tomatoes, sprouts and remaining bread slices.

NUTRITION INFORMATION PER SERVING: Serving Size: 1 Sandwich ◆ Calories: 310 ◆ Calories from Fat: 70 ◆ % DAILY VALUE: Total Fat: 8 g 12% ◆ Saturated Fat: 1 g 5% ◆ Cholesterol: 0 mg 0% ◆ Sodium: 540 mg 23% ◆ Total Carbohydrate: 47 g 16% ◆ Dietary Fiber: 10 g 40% ◆ Sugars: 4 g ◆ Protein: 13 g ◆ Vitamin A: 8% ◆ Vitamin C: 25% ◆ Calcium: 10% ◆ Iron: 20% ◆ DIETARY EXCHANGES: 3 Starch, ½ Very Lean Meat, 1 Fat OR 3 Carbohydrate, ½ Very Lean Meat, 1 Fat

Powerful Peanut Butter Sandwiches

PREP TIME: 5 MINUTES ◆ YIELD: 4 SANDWICHES

1/2 cup peanut butter
1/4 cup shredded carrot
2 tablespoons shelled sunflower seeds
2 tablespoons raisins
2 tablespoons honey or sugar
4 bagels, split, or 8 slices whole wheat bread

1. In small container, combine all ingredients except bagels; mix well.
2. Spread mixture on 4 bagel halves or bread slices; top with remaining bagel halves or bread slices.

NUTRITION INFORMATION PER SERVING: Serving Size: 1 Sandwich ◆ Calories: 480 ◆ Calories from Fat: 180 ◆ % DAILY VALUE: Total Fat: 20 g 31% ◆ Saturated Fat: 4 g 20% ◆ Cholesterol: 0 mg 0% ◆ Sodium: 560 mg 23% ◆ Total Carbohydrate: 58 g 19% ◆ Dietary Fiber: 4 g 16% ◆ Sugars: 15 g ◆ Protein: 17 g ◆ Vitamin A: 40% ◆ Vitamin C: 0% ◆ Calcium: 8% ◆ Iron: 20% ◆ DIETARY EXCHANGES: 4 Starch, 1 High-Fat Meat, 1½ Fat OR 4 Carbohydrate, 1 High-Fat Meat, 1½ Fat

Hearty Grain Burgers

PREP TIME: 20 MINUTES ◆ YIELD: 6 SANDWICHES

½ cup cornmeal
¼ cup uncooked instant rice
¼ cup quick-cooking rolled oats
¼ cup uncooked bulgur
¼ cup uncooked couscous
1 cup boiling water
½ cup low-fat cottage cheese
¼ teaspoon garlic powder
¼ teaspoon pepper
2 tablespoons soy sauce
  Nonstick cooking spray
6 burger buns, split

1. GRILL DIRECTIONS: Heat grill. In medium bowl, combine cornmeal, rice, oats, bulgur and couscous. Stir in boiling water. Cover; let stand 5 minutes.
2. Add cottage cheese, garlic powder, pepper and soy sauce; mix well. Shape into 6 patties, ½ inch thick. Spray both sides of each patty with nonstick cooking spray.
3. When ready to grill, place patties on gas grill over medium heat or on charcoal grill 4 to 6 inches from medium coals. Cook 6 to 10 minutes or until thoroughly heated, turning once. Serve in buns.

> **TIP:** To cook patties in skillet, place in sprayed large nonstick skillet. Cook 6 to 10 minutes, turning once.

NUTRITION INFORMATION PER SERVING: Serving Size: 1 Sandwich ◆ Calories: 260 ◆ Calories from Fat: 25 ◆ **% DAILY VALUE:** Total Fat: 3 g 5% ◆ Saturated Fat: 1 g 5% ◆ Cholesterol: 0 mg 0% ◆ Sodium: 670 mg 28% ◆ Total Carbohydrate: 47 g 16% ◆ Dietary Fiber: 4 g 16% ◆ Sugars: 6 g ◆ Protein: 10 g ◆ Vitamin A: 0% ◆ Vitamin C: 0% ◆ Calcium: 8% ◆ Iron: 15% ◆ **DIETARY EXCHANGES:** 3 Starch OR 3 Carbohydrate

Spicy Bean Burgers

PREP TIME: 20 MINUTES ◆ YIELD: 5 SANDWICHES

1 (15-oz.) can spicy chili beans, undrained
1 cup unseasoned dry bread crumbs
¼ cup finely chopped onion
1 egg, slightly beaten
5 burger buns, split

1. In medium bowl, mash beans. Stir in bread crumbs, onion and egg; mix well. Shape mixture into 5 patties, about 3½ inches in diameter.

2. Spray 12-inch nonstick skillet with nonstick cooking spray. Heat over medium heat until hot. Place patties in skillet; cook 6 to 8 minutes or until lightly browned, turning once. Serve burgers in buns.

NUTRITION INFORMATION PER SERVING: Serving Size: 1 Sandwich ◆ Calories: 300 ◆ Calories from Fat: 45 ◆ **% DAILY VALUE:** Total Fat: 5 g 8% ◆ Saturated Fat: 1 g 5% ◆ Cholesterol: 45 mg 15% ◆ Sodium: 750 mg 31% ◆ Total Carbohydrate: 51 g 17% ◆ Dietary Fiber: 6 g 24% ◆ Sugars: 7 g ◆ Protein: 12 g ◆ Vitamin A: 4% ◆ Vitamin C: 0% ◆ Calcium: 15% ◆ Iron: 25% ◆ **DIETARY EXCHANGES:** 3½ Starch, ½ Fat OR 3½ Carbohydrate, ½ Fat

Curried Tofu Salad Sandwiches

PREP TIME: 30 MINUTES (READY IN 1 HOUR) ◆ YIELD: 4 SANDWICHES

1 (10-oz.) pkg. firm or extra-firm tofu
¼ cup chopped celery
2 tablespoons sliced green onions
¼ cup low-fat plain yogurt
2 tablespoons sweet pickle relish
2 teaspoons sweet honey mustard
½ teaspoon curry powder
⅛ teaspoon turmeric
8 slices multi-grain bread
4 lettuce leaves
1 small tomato, sliced

1. Drain tofu if necessary; press between layers of paper towels to remove excess moisture. Place tofu in medium bowl; break up slightly with fork. Add celery and onions; mix well.
2. In medium bowl, combine yogurt, relish, mustard, curry powder and turmeric; blend well. Stir carefully into tofu mixture. Refrigerate at least 30 minutes to blend flavors.
3. Top 4 slices of bread with lettuce leaves and tomato slices. Spread tofu mixture over tomato slices; top with remaining bread slices.

NUTRITION INFORMATION PER SERVING: Serving Size: 1 Sandwich ◆ Calories: 210 ◆ Calories from Fat: 45 ◆ **% DAILY VALUE:** Total Fat: 5 g 8% ◆ Saturated Fat: 1 g 5% ◆ Cholesterol: 0 mg 0% ◆ Sodium: 360 mg 15% ◆ Total Carbohydrate: 31 g 10% ◆ Dietary Fiber: 4 g 16% ◆ Sugars: 7 g ◆ Protein: 11 g ◆ Vitamin A: 4% ◆ Vitamin C: 8% ◆ Calcium: 15% ◆ Iron: 15% ◆ **DIETARY EXCHANGES:** 2 Starch, 1 Lean Meat OR 2 Carbohydrate, 1 Lean Meat

Roasted Vegetable Sandwiches with Spicy Green Chile Dressing

PREP TIME: 55 MINUTES ♦ YIELD: 4 SANDWICHES

    1   (4.5-oz.) can chopped green chiles
    3   tablespoons red wine vinegar
    2   tablespoons oil
    1   tablespoon dried basil leaves
    ½   teaspoon coarse ground black pepper
    1   small red bell pepper, cut into 1-inch pieces
    1   small zucchini, cut into ¼-inch-thick slices
    1   small sweet potato, peeled, cut
          into ⅛-inch-thick slices
    1   small red onion, cut into wedges
    ¼   cup nonfat cream cheese (from 8-oz. tub)
    2   tablespoons buttermilk
    ⅛   teaspoon salt
    4   large French rolls or hoagie buns
          (about 6 inches long), not split in half

1. Heat oven to 450°F. Set aside 1 tablespoon green chiles for dressing. In large bowl, combine remaining green chiles, vinegar, oil, basil and pepper; mix well. Add bell pepper, zucchini, sweet potato and onion; toss gently to coat. Let stand at room temperature 15 minutes to marinate.

Roasted Vegetable Sandwiches with
Spicy Green Chile Dressing

2. With slotted spoon, remove vegetables from marinade; place on ungreased 15× 10×1-inch baking pan. Discard marinade. Bake vegetables at 450°F. for 20 to 25 minutes or until tender, stirring once.

3. Meanwhile, in small bowl, beat cream cheese until smooth. Add buttermilk, reserved 1 tablespoon green chiles and salt; mix well. Cover; refrigerate.

4. In top of each roll, starting and ending ½ inch from each end, cut a V-shaped wedge 1½ inches wide and 1½ inches deep; remove bread wedge and reserve. To assemble sandwiches, spoon 1½ tablespoons cream cheese mixture into each hollowed-out roll; top each with ¼ of vegetable mixture and reserved bread wedge.

NUTRITION INFORMATION PER SERVING: Serving Size: 1 Sandwich ♦ Calories: 340 ♦ Calories from Fat: 50 ♦ % DAILY VALUE: Total Fat: 6 g 9% ♦ Saturated Fat: 1 g 5% ♦ Cholesterol: 3 mg 1% ♦ Sodium: 820 mg 34% ♦ Total Carbohydrate: 59 g 20% ♦ Dietary Fiber: 5 g 20% ♦ Sugars: 6 g ♦ Protein: 12 g ♦ Vitamin A: 80% ♦ Vitamin C: 35% ♦ Calcium: 20% ♦ Iron: 15% ♦ DIETARY EXCHANGES: 4 Starch, 1 Fat OR 4 Carbohydrate, 1 Fat

Cheese and Veggie Wraps

PREP TIME: 15 MINUTES ♦ YIELD: 4 WRAPS

    4   (7 or 8-inch) whole wheat or flour tortillas
    2   tablespoons purchased sandwich spread
    4   (1-oz.) slices hot pepper Monterey Jack
          cheese
    4   (1-oz.) slices Cheddar cheese
    1   small cucumber, very thinly sliced
    1   small red or green bell pepper, seeded, very
          thinly sliced
    ½   cup alfalfa sprouts

1. Spread each tortilla with 1½ teaspoons of the sandwich spread to within 1 inch of edges.

2. Top with cheeses, cucumber, bell pepper and alfalfa sprouts. Roll up each tortilla.

NUTRITION INFORMATION PER SERVING: Serving Size: 1 Wrap ♦ Calories: 360 ♦ Calories from Fat: 200 ♦ % DAILY VALUE: Total Fat: 22 g 34% ♦ Saturated Fat: 12 g 60% ♦ Cholesterol: 55 mg 18% ♦ Sodium: 600 mg 25% ♦ Total Carbohydrate: 22 g 7% ♦ Dietary Fiber: 3 g 12% ♦ Sugars: 3 g ♦ Protein: 18 g ♦ Vitamin A: 25% ♦ Vitamin C: 40% ♦ Calcium: 45% ♦ Iron: 10% ♦ DIETARY EXCHANGES: 1 Starch, 1 Vegetable, 2 Medium-Fat Meat, 2½ Fat OR 1 Carbohydrate, 1 Vegetable, 2 Medium-Fat Meat, 2½ Fat

EGGS

EGGS

A lthough you may associate eggs with breakfast, they are equally suitable for lunch or dinner—chopped egg salad, quiche, frittata and savory custard, to name a few entrées. The relatively low cost per serving makes them one of the great main-dish bargains.

Hints for Handling Eggs

Eggs will separate best when cold from the refrigerator. To avoid getting a little yolk in a bowl of whites, separate each egg into a small bowl, then combine with other separated whites and yolks.

To beat egg whites to the highest volume, bring whites to room temperature by placing them in a bowl of warm water for a minute or two (refrigerate leftover yolks immediately). Keep egg whites free of any fat; a speck of egg yolk, for example, will prevent eggs from whipping. Make sure the bowl and beaters are clean and free from grease; use a metal or glass bowl instead of plastic, which can retain traces of grease despite thorough washing.

Cream of tartar may be added to increase the stability of beaten egg whites. Use ¼ teaspoon of cream of tartar for 3 eggs. Sugar also increases the stability but decreases the volume, so it should be added gradually toward the end of beating.

To keep beaten eggs from curdling when combining with a hot mixture, temper the eggs by stirring a small amount of hot liquid into the eggs, then gradually add the tempered eggs to the hot mixture.

COOK'S NOTE

ABOUT HARD-COOKED EGGS

For hard-cooked eggs that are thoroughly cooked but not rubbery, reduce the heat to a simmer after the water first comes to a boil. Immediately cool the cooked eggs, still in the shell, under cold water, to prevent a harmless but unattractive greenish color from developing around the yolk. For easiest peeling, crack the egg at the large end, which has an air pocket, and peel with the side of your thumb rather than fingertips.

Freezing Raw Eggs

Freezing eggs may be convenient when you have leftover whites or yolks after preparing a recipe.

◆ To freeze whole eggs or egg yolks, mix ⅛ teaspoon salt or 1½ teaspoons sugar into the eggs for every 4 yolks or 2 whole eggs to preserve the texture. (Use salt if you plan to use the eggs in a savory dish and sugar if you plan to use them in a sweet dish.) Freeze in a tightly covered container.

◆ Freeze egg whites in tightly covered containers labeled with the date, contents and quantity.

◆ For best quality, use frozen eggs within six months. Thaw the frozen eggs in the refrigerator or place the container under cold water; do not thaw at room temperature.

◆ 1 large whole egg = 3 tablespoons whole egg

◆ 1 large egg yolk = 1 tablespoon egg yolk

◆ 1 large egg white = 2 tablespoons egg white

◆ Freezing hard-cooked eggs or egg dishes is not recommended.

Poached Eggs

PREP TIME: 15 MINUTES

1. In skillet or saucepan, bring 2 to 3 inches water and 1 tablespoon vinegar to a boil. Reduce heat to medium-low.
2. Allow 1 egg per serving. Break each egg into shallow dish; carefully place in water. Quickly spoon hot water over each egg until film forms over yolk.
3. Simmer about 5 minutes or until eggs are of desired doneness. With slotted spoon, remove eggs from water. Season to taste with salt and pepper. If desired, serve on buttered toast or English muffin.

NUTRITION INFORMATION PER SERVING: Serving Size: 1 Egg ◆ Calories: 70 ◆ Calories from Fat: 45 ◆ % DAILY VALUE: Total Fat: 5 g 8% ◆ Saturated Fat: 2 g 10% ◆ Cholesterol: 215 mg 72% ◆ Sodium: 65 mg 3% ◆ Total Carbohydrate: 1 g 1% ◆ Dietary Fiber: 0 g 0% ◆ Sugars: 1 g ◆ Protein: 6 g ◆ Vitamin A: 6% ◆ Vitamin C: 0% ◆ Calcium: 2% ◆ Iron: 4% ◆ DIETARY EXCHANGES: 1 Medium-Fat Meat

Hard and Soft-Cooked Eggs

1. Place desired number of eggs in medium saucepan; cover with cold water. Bring to a boil.* Reduce heat to low; simmer about 15 minutes for hard-cooked eggs or 7 minutes for soft-cooked eggs.
2. Immediately drain; run cold water over eggs to stop cooking.
3. Cut soft-cooked eggs in half, spoon out of shell.** Serve in egg cups, if desired. Peel hard-cooked eggs and use as desired.

TIPS: * If water boils hard, the egg white will toughen.
** Eggs a few days old are easier to remove from the shell than very fresh eggs. For ease in shelling hard-cooked eggs, crack and peel eggs under cold water, beginning at larger end.

NUTRITION INFORMATION PER SERVING: Serving Size: 1 Egg • Calories: 70 • Calories from Fat: 45 • **% DAILY VALUE:** Total Fat: 5 g 8% • Saturated Fat: 2 g 10% • Cholesterol: 215 mg 72% • Sodium: 65 mg 3% • Total Carbohydrate: 1 g 1% • Dietary Fiber: 0 g 0% • Sugars: 1 g • Protein: 6 g • Vitamin A: 6% • Vitamin C: 0% • Calcium: 2% • Iron: 4% • **DIETARY EXCHANGES:** 1 Medium-Fat Meat

Hollandaise Sauce

PREP TIME: 20 MINUTES ✦ YIELD: ¾ CUP

> 3 egg yolks
> ⅛ teaspoon salt, if desired
>   Dash white pepper
> 4 teaspoons lemon juice
> ½ cup margarine or butter, softened

1. In small saucepan or top of double boiler, slightly beat egg yolks. Add salt, pepper, lemon juice and ¼ cup of the margarine; blend well. Cook over low heat or over hot, but not boiling, water until margarine is melted, stirring constantly.
2. Gradually add remaining margarine 1 tablespoon at a time, beating well after each addition. Continue beating until mixture is smooth and thickened. Remove from heat. Serve immediately or keep warm over hot, but not boiling, water.

TIP: If sauce curdles, add hot water 1 teaspoon at a time; beat until sauce is smooth.

NUTRITION INFORMATION PER SERVING: Serving Size: 1 Tablespoon • Calories: 80 • Calories from Fat: 80 • **% DAILY VALUE:** Total Fat: 9 g 14% • Saturated Fat: 2 g 10% • Cholesterol: 55 mg 18% • Sodium: 115 mg 5% • Total Carbohydrate: 0 g 0% • Dietary Fiber: 0 g 0% • Sugars: 0 g • Protein: 1 g • Vitamin A: 8% • Vitamin C: 0% • Calcium: 0% • Iron: 0% • **DIETARY EXCHANGES:** 2 Fat

Almost Hollandaise Sauce

PREP TIME: 10 MINUTES ✦ YIELD: ½ CUP

> ¼ cup mayonnaise or salad dressing
> ¼ cup sour cream
> 1 teaspoon lemon juice
> ½ teaspoon prepared mustard
> ¼ teaspoon grated lemon peel
> ¼ teaspoon butter flavor
>   Dash to ⅛ teaspoon ground red pepper (cayenne)

In small saucepan, combine all ingredients; blend well. Cook over medium heat until warm, stirring frequently. Store in refrigerator.

TIPS: Sauce can be reheated in microwave. Microwave on MEDIUM for 30 to 60 seconds.
If sauce becomes too thick, stir in a small amount of milk until of desired consistency.

NUTRITION INFORMATION PER SERVING: Serving Size: 1 Tablespoon • Calories: 70 • Calories from Fat: 60 • **% DAILY VALUE:** Total Fat: 7 g 11% • Saturated Fat: 2 g 10% • Cholesterol: 5 mg 2% • Sodium: 45 mg 2% • Total Carbohydrate: 1 g 1% • Dietary Fiber: 0 g 0% • Sugars: 1 g • Protein: 0 g • Vitamin A: 0% • Vitamin C: 0% • Calcium: 0% • Iron: 0% • **DIETARY EXCHANGES:** 1½ Fat

Eggs Benedict

PREP TIME: 30 MINUTES ✦ YIELD: 6 SERVINGS

>   Hollandaise Sauce, at left
> 6 slices Canadian bacon
> 3 English muffins, split, toasted
> 6 teaspoons margarine or butter
> 6 Poached Eggs, page 242

1. Place sauce over hot (not boiling) water to keep warm.
2. Spray medium skillet with nonstick cooking spray. Place Canadian bacon in sprayed skillet. Cook over medium heat about 1 minute on each side or until hot. Remove from skillet.
3. To assemble, spread each English muffin half with 1 teaspoon margarine. Place each on individual serving plate. Top each with Canadian bacon, egg and sauce.

NUTRITION INFORMATION PER SERVING: Serving Size: ⅙ of Recipe • Calories: 390 • Calories from Fat: 260 • **% DAILY VALUE:** Total Fat: 29 g 45% • Saturated Fat: 7 g 35% • Cholesterol: 335 mg 112% • Sodium: 870 mg 36% • Total Carbohydrate: 15 g 5% • Dietary Fiber: 1 g 3% • Sugars: 5 g • Protein: 16 g • Vitamin A: 25% • Vitamin C: 0% • Calcium: 10% • Iron: 10% • **DIETARY EXCHANGES:** 1 Starch, 2 Medium-Fat Meat, 3½ Fat OR 1 Carbohydrate, 2 Medium-Fat Meat, 3½ Fat

Scrambled Eggs

PREP TIME: 15 MINUTES

1. For each egg, allow 1 tablespoon milk, half-and-half or water, ⅛ teaspoon salt and 1 teaspoon margarine. In bowl, break egg(s); add milk and salt. Beat slightly with fork until uniform in color.

2. Melt margarine in skillet over medium heat; tilt pan to coat. Add egg mixture. Reduce heat to low. Cook until firm but still moist, stirring frequently.

> **TIP:** If desired, one of the following can be added during last 1 to 2 minutes of cooking: chopped chives, parsley or pimientos, hot pepper sauce, shredded or cubed cheese, diced cooked ham, crumbled cooked bacon, sliced cooked sausage, drained canned seafood (flaked crabmeat, tuna, salmon or shrimp), mushrooms, cubed cream cheese, or chopped tomato, bell pepper or green chiles.

NUTRITION INFORMATION PER SERVING: Serving Size: 1 Scrambled Egg ◆ Calories: 80 ◆ Calories from Fat: 45 ◆ **% DAILY VALUE:** Total Fat: 5 g 8% ◆ Saturated Fat: 2 g 10% ◆ Cholesterol: 215 mg 72% ◆ Sodium: 340 mg 14% ◆ Total Carbohydrate: 1 g 1% ◆ Dietary Fiber: 0 g 0% ◆ Sugars: 1 g ◆ Protein: 7 g ◆ Vitamin A: 6% ◆ Vitamin C: 0% ◆ Calcium: 4% ◆ Iron: 4% ◆ **DIETARY EXCHANGES:** 1 Medium-Fat Meat

Ham and Vegetable Scrambled Eggs

PREP TIME: 20 MINUTES ◆ YIELD: 4 SERVINGS

    8 eggs
    2 tablespoons milk
    ½ teaspoon garlic salt
    2 tablespoons margarine or butter
    ½ cup finely chopped cooked ham
    ¼ cup chopped green bell pepper
    ¼ cup chopped onion
    2 oz. (½ cup) shredded Cheddar cheese

1. In medium bowl, combine eggs, milk and garlic salt; beat well. Set aside.

2. Melt margarine in large skillet over medium heat. Add ham, bell pepper and onion; cook and stir 2 to 4 minutes or until vegetables are crisp-tender.

3. Pour egg mixture over ham mixture in skillet. Cook until eggs are firm but still moist, stirring occasionally from outside edge to center of pan. Remove from heat. Sprinkle with cheese. Cover; let stand 1 minute or until cheese is melted.

NUTRITION INFORMATION PER SERVING: Serving Size: ¼ of Recipe ◆ Calories: 280 ◆ Calories from Fat: 190 ◆ **% DAILY VALUE:** Total Fat: 21 g 32% ◆ Saturated Fat: 8 g 40% ◆ Cholesterol: 450 mg 150% ◆ Sodium: 770 mg 32% ◆ Total Carbohydrate: 3 g 1% ◆ Dietary Fiber: 0 g 0% ◆ Sugars: 2 g ◆ Protein: 20 g ◆ Vitamin A: 20% ◆ Vitamin C: 8% ◆ Calcium: 15% ◆ Iron: 10% ◆ **DIETARY EXCHANGES:** 3 Medium-Fat Meat, 1 Fat

Skillet Corn Frittata

PREP TIME: 40 MINUTES ◆ YIELD: 8 SERVINGS

    3 tablespoons margarine or butter
    1 (1-lb.) pkg. frozen whole kernel corn
    ¼ cup sliced green onions
    10 eggs
    ½ cup half-and-half
    1 teaspoon dried basil leaves
    ½ teaspoon salt
    ⅛ teaspoon pepper
    2 tomatoes, peeled, sliced
    1 green bell pepper, cut into rings
    4 oz. (1 cup) shredded Swiss cheese

1. Melt margarine in large skillet over medium heat. Add frozen corn and onions; cook and stir about 5 minutes or until vegetables are crisp-tender. Reduce heat to low.

2. In large bowl, beat eggs well. Add half-and-half, basil, salt and pepper; blend well. Pour over vegetables. Cook over low heat 6 minutes.

3. As edges set, run spatula around edge of skillet, gently lifting vegetable mixture to allow uncooked egg to flow to bottom of

Ham and Vegetable Scrambled Eggs

Skillet Corn Frittata (page 244)

are softened and thoroughly heated, stirring occasionally.

3. Meanwhile, melt margarine in large skillet over medium heat. Add eggs to skillet 1 at a time; cook 4 to 6 minutes or until yolks are cooked, occasionally spooning margarine over eggs.

4. To serve, place 1 warm tortilla on each individual serving plate. Top each with ¼ of bean mixture, 2 eggs, 2 tablespoons remaining salsa, and 1 tablespoon each feta cheese and cilantro.

NUTRITION INFORMATION PER SERVING: Serving Size: ¼ of Recipe ◆ Calories: 420 ◆ Calories from Fat: 200 ◆ **% DAILY VALUE:** Total Fat: 22 g 34% ◆ Saturated Fat: 6 g 30% ◆ Cholesterol: 435 mg 145% ◆ Sodium: 1010 mg 42% ◆ Total Carbohydrate: 34 g 11% ◆ Dietary Fiber: 6 g 24% ◆ Sugars: 5 g ◆ Protein: 21 g ◆ Vitamin A: 25% ◆ Vitamin C: 0% ◆ Calcium: 15% ◆ Iron: 15% ◆ **DIETARY EXCHANGES:** 2½ Starch, 2 Lean Meat, 2½ Fat OR 2½ Carbohydrate, 2 Lean Meat, 2½ Fat

skillet. Cover; cook an additional 6 minutes or until top is almost set. (Top will be moist.)

4. Arrange tomato slices and bell pepper rings around outer edge of frittata; sprinkle with cheese. Cover; cook an additional 5 minutes or until cheese is melted. Remove from heat; let stand 5 minutes. Cut into wedges to serve.

NUTRITION INFORMATION PER SERVING: Serving Size: ⅛ of Recipe ◆ Calories: 270 ◆ Calories from Fat: 150 ◆ **% DAILY VALUE:** Total Fat: 17 g 26% ◆ Saturated Fat: 6 g 30% ◆ Cholesterol: 285 mg 95% ◆ Sodium: 340 mg 14% ◆ Total Carbohydrate: 14 g 5% ◆ Dietary Fiber: 2 g 8% ◆ Sugars: 4 g ◆ Protein: 14 g ◆ Vitamin A: 20% ◆ Vitamin C: 20% ◆ Calcium: 20% ◆ Iron: 8% ◆ **DIETARY EXCHANGES:** 1 Starch, 1½ Medium-Fat Meat, 1½ Fat OR 1 Carbohydrate, 1½ Medium-Fat Meat, 1½ Fat

Huevos Rancheros

PREP TIME: 25 MINUTES ✦ YIELD: 4 SERVINGS

   1 tablespoon oil
½ cup chopped onion
   1 (15-oz.) can black beans, drained, rinsed
   1 cup salsa
   2 tablespoons margarine or butter
   8 eggs
   4 (6-inch) soft corn tortillas, heated
   1 oz. feta cheese, crumbled (¼ cup)
¼ cup chopped fresh cilantro

1. Heat oil in medium skillet over medium-high heat until hot. Add onion; cook 3 to 4 minutes or until softened.

2. Stir in beans and ½ cup of the salsa, mashing beans with back of spoon. (Beans will be slightly lumpy.) Reduce heat to medium; cook 6 to 8 minutes or until beans

COOK'S NOTE

FIRM OR SOFT YOLKS?

Cooking eggs to a temperature of 160°F. kills salmonella.

For safety's sake, the U.S. Department of Agriculture recommends that people at risk (the elderly, children, pregnant women and people with compromised immune systems) consume eggs only if the yolk has been cooked until completely firm. People in good health, however, can safely eat eggs that are not completely firm by following these recommendations:

✦ Cook fried eggs 2 to 3 minutes on each side or 4 minutes in a covered pan.

✦ Cook scrambled eggs until they are firm throughout.

✦ Poach eggs for 5 minutes over boiling water.

✦ Cook soft-cooked eggs (in the shell) for 7 minutes in boiling water.

✦ Custards, omelets, quiches and other foods made with eggs should be served immediately or refrigerated.

EGG SAFETY

You may have heard that eggs can be contaminated with salmonella, which is potentially very harmful. However, storing and cooking eggs properly virtually eliminates the risk.

+ Refrigeration is essential. Store eggs in their original carton (to prevent them from absorbing odors from other foods) on the refrigerator shelf, not in the door. Because the door is opened so often, the eggs are subject to too many temperature fluctuations. Do not wash eggs; washing can actually increase the chance of contamination.

+ Use raw eggs within three to five weeks. A date is often stamped on the carton. The proverbial "rotten egg" is almost unheard of nowadays, but discard any egg that has a sulfur smell when cracked open. It is a good idea to crack eggs individually into a cup or bowl before adding them to a mixing bowl. If a bit of shell falls into the egg, remove it with a clean utensil, not with a piece of the eggshell.

+ Although it is best to crack eggs just before using them, whole eggs out of the shell, cov-

ered tightly, can be safely refrigerated for up to two days. Store leftover yolks or whites in the refrigerator for no more than four days.

+ Don't eat raw unpasteurized eggs. Forgo the pleasure of "licking the spoon" from cake batter or cookie dough. Choose alternatives to homemade mayonnaise, Caesar salad dressing, eggnog and milk shakes made with raw egg.

+ Pasteurized eggs may be eaten raw. Pasteurized eggs are uncooked eggs that have been heat-treated to kill bacteria which can cause food poisoning and gastrointestinal distress. They can be found in the dairy case at large supermarkets.

+ Take care not to cross-contaminate. Wash your hands before and after handling eggs, and wash all utensils and dishes that have come in contact with raw egg in hot, soapy water before using them for anything else.

+ Keep cold egg dishes cold (40°F.). For a buffet, make sure hot egg dishes remain hot (140°F.) and do not leave them out for more than 30 minutes. Refrigerate leftovers immediately.

Fried Eggs

PREP TIME: 10 MINUTES

1. For each serving, in skillet, melt 1 teaspoon margarine, butter or bacon drippings over medium heat.
2. Break eggs, 1 at a time, into custard cup or saucer; carefully slip each egg into skillet. Reduce heat to low; cook 2 to 3 minutes on each side or until of desired doneness.

NUTRITION INFORMATION PER SERVING: Serving Size: 1 Egg ◆ Calories: 110 ◆ Calories from Fat: 80 ◆ **% DAILY VALUE:** Total Fat: 9 g 14% ◆ Saturated Fat: 2 g 10% ◆ Cholesterol: 215 mg 72% ◆ Sodium: 105 mg 4% ◆ Total Carbohydrate: 1 g 1% ◆ Dietary Fiber: 0 g 0% ◆ Sugars: 1 g ◆ Protein: 6 g ◆ Vitamin A: 10% ◆ Vitamin C: 0% ◆ Calcium: 2% ◆ Iron: 4% ◆ **DIETARY EXCHANGES:** 1 Medium-Fat Meat, 1 Fat

VARIATIONS

Sunny-Side-Up Basted Eggs: Spoon melted margarine, butter or bacon drippings over eggs; cook until whites are set and white film forms over yolks.

Sunny-Side-Up Steamed Eggs: Add 1 to 2 teaspoons water to skillet; cover and cook 3 to 5 minutes or until whites are set and white film forms over yolks.

Baked Eggs

PREP TIME: 25 MINUTES ◆ YIELD: 4 SERVINGS

    4 eggs
    4 tablespoons half-and-half or milk, if desired
    1/4 teaspoon salt
    1/8 teaspoon pepper
    1 tablespoon butter

1. Heat oven to 325°F. Butter four 6-oz. custard cups or large muffin cups. Place cups in 15 × 10 × 1-inch baking pan. Break 1 egg into each buttered cup. Add 1 tablespoon half-and-half to each. Sprinkle with salt and pepper; top with butter.
2. Bake at 325°F. for 12 to 15 minutes or until eggs are set.

NUTRITION INFORMATION PER SERVING: Serving Size: ¼ of Recipe • Calories: 120 • Calories from Fat: 90 • **% DAILY VALUE:** Total Fat: 10 g 15% • Saturated Fat: 4 g 20% • Cholesterol: 225 mg 75% • Sodium: 230 mg 10% • Total Carbohydrate: 1 g 1% • Dietary Fiber: 0 g 0% • Sugars: 1 g • Protein: 7 g • Vitamin A: 10% • Vitamin C: 0% • Calcium: 4% • Iron: 4% • **DIETARY EXCHANGES:** 1 Medium-Fat Meat, 1 Fat

VARIATIONS

Baked Eggs and Bacon: Place 1 slice cooked bacon around inside edge of each cup before adding egg. Continue as directed above.

Baked Eggs and Ham: Carefully press 1 square ham slice in bottom and up sides of each buttered cup. Prepare eggs as directed above. Cover loosely with foil. Bake as directed above. Sprinkle 1 tablespoon shredded Cheddar cheese over each baked egg. Cover; let stand until cheese is melted.

Baked Eggs and Hash: Spoon ¼ cup corned beef hash into each cup; make indentation in center. Break egg into each indentation. Continue as directed above.

Baked Eggs in Toast Cups: Remove crust from 4 bread slices. Spread butter on both sides of each slice. Press bread slice into each cup. Break egg over each bread slice. Continue as directed above. If desired, serve with Cheese Sauce, page 314.

Puffy Omelet

PREP TIME: 20 MINUTES (READY IN 40 MINUTES)
✦ YIELD: 4 SERVINGS

    6 eggs, separated
    1 teaspoon salt
    6 tablespoons water
    ⅛ teaspoon pepper
    2 tablespoons margarine or butter

1. Heat oven to 325°F. In large bowl, combine egg whites, salt and water; beat until stiff peaks form. Set aside.
2. With same beaters, in small bowl, beat egg yolks and pepper until thickened and light yellow in color. Fold into egg whites.
3. Melt margarine in 10-inch ovenproof skillet over medium heat; tilt pan to coat. Pour in egg mixture. Reduce heat to low; cook about 5 minutes or until puffy and light brown on bottom.
4. Place skillet in oven. Bake at 325°F. for 15 to 18 minutes or until knife inserted in center comes out clean. To remove from pan,

tip skillet, loosening omelet with pancake turner. Fold in half* and slip onto platter. Serve immediately with Cheese Sauce, page 314, if desired.

TIPS: * If desired, cut into wedges rather than folding in half.
For 3-egg omelet, cut all ingredients in half. Cook in 6 or 8-inch skillet until puffy and light brown. Bake 10 to 15 minutes.

NUTRITION INFORMATION PER SERVING: Serving Size: ¼ of Recipe • Calories: 160 • Calories from Fat: 120 • **% DAILY VALUE:** Total Fat: 13 g 20% • Saturated Fat: 3 g 15% • Cholesterol: 320 mg 107% • Sodium: 690 mg 29% • Total Carbohydrate: 1 g 1% • Dietary Fiber: 0 g 0% • Sugars: 1 g • Protein: 9 g • Vitamin A: 15% • Vitamin C: 0% • Calcium: 4% • Iron: 6% • **DIETARY EXCHANGES:** 1½ Medium-Fat Meat, 1 Fat

COOK'S NOTE

PURCHASING EGGS

As a rule, the larger the egg, the higher the price. However, size has no relation to quality. The recipes in this cookbook, like most others today, have been developed and tested with large eggs. You may buy small, medium or extra-large to match the appetites in your household, but for recipes use those labeled "large." The color of the shell—white or brown—has no effect on flavor or quality and is important only if you plan to dye or decorate the shells.

Grades AA and A, the grades usually available in stores, are both fine for home use. The differences have to do with appearance, not freshness, and the nutritive value is equal. The yolk is somewhat plumper in Grade AA. The yolk is also more symmetrically centered in the white, and the white is somewhat thicker. These differences might matter if you're planning to serve a plate of sunny-side-up eggs for guests but will make virtually no difference in the recipe.

Eggs should be sold in a refrigerated case. Open the carton and make sure the eggs look clean and that none of the shells is cracked or broken. Move each egg slightly with your finger to make sure it is not stuck to the carton by a bit of leaking egg.

Cheese Omelet

PREP TIME: 15 MINUTES ◆ YIELD: 2 SERVINGS

4 eggs
¼ cup milk or water
¼ teaspoon salt
Dash pepper
4 teaspoons margarine or butter
2 oz. (½ cup) shredded Cheddar cheese

1. In small bowl, combine eggs, milk, salt and pepper; beat well. Melt margarine in medium skillet over medium-low heat; tilt pan to coat. Pour egg mixture into skillet; reduce heat to low.
2. Cook, without stirring, for 3 to 4 minutes or until set, lifting edges occasionally to allow uncooked egg mixture to flow underneath. Cook until top is set but still moist. Sprinkle with cheese. With pancake turner, loosen edge of omelet and fold in half.

NUTRITION INFORMATION PER SERVING: Serving Size: ½ of Recipe ◆ Calories: 350 ◆ Calories from Fat: 250 ◆ **% DAILY VALUE:** Total Fat: 28 g 43% ◆ Saturated Fat: 11 g 55% ◆ Cholesterol: 455 mg 152% ◆ Sodium: 670 mg 28% ◆ Total Carbohydrate: 3 g 1% ◆ Dietary Fiber: 0 g 0% ◆ Sugars: 3 g ◆ Protein: 21 g ◆ Vitamin A: 25% ◆ Vitamin C: 0% ◆ Calcium: 30% ◆ Iron: 10% ◆ **DIETARY EXCHANGES:** 3 Medium-Fat Meat, 3 Fat

VARIATIONS

Asian Omelet: Cook 2 tablespoons chopped onion and 1 tablespoon chopped bell pepper in 1 tablespoon margarine over medium heat until tender. Add ⅓ cup fresh bean sprouts, ⅓ cup chopped cooked shrimp, ½ teaspoon soy sauce and dash ginger. Cook until thoroughly heated. Just before folding omelet, spoon half of shrimp mixture on half of omelet. Fold in half; top with remaining shrimp mixture.

Filled Omelet: Just before folding, top half of omelet with cooked mushrooms, crumbled cooked bacon, chopped cooked ham, shredded cheese, cottage cheese, diced tomato, jelly or marmalade, sweetened strawberries or raspberries. Fold in half as directed above.

Spanish Omelet: Cook 3 tablespoons chopped onion in 4 teaspoons margarine over medium heat until tender. Stir in 2 teaspoons flour. Stir in 1 cup chopped peeled tomato, ⅓ cup sliced ripe olives, ¼ teaspoon salt and dash pepper. Just before folding omelet, spoon half of tomato mixture on half of omelet. Fold in half; top with remaining tomato mixture.

Cheese Omelet

COOK'S NOTE

HOW TO MAKE AN OMELET

Melt margarine or butter in a skillet. Pour beaten egg mixture into skillet; reduce heat to low.

With a pancake turner, gently lift the edges as they begin to set and allow uncooked egg to flow underneath.

Continue to cook until mixture is set but top is still moist looking. If desired, spoon filling onto half of the omelet. Loosen the edges with a pancake turner and fold the omelet as you slide it from the pan to a serving dish.

Quiche Lorraine

PREP TIME: 30 MINUTES (READY IN 1 HOUR 15 MINUTES)
◆ YIELD: 6 SERVINGS

    1 refrigerated pie crust (from 15-oz. pkg.) or
        Pastry for One-Crust Filled Pie, page 385
    8 slices bacon
    8 oz. Swiss cheese, cut into thin strips (2 cups)
    2 tablespoons all-purpose flour
    4 eggs
 1½ cups half-and-half
    ¼ cup chopped onion
        Dash pepper

1. Heat oven to 350°F. Prepare pie crust for *one-crust filled pie* using 9-inch pie pan.
2. Cook bacon in large skillet over medium heat until crisp. Remove from skillet; drain on paper towels. Crumble.
3. In medium bowl, combine cheese and flour; mix well. In large bowl, beat eggs slightly. Add half-and-half, onion, pepper, bacon and cheese mixture; mix well. Spoon into crust-lined pan.
4. Bake at 350°F. for 40 to 45 minutes or until knife inserted near center comes out clean. Let stand 10 minutes before serving.

NUTRITION INFORMATION PER SERVING: Serving Size: ⅙ of Recipe ◆ Calories: 490 ◆ Calories from Fat: 310 ◆ % DAILY VALUE: Total Fat: 34 g 52% ◆ Saturated Fat: 17 g 85% ◆ Cholesterol: 215 mg 72% ◆ Sodium: 440 mg 18% ◆ Total Carbohydrate: 24 g 8% ◆ Dietary Fiber: 0 g 0% ◆ Sugars: 5 g ◆ Protein: 21 g ◆ Vitamin A: 15% ◆ Vitamin C: 45% ◆ Calcium: 45% ◆ Iron: 6% ◆ DIETARY EXCHANGES: 1½ Starch, 2½ High-Fat Meat, 2½ Fat OR 1½ Carbohydrate, 2½ High-Fat Meat, 2½ Fat

COOK'S NOTE

EGG NUTRITION

One large egg supplies about 70 calories, 6 grams of protein, 1 gram of carbohydrate, 5 grams of fat and 215 milligrams of cholesterol. This relatively high amount of dietary cholesterol, much more concentrated than in most other foods, gave eggs a bad name. Since elevated levels of blood cholesterol can predispose a person to heart trouble, doctors and dietitians began to recommend eating no more than two eggs a week. More recent research, however, suggests that it is not the dietary cholesterol intake alone that affects blood cholesterol, but rather the saturated fat in the diet. Experts believe most healthy people can include eggs as part of a balanced diet that is low in saturated fat.

Cheese Soufflé

PREP TIME: 20 MINUTES (READY IN 1 HOUR 20 MINUTES)
◆ YIELD: 6 SERVINGS

    6 tablespoons margarine or butter
    ⅔ cup all-purpose flour
    ½ teaspoon dry mustard
    ¼ teaspoon salt
 1½ cups milk
    6 oz. (1½ cups) shredded Cheddar cheese
    1 teaspoon Worcestershire sauce
    6 eggs, separated

1. Heat oven to 350°F. Grease and lightly flour 1½-quart soufflé dish or casserole. Make 4-inch band of double thickness foil 2 inches longer than top edge of dish; grease one side. Place foil, greased side in, around top edge of dish extending above edge. Secure foil with clear tape.
2. Melt margarine in large saucepan over medium heat. Add flour, dry mustard and salt; cook and stir until bubbly. Gradually add milk; cook until mixture is very thick and smooth, stirring constantly. Add cheese and Worcestershire sauce; stir until cheese melts. Remove from heat. Add egg yolks 1 at a time, beating well after each addition.
3. In medium bowl, beat egg whites just until stiff peaks form. Fold into cheese mixture. Carefully pour into greased and floured soufflé dish.
4. Bake at 350°F. for 55 to 60 minutes or until knife inserted near center comes out clean. Carefully remove foil band. Serve immediately.

TIP: For 3-egg soufflé, cut all ingredients in half. Bake in 1-quart soufflé dish or casserole for 35 to 40 minutes.

NUTRITION INFORMATION PER SERVING: Serving Size: ⅙ of Recipe ◆ Calories: 370 ◆ Calories from Fat: 240 ◆ % DAILY VALUE: Total Fat: 27 g 42% ◆ Saturated Fat: 10 g 50% ◆ Cholesterol: 245 mg 82% ◆ Sodium: 500 mg 21% ◆ Total Carbohydrate: 15 g 5% ◆ Dietary Fiber: 0 g 0% ◆ Sugars: 4 g ◆ Protein: 17 g ◆ Vitamin A: 25% ◆ Vitamin C: 0% ◆ Calcium: 30% ◆ Iron: 8% ◆ DIETARY EXCHANGES: 1 Starch, 2 Medium-Fat Meat, 3 Fat OR 1 Carbohydrate, 2 Medium-Fat Meat, 3 Fat

VARIATIONS

Bacon or Ham Soufflé: Add 6 to 8 slices crumbled, cooked bacon or 1 cup finely chopped cooked ham with cheese.
Chicken Soufflé: Add 1 cup finely chopped cooked chicken with cheese.

Fancy Baked Egg Scramble

PREP TIME: 30 MINUTES (READY IN 1 HOUR)
◆ YIELD: 12 SERVINGS

EGGS
3 tablespoons margarine or butter
¼ cup chopped onion
¼ cup chopped green bell pepper
2 cups cubed cooked ham
12 eggs, beaten
1 (4.5-oz.) jar sliced mushrooms, drained

SAUCE
2 tablespoons margarine or butter
2 tablespoons all-purpose flour
1 teaspoon chicken-flavor instant bouillon
1½ cups milk
2 oz. (1½ cups) shredded Swiss cheese
¼ cup grated Parmesan cheese

TOPPING
2 cups soft bread crumbs
¼ cup grated Parmesan cheese
¼ cup margarine or butter, melted
2 tablespoons chopped fresh parsley

1. Heat oven to 350°F. Grease 12 × 8-inch (2-quart) baking dish. Melt 3 tablespoons margarine in large skillet over medium heat. Add onion and bell pepper; cook until crisp-tender.
2. Add ham and eggs; cook until eggs are firm but still moist, stirring frequently. Stir in mushrooms. Remove from heat.
3. Melt 2 tablespoons margarine in medium saucepan. Add flour and bouillon; cook and stir until smooth and bubbly. Gradually add milk; cook until mixture boils and thickens, stirring constantly. Add Swiss cheese and ¼ cup Parmesan cheese; stir until smooth. Fold scrambled eggs into sauce. Pour into greased baking dish.*
4. In small bowl, combine all topping ingredients; sprinkle over eggs. Bake at 350°F. for 25 to 30 minutes or until light golden brown.

TIP: * To make ahead, prepare as directed to this point. Cover; refrigerate up to 3 hours. Uncover; top and bake as directed above.

NUTRITION INFORMATION PER SERVING: Serving Size: ¹⁄₁₂ of Recipe ◆ Calories: 260 ◆ Calories from Fat: 160 ◆ **% DAILY VALUE:** Total Fat: 18 g 28% ◆ Saturated Fat: 6 g 30% ◆ Cholesterol: 230 mg 77% ◆ Sodium: 710 mg 30% ◆ Total Carbohydrate: 9 g 3% ◆ Dietary Fiber: 1 g 2% ◆ Sugars: 3 g ◆ Protein: 16 g ◆ Vitamin A: 20% ◆ Vitamin C: 4% ◆ Calcium: 20% ◆ Iron: 8% ◆ **DIETARY EXCHANGES:** ½ Starch, 2 Medium-Fat Meat, 1½ Fat OR ½ Carbohydrate, 2 Medium-Fat Meat, 1½ Fat

Stuffed Eggs with Mushroom Sauce

PREP TIME: 45 MINUTES (READY IN 1 HOUR 10 MINUTES)
◆ YIELD: 8 SERVINGS

8 eggs
⅓ cup finely chopped cooked ham
⅛ teaspoon dry mustard
⅛ teaspoon onion powder
Dash pepper
¼ cup mayonnaise
⅓ cup margarine or butter
1½ cups sliced fresh mushrooms
⅓ cup all-purpose flour
¼ teaspoon dried thyme leaves
⅛ to ¼ teaspoon salt
⅛ teaspoon pepper
2 cups milk
¾ cup chicken broth
1 (2-oz.) jar chopped pimientos, drained
2 tablespoons margarine or butter, melted
½ cup unseasoned dry bread crumbs

1. Place eggs in medium saucepan; cover with cold water. Bring to a boil. Reduce heat; simmer about 15 minutes. Immediately drain; run cold water over eggs to stop cooking.
2. Remove shells from eggs; halve lengthwise. Carefully remove yolks; place in small bowl. Add ham, mustard, onion powder, pepper and mayonnaise; mix well. Fill egg white halves with yolk mixture. Set aside.
3. Heat oven to 350°F. Melt ⅓ cup margarine in medium saucepan over medium heat. Add mushrooms; cook and stir until tender. Stir in flour, thyme, salt and pepper. Cook 1 minute until smooth and bubbly, stirring constantly.
4. Gradually stir in milk and chicken broth. Cook over medium heat until slightly thickened and bubbly, stirring constantly. Stir in pimientos.
5. Spoon about 1 cup sauce mixture into bottom of ungreased 12 × 8-inch (2-quart) baking dish. Arrange egg halves over sauce. Spoon remaining sauce over egg halves.*
6. In small bowl, combine 2 tablespoons margarine and bread crumbs. Sprinkle evenly over egg mixture.
7. Bake at 350°F. for 20 to 25 minutes or until bubbly.

TIP: *To make ahead, prepare as directed to this point. Cover; refrigerate up to 24 hours. Uncover; sprinkle with bread crumb mixture. Bake as directed above.

NUTRITION INFORMATION PER SERVING: Serving Size: ⅛ of Recipe ♦ Calories: 310 ♦ Calories from Fat: 210 ♦ **% DAILY VALUE:** Total Fat: 23 g 35% ♦ Saturated Fat: 5 g 25% ♦ Cholesterol: 225 mg 75% ♦ Sodium: 680 mg 28% ♦ Total Carbohydrate: 14 g 5% ♦ Dietary Fiber: 1 g 3% ♦ Sugars: 5 g ♦ Protein: 12 g ♦ Vitamin A: 25% ♦ Vitamin C: 15% ♦ Calcium: 10% ♦ Iron: 8% ♦ **DIETARY EXCHANGES:** 1 Starch, 1 Medium-Fat Meat, 3½ Fat OR 1 Carbohydrate, 1 Medium-Fat Meat, 3½ Fat

Baked Broccoli Frittata

PREP TIME: 20 MINUTES (READY IN 40 MINUTES)
✦ YIELD: 4 SERVINGS

    1 to 1½ cups frozen cut broccoli, drained
    2 tablespoons margarine or butter
    1 cup sliced onions
    ½ cup sliced red or green bell pepper
    1 garlic clove, minced
    6 eggs
    ⅓ cup half-and-half
    ½ teaspoon dried basil leaves
    ½ teaspoon dried thyme leaves
    ½ teaspoon seasoned salt or lemon-pepper
        seasoning
    4 oz. (1 cup) shredded Monterey Jack cheese
    ½ cup grated Parmesan cheese

1. Cook broccoli as directed on package until crisp-tender. Drain.
2. Heat oven to 425°F. Generously grease 2-quart shallow casserole or 4 individual baking dishes. Melt margarine in large skillet over medium-low heat. Add onions, bell pepper and garlic; cook and stir until tender. Cool slightly.
3. In large bowl, combine eggs, half-and-half, basil, thyme and seasoned salt; beat well. Stir in onion mixture and broccoli. Pour into casserole. Sprinkle with cheeses.
4. Bake at 425°F. for 15 to 20 minutes or until set. Top will be moist. Let stand 5 minutes before serving.

NUTRITION INFORMATION PER SERVING: Serving Size: ¼ of Recipe ♦ Calories: 380 ♦ Calories from Fat: 250 ♦ **% DAILY VALUE:** Total Fat: 28 g 43% ♦ Saturated Fat: 13 g 65% ♦ Cholesterol: 360 mg 120% ♦ Sodium: 760 mg 32% ♦ Total Carbohydrate: 9 g 3% ♦ Dietary Fiber: 2 g 8% ♦ Sugars: 5 g ♦ Protein: 24 g ♦ Vitamin A: 60% ♦ Vitamin C: 60% ♦ Calcium: 50% ♦ Iron: 10% ♦ **DIETARY EXCHANGES:** 1 Vegetable, 3 Medium-Fat Meat, 3 Fat

Ham and Egg Enchiladas

PREP TIME: 30 MINUTES (READY IN 1 HOUR 10 MINUTES)
✦ YIELD: 8 SERVINGS

    1 tablespoon cornmeal
    2 cups diced cooked ham
    4 oz. (1 cup) shredded Monterey Jack cheese
    ½ cup sliced green onions
    1 (4.5-oz.) can chopped green chiles, drained
    8 (8-inch) flour tortillas
    6 eggs
    1 cup half-and-half
    1 tablespoon all-purpose flour
    3 drops hot pepper sauce
    4 oz. (1 cup) shredded Cheddar cheese
        Shredded lettuce
        Chopped tomatoes

1. Heat oven to 350°F. Grease 13 × 9-inch (3-quart) baking dish; sprinkle with cornmeal. In medium bowl, combine ham, Monterey Jack cheese, onions and green chiles. Spoon about ⅓ cup mixture down center of each tortilla. Roll up tightly; place in greased and cornmeal-coated baking dish.*
2. In medium bowl, combine eggs, half-and-half, flour and hot pepper sauce; beat well. Pour evenly over filled tortillas. Cover with foil.
3. Bake at 350°F. for 35 to 40 minutes or until eggs are set. Remove from oven; sprinkle with Cheddar cheese. Cover; let stand 5 minutes. Top with shredded lettuce and chopped tomatoes.

TIP: *To make ahead, prepare as directed to this point. Cover; refrigerate up to 24 hours. Uncover; prepare egg mixture. Continue as directed above.

NUTRITION INFORMATION PER SERVING: Serving Size: ⅛ of Recipe ♦ Calories: 380 ♦ Calories from Fat: 190 ♦ **% DAILY VALUE:** Total Fat: 21 g 32% ♦ Saturated Fat: 10 g 50% ♦ Cholesterol: 215 mg 72% ♦ Sodium: 950 mg 40% ♦ Total Carbohydrate: 25 g 8% ♦ Dietary Fiber: 2 g 8% ♦ Sugars: 3 g ♦ Protein: 23 g ♦ Vitamin A: 15% ♦ Vitamin C: 10% ♦ Calcium: 35% ♦ Iron: 15% ♦ **DIETARY EXCHANGES:** 1½ Starch, 2½ Medium-Fat Meat, 1½ Fat OR 1½ Carbohydrate, 2½ Medium-Fat Meat, 1½ Fat

NUTRITION INFORMATION PER SERVING: Serving Size: 1/12 of Recipe ♦ Calories: 190 ♦ Calories from Fat: 60 ♦ % DAILY VALUE: Total Fat: 7 g 11% ♦ Saturated Fat: 3 g 15% ♦ Cholesterol: 115 mg 38% ♦ Sodium: 420 mg 18% ♦ Total Carbohydrate: 22 g 7% ♦ Dietary Fiber: 3 g 12% ♦ Sugars: 5 g ♦ Protein: 10 g ♦ Vitamin A: 15% ♦ Vitamin C: 8% ♦ Calcium: 15% ♦ Iron: 8% ♦ DIETARY EXCHANGES: 1½ Starch, 1 Lean Meat, ½ Fat OR 1½ Carbohydrate, 1 Lean Meat, ½ Fat

Egg 'n Bagel Dijon

PREP TIME: 25 MINUTES ♦ YIELD: 4 SANDWICHES

    4 eggs
    2 tablespoons sliced green onions
  ¼ teaspoon dried basil leaves
    4 thin slices Canadian bacon
    4 bagels, split, toasted
    4 teaspoons Dijon mustard
    4 lettuce leaves
    4 tomato slices

1. In small bowl, combine eggs, onions and basil; blend well. Spray medium skillet with nonstick cooking spray. Place Canadian bacon in sprayed skillet. Cook over medium heat about 1 minute on each side or until hot; remove from skillet.

2. Add egg mixture to skillet. Cook until eggs are firm but still moist, stirring frequently. Spread 4 bagel halves with mustard. Top each with 1 lettuce leaf, 1 slice Canadian bacon, 1 slice tomato, ¼ of the egg mixture and bagel half.

NUTRITION INFORMATION PER SERVING: Serving Size: 1 Sandwich ♦ Calories: 310 ♦ Calories from Fat: 70 ♦ % DAILY VALUE: Total Fat: 8 g 12% ♦ Saturated Fat: 2 g 10% ♦ Cholesterol: 225 mg 75% ♦ Sodium: 970 mg 40% ♦ Total Carbohydrate: 40 g 13% ♦ Dietary Fiber: 2 g 8% ♦ Sugars: 2 g ♦ Protein: 20 g ♦ Vitamin A: 8% ♦ Vitamin C: 4% ♦ Calcium: 10% ♦ Iron: 20% ♦ DIETARY EXCHANGES: 2½ Starch, 1½ Medium-Fat Meat OR 2½ Carbohydrate, 1½ Medium-Fat Meat

Egg 'n Bagel Dijon

Black Bean and Corn Enchilada Egg Bake

Black Bean and Corn Enchilada Egg Bake

PREP TIME: 20 MINUTES (READY IN 5 HOURS 20 MINUTES) ♦ YIELD: 12 SERVINGS

  10 (6-inch) corn tortillas
    1 (15-oz.) can black beans, drained, rinsed
    1 (11-oz.) can vacuum-packed whole kernel corn with red and green peppers, drained
    1 (10¾-oz.) can condensed nacho cheese soup
    6 eggs
    2 cups milk
    1 teaspoon cumin
    2 oz. (½ cup) shredded Cheddar cheese
  ½ red bell pepper, if desired
    3 sprigs fresh cilantro, if desired

1. Grease 13×9-inch (3-quart) baking dish. Arrange and overlap 6 tortillas on bottom of dish. Spoon beans and corn evenly over tortillas. Spoon cheese soup evenly over vegetables. Cut remaining tortillas into 1-inch strips; arrange over top.

2. In large bowl, combine eggs, milk and cumin; beat well. Pour over tortilla strips. Cover tightly; refrigerate 4 hours or overnight.

3. Heat oven to 325°F. Uncover dish; sprinkle with cheese. Bake at 325°F. for 55 to 60 minutes or until eggs are set. Let stand 5 minutes before serving.

4. To garnish, cut five 1-inch pieces from bell pepper to resemble petals. Arrange petals in center of dish to resemble poinsettia. Tuck 2 or 3 sprigs of cilantro between petals. Or, chop bell pepper and cilantro; sprinkle over top. To serve, cut into squares. If desired, top with salsa and sour cream.

Weekend Breakfast Burritos

Weekend Breakfast Burritos

PREP TIME: 25 MINUTES (READY IN 40 MINUTES)
✦ YIELD: 6 SERVINGS

  1 tablespoon margarine or butter
  8 eggs, beaten
  ¼ teaspoon pepper
  2 cups diced Canadian bacon
  6 (8-inch) flour tortillas
  6 oz. (1½ cups) shredded Cheddar cheese

1. Heat oven to 400°F. Melt margarine in large skillet over medium-high heat. Add eggs, pepper and bacon; cook and stir about 5 minutes or until eggs are firm but still moist.
2. Spoon egg mixture evenly onto each tortilla. Top each with 1 tablespoon cheese. Roll up tortillas tightly. Place, seam side down, in ungreased 13×9-inch (3-quart) baking dish. Sprinkle remaining cheese over tortillas.
3. Bake at 400°F. for 10 to 15 minutes or until cheese is melted. If desired, serve with sour cream and salsa.

NUTRITION INFORMATION PER SERVING: Serving Size: ⅙ of Recipe ✦ Calories: 410 ✦ Calories from Fat: 220 ✦ **% DAILY VALUE:** Total Fat: 24 g 37% ✦ Saturated Fat: 10 g 50% ✦ Cholesterol: 335 mg 112% ✦ Sodium: 1080 mg 45% ✦ Total Carbohydrate: 21 g 7% ✦ Dietary Fiber: 1 g 4% ✦ Sugars: 2 g ✦ Protein: 28 g ✦ Vitamin A: 15% ✦ Vitamin C: 0% ✦ Calcium: 30% ✦ Iron: 15% ✦ **DIETARY EXCHANGES:** 1½ Starch, 3 Medium-Fat Meat, 1½ Fat OR 1½ Carbohydrate, 3 Medium-Fat Meat, 1½ Fat

Down-Home Creamed Eggs on Toasted English Muffins

PREP TIME: 35 MINUTES ✦ YIELD: 4 SERVINGS

  6 eggs
  3 cups milk
  3 tablespoons all-purpose flour
  ½ teaspoon salt
  ¼ teaspoon pepper
  4 English muffins, split, toasted

1. Place eggs in medium saucepan; cover with cold water. Bring to a boil. Reduce heat; simmer about 15 minutes. Immediately drain; run cold water over eggs to stop cooking. Peel eggs; slice thinly.
2. Pour milk into medium nonstick saucepan. Place saucepan over medium-high heat; stir in flour with wire whisk until well blended. Add salt and pepper. Cook and stir until bubbly and thickened. Remove from heat.
3. Place muffin halves, cut side up, on 4 individual plates. Arrange sliced eggs evenly over muffins, using 1½ eggs per serving. Spoon sauce evenly over eggs.

NUTRITION INFORMATION PER SERVING: Serving Size: ¼ of Recipe ✦ Calories: 350 ✦ Calories from Fat: 110 ✦ **% DAILY VALUE:** Total Fat: 12 g 18% ✦ Saturated Fat: 5 g 25% ✦ Cholesterol: 330 mg 110% ✦ Sodium: 720 mg 30% ✦ Total Carbohydrate: 40 g 13% ✦ Dietary Fiber: 2 g 8% ✦ Sugars: 17 g ✦ Protein: 20 g ✦ Vitamin A: 15% ✦ Vitamin C: 2% ✦ Calcium: 35% ✦ Iron: 15% ✦ **DIETARY EXCHANGES:** 2½ Starch, 2 Medium-Fat Meat OR 2½ Carbohydrate, 2 Medium-Fat Meat

Down-Home Creamed Eggs on Toasted English Muffins

Phyllo Sausage Egg Bake

PREP TIME: 40 MINUTES (READY IN 1 HOUR 40 MINUTES)
◆ YIELD: 12 SERVINGS

  1 tablespoon margarine or butter
  1 medium red bell pepper, chopped
  1 medium onion, chopped
  4 oz. fresh mushrooms, sliced (1½ cups)
  ½ lb. bulk Italian sausage
  5 eggs
  4 oz. (1 cup) shredded Monterey Jack cheese
  1 (9-oz.) pkg. frozen cut broccoli in a pouch,
      thawed, drained
  1 cup ricotta cheese
  1 tablespoon dried parsley flakes
 20 (17 x 12-inch) sheets frozen phyllo (filo)
      pastry, thawed
  ¾ to 1 cup butter, melted

1. Melt 1 tablespoon margarine in large skillet over medium heat. Add bell pepper, onion and mushrooms; cook until tender. Remove from skillet. Add sausage to skillet; cook over medium heat until no longer pink. Drain. Add mushroom mixture to sausage.
2. In medium bowl, beat eggs slightly; stir in Monterey Jack cheese and mushroom-sausage mixture. In another medium bowl, combine broccoli, ricotta cheese and parsley flakes.
3. Heat oven to 350°F. Unroll phyllo sheets; cover with plastic wrap or towel. Place 1 phyllo sheet in ungreased 13 × 9-inch (3-quart) baking dish, folding to fit. Brush with melted butter. Continue layering and brushing with butter 4 additional phyllo sheets.
4. Spread half of mushroom-sausage mixture evenly over phyllo dough. Layer and brush with butter 5 more phyllo sheets; spread with all of broccoli mixture. Layer and brush with butter 5 more phyllo sheets; spread with remaining mushroom-sausage mixture. Layer and brush with butter 5 remaining phyllo sheets. Score top of phyllo dough in diamond shape.*
5. Bake at 350°F. for 50 to 60 minutes or until puffed and golden brown.

TIP: * To make ahead, prepare as directed to this point. Cover; refrigerate 2 to 24 hours. Uncover; bake as directed above.

NUTRITION INFORMATION PER SERVING: Serving Size: 1/12 of Recipe ◆ Calories: 390 ◆ Calories from Fat: 250 ◆ % DAILY VALUE: Total Fat: 28 g 43% ◆ Saturated Fat: 15 g 75% ◆ Cholesterol: 155 mg 52% ◆ Sodium: 590 mg 25% ◆ Total Carbohydrate: 21 g 7% ◆ Dietary Fiber: 2 g 8% ◆ Sugars: 2 g ◆ Protein: 13 g ◆ Vitamin A: 30% ◆ Vitamin C: 25% ◆ Calcium: 15% ◆ Iron: 15% ◆ DIETARY EXCHANGES: 1½ Starch, 1 High-Fat Meat, 4 Fat OR 1½ Carbohydrate, 1 High-Fat Meat, 4 Fat

Puff Pancake with Caramelized Fruit

PREP TIME: 40 MINUTES ◆ YIELD: 4 SERVINGS

PANCAKE
  1 cup all-purpose flour
  1 cup milk
  4 eggs
  2 tablespoons margarine or butter

FRUIT MIXTURE
  1 tablespoon margarine or butter
  3 medium Gala apples, peeled, cut
      into ¼-inch-thick slices
  2 medium pears, peeled, cut
      into ¼-inch-thick slices
  ¾ cup firmly packed brown sugar
  ½ cup sweetened dried cranberries
  2 teaspoons lemon juice

1. Heat oven to 425°F. In medium bowl, combine flour, milk and eggs; beat 2 minutes at medium speed.
2. Place 2 tablespoons margarine in 9-inch glass pie pan. Heat in oven for 2 to 4 minutes or just until margarine sizzles. Remove pan from oven; tilt pan to coat bottom with melted margarine. Immediately pour batter into hot pan.
3. Bake at 425°F. for 18 to 25 minutes or until puffed and golden brown.
4. Meanwhile, melt 1 tablespoon margarine in 12-inch nonstick skillet over medium heat. Add apples and pears; cook 2 minutes, stirring occasionally. Add brown sugar, cranberries and lemon juice; mix well. Cook 8 to 10 minutes or until fruit is tender.
5. To serve, pour fruit mixture into pancake. Serve immediately.

HIGH ALTITUDE (over 3500 feet): No change.

NUTRITION INFORMATION PER SERVING: Serving Size: ¼ of Recipe ◆ Calories: 680 ◆ Calories from Fat: 140 ◆ % DAILY VALUE: Total Fat: 16 g 25% ◆ Saturated Fat: 4 g 20% ◆ Cholesterol: 215 mg 72% ◆ Sodium: 220 mg 9% ◆ Total Carbohydrate: 123 g 41% ◆ Dietary Fiber: 6 g 24% ◆ Sugars: 88 g ◆ Protein: 12 g ◆ Vitamin A: 20% ◆ Vitamin C: 10% ◆ Calcium: 15% ◆ Iron: 20% ◆ DIETARY EXCHANGES: 4 Starch, 4 Fruit, 3 Fat OR 8 Carbohydrate, 3 Fat

Classic French Toast

PREP TIME: 30 MINUTES ◆ YIELD: 18 SLICES; 6 SERVINGS

⅓ cup all-purpose flour
2 tablespoons sugar
½ teaspoon cinnamon
¼ teaspoon salt
2 cups half-and-half
1 teaspoon vanilla
6 eggs
18 (1-inch-thick) slices French bread

1. Heat large skillet or griddle over medium heat (350°F.) until hot. In large bowl, combine all ingredients except French bread slices; beat well. Dip each bread slice in egg mixture; turn to coat both sides.
2. Lightly grease heated skillet. Place bread slices in skillet. Cook 2 to 3 minutes on each side or until golden brown. If desired, sprinkle lightly with powdered sugar.

NUTRITION INFORMATION PER SERVING: Serving Size: ⅙ of Recipe ◆ Calories: 510 ◆ Calories from Fat: 160 ◆ **% DAILY VALUE:** Total Fat: 18 g 28% ◆ Saturated Fat: 8 g 40% ◆ Cholesterol: 240 mg 80% ◆ Sodium: 820 mg 34% ◆ Total Carbohydrate: 68 g 23% ◆ Dietary Fiber: 3 g 12% ◆ Sugars: 12 g ◆ Protein: 19 g ◆ Vitamin A: 15% ◆ Vitamin C: 0% ◆ Calcium: 20% ◆ Iron: 20% ◆ **DIETARY EXCHANGES:** 4 Starch, ½ Fruit, 1 High-Fat Meat, 1½ Fat OR 4½ Carbohydrate, 1 High-Fat Meat, 1½ Fat

Banana-Stuffed French Toast

PREP TIME: 35 MINUTES ◆ YIELD: 4 SERVINGS

4 eggs
⅔ cup milk
½ teaspoon cinnamon
1 teaspoon vanilla
8 (1-inch-thick) slices bread
2 medium bananas, thinly sliced
⅓ cup coconut
2 tablespoons margarine or butter

1. In shallow bowl, combine eggs, milk, cinnamon and vanilla; beat well.
2. Split each bread slice in half horizontally, leaving one side attached. Carefully pull back top layer of each bread slice. Spread 1 tablespoon of the egg mixture on bottom layer. Place ¼ of banana slices and 2 teaspoons coconut on the egg mixture in each slice.
3. Heat large skillet or griddle over medium-high heat (375°F.) until hot. Melt margarine in heated skillet. Dip each stuffed bread slice into egg mixture; turn to coat both sides. Place stuffed bread slices in skillet; cook 4 minutes on each side or until golden brown. If desired, serve with additional banana slices, toasted coconut and maple-flavored syrup.

NUTRITION INFORMATION PER SERVING: Serving Size: ¼ of Recipe ◆ Calories: 500 ◆ Calories from Fat: 150 ◆ **% DAILY VALUE:** Total Fat: 17 g 26% ◆ Saturated Fat: 6 g 30% ◆ Cholesterol: 215 mg 72% ◆ Sodium: 700 mg 29% ◆ Total Carbohydrate: 69 g 23% ◆ Dietary Fiber: 4 g 16% ◆ Sugars: 16 g ◆ Protein: 17 g ◆ Vitamin A: 15% ◆ Vitamin C: 6% ◆ Calcium: 20% ◆ Iron: 25% ◆ **DIETARY EXCHANGES:** 4 Starch, ½ Fruit, 1 Medium-Fat Meat, 2 Fat OR 4½ Carbohydrate, 1 Medium-Fat Meat, 2 Fat

Crunchy Oven French Toast

PREP TIME: 20 MINUTES (READY IN 2 HOURS 40 MINUTES) ◆ YIELD: 8 SLICES; 4 SERVINGS

3 eggs
1 cup half-and-half
2 tablespoons sugar
1 teaspoon vanilla
¼ teaspoon salt
3 cups corn flakes cereal, crushed to 1 cup
8 (¾-inch-thick) diagonally cut slices French bread
Strawberry syrup
Fresh strawberries

1. Grease 15 × 10 × 1-inch baking pan. In shallow bowl, combine eggs, half-and-half, sugar, vanilla and salt; beat well. Place crushed cereal in another shallow bowl. Dip each bread slice in egg mixture, making sure all egg mixture is absorbed. Coat each slice with crumbs. Place in greased pan; cover. Freeze 1 to 2 hours or until firm.
2. Heat oven to 425°F. Bake bread slices 15 to 20 minutes or until golden brown, turning once. Serve with syrup and strawberries. If desired, garnish with whipped topping.

NUTRITION INFORMATION PER SERVING: Serving Size: ¼ of Recipe ◆ Calories: 500 ◆ Calories from Fat: 120 ◆ **% DAILY VALUE:** Total Fat: 13 g 20% ◆ Saturated Fat: 6 g 30% ◆ Cholesterol: 180 mg 60% ◆ Sodium: 750 mg 31% ◆ Total Carbohydrate: 82 g 27% ◆ Dietary Fiber: 3 g 12% ◆ Sugars: 39 g ◆ Protein: 13 g ◆ Vitamin A: 20% ◆ Vitamin C: 35% ◆ Calcium: 15% ◆ Iron: 40% ◆ **DIETARY EXCHANGES:** 3½ Starch, 2 Fruit, ½ Medium-Fat Meat, 1½ Fat OR 5½ Carbohydrate, ½ Medium-Fat Meat, 1½ Fat

Celebration Brunch Strata

PREP TIME: 30 MINUTES (READY IN 1 HOUR 50 MINUTES)
◆ YIELD: 12 SERVINGS

½ cup margarine or butter, softened
12 slices white bread
8 oz. (2 cups) shredded Cheddar cheese
1 (9-oz.) pkg. frozen asparagus cuts in a pouch, thawed, drained
6 oz. flaked cooked crabmeat
8 eggs
2½ cups milk
3 tablespoons chopped fresh parsley or chervil
1 teaspoon salt
1 teaspoon paprika
¼ teaspoon pepper

1. Heat oven to 325°F. Spread margarine on one side of each slice of bread. Arrange 6 slices, margarine side down, in ungreased 13×9-inch (3-quart) baking dish. Layer cheese, asparagus and crabmeat over bread. Place remaining bread slices, margarine side up, over crabmeat.
2. In large bowl, combine all remaining ingredients; beat well. Pour egg mixture evenly over bread. Let stand 10 to 15 minutes.
3. Bake at 325°F. for 55 to 65 minutes or until knife inserted in center comes out clean.

NUTRITION INFORMATION PER SERVING: Serving Size: ¹⁄₁₂ of Recipe ◆ Calories: 300 ◆ Calories from Fat: 170 ◆ % DAILY VALUE: Total Fat: 19 g 29% ◆ Saturated Fat: 7 g 35% ◆ Cholesterol: 175 mg 58% ◆ Sodium: 760 mg 32% ◆ Total Carbohydrate: 17 g 6% ◆ Dietary Fiber: 1 g 4% ◆ Sugars: 4 g ◆ Protein: 16 g ◆ Vitamin A: 20% ◆ Vitamin C: 8% ◆ Calcium: 25% ◆ Iron: 10% ◆ DIETARY EXCHANGES: 1 Starch, 2 Medium-Fat Meat, 1½ Fat OR 1 Carbohydrate, 2 Medium-Fat Meat, 1½ Fat

Celebration Brunch Strata

Southwestern Egg Bake

Southwestern Egg Bake

PREP TIME: 20 MINUTES (READY IN 1 HOUR 30 MINUTES)
◆ YIELD: 6 SERVINGS

¾ lb. bulk spicy pork sausage
½ cup chopped onion
½ cup chopped green bell pepper
4 cups refrigerated or frozen hash-brown potatoes, thawed
6 oz. (1½ cups) shredded Cheddar cheese
4 eggs
¾ cup milk
1 cup chunky-style salsa

1. Heat oven to 350°F. Grease 8-inch square (2-quart) baking dish. In medium skillet, combine sausage, onion and bell pepper; cook over medium heat until browned. Drain.
2. Arrange potatoes in bottom of greased baking dish. Top with half of the cheese, all of the sausage mixture and the remaining cheese.
3. In small bowl, beat eggs slightly. Beat in milk. Pour over mixture in dish. Cover with foil.
4. Bake at 350°F. for 1 hour. Uncover baking dish; bake an additional 10 to 15 minutes or until knife inserted near center comes out clean. Let stand 5 minutes before serving. Serve topped with salsa.

NUTRITION INFORMATION PER SERVING: Serving Size: ⅙ of Recipe ◆ Calories: 390 ◆ Calories from Fat: 200 ◆ % DAILY VALUE: Total Fat: 22 g 34% ◆ Saturated Fat: 9 g 45% ◆ Cholesterol: 195 mg 65% ◆ Sodium: 1050 mg 44% ◆ Total Carbohydrate: 24 g 8% ◆ Dietary Fiber: 2 g 8% ◆ Sugars: 4 g ◆ Protein: 23 g ◆ Vitamin A: 15% ◆ Vitamin C: 20% ◆ Calcium: 25% ◆ Iron: 10% ◆ DIETARY EXCHANGES: 1½ Starch, 2½ High-Fat Meat, ½ Fat OR 1½ Carbohydrate, 2½ High-Fat Meat, ½ Fat

SALADS, VEGETABLES
& SIDES

SALADS VEGETABLES & SIDES

S alads, vegetables and side dishes bring distinctive flavor, color and textures to the menu. With flavors that awaken the palate, salads make an exotic first course or a savory and substantial main meal while vibrant vegetables create intriguing side dishes. Cold or hot, with dressing or not, this chapter hosts salads, vegetables and side dishes for every occasion.

Buying Greens

Look for signs of freshness and proper handling—bright color and healthy leaves free from blemishes and bruises. For delicate flavor and tender texture, choose young shoots and leaves. Select heads of iceberg lettuce and cabbage that are firm.

If you buy several varieties, you can combine them for contrast in flavor and texture. Many people use assertive greens such as arugula or radicchio (see "Type of Greens" chart, page 284) as an accent in a salad of milder lettuce.

Many greens are now available washed, torn and ready to dress either in grocery store salad bars or in an increasing number of prepackaged options, including romaine, coleslaw blend, mesclun (mixed young salad greens) and spinach. When purchasing packaged greens, look for packages with crisp, bright-colored leaves and avoid packages with leaves that are wilted, bruised or have rust spots.

How to Wash and Store Greens

Before washing, discard any discolored or blemished areas. Immerse the leaves in a sink filled with cool water. Swish gently to release the grit. Some greens, such as spinach, require several washings to remove all the sand particles. Drain the leaves in a colander. Dry them in a salad spinner or pat dry with paper towels.

Place washed and dried greens in a paper towel-lined plastic bag or lettuce keeper. Keep bagged greens in the refrigerator's crisper or coolest section. Iceberg and romaine keep for up to a week; plan to use more delicate varieties as soon as possible. Use unwashed leaves within 3 to 4 days.

Preparing Greens

Trim away tough ribs and stems. To remove the core of iceberg lettuce, bang the core hard against the countertop; then you can remove it easily with your fingertips.

Cutting the greens with a knife may cause the leaves to bruise or brown. Instead, tear them gently into bite-sized pieces with your fingers.

Coleslaw Deluxe

PREP TIME: 20 MINUTES ✦ YIELD: 12 (½-CUP) SERVINGS

SALAD
6 cups shredded cabbage
1½ cups (3 medium) shredded carrots
½ cup chopped green onions

DRESSING
1 cup salad dressing or mayonnaise
2 tablespoons cider vinegar
2 tablespoons sugar
1 to 2 tablespoons dill seed, if desired
½ teaspoon salt

1. In large bowl, combine all salad ingredients.
2. In small bowl, combine all dressing ingredients; blend well. Spoon dressing over salad; toss gently. Serve immediately, or cover and refrigerate until serving time.

NUTRITION INFORMATION PER SERVING: Serving Size: ½ Cup ✦ Calories: 170 ✦ Calories from Fat: 140 ✦ % DAILY VALUE: Total Fat: 15 g 23% ✦ Saturated Fat: 2 g 10% ✦ Cholesterol: 10 mg 3% ✦ Sodium: 210 mg 9% ✦ Total Carbohydrate: 7 g 2% ✦ Dietary Fiber: 2 g 8% ✦ Sugars: 5 g ✦ Protein: 1 g ✦ Vitamin A: 80% ✦ Vitamin C: 25% ✦ Calcium: 4% ✦ Iron: 4% ✦ DIETARY EXCHANGES: 1 Vegetable, 3 Fat

Dressed-Up Deli Coleslaw

PREP TIME: 5 MINUTES ◆ YIELD: 8 (½-CUP) SERVINGS

1 pint (2 cups) creamy coleslaw (from deli)
1 cup cubed fresh pineapple or 1 (8-oz.) can
    pineapple tidbits, drained
½ cup raisins
½ cup shelled sunflower seeds

In medium bowl, combine all ingredients; stir gently to coat. If desired, serve in lettuce-lined bowl.

NUTRITION INFORMATION PER SERVING: Serving Size: ½ Cup ◆ Calories: 140 ◆ Calories from Fat: 70 ◆ % DAILY VALUE: Total Fat: 8 g 12% ◆ Saturated Fat: 1 g 5% ◆ Cholesterol: 0 mg 0% ◆ Sodium: 90 mg 4% ◆ Total Carbohydrate: 16 g 5% ◆ Dietary Fiber: 2 g 8% ◆ Sugars: 10 g ◆ Protein: 2 g ◆ Vitamin A: 2% ◆ Vitamin C: 0% ◆ Calcium: 2% ◆ Iron: 4% ◆ DIETARY EXCHANGES: ½ Starch, ½ Fruit, 1½ Fat OR 1 Carbohydrate, 1½ Fat

Waldorf Coleslaw

PREP TIME: 20 MINUTES ◆ YIELD: 16 (½-CUP) SERVINGS

1 red apple, chopped
    Lemon juice
6 cups shredded cabbage
1 cup seedless red grapes
1 (20-oz.) can pineapple chunks in
    unsweetened juice, drained
1 cup sour cream
1 tablespoon sugar
1 teaspoon lemon juice
½ teaspoon salt
⅓ cup chopped walnuts, toasted*

1. In large bowl, sprinkle chopped apple with lemon juice. Add cabbage, grapes and pineapple; toss gently.
2. In small bowl, combine sour cream, sugar, 1 teaspoon lemon juice and salt; blend well. Pour sour cream mixture over cabbage mixture; toss until well coated. Serve immediately, or cover and refrigerate until serving time.
3. Just before serving, sprinkle with walnuts.

TIP: *To toast walnuts, spread on cookie sheet; bake at 350°F. for 5 to 7 minutes or until golden brown, stirring occasionally. Or spread in thin layer in microwave-safe pie pan. Microwave on HIGH for 4 to 7 minutes or until golden brown, stirring frequently.

NUTRITION INFORMATION PER SERVING: Serving Size: ½ Cup ◆ Calories: 90 ◆ Calories from Fat: 45 ◆ % DAILY VALUE: Total Fat: 5 g 8% ◆ Saturated Fat: 2 g 10% ◆ Cholesterol: 5 mg 2% ◆ Sodium: 80 mg 3% ◆ Total Carbohydrate: 9 g 3% ◆ Dietary Fiber: 1 g 4% ◆ Sugars: 8 g ◆ Protein: 1 g ◆ Vitamin A: 4% ◆ Vitamin C: 20% ◆ Calcium: 4% ◆ Iron: 2% ◆ DIETARY EXCHANGES: ½ Fruit, 1 Vegetable, 1 Fat OR ½ Carbohydrate, 1 Vegetable, 1 Fat

Asian Noodle and Vegetable Salad

PREP TIME: 25 MINUTES (READY IN 1 HOUR 25 MINUTES) ◆ YIELD: 6 (1-CUP) SERVINGS

SALAD

1 (1-lb.) pkg. frozen broccoli, carrots and
    water chestnuts
3 cups shredded cabbage
¼ cup sliced green onions

DRESSING

2 tablespoons oil
1 tablespoon cider vinegar
4 teaspoons sugar
1 (3-oz.) pkg. oriental-flavor instant ramen
    noodle soup mix
1 tablespoon sesame seed, toasted*

1. Cook vegetables as directed on package until crisp-tender. Drain; rinse with cold water to cool. In large bowl, combine vegetables, cabbage and onions.
2. In small jar with tight-fitting lid, combine oil, vinegar, sugar and seasoning packet from soup mix; shake well. Pour over vegetable mixture; toss to coat. Cover; refrigerate at least 1 hour to blend flavors.
3. Just before serving, break noodles into pieces. Add noodle pieces and sesame seed to salad; toss to combine.

TIP: *To toast sesame seed, spread in small nonstick skillet; stir over medium-high heat for 1 to 2 minutes or until light golden brown.

NUTRITION INFORMATION PER SERVING: Serving Size: 1 Cup ◆ Calories: 160 ◆ Calories from Fat: 70 ◆ % DAILY VALUE: Total Fat: 8 g 12% ◆ Saturated Fat: 2 g 10% ◆ Cholesterol: 0 mg 0% ◆ Sodium: 330 mg 14% ◆ Total Carbohydrate: 19 g 6% ◆ Dietary Fiber: 3 g 12% ◆ Sugars: 7 g ◆ Protein: 4 g ◆ Vitamin A: 40% ◆ Vitamin C: 45% ◆ Calcium: 4% ◆ Iron: 6% ◆ DIETARY EXCHANGES: ½ Starch, 2 Vegetable, 1½ Fat OR ½ Carbohydrate, 2 Vegetable, 1½ Fat

COOK'S NOTE

WATERMELON BOWL

Fresh Fruit Quantities

18½ pounds of watermelon (16 cups cubed)

4 pounds of pineapple (5 cups cubed)

3 pounds of honeydew or cantaloupe (4 cups cubed)

1 pint of strawberries, blueberries or raspberries (2 cups)

1 pound of green or red grapes (2 to 3 cups)

How to Carve a Melon Bowl

Select and wash a uniformly shaped melon. Cut off the top ⅓ of the melon. Cut

a thin slice from the bottom so the melon sits flat (do not cut into the red pulp). Scoop out the melon pulp, leaving a ½ to 1-inch shell.

Trace around a 1 to 2-inch star-shaped cookie cutter or adhesive-backed, vinyl-coated paper pattern placed at the edge of the melon. Space the stars as desired.

With a sharp, small pointed knife, cut ¾ of the way around each star, cutting out three star points.

The bowl can be carved, wrapped in plastic and refrigerated up to two days before the party.

Fill watermelon bowl with fruit just before serving. Garnish with mint leaves, if desired.

COOK'S NOTE

HOW TO CUT FRESH PINEAPPLE

Using a sharp knife, cut off the top and bottom of the pineapple.

Cut away the shell of the pineapple, one strip at a time.

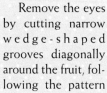

Remove the eyes by cutting narrow wedge-shaped grooves diagonally around the fruit, following the pattern of the eyes.

Cut pie-shaped wedges the length of the fruit.

To make smaller pieces, cut the wedges crosswise.

Summer Fruit Combo

PREP TIME: 30 MINUTES ◆ YIELD: 16 (½-CUP) SERVINGS

DRESSING

¼ cup frozen lemonade concentrate, thawed

¼ cup honey

½ teaspoon poppy seed

Dash salt

SALAD

2 cups seedless red grapes, halved

2 cups watermelon cubes

2 medium nectarines or peeled peaches, sliced

2 medium pears, cubed

1. In small jar with tight-fitting lid, combine all dressing ingredients; shake well.

2. In large bowl, combine all salad ingredients. Pour dressing over salad; toss gently to coat.

NUTRITION INFORMATION PER SERVING: Serving Size: ½ Cup ◆ Calories: 70 ◆ Calories from Fat: 0 ◆ **% DAILY VALUE:** Total Fat: 0 g 0% ◆ Saturated Fat: 0 g 0% ◆ Cholesterol: 0 mg 0% ◆ Sodium: 10 mg 0% ◆ Total Carbohydrate: 17 g 6% ◆ Dietary Fiber: 1 g 4% ◆ Sugars: 15 g ◆ Protein: 1 g ◆ Vitamin A: 4% ◆ Vitamin C: 10% ◆ Calcium: 0% ◆ Iron: 0% ◆ **DIETARY EXCHANGES:** 1 Fruit OR 1 Carbohydrate

ABOUT PEARS

The pears you buy at the market almost always need to ripen at home. Store them at room temperature until they yield to gentle pressure. Like apples, pears turn brown when the cut surface is exposed to air, so toss the cut-up fruit with citrus juice.

Orange Cream Squares

Orange Cream Squares

PREP TIME: 15 MINUTES (READY IN 5 HOURS)
✦ YIELD: 12 SERVINGS

GELATIN
1 (6-oz.) pkg. orange flavor gelatin
2 cups boiling water
1½ cups cold water
1 (11-oz.) can mandarin orange segments, drained, reserving liquid
1 (8-oz.) can crushed pineapple, drained, reserving liquid

TOPPING
¼ cup sugar
2 tablespoons cornstarch
1 cup reserved mandarin orange and pineapple liquid
1 egg, slightly beaten
1 cup whipping cream, whipped

1. In large bowl, dissolve gelatin in boiling water. Stir in cold water. Refrigerate until thickened but not set, about 45 minutes. Stir in orange segments and pineapple. Pour into 13 × 9-inch pan. Refrigerate until firm, about 4 hours.
2. Meanwhile, in small saucepan, combine sugar and cornstarch; stir in 1 cup reserved liquid and egg. Cook over medium heat until thickened, stirring constantly. Cover surface with plastic wrap or waxed paper; cool completely.
3. Fold whipped cream into cornstarch mixture. Spread over firm gelatin. Refrigerate until serving time.

NUTRITION INFORMATION PER SERVING: Serving Size: ⅟₁₂ of Recipe ✦ Calories: 180 ✦ Calories from Fat: 70 ✦ **% DAILY VALUE:** Total Fat: 8 g 12% ✦ Saturated Fat: 5 g 25% ✦ Cholesterol: 45 mg 15% ✦ Sodium: 50 mg 2% ✦ Total Carbohydrate: 24 g 8% ✦ Dietary Fiber: 0 g 0% ✦ Sugars: 23 g ✦ Protein: 2 g ✦ Vitamin A: 10% ✦ Vitamin C: 20% ✦ Calcium: 2% ✦ Iron: 0% ✦ **DIETARY EXCHANGES:** 1½ Fruit, 2 Fat OR 1½ Carbohydrate, 2 Fat

Cherry Cream Gelatin Squares

PREP TIME: 15 MINUTES (READY IN 4 HOURS 15 MINUTES) ✦ YIELD: 15 SERVINGS

GELATIN
1 (6-oz.) pkg. cherry flavor gelatin
2 cups boiling water
1 cup cold water
2 tablespoons lemon juice
½ teaspoon almond extract
1 (21-oz.) can cherry pie filling

TOPPING
½ cup sugar
½ cup sour cream
1 (8-oz.) pkg. cream cheese, softened

1. In large bowl, dissolve gelatin in boiling water. Stir in cold water, lemon juice, almond extract and pie filling. Pour into ungreased 13 × 9-inch (3-quart) baking dish. Refrigerate until firm, about 4 hours.
2. In small bowl, combine all topping ingredients; beat until smooth. Carefully spread over firm gelatin. Refrigerate until serving time.

NUTRITION INFORMATION PER SERVING: Serving Size: ⅟₁₅ of Recipe ✦ Calories: 190 ✦ Calories from Fat: 60 ✦ **% DAILY VALUE:** Total Fat: 7 g 11% ✦ Saturated Fat: 4 g 20% ✦ Cholesterol: 20 mg 7% ✦ Sodium: 80 mg 3% ✦ Total Carbohydrate: 29 g 10% ✦ Dietary Fiber: 0 g 0% ✦ Sugars: 27 g ✦ Protein: 2 g ✦ Vitamin A: 8% ✦ Vitamin C: 4% ✦ Calcium: 2% ✦ Iron: 0% ✦ **DIETARY EXCHANGES:** 1 Starch, 1 Fruit, 1 Fat OR 2 Carbohydrate, 1 Fat

Southern Citrus Salad

PREP TIME: 20 MINUTES ✦ YIELD: 8 SERVINGS

3 cups torn leaf lettuce
3 cups torn iceberg lettuce
2 grapefruit, peeled, sectioned
3 oranges, peeled, sectioned
1 avocado, peeled, pitted and sliced
¼ cup slivered almonds, toasted if desired*
1 cup purchased poppy seed salad dressing

In large serving bowl, combine leaf and iceberg lettuce; toss to mix. Arrange grapefruit, oranges, avocado and almonds over greens. Serve with dressing.

> **TIP:** * To toast almonds, spread on cookie sheet; bake at 350°F. for 5 to 7 minutes or until golden brown, stirring occasionally. Or spread in thin layer in microwave-safe pie pan. Microwave on HIGH for 4 to 7 minutes or until golden brown, stirring frequently.

NUTRITION INFORMATION PER SERVING: Serving Size: ⅛ of Recipe ✦ Calories: 290 ✦ Calories from Fat: 180 ✦ **% DAILY VALUE:** Total Fat: 20 g 31% ✦ Saturated Fat: 3 g 15% ✦ Cholesterol: 10 mg 3% ✦ Sodium: 230 mg 10% ✦ Total Carbohydrate: 24 g 8% ✦ Dietary Fiber: 4 g 16% ✦ Sugars: 17 g ✦ Protein: 3 g ✦ Vitamin A: 20% ✦ Vitamin C: 70% ✦ Calcium: 6% ✦ Iron: 6% ✦ **DIETARY EXCHANGES:** 1½ Fruit, 1 Vegetable, 4 Fat OR 1½ Carbohydrate, 1 Vegetable, 4 Fat

Waldorf Salad

PREP TIME: 15 MINUTES ✦ YIELD: 8 (⅔-CUP) SERVINGS

¼ cup chopped nuts
¼ cup chopped dates or raisins
2 tablespoons sugar
4 medium apples, cubed
1 stalk celery, chopped
⅔ cup mayonnaise or salad dressing*
1 teaspoon lemon juice

In large bowl, combine all ingredients; mix well. Serve immediately, or cover and refrigerate until serving time.

> **TIP:** * Sour cream or yogurt can be substituted for part of the mayonnaise.

NUTRITION INFORMATION PER SERVING: Serving Size: ⅔ Cup ✦ Calories: 230 ✦ Calories from Fat: 150 ✦ **% DAILY VALUE:** Total Fat: 17 g 26% ✦ Saturated Fat: 2 g 10% ✦ Cholesterol: 10 mg 3% ✦ Sodium: 110 mg 5% ✦ Total Carbohydrate: 19 g 6% ✦ Dietary Fiber: 3 g 12% ✦ Sugars: 17 g ✦ Protein: 1 g ✦ Vitamin A: 2% ✦ Vitamin C: 8% ✦ Calcium: 0% ✦ Iron: 2% ✦ **DIETARY EXCHANGES:** 1½ Fruit, 3 Fat OR 1½ Carbohydrate, 3 Fat

Margarita Fruit Salad

PREP TIME: 20 MINUTES ✦ YIELD: 12 (½-CUP) SERVINGS

¼ cup margarita mix (from 1-liter bottle)
¼ cup orange juice
1 tablespoon grated lime peel
1 tablespoon honey
6 cups assorted cut-up fresh fruit (such as oranges, pineapple, strawberries, grapes and/or pomegranate seeds)

1. In small bowl, combine all ingredients except fruit; blend well.
2. Place fruit in large bowl. Add margarita mixture; toss gently to combine.

NUTRITION INFORMATION PER SERVING: Serving Size: ½ Cup ✦ Calories: 45 ✦ Calories from Fat: 0 ✦ **% DAILY VALUE:** Total Fat: 0 g 0% ✦ Saturated Fat: 0 g 0% ✦ Cholesterol: 0 mg 0% ✦ Sodium: 0 mg 0% ✦ Total Carbohydrate: 11 g 4% ✦ Dietary Fiber: 1 g 4% ✦ Sugars: 9 g ✦ Protein: 0 g ✦ Vitamin A: 0% ✦ Vitamin C: 30% ✦ Calcium: 0% ✦ Iron: 0% ✦ **DIETARY EXCHANGES:** 1 Fruit OR 1 Carbohydrate

Refrigerated Fruit Salad

PREP TIME: 10 MINUTES (READY IN 4 HOURS 10 MINUTES) ✦ YIELD: 12 (½-CUP) SERVINGS

1 (21-oz.) can peach pie filling
1 (20-oz.) can pineapple chunks in unsweetened juice, drained
1 (11-oz.) can mandarin orange segments, drained
1 cup seedless red grapes, halved, or 1 cup fresh blueberries
1 cup miniature marshmallows
2 bananas, sliced

In large bowl, combine all ingredients; mix well. Cover; refrigerate at least 4 hours or overnight.

NUTRITION INFORMATION PER SERVING: Serving Size: ½ Cup ✦ Calories: 110 ✦ Calories from Fat: 0 ✦ **% DAILY VALUE:** Total Fat: 0 g 0% ✦ Saturated Fat: 0 g 0% ✦ Cholesterol: 0 mg 0% ✦ Sodium: 10 mg 0% ✦ Total Carbohydrate: 27 g 9% ✦ Dietary Fiber: 2 g 8% ✦ Sugars: 22 g ✦ Protein: 1 g ✦ Vitamin A: 6% ✦ Vitamin C: 25% ✦ Calcium: 0% ✦ Iron: 0% ✦ **DIETARY EXCHANGES:** 2 Fruit OR 2 Carbohydrate

Lemony Fruit Salad

PREP TIME: 25 MINUTES (READY IN 1 HOUR 10 MINUTES)
✦ YIELD: 20 (½-CUP) SERVINGS

    1 (2.9-oz.) pkg. lemon pudding and pie filling
      mix (not instant)
    ½ cup sugar
    ¼ cup water
    2 egg yolks
    2 cups water
    1 cup whipping cream, whipped
    1 (29-oz.) can sliced peaches, drained
    1 (20-oz.) can pineapple chunks, drained
    1 (16-oz.) can mandarin orange segments,
      drained
    1 (16-oz.) can sliced pears, drained

1. In medium saucepan, combine pudding mix, sugar and ¼ cup water. Stir in egg yolks. Add 2 cups water; mix well. Cook over medium heat until mixture comes to a full boil, stirring constantly. Cool about 45 minutes or until completely cooled, stirring occasionally.

2. Fold in whipped cream. Gently fold in drained fruits. Serve immediately, or cover and refrigerate several hours or overnight.

NUTRITION INFORMATION PER SERVING: Serving Size: ½ Cup ✦ Calories: 120 ✦ Calories from Fat: 45 ✦ % DAILY VALUE: Total Fat: 5 g 8% ✦ Saturated Fat: 3 g 15% ✦ Cholesterol: 40 mg 13% ✦ Sodium: 30 mg 1% ✦ Total Carbohydrate: 18 g 6% ✦ Dietary Fiber: 1 g 4% ✦ Sugars: 16 g ✦ Protein: 1 g ✦ Vitamin A: 10% ✦ Vitamin C: 15% ✦ Calcium: 0% ✦ Iron: 2% ✦ DIETARY EXCHANGES: 1 Fruit, 1 Fat OR 1 Carbohydrate, 1 Fat

Shimmering Sunshine Salad

PREP TIME: 15 MINUTES (READY IN 5 HOURS)
✦ YIELD: 6 SERVINGS

    1 (3-oz.) pkg. lime or lemon flavor gelatin
    1 cup boiling water
    ½ cup cold water
    1 (8¼-oz.) can crushed pineapple, undrained
    ½ cup shredded carrot

1. In medium bowl, dissolve gelatin in boiling water. Stir in cold water and pineapple. Refrigerate until thickened but not set, about 45 minutes.

2. Lightly oil six ½-cup salad molds. Stir carrot into thickened gelatin. Pour into oiled molds. Refrigerate until firm, about 4 hours.

3. To serve, unmold onto salad plates. If desired, top with mayonnaise or whipped cream.

NUTRITION INFORMATION PER SERVING: Serving Size: ⅙ of Recipe ✦ Calories: 80 ✦ Calories from Fat: 0 ✦ % DAILY VALUE: Total Fat: 0 g 0% ✦ Saturated Fat: 0 g 0% ✦ Cholesterol: 0 mg 0% ✦ Sodium: 40 mg 2% ✦ Total Carbohydrate: 20 g 7% ✦ Dietary Fiber: 1 g 2% ✦ Sugars: 19 g ✦ Protein: 1 g ✦ Vitamin A: 50% ✦ Vitamin C: 0% ✦ Calcium: 0% ✦ Iron: 0% ✦ DIETARY EXCHANGES: 1½ Fruit OR 1½ Carbohydrate

COOK'S NOTE

HOW TO MAKE MOLDED SALADS

In large bowl, add boiling water to gelatin, stirring constantly until all granules are dissolved. This may require up to 4 minutes of stirring before adding any cold liquid.

Refrigerate the clear gelatin mixture until it is the consistency of thick unbeaten egg whites and somewhat lumpy, about 45 minutes. Then stir in fruit. With slightly thickened gelatin, the fruit will be evenly distributed rather than sinking to the bottom of the mold. Pour the thickened gelatin into a lightly oiled mold and chill it at least 4 more hours.

To unmold, loosen the gelatin by running the tip of a pointed knife around the edge of the mold. Moisten the surface of the serving plate to make it easier to adjust the gelatin's position on the plate. Apply a clean, hot, moist kitchen towel to the outside of the mold for 1 minute to loosen the gelatin without overmelting it. Gently shake the mold to release the gelatin. Repeat application of the hot, moist towel, if necessary, until the gelatin slides out easily. Garnish as desired.

Fruit 'n Yogurt Pasta Salad

Molded Cranberry-Orange Salad

PREP TIME: 15 MINUTES (READY IN 5 HOURS 15 MINUTES) ◆ YIELD: 10 SERVINGS

3½ cups cranberry juice cocktail
1 (6-oz.) pkg. orange flavor gelatin
1½ cups chopped fresh or frozen cranberries
½ cup chopped walnuts
1 (11-oz.) can mandarin orange segments, drained
Lettuce leaves

Molded Cranberry-Orange Salad

1. In small saucepan, bring 1½ cups of the cranberry juice cocktail to a boil. In large bowl, dissolve gelatin in hot cranberry cocktail. Stir in remaining 2 cups cranberry cocktail. Refrigerate until thickened but not set, about 1 hour.
2. Lightly oil 6-cup ring or other mold. Stir cranberries, walnuts and orange segments into thickened gelatin. Spoon into oiled mold. Refrigerate until firm, about 4 hours.
3. To serve, line serving plate with lettuce leaves. Unmold gelatin onto serving plate.

NUTRITION INFORMATION PER SERVING: Serving Size: ¹⁄₁₀ of Recipe ◆ Calories: 180 ◆ Calories from Fat: 35 ◆ **% DAILY VALUE:** Total Fat: 4 g 6% ◆ Saturated Fat: 0 g 0% ◆ Cholesterol: 0 mg 0% ◆ Sodium: 45 mg 2% ◆ Total Carbohydrate: 34 g 11% ◆ Dietary Fiber: 2 g 8% ◆ Sugars: 31 g ◆ Protein: 2 g ◆ Vitamin A: 4% ◆ Vitamin C: 45% ◆ Calcium: 0% ◆ Iron: 2% ◆ **DIETARY EXCHANGES:** 2½ Fruit, ½ Fat OR 2½ Carbohydrate, ½ Fat

Fruit 'n Yogurt Pasta Salad

PREP TIME: 25 MINUTES (READY IN 1 HOUR 25 MINUTES) ◆ YIELD: 10 (½-CUP) SERVINGS

4 oz. (1 cup) uncooked macaroni rings or small shells
1 (11-oz.) can mandarin orange segments, drained
1 (8-oz.) can pineapple chunks, drained
1 cup halved seedless green grapes
1 (6-oz.) container low-fat lemon yogurt
1 tablespoon sugar
1 cup halved strawberries

1. Cook macaroni to desired doneness as directed on package. Drain; rinse with cold water to cool.
2. In medium bowl, combine cooked macaroni and all remaining ingredients except strawberries; mix gently to coat. Cover; refrigerate 1 to 2 hours to blend flavors.
3. Just before serving, stir in strawberries.

NUTRITION INFORMATION PER SERVING: Serving Size: ½ Cup • Calories: 110 • Calories from Fat: 10 • % DAILY VALUE: Total Fat: 1 g 2% • Saturated Fat: 0 g 0% • Cholesterol: 0 mg 0% • Sodium: 10 mg 0% • Total Carbohydrate: 21 g 7% • Dietary Fiber: 1 g 4% • Sugars: 12 g • Protein: 3 g • Vitamin A: 4% • Vitamin C: 30% • Calcium: 4% • Iron: 4% • DIETARY EXCHANGES: 1 Starch, ½ Fruit OR 1½ Carbohydrate

Tossed Salad

PREP TIME: 10 MINUTES ✦ YIELD: 6 SERVINGS

    4 cups assorted salad greens, torn into
        bite-sized pieces
    3 medium tomatoes, cut into wedges
    1 medium cucumber, sliced
    ½ teaspoon salt
        Dash pepper
    ½ cup purchased French or other favorite
        salad dressing

In large serving bowl, combine all ingredients except salad dressing. Add salad dressing; toss gently to coat.

TIP: Any type of salad greens can be used, such as:

    Bibb lettuce
    Boston lettuce
    Curly endive
    Escarole
    Iceberg lettuce
    Leaf lettuce
    Romaine lettuce
    Spinach
    Watercress

Any of the following vegetables can be added:

    Artichoke hearts
    Bamboo shoots
    Bean sprouts
    Beets, cooked, julienne-cut
    Bell pepper, sliced
    Broccoli florets
    Carrots, shredded, thinly sliced or
        julienne-cut
    Cauliflower florets
    Celery, sliced
    French fried onions
    Garbanzo beans
    Green beans, cooked
    Mushrooms, sliced or quartered
    Olives, sliced

    Onions, thinly sliced
    Pimientos, cut into strips
    Radishes, sliced
    Water chestnuts, sliced
    Zucchini, sliced

Any of the following fruit can be added:

    Apples, sliced or cubed
    Avocado, thinly sliced
    Grapefruit segments
    Grapes (seedless green or red)
    Mandarin orange segments
    Pears, sliced or cubed
    Pomegranate seeds

Any of the following meats and cheeses can be added:

    Anchovy fillets
    Beef, cooked, cubed or julienne-cut
    Cheese, cubed or shredded
    Chicken or turkey, cooked, cubed or
        julienne-cut
    Ham, cubed or julienne-cut
    Hard-cooked eggs, sliced or cut into wedges
    Salami, cubed or sliced
    Seafood, cooked or canned, or imitation
        seafood (surimi)
    Summer sausage, cubed or sliced

NUTRITION INFORMATION PER SERVING: Serving Size: ⅙ of Recipe • Calories: 120 • Calories from Fat: 80 • % DAILY VALUE: Total Fat: 9 g 14% • Saturated Fat: 2 g 10% • Cholesterol: 0 mg 0% • Sodium: 480 mg 20% • Total Carbohydrate: 9 g 3% • Dietary Fiber: 2 g 8% • Sugars: 6 g • Protein: 1 g • Vitamin A: 35% • Vitamin C: 30% • Calcium: 0% • Iron: 2% • DIETARY EXCHANGES: 1 Vegetable, 2 Fat

Tomato-Mozzarella Platter

PREP TIME: 10 MINUTES ✦ YIELD: 4 SERVINGS

    2 large beefsteak tomatoes, sliced
    ¼ teaspoon salt
    5 oz. (8 slices) fresh mozzarella cheese
    2 teaspoons olive or vegetable oil
    2 tablespoons torn fresh basil leaves
    ¼ teaspoon coarse ground black pepper

Sprinkle tomato slices with salt. Arrange tomato and cheese slices alternately on serving platter, overlapping slices. Drizzle with oil; sprinkle with basil and pepper.

NUTRITION INFORMATION PER SERVING: Serving Size: ¼ of Recipe • Calories: 150 • Calories from Fat: 90 • % DAILY VALUE: Total Fat: 10 g 15% • Saturated Fat: 5 g 25% • Cholesterol: 30 mg 10% • Sodium: 280 mg 12% • Total Carbohydrate: 6 g 2% • Dietary Fiber: 1 g 4% • Sugars: 3 g • Protein: 8 g • Vitamin A: 20% • Vitamin C: 25% • Calcium: 20% • Iron: 4% • DIETARY EXCHANGES: 1 Vegetable, 1 Medium-Fat Meat, 1 Fat

Barley Confetti Salad

PREP TIME: 25 MINUTES (READY IN 1 HOUR 25 MINUTES)
◆ YIELD: 10 (½-CUP) SERVINGS

2 cups water
¼ teaspoon garlic salt
1 cup uncooked quick-cooking barley
1 (6-oz.) jar marinated artichoke hearts,
    undrained
½ cup sliced celery
⅓ cup sliced green onions
1 small red or green bell pepper, cut into strips
½ teaspoon garlic salt
½ teaspoon dried thyme leaves

1. In large saucepan, bring water and ¼ teaspoon garlic salt to a boil. Add barley; return to a boil. Reduce heat; cover and simmer 10 to 15 minutes or until barley is tender. Drain.
2. In large bowl, combine barley and all remaining ingredients; mix well. Cover; refrigerate at least 1 hour to blend flavors.

NUTRITION INFORMATION PER SERVING: Serving Size: ½ Cup ◆ Calories: 110 ◆ Calories from Fat: 45 ◆ % DAILY VALUE: Total Fat: 5 g 8% ◆ Saturated Fat: 0 g 0% ◆ Cholesterol: 0 mg 0% ◆ Sodium: 180 mg 8% ◆ Total Carbohydrate: 13 g 4% ◆ Dietary Fiber: 2 g 8% ◆ Sugars: 1 g ◆ Protein: 2 g ◆ Vitamin A: 6% ◆ Vitamin C: 15% ◆ Calcium: 0% ◆ Iron: 0% ◆ DIETARY EXCHANGES: 1 Starch, 1 Fat OR 1 Carbohydrate, 1 Fat

Tabbouleh

PREP TIME: 25 MINUTES (READY IN 2 HOURS 25 MINUTES) ◆ YIELD: 8 (1-CUP) SERVINGS

2 cups uncooked bulgur or cracked wheat
2 cups boiling water
3 medium tomatoes, chopped
1 medium cucumber, diced (1 cup)
1 cup finely chopped fresh parsley
½ cup finely chopped green onions
1 tablespoon dried mint leaves
    or 2 tablespoons chopped fresh mint
½ cup lemon juice
½ cup olive oil
1 teaspoon salt

1. Place bulgur in large bowl; pour boiling water over bulgur. Let stand 1 hour or until bulgur is softened and most of liquid is absorbed.
2. Drain bulgur well; return to bowl. Add tomatoes, cucumber, parsley, onions and mint; mix well.
3. In small bowl, combine lemon juice, oil and salt; blend well. Add to bulgur mixture; mix well. Cover; refrigerate at least 1 hour to blend flavors.

TIP: One to 2 cups cubed cooked beef can be added for a main-dish salad.

NUTRITION INFORMATION PER SERVING: Serving Size: 1 Cup ◆ Calories: 270 ◆ Calories from Fat: 130 ◆ % DAILY VALUE: Total Fat: 14 g 22% ◆ Saturated Fat: 2 g 10% ◆ Cholesterol: 0 mg 0% ◆ Sodium: 290 mg 12% ◆ Total Carbohydrate: 31 g 10% ◆ Dietary Fiber: 8 g 32% ◆ Sugars: 3 g ◆ Protein: 5 g ◆ Vitamin A: 15% ◆ Vitamin C: 45% ◆ Calcium: 4% ◆ Iron: 10% ◆ DIETARY EXCHANGES: 2 Starch, 2½ Fat OR 2 Carbohydrate, 2½ Fat

Balsamic Couscous Salad with Sun-Dried Tomatoes and Olives

PREP TIME: 30 MINUTES ◆ YIELD: 20 (½-CUP) SERVINGS

1 (14½-oz.) can ready-to-serve fat-free
    chicken broth with ⅓ less sodium
2 cups water
½ cup dry-pack sun-dried tomatoes, cut up
2¼ cups uncooked couscous
1 cup chopped green onions
¼ cup chopped fresh basil or 4 teaspoons
    dried basil leaves
1 (5¾-oz.) jar sliced green olives, drained
    (about 1¼ cups)
¼ cup balsamic vinegar
2 tablespoons water
2 tablespoons extra-virgin olive oil

1. In medium saucepan, combine broth, 2 cups water and sun-dried tomatoes. Bring to a boil. Stir in couscous; remove from heat. Cover; let stand 5 minutes.
2. Line 1 large or 2 small cookie sheets with waxed paper. To cool couscous mixture quickly, fluff with fork; spread on lined cookie sheet. Let stand 5 minutes.
3. In large bowl, combine cooled couscous mixture, onions, basil, olives, balsamic vinegar and 2 tablespoons water; toss gently to mix well. Add oil; toss gently. Serve immediately, or cover and refrigerate until serving time.

NUTRITION INFORMATION PER SERVING: Serving Size: ½ Cup ◆ Calories: 100 ◆ Calories from Fat: 20 ◆ % DAILY VALUE: Total Fat: 2 g 3% ◆ Saturated Fat: 0 g 0% ◆ Cholesterol: 0 mg 0% ◆ Sodium: 170 mg 7% ◆ Total Carbohydrate: 17 g 6% ◆ Dietary Fiber: 1 g 4% ◆ Sugars: 1 g ◆ Protein: 3 g ◆ Vitamin A: 0% ◆ Vitamin C: 2% ◆ Calcium: 0% ◆ Iron: 2% ◆ DIETARY EXCHANGES: 1 Starch, ½ Fat OR 1 Carbohydrate, ½ Fat

Grandma's Potato Salad

PREP TIME: 30 MINUTES (READY IN 1 HOUR 30 MINUTES)
◆ YIELD: 6 (½-CUP) SERVINGS

SALAD
3 eggs
2 cups cubed peeled cooked potatoes
¾ cup sliced celery
¼ cup chopped onion

DRESSING
½ cup salad dressing or mayonnaise
1½ teaspoons cider vinegar
1 teaspoon prepared mustard
½ teaspoon sugar
¼ teaspoon salt
⅛ teaspoon pepper
Paprika

1. Place eggs in medium saucepan; cover with cold water. Bring to a boil. Reduce heat; simmer about 15 minutes. Immediately drain; run cold water over eggs to stop cooking.
2. Peel eggs. Chop 2 of the eggs; reserve 1 egg for garnish. In large bowl, combine chopped eggs, potatoes, celery and onion.
3. In small bowl, combine all dressing ingredients except paprika; blend well. Spoon dressing over salad; mix well. Cover; refrigerate at least 1 hour or until chilled.
4. Just before serving, slice reserved egg. Garnish potato salad with sliced egg; sprinkle with paprika.

NUTRITION INFORMATION PER SERVING: Serving Size: ½ Cup ◆ Calories: 170 ◆ Calories from Fat: 80 ◆ % DAILY VALUE: Total Fat: 9 g 14% ◆ Saturated Fat: 2 g 10% ◆ Cholesterol: 110 mg 37% ◆ Sodium: 280 mg 12% ◆ Total Carbohydrate: 17 g 6% ◆ Dietary Fiber: 1 g 4% ◆ Sugars: 4 g ◆ Protein: 4 g ◆ Vitamin A: 4% ◆ Vitamin C: 0% ◆ Calcium: 2% ◆ Iron: 4% ◆ DIETARY EXCHANGES: 1 Starch, 2 Fat OR 1 Carbohydrate, 2 Fat

Low-Fat Potato Salad

PREP TIME: 30 MINUTES (READY IN 1 HOUR 30 MINUTES)
◆ YIELD: 11 (½-CUP) SERVINGS

4 cups (2 lb.) cubed peeled cooked potatoes
1 cup sliced celery
½ cup sliced radishes
¼ cup sliced green onions
¾ cup low-fat plain yogurt
2 tablespoons light mayonnaise
1 teaspoon prepared mustard
½ teaspoon salt
⅛ teaspoon pepper

1. In large bowl, combine potatoes, celery, radishes and onions; toss lightly.
2. In small bowl, combine yogurt, mayonnaise, mustard, salt and pepper; blend well. Add to potato mixture; mix gently. Cover; refrigerate at least 1 hour to blend flavors.

NUTRITION INFORMATION PER SERVING: Serving Size: ½ Cup ◆ Calories: 70 ◆ Calories from Fat: 10 ◆ % DAILY VALUE: Total Fat: 1 g 2% ◆ Saturated Fat: 0 g 0% ◆ Cholesterol: 2 mg 1% ◆ Sodium: 150 mg 6% ◆ Total Carbohydrate: 14 g 5% ◆ Dietary Fiber: 1 g 4% ◆ Sugars: 2 g ◆ Protein: 2 g ◆ Vitamin A: 0% ◆ Vitamin C: 15% ◆ Calcium: 4% ◆ Iron: 0% ◆ DIETARY EXCHANGES: 1 Starch OR 1 Carbohydrate

French Potato Salad with Green Beans

PREP TIME: 25 MINUTES ◆ YIELD: 6 (1-CUP) SERVINGS

SALAD
6 medium potatoes (about 2 lb.), peeled, sliced
1 (8-oz.) pkg. frozen cut green beans*
2 tablespoons chopped red bell pepper

DRESSING
½ cup dry white wine or chicken broth
¼ cup tarragon vinegar
2 tablespoons chopped fresh parsley
1 tablespoon chopped fresh chives
    or ¼ cup thinly sliced green onions
1 teaspoon salt
¼ teaspoon pepper

1. In medium saucepan, cook potatoes in boiling water until tender, about 10 minutes. Drain. Cook green beans as directed on package. Drain.
2. Meanwhile, in jar with tight-fitting lid, combine all dressing ingredients; shake well.
3. To serve, spoon warm green beans into center of shallow serving bowl or deep platter. Arrange warm potato slices around beans. Drizzle dressing over vegetables. Sprinkle with bell pepper.

TIP: * Two cups (about ¾ lb.) fresh green beans, cut into 1½-inch pieces, can be substituted for frozen beans. Simmer covered in small amount of water for 15 to 20 minutes or until tender. Drain.

NUTRITION INFORMATION PER SERVING: Serving Size: 1 Cup ◆ Calories: 120 ◆ Calories from Fat: 0 ◆ % DAILY VALUE: Total Fat: 0 g 0% ◆ Saturated Fat: 0 g 0% ◆ Cholesterol: 0 mg 0% ◆ Sodium: 360 mg 15% ◆ Total Carbohydrate: 24 g 8% ◆ Dietary Fiber: 3 g 12% ◆ Sugars: 2 g ◆ Protein: 3 g ◆ Vitamin A: 8% ◆ Vitamin C: 40% ◆ Calcium: 2% ◆ Iron: 4% ◆ DIETARY EXCHANGES: 1½ Starch OR 1½ Carbohydrate

Mixed Potato Salad

PREP TIME: 25 MINUTES (READY IN 1 HOUR)
◆ YIELD: 24 (½-CUP) SERVINGS

SALAD
  3 lb. red potatoes
  2 lb. sweet potatoes
  1 cup chopped celery
  1 medium cucumber, peeled, seeded and
      chopped

DRESSING
  1 (8-oz.) container nonfat plain yogurt
  ¼ cup chopped fresh dill or 1 tablespoon dried
      dill weed
  ¼ cup light mayonnaise or salad dressing
  1 tablespoon lemon juice
  ¼ teaspoon salt

1. Place whole red and sweet potatoes separately in 2 Dutch ovens or large saucepans; cover with water. Bring to a boil. Reduce heat; simmer until tender. Simmer red potatoes 20 to 25 minutes; simmer sweet potatoes 30 to 35 minutes.
2. Drain potatoes; rinse with cold water to cool. Peel potatoes; cut into cubes. Place in large serving bowl. Add celery and cucumber; mix well.
3. In medium bowl, combine all dressing ingredients; blend well. Pour dressing over salad; toss gently. Serve immediately, or cover and refrigerate until serving time.

NUTRITION INFORMATION PER SERVING: Serving Size: ½ Cup ◆ Calories: 90 ◆ Calories from Fat: 10 ◆ % DAILY VALUE: Total Fat: 1 g 2% ◆ Saturated Fat: 0 g 0% ◆ Cholesterol: 0 mg 0% ◆ Sodium: 60 mg 3% ◆ Total Carbohydrate: 19 g 6% ◆ Dietary Fiber: 2 g 8% ◆ Sugars: 6 g ◆ Protein: 2 g ◆ Vitamin A: 100% ◆ Vitamin C: 25% ◆ Calcium: 2% ◆ Iron: 2% ◆ DIETARY EXCHANGES: 1 Starch OR 1 Carbohydrate

---

COOK'S NOTE

POTATO SALAD TYPES

◆ **Mayonnaise-dressed potato salads.** To reduce the fat, substitute nonfat or low-fat mayonnaise or nonfat plain yogurt for some or all of the regular mayonnaise in the recipe.

◆ **Vinaigrette-dressed potato salads.** Toss in the dressing while the potatoes are still warm, and the flavor will soak right into the potatoes. German potato salad includes crumbled bacon with a vinaigrette-style dressing.

Mixed Potato Salad

German Potato Salad

PREP TIME: 25 MINUTES ◆ YIELD: 8 (½-CUP) SERVINGS

  2 lb. (10 to 16) small new red potatoes
  4 slices bacon
  ½ cup chopped onion
  ¼ cup sugar
  2 tablespoons all-purpose flour
  ½ teaspoon salt
      Dash pepper
  1 cup water
  ⅓ cup vinegar
      Fresh parsley, if desired

1. In medium saucepan, cook potatoes in boiling water for 15 to 20 minutes or until tender. Drain. Peel potatoes; slice.
2. Meanwhile, in large skillet, cook bacon until crisp. Remove bacon from skillet; drain on paper towels. Reserve 2 tablespoons drippings in skillet. Add onion; cook and stir until crisp-tender.
3. Add sugar, flour, salt and pepper; blend well. Gradually add water and vinegar. Cook over medium-high heat until bubbly and thickened, stirring constantly.
4. Stir in potatoes; cook until thoroughly heated. Crumble bacon; sprinkle over top. Garnish with parsley.

NUTRITION INFORMATION PER SERVING: Serving Size: ½ Cup ◆ Calories: 160 ◆ Calories from Fat: 45 ◆ % DAILY VALUE: Total Fat: 5 g 8% ◆ Saturated Fat: 2 g 10% ◆ Cholesterol: 5 mg 2% ◆ Sodium: 190 mg 8% ◆ Total Carbohydrate: 25 g 8% ◆ Dietary Fiber: 2 g 8% ◆ Sugars: 7 g ◆ Protein: 3 g ◆ Vitamin A: 0% ◆ Vitamin C: 20% ◆ Calcium: 0% ◆ Iron: 2% ◆ DIETARY EXCHANGES: 1 Starch, ½ Fruit, 1 Fat OR 1½ Carbohydrate, 1 Fat

Sunny Cauliflower-Broccoli Toss

PREP TIME: 25 MINUTES ✦ YIELD: 8 (½-CUP) SERVINGS

DRESSING
- ½ cup mayonnaise or salad dressing
- 2 tablespoons sugar
- 1 tablespoon cider vinegar

SALAD
- 3 slices bacon
- 2 cups fresh cauliflower florets
- 2 cups cut-up fresh broccoli (including tender part of stalks)
- ½ cup raisins
- ¼ cup sliced green onions
- ¼ cup shelled sunflower seeds

1. In small bowl, combine all dressing ingredients; blend with wire whisk until smooth. Set aside.

2. Cook bacon until crisp. Drain on paper towels; crumble.

3. In large bowl, combine bacon and all remaining salad ingredients; toss gently. Pour dressing over salad; toss to coat. If desired, sprinkle with additional sunflower seeds.

NUTRITION INFORMATION PER SERVING: Serving Size: ½ Cup ✦ Calories: 200 ✦ Calories from Fat: 140 ✦ **% DAILY VALUE:** Total Fat: 15 g 23% ✦ Saturated Fat: 2 g 10% ✦ Cholesterol: 10 mg 3% ✦ Sodium: 160 mg 7% ✦ Total Carbohydrate: 14 g 5% ✦ Dietary Fiber: 2 g 8% ✦ Sugars: 11 g ✦ Protein: 3 g ✦ Vitamin A: 8% ✦ Vitamin C: 60% ✦ Calcium: 2% ✦ Iron: 6% ✦ **DIETARY EXCHANGES:** ½ Starch, ½ Fruit, ½ Vegetable, 3 Fat OR 1 Carbohydrate, ½ Vegetable, 3 Fat

Sunny Cauliflower-Broccoli Toss

Tuscan Panzanella Salad

Tuscan Panzanella Salad

PREP TIME: 25 MINUTES ✦ YIELD: 6 (1-CUP) SERVINGS

- 3 cups cubed dry (day-old) Italian bread
- ¼ cup balsamic vinegar
- 2 teaspoons olive oil
- ⅛ teaspoon coarse ground black pepper
- 2 medium tomatoes, seeded, diced
- 2 medium cucumbers, halved, seeded and chopped
- 1 red bell pepper, chopped
- ¼ cup sliced ripe olives
- ¼ cup thinly sliced fresh basil leaves

1. Heat oven to 350°F. Place bread cubes on ungreased cookie sheet. Toast bread at 350°F. for 5 to 10 minutes or until lightly browned.

2. Meanwhile, in small bowl, combine vinegar, oil and pepper; blend well.

3. In large bowl, combine tomatoes, cucumbers, bell pepper, olives and toasted bread cubes. Pour vinegar mixture over salad; toss gently to coat. Sprinkle with basil.

NUTRITION INFORMATION PER SERVING: Serving Size: 1 Cup ✦ Calories: 100 ✦ Calories from Fat: 25 ✦ **% DAILY VALUE:** Total Fat: 3 g 5% ✦ Saturated Fat: 0 g 0% ✦ Cholesterol: 0 mg 0% ✦ Sodium: 160 mg 7% ✦ Total Carbohydrate: 14 g 5% ✦ Dietary Fiber: 2 g 8% ✦ Sugars: 4 g ✦ Protein: 3 g ✦ Vitamin A: 25% ✦ Vitamin C: 60% ✦ Calcium: 4% ✦ Iron: 6% ✦ **DIETARY EXCHANGES:** ½ Starch, 1 Vegetable, ½ Fat OR ½ Carbohydrate, 1 Vegetable, ½ Fat

Cucumbers in Sour Cream

PREP TIME: 15 MINUTES (READY IN 45 MINUTES)
◆ YIELD: 8 (½-CUP) SERVINGS

    4 medium cucumbers, thinly sliced (4 cups)
 1½ teaspoons salt
  ¾ cup white vinegar
  ¾ cup water
    1 cup sour cream
    1 teaspoon chopped fresh dill or ¼ teaspoon
       dried dill weed
    1 teaspoon sugar
       Dash pepper

1. Place cucumbers in medium bowl; sprinkle with salt. Add vinegar and water; stir. Let stand 30 minutes, stirring occasionally. Drain well; return to bowl.

2. In small bowl, combine sour cream, dill, sugar and pepper; blend well. Add to cucumbers; mix gently. Serve immediately, or cover and refrigerate until serving time.

> **TIP:** Thinly sliced onion, separated into rings, can be added with sour cream mixture.

NUTRITION INFORMATION PER SERVING: Serving Size: ½ Cup ◆ Calories: 70 ◆ Calories from Fat: 50 ◆ **% DAILY VALUE:** Total Fat: 6 g 9% ◆ Saturated Fat: 4 g 20% ◆ Cholesterol: 15 mg 5% ◆ Sodium: 420 mg 18% ◆ Total Carbohydrate: 4 g 1% ◆ Dietary Fiber: 0 g 0% ◆ Sugars: 3 g ◆ Protein: 1 g ◆ Vitamin A: 8% ◆ Vitamin C: 6% ◆ Calcium: 4% ◆ Iron: 0% ◆ **DIETARY EXCHANGES:** 1 Vegetable, 1 Fat

Antipasto Salad

PREP TIME: 20 MINUTES (READY IN 50 MINUTES)
◆ YIELD: 6 SERVINGS

DRESSING
  ⅓ cup red wine vinegar
  ½ cup olive or vegetable oil
    1 teaspoon Dijon mustard
    1 teaspoon dried Italian seasoning
  ½ teaspoon salt
  ¼ teaspoon sugar
  ⅛ teaspoon pepper
    2 garlic cloves, minced, or 1 teaspoon chopped
       garlic in water (from 4.5-oz. jar)

SALAD
    6 cups torn leaf lettuce
 12 thin slices provolone cheese
    1 (3.5-oz.) pkg. giant-sized sliced pepperoni
    2 large tomatoes, cut into wedges
    8 large fresh mushrooms, sliced
    8 large pitted ripe olives

1. In small jar with tight-fitting lid, combine all dressing ingredients; shake well. Let stand at room temperature for 30 minutes to blend flavors.

2. To serve, place lettuce on large serving platter. Cut cheese slices in half. Roll cheese and pepperoni slices into cones. Arrange cheese and pepperoni cones, tomatoes, mushrooms and olives over lettuce. Drizzle with dressing.

NUTRITION INFORMATION PER SERVING: Serving Size: ⅙ of Recipe ◆ Calories: 390 ◆ Calories from Fat: 310 ◆ **% DAILY VALUE:** Total Fat: 34 g 52% ◆ Saturated Fat: 10 g 50% ◆ Cholesterol: 35 mg 12% ◆ Sodium: 850 mg 35% ◆ Total Carbohydrate: 8 g 3% ◆ Dietary Fiber: 2 g 8% ◆ Sugars: 4 g ◆ Protein: 13 g ◆ Vitamin A: 15% ◆ Vitamin C: 30% ◆ Calcium: 25% ◆ Iron: 10% ◆ **DIETARY EXCHANGES:** 1½ Vegetable, 1½ High-Fat Meat, 4½ Fat

Three-Bean Salad

PREP TIME: 15 MINUTES (READY IN 4 HOURS 15 MINUTES) ◆ YIELD: 12 (½-CUP) SERVINGS

SALAD
    1 (15.5 or 15-oz.) can kidney beans, drained
    1 (14.5-oz.) can cut yellow wax beans, drained
    1 (14.5-oz.) can cut green beans, drained
    1 medium red onion, sliced, separated into
       rings
    1 green bell pepper, cut into strips

DRESSING
  ¾ cup vinegar
  ½ cup sugar
  ½ cup oil
    1 tablespoon chopped fresh parsley
    1 teaspoon celery seed
  ¼ teaspoon pepper

1. In large bowl, combine all salad ingredients.

2. In jar with tight-fitting lid, combine all dressing ingredients; shake well. Pour dressing over salad; toss to coat. Cover; refrigerate at least 4 hours or overnight to blend flavors.

NUTRITION INFORMATION PER SERVING: Serving Size: ½ Cup ◆ Calories: 160 ◆ Calories from Fat: 80 ◆ **% DAILY VALUE:** Total Fat: 9 g 14% ◆ Saturated Fat: 1 g 5% ◆ Cholesterol: 0 mg 0% ◆ Sodium: 150 mg 6% ◆ Total Carbohydrate: 17 g 6% ◆ Dietary Fiber: 2 g 8% ◆ Sugars: 10 g ◆ Protein: 2 g ◆ Vitamin A: 4% ◆ Vitamin C: 15% ◆ Calcium: 4% ◆ Iron: 6% ◆ **DIETARY EXCHANGES:** 1 Starch, 2 Fat OR 1 Carbohydrate, 2 Fat

Tangy Carrot-Raisin Salad

PREP TIME: 20 MINUTES ◆ YIELD: 7 (¹/₂-CUP) SERVINGS

    3 cups shredded carrots
    1 cup raisins
    3 tablespoons oil
    2 tablespoons honey
    2 tablespoons lemon juice
    ¹/₄ teaspoon salt
    ¹/₈ teaspoon nutmeg

1. In medium bowl, combine carrots and raisins.
2. In small bowl, combine all remaining ingredients; mix well. Pour over carrot mixture; toss until well blended. Serve immediately, or cover and refrigerate until serving time.

NUTRITION INFORMATION PER SERVING: Serving Size: ¹/₂ Cup ◆ Calories: 170 ◆ Calories from Fat: 50 ◆ % DAILY VALUE: Total Fat: 6 g 9% ◆ Saturated Fat: 1 g 5% ◆ Cholesterol: 0 mg 0% ◆ Sodium: 95 mg 4% ◆ Total Carbohydrate: 29 g 10% ◆ Dietary Fiber: 2 g 8% ◆ Sugars: 23 g ◆ Protein: 1 g ◆ Vitamin A: 270% ◆ Vitamin C: 10% ◆ Calcium: 2% ◆ Iron: 4% ◆ DIETARY EXCHANGES: 2 Fruit, ¹/₂ Vegetable, 1 Fat OR 2 Carbohydrate, ¹/₂ Vegetable, 1 Fat

Black Bean and Corn Salad

PREP TIME: 15 MINUTES ◆ YIELD: 7 (¹/₂-CUP) SERVINGS

SALAD
    1 medium zucchini, halved, sliced (1 cup)
    1 (15-oz.) can black beans, drained, rinsed
    1 (7-oz.) can whole kernel corn, drained
    ¹/₄ cup chopped red onion
    ¹/₄ cup chopped fresh parsley

DRESSING
    ¹/₂ cup purchased oil and vinegar salad dressing
    3 tablespoons sugar
    ¹/₄ teaspoon seasoned salt

1. In medium bowl, combine all salad ingredients.
2. In small bowl, combine all dressing ingredients; blend well. Spoon dressing over salad; stir to coat.

NUTRITION INFORMATION PER SERVING: Serving Size: ¹/₂ Cup ◆ Calories: 190 ◆ Calories from Fat: 90 ◆ % DAILY VALUE: Total Fat: 10 g 15% ◆ Saturated Fat: 2 g 10% ◆ Cholesterol: 0 mg 0% ◆ Sodium: 350 mg 15% ◆ Total Carbohydrate: 21 g 7% ◆ Dietary Fiber: 4 g 16% ◆ Sugars: 9 g ◆ Protein: 4 g ◆ Vitamin A: 4% ◆ Vitamin C: 10% ◆ Calcium: 2% ◆ Iron: 6% ◆ DIETARY EXCHANGES: 1¹/₂ Starch, 2 Fat OR 1¹/₂ Carbohydrate, 2 Fat

Fresh Green Bean-Walnut Salad

PREP TIME: 25 MINUTES (READY IN 1 HOUR 25 MINUTES) ◆ YIELD: 8 (¹/₂-CUP) SERVINGS

SALAD
    1 lb. fresh green beans, trimmed
    ¹/₂ cup roasted red bell peppers (from 7.25-oz. jar), drained, cut into strips
    1 small onion, cut into wedges
    ¹/₄ cup coarsely chopped walnuts

DRESSING
    ¹/₄ cup olive oil
    2 tablespoons balsamic vinegar
    1 teaspoon dry mustard
    ¹/₈ teaspoon salt

1. Place green beans in medium saucepan; add just enough water to cover. Bring to a boil over medium-high heat. Cook 8 to 10 minutes or until beans are crisp-tender, stirring occasionally. Drain; rinse with cold water to cool.
2. In medium bowl, combine green beans and all remaining salad ingredients.
3. In jar with tight-fitting lid, combine all dressing ingredients; shake well. Pour over salad; toss gently to coat. Cover; refrigerate at least 1 hour to blend flavors.

NUTRITION INFORMATION PER SERVING: Serving Size: ¹/₂ Cup ◆ Calories: 110 ◆ Calories from Fat: 80 ◆ % DAILY VALUE: Total Fat: 9 g 14% ◆ Saturated Fat: 1 g 5% ◆ Cholesterol: 0 mg 0% ◆ Sodium: 35 mg 1% ◆ Total Carbohydrate: 6 g 2% ◆ Dietary Fiber: 2 g 8% ◆ Sugars: 2 g ◆ Protein: 2 g ◆ Vitamin A: 15% ◆ Vitamin C: 25% ◆ Calcium: 2% ◆ Iron: 4% ◆ DIETARY EXCHANGES: 1 Vegetable, 2 Fat

Suit Yourself Tuna Salad

PREP TIME: 25 MINUTES ✦ YIELD: 5 (1-CUP) SERVINGS

SALAD

6 oz. (2¼ cups) uncooked medium shell pasta
2 (6-oz.) cans water-packed tuna
   or 1 (14¾-oz.) can salmon, drained, flaked
½ cup diagonally sliced celery
½ cup shredded carrot

DRESSING

½ to ¾ cup mayonnaise or salad dressing
1 teaspoon Dijon mustard
¼ teaspoon sugar
¼ teaspoon salt
⅛ teaspoon pepper

1. Cook pasta to desired doneness as directed on package. Drain; rinse with cold water to cool.
2. In large bowl, combine cooked pasta and all remaining salad ingredients; toss gently.
3. In small bowl, combine all dressing ingredients; blend well. Add to salad; toss gently to coat. Serve immediately, or cover and refrigerate until serving time.

> **TIP:** For variety, add one or more of the following:
>   Apple, diced
>   Avocado, diced
>   Bacon, cooked, crumbled
>   Bell pepper, chopped
>   Cheese, shredded or diced
>   Chives, chopped
>   Cucumber, seeded, chopped
>   Dill pickle, chopped
>   Dried dill weed
>   Grapes (seedless green or red)
>   Hard-cooked eggs, chopped
>   Mandarin orange segments
>   Olives, sliced
>   Onions (green or red), sliced or chopped
>   Parsley, chopped
>   Peas, cooked
>   Pickle relish
>   Pimientos, chopped
>   Radishes, sliced
>   Shelled sunflower seeds
>   Shoestring potatoes
>   Tomatoes, seeded, diced
>   Walnuts or pecans, chopped

NUTRITION INFORMATION PER SERVING: Serving Size: 1 Cup ✦ Calories: 440 ✦ Calories from Fat: 250 ✦ **% DAILY VALUE:** Total Fat: 28 g 43% ✦ Saturated Fat: 4 g 20% ✦ Cholesterol: 35 mg 12% ✦ Sodium: 530 mg 22% ✦ Total Carbohydrate: 28 g 9% ✦ Dietary Fiber: 1 g 4% ✦ Sugars: 3 g ✦ Protein: 19 g ✦ Vitamin C: 4% ✦ Calcium: 2% ✦ Iron: 15% ✦ **DIETARY EXCHANGES:** 2 Starch, 2 Very Lean Meat, 5 Fat OR 2 Carbohydrate, 2 Very Lean Meat, 5 Fat

Quick Tortellini Salad

PREP TIME: 25 MINUTES ✦ YIELD: 3 (1⅓-CUP) SERVINGS

DRESSING

⅓ cup olive oil
3 tablespoons red wine vinegar
1 teaspoon lemon juice
½ teaspoon sugar
½ teaspoon salt
¼ teaspoon garlic powder
¼ teaspoon dried oregano leaves

SALAD

1 (9-oz.) pkg. refrigerated cheese-filled tortellini
1 cup sliced carrots
1½ cups frozen cut green beans
2 tablespoons sliced green onions

1. In jar with tight-fitting lid, combine all dressing ingredients; shake well. Set aside.
2. Cook tortellini, carrots and green beans as directed on tortellini package until tortellini is tender and vegetables are crisp-tender. Drain; return to saucepan. Cover with cold water; let stand 5 minutes. Drain well.
3. Place tortellini, carrots and green beans in medium bowl; add onions. Pour dressing over salad; toss gently to coat.

NUTRITION INFORMATION PER SERVING: Serving Size: 1⅓ Cups ✦ Calories: 450 ✦ Calories from Fat: 220 ✦ **% DAILY VALUE:** Total Fat: 24 g 37% ✦ Saturated Fat: 5 g 25% ✦ Cholesterol: 40 mg 13% ✦ Sodium: 720 mg 30% ✦ Total Carbohydrate: 48 g 16% ✦ Dietary Fiber: 6 g 24% ✦ Sugars: 7 g ✦ Protein: 11 g ✦ Vitamin A: 260% ✦ Vitamin C: 0% ✦ Calcium: 15% ✦ Iron: 15% ✦ **DIETARY EXCHANGES:** 3 Starch, 1 Vegetable, 4½ Fat OR 3 Carbohydrate, 1 Vegetable, 4½ Fat

Quick Tortellini Salad

Grilled Steak and Potato Salad

Grilled Steak and Potato Salad

PREP TIME: 30 MINUTES ✦ YIELD: 4 SERVINGS

½ lb. new red potatoes, halved
⅔ cup purchased fat-free honey Dijon salad dressing
¾ lb. boneless beef sirloin steak (¾ inch thick)
¼ teaspoon salt
¼ teaspoon coarse ground black pepper
4 cups torn romaine lettuce
2 tomatoes, cut into thin wedges
½ cup thinly sliced red onion

1. GRILL DIRECTIONS: Heat grill. Place potatoes in medium saucepan; add enough water to cover. Bring to a boil. Reduce heat to medium; cook 5 to 8 minutes or just until potatoes are fork-tender.
2. Drain potatoes; place in medium bowl. Add 2 tablespoons of the salad dressing; toss to coat evenly. Brush steak with 1 tablespoon of the salad dressing; sprinkle with salt and pepper.
3. When ready to grill, place steak and potatoes on gas grill over medium heat or on charcoal grill 4 to 6 inches from medium coals; cover grill. Cook 8 to 15 minutes or until steak is of desired doneness and potatoes are golden brown, turning once.
4. Meanwhile, arrange lettuce, tomatoes and onion on large serving platter. Slice steak into thin slices; arrange on platter. Top with potatoes. Drizzle salad with remaining salad dressing. If desired, sprinkle with additional pepper.

> **TIP:** To broil, place steak and cooked potatoes on broiler pan; broil 4 to 6 inches from heat using times above as a guide.

NUTRITION INFORMATION PER SERVING: Serving Size: ¼ of Recipe ✦ Calories: 250 ✦ Calories from Fat: 35 ✦ **% DAILY VALUE:** Total Fat: 4 g 6% ✦ Saturated Fat: 1 g 5% ✦ Cholesterol: 45 mg 15% ✦ Sodium: 660 mg 28% ✦ Total Carbohydrate: 35 g 12% ✦ Dietary Fiber: 4 g 16% ✦ Sugars: 13 g ✦ Protein: 18 g ✦ Vitamin A: 50% ✦ Vitamin C: 40% ✦ Calcium: 4% ✦ Iron: 20% ✦ **DIETARY EXCHANGES:** 1½ Starch, ½ Fruit, 1 Vegetable, 1½ Lean Meat OR 2 Carbohydrate, 1 Vegetable, 1½ Lean Meat

Curry Wild Rice Salad

PREP TIME: 10 MINUTES ✦ YIELD: 4 (½-CUP) SERVINGS

DRESSING
¼ cup nonfat plain yogurt
2 tablespoons light mayonnaise
½ teaspoon curry powder
⅛ teaspoon pepper

SALAD
1 (15-oz.) can cooked wild rice, drained*
¼ cup chopped red bell pepper
¼ cup chopped celery
2 tablespoons raisins

1. In small bowl, combine all dressing ingredients; blend well.
2. In large bowl, combine all salad ingredients; mix well. Add dressing; toss gently to mix thoroughly. Serve immediately, or cover and refrigerate until serving time.

> **TIP:** * Two cups cooked instant wild or brown rice can be substituted for the canned rice.

NUTRITION INFORMATION PER SERVING: Serving Size: ½ Cup ✦ Calories: 120 ✦ Calories from Fat: 25 ✦ **% DAILY VALUE:** Total Fat: 3 g 5% ✦ Saturated Fat: 1 g 5% ✦ Cholesterol: 3 mg 1% ✦ Sodium: 320 mg 13% ✦ Total Carbohydrate: 19 g 6% ✦ Dietary Fiber: 2 g 8% ✦ Sugars: 6 g ✦ Protein: 3 g ✦ Vitamin A: 8% ✦ Vitamin C: 20% ✦ Calcium: 4% ✦ Iron: 0% ✦ **DIETARY EXCHANGES:** 1 Starch, ½ Fruit, ½ Fat OR 1½ Carbohydrate, ½ Fat

Curry Wild Rice Salad

Taco Salad

PREP TIME: 25 MINUTES ✦ YIELD: 6 SERVINGS

- 1 lb. extra-lean ground beef
- 1 medium onion, chopped
- 1 (1¼-oz.) pkg. taco seasoning mix*
- ½ cup water
- ½ head lettuce, torn into bite-sized pieces
- 6 oz. (4 cups) corn chips
- 3 oz. (¾ cup) shredded Cheddar or American cheese
- 2 medium tomatoes, cut into wedges
- ¾ cup purchased French or Russian salad dressing

1. In large skillet, brown ground beef and onion until beef is thoroughly cooked. Drain. Stir in taco seasoning mix and water; simmer 10 minutes over low heat, stirring occasionally.
2. Line individual salad bowls or plates with lettuce. Sprinkle with corn chips. Spoon beef mixture in center of each. Sprinkle with cheese. Garnish with tomatoes. Serve with salad dressing.

TIP: *To substitute for taco seasoning mix, add ½ cup chili sauce, 1 teaspoon salt, 1 teaspoon chili powder and ¼ teaspoon hot pepper sauce when adding water to beef-onion mixture.

NUTRITION INFORMATION PER SERVING: Serving Size: ⅙ of Recipe • Calories: 530 • Calories from Fat: 320 • **% DAILY VALUE:** Total Fat: 36 g 55% • Saturated Fat: 11 g 55% • Cholesterol: 60 mg 20% • Sodium: 1280 mg 53% • Total Carbohydrate: 31 g 10% • Dietary Fiber: 3 g 12% • Sugars: 7 g • Protein: 21 g • Vitamin A: 25% • Vitamin C: 15% • Calcium: 15% • Iron: 15% • **DIETARY EXCHANGES:** 1½ Starch, 1 Vegetable, 2 Lean Meat, 6 Fat OR 1½ Carbohydrate, 1 Vegetable, 2 Lean Meat, 6 Fat

Ham and Macaroni Picnic Salad

PREP TIME: 20 MINUTES ✦ YIELD: 12 (1-CUP) SERVINGS

SALAD

- 4 eggs
- 16 oz. (4 cups) uncooked elbow macaroni
- 1 cup diced cooked ham
- 1 cup sliced celery
- ½ cup chopped green onions
- ¼ cup sweet pickle relish
- 1 (2-oz.) jar diced pimientos, drained

DRESSING

- 1 cup salad dressing or mayonnaise
- 2 tablespoons prepared mustard
- ½ teaspoon salt
- ¼ teaspoon pepper

1. Place eggs in medium saucepan; cover with cold water. Bring to a boil. Reduce heat; simmer about 15 minutes. Immediately drain; run cold water over eggs to stop cooking. Peel eggs; chop. Set aside.
2. Meanwhile, cook macaroni to desired doneness as directed on package. Drain; rinse with cold water to cool.
3. In large bowl, combine cooked macaroni, ham, celery, onions, pickle relish and pimientos.
4. In small bowl, combine all dressing ingredients; blend well. Add to salad; mix well. Gently stir in hard-cooked eggs. Serve immediately, or cover and refrigerate until serving time.

NUTRITION INFORMATION PER SERVING: Serving Size: 1 Cup • Calories: 270 • Calories from Fat: 90 • **% DAILY VALUE:** Total Fat: 10 g 15% • Saturated Fat: 2 g 10% • Cholesterol: 80 mg 27% • Sodium: 500 mg 21% • Total Carbohydrate: 36 g 12% • Dietary Fiber: 1 g 4% • Sugars: 6 g • Protein: 10 g • Vitamin A: 6% • Vitamin C: 15% • Calcium: 2% • Iron: 10% • **DIETARY EXCHANGES:** 2½ Starch, ½ Medium-Fat Meat, 1 Fat OR 2½ Carbohydrate, ½ Medium-Fat Meat, 1 Fat

Old-Fashioned Chicken Salad

PREP TIME: 15 MINUTES (READY IN 1 HOUR 15 MINUTES) ✦ YIELD: 4 SERVINGS

- 3 cups cubed cooked chicken
- 1 cup chopped celery
- 2 tablespoons chopped onion
- ¼ teaspoon salt
- ⅛ teaspoon pepper
- ½ cup mayonnaise
- 1 tablespoon lemon juice
- 4 medium tomatoes

1. In medium bowl, combine all ingredients except tomatoes; mix well. Cover; refrigerate 1 hour or until chilled.
2. To serve, cut each tomato into 6 wedges, cutting to but not through bottom. Place on individual serving plates. Spread wedges; spoon chicken salad into tomatoes. If desired, garnish with lettuce leaf and sprig of fresh parsley.

NUTRITION INFORMATION PER SERVING: Serving Size: ¼ of Recipe • Calories: 430 • Calories from Fat: 270 • **% DAILY VALUE:** Total Fat: 30 g 46% • Saturated Fat: 5 g 25% • Cholesterol: 110 mg 37% • Sodium: 420 mg 18% • Total Carbohydrate: 8 g 3% • Dietary Fiber: 2 g 8% • Sugars: 4 g • Protein: 32 g • Vitamin A: 20% • Vitamin C: 30% • Calcium: 4% • Iron: 10% • **DIETARY EXCHANGES:** 1 Vegetable, 4½ Lean Meat, 3½ Fat

Chinese Chicken Salad with Rice Vinegar Dressing

PREP TIME: 30 MINUTES ✦ YIELD: 4 (1½-CUP) SERVINGS

DRESSING
- 3 tablespoons sugar
- 1 teaspoon ginger
- ⅛ teaspoon crushed red pepper flakes
- ½ cup rice vinegar
- 4 teaspoons soy sauce

SALAD
- 3 boneless skinless chicken breast halves
- ½ small head Chinese (napa) cabbage, shredded (4 cups)
- 1 medium carrot, shredded
- 2 tablespoons sliced green onions
- ¼ cup chow mein noodles, if desired

1. In small bowl, combine all dressing ingredients; blend well. Place chicken breast halves in medium nonstick skillet. Drizzle 3 tablespoons dressing over chicken. Let stand at room temperature for 10 minutes.
2. Add 3 tablespoons water. Bring to a boil. Reduce heat; cover and simmer 10 minutes or until chicken is no longer pink. Drain; cool slightly. Shred or chop chicken.
3. In large bowl, combine chicken, cabbage, carrot and onions. Add remaining dressing; toss to coat. Top with chow mein noodles.

NUTRITION INFORMATION PER SERVING: Serving Size: 1½ Cups ✦ Calories: 180 ✦ Calories from Fat: 25 ✦ % DAILY VALUE: Total Fat: 3 g 5% ✦ Saturated Fat: 1 g 5% ✦ Cholesterol: 55 mg 18% ✦ Sodium: 460 mg 19% ✦ Total Carbohydrate: 17 g 6% ✦ Dietary Fiber: 2 g 8% ✦ Sugars: 11 g ✦ Protein: 22 g ✦ Vitamin A: 140% ✦ Vitamin C: 60% ✦ Calcium: 10% ✦ Iron: 10% ✦ DIETARY EXCHANGES: ½ Fruit, 2 Vegetable, 2½ Very Lean Meat OR ½ Carbohydrate, 2 Vegetable, 2½ Very Lean Meat

Pesto, Turkey and Pasta Salad

PREP TIME: 30 MINUTES ✦ YIELD: 6 (1½-CUP) SERVINGS

- 8 oz. (3 cups) uncooked bow tie pasta (farfalle)
- 2 cups diced cooked turkey
- ½ cup sliced marinated sun-dried tomatoes
- 1 (2¼-oz.) can sliced ripe olives, drained
- ½ cup mayonnaise
- ½ cup purchased pesto
- 4 leaves leaf lettuce
- 1 oz. (¼ cup) shredded fresh Parmesan cheese

1. Cook pasta to desired doneness as directed on package. Drain; rinse with cold water to cool.
2. In large bowl, combine cooked pasta, turkey, tomatoes and olives.
3. In small bowl, combine mayonnaise and pesto; blend well. Add to turkey mixture; toss to coat.
4. Line 4 individual plates with lettuce. Spoon turkey mixture over lettuce. Sprinkle with cheese.

NUTRITION INFORMATION PER SERVING: Serving Size: 1½ Cups ✦ Calories: 510 ✦ Calories from Fat: 280 ✦ % DAILY VALUE: Total Fat: 31 g 48% ✦ Saturated Fat: 6 g 30% ✦ Cholesterol: 55 mg 18% ✦ Sodium: 480 mg 20% ✦ Total Carbohydrate: 34 g 11% ✦ Dietary Fiber: 2 g 8% ✦ Sugars: 4 g ✦ Protein: 23 g ✦ Vitamin A: 10% ✦ Vitamin C: 20% ✦ Calcium: 15% ✦ Iron: 20% ✦ DIETARY EXCHANGES: 2½ Starch, 2 Lean Meat, 4½ Fat OR 2½ Carbohydrate, 2 Lean Meat, 4½ Fat

Cashew-Curry-Chicken Salad

PREP TIME: 20 MINUTES ✦ YIELD: 8 (1⅓-CUP) SERVINGS

SALAD
- 12 oz. (4½ cups) uncooked rotini (spiral pasta)
- 2 cups cubed cooked chicken
- 1½ cups halved red seedless grapes
- ½ cup chopped red bell pepper
- ¼ cup chopped green onions
- 2 oranges, peeled, chopped
- 1 cup cashew halves

DRESSING
- ½ cup mayonnaise or salad dressing
- ¼ cup sour cream
- 3 tablespoons orange juice
- 2 tablespoons honey
- 1 teaspoon curry powder
- ¼ teaspoon salt

1. Cook rotini to desired doneness as directed on package. Drain; rinse with cold water to cool.
2. In large bowl, combine cooked rotini and all remaining salad ingredients.
3. In small bowl, combine all dressing ingredients; blend well. Add to salad; toss to coat. Serve immediately, or cover and refrigerate until serving time.

NUTRITION INFORMATION PER SERVING: Serving Size: 1⅓ Cups ✦ Calories: 500 ✦ Calories from Fat: 220 ✦ % DAILY VALUE: Total Fat: 24 g 37% ✦ Saturated Fat: 5 g 25% ✦ Cholesterol: 45 mg 15% ✦ Sodium: 290 mg 12% ✦ Total Carbohydrate: 53 g 18% ✦ Dietary Fiber: 3 g 12% ✦ Sugars: 17 g ✦ Protein: 19 g ✦ Vitamin A: 10% ✦ Vitamin C: 60% ✦ Calcium: 6% ✦ Iron: 20% ✦ DIETARY EXCHANGES: 2½ Starch, 1 Fruit, 1½ Lean Meat, 3½ Fat OR 3½ Carbohydrate, 1½ Lean Meat, 3½ Fat

Party Caesar Salad

Party Caesar Salad

PREP TIME: 25 MINUTES ✦ YIELD: 12 (1-CUP) SERVINGS

DRESSING
- ½ cup refrigerated or frozen fat-free egg product, thawed
- ¼ cup olive oil
- 2 tablespoons lemon juice
- 1 teaspoon Dijon mustard
- 1 teaspoon anchovy paste
- 2 garlic cloves, minced

SALAD
- 1 large head romaine lettuce, torn into bite-sized pieces (10 cups)
- 4 oz. (1 cup) grated fresh Parmesan cheese
- 1½ cups croutons

1. In jar with tight-fitting lid, combine all dressing ingredients; shake well. (Dressing can be refrigerated for up to 3 days.)
2. In large bowl, combine all salad ingredients; toss gently. Pour dressing over salad; toss to coat.

NUTRITION INFORMATION PER SERVING: Serving Size: 1 Cup ✦ Calories: 110 ✦ Calories from Fat: 60 ✦ % DAILY VALUE: Total Fat: 7 g 11% ✦ Saturated Fat: 2 g 10% ✦ Cholesterol: 5 mg 2% ✦ Sodium: 230 mg 10% ✦ Total Carbohydrate: 5 g 2% ✦ Dietary Fiber: 1 g 4% ✦ Sugars: 1 g ✦ Protein: 6 g ✦ Vitamin A: 25% ✦ Vitamin C: 20% ✦ Calcium: 15% ✦ Iron: 6% ✦ DIETARY EXCHANGES: 1 Vegetable, ½ Lean Meat, 1 Fat

Seven-Layer Vegetable Salad

PREP TIME: 20 MINUTES (READY IN 4 HOURS 20 MINUTES) ✦ YIELD: 12 SERVINGS

- ½ lb. sliced bacon
- 3 cups torn iceberg lettuce
- 3 cups torn romaine lettuce
- 1 cup mayonnaise or salad dressing
- 4 teaspoons sugar
- 1 (1-lb.) pkg. frozen sweet peas, cooked, drained
- ½ cup sliced green onions
- ½ cup sliced celery
- 6 oz. (1½ cups) shredded Cheddar cheese

1. Cook bacon until crisp. Drain; set aside.
2. In 13×9-inch (3-quart) baking dish, toss iceberg and romaine lettuce. Spread with ½ cup of the mayonnaise; sprinkle with 2 teaspoons of the sugar.
3. Layer with peas, onions and celery. Spread with remaining ½ cup mayonnaise; sprinkle with remaining 2 teaspoons sugar. Sprinkle with cheese. Cover; refrigerate at least 4 hours or overnight.
4. Just before serving, crumble bacon; sprinkle over top.

NUTRITION INFORMATION PER SERVING: Serving Size: 1/12 of Recipe ✦ Calories: 260 ✦ Calories from Fat: 200 ✦ % DAILY VALUE: Total Fat: 22 g 34% ✦ Saturated Fat: 6 g 30% ✦ Cholesterol: 30 mg 10% ✦ Sodium: 330 mg 14% ✦ Total Carbohydrate: 8 g 3% ✦ Dietary Fiber: 2 g 8% ✦ Sugars: 5 g ✦ Protein: 8 g ✦ Vitamin A: 20% ✦ Vitamin C: 20% ✦ Calcium: 15% ✦ Iron: 6% ✦ DIETARY EXCHANGES: 1 Vegetable, 1 High-Fat Meat, 3 Fat

Wilted Spinach Salad

PREP TIME: 25 MINUTES ✦ YIELD: 6 SERVINGS

- 2 eggs
- 6 cups torn fresh spinach
- 2 tablespoons chopped green onions
- 3 slices bacon, cut into ½-inch pieces
- ¼ cup cider vinegar
- 2 teaspoons sugar
- ¼ teaspoon salt
- ¼ teaspoon dry mustard
- ⅛ teaspoon pepper

1. Place eggs in small saucepan; cover with cold water. Bring to a boil. Reduce heat; simmer about 15 minutes. Immediately drain; run cold water over eggs to stop cooking. Peel eggs; chop.
2. In large bowl, combine spinach, onions and eggs. Set aside.
3. In small skillet, cook bacon until crisp. Add all remaining ingredients; heat until sugar is dissolved. Pour over spinach mixture; toss gently. Serve immediately.

VARIATION

Wilted Leaf Lettuce Salad: Substitute 6 cups torn leaf lettuce for spinach.

Sesame Chicken and Wild Rice Salad

Smoked Turkey Waldorf Salad

PREP TIME: 10 MINUTES ◆ YIELD: 4 SERVINGS

2 medium red apples, chopped
½ cup chopped celery
½ lb. smoked turkey, cubed (1½ cups)
⅓ cup light mayonnaise or salad dressing
4 cups torn Bibb or Boston lettuce
¼ cup chopped walnuts, toasted if desired*

1. In medium bowl, combine apples, celery, turkey and mayonnaise; mix well.
2. Arrange lettuce on individual plates. Spoon apple mixture onto lettuce. Sprinkle with walnuts.

> **TIP:** *To toast walnuts, spread on cookie sheet; bake at 350°F. for 5 to 7 minutes or until golden brown, stirring occasionally. Or spread in thin layer in microwave-safe pie pan. Microwave on HIGH for 4 to 7 minutes or until golden brown, stirring frequently.

Smoked Turkey Waldorf Salad

Sesame Chicken and Wild Rice Salad

PREP TIME: 20 MINUTES (READY IN 2 HOURS 10 MINUTES) ◆ YIELD: 4 (1½-CUP) SERVINGS

SALAD
1 cup uncooked wild rice
2½ cups water
2 cups cubed cooked chicken
1 cup fresh snow pea pods, halved crosswise
1 (11-oz.) can mandarin orange segments, drained

DRESSING
¼ cup oil
3 tablespoons soy sauce
3 tablespoons cider vinegar
2 tablespoons sesame seed, toasted*
1½ teaspoons ginger
¼ teaspoon pepper

1. Cook wild rice in water as directed on package.
2. Meanwhile, in large bowl, combine chicken, pea pods and orange segments; mix well. Refrigerate.
3. In small jar with tight-fitting lid, combine all dressing ingredients; shake well. Refrigerate.
4. Add cooked rice to salad; toss gently. Pour dressing over salad; toss to coat. Cover; refrigerate at least 1 hour or until serving time to blend flavors.

> **TIP:** *To toast sesame seed, place in small nonstick skillet; stir over medium-high heat for 1 to 2 minutes or until light golden brown.

Niçoise Salad

PREP TIME: 35 MINUTES (READY IN 2 HOURS
35 MINUTES) ◆ YIELD: 8 SERVINGS

DRESSING
  2 tablespoons chopped green onions
  2 tablespoons chopped fresh parsley
  ½ teaspoon dried dill weed
  ¼ teaspoon garlic salt
  1 (0.7-oz.) pkg. Italian salad dressing mix
  ¾ cup oil
  ¼ cup red wine vinegar

SALAD
  4 medium potatoes, cooked, peeled and sliced
  1 lb. (3 cups) cut fresh green beans, cooked,
      drained
  3 eggs
    Lettuce leaves
  2 (9-oz.) cans water-packed tuna, drained,
      flaked*
  2 tomatoes, peeled, each cut into 8 wedges
  ½ cup pitted ripe olives, quartered

1. In jar with tight-fitting lid, combine all dressing ingredients; shake well.
2. In medium bowl, pour ¼ cup of the dressing over cooked potatoes; toss to coat. Cover; refrigerate at least 2 hours. In another bowl, pour ¼ cup of the dressing over cooked green beans; toss to coat. Cover; refrigerate 1 to 2 hours.
3. Place eggs in small saucepan; cover with cold water. Bring to a boil. Reduce heat; simmer about 15 minutes. Immediately drain; run cold water over eggs to stop cooking. Peel eggs; cut into quarters.
4. To serve, line large serving platter with lettuce leaves. Spoon potatoes onto center of plate. Arrange tuna over potatoes. Spoon green beans around potatoes. Alternately place egg quarters and tomato wedges over beans. Garnish with olives. Pour remaining dressing over salad.

> **TIP:** * One 14¾-oz. can pink salmon, drained, skin and bones removed, flaked, can be substituted for tuna.

NUTRITION INFORMATION PER SERVING: Serving Size: ⅛ of Recipe ◆ Calories: 380 ◆ Calories from Fat: 220 ◆ **% DAILY VALUE:** Total Fat: 24 g 37% ◆ Saturated Fat: 3 g 15% ◆ Cholesterol: 95 mg 32% ◆ Sodium: 650 mg 27% ◆ Total Carbohydrate: 23 g 8% ◆ Dietary Fiber: 4 g 16% ◆ Sugars: 4 g ◆ Protein: 18 g ◆ Vitamin A: 15% ◆ Vitamin C: 40% ◆ Calcium: 6% ◆ Iron: 15% ◆ **DIETARY EXCHANGES:** 1 Starch, 1 Vegetable, 2½ Lean Meat, 3 Fat OR 1 Carbohydrate, 1 Vegetable, 2½ Lean Meat, 3 Fat

Chef's Salad

PREP TIME: 30 MINUTES ◆ YIELD: 6 (1½-CUP) SERVINGS

  3 eggs
  1 garlic clove, halved
  3 cups torn iceberg lettuce
  ½ cup sliced cucumber
  ½ cup chopped celery
  ¼ cup sliced green onions
  1 carrot, shredded
  3 radishes, sliced
  1 cup julienne-cut cooked chicken or turkey
  1 cup julienne-cut cooked ham
  4 oz. (1 cup) julienne-cut Swiss or
      Cheddar cheese
  2 tomatoes, cut into wedges
  ½ cup croutons
  ½ to 1 cup favorite salad dressing

1. Place eggs in medium saucepan; cover with cold water. Bring to a boil. Reduce heat; simmer about 15 minutes. Immediately drain; run cold water over eggs to stop cooking. Peel eggs; slice.
2. Meanwhile, rub large salad bowl with cut garlic clove; discard garlic. Add lettuce, cucumber, celery, onions, carrot and radishes to salad bowl; toss to combine.
3. Arrange chicken, ham and cheese over lettuce. Top with eggs, tomatoes and croutons. Serve with dressing.

NUTRITION INFORMATION PER SERVING: Serving Size: 1½ Cups ◆ Calories: 420 ◆ Calories from Fat: 270 ◆ **% DAILY VALUE:** Total Fat: 30 g 46% ◆ Saturated Fat: 9 g 45% ◆ Cholesterol: 155 mg 52% ◆ Sodium: 1020 mg 43% ◆ Total Carbohydrate: 16 g 5% ◆ Dietary Fiber: 2 g 8% ◆ Sugars: 9 g ◆ Protein: 21 g ◆ Vitamin A: 90% ◆ Vitamin C: 0% ◆ Calcium: 25% ◆ Iron: 10% ◆ **DIETARY EXCHANGES:** ½ Fruit, 1 Vegetable, 2½ Medium-Fat Meat, 3½ Fat OR ½ Carbohydrate, 1 Vegetable, 2½ Medium-Fat Meat, 3½ Fat

SALAD DRESSING COMPARISON

DRESSING	CALORIES PER TABLESPOON	FAT (G) PER TABLESPOON
OLIVE OIL	120	14
VINAIGRETTE (*3 parts olive oil to 1 part vinegar*)	90	10
REGULAR MAYONNAISE	100	11
REDUCED-FAT MAYONNAISE	50	5
NONFAT MAYONNAISE	10	0
SOUR CREAM	30	2.5
REDUCED-FAT SOUR CREAM	22.5	1.75
NONFAT SOUR CREAM	17.5	0
REGULAR PLAIN YOGURT	10.5	.6
LOW-FAT PLAIN YOGURT	8	.25
NONFAT PLAIN YOGURT	7	0

Pasta Seafood Salad

PREP TIME: 25 MINUTES ◆ YIELD: 6 (1⅓-CUP) SERVINGS

8 oz. (3 cups) uncooked small shell pasta
½ cup frozen sweet peas
1 cup mayonnaise
¼ cup milk
2 tablespoons chopped fresh dill
    or 2 teaspoons dried dill weed
4 teaspoons lemon juice
½ teaspoon Worcestershire sauce
3 (8-oz.) pkg. imitation crabmeat (surimi),
    chopped (4 cups)
1 (8-oz.) can sliced water chestnuts, drained
1 red bell pepper, chopped
½ cup sliced green onions

1. Cook pasta to desired doneness as directed on package, adding peas during last 2 minutes of cooking time. Drain; rinse with cold water to cool.
2. Meanwhile, in large bowl, combine mayonnaise, milk, dill, lemon juice and Worcestershire sauce; mix well.
3. Add cooked macaroni and peas and all remaining ingredients to mayonnaise mixture; mix well. Serve immediately, or cover and refrigerate until serving time.

NUTRITION INFORMATION PER SERVING: Serving Size: 1⅓ Cups ◆ Calories: 570 ◆ Calories from Fat: 290 ◆ **% DAILY VALUE:** Total Fat: 32 g 49% ◆ Saturated Fat: 5 g 25% ◆ Cholesterol: 45 mg 15% ◆ Sodium: 1190 mg 50% ◆ Total Carbohydrate: 50 g 17% ◆ Dietary Fiber: 3 g 12% ◆ Sugars: 13 g ◆ Protein: 20 g ◆ Vitamin A: 20% ◆ Vitamin C: 35% ◆ Calcium: 6% ◆ Iron: 15% ◆ **DIETARY EXCHANGES:** 3 Starch, 1 Vegetable, 1½ Very Lean Meat, 6 Fat OR 3 Carbohydrate, 1 Vegetable, 1½ Very Lean Meat, 6 Fat

COOK'S NOTE

PREPARING DRESSINGS

Salad dressings range from creamy-tasting low-fat mixtures made with nonfat yogurt or nonfat mayonnaise to rich and delicious dressings made with regular mayonnaise, blue cheese, avocado or sour cream.

Many dressings can be made ahead and refrigerated. Refrigeration is important if the dressing contains dairy ingredients or chunks of garlic. Salads made of sturdy ingredients such as carrots may be marinated in vinaigrette; lettuce and other greens, however, should not be tossed with the dressing until served or the leaves will go limp. If dressings made with olive oil thicken and take on a cloudy appearance in the refrigerator, set them out at room temperature for a while before dressing the salad. The oil will clarify and become thin again.

Salmon-Broccoli Salad in Shells

PREP TIME: 35 MINUTES ◆ YIELD: 4 SERVINGS

  1 (9-oz.) pkg. frozen cut broccoli in a pouch
12 uncooked jumbo pasta shells
  1 (6-oz.) can salmon, drained, flaked
  1 cup cherry tomatoes, quartered
¼ cup sliced green onions
¼ cup purchased ranch salad dressing
¼ cup light mayonnaise
  1 tablespoon chopped fresh parsley
  4 lettuce leaves

1. Cook broccoli pouch as directed on package. Drain; cool.
2. Cook pasta shells to desired doneness as directed on package. Drain; return to saucepan. Cover with cold water to cool.
3. In medium bowl, combine cooked broccoli, salmon, tomatoes and green onions. Add salad dressing, mayonnaise and parsley; stir gently to coat.
4. Line 4 individual plates with lettuce. Drain water from cooked pasta shells. Spoon about ¼ cup salmon mixture into each shell. Arrange stuffed shells over lettuce.

NUTRITION INFORMATION PER SERVING: Serving Size: ¼ of Recipe ◆ Calories: 340 ◆ Calories from Fat: 160 ◆ **% DAILY VALUE:** Total Fat: 18 g 28% ◆ Saturated Fat: 3 g 15% ◆ Cholesterol: 25 mg 8% ◆ Sodium: 570 mg 24% ◆ Total Carbohydrate: 31 g 10% ◆ Dietary Fiber: 3 g 12% ◆ Sugars: 4 g ◆ Protein: 14 g ◆ Vitamin A: 15% ◆ Vitamin C: 45% ◆ Calcium: 6% ◆ Iron: 25% ◆ **DIETARY EXCHANGES:** 2 Starch, 1 Lean Meat, 3 Fat OR 2 Carbohydrate, 1 Lean Meat, 3 Fat

Salmon-Broccoli Salad in Shells

Seafood Salad with Crab Louis Dressing

Seafood Salad with Crab Louis Dressing

PREP TIME: 30 MINUTES ◆ YIELD: 7 SERVINGS

DRESSING
¾ cup chili sauce
¼ cup light mayonnaise
¼ cup low-fat plain yogurt

SALAD
  1 (7-oz.) pkg. (2 cups) small shell macaroni
  1 (10-oz.) pkg. frozen cooked shrimp, thawed, drained
  1 (8-oz.) pkg. imitation crabmeat (surimi), cut into ½-inch pieces
½ cup sliced celery
½ cup chopped green bell pepper
    Lettuce leaves, if desired
  6 to 8 ripe olives, quartered
  3 medium tomatoes, cut into wedges
  2 tablespoons chopped fresh parsley, if desired

1. In small bowl, combine all dressing ingredients; blend well. Set aside.
2. Cook macaroni to desired doneness as directed on package. Drain; rinse with cold water to cool.
3. In large bowl, combine cooked macaroni, shrimp, imitation crabmeat, celery and bell pepper; toss gently to mix.
4. Line 7 individual salad bowls with lettuce leaves. Place about ⅔ cup crabmeat mixture in each bowl. Garnish with olives, tomatoes and parsley. Serve with dressing.

NUTRITION INFORMATION PER SERVING: Serving Size: ⅐ of Recipe ◆ Calories: 270 ◆ Calories from Fat: 45 ◆ **% DAILY VALUE:** Total Fat: 5 g 8% ◆ Saturated Fat: 1 g 5% ◆ Cholesterol: 90 mg 30% ◆ Sodium: 880 mg 37% ◆ Total Carbohydrate: 37 g 12% ◆ Dietary Fiber: 2 g 8% ◆ Sugars: 10 g ◆ Protein: 18 g ◆ Vitamin A: 20% ◆ Vitamin C: 40% ◆ Calcium: 6% ◆ Iron: 20% ◆ **DIETARY EXCHANGES:** 2 Starch, 1 Vegetable, 1½ Very Lean Meat, ½ Fat OR 2 Carbohydrate, 1 Vegetable, 1½ Very Lean Meat, ½ Fat

Cobb Salad

PREP TIME: 45 MINUTES ✦ YIELD: 6 SERVINGS

　　2　eggs
　　6　slices bacon
　　4　cups torn salad greens
　1½　cups cubed cooked chicken
　　1　large tomato, chopped
　　¼　cup sliced green onions
　　1　avocado, peeled, sliced or cubed, tossed in
　　　　lemon juice
　　4　oz. (1 cup) crumbled blue cheese
　　½　to 1 cup purchased Thousand Island salad
　　　　dressing

1. Place eggs in small saucepan; cover with cold water. Bring to a boil. Reduce heat; simmer about 15 minutes. Immediately drain; run cold water over eggs to stop cooking. Peel eggs; coarsely chop.
2. Meanwhile, in large skillet, cook bacon until crisp. Remove bacon from skillet; drain on paper towels. Crumble bacon.
3. Arrange salad greens on large serving platter or in 13×9-inch (3-quart) baking dish. Arrange eggs, bacon and all remaining ingredients except dressing in rows. Or, arrange each serving on lettuce-lined plate. Serve with dressing or spoon dressing over each salad.

NUTRITION INFORMATION PER SERVING: Serving Size: ⅙ of Recipe ◆ Calories: 430 ◆ Calories from Fat: 300 ◆ **% DAILY VALUE:** Total Fat: 33 g 51% ◆ Saturated Fat: 9 g 45% ◆ Cholesterol: 130 mg 43% ◆ Sodium: 720 mg 30% ◆ Total Carbohydrate: 12 g 4% ◆ Dietary Fiber: 3 g 12% ◆ Sugars: 8 g ◆ Protein: 20 g ◆ Vitamin A: 20% ◆ Vitamin C: 0% ◆ Calcium: 15% ◆ Iron: 10% ◆ **DIETARY EXCHANGES:** ½ Fruit, 1 Vegetable, 2½ Medium-Fat Meat, 4 Fat OR ½ Carbohydrate, 1 Vegetable, 2½ Medium-Fat Meat, 4 Fat

Cobb Salad

Tangy French Dressing

PREP TIME: 10 MINUTES ✦ YIELD: 2¼ CUPS

　　½　cup firmly packed brown sugar
　　½　cup vinegar
　　½　cup ketchup
　　½　cup chili sauce
　　½　cup oil
　　½　teaspoon salt
　　¼　teaspoon Worcestershire sauce
　　1　garlic clove, minced
　　　　Dash hot pepper sauce

In blender container or jar with tight-fitting lid, combine all ingredients; blend at medium speed or shake until well mixed. Store in tightly covered container in refrigerator.

NUTRITION INFORMATION PER SERVING: Serving Size: 1 Tablespoon ◆ Calories: 45 ◆ Calories from Fat: 25 ◆ **% DAILY VALUE:** Total Fat: 3 g 5% ◆ Saturated Fat: 0 g 0% ◆ Cholesterol: 0 mg 0% ◆ Sodium: 120 mg 5% ◆ Total Carbohydrate: 5 g 2% ◆ Dietary Fiber: 0 g 0% ◆ Sugars: 4 g ◆ Protein: 0 g ◆ Vitamin A: 0% ◆ Vitamin C: 0% ◆ Calcium: 0% ◆ Iron: 0% ◆ **DIETARY EXCHANGES:** ½ Starch, ½ Fat OR ½ Carbohydrate, ½ Fat

Green Goddess Salad Dressing

PREP TIME: 15 MINUTES ✦ YIELD: 2 CUPS

　　¼　cup finely chopped fresh parsley
　　3　tablespoons chopped green onions
　　1　garlic clove, minced
　　½　teaspoon salt
　　⅛　teaspoon freshly ground black pepper
　　1　(2-oz.) can anchovy fillets, drained, chopped
　　1　cup mayonnaise
　　½　cup sour cream
　　2　tablespoons tarragon vinegar
　　1　tablespoon lemon juice
　　2　drops green food color

In small bowl, combine all ingredients; mix well. Store in tightly covered container in refrigerator.

NUTRITION INFORMATION PER SERVING: Serving Size: 1 Tablespoon ◆ Calories: 70 ◆ Calories from Fat: 60 ◆ **% DAILY VALUE:** Total Fat: 7 g 11% ◆ Saturated Fat: 2 g 10% ◆ Cholesterol: 10 mg 3% ◆ Sodium: 140 mg 6% ◆ Total Carbohydrate: 1 g 1% ◆ Dietary Fiber: 0 g 0% ◆ Sugars: 0 g ◆ Protein: 1 g ◆ Vitamin A: 0% ◆ Vitamin C: 0% ◆ Calcium: 0% ◆ Iron: 0% ◆ **DIETARY EXCHANGES:** 1½ Fat

Russian Dressing

PREP TIME: 10 MINUTES ◆ YIELD: 1¾ CUPS

    1 cup oil
    ⅓ cup chili sauce
    ¼ cup sugar
    ¼ cup vinegar
    2 tablespoons minced onion
    ½ teaspoon salt
    ½ teaspoon Worcestershire sauce
    1 garlic clove, minced

In blender container or jar with tight-fitting lid, combine all ingredients; blend at medium speed or shake until well mixed. Store in tightly covered container in refrigerator.

NUTRITION INFORMATION PER SERVING: Serving Size: 1 Tablespoon ◆ Calories: 80 ◆ Calories from Fat: 70 ◆ **% DAILY VALUE:** Total Fat: 8 g 12% ◆ Saturated Fat: 1 g 5% ◆ Cholesterol: 0 mg 0% ◆ Sodium: 85 mg 4% ◆ Total Carbohydrate: 3 g 1% ◆ Dietary Fiber: 0 g 0% ◆ Sugars: 2 g ◆ Protein: 0 g ◆ Vitamin A: 0% ◆ Vitamin C: 0% ◆ Calcium: 0% ◆ Iron: 0% ◆ **DIETARY EXCHANGES:** 2 Fat

Cooked Salad Dressing

PREP TIME: 15 MINUTES ◆ YIELD: 1 CUP

    2 tablespoons all-purpose flour
    2 tablespoons sugar
    1 teaspoon salt
    1 teaspoon dry or prepared mustard
    ¾ cup milk
    1 egg, slightly beaten
    3 tablespoons vinegar
    1 tablespoon margarine or butter

1. In small saucepan, combine flour, sugar, salt and mustard; mix well. Stir in milk and egg; mix until smooth. Cook over medium heat until mixture boils and thickens, stirring constantly.

2. Add vinegar and margarine; stir until well blended. Cool 1 hour or until completely cooled. Store in tightly covered container in refrigerator.

> **TIP:** For potato salad, warm dressing penetrates potatoes quicker.

NUTRITION INFORMATION PER SERVING: Serving Size: 1 Tablespoon ◆ Calories: 25 ◆ Calories from Fat: 10 ◆ **% DAILY VALUE:** Total Fat: 1 g 2% ◆ Saturated Fat: 0 g 0% ◆ Cholesterol: 15 mg 5% ◆ Sodium: 150 mg 6% ◆ Total Carbohydrate: 3 g 1% ◆ Dietary Fiber: 0 g 0% ◆ Sugars: 2 g ◆ Protein: 1 g ◆ Vitamin A: 0% ◆ Vitamin C: 0% ◆ Calcium: 0% ◆ Iron: 0% ◆ **DIETARY EXCHANGES:** ½ Fat

VARIATIONS

Cooked Fruit Dressing: Cool cooked dressing. Before adding to fruit, fold in 1 cup thawed whipped topping or ½ cup whipping cream, whipped and sweetened.

Sour Cream Cooked Dressing: Cool cooked dressing. Fold in ½ cup sour cream. Serve on meat, seafood or potato or other vegetable salads.

Thousand Island Dressing

PREP TIME: 25 MINUTES (READY IN 4 HOURS 25 MINUTES) ◆ YIELD: 1⅓ CUPS

    1 egg
    1 cup mayonnaise
    ¼ teaspoon paprika
    2 tablespoons sweet pickle relish
    1 teaspoon finely chopped onion
    2 tablespoons chili sauce
    ½ teaspoon Worcestershire sauce
      Dash hot pepper sauce

1. Place egg in small saucepan; cover with cold water. Bring to a boil. Reduce heat; simmer about 15 minutes. Immediately drain; run cold water over egg to stop cooking. Peel egg; chop.

2. In small bowl, combine egg and all remaining ingredients; mix until well combined. Cover; refrigerate at least 4 hours to blend flavors. Store in tightly covered container in refrigerator.

NUTRITION INFORMATION PER SERVING: Serving Size: 1 Tablespoon ◆ Calories: 90 ◆ Calories from Fat: 80 ◆ **% DAILY VALUE:** Total Fat: 9 g 14% ◆ Saturated Fat: 1 g 5% ◆ Cholesterol: 15 mg 5% ◆ Sodium: 95 mg 4% ◆ Total Carbohydrate: 1 g 1% ◆ Dietary Fiber: 0 g 0% ◆ Sugars: 1 g ◆ Protein: 0 g ◆ Vitamin A: 0% ◆ Vitamin C: 0% ◆ Calcium: 0% ◆ Iron: 0% ◆ **DIETARY EXCHANGES:** 2 Fat

Creamy Blue Cheese Dressing

PREP TIME: 10 MINUTES ◆ YIELD: 2⅓ CUPS

    4 oz. (1 cup) crumbled blue cheese
    ¾ cup oil
    1 cup sour cream
    1 teaspoon salt
    ½ teaspoon sugar
    ⅛ teaspoon pepper
    1 garlic clove, minced
    ¼ cup tarragon vinegar
    ½ teaspoon Worcestershire sauce

1. In small bowl, beat blue cheese at low speed. Gradually add ¼ cup of the oil, beating until smooth.

2. Gradually add remaining oil, beating continuously. Add all remaining ingredients; beat until well blended. Store in tightly covered container in refrigerator.

NUTRITION INFORMATION PER SERVING: Serving Size: 1 Tablespoon • Calories: 70 • Calories from Fat: 60 • % DAILY VALUE: Total Fat: 7 g 11% • Saturated Fat: 2 g 10% • Cholesterol: 5 mg 2% • Sodium: 105 mg 4% • Total Carbohydrate: 1 g 1% • Dietary Fiber: 0 g 0% • Sugars: 0 g • Protein: 1 g • Vitamin A: 0% • Vitamin C: 0% • Calcium: 2% • Iron: 0% • DIETARY EXCHANGES: 1½ Fat

COOK'S NOTE

OIL AND VINEGAR SALAD DRESSING

The classic ratio is three parts oil to one part vinegar, with seasoning to taste, but you can adjust the proportions to suit your taste. Add more vinegar if you like a tangier dressing or want to reduce the fat content.

Oil and vinegar have a natural tendency to separate. Mix them in a blender or shake them well in a tightly closed jar to blend them. To mix oil and vinegar by hand, begin whisking the vinegar and pour in the oil a drop or two at a time, then in a slow steady stream, all the while whisking vigorously. If a dressing separates after it has stood for a while, simply rewhisk (or shake) the mixture before tossing with the salad.

Vinegar and Oil Dressing

PREP TIME: 5 MINUTES ✦ YIELD: 1 CUP

½ cup oil
½ cup vinegar
½ teaspoon salt
½ teaspoon Worcestershire sauce
  Dash pepper

In blender container or jar with tight-fitting lid, combine all ingredients; blend at medium speed or shake until well mixed. Store in tightly covered container in refrigerator.

NUTRITION INFORMATION PER SERVING: Serving Size: 1 Tablespoon • Calories: 60 • Calories from Fat: 60 • % DAILY VALUE: Total Fat: 7 g 11% • Saturated Fat: 1 g 5% • Cholesterol: 0 mg 0% • Sodium: 70 mg 3% • Total Carbohydrate: 0 g 0% • Dietary Fiber: 0 g 0% • Sugars: 0 g • Protein: 0 g • Vitamin A: 0% • Vitamin C: 0% • Calcium: 0% • Iron: 0% • DIETARY EXCHANGES: 1½ Fat

Homemade Mayonnaise

PREP TIME: 10 MINUTES ✦ YIELD: 1¾ CUPS

1¼ cups oil
2 tablespoons lemon juice
1 tablespoon Dijon mustard
½ teaspoon salt
1 pasteurized egg*

1. In blender container, combine ¼ cup of the oil, lemon juice, mustard, salt and egg; blend until smooth.

2. With blender running at medium-high speed, slowly add remaining 1 cup oil in thin stream, scraping down sides of container as needed. Store in tightly covered container in refrigerator.

TIP: * Pasteurized eggs are uncooked eggs that have been heat-treated to kill bacteria that can cause food poisoning and gastrointestinal distress. Because the egg in this recipe is not cooked, be sure to use a pasteurized egg. They can be found in the dairy case at large supermarkets.

NUTRITION INFORMATION PER SERVING: Serving Size: 1 Tablespoon • Calories: 90 • Calories from Fat: 90 • % DAILY VALUE: Total Fat: 10 g 15% • Saturated Fat: 1 g 5% • Cholesterol: 10 mg 3% • Sodium: 55 mg 2% • Total Carbohydrate: 0 g 0% • Dietary Fiber: 0 g 0% • Sugars: 0 g • Protein: 0 g • Vitamin A: 0% • Vitamin C: 0% • Calcium: 0% • Iron: 0% • DIETARY EXCHANGES: 2 Fat

VARIATIONS

Curried Mayonnaise: Add ½ to 1 teaspoon curry powder to egg mixture.

Garlic Mayonnaise: Stir 1 garlic clove, minced, into prepared mayonnaise.

Herbed Mayonnaise: Stir 1 tablespoon chopped fresh herbs, such as parsley, basil, chervil or chives, into prepared mayonnaise. If using dried herbs, add 1 teaspoon.

TYPES OF GREENS

TYPE	DESCRIPTION
Arugula, also known as roquette or rocket	Slender, toothed leaves with a peppery bite. Especially good as an accent with milder greens.
Belgian or French endive	Smooth, elongated, compact heads of slender, crisp leaves that shade from white to very pale green. Slightly bitter flavor. Shred and serve alone or with other greens; use the leaves whole with dips.
Bibb lettuce	Small heads of tender, buttery-feeling leaves with a slightly sweet, mild flavor.
Boston lettuce	Loose heads of tender, buttery-feeling leaves with flavor similar to Bibb lettuce.
Chinese cabbage, also called celery cabbage or napa cabbage	Elongated heads that may be slender or fat; wide-ribbed, tender leaves and crisp stalks are both equally good raw or cooked. Slightly spicy flavor. Mix with American- or Asian-style salads.
Chicory, also called curly endive	Fringed, curly leaves with a sharp, bitter taste. Darker green, tougher outside leaves have a stronger flavor than the lighter inner leaves. Good cooked or as an accent with milder greens; choose a sweet dressing for contrast or an assertive one for power balance.
Escarole	Wide, crisp flat leaves with slightly curled edges. Slightly bitter flavor. As with chicory, the tender, pale inner leaves are milder in taste. Use in salads, especially with other greens.
Green cabbage	Heavy, tightly packed heads that shade from medium green on the outside to white on the inside. Shred for slaws or stir-fries, or use the leaves whole as wrappers for spicy meat or rice fillings for stuffed cabbage.
Iceberg lettuce	Large, round tightly packed heads of light green, crisp leaves. Though wilt-resistant, the flavor is rather neutral.
Leaf lettuce	Leaves—which may be ruffled or curly, green or red-tipped—are joined at the base but sprout out loosely rather than forming a compact head. Generally mild in flavor and very tender.
Mâche, also called lamb's lettuce	Dark green leaves shaped like lambs' tongues, with mild, sweet flavor and soft texture.
Radicchio	Small, compact heads of variegated red and white leaves with slightly bitter flavor. Generally more expensive than other greens, but a small amount is enough for color contrast and flavor accent.
Red cabbage	Similar in shape and flavor to green cabbage. Adding a small amount of vinegar when cooking red cabbage helps preserve the color.
Romaine lettuce	Firm, crisp leaves with a mild, sweet flavor. Inner yellow leaves are more tender and sweeter than dark-green exterior leaves. Keeps well.
Savoy cabbage	Like green cabbage, with deeper green color and crinkled leaves that are more delicate than regular cabbage. Can be used interchangeably with green cabbage.

TYPE	DESCRIPTION
Sorrel	Long, crisp, arrow-shaped leaves with a pungent, lemony flavor that is more pronounced than spinach. Sorrel is best cooked.
Spinach	Crinkled or flat, crisp leaves with a soft texture and mild flavor. Hearty enough for main-dish salads. Requires extra washing to remove grit. Spinach can be served raw or cooked.
Watercress	Delicate, spicy-flavored green. A good accent for salads and tea sandwiches.
Bags of prewashed, mixed greens	A time-saving convenience that often includes several fancier greens in addition to a workhorse lettuce such as romaine or iceberg. Store the blends in the refrigerator in the original bag.

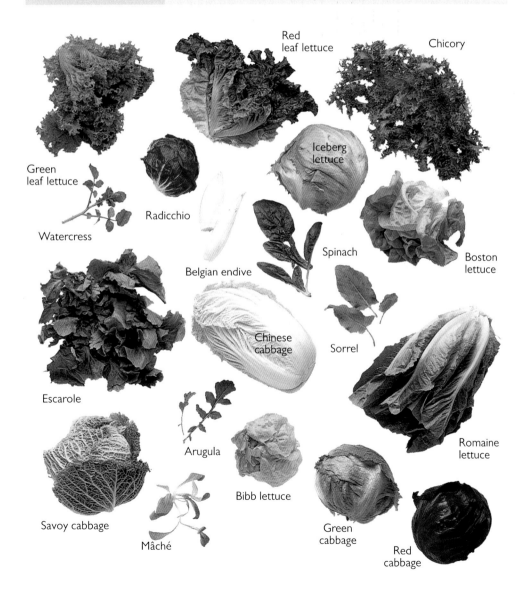

Asian Dressing

PREP TIME: 5 MINUTES ◆ YIELD: I CUP

⅓ cup oil
¼ cup rice vinegar
2 tablespoons sugar
I tablespoon grated gingerroot
3 tablespoons soy sauce
2 garlic cloves, minced

In small bowl, combine all dressing ingredients; blend well. Store in tightly covered container in refrigerator.

NUTRITION INFORMATION PER SERVING: Serving Size: 1 Tablespoon ◆ Calories: 50 ◆ Calories from Fat: 45 ◆ **% DAILY VALUE:** Total Fat: 5 g 8% ◆ Saturated Fat: 1 g 5% ◆ Cholesterol: 0 mg 0% ◆ Sodium: 190 mg 8% ◆ Total Carbohydrate: 2 g 1% ◆ Dietary Fiber: 0 g 0% ◆ Sugars: 2 g ◆ Protein: 0 g ◆ Vitamin A: 0% ◆ Vitamin C: 0% ◆ Calcium: 0% ◆ Iron: 0% ◆ **DIETARY EXCHANGES:** 1 Fat

---

COOK'S NOTE

OIL VARIETIES

Olive Oil

Virgin or extra-virgin olive oil has a strong, distinctive flavor and a color that ranges from golden to green. It is made from the first cold pressing of the olives.

Pure olive oil, made from subsequent pressings of olives, has a milder flavor and is much less expensive than virgin or extra-virgin olive oil.

Vegetable Oil

Corn oil, safflower oil and sunflower oil are all golden colored and mild. They combine well with vinegar but add little flavor to the salad dressing.

Peanut Oil

Peanut oil has a slight peanut flavor and a golden color.

Walnut Oil

Walnut oil is fairly expensive and delicate. It has a good nutty flavor. Store it in the refrigerator or in a cool place to prevent it from becoming rancid.

Sesame Oil

Sesame oil, a favorite flavoring in Asian recipes, can be dark (made from toasted sesame seeds) or light (made from untoasted seeds). Use the dark oil sparingly; its flavor is quite strong. Some "hot" sesame oils contain chiles.

Sun-Dried Tomato Vinaigrette

PREP TIME: I0 MINUTES ◆ YIELD: I CUP

½ cup olive oil
¼ cup chopped sun-dried tomatoes packed in olive oil and herbs (from 6.5-oz. jar)
3 tablespoons white wine vinegar
I teaspoon white wine Worcestershire sauce
½ teaspoon sugar
½ teaspoon salt
¼ teaspoon white pepper
I garlic clove, minced

In jar with tight-fitting lid, combine all ingredients; shake well. Store in tightly covered container in refrigerator.

NUTRITION INFORMATION PER SERVING: Serving Size: 1 Tablespoon ◆ Calories: 70 ◆ Calories from Fat: 60 ◆ **% DAILY VALUE:** Total Fat: 7 g 11% ◆ Saturated Fat: 1 g 5% ◆ Cholesterol: 0 mg 0% ◆ Sodium: 75 mg 3% ◆ Total Carbohydrate: 1 g 1% ◆ Dietary Fiber: 0 g 0% ◆ Sugars: 0 g ◆ Protein: 0 g ◆ Vitamin A: 0% ◆ Vitamin C: 4% ◆ Calcium: 0% ◆ Iron: 0% ◆ **DIETARY EXCHANGES:** 1½ Fat

Low-Fat Balsamic Vinaigrette

PREP TIME: 5 MINUTES ◆ YIELD: ¾ CUP

½ cup balsamic vinegar
I garlic clove, minced
2 tablespoons olive or vegetable oil
2 tablespoons water
I tablespoon honey
2 teaspoons chopped fresh thyme
⅛ teaspoon salt

In small bowl, combine all ingredients; mix well. Store in tightly covered container in refrigerator.

NUTRITION INFORMATION PER SERVING: Serving Size: 1 Tablespoon ◆ Calories: 25 ◆ Calories from Fat: 20 ◆ **% DAILY VALUE:** Total Fat: 2 g 3% ◆ Saturated Fat: 0 g 0% ◆ Cholesterol: 0 mg 0% ◆ Sodium: 25 mg 1% ◆ Total Carbohydrate: 2 g 1% ◆ Dietary Fiber: 0 g 0% ◆ Sugars: 1 g ◆ Protein: 0 g ◆ Vitamin A: 0% ◆ Vitamin C: 0% ◆ Calcium: 0% ◆ Iron: 0% ◆ **DIETARY EXCHANGES:** ½ Fat

Roasted Garlic Dressing

PREP TIME: 15 MINUTES ◆ YIELD: ⅓ CUP

⅓ cup oil
8 garlic cloves, peeled
2 tablespoons chopped fresh parsley
3 tablespoons vinegar
2 tablespoons grated Parmesan cheese
Dash pepper

1. In small skillet, cook 2 tablespoons of the oil and garlic over medium heat for about 10 minutes or until garlic is golden brown, stirring frequently. Cool slightly.
2. In blender container or food processor bowl with metal blade, combine garlic mixture, remaining oil, parsley, vinegar, cheese and pepper; blend at high speed until smooth. Store in tightly covered container in refrigerator.

NUTRITION INFORMATION PER SERVING: Serving Size: 1 Tablespoon ◆ Calories: 150 ◆ Calories from Fat: 140 ◆ % DAILY VALUE: Total Fat: 15 g 23% ◆ Saturated Fat: 2 g 10% ◆ Cholesterol: 0 mg 0% ◆ Sodium: 40 mg 2% ◆ Total Carbohydrate: 2 g 1% ◆ Dietary Fiber: 0 g 0% ◆ Sugars: 0 g ◆ Protein: 1 g ◆ Vitamin A: 0% ◆ Vitamin C: 6% ◆ Calcium: 4% ◆ Iron: 0% ◆ DIETARY EXCHANGES: 3 Fat

Honey-Orange-Poppy Seed Dressing

PREP TIME: 5 MINUTES ◆ YIELD: ⅔ CUP

¼ cup orange juice
¼ to ⅓ cup honey
2 tablespoons oil
2 to 4 teaspoons poppy seed

In jar with tight-fitting lid, combine all dressing ingredients; shake well. Store in tightly covered container in refrigerator.

NUTRITION INFORMATION PER SERVING: Serving Size: 1 Tablespoon ◆ Calories: 60 ◆ Calories from Fat: 25 ◆ % DAILY VALUE: Total Fat: 3 g 5% ◆ Saturated Fat: 0 g 0% ◆ Cholesterol: 0 mg 0% ◆ Sodium: 0 mg 0% ◆ Total Carbohydrate: 9 g 3% ◆ Dietary Fiber: 0 g 0% ◆ Sugars: 9 g ◆ Protein: 0 g ◆ Vitamin A: 0% ◆ Vitamin C: 4% ◆ Calcium: 0% ◆ Iron: 0% ◆ DIETARY EXCHANGES: ½ Fruit, ½ Fat OR ½ Carbohydrate, ½ Fat

Tomato-Basil Dressing

PREP TIME: 5 MINUTES ◆ YIELD: ⅔ CUP

½ cup vegetable juice cocktail
1 tablespoon powdered fruit pectin
1 tablespoon lemon juice
1½ teaspoons chopped fresh basil
1 teaspoon brown sugar
1 garlic clove, minced

In small bowl, combine all ingredients; stir until pectin is dissolved. Store in tightly covered container in refrigerator.

NUTRITION INFORMATION PER SERVING: Serving Size: 1 Tablespoon ◆ Calories: 0 ◆ Calories from Fat: 0 ◆ % DAILY VALUE: Total Fat: 0 g 0% ◆ Saturated Fat: 0 g 0% ◆ Cholesterol: 0 mg 0% ◆ Sodium: 30 mg 1% ◆ Total Carbohydrate: 1 g 1% ◆ Dietary Fiber: 0 g 0% ◆ Sugars: 1 g ◆ Protein: 0 g ◆ Vitamin A: 2% ◆ Vitamin C: 6% ◆ Calcium: 0% ◆ Iron: 0% ◆ DIETARY EXCHANGES: Free

Peppercorn-Chive Dressing

PREP TIME: 5 MINUTES ◆ YIELD: 1 CUP

¾ cup buttermilk
2 tablespoons chopped fresh chives
3 tablespoons fat-free mayonnaise or salad dressing
½ teaspoon sugar
½ teaspoon coarse ground black pepper
Dash turmeric

In small bowl, combine all ingredients; blend well. Store in tightly covered container in refrigerator.

NUTRITION INFORMATION PER SERVING: Serving Size: 1 Tablespoon ◆ Calories: 5 ◆ Calories from Fat: 0 ◆ % DAILY VALUE: Total Fat: 0 g 0% ◆ Saturated Fat: 0 g 0% ◆ Cholesterol: 0 mg 0% ◆ Sodium: 35 mg 1% ◆ Total Carbohydrate: 1 g 1% ◆ Dietary Fiber: 0 g 0% ◆ Sugars: 1 g ◆ Protein: 0 g ◆ Vitamin A: 0% ◆ Vitamin C: 0% ◆ Calcium: 0% ◆ Iron: 0% ◆ DIETARY EXCHANGES: Free

Clockwise from top: Tangy French Dressing (page 281),
Thousand Island Dressing (page 282),
Green Goddess Salad Dressing (page 281)

Sour Cream-Buttermilk Dressing

PREP TIME: 5 MINUTES ✦ YIELD: 2½ CUPS

    1 cup sour cream
    1 cup buttermilk
    ¼ cup mayonnaise or salad dressing
    ¼ cup vinegar
    2 tablespoons sugar
    1 teaspoon salt
    ½ teaspoon celery salt
    ¼ teaspoon pepper

In small bowl, combine all ingredients; beat well. Store in tightly covered container in refrigerator.

NUTRITION INFORMATION PER SERVING: Serving Size: 1 Tablespoon ✦ Calories: 20 ✦ Calories from Fat: 20 ✦ **% DAILY VALUE:** Total Fat: 2 g 3% ✦ Saturated Fat: 1 g 5% ✦ Cholesterol: 4 mg 1% ✦ Sodium: 70 mg 3% ✦ Total Carbohydrate: 1 g 1% ✦ Dietary Fiber: 0 g 0% ✦ Sugars: 1 g ✦ Protein: 0 g ✦ Vitamin A: 0% ✦ Vitamin C: 0% ✦ Calcium: 0% ✦ Iron: 0% ✦ **DIETARY EXCHANGES:** ½ Fat

Italian Dressing

PREP TIME: 10 MINUTES (READY IN 2 HOURS 10 MINUTES) ✦ YIELD: ¾ CUP

    ½ cup olive oil
    3 tablespoons white wine vinegar
    1 tablespoon chopped onion
    1 tablespoon chopped pimientos, drained
    1 tablespoon chopped fresh parsley
    1 garlic clove, halved
    ½ teaspoon dried oregano leaves or Italian
        seasoning
    ¼ teaspoon salt
    ⅛ teaspoon pepper

1. In jar with tight-fitting lid, combine all ingredients; shake well. Refrigerate at least 2 hours to blend flavors.
2. Before serving, remove garlic; shake well. Store in tightly covered container in refrigerator.

NUTRITION INFORMATION PER SERVING: Serving Size: 1 Tablespoon ✦ Calories: 80 ✦ Calories from Fat: 80 ✦ **% DAILY VALUE:** Total Fat: 9 g 14% ✦ Saturated Fat: 1 g 5% ✦ Cholesterol: 0 mg 0% ✦ Sodium: 45 mg 2% ✦ Total Carbohydrate: 0 g 0% ✦ Dietary Fiber: 0 g 0% ✦ Sugars: 0 g ✦ Protein: 0 g ✦ Vitamin A: 0% ✦ Vitamin C: 2% ✦ Calcium: 0% ✦ Iron: 0% ✦ **DIETARY EXCHANGES:** 2 Fat

VARIATION
Creamy Italian Dressing: Add ½ cup mayonnaise; mix well. YIELD: 1¼ CUPS

Low-Fat Creamy Herb Dressing

PREP TIME: 10 MINUTES ✦ YIELD: 1½ CUPS

    ¾ cup firmly packed fresh parsley
    ¼ cup firmly packed fresh basil
    1 tablespoon sugar
    1 teaspoon grated lemon peel
    ¼ teaspoon salt
    ¾ cup low-fat plain yogurt
    ¾ cup fat-free mayonnaise or salad dressing
    1 tablespoon white wine vinegar

1. In food processor bowl with metal blade or blender container, combine herbs; process until chopped.
2. Add all remaining ingredients; process until smooth, scraping down sides of bowl as needed. Store in tightly covered container in refrigerator.

NUTRITION INFORMATION PER SERVING: Serving Size: 1 Tablespoon ✦ Calories: 10 ✦ Calories from Fat: 0 ✦ **% DAILY VALUE:** Total Fat: 0 g 0% ✦ Saturated Fat: 0 g 0% ✦ Cholesterol: 0 mg 0% ✦ Sodium: 125 mg 5% ✦ Total Carbohydrate: 2 g 1% ✦ Dietary Fiber: 0 g 0% ✦ Sugars: 1 g ✦ Protein: 0 g ✦ Vitamin A: 0% ✦ Vitamin C: 0% ✦ Calcium: 0% ✦ Iron: 0% ✦ **DIETARY EXCHANGES:** Free

VINEGAR VARIETIES

Vinegar is made from fermented wine or another alcoholic liquid. With the exception of balsamic vinegar, it should look bright and unclouded.

Red Wine Vinegar

Ranging from pale to deep red, red wine vinegar has a full-bodied flavor that varies according to the grape used in processing, the amount of dilution and length of aging. It is a good choice for salads.

White Wine Vinegar

White wine vinegar has a delicate flavor and pale golden color.

Balsamic Vinegar

This Italian specialty gains its dark brown color and rich, mellow, almost sweet flavor from lengthy aging in oak casks. Good in salad dressing.

Sherry Vinegar

Pleasant with salads and poultry, sherry vinegar is made from sweet sherry and takes on a nutlike flavor when combined with lemon juice.

Cider Vinegar

Made from "hard" (fermented) apple cider, cider vinegar is sharp-flavored and golden in color. Often used in pickling, cider vinegar is usually considered too strong and raw-edged for salads.

White Vinegar

Also called distilled vinegar, white vinegar is colorless and often used in pickling. Like cider vinegar, it is usually considered too harsh for salad dressings.

Rice Vinegar

Rice vinegar, or mirin, is golden in color and slightly sweet in flavor. It is well suited to salads and side dishes prepared with Asian ingredients.

Fruit-Flavored Vinegar

Infused with the flavors of raspberries or other fruits, fruit-flavored vinegar adds excellent flavor and aroma to salad dressings.

Herb-Flavored Vinegar

These vinegars can be purchased or made at home with herbs such as tarragon, rosemary and garlic. Herb-flavored vinegars are excellent for a variety of salads.

Creamy Cucumber Dressing

PREP TIME: 10 MINUTES ◆ YIELD: 1½ CUPS

½ cup mayonnaise
½ cup sour cream
½ cup chopped cucumber
2 green onions, sliced
¼ teaspoon onion salt
¼ teaspoon dried dill weed, if desired

In small bowl, combine all ingredients; mix well. Store in tightly covered container in refrigerator.

NUTRITION INFORMATION PER SERVING: Serving Size: 1 Tablespoon ◆ Calories: 45 ◆ Calories from Fat: 45 ◆ **% DAILY VALUE:** Total Fat: 5 g 8% ◆ Saturated Fat: 1 g 5% ◆ Cholesterol: 5 mg 2% ◆ Sodium: 50 mg 2% ◆ Total Carbohydrate: 1 g 1% ◆ Dietary Fiber: 0 g 0% ◆ Sugars: 0 g ◆ Protein: 0 g ◆ Vitamin A: 0% ◆ Vitamin C: 0% ◆ Calcium: 0% ◆ Iron: 0% ◆ **DIETARY EXCHANGES:** 1 Fat

Honey-Dijon Dressing

PREP TIME: 5 MINUTES (READY IN 1 HOUR 5 MINUTES) ◆ YIELD: ¾ CUP

6 tablespoons olive or vegetable oil
2 tablespoons cider vinegar
2 tablespoons Dijon mustard
2 tablespoons honey
1 garlic clove, minced
Dash pepper

In jar with tight-fitting lid, combine all ingredients; shake well. Refrigerate at least 1 hour to blend flavors. Store in tightly covered container in refrigerator.

NUTRITION INFORMATION PER SERVING: Serving Size: 1 Tablespoon ◆ Calories: 80 ◆ Calories from Fat: 60 ◆ **% DAILY VALUE:** Total Fat: 7 g 11% ◆ Saturated Fat: 1 g 5% ◆ Cholesterol: 0 mg 0% ◆ Sodium: 65 mg 3% ◆ Total Carbohydrate: 3 g 1% ◆ Dietary Fiber: 0 g 0% ◆ Sugars: 3 g ◆ Protein: 0 g ◆ Vitamin A: 0% ◆ Vitamin C: 0% ◆ Calcium: 0% ◆ Iron: 0% ◆ **DIETARY EXCHANGES:** 1½ Fat

VEGETABLES & SIDES

Buying Vegetables

FRESH

Fresh vegetables are usually least expensive and of best quality during their peak growing season. Unlike fruits, most vegetables do not continue to ripen after harvesting.

Look for produce that is crisp, nicely colored, firm and unblemished. Avoid vegetables with wilting, bruising, spoilage or dryness.

Most vegetables lose nutrients and flavor in prolonged storage. Buy a few days' supply of vegetables at a time. Good "keepers" for longer storage include potatoes, onions, winter squash, carrots and cabbage.

The waxy coating commonly found on vegetables such as cucumbers, squash and turnips guards against spoilage and retains moisture. The wax, approved by the Food and Drug Administration, is edible but may be scrubbed off with a vegetable brush or pared away.

FROZEN

Frozen vegetables are generally of high quality because crops are harvested at the proper stage of ripeness, when flavors and nutrients are at their peak. Soon after being picked, the vegetables are blanched to retain their flavor, color and texture. Little or no salt or sugar is added unless the package contains a sauce. Block-frozen packages should feel solid. Bags of loose corn, peas or other vegetables should feel loose and shakable inside; big lumps probably indicate that the package was partially thawed and refrozen.

CANNED

Compare labels and choose cans with little or no salt or sugar. Avoid any cans that are dented or bulging. Store cans in a cool, dry place and use the oldest cans first.

DRIED

Dried vegetables such as beans, peas and lentils provide an excellent, low-cost source of protein. Dried peppers, mushrooms, tomatoes and onions are convenient to store, and add flavor and character to recipes. Store dried vegetables in a cool, dry place.

Storing Vegetables

Nutrient losses occur much more rapidly in fresh vegetables than in canned or frozen. Most fresh vegetables do best in the vegetable crisper compartment in the refrigerator, which is designed to provide optimum humidity, or in plastic bags in the refrigerator. Some vegetables, such as potatoes, sweet potatoes, onions, garlic, rutabaga and winter squash, are best stored unrefrigerated in a cool, dry, dark place. Store onions and potatoes separately to retard spoilage.

FREEZING VEGETABLES

To freeze most fresh vegetables, blanch them first to retain flavor, true color, tender texture and to prolong freezer life. (For more information, see "Fruit Freezing Chart," page 486, and "Vegetable Freezing Chart," page 488.)

Preparing Vegetables

FRESH

Wash, but do not soak, fresh vegetables before cooking. Vegetables can be boiled, steamed, microwaved, baked, stir-fried, grilled or even broiled.

Whichever preparation method you choose, use as little water as possible and avoid overcooking. To keep flavor, color and texture at their best and to preserve vitamins and minerals, cook most vegetables just until crisp-tender—tender enough to pierce with a fork, but not mushy. The color should still be bright. Potatoes, turnips, rutabaga, winter squash and beets should be tender throughout. Leafy greens should be wilted but still bright in color.

FROZEN OR CANNED

Prepare commercially frozen vegetables according to package directions. Canned vegetables need only to be placed in a saucepan and heated. They are sometimes used in salads without heating.

Cooking Fresh Vegetables

BOILING

To boil fresh vegetables, use a saucepan and about 1 cup water per pound of vegetable. Add ½ teaspoon salt per cup of water. Bring salted water to a boil over high heat; add vegetables. Return to a boil; begin timing. To preserve the natural color of green vegetables, boil uncovered for first 5 minutes. Cover pan and reduce heat; boil gently throughout the cooking time. Do not overcook. For directions on boiling specific vegetables, see the "Fresh Vegetable Cooking Reference" chart on pages 322 to 330.

GRILLING

Grill Basket: Choose vegetables with similar cooking times and of similar size, at least ¾-inch wide to prevent falling through grill basket. Brush vegetables with oil or melted butter. **Kabobs:** Choose vegetables with similar cooking times and of similar size. Brush with oil or melted butter to prevent drying. Two skewers per kabob will hold vegetables in place and prevent falling off or slipping when turning them. **Direct Grill:** Use whole vegetables, turning them for even heating. Vegetables with skins need to be pierced with a fork. Soak corn husks in water before grilling to prevent burning. **Foil Packet:** Add butter, chicken, beef or vegetable stock, or another type of liquid for moisture. Use heavy-duty foil.

C O O K ' S   N O T E

HOW TO STEAM FRESH VEGETABLES

 Place a steamer basket into a pan with ½ to 1 inch of boiling water. (The water should not touch the bottom of the basket.) Place whole vegetables into the pan or layer cut-up vegetables up to 2 inches deep. Cover the pan tightly and reduce heat so water continues to boil. Add more water during cooking if necessary. Vegetables are done when crisp-tender. For directions on steaming specific vegetables, see the "Fresh Vegetable Cooking Reference" chart on pages 322 to 330.

C O O K ' S   N O T E

HOW TO MICROWAVE FRESH VEGETABLES

 To microwave, arrange fresh vegetables in a microwave-safe dish with thicker portions toward the outside of the dish. Add 2 to 3 tablespoons of water and cover the dish with a lid or plastic wrap. Microwave the vegetables on HIGH, stirring, rearranging or turning them halfway through cooking. Remove them at the minimum time and check for doneness. See the "Fresh Vegetable Cooking Reference" chart on pages 322 to 330 or check your microwave manual for specific cooking times.

Green Bean Casserole

PREP TIME: 10 MINUTES (READY IN 35 MINUTES)
◆ YIELD: 4 SERVINGS

1 (14.5-oz.) can french-style green beans, drained
1 (10¾-oz.) can condensed cream of mushroom soup
1 (2.8-oz.) can french fried onions

1. Heat oven to 350°F. In ungreased 1½-quart casserole, combine green beans and soup; mix thoroughly.
2. Bake at 350°F. for 20 to 25 minutes or until bubbly. Top with onions during last 5 minutes of baking time.

NUTRITION INFORMATION PER SERVING: Serving Size: ¼ of Recipe ◆ Calories: 220 ◆ Calories from Fat: 140 ◆ **% DAILY VALUE:** Total Fat: 16 g 25% ◆ Saturated Fat: 4 g 20% ◆ Cholesterol: 0 mg 0% ◆ Sodium: 810 mg 34% ◆ Total Carbohydrate: 17 g 6% ◆ Dietary Fiber: 2 g 8% ◆ Sugars: 2 g ◆ Protein: 3 g ◆ Vitamin A: 4% ◆ Vitamin C: 4% ◆ Calcium: 4% ◆ Iron: 4% ◆ **DIETARY EXCHANGES:** 1 Starch, ½ Vegetable, 3 Fat OR 1 Carbohydrate, ½ Vegetable, 3 Fat

Cheesy Green Beans

PREP TIME: 15 MINUTES ◆ YIELD: 4 (½-CUP) SERVINGS

2 cups cut fresh green beans
1 teaspoon margarine or butter
2 tablespoons finely chopped onion
2 small garlic cloves, minced
2 tablespoons shredded Cheddar cheese

1. In medium saucepan, bring 1 cup water to a boil. Add green beans; cover and cook over medium heat for 6 to 8 minutes or until beans are crisp-tender. Drain; return beans to saucepan.
2. In small skillet, melt margarine over medium heat. Add onion and garlic; cook, stirring frequently, until onion begins to brown.
3. Add onion mixture to cooked beans; cook until thoroughly heated. Add cheese; toss gently to mix.

NUTRITION INFORMATION PER SERVING: Serving Size: ½ Cup ◆ Calories: 45 ◆ Calories from Fat: 20 ◆ % DAILY VALUE: Total Fat: 2 g 3% ◆ Saturated Fat: 1 g 5% ◆ Cholesterol: 4 mg 1% ◆ Sodium: 35 mg 1% ◆ Total Carbohydrate: 5 g 2% ◆ Dietary Fiber: 2 g 8% ◆ Sugars: 2 g ◆ Protein: 2 g ◆ Vitamin A: 8% ◆ Vitamin C: 10% ◆ Calcium: 4% ◆ Iron: 4% ◆ DIETARY EXCHANGES: 1 Vegetable, ½ Fat

Green Beans with Cashew Butter

PREP TIME: 10 MINUTES ◆ YIELD: 6 (½-CUP) SERVINGS

3½ cups frozen cut green beans
⅓ cup butter
⅓ cup coarsely chopped cashews

1. Cook green beans as directed on package. Drain; spoon into serving bowl.
2. Meanwhile, melt butter in small saucepan.

Green Beans with Cashew Butter

Add cashews; cook and stir over low heat for 2 minutes or until cashews are very light brown. Pour cashew butter over hot green beans.

NUTRITION INFORMATION PER SERVING: Serving Size: ½ Cup ◆ Calories: 180 ◆ Calories from Fat: 140 ◆ % DAILY VALUE: Total Fat: 15 g 23% ◆ Saturated Fat: 7 g 35% ◆ Cholesterol: 30 mg 10% ◆ Sodium: 170 mg 7% ◆ Total Carbohydrate: 9 g 3% ◆ Dietary Fiber: 2 g 8% ◆ Sugars: 2 g ◆ Protein: 3 g ◆ Vitamin A: 15% ◆ Vitamin C: 10% ◆ Calcium: 4% ◆ Iron: 6% ◆ DIETARY EXCHANGES: 1½ Vegetable, 3 Fat

Garden Beans with Hot Bacon Dressing

PREP TIME: 25 MINUTES ◆ YIELD: 8 (½-CUP) SERVINGS

4 slices bacon, cut into ½-inch pieces
1 beef bouillon cube or 1 teaspoon beef-flavor instant bouillon
⅓ cup boiling water
1 tablespoon sugar
⅛ teaspoon pepper
4 cups fresh yellow wax or green beans, cut into 2-inch pieces
½ cup chopped onion
2 tablespoons red wine vinegar
¼ cup sliced almonds

1. In large skillet, cook bacon until crisp, stirring occasionally. With slotted spoon, remove bacon from skillet; drain on paper towels. Set aside.
2. Dissolve bouillon in water. Add bouillon, sugar and pepper to bacon drippings; mix well. Add wax beans and onion; mix well. Cover; cook 4 to 6 minutes or until crisp-tender.
3. Remove skillet from heat. Stir in vinegar. Spoon into serving dish. Sprinkle with bacon and almonds.

NUTRITION INFORMATION PER SERVING: Serving Size: ½ Cup ◆ Calories: 70 ◆ Calories from Fat: 25 ◆ % DAILY VALUE: Total Fat: 3 g 5% ◆ Saturated Fat: 1 g 5% ◆ Cholesterol: 3 mg 1% ◆ Sodium: 160 mg 7% ◆ Total Carbohydrate: 7 g 2% ◆ Dietary Fiber: 2 g 8% ◆ Sugars: 3 g ◆ Protein: 3 g ◆ Vitamin A: 8% ◆ Vitamin C: 10% ◆ Calcium: 4% ◆ Iron: 4% ◆ DIETARY EXCHANGES: 1½ Vegetable, ½ Fat

Lemon-Buttered Asparagus

PREP TIME: 20 MINUTES ◆ YIELD: 4 SERVINGS

1 lb. fresh asparagus spears
3 tablespoons butter
1 tablespoon lemon juice
½ teaspoon grated lemon peel

Lemon-Buttered Asparagus (page 292)

Broccoli with Sharp Cheddar Sauce

PREP TIME: 20 MINUTES ◆ YIELD: 12 (¾-CUP) SERVINGS

 2 lb. fresh broccoli florets (about 15 cups)
2¾ cups skim milk
 ⅓ cup all-purpose flour
 5 oz. (1¼ cups) shredded reduced-fat sharp
    Cheddar cheese
 ¾ teaspoon salt
 ⅛ teaspoon ground red pepper (cayenne)
 1 teaspoon Dijon mustard
 1 tablespoon grated Parmesan cheese

1. Place about 4 cups water in Dutch oven; bring to a boil. Add broccoli; return to a boil. Reduce heat to medium; cover tightly and cook 5 to 7 minutes or until broccoli is crisp-tender, stirring once.
2. Meanwhile, place 2 cups of the milk in large nonstick saucepan; place over medium heat. In small bowl, combine remaining ¾ cup milk and flour; blend with wire whisk until smooth. Add to milk in skillet; cook 8 to 10 minutes or until thickened, stirring constantly.
3. Remove saucepan from heat. Add Cheddar cheese, salt, ground red pepper and mustard; stir until thoroughly blended.
4. Drain broccoli; place in shallow oven-proof casserole. Spoon sauce over broccoli; sprinkle with Parmesan cheese.

NUTRITION INFORMATION PER SERVING: Serving Size: ¾ Cup ◆ Calories: 100 ◆ Calories from Fat: 25 ◆ **% DAILY VALUE:** Total Fat: 3 g 5% ◆ Saturated Fat: 2 g 10% ◆ Cholesterol: 10 mg 3% ◆ Sodium: 300 mg 13% ◆ Total Carbohydrate: 10 g 3% ◆ Dietary Fiber: 2 g 8% ◆ Sugars: 4 g ◆ Protein: 8 g ◆ Vitamin A: 30% ◆ Vitamin C: 80% ◆ Calcium: 20% ◆ Iron: 4% ◆ **DIETARY EXCHANGES:** ½ Starch, 1 Vegetable, ½ Medium-Fat Meat OR ½ Carbohydrate, 1 Vegetable, ½ Medium-Fat Meat

Broccoli with Sharp Cheddar Sauce

---

1. Snap off tough ends of asparagus. In large skillet, combine asparagus spears and ½ cup water. Bring to a boil over medium heat. Cook 5 to 10 minutes or until crisp-tender. Drain.
2. Meanwhile, melt butter in small saucepan. Stir in lemon juice and lemon peel.
3. Place asparagus on serving platter; pour butter mixture over spears.

NUTRITION INFORMATION PER SERVING: Serving Size: ¼ of Recipe ◆ Calories: 110 ◆ Calories from Fat: 80 ◆ **% DAILY VALUE:** Total Fat: 9 g 14% ◆ Saturated Fat: 5 g 25% ◆ Cholesterol: 25 mg 8% ◆ Sodium: 90 mg 4% ◆ Total Carbohydrate: 5 g 2% ◆ Dietary Fiber: 2 g 8% ◆ Sugars: 2 g ◆ Protein: 2 g ◆ Vitamin A: 20% ◆ Vitamin C: 15% ◆ Calcium: 2% ◆ Iron: 4% ◆ **DIETARY EXCHANGES:** 1 Vegetable, 2 Fat

Harvard Beets

PREP TIME: 20 MINUTES ◆ YIELD: 4 SERVINGS

 1 (15-oz.) can sliced or baby whole beets
    Water
 ¼ cup sugar
 1 tablespoon cornstarch
 ¾ teaspoon salt
    Dash pepper
 3 tablespoons vinegar

1. Drain beets, reserving liquid. Measure liquid; add water to make ¾ cup. Set beets aside.
2. In medium saucepan, combine sugar, cornstarch, salt and pepper; mix well. Gradually stir beet liquid and vinegar into sugar mixture; blend until smooth. Cook until mixture boils and thickens, stirring constantly.
3. Add beets; cook until thoroughly heated.

NUTRITION INFORMATION PER SERVING: Serving Size: ¼ of Recipe ◆ Calories: 90 ◆ Calories from Fat: 0 ◆ **% DAILY VALUE:** Total Fat: 0 g 0% ◆ Saturated Fat: 0 g 0% ◆ Cholesterol: 0 mg 0% ◆ Sodium: 670 mg 28% ◆ Total Carbohydrate: 22 g 7% ◆ Dietary Fiber: 1 g 4% ◆ Sugars: 18 g ◆ Protein: 1 g ◆ Vitamin A: 0% ◆ Vitamin C: 4% ◆ Calcium: 0% ◆ Iron: 4% ◆ **DIETARY EXCHANGES:** 1 Fruit, 1 Vegetable OR 1 Carbohydrate, 1 Vegetable

WHEN VEGETABLES ARE IN THEIR PRIME

VEGETABLE	PEAK AVAILABILITY
Artichokes (*globe*)	March to May
Asparagus	March to June
Beans	April to September
Beets	June to October
Broccoli	October to May
Brussels sprouts	October to March
Cabbage	September to June
Carrots	Year-round
Cauliflower	October to November
Celery	Year-round
Chinese pea pods (*snow pea pods*)	February to June
Corn	May to August
Cucumbers	May to August
Eggplant	July to October
Garlic	Year-round
Kohlrabi	June to October
Leeks	October to May
Lettuce (*head*)	Year-round
Okra	June to August
Onions	Year-round
Parsnips	October to March
Peas	April to July
Peppers	June to September
Pumpkins	September to October
Radishes	March to June
Rutabaga	January to March
Spinach	Year-round
Squash	June to December
Sweet potatoes	June to December
Tomatoes	May to August
Turnips	October to March
Zucchini	May to August

Southern Succotash

PREP TIME: 15 MINUTES ◆ YIELD: 4 (½-CUP) SERVINGS

1 tablespoon butter
½ cup chopped red bell pepper
1 cup frozen whole kernel corn
1 (9-oz.) pkg. frozen baby lima beans in a pouch
¼ teaspoon salt
¼ teaspoon dried marjoram leaves, if desired
⅛ teaspoon pepper

1. Melt butter in medium skillet over medium heat. Add bell pepper; cook and stir 1 minute.
2. Add all remaining ingredients; mix well. Cook 3 to 5 minutes or until vegetables are crisp-tender, stirring occasionally.

NUTRITION INFORMATION PER SERVING: Serving Size: ½ Cup ◆ Calories: 160 ◆ Calories from Fat: 35 ◆ % DAILY VALUE: Total Fat: 4 g 6% ◆ Saturated Fat: 2 g 10% ◆ Cholesterol: 10 mg 3% ◆ Sodium: 200 mg 8% ◆ Total Carbohydrate: 25 g 8% ◆ Dietary Fiber: 5 g 20% ◆ Sugars: 3 g ◆ Protein: 6 g ◆ Vitamin A: 20% ◆ Vitamin C: 35% ◆ Calcium: 2% ◆ Iron: 10% ◆ DIETARY EXCHANGES: 1½ Starch, ½ Fat OR 1½ Carbohydrate, ½ Fat

Cabbage Stir-Fry

PREP TIME: 15 MINUTES ◆ YIELD: 4 (½-CUP) SERVINGS

2 tablespoons oil
1 teaspoon sesame oil
1 garlic clove, minced
1 teaspoon grated gingerroot
1 cup shredded cabbage
1 cup shredded Chinese (napa) cabbage
1 cup shredded bok choy
½ cup chopped green onions
1 tablespoon soy sauce
2 teaspoons sesame seed, toasted if desired*

1. In large skillet or wok, heat oils over high heat until hot. Add garlic and gingerroot; cook a few seconds.
2. Add cabbage, Chinese cabbage, bok choy, onions and soy sauce; mix well. Cook 2 to 3 minutes or until cabbage is crisp-tender, stirring constantly. Place in serving bowl. Sprinkle with sesame seed.

TIP: * To toast sesame seed, spread in small nonstick skillet; stir over medium-high heat for 1 to 2 minutes or until light golden brown.

NUTRITION INFORMATION PER SERVING: Serving Size: ½ Cup ◆ Calories: 110 ◆ Calories from Fat: 80 ◆ % DAILY VALUE: Total Fat: 9 g 14% ◆ Saturated Fat: 1 g 5% ◆ Cholesterol: 0 mg 0% ◆ Sodium: 290 mg 12% ◆ Total Carbohydrate: 4 g 1% ◆ Dietary Fiber: 1 g 4% ◆ Sugars: 2 g ◆ Protein: 2 g ◆ Vitamin A: 20% ◆ Vitamin C: 30% ◆ Calcium: 6% ◆ Iron: 4% ◆ DIETARY EXCHANGES: 1 Vegetable, 2 Fat

Sweet-Sour Red Cabbage

PREP TIME: 35 MINUTES ◆ YIELD: 6 SERVINGS

    6 cups shredded red cabbage
    2 tart green apples, chopped
    ¼ cup firmly packed brown sugar
    1 teaspoon salt
    ½ teaspoon caraway seed
    ⅛ teaspoon pepper
    ½ cup water
    ¼ to ⅓ cup vinegar

In large saucepan, combine all ingredients; mix gently. Cover; simmer 20 to 25 minutes or until cabbage is tender, stirring occasionally.

NUTRITION INFORMATION PER SERVING: Serving Size: ⅙ of Recipe ◆ Calories: 90 ◆ Calories from Fat: 0 ◆ **% DAILY VALUE:** Total Fat: 0 g 0% ◆ Saturated Fat: 0 g 0% ◆ Cholesterol: 0 mg 0% ◆ Sodium: 370 mg 15% ◆ Total Carbohydrate: 21 g 7% ◆ Dietary Fiber: 3 g 12% ◆ Sugars: 18 g ◆ Protein: 1 g ◆ Vitamin A: 2% ◆ Vitamin C: 30% ◆ Calcium: 4% ◆ Iron: 4% ◆ **DIETARY EXCHANGES:** 1 Fruit, 1 Vegetable OR 1 Carbohydrate, 1 Vegetable

Brussels Sprouts with Bacon and Pecans

PREP TIME: 25 MINUTES ◆ YIELD: 6 (½-CUP) SERVINGS

    1½ lb. fresh Brussels sprouts
    4 slices bacon
    1 teaspoon all-purpose flour
    1 tablespoon brown sugar
    1 tablespoon water
    1 tablespoon cider vinegar
    1 teaspoon Dijon mustard
    ¼ cup chopped pecans

1. Wash and trim Brussels sprouts. With tip of knife, cut an X in base of each. Place in large saucepan; add just enough water to cover. Bring to a boil over high heat. Reduce heat; simmer 8 to 10 minutes or until tender.
2. Meanwhile, in medium skillet, cook bacon until crisp. Drain, reserving 2 tablespoons bacon drippings in skillet; cool. Add flour to cooled drippings; cook and stir over medium-low heat until bubbly. Remove from heat.
3. In small bowl, combine brown sugar, water, vinegar and mustard; mix well. Gradually stir into bacon drippings mixture.
4. Drain Brussels sprouts; place in serving bowl. Add hot bacon dressing mixture; toss gently. Crumble bacon over Brussels sprouts. Sprinkle with pecans.

NUTRITION INFORMATION PER SERVING: Serving Size: ½ Cup ◆ Calories: 120 ◆ Calories from Fat: 70 ◆ **% DAILY VALUE:** Total Fat: 8 g 12% ◆ Saturated Fat: 2 g 10% ◆ Cholesterol: 4 mg 1% ◆ Sodium: 40 mg 2% ◆ Total Carbohydrate: 10 g 3% ◆ Dietary Fiber: 3 g 12% ◆ Sugars: 4 g ◆ Protein: 3 g ◆ Vitamin A: 10% ◆ Vitamin C: 70% ◆ Calcium: 4% ◆ Iron: 6% ◆ **DIETARY EXCHANGES:** ½ Starch, 1 Vegetable, 1½ Fat OR ½ Carbohydrate, 1 Vegetable, 1½ Fat

Apricot-Glazed Carrots

PREP TIME: 15 MINUTES ◆ YIELD: 8 (½-CUP) SERVINGS

    5 cups julienne-cut (2 x ⅛ x ⅛-inch) carrots
    ¼ teaspoon salt
    ¼ cup apricot preserves

1. In medium saucepan, combine carrots and ¾ cup water; bring to a boil. Reduce heat to low; cover and simmer until carrots are tender. Drain.
2. Add salt and apricot preserves; stir to coat. Cook over low heat for 1 to 2 minutes or until thoroughly heated.

NUTRITION INFORMATION PER SERVING: Serving Size: ½ Cup ◆ Calories: 60 ◆ Calories from Fat: 0 ◆ **% DAILY VALUE:** Total Fat: 0 g 0% ◆ Saturated Fat: 0 g 0% ◆ Cholesterol: 0 mg 0% ◆ Sodium: 100 mg 4% ◆ Total Carbohydrate: 14 g 5% ◆ Dietary Fiber: 2 g 8% ◆ Sugars: 10 g ◆ Protein: 1 g ◆ Vitamin A: 430% ◆ Vitamin C: 10% ◆ Calcium: 2% ◆ Iron: 2% ◆ **DIETARY EXCHANGES:** ½ Fruit, 1 Vegetable OR ½ Carbohydrate, 1 Vegetable

Dill Baby Carrots

PREP TIME: 15 MINUTES ◆ YIELD: 7 (½-CUP) SERVINGS

    1 lb. fresh baby carrots
    1 tablespoon margarine or butter
    1 teaspoon chopped fresh dill
        or ¼ teaspoon dried dill weed
    1 teaspoon fresh lemon juice
    ¼ teaspoon salt
    ⅛ teaspoon pepper

1. In medium saucepan, bring ¾ cup water to a boil. Add carrots; cover and cook over medium heat for 10 to 12 minutes or until tender.
2. Drain carrots; return to saucepan. Add all remaining ingredients; stir until margarine is melted.

NUTRITION INFORMATION PER SERVING: Serving Size: ½ Cup ◆ Calories: 50 ◆ Calories from Fat: 20 ◆ **% DAILY VALUE:** Total Fat: 2 g 3% ◆ Saturated Fat: 0 g 0% ◆ Cholesterol: 0 mg 0% ◆ Sodium: 120 mg 5% ◆ Total Carbohydrate: 7 g 2% ◆ Dietary Fiber: 2 g 8% ◆ Sugars: 4 g ◆ Protein: 1 g ◆ Vitamin A: 370% ◆ Vitamin C: 8% ◆ Calcium: 0% ◆ Iron: 0% ◆ **DIETARY EXCHANGES:** 1 Vegetable, ½ Fat

Corn off the Cob

Corn off the Cob

PREP TIME: 20 MINUTES ✦ YIELD: 3 (½-CUP) SERVINGS

- 6 ears corn, husked, cleaned
- 2 tablespoons margarine or butter
- 2 tablespoons chopped green onions
- ½ teaspoon salt
- ⅛ teaspoon pepper
- ¼ cup whipping cream or milk

1. With sharp knife, cut kernels of corn from cob.
2. Melt margarine in medium skillet over low heat. Add corn and all remaining ingredients except whipping cream; cook 4 to 6 minutes or until corn is crisp-tender.
3. Stir in whipping cream; cook about 2 minutes or until cream coats corn.

NUTRITION INFORMATION PER SERVING: Serving Size: ½ Cup ✦ Calories: 370 ✦ Calories from Fat: 150 ✦ **% DAILY VALUE:** Total Fat: 17 g 26% ✦ Saturated Fat: 6 g 30% ✦ Cholesterol: 25 mg 8% ✦ Sodium: 480 mg 20% ✦ Total Carbohydrate: 47 g 16% ✦ Dietary Fiber: 5 g 20% ✦ Sugars: 5 g ✦ Protein: 7 g ✦ Vitamin A: 20% ✦ Vitamin C: 15% ✦ Calcium: 2% ✦ Iron: 6% ✦ **DIETARY EXCHANGES:** 3 Starch, 3 Fat OR 3 Carbohydrate, 3 Fat

Carrots and Broccoli with Orange Browned Butter

PREP TIME: 15 MINUTES ✦ YIELD: 8 (¾-CUP) SERVINGS

- 1 (16-oz.) pkg. fresh baby carrots
- 1 (14-oz.) pkg. frozen broccoli florets
- ⅓ cup butter
- 1 teaspoon grated orange peel
- ½ teaspoon grated gingerroot
- 2 tablespoons orange juice

1. Place carrots in large saucepan; cover with water. Bring to a boil. Reduce heat; cover and simmer 3 minutes. Add broccoli; cook 2 to 3 minutes or until vegetables are crisp-tender.
2. Meanwhile, in small saucepan, cook butter over medium-high heat until golden brown; immediately remove from heat. Add orange peel, gingerroot and orange juice; mix well.
3. Drain vegetables. Pour butter sauce over vegetables; toss lightly to coat.

NUTRITION INFORMATION PER SERVING: Serving Size: ¾ Cup ✦ Calories: 120 ✦ Calories from Fat: 70 ✦ **% DAILY VALUE:** Total Fat: 8 g 12% ✦ Saturated Fat: 5 g 25% ✦ Cholesterol: 20 mg 7% ✦ Sodium: 110 mg 5% ✦ Total Carbohydrate: 9 g 3% ✦ Dietary Fiber: 3 g 12% ✦ Sugars: 5 g ✦ Protein: 2 g ✦ Vitamin A: 330% ✦ Vitamin C: 30% ✦ Calcium: 2% ✦ Iron: 2% ✦ **DIETARY EXCHANGES:** ½ Fruit, 1 Vegetable, 1½ Fat OR ½ Carbohydrate, 1 Vegetable, 1½ Fat

Scalloped Corn

PREP TIME: 20 MINUTES (READY IN 1 HOUR) ✦ YIELD: 6 (½-CUP) SERVINGS

- ¼ cup margarine or butter
- ½ cup chopped onion
- 1 green bell pepper, chopped
- 1 (15-oz.) can cream-style corn
- ½ cup Italian style dry bread crumbs
- 2 eggs, beaten

1. Heat oven to 375°F. Grease 1-quart casserole. Melt margarine in medium saucepan over medium heat. Add onion and bell pepper; cook 3 to 4 minutes or until crisp-tender.

Carrots and Broccoli with Orange Browned Butter

2. Stir in all remaining ingredients. Pour into greased casserole.

3. Bake at 375°F. for 35 to 40 minutes or until knife inserted in center comes out clean.

NUTRITION INFORMATION PER SERVING: Serving Size: ½ Cup ◆ Calories: 200 ◆ Calories from Fat: 90 ◆ **% DAILY VALUE:** Total Fat: 10 g 15% ◆ Saturated Fat: 2 g 10% ◆ Cholesterol: 70 mg 23% ◆ Sodium: 610 mg 25% ◆ Total Carbohydrate: 22 g 7% ◆ Dietary Fiber: 2 g 8% ◆ Sugars: 8 g ◆ Protein: 5 g ◆ Vitamin A: 10% ◆ Vitamin C: 15% ◆ Calcium: 2% ◆ Iron: 4% ◆ **DIETARY EXCHANGES:** 1 Starch, 1 Vegetable, 2 Fat OR 1 Carbohydrate, 1 Vegetable, 2 Fat

Savory Butter Roasted Corn

PREP TIME: 15 MINUTES (READY IN 1 HOUR 10 MINUTES) ◆ YIELD: 4 SERVINGS

    4 ears fresh corn in husks
    1 tablespoon butter, melted
    1 garlic clove, minced

1. GRILL DIRECTIONS: Place corn in husks in enough cold water to cover; soak for 30 minutes.

2. Meanwhile, heat grill. In small bowl, combine melted butter and garlic; mix well.

3. Carefully pull back husks of corn to expose silk, leaving husks attached to corn. Remove and discard silk; brush corn with garlic butter. Smooth husks over corn to enclose.

4. When ready to grill, place corn directly on gas grill over medium heat or on charcoal grill 4 to 6 inches from medium coals. Cook 20 to 30 minutes or until tender. Remove husks before serving.

COOK'S NOTE

MUSHROOMS

Mushrooms have a high water content and readily absorb more, so soaking before cooking is not recommended. Instead, clean mushrooms with a mushroom brush or wipe the cap and stem with a paper towel to loosen any pebbles or dirt. Store them in the refrigerator, uncovered or loosely wrapped in paper towels. Don't keep them tightly wrapped in plastic, which holds in too much moisture and will lead to untimely spoilage.

TIP: To bake corn, place on ungreased cookie sheet; bake at 400°F. using times above as a guide.

NUTRITION INFORMATION PER SERVING: Serving Size: ¼ of Recipe ◆ Calories: 120 ◆ Calories from Fat: 35 ◆ **% DAILY VALUE:** Total Fat: 4 g 6% ◆ Saturated Fat: 2 g 10% ◆ Cholesterol: 10 mg 3% ◆ Sodium: 45 mg 2% ◆ Total Carbohydrate: 17 g 6% ◆ Dietary Fiber: 2 g 8% ◆ Sugars: 5 g ◆ Protein: 3 g ◆ Vitamin A: 8% ◆ Vitamin C: 8% ◆ Calcium: 0% ◆ Iron: 2% ◆ **DIETARY EXCHANGES:** 1 Starch, 1 Fat OR 1 Carbohydrate, 1 Fat

Parmesan Mushrooms and Onions

PREP TIME: 15 MINUTES ◆ YIELD: 3 (⅔-CUP) SERVINGS

    2 tablespoons margarine or butter
    2 cups (6 oz.) small fresh mushrooms
    ⅓ cup sliced sweet onion
    ½ teaspoon dried marjoram leaves
    ¼ teaspoon salt
    ¼ teaspoon pepper
    1 tablespoon dry white wine
    1 to 2 tablespoons grated fresh Parmesan
        cheese

Melt margarine in small skillet over medium-high heat. Add all remaining ingredients except Parmesan cheese; cook 5 to 10 minutes or until mushrooms are tender, stirring occasionally. Remove from heat. Sprinkle with cheese.

NUTRITION INFORMATION PER SERVING: Serving Size: ⅔ Cup ◆ Calories: 120 ◆ Calories from Fat: 80 ◆ **% DAILY VALUE:** Total Fat: 9 g 14% ◆ Saturated Fat: 2 g 10% ◆ Cholesterol: 3 mg 1% ◆ Sodium: 350 mg 15% ◆ Total Carbohydrate: 5 g 2% ◆ Dietary Fiber: 1 g 4% ◆ Sugars: 1 g ◆ Protein: 3 g ◆ Vitamin A: 8% ◆ Vitamin C: 4% ◆ Calcium: 6% ◆ Iron: 6% ◆ **DIETARY EXCHANGES:** 1 Vegetable, 2 Fat

Parmesan Mushrooms and Onions

TYPES OF MUSHROOMS

TYPE	DESCRIPTION
Button mushrooms	Ordinary white grocery-store mushrooms.
Cremini	Like button mushrooms but grown indoors and have light brown caps and richer flavor.
Enoki mushrooms (cultivated and wild)	Long, skinny stems with rounded, snowy white thumbtack-sized heads. The wild form has orangy-brown, very shiny caps.
Oyster mushrooms (cultivated and wild)	The cap color varies from white to gray or brown. The flavor is fairly robust and slightly peppery but becomes milder when cooked.
Porcini	Large wild mushrooms with thick stems and reddish caps. Also called cèpes.
Portobello mushrooms	Large, meaty, brown-capped; great for grilling.
Shiitake mushrooms (cultivated and wild)	Flat brown cap with chewy texture and distinctive flavor that hints at onion. Readily available fresh and dried; fibrous stems can be discarded or used to flavor soup stalk.
Wild mushrooms	Intensely earthy flavors. Most varieties are quite expensive because availability is seasonal and depends on local foragers. Varieties you may find include chanterelles, porcini and morels.

Creamy Basil Mushrooms

PREP TIME: 25 MINUTES ♦ YIELD: 6 (½-CUP) SERVINGS

¼ cup margarine or butter, melted
1 lb. fresh mushrooms, sliced
2 tablespoons chopped green bell pepper
2 tablespoons chopped red bell pepper
½ cup whipping cream
2 tablespoons dry white wine
½ teaspoon salt
¼ teaspoon basil leaves

1. Melt margarine in large skillet over medium heat. Add mushrooms and bell peppers; cook 5 to 7 minutes or until vegetables are tender, stirring occasionally. Remove mushrooms and bell peppers from skillet; cover to keep warm.
2. In same skillet, combine cream, wine, salt and basil. Simmer over low heat for 5 to 7 minutes or until mixture thickens slightly, stirring frequently.
3. Add mushrooms and bell peppers; cook until thoroughly heated.

NUTRITION INFORMATION PER SERVING: Serving Size: ½ Cup ♦ Calories: 160 ♦ Calories from Fat: 140 ♦ % DAILY VALUE: Total Fat: 15 g 23% ♦ Saturated Fat: 6 g 30% ♦ Cholesterol: 25 mg 8% ♦ Sodium: 190 mg 8% ♦ Total Carbohydrate: 4 g 1% ♦ Dietary Fiber: 1 g 4% ♦ Sugars: 2 g ♦ Protein: 2 g ♦ Vitamin A: 15% ♦ Vitamin C: 10% ♦ Calcium: 2% ♦ Iron: 6% ♦ DIETARY EXCHANGES: 1 Vegetable, 3 Fat

Cauliflower Parmesan

PREP TIME: 25 MINUTES ♦ YIELD: 6 (½-CUP) SERVINGS

4 cups fresh cauliflower florets (1 medium head)
1 tablespoon olive oil
2 tablespoons all-purpose flour
½ cup skim milk
⅓ cup water
½ teaspoon chicken-flavor instant bouillon
¼ cup grated Parmesan cheese
¼ cup fresh bread crumbs
¼ teaspoon paprika

1. In medium nonstick saucepan, combine cauliflower and ¼ cup water. Bring to a boil. Reduce heat; cover and simmer 5 to 6 minutes or until cauliflower is crisp-tender. Drain; spoon cauliflower into ungreased 1-quart ovenproof casserole. Set aside.
2. In same saucepan, heat oil over medium

heat until hot. With wire whisk, stir in flour; cook and stir 1 minute. Add milk, ⅓ cup water and bouillon; blend well. Cook 3 minutes or until sauce boils and thickens, stirring constantly. Stir in cheese; cook and stir until cheese is melted. Pour sauce over cauliflower. Sprinkle with bread crumbs and paprika.
3. Broil 4 to 6 inches from heat for 2 minutes or until bread crumbs are golden brown.

NUTRITION INFORMATION PER SERVING: Serving Size: ½ Cup ♦ Calories: 80 ♦ Calories from Fat: 35 ♦ **% DAILY VALUE:** Total Fat: 4 g 6% ♦ Saturated Fat: 1 g 5% ♦ Cholesterol: 4 mg 1% ♦ Sodium: 125 mg 5% ♦ Total Carbohydrate: 8 g 3% ♦ Dietary Fiber: 2 g 8% ♦ Sugars: 3 g ♦ Protein: 4 g ♦ Vitamin A: 2% ♦ Vitamin C: 35% ♦ Calcium: 10% ♦ Iron: 4% ♦ **DIETARY EXCHANGES:** 1 Vegetable, 1 Fat

Fried Eggplant

PREP TIME: 30 MINUTES ✦ YIELD: 6 SERVINGS

- 2 eggs
- 1 teaspoon salt
- 2 tablespoons milk
- 1½ lb. eggplant
- 1¼ to 2 cups unseasoned dry bread crumbs
- ½ cup vegetable or olive oil

1. In small bowl, combine eggs, salt and milk; beat well. Peel eggplant. Cut into ¼-inch-thick slices or cut into strips about ½ inch wide. Dip slices in egg mixture, then in bread crumbs to coat.
2. Heat some of the oil in large skillet until hot. Add some of the eggplant slices; cook until tender and golden brown. (Eggplant will absorb oil rapidly; add oil gradually as eggplant is fried.) Drain slices on paper towels. Repeat with remaining oil and eggplant. If necessary, place eggplant slices in warm oven until serving time.

NUTRITION INFORMATION PER SERVING: Serving Size: ⅙ of Recipe ♦ Calories: 360 ♦ Calories from Fat: 200 ♦ **% DAILY VALUE:** Total Fat: 22 g 34% ♦ Saturated Fat: 3 g 15% ♦ Cholesterol: 70 mg 23% ♦ Sodium: 690 mg 29% ♦ Total Carbohydrate: 32 g 11% ♦ Dietary Fiber: 3 g 12% ♦ Sugars: 6 g ♦ Protein: 8 g ♦ Vitamin A: 4% ♦ Vitamin C: 0% ♦ Calcium: 10% ♦ Iron: 15% ♦ **DIETARY EXCHANGES:** 2 Starch, 1 Vegetable, 4 Fat OR 2 Carbohydrate, 1 Vegetable, 4 Fat

Okra-Corn Medley

PREP TIME: 20 MINUTES ✦ YIELD: 10 (½-CUP) SERVINGS

- 3 slices bacon
- 1 lb. fresh okra, sliced crosswise
- 1 (1-lb.) pkg. frozen whole kernel corn, thawed
- ½ cup chopped red bell pepper
- ¼ teaspoon salt
- ⅛ teaspoon pepper

1. In large nonstick skillet, cook bacon until crisp. Remove bacon from skillet; crumble. Set aside.
2. Drain all but 1 tablespoon bacon drippings from skillet, *or* drain off all drippings and add ¼ cup water to skillet. Add okra; cook over medium heat for 4 to 6 minutes or until crisp-tender, stirring frequently.
3. Stir in crumbled bacon, corn, bell pepper, salt and pepper; cook until thoroughly heated, stirring occasionally.

NUTRITION INFORMATION PER SERVING: Serving Size: ½ Cup ♦ Calories: 90 ♦ Calories from Fat: 25 ♦ **% DAILY VALUE:** Total Fat: 3 g 5% ♦ Saturated Fat: 1 g 5% ♦ Cholesterol: 3 mg 1% ♦ Sodium: 90 mg 4% ♦ Total Carbohydrate: 13 g 4% ♦ Dietary Fiber: 3 g 12% ♦ Sugars: 3 g ♦ Protein: 3 g ♦ Vitamin A: 15% ♦ Vitamin C: 25% ♦ Calcium: 4% ♦ Iron: 4% ♦ **DIETARY EXCHANGES:** ½ Starch, 1 Vegetable, ½ Fat OR ½ Carbohydrate, 1 Vegetable, ½ Fat

Grilled Sweet Onions

PREP TIME: 25 MINUTES ✦ YIELD: 4 SERVINGS

GLAZE
- 2 tablespoons oil
- 1 teaspoon white wine Worcestershire sauce
- ½ to 1 teaspoon sugar
- ⅛ teaspoon salt
- ⅛ teaspoon dried oregano leaves

ONIONS
- 2 sweet onions (Spanish, Bermuda, Vidalia or Walla Walla), cut into ¼-inch-thick slices

1. GRILL DIRECTIONS: Heat grill. In small bowl, combine all glaze ingredients; blend well. If desired, place onions in grill basket.
2. When ready to grill, place onions on gas grill over medium heat or on charcoal grill 4 to 6 inches from medium coals. Cook 10 to 15 minutes or until crisp-tender and lightly browned, brushing both sides with glaze and turning once.

TIP: To broil onions, place on broiler pan; broil 4 to 6 inches from heat using times above as a guide, brushing both sides with glaze and turning once.

NUTRITION INFORMATION PER SERVING: Serving Size: ¼ of Recipe ♦ Calories: 90 ♦ Calories from Fat: 60 ♦ **% DAILY VALUE:** Total Fat: 7 g 11% ♦ Saturated Fat: 1 g 5% ♦ Cholesterol: 0 mg 0% ♦ Sodium: 80 mg 3% ♦ Total Carbohydrate: 6 g 2% ♦ Dietary Fiber: 1 g 4% ♦ Sugars: 4 g ♦ Protein: 1 g ♦ Vitamin A: 0% ♦ Vitamin C: 4% ♦ Calcium: 0% ♦ Iron: 0% ♦ **DIETARY EXCHANGES:** 1 Vegetable, 1½ Fat

Root Vegetable Sauté

PREP TIME: 25 MINUTES ◆ YIELD: 8 (½-CUP) SERVINGS

  2 teaspoons margarine or butter
  ¼ cup water
  1 teaspoon dried sage leaves
  ½ teaspoon chicken-flavor instant bouillon
  2 cups cubed (½-inch) peeled parsnips
  1 cup cubed (½-inch) seeded peeled
      butternut squash
  1 cup cubed (½-inch) peeled rutabaga

1. Melt margarine in large nonstick skillet over medium-high heat. Add all remaining ingredients; mix well.
2. Reduce heat to medium; cover and cook 8 to 10 minutes or until vegetables are tender, stirring occasionally.

NUTRITION INFORMATION PER SERVING: Serving Size: ½ Cup ◆ Calories: 50 ◆ Calories from Fat: 10 ◆ % DAILY VALUE: Total Fat: 1 g 2% ◆ Saturated Fat: 0 g 0% ◆ Cholesterol: 0 mg 0% ◆ Sodium: 80 mg 3% ◆ Total Carbohydrate: 10 g 3% ◆ Dietary Fiber: 2 g 8% ◆ Sugars: 3 g ◆ Protein: 1 g ◆ Vitamin A: 30% ◆ Vitamin C: 15% ◆ Calcium: 4% ◆ Iron: 2% ◆ DIETARY EXCHANGES: ½ Starch OR ½ Carbohydrate

Peas and Mushrooms

PREP TIME: 10 MINUTES ◆ YIELD: 5 (½-CUP) SERVINGS

  2 tablespoons margarine or butter
  ¼ cup chopped celery
  2 tablespoons finely chopped onion
  1 (2.5-oz.) jar sliced mushrooms, drained
  2 cups frozen sweet peas, thawed
  1 (2-oz.) jar diced pimientos, drained

1. Melt margarine in medium saucepan over medium heat. Stir in celery and onion; cook 3 to 4 minutes or until crisp-tender.

Peas and Mushrooms

2. Stir in all remaining ingredients; cook 3 to 5 minutes or until thoroughly heated.

NUTRITION INFORMATION PER SERVING: Serving Size: ½ Cup ◆ Calories: 100 ◆ Calories from Fat: 45 ◆ % DAILY VALUE: Total Fat: 5 g 8% ◆ Saturated Fat: 1 g 5% ◆ Cholesterol: 0 mg 0% ◆ Sodium: 180 mg 8% ◆ Total Carbohydrate: 10 g 3% ◆ Dietary Fiber: 3 g 12% ◆ Sugars: 2 g ◆ Protein: 3 g ◆ Vitamin A: 15% ◆ Vitamin C: 20% ◆ Calcium: 0% ◆ Iron: 6% ◆ DIETARY EXCHANGES: 2 Vegetable, 1 Fat

Pea Pods and Peppers

PREP TIME: 15 MINUTES ◆ YIELD: 4 (½-CUP) SERVINGS

  2 teaspoons margarine or butter
  2 cups fresh snow pea pods
  ½ red bell pepper, cut into julienne strips
  ¼ teaspoon salt
  ¼ teaspoon dried basil leaves
  ⅛ teaspoon pepper
  1 (8-oz.) can sliced water chestnuts, drained

1. Melt margarine in large skillet over medium-high heat. Add pea pods and bell pepper; cook 3 to 4 minutes or until vegetables are crisp-tender, stirring occasionally.
2. Stir in all remaining ingredients; cook until thoroughly heated.

NUTRITION INFORMATION PER SERVING: Serving Size: ½ Cup ◆ Calories: 90 ◆ Calories from Fat: 20 ◆ % DAILY VALUE: Total Fat: 2 g 3% ◆ Saturated Fat: 0 g 0% ◆ Cholesterol: 0 mg 0% ◆ Sodium: 160 mg 7% ◆ Total Carbohydrate: 15 g 5% ◆ Dietary Fiber: 3 g 12% ◆ Sugars: 5 g ◆ Protein: 3 g ◆ Vitamin A: 15% ◆ Vitamin C: 70% ◆ Calcium: 4% ◆ Iron: 8% ◆ DIETARY EXCHANGES: ½ Fruit, 1½ Vegetable, ½ Fat OR ½ Carbohydrate, 1½ Vegetable, ½ Fat

Pea Pod Medley

PREP TIME: 10 MINUTES ◆ YIELD: 4 (½-CUP) SERVINGS

  1 cup frozen sweet peas
  1 cup frozen sugar snap peas
  1 tablespoon margarine or butter
  1 garlic clove, minced

MICROWAVE DIRECTIONS: In 1½-quart microwave-safe casserole, combine all ingredients; cover. Microwave on HIGH for 5 to 6 minutes or until vegetables are thoroughly heated, stirring twice during cooking.

NUTRITION INFORMATION PER SERVING: Serving Size: ½ Cup ◆ Calories: 60 ◆ Calories from Fat: 25 ◆ % DAILY VALUE: Total Fat: 3 g 5% ◆ Saturated Fat: 1 g 5% ◆ Cholesterol: 0 mg 0% ◆ Sodium: 70 mg 3% ◆ Total Carbohydrate: 6 g 2% ◆ Dietary Fiber: 2 g 8% ◆ Sugars: 2 g ◆ Protein: 2 g ◆ Vitamin A: 8% ◆ Vitamin C: 20% ◆ Calcium: 0% ◆ Iron: 4% ◆ DIETARY EXCHANGES: 1 Vegetable, ½ Fat

Roasted Peppers with Garlic

1. In jar with tight-fitting lid, combine all dressing ingredients; shake well. Set aside.
2. In medium bowl, combine pepper strips and olives. Pour dressing over pepper mixture; let stand 10 minutes.
3. Line serving platter with lettuce. Decoratively arrange peppers and olives over lettuce. Sprinkle with basil. Serve warm or at room temperature.

NUTRITION INFORMATION PER SERVING: Serving Size: ½ Cup ◆ Calories: 100 ◆ Calories from Fat: 70 ◆ % DAILY VALUE: Total Fat: 8 g 12% ◆ Saturated Fat: 1 g 5% ◆ Cholesterol: 0 mg 0% ◆ Sodium: 280 mg 12% ◆ Total Carbohydrate: 6 g 2% ◆ Dietary Fiber: 1 g 4% ◆ Sugars: 1 g ◆ Protein: 1 g ◆ Vitamin A: 35% ◆ Vitamin C: 90% ◆ Calcium: 2% ◆ Iron: 4% ◆ DIETARY EXCHANGES: 1 Vegetable, 1½ Fat

Roasted Pepper

PREP TIME: 20 MINUTES ◆ YIELD: 1 ROASTED PEPPER

1. Cut 1 large bell pepper in half; remove seeds. Place pepper, cut side down, on broiler pan. Broil 4 to 6 inches from heat for 5 to 10 minutes or until skin has blackened. Wrap pepper halves in damp paper towel and place in plastic bag. Cool 10 minutes.
2. Peel skin from pepper halves; discard skin. Use roasted pepper as directed in recipe.

> **TIP:** Several peppers can be roasted at one time with no change in broiling time. Wrap 2 pepper halves in damp paper towel and place in plastic bag; repeat for additional peppers. Continue as directed above.

NUTRITION INFORMATION PER SERVING: Serving Size: 1 Roasted Pepper ◆ Calories: 30 ◆ Calories from Fat: 0 ◆ % DAILY VALUE: Total Fat: 0 g 0% ◆ Saturated Fat: 0 g 0% ◆ Cholesterol: 0 mg 0% ◆ Sodium: 0 mg 0% ◆ Total Carbohydrate: 7 g 2% ◆ Dietary Fiber: 2 g 8% ◆ Sugars: 3 g ◆ Protein: 1 g ◆ Vitamin A: 15% ◆ Vitamin C: 150% ◆ Calcium: 0% ◆ Iron: 2% ◆ DIETARY EXCHANGES: 1 Vegetable

Roasted Peppers with Garlic

PREP TIME: 25 MINUTES ◆ YIELD: 4 (½-CUP) SERVINGS

DRESSING
- 2 garlic cloves, minced
- 2 tablespoons red wine vinegar
- 2 tablespoons olive oil
- ¼ teaspoon salt
- ¼ teaspoon freshly ground black pepper

SALAD
- 1 roasted red bell pepper, cut into strips
- 1 roasted green bell pepper, cut into strips
- 1 roasted yellow bell pepper, cut into strips
- ⅓ cup halved ripe olives
- Leaf lettuce
- 2 tablespoons chopped fresh basil

New Potatoes with Chive Butter

PREP TIME: 15 MINUTES (READY IN 40 MINUTES) ◆ YIELD: 6 SERVINGS

- 1 to 1½ lb. small new potatoes
- 1 tablespoon butter, melted
- 1 tablespoon chopped fresh chives
- ¼ to ½ teaspoon salt
- Dash pepper

1. Scrub or peel potatoes. In medium saucepan, cook potatoes in small amount of boiling water for 15 to 25 minutes or until fork-tender. Drain well. Return potatoes to saucepan or place in serving bowl.
2. Add butter, chives, salt and pepper; toss gently to coat.

NUTRITION INFORMATION PER SERVING: Serving Size: ⅙ of Recipe ◆ Calories: 150 ◆ Calories from Fat: 20 ◆ % DAILY VALUE: Total Fat: 2 g 3% ◆ Saturated Fat: 1 g 5% ◆ Cholesterol: 5 mg 2% ◆ Sodium: 210 mg 9% ◆ Total Carbohydrate: 29 g 10% ◆ Dietary Fiber: 3 g 12% ◆ Sugars: 1 g ◆ Protein: 3 g ◆ Vitamin A: 0% ◆ Vitamin C: 15% ◆ Calcium: 0% ◆ Iron: 8% ◆ DIETARY EXCHANGES: 1½ Starch, ½ Fat OR 1½ Carbohydrate, ½ Fat

New Potatoes with Chive Butter

Baked Potatoes

PREP TIME: 10 MINUTES (READY IN 1 HOUR 10 MINUTES)

1. OVEN DIRECTIONS: Heat oven to 350 to 400°F. Select medium white baking potatoes (uniform for same baking time). Scrub potatoes. If desired, rub with small amount of shortening to soften skins. Prick with fork to allow steam to escape.
2. Bake at 350°F. for about 1 hour or at 400°F. for 45 to 50 minutes or until tender.
3. Using paper towels to protect hands from heat, roll potatoes between hands to make inside potato mixture light and mealy. Cut criss-cross slit in tops; gently squeeze lower part of potato to force potato up through slit. If desired, top with margarine or butter; sprinkle with salt and pepper.

1. MICROWAVE DIRECTIONS: To microwave 1 medium white baking potato, place in center of microwave. Microwave on HIGH for 3 to 4 minutes or until tender. For each additional potato, add 2 to 3 minutes cooking time.
2. Cover; let stand 2 to 3 minutes before serving. Continue as directed above.

TIP: Baked potatoes can be served with any of the following toppings:
Bacon, cooked, crumbled
Blue cheese, crumbled
Cheddar cheese, shredded
Cheese Sauce, page 314
Garlic or onion salt
Green onions, sliced
Margarine or butter, whipped
   with 2 teaspoons lemon juice
   and 2 teaspoons chopped fresh parsley
Onion, chopped, cooked in margarine or
   butter
Sour cream and chives
Whipped cream cheese

NUTRITION INFORMATION PER SERVING: Serving Size: 1 Medium Baked Potato ◆ Calories: 140 ◆ Calories from Fat: 0 ◆ % DAILY VALUE: Total Fat: 0 g 0% ◆ Saturated Fat: 0 g 0% ◆ Cholesterol: 0 mg 0% ◆ Sodium: 10 mg 0% ◆ Total Carbohydrate: 31 g 10% ◆ Dietary Fiber: 3 g 12% ◆ Sugars: 1 g ◆ Protein: 3 g ◆ Vitamin A: 0% ◆ Vitamin C: 25% ◆ Calcium: 0% ◆ Iron: 10% ◆ DIETARY EXCHANGES: 2 Starch OR 2 Carbohydrate

VARIATIONS

Quick Baked Potatoes: Halve potatoes lengthwise; cut surfaces in criss-cross pattern (do not cut skins). Sprinkle lightly with onion salt and garlic salt. Dot with margarine or butter. Place in ungreased shallow baking pan. Bake at 425°F. for about 30 minutes or until tender. Sprinkle with paprika.

Quick Microwaved Potatoes: Halve potatoes lengthwise; cut surfaces in criss-cross pattern (do not cut skins). Sprinkle lightly with onion salt and garlic salt. Dot with margarine or butter. Place 4 potato halves in 8-inch square (2-quart) microwave-safe dish; cover with microwave-safe plastic wrap. Microwave on HIGH for 10 to 12 minutes or until potatoes begin to feel tender, rotating potatoes once during cooking. Remove from microwave. Let stand covered 2 minutes. Sprinkle with paprika.

COOK'S NOTE

POTATO POINTERS

◆ Mealy textured potatoes, commonly called Idahos or Russets, have thick brown skin and a dry, mealy texture that makes them excellent for baking, frying and mashing.

◆ Waxy potatoes, also known as all-purpose or thin-skinned potatoes, include round white- or red-skinned potatoes, long white-skinned potatoes, Yukon Gold potatoes with buttery-yellow flesh, and even purple potatoes. Waxy potatoes, so called for their moist, smooth flesh, are excellent for boiling and steaming and can also be baked or fried.

◆ New potatoes are generally small, freshly harvested thin-skinned potatoes. They are wonderful boiled in their "jackets" (unpeeled), then tossed with butter and chopped parsley.

◆ Fingerling potatoes, available in some markets, come in many shapes and sizes, though many do resemble a finger in size and shape.

◆ Sweet potatoes come in two basic varieties. Dry sweet potatoes have a pale orange flesh that is dry and mealy after cooking. Moist sweet potatoes have a bright orange flesh and are sweet and moist when cooked. Moist sweet potatoes are often incorrectly sold as "yams." However, yams, which may be found in Caribbean markets but rarely make it into mainstream supermarkets, are a different species altogether.

Baked Stuffed Potatoes

PREP TIME: 20 MINUTES (READY IN 1 HOUR 45 MINUTES)
✦ YIELD: 6 SERVINGS

6 medium baking potatoes, scrubbed, pierced
⅔ cup sour cream
¼ cup margarine or butter, softened
½ teaspoon salt
¼ teaspoon dry mustard
⅛ teaspoon pepper
1 (2-oz.) jar chopped pimientos, drained

1. Heat oven to 375°F. If desired, rub potatoes with shortening or wrap in foil. Bake at 375°F. for about 1 hour or until tender.
2. Cut a slice from top of each potato; carefully scoop out potato pulp into large bowl. Add sour cream, margarine, salt, mustard and pepper; beat until smooth and fluffy. Stir in pimientos. Spoon mixture into potato shells. Place in ungreased 13 × 9-inch pan.
3. Bake an additional 20 to 25 minutes or until lightly browned.

NUTRITION INFORMATION PER SERVING: Serving Size: ⅙ of Recipe ✦ Calories: 270 ✦ Calories from Fat: 120 ✦ **% DAILY VALUE:** Total Fat: 13 g 20% ✦ Saturated Fat: 5 g 25% ✦ Cholesterol: 10 mg 3% ✦ Sodium: 290 mg 12% ✦ Total Carbohydrate: 33 g 11% ✦ Dietary Fiber: 3 g 12% ✦ Sugars: 3 g ✦ Protein: 4 g ✦ Vitamin A: 15% ✦ Vitamin C: 35% ✦ Calcium: 4% ✦ Iron: 10% ✦ **DIETARY EXCHANGES:** 2 Starch, 2½ Fat OR 2 Carbohydrate, 2½ Fat

Au Gratin Potatoes

PREP TIME: 20 MINUTES (READY IN 1 HOUR 50 MINUTES)
✦ YIELD: 6 SERVINGS

¼ cup margarine or butter
¼ cup all-purpose flour
½ teaspoon salt
2 cups milk
4 oz. (1 cup) shredded American or Cheddar cheese
½ cup grated Parmesan cheese
5 cups (5 medium) sliced peeled potatoes
¼ cup unseasoned dry bread crumbs
1 tablespoon margarine or butter, melted

1. Heat oven to 350°F. Grease 2-quart casserole or 6 individual casserole dishes. In medium saucepan, melt ¼ cup margarine. Stir in flour and salt; add milk. Cook until mixture boils and thickens, stirring constantly.
2. Stir in cheeses and potatoes. Pour into greased casserole. Combine crumbs with 1 tablespoon margarine; sprinkle over potatoes. Cover.

3. Bake at 350°F. for 1 to 1½ hours or until potatoes are tender. If desired, garnish with chopped chives.

TIP: Potatoes can be cooked before combining with other ingredients. Reduce baking time to 30 to 35 minutes.

NUTRITION INFORMATION PER SERVING: Serving Size: ⅙ of Recipe ✦ Calories: 370 ✦ Calories from Fat: 180 ✦ **% DAILY VALUE:** Total Fat: 20 g 31% ✦ Saturated Fat: 8 g 40% ✦ Cholesterol: 30 mg 10% ✦ Sodium: 800 mg 33% ✦ Total Carbohydrate: 34 g 11% ✦ Dietary Fiber: 2 g 8% ✦ Sugars: 6 g ✦ Protein: 14 g ✦ Vitamin A: 15% ✦ Vitamin C: 15% ✦ Calcium: 35% ✦ Iron: 6% ✦ **DIETARY EXCHANGES:** 2½ Starch, 1 High-Fat Meat, 2 Fat OR 2½ Carbohydrate, 1 High-Fat Meat, 2 Fat

COOKING POTATOES

METHOD	INSTRUCTIONS
Baking	Pierce potatoes with fork and oil lightly, if desired. Place the potatoes in a baking pan, or wrap them in foil and place directly on the oven rack. Bake in 350°F. oven until tender, about 1 hour.
Microwaving	Pierce potatoes with fork and arrange spoke-fashion on a microwave-safe dinner plate. Cook on HIGH power until tender, about 6 minutes for 1 potato; 12 minutes for 2.
Steaming	Steam small potatoes whole; cut larger ones into chunks or slices. Cook in a steamer basket set over boiling water until tender.
Boiling	In a large saucepan, cover potatoes with cold water and bring to a boil. Reduce heat to a simmer and cook until tender, 15 to 25 minutes.
Grilling	Lightly oil potatoes and pierce with fork. Wrap whole or sliced potatoes in two layers of foil. Set the potatoes directly into the coals and cook until tender.

Perfect Mashed Potatoes

Perfect Mashed Potatoes

PREP TIME: 20 MINUTES (READY IN 45 MINUTES)
✦ YIELD: 8 (½-CUP) SERVINGS

    4 medium russet potatoes (about 1½ lb.),
        peeled, cut into quarters
    ¾ teaspoon salt
    1 to 2 tablespoons margarine or butter,
        if desired
       Dash pepper
    ¼ to ⅓ cup hot milk

1. Place potatoes in large saucepan; add enough water to cover. Add ½ teaspoon of the salt. Bring to a boil. Reduce heat to medium-low; cover loosely and boil gently for 15 to 20 minutes or until potatoes break apart easily when pierced with fork. Drain well.
2. Return potatoes to saucepan; shake saucepan gently over low heat for 1 to 2 minutes to evaporate any excess moisture.
3. Mash potatoes with potato masher until no lumps remain. Add margarine, pepper and remaining ¼ teaspoon salt; continue mashing, gradually adding enough milk to make potatoes smooth and creamy.

NUTRITION INFORMATION PER SERVING: Serving Size: ½ Cup ◆ Calories: 100 ◆ Calories from Fat: 25 ◆ **% DAILY VALUE:** Total Fat: 3 g 5% ◆ Saturated Fat: 1 g 5% ◆ Cholesterol: 0 mg 0% ◆ Sodium: 180 mg 8% ◆ Total Carbohydrate: 16 g 5% ◆ Dietary Fiber: 1 g 4% ◆ Sugars: 1 g ◆ Protein: 2 g ◆ Vitamin A: 2% ◆ Vitamin C: 10% ◆ Calcium: 0% ◆ Iron: 0% ◆ **DIETARY EXCHANGES:** 1 Starch, ½ Fat OR 1 Carbohydrate, ½ Fat

VARIATIONS

Cheesy Garlic and Chive Mashed Potatoes: Prepare recipe as directed except add 2 quartered garlic cloves to potato cooking water; omit salt. Continue as directed except after mashing potatoes and garlic, stir in ½ cup warm buttermilk or milk, ⅓ cup shredded Cheddar cheese, 1 tablespoon chopped fresh or 1 teaspoon freeze-dried chopped chives and ¼ teaspoon salt.

Herbed Mashed Potatoes: Prepare recipe as directed except after mashing potatoes, add 2 tablespoons chopped fresh parsley, 1 tablespoon margarine or butter, 2 teaspoons chopped fresh or ½ teaspoon dried basil leaves, and an additional ½ teaspoon salt. Continue mashing, gradually adding ¼ to ½ cup milk until potatoes are smooth and creamy.

Low-Fat French Fries

PREP TIME: 10 MINUTES (READY IN 35 MINUTES)
✦ YIELD: 6 SERVINGS

    3 large baking potatoes, unpeeled, cut
        into ⅜-inch-thick strips
    1 tablespoon oil
       Seasoned salt

1. Heat oven to 425°F. Spray large cookie sheet with nonstick cooking spray.
2. Place potatoes and oil in plastic bag; shake until well coated. Arrange in single layer on sprayed cookie sheet.
3. Bake at 425°F. for 15 minutes. Carefully turn potatoes; sprinkle lightly with seasoned salt. Bake an additional 5 minutes or until tender. If desired, broil 1 to 2 minutes for additional browning.

NUTRITION INFORMATION PER SERVING: Serving Size: ⅙ of Recipe ◆ Calories: 100 ◆ Calories from Fat: 20 ◆ **% DAILY VALUE:** Total Fat: 2 g 3% ◆ Saturated Fat: 0 g 0% ◆ Cholesterol: 0 mg 0% ◆ Sodium: 70 mg 3% ◆ Total Carbohydrate: 18 g 6% ◆ Dietary Fiber: 2 g 8% ◆ Sugars: 1 g ◆ Protein: 2 g ◆ Vitamin A: 0% ◆ Vitamin C: 10% ◆ Calcium: 0% ◆ Iron: 6% ◆ **DIETARY EXCHANGES:** 1 Starch, ½ Fat OR 1 Carbohydrate, ½ Fat

Low-Fat French Fries

Seasoned Oven Potatoes

Seasoned Oven Potatoes

PREP TIME: 10 MINUTES (READY IN 1 HOUR 10 MINUTES)
♦ YIELD: 4 SERVINGS

- ½ teaspoon dried parsley flakes
- ½ teaspoon onion powder
- ½ teaspoon salt
- 2 tablespoons oil
- 3 to 4 medium baking potatoes, cut into 1 to 1½-inch cubes (3 cups)

1. Heat oven to 350°F. In ungreased 12 × 8-inch (2-quart) baking dish, combine parsley flakes, onion powder, salt and oil; blend well. Add potatoes; toss to coat well.
2. Bake at 350°F. for 50 to 60 minutes or until tender, stirring once during baking. Drain potatoes on paper towels.

NUTRITION INFORMATION PER SERVING: Serving Size: ¼ of Recipe ♦ Calories: 200 ♦ Calories from Fat: 60 ♦ **% DAILY VALUE:** Total Fat: 7 g 11% ♦ Saturated Fat: 1 g 5% ♦ Cholesterol: 0 mg 0% ♦ Sodium: 280 mg 12% ♦ Total Carbohydrate: 31 g 10% ♦ Dietary Fiber: 3 g 12% ♦ Sugars: 1 g ♦ Protein: 3 g ♦ Vitamin A: 0% ♦ Vitamin C: 20% ♦ Calcium: 0% ♦ Iron: 10% ♦ **DIETARY EXCHANGES:** 2 Starch, 1 Fat OR 2 Carbohydrate, 1 Fat

---

C O O K ' S   N O T E

COOKING POTATOES

To cook potatoes in their skins, first scrub them and trim away soft spots or eyes and pare away any green coloration under the skin. Keep peeled or cut potatoes submerged in a bowl of cold water until cooking time to prevent discoloration. Start with potatoes that are all about the same size or cut them into uniformly sized pieces for even cooking.

Potato Pancakes

PREP TIME: 45 MINUTES ♦ YIELD: 16 PANCAKES

- 6 cups shredded peeled potatoes*
- 1 cup finely chopped onion
- ¼ cup all-purpose flour
- 6 eggs, beaten
- 2 teaspoons salt
- ¼ teaspoon pepper
- Oil

1. Place shredded potatoes in clean cloth; squeeze to remove excess moisture. In medium bowl, combine potatoes and all remaining ingredients except oil.
2. Heat ¼ inch oil in large, heavy skillet over medium heat until hot. Using about ⅓ cup potato mixture for each, form very thin pancake patties 3 to 4 inches in diameter. Fry 2 to 3 minutes on each side or until lightly browned. Drain on paper towels. If needed, add more oil to skillet to fry remaining pancakes. If desired, serve with applesauce.

TIP: * Shred potatoes into cold water to prevent darkening. Drain well.

NUTRITION INFORMATION PER SERVING: Serving Size: 1 Pancake ♦ Calories: 170 ♦ Calories from Fat: 110 ♦ **% DAILY VALUE:** Total Fat: 12 g 18% ♦ Saturated Fat: 2 g 10% ♦ Cholesterol: 80 mg 27% ♦ Sodium: 290 mg 12% ♦ Total Carbohydrate: 12 g 4% ♦ Dietary Fiber: 1 g 4% ♦ Sugars: 1 g ♦ Protein: 4 g ♦ Vitamin A: 2% ♦ Vitamin C: 8% ♦ Calcium: 0% ♦ Iron: 4% ♦ **DIETARY EXCHANGES:** 1 Starch, 2 Fat OR 1 Carbohydrate, 2 Fat

Potato Pancakes

Spuds 'n Onions

PREP TIME: 1 HOUR 15 MINUTES ◆ YIELD: 4 SERVINGS

    4 medium baking potatoes
    ¼ cup margarine or butter, softened
    2 medium mild onions
      Salt
      Pepper
      Paprika, if desired

1. GRILL DIRECTIONS: Heat grill. Cut four 12-inch-square pieces of heavy-duty foil. If desired, peel potatoes. Make 4 or 5 crosswise cuts in each potato, cutting to but not through bottom. Spread margarine between slices.
2. Cut each onion into 8 to 10 thin slices. Insert onion slice into each potato slice. Sprinkle with salt, pepper and paprika. Place each potato on square of foil. Wrap each packet securely using double-fold seals, allowing room for heat expansion.
3. When ready to grill, place packets, seam side up, on gas grill over medium-high heat or on charcoal grill 4 to 6 inches from medium-high coals. Cook 40 to 50 minutes or until vegetables are tender, turning occasionally. Open packets carefully to allow hot steam to escape.

> TIP: To bake potato packets, place, seam side up, in 15 x 10 x 1-inch baking pan; bake at 400°F. for 45 to 50 minutes.

NUTRITION INFORMATION PER SERVING: Serving Size: ¼ of Recipe ◆ Calories: 270 ◆ Calories from Fat: 110 ◆ % DAILY VALUE: Total Fat: 12 g 18% ◆ Saturated Fat: 2 g 10% ◆ Cholesterol: 0 mg 0% ◆ Sodium: 280 mg 12% ◆ Total Carbohydrate: 36 g 12% ◆ Dietary Fiber: 4 g 16% ◆ Sugars: 4 g ◆ Protein: 4 g ◆ Vitamin A: 10% ◆ Vitamin C: 25% ◆ Calcium: 2% ◆ Iron: 10% ◆ DIETARY EXCHANGES: 2 Starch, 1 Vegetable, 2 Fat OR 2 Carbohydrate, 1 Vegetable, 2 Fat

Scalloped Potatoes

PREP TIME: 20 MINUTES (READY IN 2 HOURS 20 MINUTES) ◆ YIELD: 4 SERVINGS

    4 medium potatoes, peeled, thinly sliced
    1 small onion, sliced, if desired
    2 tablespoons margarine or butter
    2 tablespoons all-purpose flour
    1 teaspoon salt
    ⅛ teaspoon pepper
    1½ cups milk

1. Heat oven to 350°F. Grease 1½ to 2-quart casserole. Place potatoes and onion in greased casserole.

2. Melt margarine in medium saucepan. Stir in flour, salt and pepper until well blended. Cook until smooth and bubbly, stirring constantly. Gradually add milk, cooking until mixture boils and thickens, stirring constantly. Pour sauce over potatoes and onion.
3. Bake at 350°F. for 1½ to 2 hours or until potatoes are tender. If desired, garnish with crumbled bacon.

> TIPS: For a layered version, place ⅓ of potatoes and half of onion slices in greased casserole. Sprinkle with 1 tablespoon all-purpose flour, ½ teaspoon salt and dash pepper; dot with 1 tablespoon margarine. Repeat layering, ending with potatoes on top. Pour milk over potatoes. Bake as directed.
>   One 10¾-oz. can condensed cream of mushroom or celery soup combined with ½ cup milk can be substituted for the white sauce.
>   For a main dish, add 1 cup cubed cooked ham.

NUTRITION INFORMATION PER SERVING: Serving Size: ¼ of Recipe ◆ Calories: 210 ◆ Calories from Fat: 70 ◆ % DAILY VALUE: Total Fat: 8 g 12% ◆ Saturated Fat: 2 g 10% ◆ Cholesterol: 5 mg 2% ◆ Sodium: 650 mg 27% ◆ Total Carbohydrate: 29 g 10% ◆ Dietary Fiber: 2 g 8% ◆ Sugars: 6 g ◆ Protein: 6 g ◆ Vitamin A: 8% ◆ Vitamin C: 15% ◆ Calcium: 10% ◆ Iron: 4% ◆ DIETARY EXCHANGES: 2 Starch, 1½ Fat OR 2 Carbohydrate, 1½ Fat

Stuffed Sweet Potatoes

PREP TIME: 45 MINUTES ◆ YIELD: 6 SERVINGS

    6 dark-orange sweet potatoes
      (about 8 oz. each)
    ⅔ cup buttermilk
    2 tablespoons sliced green onions
    ¼ teaspoon salt
    ⅛ teaspoon pepper
    3 tablespoons shredded reduced-fat sharp
      Cheddar cheese

1. MICROWAVE DIRECTIONS: Scrub potatoes; pierce several times with tip of knife. Place in microwave on microwave-safe paper towel; cover with another paper towel. Microwave on HIGH for 15 to 20 minutes or until potatoes are tender, rearranging once.
2. Spray 13 x 9-inch (3-quart) baking dish with nonstick cooking spray. Cut thin slice from top of each cooked potato. Scoop out each potato, leaving ¼-inch-thick shell. Place potato pulp in large bowl; mash with electric mixer on medium-low speed or potato masher.

3. Add buttermilk, onions, salt and pepper; mix well. Fill potato shells with mixture; place in sprayed baking dish. Sprinkle cheese over tops of potatoes.

4. Broil 4 to 6 inches from heat for about 1 minute or until cheese is melted.

NUTRITION INFORMATION PER SERVING: Serving Size: ⅙ of Recipe ◆ Calories: 270 ◆ Calories from Fat: 20 ◆ **% DAILY VALUE:** Total Fat: 2 g 3% ◆ Saturated Fat: 1 g 5% ◆ Cholesterol: 3 mg 1% ◆ Sodium: 180 mg 8% ◆ Total Carbohydrate: 57 g 19% ◆ Dietary Fiber: 7 g 28% ◆ Sugars: 14 g ◆ Protein: 6 g ◆ Vitamin A: 910% ◆ Vitamin C: 60% ◆ Calcium: 10% ◆ Iron: 8% ◆ **DIETARY EXCHANGES:** 3½ Starch OR 3½ Carbohydrate

Maple-Cinnamon Sweet Potatoes

PREP TIME: 20 MINUTES ◆ YIELD: 8 (½-CUP) SERVINGS

    4 small dark-orange sweet potatoes, peeled, cut into ¾-inch cubes (about 4 cups)
    ¼ cup real maple syrup or maple-flavored syrup
    ½ teaspoon cinnamon
    2 tablespoons finely chopped walnuts

1. In large saucepan, bring 4 cups water to a boil. Add sweet potatoes; return to a boil. Cook over medium heat for 8 to 12 minutes or until tender. Drain well. Return sweet potatoes to saucepan or place in serving bowl.

2. Meanwhile, in small bowl, combine syrup and cinnamon; mix well. Add to sweet potatoes; toss gently to coat. Just before serving, sprinkle with walnuts.

NUTRITION INFORMATION PER SERVING: Serving Size: ½ Cup ◆ Calories: 110 ◆ Calories from Fat: 10 ◆ **% DAILY VALUE:** Total Fat: 1 g 2% ◆ Saturated Fat: 0 g 0% ◆ Cholesterol: 0 mg 0% ◆ Sodium: 10 mg 0% ◆ Total Carbohydrate: 23 g 8% ◆ Dietary Fiber: 2 g 8% ◆ Sugars: 10 g ◆ Protein: 1 g ◆ Vitamin A: 260% ◆ Vitamin C: 15% ◆ Calcium: 2% ◆ Iron: 4% ◆ **DIETARY EXCHANGES:** 1 Starch, ½ Fruit OR 1½ Carbohydrate

Mashed Rutabagas

PREP TIME: 20 MINUTES (READY IN 45 MINUTES)
◆ YIELD: 6 SERVINGS

    2 to 3 medium rutabagas, peeled, cubed
    ½ teaspoon salt
    ⅛ teaspoon pepper
        Dash nutmeg, if desired
    ¼ cup warm milk
    ¼ cup margarine or butter

1. In medium saucepan, cook rutabaga cubes in boiling water for 20 to 25 minutes or until tender. Drain.

2. In large bowl, mash hot rutabagas. Add all remaining ingredients; beat until light and fluffy.

NUTRITION INFORMATION PER SERVING: Serving Size: ⅙ of Recipe ◆ Calories: 140 ◆ Calories from Fat: 70 ◆ **% DAILY VALUE:** Total Fat: 8 g 12% ◆ Saturated Fat: 2 g 10% ◆ Cholesterol: 0 mg 0% ◆ Sodium: 310 mg 13% ◆ Total Carbohydrate: 15 g 5% ◆ Dietary Fiber: 5 g 20% ◆ Sugars: 11 g ◆ Protein: 3 g ◆ Vitamin A: 30% ◆ Vitamin C: 50% ◆ Calcium: 10% ◆ Iron: 6% ◆ **DIETARY EXCHANGES:** 1 Starch, 1½ Fat OR 1 Carbohydrate, 1½ Fat

Steamed Nutmeg Spinach

PREP TIME: 15 MINUTES ◆ YIELD: 3 (½-CUP) SERVINGS

    1 tablespoon olive or vegetable oil
    1 (10-oz.) pkg. fresh prewashed spinach (about 12 cups)
    2 tablespoons apple juice
    ¼ teaspoon nutmeg

1. Heat oil in large nonstick skillet or Dutch oven over medium-high heat until hot. Add half of spinach; cook and stir 1 to 2 minutes or until spinach starts to wilt.

2. Add remaining spinach; cook and stir until wilted. Reduce heat; cover and simmer 5 to 7 minutes or until tender.

3. With slotted spoon, place spinach in serving bowl. Add apple juice and nutmeg; stir gently.

NUTRITION INFORMATION PER SERVING: Serving Size: ½ Cup ◆ Calories: 80 ◆ Calories from Fat: 45 ◆ **% DAILY VALUE:** Total Fat: 5 g 8% ◆ Saturated Fat: 1 g 5% ◆ Cholesterol: 0 mg 0% ◆ Sodium: 75 mg 3% ◆ Total Carbohydrate: 5 g 2% ◆ Dietary Fiber: 3 g 12% ◆ Sugars: 1 g ◆ Protein: 3 g ◆ Vitamin A: 130% ◆ Vitamin C: 30% ◆ Calcium: 10% ◆ Iron: 15% ◆ **DIETARY EXCHANGES:** 1 Vegetable, 1 Fat

COOK'S NOTE

SUMMER SQUASH

Summer squash has tender, edible skin that rarely needs peeling. Use zucchini and yellow squash interchangeably, or combine the two for color contrast.

Yellow summer squash
Shiny yellow skin; elongated shape with bottom slightly more bulbous. Neck may be straight or slightly crooked. Pale yellow flesh with edible seeds.

Zucchini
Dark green, elongated squash. Pale green interior with edible seeds.

Zucchini with Tomatoes and Basil

Summer Squash Sauté

PREP TIME: 20 MINUTES ✦ YIELD: 6 (⅔-CUP) SERVINGS

 1 tablespoon olive or vegetable oil
 2 small zucchini, sliced
 2 small yellow summer squash, sliced
 2 large garlic cloves, minced
 1 small onion, thinly sliced
 1½ cups (4 oz.) sliced fresh mushrooms
 1 tablespoon chopped fresh dill
 1 tablespoon chopped fresh chives
 ¼ teaspoon salt
    Dash coarse ground black pepper

1. Heat oil in large skillet over medium-high heat until hot. Add zucchini, summer squash, garlic and onion; cook 2 to 3 minutes, stirring frequently.

Summer Squash Sauté

2. Add mushrooms, dill, chives, salt and pepper; mix gently. Cook 3 to 4 minutes or until vegetables are crisp-tender, stirring occasionally.

NUTRITION INFORMATION PER SERVING: Serving Size: ⅔ Cup ✦ Calories: 60 ✦ Calories from Fat: 25 ✦ **% DAILY VALUE:** Total Fat: 3 g 5% ✦ Saturated Fat: 0 g 0% ✦ Cholesterol: 0 mg 0% ✦ Sodium: 95 mg 4% ✦ Total Carbohydrate: 7 g 2% ✦ Dietary Fiber: 3 g 12% ✦ Sugars: 3 g ✦ Protein: 2 g ✦ Vitamin A: 8% ✦ Vitamin C: 25% ✦ Calcium: 4% ✦ Iron: 6% ✦ **DIETARY EXCHANGES:** 1 Vegetable, ½ Fat

Zucchini with Tomatoes and Basil

PREP TIME: 15 MINUTES ✦ YIELD: 5 (½-CUP) SERVINGS

 4 small zucchini (½ lb.), cut
    into ½-inch-thick slices
 1 cup coarsely chopped tomatoes
 2 tablespoons chopped fresh basil
 ¼ teaspoon salt
 ⅛ teaspoon pepper
 2 teaspoons lemon juice
 2 tablespoons shredded fresh Parmesan
    cheese, if desired

1. In medium saucepan, combine zucchini and ¼ cup water. Cook over medium heat for 3 to 4 minutes or until crisp-tender. Drain well.

2. Add tomatoes, basil, salt, pepper and lemon juice; mix well. Cook and stir about 1 minute or until thoroughly heated. Sprinkle with cheese.

NUTRITION INFORMATION PER SERVING: Serving Size: ½ Cup ✦ Calories: 30 ✦ Calories from Fat: 10 ✦ **% DAILY VALUE:** Total Fat: 1 g 2% ✦ Saturated Fat: 0 g 0% ✦ Cholesterol: 0 mg 0% ✦ Sodium: 150 mg 6% ✦ Total Carbohydrate: 3 g 1% ✦ Dietary Fiber: 1 g 4% ✦ Sugars: 2 g ✦ Protein: 2 g ✦ Vitamin A: 8% ✦ Vitamin C: 15% ✦ Calcium: 4% ✦ Iron: 2% ✦ **DIETARY EXCHANGES:** 1 Vegetable

Buttercup Squash Casserole

PREP TIME: 10 MINUTES (READY IN 1 HOUR 25 MINUTES)
✦ YIELD: 4 (½-CUP) SERVINGS

    1 medium buttercup squash
    2 tablespoons brown sugar
    ¼ teaspoon salt
    ¼ teaspoon cinnamon
    ¼ teaspoon nutmeg
    2 tablespoons margarine or butter
    1 tablespoon chopped fresh chives
    ⅛ teaspoon nutmeg, if desired

1. Heat oven to 350°F. Cut squash into quarters; remove seeds. Place, cut side down, in ungreased shallow baking pan. Bake at 350°F. for 45 to 50 minutes or until tender. Cool slightly.
2. Grease 1-quart casserole. Scoop squash pulp from skin; place in medium bowl. Discard skin. Add brown sugar, salt, cinnamon, ¼ teaspoon nutmeg and margarine to squash. Mix with potato masher or fork until well blended. Spoon into greased casserole. Sprinkle with chives and ⅛ teaspoon nutmeg.
3. Bake at 350°F. for 20 to 25 minutes or until thoroughly heated.

NUTRITION INFORMATION PER SERVING: Serving Size: ½ Cup ✦ Calories: 160 ✦ Calories from Fat: 60 ✦ **% DAILY VALUE:** Total Fat: 7 g 11% ✦ Saturated Fat: 1 g 5% ✦ Cholesterol: 0 mg 0% ✦ Sodium: 210 mg 9% ✦ Total Carbohydrate: 23 g 8% ✦ Dietary Fiber: 6 g 24% ✦ Sugars: 13 g ✦ Protein: 2 g ✦ Vitamin A: 140% ✦ Vitamin C: 20% ✦ Calcium: 4% ✦ Iron: 4% ✦ **DIETARY EXCHANGES:** 1 Starch, ½ Fruit, 1 Fat OR 1½ Carbohydrate, 1 Fat

Buttercup Squash Casserole

Baked Squash with Pecan Brittle

Baked Squash with Pecan Brittle

PREP TIME: 15 MINUTES (READY IN 1 HOUR 10 MINUTES)
✦ YIELD: 4 SERVINGS

    2 tablespoons chopped pecans
    1 tablespoon brown sugar
    1 tablespoon orange juice
    2 teaspoons margarine or butter, melted
    ⅛ teaspoon cinnamon
    1 (1½-lb.) acorn squash

1. Heat oven to 350°F. Line 8-inch square pan with foil; spray foil with nonstick cooking spray.
2. In small bowl, combine all ingredients except squash. Spread in sprayed foil-lined pan. Bake at 350°F. for 8 to 10 minutes or until bubbly and deep golden brown, stirring once. Cool 15 minutes.
3. Meanwhile, quarter squash; remove seeds. Place squash, cut side up, in ungreased 13×9-inch pan. Add ½ cup water to pan; cover with foil. Bake at 350°F. for 45 to 50 minutes or until tender.
4. Arrange squash on platter. Crumble pecan mixture; sprinkle over squash.

NUTRITION INFORMATION PER SERVING: Serving Size: ¼ of Recipe ✦ Calories: 120 ✦ Calories from Fat: 35 ✦ **% DAILY VALUE:** Total Fat: 4 g 6% ✦ Saturated Fat: 1 g 5% ✦ Cholesterol: 0 mg 0% ✦ Sodium: 30 mg 1% ✦ Total Carbohydrate: 20 g 7% ✦ Dietary Fiber: 5 g 20% ✦ Sugars: 8 g ✦ Protein: 2 g ✦ Vitamin A: 10% ✦ Vitamin C: 15% ✦ Calcium: 6% ✦ Iron: 6% ✦ **DIETARY EXCHANGES:** 1 Starch, ½ Fruit, ½ Fat OR 1½ Carbohydrate, ½ Fat

COOK'S NOTE

WINTER SQUASH

Winter squash has a hard skin and keeps well. Peeling is much easier after cooking. Cut the squash in half through the stem, scoop out the seeds and bake, steam or microwave the squash until tender. The squash can be served in the skin or easily scooped out.

TYPES OF WINTER SQUASH

TYPE	DESCRIPTION
Acorn squash	Deeply ridged, round, slightly pointed on the bottom. Dark green skin with orange patches. Orange, somewhat stringy flesh. Classic sweet squash flavor.
Buttercup squash	Round shape, dark green skin. Sweet, slightly dry, smooth orange flesh. Very sweet.
Butternut squash	Shape resembles an oversized pear. Skin is beige. Flesh is bright orange, moist, very smooth and sweet.
Delicata squash	Small, oval squash. Pale yellow skin with green stripes. Dark, sweet, smooth orange flesh. Mild, slightly sweet.
Hubbard squash	Bumpy, greenish-gray skin. Sweet, yellow flesh. Often sold in wrapped, cut wedges because of its large size. Rich, sweet flavor.
Pumpkin	Dark orange skin. Paler orange flesh. For cooking, choose sugar pumpkins, which have denser, smoother flesh. The more watery, stringy field pumpkins make good jack-o'-lanterns. Mild flavors.
Spaghetti squash	Large oval squash with pale yellow skin. Stringy, dark yellow to pale orange flesh separates into strands that resemble noodles. Neutral, mild flavor.
Sweet dumpling squash	Similar to delicata, but shaped like a flattened pumpkin. Mild, sweet flavor.

Grilled Green Tomatoes

PREP TIME: 15 MINUTES ✦ YIELD: 6 SERVINGS

- ¼ teaspoon garlic powder
- ¼ teaspoon salt
- ⅛ teaspoon pepper
- 3 large green tomatoes, cut into ½-inch-thick slices*
- 1 tablespoon oil

1. GRILL DIRECTIONS: Heat grill. In small bowl, combine garlic powder, salt and pepper; mix well. Brush 1 side of each tomato slice with oil; sprinkle lightly with seasonings.
2. When ready to grill, place tomatoes, seasoned side down, on gas grill over medium heat or on charcoal grill 4 to 6 inches from medium coals. Cook 4 minutes. Brush tops with remaining oil. Turn; cook 4 minutes or until tender.

TIPS: * If green tomatoes are not available, firm red tomatoes can be substituted.
To broil tomatoes, place, seasoned side up, on oiled or sprayed broiler pan; broil 4 to 6 inches from heat using times above as a guide, brushing with oil and turning once.

NUTRITION INFORMATION PER SERVING: Serving Size: ⅙ of Recipe ✦ Calories: 35 ✦ Calories from Fat: 20 ✦ **% DAILY VALUE:** Total Fat: 2 g 3% ✦ Saturated Fat: 0 g 0% ✦ Cholesterol: 0 mg 0% ✦ Sodium: 95 mg 4% ✦ Total Carbohydrate: 3 g 1% ✦ Dietary Fiber: 1 g 3% ✦ Sugars: 1 g ✦ Protein: 1 g ✦ Vitamin A: 8% ✦ Vitamin C: 15% ✦ Calcium: 0% ✦ Iron: 0% ✦ **DIETARY EXCHANGES:** 1 Vegetable, ½ Fat

Vegetable Kabobs with Lemon Pepper

PREP TIME: 55 MINUTES ✦ YIELD: 4 SERVINGS

VEGETABLES
- 8 small new red potatoes
- 2 medium onions
- 1 medium yellow summer squash, cut into 8 pieces
- 8 medium fresh mushrooms
- 8 cherry tomatoes

SAUCE
- ½ cup margarine or butter
- ¼ cup grated Parmesan cheese
- 1 teaspoon lemon-pepper seasoning
- ¼ teaspoon garlic salt

1. GRILL DIRECTIONS: Heat grill. Remove thin strip of peel from around center of each potato. Place potatoes and onions in medium

saucepan; add enough water to cover. Bring to a boil. Cook 5 to 8 minutes or just until potatoes can be pierced with fork. Drain. Cut each onion into 4 wedges.

2. Melt margarine in small saucepan. Stir in all remaining sauce ingredients.

3. When ready to grill, alternately thread vegetables onto eight 8 to 12-inch metal skewers. Place on gas grill over medium heat or on charcoal grill 4 to 6 inches from medium coals. Cook 10 minutes or until vegetables are tender, turning and brushing frequently with sauce.

NUTRITION INFORMATION PER SERVING: Serving Size: ¼ of Recipe • Calories: 280 • Calories from Fat: 60 • **% DAILY VALUE:** Total Fat: 7 g 11% • Saturated Fat: 1 g 5% • Cholesterol: 0 mg 0% • Sodium: 170 mg 7% • Total Carbohydrate: 47 g 16% • Dietary Fiber: 7 g 28% • Sugars: 7 g • Protein: 7 g • Vitamin A: 10% • Vitamin C: 50% • Calcium: 6% • Iron: 15% • **DIETARY EXCHANGES:** 2½ Starch, 2 Vegetable, 1 Fat OR 2½ Carbohydrate, 2 Vegetable, 1 Fat

Home-Style Roasted Vegetables

PREP TIME: 15 MINUTES (READY IN 1 HOUR)
♦ YIELD: 4 SERVINGS

2 tablespoons olive or vegetable oil
1 teaspoon seasoned salt
¼ teaspoon dried marjoram leaves
¼ teaspoon pepper
4 medium baking potatoes, unpeeled, cut into 1½-inch chunks
2 medium carrots, cut into 2 x ¼ x ¼-inch strips (1 to 1½ cups)
1 to 2 parsnips, peeled, cut into 2 x ¼ x ¼-inch strips (1 to 1½ cups)
1 red onion, cut into 8 wedges
1 medium green bell pepper, cut into 8 pieces

1. Heat oven to 450°F. In large bowl, combine oil, seasoned salt, marjoram and pepper; mix well. Add all remaining ingredients; toss to coat. Spread on ungreased 15 × 10 × 1-inch baking pan.

2. Bake at 450°F. for 20 minutes. Turn and stir vegetables. Bake an additional 20 to 25 minutes or until vegetables are tender, stirring once.

NUTRITION INFORMATION PER SERVING: Serving Size: ¼ of Recipe • Calories: 270 • Calories from Fat: 60 • **% DAILY VALUE:** Total Fat: 7 g 11% • Saturated Fat: 1 g 5% • Cholesterol: 0 mg 0% • Sodium: 410 mg 17% • Total Carbohydrate: 47 g 16% • Dietary Fiber: 7 g 28% • Sugars: 8 g • Protein: 4 g • Vitamin A: 200% • Vitamin C: 50% • Calcium: 4% • Iron: 15% • **DIETARY EXCHANGES:** 2½ Starch, 1 Vegetable, 1 Fat OR 2½ Carbohydrate, 1 Vegetable, 1 Fat

COOK'S NOTE

GRILLING VEGETABLES

The grill does wonderful things to vegetables, imparting a rich concentrated flavor. Timing varies according to the thickness of the vegetables, the amount and type of fuel and the distance between the grill rack and the fire.

- *Corn.* Roasted in its husk, corn on the cob has an intense, deep corn flavor. Soak the unhusked ears in water for 30 minutes. Remove silk then bring husk back up to enclose corn and roast directly on the grill rack, turning occasionally until the corn is hot throughout.

- *Potatoes.* Scrub potatoes, lightly oil and pierce them several times with a fork. Wrap in two layers of foil and set them directly into the coals of a charcoal or wood fire, or on the grate of a gas grill. Cook until a skewer can easily pierce the flesh.

- *Summer squash.* Cut rounds approximately ½ inch thick of yellow summer squash or zucchini and thread them onto skewers. Brush lightly with oil. Grill, turning occasionally, until tender.

- *Cherry tomatoes or mushrooms.* Thread cherry tomatoes or mushrooms onto skewers and cook until the skin is slightly charred and the inside is hot.

- *Bell peppers.* Grilling brings out the mellow sweetness of peppers. Grill a large batch and save them in the refrigerator for salads, sandwiches, pasta dishes and other recipes. To grill, rinse the peppers and place them directly on the grill rack. Let the skin blacken, then turn the peppers and continue grilling and turning until the skin is evenly charred all over. Remove from the grill. When the peppers are cool enough to handle, peel off the charred skin and remove the seeds and ribs.

- *Onions.* Cut 1-inch-thick round slices of onion, brush lightly with oil and lay directly on the grill.

Swiss Vegetable Casserole

Swiss Vegetable Casserole

PREP TIME: 20 MINUTES (READY IN 50 MINUTES)
♦ YIELD: 8 (½-CUP) SERVINGS

 1 (1-lb.) pkg. frozen broccoli florets, carrots and cauliflower
 2 tablespoons margarine or butter
 6 green onions, cut into ½-inch pieces (½ cup)
 2 tablespoons all-purpose flour
 ¼ teaspoon salt
 ⅛ teaspoon pepper
1½ cups milk
 4 oz. (1 cup) shredded Swiss cheese
 ¼ cup crushed round buttery crackers

1. Heat oven to 350°F. Grease 1 to 1½-quart casserole. Cook frozen vegetables as directed on package. Drain.
2. Meanwhile, melt margarine in medium saucepan over medium heat. Add onions; cook and stir 2 to 3 minutes or until tender.
3. Stir in flour, salt and pepper; mix well. Gradually add milk, stirring constantly. Cook and stir until mixture is bubbly and thickened. Remove from heat.
4. Add ¾ cup of the cheese; stir until melted. Stir in cooked vegetables. Spoon mixture into greased casserole. Sprinkle with crushed crackers and remaining ¼ cup cheese.
5. Bake at 350°F. for 25 to 30 minutes or until topping is golden brown and casserole is bubbly.

NUTRITION INFORMATION PER SERVING: Serving Size: ½ Cup ♦ Calories: 130 ♦ Calories from Fat: 50 ♦ **% DAILY VALUE:** Total Fat: 6 g 9% ♦ Saturated Fat: 2 g 10% ♦ Cholesterol: 10 mg 3% ♦ Sodium: 190 mg 8% ♦ Total Carbohydrate: 10 g 3% ♦ Dietary Fiber: 2 g 8% ♦ Sugars: 4 g ♦ Protein: 8 g ♦ Vitamin A: 50% ♦ Vitamin C: 15% ♦ Calcium: 25% ♦ Iron: 4% ♦ **DIETARY EXCHANGES:** ½ Starch, 1 Vegetable, ½ High-Fat Meat, ½ Fat OR ½ Carbohydrate, 1 Vegetable, ½ High-Fat Meat, ½ Fat

Spicy Nuggets and Vegetables

PREP TIME: 25 MINUTES ♦ YIELD: 4 (¾-CUP) SERVINGS

4½ oz. (1½ cups) uncooked pasta nuggets (radiatore)
 2 cups frozen broccoli florets, carrots and cauliflower
 4 oz. mild Mexican pasteurized process cheese spread with jalapeño peppers, cubed (½ cup)
 1 tablespoon milk

1. In large saucepan, cook pasta nuggets as directed on package, adding vegetables during last 3 to 5 minutes of cooking time. Cook until pasta nuggets and vegetables are tender. Drain well; return to saucepan.
2. Add cheese and milk; cook over medium heat, stirring constantly, until cheese is melted and pasta and vegetables are coated.

NUTRITION INFORMATION PER SERVING: Serving Size: ¾ Cup ♦ Calories: 220 ♦ Calories from Fat: 60 ♦ **% DAILY VALUE:** Total Fat: 7 g 11% ♦ Saturated Fat: 4 g 20% ♦ Cholesterol: 15 mg 5% ♦ Sodium: 400 mg 17% ♦ Total Carbohydrate: 29 g 10% ♦ Dietary Fiber: 2 g 8% ♦ Sugars: 5 g ♦ Protein: 10 g ♦ Vitamin A: 30% ♦ Vitamin C: 15% ♦ Calcium: 20% ♦ Iron: 8% ♦ **DIETARY EXCHANGES:** 1½ Starch, 1 Vegetable, ½ High-Fat Meat, ½ Fat OR 1½ Carbohydrate, 1 Vegetable, ½ High-Fat Meat, ½ Fat

Spicy Nuggets and Vegetables

Fettuccine with Garlic-Herb Butter

Fettuccine with Garlic-Herb Butter

PREP TIME: 25 MINUTES ◆ YIELD: 4 (¾-CUP) SERVINGS

    6 oz. uncooked fettuccine
    1 teaspoon butter
    1 large garlic clove, minced
    2 to 3 tablespoons chopped fresh herbs
        (such as 1 tablespoon parsley,
        1 tablespoon basil, 1 teaspoon
        marjoram and 1 teaspoon thyme)
    1 tablespoon butter, softened
    ⅛ teaspoon salt
      Dash pepper

1. In large saucepan, cook fettuccine to desired doneness as directed on package. Drain; return to saucepan.
2. Meanwhile, in small saucepan, melt 1 teaspoon butter over medium heat. Add garlic; cook 30 to 60 seconds or until garlic begins to turn golden brown.
3. In small bowl, combine herbs, 1 tablespoon butter, salt, pepper and cooked garlic; mix well. Add to fettuccine; toss to coat.

NUTRITION INFORMATION PER SERVING: Serving Size: ¾ Cup ◆ Calories: 200 ◆ Calories from Fat: 50 ◆ % DAILY VALUE: Total Fat: 6 g 9% ◆ Saturated Fat: 3 g 15% ◆ Cholesterol: 50 mg 17% ◆ Sodium: 180 mg 8% ◆ Total Carbohydrate: 31 g 10% ◆ Dietary Fiber: 1 g 4% ◆ Sugars: 1 g ◆ Protein: 6 g ◆ Vitamin A: 6% ◆ Vitamin C: 2% ◆ Calcium: 2% ◆ Iron: 15% ◆ DIETARY EXCHANGES: 2 Starch, 1 Fat OR 2 Carbohydrate, 1 Fat

Bow Ties and Broccoli Alfredo

PREP TIME: 25 MINUTES (READY IN 55 MINUTES)
◆ YIELD: 4 (1-CUP) SERVINGS

    6 oz. (3 cups) uncooked bow tie pasta (farfalle)
    2 cups frozen broccoli florets
    ½ cup sliced purchased roasted red bell
        peppers (from 7.25-oz. jar)
    ½ teaspoon dried basil leaves
    ⅛ teaspoon pepper
    1 (10-oz.) container refrigerated Alfredo sauce
    2 tablespoons shredded fresh Parmesan
        cheese

1. Heat oven to 350°F. Grease 2-quart casserole. Cook pasta to desired doneness as directed on package, adding broccoli during last 2 to 3 minutes of cooking time. Drain.
2. In greased casserole, combine all ingredients except cheese; mix well. Cover.
3. Bake at 350°F. for 20 minutes. Uncover casserole; sprinkle with cheese. Bake, uncovered, an additional 5 to 10 minutes or until cheese is light golden brown.

NUTRITION INFORMATION PER SERVING: Serving Size: 1 Cup ◆ Calories: 420 ◆ Calories from Fat: 220 ◆ % DAILY VALUE: Total Fat: 24 g 37% ◆ Saturated Fat: 13 g 65% ◆ Cholesterol: 50 mg 17% ◆ Sodium: 370 mg 15% ◆ Total Carbohydrate: 39 g 13% ◆ Dietary Fiber: 2 g 8% ◆ Sugars: 4 g ◆ Protein: 12 g ◆ Vitamin A: 15% ◆ Vitamin C: 50% ◆ Calcium: 20% ◆ Iron: 10% ◆ DIETARY EXCHANGES: 2½ Starch, 1 Vegetable, ½ High-Fat Meat, 3½ Fat OR 2½ Carbohydrate, 1 Vegetable, ½ High-Fat Meat, 3½ Fat

Bow Ties and Broccoli Alfredo

Buttered Parmesan Noodles

PREP TIME: 25 MINUTES ◆ YIELD: 5 (½-CUP) SERVINGS

5 oz. (2½ cups) uncooked wide egg noodles
2 to 3 tablespoons butter
¼ cup grated Parmesan cheese
1½ teaspoons chopped fresh parsley
    or 1 teaspoon dried parsley flakes

1. Cook noodles to desired doneness as directed on package. Drain; cover to keep warm.
2. In same saucepan, melt butter over low heat. Gently stir in noodles. Add cheese and parsley; toss to coat.

NUTRITION INFORMATION PER SERVING: Serving Size: ½ Cup ◆ Calories: 190 ◆ Calories from Fat: 90 ◆ **% DAILY VALUE:** Total Fat: 10 g 15% ◆ Saturated Fat: 2 g 10% ◆ Cholesterol: 30 mg 10% ◆ Sodium: 180 mg 8% ◆ Total Carbohydrate: 20 g 7% ◆ Dietary Fiber: 1 g 3% ◆ Sugars: 1 g ◆ Protein: 6 g ◆ Vitamin A: 8% ◆ Vitamin C: 0% ◆ Calcium: 8% ◆ Iron: 8% ◆ **DIETARY EXCHANGES:** 1 Starch, ½ Lean Meat, 1½ Fat OR 1 Carbohydrate, ½ Lean Meat, 1½ Fat

White Sauce

PREP TIME: 10 MINUTES ◆ YIELD: 1 CUP

2 tablespoons margarine or butter
2 tablespoons all-purpose flour
¼ teaspoon salt
⅛ teaspoon white pepper
1 cup milk

1. Melt margarine in small saucepan over medium-low heat. Stir in flour, salt and pepper. Cook 1 minute, stirring constantly, until smooth and bubbly.
2. Gradually add milk, cooking and stirring constantly, until mixture is bubbly and thickened.

> TIP: For a thinner white sauce, use 1 tablespoon margarine and 1 tablespoon flour; for a thicker white sauce, use 3 tablespoons margarine and 3 tablespoons flour.

NUTRITION INFORMATION PER SERVING: Serving Size: 1 Tablespoon ◆ Calories: 30 ◆ Calories from Fat: 20 ◆ **% DAILY VALUE:** Total Fat: 2 g 3% ◆ Saturated Fat: 0 g 0% ◆ Cholesterol: 0 mg 0% ◆ Sodium: 60 mg 3% ◆ Total Carbohydrate: 2 g 1% ◆ Dietary Fiber: 0 g 0% ◆ Sugars: 1 g ◆ Protein: 1 g ◆ Vitamin A: 0% ◆ Vitamin C: 0% ◆ Calcium: 0% ◆ Iron: 0% ◆ **DIETARY EXCHANGES:** ½ Fat

Cheese Sauce

PREP TIME: 15 MINUTES ◆ YIELD: 2¼ CUPS

2 tablespoons margarine or butter
2 tablespoons all-purpose flour
¼ teaspoon salt
⅛ teaspoon pepper
2 cups milk
8 oz. (2 cups) shredded American or
    Cheddar cheese
1 teaspoon Worcestershire sauce
    Dash hot pepper sauce

1. Melt margarine in medium saucepan over medium-low heat. Stir in flour, salt and pepper. Cook 1 minute, stirring constantly, until smooth and bubbly.
2. Gradually add milk, cooking and stirring constantly, until mixture is bubbly and slightly thickened, about 7 minutes.
3. Remove from heat. Add cheese, Worcestershire sauce and hot pepper sauce; stir until cheese is melted.

NUTRITION INFORMATION PER SERVING: Serving Size: 1 Tablespoon ◆ Calories: 40 ◆ Calories from Fat: 25 ◆ **% DAILY VALUE:** Total Fat: 3 g 5% ◆ Saturated Fat: 2 g 10% ◆ Cholesterol: 5 mg 2% ◆ Sodium: 120 mg 5% ◆ Total Carbohydrate: 1 g 1% ◆ Dietary Fiber: 0 g 0% ◆ Sugars: 1 g ◆ Protein: 2 g ◆ Vitamin A: 2% ◆ Vitamin C: 0% ◆ Calcium: 6% ◆ Iron: 0% ◆ **DIETARY EXCHANGES:** ½ High-Fat Meat

COOK'S NOTE

COOKING PASTA

Bring a large pot of water, covered, to a boil over high heat. When it comes to a full rolling boil, salt generously and add the pasta. Leave the cover off for cooking.

Stir the pasta after adding it to the pot and periodically throughout cooking time to prevent clumping.

To test for doneness, remove a noodle from the pot with a slotted spoon. Run it under cold water just long enough to keep you from burning your mouth when you bite into it. For pasta that is perfectly al dente (Italian for "to the tooth"), the noodle should be tender almost all the way through, with just a tiny bit of resistance in the very center.

Drain the pasta into a colander set in a sink, shaking occasionally to shed all the moisture. Do not rinse it. Toss the noodles with a little cooking oil to prevent them from sticking together.

PASTA COOKING REFERENCE

PASTA	DRY MEASUREMENT (APPROXIMATELY)	YIELD
EGG NOODLES		
fine	4 cups	4 cups
medium	5 cups	4 cups
spinach	3¼ cups	3¾ cups
SHORT PASTA		
elbow	1¾ cups	3⅔ cups
medium shells	2¾ cups	4 cups
orzo	1¼ cups	2¾ cups
rigatoni, penne, rotini, bowties, wagon wheels	2 cups	4 cups
ring	2 cups	2⅔ cups
LONG PASTA		
spaghetti, linguine, vermicelli, capellini, fettuccine	8 ounces	4 cups

Easy Noodles Romanoff

PREP TIME: 25 MINUTES (READY IN 1 HOUR)
♦ YIELD: 6 (½-CUP) SERVINGS

    5 oz. (2½ cups) uncooked wide egg noodles
    1 cup creamed cottage cheese
    1 cup sour cream
    2 tablespoons chopped green onions
    ¼ teaspoon garlic salt
    ¼ cup unseasoned dry bread crumbs
    2 tablespoons margarine or butter, melted
    1 tablespoon dried parsley flakes
    1 teaspoon Worcestershire sauce

1. Heat oven to 350°F. Grease 1½-quart casserole. Cook noodles to desired doneness as directed on package. Drain; rinse with hot water.
2. In greased casserole, combine noodles, cottage cheese, sour cream, onions and garlic salt; blend well.
3. In small bowl, combine all remaining ingredients; mix well. Spoon over noodles.
4. Bake at 350°F. for 25 to 35 minutes or until casserole is thoroughly heated and crumbs are light golden brown.

NUTRITION INFORMATION PER SERVING: Serving Size: ½ Cup ♦ Calories: 270 ♦ Calories from Fat: 140 ♦ **% DAILY VALUE:** Total Fat: 15 g 23% ♦ Saturated Fat: 7 g 35% ♦ Cholesterol: 45 mg 15% ♦ Sodium: 340 mg 14% ♦ Total Carbohydrate: 23 g 8% ♦ Dietary Fiber: 1 g 3% ♦ Sugars: 3 g ♦ Protein: 10 g ♦ Vitamin A: 10% ♦ Vitamin C: 0% ♦ Calcium: 8% ♦ Iron: 8% ♦ **DIETARY EXCHANGES:** 1½ Starch, 1 Lean Meat, 2 Fat OR 1½ Carbohydrate, 1 Lean Meat, 2 Fat

Cashew-Rice Pilaf

PREP TIME: 10 MINUTES (READY IN 40 MINUTES)
♦ YIELD: 3 SERVINGS

    2 tablespoons margarine or butter
    2 to 3 tablespoons finely chopped onion
    ½ cup uncooked regular long-grain white rice
    1 cup chicken broth
    ¼ teaspoon salt
    ¼ cup cashews, coarsely chopped
    2 tablespoons chopped fresh parsley

1. Melt margarine in medium saucepan. Add onion; cook until tender. Add rice; stir until coated with margarine.
2. Add broth and salt. Cover; simmer 25 to 30 minutes or until rice is tender and liquid is absorbed. Stir in cashews and parsley.

NUTRITION INFORMATION PER SERVING: Serving Size: ⅓ of Recipe ♦ Calories: 280 ♦ Calories from Fat: 140 ♦ **% DAILY VALUE:** Total Fat: 15 g 23% ♦ Saturated Fat: 3 g 15% ♦ Cholesterol: 0 mg 0% ♦ Sodium: 620 mg 26% ♦ Total Carbohydrate: 31 g 10% ♦ Dietary Fiber: 1 g 4% ♦ Sugars: 2 g ♦ Protein: 6 g ♦ Vitamin A: 10% ♦ Vitamin C: 4% ♦ Calcium: 2% ♦ Iron: 15% ♦ **DIETARY EXCHANGES:** 2 Starch, 3 Fat OR 2 Carbohydrate, 3 Fat

Quick Brown Rice Pilaf

PREP TIME: 15 MINUTES ◆ YIELD: 5 (½-CUP) SERVINGS

1¼ cups chicken broth
1 tablespoon margarine or butter
1 to 1½ cups uncooked instant brown rice*
½ cup shredded carrot
⅓ cup sliced green onions
½ teaspoon dried rosemary or marjoram
    leaves

1. In medium saucepan, combine broth and margarine. Bring to a boil. Stir in all remaining ingredients. Reduce heat to low; cover and simmer 5 minutes.
2. Remove saucepan from heat; stir. Cover; let stand 5 minutes. Fluff mixture with fork before serving.

TIP: * Use amount of rice indicated on package to make 4 servings.

NUTRITION INFORMATION PER SERVING: Serving Size: ½ Cup ◆ Calories: 140 ◆ Calories from Fat: 35 ◆ **% DAILY VALUE:** Total Fat: 4 g 6% ◆ Saturated Fat: 1 g 5% ◆ Cholesterol: 0 mg 0% ◆ Sodium: 230 mg 10% ◆ Total Carbohydrate: 22 g 7% ◆ Dietary Fiber: 2 g 8% ◆ Sugars: 1 g ◆ Protein: 4 g ◆ Vitamin A: 60% ◆ Vitamin C: 2% ◆ Calcium: 0% ◆ Iron: 2% ◆ **DIETARY EXCHANGES:** 1½ Starch, ½ Fat OR 1½ Carbohydrate, ½ Fat

Quick Fried Rice

PREP TIME: 20 MINUTES ◆ YIELD: 4 (1-CUP) SERVINGS

1½ cups uncooked instant white rice
1½ cups water
1 teaspoon oil
2 eggs, beaten
4 teaspoons dark sesame oil
½ cup frozen early June peas
⅓ cup sliced green onions
1 cup fresh bean sprouts
¼ cup soy sauce

1. Cook rice in water as directed on package.
2. Meanwhile, heat 1 teaspoon oil in large nonstick skillet over medium-high heat until hot. Add beaten eggs; tilt pan to form thin layer of egg. Lift edges of egg with small spatula to let uncooked egg flow to bottom of skillet. Cover; cook 1 minute or until set. Slide egg from skillet onto cutting board. Set aside.

3. In same skillet, heat 4 teaspoons sesame oil over medium-high heat until hot. Add peas and onions; cook and stir 1 to 2 minutes or until vegetables are crisp-tender.
4. Add cooked rice, sprouts and soy sauce; cook and stir until rice is thoroughly heated.
5. Roll up egg; cut into small strips. Cut strips into 2-inch lengths; fold into rice mixture. Heat thoroughly. If desired, serve with additional soy sauce.

NUTRITION INFORMATION PER SERVING: Serving Size: 1 Cup ◆ Calories: 250 ◆ Calories from Fat: 70 ◆ **% DAILY VALUE:** Total Fat: 8 g 12% ◆ Saturated Fat: 2 g 10% ◆ Cholesterol: 105 mg 35% ◆ Sodium: 1090 mg 45% ◆ Total Carbohydrate: 36 g 12% ◆ Dietary Fiber: 2 g 8% ◆ Sugars: 3 g ◆ Protein: 9 g ◆ Vitamin A: 6% ◆ Vitamin C: 8% ◆ Calcium: 4% ◆ Iron: 15% ◆ **DIETARY EXCHANGES:** 2 Starch, 1 Vegetable, 1½ Fat OR 2 Carbohydrate, 1 Vegetable, 1½ Fat

Quick Fried Rice

Wild Rice and Mushrooms

PREP TIME: 15 MINUTES (READY IN 2 HOURS)
◆ YIELD: 8 (½-CUP) SERVINGS

3 tablespoons margarine or butter
1 (5-oz.) pkg. fresh brown mushrooms
    (such as crimini) or white button
    mushrooms, sliced
½ cup slivered almonds
1 cup uncooked wild rice
½ cup sliced green onions
3 cups chicken broth

1. Heat oven to 350°F. Grease 1½-quart casserole. Melt margarine in large skillet over medium heat. Add mushrooms and almonds; cook and stir 3 minutes or until mushrooms are tender and almonds begin to brown.
2. Add wild rice; cook 10 minutes, stirring frequently. Stir in onions and broth. Bring to a boil. Pour into greased casserole; cover.
3. Bake at 350°F. for 45 minutes. Uncover; bake an additional 45 to 60 minutes or until rice is tender and liquid is absorbed.

NUTRITION INFORMATION PER SERVING: Serving Size: ½ Cup ◆ Calories: 180 ◆ Calories from Fat: 80 ◆ **% DAILY VALUE:** Total Fat: 9 g 14% ◆ Saturated Fat: 1 g 5% ◆ Cholesterol: 0 mg 0% ◆ Sodium: 350 mg 15% ◆ Total Carbohydrate: 18 g 6% ◆ Dietary Fiber: 2 g 8% ◆ Sugars: 1 g ◆ Protein: 7 g ◆ Vitamin A: 4% ◆ Vitamin C: 2% ◆ Calcium: 4% ◆ Iron: 6% ◆ **DIETARY EXCHANGES:** 1 Starch, 1 Vegetable, 1½ Fat OR 1 Carbohydrate, 1 Vegetable, 1½ Fat

Rice and Barley Medley

PREP TIME: 30 MINUTES ◆ YIELD: 7 (½-CUP) SERVINGS

2 teaspoons olive oil
½ cup sliced fresh mushrooms
¼ cup chopped onion
1 garlic clove, minced
1 (14½-oz.) can ready-to-serve vegetable
    broth
½ cup uncooked quick-cooking barley
½ cup uncooked instant brown rice
½ cup chopped fresh broccoli
¼ cup shredded carrot

1. Heat oil in medium nonstick skillet over high heat until hot. Add mushrooms, onion and garlic; cook until tender.
2. Add broth; bring to a boil. Stir in barley and rice. Reduce heat; cover and simmer 10 to 12 minutes or until most of liquid is absorbed, adding broccoli and carrot during last 5 minutes of cooking time.
3. Remove skillet from heat; let stand 5 minutes. Fluff mixture with fork before serving.

NUTRITION INFORMATION PER SERVING: Serving Size: ½ Cup ◆ Calories: 90 ◆ Calories from Fat: 20 ◆ **% DAILY VALUE:** Total Fat: 2 g 3% ◆ Saturated Fat: 0 g 0% ◆ Cholesterol: 0 mg 0% ◆ Sodium: 270 mg 11% ◆ Total Carbohydrate: 15 g 5% ◆ Dietary Fiber: 2 g 8% ◆ Sugars: 1 g ◆ Protein: 2 g ◆ Vitamin A: 25% ◆ Vitamin C: 8% ◆ Calcium: 0% ◆ Iron: 2% ◆ **DIETARY EXCHANGES:** 1 Starch OR 1 Carbohydrate

---

COOK'S NOTE

KNOW YOUR RICE

Store rice in an airtight container in a cool, dark, dry place.

- White rice, sometimes called polished rice, has had the husk, bran and germ removed. It keeps almost indefinitely. Varieties of white rice include fragrant jasmine rice, available at Asian markets and specialty food shops; basmati (or Texmati) rice, sold in supermarkets, Indian groceries and gourmet food stores; and Arborio rice, a short-grain Italian rice used for risotto, available in Italian markets and specialty food shops.
- Brown rice is the whole grain with only the outer, inedible husk removed. Because the bran contains oil, use brown rice within 6 months to prevent it from becoming rancid. The high-fiber bran coating gives brown rice its tan color and nutty flavor. It takes about 45 minutes for brown rice to cook on the stovetop.
- Converted rice is white rice that has been parboiled, then dried. When cooked to completion, its kernels are fluffier and more separated than those of regular white rice. Cooking time is similar to that of white rice.
- Instant or quick rice has been partially cooked and dehydrated. Both white and brown varieties cook quickly, usually in about 5 minutes.
- Wild rice is actually a marsh grass seed, native to the northern Great Lakes, that has a nutty flavor when cooked. During cooking, which takes 45 to 60 minutes, the dark seeds burst, giving the cooked rice an attractive dark-and-light appearance.

Spanish Rice

PREP TIME: 10 MINUTES (READY IN 1 HOUR 55 MINUTES)
◆ YIELD: 6 SERVINGS

    6 slices bacon
    1 cup uncooked regular long-grain white or
        brown rice*
  1/4 cup chopped green bell pepper
    1 medium onion, sliced
    1 teaspoon salt
  1/8 teaspoon pepper
    2 cups water
  1/4 cup ketchup
    1 (14.5 or 16-oz.) can tomatoes, undrained,
        cut up

1. In large skillet, cook bacon until crisp. Drain on paper towel; crumble. Reserve 2 tablespoons drippings in skillet.
2. Add rice, bell pepper and onion to drippings. Cook until onion is tender. Add crumbled bacon and all remaining ingredients. Cover; simmer 30 to 45 minutes or until rice is tender and liquid is absorbed.

> **TIP:** * If using instant rice, cook bell pepper and onion in drippings. Add all remaining ingredients except rice. Cover; simmer 10 minutes. Add 2½ cups instant rice. Remove from heat; let stand 5 minutes. Fluff with fork before serving.

NUTRITION INFORMATION PER SERVING: Serving Size: ⅙ of Recipe ◆ Calories: 230 ◆ Calories from Fat: 70 ◆ **% DAILY VALUE:** Total Fat: 8 g 12% ◆ Saturated Fat: 3 g 15% ◆ Cholesterol: 10 mg 3% ◆ Sodium: 550 mg 23% ◆ Total Carbohydrate: 34 g 11% ◆ Dietary Fiber: 2 g 8% ◆ Sugars: 4 g ◆ Protein: 5 g ◆ Vitamin A: 10% ◆ Vitamin C: 15% ◆ Calcium: 4% ◆ Iron: 10% ◆ **DIETARY EXCHANGES:** 1½ Starch, ½ Fruit, 1 Vegetable, 1½ Fat OR 2 Carbohydrate, 1 Vegetable, 1½ Fat

Quick Mushroom Risotto

PREP TIME: 20 MINUTES ◆ YIELD: 8 (½-CUP) SERVINGS

    2 tablespoons butter
  1/2 cup chopped onion
    1 (4.5-oz.) jar sliced mushrooms, drained
    2 cups uncooked instant white rice
    1 teaspoon garlic powder
  1/4 teaspoon pepper
    2 (14½-oz.) cans ready-to-serve chicken broth
  1/3 cup whipping cream or half-and-half
  1/3 cup grated Parmesan cheese
    1 tablespoon grated Parmesan cheese, if
        desired

1. In large skillet, melt butter over medium-high heat. Add onion and mushrooms; cook and stir 3 minutes. Add rice, garlic powder and pepper; cook 2 minutes.
2. Stir in 1 can of the broth; cook 4 minutes, stirring constantly. Gradually stir in remaining can of broth; cook 7 minutes or until liquid is almost absorbed, stirring frequently.
3. Stir in whipping cream. Remove from heat. Stir in ⅓ cup cheese. Spoon into serving dish; sprinkle with 1 tablespoon cheese.

NUTRITION INFORMATION PER SERVING: Serving Size: ½ Cup ◆ Calories: 200 ◆ Calories from Fat: 80 ◆ **% DAILY VALUE:** Total Fat: 9 g 14% ◆ Saturated Fat: 5 g 25% ◆ Cholesterol: 25 mg 8% ◆ Sodium: 500 mg 21% ◆ Total Carbohydrate: 23 g 8% ◆ Dietary Fiber: 1 g 4% ◆ Sugars: 1 g ◆ Protein: 7 g ◆ Vitamin A: 6% ◆ Vitamin C: 0% ◆ Calcium: 8% ◆ Iron: 8% ◆ **DIETARY EXCHANGES:** 1½ Starch, 2 Fat OR 1½ Carbohydrate, 2 Fat

RICE COOKING REFERENCE

RICE (1 CUP UNCOOKED)	BOILING WATER	SALT (OPTIONAL)	SIMMERING TIME	YIELD
BROWN RICE	2½ cups	1 teaspoon	45 to 50 minutes	3 cups
CONVERTED RICE	2¼ cups	1 teaspoon	20 minutes	4 cups
INSTANT RICE	1 cup	1 teaspoon	Add rice to boiling water and remove from heat. Do not simmer.	2 cups
REGULAR LONG-GRAIN WHITE RICE	2 cups	1 teaspoon	15 to 20 minutes	3 cups
WILD RICE	4 cups	1 teaspoon	45 to 60 minutes	4 cups

TO COOK RICE

+ Bring water to a boil.
+ Add rice, stir and cover tightly; reduce heat and simmer until the liquid has been absorbed and the grains are tender. See "Rice Cooking Reference," page 318, or follow package instructions for specific times.
+ Remove from heat and fluff with fork; cover and let stand 5 minutes.
+ Lifting the lid during cooking and over-cooking can cause gummy, unattractive results.
+ If possible, follow package directions for specifics about cooking each type of rice. One type of rice may be substituted for another, but adjustments must be made in the amount of liquid and the cooking time.

Easy Cheesy Savory Polenta

PREP TIME: 45 MINUTES (READY IN 1 HOUR)
+ YIELD: 6 SERVINGS

    3 cups water
    1 cup yellow cornmeal
    2 teaspoons chicken-flavor instant bouillon
    1/2 teaspoon garlic powder
    1/2 teaspoon dried basil leaves
    1/4 teaspoon hot pepper sauce
    1 tablespoon margarine or butter, melted
    2 oz. (1/2 cup) shredded provolone cheese

1. Spray 9-inch pie pan with nonstick cooking spray. In large saucepan, combine 1 cup of the water and cornmeal; mix until smooth. Stir in remaining 2 cups water, bouillon, garlic powder, basil and hot pepper sauce.
2. Bring to a boil over medium-high heat. Reduce heat to low; cook 10 to 15 minutes or until very thick, stirring frequently. Pour polenta into sprayed pie pan. Let stand 15 minutes.
3. Cut polenta into wedges; place on broiler pan. Drizzle wedges lightly with half of margarine. Broil 4 to 6 inches from heat for 5 to 7 minutes or until bubbly.

4. Turn wedges. Drizzle with remaining margarine; sprinkle with cheese. Broil an additional 3 to 5 minutes or until cheese is bubbly and golden brown.

NUTRITION INFORMATION PER SERVING: Serving Size: 1/6 of Recipe ◆ Calories: 130 ◆ Calories from Fat: 45 ◆ **% DAILY VALUE:** Total Fat: 5 g 8% ◆ Saturated Fat: 2 g 10% ◆ Cholesterol: 5 mg 2% ◆ Sodium: 440 mg 18% ◆ Total Carbohydrate: 16 g 5% ◆ Dietary Fiber: 2 g 8% ◆ Sugars: 1 g ◆ Protein: 4 g ◆ Vitamin A: 6% ◆ Vitamin C: 0% ◆ Calcium: 8% ◆ Iron: 4% ◆ **DIETARY EXCHANGES:** 1 Starch, 1 Fat OR 1 Carbohydrate, 1 Fat

Cheesy Garlic Grits

PREP TIME: 20 MINUTES (READY IN 40 MINUTES)
+ YIELD: 10 (1/2-CUP) SERVINGS

    4 cups water
    1 cup uncooked quick-cooking grits
    1/2 teaspoon garlic salt
    1 (10¾-oz.) can condensed Cheddar cheese soup
    2 tablespoons margarine or butter
    1/8 teaspoon hot pepper sauce, if desired
    2 oz. (1/2 cup) shredded sharp Cheddar cheese
    Dash paprika

1. Heat oven to 350°F. Spray 12×8-inch (2-quart) baking dish with nonstick cooking spray.
2. In large saucepan, bring water to a boil. Stir in grits and garlic salt. Reduce heat to medium-low; cover and cook 5 to 7 minutes or until thickened, stirring occasionally.
3. Stir in soup, margarine and hot pepper sauce; mix well. Spread mixture evenly in sprayed dish. Sprinkle with cheese and paprika.
4. Bake at 350°F. for 15 to 20 minutes or until grits are bubbly around edges and cheese is melted.

NUTRITION INFORMATION PER SERVING: Serving Size: 1/2 Cup ◆ Calories: 140 ◆ Calories from Fat: 60 ◆ **% DAILY VALUE:** Total Fat: 7 g 11% ◆ Saturated Fat: 3 g 15% ◆ Cholesterol: 15 mg 5% ◆ Sodium: 380 mg 16% ◆ Total Carbohydrate: 15 g 5% ◆ Dietary Fiber: 0 g 0% ◆ Sugars: 1 g ◆ Protein: 4 g ◆ Vitamin A: 8% ◆ Vitamin C: 0% ◆ Calcium: 8% ◆ Iron: 4% ◆ **DIETARY EXCHANGES:** 1 Starch, 1½ Fat OR 1 Carbohydrate, 1½ Fat

Savory Couscous

Boston Baked Beans

PREP TIME: 30 MINUTES (READY IN 18 HOURS)
✦ YIELD: 8 (1-CUP) SERVINGS

- 1 (16-oz.) pkg. (about 2⅓ cups) dried great northern or navy beans, rinsed, sorted
- 2 quarts (8 cups) water
- 1 lb. smoked pork shank
- ½ cup chopped onion
- ½ cup molasses
- 2 tablespoons brown sugar
- ½ teaspoon dry mustard
- ¼ teaspoon ginger
- ¼ teaspoon allspice

Savory Couscous

PREP TIME: 20 MINUTES ✦ YIELD: 4 (1-CUP) SERVINGS

- 1 tablespoon margarine or butter
- ¼ cup chopped red onion
- 2 cups water
- 1 teaspoon dried parsley flakes
- ½ teaspoon seasoned salt
- ¼ teaspoon dried sage leaves
- ¼ teaspoon dried thyme leaves
- 1⅓ cups uncooked couscous

1. Melt margarine in medium saucepan over medium-high heat. Add onion; cook 1 minute or until tender, stirring occasionally.

2. Add water, parsley, seasoned salt, sage and thyme. Increase heat to high; bring to a boil. Stir in couscous. Remove from heat; cover and let stand 5 minutes. Fluff lightly with fork before serving.

NUTRITION INFORMATION PER SERVING: Serving Size: 1 Cup ✦ Calories: 260 ✦ Calories from Fat: 25 ✦ **% DAILY VALUE:** Total Fat: 3 g 5% ✦ Saturated Fat: 1 g 5% ✦ Cholesterol: 0 mg 0% ✦ Sodium: 230 mg 10% ✦ Total Carbohydrate: 49 g 16% ✦ Dietary Fiber: 4 g 16% ✦ Sugars: 2 g ✦ Protein: 8 g ✦ Vitamin A: 4% ✦ Vitamin C: 0% ✦ Calcium: 4% ✦ Iron: 10% ✦ **DIETARY EXCHANGES:** 3 Starch, ½ Fat OR 3 Carbohydrate, ½ Fat

COOK'S NOTE

PREPARING LEGUMES

Although there are differences in color and flavor, peas and beans of a similar type can be used interchangeably or combined for contrast. Canned beans are inexpensive and easy to use—open a can, rinse the beans and add them to cold salad, soup, chili and more.

Packages of dried legumes are even less expensive, and some cooks prefer their firmer texture to that of canned beans. Preparation is easy. Most need to be soaked before cooking. Lentils and split peas are the exception because of their small size and lack of skin; they are added dry to recipes.

Before soaking or cooking, rinse the beans or peas in a colander and pick out any pebbles. To soak, let the legumes stand covered in water at room temperature overnight or for about 12 hours. Or use the short-cut method: Combine beans or peas and water; heat to boiling and let boil 2 minutes. Remove the pot from the heat, cover and let stand 1 hour.

To cook, heat the beans and the soaking liquid to boiling over high heat. Reduce heat; cover and simmer over low heat until tender. To keep the water from foaming, add 1 tablespoon oil during cooking. Salt, wine, tomatoes or other acidic foods tend to toughen the skins of beans and peas and keep them from becoming tender; add acidic foods toward the end of cooking.

1. In Dutch oven or large saucepan, cover beans with water. Soak at least 12 hours.
2. DO NOT DRAIN. Add pork shank and onion to beans; bring to a boil. Simmer 1 hour.
3. Heat oven to 300°F. Drain bean mixture, reserving 2 cups liquid. Place drained beans and pork in ungreased 3-quart casserole or bean pot. In small bowl, combine all remaining ingredients; stir in reserved liquid. Pour over beans; cover.
4. Bake at 300°F. for 3 to 3½ hours or until beans are tender.
5. Remove pork shank; trim meat off bone and return meat to casserole. Bake, uncovered, an additional 30 to 60 minutes or until liquid is absorbed and beans are tender.

NUTRITION INFORMATION PER SERVING: Serving Size: 1 Cup ✦ Calories: 270 ✦ Calories from Fat: 20 ✦ % DAILY VALUE: Total Fat: 2 g 3% ✦ Saturated Fat: 1 g 5% ✦ Cholesterol: 15 mg 5% ✦ Sodium: 390 mg 16% ✦ Total Carbohydrate: 47 g 16% ✦ Dietary Fiber: 10 g 40% ✦ Sugars: 17 g ✦ Protein: 17 g ✦ Vitamin A: 0% ✦ Vitamin C: 2% ✦ Calcium: 15% ✦ Iron: 25% ✦ DIETARY EXCHANGES: 2 Starch, 1 Fruit, 1½ Very Lean Meat OR 3 Carbohydrate, 1½ Very Lean Meat

Slow-Cooked Beans

PREP TIME: 15 MINUTES (READY IN 8 HOURS 15 MINUTES) ✦ YIELD: 18 (½-CUP) SERVINGS

½ lb. bacon, diced
½ cup firmly packed brown sugar
¼ cup cornstarch
1 teaspoon dry mustard
½ cup molasses
1 tablespoon vinegar

COOK'S NOTE

LEGUMES

The legume family includes lentils, peanuts, lima beans, black-eyed peas, soybeans, navy beans, split peas, kidney beans and pinto beans. Legumes are a staple all over the world. They are affectionately referred to as "the perfect food" because they are low in fat (with the exception of peanuts), high in protein, rich in dietary fiber and inexpensive. Legumes are excellent sources of iron, potassium, thiamine, riboflavin and niacin.

4 (16-oz.) cans baked beans
1 medium onion, chopped
1 green bell pepper, chopped

1. In large skillet, cook bacon over medium heat until crisp. Drain, reserving 2 tablespoons drippings.
2. In 3½ to 4-quart slow cooker, combine cooked bacon, reserved 2 tablespoons drippings and all remaining ingredients; mix well.
3. Cover; cook on high setting for 1 hour.
4. Reduce heat to low setting; cook an additional 5 to 7 hours.

NUTRITION INFORMATION PER SERVING: Serving Size: ½ Cup ✦ Calories: 200 ✦ Calories from Fat: 35 ✦ % DAILY VALUE: Total Fat: 4 g 6% ✦ Saturated Fat: 1 g 5% ✦ Cholesterol: 4 mg 1% ✦ Sodium: 460 mg 19% ✦ Total Carbohydrate: 35 g 12% ✦ Dietary Fiber: 5 g 20% ✦ Sugars: 17 g ✦ Protein: 6 g ✦ Vitamin A: 4% ✦ Vitamin C: 8% ✦ Calcium: 8% ✦ Iron: 6% ✦ DIETARY EXCHANGES: 2 Starch, ½ Fruit, ½ Fat OR 2½ Carbohydrate, ½ Fat

DRIED LEGUMES COOKING REFERENCE

LEGUME (1 CUP [½ LB.] UNCOOKED)	WATER	SOAK	COOKING TIME	YIELD
BEANS OR BLACK-EYED PEAS	2½ to 3 cups	Yes	1½ to 2 hours	2½ cups
LENTILS	2 cups	No	30 to 35 minutes	2½ cups
SOYBEANS	4 cups	Yes	2 to 2½ hours	2½ cups
SPLIT PEAS	2 cups	No	30 to 45 minutes	2½ cups
WHOLE PEAS	2½ to 3 cups	Yes	1 to 1⅓ hours	2½ cups

FRESH VEGETABLE COOKING REFERENCE

Use the following chart and general cooking instructions as a guide for preparing and cooking fresh vegetables. Cooking times are based on 4 servings. Vary cooking times slightly to suit individual preference.

VEGETABLE	PREPARATION	COOKING TIME	SEASONING AND SERVING SUGGESTIONS
ARTICHOKES 2 medium	Wash and peel. Leave whole or slice. To keep from darkening before cooking, place in 1 quart water with 3 tablespoons lemon juice added. Remove stem and slightly open leaves or cut in half. To grill, place on grill rack, brush with oil.	**Boil:** Whole, 10 to 20 minutes. Slices, 5 to 10 minutes. **Steam:** Whole, 15 to 20 minutes.Slices, 12 to 15 minutes. **Microwave:** Whole or slices, 6 to 7 minutes, let stand 1 minute. **Grill:** Whole, 20 to 30 minutes, or precook slightly in oil to soften and reduce time.	Season with lemon. Serve with butter, margarine or white sauce.
ASPARAGUS 1 lb.	Wash and snap off base of stalks (they will snap just between the tender and tough portions). Leave whole or cut into 1-inch pieces. Tips will cook faster than stalks. A bundle of spears can be placed upright so tips are above water. To grill, use grill basket, brush with oil.	**Boil:** Whole, 10 to 15 minutes. Pieces, 5 to 8 minutes. **Steam:** Whole, 12 to 20 minutes. **Microwave:** Whole or pieces, 6 to 7 minutes, let stand 1 minute. **Grill:** Whole, 6 to 8 minutes, medium coals.	Season with lemon, marjoram, thyme or tarragon. Serve with butter, margarine, hollandaise sauce, fresh lemon, toasted almonds, grated Parmesan cheese or Italian salad dressing. Marinate cooked asparagus in French dressing or vinegar and oil dressing and chill.
BEANS (*green and wax*) 1 lb.	Wash and trim off ends. Leave whole, slice diagonally into 1-inch pieces or slice lengthwise (French-style). To grill, use grill basket, brush with oil.	**Boil:** Whole or pieces, 8 to 15 minutes.French-style, 10 to 12 minutes. **Steam:** Whole or pieces, 15 to 20 minutes. **Microwave:** Whole or pieces, 11 to 16 minutes, let stand 1 minute. **Grill:** Whole, 8 to 10 minutes, medium coals, turn once.	Season with Italian seasoning, basil leaves or add chopped onions during cooking. Serve with cheese sauce, sour cream and dill. Marinate cooked beans in Italian dressing and chill.
BEANS (*lima*) 3 lb. unshelled, 1 lb. shelled	Shell and wash.	**Boil:** 12 to 20 minutes. **Steam:** 20 to 25 minutes. **Microwave:** 16 to 18 minutes, stir twice. Let stand 1 minute.	Season with oregano, savory, tarragon or thyme. Serve with butter. margarine or white sauce.

VEGETABLE	PREPARATION	COOKING TIME	SEASONING AND SERVING SUGGESTIONS
BEETS 1 lb. (4 medium)	Wash and leave root ends and 2 inches of beet tops attached. Do not peel before cooking. Skins will easily slip off after cooking. Slice, dice, shred or leave whole. For boiling, use enough water to cover. Add 1 tablespoon vinegar or lemon juice to preserve color. To grill, place ½-inch thick slices on grill rack, brush with oil.	**Boil:** Whole, 35 to 40 minutes. **Steam:** Whole, 40 to 50 minutes. **Microwave:** Whole, 15 to 20 minutes, stir every 5 minutes. Let stand 3 to 5 minutes. **Grill:** Slices, 20 to 25 minutes, medium coals, turn often.	Season with cloves or thyme. Serve with butter, margarine, sour cream or orange sauce.
BELGIAN ENDIVE ½ to 1 lb.	Wash well and leave whole. To grill, place on grill rack, brush with oil.	**Boil:** Whole, 15 to 20 minutes. **Steam:** Whole, 20 to 25 minutes. **Panfry:** Whole, 10 to 12 minutes. **Grill:** Whole, 7 to 10 minutes, medium coals, turn once.	Season with lemon, pepper or thyme. Serve with butter, margarine or crumbled cooked bacon.
BOK CHOY 1 lb. (medium head)	Wash well and cut in half or slice. To grill, cut in half lengthwise, place on grill rack, brush with oil.	**Boil:** Halves, 4 to 5 minutes. **Steam:** Halves, 4 to 6 minutes. **Microwave:** Halves, 5 to 8 minutes, let stand 3 minutes. **Grill:** Halves, 10 to 12 minutes, medium coals, turn once.	Season with ginger. Serve with butter, margarine, soy sauce or stir-fry sauce.
BROCCOLI 1 lb. (4 to 5 cups pieces)	Wash and remove larger outer leaves and tough portion of stalk. For uniform cooking, cut pieces of similar sizes, split larger ones if necessary. Stalks take longer to cook than florets. Place in grill basket or on grill rack, brush with oil.	**Boil:** Whole with stem or florets, 7 to 12 minutes. **Steam:** Whole with stem or florets, 12 to 14 minutes. **Microwave:** Whole with stem or florets, 8 to 12 minutes, let stand 2 to 3 minutes. **Grill:** Whole with stem or florets, 15 to 20 minutes, medium coals, turn often.	Serve with butter, margarine, hollandaise sauce, sour cream, cheese or mustard sauce, buttered bread crumbs, grated Parmesan cheese, crumbled cooked bacon or toasted almonds.
BRUSSELS SPROUTS	Wash and remove wilted outer leaves, trim stems.	**Boil:** 7 to 15 minutes. **Steam:** 15 to 20 minutes.	Season with curry powder, nutmeg or sage.

VEGETABLE	PREPARATION	COOKING TIME	SEASONING AND SERVING SUGGESTIONS
BRUSSELS SPROUTS *(cont.)* 1 lb. (4 cups)	To grill, use grill basket or kabobs, brush with oil.	**Microwave:** 6 to 9 minutes, let stand 3 minutes. **Grill:** 15 to 20 minutes, medium coals, turn once or twice.	Serve with butter, margarine, white sauce, cheese or mustard sauce, hollandaise sauce, buttered bread crumbs, grated Parmesan cheese or chopped hard-cooked egg.
CABBAGE *(savoy, green or red)* 1 medium head	Wash and remove wilted outer leaves. Cut into wedges or shred. Discard core. Add 1 tablespoon vinegar or lemon juice to preserve color. To grill, cut into wedges, place in grill basket or on grill rack, brush with oil.	**Boil:** Wedges, 8 to 12 minutes. Shredded, 3 to 7 minutes. **Steam:** Wedges, 9 to 14 minutes. Shredded, 5 to 8 minutes. **Microwave:** Wedges or shredded, 6 to 13 minutes, let stand 3 minutes. **Grill:** Wedges, 10 to 15 minutes, medium coals, turn often.	Season with caraway, dill, nutmeg or oregano. Serve with sour cream, butter, margarine, crumbled cooked bacon, cheese or white sauce.
CARROTS *(baby or regular)* 1 lb. (2½ cups sliced or 3 cups shredded)	Wash and peel with vegetable peeler to remove thin outer layer of skin. Remove ends and rinse. Cut into slices or strips or shred. Leave baby carrots whole. To grill, cut in ½-inch thick strips or use baby carrots. Use grill basket, brush with oil.	**Boil:** Whole, 15 to 20 minutes. Slices, strips or baby, 8 to 13 minutes. **Steam:** Whole, 20 to 30 minutes. Slices, strips or baby, 8 to 11 minutes. **Microwave:** Whole, 7 to 12 minutes, let stand 3 minutes. **Grill:** Strips or baby, 10 to 15 minutes, medium coals, turn often.	Season with mint, cinnamon, ginger, nutmeg, chives or add raisins or chopped apples during cooking. Serve with butter, margarine, parsley, cheese sauce, honey, brown sugar, crumbled cooked bacon or sour cream.
CAULIFLOWER 1 to 1½ lb. (medium head)	Wash and remove outer leaves and excess portion of stem. Leave whole or cut into florets. To cook whole, place stem side down. To grill, use grill basket or kabobs, brush with oil.	**Boil:** Whole, 15 to 20 minutes. Florets, 8 to 15 minutes. **Steam:** Whole, 20 to 25 minutes. Florets, 10 to 18 minutes. **Microwave:** Whole, 8 to 15 minutes, let stand 3 minutes. Florets, 7 to 13 minutes, let stand 3 minutes. **Grill:** Whole or florets, 10 to 15 minutes, medium coals, turn once or twice.	Season with nutmeg, rosemary, basil, caraway or tarragon. Serve with cheese, hollandaise or mustard sauce, Parmesan cheese, buttered bread crumbs or sour cream.
CELERIAC 1 lb. (2½ cups julienne strips)	Wash and trim off leaves and ends. Peel off brown skin. Cut into julienne strips.	**Boil:** 5 to 6 minutes. **Steam:** 5 minutes. **Microwave:** 3 to 5 minutes.	Season with thyme or marjoram. Serve hot with butter, margarine or white sauce.

VEGETABLE	PREPARATION	COOKING TIME	SEASONING AND SERVING SUGGESTIONS
CELERY 1½ lb. (1 medium stalk or 4 cups sliced)	Wash and separate ribs. Cut off bottoms, leaves and any blemishes. If outer ribs are especially stringy, remove larger strings with a vegetable peeler. Cut ribs into slices or 1-inch pieces.	**Boil:** 5 to 10 minutes. **Steam:** 18 to 20 minutes. **Microwave:** 3 to 6 minutes, let stand 3 minutes.	Season with bouillon, onion or dill. Serve with margarine, butter, cheese sauce, toasted almonds or grated Parmesan cheese.
CHILES *(includes jalapeño, Anaheim, poblano, serrano and more than 200 other varieties)*	When handling chiles, wear rubber or plastic gloves to protect hands from the chile oil or capsaicin. Remove stems and seeds, then rinse with cold water. To grill, place on grill rack or in grill basket.	**Grill:** 8 to 10 minutes, medium coals, turn once or twice.	Generally used as an ingredient in recipes. Add to soups, stews, entrées and dips.
CHINESE (NAPA) CABBAGE *(celery cabbage)* 1½ lb. (medium head)	Wash and remove wilted outer leaves. Cut off base and slice crosswise. To grill, cut into quarters, place on grill rack.	**Boil:** 4 to 5 minutes. **Steam:** 4 to 6 minutes. **Microwave:** 5 to 8 minutes, let stand 3 minutes. **Grill:** 10 to 15 minutes, medium coals, turn often.	Season with ginger, garlic, onions or soy sauce. Serve with butter, margarine or sour cream.
CORN 4 large ears (2 to 3 cups kernels)	Remove husks and silk and trim ends. Leave corn on cob or cut off kernels with sharp knife. To cook in husk, strip back husk to remove silk, then pull husk back over corn. To microwave, leave husk on, or wrap each ear in waxed paper. To grill, leave husk on. If husk is removed, brush with oil. Place on grill rack.	**Boil:** Ears, 5 to 8 minutes. Kernels, 4 to 6 minutes. **Steam:** Ears, 5 to 9 minutes. Kernels, 4 to 8 minutes. **Microwave:** 3 to 4 minutes per ear, let stand 2 minutes. Kernels, 5 to 9 minutes, let stand 1 minute. **Grill:** Ears, 25 to 30 minutes, turn often.	Season with sugar, curry powder, basil or pepper. Serve with butter, margarine, seasoned butter, grated Parmesan cheese, onion or chili sauce.
EGGPLANT 1½ lb. (1 medium or 4 cups cubed)	Wash and peel if skin is tough. Cut off stem. Slice, cube or cut into strips. Dip in lemon juice to prevent darkening. Cut into ½-inch thick slices to pan-fry or grill. To grill, place on grill rack or in grill basket, brush with oil.	**Boil:** 5 to 8 minutes. **Steam:** 5 to 9 minutes. **Panfry:** 10 to 12 minutes. **Microwave:** 5 to 7 minutes, stir every 2 minutes, let stand 2 minutes. **Grill:** 15 to 20 minutes, medium coals, turn often.	Season with garlic, oregano, basil, thyme, rosemary, allspice, nutmeg or curry. Serve with grated Parmesan or shredded mozzarella cheese.

VEGETABLE	PREPARATION	COOKING TIME	SEASONING AND SERVING SUGGESTIONS

FENNEL 1 lb.	Cut off and discard woody stems. Cut into slices.
	     To grill, use grill basket or place on grill rack.
		Boil: 15 to 20 minutes.
		Steam: 15 to 20 minutes.
		Panfry: 8 to 10 minutes.
		Bake: 30 to 35 minutes.
		Microwave: 7 to 9 minutes.
		Grill: 15 to 20 minutes, medium coals, turn often.
			Season with chives, savory or pepper.
			     Serve with butter, margarine or olive oil.

GARLIC whole heads	Remove most of paper covering, place whole heads on foil. Brush with oil.	**Bake**: 20 to 30 minutes. **Grill**: 35 to 40 minutes, medium coals.	Season with lemon-pepper or basil.

JERUSALEM ARTICHOKES *(sunchoke)* 1 lb.	Wash and peel. Leave whole or slice. To preserve color before cooking, place in 1 quart water with 3 tablespoons lemon juice.
	     To grill, use grill basket.
		Boil: Whole, 10 to 20 minutes. Slices, 5 to 10 minutes.
		Steam: Whole, 15 to 20 minutes. Slices, 12 to 15 minutes.
		Microwave: Slices, 6 to 7 minutes, let stand 1 minute.
		Grill: Whole or slices, 10 to 20 minutes, medium coals, turn once.
			Season with lemon, chives or marjoram.
			     Serve hot with butter, margarine or white sauce.

KOHLRABI 1½ lb. (4 small to medium)	Remove root ends, tough outer leaves and tops, leaving 2 inches of dark leaves. Split lengthwise and wash thoroughly.
	     To grill, place on grill rack, brush with oil.
		Boil: 20 to 25 minutes.
		Steam: 20 to 25 minutes.
		Microwave: 10 to 12 minutes, stir twice. Let stand 5 minutes.
		Grill: 15 to 20 minutes, medium coals, turn once or twice.
			Season with nutmeg, garlic, basil, dill or chives.
			     Serve with Parmesan cheese, cheese sauce, sour cream, butter or margarine.

LEEKS 1½ lb.	Remove root ends, tough outer leaves and tops, leaving 2 inches of dark leaves. Split lengthwise and wash thoroughly.
	     To grill, place on grill rack, brush with oil.
		Boil: 10 to 15 minutes.
		Steam: 10 to 15 minutes.
		Microwave: 4 to 7 minutes, let stand 3 minutes.
		Grill: 4 to 6 minutes, medium coals, turn once or twice.
			Season with dill, basil, thyme or rosemary.
			     Serve with seasoned butter, crumbled cooked bacon or grated Parmesan cheese.

MUSHROOMS 1 lb.	Wash and pat dry. Cut off tips of stems. Leave whole or slice.
	     To grill, use grill basket or kabobs, brush with oil.
		Panfry: 4 to 5 minutes in 2 to 3 tablespoons butter.
		Broil: 8 to 10 minutes, 4 to 5 inches from heat, brush with butter.
			Season with white wine, garlic, green onions or chives.
			     Serve with toasted almonds, dill or sour cream.

VEGETABLE	PREPARATION	COOKING TIME	SEASONING AND SERVING SUGGESTIONS
MUSHROOMS (*cont.*)		**Microwave:** 4 to 6 minutes with 2 table-spoons butter, let stand 2 minutes. **Grill:** 6 to 8 minutes, medium coals.	
OKRA 1 lb.	Wash thoroughly and cut off ends. Leave whole or slice. To grill, place in grill basket, brush with oil.	**Boil:** 5 to 10 minutes. **Steam:** 15 to 20 minutes. **Microwave:** 7 to 10 minutes, let stand 3 minutes. **Grill:** 10 to 20 minutes, medium coals.	Season with thyme, ground red pepper or oregano. Serve with butter, margarine, buttered bread crumbs, tomato sauce, grated Parmesan cheese, crumbled cooked bacon, French dressing or sour cream.
ONIONS (*white, yellow or red*) 1 lb. (2 large, 4 medium or 8 small)	Trim stem and root ends and wash. Peel and cut large onions into quar-ters or slices; leave small onions whole. To grill, place slices in grill basket, foil or kabobs; brush with oil.	**Boil:** Small whole, 15 to 20 minutes. Large whole, 20 to 30 minutes. **Steam:** Small whole, 20 to 25 minutes. Large whole, 35 to 40 minutes. **Microwave:** Small whole, 4 to 6 minutes, let stand 5 minutes. Large, cut into quarters, 5 to 6 minutes, let stand 5 minutes. **Grill:** 10 to 15 minutes, turn once or twice.	Season with chicken broth, curry, caraway or parsley. Serve with white sauce, buttered bread crumbs or grated Parmesan cheese.
PARSNIPS 1¼ lb. (4 to 5 medium)	Wash and peel. Cut off ends. Leave whole or cut in half, quarters, slices or thin strips. To grill, place strips or slices in grill basket, brush with oil.	**Boil:** Whole, 10 to 20 minutes. Slices, 8 to 15 minutes. **Steam:** Whole, 15 to 25 minutes. Slices, 11 to 17 minutes. **Microwave:** 5 to 7 min-utes, let stand 1 minute. **Grill:** 10 to 15 minutes, turn once or twice.	Season with nutmeg, onions or parsley. Serve with butter, margarine, brown sugar, honey, jelly, cheese or white sauce.
PEA PODS (*snow peas, Chi-nese pea pods or sugar snap peas*) 1 lb.	Wash and remove tips and strings along both sides of pod. To grill, place in grill basket, brush with oil.	**Boil:** 2 to 3 minutes. **Steam:** 3 to 5 minutes. **Microwave:** 4 to 6 min-utes, let stand 1 minute. **Grill:** 8 to 10 minutes, medium coals.	Season with garlic, ginger, bouillon or lemon. Serve with mush-rooms, water chest-nuts, soy sauce, toasted almonds or bean sprouts. Add to stir-fry mixtures.

VEGETABLE	PREPARATION	COOKING TIME	SEASONING AND SERVING SUGGESTIONS
PEAS 2 lb. unshelled, 2 cups shelled	Shell and wash.	**Boil**: 20 to 25 minutes. **Steam**: 20 to 30 minutes. **Microwave**: 14 to 18 minutes, let stand 5 minutes.	Season with marjoram, savory, mint, dill, basil or rosemary. Serve with butter, margarine, cheese or white sauce, crumbled cooked bacon, mushrooms, toasted almonds or sour cream.
PEAS *(black-eyed)* 2 lb. unshelled, 1 lb. shelled	Shell and wash.	**Boil**: 20 to 25 minutes. **Steam**: 20 to 30 minutes. **Microwave**: 14 to 18 minutes, let stand 5 minutes.	Season with garlic, ground red pepper, cumin, chili powder or basil. Serve with butter, margarine, bell pepper, cream or tomato sauce.
PEPPERS/BELL *(green, red or yellow)* 4 peppers	Wash and remove stem, white membrane and seeds. Leave whole, cut in half, rings or strips or chop. To grill, place halves or quarters on grill rack, in grill basket or on kabobs, brush with oil.	**Boil**: Whole or halves, 3 to 5 minutes to partially cook for stuffing. **Steam**: Whole or halves, 10 to 15 minutes. Rings or strips, 8 to 10 minutes. **Panfry**: 6 to 8 minutes. **Microwave**: Whole or halves, 4 to 6 minutes. **Grill**: Whole or halves, 8 to 10 minutes, medium coals, turn once or twice.	Season with basil, oregano, marjoram, onion or garlic. Serve with tomatoes, corn or shredded cheese.
POTATOES 1½ to 2 lb.	Wash and peel if desired. Leave whole or cut into quarters, slices or chunks. To prevent peeled or cut edges from darkening before cooking, submerge in cold water. To bake or microwave, pierce whole potatoes with fork several times. To microwave, place at least 1 inch apart on paper towels in oven. To grill, place whole potatoes on grill rack or place slices in grill basket, brush with oil. Or wrap in foil and place on grill rack.	**Boil**: Whole, 25 to 40 minutes. Quarters, 20 to 25 minutes. Slices or pieces, 15 to 20 minutes. **Steam**: Whole, 30 to 35 minutes. Quarters, 20 to 25 minutes. **Panfry**: ¼-inch thick slices for 20 to 25 minutes. **Bake**: At 350°F. for 1 to 1½ hours or at 400°F. for 45 minutes to 1¼ hours. **Microwave**: 4 whole, 10 to 12 minutes, turn once or twice. **Grill**: 25 to 30 minutes, turn once.	Season with onion, chives or rosemary. Serve with white or cheese sauce, butter or margarine, sour cream, chives, grated cheese or crumbled cooked bacon.

VEGETABLE	PREPARATION	COOKING TIME	SEASONING AND SERVING SUGGESTIONS
POTATOES/ NEW 1½ lb. (10 to 12 small)	Wash and leave whole with skins on. If desired, peel a narrow strip around center of each potato. To microwave, cut potatoes into quarters. To grill, wrap slices in foil or place in grill basket, brush with oil.	**Boil:** 15 to 25 minutes. **Steam:** 18 to 22 minutes. **Panfry:** ¼-inch thick slices for 20 to 25 minutes. **Bake:** 40 to 45 minutes. **Microwave:** 8 to 12 minutes, let stand 3 minutes. **Grill:** 20 to 30 minutes, medium coals.	Season with dill, chives, parsley or lemon peel. Serve with butter, margarine, sour cream, Italian dressing or grated Parmesan cheese.
RUTABAGAS (*yellow turnips*) 2 lb. (1 large or 2 medium)	Wash and peel. Slice, cube or cut into 2-inch pieces. To grill, place in grill basket, brush with oil.	**Boil:** Cubes or pieces, 20 to 30 minutes. **Steam:** Cubes or pieces, 25 to 30 minutes. **Microwave:** Cubes, 14 to 18 minutes, stir every 3 minutes. Let stand 3 minutes. **Grill:** 15 to 20 minutes, medium coals, turn once.	Season with dill, cinnamon or nutmeg. Serve with brown sugar, maple syrup, butter or margarine.
SPINACH AND OTHER GREENS (*beet tops, collards, turnip greens, mustard greens, kale, Swiss chard*) 1½ to 2 lb.	Wash and drain leaves several times. Remove tough stems and wilted leaves. Tear large leaves into bite-sized pieces. To grill, place in grill basket, brush with oil.	**Boil:** Spinach, 3 to 5 minutes. Other greens, 9 to 12 minutes. **Steam:** Spinach, 5 to 12 minutes. Other greens, 10 to 15 minutes. **Microwave:** Spinach, 4 to 7 minutes. Other greens, 7 to 9 minutes. **Grill:** 8 to 10 minutes, medium coals, turn once.	Season with garlic, onion, nutmeg, lemon or lime juice. Serve with crumbled cooked bacon, vinegar, soy sauce, white sauce, toasted sesame seed, sour cream or French dressing.
SUMMER SQUASH (*pattypan, zucchini, straight-neck, yellow, crookneck and cocozelle*) 2 lb.	Wash but do not peel. Cut off stem and blossom end. If necessary, remove seeds and fibers. Slice or cube. To grill, cut into strips lengthwise. Use grill basket, kabobs or place on grill rack, brush with oil.	**Boil:** 5 to 10 minutes. **Steam:** 5 to 10 minutes. **Microwave:** 7 to 11 minutes, let stand 3 minutes. **Grill:** 5 to 10 minutes, medium coals, turn once.	Season with oregano, basil, dill, nutmeg, ginger, allspice or rosemary. Serve with sour cream, butter, margarine, grated Parmesan cheese, parsley or crumbled cooked bacon.
SWEET POTATOES OR YAMS 1½ to 2 lb.	Wash but do not peel. After cooking, remove skins and slice or mash. To bake or microwave, pierce with a fork several times. To grill, leave whole, cut into ½-inch thick	**Boil:** Whole, 20 to 30 minutes. **Steam:** 30 to 40 minutes. **Bake:** At 400°F. for 45 to 60 minutes. **Microwave:** 8 to 12 minutes, let stand 1 minute.	Season with cinnamon, allspice or nutmeg. Serve with butter, margarine, brown sugar, maple syrup or honey.

VEGETABLE	PREPARATION	COOKING TIME	SEASONING AND SERVING SUGGESTIONS
SWEET POTATOES OR YAMS *(cont.)*	slices. Place in grill basket or wrap in foil.	**Grill:** Whole, 50 to 60 minutes. Slices, 25 to 30 minutes, medium coals, turn once.	
TOMATOES 1½ lb. (5 medium)	Wash and cut out stem. Peel if desired. (Dip tomato into boiling water for 30 seconds, remove and dip into cold water, peel.) To grill, plum tomatoes can be placed on kabobs. Large tomatoes can be sliced and placed on grill rack, brush with oil.	**Boil:** Slices or wedges without additional liquid, 7 to 15 minutes over low heat. **Microwave:** Slices or wedges without additional liquid, 5 to 8 minutes, let stand 1 minute. **Grill:** 8 to 10 minutes, medium coals, turn once.	Season with basil, oregano, thyme, marjoram, sage or tarragon. Serve with sour cream, vinaigrette dressing, grated Parmesan cheese or chives.
TURNIPS 1 lb.	Wash and peel. Leave whole or cut into slices or cubes. To grill, place slices in grill basket or on grill rack, brush with oil.	**Boil:** Whole, 20 to 30 minutes. Slices, 10 to 15 minutes. **Steam:** Whole, 25 to 35 minutes. Slices, 20 to 25 minutes. **Microwave:** 9 to 14 minutes, let stand 3 minutes. **Grill:** 15 to 20 minutes, medium coals, turn once or twice.	Season with basil, dill, thyme or chives. Serve with butter, margarine, onion, crumbled cooked bacon or brown sugar.
WINTER SQUASH *(banana, butternut, buttercup, hubbard, acorn, spaghetti, delicata, sweet dumpling, sugar pumpkin)* 3 lb.	To boil or steam, peel and cut into cubes or slices. To bake or microwave, cut in half or in serving-sized pieces. To bake, place cut side up in shallow baking dish or pan. Add ¼ cup water. Top with butter or margarine. Cover with foil. To microwave, do not use water. Spread cut surfaces with butter and place in dish; cover with plastic wrap. Remove seeds and fiber. To grill, peel and cut into slices. Place on grill rack, brush with oil.	**Boil:** Slices, 7 to 9 minutes. Cubes, 6 to 8 minutes. Spaghetti squash, place cut side up, boil 25 to 30 minutes. **Steam:** Slices, 9 to 12 minutes. Cubes, 7 to 10 minutes. **Bake:** For acorn, buttercup, butternut, hubbard or spaghetti squash, bake at 400°F. for 30 to 50 minutes. Banana, 20 to 30 minutes. **Microwave:** 10 to 13 minutes, let stand 5 minutes. **Grill:** 35 to 40 minutes, medium coals, turn once or twice.	Season with curry, nutmeg or sage. Serve with honey, brown sugar, maple syrup, cooked crumbled bacon, orange juice, butter or margarine. Tuck several unpeeled cloves of garlic and a sprig of fresh thyme into each halfsquash before microwaving or baking.

DESSERTS, CAKES
& PIES

DESSERTS, CAKES & PIES

There are those who insist that no meal is complete without a sweet finale. And then there are those who would prefer to skip the meal and go directly to dessert. With its collection of creamy cheesecakes, home-style puddings, delicious cakes and exquisite pies and tarts, this chapter will delight all lovers of sweets. Whether as the centerpiece for a special celebration, or as the luscious conclusion to a meal, each one is worth saving room for.

Blueberry Crumble

PREP TIME: 10 MINUTES (READY IN 40 MINUTES)
♦ YIELD: 6 SERVINGS

FRUIT MIXTURE
4 cups fresh or frozen blueberries
¼ cup raisins
2 tablespoons cornstarch
1 teaspoon grated lemon peel
1 tablespoon lemon juice
⅓ cup apricot preserves

TOPPING
½ cup all-purpose flour
½ cup firmly packed brown sugar
1 teaspoon cinnamon
¼ cup margarine or butter, softened

1. Heat oven to 400°F. Grease 10×6-inch (1½-quart) or 8-inch square (2-quart) baking dish. In large bowl, combine blueberries, raisins, cornstarch, lemon peel and lemon juice; mix well. Spoon mixture evenly into greased baking dish. Dot with apricot preserves.
2. In medium bowl, combine flour, brown sugar and cinnamon; mix well. With pastry blender or fork, cut in margarine until mixture is crumbly. Sprinkle topping evenly over fruit mixture.
3. Bake at 400°F. for 20 to 30 minutes or until topping is golden brown. Serve warm or at room temperature. If desired, top with whipped topping or ice cream.

NUTRITION INFORMATION PER SERVING: Serving Size: ⅙ of Recipe ♦ Calories: 320 ♦ Calories from Fat: 70 ♦ % DAILY VALUE: Total Fat: 8 g 12% ♦ Saturated Fat: 1 g 5% ♦ Cholesterol: 0 mg 0% ♦ Sodium: 110 mg 5% ♦ Total Carbohydrate: 59 g 20% ♦ Dietary Fiber: 4 g 16% ♦ Sugars: 38 g ♦ Protein: 2 g ♦ Vitamin A: 8% ♦ Vitamin C: 20% ♦ Calcium: 4% ♦ Iron: 8% ♦ DIETARY EXCHANGES: 1 Starch, 3 Fruit, 1½ Fat OR 4 Carbohydrate, 1½ Fat

Apple Brown Betty

PREP TIME: 10 MINUTES (READY IN 1 HOUR 20 MINUTES) ♦ YIELD: 8 SERVINGS

5 cups (5 medium) sliced peeled apples
½ cup firmly packed brown sugar
1 teaspoon grated lemon peel
¼ teaspoon nutmeg
1 tablespoon lemon juice
1 cup unseasoned dry bread crumbs
½ cup margarine or butter, melted
   Half-and-half, if desired

1. Heat oven to 375°F. Grease 8-inch square (2-quart) baking dish. In large bowl, combine apples, brown sugar, lemon peel, nutmeg and lemon juice; mix well.
2. In medium bowl, combine bread crumbs and margarine; sprinkle ½ cup bread crumb mixture in greased baking dish. Spoon apple mixture over crumb mixture; top with remaining bread crumb mixture. Cover with foil.
3. Bake at 375°F. for 45 to 50 minutes or until apples are almost tender. Uncover; bake an additional 15 to 20 minutes or until top is crisp and golden brown. Serve warm with half-and-half.

NUTRITION INFORMATION PER SERVING: Serving Size: ⅛ of Recipe ♦ Calories: 300 ♦ Calories from Fat: 140 ♦ % DAILY VALUE: Total Fat: 16 g 25% ♦ Saturated Fat: 5 g 25% ♦ Cholesterol: 10 mg 3% ♦ Sodium: 270 mg 11% ♦ Total Carbohydrate: 35 g 12% ♦ Dietary Fiber: 2 g 8% ♦ Sugars: 23 g ♦ Protein: 3 g ♦ Vitamin A: 15% ♦ Vitamin C: 4% ♦ Calcium: 8% ♦ Iron: 6% ♦ DIETARY EXCHANGES: 1 Starch, 1½ Fruit, 3 Fat OR 2½ Carbohydrate, 3 Fat

COOK'S NOTE

**APPLE BROWN BETTY
VS. APPLE CRISP**

How can you tell the two apart? Apple Brown Betty's (page 332) topping is made with flour or bread crumbs, butter, sugar and spices; Apple Crisp (see Fresh Fruit Crisp on page 334) is a baked, deep-dish apple dessert made with a crumb or streusel topping.

Strawberry Shortcake

PREP TIME: 25 MINUTES (READY IN 1 HOUR)
◆ YIELD: 8 SERVINGS

SHORTCAKE
2 cups all-purpose flour
1/2 cup sugar
3 teaspoons baking powder
1/2 teaspoon salt
1/2 cup margarine or butter
3/4 cup milk
2 eggs, slightly beaten

FRUIT
2 pints (4 cups) fresh strawberries, sliced
1/2 cup sugar

TOPPING
1 cup whipping cream
2 tablespoons powdered sugar
1/2 teaspoon vanilla

1. Heat oven to 375°F. Grease and flour 8 or 9-inch round cake pan. In large bowl, combine flour, 1/2 cup sugar, baking powder and salt; mix well. With pastry blender or fork, cut in margarine until mixture resembles coarse crumbs. Add milk and eggs, stirring just until dry ingredients are moistened. Spoon into greased and floured pan.
2. Bake at 375°F. for 25 to 30 minutes or until toothpick inserted in center comes out clean. Cool 10 minutes.
3. Meanwhile, in medium bowl, combine strawberries and 1/2 cup sugar; mix well. Refrigerate 30 minutes or until serving time.
4. Just before serving, in small bowl, beat whipping cream until soft peaks form. Add powdered sugar and vanilla; beat until stiff peaks form.

5. Invert shortcake onto serving platter. If desired, split shortcake into 2 layers. Serve shortcake topped with strawberries and whipped cream. Store in refrigerator.

HIGH ALTITUDE (*above 3500 feet*)**:** Increase flour to 2 cups plus 2 tablespoons; decrease baking powder to 2 1/2 teaspoons. Bake at 375°F. for 30 to 35 minutes.

NUTRITION INFORMATION PER SERVING: Serving Size: 1/8 of Recipe ◆ Calories: 490 ◆ Calories from Fat: 230 ◆ **% DAILY VALUE:** Total Fat: 25 g 38% ◆ Saturated Fat: 10 g 50% ◆ Cholesterol: 95 mg 32% ◆ Sodium: 490 mg 20% ◆ Total Carbohydrate: 59 g 20% ◆ Dietary Fiber: 3 g 12% ◆ Sugars: 34 g ◆ Protein: 7 g ◆ Vitamin A: 20% ◆ Vitamin C: 60% ◆ Calcium: 20% ◆ Iron: 10% ◆ **DIETARY EXCHANGES:** 2 Starch, 2 Fruit, 4 1/2 Fat OR 4 Carbohydrate, 4 1/2 Fat

Strawberry Celebration Dessert

PREP TIME: 25 MINUTES (READY IN 2 HOURS 55 MINUTES) ◆ YIELD: 16 SERVINGS

CRUST
1 1/2 cups graham cracker crumbs (24 squares)
1/4 cup sugar
1/3 cup margarine or butter, melted

FILLING
3 cups miniature marshmallows
1/2 cup orange juice
1 pint (2 cups) whipping cream, whipped
1/4 teaspoon almond extract
2 pints (4 cups) fresh strawberries, sliced

1. In small bowl, combine all crust ingredients; mix well. Press in bottom of ungreased 13×9-inch pan. Refrigerate to cool.
2. Meanwhile, in medium saucepan, combine marshmallows and orange juice; cook over low heat until marshmallows are melted, stirring constantly. Cool 30 minutes.
3. Fold whipped cream and almond extract into marshmallow mixture. Spoon half of whipped cream mixture over crust. Arrange strawberries evenly over whipped cream mixture. Top with remaining whipped cream mixture. Refrigerate 2 to 3 hours to blend flavors.
4. To serve, cut into squares. If desired, garnish each serving with additional strawberries. Store in refrigerator.

NUTRITION INFORMATION PER SERVING: Serving Size: 1/16 of Recipe ◆ Calories: 240 ◆ Calories from Fat: 140 ◆ **% DAILY VALUE:** Total Fat: 16 g 25% ◆ Saturated Fat: 8 g 40% ◆ Cholesterol: 40 mg 13% ◆ Sodium: 105 mg 4% ◆ Total Carbohydrate: 21 g 7% ◆ Dietary Fiber: 1 g 4% ◆ Sugars: 14 g ◆ Protein: 2 g ◆ Vitamin A: 15% ◆ Vitamin C: 35% ◆ Calcium: 4% ◆ Iron: 2% ◆ **DIETARY EXCHANGES:** 1/2 Starch, 1 Fruit, 3 Fat OR 1 1/2 Carbohydrate, 3 Fat

Simple Fruit Crisp (page 335)

Maple Baked Apples

PREP TIME: 20 MINUTES (READY IN 1 HOUR 10 MINUTES)
◆ YIELD: 6 SERVINGS

    6 large baking apples
    2 tablespoons lemon juice
  ½ cup raisins
  ½ teaspoon cinnamon
    1 cup real maple or maple-flavored syrup
  ¼ cup water

1. Heat oven to 350°F. Core apples and remove a 1-inch strip of peel around top to prevent splitting. Brush tops and insides with lemon juice. Place apples in ungreased 8-inch square (2-quart) baking dish.
2. In small bowl, combine raisins and cinnamon; fill center of each apple with mixture. Pour maple syrup over apples. Add ¼ cup water to baking dish.
3. Bake at 350°F. for 45 to 50 minutes or until apples are tender, occasionally spooning syrup mixture over apples.

NUTRITION INFORMATION PER SERVING: Serving Size: ⅙ of Recipe ◆ Calories: 320 ◆ Calories from Fat: 10 ◆ **% DAILY VALUE:** Total Fat: 1 g 2% ◆ Saturated Fat: 0 g 0% ◆ Cholesterol: 0 mg 0% ◆ Sodium: 5 mg 0% ◆ Total Carbohydrate: 78 g 26% ◆ Dietary Fiber: 6 g 24% ◆ Sugars: 70 g ◆ Protein: 1 g ◆ Vitamin A: 2% ◆ Vitamin C: 15% ◆ Calcium: 6% ◆ Iron: 8% ◆ **DIETARY EXCHANGES:** 5½ Fruit OR 5½ Carbohydrate

Maple Baked Apples

Fresh Fruit Crisp

PREP TIME: 15 MINUTES (READY IN 50 MINUTES)
◆ YIELD: 12 (½-CUP) SERVINGS

FRUIT MIXTURE
    6 cups sliced apples, peaches, nectarines, pears, plums and/or apricots, peeled if desired
    1 teaspoon cinnamon, if desired
    1 tablespoon water
    1 teaspoon lemon juice

TOPPING
    1 cup rolled oats
  ¾ cup all-purpose flour
  ¾ cup firmly packed brown sugar
  ½ cup margarine or butter, softened

1. Heat oven to 375°F. Place fruit in ungreased 2-quart casserole. Sprinkle with cinnamon, water and lemon juice.
2. In large bowl, combine all topping ingredients. With pastry blender or fork, mix until crumbly. Sprinkle evenly over fruit.
3. Bake at 375°F. for 25 to 35 minutes or until fruit is tender and topping is golden brown. Serve warm with cream, ice cream or whipped cream, if desired.

1. MICROWAVE DIRECTIONS: Prepare recipe as directed above, using 8-inch square (2-quart) microwave-safe dish.
2. Microwave on HIGH for 12 to 14 minutes or until fruit is tender, rotating dish ¼ turn halfway through cooking.

NUTRITION INFORMATION PER SERVING: Serving Size: ½ Cup ◆ Calories: 210 ◆ Calories from Fat: 70 ◆ **% DAILY VALUE:** Total Fat: 8 g 12% ◆ Saturated Fat: 2 g 10% ◆ Cholesterol: 0 mg 0% ◆ Sodium: 95 mg 4% ◆ Total Carbohydrate: 32 g 11% ◆ Dietary Fiber: 2 g 8% ◆ Sugars: 20 g ◆ Protein: 2 g ◆ Vitamin A: 8% ◆ Vitamin C: 0% ◆ Calcium: 2% ◆ Iron: 6% ◆ **DIETARY EXCHANGES:** 1 Starch, 1 Fruit, 1½ Fat OR 2 Carbohydrate, 1½ Fat

Simple Fruit Crisp

PREP TIME: 10 MINUTES (READY IN 40 MINUTES)
+ YIELD: 8 SERVINGS

FRUIT
  1 (21-oz.) can fruit pie filling (apple, apricot, cherry, blueberry, peach or raspberry)

TOPPING
  ¾ cup all-purpose flour
  ⅓ cup firmly packed brown sugar
  ½ teaspoon cinnamon, if desired
  ½ teaspoon nutmeg, if desired
  ¼ cup margarine or butter, softened

1. Heat oven to 375°F. Spread pie filling in ungreased 8-inch square (2-quart) baking dish.

2. In medium bowl, combine all topping ingredients; mix until crumbly. Sprinkle over pie filling.

3. Bake at 375°F. for 25 to 30 minutes or until bubbly and golden brown. If desired, serve warm with frozen yogurt or whipped topping.

NUTRITION INFORMATION PER SERVING: Serving Size: ⅛ of Recipe + Calories: 220 + Calories from Fat: 50 + % DAILY VALUE: Total Fat: 6 g 9% + Saturated Fat: 1 g 5% + Cholesterol: 0 mg 0% + Sodium: 75 mg 3% + Total Carbohydrate: 40 g 13% + Dietary Fiber: 1 g 3% + Sugars: 28 g + Protein: 2 g + Vitamin A: 8% + Vitamin C: 4% + Calcium: 2% + Iron: 6% + DIETARY EXCHANGES: 1 Starch, 1½ Fruit, 1 Fat OR 2½ Carbohydrate, 1 Fat

Old-Fashioned Berry Cobbler

PREP TIME: 35 MINUTES (READY IN 1 HOUR 10 MINUTES)
+ YIELD: 8 SERVINGS

FRUIT MIXTURE
  4 cups fresh or frozen berries (raspberries, blackberries, boysenberries and/or loganberries)
  ½ cup seedless raspberry jam
  2 tablespoons quick-cooking tapioca or cornstarch
  ⅓ cup sugar
  1 tablespoon margarine or butter, cut into small pieces

BISCUITS
  1 cup all-purpose flour
  2 tablespoons sugar
  2 teaspoons baking powder
  ¼ teaspoon salt
  ¼ cup margarine or butter
  1 egg
  2 to 4 tablespoons milk
  1 teaspoon sugar

Old-Fashioned Berry Cobbler

1. Heat oven to 425°F. Spray 8-inch square (2-quart) baking dish with nonstick cooking spray.

2. In large bowl, combine berries, jam, tapioca and ⅓ cup sugar; mix gently. Spread in sprayed baking dish. Top with 1 tablespoon margarine.

3. Bake at 425°F. for 20 to 30 minutes or until berry mixture begins to bubble and is thickened and clear, stirring every 10 minutes.

4. Meanwhile, in large bowl, combine flour, 2 tablespoons sugar, baking powder and salt; mix well. With pastry blender or fork, cut in ¼ cup margarine until crumbly. In small bowl, combine egg and 2 tablespoons milk; beat well. Stir into flour mixture until a stiff dough forms, adding additional milk if necessary.

5. On lightly floured surface, roll out dough to ½-inch thickness. With 2-inch cookie cutter, cut out hearts, rounds or diamonds. Stir hot fruit mixture; top with dough cutouts. Sprinkle cutouts with 1 teaspoon sugar.

6. Bake at 425°F. for 10 to 20 minutes or until fruit bubbles around edges and biscuits are light golden brown. Cool at least 15 minutes.

HIGH ALTITUDE (*above 3500 feet*): No change.

NUTRITION INFORMATION PER SERVING: Serving Size: ⅛ of Recipe + Calories: 280 + Calories from Fat: 70 + % DAILY VALUE: Total Fat: 8 g 12% + Saturated Fat: 2 g 10% + Cholesterol: 25 mg 8% + Sodium: 290 mg 12% + Total Carbohydrate: 48 g 16% + Dietary Fiber: 4 g 16% + Sugars: 26 g + Protein: 4 g + Vitamin A: 10% + Vitamin C: 20% + Calcium: 10% + Iron: 8% + DIETARY EXCHANGES: 1 Starch, 2 Fruit, 1½ Fat OR 3 Carbohydrate, 1½ Fat

Cherries Jubilee

PREP TIME: 10 MINUTES ◆ YIELD: 8 SERVINGS

1 (16-oz.) can (2 cups) pitted dark sweet
　cherries
1 tablespoon cornstarch
¼ cup brandy
1 quart (4 cups) fat-free vanilla frozen yogurt
　or ice cream

1. Drain cherries, reserving liquid. In chafing dish or skillet, combine cornstarch and liquid from cherries; blend well. Add cherries; heat until mixture boils and thickens, stirring occasionally.
2. Heat brandy in small saucepan; pour over cherries. Carefully ignite. Serve over frozen yogurt or ice cream.

NUTRITION INFORMATION PER SERVING: Serving Size: ⅛ of Recipe ◆ Calories: 150 ◆ Calories from Fat: 0 ◆ % DAILY VALUE: Total Fat: 0 g 0% ◆ Saturated Fat: 0 g 0% ◆ Cholesterol: 0 mg 0% ◆ Sodium: 70 mg 3% ◆ Total Carbohydrate: 30 g 10% ◆ Dietary Fiber: 1 g 3% ◆ Sugars: 17 g ◆ Protein: 4 g ◆ Vitamin A: 0% ◆ Vitamin C: 0% ◆ Calcium: 10% ◆ Iron: 0% ◆ DIETARY EXCHANGES: 1 Starch, 1 Fruit OR 2 Carbohydrate

Peach Melba

PREP TIME: 20 MINUTES (READY IN 1 HOUR 5 MINUTES) ◆ YIELD: 6 SERVINGS

2 teaspoons cornstarch
½ cup currant jelly
1 (10-oz.) pkg. frozen raspberries in syrup,
　thawed
1 (29-oz.) can peach halves, drained, or 6 fresh
　peach halves, peeled
1 quart (4 cups) vanilla ice cream

1. In medium saucepan, combine cornstarch, jelly and raspberries with liquid. Cook over medium heat until mixture boils and thickens, stirring frequently.
2. If desired, place strainer over medium bowl; pour berry mixture into strainer. Press mixture with back of spoon through strainer to remove seeds; discard seeds. Cool 40 to 45 minutes or until completely cooled.
3. To serve, place peach half in each dessert dish. Top with ice cream; spoon cooled raspberry sauce over ice cream.

NUTRITION INFORMATION PER SERVING: Serving Size: ⅙ of Recipe ◆ Calories: 340 ◆ Calories from Fat: 90 ◆ % DAILY VALUE: Total Fat: 10 g 15% ◆ Saturated Fat: 6 g 30% ◆ Cholesterol: 40 mg 13% ◆ Sodium: 85 mg 4% ◆ Total Carbohydrate: 59 g 20% ◆ Dietary Fiber: 4 g 16% ◆ Sugars: 42 g ◆ Protein: 4 g ◆ Vitamin A: 20% ◆ Vitamin C: 15% ◆ Calcium: 10% ◆ Iron: 4% ◆ DIETARY EXCHANGES: 1 Starch, 3 Fruit, 2 Fat OR 4 Carbohydrate, 2 Fat

---

COOK'S NOTE

DESSERTS WITH A FLARE

For best results, heat the brandy just until it begins to release fumes—the fumes are actually what will burn. Do not allow brandy to boil or it may catch fire on its own. Follow the steps to flambé as outlined in the recipe, and don't forget to tie back loose hair and clothing.

Baked Custard

PREP TIME: 10 MINUTES (READY IN 1 HOUR 5 MINUTES) ◆ YIELD: 6 SERVINGS

3 eggs, slightly beaten
¼ cup sugar
⅛ teaspoon salt
1 teaspoon vanilla
2½ cups milk
　Dash nutmeg

1. Heat oven to 350°F. In large bowl, combine eggs, sugar, salt and vanilla; blend well. Gradually stir in milk. Pour into 6 ungreased 6-oz. custard cups. Sprinkle with nutmeg. Place custard cups in 13×9-inch pan; place in oven. Pour boiling water into pan around custard cups to a depth of 1 inch.
2. Bake at 350°F. for 45 to 55 minutes or until knife inserted near center comes out clean. Serve warm or cold. Store in refrigerator.

TIP: If desired, pour mixture into 1 or 1½-quart casserole. Place in 13×9-inch pan; pour boiling water into pan around casserole to a depth of 1 inch. Bake at 350°F. for 50 to 60 minutes.

NUTRITION INFORMATION PER SERVING: Serving Size: ⅙ of Recipe ◆ Calories: 120 ◆ Calories from Fat: 35 ◆ % DAILY VALUE: Total Fat: 4 g 6% ◆ Saturated Fat: 2 g 10% ◆ Cholesterol: 115 mg 38% ◆ Sodium: 125 mg 5% ◆ Total Carbohydrate: 14 g 5% ◆ Dietary Fiber: 0 g 0% ◆ Sugars: 14 g ◆ Protein: 7 g ◆ Vitamin A: 8% ◆ Vitamin C: 0% ◆ Calcium: 15% ◆ Iron: 2% ◆ DIETARY EXCHANGES: 1 Starch, ½ Medium-Fat Meat OR 1 Carbohydrate, ½ Medium-Fat Meat

Mom's Apple Dumplings

PREP TIME: 25 MINUTES (READY IN 1 HOUR 15 MINUTES) ◆ YIELD: 6 SERVINGS

SAUCE

1½ cups sugar
1½ cups water
¼ cup red cinnamon candies
¼ teaspoon cinnamon
¼ teaspoon nutmeg

DUMPLINGS

2 cups all-purpose flour
2 teaspoons baking powder
1 teaspoon salt
⅔ cup shortening
½ to ⅔ cup cold milk
6 small (2½-inch diameter) baking apples, peeled, cored
3 tablespoons margarine or butter
1 egg white, beaten
1 tablespoon sugar

1. In medium saucepan, combine all sauce ingredients. Bring to a full rolling boil, stirring occasionally. Set aside.

2. Heat oven to 375°F. In large bowl, combine flour, baking powder and salt. With pastry blender or fork, cut in shortening until mixture resembles coarse crumbs. Sprinkle flour mixture with milk while tossing and mixing lightly with fork, adding enough milk to form a soft dough. Shape dough into ball.

3. On lightly floured surface, roll dough into 18 × 12-inch rectangle. Cut rectangle into 6 squares. Place 1 apple in center of each pastry square; dot with margarine. Bring corners of pastry squares up to top of apples; press edges to seal. Place in ungreased 13 × 9-inch pan. Pour sauce in pan evenly around dumplings. Brush dumplings with egg white; sprinkle with 1 tablespoon sugar.

4. Bake at 375°F. for 40 to 50 minutes or until dumplings are light golden brown and apples are tender. Serve dumplings warm or cool with sauce and, if desired, half-and-half.

TIP: If desired, prepare 5 dumplings, omitting 1 apple and reserving remaining pastry square for decorative cutouts. Garnish sealed dumplings with cutouts before baking.

HIGH ALTITUDE (*above 3500 feet*)**:** No change.

NUTRITION INFORMATION PER SERVING: Serving Size: 1 Dumpling ◆ Calories: 730 ◆ Calories from Fat: 260 ◆ **% DAILY VALUE:** Total Fat: 29 g 45% ◆ Saturated Fat: 7 g 35% ◆ Cholesterol: 2 mg 1% ◆ Sodium: 610 mg 25% ◆ Total Carbohydrate: 110 g 37% ◆ Dietary Fiber: 3 g 12% ◆ Sugars: 71 g ◆ Protein: 6 g ◆ Vitamin A: 8% ◆ Vitamin C: 4% ◆ Calcium: 15% ◆ Iron: 15% ◆ **DIETARY EXCHANGES:** 2 Starch, 5½ Fruit, 5½ Fat OR 7½ Carbohydrate, 5½ Fat

Caramel Flan (Crème Caramel)

PREP TIME: 15 MINUTES (READY IN 5 HOURS 45 MINUTES) ◆ YIELD: 8 SERVINGS

1 cup sugar
5 eggs
2½ cups milk
1 teaspoon vanilla
3 cups fresh fruit (sliced strawberries, sliced kiwi fruit, seedless grapes and/or pineapple cubes)

1. Heat oven to 325°F. In heavy small skillet, heat ½ cup of the sugar over medium heat until sugar melts and turns a rich golden-brown color, stirring constantly. Immediately pour sugar into 8-inch ring mold. Holding ring mold with pot holders, swirl so sugar coats bottom and sides.

2. In large bowl, slightly beat eggs. Stir in milk, remaining ½ cup sugar and vanilla. Place sugar-coated ring mold in shallow baking pan; place in oven. Pour egg mixture over sugar in mold. Pour very hot water into pan around mold to a depth of 1 inch.

3. Bake at 325°F. for 55 to 60 minutes or until knife inserted halfway between center and edge comes out clean. Remove mold from hot water; place on wire rack. Cool 1 hour or until completely cooled. Refrigerate at least 3½ hours.

4. To unmold, run knife around edge of custard to loosen; invert onto serving platter. Spoon any caramel that remains in mold over custard. Serve with fruit. Store in refrigerator.

NUTRITION INFORMATION PER SERVING: Serving Size: ⅛ of Recipe ◆ Calories: 210 ◆ Calories from Fat: 45 ◆ **% DAILY VALUE:** Total Fat: 5 g 8% ◆ Saturated Fat: 2 g 10% ◆ Cholesterol: 140 mg 47% ◆ Sodium: 80 mg 3% ◆ Total Carbohydrate: 33 g 11% ◆ Dietary Fiber: 1 g 4% ◆ Sugars: 32 g ◆ Protein: 7 g ◆ Vitamin A: 8% ◆ Vitamin C: 40% ◆ Calcium: 10% ◆ Iron: 4% ◆ **DIETARY EXCHANGES:** 2 Starch, 1 Fat OR 2 Carbohydrate, 1 Fat

Apple-Cranberry Strudel

Apple-Cranberry Strudel

PREP TIME: 35 MINUTES (READY IN 1 HOUR 15 MINUTES)
✦ YIELD: 8 SERVINGS

 2 apples, chopped (about 2 cups)
½ cup fresh or frozen cranberries
½ cup sugar
½ cup finely chopped walnuts
 1 teaspoon grated lemon peel
 2 teaspoons lemon juice
 8 (17 x 12-inch) sheets frozen phyllo (filo)
    pastry, thawed
⅓ to ½ cup butter, melted
 4 tablespoons unseasoned dry bread crumbs

1. Heat oven to 375°F. Grease 15 × 10 × 1-inch baking pan. In medium bowl, combine apples, cranberries, sugar, walnuts, lemon peel and lemon juice; toss to coat.
2. Unroll phyllo sheets; cover with plastic wrap or towel. Place 1 phyllo sheet on piece of plastic wrap. Brush with butter; sprinkle with 1 tablespoon bread crumbs. Repeat layering with remaining phyllo sheets and butter, sprinkling 1 tablespoon bread crumbs on every other sheet. (Top phyllo sheet should be brushed with butter only.)
3. Spoon apple mixture over phyllo stack to within 2 inches of each edge; press lightly. Fold shorter sides of phyllo up over filling. Starting with longer side and using plastic wrap, lift phyllo and carefully roll up jelly-roll fashion. Place, seam side down, in greased pan. Make several crosswise cuts in top of roll. Brush top with any remaining butter.
4. Bake at 375°F. for 20 to 25 minutes or until golden brown. Cool at least 15 minutes before serving. To serve, cut into slices.

NUTRITION INFORMATION PER SERVING: Serving Size: ⅛ of Recipe ✦ Calories: 300 ✦ Calories from Fat: 160 ✦ **% DAILY VALUE:** Total Fat: 18 g 28% ✦ Saturated Fat: 8 g 40% ✦ Cholesterol: 30 mg 10% ✦ Sodium: 230 mg 10% ✦ Total Carbohydrate: 32 g 11% ✦ Dietary Fiber: 2 g 8% ✦ Sugars: 18 g ✦ Protein: 3 g ✦ Vitamin A: 10% ✦ Vitamin C: 4% ✦ Calcium: 0% ✦ Iron: 6% ✦ **DIETARY EXCHANGES:** 1 Starch, 1 Fruit, 3½ Fat OR 2 Carbohydrate, 3½ Fat

C O O K ' S   N O T E

HOW TO HANDLE PHYLLO (FILO) DOUGH

Traditional Greek and Middle Eastern bakers prepare phyllo from scratch, stretching the dough to an incredibly paper-thin leaf. Frozen phyllo from the supermarket is an excellent and infinitely easier alternative. Phyllo is used for both sweet and savory dishes.

Before you begin using phyllo, lay a piece of plastic wrap (larger than the phyllo dough) onto the counter. Unroll phyllo sheets onto the plastic wrap. To keep the paper-thin sheets of phyllo from drying out, which can happen in minutes, cover the dough with plastic wrap or a damp towel, replacing the wrap immediately after you remove each sheet.

The remaining phyllo dough can be rolled up, sealed tightly in plastic wrap and stored in the freezer.

Individual Hot Fudge Sundae Cakes

PREP TIME: 10 MINUTES (READY IN 35 MINUTES)
✦ YIELD: 6 SERVINGS

 1 cup all-purpose flour
½ cup sugar
 2 tablespoons unsweetened cocoa
1½ teaspoons baking powder
⅔ cup skim milk

2 tablespoons margarine or butter, melted
1 teaspoon vanilla
¾ cup firmly packed brown sugar
¼ cup unsweetened cocoa
1½ cups hot water

1. Heat oven to 350°F. In small bowl, combine flour, sugar, 2 tablespoons cocoa and baking powder; mix well. Add milk, margarine and vanilla; blend well. Spoon evenly into 6 ungreased 10-oz. custard cups. Place cups in 15 × 10 × 1-inch baking pan.
2. In small bowl, combine brown sugar and ¼ cup cocoa; mix well. Spoon 2 to 3 tablespoons mixture evenly over batter in each cup. Pour ¼ cup hot water evenly over sugar mixture in each cup.
3. Bake at 350°F. for 20 to 25 minutes or until center is set and firm to the touch. Serve warm. If desired, sprinkle with powdered sugar, or serve with nonfat frozen yogurt or light whipped topping.*

> **TIP:** * To decorate top of each dessert with powdered sugar, cut stencil of favorite holiday shape from paper, or use paper doily. Place stencil on dessert; dust with powdered sugar. Remove stencil.

HIGH ALTITUDE (*above 3500 feet*)**:** No change.

Old-Fashioned Bread Pudding with Brandy Hard Sauce

NUTRITION INFORMATION PER SERVING: Serving Size: ⅙ of Recipe ◆ Calories: 320 ◆ Calories from Fat: 45 ◆ **% DAILY VALUE:** Total Fat: 5 g 8% ◆ Saturated Fat: 1 g 5% ◆ Cholesterol: 0 mg 0% ◆ Sodium: 150 mg 6% ◆ Total Carbohydrate: 64 g 21% ◆ Dietary Fiber: 2 g 8% ◆ Sugars: 45 g ◆ Protein: 4 g ◆ Vitamin A: 4% ◆ Vitamin C: 0% ◆ Calcium: 10% ◆ Iron: 15% ◆ **DIETARY EXCHANGES:** 1½ Starch, 2½ Fruit, 1 Fat OR 4 Carbohydrate, 1 Fat

Old-Fashioned Bread Pudding with Brandy Hard Sauce

PREP TIME: 15 MINUTES (READY IN 1 HOUR 10 MINUTES) ◆ YIELD: 10 SERVINGS

PUDDING
5 cups cubed white and whole wheat bread*
2½ cups warm milk
½ cup sugar
1 teaspoon cinnamon
¾ teaspoon nutmeg
1 teaspoon vanilla
2 eggs, beaten
1 cup raisins
¼ cup chopped nuts

HARD SAUCE
2 cups powdered sugar
½ cup butter, softened
1 tablespoon hot water
2 tablespoons brandy or 2 teaspoons brandy extract

1. Heat oven to 350°F. Grease 2-quart casserole. In greased casserole, combine bread cubes and milk. In medium bowl, combine sugar, cinnamon, nutmeg, vanilla and eggs; mix well. Stir in raisins and nuts. Add egg mixture to soaked bread cubes; blend well.
2. Bake at 350°F. for 50 to 60 minutes or until pudding is set.
3. Meanwhile, in small bowl, combine all hard sauce ingredients. Beat at high speed until well blended. Cover; refrigerate until serving time. Serve hard sauce over warm pudding.

> **TIP:** * Four slices white bread and four slices whole wheat bread yield about 5 cups bread cubes.

NUTRITION INFORMATION PER SERVING: Serving Size: ⅒ of Recipe ◆ Calories: 390 ◆ Calories from Fat: 130 ◆ **% DAILY VALUE:** Total Fat: 14 g 22% ◆ Saturated Fat: 7 g 35% ◆ Cholesterol: 70 mg 23% ◆ Sodium: 250 mg 10% ◆ Total Carbohydrate: 59 g 20% ◆ Dietary Fiber: 2 g 8% ◆ Sugars: 46 g ◆ Protein: 6 g ◆ Vitamin A: 10% ◆ Vitamin C: 0% ◆ Calcium: 10% ◆ Iron: 8% ◆ **DIETARY EXCHANGES:** 2 Starch, 2 Fruit, 2½ Fat OR 4 Carbohydrate, 2½ Fat

Baked Rice Pudding

PREP TIME: 30 MINUTES (READY IN 1 HOUR 40 MINUTES)
♦ YIELD: 9 SERVINGS

RICE MIXTURE
½ cup uncooked regular long-grain white rice
2 tablespoons sugar
2 cups milk
1 tablespoon margarine or butter

PUDDING
6 eggs
1 cup sugar
½ teaspoon cinnamon
¼ teaspoon salt
¼ teaspoon nutmeg
½ cup raisins
2 cups milk

1. In medium saucepan, combine all rice mixture ingredients. Bring to a boil. Reduce heat to low; cook uncovered 20 to 25 minutes or until creamy, stirring occasionally. Remove from heat; cool 10 minutes.
2. Heat oven to 350°F. Lightly grease 8-inch square (2-quart) baking dish. In large bowl, beat eggs; stir in all remaining pudding ingredients and rice mixture. Pour into greased baking dish.
3. Bake at 350°F. for 55 to 60 minutes or until set. Serve warm or cold. If desired, serve with cream or whipped cream. Store in refrigerator.

NUTRITION INFORMATION PER SERVING: Serving Size: ⅑ of Recipe ♦ Calories: 280 ♦ Calories from Fat: 60 ♦ % DAILY VALUE: Total Fat: 7 g 11% ♦ Saturated Fat: 3 g 15% ♦ Cholesterol: 150 mg 50% ♦ Sodium: 170 mg 7% ♦ Total Carbohydrate: 45 g 15% ♦ Dietary Fiber: 1 g 2% ♦ Sugars: 36 g ♦ Protein: 9 g ♦ Vitamin A: 10% ♦ Vitamin C: 0% ♦ Calcium: 15% ♦ Iron: 6% ♦ DIETARY EXCHANGES: 3 Starch, 1 Fat OR 3 Carbohydrate, 1 Fat

Chocolate Mousse

PREP TIME: 20 MINUTES (READY IN 1 HOUR 20 MINUTES)
♦ YIELD: 8 (½-CUP) SERVINGS

¼ cup butter
8 oz. semisweet chocolate, cut into pieces
1 teaspoon vanilla
1 (8-oz.) carton (1 cup) refrigerated or frozen fat-free egg product, thawed
¼ cup sugar
1 cup whipping cream, whipped

1. In medium saucepan, melt butter and chocolate over low heat, stirring constantly. Remove from heat; stir in vanilla.
2. In large bowl, beat egg product until foamy; gradually beat in sugar. With wire whisk, gradually add chocolate mixture, blending well.
3. Fold in whipped cream. Refrigerate at least 1 hour. If desired, serve with additional whipped cream.

NUTRITION INFORMATION PER SERVING: Serving Size: ½ Cup ♦ Calories: 350 ♦ Calories from Fat: 230 ♦ % DAILY VALUE: Total Fat: 25 g 38% ♦ Saturated Fat: 15 g 75% ♦ Cholesterol: 55 mg 18% ♦ Sodium: 120 mg 5% ♦ Total Carbohydrate: 25 g 8% ♦ Dietary Fiber: 2 g 8% ♦ Sugars: 24 g ♦ Protein: 5 g ♦ Vitamin A: 15% ♦ Vitamin C: 0% ♦ Calcium: 4% ♦ Iron: 8% ♦ DIETARY EXCHANGES: ½ Starch, 1 Fruit, ½ Very Lean Meat, 5 Fat OR 1½ Carbohydrate, ½ Very Lean Meat, 5 Fat

Chocolate Soufflé

PREP TIME: 15 MINUTES (READY IN 1 HOUR 5 MINUTES)
♦ YIELD: 10 SERVINGS

½ cup sugar
2 tablespoons cornstarch
¼ teaspoon salt
¾ cup milk
2 oz. unsweetened chocolate or 2 envelopes premelted unsweetened chocolate
3 tablespoons margarine or butter
1 teaspoon vanilla
4 eggs, separated
¼ teaspoon cream of tartar
Whipped cream or topping, if desired

1. Heat oven to 350°F. Prepare 4 to 5-cup soufflé dish or casserole with foil band by cutting 3-inch strip of foil to go around top of dish. Lightly grease dish and strip of foil. With greased side toward inside of dish, secure foil band around top of dish, letting it extend 2 inches above edge of dish.
2. In medium saucepan, combine sugar, cornstarch and salt. Stir in milk. Cook over medium heat until mixture boils and thickens, stirring constantly. Remove from heat; stir in chocolate and margarine until melted. Stir in vanilla. Add egg yolks 1 at a time, beating well after each addition.

COOK'S NOTE

ABOUT SOUFFLÉS

A baked soufflé waits for no one. Serve it directly from the oven before it loses its height and characteristic light texture. As the soufflé bakes, watch it carefully to make sure it's done because an underdone soufflé will collapse prematurely. Soufflés do not freeze well.

3. In large bowl, beat egg whites with cream of tartar until soft peaks form. Gently fold in chocolate mixture. Pour into greased soufflé dish.*

4. Bake at 350°F. for 45 to 50 minutes or until knife inserted near center comes out clean. Remove foil band. Immediately serve soufflé with whipped cream or topping.

> **TIP:** * Soufflé can stand at room temperature, loosely covered, up to 1 hour before baking.

NUTRITION INFORMATION PER SERVING: Serving Size: ¹⁄₁₀ of Recipe • Calories: 190 • Calories from Fat: 120 • **% DAILY VALUE:** Total Fat: 13 g 20% • Saturated Fat: 6 g 30% • Cholesterol: 100 mg 33% • Sodium: 135 mg 6% • Total Carbohydrate: 15 g 5% • Dietary Fiber: 1 g 4% • Sugars: 11 g • Protein: 4 g • Vitamin A: 10% • Vitamin C: 0% • Calcium: 4% • Iron: 4% • **DIETARY EXCHANGES:** 1 Starch, 2½ Fat OR 1 Carbohydrate, 2½ Fat

VARIATION

Chocolate Mocha Soufflé: Add 1 teaspoon instant coffee granules or crystals with cornstarch.

Cheesecake

PREP TIME: 15 MINUTES (READY IN 3 HOURS 40 MINUTES) ◆ YIELD: 16 SERVINGS

CRUST
2 cups graham cracker crumbs (32 squares)
½ cup margarine or butter, melted

FILLING
3 eggs
2 (8-oz.) pkg. cream cheese, softened
1 cup sugar
¼ teaspoon salt
2 teaspoons vanilla
3 cups sour cream

1. Heat oven to 350°F. In medium bowl, combine crust ingredients; mix well. Press mixture in bottom and 1½ inches up sides of ungreased 10-inch springform pan.*

2. In large bowl, beat eggs. Add cream cheese, sugar, salt and vanilla; beat until smooth. Add sour cream; blend well. Pour into crust-lined pan.

3. Bake at 350°F. for 60 to 70 minutes or until edges are set; center of cheesecake will be soft. Cool in pan 15 minutes. Carefully remove sides of pan. Cool 2 hours or until completely cooled. Store in refrigerator.

> **TIP:** * If desired, cheesecake can be baked in two ungreased 8-inch round cake pans. Bake at 375°F. for 25 to 30 minutes or until set.

NUTRITION INFORMATION PER SERVING: Serving Size: ¹⁄₁₆ of Recipe • Calories: 360 • Calories from Fat: 240 • **% DAILY VALUE:** Total Fat: 27 g 42% • Saturated Fat: 14 g 70% • Cholesterol: 90 mg 30% • Sodium: 280 mg 12% • Total Carbohydrate: 23 g 8% • Dietary Fiber: 0 g 0% • Sugars: 17 g • Protein: 6 g • Vitamin A: 20% • Vitamin C: 0% • Calcium: 8% • Iron: 6% • **DIETARY EXCHANGES:** 1½ Starch, 5½ Fat OR 1½ Carbohydrate, 5½ Fat

No-Bake Fruit-Topped Cheesecake

PREP TIME: 30 MINUTES (READY IN 3 HOURS 50 MINUTES) ◆ YIELD: 10 SERVINGS

CRUST
¾ cup graham cracker crumbs (12 squares)
2 tablespoons margarine or butter, melted

FILLING
1 cup boiling water
1 (3-oz.) pkg. lemon flavor gelatin
¼ cup orange juice
1 (15-oz.) container light ricotta cheese
1 (8-oz.) container low-fat lemon yogurt
3 tablespoons sugar

TOPPING
2 tablespoons orange marmalade
½ teaspoon lemon juice
1 cup fresh fruit (blueberries, raspberries and/or strawberries)

1. Spray bottom of 8 or 9-inch springform pan with nonstick cooking spray. In small bowl, combine crust ingredients; mix well. Press in bottom of sprayed pan. Refrigerate.

2. In medium bowl, combine boiling water and gelatin; stir until dissolved. Stir in orange juice. Refrigerate 20 to 30 minutes or until lukewarm.

3. In food processor bowl with metal blade or blender container, combine ricotta cheese, yogurt and sugar; process until smooth. Gradually add to gelatin mixture in bowl, folding together until completely mixed. Pour into crust-lined pan. Refrigerate 2½ to 3 hours or until firm.

4. Just before serving, run sharp knife around edge of pan. Carefully remove sides of pan. In small bowl, combine orange marmalade and lemon juice; spread over top of cheesecake. Arrange fruit on top. Store in refrigerator.

NUTRITION INFORMATION PER SERVING: Serving Size: ¹⁄₁₀ of Recipe • Calories: 210 • Calories from Fat: 60 • **% DAILY VALUE:** Total Fat: 7 g 11% • Saturated Fat: 3 g 15% • Cholesterol: 15 mg 5% • Sodium: 160 mg 7% • Total Carbohydrate: 28 g 9% • Dietary Fiber: 1 g 3% • Sugars: 20 g • Protein: 8 g • Vitamin A: 6% • Vitamin C: 6% • Calcium: 20% • Iron: 4% • **DIETARY EXCHANGES:** ½ Starch, 1½ Fruit, 1 Medium-Fat Meat OR 2 Carbohydrate, 1 Medium-Fat Meat

Chocolate Cheesecake

PREP TIME: 15 MINUTES (READY IN 7 HOURS
20 MINUTES) ◆ YIELD: 16 SERVINGS

CRUST
  1 (9-oz.) pkg. chocolate wafer cookies,
    crushed (1¾ cups)
  6 tablespoons margarine or butter, melted

FILLING
  2 (8-oz.) pkg. cream cheese, softened
  ⅔ cup sugar
  3 eggs
  1 (12-oz.) pkg. (2 cups) semisweet chocolate
    chips, melted
  1 cup whipping cream
  2 tablespoons margarine or butter, melted
  1 teaspoon vanilla

1. Heat oven to 325°F. In medium bowl, combine crust ingredients; reserve 1 tablespoon crumbs for garnish. Press remaining crumbs in bottom and 2 inches up sides of ungreased 10-inch springform pan. Refrigerate.
2. In large bowl, combine cream cheese and sugar; beat until smooth. Add eggs 1 at a time, beating well after each addition. Add melted chocolate; beat well. Add all remaining filling ingredients; beat until smooth. Pour into crust-lined pan.
3. Bake at 325°F. for 55 to 65 minutes or until edges are set; center of cheesecake will be soft. (To minimize cracking, place shallow pan half full of hot water on lower oven rack during baking.) Cool in pan 5 minutes.
4. Carefully remove sides of pan. Cool 2 hours or until completely cooled. Garnish with reserved crumbs. Refrigerate at least 4 hours or overnight. Store in refrigerator.

NUTRITION INFORMATION PER SERVING: Serving Size: ¹⁄₁₆ of Recipe ◆ Calories: 440 ◆ Calories from Fat: 280 ◆ % DAILY VALUE: Total Fat: 31 g 48% ◆ Saturated Fat: 15 g 75% ◆ Cholesterol: 90 mg 30% ◆ Sodium: 260 mg 11% ◆ Total Carbohydrate: 34 g 11% ◆ Dietary Fiber: 2 g 8% ◆ Sugars: 28 g ◆ Protein: 6 g ◆ Vitamin A: 20% ◆ Vitamin C: 0% ◆ Calcium: 6% ◆ Iron: 10% ◆ DIETARY EXCHANGES: 2 Starch, 6 Fat OR 2 Carbohydrate, 6 Fat

Chocolate Cheesecake

White Chocolate Cheesecake

PREP TIME: 25 MINUTES (READY IN 1 HOUR 55 MINUTES)
◆ YIELD: 16 SERVINGS

CRUST
  1 cup (about 20) crushed chocolate cookie
    wafers
  2 tablespoons margarine or butter, melted

FILLING
  1 envelope unflavored gelatin
  ½ cup water
  ½ cup sugar
  1 (8-oz.) pkg. cream cheese, softened
  1 cup sour cream
  6 oz. white chocolate baking bar or vanilla-
    flavored candy coating (almond bark), cut
    into pieces, melted*
  1 cup whipping cream
  ½ teaspoon vanilla

TOPPING
  1 cup sliced fresh strawberries
  1 kiwi fruit, peeled, sliced

1. In small bowl, combine crust ingredients; mix well. Press in bottom of 8-inch springform pan. Set aside.
2. In small saucepan, combine gelatin and water; let stand 1 minute. Add sugar; stir over medium heat until mixture is hot and gelatin and sugar are dissolved.
3. In large bowl, beat cream cheese and sour cream until creamy. Gradually add melted baking bar, gelatin mixture, whipping cream

White Chocolate Cheesecake (page 342)

1. Heat oven to 350°F. Grease 1-quart casserole. In small bowl, beat egg yolks; stir in milk, lemon juice and lemon peel. Add sugar, flour and salt; beat until smooth.

2. In another small bowl, beat egg whites until stiff peaks form. Gently fold yolk mixture into beaten egg whites. DO NOT OVERMIX. Pour into greased casserole. Place casserole in 13 × 9-inch pan; place in oven. Pour hot water into pan around casserole to a depth of 1 inch.

3. Bake at 350°F. for 25 to 35 minutes or until light golden brown. Serve warm or cool.

NUTRITION INFORMATION PER SERVING: Serving Size: ½ Cup ◆ Calories: 140 ◆ Calories from Fat: 25 ◆ % DAILY VALUE: Total Fat: 3 g 5% ◆ Saturated Fat: 1 g 5% ◆ Cholesterol: 110 mg 37% ◆ Sodium: 90 mg 4% ◆ Total Carbohydrate: 24 g 8% ◆ Dietary Fiber: 0 g 0% ◆ Sugars: 18 g ◆ Protein: 5 g ◆ Vitamin A: 4% ◆ Vitamin C: 4% ◆ Calcium: 4% ◆ Iron: 4% ◆ DIETARY EXCHANGES: ½ Starch, 1 Fruit, ½ Medium-Fat Meat OR 1½ Carbohydrate, ½ Medium-Fat Meat

and vanilla; beat until smooth. Pour into crust-lined pan. Cover; refrigerate 1½ to 2½ hours or until firm.

4. Just before serving, run knife around edge of pan to loosen cheesecake. Carefully remove sides of pan. Arrange fruit over cheesecake. Store in refrigerator.

TIP: * To melt baking bar, place in 1-quart microwave-safe bowl. Microwave on MEDIUM for 2½ to 3 minutes, stirring once halfway through cooking. Stir until smooth.

NUTRITION INFORMATION PER SERVING: Serving Size: ¹⁄₁₆ of Recipe ◆ Calories: 260 ◆ Calories from Fat: 170 ◆ % DAILY VALUE: Total Fat: 19 g 29% ◆ Saturated Fat: 11 g 55% ◆ Cholesterol: 45 mg 15% ◆ Sodium: 125 mg 5% ◆ Total Carbohydrate: 20 g 7% ◆ Dietary Fiber: 1 g 3% ◆ Sugars: 18 g ◆ Protein: 3 g ◆ Vitamin A: 10% ◆ Vitamin C: 20% ◆ Calcium: 6% ◆ Iron: 4% ◆ DIETARY EXCHANGES: 1 Starch, ½ Fruit, 3½ Fat OR 1½ Carbohydrate, 3½ Fat

Lemon Pudding Cake

PREP TIME: 15 MINUTES (READY IN 50 MINUTES)
◆ YIELD: 6 (½-CUP) SERVINGS

  3 eggs, separated
½ cup milk
¼ cup lemon juice
  1 teaspoon grated lemon peel
½ cup sugar
⅓ cup all-purpose flour
⅛ teaspoon salt

COOK'S NOTE

AVOIDING A CRACKED CHEESECAKE SURFACE

If the baked cheesecake will be topped with fruit or sauce, it may not matter if the top cracks during baking. If you prefer a smoother top, try these tips:

◆ Bring the eggs and the cream cheese to room temperature before mixing the batter.

◆ Use an electric mixer or food processor to beat the filling. Beat at medium speed just until smooth. Overbeating or mixing at high speed can cause cracks to form during baking.

◆ Place a shallow pan half full of hot water on the lower oven rack during baking. The resulting steam will help prevent cracks.

◆ Let the cheesecake cool gradually after baking. Unless the recipe specifies otherwise, when the cheesecake is done, turn off the oven and open the door. Let the cheesecake remain in the oven for 30 minutes, then transfer it to a cooling rack in a draft-free place until it reaches room temperature. When it is completely cool, remove the sides of the pan and refrigerate the cheesecake.

Easy-Method Puff Pastry

PREP TIME: 35 MINUTES (READY IN 1 HOUR 35 MINUTES)

    4 cups all-purpose flour
  ½ teaspoon salt
    2 cups cold butter
1¼ cups ice water
    1 teaspoon lemon juice

1. In large bowl, combine flour and salt. Cut butter into ½-inch slices; add to flour mixture. Toss until butter is thoroughly coated with flour and slices are separated. In small bowl, combine ice water and lemon juice. Pour over flour mixture. With large spoon, quickly stir together. (Butter will remain in slices and flour will not be completely moistened.)

2. On lightly floured surface, knead dough about 10 times or until a very rough looking ball forms. Shape dough into rectangle. (Dough will have dry-looking areas.) Flatten dough slightly, making corners square.

3. On well-floured surface, roll dough to 15 × 12-inch rectangle, keeping corners square. Fold dough crosswise into thirds forming 12 × 5-inch rectangle. Give dough quarter turn and repeat folding crosswise into thirds, forming 5 × 4-inch rectangle. Cover tightly with plastic wrap; refrigerate 20 minutes.

4. Repeat the rolling, folding, turning and folding steps, forming 5 × 4-inch rectangle. Cover tightly with plastic wrap; refrigerate 20 minutes.

5. Repeat the rolling, folding, turning and folding steps forming 5 × 4-inch rectangle. Cover tightly with plastic wrap; refrigerate at least 20 minutes.

6. Shape and bake puff pastry as directed in the following 2 recipes: Palmiers and Patty Shells.

NUTRITION INFORMATION PER SERVING: Serving Size: 1 Pastry • Calories: 290 • Calories from Fat: 190 • % DAILY VALUE: Total Fat: 21 g 32% • Saturated Fat: 13 g 65% • Cholesterol: 55 mg 18% • Sodium: 270 mg 11% • Total Carbohydrate: 21 g 7% • Dietary Fiber: 1 g 3% • Sugars: 0 g • Protein: 3 g • Vitamin A: 15% • Vitamin C: 0% • Calcium: 0% • Iron: 8% • DIETARY EXCHANGES: 1½ Starch, 4 Fat OR 1½ Carbohydrate, 4 Fat

Palmiers

PREP TIME: 30 MINUTES (READY IN 1 HOUR 10 MINUTES)
♦ YIELD: 56 PALMIERS

    1 recipe Easy-Method Puff Pastry, this page
  ½ cup sugar
    1 teaspoon cinnamon

1. Line cookie sheets with parchment paper. With sharp knife, cut dough crosswise in half. Cover half of dough with plastic wrap; return to refrigerator.

2. Heat oven to 375°F. In small bowl, combine sugar and cinnamon; mix well. On lightly floured surface, roll half of dough into 14 × 10-inch rectangle. Sprinkle with half of sugar-cinnamon mixture; press lightly into dough. Starting from 2 shortest sides, roll sides to meet in center. With sharp knife, cut into about ⅜-inch slices. Place 2 inches apart on paper-lined cookie sheets.

3. Bake at 375°F. for 15 to 20 minutes or until golden brown. Remove from paper; cool on wire rack. Repeat with remaining half of dough and sugar-cinnamon mixture.

NUTRITION INFORMATION PER SERVING: Serving Size: 1 Palmier • Calories: 100 • Calories from Fat: 60 • % DAILY VALUE: Total Fat: 7 g 11% • Saturated Fat: 4 g 20% • Cholesterol: 20 mg 7% • Sodium: 85 mg 4% • Total Carbohydrate: 9 g 3% • Dietary Fiber: 0 g 0% • Sugars: 2 g • Protein: 1 g • Vitamin A: 4% • Vitamin C: 0% • Calcium: 0% • Iron: 2% • DIETARY EXCHANGES: ½ Starch, 1½ Fat OR ½ Carbohydrate, 1½ Fat

Patty Shells

PREP TIME: 30 MINUTES (READY IN 1 HOUR 10 MINUTES)
♦ YIELD: 18 PATTY SHELLS

    1 recipe Easy-Method Puff Pastry, this page

1. Line cookie sheets with parchment paper. With sharp knife, cut dough crosswise in half. Cover half of dough with plastic wrap; return to refrigerator.

2. Heat oven to 425°F. On lightly floured surface, roll half of dough into 12-inch square. Cut dough with floured 3½-inch round cookie cutter. Do not twist cutter. Dip cutter in flour between cuts. With floured 2½-inch round cutter, cut into centers of 3½-inch rounds by cutting to but not completely through pastry. (This will create center portion to be removed after baking.) Place 2 inches apart on paper-lined cookie sheets.

3. Bake at 425°F. for 15 to 20 minutes or until golden brown. Remove from paper.

With fork, remove centers from patty shells; cool on wire rack. Repeat with remaining half of dough. Fill with favorite pudding or fruit filling.*

TIP: * Patty shells can also be used in Chicken à la King (page 173), Lobster Newburg (page 216), or Salmon à la King (page 194).

NUTRITION INFORMATION PER SERVING: Serving Size: 1 Patty Shell ◆ Calories: 290 ◆ Calories from Fat: 190 ◆ **% DAILY VALUE:** Total Fat: 21 g 32% ◆ Saturated Fat: 13 g 65% ◆ Cholesterol: 55 mg 18% ◆ Sodium: 270 mg 11% ◆ Total Carbohydrate: 21 g 7% ◆ Dietary Fiber: 1 g 3% ◆ Sugars: 0 g ◆ Protein: 3 g ◆ Vitamin A: 15% ◆ Vitamin C: 0% ◆ Calcium: 0% ◆ Iron: 8% ◆ **DIETARY EXCHANGES:** 1½ Starch, 4 Fat OR 1½ Carbohydrate, 4 Fat

Cream Puffs

PREP TIME: 15 MINUTES (READY IN 1 HOUR 55 MINUTES)
◆ YIELD: 6 CREAM PUFFS

½ cup water
¼ cup margarine or butter
½ cup all-purpose flour
¼ teaspoon salt
2 eggs

1. Heat oven to 425°F. Grease cookie sheet. In medium saucepan, combine water and margarine. Bring to a boil over medium heat. Stir in flour and salt; cook, stirring vigorously until mixture leaves sides of pan in smooth ball. Remove from heat.
2. Add eggs 1 at a time, beating vigorously after each addition until mixture is smooth and glossy.* Spoon 6 mounds of dough (about ¼ cup each) 3 inches apart onto greased cookie sheet.
3. Bake at 425°F. for 30 to 40 minutes or until golden brown. Remove from oven; prick puffs with sharp knife to allow steam to escape. Remove from cookie sheet; cool 1 hour or until completely cooled.
4. Split cream puffs; if desired, remove any filaments of soft dough. Fill with ice cream, whipped cream or pudding. If desired, top with chocolate sauce.

TIP: * An electric mixer at medium speed can be used to beat in eggs. Beat for 1 minute after each addition until smooth and glossy. DO NOT OVERBEAT.

NUTRITION INFORMATION PER SERVING: Serving Size: ⅙ of Recipe ◆ Calories: 130 ◆ Calories from Fat: 80 ◆ **% DAILY VALUE:** Total Fat: 9 g 14% ◆ Saturated Fat: 2 g 10% ◆ Cholesterol: 70 mg 23% ◆ Sodium: 200 mg 8% ◆ Total Carbohydrate: 8 g 3% ◆ Dietary Fiber: 0 g 0% ◆ Sugars: 0 g ◆ Protein: 3 g ◆ Vitamin A: 8% ◆ Vitamin C: 0% ◆ Calcium: 0% ◆ Iron: 4% ◆ **DIETARY EXCHANGES:** ½ Starch, 2 Fat OR ½ Carbohydrate, 2 Fat

VARIATIONS

Eclairs: Drop dough into 12 long ovals about 1 inch wide. Bake at 425°F. for 20 to 25 minutes. When cool, fill with prepared vanilla pudding and drizzle with Chocolate Glaze (page 382).
YIELD: 12 ECLAIRS

Miniature Cream Puffs: Drop dough by tablespoons, making 20 small cream puffs. Bake at 425°F. for 15 to 20 minutes.
YIELD: 20 CREAM PUFFS

Praline Cream Puffs: Prepare and bake 6 cream puffs as directed above. When cool, fill with vanilla ice cream. Drizzle with warm caramel ice cream topping; sprinkle with chopped pecans.

COOK'S NOTE

ABOUT CREAM PUFFS

Although they evoke the mystique of fine bakeries, it's actually easy to make cream puffs successfully at home. They are made with what the French call *choux* pastry, which translates as "cabbage pastry" and refers to the way the cooked pastry separates into layers that resemble leaves. Choux pastry is cooked on the stove before baking. The batter can be formed into shapes by dropping it from a spoon or piping it from a pastry tube, using any large fluted tip. Make sure the puffs are fully baked; if underbaked, they may collapse. Add the creamy filling as close to serving time as possible to preserve the crisp texture of the exterior. Store unfilled puffs in an airtight container overnight or for up to three months in the freezer.

Rich Tiramisu

PREP TIME: 25 MINUTES (READY IN 4 HOURS 55 MINUTES) ◆ YIELD: 15 SERVINGS

CAKE
¼ cup margarine or butter
¼ cup milk
2 eggs
¾ cup sugar
¾ cup all-purpose flour
1 teaspoon baking powder
¼ teaspoon salt
¼ teaspoon vanilla
¾ cup hot strong coffee
1 tablespoon sugar

TOPPING
1 (8-oz.) pkg. cream cheese, softened
1 (8-oz.) container mascarpone cheese
⅓ cup powdered sugar
2 tablespoons Marsala wine or dark rum
1 pint (2 cups) whipping cream
Grated semisweet chocolate (about ½ oz.)

1. Heat oven to 375°F. Spray 13×9-inch pan with nonstick cooking spray. In small saucepan or 2-cup microwave-safe measuring cup, heat margarine and milk until steaming hot (about 1 minute on HIGH in microwave).

2. Meanwhile, in large bowl, beat eggs at high speed until light. Gradually beat in ¾ cup sugar; beat an additional 2 minutes.

3. Add flour, baking powder, salt, vanilla and hot milk mixture; beat at low speed until smooth. Pour into sprayed pan.

Rich Tiramisu

4. Bake at 375°F. for 14 to 16 minutes or until cake springs back when touched lightly in center. In 1-cup measuring cup, combine coffee and 1 tablespoon sugar; mix well. Drizzle over warm cake. Cool 30 minutes or until completely cooled.

5. In large bowl, combine cream cheese and mascarpone cheese; beat at medium speed until smooth and creamy. Beat in powdered sugar and wine.

6. In large bowl, beat whipping cream until stiff peaks form. Fold into cream cheese mixture until combined. Spread evenly on cake. Sprinkle grated chocolate over top of cake. Cover; refrigerate at least 4 hours or overnight. To serve, cut into squares. Store in refrigerator.

HIGH ALTITUDE *(above 3500 feet)*: Increase flour to 1 cup. Bake as directed above.

NUTRITION INFORMATION PER SERVING: Serving Size: ¹⁄₁₅ of Recipe ◆ Calories: 350 ◆ Calories from Fat: 240 ◆ **% DAILY VALUE:** Total Fat: 27 g 42% ◆ Saturated Fat: 15 g 75% ◆ Cholesterol: 110 mg 37% ◆ Sodium: 180 mg 8% ◆ Total Carbohydrate: 21 g 7% ◆ Dietary Fiber: 0 g 0% ◆ Sugars: 16 g ◆ Protein: 4 g ◆ Vitamin A: 20% ◆ Vitamin C: 0% ◆ Calcium: 8% ◆ Iron: 4% ◆ **DIETARY EXCHANGES:** 1½ Starch, 5 Fat OR 1½ Carbohydrate, 5 Fat

Fanciful Fruit Pizza

PREP TIME: 20 MINUTES (READY IN 1 HOUR 45 MINUTES) ◆ YIELD: 12 SERVINGS

1 (18-oz.) pkg. refrigerated sugar cookies
1 (8-oz.) pkg. cream cheese, softened
⅓ cup sugar
½ teaspoon vanilla
1 cup fresh or canned peach slices, drained*
1 cup whole strawberries, cut in half*
1 cup fresh or frozen blueberries*
¼ cup orange marmalade
1 tablespoon water

1. Heat oven to 350°F. Slice cookie dough as directed on package. Arrange slices in bottom of ungreased 15×10×1-inch baking pan or 14-inch pizza pan. With floured fingers, press dough evenly in pan.

2. Bake at 350°F. for 12 to 15 minutes or until golden brown. Cool 15 minutes or until completely cooled.

3. In small bowl, combine cream cheese, sugar and vanilla; beat until fluffy. Spread mixture over cooled cookie crust. Arrange fruit over cream cheese.

4. In another small bowl, combine orange marmalade and water; blend well. Spoon

Fanciful Fruit Pizza (page 346)

marmalade mixture over fruit. Refrigerate at least 1 hour before serving. Cut into squares or wedges. Store in refrigerator.

TIP: * Other fruit such as fresh or canned pineapple slices, maraschino cherries, mandarin orange segments or sliced peeled kiwi fruit can be used.

NUTRITION INFORMATION PER SERVING: Serving Size: ¹⁄₁₂ of Recipe ◆ Calories: 310 ◆ Calories from Fat: 130 ◆ **% DAILY VALUE:** Total Fat: 14 g 22% ◆ Saturated Fat: 6 g 30% ◆ Cholesterol: 25 mg 8% ◆ Sodium: 230 mg 10% ◆ Total Carbohydrate: 41 g 14% ◆ Dietary Fiber: 1 g 4% ◆ Sugars: 26 g ◆ Protein: 4 g ◆ Vitamin A: 8% ◆ Vitamin C: 20% ◆ Calcium: 2% ◆ Iron: 6% ◆ **DIETARY EXCHANGES:** 1½ Starch, 1 Fruit, 3 Fat OR 2½ Carbohydrate, 3 Fat

Mint Chocolate Mousse Dessert

PREP TIME: 50 MINUTES (READY IN 5 HOURS 50 MINUTES) ◆ YIELD: 18 SERVINGS

CRUST
   2 cups vanilla wafer crumbs (40 wafers)
   ⅓ cup margarine or butter, melted

FILLING
   1 (8-oz.) pkg. cream cheese, softened
   2 cups powdered sugar
   3 oz. unsweetened chocolate, melted
   3 eggs
   ½ gallon (8 cups) pink peppermint or green mint ice cream, slightly softened

SAUCE
   4 oz. semisweet chocolate, chopped
   ⅓ cup margarine or butter
   1½ cups powdered sugar
   1 (5-oz.) can (⅔ cup) evaporated milk
   1 teaspoon vanilla

1. Heat oven to 350°F. In small bowl, combine crust ingredients; mix well. Press in bottom of ungreased 13 × 9-inch pan. Bake at 350°F. for 10 minutes or until light golden brown.

2. Meanwhile, in small bowl, beat cream cheese until fluffy. Add 2 cups powdered sugar; beat until smooth. Add melted chocolate; beat well. Add eggs 1 at a time, beating well after each addition. Pour over partially baked crust.

3. Bake at 350°F. for 12 to 15 minutes or until filling is set. Cool 1 hour or until completely cooled.

4. Spread ice cream over chocolate layer. Cover with foil; freeze 4 hours or until firm.

5. Just before serving, in heavy medium saucepan, combine all sauce ingredients except vanilla; mix well. Bring to a boil over medium heat, stirring constantly. Reduce heat to low; cook 5 minutes, stirring constantly. Remove from heat; stir in vanilla.

6. To serve, let dessert stand at room temperature for 10 minutes. Cut into squares; place on individual dessert plates. Drizzle warm sauce over each serving.

NUTRITION INFORMATION PER SERVING: Serving Size: ¹⁄₁₈ of Recipe ◆ Calories: 470 ◆ Calories from Fat: 230 ◆ **% DAILY VALUE:** Total Fat: 26 g 40% ◆ Saturated Fat: 15 g 75% ◆ Cholesterol: 95 mg 32% ◆ Sodium: 220 mg 9% ◆ Total Carbohydrate: 53 g 18% ◆ Dietary Fiber: 1 g 4% ◆ Sugars: 42 g ◆ Protein: 6 g ◆ Vitamin A: 15% ◆ Vitamin C: 0% ◆ Calcium: 10% ◆ Iron: 6% ◆ **DIETARY EXCHANGES:** 2 Starch, 1½ Fruit, 5 Fat OR 3½ Carbohydrate, 5 Fat

Mint Chocolate Mousse Dessert

Vanilla Custard Ice Cream

PREP TIME: 20 MINUTES (READY IN 5 HOURS)
◆ YIELD: 10 (½-CUP) SERVINGS

¾ cup sugar
2 cups milk
2 eggs, slightly beaten
1 pint (2 cups) whipping cream
2 to 3 teaspoons vanilla

1. In medium saucepan, combine sugar, milk and eggs; mix well. Cook over medium heat for about 12 minutes or until mixture is slightly thickened and coats a metal spoon, stirring constantly. DO NOT BOIL. Cool 30 minutes.*
2. Add whipping cream and vanilla; blend well. Refrigerate at least 4 hours or until ready to freeze.
3. When ready to freeze, place mixture in ice cream maker; freeze according to manufacturer's directions.

> TIP: *To make ahead, prepare recipe to this point. Cover; refrigerate up to 24 hours. When ready to freeze, continue as directed.

NUTRITION INFORMATION PER SERVING: Serving Size: ½ Cup ◆ Calories: 270 ◆ Calories from Fat: 180 ◆ % DAILY VALUE: Total Fat: 20 g 31% ◆ Saturated Fat: 12 g 60% ◆ Cholesterol: 110 mg 37% ◆ Sodium: 55 mg 2% ◆ Total Carbohydrate: 19 g 6% ◆ Dietary Fiber: 0 g 0% ◆ Sugars: 19 g ◆ Protein: 4 g ◆ Vitamin A: 15% ◆ Vitamin C: 0% ◆ Calcium: 10% ◆ Iron: 0% ◆ DIETARY EXCHANGES: 1 Starch, 4 Fat OR 1 Carbohydrate, 4 Fat

VARIATION

Rum Raisin Ice Cream: In small bowl, combine ¾ cup raisins and 3 tablespoons dark rum; soak at least 8 hours. Add to ice cream in middle of freezing process.

Cherries 'n Cream Dessert Squares

PREP TIME: 25 MINUTES (READY IN 3 HOURS 25 MINUTES) ◆ YIELD: 15 SERVINGS

CRUST
1½ cups vanilla wafer or graham cracker crumbs
2 tablespoons powdered sugar
⅓ cup margarine or butter, melted

FILLING
1 (8-oz.) pkg. cream cheese, softened
1 cup powdered sugar
1 teaspoon vanilla
2 cups miniature marshmallows
1 cup whipping cream, whipped
1 (21-oz.) can cherry pie filling
½ teaspoon almond extract

1. In medium bowl, combine all crust ingredients; blend well. Press in bottom of ungreased 13×9-inch pan; refrigerate while preparing filling.
2. In large bowl, beat cream cheese, 1 cup powdered sugar and vanilla until light and fluffy. Fold in marshmallows and whipped cream. Spread mixture over crust.
3. In small bowl, combine pie filling and almond extract. Carefully spread over cream layer. Refrigerate 3 hours or until firm. Store in refrigerator.

NUTRITION INFORMATION PER SERVING: Serving Size: 1/15 of Recipe ◆ Calories: 290 ◆ Calories from Fat: 150 ◆ % DAILY VALUE: Total Fat: 17 g 26% ◆ Saturated Fat: 8 g 40% ◆ Cholesterol: 40 mg 13% ◆ Sodium: 130 mg 5% ◆ Total Carbohydrate: 32 g 11% ◆ Dietary Fiber: 0 g 0% ◆ Sugars: 25 g ◆ Protein: 2 g ◆ Vitamin A: 15% ◆ Vitamin C: 2% ◆ Calcium: 4% ◆ Iron: 2% ◆ DIETARY EXCHANGES: 1 Starch, 1 Fruit, 3 Fat OR 2 Carbohydrate, 3 Fat

Vanilla Pudding

PREP TIME: 20 MINUTES (READY IN 35 MINUTES)
◆ YIELD: 4 (½-CUP) SERVINGS

⅓ cup sugar
2 tablespoons cornstarch
⅛ teaspoon salt
2 cups milk
2 egg yolks, slightly beaten
1 tablespoon margarine or butter
1 teaspoon vanilla

1. In medium saucepan, combine sugar, cornstarch and salt. Gradually stir in milk. Cook over medium heat until mixture boils and thickens, stirring constantly. Boil 1 minute.
2. In small bowl, stir about ⅓ of hot mixture into egg yolks. Stir yolk mixture into hot mixture; blend well. Cook until mixture bubbles, stirring constantly. Remove from heat; stir in margarine and vanilla. If desired, spoon into individual dessert dishes. Cool 15 minutes before serving. Store in refrigerator.

NUTRITION INFORMATION PER SERVING: Serving Size: ½ Cup ◆ Calories: 200 ◆ Calories from Fat: 70 ◆ % DAILY VALUE: Total Fat: 8 g 12% ◆ Saturated Fat: 3 g 15% ◆ Cholesterol: 120 mg 40% ◆ Sodium: 170 mg 7% ◆ Total Carbohydrate: 26 g 9% ◆ Dietary Fiber: 0 g 0% ◆ Sugars: 23 g ◆ Protein: 6 g ◆ Vitamin A: 10% ◆ Vitamin C: 0% ◆ Calcium: 15% ◆ Iron: 2% ◆ DIETARY EXCHANGES: 2 Starch, 1 Fat OR 2 Carbohydrate, 1 Fat

VARIATIONS

Butterscotch Pudding: Substitute ½ cup firmly packed brown sugar for sugar.

Chocolate Pudding: Increase sugar to ½ cup and cornstarch to 3 tablespoons. Add 1 oz. unsweetened chocolate with milk. After cooking pudding, beat until smooth. Omit margarine.

Triple Chocolate Pudding

PREP TIME: 25 MINUTES (READY IN 2 HOURS 40 MINUTES) ♦ YIELD: 6 (½-CUP) SERVINGS

PUDDING
2¼ cups milk
  2 oz. semisweet chocolate, finely chopped
  ½ cup sugar*
  2 tablespoons cornstarch
  ¼ cup unsweetened cocoa
  2 eggs
  2 tablespoons margarine or butter
  I teaspoon vanilla

TOPPING
  ½ cup whipping cream
  2 tablespoons powdered sugar
  I (2.1-oz.) chocolate-covered peanut butter
    candy bar, chopped

1. In heavy medium saucepan, bring 2 cups of the milk to a boil. Remove from heat; stir in semisweet chocolate. Set aside.
2. In small bowl, combine sugar, cornstarch and cocoa; mix well. Stir in remaining ¼ cup milk.
3. With wire whisk, beat chocolate milk mixture until all chocolate is melted. Add cocoa mixture, beating until well blended. Bring to a boil over medium heat, beating constantly. Reduce heat; simmer 1 minute. Remove saucepan from heat.
4. In small bowl, beat eggs. Slowly beat in about 1 cup chocolate mixture. Add egg mixture to saucepan; cook over medium heat until mixture thickens and just begins to boil, beating constantly. Remove from heat; beat in margarine and vanilla. Place waxed paper or plastic wrap over surface of pudding. Cool 15 minutes. Refrigerate 2 hours or until cold.
5. In small bowl, beat whipping cream and powdered sugar until stiff peaks form. Fold in half of candy pieces.

6. To serve, spoon pudding into parfait glasses or dessert dishes. Top each with whipped cream mixture; sprinkle with remaining half of candy pieces. Store in refrigerator.

> **TIP:** * For sweeter pudding, increase sugar to ⅔ cup.

NUTRITION INFORMATION PER SERVING: Serving Size: ½ Cup ♦ Calories: 380 ♦ Calories from Fat: 190 ♦ **% DAILY VALUE:** Total Fat: 21 g 32% ♦ Saturated Fat: 10 g 50% ♦ Cholesterol: 105 mg 35% ♦ Sodium: 150 mg 6% ♦ Total Carbohydrate: 40 g 13% ♦ Dietary Fiber: 2 g 8% ♦ Sugars: 33 g ♦ Protein: 8 g ♦ Vitamin A: 15% ♦ Vitamin C: 0% ♦ Calcium: 15% ♦ Iron: 6% ♦ **DIETARY EXCHANGES:** 2½ Starch, 4 Fat OR 2½ Carbohydrate, 4 Fat

Tapioca Pudding

PREP TIME: 25 MINUTES (READY IN 55 MINUTES) ♦ YIELD: 8 (½-CUP) SERVINGS

  2 eggs, separated
  2 tablespoons sugar
  ¼ cup sugar
  2 tablespoons quick-cooking tapioca
    Dash salt
  2 cups milk
  I teaspoon vanilla

1. In small bowl, beat egg whites until foamy. Gradually add 2 tablespoons sugar, beating until stiff peaks form. Set aside.
2. In medium saucepan, combine ¼ cup sugar, tapioca and salt; mix well. Stir in milk and egg yolks. Cook over medium heat for 10 to 15 minutes or until mixture comes to a full boil, stirring constantly.
3. Remove from heat; stir in vanilla. Stir in egg white mixture until well blended. Spoon into individual dessert dishes. Cool at least 30 minutes before serving. Store in refrigerator.

> **TIP:** If desired, ½ cup finely chopped dates, peaches, apricots, strawberries, raspberries or other desired fruit can be folded into pudding before spooning into dishes.

NUTRITION INFORMATION PER SERVING: Serving Size: ⅓ Cup ♦ Calories: 90 ♦ Calories from Fat: 20 ♦ **% DAILY VALUE:** Total Fat: 2 g 3% ♦ Saturated Fat: 1 g 5% ♦ Cholesterol: 60 mg 20% ♦ Sodium: 65 mg 3% ♦ Total Carbohydrate: 15 g 5% ♦ Dietary Fiber: 0 g 0% ♦ Sugars: 12 g ♦ Protein: 4 g ♦ Vitamin A: 4% ♦ Vitamin C: 0% ♦ Calcium: 8% ♦ Iron: 0% ♦ **DIETARY EXCHANGES:** 1 Starch OR 1 Carbohydrate

Charlotte Russe de Raspberry

Charlotte Russe de Raspberry

PREP TIME: 40 MINUTES (READY IN 4 HOURS 40 MINUTES) ✦ YIELD: 12 SERVINGS

DESSERT
  18 ladyfingers
  ¼ cup orange-flavored liqueur
  ⅔ cup water
  2 envelopes unflavored gelatin
  ¼ cup sugar
  3 tablespoons lemon juice
  1 (10-oz.) pkg. frozen raspberries in syrup, thawed
  1 pint (2 cups) whipping cream, whipped

TOPPING
  1 tablespoon butter
  ½ cup sliced almonds
  2 tablespoons sugar
  ½ cup whipping cream
  2 tablespoons powdered sugar

1. Grease 9-inch springform pan with butter. Split ladyfingers lengthwise. Sprinkle cut surfaces with liqueur. Place ladyfingers around sides and in bottom of buttered pan (cut sides facing center and top of pan).
2. In small saucepan, combine water and gelatin; let stand 2 minutes to soften. Heat mixture over low heat until gelatin dissolves, stirring occasionally. Remove from heat. Stir in ¼ cup sugar, lemon juice and raspberries; beat with wire whisk until frothy. Refrigerate 15 minutes or just until mixture begins to thicken.
3. Gently fold cooled raspberry mixture into whipped cream. Pour into ladyfinger-lined pan. Refrigerate 4 hours or until mixture is set.

4. Meanwhile, heat oven to 350°F. Place butter in shallow baking pan. Place pan in oven for 1 to 2 minutes or until butter is melted. Add almonds; stir until well coated. Bake at 350°F. for 8 to 10 minutes or until almonds are light golden brown, stirring occasionally. Remove from oven. Sprinkle with 2 tablespoons sugar; stir to coat. Cool completely.
5. In small bowl, combine ½ cup whipping cream and 2 tablespoons powdered sugar; beat at high speed until stiff peaks form. Garnish top of dessert with whipped cream and sugared almonds. Store in refrigerator.

NUTRITION INFORMATION PER SERVING: Serving Size: ¹⁄₁₂ of Recipe ✦ Calories: 350 ✦ Calories from Fat: 210 ✦ **% DAILY VALUE:** Total Fat: 23 g 35% ✦ Saturated Fat: 13 g 65% ✦ Cholesterol: 130 mg 43% ✦ Sodium: 55 mg 2% ✦ Total Carbohydrate: 28 g 9% ✦ Dietary Fiber: 1 g 4% ✦ Sugars: 23 g ✦ Protein: 5 g ✦ Vitamin A: 15% ✦ Vitamin C: 10% ✦ Calcium: 6% ✦ Iron: 6% ✦ **DIETARY EXCHANGES:** 1½ Starch, ½ Fruit, 4½ Fat OR 2 Carbohydrate, 4½ Fat

Fresh Fruit Trifle

PREP TIME: 15 MINUTES (READY IN 2 HOURS 15 MINUTES) ✦ YIELD: 10 SERVINGS

  1¼ cups skim milk
  ½ cup low-fat plain yogurt
  1 teaspoon grated orange peel
  1 (3.4-oz.) pkg. instant vanilla pudding and pie filling mix
  8 cups angel food cake cubes
  4 cups fresh fruit (seedless grapes, halved strawberries, sliced nectarines, mandarin orange segments and/or pineapple tidbits)

Fresh Fruit Trifle

1. In medium bowl, combine milk, yogurt and orange peel; blend well. Add pudding mix; beat until well blended. Let stand 5 minutes.

2. In large serving bowl, layer half of cake cubes, ⅓ of fruit and half of pudding mixture. Repeat layers. Arrange remaining fruit over top. Cover; refrigerate at least 2 hours or up to 6 hours before serving.

NUTRITION INFORMATION PER SERVING: Serving Size: ¹⁄₁₀ of Recipe ✦ Calories: 180 ✦ Calories from Fat: 10 ✦ **% DAILY VALUE:** Total Fat: 1 g 2% ✦ Saturated Fat: 0 g 0% ✦ Cholesterol: 0 mg 0% ✦ Sodium: 420 mg 18% ✦ Total Carbohydrate: 39 g 13% ✦ Dietary Fiber: 2 g 8% ✦ Sugars: 37 g ✦ Protein: 4 g ✦ Vitamin A: 4% ✦ Vitamin C: 35% ✦ Calcium: 10% ✦ Iron: 0% ✦ **DIETARY EXCHANGES:** 1½ Starch, 1 Fruit OR 2½ Carbohydrate

Triple Berry Ice Milk

Triple Berry Ice Milk

PREP TIME: 25 MINUTES ✦ YIELD: 6 (½-CUP) SERVINGS

½ cup fresh or frozen raspberries
½ cup fresh or frozen blueberries
½ cup fresh or frozen blackberries
1 (12-oz.) can lite evaporated skimmed milk
⅔ cup sugar

1. In food processor bowl with metal blade or blender container, process berries and ¼ cup of the milk until pureed. Add sugar; process until well mixed. Add remaining milk; process until sugar is dissolved.

2. Place mixture in ice cream maker; freeze according to manufacturer's directions for 15 to 20 minutes.

NUTRITION INFORMATION PER SERVING: Serving Size: ½ Cup ✦ Calories: 150 ✦ Calories from Fat: 0 ✦ **% DAILY VALUE:** Total Fat: 0 g 0% ✦ Saturated Fat: 0 g 0% ✦ Cholesterol: 0 mg 0% ✦ Sodium: 65 mg 3% ✦ Total Carbohydrate: 33 g 11% ✦ Dietary Fiber: 1 g 4% ✦ Sugars: 31 g ✦ Protein: 4 g ✦ Vitamin A: 6% ✦ Vitamin C: 0% ✦ Calcium: 15% ✦ Iron: 0% ✦ **DIETARY EXCHANGES:** 1 Starch, 1 Fruit OR 2 Carbohydrate

Lemon Granita

PREP TIME: 10 MINUTES (READY IN 2 HOURS 40 MINUTES) ✦ YIELD: 7 (1-CUP) SERVINGS

¾ cup sugar
1 teaspoon grated lemon peel
3 cups water
½ cup fresh lemon juice

1. Place 13 × 9-inch metal pan in freezer to chill. Meanwhile, in medium bowl, combine all ingredients; blend well. Pour mixture into chilled pan. Freeze 30 minutes.

2. When ice crystals begin to form at edges of pan, stir mixture with fork. Return to freezer; freeze about 2 hours or until completely frozen, stirring every 30 minutes.

3. To serve, scoop into individual dessert dishes.

NUTRITION INFORMATION PER SERVING: Serving Size: 1 Cup ✦ Calories: 90 ✦ Calories from Fat: 0 ✦ **% DAILY VALUE:** Total Fat: 0 g 0% ✦ Saturated Fat: 0 g 0% ✦ Cholesterol: 0 mg 0% ✦ Sodium: 0 mg 0% ✦ Total Carbohydrate: 23 g 8% ✦ Dietary Fiber: 0 g 0% ✦ Sugars: 22 g ✦ Protein: 0 g ✦ Vitamin A: 0% ✦ Vitamin C: 15% ✦ Calcium: 0% ✦ Iron: 0% ✦ **DIETARY EXCHANGES:** 1½ Fruit OR 1½ Carbohydrate

Lemon Granita

Crème Anglaise

PREP TIME: 20 MINUTES (READY IN 50 MINUTES)
◆ YIELD: 1½ CUPS

  1 cup whipping cream
  2 egg yolks
  ⅓ cup sugar

1. In medium saucepan, bring cream just to a boil over low heat. In small bowl, combine egg yolks and sugar; beat well.
2. Blend a small amount of hot cream into yolks. Blend yolk mixture into cream in saucepan; cook over low heat about 10 minutes or until custard coats a spoon, stirring constantly. DO NOT BOIL.
3. Remove from heat. Cool 30 minutes or until room temperature. Refrigerate until serving time. Store in refrigerator.

NUTRITION INFORMATION PER SERVING: Serving Size: 1 Tablespoon ◆ Calories: 50 ◆ Calories from Fat: 35 ◆ **% DAILY VALUE:** Total Fat: 4 g 6% ◆ Saturated Fat: 2 g 10% ◆ Cholesterol: 30 mg 10% ◆ Sodium: 0 mg 0% ◆ Total Carbohydrate: 3 g 1% ◆ Dietary Fiber: 0 g 0% ◆ Sugars: 3 g ◆ Protein: 0 g ◆ Vitamin A: 4% ◆ Vitamin C: 0% ◆ Calcium: 0% ◆ Iron: 0% ◆ **DIETARY EXCHANGES:** 1 Fat

Hot Caramel Sauce

PREP TIME: 15 MINUTES ◆ YIELD: 2 CUPS

1½ cups sugar
  1 cup half-and-half
  ½ cup light corn syrup
  6 tablespoons butter
  ½ teaspoon vanilla

1. In medium saucepan, combine sugar, ½ cup of the half-and-half, corn syrup and butter; mix well. Bring to a full rolling boil.
2. Gradually add remaining half-and-half, being sure boiling does not stop. Cook over medium heat until thermometer reaches soft-ball stage (234°F.), stirring occasionally. Remove from heat; stir in vanilla. Serve warm. Store in refrigerator.

NUTRITION INFORMATION PER SERVING: Serving Size: 1 Tablespoon ◆ Calories: 80 ◆ Calories from Fat: 25 ◆ **% DAILY VALUE:** Total Fat: 3 g 5% ◆ Saturated Fat: 2 g 10% ◆ Cholesterol: 10 mg 3% ◆ Sodium: 30 mg 1% ◆ Total Carbohydrate: 14 g 5% ◆ Dietary Fiber: 0 g 0% ◆ Sugars: 12 g ◆ Protein: 0 g ◆ Vitamin A: 2% ◆ Vitamin C: 0% ◆ Calcium: 0% ◆ Iron: 0% ◆ **DIETARY EXCHANGES:** 1 Fruit, ½ Fat OR 1 Carbohydrate, ½ Fat

Hot Fudge Sauce

PREP TIME: 15 MINUTES ◆ YIELD: 1¼ CUPS

  3 oz. semisweet chocolate, cut into pieces, or ½ cup semisweet chocolate chips
  ⅔ cup sugar
  Dash salt
  1 (5-oz.) can (⅔ cup) evaporated milk

1. Melt chocolate in small saucepan over very low heat, stirring constantly. Stir in sugar and salt.
2. Gradually add evaporated milk, stirring constantly. Cook until thickened and hot, stirring constantly. Serve warm. Store in refrigerator.

NUTRITION INFORMATION PER SERVING: Serving Size: 1 Tablespoon ◆ Calories: 60 ◆ Calories from Fat: 20 ◆ **% DAILY VALUE:** Total Fat: 2 g 3% ◆ Saturated Fat: 1 g 5% ◆ Cholesterol: 2 mg 1% ◆ Sodium: 15 mg 1% ◆ Total Carbohydrate: 10 g 3% ◆ Dietary Fiber: 0 g 0% ◆ Sugars: 10 g ◆ Protein: 1 g ◆ Vitamin A: 0% ◆ Vitamin C: 0% ◆ Calcium: 0% ◆ Iron: 0% ◆ **DIETARY EXCHANGES:** ½ Starch, ½ Fat OR ½ Carbohydrate, ½ Fat

White Chocolate Sauce

PREP TIME: 15 MINUTES ◆ YIELD: 2 CUPS

1½ cups whipping cream
  ¼ cup powdered sugar
  4 oz. white chocolate baking bar or vanilla-flavored candy coating (almond bark), cut into pieces
  2 tablespoons rum

1. In medium saucepan, combine cream and powdered sugar; mix well. Bring to a boil over medium heat, stirring constantly. Reduce heat; simmer 3 to 4 minutes, stirring occasionally.
2. Remove from heat; stir in baking bar and rum until chocolate is melted and sauce is smooth. Serve warm or cool. Store in refrigerator.

NUTRITION INFORMATION PER SERVING: Serving Size: 1 Tablespoon ◆ Calories: 60 ◆ Calories from Fat: 45 ◆ **% DAILY VALUE:** Total Fat: 5 g 8% ◆ Saturated Fat: 3 g 15% ◆ Cholesterol: 15 mg 5% ◆ Sodium: 5 mg 0% ◆ Total Carbohydrate: 3 g 1% ◆ Dietary Fiber: 0 g 0% ◆ Sugars: 3 g ◆ Protein: 0 g ◆ Vitamin A: 4% ◆ Vitamin C: 0% ◆ Calcium: 0% ◆ Iron: 0% ◆ **DIETARY EXCHANGES:** ½ Fruit, 1 Fat OR ½ Carbohydrate, 1 Fat

Lemon Sauce

PREP TIME: 15 MINUTES ✦ YIELD: 1½ CUPS

    ½ cup sugar
    2 tablespoons cornstarch
      Dash salt
    1 cup water
    2 tablespoons lemon juice
    2 tablespoons margarine or butter
    2 teaspoons grated lemon peel

1. In medium saucepan, combine sugar, cornstarch and salt; mix well. Stir in water until well blended.
2. Cook over medium heat for about 7 minutes or until mixture boils and is slightly thickened and clear, stirring constantly.
3. Remove from heat; stir in lemon juice, margarine and lemon peel. Serve immediately, or cover and refrigerate until serving time. Store in refrigerator.

NUTRITION INFORMATION PER SERVING: Serving Size: 1 Tablespoon ✦ Calories: 30 ✦ Calories from Fat: 10 ✦ **% DAILY VALUE:** Total Fat: 1 g 2% ✦ Saturated Fat: 0 g 0% ✦ Cholesterol: 0 mg 0% ✦ Sodium: 15 mg 1% ✦ Total Carbohydrate: 5 g 2% ✦ Dietary Fiber: 0 g 0% ✦ Sugars: 4 g ✦ Protein: 0 g ✦ Vitamin A: 0% ✦ Vitamin C: 0% ✦ Calcium: 0% ✦ Iron: 0% ✦ **DIETARY EXCHANGES:** ½ Fruit OR ½ Carbohydrate

Ruby Raspberry Sauce

PREP TIME: 10 MINUTES ✦ YIELD: 1½ CUPS

    1 (10-oz.) pkg. frozen raspberries in syrup, thawed
    2 tablespoons sugar
    2 tablespoons orange-flavored liqueur

1. In blender container or food processor bowl with metal blade, combine all ingredients. Cover; blend until smooth.
2. If desired, place strainer over medium bowl; pour berry mixture into strainer. Press mixture with back of spoon through strainer to remove seeds; discard seeds. Store in refrigerator.

NUTRITION INFORMATION PER SERVING: Serving Size: ¼ Cup ✦ Calories: 80 ✦ Calories from Fat: 0 ✦ **% DAILY VALUE:** Total Fat: 0 g 0% ✦ Saturated Fat: 0 g 0% ✦ Cholesterol: 0 mg 0% ✦ Sodium: 0 mg 0% ✦ Total Carbohydrate: 18 g 6% ✦ Dietary Fiber: 2 g 8% ✦ Sugars: 16 g ✦ Protein: 0 g ✦ Vitamin A: 0% ✦ Vitamin C: 10% ✦ Calcium: 0% ✦ Iron: 0% ✦ **DIETARY EXCHANGES:** 1½ Fruit OR 1½ Carbohydrate

Triple Berry Dessert Topping

PREP TIME: 10 MINUTES ✦ YIELD: 8 (½-CUP) SERVINGS

    1½ cups fresh blackberries
    1½ cups fresh raspberries
    1½ cups sliced fresh strawberries
    ⅓ cup seedless raspberry jam
    ⅓ cup frozen raspberry or mixed berry juice concentrate, thawed

1. In medium bowl, combine blackberries, raspberries and strawberries.
2. In small bowl, combine raspberry jam and juice concentrate; mix well. Pour jam mixture over berries; toss gently to mix. Serve immediately, or cover and refrigerate until serving time. Store in refrigerator.

NUTRITION INFORMATION PER SERVING: Serving Size: ½ Cup ✦ Calories: 100 ✦ Calories from Fat: 0 ✦ **% DAILY VALUE:** Total Fat: 0 g 0% ✦ Saturated Fat: 0 g 0% ✦ Cholesterol: 0 mg 0% ✦ Sodium: 15 mg 1% ✦ Total Carbohydrate: 24 g 8% ✦ Dietary Fiber: 3 g 12% ✦ Sugars: 18 g ✦ Protein: 1 g ✦ Vitamin A: 0% ✦ Vitamin C: 60% ✦ Calcium: 2% ✦ Iron: 2% ✦ **DIETARY EXCHANGES:** 1½ Fruit OR 1½ Carbohydrate

Sweetened Whipped Cream

PREP TIME: 10 MINUTES ✦ YIELD: 2 CUPS

    1 cup whipping cream
    2 tablespoons powdered sugar
    ½ teaspoon vanilla*

In small bowl, beat cream until soft peaks form. Blend in sugar and vanilla; beat until stiff peaks form. Store in refrigerator.

TIP: * One to 2 tablespoons brandy, rum or flavored liqueur can be substituted for vanilla.

NUTRITION INFORMATION PER SERVING: Serving Size: 1 Tablespoon ✦ Calories: 30 ✦ Calories from Fat: 25 ✦ **% DAILY VALUE:** Total Fat: 3 g 5% ✦ Saturated Fat: 2 g 10% ✦ Cholesterol: 10 mg 3% ✦ Sodium: 0 mg 0% ✦ Total Carbohydrate: 1 g 1% ✦ Dietary Fiber: 0 g 0% ✦ Sugars: 1 g ✦ Protein: 0 g ✦ Vitamin A: 2% ✦ Vitamin C: 0% ✦ Calcium: 0% ✦ Iron: 0% ✦ **DIETARY EXCHANGES:** ½ Fat

VARIATIONS

Chocolate Whipped Cream: Add 2 tablespoons unsweetened cocoa and dash salt to cream before beating; increase sugar to 4 tablespoons.
Spicy Whipped Cream: Add ¼ teaspoon cinnamon (or ⅛ teaspoon cinnamon and ⅛ teaspoon nutmeg) with sugar and vanilla.

Frozen Key Lime Torte

PREP TIME: 15 MINUTES (READY IN 4 HOURS
30 MINUTES) ◆ YIELD: 10 SERVINGS

  1 pint (2 cups) lime sherbet
  1 pint (2 cups) lemon sorbet
  1 pint (2 cups) vanilla frozen yogurt
1¼ cups graham cracker crumbs (20 squares)
  2 tablespoons sugar
  ¼ cup margarine or butter, melted
  1 tablespoon Key lime juice
  ¼ cup coconut, toasted*

1. Place sherbet, sorbet and frozen yogurt in refrigerator to soften while preparing crust.
2. In small bowl, combine graham cracker crumbs, sugar and margarine; mix well. Press mixture in bottom of ungreased 9-inch springform pan. Freeze 15 minutes.
3. Spoon or scoop softened sherbet, sorbet and frozen yogurt into large bowl. Add lime juice; stir gently to mix. Spoon mixture over crust in pan, spreading evenly. Sprinkle with coconut; press lightly. Freeze at least 4 hours or until firm.
4. To serve, let stand at room temperature for 15 minutes. Cut into wedges.

> TIP: * To toast coconut, spread on cookie sheet; bake at 350°F. for 7 to 8 minutes or until light golden brown, stirring occasionally.

NUTRITION INFORMATION PER SERVING: Serving Size: ¹⁄₁₀ of Recipe ◆ Calories: 270 ◆ Calories from Fat: 60 ◆ % DAILY VALUE: Total Fat: 7 g 11% ◆ Saturated Fat: 2 g 10% ◆ Cholesterol: 4 mg 1% ◆ Sodium: 160 mg 7% ◆ Total Carbohydrate: 47 g 16% ◆ Dietary Fiber: 1 g 3% ◆ Sugars: 32 g ◆ Protein: 4 g ◆ Vitamin A: 6% ◆ Vitamin C: 4% ◆ Calcium: 10% ◆ Iron: 4% ◆ DIETARY EXCHANGES: 1½ Starch, 2 Fruit, 2½ Fat OR 3½ Carbohydrate, 2½ Fat

Frozen Key Lime Torte

Caramel-Banana Ice Cream Dessert

Caramel-Banana Ice Cream Dessert

PREP TIME: 15 MINUTES (READY IN 2 HOURS
15 MINUTES) ◆ YIELD: 12 SERVINGS

  ½ cup coarsely chopped pecans
1½ quarts (6 cups) fat-free vanilla ice cream, slightly softened
  4 ripe medium bananas, sliced
 25 vanilla wafers, coarsely crushed
  ¼ cup fat-free caramel ice cream topping
  ¼ cup chocolate-flavored syrup

1. Heat oven to 375°F. Line cookie sheet with foil; place pecans in single layer on foil. Bake at 375°F. for 3 to 5 minutes or until golden brown. Remove pecans from foil; set aside to cool.*
2. Scoop ice cream into 13×9-inch (3-quart) baking dish; gently spread over bottom of dish.** Top with banana slices. Sprinkle evenly with crushed wafers.
3. Heat caramel topping in microwave on HIGH for about 10 seconds or until warmed to pourable consistency but not hot. Repeat to warm chocolate-flavored syrup. Drizzle caramel and chocolate over crushed wafers. Sprinkle evenly with pecans. Cover tightly with sprayed plastic wrap; freeze at least 2 hours before serving. To serve, cut into squares.

> TIPS: * If desired, pecans can be broiled instead of baked. Line broiler pan with foil; place pecans in single layer on foil. Broil 4 to 6 inches from heat for about 1 minute or just until pecans begin to brown, being careful not to burn them.
> ** If desired, spray sheet of plastic wrap with nonstick cooking spray; place over scoops of ice cream. With hand, spread ice cream evenly; remove plastic wrap.

NUTRITION INFORMATION PER SERVING: Serving Size: ¹⁄₁₂ of Recipe ♦ Calories: 290 ♦ Calories from Fat: 70 ♦ % DAILY VALUE: Total Fat: 8 g 12% ♦ Saturated Fat: 1 g 5% ♦ Cholesterol: 0 mg 0% ♦ Sodium: 130 mg 5% ♦ Total Carbohydrate: 49 g 16% ♦ Dietary Fiber: 2 g 8% ♦ Sugars: 30 g ♦ Protein: 6 g ♦ Vitamin A: 8% ♦ Vitamin C: 4% ♦ Calcium: 30% ♦ Iron: 4% ♦ DIETARY EXCHANGES: 2 Starch, 1½ Fruit, 1 Fat OR 3½ Carbohydrate, 1 Fat

Creamy Rum Butter Sauce

PREP TIME: 15 MINUTES ♦ YIELD: 1½ CUPS

1 cup sugar
¾ cup half-and-half or evaporated milk
½ cup butter
¼ to ½ teaspoon rum extract, if desired

In small saucepan, combine all ingredients; mix well. Bring just to a boil, stirring occasionally. Serve warm. Store in refrigerator.

NUTRITION INFORMATION PER SERVING: Serving Size: 1 Tablespoon ♦ Calories: 80 ♦ Calories from Fat: 45 ♦ % DAILY VALUE: Total Fat: 5 g 8% ♦ Saturated Fat: 3 g 15% ♦ Cholesterol: 15 mg 5% ♦ Sodium: 40 mg 2% ♦ Total Carbohydrate: 9 g 3% ♦ Dietary Fiber: 0 g 0% ♦ Sugars: 9 g ♦ Protein: 0 g ♦ Vitamin A: 4% ♦ Vitamin C: 0% ♦ Calcium: 0% ♦ Iron: 0% ♦ DIETARY EXCHANGES: ½ Fruit, 1 Fat OR ½ Carbohydrate, 1 Fat

Brandied Cherry Sauce

PREP TIME: 10 MINUTES ♦ YIELD: 2 CUPS

1 (16-oz.) can (2 cups) pitted dark sweet cherries
About ¼ cup orange juice
¼ cup sugar
1 tablespoon cornstarch
2 tablespoons brandy, if desired

Brandied Cherry Sauce

1. Drain cherry liquid into 1-cup measuring cup; add orange juice to liquid to make 1 cup. Set cherries aside.
2. In small saucepan, combine liquid, sugar and cornstarch; mix well. Cook over medium heat until mixture comes to a boil, stirring constantly. Stir in brandy and cherries. Serve warm or cool. Store in refrigerator.

NUTRITION INFORMATION PER SERVING: Serving Size: ¼ Cup ♦ Calories: 90 ♦ Calories from Fat: 0 ♦ % DAILY VALUE: Total Fat: 0 g 0% ♦ Saturated Fat: 0 g 0% ♦ Cholesterol: 0 mg 0% ♦ Sodium: 0 mg 0% ♦ Total Carbohydrate: 20 g 7% ♦ Dietary Fiber: 1 g 4% ♦ Sugars: 18 g ♦ Protein: 0 g ♦ Vitamin A: 0% ♦ Vitamin C: 6% ♦ Calcium: 0% ♦ Iron: 0% ♦ DIETARY EXCHANGES: 1½ Fruit OR 1½ Carbohydrate

Classic Hard Sauce

PREP TIME: 10 MINUTES ♦ YIELD: ¾ CUP

1 cup powdered sugar
¼ cup butter, softened
2 teaspoons hot water
1 tablespoon brandy, bourbon or rum, or 1 teaspoon brandy or rum extract

In small bowl, combine all ingredients; beat at high speed until well blended. Serve immediately, or cover and refrigerate until serving time. Serve over warm dessert. Store in refrigerator.

NUTRITION INFORMATION PER SERVING: Serving Size: 1 Tablespoon ♦ Calories: 80 ♦ Calories from Fat: 35 ♦ % DAILY VALUE: Total Fat: 4 g 6% ♦ Saturated Fat: 2 g 10% ♦ Cholesterol: 10 mg 3% ♦ Sodium: 40 mg 2% ♦ Total Carbohydrate: 10 g 3% ♦ Dietary Fiber: 0 g 0% ♦ Sugars: 10 g ♦ Protein: 0 g ♦ Vitamin A: 2% ♦ Vitamin C: 0% ♦ Calcium: 0% ♦ Iron: 0% ♦ DIETARY EXCHANGES: ½ Fruit, 1 Fat OR ½ Carbohydrate, 1 Fat

Easy Crème Fraîche

PREP TIME: 10 MINUTES (READY IN 1 HOUR 10 MINUTES) ♦ YIELD: 1½ CUPS

1 cup sour cream
2 tablespoons brown sugar
Dash salt
½ cup whipping cream

1. In small bowl, sprinkle sour cream with brown sugar and salt; let stand 2 minutes.
2. Gently fold in cream 1 tablespoon at a time, until thoroughly blended. Cover; refrigerate at least 1 hour or until serving time. Store in refrigerator.

NUTRITION INFORMATION PER SERVING: Serving Size: 1 Tablespoon ♦ Calories: 45 ♦ Calories from Fat: 35 ♦ % DAILY VALUE: Total Fat: 4 g 6% ♦ Saturated Fat: 2 g 10% ♦ Cholesterol: 10 mg 3% ♦ Sodium: 15 mg 1% ♦ Total Carbohydrate: 2 g 1% ♦ Dietary Fiber: 0 g 0% ♦ Sugars: 2 g ♦ Protein: 0 g ♦ Vitamin A: 4% ♦ Vitamin C: 0% ♦ Calcium: 0% ♦ Iron: 0% ♦ DIETARY EXCHANGES: 1 Fat

CAKES, FROSTINGS & FILLINGS

Before You Begin

Read through the entire recipe.
Assemble all ingredients, mixing bowls, utensils and measuring equipment.
Prepare the baking pan(s).
Preheat the oven.

Recipe for Success

Unless you're an expert baker, stick precisely with the recipe. It really does matter whether you:

+ Preheat the oven to the right temperature.
+ Use the specified size or shape of cake pan.
+ Measure ingredients accurately and add them in the correct order.
+ Over- or underbeat, which can cause problems with the cake's texture and structure.
+ Follow instructions for cooling the cake and removing it from the pan.

Altitude Adjustments

Baking is as much science as art, a fact that becomes apparent when you bake a tried-and-true cake recipe at high altitude (more than 3,500 feet above sea level). As the altitude increases, air pressure decreases and the boiling point decreases, altering the way leavening agents, sweeteners and liquids interact.

Since cakes are especially sensitive to altitude, the recipes in this chapter indicate specific changes for highland bakers. If you have trouble with a recipe that does not specify altitude adjustments, try adding 2 to 4 tablespoons of flour or reducing the sugar by 3 tablespoons per cup.

Tips for Better Cakes

+ Shiny metal cake pans aid in delicate browning and produce a tender exterior.
+ Bake a single cake in the center of the oven. Arrange multiple pans on one or more racks, making sure the pans do not touch each other or the oven sides.
+ Test the cake for doneness at the minimum suggested baking time.
+ Cakes left in the pan too long may stick; if this

happens, reheat the cake in the oven for one minute.

+ Cool cakes on wire racks to allow for air circulation.
+ Wait until the cake has cooled completely (1 to 2 hours) before filling or frosting, unless the recipe has different instructions.

Storing Cake

+ Wait until cake has cooled completely before wrapping and storing it.
+ Refrigerate any cake containing dairy products in its filling or frosting.
+ Store layer or tube cakes under a cake dome or improvise one with an inverted mixing bowl.
+ Serve cakes with fluffy frosting as soon as possible, as the cake tends to absorb the frosting after a day or two. Store leftovers under a cake cover, but slip a knife under the edge so the container is not completely airtight. Moisture collects between the cake and the frosting if leftovers are stored airtight.
+ Freeze frosted or unfrosted cakes unwrapped on a plate. When the cake is firm, wrap it securely in heavy-duty plastic or foil and keep it frozen for up to six months. Cakes with cream or fruit filling, or with whipped cream or fluffy frosting, do not freeze well.
+ Thaw unfrosted cakes, wrapped, at room temperature. Frosted cakes, on the other hand, should be unwrapped as soon as you remove them from the freezer; then let them thaw at room temperature.

Two Types of Cake

All cakes fall into one of two categories. Butter cake includes the basic white, yellow, chocolate and pound cakes. Foam cake, which gets its lightness from beaten egg white, includes the fat-free angel food and sponge cakes as well as chiffon cake made with oil.

COOK'S NOTE

FOR BUTTER CAKE

+ Butter cakes can be made with butter, shortening or margarine.
+ When the recipe calls for butter or margarine, use the solid form, not whipped spreads.
+ Cut the cake with a thin, sharp knife in a gentle sawing motion.

White Cake

PREP TIME: 15 MINUTES (READY IN 2 HOURS)
✦ YIELD: 12 SERVINGS

    2 cups all-purpose flour
1½ cups sugar
    3 teaspoons baking powder
½ teaspoon salt
    1 cup milk
½ cup shortening
    1 teaspoon vanilla or ½ teaspoon almond
        extract
    5 egg whites

1. Heat oven to 350°F. Grease and flour two 9-inch round cake pans.* In large bowl, combine flour, sugar, baking powder, salt, milk and shortening; beat at low speed until moistened. Beat 2 minutes at medium speed. Add vanilla and egg whites; beat an additional 2 minutes. Pour into greased and floured pans.
2. Bake at 350°F. for 27 to 35 minutes or until toothpick inserted in center comes out clean. Cool 10 minutes. Remove from pans. Cool 1 hour or until completely cooled. Fill and frost as desired.

> **TIP:** * Cake can be baked in greased and floured 13×9-inch pan. Bake at 350°F. for 33 to 40 minutes. Cool 1 hour or until completely cooled.

HIGH ALTITUDE (*above 3500 feet*): Decrease sugar to 1¼ cups. Bake as directed above.

COOK'S NOTE

TESTING FOR DONENESS

The range of baking times suggested for each recipe is only an estimate; your oven may vary from that in our test kitchen.

Most layer cakes are done when:

✦ The top of the cake springs back, leaving no impression, when gently pressed with a fingertip.
✦ A toothpick, knife or cake tester inserted into the center comes out clean, without any crumbs or batter.
✦ The top is golden brown (for non-chocolate batter).

NUTRITION INFORMATION PER SERVING: Serving Size: ¹⁄₁₂ of Recipe ✦ Calories: 270 ✦ Calories from Fat: 80 ✦ **% DAILY VALUE:** Total Fat: 9 g 14% ✦ Saturated Fat: 2 g 10% ✦ Cholesterol: 0 mg 0% ✦ Sodium: 240 mg 10% ✦ Total Carbohydrate: 42 g 14% ✦ Dietary Fiber: 1 g 2% ✦ Sugars: 26 g ✦ Protein: 4 g ✦ Vitamin A: 0% ✦ Vitamin C: 0% ✦ Calcium: 10% ✦ Iron: 6% ✦ **DIETARY EXCHANGES:** 1½ Starch, 1½ Fruit, 1½ Fat OR 3 Carbohydrate, 1½ Fat

VARIATIONS

Coconut Cake: Stir 1 cup flaked coconut into batter before pouring into greased and floured pans.
Poppy Seed Cake: Combine ¼ cup poppy seed with an additional ¼ cup milk; let stand 30 minutes. Add to batter with vanilla and egg whites.

HOW MUCH BATTER

PAN SIZE	AMOUNT OF BATTER	BAKING TIME
6-inch round layer	2 cups	45 to 55 minutes
8-inch round layer	4 cups	50 to 60 minutes
10-inch round layer	6 cups	50 to 60 minutes
12-inch round layer	8 cups	50 to 60 minutes
14-inch round layer	11 cups	50 to 60 minutes
16 × 11 × 1½-inch sheet cake	9 cups (two mixes)	30 to 40 minutes

Yellow Cake

Yellow Cake

PREP TIME: 20 MINUTES (READY IN 1 HOUR 55 MINUTES)
♦ YIELD: 12 SERVINGS

    2½ cups all-purpose flour
     3 teaspoons baking powder
    ¼ teaspoon salt
    1¼ cups sugar
    ¾ cup margarine or butter, softened
     1 teaspoon vanilla
     3 eggs
     1 cup milk

1. Heat oven to 350°F. Grease and flour two 8 or 9-inch round cake pans.* In medium bowl, combine flour, baking powder and salt; mix well.
2. In large bowl, combine sugar and margarine; beat until light and fluffy. Add vanilla and eggs; blend well. Alternately add dry ingredients and milk, beating well after each addition. Pour batter into greased and floured pans.
3. Bake at 350°F. for 27 to 35 minutes or until toothpick inserted in center comes out clean. Cool 10 minutes. Remove from pans. Cool 1 hour or until completely cooled. Fill and frost as desired.

TIP: * Cake can be baked in greased and floured 13 x 9-inch pan. Bake at 350°F. for 33 to 40 minutes. Cool 1 hour or until completely cooled.

HIGH ALTITUDE (*above 3500 feet*)**:** Decrease sugar to 1 cup. Bake as directed above.

NUTRITION INFORMATION PER SERVING: Serving Size: ¹⁄₁₂ of Recipe ♦ Calories: 310 ♦ Calories from Fat: 120 ♦ **% DAILY VALUE:** Total Fat: 13 g 20% ♦ Saturated Fat: 3 g 15% ♦ Cholesterol: 55 mg 18% ♦ Sodium: 330 mg 14% ♦ Total Carbohydrate: 42 g 14% ♦ Dietary Fiber: 1 g 3% ♦ Sugars: 22 g ♦ Protein: 5 g ♦ Vitamin A: 15% ♦ Vitamin C: 0% ♦ Calcium: 10% ♦ Iron: 8% ♦ **DIETARY EXCHANGES:** 1½ Starch, 1½ Fruit, 2 Fat OR 3 Carbohydrate, 2 Fat

Black Forest Cake

PREP TIME: 30 MINUTES (READY IN 2 HOURS 30 MINUTES) ♦ YIELD: 12 SERVINGS

CAKE
     1 (1 lb. 2.25-oz.) pkg. pudding-included dark chocolate cake mix
    1¼ cups water
    ⅓ cup oil
     3 eggs
FILLING
     1 (21-oz.) can cherry pie filling
    ½ teaspoon almond extract
FROSTING
     1 pint (2 cups) whipping cream
    ½ cup powdered sugar
     2 tablespoons brandy
       Chocolate curls, if desired

1. Heat oven to 350°F. Grease and flour two 8 or 9-inch round cake pans. In large bowl, combine all cake ingredients; beat at low speed until moistened. Beat 2 minutes at medium speed. Pour batter into greased and floured pans.
2. Bake at 350°F. Bake 8-inch pans 30 to 40 minutes; bake 9-inch pans 25 to 35 minutes or until cake springs back when touched lightly in center. Cool 15 minutes. Remove from pans. Cool 1 hour or until completely cooled.
3. In small bowl, combine filling ingredients; mix well.

Black Forest Cake

4. In medium bowl, beat whipping cream at high speed until soft peaks form. Gradually add powdered sugar, beating until stiff peaks form. Fold in brandy.

5. Place 1 cake layer, top side down, on serving plate. Spread 1 cup filling to within 1 inch of edge. Top with second cake layer, top side up. Frost sides and top with whipped cream. Spoon remaining filling in center of top of cake. Garnish with chocolate curls. Store in refrigerator.

HIGH ALTITUDE *(above 3500 feet)***:** Add ¼ cup flour to dry cake mix; increase water to 1⅓ cups. Bake as directed above.

NUTRITION INFORMATION PER SERVING: Serving Size: ¹⁄₁₂ of Recipe ◆ Calories: 480 ◆ Calories from Fat: 230 ◆ **% DAILY VALUE:** Total Fat: 26 g 40% ◆ Saturated Fat: 11 g 55% ◆ Cholesterol: 110 mg 37% ◆ Sodium: 420 mg 18% ◆ Total Carbohydrate: 55 g 18% ◆ Dietary Fiber: 2 g 8% ◆ Sugars: 42 g ◆ Protein: 5 g ◆ Vitamin A: 15% ◆ Vitamin C: 2% ◆ Calcium: 10% ◆ Iron: 8% ◆ **DIETARY EXCHANGES:** 1 Starch, 2½ Fruit, 5½ Fat OR 3½ Carbohydrate, 5½ Fat

Chocolate Praline Layer Cake

PREP TIME: 25 MINUTES (READY IN 2 HOURS 15 MINUTES) ◆ YIELD: 16 SERVINGS

CAKE
- ½ cup butter
- ¼ cup whipping cream
- 1 cup firmly packed brown sugar
- ¾ cup coarsely chopped pecans
- 1 (1 lb. 2.25-oz.) pkg. pudding-included devil's food cake mix
- 1¼ cups water
- ⅓ cup oil
- 3 eggs

TOPPING
- 1¾ cups whipping cream
- ¼ cup powdered sugar
- ¼ teaspoon vanilla
- 16 whole pecans, if desired
- 16 chocolate curls, if desired

1. Heat oven to 325°F. In heavy small saucepan, combine butter, ¼ cup whipping cream and brown sugar. Cook over low heat just until butter is melted, stirring occasionally. Pour into two 9 or 8-inch round cake pans; sprinkle evenly with chopped pecans.*

2. In large bowl, combine cake mix, water, oil and eggs; beat at low speed until moistened. Beat 2 minutes at medium speed. Carefully spoon batter over pecan mixture.

3. Bake at 325°F. for 35 to 45 minutes or until cake springs back when touched lightly in center. Cool 5 minutes. Remove from pans. Cool 1 hour or until completely cooled.

4. In small bowl, beat 1¾ cups whipping cream until soft peaks form. Gradually add powdered sugar and vanilla; beat until stiff peaks form.

5. To assemble cake, place 1 layer on serving plate, praline side up. Spread with half of whipped cream. Top with second layer, praline side up. Spread top with remaining whipped cream. Garnish with whole pecans and chocolate curls. Store in refrigerator.

> **TIP:** * Cake can be baked in 13x9-inch pan. Bake at 325°F. for 50 to 60 minutes or until cake springs back when touched lightly in center. Cool 5 minutes. Invert onto serving platter. Cool completely. Frost cake or pipe with whipped cream. Garnish with pecan halves and chocolate curls. Serve with any remaining whipped cream. Store in refrigerator.

HIGH ALTITUDE *(above 3500 feet)***:** Add ⅓ cup flour to dry cake mix; increase water to 1⅓ cups. Bake at 350°F. for 30 to 35 minutes. Immediately remove from pans.

NUTRITION INFORMATION PER SERVING: Serving Size: ¹⁄₁₆ of Recipe ◆ Calories: 460 ◆ Calories from Fat: 270 ◆ **% DAILY VALUE:** Total Fat: 30 g 46% ◆ Saturated Fat: 13 g 65% ◆ Cholesterol: 95 mg 32% ◆ Sodium: 330 mg 14% ◆ Total Carbohydrate: 43 g 14% ◆ Dietary Fiber: 2 g 8% ◆ Sugars: 30 g ◆ Protein: 4 g ◆ Vitamin A: 15% ◆ Vitamin C: 0% ◆ Calcium: 6% ◆ Iron: 10% ◆ **DIETARY EXCHANGES:** 1½ Starch, 1½ Fruit, 5½ Fat OR 3 Carbohydrate, 5½ Fat

Chocolate Praline Layer Cake

CUTTING AND SERVING A ROUND CAKE

Cutting wedges works fine for smaller round cakes, but cakes 10 inches or more in diameter need a different approach.

+ Straight-cut method: Cut the layer into parallel strips about an inch wide, slicing each strip into serving-sized pieces as you go.
+ Concentric-cut method: Cut a circle 2 inches from the outside edge. Slice this outer ring into pieces 1 inch wide. Move in 2 more inches from the cut edges and cut a second circle; again, slice it into inch-wide pieces. When the inside core is of a manageable size, cut it into serving-sized wedges.

Chocolate Sour Cream Cake

PREP TIME: 20 MINUTES (READY IN 2 HOURS 10 MINUTES) + YIELD: 12 SERVINGS

    2 cups all-purpose flour
    2 cups sugar
1 ¼ teaspoons baking soda
    1 teaspoon salt
    ½ teaspoon baking powder
    1 cup water
    ¾ cup sour cream
    ¼ cup shortening
    1 teaspoon vanilla
    2 eggs
    4 oz. unsweetened chocolate, cut into pieces, melted, cooled

1. Heat oven to 350°F. Grease and flour two 8 or 9-inch round cake pans; line bottom of pans with waxed paper. In medium bowl, combine flour, sugar, baking soda, salt and baking powder; mix well.
2. In large bowl, combine all remaining ingredients; blend well. Add dry ingredients; blend at low speed until moistened. Beat 3 minutes at high speed. Pour batter into greased, floured and lined pans.
3. Bake at 350°F. for 30 to 40 minutes or until toothpick inserted in center comes out clean. Cool 10 minutes. Remove from pans.

Cool 1 hour or until completely cooled. Fill and frost as desired.

HIGH ALTITUDE (*above 3500 feet*)**:** Decrease sugar to 1¾ cups; omit baking powder. Bake at 375°F. for 25 to 35 minutes.

NUTRITION INFORMATION PER SERVING: Serving Size: ¹⁄₁₂ of Recipe • Calories: 360 • Calories from Fat: 130 • % DAILY VALUE: Total Fat: 14 g 22% • Saturated Fat: 6 g 30% • Cholesterol: 40 mg 13% • Sodium: 350 mg 15% • Total Carbohydrate: 53 g 18% • Dietary Fiber: 2 g 8% • Sugars: 34 g • Protein: 5 g • Vitamin A: 4% • Vitamin C: 0% • Calcium: 4% • Iron: 10% • DIETARY EXCHANGES: 2 Starch, 1½ Fruit, 2½ Fat OR 3½ Carbohydrate, 2½ Fat

Chocolate Zucchini Cake

PREP TIME: 15 MINUTES (READY IN 2 HOURS) + YIELD: 12 SERVINGS

    1 (1 lb. 2.25-oz.) pkg. pudding-included devil's food cake mix
    1 teaspoon cinnamon
    ¼ teaspoon cloves
    2 cups shredded unpeeled zucchini
    ½ cup buttermilk
    ⅓ cup oil
    3 eggs
    ½ cup chopped nuts
    ½ cup semisweet chocolate chips

BIRTHDAY CAKE IDEAS

+ Create a border by drizzling melted chocolate around the top edges of the cake.
+ Sift powdered sugar onto an unfrosted cake. To make a beautiful lacy pattern, place a paper doily on top of the cake. Sprinkle powdered sugar over the top of the entire doily. Carefully remove the doily by lifting straight up. Vary this idea by cutting shapes or names from waxed paper to make a stencil.
+ Coat the entire cake or just the top or sides with chopped nuts, colored sugar, sprinkles, miniature chocolate chips or miniature candy-coated chocolate pieces.
+ Use a cookie cutter or stencil to mark a design on a frosted cake. Fill in with colored sugar, candy sprinkles or minced nuts.

CONVERTING TO CUPCAKES

Most layer cake batters work well for cupcakes. Batter for a one-layer cake yields 12 to 15 cupcakes; for a two-layer cake, 24 to 30 cupcakes. Line muffin cups with paper baking cups or generously grease and flour the cups. In a pinch, you can set foil baking cups on a cookie sheet. Fill the cups ⅔ full of batter and bake at 350°F. for 15 to 20 minutes or until tops spring back when lightly touched. Immediately remove cupcakes from the pan and transfer them to a wire rack to cool.

1. Heat oven to 350°F. Grease and flour 13 × 9-inch pan. In large bowl, combine cake mix, cinnamon, cloves, zucchini, buttermilk, oil and eggs; beat at low speed until moistened. Beat 2 minutes at high speed. Pour into greased and floured pan. Sprinkle with nuts and chocolate chips.
2. Bake at 350°F. for 35 to 40 minutes or until toothpick inserted in center comes out clean. Cool 1 hour or until completely cooled.

HIGH ALTITUDE (*above 3500 feet*)**:** Add 2 tablespoons flour to dry cake mix. Bake at 375°F. for 30 to 40 minutes.

NUTRITION INFORMATION PER SERVING: Serving Size: ¹⁄₁₂ of Recipe ♦ Calories: 330 ♦ Calories from Fat: 150 ♦ **% DAILY VALUE:** Total Fat: 17 g 26% ♦ Saturated Fat: 4 g 20% ♦ Cholesterol: 55 mg 18% ♦ Sodium: 360 mg 15% ♦ Total Carbohydrate: 40 g 13% ♦ Dietary Fiber: 2 g 8% ♦ Sugars: 22 g ♦ Protein: 5 g ♦ Vitamin A: 4% ♦ Vitamin C: 2% ♦ Calcium: 4% ♦ Iron: 10% ♦ **DIETARY EXCHANGES:** 2 Starch, ½ Fruit, 3 Fat OR 2½ Carbohydrate, 3 Fat

Devil's Food Cake

PREP TIME: 15 MINUTES (READY IN 2 HOURS)
♦ YIELD: 12 SERVINGS

          2 cups all-purpose flour
     1¼ teaspoons baking soda
          ½ teaspoon salt
     1½ cups sugar
          ½ cup margarine or butter, softened
          1 teaspoon vanilla
          2 eggs
          4 oz. unsweetened chocolate, cut into pieces, melted
          1 cup milk

1. Heat oven to 350°F. Grease and flour two 8 or 9-inch round cake pans.* In medium bowl, combine flour, baking soda and salt; mix well.
2. In large bowl, combine sugar and margarine; beat until light and fluffy. Add vanilla and eggs; blend well. Stir in chocolate. Alternately add dry ingredients and milk, beating well after each addition. Pour batter into greased and floured pans.
3. Bake at 350°F. for 27 to 35 minutes or until toothpick inserted in center comes out clean. Cool 10 minutes. Remove from pans. Cool 1 hour or until completely cooled. Fill and frost as desired.

TIP: * Cake can be baked in greased and floured 13×9-inch pan. Bake at 350°F. for 33 to 40 minutes. Cool 1 hour or until completely cooled.

HIGH ALTITUDE (*above 3500 feet*)**:** Decrease sugar to 1¼ cups. Bake as directed above.

NUTRITION INFORMATION PER SERVING: Serving Size: ¹⁄₁₂ of Recipe ♦ Calories: 330 ♦ Calories from Fat: 130 ♦ **% DAILY VALUE:** Total Fat: 14 g 22% ♦ Saturated Fat: 5 g 25% ♦ Cholesterol: 35 mg 12% ♦ Sodium: 330 mg 14% ♦ Total Carbohydrate: 45 g 15% ♦ Dietary Fiber: 2 g 8% ♦ Sugars: 26 g ♦ Protein: 5 g ♦ Vitamin A: 8% ♦ Vitamin C: 0% ♦ Calcium: 4% ♦ Iron: 10% ♦ **DIETARY EXCHANGES:** 1½ Starch, 1½ Fruit, 2½ Fat OR 3 Carbohydrate, 2½ Fat

TIPS FOR SHAPED CAKE PANS

Specialty cake pans in the shape of a favorite storybook character or holiday motif are fun to use. The batter should reach about halfway up the side of the pan. To calculate, measure the amount of water needed to fill the empty pan; use half that amount of cake batter. Using solid shortening, grease and flour the pans carefully.

German Chocolate Cake with Coconut-Pecan Frosting

PREP TIME: 30 MINUTES (READY IN 2 HOURS 50 MINUTES) ◆ YIELD: 16 SERVINGS

CAKE
4 oz. sweet cooking chocolate, cut into pieces
½ cup water
2 cups sugar
1 cup margarine or butter, softened
4 eggs
2½ cups all-purpose flour
1 teaspoon baking soda
½ teaspoon salt
1 cup buttermilk
1 teaspoon vanilla

FROSTING
1 cup sugar
1 cup evaporated milk
½ cup margarine or butter
3 eggs, beaten
1⅓ cups flaked coconut
1 cup chopped pecans or walnuts
1 teaspoon vanilla

1. Heat oven to 350°F. Grease and lightly flour three 9-inch round cake pans. In small saucepan, melt chocolate with water over low heat. Cool.
2. In large bowl, combine 2 cups sugar and 1 cup margarine; beat until light and fluffy. Add 4 eggs, one at a time, beating well after each addition. Stir in chocolate mixture. Add all remaining cake ingredients; beat at low speed until well combined. Pour batter into greased and floured pans.
3. Bake at 350°F. for 35 to 45 minutes or until toothpick inserted in center comes out clean. Cool 5 minutes. Remove from pans. Cool 1 hour or until completely cooled.
4. In medium saucepan, combine 1 cup sugar, evaporated milk, ½ cup margarine and 3 eggs; mix well. Cook over medium heat until mixture begins to bubble, stirring constantly. Remove saucepan from heat. Stir in coconut, pecans and 1 teaspoon vanilla. Cool 30 minutes or until completely cooled.
5. Place 1 cake layer, top side down, on serving plate. Spread with ⅓ of frosting. Repeat with remaining cake layers and frosting, ending with frosting.

HIGH ALTITUDE (*above 3500 feet*)**:** Decrease sugar in cake to 1¾ cups; decrease baking soda to ¾ teaspoon. Bake at 375°F. for 25 to 30 minutes.

NUTRITION INFORMATION PER SERVING: Serving Size: ¹⁄₁₆ of Recipe ◆ Calories: 560 ◆ Calories from Fat: 270 ◆ **% DAILY VALUE:** Total Fat: 30 g 46% ◆ Saturated Fat: 8 g 40% ◆ Cholesterol: 100 mg 33% ◆ Sodium: 420 mg 18% ◆ Total Carbohydrate: 64 g 21% ◆ Dietary Fiber: 2 g 8% ◆ Sugars: 46 g ◆ Protein: 8 g ◆ Vitamin A: 20% ◆ Vitamin C: 0% ◆ Calcium: 8% ◆ Iron: 10% ◆ **DIETARY EXCHANGES:** 3 Starch, 1½ Fruit, 5 Fat OR 4½ Carbohydrate, 5 Fat

Tunnel of Fudge Cake

PREP TIME: 35 MINUTES (READY IN 4 HOURS 30 MINUTES) ◆ YIELD: 16 SERVINGS

CAKE
1¾ cups sugar
1¾ cups margarine or butter, softened
6 eggs
2 cups powdered sugar
2¼ cups all-purpose flour
¾ cup unsweetened cocoa
2 cups chopped walnuts*

GLAZE
¾ cup powdered sugar
¼ cup unsweetened cocoa
4 to 6 teaspoons milk

1. Heat oven to 350°F. Grease and flour 12-cup Bundt® pan or 10-inch tube pan. In large bowl, combine sugar and margarine; beat until light and fluffy. Add eggs 1 at a

Tunnel of Fudge Cake

time, beating well after each addition. Gradually add 2 cups powdered sugar; blend well. By hand, stir in flour and remaining cake ingredients until well blended. Spoon batter into greased and floured pan; spread evenly.

2. Bake at 350°F. for 45 to 50 minutes or until top is set and edges are beginning to pull away from edge of pan.** Cool upright in pan on wire rack for 1½ hours. Invert cake onto serving plate; cool at least 2 hours.

3. In small bowl, combine all glaze ingredients, adding enough milk for desired drizzling consistency. Spoon over top of cake, allowing some to run down sides. Store tightly covered.

TIPS: * Nuts are essential for success of recipe. ** Since cake has soft filling, ordinary doneness tests cannot be used. Accurate oven temperature and baking times are essential.

HIGH ALTITUDE (*above 3500 feet*)**:** Increase flour to 1¾ cups plus 3 tablespoons. Bake as directed above.

NUTRITION INFORMATION PER SERVING: Serving Size: ⅟₁₆ of Recipe ♦ Calories: 570 ♦ Calories from Fat: 290 ♦ **% DAILY VALUE:** Total Fat: 32 g 49% ♦ Saturated Fat: 6 g 30% ♦ Cholesterol: 80 mg 27% ♦ Sodium: 260 mg 11% ♦ Total Carbohydrate: 62 g 21% ♦ Dietary Fiber: 3 g 12% ♦ Sugars: 43 g ♦ Protein: 8 g ♦ Vitamin A: 20% ♦ Vitamin C: 0% ♦ Calcium: 4% ♦ Iron: 10% ♦ **DIETARY EXCHANGES:** 3 Starch, 1 Fruit, 6 Fat OR 4 Carbohydrate, 6 Fat

Macadamia Fudge Torte

PREP TIME: 30 MINUTES (READY IN 3 HOURS) ♦ YIELD: 12 SERVINGS

FILLING
⅓ cup low-fat sweetened condensed milk (not evaporated)
½ cup semisweet chocolate chips

CAKE
1 (1 lb. 2.25-oz.) pkg. pudding-included devil's food cake mix
1½ teaspoons cinnamon
⅓ cup oil
1 (16-oz.) can sliced pears in light syrup, drained
2 eggs
⅓ cup chopped macadamia nuts or pecans
2 teaspoons water

SAUCE
1 (17-oz.) jar butterscotch caramel fudge ice cream topping
⅓ cup milk

Macadamia Fudge Torte

1. Heat oven to 350°F. Spray 9 or 10-inch springform pan with nonstick cooking spray. In small saucepan, combine filling ingredients. Cook over medium-low heat until chocolate is melted, stirring occasionally.

2. In large bowl, combine cake mix, cinnamon and oil; blend at low speed for 20 to 30 seconds or until crumbly. (Mixture will be dry.)

3. Place pears in blender container or food processor bowl with metal blade; cover and blend until smooth.

4. In another large bowl, combine 2½ cups of the cake mix mixture, pureed pears and eggs; beat at low speed until moistened. Beat 2 minutes at medium speed. Spread batter evenly in sprayed pan. Drop filling by spoonfuls over batter. Stir nuts and water into remaining cake mix mixture. Sprinkle over filling.

5. Bake at 350°F. for 45 to 50 minutes or until top springs back when touched lightly in center. Cool 10 minutes. Remove sides of pan. Cool 1½ hours or until completely cooled.

6. In small saucepan, combine sauce ingredients. Cook over medium-low heat for 3 to 4 minutes or until well blended, stirring occasionally. Just before serving, spoon 2 tablespoons warm sauce onto each serving plate; top with wedge of torte. If desired, serve with vanilla ice cream or frozen yogurt and garnish with chocolate curls.

HIGH ALTITUDE (*above 3500 feet*)**:** Add ⅓ cup flour to dry cake mix. Bake as directed above.

NUTRITION INFORMATION PER SERVING: Serving Size: ⅟₁₂ of Recipe ♦ Calories: 460 ♦ Calories from Fat: 140 ♦ **% DAILY VALUE:** Total Fat: 16 g 25% ♦ Saturated Fat: 4 g 20% ♦ Cholesterol: 35 mg 12% ♦ Sodium: 490 mg 20% ♦ Total Carbohydrate: 73 g 24% ♦ Dietary Fiber: 3 g 12% ♦ Sugars: 49 g ♦ Protein: 5 g ♦ Vitamin A: 2% ♦ Vitamin C: 0% ♦ Calcium: 6% ♦ Iron: 10% ♦ **DIETARY EXCHANGES:** 1½ Starch, 3½ Fruit, 3 Fat OR 5 Carbohydrate, 3 Fat

Old-Fashioned Oatmeal Cake with Broiled Topping

PREP TIME: 30 MINUTES (READY IN 2 HOURS 15 MINUTES) ◆ YIELD: 16 SERVINGS

CAKE
1½ cups quick-cooking rolled oats
1¼ cups boiling water
1 cup sugar
1 cup firmly packed brown sugar
½ cup margarine or butter, softened
1 teaspoon vanilla
3 eggs
1½ cups all-purpose flour
1 teaspoon baking soda
½ teaspoon baking powder
½ teaspoon salt
1½ teaspoons cinnamon
½ teaspoon nutmeg

TOPPING
⅔ cup firmly packed brown sugar
¼ cup margarine or butter, melted
3 tablespoons half-and-half or milk
1 cup coconut
½ cup chopped nuts

1. In small bowl, combine rolled oats and boiling water; let stand 20 minutes.
2. Meanwhile, heat oven to 350°F. Grease and flour 13×9-inch pan. In large bowl, combine sugar, 1 cup brown sugar and ½ cup margarine; beat until light and fluffy. Add vanilla and eggs; blend well. Add oatmeal and all remaining cake ingredients; mix well. Pour batter into greased and floured pan.
3. Bake at 350°F. for 35 to 45 minutes or until toothpick inserted in center comes out clean.
4. In small bowl, combine ⅔ cup brown sugar, ¼ cup margarine and half-and-half; beat at high speed until smooth. Stir in coconut and nuts. Spoon over warm cake; spread to cover.
5. Broil 4 to 6 inches from heat for 1 to 2 minutes or until bubbly and light golden brown. Cool 1 hour or until completely cooled.

HIGH ALTITUDE (*above 3500 feet*)**:** Decrease brown sugar in cake to ¾ cup; increase flour to 1½ cups plus 3 tablespoons. Bake at 375°F. for 30 to 40 minutes.

NUTRITION INFORMATION PER SERVING: Serving Size: ¹⁄₁₆ of Recipe ◆ Calories: 350 ◆ Calories from Fat: 130 ◆ **% DAILY VALUE:** Total Fat: 14 g 22% ◆ Saturated Fat: 4 g 20% ◆ Cholesterol: 40 mg 13% ◆ Sodium: 300 mg 13% ◆ Total Carbohydrate: 52 g 17% ◆ Dietary Fiber: 2 g 8% ◆ Sugars: 37 g ◆ Protein: 4 g ◆ Vitamin A: 10% ◆ Vitamin C: 0% ◆ Calcium: 6% ◆ Iron: 10% ◆ **DIETARY EXCHANGES:** 1½ Starch, 2 Fruit, 2½ Fat OR 3½ Carbohydrate, 2½ Fat

Whole Wheat Apple Ring Cake

PREP TIME: 35 MINUTES (READY IN 2 HOURS 40 MINUTES) ◆ YIELD: 16 SERVINGS

CAKE
3 cups whole wheat flour
2 teaspoons baking powder
1 teaspoon cinnamon
½ teaspoon salt
2 cups firmly packed brown sugar
1¼ cups oil
2 teaspoons vanilla
4 eggs
2 cups shredded peeled apples

COOK'S NOTE

VARIATIONS FOR CAKES FROM SCRATCH OR MIXES

◆ Before mixing the batter, add a flavoring such as:
  1 tablespoon finely grated lemon or orange peel
  1 to 2 teaspoons of flavored extract, such as vanilla, almond, orange or lemon.
  1 teaspoon cinnamon, ½ teaspoon nutmeg and ½ teaspoon cloves
◆ Replace the water with the same amount of a flavorful liquid such as fruit juice, coffee or flavored soda. This will also change the texture.
◆ Replace part of the water with up to ¼ cup of liqueur or liquor.
◆ Add a stir-in after the batter is mixed, such as:
  2 to 4 ounces finely grated milk chocolate or semisweet chocolate
  1 cup chopped nuts
  1 cup coconut
  2 tablespoons poppy seed
  ½ cup grated apple or thinly sliced peach
  ½ cup raisins or other chopped, dried fruit

GLAZE
½ cup firmly packed brown sugar
1 tablespoon light corn syrup
1 tablespoon margarine or butter
1 tablespoon milk

1. Heat oven to 350°F. Grease and flour 12-cup Bundt® pan. In medium bowl, combine whole wheat flour, baking powder, cinnamon and salt; mix well.
2. In large bowl, combine brown sugar, oil, vanilla and eggs; beat well. Add flour mixture; blend well. Fold in apples. Spoon batter into greased and floured pan.
3. Bake at 350°F. for 45 to 55 minutes or until toothpick inserted in center comes out clean. Cool upright in pan 10 minutes. Invert cake onto serving plate. Cool 1 hour or until completely cooled.
4. In small saucepan, combine all glaze ingredients; mix well. Bring to a boil. Boil 1 minute, stirring constantly. Cool 5 to 10 minutes or until of desired drizzling consistency. Drizzle glaze over cooled cake.

HIGH ALTITUDE (*above 3500 feet*): Decrease brown sugar in cake to 1¾ cups. Bake at 375°F. for 35 to 45 minutes.

NUTRITION INFORMATION PER SERVING: Serving Size: ¹⁄₁₆ of Recipe • Calories: 420 • Calories from Fat: 180 • % DAILY VALUE: Total Fat: 20 g 31% • Saturated Fat: 3 g 15% • Cholesterol: 55 mg 18% • Sodium: 170 mg 7% • Total Carbohydrate: 54 g 18% • Dietary Fiber: 3 g 12% • Sugars: 37 g • Protein: 5 g • Vitamin A: 2% • Vitamin C: 0% • Calcium: 8% • Iron: 10% • DIETARY EXCHANGES: 2 Starch, 1½ Fruit, 4 Fat OR 3½ Carbohydrate, 4 Fat

Pineapple Upside-Down Cake

PREP TIME: 20 MINUTES (READY IN 1 HOUR)
◆ YIELD: 6 SERVINGS

½ cup firmly packed brown sugar
¼ cup margarine or butter, melted
6 canned pineapple slices, drained
6 maraschino cherries
2 eggs, separated
½ cup sugar
¾ cup all-purpose flour
½ teaspoon baking powder
¼ teaspoon salt
¼ cup pineapple juice
   Whipped cream

1. Heat oven to 350°F. In small bowl, combine brown sugar and margarine; blend well. Spread in bottom of ungreased 9-inch round cake pan. Arrange pineapple slices and maraschino cherries over brown sugar mixture. Set aside.
2. In small bowl, beat egg yolks until thick and lemon colored. Gradually add sugar; beat well. Add flour, baking powder, salt and pineapple juice; mix well.
3. In another small bowl, beat egg whites until stiff peaks form. Fold into batter. Pour batter evenly over pineapple slices and cherries.
4. Bake at 350°F. for 30 to 35 minutes or until toothpick inserted in center comes out clean. Cool upright in pan 2 minutes. Invert cake onto serving plate. Serve warm with whipped cream.

HIGH ALTITUDE (*above 3500 feet*): Increase flour to ¾ cup plus 3 tablespoons. Bake at 375°F. for 30 to 35 minutes.

NUTRITION INFORMATION PER SERVING: Serving Size: ⅙ of Recipe • Calories: 370 • Calories from Fat: 140 • % DAILY VALUE: Total Fat: 15 g 23% • Saturated Fat: 5 g 25% • Cholesterol: 90 mg 30% • Sodium: 250 mg 10% • Total Carbohydrate: 55 g 18% • Dietary Fiber: 1 g 4% • Sugars: 43 g • Protein: 4 g • Vitamin A: 15% • Vitamin C: 6% • Calcium: 8% • Iron: 10% • DIETARY EXCHANGES: 1 Starch, 2½ Fruit, 3 Fat OR 3½ Carbohydrate, 3 Fat

COOK'S NOTE

GARNISHING CAKE SLICES

✦ Before adding a slice of cake, drizzle the plate with raspberry puree (ice cream topping), chocolate syrup or melted chocolate chips, Crème Anglaise (page 352) or thinned vanilla pudding. Make swirls, zigzags, polka dots or other designs, then set a slice of cake on the decorated plate.
✦ Sift powdered sugar or cocoa over and around the slice.
✦ Serve with a scoop of ice cream, sorbet or frozen yogurt garnished with a fresh mint sprig and sliced berry.
✦ Pipe a border around the slice with whipped cream and grate bittersweet chocolate over all.

Banana Crunch Cake

PREP TIME: 25 MINUTES (READY IN 2 HOURS
40 MINUTES) ◆ YIELD: 16 SERVINGS

½ cup all-purpose flour
1 cup coconut
1 cup rolled oats
¾ cup firmly packed brown sugar
½ cup chopped pecans
½ cup margarine or butter
1½ cups (2 large) sliced *very ripe* bananas
½ cup sour cream
4 eggs
1 (1 lb. 2.25-oz.) pkg. pudding-included yellow
   cake mix

1. Heat oven to 350°F. Grease and flour 10-inch tube pan. In medium bowl, combine flour, coconut, rolled oats, brown sugar and pecans; mix well. With fork or pastry blender, cut in margarine until mixture is crumbly. Set aside.
2. In large bowl, combine bananas, sour cream and eggs; beat at low speed until smooth. Add cake mix; beat 2 minutes at high speed. Spread ⅓ of batter in greased and floured pan; sprinkle with ⅓ of coconut mixture. Repeat layers 2 more times using remaining batter and coconut mixture, ending with coconut mixture.
3. Bake at 350°F. for 50 to 60 minutes or until toothpick inserted near center comes out clean. Cool upright in pan 15 minutes. Remove cake from pan; place on serving plate, coconut side up. Cool 1 hour or until completely cooled.

HIGH ALTITUDE *(above 3500 feet)*: Add 3 tablespoons flour to dry cake mix. Bake at 375°F. for 45 to 55 minutes.

Banana Crunch Cake

Carrot Cake with Creamy Coconut Frosting

NUTRITION INFORMATION PER SERVING: Serving Size: ¹⁄₁₆ of Recipe ◆ Calories: 360 ◆ Calories from Fat: 140 ◆ **% DAILY VALUE:** Total Fat: 16 g 25% ◆ Saturated Fat: 5 g 25% ◆ Cholesterol: 55 mg 18% ◆ Sodium: 310 mg 13% ◆ Total Carbohydrate: 49 g 16% ◆ Dietary Fiber: 2 g 8% ◆ Sugars: 29 g ◆ Protein: 5 g ◆ Vitamin A: 8% ◆ Vitamin C: 0% ◆ Calcium: 4% ◆ Iron: 8% ◆ **DIETARY EXCHANGES:** 1½ Starch, 2 Fruit, 3 Fat OR 3½ Carbohydrate, 3 Fat

Carrot Cake with Creamy Coconut Frosting

PREP TIME: 30 MINUTES (READY IN 2 HOURS
30 MINUTES) ◆ YIELD: 24 SERVINGS

CAKE
2½ cups all-purpose flour
2 teaspoons baking soda
1 teaspoon salt
1 teaspoon cinnamon, if desired
2 cups sugar
1 cup oil
2 teaspoons vanilla
2 eggs
2 cups shredded carrots
1 (8¼-oz.) can crushed pineapple, well drained
½ cup raisins
½ cup chopped nuts

FROSTING
1 (8-oz.) pkg. cream cheese, softened
2½ cups powdered sugar
6 tablespoons margarine or butter, softened
2 teaspoons vanilla
1 cup coconut
½ cup chopped nuts

1. Heat oven to 350°F. Grease and flour 13×9-inch pan. In medium bowl, combine flour, baking soda, salt and cinnamon; mix well.
2. In large bowl, combine sugar, oil, 2 teaspoons vanilla and eggs; beat well. Add flour

mixture; mix well. Stir in carrots, pineapple, raisins and ½ cup nuts. Pour and spread batter into greased and floured pan.

3. Bake at 350°F. for 50 to 60 minutes or until cake springs back when touched lightly in center. Cool 1 hour or until completely cooled.

4. In large bowl, combine cream cheese, powdered sugar, margarine and 2 teaspoons vanilla; beat until smooth. Stir in coconut and ½ cup nuts. Spread over cooled cake.

HIGH ALTITUDE *(above 3500 feet)*: Increase flour to 2¾ cups; decrease sugar in cake to 1½ cups. Bake as directed above.

NUTRITION INFORMATION PER SERVING: Serving Size: ¹⁄₂₄ of Recipe ♦ Calories: 380 ♦ Calories from Fat: 180 ♦ **% DAILY VALUE:** Total Fat: 20 g 31% ♦ Saturated Fat: 5 g 25% ♦ Cholesterol: 30 mg 10% ♦ Sodium: 270 mg 11% ♦ Total Carbohydrate: 46 g 15% ♦ Dietary Fiber: 1 g 4% ♦ Sugars: 34 g ♦ Protein: 4 g ♦ Vitamin A: 60% ♦ Vitamin C: 2% ♦ Calcium: 2% ♦ Iron: 6% ♦ **DIETARY EXCHANGES:** 1 Starch, 2 Fruit, 4 Fat OR 3 Carbohydrate, 4 Fat

Coconut Cake with Lemon Filling

PREP TIME: 30 MINUTES (READY IN 2 HOURS 10 MINUTES) ♦ YIELD: 12 SERVINGS

CAKE
   2 cups all-purpose flour
1½ cups sugar
   3 teaspoons baking powder
   1 teaspoon salt
   1 cup milk
   ½ cup shortening
   2 teaspoons coconut extract or vanilla
   4 egg whites

FILLING
   ¾ cup sugar
   3 tablespoons cornstarch
   ¼ teaspoon salt
   ⅔ cup cold water
   2 egg yolks
   1 tablespoon margarine or butter
   2 teaspoons grated lemon peel
   3 tablespoons lemon juice

FROSTING
   ½ cup sugar
   2 tablespoons water
   2 egg whites
   1 (7-oz.) jar (1½ cups) marshmallow creme
   1 cup coconut

1. Heat oven to 350°F. Grease and flour two 9-inch round cake pans. In large bowl, combine flour, 1½ cups sugar, baking powder, 1 teaspoon salt, milk and shortening; beat at

Coconut Cake with Lemon Filling

low speed until moistened. Beat 2 minutes at medium speed. Add coconut extract and 4 egg whites; beat an additional 2 minutes. Pour into greased and floured pans.

2. Bake at 350°F. for 20 to 30 minutes or until toothpick inserted in center comes out clean. Cool 10 minutes. Remove from pans. Cool 1 hour or until completely cooled.

3. Meanwhile, in small saucepan, combine ¾ cup sugar, cornstarch and ¼ teaspoon salt. Gradually stir in water until smooth. Cook over medium heat, stirring constantly, until mixture boils. Boil 1 minute, stirring constantly. Remove saucepan from heat.

4. In small bowl, beat egg yolks. Stir about ¼ cup of hot mixture into egg yolks. Gradually stir yolk mixture into hot mixture. Cook over medium heat until mixture boils. Boil 1 minute, stirring constantly. Remove saucepan from heat. Stir in margarine, lemon peel and lemon juice. Cool 30 minutes or until completely cooled.

5. In medium saucepan, combine ½ cup sugar, 2 tablespoons water and 2 egg whites. Cook over low heat, beating continuously with electric hand mixer at high speed until soft peaks form. Add marshmallow creme; beat until stiff peaks form.

6. Place 1 cake layer, top side down, on serving plate. Spread with cooled filling. Top with second cake layer, top side up. Frost sides and top of cake with frosting. Sprinkle coconut over top of cake.

HIGH ALTITUDE *(above 3500 feet)*: Decrease flour to 1¾ cups; decrease sugar in cake to 1¼ cups. Bake at 375°F. for 25 to 30 minutes.

NUTRITION INFORMATION PER SERVING: Serving Size: ¹⁄₁₂ of Recipe ♦ Calories: 470 ♦ Calories from Fat: 120 ♦ **% DAILY VALUE:** Total Fat: 13 g 20% ♦ Saturated Fat: 5 g 25% ♦ Cholesterol: 40 mg 13% ♦ Sodium: 420 mg 18% ♦ Total Carbohydrate: 81 g 27% ♦ Dietary Fiber: 1 g 4% ♦ Sugars: 61 g ♦ Protein: 6 g ♦ Vitamin A: 2% ♦ Vitamin C: 2% ♦ Calcium: 10% ♦ Iron: 8% ♦ **DIETARY EXCHANGES:** 2 Starch, 3½ Fruit, 2 Fat OR 5½ Carbohydrate, 2 Fat

Sour Cream Pound Cake

PREP TIME: 15 MINUTES (READY IN 2 HOURS
35 MINUTES) ◆ YIELD: 16 SERVINGS

2¾ cups sugar
1½ cups butter, softened
1 teaspoon vanilla
6 eggs
3 cups all-purpose flour
1 teaspoon grated orange or lemon peel
½ teaspoon baking powder
½ teaspoon salt
1 cup sour cream

1. Heat oven to 350°F. Generously grease and flour 12-cup Bundt® pan. In large bowl, combine sugar and butter; beat until light and fluffy. Beat in vanilla. Add eggs 1 at a time, beating well after each addition.
2. In medium bowl, combine flour, orange peel, baking powder and salt; mix well. Add dry ingredients alternately with sour cream, beating well after each addition. Pour batter into greased and floured pan.
3. Bake at 350°F. for 55 to 65 minutes or until toothpick inserted in center comes out clean. Cool 15 minutes. Invert onto serving plate. Cool 1 hour or until completely cooled.

HIGH ALTITUDE (*above 3500 feet*): Decrease sugar to 2½ cups. Bake at 375°F. for 55 to 65 minutes.

NUTRITION INFORMATION PER SERVING: Serving Size: ¹⁄₁₆ of recipe ◆ Calories: 440 ◆ Calories from Fat: 210 ◆ **% DAILY VALUE:** Total Fat: 23 g 35% ◆ Saturated Fat: 13 g 65% ◆ Cholesterol: 135 mg 45% ◆ Sodium: 290 mg 12% ◆ Total Carbohydrate: 53 g 18% ◆ Dietary Fiber: 1 g 3% ◆ Sugars: 36 g ◆ Protein: 5 g ◆ Vitamin A: 20% ◆ Vitamin C: 0% ◆ Calcium: 4% ◆ Iron: 8% ◆ **DIETARY EXCHANGES:** 1½ Starch, 2 Fruit, 4½ Fat OR 3½ Carbohydrate, 4½ Fat

---

COOK'S NOTE

FREEZING LEFTOVER EGG WHITES

Beat the whites lightly and spoon them into ice cube trays so you can easily calculate the amount needed. Thaw egg whites in the refrigerator and use them as you would fresh whites. One egg white equals about 2 tablespoons.

Lemon Delight Pound Cake

PREP TIME: 40 MINUTES (READY IN 2 HOURS
30 MINUTES) ◆ YIELD: 16 SERVINGS

CAKE
2½ cups all-purpose flour
1½ cups sugar
3 teaspoons baking powder
½ teaspoon salt
¾ cup apricot nectar or orange juice
¾ cup oil
2 teaspoons lemon extract
4 eggs

GLAZE
1½ cups powdered sugar
½ cup lemon juice

1. Heat oven to 325°F. Generously grease and flour 12-cup Bundt® pan. In large bowl, combine all cake ingredients; beat at low speed until moistened. Beat 3 minutes at medium speed. Pour batter into greased and floured pan.
2. Bake at 325°F. for 40 to 50 minutes or until toothpick inserted in center comes out clean.
3. Remove cake from oven. With long-tined fork, poke deep holes in cake every inch. In small bowl, blend glaze ingredients until smooth. Spoon half of glaze over hot cake in pan. Let stand upright in pan 10 minutes.
4. Invert cake onto serving plate. Spoon remaining glaze over cake. Cool 1 hour or until completely cooled.

HIGH ALTITUDE (*above 3500 feet*): Decrease baking powder to 2½ teaspoons. Bake at 350°F. for 40 to 50 minutes.

NUTRITION INFORMATION PER SERVING: Serving Size: ¹⁄₁₆ of Recipe ◆ Calories: 310 ◆ Calories from Fat: 110 ◆ **% DAILY VALUE:** Total Fat: 12 g 18% ◆ Saturated Fat: 2 g 10% ◆ Cholesterol: 55 mg 18% ◆ Sodium: 180 mg 8% ◆ Total Carbohydrate: 47 g 16% ◆ Dietary Fiber: 1 g 3% ◆ Sugars: 32 g ◆ Protein: 4 g ◆ Vitamin A: 4% ◆ Vitamin C: 2% ◆ Calcium: 6% ◆ Iron: 6% ◆ **DIETARY EXCHANGES:** 1½ Starch, 1½ Fruit, 2 Fat OR 3 Carbohydrate, 2 Fat

Sponge Cake

PREP TIME: 15 MINUTES (READY IN 2 HOURS)
✦ YIELD: 12 SERVINGS

  6 eggs, separated
  ¾ teaspoon cream of tartar
1½ cups sugar
1½ cups all-purpose flour
  1 tablespoon grated orange peel
  1 teaspoon baking powder
  ½ teaspoon salt
  ½ cup apricot nectar or water
  1 teaspoon rum extract or vanilla

1. Heat oven to 350°F. In large bowl, combine egg whites and cream of tartar; beat until soft peaks form. Gradually add ¾ cup of the sugar, beating at high speed until stiff peaks form.
2. In small bowl, combine egg yolks, remaining ¾ cup sugar, flour, orange peel, baking powder, salt, nectar and rum extract; beat at low speed until moistened. Beat 1 minute at medium speed. Pour over egg white mixture; fold in gently just until blended. Pour batter into ungreased 10-inch tube pan.
3. Bake at 350°F. for 35 to 45 minutes or until top springs back when lightly touched. Immediately invert cake onto funnel or soft drink bottle; let hang 1 hour or until completely cooled. To remove cake from pan, run edge of knife around outer edge of pan and tube.

COOK'S NOTE

FOR BETTER FOAM CAKE

- ✦ For the fluffiest results, start with the egg whites at room temperature. Use a glass or ceramic bowl; plastic may retain traces of grease. Any trace of fat will prevent the whites from whipping properly.
- ✦ Bake the cake in an ungreased pan to give the batter something to cling to as it rises.
- ✦ Turn the baked cake upside down to prevent it from collapsing while it cools. Balance it on a bottle or funnel if the cake pan does not have its own prongs to rest on. Keep the cake upside down until completely cool.
- ✦ Cut the finished cake with a long, serrated knife in a gentle sawing motion to prevent it from being compressed.

HIGH ALTITUDE (*above 3500 feet*)**:** Decrease total sugar to 1¼ cups. Bake at 375°F. for 35 to 45 minutes.

NUTRITION INFORMATION PER SERVING: Serving Size: ¹⁄₁₂ of Recipe ✦ Calories: 160 ✦ Calories from Fat: 25 ✦ **% DAILY VALUE:** Total Fat: 3 g 5% ✦ Saturated Fat: 1 g 5% ✦ Cholesterol: 105 mg 35% ✦ Sodium: 160 mg 7% ✦ Total Carbohydrate: 27 g 9% ✦ Dietary Fiber: 1 g 2% ✦ Sugars: 14 g ✦ Protein: 5 g ✦ Vitamin A: 6% ✦ Vitamin C: 0% ✦ Calcium: 4% ✦ Iron: 6% ✦ **DIETARY EXCHANGES:** 1 Starch, 1 Fruit, ½ Fat OR 2 Carbohydrate, ½ Fat

Chiffon Cake

PREP TIME: 30 MINUTES (READY IN 2 HOURS 45 MINUTES) ✦ YIELD: 12 SERVINGS

  2 cups all-purpose flour
1½ cups sugar
  3 teaspoons baking powder
  ¼ teaspoon salt
  ¾ cup cold water
  ½ cup oil
  7 eggs, separated
  ½ teaspoon vanilla
  4 teaspoons finely grated lemon peel
  ½ teaspoon cream of tartar

1. Heat oven to 325°F. In large bowl, combine flour, sugar, baking powder and salt; mix well. Add water, oil, egg yolks and vanilla; beat at low speed until moistened. Beat at high speed for 5 minutes or until very smooth, scraping sides of bowl occasionally. Fold in lemon peel. Transfer to another large bowl. Thoroughly wash bowl and beaters.
2. In same large bowl, combine egg whites and cream of tartar; beat 3 minutes or until stiff peaks form. Gradually add egg yolk mixture to egg whites, folding gently to combine. Pour into ungreased 10-inch tube pan.
3. Bake at 325°F. for 60 to 75 minutes or until top springs back when lightly touched. Immediately invert cake onto funnel or soft drink bottle; let hang 1 hour or until completely cooled. To remove cake from pan, run edge of knife around outer edge of pan and tube.

HIGH ALTITUDE (*above 3500 feet*)**:** Bake at 350°F. for 55 to 60 minutes.

NUTRITION INFORMATION PER SERVING: Serving Size: ¹⁄₁₂ of Recipe ✦ Calories: 300 ✦ Calories from Fat: 110 ✦ **% DAILY VALUE:** Total Fat: 12 g 18% ✦ Saturated Fat: 2 g 10% ✦ Cholesterol: 125 mg 42% ✦ Sodium: 200 mg 8% ✦ Total Carbohydrate: 42 g 14% ✦ Dietary Fiber: 1 g 3% ✦ Sugars: 26 g ✦ Protein: 6 g ✦ Vitamin A: 4% ✦ Vitamin C: 0% ✦ Calcium: 8% ✦ Iron: 8% ✦ **DIETARY EXCHANGES:** 2 Starch, 1 Fruit, 2 Fat OR 3 Carbohydrate, 2 Fat

Sugar-Crusted Lime Cake

Sugar-Crusted Lime Cake

PREP TIME: 15 MINUTES (READY IN 1 HOUR 35 MINUTES) ✦ YIELD: 8 SERVINGS

CAKE
    2 egg whites, room temperature*
 ½ teaspoon baking powder
 1 cup all-purpose flour
 ¾ cup sugar
 1 tablespoon grated lime peel
 1 teaspoon baking powder
 ¼ teaspoon salt
 ⅓ cup milk
 ¼ cup shortening
 2 tablespoons lime juice

TOPPING
 ¼ cup sugar
 1 tablespoon lime juice

1. Heat oven to 350°F. Spray 9-inch round cake pan with nonstick cooking spray; sprinkle lightly with flour.
2. In small bowl, combine egg whites and ½ teaspoon baking powder; beat until stiff peaks form. Set aside.
3. In large bowl, combine all remaining cake ingredients; beat at low speed until moistened. Beat 2 minutes at medium speed. Gently fold stiffly beaten egg whites into batter. Pour into sprayed and floured pan.
4. Bake at 350°F. for 27 to 35 minutes or until toothpick inserted in center comes out clean.
5. In small bowl, combine topping ingredients; mix well. Spread over hot cake. Cool 45 minutes or until completely cooled.

TIP: * For higher volume, bring egg whites to room temperature before beating. Set bowl of egg whites in large bowl of very warm water; stir gently for 2 to 3 minutes.

HIGH ALTITUDE *(above 3500 feet)*: Decrease sugar in cake to ⅔ cup. Bake as directed above.

NUTRITION INFORMATION PER SERVING: Serving Size: ⅛ of Recipe ✦ Calories: 220 ✦ Calories from Fat: 50 ✦ % DAILY VALUE: Total Fat: 6 g 9% ✦ Saturated Fat: 2 g 10% ✦ Cholesterol: 0 mg 0% ✦ Sodium: 180 mg 8% ✦ Total Carbohydrate: 38 g 13% ✦ Dietary Fiber: 1 g 2% ✦ Sugars: 26 g ✦ Protein: 3 g ✦ Vitamin A: 0% ✦ Vitamin C: 0% ✦ Calcium: 6% ✦ Iron: 4% ✦ DIETARY EXCHANGES: 1 Starch, 1½ Fruit, 1 Fat OR 2½ Carbohydrate, 1 Fat

S'More Snack Cake

PREP TIME: 25 MINUTES (READY IN 2 HOURS 15 MINUTES) ✦ YIELD: 16 SERVINGS

 1 cup all-purpose flour
 1½ cups graham cracker crumbs (24 squares)
 1 teaspoon baking powder
 ½ teaspoon baking soda
 ½ teaspoon salt
 1 cup firmly packed brown sugar
 ½ cup shortening
 3 eggs
 1 cup milk
 1 cup miniature semisweet chocolate chips
 1 (7-oz.) jar (1½ cups) marshmallow creme

1. Heat oven to 350°F. Grease and flour 13×9-inch pan. In medium bowl, combine flour, graham cracker crumbs, baking powder, baking soda and salt; mix well.
2. In large bowl, combine brown sugar, shortening and eggs; beat until well blended. Add dry ingredients and milk; beat at low speed until well blended. Beat 1 minute at medium speed. Stir in ⅔ cup of the chocolate

S'More Snack Cake

chips. Spoon and spread batter evenly into greased and floured pan.

3. Bake at 350°F. for 25 to 35 minutes or until toothpick inserted in center comes out clean. Cool 15 minutes.

4. Meanwhile, in small saucepan, melt remaining ⅓ cup chocolate chips over low heat. Spoon teaspoonfuls of marshmallow creme onto top of warm cake; carefully spread with knife dipped in hot water. Drizzle with melted chocolate; swirl chocolate through marshmallow creme to marble. Cool 1 hour or until completely cooled.

HIGH ALTITUDE *(above 3500 feet)*: Increase flour to 1 cup plus 2 tablespoons. Bake at 375°F. for 20 to 30 minutes.

NUTRITION INFORMATION PER SERVING: Serving Size: ¹⁄₁₆ of Recipe ◆ Calories: 300 ◆ Calories from Fat: 110 ◆ **% DAILY VALUE:** Total Fat: 12 g 18% ◆ Saturated Fat: 4 g 20% ◆ Cholesterol: 40 mg 13% ◆ Sodium: 220 mg 9% ◆ Total Carbohydrate: 43 g 14% ◆ Dietary Fiber: 1 g 4% ◆ Sugars: 30 g ◆ Protein: 4 g ◆ Vitamin A: 0% ◆ Vitamin C: 0% ◆ Calcium: 6% ◆ Iron: 8% ◆ **DIETARY EXCHANGES:** 1½ Starch, 1½ Fruit, 2 Fat OR 3 Carbohydrate, 2 Fat

Dixie Spice Cake with Caramel Frosting

PREP TIME: 30 MINUTES (READY IN 2 HOURS 15 MINUTES) ◆ YIELD: 12 SERVINGS

CAKE
2¼ cups all-purpose flour
1¼ cups firmly packed brown sugar
½ cup sugar
1 teaspoon baking soda
½ teaspoon salt
½ teaspoon nutmeg
½ teaspoon allspice
1 cup buttermilk
⅔ cup shortening
1 teaspoon vanilla
3 eggs
1 cup chopped walnuts or pecans

FROSTING
½ cup margarine or butter
1 cup firmly packed brown sugar
¼ cup milk
3 cups powdered sugar
½ teaspoon vanilla

1. Heat oven to 350°F. Generously grease and flour bottom only of 13×9-inch pan. In large bowl, combine all cake ingredients except walnuts; beat at low speed until

moistened. Beat 3 minutes at medium speed. Stir in walnuts. Pour batter into greased and floured pan.

2. Bake at 350°F. for 40 to 45 minutes or until top springs back when touched lightly in center. Cool 1 hour or until completely cooled.

3. In medium saucepan, melt margarine. Add brown sugar; cook over low heat for 2 minutes, stirring constantly. Add milk; continue cooking until mixture comes to a rolling boil. Remove from heat. Gradually add powdered sugar and vanilla; mix well. If needed, add a few drops of milk for desired spreading consistency. Spread over cooled cake.

HIGH ALTITUDE *(above 3500 feet)*: Increase flour to 2¼ cups plus 3 tablespoons; decrease brown sugar in cake to 1 cup. Bake at 375°F. for 35 to 40 minutes.

NUTRITION INFORMATION PER SERVING: Serving Size: ¹⁄₁₂ of Recipe ◆ Calories: 670 ◆ Calories from Fat: 240 ◆ **% DAILY VALUE:** Total Fat: 27 g 42% ◆ Saturated Fat: 5 g 25% ◆ Cholesterol: 55 mg 18% ◆ Sodium: 340 mg 14% ◆ Total Carbohydrate: 100 g 33% ◆ Dietary Fiber: 1 g 4% ◆ Sugars: 79 g ◆ Protein: 6 g ◆ Vitamin A: 8% ◆ Vitamin C: 0% ◆ Calcium: 8% ◆ Iron: 15% ◆ **DIETARY EXCHANGES:** 2 Starch, 4½ Fruit, 5½ Fat OR 6½ Carbohydrate, 5½ Fat

VARIATION

Dixie Spice Cupcakes: Fill 24 to 30 paper-lined muffin cups ⅔ full with batter. Bake at 350°F. for 20 to 25 minutes. Frost with caramel frosting.

Top to bottom: German Chocolate Cake with Coconut-Pecan Frosting (page 362), Dixie Spice Cake with Caramel Frosting

Delicious White Fruitcake

PREP TIME: 15 MINUTES (READY IN 3 HOURS
15 MINUTES) ♦ YIELD: 2 (20-SLICE) LOAVES

1¾ cups all-purpose flour
 1 cup sugar
 ½ teaspoon salt
 ½ teaspoon baking powder
1½ cups margarine or butter, softened
 1 tablespoon vanilla
 1 tablespoon lemon extract
 5 eggs
 1 lb. (4 cups) pecan halves
 1 lb. (2 cups) cut-up candied pineapple
 ¾ lb. (1½ cups) whole or cut-up candied
    cherries

1. Heat oven to 300°F. Generously grease and lightly flour two 8×4-inch loaf pans. In large bowl, combine all ingredients except pecans and fruit; beat at low speed until moistened. Beat 2 minutes at medium speed. Stir in pecans and fruit. Spoon and spread batter into greased and floured pans.
2. Bake at 300°F. for 1¼ to 1¾ hours or until toothpick inserted in center comes out clean. Cool 15 minutes. Remove from pans. Cool 1 hour or until completely cooled.
3. Wrap tightly in plastic wrap or foil. Store in refrigerator for up to 1 month or in freezer for up to 3 months.

> **TIP:** Fruitcake can be wrapped in cheesecloth that has been soaked in brandy or fruit juice. Wrap with plastic wrap or foil. Store in refrigerator. Moisten cloth every 2 weeks.

HIGH ALTITUDE (*above 3500 feet*)**:** No change.

NUTRITION INFORMATION PER SERVING: Serving Size: 1 Slice ♦ Calories: 260 ♦ Calories from Fat: 140 ♦ **% DAILY VALUE:** Total Fat: 15 g 23% ♦ Saturated Fat: 2 g 10% ♦ Cholesterol: 25 mg 8% ♦ Sodium: 180 mg 8% ♦ Total Carbohydrate: 28 g 9% ♦ Dietary Fiber: 1 g 4% ♦ Sugars: 17 g ♦ Protein: 2 g ♦ Vitamin A: 8% ♦ Vitamin C: 0% ♦ Calcium: 4% ♦ Iron: 4% ♦ **DIETARY EXCHANGES:** ½ Starch, 1½ Fruit, 3 Fat OR 2 Carbohydrate, 3 Fat

Gingerbread with Lemon Sauce

PREP TIME: 20 MINUTES (READY IN 50 MINUTES)
♦ YIELD: 9 SERVINGS

GINGERBREAD
 1 cup all-purpose flour
 ⅓ cup wheat germ
 ¼ cup firmly packed brown sugar
 ½ teaspoon baking powder
 ½ teaspoon baking soda
 ¾ teaspoon ginger
 ¾ teaspoon cinnamon
 ½ teaspoon allspice
 ½ cup unsweetened apple juice
 ⅓ cup molasses
 ¼ cup oil
 1 egg
SAUCE
 ¼ cup sugar
 2 teaspoons cornstarch
 ½ cup hot water
 1 tablespoon lemon juice
 1 teaspoon grated lemon peel

1. Heat oven to 350°F. Grease bottom only of 8-inch square pan. In large bowl, combine flour, wheat germ, brown sugar, baking powder, baking soda, ginger, cinnamon and allspice; mix well. Add all remaining gingerbread ingredients; blend well. Pour into greased pan.
2. Bake at 350°F. for 30 to 40 minutes or until toothpick inserted in center comes out clean.
3. Meanwhile, in medium saucepan, combine sugar and cornstarch. Gradually stir in hot water. Cook over medium heat until mixture comes to a boil and is slightly thickened and clear, stirring constantly. Stir in lemon juice and lemon peel. Serve warm sauce over warm gingerbread.

HIGH ALTITUDE (*above 3500 feet*)**:** Increase flour to 1 cup plus 2 tablespoons. Bake as directed above.

NUTRITION INFORMATION PER SERVING: Serving Size: ⅑ of Recipe ♦ Calories: 220 ♦ Calories from Fat: 60 ♦ **% DAILY VALUE:** Total Fat: 7 g 11% ♦ Saturated Fat: 1 g 5% ♦ Cholesterol: 25 mg 8% ♦ Sodium: 115 mg 5% ♦ Total Carbohydrate: 35 g 12% ♦ Dietary Fiber: 1 g 4% ♦ Sugars: 20 g ♦ Protein: 3 g ♦ Vitamin A: 0% ♦ Vitamin C: 0% ♦ Calcium: 6% ♦ Iron: 10% ♦ **DIETARY EXCHANGES:** 1 Starch, 1½ Fruit, 1 Fat OR 2½ Carbohydrate, 1 Fat

Amaretto Petits Fours

PREP TIME: 50 MINUTES (READY IN 3 HOURS)
♦ YIELD: 24 PETITS FOURS

CAKE
    2 cups all-purpose flour
1½ cups sugar
    3 teaspoons baking powder
 ½ teaspoon salt
    I cup milk
 ½ cup shortening
 ½ teaspoon almond extract or I teaspoon
        vanilla
    5 egg whites
    2 tablespoons amaretto

GLAZE AND GARNISH
    3 cups powdered sugar
 ¼ cup water
    3 tablespoons light corn syrup
    2 tablespoons margarine or butter, melted
 ½ teaspoon vanilla
 ¼ teaspoon almond extract
 ½ recipe Buttercream Frosting (page 377)
        Food colors

1. Heat oven to 350°F. Grease and flour 15×10×1-inch baking pan. In large bowl, combine flour, sugar, baking powder, salt, milk and shortening; beat at low speed until moistened. Beat 2 minutes at medium speed. Add almond extract and egg whites; continue beating an additional 2 minutes. Pour into greased and floured pan.

2. Bake at 350°F. for 18 to 23 minutes or until toothpick inserted in center comes out clean. Cool 45 minutes or until completely cooled.

3. Brush top of cake with amaretto. To avoid cake crumbs, freeze cake 1 hour before cutting.

4. Cut cake into squares, diamonds or desired shapes using 1½ to 2-inch cookie cutters. Set cake pieces on wire rack over waxed paper.

5. In small bowl, combine powdered sugar, water, corn syrup, margarine, vanilla and almond extract; beat at low speed until powdered sugar is moistened. Beat at high speed until smooth. If necessary, add 2 to 3 teaspoons water until glaze is of desired consistency. Spoon glaze evenly over top and sides of cake pieces. (Glaze that drips off can be reused.)

6. Tint Buttercream Frosting using desired food colors. With decorating bag fitted with desired tips, decorate petits fours.

HIGH ALTITUDE (*above 3500 feet*)**:** Decrease sugar to 1¼ cups. Bake as directed above.

NUTRITION INFORMATION PER SERVING: Serving Size: 1 Petit Four ♦ Calories: 270 ♦ Calories from Fat: 70 ♦ **% DAILY VALUE:** Total Fat: 8 g 12% ♦ Saturated Fat: 3 g 15% ♦ Cholesterol: 10 mg 3% ♦ Sodium: 160 mg 7% ♦ Total Carbohydrate: 48 g 16% ♦ Dietary Fiber: 0 g 0% ♦ Sugars: 39 g ♦ Protein: 2 g ♦ Vitamin A: 4% ♦ Vitamin C: 0% ♦ Calcium: 6% ♦ Iron: 4% ♦ **DIETARY EXCHANGES:** 1 Starch, 2 Fruit, 1½ Fat OR 3 Carbohydrate, 1½ Fat

Lemon-Orange Picnic Cake

PREP TIME: 15 MINUTES (READY IN 1 HOUR 35 MINUTES)
♦ YIELD: 9 SERVINGS

CAKE
    I cup all-purpose flour
 ¾ cup sugar
1½ teaspoons grated orange peel
    I teaspoon grated lemon peel
    I teaspoon baking powder
 ¼ teaspoon salt
 ⅓ cup milk
 ¼ cup shortening
    2 tablespoons orange juice
    3 egg whites

TOPPING
 ¼ cup sugar
    2 teaspoons lemon juice
    I teaspoon orange juice

1. Heat oven to 350°F. Spray bottom only of 8-inch square pan with nonstick cooking spray. In large bowl, combine all cake ingredients; beat at low speed until moistened. Beat 2 minutes at medium speed. Pour into sprayed pan.

2. Bake at 350°F. for 25 to 32 minutes or until cake is light golden brown and toothpick inserted in center comes out clean.

3. In small bowl, combine all topping ingredients; mix well. Spread over warm cake. Cool 45 minutes or until completely cooled.

HIGH ALTITUDE (*above 3500 feet*)**:** Decrease sugar in cake to ⅔ cup. Bake as directed above.

NUTRITION INFORMATION PER SERVING: Serving Size: ⅑ of Recipe ♦ Calories: 200 ♦ Calories from Fat: 50 ♦ **% DAILY VALUE:** Total Fat: 6 g 9% ♦ Saturated Fat: 1 g 5% ♦ Cholesterol: 0 mg 0% ♦ Sodium: 135 mg 6% ♦ Total Carbohydrate: 34 g 11% ♦ Dietary Fiber: 0 g 0% ♦ Sugars: 23 g ♦ Protein: 3 g ♦ Vitamin A: 0% ♦ Vitamin C: 4% ♦ Calcium: 4% ♦ Iron: 4% ♦ **DIETARY EXCHANGES:** 1 Starch, 1 Fruit, 1 Fat OR 2 Carbohydrate, 1 Fat

Angel Food Cake

PREP TIME: 20 MINUTES (READY IN 2 HOURS)
◆ YIELD: 12 SERVINGS

¾ cup all-purpose flour
¾ cup sugar
1½ cups (about 12) egg whites, room
temperature
1½ teaspoons cream of tartar
¼ teaspoon salt
1½ teaspoons vanilla
½ teaspoon almond extract
¾ cup sugar

1. Place oven rack at lowest position. Heat oven to 375°F. In small bowl, combine flour and ¾ cup sugar.

2. In large bowl, combine egg whites, cream of tartar, salt, vanilla and almond extract; beat until mixture forms soft peaks. Gradually add ¾ cup sugar, beating at high speed until stiff peaks form. Spoon flour-sugar mixture ¼ cup at a time over beaten egg whites; gently fold in just until blended. Pour batter into ungreased 10-inch tube pan. With knife, cut gently through batter to remove large air bubbles.

3. Bake at 375°F. on lowest oven rack for 30 to 40 minutes or until crust is golden brown and cracks are very dry. Immediately invert cake onto funnel or soft drink bottle; let hang 1 hour or until completely cooled. To remove cake from pan, run edge of knife around outer edge of pan and tube.

Chocolate-Cherry Angel Food Cake

TIP: To make loaves, bake in 2 ungreased 9×5-inch loaf pans for 25 to 30 minutes.

HIGH ALTITUDE *(above 3500 feet)*: Increase flour to 1 cup; increase egg whites to 1¾ cups (about 13). Bake at 400°F. for 30 to 35 minutes.

NUTRITION INFORMATION PER SERVING: Serving Size: ¹⁄₁₂ of Recipe ◆ Calories: 140 ◆ Calories from Fat: 0 ◆ % DAILY VALUE: Total Fat: 0 g 0% ◆ Saturated Fat: 0 g 0% ◆ Cholesterol: 0 mg 0% ◆ Sodium: 100 mg 4% ◆ Total Carbohydrate: 32 g 11% ◆ Dietary Fiber: 0 g 0% ◆ Sugars: 25 g ◆ Protein: 4 g ◆ Vitamin A: 0% ◆ Vitamin C: 0% ◆ Calcium: 0% ◆ Iron: 2% ◆ DIETARY EXCHANGES: 1 Starch, 1 Fruit OR 2 Carbohydrate

VARIATION

Chocolate-Cherry Angel Food Cake:
Fold ⅓ cup well-drained, chopped maraschino cherries and 1 oz. grated semisweet chocolate into batter. Bake as directed above. In small saucepan over low heat, melt 2 tablespoons margarine or butter and 1 oz. semisweet chocolate with 1 tablespoon corn syrup. Stir in 1 cup powdered sugar and 2 to 3 tablespoons maraschino cherry liquid until smooth and of desired drizzling consistency. Immediately drizzle over cooled cake.

Jelly Roll

PREP TIME: 30 MINUTES (READY IN 1 HOUR 45 MINUTES)
◆ YIELD: 10 SERVINGS

2 teaspoons powdered sugar
4 eggs
¾ cup sugar
¼ cup cold water
1 teaspoon vanilla
1 cup all-purpose flour
1 teaspoon baking powder
¼ teaspoon salt
¾ cup any flavor jelly or preserves

1. Heat oven to 375°F. Lightly sprinkle clean towel with powdered sugar; set aside. Generously grease and lightly flour 15× 10×1-inch baking pan.
2. In large bowl, beat eggs at high speed for 5 minutes or until thick and lemon colored. Gradually add sugar, beating until light and fluffy. Stir in water and vanilla. Add flour, baking powder and salt; blend at low speed just until dry ingredients are moistened. Spread batter evenly in greased and floured pan.
3. Bake at 375°F. for 8 to 12 minutes or until cake springs back when touched lightly in

Jelly Roll (page 374)

center. Loosen edges of cake; immediately invert onto sugared side of towel. Remove pan.

4. Starting with short side, roll up cake in towel; cool on wire rack for 1 hour or until completely cooled.

5. Unroll cake; remove towel. Spread cake with jelly; re-roll loosely to incorporate filling. Wrap in foil or waxed paper. Store in refrigerator. If desired, sprinkle with powdered sugar just before serving.

HIGH ALTITUDE *(above 3500 feet)***:** No change.

NUTRITION INFORMATION PER SERVING: Serving Size: ¹⁄₁₀ of Recipe ♦ Calories: 200 ♦ Calories from Fat: 20 ♦ **% DAILY VALUE:** Total Fat: 2 g 3% ♦ Saturated Fat: 1 g 5% ♦ Cholesterol: 85 mg 28% ♦ Sodium: 135 mg 6% ♦ Total Carbohydrate: 41 g 14% ♦ Dietary Fiber: 1 g 2% ♦ Sugars: 28 g ♦ Protein: 4 g ♦ Vitamin A: 2% ♦ Vitamin C: 2% ♦ Calcium: 4% ♦ Iron: 6% ♦ **DIETARY EXCHANGES:** 1½ Starch, 1 Fruit, ½ Fat OR 2½ Carbohydrate, ½ Fat

Holiday Fruitcake

PREP TIME: 30 MINUTES (READY IN 11 HOURS 30 MINUTES) ♦ YIELD: 36 SERVINGS

     2 cups water
 ¼ cup oil
     2 eggs
     2 (1 lb. 0.6 or 15.4-oz.) pkg. date or nut quick
        bread mix
     2 cups pecans (halves or chopped)
     2 cups raisins
     2 cups (12 to 13 oz.) candied cherries, halved
     1 cup cut-up candied pineapple
        Corn syrup, if desired

1. Heat oven to 350°F. Grease and flour bottom and sides of 12-cup Bundt® pan or 10-inch tube pan. In large bowl, combine water, oil and eggs; beat well. Add all remaining ingredients except corn syrup; stir by hand until combined. Pour into greased and floured pan.

2. Bake at 350°F. for 80 to 90 minutes or until toothpick inserted in center comes out clean. Cool 30 minutes. Loosen edges of fruitcake; remove from pan. Cool 1 hour or until completely cooled.

3. Wrap tightly in plastic wrap or foil; refrigerate at least 8 hours. Store in refrigerator for up to 2 weeks or in freezer for up to 3 months.

4. Before serving, heat corn syrup until warm. Brush over fruitcake. If desired, decorate with additional candied fruits and nuts or as desired.

HIGH ALTITUDE *(above 3500 feet)***:** Add ¼ cup flour to dry quick bread mix. Bake as directed above.

NUTRITION INFORMATION PER SERVING: Serving Size: ¹⁄₃₆ of Recipe ♦ Calories: 240 ♦ Calories from Fat: 60 ♦ **% DAILY VALUE:** Total Fat: 7 g 11% ♦ Saturated Fat: 1 g 5% ♦ Cholesterol: 10 mg 3% ♦ Sodium: 140 mg 6% ♦ Total Carbohydrate: 42 g 14% ♦ Dietary Fiber: 2 g 8% ♦ Sugars: 26 g ♦ Protein: 2 g ♦ Vitamin A: 0% ♦ Vitamin C: 0% ♦ Calcium: 0% ♦ Iron: 6% ♦ **DIETARY EXCHANGES:** 1 Starch, 2 Fruit, 1 Fat OR 3 Carbohydrate, 1 Fat

Holiday Fruitcake

Black Bottom Cups

PREP TIME: 20 MINUTES (READY IN 1 HOUR 35 MINUTES)
◆ YIELD: 18 CUPCAKES

2 (3-oz.) pkg. cream cheese, softened
⅓ cup sugar
1 egg
1 (6-oz.) pkg. (1 cup) semisweet chocolate
   chips
1½ cups all-purpose flour
1 cup sugar
¼ cup unsweetened cocoa
1 teaspoon baking soda
½ teaspoon salt
1 cup water
⅓ cup oil
1 tablespoon vinegar
1 teaspoon vanilla
½ cup chopped almonds, if desired
2 tablespoons sugar, if desired

1. Heat oven to 350°F. Line 18 muffin cups with paper baking cups. In small bowl, combine cream cheese, ⅓ cup sugar and egg; blend well. Stir in chocolate chips. Set aside.
2. In large bowl, combine flour, 1 cup sugar, cocoa, baking soda and salt; mix well. Add water, oil, vinegar and vanilla; beat 2 minutes at medium speed.
3. Fill paper-lined muffin cups half full. Top each with 1 tablespoon cream cheese mixture. Combine almonds and 2 tablespoons sugar; sprinkle evenly over cream cheese mixture.
4. Bake at 350°F. for 20 to 30 minutes or until cream cheese mixture is light golden brown. Cool 15 minutes. Remove from pans. Cool 30 minutes or until completely cooled. Store in refrigerator.

HIGH ALTITUDE (*above 3500 feet*)**:** No change.

NUTRITION INFORMATION PER SERVING: Serving Size: 1 Cupcake ◆ Calories: 260 ◆ Calories from Fat: 120 ◆ **% DAILY VALUE:** Total Fat: 13 g 20% ◆ Saturated Fat: 5 g 25% ◆ Cholesterol: 20 mg 7% ◆ Sodium: 160 mg 7% ◆ Total Carbohydrate: 32 g 11% ◆ Dietary Fiber: 2 g 8% ◆ Sugars: 22 g ◆ Protein: 3 g ◆ Vitamin A: 4% ◆ Vitamin C: 0% ◆ Calcium: 2% ◆ Iron: 6% ◆ **DIETARY EXCHANGES:** 1 Starch, 1 Fruit, 2½ Fat OR 2 Carbohydrate, 2½ Fat

Pumpkin Chocolate Chip Cupcakes

PREP TIME: 25 MINUTES (READY IN 1 HOUR 25 MINUTES)
◆ YIELD: 24 CUPCAKES

CUPCAKES
1 (1 lb. 2.25-oz.) pkg. pudding-included
   yellow cake mix
1 cup canned pumpkin
1/2 cup water
1/3 cup oil
3 eggs
1 teaspoon cinnamon
1/2 teaspoon nutmeg
1 cup miniature semisweet chocolate chips

CINNAMON FROSTING
2 teaspoons cinnamon
1 (16-oz.) can vanilla frosting

1. Heat oven to 350°F. Line 24 muffin cups with paper baking cups. In large bowl, combine all cupcake ingredients except chocolate chips; beat at low speed until moistened. Beat 2 minutes at high speed. Fold in chocolate chips. Fill paper-lined muffin cups ¾ full.
2. Bake at 350°F. for 15 to 20 minutes or until toothpick inserted in center comes out clean. Cool in pan 5 minutes. Remove from pan; cool 20 minutes or until completely cooled.
3. Stir cinnamon into vanilla frosting. Frost cooled cupcakes.

HIGH ALTITUDE (*above 3500 feet*)**:** Add ½ cup flour to dry cake mix. Bake as directed above.

NUTRITION INFORMATION PER SERVING: Serving Size: 1 Cupcake ◆ Calories: 250 ◆ Calories from Fat: 100 ◆ **% DAILY VALUE:** Total Fat: 11 g 17% ◆ Saturated Fat: 3 g 15% ◆ Cholesterol: 25 mg 8% ◆ Sodium: 180 mg 8% ◆ Total Carbohydrate: 36 g 12% ◆ Dietary Fiber: 1 g 4% ◆ Sugars: 25 g ◆ Protein: 2 g ◆ Vitamin A: 45% ◆ Vitamin C: 0% ◆ Calcium: 0% ◆ Iron: 6% ◆ **DIETARY EXCHANGES:** ½ Starch, 2 Fruit, 2 Fat OR 2½ Carbohydrate, 2 Fat

Peanut Butter Cups

PREP TIME: 25 MINUTES (READY IN 1 HOUR 40 MINUTES)
◆ YIELD: 24 CUPCAKES

1¾ cups all-purpose flour
1¼ cups firmly packed brown sugar
  3 teaspoons baking powder
  1 teaspoon salt
  1 cup milk
  ⅓ cup shortening
  ⅓ cup peanut butter
  1 teaspoon vanilla
  2 eggs
 24 miniature milk chocolate-covered peanut
      butter cups, unwrapped

1. Heat oven to 350°F. Line 24 muffin cups with paper baking cups. In large bowl, combine all ingredients except peanut butter cups; beat at low speed until moistened. Beat 2 minutes at medium speed.
2. Fill paper-lined muffin cups ⅔ full. Press 1 peanut butter cup into batter in each cup until top edge of candy is even with batter.
3. Bake at 350°F. for 18 to 28 minutes or until tops spring back when touched lightly in center. Cool 5 minutes. Remove from pans. Serve warm or cool.

HIGH ALTITUDE (*above 3500 feet*)**:** No change.

NUTRITION INFORMATION PER SERVING: Serving Size: 1 Cupcake ◆ Calories: 160 ◆ Calories from Fat: 60 ◆ **% DAILY VALUE:** Total Fat: 7 g 11% ◆ Saturated Fat: 2 g 10% ◆ Cholesterol: 20 mg 7% ◆ Sodium: 200 mg 8% ◆ Total Carbohydrate: 22 g 7% ◆ Dietary Fiber: 1 g 2% ◆ Sugars: 14 g ◆ Protein: 3 g ◆ Vitamin A: 0% ◆ Vitamin C: 0% ◆ Calcium: 6% ◆ Iron: 4% ◆ **DIETARY EXCHANGES:** 1 Starch, ½ Fruit, 1 Fat OR 1½ Carbohydrate, 1 Fat

---

COOK'S NOTE

FROSTINGS AND FILLINGS

◆ Glazes contain powdered sugar, liquid and little or no butter or shortening.
◆ There are cooked and uncooked buttercream frostings. Uncooked buttercream frosting gets its smooth, rich texture from butter, powdered sugar, flavoring and milk and is used most often.
◆ Cream cheese frosting is a tangy variation on buttercream.
◆ Whipped cream or whipped topping gives a velvety finish.
◆ Broiled topping takes a brief stint under the heat to caramelize the sugar-butter mixture.
◆ Cooked fillings add a puddinglike smoothness.

Buttercream Frosting

PREP TIME: 10 MINUTES ◆ YIELD: FROSTS 2-LAYER OR 13 X 9-INCH CAKE

  ⅔ cup butter, softened
  4 cups powdered sugar
  1 teaspoon vanilla
  2 to 4 tablespoons half-and-half or milk

1. In large bowl, beat butter until light and fluffy. Gradually add powdered sugar, beating well.
2. Beat in vanilla and enough half-and-half for desired spreading consistency.

NUTRITION INFORMATION PER SERVING: Serving Size: ¹⁄₁₂ of Recipe ◆ Calories: 260 ◆ Calories from Fat: 100 ◆ **% DAILY VALUE:** Total Fat: 11 g 17% ◆ Saturated Fat: 7 g 35% ◆ Cholesterol: 30 mg 10% ◆ Sodium: 105 mg 4% ◆ Total Carbohydrate: 40 g 13% ◆ Dietary Fiber: 0 g 0% ◆ Sugars: 39 g ◆ Protein: 0 g ◆ Vitamin A: 8% ◆ Vitamin C: 0% ◆ Calcium: 0% ◆ Iron: 0% ◆ **DIETARY EXCHANGES:** 2½ Fruit, 2½ Fat OR 2½ Carbohydrate, 2½ Fat

VARIATIONS

Browned Butter Frosting: In large saucepan, cook butter over medium heat until light golden brown, stirring constantly. Gradually add powdered sugar, beating well. Continue as directed above.
Chocolate Buttercream Frosting: Add ⅓ cup unsweetened cocoa, 2 envelopes premelted unsweetened chocolate or 2 oz. unsweetened chocolate, melted, to butter; blend well. Continue as directed above.
Chocolate-Cherry Buttercream Frosting: Add 3 tablespoons drained chopped maraschino cherries to Chocolate Buttercream Frosting; mix well.
Coffee Buttercream Frosting: Dissolve 1½ teaspoons instant coffee granules or crystals in 2 tablespoons of the half-and-half.
Lemon Buttercream Frosting: Substitute 2 to 4 tablespoons lemon juice for the half-and-half and 1 teaspoon grated lemon peel for the vanilla.
Nut Buttercream Frosting: Stir in ¼ cup chopped nuts.
Orange Buttercream Frosting: Substitute 2 to 4 tablespoons orange juice for the half-and-half and 1 teaspoon grated orange peel for the vanilla.
Peanut Butter Frosting: Add 3 tablespoons peanut butter to the butter; blend well. Continue as directed above.

Fudge Frosting

PREP TIME: 20 MINUTES (READY IN 50 MINUTES)
♦ YIELD: FROSTS 2-LAYER OR 13 X 9-INCH CAKE

    2 cups sugar
    ¾ cup half-and-half
    2 oz. unsweetened chocolate or 2 envelopes
        premelted unsweetened chocolate
    2 tablespoons light corn syrup
    ⅛ teaspoon salt
    2 tablespoons margarine or butter
    I teaspoon vanilla

1. In large saucepan, combine sugar, half-and-half, chocolate, corn syrup and salt. Cook over low heat, stirring just until sugar is dissolved. Cover; cook over medium heat for 2 minutes. Uncover; cook without stirring until candy thermometer reaches softball stage (234°F.), about 5 minutes.
2. Remove saucepan from heat. Stir in margarine. Cool about 30 minutes or until lukewarm (110°F.). Additional cooling may cause frosting to harden too soon.
3. Add vanilla; beat until frosting begins to thicken and loses its gloss. If necessary, thin with a few drops of half-and-half.

NUTRITION INFORMATION PER SERVING: Serving Size: ¹⁄₁₂ of Recipe ♦ Calories: 210 ♦ Calories from Fat: 50 ♦ **% DAILY VALUE:** Total Fat: 6 g 9% ♦ Saturated Fat: 3 g 15% ♦ Cholesterol: 5 mg 2% ♦ Sodium: 55 mg 2% ♦ Total Carbohydrate: 38 g 13% ♦ Dietary Fiber: 1 g 3% ♦ Sugars: 35 g ♦ Protein: 1 g ♦ Vitamin A: 4% ♦ Vitamin C: 0% ♦ Calcium: 2% ♦ Iron: 0% ♦ **DIETARY EXCHANGES:** 2½ Fruit, 1½ Fat OR 2½ Carbohydrate, 1½ Fat

---

COOK'S NOTE

IN PRAISE OF GLAZE

A sweet glaze—a thin, simple frosting typically made of powdered sugar mixed with liquid—is a good quick finish for any cake, but especially for those baked in a tube pan. Sift the powdered sugar to remove lumps, then gradually mix in a liquid such as milk, liqueur, lemon or orange juice and peel, or coffee. The glaze should be thin enough to pour or drizzle but thick enough so that most stays on the cake rather than puddling on the plate. For the neatest results, brush loose crumbs from the surface of the cake before glazing. Spread the glaze on top, allowing some to run down the sides of the cake.

VARIATIONS
Marshmallow Nut Fudge Frosting: Add 1 cup miniature marshmallows and ½ cup chopped nuts to frosting just before spreading.
Peanut Butter Fudge Frosting: Add ¼ cup creamy peanut butter with margarine.

COOK'S NOTE

FROSTING FINISHES

* Dip a knife into milk (or the liquid used in the frosting) and spread it over the frosted cake for a sleek, shiny finish.
* Work a knife over the top and sides of the cake in small circular motions to create a swirled top.
* Use a rubber scraper or the back of a spoon to gently smooth spirals or trace crisscross or zigzag patterns.
* For soft or fluffy frosting, use the back of a teaspoon or the tip of a butter knife to lift frosting into peaks at regular intervals.
* Drag a fork across the sides of the cake, alternating horizontal and vertical strokes to create a basket weave effect.

Fluffy Marshmallow Frosting

PREP TIME: 15 MINUTES ♦ YIELD: FROSTS 2-LAYER OR 13 X 9-INCH CAKE

    ½ cup sugar
    2 tablespoons water
    2 egg whites
    I (7-oz.) jar (1½ cups) marshmallow creme
    I teaspoon vanilla

1. In medium saucepan, combine sugar, water and egg whites. Cook over low heat, beating continuously with electric hand mixer at high speed until soft peaks form.
2. Add marshmallow creme; beat until stiff peaks form. Remove saucepan from heat. Beat in vanilla.

NUTRITION INFORMATION PER SERVING: Serving Size: ¹⁄₁₂ of Recipe ♦ Calories: 90 ♦ Calories from Fat: 0 ♦ **% DAILY VALUE:** Total Fat: 0 g 0% ♦ Saturated Fat: 0 g 0% ♦ Cholesterol: 0 mg 0% ♦ Sodium: 15 mg 1% ♦ Total Carbohydrate: 21 g 7% ♦ Dietary Fiber: 0 g 0% ♦ Sugars: 20 g ♦ Protein: 1 g ♦ Vitamin A: 0% ♦ Vitamin C: 0% ♦ Calcium: 0% ♦ Iron: 0% ♦ **DIETARY EXCHANGES:** 1½ Fruit OR 1½ Carbohydrate

COOK'S NOTE

HOW TO FROST A TWO-LAYER CAKE

◆ Cool cake layers completely. Brush loose crumbs from the sides.

◆ Place one cake layer, top side down, on a serving plate. Tuck strips of waxed paper under the edge of the cake to keep the serving plate clean. Spread about ¼ of the frosting evenly over the first layer to within ½ inch of the edge.

◆ Place the other cake layer, top side up, on the frosted layer. Spread the side of the cake with a very thin coat of frosting to seal in the crumbs.

◆ Use about ⅔ of the remaining frosting to spread a thicker layer over the sides. Use upward strokes to create the best shape.

◆ Spread the remaining frosting over the top of the cake just to the frosted sides. Carefully remove the waxed paper strips from under the cake.

Sour Cream Chocolate Frosting

PREP TIME: 10 MINUTES ◆ YIELD: FROSTS 2-LAYER OR 13 X 9-INCH CAKE

2 cups powdered sugar
½ cup sour cream
1 tablespoon margarine or butter, softened
1 (6-oz.) pkg. (1 cup) semisweet chocolate chips, melted, cooled
1 teaspoon vanilla
Milk, if needed

1. In small bowl, combine powdered sugar, sour cream and margarine; beat at medium speed until light and fluffy.
2. Add chocolate and vanilla; blend at low speed until smooth. If necessary, add milk a teaspoon at a time until of desired spreading consistency. Store in refrigerator.

NUTRITION INFORMATION PER SERVING: Serving Size: ½₂ of Recipe ◆ Calories: 180 ◆ Calories from Fat: 60 ◆ % DAILY VALUE: Total Fat: 7 g 11% ◆ Saturated Fat: 4 g 20% ◆ Cholesterol: 4 mg 1% ◆ Sodium: 20 mg 1% ◆ Total Carbohydrate: 29 g 10% ◆ Dietary Fiber: 1 g 3% ◆ Sugars: 28 g ◆ Protein: 1 g ◆ Vitamin A: 2% ◆ Vitamin C: 0% ◆ Calcium: 0% ◆ Iron: 2% ◆ DIETARY EXCHANGES: 2 Fruit, 1½ Fat OR 2 Carbohydrate, 1½ Fat

Chocolate Whipped Cream Frosting

PREP TIME: 10 MINUTES ◆ YIELD: FROSTS 2-LAYER OR 13 X 9-INCH CAKE

1 cup whipping cream
⅓ cup chocolate-flavored syrup

1. In small bowl, beat whipping cream at high speed just until it begins to thicken.
2. Gradually add syrup, beating until soft peaks form. Frost cake and serve immediately. Store in refrigerator.

NUTRITION INFORMATION PER SERVING: Serving Size: ½₂ of Recipe ◆ Calories: 100 ◆ Calories from Fat: 70 ◆ % DAILY VALUE: Total Fat: 8 g 12% ◆ Saturated Fat: 5 g 25% ◆ Cholesterol: 25 mg 8% ◆ Sodium: 40 mg 2% ◆ Total Carbohydrate: 6 g 2% ◆ Dietary Fiber: 0 g 0% ◆ Sugars: 4 g ◆ Protein: 1 g ◆ Vitamin A: 6% ◆ Vitamin C: 0% ◆ Calcium: 2% ◆ Iron: 0% ◆ DIETARY EXCHANGES: ½ Fruit, 1½ Fat OR ½ Carbohydrate, 1½ Fat

Ganache

PREP TIME: 15 MINUTES (READY IN 1 HOUR 15 MINUTES) ◆ YIELD: FROSTS 2-LAYER OR 13 X 9-INCH CAKE

6 oz. semisweet chocolate, cut into pieces, or 1 cup semisweet chocolate chips
½ cup whipping cream
1 tablespoon butter

1. In small saucepan, combine chocolate and whipping cream; heat over low heat until chocolate is melted and mixture is smooth and creamy, stirring constantly. Remove saucepan from heat. Stir in butter. Refrigerate 1 to 1½ hours or until cold, stirring occasionally.
2. With wooden spoon or electric hand mixer, beat chilled mixture until thick and creamy and of desired spreading consistency.

NUTRITION INFORMATION PER SERVING: Serving Size: ½₂ of Recipe ◆ Calories: 120 ◆ Calories from Fat: 80 ◆ % DAILY VALUE: Total Fat: 9 g 14% ◆ Saturated Fat: 5 g 25% ◆ Cholesterol: 15 mg 5% ◆ Sodium: 15 mg 1% ◆ Total Carbohydrate: 9 g 3% ◆ Dietary Fiber: 1 g 3% ◆ Sugars: 8 g ◆ Protein: 1 g ◆ Vitamin A: 4% ◆ Vitamin C: 0% ◆ Calcium: 0% ◆ Iron: 2% ◆ DIETARY EXCHANGES: ½ Starch, 2 Fat OR ½ Carbohydrate, 2 Fat

Caramel Frosting

PREP TIME: 15 MINUTES ◆ YIELD: FROSTS 2-LAYER OR
13 X 9-INCH CAKE

$\frac{1}{2}$ cup margarine or butter
1 cup firmly packed brown sugar
$\frac{1}{4}$ cup milk
3 cups powdered sugar
$\frac{1}{2}$ teaspoon vanilla

1. In medium saucepan, melt margarine.
Add brown sugar; cook over low heat for
2 minutes, stirring constantly. Add milk; continue cooking until mixture comes to a
rolling boil. Remove saucepan from heat.
2. Gradually add powdered sugar and
vanilla, mixing well after each addition. If
needed, add a few drops of milk for desired
spreading consistency.

NUTRITION INFORMATION PER SERVING: Serving Size: $\frac{1}{12}$ of
Recipe ◆ Calories: 260 ◆ Calories from Fat: 70 ◆ **% DAILY VALUE:**
Total Fat: 8 g 12% ◆ Saturated Fat: 1 g 5% ◆ Cholesterol: 0 mg 0%
◆ Sodium: 100 mg 4% ◆ Total Carbohydrate: 48 g 16% ◆ Dietary
Fiber: 0 g 0% ◆ Sugars: 47 g ◆ Protein: 0 g ◆ Vitamin A: 6% ◆ Vitamin C: 0% ◆ Calcium: 2% ◆ Iron: 2% ◆ **DIETARY EXCHANGES:**
3 Fruit, 1½ Fat OR 3 Carbohydrate, 1½ Fat

Coconut Pecan Frosting

PREP TIME: 15 MINUTES ◆ YIELD: FROSTS 2-LAYER OR
13 X 9-INCH CAKE

1 cup sugar
1 cup evaporated milk
$\frac{1}{2}$ cup margarine or butter, softened
3 eggs, beaten
1$\frac{1}{3}$ cups flaked coconut
1 cup chopped pecans or almonds
1 teaspoon vanilla

1. In medium saucepan, combine sugar,
milk, margarine and eggs. Cook over medium
heat until mixture begins to bubble, stirring
constantly.
2. Stir in all remaining ingredients. Cool
until of desired spreading consistency.

NUTRITION INFORMATION PER SERVING: Serving Size: $\frac{1}{12}$ of
Recipe ◆ Calories: 290 ◆ Calories from Fat: 170 ◆ **% DAILY VALUE:**
Total Fat: 19 g 29% ◆ Saturated Fat: 6 g 30% ◆ Cholesterol:
60 mg 20% ◆ Sodium: 150 mg 6% ◆ Total Carbohydrate: 25 g 8% ◆
Dietary Fiber: 1 g 4% ◆ Sugars: 22 g ◆ Protein: 4 g ◆ Vitamin A: 10%
◆ Vitamin C: 0% ◆ Calcium: 6% ◆ Iron: 4% ◆ **DIETARY EXCHANGES:**
1 Starch, ½ Fruit, 4 Fat OR 1½ Carbohydrate, 4 Fat

Vanilla Cream Filling

PREP TIME: 15 MINUTES (READY IN 45 MINUTES)
◆ YIELD: 1$\frac{1}{3}$ CUPS; FILLS 2-LAYER CAKE OR 1 JELLY ROLL

$\frac{1}{2}$ cup sugar
3 tablespoons all-purpose flour
$\frac{1}{4}$ teaspoon salt
1$\frac{1}{4}$ cups milk
2 egg yolks or 1 egg
1 tablespoon margarine or butter
1 teaspoon vanilla

1. In small saucepan, combine sugar, flour
and salt; mix well. Gradually stir in milk until
smooth. Cook over medium heat, stirring
constantly, until mixture boils. Boil 1 minute,
stirring constantly. Remove saucepan from
heat.
2. In small bowl, beat egg yolks. Stir about
$\frac{1}{4}$ cup hot mixture into egg yolks. Gradually
stir yolk mixture into hot mixture in saucepan. Cook over low heat, stirring constantly,
until mixture boils.
3. Remove saucepan from heat. Stir in
margarine and vanilla. Cover; cool 30 minutes or until completely cooled, stirring
occasionally.

NUTRITION INFORMATION PER SERVING: Serving Size: $\frac{1}{12}$ of
Recipe ◆ Calories: 70 ◆ Calories from Fat: 20 ◆ **% DAILY VALUE:**
Total Fat: 2 g 3% ◆ Saturated Fat: 1 g 5% ◆ Cholesterol: 40 mg 13%
◆ Sodium: 70 mg 3% ◆ Total Carbohydrate: 11 g 4% ◆ Dietary
Fiber: 0 g 0% ◆ Sugars: 10 g ◆ Protein: 2 g ◆ Vitamin A: 2% ◆ Vitamin C: 0% ◆ Calcium: 4% ◆ Iron: 0% ◆ **DIETARY EXCHANGES:**
½ Starch, ½ Fruit OR 1 Carbohydrate

VARIATIONS
Butterscotch Cream Filling: Substitute
$\frac{2}{3}$ cup firmly packed brown sugar for sugar
YIELD: 1$\frac{2}{3}$ CUPS
Chocolate Cream Filling: Increase sugar
to $\frac{3}{4}$ cup and add 1 oz. unsweetened
chocolate, melted, or 1 envelope premelted unsweetened chocolate with the
sugar. YIELD: 1$\frac{2}{3}$ CUPS
Coconut Cream Filling: Stir in $\frac{1}{3}$ cup
flaked coconut with vanilla. YIELD: 1$\frac{2}{3}$ CUPS

Lemon Filling

PREP TIME: 15 MINUTES (READY IN 45 MINUTES)
◆ YIELD: 1⅓ CUPS; FILLS 2-LAYER CAKE OR 1 JELLY ROLL

¾ cup sugar
3 tablespoons cornstarch
¼ teaspoon salt
¾ cup cold water
2 egg yolks
1 tablespoon margarine or butter
2 teaspoons grated lemon peel
3 tablespoons lemon juice

1. In small saucepan, combine sugar, corn-starch and salt; mix well. Gradually stir in cold water until smooth. Cook over medium heat, stirring constantly, until mixture boils. Boil 1 minute, stirring constantly. Remove from heat.
2. In small bowl, beat egg yolks. Stir about ¼ cup hot mixture into egg yolks. Gradually stir yolk mixture into hot mixture. Cook over low heat, stirring constantly, until mixture boils. Boil 1 minute, stirring constantly.
3. Remove saucepan from heat. Stir in margarine, lemon peel and lemon juice. Cool 30 minutes or until completely cooled, stirring occasionally.

NUTRITION INFORMATION PER SERVING: Serving Size: ½₂ of Recipe ◆ Calories: 80 ◆ Calories from Fat: 20 ◆ % DAILY VALUE: Total Fat: 2 g 3% ◆ Saturated Fat: 1 g 5% ◆ Cholesterol: 35 mg 12% ◆ Sodium: 60 mg 3% ◆ Total Carbohydrate: 14 g 5% ◆ Dietary Fiber: 1 g 4% ◆ Sugars: 13 g ◆ Protein: 1 g ◆ Vitamin A: 4% ◆ Vitamin C: 2% ◆ Calcium: 4% ◆ Iron: 6% ◆ DIETARY EXCHANGES: 1 Fruit, ½ Fat OR 1 Carbohydrate, ½ Fat

VARIATIONS

Orange Filling: Omit lemon peel and lemon juice. Substitute orange juice for water and add 1 tablespoon grated orange peel with margarine. YIELD: 1⅓ CUPS
Pineapple Filling: Omit lemon peel and lemon juice. Drain liquid from 1 (8-oz.) can (1 cup) crushed pineapple; add water to liquid to make ¾ cup. Substitute pineapple liquid for cold water. Add pineapple after stirring yolk mixture into hot mixture. YIELD: 1½ CUPS

Broiled Coconut Topping

PREP TIME: 15 MINUTES ◆ YIELD: FROSTS 13 X 9-INCH CAKE

¼ cup margarine or butter
1 cup flaked or shredded coconut
⅔ cup firmly packed brown sugar
½ cup chopped nuts
3 tablespoons half-and-half or milk

1. In small saucepan, melt margarine. Stir in all remaining ingredients. Spread over warm cake.
2. Broil 4 to 6 inches from heat for 1 to 2 minutes or until bubbly and light golden brown. (Watch carefully, mixture burns easily.)

NUTRITION INFORMATION PER SERVING: Serving Size: ½₂ of Recipe ◆ Calories: 150 ◆ Calories from Fat: 80 ◆ % DAILY VALUE: Total Fat: 9 g 14% ◆ Saturated Fat: 3 g 15% ◆ Cholesterol: 0 mg 0% ◆ Sodium: 65 mg 3% ◆ Total Carbohydrate: 16 g 5% ◆ Dietary Fiber: 1 g 2% ◆ Sugars: 14 g ◆ Protein: 1 g ◆ Vitamin A: 4% ◆ Vitamin C: 0% ◆ Calcium: 2% ◆ Iron: 2% ◆ DIETARY EXCHANGES: 1 Fruit, 2 Fat OR 1 Carbohydrate, 2 Fat

COOK'S NOTE

DECORATING THE CAKE

- ✦ Buttery Decorator Icing (page 382) works well for decorating.
- ✦ To adjust the consistency of frosting, stir in a small amount of liquid or additional powdered sugar.
- ✦ Tinted frosting darkens slightly as it dries. Tint enough frosting at the start.
- ✦ Cover the frosting bowl with a damp cloth to prevent drying.
- ✦ Pack frosting to the end of the decorating bag. Squeeze out a little frosting before starting.
- ✦ The frosted surface to be decorated should be smooth and even.
- ✦ With a toothpick, mark the design on the cake before starting.
- ✦ Frosting made with butter or margarine may soften from the heat of your hand. If it becomes too soft, chill it for a few minutes.

HOW MUCH FROSTING?

TO FROST A PAIR OF:	BETWEEN LAYERS	SIDES AND TOP
6-inch round layers	1/3 cup	2 cups
8-inch round layers	3/4 cup	2 1/2 cups
10-inch round layers	1 1/4 cups	3 1/2 cups
12-inch round layers	1 3/4 cups	4 1/2 cups
14-inch round layers	2 cups	6 cups
16 × 11 × 1 1/2-inch sheet cake	NA	8 cups

Buttery Decorator Icing

PREP TIME: 10 MINUTES ◆ YIELD: 3 CUPS

1/2 cup butter, softened
1/4 cup shortening
1 teaspoon vanilla
1/8 teaspoon salt
4 cups powdered sugar
2 to 4 tablespoons milk

1. In large bowl, combine butter and shortening; beat until light and fluffy. Add vanilla and salt; mix well.
2. Add powdered sugar 1 cup at a time, beating well after each addition. Beat in enough milk at high speed until light and fluffy and of desired spreading consistency.

> **TIP:** Icing can be made up to 2 weeks in advance and stored in tightly covered container in refrigerator. Bring to room temperature and rewhip before using.

NUTRITION INFORMATION PER SERVING: Serving Size: 1/12 of Recipe ◆ Calories: 270 ◆ Calories from Fat: 110 ◆ **% DAILY VALUE:** Total Fat: 12 g 18% ◆ Saturated Fat: 6 g 30% ◆ Cholesterol: 20 mg 7% ◆ Sodium: 105 mg 4% ◆ Total Carbohydrate: 40 g 13% ◆ Dietary Fiber: 0 g 0% ◆ Sugars: 39 g ◆ Protein: 0 g ◆ Vitamin A: 6% ◆ Vitamin C: 0% ◆ Calcium: 0% ◆ Iron: 0% ◆ **DIETARY EXCHANGES:** 2 1/2 Fruit, 2 1/2 Fat OR 2 1/2 Carbohydrate, 2 1/2 Fat

Basic Powdered Sugar Glaze

PREP TIME: 10 MINUTES ◆ YIELD: 1 1/2 CUPS

2 cups powdered sugar
2 tablespoons margarine or butter, softened
1 teaspoon vanilla
3 to 4 tablespoons milk or half-and-half

1. In medium bowl, combine all ingredients until smooth, adding enough milk for desired glaze consistency.
2. Use to glaze cakes, coffee cakes or pastries.

NUTRITION INFORMATION PER SERVING: Serving Size: 1/12 of Recipe ◆ Calories: 100 ◆ Calories from Fat: 20 ◆ **% DAILY VALUE:** Total Fat: 2 g 3% ◆ Saturated Fat: 0 g 0% ◆ Cholesterol: 0 mg 0% ◆ Sodium: 25 mg 1% ◆ Total Carbohydrate: 20 g 7% ◆ Dietary Fiber: 0 g 0% ◆ Sugars: 19 g ◆ Protein: 0 g ◆ Vitamin A: 0% ◆ Vitamin C: 0% ◆ Calcium: 0% ◆ Iron: 0% ◆ **DIETARY EXCHANGES:** 1 1/2 Fruit, 1/2 Fat OR 1 1/2 Carbohydrate, 1/2 Fat

VARIATIONS

Chocolate Glaze: Add 2 oz. unsweetened chocolate, melted, or 2 envelopes premelted unsweetened chocolate.
Coffee Glaze: Substitute hot water for milk. Dissolve 1 teaspoon instant coffee granules or crystals in the hot water.
Lemon Glaze: Substitute 2 tablespoons lemon juice for part of milk and add 1 teaspoon grated lemon peel.
Maple Glaze: Add 1/2 teaspoon maple extract or flavor.
Orange Glaze: Substitute orange juice for milk and add 1 teaspoon grated orange peel.
Spice Glaze: Combine 1/4 teaspoon cinnamon and 1/8 teaspoon nutmeg with powdered sugar.

Almond Bark Buttercream Frosting

PREP TIME: 15 MINUTES (READY IN 45 MINUTES)
◆ YIELD: FROSTS 2-LAYER OR 13 X 9-INCH CAKE

    6 oz. vanilla-flavored candy coating (almond
        bark), cut into pieces
    3 to 4 tablespoons chocolate-flavored liqueur
    ¾ cup butter, softened
    ¼ cup powdered sugar

1. In small saucepan, melt candy coating over low heat, stirring constantly. Remove saucepan from heat. Stir in liqueur. Cool 30 minutes.
2. In small bowl, combine butter and powdered sugar; beat until light and fluffy. Gradually beat in cooled candy coating mixture until smooth.

NUTRITION INFORMATION PER SERVING: Serving Size: ¹⁄₁₂ of Recipe ◆ Calories: 200 ◆ Calories from Fat: 140 ◆ **% DAILY VALUE:** Total Fat: 16 g 25% ◆ Saturated Fat: 10 g 50% ◆ Cholesterol: 35 mg 12% ◆ Sodium: 130 mg 5% ◆ Total Carbohydrate: 13 g 4% ◆ Dietary Fiber: 0 g 0% ◆ Sugars: 14 g ◆ Protein: 1 g ◆ Vitamin A: 8% ◆ Vitamin C: 0% ◆ Calcium: 4% ◆ Iron: 0% ◆ **DIETARY EXCHANGES:** ½ Starch, ½ Fruit, 3 Fat OR 1 Carbohydrate, 3 Fat

Decorating with Decorating Bags and Tips

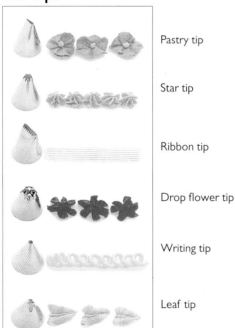

Pastry tip

Star tip

Ribbon tip

Drop flower tip

Writing tip

Leaf tip

Cream Cheese Frosting

PREP TIME: 10 MINUTES ◆ YIELD: FROSTS 2-LAYER OR 13 X 9-INCH CAKE

    3 cups powdered sugar
    1 (8-oz.) pkg. cream cheese, softened
    2 tablespoons margarine or butter, melted
    1 teaspoon vanilla

In large bowl, combine all ingredients; beat until smooth.

NUTRITION INFORMATION PER SERVING: Serving Size: ¹⁄₁₂ of Recipe ◆ Calories: 210 ◆ Calories from Fat: 80 ◆ **% DAILY VALUE:** Total Fat: 9 g 14% ◆ Saturated Fat: 5 g 25% ◆ Cholesterol: 20 mg 7% ◆ Sodium: 80 mg 3% ◆ Total Carbohydrate: 30 g 10% ◆ Dietary Fiber: 0 g 0% ◆ Sugars: 29 g ◆ Protein: 1 g ◆ Vitamin A: 8% ◆ Vitamin C: 0% ◆ Calcium: 0% ◆ Iron: 0% ◆ **DIETARY EXCHANGES:** 2 Fruit, 2 Fat OR 2 Carbohydrate, 2 Fat

C O O K ' S   N O T E

MAKING A DECORATING BAG

You don't need a special device to squeeze frosting through a decorating tip. If you're using several different decorating colors, you can make your own tubes. Fold a square sheet of waxed paper or parchment in half diagonally. Starting with the longest edge, roll it into a cone shape. Cut off the pointed end and push the decorating tip down the cone and into the opening. Fill the cone with frosting, roll down the open end and squeeze with even pressure. Practice on a plate or scrap of waxed paper before working directly on the cake.

C O O K ' S   N O T E

USING A DECORATING BAG AND TIP

You can add elegance or whimsy to a cake by decorating it with whipped cream or frosting using decorating bags and tips.

Choose larger tips for whipped cream. After decorating, refrigerate the cake until serving time.

PIES & TARTS

TIPS FOR SUCCESSFUL PASTRIES AND PIE CRUSTS

+ Pie pastry gains its characteristic flakiness from careful handling. The ingredients are mixed just enough to hold together, but not so much as to break down the pieces of shortening (or other fat) entirely. In the oven, the water in the bits of shortening turns to steam, pushing up the floury dough and creating tender flaky layers.

+ Pastry success depends upon accurate measurements.

+ Stir together the flour and salt thoroughly before adding shortening and water.

+ Work chilled shortening into the flour mixture with a pastry blender, two butter knives or a fork. Cut just until the mixture resembles coarse crumbs with a few pea-sized morsels remaining.

floured pastry cloth and a rolling pin covered with a cloth sleeve are best. With light strokes, roll pastry into an 11-inch circle. Fold dough in half or quarters; transfer to pan and unfold without stretching.

+ Make sure the liquid you add is ice-cold (again, to prevent the shortening from melting) and add the minimum necessary for the dough to stick together. Mix it in gently, a tablespoon at a time; vigorous mixing toughens the dough.

+ For easier handling, press the dough into a disc shape, wrap it in plastic wrap or waxed paper and chill it at least 30 minutes before rolling it out. When you remove the dough from the refrigerator, you may need to let it stand for a few minutes to prevent crumbling.

+ Sparingly flour the work surface and rolling pin to keep the dough from sticking, but use as little as possible to avoid toughening the dough. A surface covered with a lightly

+ An ovenproof, glass pie plate is best for even baking and browning; second-best is an aluminum pan with a dull finish.

+ For two-crust pie, trim bottom pastry even with pie plate edge; add filling. Cover with top pastry, allowing 1-inch overlap; fold over. Seal and flute.

+ Place the pie in the center of the preheated oven. If two pies are baking side by side, arrange them so they do not touch the sides of the oven or each other. If two pies are baking on separate shelves, stagger the placement so the pies are not directly over each other.

+ Heat circulation varies among ovens. If the edges of the crust start to brown before the center is done, cover the edges with 2-inch-wide strips of foil. If the whole top is over-browning, drape a sheet of foil over the top.

Pastry for Pies and Tarts

PREP TIME: 20 MINUTES ♦ YIELD: ONE-CRUST
OR TWO-CRUST PASTRY

ONE-CRUST PIE
 1 cup all-purpose flour
 ½ teaspoon salt
 ⅓ cup shortening
 2 to 4 tablespoons ice water

1. In medium bowl, combine flour and salt; mix well. With pastry blender or fork, cut in shortening until mixture resembles coarse crumbs. Sprinkle with water 1 tablespoon at a time, while tossing and mixing lightly with fork. Add water until dough is just moist enough to form a ball when lightly pressed together. (Too much water causes dough to become sticky and tough; too little water causes edges to crack and pastry to tear easily while rolling.)

2. Shape dough into ball. Flatten ball to ½-inch thickness, rounding and smoothing edges. On floured surface, roll lightly from center to edge into 11-inch round. Fold pastry in half; place in 9-inch pie pan, or 9 or 10-inch tart pan. Unfold; gently press in bottom and up sides of pan. Do not stretch.

3. If using pie pan, fold edge under to form a standing rim; flute edge. If using tart pan, trim pastry edge if necessary.

For One-Crust Filled Pie: Fill and bake as directed in recipe.

For One-Crust Baked Pie Shell (Unfilled): Prick bottom and sides of pastry generously with fork. Bake at 450°F. for 9 to 12 minutes or until light golden brown. Cool 30 minutes or until completely cooled. Continue as directed in pie recipe.

NUTRITION INFORMATION PER SERVING: Serving Size: ⅛ of Recipe ♦ Calories: 140 ♦ Calories from Fat: 80 ♦ **% DAILY VALUE:** Total Fat: 9 g 14% ♦ Saturated Fat: 2 g 10% ♦ Cholesterol: 0 mg 0% ♦ Sodium: 135 mg 6% ♦ Total Carbohydrate: 12 g 4% ♦ Dietary Fiber: 0 g 0% ♦ Sugars: 0 g ♦ Protein: 2 g ♦ Vitamin A: 0% ♦ Vitamin C: 0% ♦ Calcium: 0% ♦ Iron: 4% ♦ **DIETARY EXCHANGES:** 1 Starch, 1½ Fat OR 1 Carbohydrate, 1½ Fat

TWO-CRUST PIE
 2 cups all-purpose flour
 1 teaspoon salt
 ⅔ cup shortening
 5 to 7 tablespoons ice water

1. In medium bowl, combine flour and salt; mix well. With pastry blender or fork, cut in shortening until mixture resembles coarse crumbs. Sprinkle with water 1 tablespoon at a time, while tossing and mixing lightly with fork. Add water until dough is just moist enough to form a ball when lightly pressed together. (Too much water causes dough to become sticky and tough; too little water causes edges to crack and pastry to tear easily while rolling.)

2. Shape dough into 2 balls. Flatten 1 ball to ½-inch thickness, rounding and smoothing edges. On floured surface, roll lightly from center to edge into 11-inch round. Fold pastry in half; place in 9-inch pie pan, or 9 or 10-inch tart pan. Unfold; gently press in bottom and up sides of pan. Do not stretch.

3. Trim pastry even with pan edge. Roll out remaining pastry; set aside. Continue as directed in pie recipe.

NUTRITION INFORMATION PER SERVING: Serving Size: ⅛ of Recipe ♦ Calories: 260 ♦ Calories from Fat: 150 ♦ **% DAILY VALUE:** Total Fat: 17 g 26% ♦ Saturated Fat: 4 g 20% ♦ Cholesterol: 0 mg 0% ♦ Sodium: 270 mg 11% ♦ Total Carbohydrate: 24 g 8% ♦ Dietary Fiber: 1 g 3% ♦ Sugars: 1 g ♦ Protein: 3 g ♦ Vitamin A: 0% ♦ Vitamin C: 0% ♦ Calcium: 0% ♦ Iron: 8% ♦ **DIETARY EXCHANGES:** 1½ Starch, 3 Fat OR 1½ Carbohydrate, 3 Fat

VARIATIONS

Cheese Pastry: For one-crust pastry, add ¼ to ½ cup shredded Cheddar or American cheese to flour. Omit salt. (For two-crust pastry, use ½ to 1 cup.)

Extra Flaky Pastry: For one-crust pastry, add 1 teaspoon sugar with flour and 1 teaspoon vinegar with water. (For two-crust pastry, use 2 teaspoons sugar and 2 teaspoons vinegar.)

Whole Wheat Pastry: For one-crust pastry, substitute up to ½ cup whole wheat flour for all-purpose flour. Additional water may be necessary. (For two-crust pastry, use up to 1 cup whole wheat flour.)

Press-in-the-Pan Oil Pie Crust

PREP TIME: 10 MINUTES (READY IN 1 HOUR)
◆ YIELD: 9-INCH BAKED PIE CRUST

1¾ cups all-purpose flour
1 teaspoon sugar
1 teaspoon salt
½ cup oil
¼ cup milk

1. Heat oven to 425°F. In medium bowl, combine flour, sugar and salt; mix well. In small bowl, combine oil and milk; blend well. Pour over flour mixture. Stir with fork until well mixed. Press in bottom and up sides of 9-inch pie pan; flute edge. (If desired, crust can be rolled out between 2 sheets of waxed paper.) Prick bottom and sides of crust generously with fork.
2. Bake at 425°F. for 12 to 17 minutes or until light golden brown. Cool 30 minutes or until completely cooled. Continue as directed in pie recipe.

NUTRITION INFORMATION PER SERVING: Serving Size: ⅛ of Recipe ◆ Calories: 230 ◆ Calories from Fat: 130 ◆ **% DAILY VALUE:** Total Fat: 14 g 22% ◆ Saturated Fat: 2 g 10% ◆ Cholesterol: 0 mg 0% ◆ Sodium: 270 mg 11% ◆ Total Carbohydrate: 22 g 7% ◆ Dietary Fiber: 1 g 3% ◆ Sugars: 1 g ◆ Protein: 3 g ◆ Vitamin A: 0% ◆ Vitamin C: 0% ◆ Calcium: 0% ◆ Iron: 8% ◆ **DIETARY EXCHANGES:** 1½ Starch, 2½ Fat OR 1½ Carbohydrate, 2½ Fat

Perfect Apple Pie

PREP TIME: 35 MINUTES (READY IN 1 HOUR 20 MINUTES)
◆ YIELD: 8 SERVINGS

CRUST
1 (15-oz.) pkg. refrigerated pie crusts or Pastry for Two-Crust Pie (page 385)

FILLING*
¾ cup sugar
2 tablespoons all-purpose flour
¾ teaspoon cinnamon
¼ teaspoon salt
⅛ teaspoon nutmeg
1 tablespoon lemon juice, if desired
6 cups (6 medium) thinly sliced, peeled apples

1. Prepare pie crust for *two-crust pie* using 9-inch pie pan.
2. Heat oven to 425°F. In large bowl, combine all filling ingredients except lemon juice and apples; mix well. Add lemon juice and apples; toss gently to mix. Spoon into crust-lined pan. Top with second crust; seal edges

Perfect Apple Pie

and flute. Cut slits or shapes in several places in top crust.
3. Bake at 425°F. for 40 to 45 minutes or until apples are tender and crust is golden brown.

TIP: *Two 21-oz. cans apple pie filling can be substituted for filling.

NUTRITION INFORMATION PER SERVING: Serving Size: ⅛ of Recipe ◆ Calories: 370 ◆ Calories from Fat: 130 ◆ **% DAILY VALUE:** Total Fat: 14 g 22% ◆ Saturated Fat: 6 g 30% ◆ Cholesterol: 15 mg 5% ◆ Sodium: 270 mg 11% ◆ Total Carbohydrate: 59 g 20% ◆ Dietary Fiber: 2 g 8% ◆ Sugars: 30 g ◆ Protein: 2 g ◆ Vitamin A: 0% ◆ Vitamin C: 4% ◆ Calcium: 0% ◆ Iron: 4% ◆ **DIETARY EXCHANGES:** 1 Starch, 3 Fruit, 2½ Fat OR 4 Carbohydrate, 2½ Fat

VARIATIONS
Caramel Pecan Apple Pie: Immediately after removing pie from oven, drizzle with ⅓ cup caramel ice cream topping. Sprinkle with 2 to 4 tablespoons chopped pecans.
Cheese Crust Apple Pie: Substitute Cheese Pastry (page 385) for crust.

Topsy Turvy Apple Pie

PREP TIME: 45 MINUTES (READY IN 1 HOUR 30 MINUTES)
◆ YIELD: 8 SERVINGS

GLAZE AND CRUST
¼ cup firmly packed brown sugar
1 tablespoon margarine or butter, melted
1 tablespoon corn syrup
¼ cup pecan halves
1 (15-oz.) pkg. refrigerated pie crusts or Pastry for Two-Crust Pie (page 385)

FILLING
⅔ cup sugar
2 tablespoons all-purpose flour
½ teaspoon cinnamon
4 cups (4 medium) sliced peeled apples

GARNISH
Whipped cream, if desired

Topsy Turvy Apple Pie (page 386)

1. In 9-inch pie pan, combine brown sugar, margarine and corn syrup; mix well. Spread evenly in bottom of pan. Arrange pecans over mixture in pan. Prepare pie crust for *two-crust pie;* place bottom crust over mixture in pan. Heat oven to 425°F.

2. In small bowl, combine sugar, flour and cinnamon; mix well. Arrange half of apple slices in crust-lined pan. Sprinkle with half of sugar mixture. Repeat with remaining apple slices and sugar mixture. Top with second crust; seal edges and flute. Cut slits in several places in top crust.

3. Bake at 425°F. for 8 minutes. Reduce oven temperature to 350°F.; bake an additional 25 to 35 minutes or until apples are tender and crust is golden brown. (Place pan on foil or cookie sheet during baking to catch any spills.)

4. Loosen edge of pie; carefully invert onto serving plate. Serve warm or cool with whipped cream.

NUTRITION INFORMATION PER SERVING: Serving Size: ⅛ of Recipe ♦ Calories: 460 ♦ Calories from Fat: 210 ♦ % DAILY VALUE: Total Fat: 23 g 35% ♦ Saturated Fat: 9 g 45% ♦ Cholesterol: 35 mg 12% ♦ Sodium: 230 mg 10% ♦ Total Carbohydrate: 62 g 21% ♦ Dietary Fiber: 2 g 8% ♦ Sugars: 33 g ♦ Protein: 2 g ♦ Vitamin A: 6% ♦ Vitamin C: 2% ♦ Calcium: 4% ♦ Iron: 4% ♦ DIETARY EXCHANGES: 1 Starch, 3 Fruit, 4½ Fat OR 4 Carbohydrate, 4½ Fat

Easy Apple Pie Foldover

PREP TIME: 25 MINUTES (READY IN 1 HOUR 20 MINUTES) ♦ YIELD: 4 SERVINGS

1½ cups (2 medium) thinly sliced, peeled apples
¼ cup firmly packed brown sugar
1 tablespoon water
1 teaspoon lemon juice
1 tablespoon all-purpose flour
1 tablespoon sugar
¼ teaspoon salt

½ teaspoon vanilla
1 tablespoon margarine or butter
1 refrigerated pie crust (from 15-oz. pkg.)
1 tablespoon water
1 egg

1. In medium saucepan, combine apples, brown sugar, 1 tablespoon water and lemon juice. Cook over medium heat until bubbly, stirring occasionally. Reduce heat to low; cover and cook 6 to 8 minutes or until apples are tender, stirring occasionally.

2. In small bowl, combine flour, sugar and salt; stir into apple mixture. Cook until mixture thickens, stirring constantly. Remove from heat; stir in vanilla and margarine. Cool 15 to 20 minutes.

3. Meanwhile, heat oven to 375°F. Let pie crust pouch stand at room temperature for 15 to 20 minutes.

4. Remove pie crust from pouch. Unfold crust; place on ungreased cookie sheet. Press out fold lines.

5. Spoon fruit mixture evenly on half of crust to within ½ inch of edge. In small bowl, beat 1 tablespoon water and egg; brush over edges of crust. Fold remaining side of crust over fruit, turnover fashion; press edges firmly to seal.* Flute edge; cut small slits in top crust. Brush top with egg mixture.

6. Bake at 375°F. for 25 to 35 minutes or until crust is golden brown. Serve warm or cool.

> **TIP:** * If desired, cut out decorative shapes from remaining side of crust before folding crust over fruit. Omit slits in crust.

NUTRITION INFORMATION PER SERVING: Serving Size: ¼ of Recipe ♦ Calories: 380 ♦ Calories from Fat: 160 ♦ % DAILY VALUE: Total Fat: 18 g 28% ♦ Saturated Fat: 6 g 30% ♦ Cholesterol: 65 mg 22% ♦ Sodium: 390 mg 16% ♦ Total Carbohydrate: 51 g 17% ♦ Dietary Fiber: 1 g 4% ♦ Sugars: 23 g ♦ Protein: 3 g ♦ Vitamin A: 4% ♦ Vitamin C: 4% ♦ Calcium: 4% ♦ Iron: 6% ♦ DIETARY EXCHANGES: 1 Starch, 2½ Fruit, 3½ Fat OR 3½ Carbohydrate, 3½ Fat

Easy Apple Pie Foldover

Apple-Blueberry Pie

PREP TIME: 25 MINUTES (READY IN 3 HOURS 35 MINUTES) ✦ YIELD: 8 SERVINGS

CRUST
  1 refrigerated pie crust (from 15-oz. pkg.) or Pastry for One-Crust Pie (page 385)

FILLING
  4 cups (4 medium) sliced peeled baking apples
  2 cups fresh blueberries
  ¾ cup sugar
  ¼ cup all-purpose flour
  ½ teaspoon cinnamon
  1 tablespoon lemon juice

TOPPING
  1 cup all-purpose flour
  ½ cup firmly packed brown sugar
  ¼ teaspoon nutmeg
  ⅓ cup margarine or butter, softened

1. Place sheet of foil on oven rack below middle baking rack to catch drips. Heat oven to 425°F. Prepare pie crust for *one-crust filled pie* using 9-inch pie pan.

2. In large bowl, combine all filling ingredients; mix well. Set aside.

3. In medium bowl, combine all topping ingredients; mix with fork or pastry blender until crumbly. Spoon fruit into crust-lined pan. Spoon topping evenly over fruit.

4. Bake at 425°F. for 50 to 70 minutes or until apples are tender and edges are bubbly.

NUTRITION INFORMATION PER SERVING: Serving Size: ⅛ of Recipe ✦ Calories: 440 ✦ Calories from Fat: 140 ✦ % DAILY VALUE: Total Fat: 15 g 23% ✦ Saturated Fat: 4 g 20% ✦ Cholesterol: 5 mg 2% ✦ Sodium: 200 mg 8% ✦ Total Carbohydrate: 74 g 25% ✦ Dietary Fiber: 3 g 12% ✦ Sugars: 42 g ✦ Protein: 3 g ✦ Vitamin A: 8% ✦ Vitamin C: 8% ✦ Calcium: 2% ✦ Iron: 8% ✦ DIETARY EXCHANGES: 1 Starch, 4 Fruit, 3 Fat OR 5 Carbohydrate, 3 Fat

Apple-Raisin Crumb Pie

PREP TIME: 30 MINUTES (READY IN 1 HOUR 15 MINUTES) ✦ YIELD: 8 SERVINGS

CRUST
  1 refrigerated pie crust (from 15-oz. pkg.) or Pastry for One-Crust Pie (page 385)

FILLING
  6 cups (6 medium) thinly sliced, peeled apples
  ½ cup raisins
  ½ cup sugar
  2 tablespoons all-purpose flour
  ¾ teaspoon cinnamon

TOPPING
  ⅓ cup sugar
  ¾ cup all-purpose flour
  6 tablespoons margarine or butter, softened

1. Prepare pie crust for *one-crust filled pie* using 9-inch pie pan.

2. Heat oven to 400°F. In large bowl, combine all filling ingredients; toss lightly. Spoon into crust-lined pan.

3. In small bowl, combine ⅓ cup sugar and ¾ cup flour; mix well. With fork or pastry blender, cut in margarine until crumbly. Sprinkle over apples.

4. Bake at 400°F. for 35 to 45 minutes or until apples are tender and crust is golden brown.

NUTRITION INFORMATION PER SERVING: Serving Size: ⅛ of Recipe ✦ Calories: 410 ✦ Calories from Fat: 140 ✦ % DAILY VALUE: Total Fat: 16 g 25% ✦ Saturated Fat: 4 g 20% ✦ Cholesterol: 5 mg 2% ✦ Sodium: 200 mg 8% ✦ Total Carbohydrate: 64 g 21% ✦ Dietary Fiber: 3 g 12% ✦ Sugars: 37 g ✦ Protein: 3 g ✦ Vitamin A: 8% ✦ Vitamin C: 4% ✦ Calcium: 2% ✦ Iron: 6% ✦ DIETARY EXCHANGES: 1 Starch, 3½ Fruit, 3 Fat OR 4½ Carbohydrate, 3 Fat

CRUMB PIE CRUSTS

Prep Time: 20 minutes (Ready in 50 minutes)

Graham cracker crumbs are the classic choice; but here are some tasty variations. To make the crumbs, place broken cookies or crackers in a plastic bag and roll with a rolling pin until the crumbs are finely crushed or crush them in a food processor.

1. Heat oven to 375°F. In medium bowl, combine crumbs, sugar and melted butter; blend well. Press mixture firmly in bottom and up sides of 8 or 9-inch pie pan or in bottom of 9-inch springform pan.

2. Bake at 375°F. for 8 to 10 minutes. Cool at least 30 minutes or until completely cooled. Fill with ice cream or pudding. Freeze or refrigerate.

COOKIE OR CRACKER	AMOUNT OF CRUMBS	SUGAR	BUTTER OR MARGARINE, MELTED
CHOCOLATE WAFER	1¼ cups (20 wafers)	¼ cup	¼ cup
CREAM-FILLED VANILLA OR CHOCOLATE COOKIE	1½ cups (15 cookies)	None	¼ cup
CRISP MACAROON COOKIE	1½ cups	None	¼ cup
GINGERSNAP COOKIE	1½ cups	None	¼ cup
GRAHAM CRACKER*	1½ cups (24 squares)	¼ cup	⅓ cup
GRANOLA (coarsely crushed)	1½ cups	None	¼ cup
PRETZEL**	1¼ cups	¼ cup	½ cup
VANILLA WAFER	1½ cups (30 wafers)	None	¼ cup

*Add ½ teaspoon cinnamon, if desired.
**For easier serving, butter pan before preparing pretzel crust.

Cherry Pie

PREP TIME: 30 MINUTES (READY IN 1 HOUR 15 MINUTES)
◆ YIELD: 8 SERVINGS

CRUST
1 (15-oz.) pkg. refrigerated pie crusts or Pastry for Two-Crust Pie (page 385)

FILLING*
2 (16-oz.) cans pitted tart red cherries in syrup, drained**
1¼ cups sugar
¼ cup all-purpose flour
2 tablespoons margarine or butter

1. Prepare pie crust for *two-crust pie* using 9-inch pie pan.
2. Heat oven to 425°F. In large bowl, combine cherries, sugar and flour; toss gently to mix. Spoon into crust-lined pan. Dot with margarine. Top with second crust; seal edges and flute. Cut slits in several places in top crust.
3. Bake at 425°F. for 35 to 45 minutes or until juice begins to bubble through slits in crust.

TIPS: * Two 21-oz. cans cherry pie filling can be substituted for filling.
** Four cups pitted fresh tart red cherries can be substituted for canned cherries.
    If desired, sprinkle cherries with ¼ teaspoon almond extract before dotting with margarine.

NUTRITION INFORMATION PER SERVING: Serving Size: ⅛ of Recipe ◆ Calories: 450 ◆ Calories from Fat: 150 ◆ % DAILY VALUE: Total Fat: 17 g 26% ◆ Saturated Fat: 6 g 30% ◆ Cholesterol: 15 mg 5% ◆ Sodium: 250 mg 10% ◆ Total Carbohydrate: 70 g 23% ◆ Dietary Fiber: 2 g 8% ◆ Sugars: 42 g ◆ Protein: 3 g ◆ Vitamin A: 20% ◆ Vitamin C: 2% ◆ Calcium: 2% ◆ Iron: 10% ◆ DIETARY EXCHANGES: 1 Starch, 3½ Fruit, 3½ Fat OR 4½ Carbohydrate, 3½ Fat

FINISHING TOUCHES FOR PIES

Woven Lattice

Topping a pie with crisscrossed strips of dough allows the filling to peek through. To make a lattice crust, roll out the bottom crust as directed and place it in the pie pan, letting ½ inch of dough extend over the edges. Roll out the remaining dough as if you were making a top crust, then cut the dough into strips ½ inch wide, using either a knife or a plain or fluted pastry cutter. For a woven lattice top, lift every other strip as the cross strips are added to create an over-and-under weave. Trim the ends even with the edge of the dough. Form a stand-up rim; flute.

Easy Lattice

Follow directions for Woven Lattice but do not weave lattice strips. Lay half the strips in 1 direction. Rotate pan 1 quarter turn and lay remaining strips at right angles directly over the first strips. Trim the ends even with the edge of the dough. Form a stand-up rim; flute.

FLUTING TECHNIQUES

Herringbone Pattern

Trim dough even with edge of pan. Dip fork tines in flour; press fork tines into edge of dough. Press next to first set of marks, creating pattern. Continue around the rim.

Pinched Crust

Place thumb on stand-up rim at an angle; press pastry against thumb with knuckle of index finger. Repeat pattern diagonally around edge on rim of pie pan.

Scalloped Edge

Place index finger on inside rim of pastry. Make flutes about ½ inch apart by pushing pastry into the V shaped by the right thumb and index finger outside of the rim. Pinch points to make definite edge.

Raspberry-Cherry Pie

Raspberry-Cherry Pie

PREP TIME: 30 MINUTES (READY IN 1 HOUR 15 MINUTES)
◆ YIELD: 8 SERVINGS

CRUST
    1 (15-oz.) pkg. refrigerated pie crusts or Pastry
        for Two-Crust Pie (page 385)

FILLING
    2 cups fresh or frozen whole raspberries
        (do not thaw)
    ¼ to ½ cup sugar
    1 tablespoon all-purpose flour
    1 (21-oz.) can cherry pie filling

1. Prepare pie crust for *two-crust pie* using 9-inch pie pan.
2. Heat oven to 400°F. In large bowl, combine all filling ingredients; stir gently to mix.

Spoon into crust-lined pan. Top with second crust; seal edges and flute. Cut slits or shapes in several places in top crust.

3. Bake at 400°F. for 40 to 45 minutes or until crust is golden brown and filling is bubbly. (Place foil or cookie sheet on oven rack in lowest position during baking to catch any spills.)

NUTRITION INFORMATION PER SERVING: Serving Size: ⅛ of Recipe • Calories: 390 • Calories from Fat: 130 • **% DAILY VALUE:** Total Fat: 14 g 22% • Saturated Fat: 6 g 30% • Cholesterol: 15 mg 5% • Sodium: 210 mg 9% • Total Carbohydrate: 65 g 22% • Dietary Fiber: 2 g 8% • Sugars: 35 g • Protein: 2 g • Vitamin A: 4% • Vitamin C: 10% • Calcium: 2% • Iron: 4% • **DIETARY EXCHANGES:** 1 Starch, 3½ Fruit, 2½ Fat OR 4½ Carbohydrate, 2½ Fat

---

COOK'S NOTE

CATCH THE OVERFLOWS

Sometimes, despite the most carefully sealed crust, fruit filling bubbles up over the edges or through steam vents in the top crust. As the drips burn, they can smell unpleasant and create a mess in the oven. Prevent this by placing a piece of foil on the lower oven rack to catch the drips.

Berry-Cherry Pie

PREP TIME: 30 MINUTES (READY IN 3 HOURS) ✦ YIELD: 8 SERVINGS

CRUST
1 refrigerated pie crust (from 15-oz. pkg.) or Pastry for One-Crust Pie (page 385)

FILLING
1 (8-oz.) pkg. cream cheese, softened
⅓ cup sugar
1 teaspoon vanilla
½ teaspoon grated lemon peel
1 pint (2 cups) fresh whole strawberries
1 (21-oz.) can cherry pie filling

1. Heat oven to 450°F. Prepare pie crust for *one-crust baked shell* using 9-inch pie pan. Bake at 450°F. for 9 to 11 minutes or until light golden brown. Cool 30 minutes or until completely cooled.

2. In small bowl, combine cream cheese, sugar, vanilla and lemon peel; beat until smooth and well blended. Spread evenly in cooled baked shell.

3. Arrange strawberries over cream cheese mixture; press in lightly. Spoon pie filling over strawberries. Refrigerate at least 2 hours before serving. If desired, garnish with whipped cream. Store in refrigerator.

NUTRITION INFORMATION PER SERVING: Serving Size: ⅛ of Recipe • Calories: 350 • Calories from Fat: 150 • **% DAILY VALUE:** Total Fat: 17 g 26% • Saturated Fat: 9 g 45% • Cholesterol: 40 mg 13% • Sodium: 190 mg 8% • Total Carbohydrate: 47 g 16% • Dietary Fiber: 2 g 8% • Sugars: 30 g • Protein: 3 g • Vitamin A: 10% • Vitamin C: 45% • Calcium: 4% • Iron: 4% • **DIETARY EXCHANGES:** 1 Starch, 2 Fruit, 3½ Fat OR 3 Carbohydrate, 3½ Fat

Fresh Raspberry Lattice Pie

PREP TIME: 50 MINUTES (READY IN 2 HOURS 35 MINUTES) ✦ YIELD: 8 SERVINGS

FILLING
4½ cups fresh raspberries*
1¼ cups sugar
5 tablespoons cornstarch
Dash salt
1 tablespoon margarine or butter

CRUST
1 (15-oz.) pkg. refrigerated pie crusts or Pastry for Two-Crust Pie (page 385)

1. In medium saucepan, combine raspberries, sugar, cornstarch and salt. Cook over medium heat for about 15 minutes or until mixture boils and thickens, stirring constantly. Refrigerate 1 hour or until completely cooled.

2. Prepare pie crust for *two-crust pie* using 9-inch pie pan. Heat oven to 425°F. Pour filling into crust-lined pan. Dot with margarine.

3. To make lattice top, cut second crust into ½-inch-wide strips. Arrange strips in lattice design over filling. Trim edges and flute. With any remaining crust, form small pea-sized balls; place over crossings in lattice pattern.

4. Bake at 425°F. for 35 to 45 minutes or until golden brown. If desired, sprinkle with powdered sugar before serving.

TIP: * Frozen whole raspberries, thawed and well drained, can be substituted for fresh raspberries.

NUTRITION INFORMATION PER SERVING: Serving Size: ⅛ of Recipe • Calories: 420 • Calories from Fat: 140 • **% DAILY VALUE:** Total Fat: 15 g 23% • Saturated Fat: 6 g 30% • Cholesterol: 15 mg 5% • Sodium: 240 mg 10% • Total Carbohydrate: 70 g 23% • Dietary Fiber: 4 g 16% • Sugars: 38 g • Protein: 2 g • Vitamin A: 4% • Vitamin C: 20% • Calcium: 2% • Iron: 4% • **DIETARY EXCHANGES:** ½ Starch, 4 Fruit, 3 Fat OR 4½ Carbohydrate, 3 Fat

Fresh Blueberry Pie

PREP TIME: 35 MINUTES (READY IN 1 HOUR 30 MINUTES)
◆ YIELD: 8 SERVINGS

CRUST
  1 (15-oz.) pkg. refrigerated pie crusts or Pastry
    for Two-Crust Pie (page 385)

FILLING
  4 cups fresh blueberries*
  ¾ cup sugar
  ¼ cup all-purpose flour
  ¼ teaspoon cinnamon
  2 teaspoons lemon juice
  2 tablespoons margarine or butter

TOPPING
  1 to 2 tablespoons milk
  2 teaspoons sugar
  Dash cinnamon

1. Prepare pie crust for *two-crust pie* using 9-inch pie pan.
2. Heat oven to 425°F. In large bowl, combine blueberries, ¾ cup sugar, flour, ¼ teaspoon cinnamon and lemon juice; toss gently to mix. Spoon into crust-lined pan. Dot with margarine. Top with second crust; seal edges and flute. Cut slits in several places in top crust. Brush crust with milk; sprinkle with 2 teaspoons sugar and dash cinnamon.
3. Bake at 425°F. for 45 to 55 minutes or until crust is golden brown. Cover edge of crust with strips of foil after 15 to 20 minutes of baking to prevent excessive browning.

TIP: * Frozen blueberries, thawed and well drained, can be substituted for fresh blueberries.

NUTRITION INFORMATION PER SERVING: Serving Size: ⅛ of Recipe ◆ Calories: 400 ◆ Calories from Fat: 150 ◆ % DAILY VALUE: Total Fat: 17 g 26% ◆ Saturated Fat: 6 g 30% ◆ Cholesterol: 15 mg 5% ◆ Sodium: 240 mg 10% ◆ Total Carbohydrate: 59 g 20% ◆ Dietary Fiber: 3 g 12% ◆ Sugars: 27 g ◆ Protein: 2 g ◆ Vitamin A: 4% ◆ Vitamin C: 10% ◆ Calcium: 2% ◆ Iron: 4% ◆ DIETARY EXCHANGES: ½ Starch, 3½ Fruit, 3½ Fat OR 4 Carbohydrate, 3½ Fat

Vanilla Cream Pie

PREP TIME: 30 MINUTES (READY IN 4 HOURS)
◆ YIELD: 8 SERVINGS

CRUST
  1 refrigerated pie crust (from 15-oz. pkg.) or
    Pastry for One-Crust Pie (page 385)

FILLING
  ¾ cup sugar
  ¼ cup cornstarch
  ¼ teaspoon salt
  3 cups milk
  3 egg yolks, slightly beaten
  2 tablespoons margarine or butter
  2 teaspoons vanilla

1. Heat oven to 450°F. Prepare pie crust for *one-crust baked shell* using 9-inch pie pan. Bake at 450°F. for 9 to 11 minutes or until light golden brown. Cool 30 minutes or until completely cooled.
2. In medium saucepan, combine sugar, cornstarch and salt; mix well. Stir in milk until smooth. Cook over medium heat until mixture boils and thickens, stirring constantly. Boil 2 minutes. Remove from heat.
3. Stir about ¼ cup hot mixture into egg yolks. Gradually stir yolk mixture into hot mixture in saucepan. Cook just until mixture begins to bubble, stirring constantly.
4. Remove from heat; stir in margarine and vanilla. Pour into cooled baked shell. Refrigerate 3 hours or until set. If desired, top with whipped cream. Store in refrigerator.

NUTRITION INFORMATION PER SERVING: Serving Size: ⅛ of Recipe ◆ Calories: 300 ◆ Calories from Fat: 120 ◆ % DAILY VALUE: Total Fat: 13 g 20% ◆ Saturated Fat: 5 g 25% ◆ Cholesterol: 95 mg 32% ◆ Sodium: 250 mg 10% ◆ Total Carbohydrate: 40 g 13% ◆ Dietary Fiber: 0 g 0% ◆ Sugars: 24 g ◆ Protein: 5 g ◆ Vitamin A: 8% ◆ Vitamin C: 0% ◆ Calcium: 15% ◆ Iron: 2% ◆ DIETARY EXCHANGES: 1½ Starch, 1 Fruit, 2½ Fat OR 2½ Carbohydrate, 2½ Fat

VARIATIONS

Banana Cream Pie: Cool filling in saucepan to lukewarm. Slice 2 or 3 bananas into cooled baked shell. Pour filling over bananas.

Butterscotch Cream Pie: Substitute firmly packed brown sugar for sugar.

Chocolate Cream Pie: Increase sugar to 1 cup and add 2 oz. unsweetened chocolate to filling mixture before cooking.

Coconut Cream Pie: Stir 1 cup coconut into cooked filling with margarine and vanilla.

Crunchy Mincemeat Pie

PREP TIME: 30 MINUTES (READY IN 1 HOUR 15 MINUTES)
♦ YIELD: 8 SERVINGS

CRUST
  1 (15-oz.) pkg. refrigerated pie crusts or Pastry for Two-Crust Pie (page 385)

FILLING
  1 (28-oz.) jar mincemeat
  1½ cups chopped peeled apples
  ⅓ cup chopped nuts
  2 teaspoons grated lemon peel, if desired
  1 tablespoon fresh lemon juice

1. Prepare pie crust for *two-crust pie* using 9-inch pie pan.
2. Heat oven to 425°F. In large bowl, combine all filling ingredients; toss gently to mix. Spoon into crust-lined pan. Top with second crust; seal edges and flute. Cut slits in several places in top crust.
3. Bake at 425°F. for 35 to 45 minutes or until golden brown. Cover edge of crust with strips of foil after 15 to 20 minutes of baking to prevent excessive browning.

NUTRITION INFORMATION PER SERVING: Serving Size: ⅛ of Recipe ♦ Calories: 630 ♦ Calories from Fat: 160 ♦ **% DAILY VALUE:** Total Fat: 18 g 28% ♦ Saturated Fat: 7 g 35% ♦ Cholesterol: 15 mg 5% ♦ Sodium: 740 mg 31% ♦ Total Carbohydrate: 114 g 38% ♦ Dietary Fiber: 3 g 12% ♦ Sugars: 76 g ♦ Protein: 2 g ♦ Vitamin A: 0% ♦ Vitamin C: 2% ♦ Calcium: 6% ♦ Iron: 8% ♦ **DIETARY EXCHANGES:** 1 Starch, 6½ Fruit, 3½ Fat OR 7½ Carbohydrate, 3½ Fat

---

COOK'S NOTE

IF THE EDGES BROWN TOO FAST

Sometimes the edges of the pie turn golden brown before the filling is fully cooked. To prevent the edges from burning, cover them with thin strips of aluminum foil.

Cranberry-Apricot Pie

PREP TIME: 30 MINUTES (READY IN 3 HOURS 20 MINUTES) ♦ YIELD: 8 SERVINGS

CRUST
  1 (15-oz.) pkg. refrigerated pie crusts or Pastry for Two-Crust Pie (page 385)

FILLING
  ½ cup sugar
  1 tablespoon cornstarch
  1 (21-oz.) can apricot pie filling
  1½ cups fresh or frozen cranberries
  ½ teaspoon cinnamon

GARNISH
  Water
  2 teaspoons sugar

1. Prepare pie crust for *two-crust pie* using 9-inch pie pan.
2. Heat oven to 425°F. In large bowl, combine ½ cup sugar and cornstarch; mix well. Stir in pie filling, cranberries and cinnamon until well mixed. Spoon into crust-lined pan.
3. With fluted pastry wheel, cut remaining pie crust into ½-inch-wide strips. Place strips over filling, overlapping to make a lattice design; flute edge. Brush with water; sprinkle with 2 teaspoons sugar.
4. Bake at 425°F. for 40 to 50 minutes or until crust is golden brown. Cover edge of crust with strips of foil after 15 to 20 minutes of baking to prevent excessive browning. Cool 2 hours or until completely cooled.

NUTRITION INFORMATION PER SERVING: Serving Size: ⅛ of Recipe ♦ Calories: 390 ♦ Calories from Fat: 130 ♦ **% DAILY VALUE:** Total Fat: 14 g 22% ♦ Saturated Fat: 6 g 30% ♦ Cholesterol: 15 mg 5% ♦ Sodium: 210 mg 9% ♦ Total Carbohydrate: 64 g 21% ♦ Dietary Fiber: 3 g 12% ♦ Sugars: 31 g ♦ Protein: 1 g ♦ Vitamin A: 25% ♦ Vitamin C: 20% ♦ Calcium: 4% ♦ Iron: 10% ♦ **DIETARY EXCHANGES:** ½ Starch, 4 Fruit, 2½ Fat OR 4½ Carbohydrate, 2½ Fat

Streusel-Topped Peach-Blueberry Pie

VARIATION
Streusel-Topped Peach-Blueberry Pie:
Substitute 1 cup blueberries for 1 cup of
the peaches.

Fresh Strawberry Pie

PREP TIME: 30 MINUTES (READY IN 4 HOURS)
◆ YIELD: 8 SERVINGS

CRUST
    1 refrigerated pie crust (from 15-oz. pkg.) or
       Pastry for One-Crust Pie (page 385)

FILLING
    3 pints (6 cups) fresh whole strawberries
    1 cup sugar
    3 tablespoons cornstarch
    ½ cup water
    4 to 5 drops red food color, if desired

TOPPING
    ½ cup whipping cream, whipped, sweetened

1. Heat oven to 450°F. Prepare pie crust for *one-crust baked shell* using 9-inch pie pan. Bake at 450°F. for 9 to 11 minutes or until light golden brown. Cool completely.
2. Meanwhile, in small bowl, crush enough strawberries to make 1 cup. In medium saucepan, combine sugar and cornstarch; add crushed strawberries and water. Cook until mixture boils and thickens, stirring constantly. Stir in food color. Cool 30 minutes or until completely cooled.
3. Place remaining strawberries, whole or sliced, in cooled baked shell. Pour cooked strawberry mixture evenly over berries. Refrigerate 3 hours or until set. To serve, top with whipped cream. Store in refrigerator.

NUTRITION INFORMATION PER SERVING: Serving Size: ⅛ of Recipe ◆ Calories: 340 ◆ Calories from Fat: 120 ◆ **% DAILY VALUE:** Total Fat: 13 g 20% ◆ Saturated Fat: 6 g 30% ◆ Cholesterol: 25 mg 8% ◆ Sodium: 110 mg 5% ◆ Total Carbohydrate: 53 g 18% ◆ Dietary Fiber: 3 g 12% ◆ Sugars: 36 g ◆ Protein: 2 g ◆ Vitamin A: 6% ◆ Vitamin C: 80% ◆ Calcium: 4% ◆ Iron: 4% ◆ **DIETARY EXCHANGES:** ½ Starch, 3 Fruit, 2½ Fat OR 3½ Carbohydrate, 2½ Fat

VARIATIONS
Fresh Peach Pie: Substitute sliced fresh peaches for strawberries. Omit red food color.
Fresh Raspberry Pie: Substitute fresh raspberries for strawberries.

Streusel-Topped Peach Pie

PREP TIME: 35 MINUTES (READY IN 1 HOUR 20 MINUTES)
◆ YIELD: 8 SERVINGS

CRUST
    1 refrigerated pie crust (from 15-oz. pkg.) or
       Pastry for One-Crust Pie (page 385)

FILLING
    4 cups sliced peeled peaches or 2 (29-oz.)
       cans peach slices, well drained
    ½ cup powdered sugar
    ⅓ cup all-purpose flour
    ½ teaspoon cinnamon

TOPPING
    ¾ cup all-purpose flour
    ½ cup firmly packed brown sugar
    ½ teaspoon cinnamon
    ⅓ cup margarine or butter

1. Prepare pie crust for *one-crust filled pie* using 9-inch pie pan.
2. Heat oven to 375°F. In large bowl, combine all filling ingredients; mix well. Spoon into crust-lined pan.
3. In medium bowl, combine all topping ingredients; mix with fork or pastry blender until crumbly. Sprinkle over filling.
4. Bake at 375°F. for 40 to 45 minutes or until topping is golden brown. Cover edge of crust with strips of foil after 15 or 20 minutes of baking to prevent excessive browning.

NUTRITION INFORMATION PER SERVING: Serving Size: ⅛ of Recipe ◆ Calories: 380 ◆ Calories from Fat: 140 ◆ **% DAILY VALUE:** Total Fat: 15 g 23% ◆ Saturated Fat: 4 g 20% ◆ Cholesterol: 5 mg 2% ◆ Sodium: 200 mg 8% ◆ Total Carbohydrate: 57 g 19% ◆ Dietary Fiber: 3 g 12% ◆ Sugars: 29 g ◆ Protein: 3 g ◆ Vitamin A: 15% ◆ Vitamin C: 6% ◆ Calcium: 2% ◆ Iron: 8% ◆ **DIETARY EXCHANGES:** 1 Starch, 3 Fruit, 3 Fat OR 4 Carbohydrate, 3 Fat

Fresh Pear Crostata

Fresh Pear Crostata

PREP TIME: 25 MINUTES (READY IN 1 HOUR)
♦ YIELD: 8 SERVINGS

    1 refrigerated pie crust (from 15-oz. pkg.)
    ½ cup sugar
    3 tablespoons all-purpose flour
    4 cups chopped peeled ripe pears
    1 teaspoon sugar
    2 tablespoons sliced almonds

1. Let pie crust pouch stand at room temperature for 15 to 20 minutes.
2. Meanwhile, heat oven to 450°F. In medium bowl, combine ½ cup sugar and flour; blend well. Add pears; toss gently.
3. Remove pie crust from pouch. Unfold crust; place in ungreased 15 × 10 × 1-inch baking pan. Press out fold lines.
4. Spoon pear mixture onto center of crust, leaving 2-inch border. Fold edge of crust 2 inches over pear mixture; crimp crust slightly. Sprinkle crust edge with 1 teaspoon sugar.
5. Bake at 450°F. for 14 to 20 minutes or until crust is golden brown and pears are tender, sprinkling almonds over pear mixture during last 5 minutes of baking time. Cool at least 15 minutes before serving.

NUTRITION INFORMATION PER SERVING: Serving Size: ⅛ of Recipe
♦ Calories: 240 ♦ Calories from Fat: 70 ♦ % DAILY VALUE: Total Fat: 8 g 12% ♦ Saturated Fat: 3 g 15% ♦ Cholesterol: 5 mg 2% ♦ Sodium: 105 mg 4% ♦ Total Carbohydrate: 40 g 13% ♦ Dietary Fiber: 2 g 8% ♦ Sugars: 22 g ♦ Protein: 2 g ♦ Vitamin A: 0% ♦ Vitamin C: 4% ♦ Calcium: 0% ♦ Iron: 4% ♦ DIETARY EXCHANGES: ½ Starch, 2 Fruit, 1½ Fat OR 2½ Carbohydrate, 1½ Fat

Margarita Pie

PREP TIME: 30 MINUTES (READY IN 2 HOURS 30 MINUTES) ♦ YIELD: 8 SERVINGS

    2 cups miniature pretzel twists
    2 tablespoons sugar
    2 tablespoons margarine or butter
    1 (6-oz.) can frozen limeade concentrate
    1 quart (4 cups) low-fat vanilla ice cream, slightly softened
    1 teaspoon grated lime peel
    3 tablespoons tequila
    1 tablespoon orange-flavored liqueur

1. Heat oven to 375°F. Spray 9-inch pie pan with nonstick cooking spray.
2. In food processor bowl with metal blade or blender container, process pretzels until crumbs form. Add sugar; process with on/off pulses to mix. Add margarine; mix well. With machine running, add 2 tablespoons of the limeade concentrate, processing until well mixed. Place mixture in sprayed pan. With back of spoon, press mixture firmly in bottom and up sides of pan.
3. Bake at 375°F. for 5 to 7 minutes or until set. Cool baked shell in freezer or refrigerator for 10 to 15 minutes.
4. Meanwhile, in food processor bowl with metal blade or large bowl for electric mixer, combine remaining limeade concentrate, ice cream, lime peel, tequila and liqueur; process or mix just until blended. Spoon into cooled baked shell. Freeze 2 hours or until firm.

NUTRITION INFORMATION PER SERVING: Serving Size: ⅛ of Recipe ♦ Calories: 280 ♦ Calories from Fat: 70 ♦ % DAILY VALUE: Total Fat: 8 g 12% ♦ Saturated Fat: 3 g 15% ♦ Cholesterol: 25 mg 8% ♦ Sodium: 380 mg 16% ♦ Total Carbohydrate: 43 g 14% ♦ Dietary Fiber: 1 g 3% ♦ Sugars: 26 g ♦ Protein: 5 g ♦ Vitamin A: 6% ♦ Vitamin C: 4% ♦ Calcium: 8% ♦ Iron: 6% ♦ DIETARY EXCHANGES: 1½ Starch, 1½ Fruit, 1½ Fat OR 3 Carbohydrate, 1½ Fat

Margarita Pie

Fresh Strawberry-Rhubarb Pie

PREP TIME: 30 MINUTES (READY IN 1 HOUR 30 MINUTES)
◆ YIELD: 8 SERVINGS

CRUST
  1 (15-oz.) pkg. refrigerated pie crusts or Pastry
    for Two-Crust Pie (page 385)

FILLING
  1 pint (2 cups) fresh whole strawberries
  3 cups cut-up fresh rhubarb*
  1 cup sugar
  ¼ cup cornstarch

1. Prepare pie crust for *two-crust pie* using 9-inch pie pan.
2. Heat oven to 400°F. In large bowl, combine all filling ingredients; mix gently. Spoon into crust-lined pan. Top with second crust; seal edges and flute. Cut slits in several places in top crust.
3. Bake at 400°F. for 45 to 60 minutes or until golden brown. (Place pan on foil or cookie sheet during last 15 minutes of baking to catch any spills.) If desired, serve with whipped cream and additional strawberries.

TIP: * One 16-oz. pkg. frozen sliced rhubarb, thawed and well drained, can be substituted for fresh rhubarb.

NUTRITION INFORMATION PER SERVING: Serving Size: ⅛ of Recipe ◆ Calories: 370 ◆ Calories from Fat: 130 ◆ % DAILY VALUE: Total Fat: 14 g 22% ◆ Saturated Fat: 6 g 30% ◆ Cholesterol: 15 mg 5% ◆ Sodium: 210 mg 9% ◆ Total Carbohydrate: 59 g 20% ◆ Dietary Fiber: 2 g 8% ◆ Sugars: 29 g ◆ Protein: 2 g ◆ Vitamin A: 0% ◆ Vitamin C: 30% ◆ Calcium: 6% ◆ Iron: 4% ◆ DIETARY EXCHANGES: 1 Starch, 3 Fruit, 2½ Fat OR 4 Carbohydrate, 2½ Fat

Strawberries and Cream Pie

PREP TIME: 30 MINUTES (READY IN 2 HOURS)
◆ YIELD: 10 SERVINGS

CRUST
  1 refrigerated pie crust (from 15-oz. pkg.) or
    Pastry for One-Crust Pie (page 385)

FILLING
  1 (8-oz.) pkg. cream cheese, softened
  ⅓ cup sugar
  ¼ to ½ teaspoon almond extract
  1 cup whipping cream, whipped
  2 pints (4 cups) fresh whole strawberries

GARNISH
  ½ cup semisweet chocolate chips
  1 tablespoon shortening

1. Heat oven to 450°F. Prepare pie crust for *one-crust baked shell* using 9-inch pie pan or 10-inch tart pan with removable bottom. Bake at 450°F. for 9 to 11 minutes or until light golden brown. Cool 30 minutes or until completely cooled.
2. In large bowl, beat cream cheese until fluffy. Gradually add sugar and almond extract, blending well. Fold in whipped cream. Spoon into cooled baked shell. Arrange strawberries, pointed side up, over filling. Refrigerate.
3. In small saucepan, melt chocolate chips and shortening over low heat, stirring constantly until smooth. Drizzle over strawberries and filling. Refrigerate 1 hour or until set. Store in refrigerator.

NUTRITION INFORMATION PER SERVING: Serving Size: ¹⁄₁₀ of Recipe ◆ Calories: 360 ◆ Calories from Fat: 230 ◆ % DAILY VALUE: Total Fat: 26 g 40% ◆ Saturated Fat: 15 g 75% ◆ Cholesterol: 65 mg 22% ◆ Sodium: 160 mg 7% ◆ Total Carbohydrate: 28 g 9% ◆ Dietary Fiber: 2 g 8% ◆ Sugars: 17 g ◆ Protein: 3 g ◆ Vitamin A: 15% ◆ Vitamin C: 60% ◆ Calcium: 4% ◆ Iron: 6% ◆ DIETARY EXCHANGES: 1 Starch, 1 Fruit, 5 Fat OR 2 Carbohydrate, 5 Fat

Rhubarb Cream Pie

PREP TIME: 30 MINUTES (READY IN 2 HOURS 35 MINUTES) ◆ YIELD: 8 SERVINGS

CRUST
  1 refrigerated pie crust (from 15-oz. pkg.) or
    Pastry for One-Crust Pie (page 385)

FILLING
  2 cups cut-up fresh rhubarb (do not use
    frozen rhubarb)
  3 egg yolks
  ½ cup half-and-half
  1 cup sugar
  2 tablespoons all-purpose flour
  ½ teaspoon salt

MERINGUE
  3 egg whites
  ¼ teaspoon cream of tartar
  ½ teaspoon vanilla
  6 tablespoons sugar

1. Prepare pie crust for *one-crust filled pie* using 9-inch pie pan.
2. Heat oven to 400°F. Place rhubarb in crust-lined pan. In small bowl, beat egg yolks until thick and lemon-colored. Stir in half-and-half. Add all remaining filling ingredients; blend well. Pour egg mixture over rhubarb.
3. Bake at 400°F. for 10 minutes. Reduce oven temperature to 350°F.; bake an additional 40 minutes.

4. In small deep bowl, combine egg whites, cream of tartar and vanilla; beat at medium speed until soft peaks form. Add 6 table-spoons sugar 1 tablespoon at a time, beating at high speed until stiff glossy peaks form and sugar is dissolved. Spoon meringue onto hot filling; spread to edge of crust to seal well and prevent shrinkage.

5. Bake at 350°F. for 15 to 20 minutes or until meringue is light golden brown. Cool 1 hour or until completely cooled. Store in refrigerator.

NUTRITION INFORMATION PER SERVING: Serving Size: ⅛ of Recipe ◆ Calories: 320 ◆ Calories from Fat: 100 ◆ **% DAILY VALUE:** Total Fat: 11 g 17% ◆ Saturated Fat: 4 g 20% ◆ Cholesterol: 95 mg 32% ◆ Sodium: 270 mg 11% ◆ Total Carbohydrate: 51 g 17% ◆ Dietary Fiber: 1 g 3% ◆ Sugars: 36 g ◆ Protein: 4 g ◆ Vitamin A: 4% ◆ Vitamin C: 2% ◆ Calcium: 6% ◆ Iron: 4% ◆ **DIETARY EXCHANGES:** 1½ Starch, 2 Fruit, 2 Fat OR 3½ Carbohydrate, 2 Fat

Golden Pecan Pie

PREP TIME: 30 MINUTES (READY IN 3 HOURS 20 MINUTES) ◆ YIELD: 8 SERVINGS

CRUST
   1 refrigerated pie crust (from 15-oz. pkg.) or
     Pastry for One-Crust Pie (page 385)

FILLING
   ⅓ cup firmly packed brown sugar
   1½ teaspoons all-purpose flour
   1¼ cups light corn syrup
   1¼ teaspoons vanilla
   3 eggs
   1½ cups pecan halves or broken pecans
   2 tablespoons margarine or butter, melted

1. Prepare pie crust for *one-crust filled pie* using 9-inch pie pan.

2. Heat oven to 375°F. In large bowl, combine brown sugar, flour, corn syrup, vanilla and eggs; beat well. Stir in pecans and margarine. Pour into crust-lined pan.

3. Bake at 375°F. for 40 to 50 minutes or until filling is puffed and pie is golden brown. Cool 2 hours or until completely cooled. Store in refrigerator.

NUTRITION INFORMATION PER SERVING: Serving Size: ⅛ of Recipe ◆ Calories: 510 ◆ Calories from Fat: 230 ◆ **% DAILY VALUE:** Total Fat: 25 g 38% ◆ Saturated Fat: 5 g 25% ◆ Cholesterol: 85 mg 28% ◆ Sodium: 230 mg 10% ◆ Total Carbohydrate: 66 g 22% ◆ Dietary Fiber: 2 g 8% ◆ Sugars: 30 g ◆ Protein: 5 g ◆ Vitamin A: 6% ◆ Vitamin C: 0% ◆ Calcium: 4% ◆ Iron: 6% ◆ **DIETARY EXCHANGES:** 1½ Starch, 3 Fruit, 5 Fat OR 4½ Carbohydrate, 5 Fat

VARIATION

Orange Pecan Pie: Add ½ teaspoon grated orange peel to filling. If desired, garnish with candied orange peel.

Chocolate Mousse Angel Pie

PREP TIME: 30 MINUTES (READY IN 3 HOURS) ◆ YIELD: 8 SERVINGS

MERINGUE SHELL
   3 egg whites, room temperature
   ¼ teaspoon cream of tartar
     Dash salt
   ¾ cup sugar
   ½ teaspoon vanilla

FILLING
   1 (6-oz.) pkg. (1 cup) semisweet chocolate
     chips
   ¼ cup water
   ⅛ to ¼ teaspoon almond extract
   1½ cups whipping cream, whipped
     Sliced almonds, toasted*

1. Heat oven to 275°F. Generously butter 9-inch pie pan. In small bowl, combine egg whites, cream of tartar and salt; beat until soft peaks form. Gradually add sugar, beating until stiff peaks form. Add vanilla; beat well.

2. With metal spatula, spread meringue in bottom and up sides of buttered pan, building up sides as high as possible.

3. Bake at 275°F. for 1 hour. Turn oven off; let stand in oven with door ajar for 1 hour. Remove meringue shell from oven.

4. In small saucepan, combine chocolate chips and water; cook over low heat, stirring constantly until smooth. Remove from heat; stir in almond extract. Cool 30 minutes.

5. Fold chocolate mixture into 2 cups of the whipped cream. Spread filling in cooled meringue shell. Store in refrigerator. When ready to serve, garnish with remaining whipped cream and toasted sliced almonds.

TIP: * To toast almonds, spread on cookie sheet; bake at 350°F. for 5 to 7 minutes or until light golden brown, stirring occasionally. Or spread in thin layer in microwave-safe pie pan. Microwave on HIGH for 4 to 7 minutes or until light golden brown, stirring frequently.

NUTRITION INFORMATION PER SERVING: Serving Size: ⅛ of Recipe ◆ Calories: 360 ◆ Calories from Fat: 210 ◆ **% DAILY VALUE:** Total Fat: 23 g 35% ◆ Saturated Fat: 14 g 70% ◆ Cholesterol: 60 mg 20% ◆ Sodium: 55 mg 2% ◆ Total Carbohydrate: 34 g 11% ◆ Dietary Fiber: 1 g 4% ◆ Sugars: 32 g ◆ Protein: 3 g ◆ Vitamin A: 15% ◆ Vitamin C: 0% ◆ Calcium: 4% ◆ Iron: 4% ◆ **DIETARY EXCHANGES:** 1 Starch, 1½ Fruit, 4½ Fat OR 2½ Carbohydrate, 4½ Fat

Chocolate Cashew Pie

PREP TIME: 35 MINUTES (READY IN 3 HOURS
30 MINUTES) ◆ YIELD: 10 SERVINGS

CRUST
1 refrigerated pie crust (from 15-oz. pkg.) or
   Pastry for One-Crust Pie (page 385)

FILLING AND TOPPING
¾ cup light corn syrup
½ cup sugar
3 tablespoons margarine or butter, melted
1 teaspoon vanilla
3 eggs
1 (6-oz.) pkg. (1 cup) semisweet chocolate
   chips
1 cup cashew halves
10 whole cashews
   Whipped cream, if desired*

1. Prepare pie crust for *one-crust filled pie* using
9-inch pie pan.
2. Heat oven to 325°F. In large bowl, combine corn syrup, sugar, margarine, vanilla and
eggs; beat with wire whisk until well
blended. Reserve 2 tablespoons chocolate
chips for topping. Stir in remaining chocolate chips and cashew halves. Spread evenly
in crust-lined pan.
3. Bake at 325°F. for 45 to 55 minutes or
until pie is deep golden brown and filling is
set. Cover edge of crust with strips of foil
after 15 to 20 minutes of baking to prevent
excessive browning. Cool 2 hours or until
completely cooled.
4. Meanwhile, line cookie sheet with waxed
paper. In small saucepan, melt reserved
2 tablespoons chocolate chips over low heat.
Dip each whole cashew in chocolate. Place
on lined cookie sheet. Refrigerate 15 to
20 minutes or until chocolate is set. Garnish
pie with whipped cream and chocolate-
dipped cashews. Store in refrigerator.

> **TIP:** *To flavor whipped cream, fold in sweet-
> ened cocoa mix, grated citrus peel, spices or a
> favorite liqueur.

NUTRITION INFORMATION PER SERVING: Serving Size: ⅒ of
Recipe ◆ Calories: 500 ◆ Calories from Fat: 250 ◆ % DAILY VALUE:
Total Fat: 28 g 43% ◆ Saturated Fat: 11 g 55% ◆ Cholesterol:
90 mg 30% ◆ Sodium: 260 mg 11% ◆ Total Carbohydrate:
55 g 18% ◆ Dietary Fiber: 2 g 8% ◆ Sugars: 31 g ◆ Protein: 6 g ◆ Vitamin A: 10% ◆ Vitamin C: 0% ◆ Calcium: 4% ◆ Iron: 10% ◆
DIETARY EXCHANGES: 2 Starch, 1½ Fruit, 5½ Fat OR 3½ Carbohydrate, 5½ Fat

Crumbleberry Pear Pie

Crumbleberry Pear Pie

PREP TIME: 30 MINUTES (READY IN 1 HOUR 30 MINUTES)
◆ YIELD: 8 SERVINGS

CRUST
1 refrigerated pie crust (from 15-oz. pkg.) or
   Pastry for One-Crust Pie (page 385)

FILLING
½ cup butter
½ cup sugar
2 eggs
1 cup finely ground almonds
¼ cup all-purpose flour
1 firm large pear, peeled, thinly sliced
1 cup fresh or frozen raspberries and/or
   blueberries, thawed

TOPPING
¾ cup all-purpose flour
⅓ cup firmly packed brown sugar
½ teaspoon almond extract
⅓ cup butter

1. Prepare pie crust for *one-crust filled pie* using
9-inch pie pan.
2. Heat oven to 350°F. In large bowl, combine ½ cup butter and sugar; beat until light
and fluffy. Add eggs 1 at a time, beating well
after each addition. Stir in almonds and
¼ cup flour just until evenly moistened.
Spread mixture in crust-lined pan. Arrange
pear slices on top of filling, overlapping
slightly.
3. Bake at 350°F. for 20 to 30 minutes or
until filling and pears are light golden brown.

4. Meanwhile, in medium bowl, combine ¾ cup flour, brown sugar and almond extract; mix well. With pastry blender or fork, cut in ⅓ cup butter until mixture resembles coarse crumbs.

5. Remove pie from oven. Sprinkle raspberries over pears; sprinkle with topping. Return to oven; bake an additional 18 to 28 minutes or until topping is golden brown. Serve warm. Store in refrigerator.

NUTRITION INFORMATION PER SERVING: Serving Size: ⅛ of Recipe ♦ Calories: 550 ♦ Calories from Fat: 310 ♦ **% DAILY VALUE:** Total Fat: 34 g 52% ♦ Saturated Fat: 16 g 80% ♦ Cholesterol: 110 mg 37% ♦ Sodium: 320 mg 13% ♦ Total Carbohydrate: 55 g 18% ♦ Dietary Fiber: 3 g 12% ♦ Sugars: 27 g ♦ Protein: 7 g ♦ Vitamin A: 15% ♦ Vitamin C: 6% ♦ Calcium: 6% ♦ Iron: 10% ♦ **DIETARY EXCHANGES:** 2½ Starch, 1 Fruit, 6½ Fat OR 3½ Carbohydrate, 6½ Fat

Custard Pie

PREP TIME: 30 MINUTES (READY IN 1 HOUR 30 MINUTES) ♦ YIELD: 8 SERVINGS

CRUST
  1 refrigerated pie crust (from 15-oz. pkg.) or Pastry for One-Crust Pie (page 385)

FILLING
  3 eggs
  ¾ cup sugar
  ¼ teaspoon salt
  ¼ teaspoon nutmeg or cinnamon
  1 teaspoon vanilla
2½ cups hot milk

1. Prepare pie crust for *one-crust filled pie* using 9-inch pie pan.

Chocolate Cashew Pie (page 398)

2. Heat oven to 400°F. In large bowl, beat eggs. Add sugar, salt, nutmeg and vanilla; mix well. Gradually blend in hot milk. Pour into crust-lined pan.

3. Bake at 400°F. for 25 to 30 minutes or until knife inserted near center comes out clean. Cool 30 minutes. Serve slightly warm or cold. Store in refrigerator.

NUTRITION INFORMATION PER SERVING: Serving Size: ⅛ of Recipe ♦ Calories: 260 ♦ Calories from Fat: 90 ♦ **% DAILY VALUE:** Total Fat: 10 g 15% ♦ Saturated Fat: 4 g 20% ♦ Cholesterol: 90 mg 30% ♦ Sodium: 230 mg 10% ♦ Total Carbohydrate: 36 g 12% ♦ Dietary Fiber: 0 g 0% ♦ Sugars: 23 g ♦ Protein: 6 g ♦ Vitamin A: 6% ♦ Vitamin C: 0% ♦ Calcium: 10% ♦ Iron: 2% ♦ **DIETARY EXCHANGES:** 2 Starch, ½ Fruit, 2 Fat OR 2½ Carbohydrate, 2 Fat

Sweet Potato Pie

PREP TIME: 30 MINUTES (READY IN 2 HOURS 10 MINUTES) ♦ YIELD: 8 SERVINGS

CRUST
  1 refrigerated pie crust (from 15-oz. pkg.) or Pastry for One-Crust Pie (page 385)

FILLING
1½ cups mashed canned sweet potatoes
  ⅔ cup firmly packed brown sugar
  1 cup half-and-half
  1 teaspoon cinnamon
  ½ teaspoon allspice
  1 tablespoon dry sherry or lemon juice
  2 eggs, beaten

TOPPING
  1 cup whipping cream
  2 tablespoons sugar
  1 teaspoon vanilla
    Pecan halves

1. Prepare pie crust for *one-crust filled pie* using 9-inch pie pan.

2. Heat oven to 425°F. In blender container or food processor bowl with metal blade, combine all filling ingredients; blend well. Pour into crust-lined pan.

3. Bake at 425°F. for 15 minutes. Reduce oven temperature to 350°F.; bake an additional 30 to 40 minutes or until center is set. Cool 45 minutes or until completely cooled.

4. In small bowl, combine whipping cream, sugar and vanilla; beat until soft peaks form. Garnish pie with whipped cream and pecan halves. Store in refrigerator.

NUTRITION INFORMATION PER SERVING: Serving Size: ⅛ of Recipe ♦ Calories: 430 ♦ Calories from Fat: 220 ♦ **% DAILY VALUE:** Total Fat: 24 g 37% ♦ Saturated Fat: 12 g 60% ♦ Cholesterol: 110 mg 37% ♦ Sodium: 200 mg 8% ♦ Total Carbohydrate: 48 g 16% ♦ Dietary Fiber: 1 g 4% ♦ Sugars: 32 g ♦ Protein: 5 g ♦ Vitamin A: 160% ♦ Vitamin C: 4% ♦ Calcium: 10% ♦ Iron: 8% ♦ **DIETARY EXCHANGES:** 1½ Starch, 1½ Fruit, 4½ Fat OR 3 Carbohydrate, 4½ Fat

Lemon Chess Pie

PREP TIME: 30 MINUTES (READY IN 4 HOURS 40 MINUTES) ◆ YIELD: 8 SERVINGS

CRUST
 1 refrigerated pie crust (from 15-oz. pkg.) or Pastry for One-Crust Pie (page 385)

FILLING
 ⅓ cup margarine or butter, softened
 1 cup sugar
 3 eggs
 2 tablespoons all-purpose flour
 1 tablespoon grated lemon peel
 ¼ cup fresh lemon juice
 ½ cup milk
 ¼ teaspoon nutmeg

1. Heat oven to 450°F. Prepare pie crust for *one-crust filled pie* using 9-inch pie pan. Bake at 450°F. for 5 to 8 minutes or until light brown. Reduce oven temperature to 325°F.
2. Meanwhile, in large bowl, combine margarine, sugar and eggs; beat well. Add flour, lemon peel, lemon juice and milk; blend well. (Mixture may look curdled.) Pour into partially baked crust. Sprinkle with nutmeg.
3. Bake at 325°F. for 40 to 45 minutes or until edge of filling begins to brown and center is almost set. Cover edge of crust with strips of foil after 15 to 20 minutes of baking to prevent excessive browning. Cool 30 minutes. Refrigerate at least 3 hours before serving. If desired, serve with whipped cream. Store in refrigerator.

NUTRITION INFORMATION PER SERVING: Serving Size: ⅛ of Recipe ◆ Calories: 330 ◆ Calories from Fat: 150 ◆ **% DAILY VALUE:** Total Fat: 17 g 26% ◆ Saturated Fat: 5 g 25% ◆ Cholesterol: 85 mg 28% ◆ Sodium: 230 mg 10% ◆ Total Carbohydrate: 41 g 14% ◆ Dietary Fiber: 0 g 0% ◆ Sugars: 27 g ◆ Protein: 4 g ◆ Vitamin A: 10% ◆ Vitamin C: 4% ◆ Calcium: 4% ◆ Iron: 4% ◆ **DIETARY EXCHANGES:** 1 Starch, 1½ Fruit, 3½ Fat OR 2½ Carbohydrate, 3½ Fat

Black Bottom Pie

PREP TIME: 40 MINUTES (READY IN 3 HOURS 35 MINUTES) ◆ YIELD: 10 SERVINGS

CRUST
 1 refrigerated pie crust (from 15-oz. pkg.) or Pastry for One-Crust Pie (page 385)

CHOCOLATE LAYER
 ½ cup sugar
 ⅓ cup unsweetened cocoa
 ½ cup light corn syrup
 1 teaspoon vanilla
 3 eggs
 ¼ cup margarine or butter, melted

CUSTARD LAYER
 ⅓ cup sugar
 2 tablespoons cornstarch
 Dash salt
 2 cups milk
 4 eggs, well beaten
 ½ teaspoon vanilla
 2 teaspoons rum extract*

TOPPING
 1 cup whipping cream, whipped
 Chocolate curls, if desired

1. Prepare pie crust for *one-crust filled pie* using 9-inch pie pan.
2. Heat oven to 350°F. In large bowl, combine ½ cup sugar and cocoa. Add corn syrup, 1 teaspoon vanilla and 3 eggs; beat well. Stir in margarine. Pour into crust-lined pan. Bake at 350°F. for 30 to 40 minutes or until center is set. (Chocolate layer will be puffy when removed from oven.) Cool 45 minutes or until completely cooled.
3. Meanwhile, in small saucepan, combine ⅓ cup sugar, cornstarch, salt, milk and 4 eggs; mix well. Cook over medium heat, stirring constantly, until mixture boils and thickens. Remove from heat; stir in vanilla and rum extract. Cover with plastic wrap; cool 30 minutes.
4. Spoon cooled custard over cooled chocolate layer. Refrigerate at least 1 hour before serving. Top with whipped cream; garnish with chocolate curls. Store in refrigerator.

TIP: * If desired, substitute 2 to 4 tablespoons light rum, bourbon, brandy or Irish whiskey.

NUTRITION INFORMATION PER SERVING: Serving Size: ¹⁄₁₀ of Recipe ◆ Calories: 430 ◆ Calories from Fat: 220 ◆ **% DAILY VALUE:** Total Fat: 24 g 37% ◆ Saturated Fat: 10 g 50% ◆ Cholesterol: 190 mg 63% ◆ Sodium: 250 mg 10% ◆ Total Carbohydrate: 46 g 15% ◆ Dietary Fiber: 1 g 4% ◆ Sugars: 27 g ◆ Protein: 8 g ◆ Vitamin A: 15% ◆ Vitamin C: 0% ◆ Calcium: 10% ◆ Iron: 6% ◆ **DIETARY EXCHANGES:** 1 Starch, 2 Fruit, ½ Medium-Fat Meat, 4½ Fat OR 3 Carbohydrate, ½ Medium-Fat Meat, 4½ Fat

Sour Cream Raisin Pie

PREP TIME: 30 MINUTES (READY IN 3 HOURS)
◆ YIELD: 8 SERVINGS

CRUST
 1 refrigerated pie crust (from 15-oz. pkg.) or
   Pastry for One-Crust Pie (page 385)

FILLING
 1½ cups raisins
  ¾ cup sugar
  ¼ cup cornstarch
  ½ teaspoon cinnamon
  ¼ teaspoon salt
  ¼ teaspoon nutmeg
   2 cups milk
   3 egg yolks, beaten
   1 cup sour cream
   1 tablespoon lemon juice

TOPPING
 1 cup whipping cream, whipped

1. Heat oven to 450°F. Prepare pie crust for *one-crust baked shell* using 9-inch pie pan. Bake at 450°F. for 9 to 11 minutes or until light golden brown. Cool 30 minutes or until completely cooled.
2. Meanwhile, in medium saucepan, combine raisins, sugar, cornstarch, cinnamon, salt and nutmeg; mix well. Stir in milk until smooth. Cook over medium heat until mixture boils, stirring constantly. Boil 1 minute. Remove from heat.
3. Stir about ¼ cup hot raisin mixture into egg yolks. Gradually stir yolk mixture into hot mixture in saucepan. Add sour cream; mix well. Cook just until mixture begins to bubble, stirring constantly.
4. Remove from heat; stir in lemon juice. Cool 10 minutes. Pour into cooled baked shell. Refrigerate 2 hours or until set. Top with whipped cream. Store in refrigerator.

NUTRITION INFORMATION PER SERVING: Serving Size: ⅛ of Recipe ◆ Calories: 520 ◆ Calories from Fat: 240 ◆ **% DAILY VALUE:** Total Fat: 27 g 42% ◆ Saturated Fat: 15 g 75% ◆ Cholesterol: 145 mg 48% ◆ Sodium: 230 mg 10% ◆ Total Carbohydrate: 62 g 21% ◆ Dietary Fiber: 1 g 4% ◆ Sugars: 43 g ◆ Protein: 6 g ◆ Vitamin A: 20% ◆ Vitamin C: 2% ◆ Calcium: 15% ◆ Iron: 6% ◆ **DIETARY EXCHANGES:** 2 Starch, 2 Fruit, 5½ Fat OR 4 Carbohydrate, 5½ Fat

VARIATION
Sour Cream Raisin Meringue Pie: Heat oven to 350°F. Substitute meringue for 1 cup whipping cream. After pouring filling into cooled baked shell, in small bowl, combine 3 egg whites and ¼ teaspoon cream of tartar; beat at medium speed for about 1 minute or until soft peaks form. Gradually add ¼ cup sugar 1 tablespoon at a time, beating at high speed until stiff peaks form and sugar is dissolved. Spoon meringue onto hot filling; spread to edge of crust to seal well and prevent shrinkage. Bake at 350°F. for 10 to 15 minutes or until meringue is light golden brown. Cool completely. Store in refrigerator.

Rum-Coconut-Key Lime Pie

PREP TIME: 20 MINUTES (READY IN 3 HOURS 50 MINUTES) ◆ YIELD: 10 SERVINGS

CRUST
 1 cup coconut, toasted*
 6 tablespoons margarine or butter, melted
 12 creme-filled vanilla sandwich cookies, finely
    crushed (about 1½ cups)

FILLING
 1 (14-oz.) can sweetened condensed milk
   (not evaporated)
 1 (8-oz.) pkg. cream cheese, softened
 ½ cup Key lime juice or lime juice
 ½ teaspoon rum extract

1. Reserve 1 tablespoon toasted coconut for topping. In 9-inch pie pan, combine remaining coconut, margarine and cookie crumbs; mix well. Press in bottom and up sides of pan. Refrigerate 30 minutes or until set.
2. In large bowl, combine sweetened condensed milk and cream cheese; beat until smooth and fluffy. Add lime juice and rum extract; mix well. Pour into crust-lined pan. Top with reserved coconut. Refrigerate at least 3 hours or until set. Store in refrigerator.

> **TIP:** *To toast coconut, spread on cookie sheet; bake at 350°F. for 6 to 8 minutes or until light golden brown, stirring occasionally.

NUTRITION INFORMATION PER SERVING: Serving Size: ¹⁄₁₀ of Recipe ◆ Calories: 380 ◆ Calories from Fat: 220 ◆ **% DAILY VALUE:** Total Fat: 24 g 37% ◆ Saturated Fat: 12 g 60% ◆ Cholesterol: 40 mg 13% ◆ Sodium: 240 mg 10% ◆ Total Carbohydrate: 35 g 12% ◆ Dietary Fiber: 1 g 4% ◆ Sugars: 25 g ◆ Protein: 6 g ◆ Vitamin A: 15% ◆ Vitamin C: 4% ◆ Calcium: 15% ◆ Iron: 6% ◆ **DIETARY EXCHANGES:** 2 Starch, ½ Fruit, 4½ Fat OR 2½ Carbohydrate, 4½ Fat

French Silk Chocolate Pie

PREP TIME: 50 MINUTES (READY IN 2 HOURS 50 MINUTES) ◆ YIELD: 10 SERVINGS

CRUST
- 1 refrigerated pie crust (from 15-oz. pkg.) or Pastry for One-Crust Pie (page 385)

FILLING
- 3 oz. unsweetened chocolate, cut into pieces
- 1 cup butter, softened (do not use margarine)
- 1 cup sugar
- ½ teaspoon vanilla
- 4 pasteurized eggs* or 1 cup refrigerated or frozen fat-free egg product, thawed

TOPPING
- ½ cup sweetened whipped cream
- Chocolate curls, if desired

1. Heat oven to 450°F. Prepare pie crust for *one-crust baked shell* using 9-inch pie pan. Bake at 450°F. for 9 to 11 minutes or until light golden brown. Cool 30 minutes or until completely cooled.

2. Melt chocolate in small saucepan over low heat; cool. In small bowl, beat butter until fluffy. Gradually add sugar, beating until light and fluffy. Add cooled chocolate and vanilla; blend well.

3. Add eggs 1 at a time, beating at high speed for 2 minutes after each addition. Beat until mixture is smooth and fluffy. Pour into cooled baked shell. Refrigerate at least 2 hours before serving. Top with whipped cream and chocolate curls. Store in refrigerator.

French Silk Chocolate Pie

Lemon Meringue Pie

TIP: * Pasteurized eggs are uncooked eggs that have been heat-treated to kill bacteria that can cause food poisoning and gastrointestinal distress. Because the eggs in this recipe are not cooked, be sure to use pasteurized eggs. They can be found in the dairy case at large supermarkets.

NUTRITION INFORMATION PER SERVING: Serving Size: ⅟₁₀ of Recipe ◆ Calories: 470 ◆ Calories from Fat: 320 ◆ % DAILY VALUE: Total Fat: 35 g 54% ◆ Saturated Fat: 20 g 100% ◆ Cholesterol: 155 mg 52% ◆ Sodium: 300 mg 13% ◆ Total Carbohydrate: 34 g 11% ◆ Dietary Fiber: 1 g 4% ◆ Sugars: 22 g ◆ Protein: 4 g ◆ Vitamin A: 20% ◆ Vitamin C: 0% ◆ Calcium: 4% ◆ Iron: 6% ◆ DIETARY EXCHANGES: 1 Starch, 1½ Fruit, 7 Fat OR 2½ Carbohydrate, 7 Fat

Lemon Meringue Pie

PREP TIME: 1 HOUR (READY IN 5 HOURS 15 MINUTES) ◆ YIELD: 8 SERVINGS

CRUST
- 1 refrigerated pie crust (from 15-oz. pkg.) or Pastry for One-Crust Pie (page 385)

FILLING
- 1¼ cups sugar
- ⅓ cup cornstarch
- ½ teaspoon salt
- 1½ cups cold water
- 3 egg yolks
- 2 tablespoons margarine or butter
- 1 tablespoon grated lemon peel
- ½ cup fresh lemon juice

MERINGUE
- 3 egg whites
- ¼ teaspoon cream of tartar
- ½ teaspoon vanilla
- ¼ cup sugar

1. Heat oven to 450°F. Prepare pie crust for *one-crust baked shell* using 9-inch pie pan. Bake at 450°F. for 9 to 11 minutes or until light golden brown. Cool 30 minutes or until completely cooled.

2. Meanwhile, in medium saucepan, combine 1¼ cups sugar, cornstarch and salt; mix well. Gradually stir in cold water until

smooth. Cook over medium heat until mixture boils, stirring constantly. Boil 1 minute, stirring constantly. Remove from heat.

3. In small bowl, beat egg yolks. Stir about ¼ cup of hot mixture into egg yolks. Gradually stir yolk mixture into hot mixture in saucepan. Cook over low heat until mixture boils, stirring constantly. Boil 1 minute, stirring constantly.

4. Remove from heat; stir in margarine, lemon peel and lemon juice. Cool 15 minutes or until slightly cooled. Pour into cooled baked shell.

5. Reduce oven temperature to 350°F. In small, deep bowl, combine egg whites, cream of tartar and vanilla; beat at medium speed for about 1 minute or until soft peaks form. Add sugar 1 tablespoon at a time, beating at high speed until stiff glossy peaks form and sugar is dissolved. Spoon meringue onto hot filling; spread to edge of crust to seal well and prevent shrinkage.

6. Bake at 350°F. for 12 to 15 minutes or until meringue is light golden brown. Cool 1 hour or until completely cooled. Refrigerate 3 hours or until filling is set. Store in refrigerator.

NUTRITION INFORMATION PER SERVING: Serving Size: ⅛ of Recipe ♦ Calories: 350 ♦ Calories from Fat: 110 ♦ **% DAILY VALUE:** Total Fat: 12 g 18% ♦ Saturated Fat: 4 g 20% ♦ Cholesterol: 90 mg 30% ♦ Sodium: 290 mg 12% ♦ Total Carbohydrate: 57 g 19% ♦ Dietary Fiber: 0 g 0% ♦ Sugars: 39 g ♦ Protein: 3 g ♦ Vitamin A: 6% ♦ Vitamin C: 10% ♦ Calcium: 0% ♦ Iron: 2% ♦ **DIETARY EXCHANGES:** 1 Starch, 3 Fruit, 2 Fat OR 4 Carbohydrate, 2 Fat

COOK'S NOTE

HOW TO MAKE MERINGUE

Beat egg whites at high speed until soft  peaks form. At the soft peak stage, egg whites will curl down when beaters are lifted. Then, gradually add sugar, 1 tablespoon at a time, beating continually until the sugar is completely dissolved.

 Continue beating until stiff peaks form. At this stage, the egg whites remain upright when the beaters are lifted out of the mixture.

Old-Fashioned Pumpkin Pie

Old-Fashioned Pumpkin Pie

PREP TIME: 25 MINUTES (READY IN 4 HOURS)
♦ YIELD: 8 SERVINGS

CRUST
  1 refrigerated pie crust (from 15-oz. pkg.) or Pastry for One-Crust Pie (page 385)

FILLING
  ¾ cup sugar
  1½ teaspoons pumpkin pie spice
  ½ teaspoon salt
  1 (16-oz.) can (2 cups) pumpkin
  1 (12-oz.) can (1½ cups) evaporated milk
  2 eggs, beaten

TOPPING
  ½ cup whipping cream, whipped

1. Prepare pie crust for *one-crust filled pie* using 9-inch pie pan.

2. Heat oven to 425°F. In large bowl, combine all filling ingredients; blend well. Pour into crust-lined pan.

3. Bake at 425°F. for 15 minutes. Reduce oven temperature to 350°F.; bake an additional 40 to 50 minutes or until knife inserted near center comes out clean. Cool 30 minutes. Refrigerate at least 2 hours or until serving time. Just before serving, top with whipped cream. Store in refrigerator.

NUTRITION INFORMATION PER SERVING: Serving Size: ⅛ of Recipe ♦ Calories: 340 ♦ Calories from Fat: 150 ♦ **% DAILY VALUE:** Total Fat: 17 g 26% ♦ Saturated Fat: 9 g 45% ♦ Cholesterol: 90 mg 30% ♦ Sodium: 310 mg 13% ♦ Total Carbohydrate: 41 g 14% ♦ Dietary Fiber: 2 g 8% ♦ Sugars: 26 g ♦ Protein: 6 g ♦ Vitamin A: 260% ♦ Vitamin C: 4% ♦ Calcium: 15% ♦ Iron: 8% ♦ **DIETARY EXCHANGES:** 2 Starch, ½ Fruit, 3½ Fat OR 2½ Carbohydrate, 3½ Fat

VARIATION

Maple Pumpkin Pie: Substitute ½ cup maple-flavored syrup for ½ cup of the evaporated milk.

Pineapple-Macadamia Nut Tart

PREP TIME: 30 MINUTES (READY IN 3 HOURS 20 MINUTES) ◆ YIELD: 10 SERVINGS

CRUST
1 refrigerated pie crust (from 15-oz. pkg.) or Pastry for One-Crust Pie (page 385)

FILLING
2 tablespoons margarine or butter
¼ cup sugar
1 cup dark corn syrup
½ teaspoon rum extract
3 eggs
1 cup macadamia nuts
1 (8-oz.) can pineapple slices, drained, halved

1. Place cookie sheet in oven on middle rack to heat. Heat oven to 375°F. Prepare pie crust for *one-crust filled pie* using 10-inch tart pan with removable bottom.
2. In medium saucepan, melt margarine over low heat; remove from heat. Add sugar, corn syrup, rum extract and eggs; beat with wire whisk until well blended.
3. Arrange macadamia nuts in bottom of crust-lined pan. Arrange pineapple around edge of tart over nuts. Carefully pour egg mixture over pineapple and nuts.
4. Place tart in oven on heated cookie sheet. Bake at 375°F. for 40 to 50 minutes or until top of tart is deep golden brown. Cool 2 hours or until completely cooled. Store in refrigerator.

NUTRITION INFORMATION PER SERVING: Serving Size: ¹⁄₁₀ of Recipe ◆ Calories: 360 ◆ Calories from Fat: 170 ◆ **% DAILY VALUE:** Total Fat: 19 g 29% ◆ Saturated Fat: 5 g 25% ◆ Cholesterol: 70 mg 23% ◆ Sodium: 180 mg 8% ◆ Total Carbohydrate: 44 g 15% ◆ Dietary Fiber: 2 g 8% ◆ Sugars: 18 g ◆ Protein: 4 g ◆ Vitamin A: 4% ◆ Vitamin C: 2% ◆ Calcium: 4% ◆ Iron: 6% ◆ **DIETARY EXCHANGES:** 1 Starch, 2 Fruit, 3½ Fat OR 3 Carbohydrate, 3½ Fat

Triple Chocolate-Raspberry Tart

PREP TIME: 25 MINUTES ◆ YIELD: 8 SERVINGS

1¼ cups chocolate wafer cookie crumbs (20 cookies)
5 tablespoons raspberry spreadable fruit, melted
2 tablespoons semisweet chocolate chips
½ teaspoon oil
2 tablespoons white vanilla chips
2 cups fresh raspberries

1. Heat oven to 400°F. Spray 9-inch tart pan with removable bottom with nonstick cooking spray. In small bowl, combine cookie crumbs and 2 tablespoons of the melted spreadable fruit; mix well. Spray hands with nonstick cooking spray. Press mixture evenly in bottom of sprayed pan.
2. Bake at 400°F. for 5 minutes. Remove from oven; spread remaining 3 tablespoons spreadable fruit over crust. Freeze 5 to 8 minutes or until cool.
3. While crust is cooling, in small microwave-safe cup, combine chocolate chips and ¼ teaspoon of the oil.* Microwave on HIGH for 40 to 60 seconds or until melted. In another microwave-safe cup, combine vanilla chips and remaining ¼ teaspoon oil. Microwave on HIGH for 30 to 40 seconds or until melted.
4. Arrange raspberries over cooled crust; drizzle with melted chocolate chips and vanilla chips. Serve immediately or refrigerate until serving time.
5. To serve, remove outer ring from tart pan; do not remove bottom of pan.

> TIP: *To melt chips in separate small saucepans, combine each kind of chip with ¼ teaspoon oil; heat and stir over low heat until melted.

NUTRITION INFORMATION PER SERVING: Serving Size: ⅛ of Recipe ◆ Calories: 150 ◆ Calories from Fat: 35 ◆ **% DAILY VALUE:** Total Fat: 4 g 6% ◆ Saturated Fat: 2 g 10% ◆ Cholesterol: 0 mg 0% ◆ Sodium: 95 mg 4% ◆ Total Carbohydrate: 26 g 9% ◆ Dietary Fiber: 2 g 8% ◆ Sugars: 19 g ◆ Protein: 2 g ◆ Vitamin A: 0% ◆ Vitamin C: 8% ◆ Calcium: 0% ◆ Iron: 6% ◆ **DIETARY EXCHANGES:** ½ Starch, 1 Fruit, 1 Fat OR 1½ Carbohydrate, 1 Fat

Pumpkin Tart with Caramel-Rum-Raisin Sauce

PREP TIME: 35 MINUTES (READY IN 2 HOURS
25 MINUTES) ◆ YIELD: 12 SERVINGS

CRUST
 1 refrigerated pie crust (from 15-oz. pkg.) or
  Pastry for One-Crust Pie (page 385)

FILLING
 ¾ cup sugar
 ½ teaspoon ginger
 ¾ teaspoon cinnamon
 ⅛ teaspoon cloves
 ½ cup milk
 1 (15-oz.) can pumpkin
 2 eggs

SAUCE
 1 cup firmly packed brown sugar
 ¼ cup whipping cream
 ¼ cup dark rum
 ¼ cup dark corn syrup
 ½ cup raisins

1. Place cookie sheet in oven on middle rack to heat. Heat oven to 450°F. Prepare pie crust for *one-crust filled pie* using 10-inch tart pan with removable bottom.
2. In large bowl, combine all filling ingredients; blend well. Pour into crust-lined pan.
3. Place tart in oven on heated cookie sheet. Bake at 450°F. for 35 to 50 minutes or until crust is deep golden brown. Cool 1 hour.
4. In medium saucepan, combine all sauce ingredients; mix well. Cook over medium heat, stirring constantly, until mixture comes to a boil. Reduce heat to low; simmer 5 minutes, stirring constantly. Serve sauce with tart. Store in refrigerator.

NUTRITION INFORMATION PER SERVING: Serving Size: ¹⁄₁₂ of Recipe ◆ Calories: 310 ◆ Calories from Fat: 70 ◆ **% DAILY VALUE:** Total Fat: 8 g 12% ◆ Saturated Fat: 3 g 15% ◆ Cholesterol: 45 mg 15% ◆ Sodium: 105 mg 4% ◆ Total Carbohydrate: 53 g 18% ◆ Dietary Fiber: 1 g 4% ◆ Sugars: 39 g ◆ Protein: 3 g ◆ Vitamin A: 160% ◆ Vitamin C: 2% ◆ Calcium: 6% ◆ Iron: 8% ◆ **DIETARY EXCHANGES:** 1 Starch, 2½ Fruit, 1½ Fat OR 3½ Carbohydrate, 1½ Fat

White Chocolate-Cranberry-Pecan Tart

PREP TIME: 30 MINUTES (READY IN 3 HOURS
15 MINUTES) ◆ YIELD: 12 SERVINGS

CRUST
 1 refrigerated pie crust (from 15-oz. pkg.) or
  Pastry for One-Crust Pie (page 385)

FILLING
 1 cup fresh or frozen cranberries
 1 cup pecan halves
 1 cup white vanilla chips
 3 eggs
 ¾ cup firmly packed brown sugar
 ¾ cup light corn syrup
 2 tablespoons all-purpose flour
 1 teaspoon grated orange peel

1. Place cookie sheet in oven on middle rack to heat. Heat oven to 400°F. Prepare pie crust for *one-crust filled pie* using 10-inch tart pan with removable bottom.
2. Layer cranberries, pecans and white vanilla chips in crust-lined pan. In large bowl, beat eggs. Add brown sugar, corn syrup, flour and orange peel; blend well. Pour over cranberry mixture.
3. Place tart in oven on heated cookie sheet. Bake at 400°F. for 35 to 45 minutes or until crust is golden brown and filling is set in center. Cover with spray-coated foil after 25 minutes of baking. Cool 2 hours or until completely cooled. If desired, serve with whipped cream. Store in refrigerator.

NUTRITION INFORMATION PER SERVING: Serving Size: ¹⁄₁₂ of Recipe ◆ Calories: 360 ◆ Calories from Fat: 140 ◆ **% DAILY VALUE:** Total Fat: 16 g 25% ◆ Saturated Fat: 5 g 25% ◆ Cholesterol: 60 mg 20% ◆ Sodium: 125 mg 5% ◆ Total Carbohydrate: 50 g 17% ◆ Dietary Fiber: 1 g 4% ◆ Sugars: 31 g ◆ Protein: 4 g ◆ Vitamin A: 2% ◆ Vitamin C: 0% ◆ Calcium: 6% ◆ Iron: 4% ◆ **DIETARY EXCHANGES:** 1 Starch, 2½ Fruit, 3 Fat OR 3½ Carbohydrate, 3 Fat

Frozen Cappuccino Pie

Frozen Cappuccino Pie

PREP TIME: 20 MINUTES (READY IN 1 HOUR 20 MINUTES)
◆ YIELD: 8 SERVINGS

    2 tablespoons instant espresso powder or
        dark-roast coffee granules
    1 tablespoon boiling water
    15 chocolate wafer cookies
    6 fat-free devil's food cookie cakes, cut up
    1 quart (4 cups) frozen nonfat vanilla yogurt
    ¼ cup powdered sugar
        Dash nutmeg or cinnamon, if desired

1. Heat oven to 375°F. Spray 9-inch pie pan with nonstick cooking spray. In small bowl, dissolve espresso powder in boiling water. Set aside to cool.

2. Place wafer cookies in food processor bowl with metal blade; process 10 to 15 seconds or until fine crumbs form. Add cut-up cookie cakes; process 10 to 15 seconds or until fine. Place crumbs in sprayed pan. With spoon, press in bottom and up sides of pan. Bake at 375°F. for 5 minutes. Cool in freezer or refrigerator.

3. Meanwhile, spoon frozen yogurt and powdered sugar into food processor bowl with metal blade; process 10 to 15 seconds or until yogurt is slightly softened. While machine is running, gradually pour dissolved espresso through feed tube and process an additional 10 seconds or just until blended.

4. Quickly spoon mixture into cooled crust; spread evenly. Sprinkle with nutmeg. Freeze at least 1 hour or until firm. If desired, garnish with chocolate coffee beans.

NUTRITION INFORMATION PER SERVING: Serving Size: ⅛ of Recipe
◆ Calories: 210 ◆ Calories from Fat: 20 ◆ **% DAILY VALUE:** Total Fat: 2 g 3% ◆ Saturated Fat: 0 g 0% ◆ Cholesterol: 0 mg 0% ◆ Sodium: 150 mg 6% ◆ Total Carbohydrate: 43 g 14% ◆ Dietary Fiber: 1 g 3% ◆ Sugars: 32 g ◆ Protein: 5 g ◆ Vitamin A: 0% ◆ Vitamin C: 0% ◆ Calcium: 10% ◆ Iron: 2% ◆ **DIETARY EXCHANGES:** 1½ Starch, 1½ Fruit OR 3 Carbohydrate

Cream Cheese Jewel Tart

PREP TIME: 30 MINUTES (READY IN 3 HOURS)
◆ YIELD: 8 SERVINGS

CRUST
    1 refrigerated pie crust (from 15-oz. pkg.) or
        Pastry for One-Crust Pie (page 385)
FILLING
    1 (8-oz.) pkg. cream cheese, softened
    ⅓ cup sugar
    1 tablespoon orange-flavored liqueur or
        orange juice
    4 cups assorted fresh whole berries (small
        strawberries, blueberries, raspberries
        and/or blackberries)
    ⅓ cup red currant jelly, melted

1. Heat oven to 450°F. Prepare pie crust for *one-crust baked shell* using 9-inch tart pan with removable bottom. Bake at 450°F. for 9 to 11 minutes or until light golden brown. Cool 30 minutes or until completely cooled.

2. In small bowl, combine cream cheese, sugar and liqueur; beat until smooth and well blended. Spread cream cheese mixture evenly in cooled baked shell.

3. Top with berries; brush berries with melted jelly to glaze. Refrigerate at least 2 hours before serving. Store in refrigerator.

NUTRITION INFORMATION PER SERVING: Serving Size: ⅛ of Recipe
◆ Calories: 320 ◆ Calories from Fat: 150 ◆ **% DAILY VALUE:** Total Fat: 17 g 26% ◆ Saturated Fat: 9 g 45% ◆ Cholesterol: 40 mg 13% ◆ Sodium: 190 mg 8% ◆ Total Carbohydrate: 39 g 13% ◆ Dietary Fiber: 3 g 12% ◆ Sugars: 20 g ◆ Protein: 3 g ◆ Vitamin A: 10% ◆ Vitamin C: 25% ◆ Calcium: 4% ◆ Iron: 4% ◆ **DIETARY EXCHANGES:** 1 Starch, 1½ Fruit, 3½ Fat OR 2½ Carbohydrate, 3½ Fat

Cream Cheese Jewel Tart

COOKIES
& CANDIES

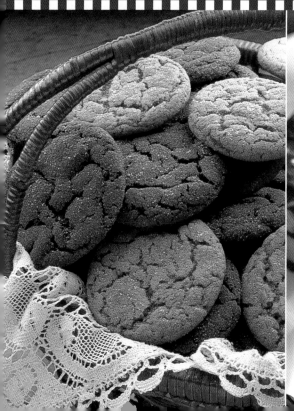

COOKIES & CANDIES

ookie jars, lunch boxes and dessert trays will all be the richer as you cook and bake your way through this special collection. You will find not only the traditional favorites—all-American chocolate chip cookies, fudgy brownies, rolled sugar cookies—but nearly four dozen treasured treats from around the world.

Chocolate Chip Cookies

PREP TIME: 40 MINUTES ✦ YIELD: 3 DOZEN COOKIES

- ¾ cup firmly packed brown sugar
- ½ cup sugar
- ½ cup margarine or butter, softened
- ½ cup shortening
- 1½ teaspoons vanilla
- 1 egg
- 1¾ cups all-purpose flour
- 1 teaspoon baking soda
- ½ teaspoon salt
- 1 (6-oz.) pkg. (1 cup) semisweet chocolate chips
- ½ cup chopped nuts or shelled sunflower seeds, if desired

1. Heat oven to 375°F. In large bowl, combine brown sugar, sugar, margarine and shortening; beat until light and fluffy. Add vanilla and egg; blend well.

2. Add flour, baking soda and salt; mix well. Stir in chocolate chips and nuts. Drop dough by rounded teaspoonfuls 2 inches apart onto ungreased cookie sheets.

3. Bake at 375°F. for 8 to 10 minutes or until light golden brown. Cool 1 minute; remove from cookie sheets.

HIGH ALTITUDE (*above 3500 feet*)**:** No change.

NUTRITION INFORMATION PER SERVING: Serving Size: 1 Cookie ◆ Calories: 140 ◆ Calories from Fat: 70 ◆ **% DAILY VALUE:** Total Fat: 8 g 12% ◆ Saturated Fat: 2 g 10% ◆ Cholesterol: 5 mg 2% ◆ Sodium: 100 mg 4% ◆ Total Carbohydrate: 15 g 5% ◆ Dietary Fiber: 1 g 2% ◆ Sugars: 10 g ◆ Protein: 1 g ◆ Vitamin A: 2% ◆ Vitamin C: 0% ◆ Calcium: 0% ◆ Iron: 4% ◆ **DIETARY EXCHANGES:** ½ Starch, ½ Fruit, 1½ Fat OR 1 Carbohydrate, 1½ Fat

VARIATIONS

Chocolate Chip Cookie Bars: Spread dough in ungreased 13 × 9-inch pan. Bake at 375°F. for 15 to 25 minutes or until light golden brown. Cool completely. Cut into bars. YIELD: 36 BARS

Chocolate Chip-Ice Cream Cookiewiches: Drop dough by heaping teaspoonfuls 3 inches apart onto ungreased cookie sheets. Bake at 375°F. for 9 to 14 minutes or until light golden brown. Cool 1 minute; remove from cookie sheets. Cool completely. To assemble each cookiewich, place scoop of favorite flavor ice cream on bottom side of 1 cookie; flatten ice cream slightly. Place another cookie, bottom side down, on top of ice cream. Gently press cookies together in center to form ice cream sandwich. Quickly wrap in foil. Freeze. YIELD: 12 COOKIEWICHES

Chocolate-Chocolate Chip Cookies: Use 1 cup margarine or butter; omit shortening. Decrease vanilla to 1 teaspoon. Add ¼ cup unsweetened cocoa with flour. Drop dough by teaspoonfuls 2 inches apart onto ungreased cookie sheets. Bake at 375°F. for 7 to 11 minutes or until set. Cool 1 minute; remove from cookie sheets. YIELD: 4 DOZEN COOKIES

Chocolate Chunk Cookies: Substitute 8 oz. coarsely chopped semisweet chocolate for chocolate chips. Drop dough by tablespoonfuls 3 inches apart onto ungreased cookie sheets. Bake at 375°F. for 9 to 12 minutes or until light golden brown. Immediately remove from cookie sheets. YIELD: 3 DOZEN COOKIES

Jumbo Candy Cookies: Omit ½ cup sugar and 1 cup semisweet chocolate chips, increase vanilla to 2 teaspoons. Stir 1 cup candy-coated chocolate pieces into dough. If necessary, refrigerate dough for easier handling. Shape dough into 2-inch balls. Place 4 inches apart on ungreased cookie sheets. Press an additional ½ cup candy-coated chocolate pieces into balls to decorate tops of cookies. Bake at 350°F. for 15 to 20 minutes or until light golden brown. Cool 2 minutes; remove from cookie sheets.

YIELD: 14 COOKIES

Maxi Chippers: For each cookie, use ⅓ cup of dough; place 4 inches apart on ungreased cookie sheets. Bake at 375°F. for 12 to 18 minutes or until light golden brown. Cool 1 minute; remove from cookie sheets.

YIELD: 10 COOKIES

Mini Chippers: Drop dough by ½ teaspoonfuls 1 inch apart onto ungreased cookie sheets. Bake at 375°F. for 5 to 7 minutes or until light golden brown. Immediately remove from cookie sheets.

YIELD: 12½ DOZEN COOKIES

COOK'S NOTE

TIPS FOR MAKING DROP COOKIES

The dough is spooned directly from the mixing bowl onto the cookie sheet. Use a teaspoon or tablespoon to scoop up some dough, then transfer it onto the baking sheet with a second spoon or a narrow rubber scraper. Keep the dough uniformly sized so cookies will bake evenly. Space them as the recipe directs to prevent them from running together. For giant cookies, try shaping the dough with an ice-cream scoop. Widen the spacing accordingly.

Double Chocolate Chip Cookies

PREP TIME: 30 MINUTES ♦ YIELD: 24 COOKIES

½ cup firmly packed brown sugar
¼ cup margarine or butter, softened
½ teaspoon vanilla
1 egg white
1 cup all-purpose flour
3 tablespoons unsweetened cocoa
½ teaspoon baking soda
⅛ teaspoon salt
½ cup semisweet chocolate chips

1. Heat oven to 375°F. In large bowl, combine brown sugar and margarine; beat until light and fluffy. Add vanilla and egg white; blend well.

2. Add flour, cocoa, baking soda and salt; mix well. Stir in chocolate chips. Drop dough by teaspoonfuls 2 inches apart onto ungreased cookie sheets.

3. Bake at 375°F. for 8 to 9 minutes or until set. DO NOT OVERBAKE. Cool 1 minute; remove from cookie sheets.

TIP: If desired, cookies can be glazed. In small bowl, combine ½ cup powdered sugar, 1½ teaspoons milk, 2 drops vanilla and, if desired, 2 drops butter flavor; stir to blend. Drizzle glaze over cookies.

HIGH ALTITUDE (*above 3500 feet*): Increase flour to 1 cup plus 2 tablespoons. Bake as directed above.

NUTRITION INFORMATION PER SERVING: Serving Size: 1 Cookie ♦ Calories: 70 ♦ Calories from Fat: 25 ♦ % DAILY VALUE: Total Fat: 3 g 5% ♦ Saturated Fat: 1 g 5% ♦ Cholesterol: 0 mg 0% ♦ Sodium: 65 mg 3% ♦ Total Carbohydrate: 11 g 4% ♦ Dietary Fiber: 1 g 2% ♦ Sugars: 7 g ♦ Protein: 1 g ♦ Vitamin A: 0% ♦ Vitamin C: 0% ♦ Calcium: 0% ♦ Iron: 2% ♦ DIETARY EXCHANGES: ½ Starch, ½ Fruit, ½ Fat OR 1 Carbohydrate, ½ Fat

---

COOK'S NOTE

ARRANGING AND BAKING THE BATCH

Begin each batch with a cool cookie sheet to prevent the cookies from spreading too much.

Arrange the dough on the cookie sheet with enough space between each cookie, as directed in the recipe, to allow for spreading as the cookies bake. Place the cookie sheet on a rack in the center of the oven, leaving space on all sides for air circulation.

In a conventional oven, it's best to bake just one sheet at a time. If you must do two at once, swap shelves and rotate trays halfway through the baking time. In a convection oven, which uses a fan to circulate air, you can bake several sheets at once. Convection baking will reduce baking time by several minutes; watch the cookies closely until you are sure how long to bake them.

German Chocolate Cake Mix Cookies

PREP TIME: 50 MINUTES ◆ YIELD: 4 DOZEN COOKIES

1 (1 lb. 2.25-oz.) pkg. pudding-included
   German chocolate cake mix
1 (6-oz.) pkg. (1 cup) semisweet chocolate
   chips
½ cup rolled oats
½ cup raisins
½ cup oil
2 eggs, slightly beaten

1. Heat oven to 350°F. In large bowl, combine all ingredients; blend well. Drop dough by rounded teaspoonfuls 2 inches apart onto ungreased cookie sheets.
2. Bake at 350°F. for 8 to 10 minutes or until set. Cool 1 minute; remove from cookie sheets.

HIGH ALTITUDE (*above 3500 feet*): Add ¼ cup flour to dry cake mix. Bake as directed above.

NUTRITION INFORMATION PER SERVING: Serving Size: 1 Cookie ◆ Calories: 100 ◆ Calories from Fat: 45 ◆ **% DAILY VALUE:** Total Fat: 5 g 8% ◆ Saturated Fat: 1 g 5% ◆ Cholesterol: 10 mg 3% ◆ Sodium: 70 mg 3% ◆ Total Carbohydrate: 13 g 4% ◆ Dietary Fiber: 1 g 2% ◆ Sugars: 7 g ◆ Protein: 1 g ◆ Vitamin A: 0% ◆ Vitamin C: 0% ◆ Calcium: 0% ◆ Iron: 2% ◆ **DIETARY EXCHANGES:** 1 Fruit, 1 Fat OR 1 Carbohydrate, 1 Fat

German Chocolate Cake Mix Cookies

Oatmeal Raisin Cookies

Oatmeal Raisin Cookies

PREP TIME: 45 MINUTES ◆ YIELD: 3½ DOZEN COOKIES

¾ cup sugar
¼ cup firmly packed brown sugar
½ cup margarine or butter, softened
½ teaspoon vanilla
1 egg
¾ cup all-purpose flour
½ teaspoon baking soda
½ teaspoon cinnamon
¼ teaspoon salt
1½ cups quick-cooking rolled oats
½ cup raisins
½ cup chopped nuts

1. Heat oven to 375°F. Grease cookie sheets. In large bowl, combine sugar, brown sugar and margarine; beat until light and fluffy. Add vanilla and egg; blend well.
2. Add flour, baking soda, cinnamon and salt; mix well. Stir in oats, raisins and nuts. Drop dough by rounded teaspoonfuls 2 inches apart onto greased cookie sheets.
3. Bake at 375°F. for 7 to 10 minutes or until edges are light golden brown. Cool 1 minute; remove from cookie sheets.

HIGH ALTITUDE (*above 3500 feet*): Increase flour to 1 cup. Bake as directed above.

NUTRITION INFORMATION PER SERVING: Serving Size: 1 Cookie ◆ Calories: 70 ◆ Calories from Fat: 25 ◆ **% DAILY VALUE:** Total Fat: 3 g 5% ◆ Saturated Fat: 0 g 0% ◆ Cholesterol: 5 mg 2% ◆ Sodium: 55 mg 2% ◆ Total Carbohydrate: 10 g 3% ◆ Dietary Fiber: 0 g 0% ◆ Sugars: 6 g ◆ Protein: 1 g ◆ Vitamin A: 2% ◆ Vitamin C: 0% ◆ Calcium: 0% ◆ Iron: 0% ◆ **DIETARY EXCHANGES:** ½ Starch, ½ Fat OR ½ Carbohydrate, ½ Fat

Giant Confetti Oatmeal Cookies

PREP TIME: 1 HOUR 25 MINUTES ✦ YIELD: 2 DOZEN LARGE COOKIES

¾ cup sugar
¾ cup firmly packed brown sugar
1 cup margarine or butter, softened
2 teaspoons vanilla
2 eggs
1⅔ cups all-purpose flour
1 teaspoon baking soda
½ teaspoon salt
2 cups rolled oats
2 cups miniature candy-coated chocolate
    pieces
1 cup raisins

1. Heat oven to 325°F. In large bowl, combine sugar, brown sugar and margarine; beat until light and fluffy. Add vanilla and eggs; blend well.
2. Add flour, baking soda and salt; mix well. Stir in oats, chocolate pieces and raisins; mix well. Drop dough by ¼ cupfuls about 3 inches apart onto ungreased cookie sheets.
3. Bake at 325°F. for 18 to 22 minutes or until golden brown. Cool 2 minutes; remove from cookie sheets.

HIGH ALTITUDE (*above 3500 feet*)**:** Increase flour to 2 cups. Bake as directed above.

NUTRITION INFORMATION PER SERVING: Serving Size: 1 Large Cookie ✦ Calories: 290 ✦ Calories from Fat: 110 ✦ **% DAILY VALUE:** Total Fat: 12 g 18% ✦ Saturated Fat: 4 g 20% ✦ Cholesterol: 20 mg 7% ✦ Sodium: 210 mg 9% ✦ Total Carbohydrate: 41 g 14% ✦ Dietary Fiber: 2 g 8% ✦ Sugars: 28 g ✦ Protein: 4 g ✦ Vitamin A: 8% ✦ Vitamin C: 0% ✦ Calcium: 4% ✦ Iron: 6% ✦ **DIETARY EXCHANGES:** 1 Starch, 1½ Fruit, 2½ Fat OR 2½ Carbohydrate, 2½ Fat

Giant Confetti Oatmeal Cookies

A BIT ABOUT SHORTENINGS

Shortenings (solid vegetable shortening, butter and margarine) give cookies tenderness and moistness. Butter offers more flavor and usually gives a crisper cookie, but the cookie and bar recipes in this chapter will all yield excellent results when made with regular butter or regular margarine.

For best results, do not use whipped margarines or butters and low-fat spreads. Their behavior in baking is unpredictable because they contain a higher proportion of water and air to make them more spreadable.

Vegetable oil does not allow the dough to incorporate air during beating. Do not use it as a substitution when the cookie recipe calls for solid shortening.

Coconut Macaroons

PREP TIME: 30 MINUTES ✦ YIELD: 12 COOKIES

2 egg whites
⅓ cup sugar
2 tablespoons all-purpose flour
    Dash salt
¼ teaspoon almond extract
2 cups coconut

1. Heat oven to 325°F. Grease and lightly flour cookie sheet. In medium bowl, beat egg whites until frothy. Add sugar, flour, salt and almond extract; mix well. Stir in coconut. Drop dough by tablespoonfuls 2 inches apart onto greased and floured cookie sheet.
2. Bake at 325°F. for 13 to 17 minutes or until set and light golden brown. Immediately remove from cookie sheet.

HIGH ALTITUDE (*above 3500 feet*)**:** No change.

NUTRITION INFORMATION PER SERVING: Serving Size: 1 Cookie ✦ Calories: 90 ✦ Calories from Fat: 35 ✦ **% DAILY VALUE:** Total Fat: 4 g 6% ✦ Saturated Fat: 4 g 20% ✦ Cholesterol: 0 mg 0% ✦ Sodium: 50 mg 2% ✦ Total Carbohydrate: 12 g 4% ✦ Dietary Fiber: 1 g 2% ✦ Sugars: 10 g ✦ Protein: 1 g ✦ Vitamin A: 0% ✦ Vitamin C: 0% ✦ Calcium: 0% ✦ Iron: 0% ✦ **DIETARY EXCHANGES:** ½ Starch, ½ Fruit, ½ Fat OR 1 Carbohydrate, ½ Fat

Frosted Maple Walnut Cookies

PREP TIME: 1 HOUR 30 MINUTES ◆ YIELD: 4½ DOZEN COOKIES

COOKIES
    2 cups firmly packed brown sugar
    1 cup margarine or butter, softened
    1 to 2 teaspoons maple flavor or extract
    3 eggs
2½ cups all-purpose flour
    1 cup whole wheat flour
    1 teaspoon baking soda
      Dash salt
1½ cups chopped walnuts

FROSTING
    4 cups powdered sugar
    3 to 4 tablespoons milk
    2 tablespoons margarine or butter, softened
    2 teaspoons maple flavor or extract

1. Heat oven to 350°F. In large bowl, combine brown sugar and 1 cup margarine; beat until light and fluffy. Add 1 to 2 teaspoons maple flavor and eggs; blend well.
2. Add all-purpose flour, whole wheat flour, baking soda and salt; mix well. Stir in walnuts. Drop by rounded tablespoonfuls 2 inches apart onto ungreased cookie sheets.
3. Bake at 350°F. for 7 to 9 minutes or until light golden brown. Cool 2 minutes; remove from cookie sheets. Cool 5 minutes or until completely cooled.
4. In medium bowl, combine all frosting ingredients; beat until smooth. Spread each cooled cookie with frosting.

HIGH ALTITUDE (*above 3500 feet*)**:** Increase all-purpose flour to 2¾ cups. Bake as directed above.

NUTRITION INFORMATION PER SERVING: Serving Size: 1 Cookie ◆ Calories: 160 ◆ Calories from Fat: 50 ◆ **% DAILY VALUE:** Total Fat: 6 g 9% ◆ Saturated Fat: 1 g 5% ◆ Cholesterol: 10 mg 3% ◆ Sodium: 80 mg 3% ◆ Total Carbohydrate: 24 g 8% ◆ Dietary Fiber: 1 g 2% ◆ Sugars: 17 g ◆ Protein: 2 g ◆ Vitamin A: 4% ◆ Vitamin C: 0% ◆ Calcium: 0% ◆ Iron: 4% ◆ **DIETARY EXCHANGES:** 1 Starch, ½ Fruit, 1 Fat OR 1½ Carbohydrate, 1 Fat

---

COOK'S NOTE

STORING NUTS

To keep shelled nuts fresh, store them in the refrigerator or freezer in an airtight container or resealable plastic bag.

Peanut Butter Cookies

PREP TIME: 45 MINUTES ◆ YIELD: 4 DOZEN COOKIES

    ½ cup sugar
    ½ cup firmly packed brown sugar
    ½ cup margarine or butter, softened
    ½ cup peanut butter
    1 teaspoon vanilla
    1 egg
1¼ cups all-purpose flour
    1 teaspoon baking soda
    ½ teaspoon salt
    4 teaspoons sugar

1. Heat oven to 375°F. In large bowl, combine ½ cup sugar, brown sugar and margarine; beat until light and fluffy. Add peanut butter, vanilla and egg; blend well.
2. Add flour, baking soda and salt; mix well. Shape dough into 1-inch balls. Place 2 inches apart on ungreased cookie sheets. With fork dipped in 4 teaspoons sugar, flatten balls in crisscross pattern.
3. Bake at 375°F. for 6 to 9 minutes or until set and golden brown. Immediately remove from cookie sheets.

HIGH ALTITUDE (*above 3500 feet*)**:** Increase flour to 1½ cups. Bake as directed above.

NUTRITION INFORMATION PER SERVING: Serving Size: 1 Cookie ◆ Calories: 60 ◆ Calories from Fat: 25 ◆ **% DAILY VALUE:** Total Fat: 3 g 5% ◆ Saturated Fat: 1 g 5% ◆ Cholesterol: 4 mg 1% ◆ Sodium: 85 mg 4% ◆ Total Carbohydrate: 8 g 3% ◆ Dietary Fiber: 0 g 0% ◆ Sugars: 5 g ◆ Protein: 1 g ◆ Vitamin A: 0% ◆ Vitamin C: 0% ◆ Calcium: 0% ◆ Iron: 0% ◆ **DIETARY EXCHANGES:** ½ Starch, ½ Fat OR ½ Carbohydrate, ½ Fat

VARIATIONS
Chocolate Chip-Peanut Butter Cookies: Stir in 1 (6-oz.) pkg. (1 cup) semisweet chocolate chips.
YIELD: 4½ DOZEN COOKIES

Chocolate-Peanut Butter Crunch Bars: Omit 4 teaspoons sugar. Stir in ½ cup crisp rice cereal. Press dough in ungreased 15 × 10 × 1-inch baking pan. Bake at 350°F. for 12 to 17 minutes or until golden brown. Cool 15 minutes. In medium saucepan, melt 1 (6-oz.) pkg. (1 cup) semisweet chocolate chips and ½ cup peanut butter over low heat. Stir in 1½ cups crisp rice cereal. Spoon mixture evenly over slightly cooled bars; spread gently. Cool completely. Cut into bars.
YIELD: 48 BARS

Giant Peanut Butter-Candy Cookies:
Omit 4 teaspoons sugar. Stir in 1 cup candy-coated chocolate pieces. Using ¼ cup dough per cookie, place cookies 4 inches apart on ungreased cookie sheets. Flatten to 4-inch diameter. Bake at 350°F. for 8 to 12 minutes or until golden brown. Cool 1 minute; remove from cookie sheets.

YIELD: 14 COOKIES

Nutty Peanut Butter Cookies: Stir in 1 cup chopped peanuts.

YIELD: 4½ DOZEN COOKIES

Oatmeal-Peanut Butter Cookies:
Decrease flour to ¾ cup and add ¾ cup rolled oats. Cover dough with plastic wrap; refrigerate 2 hours for easier handling. Shape and flatten balls as directed. Bake at 375°F. for 6 to 10 minutes or until golden brown. Immediately remove from cookie sheets.

YIELD: 4 DOZEN COOKIES

Peanut Blossoms: Increase 4 teaspoons sugar to ¼ cup; roll balls in sugar. Place 1 inch apart on ungreased cookie sheets. Bake as directed. Immediately top each cookie with 1 milk chocolate candy kiss, pressing down firmly so cookie cracks around edge. Remove from cookie sheets.

YIELD: 3½ DOZEN COOKIES

Peanut Butter and Jelly Thumbprints:
Increase 4 teaspoons sugar to ¼ cup; roll balls in sugar. Place 1 inch apart on ungreased cookie sheets. With thumb or handle of wooden spoon, make deep indentation in center of each cookie. Bake as directed. Remove from cookie sheets. Cool completely. Spoon ½ teaspoon jelly, jam or preserves into center of each cookie.

YIELD: 4 DOZEN COOKIES

Peanut Butter-Brickle Cookies: Stir in 1 cup peanut butter chips and ⅔ cup almond brickle baking chips.

YIELD: 5 DOZEN COOKIES

Peanut Butter-Raisin Cookie Pops: Stir in 1 cup chocolate-covered raisins. Shape dough into 1½-inch balls. Place 4 cookies on each ungreased cookie sheet. With fork dipped in sugar, flatten balls in crisscross pattern. Insert wooden stick into side of each cookie. Bake at 350°F. for 7 to 12 minutes or until golden brown. Cool 1 minute; remove from cookie sheets.

YIELD: 22 COOKIE POPS

C O O K ' S   N O T E

TESTING FOR DONENESS
Most recipes give a range of baking times to compensate for variations in ovens, ingredients, size of the cookies and so on. Check at the minimum time, looking for cookies that are firmly set or browned according to recipe directions.

No-Roll Sugar Cookies

PREP TIME: 1 HOUR 20 MINUTES (READY IN 3 HOURS 20 MINUTES) ♦ YIELD: 10 DOZEN COOKIES

    1   cup sugar
    1   cup powdered sugar
    1   cup margarine or butter, softened
    1   cup oil
    1   teaspoon vanilla
    2   eggs
  4¼   cups all-purpose flour
    1   teaspoon baking soda
    1   teaspoon cream of tartar
    1   teaspoon salt

1. In large bowl, combine sugar, powdered sugar and margarine; beat until light and fluffy. Add oil, vanilla and eggs; blend well. Add flour, baking soda, cream of tartar and salt; mix well. Cover with plastic wrap; refrigerate at least 2 hours or overnight for easier handling.

2. Heat oven to 375°F. Shape dough into 1-inch balls. Place 2 inches apart on ungreased cookie sheets. Flatten with bottom of glass dipped in sugar.

3. Bake at 375°F. for 5 to 8 minutes or until set but not brown. Immediately remove from cookie sheets.

HIGH ALTITUDE *(above 3500 feet)*: No change.

NUTRITION INFORMATION PER SERVING: Serving Size: 1 Cookie ♦ Calories: 50 ♦ Calories from Fat: 25 ♦ **% DAILY VALUE:** Total Fat: 3 g 5% ♦ Saturated Fat: 1 g 5% ♦ Cholesterol: 4 mg 1% ♦ Sodium: 45 mg 2% ♦ Total Carbohydrate: 6 g 2% ♦ Dietary Fiber: 0 g 0% ♦ Sugars: 3 g ♦ Protein: 1 g ♦ Vitamin A: 0% ♦ Vitamin C: 0% ♦ Calcium: 0% ♦ Iron: 0% ♦ **DIETARY EXCHANGES:** ½ Starch, ½ Fat OR ½ Carbohydrate, ½ Fat

VARIATIONS
Almond Sugar Cookies: Add 1 teaspoon almond extract with vanilla.
Orange Sugar Cookies: Add 2 teaspoons grated orange peel and 1 teaspoon cinnamon with flour.

Stamped Shortbread Cookies

PREP TIME: I HOUR I5 MINUTES ♦ YIELD: 18 COOKIES

½ cup sugar
1 cup butter, softened
2 cups all-purpose flour
¼ cup cornstarch
3 tablespoons sugar

1. Heat oven to 350°F. In large bowl, combine ½ cup sugar and butter; beat until light and fluffy. Add flour and cornstarch; mix well.
2. Divide dough into 18 equal pieces; shape into balls. Roll balls in 3 tablespoons sugar. Place 2 inches apart on ungreased cookie sheets. For each cookie, flatten ball of dough firmly with cookie stamp.
3. Bake at 350°F. for 9 to 12 minutes or until bottoms are very light golden brown. Cool 1 minute; remove from cookie sheets.

HIGH ALTITUDE (*above 3500 feet*): No change.

NUTRITION INFORMATION PER SERVING: Serving Size: 1 Cookie ♦ Calories: 180 ♦ Calories from Fat: 90 ♦ **% DAILY VALUE:** Total Fat: 10 g 15% ♦ Saturated Fat: 6 g 30% ♦ Cholesterol: 30 mg 10% ♦ Sodium: 105 mg 4% ♦ Total Carbohydrate: 20 g 7% ♦ Dietary Fiber: 0 g 0% ♦ Sugars: 8 g ♦ Protein: 2 g ♦ Vitamin A: 8% ♦ Vitamin C: 0% ♦ Calcium: 0% ♦ Iron: 4% ♦ **DIETARY EXCHANGES:** ½ Starch, 1 Fruit, 2 Fat OR 1½ Carbohydrate, 2 Fat

Stamped Shortbread Cookies

Crisp Chocolate Snaps

PREP TIME: I HOUR I5 MINUTES (READY IN 2 HOURS I5 MINUTES) ♦ YIELD: 6 DOZEN COOKIES

2 cups sugar
1 cup firmly packed brown sugar
1½ cups margarine or butter, softened
6 oz. unsweetened chocolate, melted, cooled
2 teaspoons vanilla
½ teaspoon red food color, if desired
3 eggs
4 cups all-purpose flour
2 teaspoons baking soda
1 teaspoon salt
¼ cup sugar

1. In large bowl, combine 2 cups sugar, brown sugar and margarine; beat until light and fluffy. Add chocolate, vanilla, food color and eggs; blend well. Add flour, baking soda and salt; mix well. Cover with plastic wrap; refrigerate 1 to 2 hours for easier handling.
2. Heat oven to 350°F. Lightly grease cookie sheets. Shape dough into 1½-inch balls; roll in ¼ cup sugar. Place 3 inches apart on greased cookie sheets.
3. Bake at 350°F. for 8 to 12 minutes or until set. (Cookies will puff up, then flatten during baking.) Cool 1 minute; remove from cookie sheets.

HIGH ALTITUDE (*above 3500 feet*): No change.

NUTRITION INFORMATION PER SERVING: Serving Size: 1 Cookie ♦ Calories: 110 ♦ Calories from Fat: 45 ♦ **% DAILY VALUE:** Total Fat: 5 g 8% ♦ Saturated Fat: 2 g 10% ♦ Cholesterol: 10 mg 3% ♦ Sodium: 115 mg 5% ♦ Total Carbohydrate: 15 g 5% ♦ Dietary Fiber: 1 g 4% ♦ Sugars: 9 g ♦ Protein: 1 g ♦ Vitamin A: 4% ♦ Vitamin C: 0% ♦ Calcium: 0% ♦ Iron: 4% ♦ **DIETARY EXCHANGES:** ½ Starch, ½ Fruit, 1 Fat OR 1 Carbohydrate, 1 Fat

Ginger Snaps

PREP TIME: I HOUR I5 MINUTES (READY IN 2 HOURS I5 MINUTES) ♦ YIELD: 5 DOZEN COOKIES

1 cup sugar
¾ cup margarine or butter, softened
¼ cup molasses
1 egg
2¼ cups all-purpose flour
2 teaspoons baking soda
1 teaspoon cinnamon
½ teaspoon salt
½ teaspoon ginger
½ teaspoon cloves
¼ teaspoon nutmeg
¼ cup sugar

1. In large bowl, combine 1 cup sugar, margarine, molasses and egg; beat until light and fluffy.

2. Add flour, baking soda, cinnamon, salt, ginger, cloves and nutmeg; mix well. Cover with plastic wrap; refrigerate 1 hour for easier handling.

3. Heat oven to 350°F. Shape dough into 1-inch balls; roll in ¼ cup sugar. Place 2 inches apart on ungreased cookie sheets.

4. Bake at 350°F. for 8 to 12 minutes or until set. (Cookies will puff up, then flatten during baking.) Cool 1 minute; remove from cookie sheets.

HIGH ALTITUDE (*above 3500 feet*)**:** Decrease baking soda to 1½ teaspoons. Bake as directed above.

NUTRITION INFORMATION PER SERVING: Serving Size: 1 Cookie ♦ Calories: 60 ♦ Calories from Fat: 20 ♦ **% DAILY VALUE:** Total Fat: 2 g 3% ♦ Saturated Fat: 0 g 0% ♦ Cholesterol: 4 mg 1% ♦ Sodium: 90 mg 4% ♦ Total Carbohydrate: 9 g 3% ♦ Dietary Fiber: 0 g 0% ♦ Sugars: 5 g ♦ Protein: 1 g ♦ Vitamin A: 2% ♦ Vitamin C: 0% ♦ Calcium: 0% ♦ Iron: 0% ♦ **DIETARY EXCHANGES:** ½ Starch, ½ Fat OR ½ Carbohydrate, ½ Fat

Whole Wheat Sugar Cookies

PREP TIME: 45 MINUTES (READY IN 1 HOUR 15 MINUTES)
♦ YIELD: 3 DOZEN COOKIES

   1 cup sugar
   ½ cup margarine or butter, softened
   2 tablespoons milk
   1 teaspoon grated lemon peel
   1 teaspoon vanilla
   1 egg
1¾ cups whole wheat flour
   1 teaspoon baking powder
   ½ teaspoon baking soda
   ½ teaspoon salt
   ½ teaspoon nutmeg
   2 tablespoons sugar
   ½ teaspoon cinnamon

1. In large bowl, combine 1 cup sugar and margarine; beat until light and fluffy. Add milk, lemon peel, vanilla and egg; blend well. Add flour, baking powder, baking soda, salt and nutmeg; mix well. Cover with plastic wrap; refrigerate 30 minutes for easier handling.

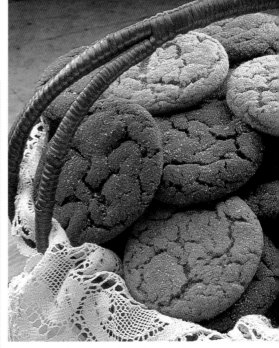

Ginger Snaps (page 414), Crisp Chocolate Snaps (page 414)

2. Heat oven to 375°F. In small bowl, combine 2 tablespoons sugar and cinnamon. Shape dough into 1-inch balls; roll in sugar-cinnamon mixture. Place 2 inches apart on ungreased cookie sheets.

3. Bake at 375°F. for 7 to 10 minutes or until light golden brown. Cool 1 minute; remove from cookie sheets.

HIGH ALTITUDE (*above 3500 feet*)**:** Increase flour to 2 cups. Bake as directed above.

NUTRITION INFORMATION PER SERVING: Serving Size: 1 Cookie ♦ Calories: 80 ♦ Calories from Fat: 25 ♦ **% DAILY VALUE:** Total Fat: 3 g 5% ♦ Saturated Fat: 1 g 5% ♦ Cholesterol: 5 mg 2% ♦ Sodium: 95 mg 4% ♦ Total Carbohydrate: 11 g 4% ♦ Dietary Fiber: 1 g 3% ♦ Sugars: 6 g ♦ Protein: 1 g ♦ Vitamin A: 2% ♦ Vitamin C: 0% ♦ Calcium: 0% ♦ Iron: 0% ♦ **DIETARY EXCHANGES:** ½ Fruit, 1 Fat OR ½ Carbohydrate, 1 Fat

Whole Wheat Sugar Cookies

Funfetti Cookies

PREP TIME: 40 MINUTES ♦ YIELD: 3 DOZEN COOKIES

- 1 (1 lb. 2.9-oz.) pkg. pudding-included white cake mix with candy bits
- 1/3 cup oil
- 2 eggs
- 1/2 (15.6-oz.) can pink vanilla frosting with candy bits

1. Heat oven to 375°F. In large bowl, combine cake mix, oil and eggs; stir with spoon until thoroughly moistened. Shape dough into 1-inch balls; place 2 inches apart on ungreased cookie sheets. With bottom of glass dipped in flour, flatten to 1/4-inch thickness.
2. Bake at 375°F. for 6 to 8 minutes or until edges are light golden brown. Cool 1 minute; remove from cookie sheets.
3. Spread frosting over warm cookies. Immediately sprinkle each with candy bits from frosting. Let frosting set before storing. Store in tightly covered container.

HIGH ALTITUDE (*above 3500 feet*)**:** Add 1/2 cup flour to dry cake mix. Bake as directed above.

NUTRITION INFORMATION PER SERVING: Serving Size: 1 Cookie ♦ Calories: 110 ♦ Calories from Fat: 45 ♦ **% DAILY VALUE:** Total Fat: 5 g 8% ♦ Saturated Fat: 1 g 5% ♦ Cholesterol: 10 mg 3% ♦ Sodium: 105 mg 4% ♦ Total Carbohydrate: 16 g 5% ♦ Dietary Fiber: 0 g 0% ♦ Sugars: 11 g ♦ Protein: 1 g ♦ Vitamin A: 0% ♦ Vitamin C: 0% ♦ Calcium: 0% ♦ Iron: 2% ♦ **DIETARY EXCHANGES:** 1/2 Starch, 1/2 Fruit, 1 Fat OR 1 Carbohydrate, 1 Fat

Mexican Wedding Cakes

PREP TIME: 1 HOUR ♦ YIELD: 5 DOZEN COOKIES

- 1/2 cup powdered sugar
- 1 cup butter, softened
- 2 teaspoons vanilla
- 2 cups all-purpose flour
- 1 cup finely chopped or ground almonds or pecans
- 1/4 teaspoon salt
- 1/2 cup powdered sugar

1. Heat oven to 325°F. In large bowl, combine 1/2 cup powdered sugar, butter and vanilla; beat until light and fluffy. Add flour, almonds and salt; mix until dough forms. Shape into 1-inch balls. Place 1 inch apart on ungreased cookie sheets.
2. Bake at 325°F. for 15 to 20 minutes or until set but not brown. Immediately remove from cookie sheets. Cool slightly; roll in 1/2 cup powdered sugar. Cool 15 minutes or until completely cooled. Re-roll in powdered sugar.

HIGH ALTITUDE (*above 3500 feet*)**:** No change.

NUTRITION INFORMATION PER SERVING: Serving Size: 1 Cookie ♦ Calories: 60 ♦ Calories from Fat: 35 ♦ **% DAILY VALUE:** Total Fat: 4 g 6% ♦ Saturated Fat: 2 g 10% ♦ Cholesterol: 10 mg 3% ♦ Sodium: 40 mg 2% ♦ Total Carbohydrate: 6 g 2% ♦ Dietary Fiber: 0 g 0% ♦ Sugars: 2 g ♦ Protein: 1 g ♦ Vitamin A: 2% ♦ Vitamin C: 0% ♦ Calcium: 0% ♦ Iron: 0% ♦ **DIETARY EXCHANGES:** 1/2 Starch, 1/2 Fat OR 1/2 Carbohydrate, 1/2 Fat

Snickerdoodles

PREP TIME: 45 MINUTES ♦ YIELD: 4 DOZEN COOKIES

- 1 1/2 cups sugar
- 1/2 cup margarine or butter, softened
- 1 teaspoon vanilla
- 2 eggs
- 2 3/4 cups all-purpose flour
- 1 teaspoon cream of tartar
- 1/2 teaspoon baking soda
- 1/4 teaspoon salt
- 2 tablespoons sugar
- 2 teaspoons cinnamon

1. Heat oven to 400°F. In large bowl, combine 1 1/2 cups sugar and margarine; beat until light and fluffy. Add vanilla and eggs; blend well. Add flour, cream of tartar, baking soda and salt; mix well.
2. In small bowl, combine 2 tablespoons sugar and cinnamon. Shape dough into

1-inch balls; roll in sugar-cinnamon mixture. Place 2 inches apart on ungreased cookie sheets.

3. Bake at 400°F. for 8 to 10 minutes or until set. Immediately remove from cookie sheets.

HIGH ALTITUDE (*above 3500 feet*)**:** No change.

NUTRITION INFORMATION PER SERVING: Serving Size: 1 Cookie ◆ Calories: 70 ◆ Calories from Fat: 20 ◆ **% DAILY VALUE:** Total Fat: 2 g 3% ◆ Saturated Fat: 0 g 0% ◆ Cholesterol: 10 mg 3% ◆ Sodium: 50 mg 2% ◆ Total Carbohydrate: 12 g 4% ◆ Dietary Fiber: 0 g 0% ◆ Sugars: 7 g ◆ Protein: 1 g ◆ Vitamin A: 0% ◆ Vitamin C: 0% ◆ Calcium: 0% ◆ Iron: 2% ◆ **DIETARY EXCHANGES:** ½ Starch, ½ Fat OR ½ Carbohydrate, ½ Fat

VARIATIONS

Chocolate Snickerdoodles: Substitute ½ cup unsweetened cocoa for ½ cup of the flour. Bake at 400°F. for 6 to 9 minutes or until set. Immediately remove from cookie sheets.

Whole Wheat Snickerdoodles: Substitute 1 cup whole wheat flour for 1 cup of the all-purpose flour.

WHEN THE COOKIE CRUMBLES

Measure all ingredients accurately and mix according to recipe directions. If you run into problems, here are some common solutions.

PROBLEM	SOLUTION
Burned cookie bottoms	Use an aluminum silver-colored cookie sheet rather than a dark one. Watch cooking times carefully. Bake one pan at a time, on the center rack of the oven.
Soft cookies	Increase baking time slightly.
Unevenly baked cookies	Size and space the cookie dough evenly. Bake only one pan at a time, in the center of the oven, and rotate the cookie sheet halfway through cooking time.
Sticky, unworkable cookie dough	Refrigerate the dough until it is firm, usually about an hour. If it is still too sticky, work in additional flour, 1 tablespoon at a time, until the texture improves.
Crumbly cookie dough	Work in an additional tablespoon or two of milk (or another liquid from the recipe) or softened butter.
Cookies run together	Space dough farther apart for subsequent batches. Use cooled cookie sheets.
Overly flat, thin cookies	Begin with a cool cookie sheet. Do not grease the cookie sheet unless specified in the recipe. Use butter or margarine as specified in the recipe; do not substitute with low-fat or nonfat spreads.
Tough rolled cookies	Handle dough gently, use as little flour as possible on the rolling pin and work surface, and avoid re-rolling scraps more than twice.
Baked cookies stick to the pan	Return the cookie sheet to the oven for a few seconds to rewarm and loosen the cookies. Remove crumbs before the next batch, lightly regrease cookie sheets (only if the recipe calls for greased sheets) or start over with a clean sheet.
Cookies break when removed from the pan	Let cookies cool and firm up for an additional minute or two before removing them from the pan. Use a pancake turner with a wide, thin metal blade to get under the cookie easily and support it fully.
Cookie jar is mysteriously empty	Make double batches and keep wrapped "logs" of dough in the freezer for cookie emergencies.

Peanut Blossoms

PREP TIME: 1 HOUR ◆ YIELD: 4 DOZEN COOKIES

1¾ cups all-purpose flour
½ cup sugar
½ cup firmly packed brown sugar
1 teaspoon baking soda
½ teaspoon salt
½ cup shortening
½ cup peanut butter
2 tablespoons milk
1 teaspoon vanilla
1 egg
    Sugar
48 milk chocolate cone-shaped candy,
    unwrapped

1. Heat oven to 375°F. In large bowl, combine flour, ½ cup sugar, brown sugar, baking soda, salt, shortening, peanut butter, milk, vanilla and egg; mix at low speed until stiff dough forms. Shape dough into 1-inch balls; roll in sugar. Place 2 inches apart on ungreased cookie sheets.
2. Bake at 375°F. for 10 to 12 minutes or until golden brown. Immediately top each cookie with 1 candy, pressing down firmly so cookie cracks around edge; remove from cookie sheets.

HIGH ALTITUDE *(above 3500 feet):* No change.

NUTRITION INFORMATION PER SERVING: Serving Size: 1 Cookie ◆ Calories: 100 ◆ Calories from Fat: 45 ◆ **% DAILY VALUE:** Total Fat: 5 g 8% ◆ Saturated Fat: 2 g 10% ◆ Cholesterol: 5 mg 2% ◆ Sodium: 65 mg 3% ◆ Total Carbohydrate: 12 g 4% ◆ Dietary Fiber: 0 g 0% ◆ Sugars: 8 g ◆ Protein: 2 g ◆ Vitamin A: 0% ◆ Vitamin C: 0% ◆ Calcium: 0% ◆ Iron: 2% ◆ **DIETARY EXCHANGES:** 1 Fruit, 1 Fat OR 1 Carbohydrate, 1 Fat

HERSHEY'S KISSES and the conical configuration are registered trademarks.

Peanut Blossoms

Ginger Butter Cookies

PREP TIME: 1 HOUR 15 MINUTES ◆ YIELD: 3½ DOZEN COOKIES

⅔ cup firmly packed brown sugar
⅓ cup sugar
1 cup butter, softened
1 teaspoon vanilla
2 cups all-purpose flour
1 teaspoon ginger
½ teaspoon salt
1 (2-oz.) jar (⅓ cup) finely chopped
    crystallized ginger
⅓ cup sugar

1. Heat oven to 350°F. In medium bowl, combine brown sugar, ⅓ cup sugar and but-

---

COOK'S NOTE

COOKIE SHEETS

With three sheets, you can bake one pan while you prepare another and cool a third. Cookie sheets come in four basic styles.

- ◆ Shiny: Silver-colored aluminum sheets without sides produce the best results. The shiny metal reflects heat, so cookies do not burn as easily.
- ◆ Double-layer: Cookie sheets with an insulating "cushion of air" between two sheets of metal are more expensive. Cookies do not brown as much on the bottom, so cooking time increases slightly and doneness can be harder to judge.
- ◆ Black or dark surface: Cookies bake faster on a dark, nonreflective surface that absorbs heat. Watch closely to prevent the bottoms from burning.
- ◆ Nonstick: While many cookies have enough shortening to prevent sticking, nonstick pans are still convenient for cleanup. Use only plastic utensils to avoid marring the finish. If the surface color is dark, watch closely to prevent the cookie bottoms from burning.

ter; beat until light and fluffy. Add vanilla; blend well.

2. Add flour, ginger and salt; mix well. Stir in crystallized ginger. Shape dough into 1-inch balls; roll in ⅓ cup sugar. Place 2 inches apart on ungreased cookie sheets. Flatten with bottom of glass dipped in sugar.

3. Bake at 350°F. for 7 to 10 minutes or until edges are light golden brown. Cool 2 minutes; remove from cookie sheets.

HIGH ALTITUDE (*above 3500 feet*)**:** Decrease brown sugar to ½ cup; increase flour to 2¼ cups. Bake as directed above.

NUTRITION INFORMATION PER SERVING: Serving Size: 1 Cookie ♦ Calories: 90 ♦ Calories from Fat: 35 ♦ **% DAILY VALUE:** Total Fat: 4 g 6% ♦ Saturated Fat: 3 g 15% ♦ Cholesterol: 10 mg 3% ♦ Sodium: 70 mg 3% ♦ Total Carbohydrate: 12 g 4% ♦ Dietary Fiber: 0 g 0% ♦ Sugars: 8 g ♦ Protein: 1 g ♦ Vitamin A: 4% ♦ Vitamin C: 0% ♦ Calcium: 0% ♦ Iron: 0% ♦ **DIETARY EXCHANGES:** ½ Starch, ½ Fruit, ½ Fat OR 1 Carbohydrate, ½ Fat

Fudgy Bonbons

PREP TIME: 1 HOUR 10 MINUTES ♦ YIELD: 5 DOZEN COOKIES

1	(12-oz.) pkg. (2 cups) semisweet chocolate chips
¼	cup margarine or butter
1	(14-oz.) can sweetened condensed milk (not evaporated)
2	cups all-purpose flour
½	cup finely chopped nuts, if desired
1	teaspoon vanilla
60	milk chocolate candy kisses or white and chocolate striped candy kisses, unwrapped
2	oz. white chocolate baking bar or vanilla-flavored candy coating (almond bark)
1	teaspoon shortening or oil

1. Heat oven to 350°F. In medium saucepan, combine chocolate chips and margarine; cook and stir over very low heat until chips are melted and smooth. (Mixture will be stiff.) Add condensed milk; mix well.

2. In large bowl, combine flour, nuts, chocolate mixture and vanilla; mix well. Shape 1 tablespoon dough (use measuring spoon) around each candy kiss, covering completely. Place 1 inch apart on ungreased cookie sheets.

3. Bake at 350°F. for 6 to 8 minutes. DO NOT OVERBAKE. Cookies will be soft and appear shiny but will become firm as they cool. Remove from cookie sheets. Cool 15 minutes or until completely cooled.

MELTING CHOCOLATE

Melt chocolate over very low heat in a heavy saucepan, in the top of a double boiler over simmering (not boiling) water or in the microwave on HIGH. Break up chocolate bars for faster melting.

Start with dry utensils and equipment. A drop of water can turn melted chocolate into a stiff, unworkable mass.

If the chocolate becomes hard or brittle, add 1 teaspoon of vegetable shortening or oil (not butter) per ounce of chocolate. Stir over low heat until the texture returns to normal.

4. Meanwhile, in small saucepan, combine baking bar and shortening; cook and stir over low heat until melted and smooth. Drizzle over cooled cookies. Let stand until set. Store in tightly covered container.

HIGH ALTITUDE (*above 3500 feet*)**:** Increase flour to 2¼ cups. Bake as directed above.

NUTRITION INFORMATION PER SERVING: Serving Size: 1 Cookie ♦ Calories: 120 ♦ Calories from Fat: 50 ♦ **% DAILY VALUE:** Total Fat: 6 g 9% ♦ Saturated Fat: 3 g 15% ♦ Cholesterol: 5 mg 2% ♦ Sodium: 20 mg 1% ♦ Total Carbohydrate: 14 g 5% ♦ Dietary Fiber: 1 g 3% ♦ Sugars: 10 g ♦ Protein: 2 g ♦ Vitamin A: 0% ♦ Vitamin C: 0% ♦ Calcium: 4% ♦ Iron: 2% ♦ **DIETARY EXCHANGES:** ½ Starch, ½ Fruit, 1 Fat OR 1 Carbohydrate, 1 Fat

Top to bottom: Salted Peanut Chews (page 433), Fudgy Bonbons

Thumbprints

PREP TIME: I HOUR 15 MINUTES (READY IN I HOUR
45 MINUTES) ◆ YIELD: 3½ DOZEN COOKIES

½ cup sugar
1 cup margarine or butter, softened
1 teaspoon vanilla
2 egg yolks
2¼ cups all-purpose flour
1 teaspoon baking powder
¼ cup any flavor jam or preserves

1. In medium bowl, combine sugar, margarine, vanilla and egg yolks; beat until light and fluffy. Gradually add flour and baking powder; mix well. Cover with plastic wrap; refrigerate 30 minutes for easier handling.
2. Heat oven to 350°F. Shape dough into 1-inch balls; place 2 inches apart on ungreased cookie sheets. With thumb, make indentation in center of each cookie.
3. Bake at 350°F. for 11 to 14 minutes or until light golden brown around edges. Immediately remove from cookie sheets. Spoon about ¼ teaspoon jam into each baked cookie.

HIGH ALTITUDE (*above 3500 feet*): No change.

NUTRITION INFORMATION PER SERVING: Serving Size: 1 Cookie ◆ Calories: 80 ◆ Calories from Fat: 45 ◆ % DAILY VALUE: Total Fat: 5 g 8% ◆ Saturated Fat: 1 g 5% ◆ Cholesterol: 10 mg 3% ◆ Sodium: 65 mg 3% ◆ Total Carbohydrate: 9 g 3% ◆ Dietary Fiber: 0 g 0% ◆ Sugars: 3 g ◆ Protein: 1 g ◆ Vitamin A: 4% ◆ Vitamin C: 0% ◆ Calcium: 0% ◆ Iron: 2% ◆ DIETARY EXCHANGES: ½ Starch, 1 Fat OR ½ Carbohydrate, 1 Fat

VARIATIONS

Custard-Filled Thumbprints: Prepare and shape dough as directed in recipe; do not bake. In small saucepan, combine 1 tablespoon sugar, 1 tablespoon flour and ¼ teaspoon almond extract. Gradually add ½ cup whipping cream or half-and-half; cook over low heat until smooth and thickened, stirring constantly. In small bowl, blend 2 tablespoons hot mixture into 1 slightly beaten egg yolk. Return to saucepan; blend well. Cook just until mixture bubbles, stirring constantly. Cool filling slightly. Spoon ½ teaspoon filling into each *unbaked* cookie. Bake as directed above, omitting jam. Store cookies in refrigerator.
Lemon-Filled Thumbprints: Bake cookies as directed in recipe, omitting jam. In medium saucepan, combine 1 beaten egg, ⅔ cup sugar, 2 to 3 teaspoons grated lemon peel, 1 teaspoon cornstarch, ¼ teaspoon salt, 3 tablespoons lemon juice and 1 tablespoon margarine or butter. Cook over low heat until smooth and thickened, stirring constantly. Cool filling slightly. Spoon ¼ teaspoon filling into each *baked* cookie. Sprinkle with powdered sugar or coconut. Store cookies in refrigerator.

C O O K ' S   N O T E

STORING COOKIES

Use a separate container for each cookie variety to avoid mingling the flavors and changing the texture.

◆ Soft cookies: Use a tightly closed container; place waxed paper between cookie layers to prevent sticking. If the cookies are frosted or filled, store them in a single layer. Good choices include airtight plastic containers, cookie tins with tight-fitting lids and resealable plastic bags.

◆ Crisp cookies: A container with a loose-fitting cover, such as a cookie tin or glass baking dish, is best unless the weather is very humid, in which case they should be tightly sealed. To revive crisp cookies that have gone limp, reheat them on a cookie sheet in a 300°F. oven for 3 to 5 minutes; cool on a wire rack.

◆ Freezing: Place unfrosted, baked cookies in containers with tight-fitting lids and freeze for up to 12 months. For frosted cookies, first freeze them uncovered on a baking sheet, then package the frozen cookies between layers of waxed paper in a rigid container for up to 2 months.

◆ Thawing: Thaw soft-textured cookies in the container at room temperature or place them briefly in a microwave oven. Crisp-textured cookies should be removed from the container before thawing.

Sauces

~ As good as homemade - prepared in less than 5 minutes
~ Try our Bearnaise Sauce on Filet Steaks or Fish
~ Try our Hollandaise Sauce on Vegetables or Eggs Benedict
~ Try our Hunter Sauce on Pork, Beef or Veal

Look for the dark green packages in our color - coded Meal Idea Center

Gravies

~ Delicious gravies - quickly prepared
~ Our gravies are low in fat - always have been
~ An easy way to spruce up holiday leftovers

Look for the brown packages in our color - coded Meal Idea Center

730123

Cherry Winks

PREP TIME: 1 HOUR 20 MINUTES ✦ YIELD: 5 DOZEN COOKIES

    1   cup sugar
    ¾   cup shortening
    2   tablespoons milk
    1   teaspoon vanilla
    2   eggs
  2¼   cups all-purpose flour
    1   teaspoon baking powder
    ½   teaspoon baking soda
    ½   teaspoon salt
    1   cup chopped pecans
    1   cup chopped dates
    ⅓   cup chopped maraschino cherries, well
          drained
  1½   cups coarsely crushed corn flakes cereal
   15   maraschino cherries, quartered

1. In large bowl, combine sugar and short-ening; beat well. Add milk, vanilla and eggs; mix well. Add flour, baking powder, baking soda and salt; mix well. Stir in pecans, dates and ⅓ cup chopped cherries. If necessary, cover with plastic wrap; refrigerate 15 min-utes for easier handling.
2. Heat oven to 375°F. Grease cookie sheets. Drop dough by rounded teaspoonfuls into cereal; thoroughly coat. Shape into balls. Place 2 inches apart on greased cookie sheets. Lightly press maraschino cherry quarter into top of each ball.
3. Bake at 375°F. for 10 to 15 minutes or until light golden brown. Remove from cookie sheets.

HIGH ALTITUDE *(above 3500 feet)*: No change.

NUTRITION INFORMATION PER SERVING: Serving Size: 1 Cookie ✦ Calories: 90 ✦ Calories from Fat: 35 ✦ **% DAILY VALUE:** Total Fat: 4 g 6% ✦ Saturated Fat: 1 g 5% ✦ Cholesterol: 5 mg 2% ✦ Sodium: 70 mg 3% ✦ Total Carbohydrate: 12 g 4% ✦ Dietary Fiber: 1 g 2% ✦ Sugars: 6 g ✦ Protein: 1 g ✦ Vitamin A: 0% ✦ Vitamin C: 0% ✦ Cal-cium: 0% ✦ Iron: 6% ✦ **DIETARY EXCHANGES:** ½ Starch, ½ Fruit, ½ Fat OR 1 Carbohydrate, ½ Fat

Split Seconds

PREP TIME: 1 HOUR 15 MINUTES ✦ YIELD: 4 DOZEN COOKIES

    ⅔   cup sugar
    ¾   cup margarine or butter, softened
    2   teaspoons vanilla
    1   egg
    2   cups all-purpose flour
    ½   teaspoon baking powder
    ½   cup red jelly or preserves

1. Heat oven to 350°F. In large bowl, com-bine sugar and margarine; beat until light and fluffy. Add vanilla and egg; blend well. Add flour and baking powder; mix well.
2. Divide dough into 4 equal parts. On lightly floured surface, shape each part into 12 × ¾-inch roll; place on ungreased cookie sheets. Using handle of wooden spoon or finger, make depression about ½ inch wide and ¼ inch deep lengthwise down center of each roll. Fill each roll with 2 tablespoons jelly.
3. Bake at 350°F. for 15 to 20 minutes or until light golden brown. Cool slightly. Cut each baked roll diagonally into 12 cookies. Remove from cookie sheets; cool on wire racks.

HIGH ALTITUDE *(above 3500 feet)*: No change.

NUTRITION INFORMATION PER SERVING: Serving Size: 1 Cookie ✦ Calories: 70 ✦ Calories from Fat: 25 ✦ **% DAILY VALUE:** Total Fat: 3 g 5% ✦ Saturated Fat: 1 g 5% ✦ Cholesterol: 4 mg 1% ✦ Sodium: 40 mg 2% ✦ Total Carbohydrate: 9 g 3% ✦ Dietary Fiber: 0 g 0% ✦ Sugars: 4 g ✦ Protein: 1 g ✦ Vitamin A: 2% ✦ Vitamin C: 0% ✦ Cal-cium: 0% ✦ Iron: 0% ✦ **DIETARY EXCHANGES:** ½ Starch, ½ Fat OR ½ Carbohydrate, ½ Fat

COOK'S NOTE

MAILING COOKIES

Choose moist, firm-textured cookies that will remain fresh and intact during trans-port. Good choices include drop cookies, unfrosted bars, fudgy brownies or other sturdy treats. Delicate, intricately shaped specialties are best reserved for personal delivery.

Pack the cookies into a firm-sided cardboard, metal or plastic container lined with plastic wrap or foil. Insulate the sides of the container with a "wall" of crumpled waxed paper. Place waxed paper between each layer or wrap cookies in pairs, flat sides together.

For extra protection, place the con-tainer in a larger box padded on all sides with crumpled paper or packing material. Wrap the box securely, mark it "perish-able" and send it the fastest way possible.

Double Chocolate-Orange Biscotti

PREP TIME: 1 HOUR 45 MINUTES (READY IN 2 HOURS)
◆ YIELD: 6½ DOZEN COOKIES

COOKIES
  3 cups all-purpose flour
  ½ cup sugar
  ½ cup firmly packed brown sugar
  3 teaspoons baking powder
  ½ teaspoon salt
  4 oz. unsweetened chocolate, melted, cooled
  1 tablespoon grated orange peel
  ⅓ cup olive or vegetable oil
  ¼ cup orange juice
  2 teaspoons vanilla
  3 eggs
  6 oz. white chocolate baking bar, chopped

TOPPING
  4 oz. white chocolate baking bar, chopped
  1 tablespoon shortening

1. Heat oven to 350°F. Lightly grease 2 cookie sheets. In large bowl, combine flour, sugar, brown sugar, baking powder and salt; mix well. Add melted chocolate, orange peel, oil, orange juice, vanilla and eggs; blend well. (Dough will be stiff.) Add 6 oz. chopped baking bar; gently knead into dough.
2. Divide dough into 4 equal parts; shape each part into roll 14 inches long. Place 2 rolls on each cookie sheet; flatten each roll to 2½-inch width. Bake at 350°F. for 18 to 20 minutes or until firm to the touch.

Double Chocolate-Orange Biscotti

3. Remove cookie sheets from oven. Reduce oven temperature to 300°F. Cool rolls on cookie sheets for 10 minutes.
4. Cut rolls diagonally into ½-inch-thick slices. Place slices, cut side up, on same cookie sheets. Bake at 300°F. for 7 to 9 minutes or until top surface is dry.
5. Turn cookies over; bake an additional 7 to 9 minutes. Remove from cookie sheets. Cool 15 minutes or until completely cooled.
6. In small saucepan, melt topping ingredients over low heat, stirring until smooth. Drizzle over cookies.

HIGH ALTITUDE (*above 3500 feet*)**:** No change.

NUTRITION INFORMATION PER SERVING: Serving Size: 1 Cookie ◆ Calories: 70 ◆ Calories from Fat: 25 ◆ **% DAILY VALUE:** Total Fat: 3 g 5% ◆ Saturated Fat: 1 g 5% ◆ Cholesterol: 10 mg 3% ◆ Sodium: 40 mg 2% ◆ Total Carbohydrate: 9 g 3% ◆ Dietary Fiber: 0 g 0% ◆ Sugars: 5 g ◆ Protein: 1 g ◆ Vitamin A: 0% ◆ Vitamin C: 0% ◆ Calcium: 2% ◆ Iron: 2% ◆ **DIETARY EXCHANGES:** ½ Vegetable, ½ Fat OR ½ Carbohydrate, ½ Fat

Lemon-Glazed Cashew Shortbread

PREP TIME: 30 MINUTES (READY IN 1 HOUR 30 MINUTES)
◆ YIELD: 4 DOZEN COOKIES

COOKIES
  ¾ cup powdered sugar
  1¼ cups butter, softened
  3 cups all-purpose flour
  ½ cup finely chopped cashews
  1 teaspoon ginger
  ½ cup coarsely chopped cashews

GLAZE
  1 cup powdered sugar
  1 teaspoon grated lemon peel
  4 to 6 teaspoons lemon juice

1. Heat oven to 325°F. In large bowl, combine ¾ cup powdered sugar and butter; beat until light and fluffy. Add flour, ½ cup finely chopped cashews and ginger; mix well. Press dough evenly in ungreased 15 × 10 × 1-inch baking pan. Sprinkle with coarsely chopped cashews; press lightly into dough.
2. Bake at 325°F. for 20 to 30 minutes or until edges are light golden brown. Place pan on wire rack. Immediately cut into 2½-inch squares. Cut each square diagonally in half. Cool in pan 30 minutes or until completely cooled.
3. In small bowl, combine all glaze ingredients, adding enough lemon juice for desired

drizzling consistency. Remove cooled cookies from pan; place on waxed paper. Drizzle with glaze.

HIGH ALTITUDE *(above 3500 feet)*: Decrease flour to 2¾ cups. Bake as directed above.

Rolled Sugar Cookies

PREP TIME: 1 HOUR 25 MINUTES (READY IN 2 HOURS 25 MINUTES) ♦ YIELD: 6 DOZEN COOKIES

    1   cup sugar
    1   cup margarine or butter, softened
    3   tablespoons milk
    1   teaspoon vanilla
    1   egg
    3   cups all-purpose flour
 1½   teaspoons baking powder
   ½   teaspoon salt
        Sugar or Buttery Decorator Icing (page 382)

1. In large bowl, combine 1 cup sugar, margarine, milk, vanilla and egg; blend well. Add flour, baking powder and salt; mix well. Cover with plastic wrap; refrigerate 1 hour for easier handling.
2. Heat oven to 400°F. On lightly floured surface, roll out ⅓ of dough at a time to ⅛-inch thickness. Keep remaining dough refrigerated. Cut with floured cookie cutter. Place 1 inch apart on ungreased cookie sheets. If desired, sprinkle with sugar.
3. Bake at 400°F. for 5 to 9 minutes or until

Rolled Sugar Cookies

edges are light brown. Immediately remove from cookie sheets. Decorate as desired.

HIGH ALTITUDE *(above 3500 feet)*: Increase flour to 3 cups plus 2 tablespoons. Bake as directed above.

COOK'S NOTE

TIPS FOR SHAPING COOKIES

Using cookie cutters is delightful when you have the time, but there are other ways to shape rolled dough into good-looking cookies. Some ideas:

+ Cut across the entire surface of the dough in two directions to create rectangles, squares or diamonds.
+ Make another cut across diamonds or squares to form triangles.
+ Cut circles with a drinking glass dipped in flour.
+ Use everyday kitchen objects to stamp a design on the top. For instance, gently press dough with the bottom of a cut-glass sugar bowl or a meat mallet.
+ Crimp the edges with a fork dipped in sugar.

Lemon-Glazed Cashew Shortbread (page 422)

Date-Filled Whole Wheat Cookies

PREP TIME: 1 HOUR (READY IN 2 HOURS)
◆ YIELD: 4½ DOZEN COOKIES

COOKIES
 1 cup firmly packed brown sugar
 ¾ cup margarine or butter, softened
 1 teaspoon vanilla
 1 egg
 1¼ cups all-purpose flour
 1 cup whole wheat flour
 1½ teaspoons baking powder
 1 teaspoon cinnamon
 ⅛ teaspoon salt

FILLING
 ¼ cup firmly packed brown sugar
 ¼ cup slivered almonds
 ⅓ cup orange juice
 1 (8-oz.) pkg. (1½ cups) chopped pitted dates

1. In large bowl, combine 1 cup brown sugar and margarine; beat until light and fluffy. Add vanilla and egg; blend well. Add all-purpose flour, whole wheat flour, baking powder, cinnamon and salt; mix well. Cover with plastic wrap; refrigerate 1 to 2 hours for easier handling.
2. Meanwhile, in food processor bowl with metal blade or blender container, combine all filling ingredients; process 1 to 2 minutes or until thickened.
3. Heat oven to 375°F. On lightly floured surface, roll out ⅓ of dough at a time to ⅛-inch thickness. (Keep remaining dough refrigerated.) Cut with floured 2½-inch round cookie cutter. Place rounds ½ inch apart on ungreased cookie sheets. Spoon scant 1 teaspoon filling onto center of each round. Fold half of each round over filling, forming half moon shape. Seal edges with fork.
4. Bake at 375°F. for 5 to 10 minutes or until edges are golden brown. Immediately remove from cookie sheets.

HIGH ALTITUDE (*above 3500 feet*): Increase all-purpose flour to 1½ cups. Bake as directed above.

NUTRITION INFORMATION PER SERVING: Serving Size: 1 Cookie ◆ Calories: 80 ◆ Calories from Fat: 25 ◆ **% DAILY VALUE:** Total Fat: 3 g 5% ◆ Saturated Fat: 1 g 5% ◆ Cholesterol: 4 mg 1% ◆ Sodium: 50 mg 2% ◆ Total Carbohydrate: 12 g 4% ◆ Dietary Fiber: 1 g 3% ◆ Sugars: 8 g ◆ Protein: 1 g ◆ Vitamin A: 2% ◆ Vitamin C: 0% ◆ Calcium: 0% ◆ Iron: 2% ◆ **DIETARY EXCHANGES:** ½ Starch, ½ Fruit, ½ Fat OR 1 Carbohydrate, ½ Fat

---

> COOK'S NOTE
>
> **TIPS FOR MAKING SHAPED COOKIES**
>
> The dough can be rolled out and cut into shapes or molded by hand. In either case, the dough is usually refrigerated for about an hour to make it less sticky and easier to handle. Roll a little bit at a time, keeping the rest chilled. Dust the work surface, your hands and the rolling pin with a little flour—just enough to prevent sticking without toughening the dough. Cut shapes as closely together as possible to minimize scraps. Chill the scraps before re-rolling, and try not to re-roll more than once or twice so the cookies do not become tough.

Ginger Cookie Cutouts

PREP TIME: 1 HOUR 15 MINUTES (READY IN 3 HOURS 15 MINUTES) ◆ YIELD: 5 DOZEN COOKIES

 ¾ cup sugar
 ½ cup shortening
 ½ cup molasses
 ¼ cup warm coffee
 1 teaspoon vanilla
 1 egg
 2½ cups all-purpose flour
 1 teaspoon baking soda
 ½ teaspoon ginger
 ½ teaspoon cinnamon
 ½ teaspoon allspice
 ¼ teaspoon salt
  Sugar

1. In large bowl, combine ¾ cup sugar and shortening; beat until light and fluffy. Add molasses, coffee, vanilla and egg; blend well. (Mixture may appear curdled.) Add flour, baking soda, ginger, cinnamon, allspice and salt; mix well. Cover with plastic wrap; refrigerate at least 2 hours for easier handling.
2. Heat oven to 350°F. On well-floured surface, roll out dough to ⅛ to ¼-inch thickness.* Cut with floured 2-inch cookie cutter. Place 1 inch apart on ungreased cookie sheets. Sprinkle lightly with sugar.

3. Bake at 350°F. for 8 to 12 minutes or until set. Immediately remove from cookie sheets.

> **TIP:** * Rolling dough ⅛ inch thick will yield a thin, crisp cookie; rolling to ¼-inch thickness will yield a more cakelike cookie.

HIGH ALTITUDE *(above 3500 feet)*: No change.

NUTRITION INFORMATION PER SERVING: Serving Size: 1 Cookie ♦ Calories: 60 ♦ Calories from Fat: 20 ♦ **% DAILY VALUE:** Total Fat: 2 g 3% ♦ Saturated Fat: 0 g 0% ♦ Cholesterol: 4 mg 1% ♦ Sodium: 30 mg 1% ♦ Total Carbohydrate: 9 g 3% ♦ Dietary Fiber: 0 g 0% ♦ Sugars: 5 g ♦ Protein: 1 g ♦ Vitamin A: 0% ♦ Vitamin C: 0% ♦ Calcium: 0% ♦ Iron: 2% ♦ **DIETARY EXCHANGES:** ½ Starch, ½ Fat OR ½ Carbohydrate, ½ Fat

Basic Refrigerator Cookies

PREP TIME: 1 HOUR (READY IN 3 HOURS)
♦ YIELD: 7½ DOZEN COOKIES

¾ cup sugar
¾ cup firmly packed brown sugar
1 cup margarine or butter, softened
1½ teaspoons vanilla
2 eggs
3 cups all-purpose flour
1½ teaspoons baking powder
¾ teaspoon salt
1 cup finely chopped nuts

1. In large bowl, combine sugar, brown sugar, margarine, vanilla and eggs; beat well. Add flour, baking powder and salt; mix well. Stir in nuts. Divide dough into 3 equal parts. Shape each into roll 1½ inches in diameter. Wrap each roll in plastic wrap; refrigerate 2 hours or until firm.
2. Heat oven to 425°F. Cut dough into ¼-inch slices. Place slices 1 inch apart on ungreased cookie sheets.
3. Bake at 425°F. for 5 to 7 minutes or until light golden brown. Immediately remove from cookie sheets.

> **TIP:** Cookie dough can be stored in refrigerator for up to 2 weeks or in freezer for up to 6 weeks. Slice and bake frozen dough as directed above.

HIGH ALTITUDE *(above 3500 feet)*: Add 3 tablespoons milk to sugar mixture. Bake as directed above.

NUTRITION INFORMATION PER SERVING: Serving Size: 1 Cookie ♦ Calories: 60 ♦ Calories from Fat: 25 ♦ **% DAILY VALUE:** Total Fat: 3 g 5% ♦ Saturated Fat: 0 g 0% ♦ Cholesterol: 5 mg 2% ♦ Sodium: 50 mg 2% ♦ Total Carbohydrate: 7 g 2% ♦ Dietary Fiber: 0 g 0% ♦ Sugars: 4 g ♦ Protein: 1 g ♦ Vitamin A: 0% ♦ Vitamin C: 0% ♦ Calcium: 0% ♦ Iron: 0% ♦ **DIETARY EXCHANGES:** ½ Starch, ½ Fat OR ½ Carbohydrate, ½ Fat

VARIATIONS
Coconut Refrigerator Cookies: Add 1 cup coconut with nuts.
Lemon Refrigerator Cookies: Add 1 tablespoon grated lemon peel with flour.
Orange Refrigerator Cookies: Add 1 tablespoon grated orange peel with flour.
Spice Refrigerator Cookies: Add 1 teaspoon cinnamon, ½ teaspoon nutmeg and ¼ to ½ teaspoon cloves with flour.

COOK'S NOTE

TIPS FOR MAKING REFRIGERATOR COOKIES

These are ideal when you have limited baking time, need only a few cookies at a time, or want to be ready to serve warm-from-the-oven cookies at a moment's notice. The dough is mixed in advance and chilled, then sliced as needed for baking.

To store the dough, mold it into logs and wrap them in plastic wrap or waxed paper. Twist the ends of the wrap tightly to secure it. Depending on the softness of the dough, shaping and wrapping may be easier if you chill the dough for about an hour in the mixing bowl first. You may refrigerate the rolls for up to a week. For longer-term storage, place the rolls in a labeled, resealable freezer bag.

To bake refrigerator cookies, unwrap the dough and slice it with a thin, sharp knife, rotating the roll after every few slices to keep it from flattening. Frozen logs may be sliced and baked without thawing; increase the baking time slightly.

Spritz Cookies

Spritz Cookies

PREP TIME: I HOUR ✦ YIELD: 5 DOZEN COOKIES

    I cup powdered sugar
    I cup butter, softened
    ½ teaspoon vanilla
    I egg
    2⅓ cups all-purpose flour
    ¼ teaspoon salt

1. Heat oven to 400°F. In large bowl, combine powdered sugar, butter, vanilla and egg; beat until light and fluffy. Add flour and salt; mix well.

2. Fit cookie press with desired template. Fill cookie press; press dough onto ungreased cookie sheets.

3. Bake at 400°F. for 5 to 7 minutes or until edges are firm but not brown. Immediately remove from cookie sheets.

HIGH ALTITUDE (*above 3500 feet*): No change.

NUTRITION INFORMATION PER SERVING: Serving Size: 1 Cookie ✦ Calories: 50 ✦ Calories from Fat: 25 ✦ **% DAILY VALUE:** Total Fat: 3 g 5% ✦ Saturated Fat: 2 g 10% ✦ Cholesterol: 10 mg 3% ✦ Sodium: 40 mg 2% ✦ Total Carbohydrate: 6 g 2% ✦ Dietary Fiber: 0 g 0% ✦ Sugars: 2 g ✦ Protein: 1 g ✦ Vitamin A: 2% ✦ Vitamin C: 0% ✦ Calcium: 0% ✦ Iron: 0% ✦ **DIETARY EXCHANGES:** ½ Starch, ½ Fat OR ½ Carbohydrate, ½ Fat

VARIATIONS

Chocolate Spritz Cookies: Add 2 oz. melted unsweetened chocolate to powdered sugar mixture.

Eggnog Spritz Cookies: Substitute 1 teaspoon rum extract for vanilla and add ¼ teaspoon nutmeg with flour.

Orange Spritz Cookies: Add 1 tablespoon grated orange peel with flour.

COOKIE PRESSES

Cookie presses, sometimes called cookie guns, make it easy to turn out professional-looking spritz cookies at home. The device, available in kitchen specialty shops or department stores, consists of a metal or plastic cylinder that holds the dough and a handle that fits into one end. After the dough is "loaded" into the cylinder, a disk with a stamped-out design fits into the front end of the press. Turning or pressing the handle forces the dough through the disk, yielding cookies of uniform size and shape. Cookie-press dough must be firm enough so it doesn't stick to the inside of the press during shaping and stable enough to hold its shape when baked. For best results, use a spritz recipe or another recipe specifically formulated for a cookie press.

Pumpkin Bars

PREP TIME: 25 MINUTES (READY IN I HOUR 55 MINUTES) ✦ YIELD: 48 BARS

BARS
    2 cups all-purpose flour
    2 cups sugar
    2 teaspoons baking powder
    I teaspoon baking soda
    I teaspoon cinnamon
    I teaspoon nutmeg
    ½ teaspoon salt
    ½ teaspoon cloves
    I cup oil
    I (16-oz.) can (2 cups) pumpkin
    4 eggs
    ½ cup chopped nuts
    ½ cup raisins

FROSTING

2 cups powdered sugar
⅓ cup margarine or butter, softened
1 (3-oz.) pkg. cream cheese, softened
1 tablespoon milk
1 teaspoon vanilla

1. Heat oven to 350°F. Grease 15 × 10 × 1-inch baking pan. In large bowl, combine all bar ingredients except nuts and raisins; beat at low speed until moistened. Beat 2 minutes at medium speed. Stir in nuts and raisins. Pour into greased pan.
2. Bake at 350°F. for 25 to 30 minutes or until toothpick inserted in center comes out clean. Cool 1 hour or until completely cooled.
3. In small bowl, combine all frosting ingredients; beat until smooth. Spread over cooled bars. Cut into bars. Store in refrigerator.

HIGH ALTITUDE *(above 3500 feet)***:** Decrease baking soda to ½ teaspoon. Bake at 375°F. for 30 to 35 minutes.

NUTRITION INFORMATION PER SERVING: Serving Size: 1 Bar ◆ Calories: 160 ◆ Calories from Fat: 70 ◆ **% DAILY VALUE:** Total Fat: 8 g 12% ◆ Saturated Fat: 1 g 5% ◆ Cholesterol: 20 mg 7% ◆ Sodium: 95 mg 4% ◆ Total Carbohydrate: 20 g 7% ◆ Dietary Fiber: 1 g 2% ◆ Sugars: 15 g ◆ Protein: 2 g ◆ Vitamin A: 45% ◆ Vitamin C: 0% ◆ Calcium: 2% ◆ Iron: 4% ◆ **DIETARY EXCHANGES:** ½ Starch, 1 Fruit, 1½ Fat OR 1½ Carbohydrate, 1½ Fat

Chocolate Cherry Bars

PREP TIME: 15 MINUTES (READY IN 2 HOURS)
◆ YIELD: 48 BARS

BARS

1 (1 lb. 2.25-oz.) pkg. pudding-included devil's food cake mix
1 (21-oz.) can cherry pie filling
1 teaspoon almond extract
2 eggs, beaten

FROSTING

1 cup sugar
⅓ cup milk
5 tablespoons margarine or butter
1 (6-oz.) pkg. (1 cup) semisweet chocolate chips

1. Heat oven to 350°F. Grease and flour 15 × 10 × 1-inch baking pan or 13 × 9-inch pan. In large bowl, combine all bar ingredients; stir until well blended. Spread in greased and floured pan.
2. Bake at 350°F. until toothpick inserted in center comes out clean. For 15 × 10 × 1-inch pan, bake 20 to 30 minutes; for 13 × 9-inch pan, bake 25 to 30 minutes.
3. In small saucepan, combine sugar, milk and margarine; mix well. Bring to a boil. Boil 1 minute, stirring constantly. Remove from heat; stir in chocolate chips until smooth. Pour and spread over warm bars. Cool 1¼ hours or until completely cooled. Cut into bars.

HIGH ALTITUDE *(above 3500 feet)***:** For either size pan, bake at 375°F. for 25 to 30 minutes.

NUTRITION INFORMATION PER SERVING: Serving Size: 1 Bar ◆ Calories: 110 ◆ Calories from Fat: 35 ◆ **% DAILY VALUE:** Total Fat: 4 g 6% ◆ Saturated Fat: 1 g 5% ◆ Cholesterol: 10 mg 3% ◆ Sodium: 100 mg 4% ◆ Total Carbohydrate: 18 g 6% ◆ Dietary Fiber: 1 g 2% ◆ Sugars: 14 g ◆ Protein: 1 g ◆ Vitamin A: 0% ◆ Vitamin C: 0% ◆ Calcium: 0% ◆ Iron: 4% ◆ **DIETARY EXCHANGES:** ½ Starch, ½ Fruit, 1 Fat OR 1 Carbohydrate, 1 Fat

Chocolate Cherry Bars

COOK'S NOTE

COOLING COOKIES

Cool cookies on the cookie sheet a minute or two for easier handling, then use a pancake turner to transfer individual cookies from cookie sheets to a wire rack to cool completely. For bar cookies and brownies, set the entire pan on a wire rack to cool for better air circulation.

Whole Wheat Zucchini Bars

PREP TIME: 20 MINUTES (READY IN 2 HOURS 10 MINUTES) ◆ YIELD: 36 BARS

BARS
  3 eggs
1½ cups sugar
  1 cup oil
1½ cups whole wheat flour
  ½ cup all-purpose flour
  1 teaspoon baking powder
  ½ teaspoon salt
  1 teaspoon cinnamon
  2 cups shredded zucchini
  1 cup dried currants or raisins

GLAZE
  1 cup powdered sugar
  ¼ teaspoon cinnamon
  2 tablespoons margarine or butter, melted
  2 tablespoons milk

1. Heat oven to 350°F. Grease 13×9-inch pan. In large bowl, beat eggs. Add sugar and oil; beat well. In medium bowl, combine whole wheat flour, all-purpose flour, baking powder, salt and 1 teaspoon cinnamon; mix well. Add to egg mixture; mix well. Stir in zucchini and currants. Spread in greased pan.
2. Bake at 350°F. for 40 to 50 minutes or until toothpick inserted in center comes out clean. Cool 1 hour or until completely cooled.
3. In small bowl, combine all glaze ingredients until smooth. Spread evenly over cooled bars. Cut into bars.

HIGH ALTITUDE (*above 3500 feet*): No change.

NUTRITION INFORMATION PER SERVING: Serving Size: 1 Bar ◆ Calories: 150 ◆ Calories from Fat: 60 ◆ **% DAILY VALUE:** Total Fat: 7 g 11% ◆ Saturated Fat: 1 g 5% ◆ Cholesterol: 20 mg 7% ◆ Sodium: 55 mg 2% ◆ Total Carbohydrate: 20 g 7% ◆ Dietary Fiber: 1 g 4% ◆ Sugars: 14 g ◆ Protein: 2 g ◆ Vitamin A: 0% ◆ Vitamin C: 0% ◆ Calcium: 0% ◆ Iron: 4% ◆ **DIETARY EXCHANGES:** 1 Starch, ½ Fruit, 1 Fat OR 1½ Carbohydrate, 1 Fat

Rocky Road Fudge Bars

PREP TIME: 25 MINUTES (READY IN 2 HOURS 10 MINUTES) ◆ YIELD: 48 BARS

BASE
  ½ cup margarine or butter
  1 oz. unsweetened chocolate, cut up
  1 cup all-purpose flour
  1 cup sugar
  1 teaspoon baking powder
  1 teaspoon vanilla
  2 eggs
  ¾ cup chopped nuts

FILLING
  1 (8-oz.) pkg. cream cheese, softened, reserving 2 oz. for frosting
  ¼ cup margarine or butter, softened
  ½ cup sugar
  2 tablespoons all-purpose flour
  ½ teaspoon vanilla
  1 egg
  ¼ cup chopped nuts
  1 (6-oz.) pkg. (1 cup) semisweet chocolate chips
  2 cups miniature marshmallows

FROSTING
  ¼ cup margarine or butter
  ¼ cup milk
  1 oz. unsweetened chocolate, cut up
    Reserved cream cheese
  3 cups powdered sugar
  1 teaspoon vanilla

1. Heat oven to 350°F. Grease and flour 13×9-inch pan. In large saucepan, melt ½ cup margarine and 1 oz. unsweetened chocolate over low heat, stirring until smooth. Add all remaining base ingredients; mix well. Spread in greased and floured pan.
2. In small bowl, combine 6 oz. of the cream cheese, ¼ cup margarine, ½ cup sugar, 2 tablespoons flour, ½ teaspoon vanilla and 1 egg; beat 1 minute at medium speed until smooth and fluffy. Stir in ¼ cup nuts. Spread over chocolate mixture; sprinkle evenly with chocolate chips.
3. Bake at 350°F. for 25 to 35 minutes or until toothpick inserted in center comes out clean. Remove from oven; immediately sprinkle with marshmallows. Return to oven; bake an additional 2 minutes.
4. While marshmallows are baking, in large saucepan, combine ¼ cup margarine, milk, 1 oz. unsweetened chocolate and reserved

2 oz. cream cheese. Cook over low heat, stirring until well blended. Remove from heat; stir in powdered sugar and 1 teaspoon vanilla until smooth. Immediately pour frosting over puffed marshmallows and lightly swirl with knife to marble. Refrigerate 1 hour or until firm. Cut into bars. Store in refrigerator.

HIGH ALTITUDE (*above 3500 feet*): No change.

NUTRITION INFORMATION PER SERVING: Serving Size: 1 Bar • Calories: 170 • Calories from Fat: 80 • **% DAILY VALUE:** Total Fat: 9 g 14% • Saturated Fat: 3 g 15% • Cholesterol: 20 mg 7% • Sodium: 75 mg 3% • Total Carbohydrate: 21 g 7% • Dietary Fiber: 1 g 2% • Sugars: 17 g • Protein: 2 g • Vitamin A: 6% • Vitamin C: 0% • Calcium: 0% • Iron: 2% • **DIETARY EXCHANGES:** 1 Starch, ½ Fruit, 1½ Fat OR 1½ Carbohydrate, 1½ Fat

Chocolate Caramel Layer Bars

PREP TIME: 30 MINUTES (READY IN 1 HOUR 55 MINUTES) ✦ YIELD: 32 BARS

 1 (1 lb. 2.25-oz.) pkg. pudding-included chocolate cake mix
 ½ cup margarine or butter, melted
 1 cup evaporated milk
 35 vanilla caramels, unwrapped
 1 (12-oz.) pkg. (1⅔ cups) miniature semisweet candy-coated chocolate pieces

1. Heat oven to 350°F. Grease 13 × 9-inch pan. In large bowl, combine cake mix, margarine and ⅔ cup of the milk; mix well. Spread half of batter (about 2 cups) in greased pan. Bake at 350°F. for 15 minutes.
2. Meanwhile, in small saucepan, heat caramels with remaining ⅓ cup milk over low heat until melted, stirring constantly.
3. Remove pan from oven; sprinkle with 1 cup of the candy-coated pieces. Drizzle with caramel mixture. Drop remaining batter by heaping teaspoonfuls over caramel mixture. Sprinkle with remaining ⅔ cup of candy-coated pieces.
4. Return to oven; bake at 350°F. for an additional 20 to 24 minutes or until center is set. Cool 1 hour or until completely cooled. Cut into bars.

HIGH ALTITUDE (*above 3500 feet*): Add ¼ cup flour to dry cake mix. Bake as directed above.

NUTRITION INFORMATION PER SERVING: Serving Size: 1 Bar • Calories: 190 • Calories from Fat: 70 • **% DAILY VALUE:** Total Fat: 8 g 12% • Saturated Fat: 3 g 15% • Cholesterol: 4 mg 1% • Sodium: 170 mg 7% • Total Carbohydrate: 28 g 9% • Dietary Fiber: 1 g 3% • Sugars: 19 g • Protein: 2 g • Vitamin A: 4% • Vitamin C: 0% • Calcium: 4% • Iron: 2% • **DIETARY EXCHANGES:** ½ Starch, 1½ Fruit, 1½ Fat OR 2 Carbohydrate, 1½ Fat

Maple Walnut Bars

PREP TIME: 25 MINUTES (READY IN 2 HOURS 10 MINUTES) ✦ YIELD: 36 BARS

BASE
 1½ cups all-purpose flour
 ¼ cup firmly packed brown sugar
 ¼ teaspoon salt
 ½ cup margarine or butter, softened

FILLING
 ¾ cup sugar
 2 tablespoons all-purpose flour
 ¾ cup maple-flavored syrup
 2 tablespoons margarine or butter, melted
 1 teaspoon maple flavor or extract
 3 eggs
 1½ cups chopped walnuts

GLAZE
 1 cup powdered sugar
 ½ teaspoon maple flavor or extract
 1 to 2 tablespoons milk

1. Heat oven to 350°F. Grease 13 × 9-inch pan. In large bowl, combine all base ingredients; beat at low speed until crumbly. Press mixture in bottom of greased pan. Bake at 350°F. for 12 to 14 minutes or until light brown.
2. Meanwhile, in small bowl, combine all filling ingredients except walnuts; beat until well combined. Stir in walnuts.
3. Remove pan from oven; pour filling evenly over warm base. Return to oven; bake at 350°F. for an additional 20 to 30 minutes or until filling is set. Cool 1 hour or until completely cooled.
4. In small bowl, combine all glaze ingredients; blend until smooth, adding enough milk for desired drizzling consistency. Drizzle evenly over bars. Cut into bars. Store in refrigerator.

HIGH ALTITUDE (*above 3500 feet*): No change.

NUTRITION INFORMATION PER SERVING: Serving Size: 1 Bar • Calories: 150 • Calories from Fat: 60 • **% DAILY VALUE:** Total Fat: 7 g 11% • Saturated Fat: 1 g 5% • Cholesterol: 20 mg 7% • Sodium: 65 mg 3% • Total Carbohydrate: 19 g 6% • Dietary Fiber: 0 g 0% • Sugars: 12 g • Protein: 2 g • Vitamin A: 4% • Vitamin C: 0% • Calcium: 0% • Iron: 2% • **DIETARY EXCHANGES:** 1½ Fruit, 1½ Fat OR 1½ Carbohydrate, 1½ Fat

Oatmeal Carmelitas

PREP TIME: 30 MINUTES (READY IN 2 HOURS
55 MINUTES) ◆ YIELD: 36 BARS

CRUST
2 cups all-purpose flour
2 cups quick-cooking rolled oats
1½ cups firmly packed brown sugar
1 teaspoon baking soda
½ teaspoon salt
1¼ cups margarine or butter, softened

FILLING
1 (12.5-oz.) jar (1 cup) caramel ice cream
topping
3 tablespoons all-purpose flour
1 (6-oz.) pkg. (1 cup) semisweet chocolate
chips
½ cup chopped nuts

1. Heat oven to 350°F. Grease 13 × 9-inch pan. In large bowl, combine all crust ingredients; mix at low speed until crumbly. Reserve half of crumb mixture (about 3 cups) for topping. Press remaining crumb mixture in bottom of greased pan. Bake at 350°F. for 10 minutes.

*Top to bottom: Oatmeal Carmelitas,
Chocolate Chunk Cookies (page 408)*

2. Meanwhile, in small bowl, combine caramel topping and 3 tablespoons flour; blend well.
3. Remove partially baked crust from oven; sprinkle with chocolate chips and nuts. Drizzle evenly with caramel mixture; sprinkle with reserved crumb mixture.
4. Return to oven; bake an additional 18 to 22 minutes or until golden brown. Cool 1 hour or until completely cooled. Refrigerate 1 to 2 hours or until filling is set. Cut into bars.

HIGH ALTITUDE *(above 3500 feet)*: No change.

NUTRITION INFORMATION PER SERVING: Serving Size: 1 Bar ◆ Calories: 200 ◆ Calories from Fat: 80 ◆ % DAILY VALUE: Total Fat: 9 g 14% ◆ Saturated Fat: 2 g 10% ◆ Cholesterol: 0 mg 0% ◆ Sodium: 180 mg 8% ◆ Total Carbohydrate: 28 g 9% ◆ Dietary Fiber: 1 g 4% ◆ Sugars: 17 g ◆ Protein: 2 g ◆ Vitamin A: 6% ◆ Vitamin C: 0% ◆ Calcium: 2% ◆ Iron: 6% ◆ DIETARY EXCHANGES: 1 Starch, 1 Fruit, 1½ Fat OR 2 Carbohydrate, 1½ Fat

Homemade Chewy Granola Bars

PREP TIME: 15 MINUTES (READY IN 1 HOUR 30 MINUTES)
◆ YIELD: 24 BARS

1 cup firmly packed brown sugar
⅔ cup peanut butter
½ cup light corn syrup
½ cup margarine or butter, melted
2 teaspoons vanilla
3 cups quick-cooking rolled oats
½ cup coconut
½ cup shelled sunflower seeds
½ cup raisins
⅓ cup wheat germ
2 tablespoons sesame seed
1 (6-oz.) pkg. (1 cup) semisweet chocolate
chips or carob chips, if desired

1. Heat oven to 350°F. Grease 13 × 9-inch pan. In large bowl, combine brown sugar, peanut butter, corn syrup, margarine and vanilla; blend well. Add all remaining ingredients; mix well. Press evenly in greased pan.
2. Bake at 350°F. for 15 to 20 minutes or until light golden brown. Cool 1 hour or until completely cooled. Cut into bars.

HIGH ALTITUDE *(above 3500 feet)*: No change.

NUTRITION INFORMATION PER SERVING: Serving Size: 1 Bar ◆ Calories: 270 ◆ Calories from Fat: 120 ◆ % DAILY VALUE: Total Fat: 13 g 20% ◆ Saturated Fat: 3 g 15% ◆ Cholesterol: 0 mg 0% ◆ Sodium: 95 mg 4% ◆ Total Carbohydrate: 32 g 11% ◆ Dietary Fiber: 3 g 12% ◆ Sugars: 19 g ◆ Protein: 5 g ◆ Vitamin A: 4% ◆ Vitamin C: 0% ◆ Calcium: 2% ◆ Iron: 8% ◆ DIETARY EXCHANGES: 1½ Starch, ½ Fruit, 2½ Fat OR 2 Carbohydrate, 2½ Fat

Sunburst Lemon Bars

NUTRITION INFORMATION PER SERVING: Serving Size: 1 Bar ♦ Calories: 150 ♦ Calories from Fat: 50 ♦ **% DAILY VALUE:** Total Fat: 6 g 9% ♦ Saturated Fat: 1 g 5% ♦ Cholesterol: 25 mg 8% ♦ Sodium: 80 mg 3% ♦ Total Carbohydrate: 22 g 7% ♦ Dietary Fiber: 0 g 0% ♦ Sugars: 16 g ♦ Protein: 2 g ♦ Vitamin A: 6% ♦ Vitamin C: 0% ♦ Calcium: 0% ♦ Iron: 2% ♦ **DIETARY EXCHANGES:** 1 Starch, ½ Fruit, 1 Fat OR 1½ Carbohydrate, 1 Fat

Quick Cranberry-Orange Bars

PREP TIME: 20 MINUTES (READY IN 1 HOUR 55 MINUTES) ♦ YIELD: 16 BARS

BASE
  1 (15.6-oz.) pkg. cranberry quick bread mix
  ⅓ cup margarine or butter, softened
  1 egg

FILLING
  1 (16-oz.) can whole berry cranberry sauce
  1 tablespoon grated orange peel
  1 tablespoon cornstarch

1. Heat oven to 350°F. Grease 9-inch square pan. In large bowl, combine all base ingredients; mix well with pastry blender or fork until crumbly. Reserve 1 cup mixture for topping. Press remaining mixture evenly in bottom of greased pan.
2. In medium bowl, combine all filling ingredients; blend well. Spread filling evenly over base. Sprinkle evenly with reserved crumb mixture; press lightly.
3. Bake at 350°F. for 30 to 35 minutes or until top is golden brown. Cool 1 hour or until completely cooled. Cut into bars.

HIGH ALTITUDE *(above 3500 feet)*: No change.

NUTRITION INFORMATION PER SERVING: Serving Size: 1 Bar ♦ Calories: 190 ♦ Calories from Fat: 45 ♦ **% DAILY VALUE:** Total Fat: 5 g 8% ♦ Saturated Fat: 1 g 5% ♦ Cholesterol: 15 mg 5% ♦ Sodium: 170 mg 7% ♦ Total Carbohydrate: 34 g 11% ♦ Dietary Fiber: 1 g 4% ♦ Sugars: 22 g ♦ Protein: 2 g ♦ Vitamin A: 4% ♦ Vitamin C: 0% ♦ Calcium: 0% ♦ Iron: 6% ♦ **DIETARY EXCHANGES:** ½ Starch, 2 Fruit, 1 Fat OR 2½ Carbohydrate, 1 Fat

Quick Cranberry-Orange Bars

Sunburst Lemon Bars

PREP TIME: 15 MINUTES (READY IN 2 HOURS) ♦ YIELD: 36 BARS

BASE
  2 cups all-purpose flour
  ½ cup powdered sugar
  1 cup margarine or butter, softened

FILLING
  4 eggs, slightly beaten
  2 cups sugar
  ¼ cup all-purpose flour
  1 teaspoon baking powder
  ¼ cup lemon juice

FROSTING
  1 cup powdered sugar
  2 to 3 tablespoons lemon juice

1. Heat oven to 350°F. In large bowl, combine all base ingredients; beat at low speed until crumbly. Press mixture evenly in bottom of ungreased 13×9-inch pan. Bake at 350°F. for 20 to 30 minutes or until light golden brown.
2. Meanwhile, in large bowl, combine all filling ingredients except lemon juice; blend well. Stir in ¼ cup lemon juice.
3. Remove pan from oven. Pour filling over warm base. Bake an additional 25 to 30 minutes or until light golden brown. Cool 1 hour or until completely cooled.
4. In small bowl, combine 1 cup powdered sugar and enough lemon juice for desired spreading consistency; blend until smooth. Frost cooled bars. Cut into bars. If desired, sprinkle with powdered sugar; garnish with lemon peel.

HIGH ALTITUDE *(above 3500 feet)*: No change.

Double Date Bars

PREP TIME: 25 MINUTES (READY IN 1 HOUR 20 MINUTES)
◆ YIELD: 32 BARS

FILLING
    1 (8-oz.) pkg. (1½ cups) chopped pitted dates
    ½ cup raisins
    ¼ cup sugar
    1 cup water
    1 teaspoon vanilla

BASE
    1 (1 lb. 0.6-oz.) pkg. date quick bread mix
    ½ cup margarine or butter, softened
    ½ cup chopped walnuts
    ¼ cup quick-cooking rolled oats

1. Heat oven to 375°F. Grease 13×9-inch pan. In medium saucepan, combine all filling ingredients except vanilla; mix well. Bring to a boil. Reduce heat to low; cook 10 minutes or until thickened, stirring occasionally. Remove from heat; stir in vanilla.
2. Meanwhile, place quick bread mix in large bowl. With pastry blender or fork, cut in margarine until crumbly. Stir in walnuts. Reserve 1 cup mixture for topping. Press remaining mixture in bottom of greased pan.
3. Carefully spread filling over base. In small bowl, combine reserved 1 cup of base mixture and oats; mix well. Sprinkle over filling.
4. Bake at 375°F. for 18 to 23 minutes or until top is golden brown. Cool 30 minutes or until completely cooled. Cut into bars.

HIGH ALTITUDE *(above 3500 feet)*: No change.

NUTRITION INFORMATION PER SERVING: Serving Size: 1 Bar ◆ Calories: 130 ◆ Calories from Fat: 45 ◆ % DAILY VALUE: Total Fat: 5 g 8% ◆ Saturated Fat: 1 g 5% ◆ Cholesterol: 0 mg 0% ◆ Sodium: 90 mg 4% ◆ Total Carbohydrate: 21 g 7% ◆ Dietary Fiber: 1 g 4% ◆ Sugars: 15 g ◆ Protein: 1 g ◆ Vitamin A: 2% ◆ Vitamin C: 0% ◆ Calcium: 0% ◆ Iron: 4% ◆ DIETARY EXCHANGES: 1½ Fruit, 1 Fat OR 1½ Carbohydrate, 1 Fat

Cinnamon Toffee Bars

PREP TIME: 20 MINUTES (READY IN 1 HOUR 45 MINUTES) ◆ YIELD: 48 BARS

BARS
    1 cup firmly packed brown sugar
    1 cup butter, softened
    1 egg, separated
    2 cups all-purpose flour
    1 teaspoon cinnamon
    1 cup chopped nuts

GLAZE
    ½ cup semisweet chocolate chips
    2 teaspoons shortening

1. Heat oven to 350°F. In large bowl, combine brown sugar and butter; beat until light and fluffy. Add egg yolk; blend well. Add flour and cinnamon; mix well. Press dough in ungreased 15×10×1-inch baking pan.
2. In small bowl, slightly beat egg white; brush over dough. Sprinkle with nuts; press lightly into dough.
3. Bake at 350°F. for 12 to 22 minutes or until light golden brown. Cool 30 minutes or until completely cooled.

4. In small saucepan, melt chocolate chips and shortening over low heat, stirring constantly until smooth. Drizzle over cooled bars. Let stand until set, about 30 minutes. Cut into bars.

HIGH ALTITUDE (*above 3500 feet*): No change.

NUTRITION INFORMATION PER SERVING: Serving Size: 1 Bar ✦ Calories: 100 ✦ Calories from Fat: 50 ✦ **% DAILY VALUE:** Total Fat: 6 g 9% ✦ Saturated Fat: 3 g 15% ✦ Cholesterol: 15 mg 5% ✦ Sodium: 45 mg 2% ✦ Total Carbohydrate: 10 g 3% ✦ Dietary Fiber: 0 g 0% ✦ Sugars: 6 g ✦ Protein: 1 g ✦ Vitamin A: 4% ✦ Vitamin C: 0% ✦ Calcium: 0% ✦ Iron: 2% ✦ **DIETARY EXCHANGES:** ½ Starch, 1 Fat OR ½ Carbohydrate, 1 Fat

Salted Peanut Chews

PREP TIME: 35 MINUTES (READY IN 1 HOUR 35 MINUTES) ✦ YIELD: 36 BARS

CRUST
1½ cups all-purpose flour
⅔ cup firmly packed brown sugar
½ teaspoon baking powder
½ teaspoon salt
¼ teaspoon baking soda
½ cup margarine or butter, softened
1 teaspoon vanilla
2 egg yolks
3 cups miniature marshmallows

TOPPING
⅔ cup corn syrup
¼ cup margarine or butter
2 teaspoons vanilla
1 (10-oz.) pkg. peanut butter chips
2 cups crisp rice cereal
2 cups salted peanuts

1. Heat oven to 350°F. In large bowl, combine all crust ingredients except marshmallows at low speed until crumbly. Press firmly in bottom of ungreased 13 × 9-inch pan.
2. Bake at 350°F. for 12 to 15 minutes or until light golden brown. Remove from oven; immediately sprinkle with marshmallows. Return to oven; bake an additional 1 to 2 minutes or until marshmallows just begin to puff. Cool while preparing topping.
3. In large saucepan, combine all topping ingredients except cereal and peanuts. Heat just until chips are melted and mixture is smooth, stirring constantly. Remove from heat; stir in cereal and peanuts. Immediately spoon warm topping over marshmallows; spread to cover. Refrigerate 45 minutes or until firm. Cut into bars.

HIGH ALTITUDE (*above 3500 feet*): No change.

NUTRITION INFORMATION PER SERVING: Serving Size: 1 Bar ✦ Calories: 200 ✦ Calories from Fat: 90 ✦ **% DAILY VALUE:** Total Fat: 10 g 15% ✦ Saturated Fat: 2 g 10% ✦ Cholesterol: 10 mg 3% ✦ Sodium: 170 mg 7% ✦ Total Carbohydrate: 23 g 8% ✦ Dietary Fiber: 2 g 8% ✦ Sugars: 13 g ✦ Protein: 4 g ✦ Vitamin A: 4% ✦ Vitamin C: 0% ✦ Calcium: 2% ✦ Iron: 4% ✦ **DIETARY EXCHANGES:** 1 Starch, ½ Fruit, 2 Fat OR 1½ Carbohydrate, 2 Fat

Cashew Caramel Brownies

PREP TIME: 20 MINUTES (READY IN 2 HOURS 10 MINUTES) ✦ YIELD: 48 BROWNIES

BROWNIES
1½ cups firmly packed brown sugar
¾ cup unsalted or regular butter, softened
3 eggs
3 oz. unsweetened chocolate, melted, cooled
1 tablespoon vanilla
1¼ cups all-purpose flour
¼ teaspoon salt
1½ cups semisweet chocolate chips
1 cup chopped cashews

TOPPING
16 caramels, unwrapped
3 tablespoons milk

1. Heat oven to 325°F. Line two 9-inch square pans with foil so foil extends over sides of pan; lightly grease foil.
2. In large bowl, combine brown sugar and butter; beat until light and fluffy. Add eggs 1 at a time, beating well after each addition. Add cooled unsweetened chocolate and vanilla; blend well.
3. Add flour and salt; mix well. Fold in chocolate chips. Pour batter into greased foil-lined pans. Sprinkle cashews evenly over batter; press lightly.
4. Bake at 325°F. for 20 to 25 minutes or until firm to the touch. Cool 30 minutes.
5. In small saucepan, combine topping ingredients; cook over low heat, stirring frequently, until melted and smooth. Drizzle over brownies. Cool 1 hour or until completely cooled. Remove from pan by lifting foil; remove foil. Cut into bars.

HIGH ALTITUDE (*above 3500 feet*): Increase flour to 1½ cups; decrease brown sugar to 1¼ cups. Bake as directed above.

NUTRITION INFORMATION PER SERVING: Serving Size: 1 Brownie ✦ Calories: 150 ✦ Calories from Fat: 70 ✦ **% DAILY VALUE:** Total Fat: 8 g 12% ✦ Saturated Fat: 4 g 20% ✦ Cholesterol: 20 mg 7% ✦ Sodium: 30 mg 1% ✦ Total Carbohydrate: 17 g 6% ✦ Dietary Fiber: 1 g 3% ✦ Sugars: 12 g ✦ Protein: 2 g ✦ Vitamin A: 2% ✦ Vitamin C: 0% ✦ Calcium: 0% ✦ Iron: 4% ✦ **DIETARY EXCHANGES:** ½ Starch, ½ Fruit, 1½ Fat OR 1 Carbohydrate, 1½ Fat

Gourmet Mint Brownies

Gourmet Mint Brownies

PREP TIME: 30 MINUTES (READY IN 2 HOURS 15 MINUTES) ✦ YIELD: 36 BROWNIES

FILLING

1 (8-oz.) pkg. cream cheese, softened
¼ cup sugar
1 egg
1 teaspoon mint extract
4 drops green food color

BROWNIES

1 cup margarine or butter
4 oz. unsweetened chocolate, cut into pieces
2 cups sugar
2 teaspoons vanilla
4 eggs
1 cup all-purpose flour

FROSTING

2 tablespoons margarine or butter
2 tablespoons corn syrup
2 tablespoons water
2 oz. unsweetened chocolate, cut into pieces
1 teaspoon vanilla
1 cup powdered sugar

1. Heat oven to 350°F. Grease and flour 13×9-inch pan. In small bowl, combine cream cheese and ¼ cup sugar; beat until smooth. Add 1 egg, mint extract and food color; mix well. Set aside.

2. In large saucepan, melt 1 cup margarine and 4 oz. chocolate over very low heat, stirring constantly. Remove from heat; cool 15 minutes or until slightly cooled.

3. Stir 2 cups sugar and 2 teaspoons vanilla into chocolate mixture. Add 4 eggs one at a time, beating well after each addition. Stir in flour; mix well. Spread in greased and floured pan. Carefully spoon filling over brownie mixture. Lightly swirl filling into brownie mixture.

4. Bake at 350°F. for 45 to 50 minutes or until set. Cool 1 hour or until completely cooled.

5. In medium saucepan, combine 2 tablespoons margarine, corn syrup and water; bring to a rolling boil. Remove from heat. Add 2 oz. chocolate; stir until melted. Stir in 1 teaspoon vanilla and powdered sugar; beat until smooth. Frost cooled brownies. Cut into bars. Store in refrigerator.

HIGH ALTITUDE *(above 3500 feet)*: No change.

NUTRITION INFORMATION PER SERVING: Serving Size: 1 Brownie ✦ Calories: 190 ✦ Calories from Fat: 100 ✦ **% DAILY VALUE:** Total Fat: 11 g 17% ✦ Saturated Fat: 4 g 20% ✦ Cholesterol: 35 mg 12% ✦ Sodium: 95 mg 4% ✦ Total Carbohydrate: 21 g 7% ✦ Dietary Fiber: 1 g 3% ✦ Sugars: 16 g ✦ Protein: 2 g ✦ Vitamin A: 8% ✦ Vitamin C: 0% ✦ Calcium: 0% ✦ Iron: 4% ✦ **DIETARY EXCHANGES:** ½ Starch, 1 Fruit, 2 Fat OR 1½ Carbohydrate, 2 Fat

Top to bottom: Chocolate Caramel Layer Bars (page 429), Espresso Brownies (page 435)

Espresso Brownies

PREP TIME: 10 MINUTES (READY IN 1 HOUR 45 MINUTES)
◆ YIELD: 24 BARS

 1 (1 lb. 3.5-oz.) pkg. fudge brownie mix
 2 tablespoons instant espresso coffee powder
 ½ cup oil
 ¼ cup water
 2 eggs
 4 oz. (¾ cup) mocha candy beans

1. Heat oven to 350°F. Grease bottom only of 13×9-inch pan. In large bowl, combine brownie mix, espresso powder, oil, water and eggs; beat 50 strokes with spoon. Spread batter in greased pan. Sprinkle evenly with mocha candy beans.
2. Bake at 350°F. for 28 to 30 minutes. DO NOT OVERBAKE. Cool 1 hour or until completely cooled. Cut into bars.

HIGH ALTITUDE (*above 3500 feet*)**:** See package for directions.

NUTRITION INFORMATION PER SERVING: Serving Size: 1 Bar ◆ Calories: 180 ◆ Calories from Fat: 60 ◆ **% DAILY VALUE:** Total Fat: 7 g 11% ◆ Saturated Fat: 1 g 5% ◆ Cholesterol: 20 mg 7% ◆ Sodium: 70 mg 3% ◆ Total Carbohydrate: 26 g 9% ◆ Dietary Fiber: 1 g 3% ◆ Sugars: 17 g ◆ Protein: 2 g ◆ Vitamin A: 0% ◆ Vitamin C: 0% ◆ Calcium: 0% ◆ Iron: 4% ◆ **DIETARY EXCHANGES:** ½ Starch, 1 Fruit, 1½ Fat OR 1½ Carbohydrate, 1½ Fat

Pecan Blondies with Browned Butter Frosting

PREP TIME: 30 MINUTES (READY IN 1 HOUR 55 MINUTES)
◆ YIELD: 36 BARS

BARS
 1 cup sugar
 ½ cup firmly packed brown sugar
 ½ cup butter, softened
 1 teaspoon vanilla
 2 eggs
 1½ cups all-purpose flour
 1 teaspoon baking powder
 ½ teaspoon salt
 ½ cup chopped pecans

FROSTING*
 2 tablespoons butter (do not use margarine)
 2 cups powdered sugar
 ¼ teaspoon vanilla
 2 to 4 tablespoons milk

GARNISH
 36 pecan halves, if desired

1. Heat oven to 350°F. Grease 13×9-inch pan. In large bowl, combine sugar, brown sugar and ½ cup butter; beat until light and fluffy. Add 1 teaspoon vanilla and eggs; blend well. Add flour, baking powder and salt; mix well. Stir in ½ cup pecans. Spread in bottom of greased pan.
2. Bake at 350°F. for 23 to 33 minutes or until toothpick inserted in center comes out clean. Cool 1 hour or until completely cooled.
3. Heat 2 tablespoons butter in medium saucepan over medium heat until light golden brown. Remove from heat. Stir in powdered sugar, ¼ teaspoon vanilla and enough milk for desired spreading consistency; blend until smooth. Spread over cooled bars. Arrange pecan halves over frosting. Cut into bars.

> **TIP:** * If desired, omit frosting and pecan halves. When bars are cool, sprinkle with powdered sugar.

HIGH ALTITUDE (*above 3500 feet*)**:** Increase flour to 1¾ cups; decrease granulated sugar to ½ cup. Bake as directed above.

NUTRITION INFORMATION PER SERVING: Serving Size: 1 Bar ◆ Calories: 130 ◆ Calories from Fat: 45 ◆ **% DAILY VALUE:** Total Fat: 5 g 8% ◆ Saturated Fat: 2 g 10% ◆ Cholesterol: 20 mg 7% ◆ Sodium: 80 mg 3% ◆ Total Carbohydrate: 20 g 7% ◆ Dietary Fiber: 0 g 0% ◆ Sugars: 15 g ◆ Protein: 1 g ◆ Vitamin A: 2% ◆ Vitamin C: 0% ◆ Calcium: 0% ◆ Iron: 2% ◆ **DIETARY EXCHANGES:** 1½ Fruit, 1 Fat OR 1½ Carbohydrate, 1 Fat

Pecan Blondies with Browned Butter Frosting

Fudgy Brownies

PREP TIME: 30 MINUTES (READY IN 2 HOURS)
◆ YIELD: 24 BROWNIES

BROWNIES
4 oz. unsweetened chocolate
½ cup margarine or butter
2 cups sugar
2 teaspoons vanilla
4 eggs
1 cup all-purpose flour
¼ teaspoon salt

GLAZE
½ cup semisweet chocolate chips
1 tablespoon margarine or butter

1. Heat oven to 350°F. Grease 13×9-inch pan. In small saucepan, melt chocolate and ½ cup margarine over low heat, stirring constantly until smooth. Remove from heat; cool 10 minutes or until slightly cooled.
2. In medium bowl, combine sugar, vanilla and eggs; beat until light and fluffy. Add flour, salt and chocolate mixture; blend well. Spread in greased pan.
3. Bake at 350°F. for 30 to 38 minutes. DO NOT OVERBAKE. Cool 1 hour or until completely cooled.
4. In small saucepan, melt glaze ingredients over low heat, stirring constantly until smooth. Drizzle glaze over cooled brownies. Let stand until set. Cut into bars.

HIGH ALTITUDE (*above 3500 feet*): No change.

NUTRITION INFORMATION PER SERVING: Serving Size: 1 Brownie ◆ Calories: 190 ◆ Calories from Fat: 80 ◆ **% DAILY VALUE:** Total Fat: 9 g 14% ◆ Saturated Fat: 3 g 15% ◆ Cholesterol: 35 mg 12% ◆ Sodium: 85 mg 4% ◆ Total Carbohydrate: 24 g 8% ◆ Dietary Fiber: 1 g 4% ◆ Sugars: 19 g ◆ Protein: 2 g ◆ Vitamin A: 4% ◆ Vitamin C: 0% ◆ Calcium: 0% ◆ Iron: 4% ◆ **DIETARY EXCHANGES:** ½ Starch, 1 Fruit, 2 Fat OR 1½ Carbohydrate, 2 Fat

---

COOK'S NOTE

MELTING CHOCOLATE IN THE MICROWAVE

Place chocolate pieces in a microwave-safe container. If possible, melt the chocolate right in the mixing bowl before adding other ingredients. Watch closely: Most chocolate melted by microwave will retain its original shape somewhat even when melted. Look for a glossy appearance and stir the chocolate to judge whether more time is needed.

1 oz. baking chocolate:
1 to 2 minutes on HIGH; stir
Add 10 to 20 seconds at a time until chocolate can be stirred smooth

2 oz. baking chocolate:
1 to 2 minutes on HIGH; stir
Add 10 to 20 seconds at a time until chocolate can be stirred smooth

6 oz. (1 cup) semisweet chocolate chips:
1 minute on HIGH; stir
Add 10 to 20 seconds at a time until chocolate can be stirred smooth

12 oz. (2 cups) semisweet chocolate chips:
1 minute on HIGH; stir
Add 10 to 20 seconds at a time until chocolate can be stirred smooth

---

Pecan Toffee Squares

PREP TIME: 20 MINUTES (READY IN 1 HOUR 50 MINUTES) ◆ YIELD: 36 BARS

BASE
1 (1 lb. 2.25-oz.) pkg. pudding-included yellow cake mix
½ cup margarine or butter, softened
1 egg

FILLING
1 (14-oz.) can sweetened condensed milk (not evaporated)
1 teaspoon vanilla
1 egg
1 (6-oz.) pkg. chocolate-coated toffee bits
1 cup chopped pecans

1. Heat oven to 350°F. Grease 13×9-inch pan. In large bowl, combine cake mix, margarine and 1 egg; mix well with pastry blender or fork. Press mixture in bottom of greased pan. Bake at 350°F. for 7 minutes.
2. Meanwhile, in medium bowl, combine condensed milk, vanilla and 1 egg; mix well. Stir in toffee bits and pecans.
3. Remove pan from oven; pour filling evenly over warm base. Return to oven; bake an additional 22 to 30 minutes or until filling is set. Cool 1 hour or until completely cooled. Cut into bars. Store in refrigerator.

HIGH ALTITUDE (*above 3500 feet*): No change.

NUTRITION INFORMATION PER SERVING: Serving Size: 1 Bar ◆ Calories: 170 ◆ Calories from Fat: 80 ◆ **% DAILY VALUE:** Total Fat: 9 g 14% ◆ Saturated Fat: 3 g 15% ◆ Cholesterol: 20 mg 7% ◆ Sodium: 160 mg 7% ◆ Total Carbohydrate: 21 g 7% ◆ Dietary Fiber: 1 g 4% ◆ Sugars: 15 g ◆ Protein: 2 g ◆ Vitamin A: 4% ◆ Vitamin C: 0% ◆ Calcium: 4% ◆ Iron: 2% ◆ **DIETARY EXCHANGES:** ½ Starch, 1 Fruit, 1½ Fat OR 1½ Carbohydrate, 1½ Fat

HOW TO CUT BARS AND CANDIES PERFECTLY

Lining a pan with foil makes it easier to cut bars into even portions. Before putting the dough in the baking pan, turn the pan upside down. Cut a piece of foil 4 inches longer than the baking pan and form the foil over the outside bottom of the pan. Set the foil aside.

Turn the pan right side up. Dampen the bottom of the inside of the pan to hold the foil in place.

Position the preformed foil inside the pan. Grease the foil if recommended in the recipe, add the batter and bake as directed.

Cool and refrigerate the baked bars for about 30 minutes. Lift the bars from the pan. Remove the foil, place the brownies on a flat surface and cut the bars into serving pieces with a sharp knife.

TIPS FOR MAKING CANDY

Homemade Candy

Long before prepackaged sweets lined every checkout counter, home cooks concocted super-rich fudge, nut-studded brittle and chewy caramel right in their own kitchens. Today, candy thermometers let you avoid much of the guesswork that once made novice candy makers uncertain of success. If you've never tasted homemade confections rich with fresh butter, cream and other indulgences, you're in for a real treat.

Candy making depends in large part on the sugar reaching a precise temperature that determines the final texture. To make sure the operation goes like clockwork, follow these hints.

- Before you begin, assemble and accurately measure all ingredients. Set out and prepare the pan or paper needed for the finished candy.
- Use a heavy saucepan to prevent scorching. Make sure it's large enough to accommodate the bubbling up that occurs during candy making.
- If you want twice as much candy, prepare the recipe twice. Making a double batch can throw off the timing and the results.
- Verify the temperature of the sugar syrup mixture with a candy thermometer.
- Stir as directed to prevent sugar crystals from forming and giving the candy a grainy texture. Do not scrape the undissolved crystals into the pan or the candy will become grainy.

   Caution: Sugar syrup gets very hot, much hotter than boiling water, and can cause serious burns. Use a large pot to prevent boil-overs and be aware that the mixture will foam up when baking soda is added.
- Unless otherwise directed, heat sugar over moderate heat so it doesn't come to a boil too rapidly.
- In humid weather or on rainy days, cook candy to a temperature 1 or 2 degrees higher than specified in the recipe.

Divinity

PREP TIME: 40 MINUTES ✦ YIELD: 24 CANDIES

2 cups sugar
¼ teaspoon salt
½ cup water
⅓ cup light corn syrup
2 egg whites
1 teaspoon vanilla
½ to 1 cup chopped nuts

1. Line cookie sheet with waxed paper. In heavy medium saucepan, combine sugar, salt, water and corn syrup; cook and stir until sugar is dissolved. Bring to a full boil, stirring constantly. Cook uncovered without stirring until candy thermometer reaches hard-ball stage (250°F.).
2. Meanwhile, in large bowl, beat egg whites until stiff peaks form. Pour syrup over egg whites in steady thin stream, beating continuously until mixture holds its shape and begins to lose its gloss. Stir in vanilla and nuts.
3. Drop by teaspoonfuls onto waxed paper-lined cookie sheet. Store in tightly covered container.

HIGH ALTITUDE (above 3500 feet): Cook until candy thermometer reaches 240°F.

NUTRITION INFORMATION PER SERVING: Serving Size: 1 Candy ✦ Calories: 120 ✦ Calories from Fat: 25 ✦ **% DAILY VALUE:** Total Fat: 3 g 5% ✦ Saturated Fat: 0 g 0% ✦ Cholesterol: 0 mg 0% ✦ Sodium: 35 mg 1% ✦ Total Carbohydrate: 21 g 7% ✦ Dietary Fiber: 0 g 0% ✦ Sugars: 19 g ✦ Protein: 1 g ✦ Vitamin A: 0% ✦ Vitamin C: 0% ✦ Calcium: 0% ✦ Iron: 0% ✦ **DIETARY EXCHANGES:** 1½ Fruit, ½ Fat OR 1½ Carbohydrate, ½ Fat

Top to bottom: Divinity, Cherry Almond Bark

Candy-Coated Pretzels

PREP TIME: 30 MINUTES ✦ YIELD: 24 PRETZELS

8 oz. chocolate-flavored or vanilla-flavored candy coating (almond bark), cut into pieces
24 (4 oz.) small pretzel twists

1. Line cookie sheet with waxed paper. Melt candy coating in medium saucepan over low heat, stirring constantly. Keep mixture warm.
2. Dip pretzels into coating; allow excess to drip off. Place on waxed paper-lined cookie sheet.

NUTRITION INFORMATION PER SERVING: Serving Size: 1 Pretzel ✦ Calories: 70 ✦ Calories from Fat: 25 ✦ **% DAILY VALUE:** Total Fat: 3 g 5% ✦ Saturated fat: 3 g 15% ✦ Cholesterol: 0 mg 0% ✦ Sodium: 90 mg 4% ✦ Total Carbohydrate: 10 g 3% ✦ Dietary Fiber: 0 g 0% ✦ Sugars: 6 g ✦ Protein: 1 g ✦ Vitamin A: 0% ✦ Vitamin C: 0% ✦ Calcium: 0% ✦ Iron: 0% ✦ **DIETARY EXCHANGES:** ½ Starch, ½ Fat OR ½ Carbohydrate, ½ Fat

Cherry Almond Bark

PREP TIME: 20 MINUTES (READY IN 50 MINUTES)
✦ YIELD: 10 DOZEN (2-INCH) PIECES (2½ POUNDS)

1 (10-oz.) jar maraschino cherries, drained, chopped
1 (24-oz.) pkg. vanilla-flavored candy coating (almond bark), coarsely chopped
1 cup chopped blanched almonds
½ teaspoon almond extract

1. Line 2 large cookie sheets with waxed paper. Spread chopped cherries on several layers of paper towels to drain completely.
2. Melt candy coating in heavy large saucepan over very low heat, stirring constantly. Stir in cherries, almonds and almond extract. Spread mixture thinly on waxed paper-lined cookie sheets. Let stand until set, about 30 minutes.
3. Break candy into pieces. Store in tightly covered container in refrigerator or cool, dry place.

NUTRITION INFORMATION PER SERVING: Serving Size: 1 Piece ✦ Calories: 35 ✦ Calories from Fat: 20 ✦ **% DAILY VALUE:** Total Fat: 2 g 3% ✦ Saturated Fat: 1 g 5% ✦ Cholesterol: 0 mg 0% ✦ Sodium: 5 mg 0% ✦ Total Carbohydrate: 4 g 1% ✦ Dietary Fiber: 0 g 0% ✦ Sugars: 4 g ✦ Protein: 1 g ✦ Vitamin A: 0% ✦ Vitamin C: 0% ✦ Calcium: 0% ✦ Iron: 0% ✦ **DIETARY EXCHANGES:** ½ Fruit, ½ Fat OR ½ Carbohydrate, ½ Fat

Penuche

PREP TIME: 50 MINUTES (READY IN 4 HOURS 20 MINUTES) ◆ YIELD: 64 SQUARES

1½ cups sugar
1½ cups firmly packed brown sugar
  1 cup milk
  2 tablespoons corn syrup
  ¼ teaspoon salt
  2 tablespoons butter
  1 teaspoon vanilla
  ½ cup chopped nuts

1. Line 9 or 8-inch square pan with foil so foil extends over sides of pan; butter foil.
2. In heavy large saucepan, combine sugar, brown sugar, milk, corn syrup and salt; stir to mix well. Cook over medium-high heat, stirring frequently, until mixture comes to a boil. Continue cooking about 15 minutes or until mixture reaches soft-ball stage (234°F.).
3. Remove saucepan from heat; stir in butter until melted. Cool about 30 minutes or until lukewarm (110°F.). Stir in vanilla. Beat until creamy and light brown color. Stir in nuts until well mixed. Pour into buttered foil-lined pan, spreading evenly. Cover; refrigerate at least 3 hours or overnight.
4. Remove candy from pan by lifting foil; remove foil from sides of candy. With knife dipped in warm water, cut candy into squares. Store in refrigerator.

HIGH ALTITUDE (*above 3500 feet*)**:** Cook until candy thermometer reaches 224°F.

NUTRITION INFORMATION PER SERVING: Serving Size: 1 Square ◆ Calories: 50 ◆ Calories from Fat: 10 ◆ **% DAILY VALUE:** Total Fat: 1 g 2% ◆ Saturated Fat: 0 g 0% ◆ Cholesterol: 0 mg 0% ◆ Sodium: 15 mg 1% ◆ Total Carbohydrate: 11 g 4% ◆ Dietary Fiber: 0 g 0% ◆ Sugars: 10 g ◆ Protein: 0 g ◆ Vitamin A: 0% ◆ Vitamin C: 0% ◆ Calcium: 0% ◆ Iron: 0% ◆ **DIETARY EXCHANGES:** 1 Fruit OR 1 Carbohydrate

Old-Fashioned Caramels

PREP TIME: 1 HOUR (READY IN 1 HOUR 30 MINUTES) ◆ YIELD: 48 SQUARES

  1 cup butter
2¼ cups firmly packed brown sugar
  1 cup light corn syrup
  1 (14-oz.) can sweetened condensed milk (not evaporated)
1½ teaspoons vanilla

1. Line 9-inch square pan with foil so foil extends over sides of pan; lightly butter foil.
2. In heavy 3-quart saucepan, melt butter. Add brown sugar; mix well. Stir in corn syrup. Cook over medium-low heat until sugar dissolves and mixture is well blended.
3. Remove saucepan from heat; stir in sweetened condensed milk. Cook over medium heat for 20 to 30 minutes, stirring constantly, until candy thermometer reaches firm-ball stage (244°F.).
4. Remove saucepan from heat; stir in vanilla. Pour into buttered foil-lined pan. Cool about 30 minutes.
5. When candy has completely set, carefully remove from pan by lifting foil; remove foil sides of candy. With thin-bladed knife, cut candy into pieces, using a light sawing motion. Wrap individual pieces in waxed paper. Store in refrigerator.

HIGH ALTITUDE (*above 3500 feet*)**:** Cook until candy thermometer reaches 234°F.

NUTRITION INFORMATION PER SERVING: Serving Size: 1 Square ◆ Calories: 130 ◆ Calories from Fat: 45 ◆ **% DAILY VALUE:** Total Fat: 5 g 8% ◆ Saturated Fat: 3 g 15% ◆ Cholesterol: 15 mg 5% ◆ Sodium: 60 mg 3% ◆ Total Carbohydrate: 20 g 7% ◆ Dietary Fiber: 0 g 0% ◆ Sugars: 17 g ◆ Protein: 1 g ◆ Vitamin A: 4% ◆ Vitamin C: 0% ◆ Calcium: 4% ◆ Iron: 0% ◆ **DIETARY EXCHANGES:** 1½ Fruit, 1 Fat OR 1½ Carbohydrate, 1 Fat

VARIATION

Chocolate Caramels: After stirring in sweetened condensed milk, cook over medium heat for about 20 minutes, stirring constantly, until candy thermometer reaches 230°F. Stir in 2 oz. unsweetened chocolate, coarsely chopped; continue cooking and stirring for about 15 minutes or until mixture reaches 240°F. Continue as directed above.

Quick Fondant

PREP TIME: 15 MINUTES

  1 tablespoon light corn syrup
  ⅔ cup sweetened condensed milk
    (not evaporated)
  4½ to 5 cups powdered sugar

In large bowl, combine corn syrup and condensed milk; mix well. Add powdered sugar gradually, stirring to form a stiff, smooth dough. (If all powdered sugar cannot be stirred in, place fondant on cookie sheet and knead in powdered sugar.) Divide fondant in half. Shape each half as directed in Cherry Almond Fondant and Classic Neapolitan Fondant Slices recipes.

Cherry Almond Fondant

PREP TIME: 15 MINUTES (READY IN 3 HOURS 15 MINUTES) ✦ YIELD: 4 DOZEN CANDIES

  ½ recipe prepared Quick Fondant (above)
  ⅓ cup chopped candied cherries
  ¼ teaspoon almond extract
  1 drop red food color
    Toasted sliced almonds, if desired

1. In medium bowl, combine half recipe of fondant, cherries, almond extract and food color; knead on cookie sheet until well blended.
2. Roll fondant into rope about 1 inch thick. Cut into ¼-inch slices; place on cookie sheet. Cover with waxed paper; let dry at least 3 hours. Garnish with almond slices. Store in tightly covered container in cool, dry place.

NUTRITION INFORMATION PER SERVING: Serving Size: 1 Candy ✦ Calories: 35 ✦ Calories from Fat: 0 ✦ **% DAILY VALUE:** Total Fat: 0 g 0% ✦ Saturated Fat: 0 g 0% ✦ Cholesterol: 0 mg 0% ✦ Sodium: 5 mg 0% ✦ Total Carbohydrate: 9 g 3% ✦ Dietary Fiber: 0 g 0% ✦ Sugars: 8 g ✦ Protein: 0 g ✦ Vitamin A: 0% ✦ Vitamin C: 0% ✦ Calcium: 0% ✦ Iron: 0% ✦ **DIETARY EXCHANGES:** ½ Fruit OR ½ Carbohydrate

Classic Neapolitan Fondant Slices

PREP TIME: 30 MINUTES (READY IN 3 HOURS 30 MINUTES) ✦ YIELD: 4½ DOZEN CANDIES

  ½ recipe prepared Quick Fondant (left)
  ⅛ teaspoon peppermint extract
  2 drops red food color
  2 tablespoons finely chopped almonds
  2 tablespoons semisweet chocolate chips,
    melted

1. Divide half recipe of fondant into 3 equal parts. To 1 part, add peppermint extract and red food color; knead on cookie sheet until well blended. To second part, add almonds; knead gently to distribute almonds. In small bowl, combine third part with melted chocolate chips; stir or knead until blended.
2. Sprinkle powdered sugar on work surface. With rolling pin, roll each part of fondant to a 12 × 1-inch strip, about ½ inch thick. Moisten top of pink strip with water; place white strip on top. Moisten top of white strip with water; place chocolate strip on top.
3. With rolling pin, lightly roll lengthwise over sandwiched strips. Set candy on edge so that 3 layers are visible on top. Roll again lengthwise with rolling pin until candy is 1 inch high and 1 inch wide. Cut candy into ¼-inch-thick slices; place on cookie sheet. Cover with waxed paper; let dry at least 3 hours. Store in tightly covered container in cool, dry place.

NUTRITION INFORMATION PER SERVING: Serving Size: 1 Candy ✦ Calories: 30 ✦ Calories from Fat: 0 ✦ **% DAILY VALUE:** Total Fat: 0 g 0% ✦ Saturated Fat: 0 g 0% ✦ Cholesterol: 0 mg 0% ✦ Sodium: 0 mg 0% ✦ Total Carbohydrate: 7 g 2% ✦ Dietary Fiber: 0 g 0% ✦ Sugars: 7 g ✦ Protein: 0 g ✦ Vitamin A: 0% ✦ Vitamin C: 0% ✦ Calcium: 0% ✦ Iron: 0% ✦ **DIETARY EXCHANGES:** ½ Fruit OR ½ Carbohydrate

COOK'S NOTE

TESTING A CANDY THERMOMETER

Test for accuracy before first using a candy thermometer and periodically thereafter. To test, insert the thermometer into a pan of water and bring it to boiling. After the water has boiled for 10 minutes, check the gauge. It should register 212°F. at sea level (1 degree less for each 500 feet above sea level).

Taffy

PREP TIME: 1 HOUR 10 MINUTES ♦ YIELD: 4 DOZEN
PIECES (1½ POUNDS)

    1½ cups sugar
     2 cups light corn syrup
    ¼ cup butter
    ½ teaspoon salt
     2 teaspoons vanilla

1. Grease 15×10×1-inch baking pan. In
large saucepan, combine sugar and corn
syrup. Bring to a boil, stirring constantly.
Add butter; stir until melted. Cook, without
stirring, until candy thermometer reaches
hard-ball stage (250°F.). Remove saucepan
from heat; stir in salt and vanilla. Pour into
greased pan. Cool slightly, folding edges
toward center to cool evenly.
2. When taffy is just cool enough to handle,
divide into 4 or 5 pieces. With buttered
hands, pull and fold taffy for 10 to 20 minutes or until taffy turns opaque and stiff. (If
candy becomes too stiff to work with, warm
briefly in oven at 350°F.)
3. Pull taffy into long rope about ½ inch
wide; cut into 1-inch pieces while still warm.
Wrap individual pieces in waxed paper. Store
in cool, dry place.

HIGH ALTITUDE *(above 3500 feet)*: Cook until
candy thermometer reaches 240°F.

NUTRITION INFORMATION PER SERVING: Serving Size: 1 Piece ♦
Calories: 80 ♦ Calories from Fat: 10 ♦ **% DAILY VALUE:** Total Fat:
1 g 2% ♦ Saturated Fat: 1 g 5% ♦ Cholesterol: 3 mg 1% ♦ Sodium:
50 mg 2% ♦ Total Carbohydrate: 17 g 6% ♦ Dietary Fiber: 0 g 0% ♦
Sugars: 11 g ♦ Protein: 0 g ♦ Vitamin A: 0% ♦ Vitamin C: 0% ♦ Calcium: 0% ♦ Iron: 0% ♦ **DIETARY EXCHANGES:** 1 Fruit, ½ Fat OR
1 Carbohydrate, ½ Fat

VARIATION

Peppermint Taffy: Substitute peppermint
extract for vanilla and add 4 to 6 drops red
food color.

Holiday Peppermints

PREP TIME: 30 MINUTES (READY IN 24 HOURS
30 MINUTES) ♦ YIELD: 5 DOZEN CANDIES

    3½ cups powdered sugar
     3 tablespoons water
     3 tablespoons light corn syrup
    ⅛ to ¼ teaspoon peppermint extract
     2 to 3 drops any color food color, if desired
       Decorator icing

1. Line cookie sheets with waxed paper. In
medium saucepan, combine powdered sugar,
water and corn syrup; mix well. Cook over
low heat until sugar dissolves and mixture is
smooth.
2. Remove saucepan from heat. Stir in peppermint extract and food color. Place
saucepan in bowl of hot water. Quickly drop
mixture by teaspoonfuls onto waxed paper-
lined cookie sheets, forming ¾-inch patties.
3. Using icing with desired tip, pipe on dec-
oration. Let stand at least 24 hours or until
firm. Store in tightly covered container with
waxed paper between layers.

NUTRITION INFORMATION PER SERVING: Serving Size: 1 Candy ♦
Calories: 30 ♦ Calories from Fat: 0 ♦ **% DAILY VALUE:** Total Fat:
0 g 0% ♦ Saturated Fat: 0 g 0% ♦ Cholesterol: 0 mg 0% ♦ Sodium:
0 mg 0% ♦ Total Carbohydrate: 8 g 3% ♦ Dietary Fiber: 0 g 0% ♦
Sugars: 7 g ♦ Protein: 0 g ♦ Vitamin A: 0% ♦ Vitamin C: 0% ♦
Calcium: 0% ♦ Iron: 0% ♦ **DIETARY EXCHANGES:** ½ Fruit OR
½ Carbohydrate

Cashew Clusters

PREP TIME: 15 MINUTES (READY IN 45 MINUTES)
♦ YIELD: 3 DOZEN CANDIES

     1 (12-oz.) pkg. (2 cups) semisweet chocolate
       chips
     1 oz. unsweetened chocolate
     2 cups cashews

1. Line cookie sheets with waxed paper. In
large saucepan, melt chocolate chips and
chocolate over low heat, stirring constantly
until smooth. Stir in cashews.
2. Drop by teaspoonfuls onto waxed paper-
lined cookie sheets. Refrigerate about
30 minutes or until set. Store in tightly covered container in refrigerator.

1. MICROWAVE DIRECTIONS: Line
cookie sheets with waxed paper. In 1-quart
microwave-safe casserole, combine chocolate chips and chocolate.
2. Microwave on HIGH for 2½ to 3½ minutes or until melted, stirring once halfway
during cooking. Continue as directed above.

NUTRITION INFORMATION PER SERVING: Serving Size: 1 Candy ♦
Calories: 110 ♦ Calories from Fat: 60 ♦ **% DAILY VALUE:** Total Fat:
7 g 11% ♦ Saturated Fat: 3 g 15% ♦ Cholesterol: 0 mg 0% ♦ Sodium:
50 mg 2% ♦ Total Carbohydrate: 9 g 3% ♦ Dietary Fiber: 1 g 4% ♦
Sugars: 6 g ♦ Protein: 2 g ♦ Vitamin A: 0% ♦ Vitamin C: 0% ♦ Calcium: 0% ♦ Iron: 4% ♦ **DIETARY EXCHANGES:** ½ Starch, 1½ Fat OR
½ Carbohydrate, 1½ Fat

Microwave Peanut Brittle

PREP TIME: 25 MINUTES (READY IN 55 MINUTES)
♦ YIELD: 16 PIECES (1 POUND)

    1 cup sugar
    ½ cup light corn syrup
    1 cup roasted salted peanuts
    1 teaspoon margarine or butter
    1 teaspoon vanilla
    1 teaspoon baking soda

1. MICROWAVE DIRECTIONS: Butter cookie sheet. In 1½-quart microwave-safe casserole, combine sugar and corn syrup; mix well. Microwave on HIGH for 4 minutes.
2. Stir in peanuts. Microwave on HIGH for 3 to 5 minutes or until light brown.
3. Stir in margarine and vanilla; blend well. Microwave on HIGH for 1 to 2 minutes. (Peanuts should be lightly browned.)
4. Add baking soda; stir gently until light and foamy. Pour onto buttered cookie sheet. Cool 30 minutes. Break into pieces.

NUTRITION INFORMATION PER SERVING: Serving Size: 1 Piece ♦ Calories: 140 ♦ Calories from Fat: 45 ♦ % DAILY VALUE: Total Fat: 5 g 8% ♦ Saturated Fat: 1 g 5% ♦ Cholesterol: 0 mg 0% ♦ Sodium: 135 mg 6% ♦ Total Carbohydrate: 22 g 7% ♦ Dietary Fiber: 1 g 3% ♦ Sugars: 17 g ♦ Protein: 2 g ♦ Vitamin A: 0% ♦ Vitamin C: 0% ♦ Calcium: 0% ♦ Iron: 0% ♦ DIETARY EXCHANGES: ½ Starch, 1 Fruit, 1 Fat OR 1½ Carbohydrate, 1 Fat

---

COOK'S NOTE

MICROWAVE CANDY MAKING

To avoid boil-overs, choose microwave-safe bowls two to three times larger than the amount of the candy mixture. Follow stirring instructions carefully to equalize heat throughout the mixture. As with stovetop candy making, remember that boiling sugar syrup is extremely hot and potentially dangerous. Beware of steam burns when you open the microwave oven or uncover a microwave dish.

COOK'S NOTE

BUTTER MAKES BETTER CANDY

Although most of the recipes in this chapter technically can be made with margarine, real butter gives candy a flavor that cannot be imitated.

Kahlúa Cream Truffles

PREP TIME: 30 MINUTES (READY IN 1 HOUR)
♦ YIELD: 3 DOZEN TRUFFLES

    6 oz. semisweet chocolate, cut into pieces
    ¼ cup whipping cream
    2 tablespoons coffee-flavored liqueur
    3 tablespoons butter
    2 tablespoons powdered sugar
    2 tablespoons unsweetened cocoa or sifted powdered sugar

1. In small saucepan, combine all ingredients except unsweetened cocoa; mix well. Cook over low heat until chocolate is melted and mixture is smooth, stirring constantly. Place saucepan in bowl of ice water to speed chilling, stirring mixture occasionally. With small strainer, sift light layer of cocoa on cookie sheet.
2. When chocolate mixture is cooled and slightly thickened, spoon into decorating bag fitted with desired decorative tip.* Squeeze small 1-inch truffles onto cocoa-dusted cookie sheet. Sift remaining cocoa over truffles. Store in tightly covered container in refrigerator. Let truffles stand at room temperature for 30 minutes before serving.

TIP: * Truffles can be dropped by teaspoonfuls onto cocoa-dusted cookie sheets and rolled with hands to form balls.

NUTRITION INFORMATION PER SERVING: Serving Size: 1 Truffle ♦ Calories: 45 ♦ Calories from Fat: 25 ♦ % DAILY VALUE: Total Fat: 3 g 5% ♦ Saturated Fat: 2 g 10% ♦ Cholesterol: 5 mg 2% ♦ Sodium: 10 mg 0% ♦ Total Carbohydrate: 4 g 1% ♦ Dietary Fiber: 0 g 0% ♦ Sugars: 3 g ♦ Protein: 0 g ♦ Vitamin A: 0% ♦ Vitamin C: 0% ♦ Calcium: 0% ♦ Iron: 0% ♦ DIETARY EXCHANGES: ½ Fruit, ½ Fat OR ½ Carbohydrate, ½ Fat

Sugared 'n Spiced Nuts

PREP TIME: 20 MINUTES (READY IN 50 MINUTES)
✦ YIELD: 4½ CUPS

    3 cups pecan or walnut halves
    1 cup sugar
    ⅓ cup water
    3 teaspoons cinnamon
    ½ teaspoon salt
    ½ teaspoon cloves
    1½ teaspoons vanilla

1. Heat oven to 275°F. Grease cookie sheet. Spread pecans on greased cookie sheet. Bake at 275°F. for 10 minutes.
2. In medium saucepan, combine sugar, water, cinnamon, salt and cloves; mix well. Bring to a boil. Cook 2 minutes, stirring occasionally. Remove saucepan from heat; stir in vanilla and pecans.
3. With slotted spoon, place pecans on foil or waxed paper. Separate with fork. Cool 30 minutes. Store in tightly covered container in cool, dry place.

NUTRITION INFORMATION PER SERVING: Serving Size: 2 Tablespoons ✦ Calories: 90 ✦ Calories from Fat: 50 ✦ % DAILY VALUE: Total Fat: 6 g 9% ✦ Saturated Fat: 0 g 0% ✦ Cholesterol: 0 mg 0% ✦ Sodium: 30 mg 1% ✦ Total Carbohydrate: 8 g 3% ✦ Dietary Fiber: 1 g 4% ✦ Sugars: 6 g ✦ Protein: 1 g ✦ Vitamin A: 0% ✦ Vitamin C: 0% ✦ Calcium: 0% ✦ Iron: 0% ✦ DIETARY EXCHANGES: ½ Starch, 1 Fat OR ½ Carbohydrate, 1 Fat

Maple Nut Goodie Bars

PREP TIME: 50 MINUTES (READY IN 4 HOURS 20 MINUTES) ✦ YIELD: 64 BARS

    1 (12-oz.) pkg. (2 cups) semisweet chocolate chips
    1 (11.5-oz.) pkg. (2 cups) milk chocolate chips
    2 cups margarine or butter
    1 cup peanut butter
    1 (12-oz.) can (2½ cups) cocktail peanuts
    ½ cup evaporated milk
    1 (3-oz.) pkg. vanilla pudding and pie filling mix (not instant)
    1 (2-lb.) pkg. (7½ cups) powdered sugar
    2 teaspoons maple flavor

1. Line 15×10×1-inch baking pan with foil. Butter or spray foil with nonstick cooking spray. In large saucepan, melt chocolate chips and 1 cup of the margarine over low heat, stirring frequently. Remove saucepan from heat. Add peanut butter; mix well. Spread half of mixture in buttered foil-lined pan. Freeze 10 minutes or until set. Place pan in refrigerator.
2. Meanwhile, stir peanuts into remaining chocolate mixture. Set aside.
3. Melt remaining 1 cup margarine in large saucepan over low heat. Gradually stir in evaporated milk. Stir in pudding mix. Cook until mixture is slightly thickened, stirring constantly. DO NOT BOIL. Remove saucepan from heat. Add powdered sugar and maple flavor; mix well. Cool about 10 minutes or until slightly cooled.
4. Carefully spread pudding mixture over chilled chocolate layer. Refrigerate 30 minutes.
5. Stir reserved chocolate-peanut mixture. Drop by spoonfuls onto chilled pudding layer; spread to cover. Refrigerate at least 3 hours or until firm. Cut into bars. Store in refrigerator.

NUTRITION INFORMATION PER SERVING: Serving Size: 1 Bar ✦ Calories: 230 ✦ Calories from Fat: 130 ✦ % DAILY VALUE: Total Fat: 14 g 22% ✦ Saturated Fat: 4 g 20% ✦ Cholesterol: 0 mg 0% ✦ Sodium: 125 mg 5% ✦ Total Carbohydrate: 24 g 8% ✦ Dietary Fiber: 1 g 4% ✦ Sugars: 21 g ✦ Protein: 3 g ✦ Vitamin A: 6% ✦ Vitamin C: 0% ✦ Calcium: 2% ✦ Iron: 2% ✦ DIETARY EXCHANGES: 1½ Fruit, ½ High-Fat Meat, 2 Fat OR 1½ Carbohydrate, ½ High-Fat Meat, 2 Fat

Maple Nut Goodie Bars

CANDY-COOKING STAGES

Sugar goes through several distinct steps as it gets hotter. If you don't have a candy thermometer, you can use the traditional method. Dip a teaspoon into the hot syrup and drop a small amount of syrup into a cup filled with very cold water.

STAGE	SYRUP TEMPERATURE	RESULT WHEN DROPPED INTO VERY COLD WATER
Thread	230 to 234°F.	Syrup forms a single 2-inch thread.
Soft-ball	234 to 240°F.	Syrup forms a soft ball that flattens when removed from water.
Firm-ball	244 to 248°F.	Syrup forms a firm ball that does not flatten when removed from water.
Hard-ball	250 to 266°F.	Syrup forms a ball that is hard enough to hold its shape, yet is pliable.
Soft-crack	270 to 290°F.	Syrup separates into threads that are hard but not brittle.
Hard-crack	300 to 310°F.	Syrup separates into threads that are hard and brittle.

Caramel Corn

PREP TIME: 15 MINUTES ♦ YIELD: 6 (1-CUP) SERVINGS

  6 cups popped popcorn
½ cup toasted slivered almonds, if desired*
¾ cup firmly packed brown sugar
½ cup butter
  2 tablespoons light corn syrup
⅛ teaspoon salt
¼ teaspoon baking soda

1. MICROWAVE DIRECTIONS: In large microwave-safe bowl, combine popcorn and almonds. In 4-cup microwave-safe measuring cup, combine brown sugar, butter, corn syrup and salt; mix well.
2. Microwave on HIGH for 2 minutes. Stir; microwave on HIGH for an additional 2 to 3 minutes or until mixture comes to a rolling boil.
3. Stir in baking soda until well mixed. Immediately pour over popcorn and almonds; toss until coated.
4. Microwave on HIGH for 2 minutes. Immediately spread on foil or waxed paper to cool.

1. CONVENTIONAL DIRECTIONS: Heat oven to 250°F. Spread popcorn in 15 × 10 × 1-inch baking pan; sprinkle almonds over popcorn.
2. In large saucepan, combine brown sugar, margarine, 2 *tablespoons water,* corn syrup and salt; mix well. Bring to a boil over medium heat. Boil 2 minutes, stirring constantly.
3. Remove saucepan from heat. Stir in baking soda until well mixed. Immediately pour over popcorn and almonds; toss until coated.
4. Bake at 250°F. for 15 minutes. Stir; bake an additional 15 minutes. Stir; bake 5 minutes. Immediately spread on foil or waxed paper to cool.

TIP: *To toast almonds, spread in thin layer in microwave-safe pie pan. Microwave on HIGH for 4 to 7 minutes or until golden brown, stirring frequently. Or spread on cookie sheet; bake at 350°F. for 5 to 7 minutes or until golden brown, stirring occasionally.

NUTRITION INFORMATION PER SERVING: Serving Size: 1 Cup ♦ Calories: 380 ♦ Calories from Fat: 210 ♦ % DAILY VALUE: Total Fat: 23 g 35% ♦ Saturated Fat: 11 g 55% ♦ Cholesterol: 40 mg 13% ♦ Sodium: 530 mg 22% ♦ Total Carbohydrate: 40 g 13% ♦ Dietary Fiber: 2 g 8% ♦ Sugars: 30 g ♦ Protein: 3 g ♦ Vitamin A: 10% ♦ Vitamin C: 0% ♦ Calcium: 6% ♦ Iron: 8% ♦ DIETARY EXCHANGES: 1 Starch, 1½ Fruit, 4½ Fat OR 2½ Carbohydrate, 4½ Fat

Candy and Popcorn Balls

PREP TIME: 50 MINUTES ✦ YIELD: 10 POPCORN BALLS

10 cups popped popcorn
1½ cups small gumdrops
½ cup sugar
½ cup light corn syrup
2 tablespoons margarine or butter
¼ teaspoon salt

1. Line cookie sheet with waxed paper. In large bowl, combine popcorn and gumdrops.
2. In medium saucepan, combine sugar, corn syrup, margarine and salt; mix well. Bring to a boil. Cook over medium-high heat for 2 minutes, stirring constantly. Remove from heat. Add to popcorn mixture; mix well.
3. With hands dipped in cold water, shape mixture into 2½-inch balls. Place on waxed paper-lined cookie sheets. Cool 15 minutes. Wrap individually in plastic wrap.

NUTRITION INFORMATION PER SERVING: Serving Size: 1 Popcorn Ball ✦ Calories: 180 ✦ Calories from Fat: 20 ✦ **% DAILY VALUE:** Total Fat: 2 g 3% ✦ Saturated: 1 g 5% ✦ Cholesterol: 2 mg 1% ✦ Sodium: 95 mg 4% ✦ Total Carbohydrate: 41 g 14% ✦ Dietary Fiber: 0 g 0% ✦ Sugars: 29 g ✦ Protein: 0 g ✦ Vitamin A: 0% ✦ Vitamin C: 0% ✦ Calcium: 0% ✦ Iron: 0% ✦ **DIETARY EXCHANGES:** 2½ Fruit, ½ Fat OR 2½ Carbohydrate, ½ Fat

COOK'S NOTE

HIGH ALTITUDE CANDY COOKING

Liquids evaporate more rapidly at high altitudes, so candies and syrups should be cooked for a shorter amount of time. Syrup will become too concentrated, and candy too hard, by the time prescribed sea level temperatures are reached.

To prevent excessive evaporation of liquid, decrease the final cooking temperature by 1°F. for each 500 feet in elevation (or 2°F. for each 1000 feet) above sea level. The cold water test is the surest way to determine the correct amount of cooking for candies. (See "Candy-Cooking Stages" chart on page 444.)

Sherried Pecan Pralines

PREP TIME: 45 MINUTES (READY IN 1 HOUR 15 MINUTES) ✦ YIELD: 4 DOZEN PRALINES

2¼ cups firmly packed brown sugar
1 cup whipping cream
1 tablespoon butter
2 tablespoons dry sherry
1½ cups pecan pieces, lightly toasted*

1. In heavy 2-quart saucepan, combine brown sugar, whipping cream and butter; mix well. Cook until bubbly, stirring occasionally. Cook uncovered, without stirring, until soft-ball stage (234°F.). Remove saucepan from heat; cool 5 minutes.
2. Add sherry; beat with wooden spoon until thick and creamy. Quickly stir in pecans. Drop by teaspoonfuls onto waxed paper, forming 2-inch candies.
3. Let stand at room temperature for 30 minutes or until firm. Store in tightly covered container in a cool, dry place.

TIP: * To toast pecans, spread on cookie sheet; bake at 350°F. for 4 to 6 minutes or until light golden brown, stirring occasionally.

HIGH ALTITUDE (*above 3500 feet*): Cook until candy thermometer reaches 224°F.

NUTRITION INFORMATION PER SERVING: Serving Size: 1 Praline ✦ Calories: 80 ✦ Calories from Fat: 35 ✦ **% DAILY VALUE:** Total Fat: 4 g 6% ✦ Saturated Fat: 1 g 5% ✦ Cholesterol: 5 mg 2% ✦ Sodium: 10 mg 0% ✦ Total Carbohydrate: 11 g 4% ✦ Dietary Fiber: 0 g 0% ✦ Sugars: 10 g ✦ Protein: 0 g ✦ Vitamin A: 0% ✦ Vitamin C: 0% ✦ Calcium: 0% ✦ Iron: 0% ✦ **DIETARY EXCHANGES:** ½ Fruit, 1 Fat OR ½ Carbohydrate, 1 Fat

Triple Chocolate Fudge

PREP TIME: 40 MINUTES (READY IN 1 HOUR 40 MINUTES)
◆ YIELD: 60 SQUARES

4½ cups sugar
½ cup butter
1 (12-oz.) can (1½ cups) evaporated milk
4½ cups miniature marshmallows
1 (12-oz.) pkg. (2 cups) semisweet chocolate chips
12 oz. sweet baking chocolate, cut into pieces
2 oz. unsweetened chocolate, cut into pieces
2 teaspoons vanilla
¼ teaspoon almond extract
1 cup chopped walnuts or pecans
Colored sugar, if desired

1. Line 15×10×1-inch baking pan with foil so foil extends over sides of pan; grease foil. In large saucepan, combine sugar, butter and evaporated milk; cook and stir over medium heat until sugar is dissolved. Bring to a full boil, stirring constantly. Boil over medium heat, without stirring, for 5 minutes.
2. Remove saucepan from heat. Add marshmallows; stir until melted. Add chocolate chips, sweet chocolate and unsweetened chocolate, stirring constantly until all chocolate is melted and mixture is smooth.
3. Stir in vanilla, almond extract and walnuts. Quickly spread mixture in greased foil-lined pan. Sprinkle with colored sugar. Cool 1 hour or until completely cooled.
4. Remove fudge from pan by lifting foil; remove foil from sides of fudge. With long knife, cut fudge into squares. Store in refrigerator.

NUTRITION INFORMATION PER SERVING: Serving Size: 1 Square ◆ Calories: 170 ◆ Calories from Fat: 60 ◆ **% DAILY VALUE:** Total Fat: 7 g 11% ◆ Saturated Fat: 4 g 20% ◆ Cholesterol: 5 mg 2% ◆ Sodium: 25 mg 1% ◆ Total Carbohydrate: 26 g 9% ◆ Dietary Fiber: 1 g 4% ◆ Sugars: 24 g ◆ Protein: 1 g ◆ Vitamin A: 0% ◆ Vitamin C: 0% ◆ Calcium: 2% ◆ Iron: 2% ◆ **DIETARY EXCHANGES:** ½ Starch, 1 Fruit, 1½ Fat OR 1½ Carbohydrate, 1½ Fat

Vanilla Fudge

PREP TIME: 40 MINUTES (READY IN 2 HOURS 10 MINUTES) ◆ YIELD: 36 SQUARES

2½ cups sugar
½ cup butter
1 (5-oz.) can (⅔ cup) evaporated milk
1 (7-oz.) jar (2 cups) marshmallow creme
8 oz. vanilla-flavored candy coating (almond bark), cut into pieces

1 teaspoon vanilla
¾ cup chopped walnuts

1. Line 9-inch square or 13×9-inch pan with foil so foil extends over sides of pan; butter foil. In large saucepan, combine sugar, butter and evaporated milk; cook and stir over medium heat until sugar is dissolved. Bring to a full boil, stirring constantly. Boil over medium heat for 5 minutes, stirring constantly.
2. Remove saucepan from heat. Add marshmallow creme and candy coating; stir until candy coating is melted and mixture is smooth. Stir in vanilla and walnuts. Pour into buttered foil-lined pan, spreading evenly. Cool 1 hour or until completely cooled.
3. Score fudge into 36 squares. Refrigerate until firm, about 30 minutes.
4. Remove fudge from pan by lifting foil; remove foil from sides of fudge. With long knife, cut through scored lines. Store in refrigerator.

NUTRITION INFORMATION PER SERVING: Serving Size: 1 Square ◆ Calories: 150 ◆ Calories from Fat: 50 ◆ **% DAILY VALUE:** Total Fat: 6 g 9% ◆ Saturated Fat: 3 g 15% ◆ Cholesterol: 10 mg 3% ◆ Sodium: 40 mg 2% ◆ Total Carbohydrate: 23 g 8% ◆ Dietary Fiber: 0 g 0% ◆ Sugars: 21 g ◆ Protein: 1 g ◆ Vitamin A: 2% ◆ Vitamin C: 0% ◆ Calcium: 2% ◆ Iron: 0% ◆ **DIETARY EXCHANGES:** 1½ Fruit, 1½ Fat OR 1½ Carbohydrate, 1½ Fat

VARIATIONS

Christmas Fudge: Substitute ½ cup chopped almonds for walnuts and ¼ teaspoon almond extract for vanilla. Stir in ½ cup chopped dates and ½ cup chopped red candied cherries with almonds and almond extract.

Eggnog Fudge: Substitute ⅔ cup eggnog for evaporated milk and ½ to 1 teaspoon rum extract for vanilla.

Peanut Butter Fudge: Use 6 oz. vanilla candy coating (almond bark) and add ½ cup peanut butter with marshmallow creme and candy coating. Substitute ¾ cup chopped dry-roasted peanuts for walnuts.

Peppermint Candy Fudge: Substitute ½ cup finely crushed peppermint candy for walnuts. Omit vanilla and add desired amount of red food color with crushed candies.

Pistachio Fudge: Substitute shelled pistachios for walnuts and add desired amount of green food color with pistachios.

CANNING
& COOKING BASICS

CANNING & COOKING BASICS

anning and Cooking Basics is a collection of helpful information from how to use spices and herbs to very specific directions and recipes for canning.

KEYS TO SUCCESSFUL CANNING

Canning Fruits and Tomatoes

Fruits and tomatoes, which are relatively high in acid, need to reach boiling temperature (212°F.) to kill any organisms that could cause spoilage. For the boiling water bath method, fill jars with the ingredient to be canned. Use a pot large enough for the canning jars to be fully surrounded in and covered by one to two inches of boiling water.

A pressure cooker may also be used for canning acid foods; 6 pounds of pressure is recommended for a dial-gauge canner; 10 pounds of pressure is recommended for a weighted gauge. In either case, the time needed is shorter than in a boiling water bath, which may be important if you are canning large quantities during the hot summer. The open-kettle method is no longer recommended for any fruits or tomatoes because it is impossible to prevent contamination at the time the jar is filled.

Canning Vegetables

Because vegetables are lower in acid than fruit is, they must reach a temperature higher than boiling water. They cannot safely be processed in a boiling water bath; they must be pressure-cooked to assure safe canning without danger of botulism. Follow manufacturer's directions carefully when using a pressure canner.

Preparing Canning Jars

+ Use standard canning jars that are specifically designed to withstand sudden changes in temperature or the high temperatures of pressure cooking.
+ Select jars without nicks, cracks or rough spots on rim where lid will provide seal. Wash jars in hot soapy water, rinse well and let stand with hot water in them to warm the jars and prevent breakage when hot syrup is added. (Dishwasher may be used.)
+ Vacuum-seal lids with metal screw bands are the easiest and most convenient to use.

(NOTE: Screw bands and jars can be reused, but LIDS ARE USED ONLY ONCE.) The seal can be checked at a glance by noting a depressed center of the lid when the jar is cooled. When using vacuum-seal lids, place the lids in a pan with water to cover; heat to boiling and keep hot during canning process.

Canning Fruits and Tomatoes Using Pressure Cooker Method

Follow directions for Canning Vegetables, using 6 pounds of pressure for a dial-gauge canner and 10 pounds of pressure for a weighted gauge. See "Timetable for Canning Fruits and Tomatoes" on page 452.

Canning Vegetables Using a Pressure Cooker

+ Prepare vegetables and pack into jars according to the "Timetable for Canning Vegetables" on page 456. Add boiling water, or the boiling water in which vegetables were heated, for packing as directed.
+ Wipe the rim of each jar with a clean cloth to remove food particles that would prevent sealing.
+ Follow the manufacturer's directions in preparing lids for use.
+ Place sealing-compound rim of vacuum-seal lid on the clean jar rim. Screw metal bands down fingertip tight, following manufacturer's directions.
+ Place filled jars on rack in pressure canner containing 2 or 3 inches of hot water or the amount recommended by canner manufacturer.
+ Place canner over high heat. Lock cover according to manufacturer's directions. Leave petcock or vent open for steam to escape.
+ After steam has escaped for 10 minutes, close petcock or vent and let pressure rise to desired pounds. Start counting processing time after it has reached desired pounds. Watch heat to keep pressure steady during processing time. (Fluctuating pressure causes the liquid to cook out of the jars.)

When time is up, remove from heat and allow pressure to fall slowly to zero before opening. Never cool the canner with running water. Slowly open the petcock; if steam escapes, the pressure is not down yet. After petcock is open, remove cover.

+ Remove jars from canner and cool them upright 2 to 3 inches apart on a wooden board, newspapers or several layers of cloth. Protect them from any draft, which could cause hot jars to break.

+ About 12 hours after processing, remove metal bands and make sure the top of each lid is depressed, which means the jar is sealed. (Lids are used only once; bands can be reused.) If jars are not sealed, store them in the refrigerator and use contents within a few days. Or check the jar top again for food particles, top with a new lid and process for the original canning time.

Safety Note: Before eating home-canned vegetables, bring the vegetables to a full boil, then cover and boil for 10 minutes. Boil corn 20 minutes. This is a safety precaution in case any phase of the canning process was not correct. The boiling destroys botulism toxins. If using home-canned vegetables for a salad, boil and cool before using.

Canning Fruits and Tomatoes Using a Boiling Water Bath

+ Prepare fruit and pack into jars according to "Timetable for Canning Fruits and Tomatoes" on page 452. If fruits tend to darken, use ascorbic acid, according to manufacturer's directions. Add hot sugar syrup for fruit (see recipe on page 485) or water as directed. Run knife between fruit and jar to remove any air bubbles. Add additional syrup if necessary.

+ To seal, wipe the rim of each jar with a clean cloth to remove food particles that would prevent sealing. Follow manufacturer's instructions in preparing lids for use. Place sealing-compound rim of vacuum-seal lid on clean jar rim. Screw metal bands down fingertip tight, following manufacturer's directions.

+ Place filled jars on a rack in a canner one-third full of hot water. Add more hot water as needed to cover jars 1 to 2 inches.

+ Cover canner and heat water to boiling. Begin timing the processing when water boils. Reduce heat to hold water at a steady but gentle boil.

+ Remove jars from canner and cool upright, 2 to 3 inches apart, on a wooden board, newspa-

pers or several layers of cloth. Protect them from any draft that could cause hot jars to break.

+ About 12 hours after processing, remove metal bands and make sure each lid is depressed, which means the jar is sealed. Do not retighten bands. (Lids are used only once; bands can be reused.) If jars are not sealed, store them in refrigerator and use contents within a few days. Or, check jar rim again for food particles; top with a new lid and process again for 15 minutes.

+ Store in a dark, cool area.

Leave Room at the Top

When you are canning, be sure to leave the recommended head space (empty space at the top of the jar). This allows room for foods to expand during the heating process, preventing jars from bursting.

Sugar-Free Peach Freezer Jam

PREP TIME: 45 MINUTES (READY IN 27 HOURS 45 MINUTES) + YIELD: 5 CUPS

> 6 cups (8 to 10 medium) coarsely chopped peeled peaches
> 1 (12-oz.) can frozen unsweetened apple juice concentrate
> 2 tablespoons fresh lemon juice
> 1 tablespoon unflavored gelatin

1. In 3-quart saucepan, combine all ingredients. Bring to a boil over medium-high heat. Reduce heat to medium; cover loosely and cook 15 minutes. Remove from heat. Skim foam from top.

2. Ladle mixture into 5 clean, hot 8-oz. jars or moisture-vaporproof freezer containers, leaving ½-inch headspace; cover with tight-fitting lids. Cool at least 3 hours or until room temperature. Refrigerate 24 hours. (Preserves will thicken during refrigeration.) Store in freezer until ready to use. Thaw in refrigerator several hours before serving. Store in refrigerator for up to 3 weeks or in freezer for up to 3 months.

NUTRITION INFORMATION PER SERVING: Serving Size: 1 Tablespoon + Calories: 15 + Calories from Fat: 0 + **% DAILY VALUE:** Total Fat: 0 g 0% + Saturated Fat: 0 g 0% + Cholesterol: 0 mg 0% + Sodium: 0 mg 0% + Total Carbohydrate: 4 g 1% + Dietary Fiber: 0 g 0% + Sugars: 3 g + Protein: 0 g + Vitamin A: 0% + Vitamin C: 0% + Calcium: 0% + Iron: 0% + **DIETARY EXCHANGES:** Free

Apple-Sweetened Cherry Preserves

Apple-Sweetened Cherry Preserves

PREP TIME: 30 MINUTES (READY IN 26 HOURS 30 MINUTES) ◆ YIELD: 7 CUPS

  6 cups coarsely chopped pitted sweet
     cherries*
  1 (12-oz.) can frozen unsweetened
     apple juice concentrate
¾ cup water
  1 tablespoon unflavored gelatin
  1 teaspoon almond extract

1. In large saucepan, combine all ingredients except almond extract. Bring to a boil over medium-high heat. Cook and stir 3 minutes. Remove from heat. Skim foam from top. Stir in almond extract.
2. Ladle mixture into 7 clean, hot 8-oz. jars; cover with tight-fitting lids. Cool 2 hours or until room temperature. Refrigerate 24 hours. (Preserves will thicken during refrigeration.) Store in refrigerator for up to 1 month.

TIP: * Frozen unsweetened pitted sweet cherries can be substituted for fresh cherries. Thaw slightly before chopping.

NUTRITION INFORMATION PER SERVING: Serving Size: 1 Tablespoon ◆ Calories: 10 ◆ Calories from Fat: 0 ◆ **% DAILY VALUE:** Total Fat: 0 g 0% ◆ Saturated Fat: 0 g 0% ◆ Cholesterol: 0 mg 0% ◆ Sodium: 0 mg 0% ◆ Total Carbohydrate: 3 g 1% ◆ Dietary Fiber: 0 g 0% ◆ Sugars: 3 g ◆ Protein: 0 g ◆ Vitamin A: 0% ◆ Vitamin C: 0% ◆ Calcium: 0% ◆ Iron: 0% ◆ **DIETARY EXCHANGES:** Free

Easy Rhubarb-Pineapple Jam

PREP TIME: 30 MINUTES ◆ YIELD: 4½ CUPS

  5 cups chopped fresh rhubarb
2½ cups sugar
  1 tablespoon grated orange peel
  1 (8-oz.) can crushed pineapple in
     unsweetened juice, undrained
  1 (3-oz.) pkg. strawberry flavor gelatin

1. In Dutch oven or large saucepan, combine rhubarb, sugar, orange peel and pineapple; mix well. Bring to a boil. Boil 10 minutes, stirring constantly. Remove from heat; cool 30 minutes.
2. Stir gelatin into cooled rhubarb mixture until dissolved.
3. Ladle mixture into 5 clean, hot 8-oz. jars or moisture-vaporproof freezer containers, leaving ½-inch headspace; cover with tight-fitting lids. Store in freezer until ready to use. Thaw in refrigerator several hours before serving. Store in refrigerator for up to 1 month.

NUTRITION INFORMATION PER SERVING: Serving Size: 1 Tablespoon ◆ Calories: 35 ◆ Calories from Fat: 0 ◆ **% DAILY VALUE:** Total Fat: 0 g 0% ◆ Saturated Fat: 0 g 0% ◆ Cholesterol: 0 mg 0% ◆ Sodium: 0 mg 0% ◆ Total Carbohydrate: 9 g 3% ◆ Dietary Fiber: 0 g 0% ◆ Sugars: 9 g ◆ Protein: 0 g ◆ Vitamin A: 0% ◆ Vitamin C: 0% ◆ Calcium: 0% ◆ Iron: 0% ◆ **DIETARY EXCHANGES:** ½ Fruit OR ½ Carbohydrate

Razzle-Dazzle Quick Jam

PREP TIME: 30 MINUTES (READY IN 3 HOURS
30 MINUTES) ◆ YIELD: 8 CUPS

1½ pints (3 cups) fresh raspberries or frozen
    raspberries without syrup, thawed,
    drained
1 (16-oz.) can sweet cherries, drained,
    reserving liquid
4 cups sugar
½ cup light corn syrup
1 tablespoon lemon juice
1 (1¾-oz.) pkg. powdered fruit pectin

1. In medium bowl, crush raspberries to
measure 2 cups. Finely chop cherries to measure 1 cup.
2. In 4-quart bowl, combine crushed raspberries, chopped cherries, sugar, corn syrup
and lemon juice; mix well. Let stand 10 minutes, stirring occasionally.
3. Meanwhile, add water to reserved cherry
liquid to measure ¾ cup. In small saucepan,
combine cherry liquid mixture and pectin;
blend well. Cook over medium-high heat
until mixture comes to a full rolling boil. Boil
1 minute, stirring constantly. Pour over fruit;
stir vigorously 3 minutes.
4. Ladle mixture into 8 clean, hot 8-oz. jars
or moisture-vaporproof freezer containers,
leaving ½-inch headspace; cover with tight-
fitting lids. Cool at least 3 hours or until
room temperature and set. Store in refrigerator for up to 3 weeks or in freezer for up to
3 months.

NUTRITION INFORMATION PER SERVING: Serving Size: 1 Tablespoon ◆ Calories: 30 ◆ Calories from Fat: 0 ◆ **% DAILY VALUE:** Total
Fat: 0 g 0% ◆ Saturated Fat: 0 g 0% ◆ Cholesterol: 0 mg 0% ◆
Sodium: 0 mg 0% ◆ Total Carbohydrate: 8 g 3% ◆ Dietary Fiber:
0 g 0% ◆ Sugars: 8 g ◆ Protein: 0 g ◆ Vitamin A: 0% ◆ Vitamin C: 0%
◆ Calcium: 0% ◆ Iron: 0% ◆ **DIETARY EXCHANGES:** ½ Fruit OR
½ Carbohydrate

Cranberry-Apple Spiced Jelly

PREP TIME: 30 MINUTES (READY IN 3 HOURS
30 MINUTES) ◆ YIELD: 4 CUPS

3½ cups sugar
1½ cups cranberry-apple drink
½ cup apple cider or apple juice
⅛ teaspoon cinnamon
⅛ teaspoon cloves
1 (3-oz.) pkg. liquid fruit pectin

1. In large saucepan, combine sugar,
cranberry-apple drink, apple cider, cinnamon and cloves. Bring to a full rolling boil,
stirring to dissolve sugar. Boil 1 minute, stirring constantly. Remove from heat; stir in
pectin. Skim foam from top.
2. Ladle mixture into 4 clean, hot 8-oz. jars
or moisture-vaporproof freezer containers,
leaving ½-inch headspace. Cool slightly;
cover with tight-fitting lids. Cool at least
3 hours or until room temperature and set.
Store in refrigerator for up to 3 weeks or in
freezer for up to 3 months.

NUTRITION INFORMATION PER SERVING: Serving Size: 1 Tablespoon ◆ Calories: 50 ◆ Calories from Fat: 0 ◆ **% DAILY VALUE:** Total
Fat: 0 g 0% ◆ Saturated Fat: 0 g 0% ◆ Cholesterol: 0 mg 0% ◆
Sodium: 0 mg 0% ◆ Total Carbohydrate: 12 g 4% ◆ Dietary Fiber:
0 g 0% ◆ Sugars: 12 g ◆ Protein: 0 g ◆ Vitamin A: 0% ◆ Vitamin C:
2% ◆ Calcium: 0% ◆ Iron: 0% ◆ **DIETARY EXCHANGES:** 1 Fruit OR
1 Carbohydrate

Cranberry-Apple Spiced Jelly

TIMETABLE FOR CANNING FRUITS AND TOMATOES

FRUIT	AMOUNT TO YIELD 1 QUART	BASIC PREPARATION	BOILING WATER BATH PINTS	QUARTS	TIME IN DIAL-GAUGE PRESSURE COOKER WITH 6 POUNDS PRESSURE (OR 10 POUNDS IN WEIGHTED GAUGE PRESSURE COOKER) PINTS	QUARTS
APPLES	2½ lb. or 8 medium	Wash, peel, core and slice. Boil 5 minutes in syrup. Pack in jars leaving ½ inch at top.	25 min.	25 min.	8 min.	8 min.
APPLESAUCE	3 lb. or 10 medium	Prepare applesauce. Pack hot into jars leaving ½ inch at top.	20 min.	25 min.	8 min.	10 min.
APRICOTS	2½ lb. or 24 medium	Wash, halve and pit. Pack into jars; add hot syrup leaving ½ inch at top.	Hot: 25 min. Raw: 30 min.	30 min. 35 min.	8 min.	10 min.
BERRIES (except strawberries, cranberries)	1½ quarts	Wash, stem and pack into jars; add hot syrup leaving ½ inch at top.	20 min.	25 min.	8 min. Raw: 10 min.	8 min.
CHERRIES	2½ lb. unpitted	Wash, stem and pit if desired. Pack into jars; add hot syrup leaving ½ inch at top.	Hot: 20 min. Raw: 30 min.	25 min. 30 min.	Hot: 8 min. Raw: 10 min.	10 min. 10 min.
CRANBERRIES	2 lb. or 1½ quarts	Wash, stem and heat to boiling in heavy syrup. Pack into jars leaving ½ inch at top.	20 min.	20 min.	Hot: 8 min. Raw: 10 min.	8 min. 10 min.
PEACHES	2 lb. or 8 medium	Peel by dipping fruit into boiling water a few seconds to loosen skin. Halve or slice and pit. Pack into jars; add hot syrup leaving ½ inch at top.	Hot: 25 min. Raw: 30 min.	30 min. 35 min.	10 min.	10 min.

FRUIT	AMOUNT TO YIELD 1 QUART	BASIC PREPARATION	BOILING WATER BATH		TIME IN DIAL-GAUGE PRESSURE COOKER WITH 6 POUNDS PRESSURE (OR 10 POUNDS IN WEIGHTED GAUGE PRESSURE COOKER)	
			PINTS	QUARTS	PINTS	QUARTS
PEARS	2 lb. or 8 medium	Peel, halve or slice and core. Pack into jars; add hot syrup leaving ½ inch at top.	25 min.	30 min.	10 min.	10 min.
PLUMS	2 lb. or 20 medium	Wash, prick skins if canning whole or cut in half and pit. Pack into jars; add hot syrup leaving ½ inch at top.	25 min.	30 min.	10 min.	10 min.
RHUBARB	1½ lb. or 10 stalks	Wash; cut into pieces. Cook in heavy syrup until tender. Pack into jars leaving ½ inch at top.	20 min.	20 min.	8 min.	8 min.
TOMATOES*	3 lb. or 12 small	Peel by dipping tomatoes into boiling water a few seconds to loosen skin. Core and quarter. Pack into jars, pressing in to form juice; add 1 teaspoon salt per quart. Leave ½ inch at top.	90 min.	90 min.	40 min. (or 25 min. at 11 or 15 pounds per square inch [psi])	40 min.

*Acid level of tomatoes varies. The USDA recommends any of the following additions to "low acid" tomatoes: ¼ teaspoon per pint citric acid (available at drugstores), 1 tablespoon lemon juice or 5% vinegar per pint.

HIGH ALTITUDE: As altitude increases, the processing times stays the same but the canner pressure must be increased.

In a Dial-Gauge Pressure Canner:

At altitudes of 0–2000 feet, process at 6 pounds pressure.

At altitudes of 2001–4000 feet, process at 7 pounds pressure.

At altitudes of 4001–6000 feet, process at 8 pounds pressure.

At altitudes of 6001–8000 feet, process at 9 pounds pressure.

In a Weighted-Gauge Pressure Canner:

At altitudes of 0–1000 feet, process at 5 pounds pressure.

At altitudes above 1000 feet, process at 10 pounds pressure.

Source: The State Department of Agriculture

Microwave Apple Butter

PREP TIME: I HOUR I5 MINUTES ◆ YIELD: 4 CUPS

8 cups (8 medium) quartered peeled apples
2 cups apple cider or apple juice
1½ cups sugar
¾ teaspoon cinnamon
¼ teaspoon cloves
¼ teaspoon allspice

1. MICROWAVE DIRECTIONS: In 3-quart microwave-safe casserole, combine apples and cider. Microwave on HIGH for 12 to 15 minutes or until apples are tender, stirring twice during cooking.
2. In food processor bowl with metal blade or blender container, process apple mixture until smooth. Return to casserole. Add sugar, cinnamon, cloves and allspice; blend well.
3. Microwave on HIGH for 25 to 35 minutes or until thickened and dark brown, stirring once halfway through cooking. (Mixture will thicken as it cools.)
4. Spoon into 4 clean, hot 8-oz. jars or moisture-vaporproof containers, leaving ½-inch headspace; cover with tight-fitting lids. Store in refrigerator for up to 3 weeks or in freezer for up to 3 months.

NUTRITION INFORMATION PER SERVING: Serving Size: 1 Tablespoon ◆ Calories: 30 ◆ Calories from Fat: 0 ◆ **% DAILY VALUE:** Total Fat: 0 g 0% ◆ Saturated Fat: 0 g 0% ◆ Cholesterol: 0 mg 0% ◆ Sodium: 0 mg 0% ◆ Total Carbohydrate: 8 g 3% ◆ Dietary Fiber: 0 g 0% ◆ Sugars: 7 g ◆ Protein: 0 g ◆ Vitamin A: 0% ◆ Vitamin C: 0% ◆ Calcium: 0% ◆ Iron: 0% ◆ **DIETARY EXCHANGES:** ½ Fruit OR ½ Carbohydrate

Applesauce

PREP TIME: I HOUR ◆ YIELD: 6 (⅔-CUP) SERVINGS

6 to 8 medium apples, peeled, quartered
½ cup water
½ to ¾ cup sugar or firmly packed brown sugar
1 to 2 tablespoons red cinnamon candies or 1 teaspoon cinnamon

1. In large saucepan, combine apples and water.* Bring to a boil. Reduce heat to low; cover and simmer 15 to 20 minutes or until apples are tender, stirring occasionally.
2. Stir in sugar and candies; mix well. Cook until mixture is thoroughly heated and candies are dissolved, stirring occasionally.

3. Ladle mixture into clean jar or moisture-vaporproof containers. Cool 15 minutes. Cover with tight-fitting lids. Store in refrigerator.

> **TIP:** * For chunky applesauce, combine sugar and water. Add apples; mix well. Cook as directed above.

NUTRITION INFORMATION PER SERVING: Serving Size: ⅔ Cup ◆ Calories: 230 ◆ Calories from Fat: 10 ◆ **% DAILY VALUE:** Total Fat: 1 g 2% ◆ Saturated Fat: 0 g 0% ◆ Cholesterol: 0 mg 0% ◆ Sodium: 0 mg 0% ◆ Total Carbohydrate: 55 g 18% ◆ Dietary Fiber: 3 g 12% ◆ Sugars: 47 g ◆ Protein: 0 g ◆ Vitamin A: 0% ◆ Vitamin C: 8% ◆ Calcium: 0% ◆ Iron: 0% ◆ **DIETARY EXCHANGES:** 3½ Fruit OR 3½ Carbohydrate

Orange-Pear Conserve

PREP TIME: I HOUR ◆ YIELD: 4½ CUPS

5 firm ripe pears
1 large thin-skinned orange (such as Valencia or Temple)
1½ cups water
1½ cups sugar
2 tablespoons grated orange peel
1½ teaspoons ginger
2 tablespoons cold water
1 tablespoon cornstarch

1. Peel, core and dice pears. Cut unpeeled orange into fourths and slice each fourth into ¼-inch slices; remove seeds.
2. In large saucepan, combine pears, orange and 1½ cups water. Cook over medium heat until fruit is tender, about 7 minutes. Stir in sugar. Bring to a boil. Boil 15 minutes, stirring occasionally. Stir in orange peel and ginger.
3. In small bowl, combine 2 tablespoons cold water and cornstarch; add to hot fruit mixture. Simmer 5 minutes or until mixture thickens slightly.
4. Ladle mixture into 5 clean, hot 8-oz. jars or moisture-vaporproof freezer containers, leaving ½-inch headspace. Cool 15 minutes; cover with tight-fitting lids. Store in refrigerator for up to 3 weeks or in freezer for up to 3 months.

NUTRITION INFORMATION PER SERVING: Serving Size: 1 Tablespoon ◆ Calories: 25 ◆ Calories from Fat: 0 ◆ **% DAILY VALUE:** Total Fat: 0 g 0% ◆ Saturated Fat: 0 g 0% ◆ Cholesterol: 0 mg 0% ◆ Sodium: 0 mg 0% ◆ Total Carbohydrate: 6 g 2% ◆ Dietary Fiber: 0 g 0% ◆ Sugars: 6 g ◆ Protein: 0 g ◆ Vitamin A: 0% ◆ Vitamin C: 4% ◆ Calcium: 0% ◆ Iron: 0% ◆ **DIETARY EXCHANGES:** ½ Fruit OR ½ Carbohydrate

Citrus Marmalade

PREP TIME: 1 HOUR (READY IN 4 HOURS)
◆ YIELD: 3 CUPS

   1 medium orange
   1 medium tangerine
   1 medium lemon
1½ cups water
  ⅛ teaspoon baking soda
   3 cups sugar
   1 (3-oz.) pkg. liquid fruit pectin

1. MICROWAVE DIRECTIONS: Score outer peel of fruit into quarters. Remove thin layer of peel a quarter at a time. Discard white membrane from peel and fruit. Cut peel into very thin strips.
2. In 2-quart microwave-safe bowl, combine peel, water and baking soda. Cover; microwave on HIGH for 5 to 8 minutes or until mixture comes to a full rolling boil. Continue to boil for 10 minutes, stirring once halfway through cooking.
3. Meanwhile, in shallow bowl, finely chop fruit, being careful not to lose any juice. Add fruit with juice to peel mixture. Cover; microwave on HIGH for 3 to 4 minutes or until mixture comes to full rolling boil. Continue to boil for 10 minutes, stirring once halfway through cooking.
4. Remove all but 2 cups fruit mixture from bowl; discard removed fruit. Add sugar and pectin to 2 cups fruit mixture; mix well. Microwave on HIGH for 6½ to 9 minutes or until mixture comes to full rolling boil, stirring twice during cooking. Continue to boil for 1 minute.
5. Spoon mixture into 3 clean, hot 8-oz. jars or moisture-vaporproof containers, leaving ½-inch headspace; cover with tight-fitting lids. Cool at least 3 hours. Store in refrigerator for up to 3 weeks or in freezer for up to 3 months.

NUTRITION INFORMATION: Not possible to calculate because of recipe variables.

Hot and Spicy Tomato Salsa

PREP TIME: 30 MINUTES ◆ YIELD: 4 CUPS

   6 medium tomatoes, coarsely chopped
     (3 cups)
   1 (15-oz.) can (1¾ cups) tomato puree
   6 garlic cloves, minced
   2 small jalapeño chiles, seeded, finely chopped
   3 tablespoons finely chopped onion
  ⅓ cup dry white wine or unsweetened apple juice
  ¼ cup lemon juice
  ½ to 1 teaspoon ground red pepper (cayenne)
  ½ teaspoon salt
  ½ teaspoon pepper
   1 teaspoon olive oil
  ¼ cup chopped fresh cilantro

1. In medium saucepan, combine all ingredients except cilantro. Bring to a boil over high heat. Reduce heat to medium; cook 15 minutes, stirring occasionally.
2. Stir in cilantro. Ladle mixture into clean jars or nonmetal containers; cover with tight-fitting lids. Store in refrigerator for up to 5 days or in freezer for up to 2 months. Serve hot as a relish or sauce, or cold as a dip for chips.

NUTRITION INFORMATION PER SERVING: Serving Size: ¼ Cup ◆ Calories: 40 ◆ Calories from Fat: 10 ◆ % DAILY VALUE: Total Fat: 1 g 2% ◆ Saturated Fat: 0 g 0% ◆ Cholesterol: 0 mg 0% ◆ Sodium: 180 mg 8% ◆ Total Carbohydrate: 6 g 2% ◆ Dietary Fiber: 1 g 4% ◆ Sugars: 3 g ◆ Protein: 1 g ◆ Vitamin A: 15% ◆ Vitamin C: 30% ◆ Calcium: 0% ◆ Iron: 4% ◆ DIETARY EXCHANGES: 1 Vegetable, ½ Fat

Hot and Spicy Tomato Salsa

TIMETABLE FOR CANNING VEGETABLES

VEGETABLE	AMOUNT TO YIELD 1 QUART	BASIC PREPARATION (IF DESIRED, ADD ½ TEASPOON SALT PER PINT.)	TIME IN DIAL-GAUGE PRESSURE COOKER WITH 11 POUNDS PRESSURE (OR 15 POUNDS IN WEIGHTED-GAUGE PRESSURE COOKER)	
			PINTS	QUARTS
ASPARAGUS	About 48 spears or 3 lb.	Wash and trim, break or cut into 1-inch pieces. Pack tightly into jars leaving 1 inch at top. Cover with boiling water leaving 1 inch at top.	30 min.	40 min.
BEANS, GREEN OR WAX	2 lb.	Wash and trim, break or cut into 1-inch pieces. Pack tightly into jars leaving 1 inch at top. Cover with boiling water leaving 1 inch at top.	20 min.	25 min.
BEANS, LIMA OR BUTTER	4 lb. (in pod)	Shell and wash. Pack into jars. For small beans, leave 1 inch at top for pints and 1½ inches at top for quarts. For large beans, leave ¾ inch at top for pints and 1¼ inches for quarts. Cover with boiling water leaving 1 inch at top.	40 min.	50 min.
BEETS	2 lb.	Wash; cut off tops leaving 1-inch stem. Boil covered with water until skins can be slipped. Remove skins; leave whole, slice or dice. Pack into jars leaving 1 inch at top. Cover with boiling water leaving 1 inch at top.	30 min.	35 min.
CARROTS	2½ lb.	Discard tops; wash and peel. Slice, dice or leave whole. Pack into jars leaving 1 inch at top. Cover with boiling water leaving 1 inch at top.	25 min.	30 min.
CORN, WHOLE KERNEL	12 to 14 ears	Husk, remove silk and trim. Cut corn from cob. Pack loosely into jars leaving 1 inch at top. Cover with boiling water leaving 1 inch at top.	55 min.	85 min.*

VEGETABLE	AMOUNT TO YIELD 1 QUART	BASIC PREPARATION (IF DESIRED, ADD ½ TEASPOON SALT PER PINT.)	TIME IN DIAL-GAUGE PRESSURE COOKER WITH 11 POUNDS PRESSURE (OR 15 POUNDS IN WEIGHTED-GAUGE PRESSURE COOKER) PINTS	QUARTS
OKRA	1½ lb.	Wash and trim; leave whole or slice. Cover with hot water and boil 2 minutes. Pack into jars leaving 1 inch at top. Cover with cooking liquid leaving ½ inch at top.	25 min.	40 min.
PEAS, GREEN	4 lb. (in pod)	Shell and wash. Pack peas lightly in jars leaving 1 inch at top. Cover with boiling water leaving 1 inch at top.	40 min.	40 min.
PUMPKIN, SEE WINTER SQUASH				
SUMMER SQUASH OR ZUCCHINI	2 or 3 lb.	Wash and slice squash. Cover with water and boil 2 minutes. Pack into jars leaving ½ inch at top. Cover with cooking liquid leaving 1 inch at top.	25 min.	30 min.
SQUASH, WINTER	2 lb.	Wash, remove seeds, peel and cube.** Cover with water and heat to boiling. Pack into jars leaving ½ inch at top. Cover with cooking liquid leaving ½ inch at top.	55 min.	90 min.
TOMATOES, SEE TIMETABLE FOR CANNING FRUITS AND TOMATOES				

*The USDA recommends that all corn be canned in pints because the long processing time for quarts tends to darken it.

**Straining or mashing squash or pumpkin should be done at time of use, not before processing.

HIGH ALTITUDE: The processing times given for canning vegetables are for altitudes of 0–1000 feet. If you are canning at higher altitude, the processing times stay the same, but you must make the following adjustments:

In a Dial-Gauge Pressure Canner:

At altitudes of 1001–2000 feet, the pressure is not increased; process at 11 pounds pressure.

At altitudes of 2001–4000 feet, process at 12 pounds pressure.

At altitudes of 4001–6000 feet, process at 13 pounds pressure.

At altitudes of 6001–8000 feet, process at 14 pounds pressure.

In a Weighted-Gauge Pressure Canner:

At altitudes above 1000 feet, process at 15 pounds pressure.

Source: The State Department of Agriculture

Homemade Tomato Sauce

PREP TIME: I HOUR 15 MINUTES ✦ YIELD: 10 CUPS

⅓ cup olive oil
2 cups (2 large) chopped onions
2 garlic cloves, minced
8 cups (16 medium) coarsely chopped, peeled
    tomatoes
1 tablespoon dried oregano leaves
1 teaspoon sugar
1 teaspoon dried basil leaves
1 teaspoon crushed dried rosemary leaves
½ teaspoon salt
¼ teaspoon pepper
2 cups water
1 (12-oz.) can tomato paste

1. Heat oil in 4-quart saucepan or Dutch oven over medium heat until hot. Add onions and garlic; cook until onions are tender.
2. Add all remaining ingredients; mix well. Bring to a boil, stirring occasionally. Reduce heat; simmer 1 hour, stirring occasionally.
3. Ladle mixture into clean jars or nonmetal containers; cover with tight-fitting lids. Store in refrigerator for up to 1 week or in freezer for up to 3 months.

NUTRITION INFORMATION PER SERVING: Serving Size: ½ Cup ✦ Calories: 70 ✦ Calories from Fat: 35 ✦ % DAILY VALUE: Total Fat: 4 g 6% ✦ Saturated Fat: 1 g 5% ✦ Cholesterol: 0 mg 0% ✦ Sodium: 190 mg 8% ✦ Total Carbohydrate: 8 g 3% ✦ Dietary Fiber: 2 g 8% ✦ Sugars: 3 g ✦ Protein: 1 g ✦ Vitamin A: 15% ✦ Vitamin C: 25% ✦ Calcium: 0% ✦ Iron: 4% ✦ DIETARY EXCHANGES: 1 Vegetable, 1 Fat

Left to right: Spiced Pear Chutney (page 460), Jalapeño Cranberry Relish (page 460), Spiced Vinegar (page 459), Spiced Vinegar Salad Dressing (page 459)

COOK'S NOTE

HOW TO CAN TOMATOES

Scalding

With a paring knife, cut a small **X** in the bottom of each tomato. Dip or scald clean, ripe tomatoes in boiling water about 30 seconds to loosen skins.

Peeling

Peel off skins. Core and quarter-large tomatoes; pack small tomatoes whole.

Packing Jars

Pack into hot jars, pressing tomatoes to form juice to fill spaces; leave ½ inch space at top of jar. If desired, add 1 teaspoon salt per quart. Wipe jar rim;  put lid in place and screw metal bands down "fingertip" tight, following manufacturer's directions.

Processing Jars

Place jars on a rack in hot water in canner. Add additional hot water to cover the jars by 1 to 2 inches. Cover canner; heat water to boiling. Begin  timing when water boils; reduce heat to hold water at gentle, steady boil.

Spiced Vinegar

PREP TIME: 15 MINUTES (READY IN 3 WEEKS)
✦ YIELD: 4 CUPS

   2 cups sweet red wine
   2 cups white vinegar
   3 (3-inch) strips orange peel
   2 (4-inch) cinnamon sticks
   2 whole cloves

1. In medium saucepan, combine wine, vinegar, orange peel strips and cinnamon sticks. Bring to a boil. Simmer 3 minutes. Strain into 2 clean 1-pint bottles.
2. Add 1 whole clove to each bottle. Place 1 of the orange strips and 1 of the cinnamon sticks in each bottle. (Discard remaining orange peel.) Cork or seal tightly.
3. Let stand in cool dark place for 3 weeks to develop flavor. Gently turn bottles occasionally to mix contents. Use to make Spiced Vinegar Salad Dressing, below.

NUTRITION INFORMATION PER SERVING: Serving Size: 1 Tablespoon ✦ Calories: 5 ✦ Calories from Fat: 0 ✦ **% DAILY VALUE:** Total Fat: 0 g 0% ✦ Saturated Fat: 0 g 0% ✦ Cholesterol: 0 mg 0% ✦ Sodium: 0 mg 0% ✦ Total Carbohydrate: 1 g 1% ✦ Dietary Fiber: 0 g 0% ✦ Sugars: 0 g ✦ Protein: 0 g ✦ Vitamin A: 0% ✦ Vitamin C: 0% ✦ Calcium: 0% ✦ Iron: 0% ✦ **DIETARY EXCHANGES:** Free

Spiced Vinegar Salad Dressing

PREP TIME: 5 MINUTES ✦ YIELD: 1 CUP

   ½ cup oil
   ½ cup Spiced Vinegar (above)
   2 teaspoons sugar

In jar with tight-fitting lid, combine all ingredients; shake to blend.

NUTRITION INFORMATION PER SERVING: Serving Size: 1 Tablespoon ✦ Calories: 70 ✦ Calories from Fat: 60 ✦ **% DAILY VALUE:** Total Fat: 7 g 11% ✦ Saturated Fat: 1 g 5% ✦ Cholesterol: 0 mg 0% ✦ Sodium: 0 mg 0% ✦ Total Carbohydrate: 1 g 1% ✦ Dietary Fiber: 0 g 0% ✦ Sugars: 1 g ✦ Protein: 0 g ✦ Vitamin A: 0% ✦ Vitamin C: 0% ✦ Calcium: 0% ✦ Iron: 0% ✦ **DIETARY EXCHANGES:** 1½ Fat

Refrigerator Pickle Medley

Refrigerator Pickle Medley

PREP TIME: 30 MINUTES (READY IN 27 HOURS 30 MINUTES) ✦ YIELD: 4 CUPS

   3 cups thinly sliced, unpeeled cucumbers
   ¾ cup sliced 1-inch-long green onion pieces
   ½ cup diagonally sliced celery
   ½ cup thinly sliced carrot
   1 small red bell pepper, cut into strips
   1 garlic clove, crushed
   1 teaspoon salt
   8 cups ice cubes
   ½ to ⅔ cup sugar
   1 teaspoon mustard seed
   1 teaspoon dried dill weed
   ¼ teaspoon celery seed
   ½ cup white vinegar

1. MICROWAVE DIRECTIONS: In large bowl, combine cucumbers, onions, celery, carrots, bell pepper, garlic and salt. Add ice cubes; mix thoroughly. Let stand at room temperature for 3 hours.
2. Using colander, drain well. Remove any remaining ice. In clean 1-quart jar, pack drained vegetables.
3. In 4-cup microwave-safe measuring cup, combine all remaining ingredients. Microwave on HIGH for 2 to 3 minutes or until mixture boils. Stir to dissolve sugar. Pour hot vinegar mixture over vegetables; cover with tight-fitting lid. Invert jar; then turn upright to distribute spices evenly. Refrigerate at least 24 hours to blend flavors. Store in refrigerator.

NUTRITION INFORMATION: Not possible to calculate because of recipe variables.

Spiced Pear Chutney

PREP TIME: 25 MINUTES (READY IN 4 HOURS
10 MINUTES) ✦ YIELD: 4 CUPS

¾ cup firmly packed brown sugar
¾ cup cider vinegar
3 firm large pears (1½ lb.), chopped
½ cup chopped onion
½ cup chopped red bell pepper
¼ cup golden or dark raisins
1 tablespoon grated gingerroot
½ teaspoon cinnamon
½ teaspoon coriander

1. In large saucepan, combine brown sugar and vinegar. Bring to a boil. Reduce heat; simmer 10 minutes.
2. Stir in all remaining ingredients. Return to a boil. Reduce heat; simmer 45 minutes or until thickened.
3. Refrigerate at least 3 hours or until chilled. Spoon into decorative crock or jar. Store in refrigerator for up to 2 weeks.

NUTRITION INFORMATION PER SERVING: Serving Size: 2 Tablespoons ✦ Calories: 40 ✦ Calories from Fat: 0 ✦ **% DAILY VALUE:** Total Fat: 0 g 0% ✦ Saturated Fat: 0 g 0% ✦ Cholesterol: 0 mg 0% ✦ Sodium: 0 mg 0% ✦ Total Carbohydrate: 10 g 3% ✦ Dietary Fiber: 1 g 3% ✦ Sugars: 8 g ✦ Protein: 0 g ✦ Vitamin A: 0% ✦ Vitamin C: 4% ✦ Calcium: 0% ✦ Iron: 0% ✦ **DIETARY EXCHANGES:** ½ Fruit OR ½ Carbohydrate

Jalapeño Cranberry Relish

PREP TIME: 35 MINUTES (READY IN 1 HOUR 35 MINUTES) ✦ YIELD: 4 CUPS

1 (12-oz.) pkg. fresh or frozen cranberries
1 to 2 jalapeño chiles, quartered, seeded
1 tart apple, peeled, finely chopped
½ cup finely chopped peeled jicama
½ cup orange marmalade
⅔ cup sugar
⅓ cup pomegranate seeds
⅓ cup chopped fresh cilantro
1 tablespoon lemon juice
1 tablespoon Dijon mustard

1. In food processor bowl with metal blade or blender container, coarsely grind cranberries and chiles.
2. In large bowl, combine all remaining ingredients. Stir in cranberry mixture; blend well. Refrigerate at least 1 hour or until chilled.
3. Spoon mixture into decorative crock or jar. Store in refrigerator for up to 1 week.

NUTRITION INFORMATION PER SERVING: Serving Size: 2 Tablespoons ✦ Calories: 40 ✦ Calories from Fat: 0 ✦ **% DAILY VALUE:** Total Fat: 0 g 0% ✦ Saturated Fat: 0 g 0% ✦ Cholesterol: 0 mg 0% ✦ Sodium: 15 mg 1% ✦ Total Carbohydrate: 10 g 3% ✦ Dietary Fiber: 1 g 3% ✦ Sugars: 8 g ✦ Protein: 0 g ✦ Vitamin A: 0% ✦ Vitamin C: 10% ✦ Calcium: 0% ✦ Iron: 0% ✦ **DIETARY EXCHANGES:** ½ Fruit OR ½ Carbohydrate

Marinated Vegetables with Olives

PREP TIME: 30 MINUTES (READY IN 28 HOURS
30 MINUTES) ✦ YIELD: 4 CUPS

1⅓ cups oil
1 cup white vinegar
2 teaspoons dried rosemary leaves
1 teaspoon dried thyme leaves
4 garlic cloves, minced
½ cup diagonally sliced 1-inch-long green
        onion pieces
1 (6-oz.) can pitted large ripe olives, drained
1 cup thin diagonally sliced carrots
1 cup fresh cauliflower florets
1 medium red bell pepper, cut into
        1-inch pieces

1. In medium saucepan, combine oil, vinegar, rosemary, thyme and garlic. Bring to a boil. In medium bowl, combine onions and olives; add hot oil mixture. Cover; refrigerate 4 hours, stirring twice.
2. Drain onions and olives, reserving liquid. In medium bowl, combine onions, olives, carrots, cauliflower and bell pepper. Spoon vegetables into 3 clean, hot 1-pint jars. Pour reserved liquid over vegetables; cover with tight-fitting lids. Refrigerate at least 24 hours. Store in refrigerator for up to 1 month.

NUTRITION INFORMATION: Not possible to calculate because of recipe variables.

COOK'S NOTE

NUTRITION PER SERVING FOR HOME-PRESERVED FOODS

Salt added to water and vinegar becomes a brine that flavors and preserves food. It is difficult to determine exactly how much salt enters the food and how much remains in the brine of home-preserved foods. Because of this variable in salt content, nutrition information is not provided for all pickling recipes.

Sweet Hot Pickled Vegetables

PREP TIME: 30 MINUTES (READY IN 10 HOURS 30 MINUTES) ♦ YIELD: 4 CUPS

VEGETABLES
  1 cup thinly sliced carrots
  1½ cups cooked sugar snap peas or thawed
      frozen sugar snap peas
  1½ cups thinly sliced cucumbers
  1 to 2 banana peppers, thinly sliced
  2 garlic cloves

PICKLING MIXTURE
  ¾ cup sugar
  1½ teaspoons salt
  ½ teaspoon celery seed
  ½ teaspoon mustard seed
  ¼ teaspoon ginger
  ⅛ teaspoon turmeric
  4 peppercorns
  1 cup white vinegar
  ¾ cup water

1. Bring 1 inch water to a boil in medium saucepan. Add carrots. Reduce heat to low; cover and simmer 2 to 4 minutes or until carrots are just crisp-tender. Drain.
2. Layer sugar snap peas, cooked carrots, cucumbers, banana peppers and garlic in clean, hot 1-quart jar.
3. In small saucepan, combine all pickling mixture ingredients. Bring to a boil. Reduce heat; simmer 5 minutes. Pour over vegetables. Run knife down sides of jar to remove air bubbles; cover with tight-fitting lid. Cool 2 hours or until room temperature. Refrigerate at least 8 hours before serving to blend flavors. Store in refrigerator for up to 6 weeks.

NUTRITION INFORMATION: Not possible to calculate because of recipe variables.

Dill-Pickled Beets

PREP TIME: 30 MINUTES ♦ YIELD: 4 CUPS

  1½ cups white vinegar
  ½ cup water
  2 garlic cloves, cut in half
  2 tablespoons chopped fresh dill
      or 2 teaspoons dried dill weed
  1 to 2 tablespoons sugar
  ½ teaspoon salt
  6 peppercorns
  2 lb. cooked beets, cubed, or 2 (16-oz.) cans
      diced beets, drained
  1 small onion, sliced, separated into rings

1. In medium saucepan, combine vinegar, water, garlic, dill, sugar, salt and peppercorns. Bring to a boil.
2. Meanwhile, place beets and onion rings in 4 clean, hot 8-oz. jars.
3. Pour hot vinegar mixture over beets; cover with tight-fitting lids. Store in refrigerator.

NUTRITION INFORMATION: Not possible to calculate because of recipe variables.

COOK'S NOTE

PRESERVING PICKLES, RELISHES AND SAUCES

Pickles, relish, chutney, salsa and sauce give a burst of tangy flavor to sandwiches, meats and salads.

Use produce at peak ripeness and wash it under cold running water or through several changes of water.

Vinegar provides the acid solution to preserve pickles and relishes. Some of our recipes call for cider vinegar, which has a more mellow flavor than distilled white vinegar. Others use distilled white vinegar for its sharper flavor and lighter color.

Pickling salt is used because iodized salt causes pickles to darken or makes the brine cloudy.

Dilled Green Beans and Cauliflower

PREP TIME: 30 MINUTES (READY IN 2 WEEKS)
◆ YIELD: 8 CUPS

VEGETABLE MIXTURE
1 lb. (2 cups) fresh whole green beans
2 cups fresh cauliflower florets
8 garlic cloves
¼ cup chopped fresh dill
4 teaspoons mustard seed
¼ teaspoon celery seed
8 peppercorns

PICKLING MIXTURE
2½ cups white vinegar
2½ cups water
¼ cup sugar
2 tablespoons salt

1. Bring 1 inch water to a boil in medium saucepan. Add green beans and cauliflower. Reduce heat to low; cover and simmer 2 to 4 minutes or until beans are just crisp-tender. Drain.
2. Divide green beans and remaining vegetable mixture ingredients evenly into 2 clean, hot 1-quart jars.
3. In small saucepan, combine all pickling mixture ingredients. Bring to a boil. Pour over vegetables. Run knife down sides of each jar to remove air bubbles; cover with tight-fitting lids. Refrigerate 2 weeks before serving to blend flavors. Store in refrigerator for up to 1 month.

NUTRITION INFORMATION: Not possible to calculate because of recipe variables.

Dill Pickles

Dill Pickles

PREP TIME: 45 MINUTES (READY IN 1 WEEK)
◆ YIELD: 4 QUARTS

24 to 30 cucumbers, 3 inches long
12 to 16 sprigs fresh dill
4 teaspoons mustard seed
4 cups (1 qt.) water
2 cups cider vinegar
2 tablespoons pickling salt

1. Wash cucumbers; pack in clean, hot 1-quart jars. To each jar, add 3 or 4 sprigs fresh dill and 1 teaspoon mustard seed.
2. In large saucepan, combine water, vinegar and salt. Bring to a boil. Fill jars leaving ½-inch headspace. Seal jars.
3. Process in boiling water bath for 10 minutes. Let stand 1 week before serving to blend flavors.

TIP: A peeled garlic clove can be added to each jar along with dill.

NUTRITION INFORMATION: Not possible to calculate because of recipe variables.

Tri-Colored Pickled Peppers

PREP TIME: 30 MINUTES (READY IN 1 WEEK)
◆ YIELD: 1 QUART

1 tablespoon sugar
1 tablespoon salt
2 cups water
1 cup white vinegar
1 red bell pepper, cut into 6 pieces
1 yellow bell pepper, cut into 6 pieces
1 green bell pepper, cut into 6 pieces
1 small onion, sliced, separated into rings
2 garlic cloves, halved
1 sprig fresh tarragon or ¼ teaspoon dried tarragon leaves

1. MICROWAVE DIRECTIONS: In 2-quart microwave-safe bowl, combine sugar, salt, water and vinegar. Microwave on HIGH for 8 to 14 minutes or until mixture boils. Stir to dissolve sugar.
2. In clean, hot 1-quart jar, pack all remaining ingredients. Pour hot vinegar mixture over vegetables; cover with tight-fitting lid. Refrigerate at least 1 week before serving to blend flavors. Store in refrigerator.

NUTRITION INFORMATION: Not possible to calculate because of recipe variables.

Bread and Butter Pickles

PREP TIME: 45 MINUTES (READY IN 8 HOURS
45 MINUTES) ♦ YIELD: 8 PINTS

    5 quarts (20 cups) thinly sliced, unpeeled
        cucumbers
    6 medium onions, thinly sliced
    3 medium green bell peppers, cut into thin
        strips
    3 garlic cloves
    ⅓ cup pickling salt
    8 cups ice cubes
    4½ cups sugar
    2 cups white vinegar
    2 tablespoons mustard seed
    1½ teaspoons celery seed
    1½ teaspoons turmeric

1. In large bowl, combine cucumbers, onions, bell peppers, garlic and salt. Add ice cubes; mix thoroughly. Let stand at room temperature for 3 hours.
2. Using colander, drain well. Remove garlic and any remaining ice.
3. In large saucepan, combine all remaining ingredients. Bring to a boil. Fill clean, hot jars with vegetables and syrup, leaving ½-inch headspace. Seal jars. Process in boiling water bath for 10 minutes. Let stand at least 8 hours before serving to blend flavors.

NUTRITION INFORMATION: Not possible to calculate because of recipe variables.

Refrigerator Cucumber Pickles

PREP TIME: 30 MINUTES (READY IN 9 HOURS)
♦ YIELD: 3 QUARTS

    12 cups (7 medium) thinly sliced, unpeeled
        cucumbers
    1 tablespoon pickling salt
    2 medium onions, thinly sliced (2 cups)
    1 cup chopped green bell pepper
    2 cups sugar
    1 tablespoon celery seed
    1 tablespoon mustard seed
    1 cup white vinegar

1. In large bowl, combine cucumbers and salt; mix well. Let stand at room temperature for 30 minutes.
2. Using colander, drain well. Stir in onions and bell pepper.

3. In small bowl, combine all remaining ingredients. Pour vinegar mixture over vegetables; mix well. Ladle mixture into clean, hot jars; cover with tight-fitting lids. Refrigerate at least 8 hours before serving to blend flavors. Store in refrigerator for up to 3 months.

NUTRITION INFORMATION: Not possible to calculate because of recipe variables.

Quick Pickles

PREP TIME: 30 MINUTES (READY IN 27 HOURS
30 MINUTES) ♦ YIELD: 1 QUART

    3 cups thinly sliced, unpeeled cucumbers
    1 medium onion, sliced
    1 small green bell pepper, cut into strips
    1 small red bell pepper, cut into strips
    1 small carrot, thinly sliced
    1 garlic clove, crushed
    1 teaspoon salt
    8 cups ice cubes
    ¾ cup sugar
    1 teaspoon mustard seed
    ¼ teaspoon celery seed
    ⅛ teaspoon turmeric
    ½ cup white vinegar

1. MICROWAVE DIRECTIONS: In large bowl, combine cucumbers, onion, bell peppers, carrot, garlic and salt. Add ice cubes; mix thoroughly. Let stand at room temperature for 3 hours.
2. Using colander, drain well. Remove any remaining ice. In clean, hot 1-quart jar, pack drained vegetables.
3. In 4-cup microwave-safe measuring cup, combine all remaining ingredients. Microwave on HIGH for 2 to 5 minutes or until mixture boils. Stir to dissolve sugar. Pour hot vinegar mixture over vegetables; cover with tight-fitting lid. Twist jar; then turn upright to distribute spices evenly. Refrigerate at least 24 hours before serving to blend flavors. Store in refrigerator.

TIP: Two 1-pint or four 8-oz. jars can be substituted for 1-quart jar.

NUTRITION INFORMATION: Not possible to calculate because of recipe variables.

GENERAL NUTRITION INFORMATION

The Food Guide Pyramid

In 1992, the U.S. Department of Agriculture, in cooperation with the Department of Health and Human Services, unveiled the "Food Guide Pyramid" to illustrate guidelines for a healthy diet. The pyramid replaced the older notion of the "Basic Four Food Groups" (later the Basic Five), which had been in use since the 1950s.

In a shift from decades past, the pyramid does not use meat as the centerpiece of a healthy diet. Instead, it emphasizes grain products, fruits and vegetables. Meat and dairy products are still important, but play more of a supporting role. The tip of the pyramid serves as a reminder that sugars and fats should be used sparingly.

Serving Sizes

The amount that constitutes a "serving" varies depending on the nutrients a food provides, as shown in the examples below. You may be surprised that you're getting several servings from different food groups with one food. One large piece of vegetable pizza, for example, may actually be two servings from the bread group, one serving from the vegetable group and one serving from the milk and cheese group.

BREAD, CEREAL, RICE AND PASTA GROUP
◆ 1 slice of bread
◆ 1 oz. of ready-to-eat cereal
◆ ½ cup of cooked cereal, rice or pasta

VEGETABLE GROUP
◆ 1 cup of raw leafy vegetables
◆ ½ cup of other vegetables, cooked or chopped raw
◆ ¾ cup of vegetable juice

HOW MANY SERVINGS DO YOU NEED EACH DAY?

	CHILDREN, MANY WOMEN, OLDER ADULTS	TEEN GIRLS, ACTIVE WOMEN, MOST MEN	TEEN BOYS, ACTIVE MEN
CALORIE LEVEL*	ABOUT 1,600	ABOUT 2,000	ABOUT 2,800
BREAD GROUP	6	9	11
VEGETABLE GROUP	3	4	5
FRUIT GROUP	2	3	4
MILK GROUP	2 to 3*	2 to 3*	2 to 3*
MEAT GROUP	5 oz.	6 oz.	7 oz.

Women who are pregnant or breast-feeding, teenagers and young adults to age 24 need 3 servings.

Source: U.S. Department of Agriculture

Food Guide Pyramid

A Guide to Daily Food Choices

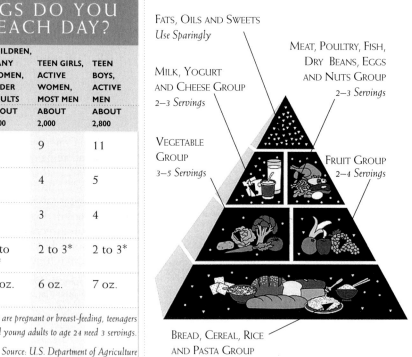

FATS, OILS AND SWEETS
Use Sparingly

MEAT, POULTRY, FISH, DRY BEANS, EGGS AND NUTS GROUP
2–3 Servings

MILK, YOGURT AND CHEESE GROUP
2–3 Servings

VEGETABLE GROUP
3–5 Servings

FRUIT GROUP
2–4 Servings

BREAD, CEREAL, RICE AND PASTA GROUP
6–11 Servings

SEVEN STEPS TO A HEALTHY DIET

These guidelines offer advice for healthy Americans about food choices that promote health and help prevent disease.

1. **Eat a variety of foods** to get the energy, protein, vitamins, minerals and fiber you need for good health. No single food can provide everything you need. Consult the "Food Guide Pyramid" on page 464 to help you plan your choices.

2. **Balance the foods you eat with physical activity** to maintain or improve a healthy weight. Weight gain increases your risk of developing high blood pressure, heart disease, stroke, certain cancers and other illnesses.

3. **Choose a diet low in fat, saturated fat and cholesterol** to reduce your risk of heart attack and certain types of cancer. Because fat contains more than twice the calories of an equal amount of carbohydrates or protein, a diet low in fat can help you maintain a healthy weight.

4. **Choose a diet with plenty of vegetables, fruits and grain products.** Most of the calories in your diet should come from these foods, which provide needed vitamins, minerals, fiber and complex carbohydrates and can help you lower your intake of fat.

5. **Use sugars only in moderation.** A diet with lots of sugars has too many calories and too few nutrients for most people and can contribute to tooth decay.

6. **Use salt and sodium only in moderation** to help reduce your risk of high blood pressure. While sodium occurs naturally in foods, the amount present in fruits and vegetables is usually very small. Read the Nutrition Facts label on prepared foods to identify those lower in sodium.

7. **If you drink alcoholic beverages, do so in moderation,** with meals and only when consumption does not put you and others at risk. Alcoholic beverages supply calories, but little or no nutrients. Moderate consumption has been associated with a lower risk for heart disease, but too much alcohol may cause many health problems and accidents and can lead to addiction.

Source: U.S. Department of Agriculture and the Department of Health and Human Services.

FRUIT GROUP
+ I medium apple, banana or orange
+ ½ cup of chopped, cooked or canned fruit
+ ¾ cup of fruit juice

MILK, YOGURT AND CHEESE GROUP
+ I cup of milk or yogurt
+ I½ oz. of natural cheese
+ 2 oz. of processed cheese

MEAT, POULTRY, FISH, DRY BEANS, EGGS AND NUTS GROUP
+ 2 to 3 oz. of cooked lean meat, poultry or fish
+ ½ cup of cooked dry beans, I egg or 2 tablespoons of peanut butter count as I oz. of lean meat

How to Use Our Nutrition Information

The detailed nutrition information that accompanies each recipe in this book can help you estimate how specific recipes contribute to your overall meal plan. At the end of each recipe we list calories, fat, cholesterol, sodium, carbohydrate, dietary fiber, sugars and protein in grams and in percent daily value. Percent daily value is provided for vitamins A and C, calcium and iron.

Each recipe also lists Percent Daily Values (%DVs), which tell you how much the nutrients in one serving of food contribute to a 2,000-calorie diet. For example, if the DV for total fat is 10%, this means one serving of this food contributes 10% of the daily total fat suggested for a person on a 2,000-calorie-a-day diet. (When the labeling guidelines were developed by the government, 2,000 calories was designated as an average level. It's about right for most moderately

YOUR DAILY NUTRITIONAL REQUIREMENTS

This chart outlines average daily nutritional needs for healthy adults age 25 to 50. Since your age, size, activity level and health all affect dietary considerations, your requirements may be different.

	MEN	WOMEN
CALORIES	2400	1850
TOTAL FAT	80 g or less	62 g or less
SATURATED FAT	27 g or less	20 g or less
CHOLESTEROL	300 mg or less	300 mg or less
SODIUM	2400 mg	2400 mg
TOTAL CARBOHYDRATE	360 g	275 g
DIETARY FIBER	20 to 30 g	20 to 30 g
PROTEIN	63 g	50 g
CALCIUM	1000 mg	1000 mg
IRON	10 mg	15 mg

Source: National Academy of Sciences, National Research Council, Recommended Dietary Allowances (10th edition, 1989).

active women, teenage girls and sedentary men. Older adults, sedentary women and young children need less; many men, teenage boys and active women may need more.)

In addition, you'll find dietary exchanges, the nutritional planning system commonly used by people with diabetes. This information is based on 1995 *Exchange Lists for Meal Planning* by the American Diabetes Association and the American Dietetic Association; they are not the same as Weight Watchers exchanges. For many recipes, two lists of exchanges are provided: The first option is based on the traditional method of figuring dietary exchanges; the second option reflects the newer system of carbohydrate counting. If you use the exchanges, consult your doctor or registered dietitian if you have questions, or call the American Dietetic Association at 1-800-366-1655.

HOW WE DETERMINE NUTRITION INFORMATION

✦ When the recipe gives options, we base the analysis on the *first* ingredient mentioned. For example, if "egg product or egg" is listed, egg product would be calculated.

✦ When there's a range for amounts of ingredients, we use the *larger* amount.
✦ When garnishes or "if desired" ingredients are included in the ingredient list, we *include* them in the analysis.
✦ When a recipe uses a marinade, the nutritional analysis includes the estimated amount of marinade *absorbed* during preparation.

OUR EXPERTS BEHIND THE SCENES

Our team of professionals, including registered dietitians and home economists, experienced recipe developers and test cooks, is dedicated to delivering comprehensive nutrition information. We continually update our nutrition database to include new information from the USDA and food manufacturers' labels.

READING A NUTRITION LABEL

Commercially packaged foods carry a Nutrition Facts label. The label must identify the serving size, number of calories per serving and the percentage of calories from fat. Also listed are quantities (in grams or milligrams) of total fat, cholesterol, sodium, potassium, carbohydrate and protein, which is translated into the "Percent Daily Value."

Many labels include information on vitamins and minerals.

When you compare labels, keep in mind:

◆ Ingredients are listed in order from largest percentage to smallest.
◆ The serving size listed on the label may be different from the amount you eat at a sitting. If you eat double the serving size listed, you need to double the nutrient and calorie values.
◆ Don't confuse "no cholesterol" with low-fat. Cholesterol is an animal product, so peanut butter has none—but it is still high in fat. Research has shown that the amount of total fat—especially saturated—in the diet, is the critical factor in your blood cholesterol level.
◆ Products labeled "low-fat" may compensate for the lack of fat by using extra sugar or salt.

If you have any nutrition questions related to the recipes in this book, please write to: Pillsbury Publications
Pillsbury Center
200 South Sixth Street, MS 28M7
Minneapolis, MN 55402

Kitchen Basics

Kitchen Basics is a collection of information designed for cooks of all experience levels. In this section you'll find general nutrition guidelines, information on cooking equipment, canning and condiment information and recipes, emergency substitutions, detailed ingredient charts, important food safety instructions for handling and storing food and much more. At the end of the chapter, you'll also find a complete glossary of food and cooking terms used throughout the book.

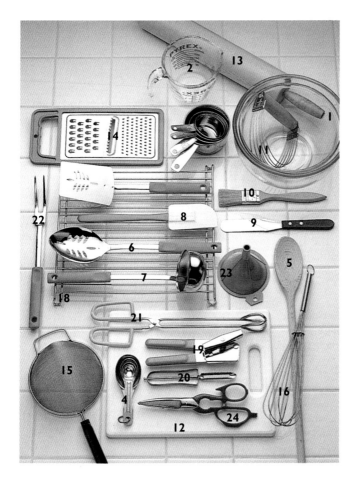

UTENSILS

1. Mixing bowls
2. Standard liquid measuring cup
3. Standard dry measuring cup set
4. Standard measuring spoon set
5. Mixing spoon
6. Slotted spoon
7. Ladle
8. Rubber scraper
9. Metal spatula
10. Pastry brush
11. Pastry blender
12. Chopping board
13. Rolling pin
14. Shredder
15. Strainer or colander
16. Wire whisk
17. Pancake turner
18. Wire rack
19. Can opener
20. Vegetable peeler
21. Tongs
22. Meat fork
23. Funnel
24. Kitchen scissors

Equipment for Good Cooking

Having the right tools makes cooking more enjoyable and successful. The bakeware and utensils we suggest are the standard sizes called for in most recipes. If you do a lot of cooking, you may want duplicates of frequently used utensils and cookware.

BAKEWARE

13 x 9-inch baking pans
Two 8-inch square baking pans
15 x 10 x 1-inch baking pan
Two 9-inch round cake pans
Two 9-inch pie pans
Two 12-cup muffin pans
Two 9 x 5-inch loaf pans
Two cookie sheets (without sides)
13 x 9-inch (3-quart) baking dish
8-inch square (2-quart) baking dish
Casserole or soufflé dish
Large shallow roasting pan

COOKWARE

Saucepans with covers in various sizes
10 or 12-inch skillet with cover
5-quart Dutch oven
Stockpot
Pancake griddle
Omelet pan
Wok

CUTLERY

A set of good cutlery is an indispensable kitchen investment.

MAINTENANCE, STORAGE AND CARE OF CUTLERY

Wash and dry knives by hand, not in the dishwasher. Store them in a wooden block, wall rack or in a drawer with the blades separated and protected. Maintain the sharpness of the blade by regular use of a sharpening steel:

1. While applying slight pressure and holding the knife blade at a 20 to 30-degree angle, draw the knife across the top of the steel in a curved motion.

2. Repeat the action with the knife blade under the steel. Alternate these two steps until the knife has been drawn across the steel 5 or 6 times. Wipe the blade clean with a paper towel to remove any tiny metal particles loosened by sharpening.

3. A sharpening steel will not cure blades that are dull. Resharpen dull knives on a whetstone or knife sharpener.

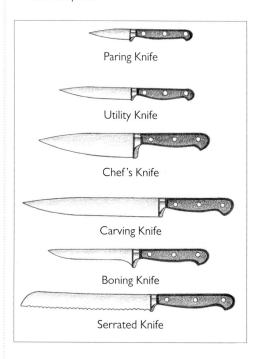

Paring Knife

Utility Knife

Chef's Knife

Carving Knife

Boning Knife

Serrated Knife

PARING KNIFE
Use for peeling and slicing fruits and vegetables, sculpting garnishes or chopping small amounts of herbs.

UTILITY KNIFE
Bigger than a paring knife, the utility knife handles similar tasks and is also handy for boning chicken.

CHEF'S KNIFE
The large, relatively heavy blade gives good leverage for chopping, slicing, dicing and mincing. It is often used with a rocking motion.

CARVING KNIFE
The blade is long, but a bit thinner than a chef's knife. Use it to cut roast beef and whole roasted poultry.

BONING KNIFE
The narrow, tapered blade offers the best maneuverability when removing bones.

SERRATED KNIFE
Use it for foods such as bread or angel food cake that might be compressed by a regular knife blade. The best technique is a back-and-forth sawing motion with light downward pressure.

BASIC CUTS

* ✦ Chop: Cut roughly into finely chopped pieces of more or less uniform size.
* ✦ Mince: Cut into tiny pieces.
* ✦ Dice: Cut into squares of uniform size, ⅛ to ¼ inches.
* ✦ Cube: Cut into squares of uniform size, usually bigger than diced; the recipe may specify the dimensions.
* ✦ Julienne: Cut into matchstick-sized pieces (approximately 2 inches × ⅛ inch × ⅛ inch).

HOW TO MEASURE LIQUIDS AND SOLIDS

Measuring Liquids

Standard liquid measuring cups are available in 1, 2 and 4-cup sizes with a pouring spout.

1. Pour the liquid into a glass measuring cup.
2. Set the measuring cup on a level surface and allow the liquid to settle.
3. Read the measurement at eye level and adjust as necessary.

Measuring Dry Ingredients

Purchase a set of standard dry measuring cups including 1 cup, ½ cup, ⅓ cup and ¼ cup. A ⅛-cup measure is also helpful because it equals 2 tablespoons, a standard coffee measure. For dense ingredients such as granulated sugar, wheat germ, dry rice and rolled oats, dip a standard dry measuring cup into the ingredient and level off the top with a spatula or knife. Fluffier ingredients, such as flour, dry baking mixes or powdered sugar, should not be measured by the dipping method because it compacts and your measurement will be inaccurate.

1. To measure flour or powdered sugar, lightly spoon the ingredient into a standard dry measuring cup.
2. Level off the top with a spatula or the flat side of a table knife. You do not need to sift flour before measuring.

Measuring Solid Fat and Brown Sugar

Sticks of butter and margarine are easily measured by using the lines printed on the wrapper. Each ¼-pound stick equals ½ cup or 8 tablespoons.

To measure brown sugar or solid shortening from a large can:

1. Press the shortening or brown sugar firmly into a standard dry measuring cup.
2. Level off at the top with a spatula or the flat side of a table knife.

Measuring by the Spoonful

The teaspoons and tablespoons you eat with may vary in size; measure flavoring extracts, leaveners and other small quantities of liquid and dry ingredients with a set of standard measuring spoons. They usually come in sets of ¼, ½, and 1 teaspoon, and 1 tablespoon.

* ✦ Pour extracts and other liquids directly into the bowl of the measuring spoon, filling it to the rim.
* ✦ Scoop up baking powder and other dry ingredients, then level the top with a spatula or the flat side of a table knife.

Equivalent Measures and Weight

dash = less than ⅛ teaspoon
3 teaspoons = 1 tablespoon
2 tablespoons = ⅛ cup or 1 fluid ounce
4 tablespoons = ¼ cup or 2 fluid ounces
5⅓ tablespoons = ⅓ cup or 2.67 fluid ounces
8 tablespoons = ½ cup or 4 fluid ounces
12 tablespoons = ¾ cup or 6 fluid ounces
16 tablespoons = 1 cup or 8 fluid ounces
1 cup = 8 fluid ounces
2 cups = 1 pint or 16 fluid ounces
4 cups = 1 quart
2 pints = 1 quart or 32 fluid ounces
4 quarts = 1 gallon
8 quarts = 1 peck
4 pecks = 1 bushel
16 ounces = 1 pound
1 ounce = 28.35 grams
1 liter = 1.06 quarts

MICROWAVE COOKING

Recipes in this cookbook have been tested in a 650-watt microwave oven. If the wattage of your oven is different, adjust the cooking time accordingly.

Microwave Cookware

+ Use only microwave-safe dishes and utensils. Glass, glass-ceramic, paper, dishwasher-safe plastic and pottery are generally acceptable.
+ Avoid metal containers, dishes with metal trim (even painted gold embellishments), metal twist-ties and conventional meat and candy thermometers. Use foil only as the oven manufacturer directs.
+ For foods that may bubble up, use a cooking dish large enough so that you can fill it only one-half to two-thirds full. Ring-shaped dishes are ideal for foods that cannot be stirred, and round shapes cook more evenly than square.

Microwave Cooking Techniques

Many microwave ovens have preset programs for commonly microwaved foods. Even so, you must watch carefully to allow for variations in the shape, quantity, density and size of foods.

+ Arrange food for more even cooking. Foods of similar size (such as whole potatoes) should be arranged in a ring. When foods have uneven thickness (such as fish and chicken pieces), place smaller pieces and thinner areas to the center of the dish so dense portions can receive the most microwave energy.
+ Cover foods with glass lids or microwave-safe plastic wrap to retain moisture and speed cooking. When using plastic wrap, fold back one corner to prevent excessive steam buildup. Paper towels and napkins absorb moisture and grease and prevent spattering; waxed paper also prevents spattering.
+ To promote even cooking, stir foods from the outside edges to the inside to mix heated portions with unheated portions. Rotate the dish one-quarter turn when stirring is not possible, or rearrange or turn over foods according to recipe directions.
+ Prick foods with thick skins such as potatoes to allow steam to escape, or they may burst.

Cooking Time

+ Small pieces cook faster than larger ones.
+ The larger the amount, the longer it takes to heat.
+ Using less liquid leads to faster cooking.
+ Test food for doneness at the shortest time listed, and return for additional time if necessary. Microwaved foods continue to cook during standing time.
+ Use a microwave thermometer to test doneness of meats and other foods, or remove meat from the microwave and test with a conventional thermometer.

Microwave Defrosting (Thawing)

+ Many microwave ovens have automatic defrosting features. You simply choose the type and weight of food to be defrosted. The manufacturer's instructions may also give suggestions.
+ In general, food should be defrosted at a medium or low setting to avoid letting the outside begin to cook while the inside is still frozen.
+ Place unwrapped food on a microwave-safe rack or plate. If you are defrosting several items, such as hamburger patties, arrange them in a ring shape. Arrange foods of uneven thickness (such as fish fillets or chicken drumsticks), spoke-fashion, with the thinner portion toward the center of the plate.
+ Break up or separate pieces of food as soon as possible during defrosting.
+ Turn foods once or twice during defrosting to compensate for any hot spots in the oven.
+ If thin or small food areas begin to cook, if possible, remove defrosted portions and continue to defrost the remainder, or cover the area that is beginning to cook.
+ Cook microwave-defrosted foods at once.

Do Not Microwave These

Regular popcorn
Liquor or liqueurs not combined with other ingredients
Eggs in the shell
Crusty bread
Crispy fried food
Foam cakes
Dried legumes

USES FOR THE MICROWAVE

USES	TIPS
Defrost frozen foods	Use microwave-defrosted meats at once.
Cook fresh and frozen vegetables	Add water sparingly for high-moisture foods like vegetables. Too much water drains color, flavor and nutrients and slows cooking.
Soften cream cheese	Remove foil wrappers and heat just long enough to soften but not melt the cream cheese.
Soften ice cream	Try low power for 10 or 15 seconds, just enough to soften the edges for easier scooping.
Soften or melt butter or margarine	Cover the dish with microwave-safe waxed paper to prevent spatters.
Melt jam for glazes	Handle carefully; melted sugar is very hot.
Soften chopped vegetables for casseroles and stuffing	Ideal for fat-free "sautéing" of onions, garlic, bell pepper and the like; soften the vegetables in water, broth, juice or wine.
Reheat soups, casseroles and main dishes	Single servings cook faster than family-sized dishes. Cover with a glass lid (the lid of a casserole or slow cooker is ideal) or microwave-safe plastic wrap to hold in moisture and speed reheating.
Plump raisins and other dried fruits, dried mushrooms or sun-dried tomatoes	Cover the dried food with water or fruit juice and cook on high power for a minute or two; let the fruit stand until soft. Drain and squeeze out liquid before using in recipes. Flavorful liquid can be reserved for compotes, baked goods or rice dishes.
Melt chocolate	Melt on medium or low power. Chocolate melted in the microwave oven tends to retain its shape, so stir it to check the degree of melting.
Partially cook foods to be finished in conventional oven or on the grill	Transfer food immediately from the microwave oven to grill or conventional oven; do not hold for later cooking.
Freshen stale muffins and soft-textured baked goods	Try about 15 seconds to add moisture to day-old baked goods. Do not microwave crusty breads or flaky pastry, which will become soggy. High-sugar fillings and frostings heat very quickly. Watch carefully to prevent overheating.
Reheat frozen dinners or prepared entrées	Follow package instructions, but check doneness at the minimum suggested cooking time. Most are sufficiently cooked when the food is piping hot throughout.
Heat milk for cocoa or a mock cappuccino	Heat 1 cup of milk for about 2½ minutes on high power, using a container with at least a 2-cup capacity to prevent boilovers. For foam, whip with a wire whisk.
Prepare single servings of hot cereal	Use milk instead of water for extra richness and calcium.

GRILLING

The great American summer pastime has become a year-round technique for restaurants chefs and home cooks equipped with indoor electric or gas grills.

Estimating Grilling Time

Grilling meat is an art that requires you to rely on your senses rather than the clock. While recipes suggest cooking times, the actual time will vary depending on the type and amount of fuel, the size and shape of the meat, the distance between the food and the flame, the shape of the grill and position of vent holes on the bottom and top.

The following guidelines assume that the meat is on a grill rack 4 to 6 inches from the coals.

✦ *Boneless skinless chicken breast halves.* These cook in 10 to 12 minutes over medium-high coals. Look for a golden brown exterior, then gently cut into the center of the breast. Escaping juices (and there should be some—don't

wait until the chicken is dry) should run clear rather than pink, and the meat should be tender and white all the way through.

✦ *Bone-in chicken breasts.* Cooking with the bone in helps retain flavor and juiciness but takes longer than for boneless breasts, 15 to 17 minutes over medium-high coals. To test for doneness, cut into the breast near the bone and look for clear juices and evenly white meat with no sign of pink.

✦ *Boneless steak.* A 1-pound steak, depending on the thickness, will cook in 9 to 12 minutes over medium-high coals. To retain juiciness, try not to turn the meat more than once. To test for doneness, cut a small slit in the center. Even if you prefer pink in the middle, make sure the center is warm and has lost its shiny translucent quality.

✦ *Beef chunks in kabobs.* Skewering a combination of foods is attractive, but it can be tricky to coordinate so that all the ingredients are done at the same time. Precook or parboil hard ingredients such as carrots or bell peppers. Beef chunks cook in 6 to 8 minutes over

TYPES OF CHARCOAL

TYPE	DESCRIPTION
Charcoal briquets	Pressed from chips of burned hardwood. Readily available and relatively inexpensive. The lighter fluid commonly used for charcoal fires gives the coals a quick start but is not necessary if you use kindling or paper.
Self-lighting charcoal *(briquets that have been impregnated with a flammable substance)*	Light easily without kindling or use of lighter fluid. The coals may emit an unpleasant smell due to the flammable substance.
Hardwood charcoal *(irregular chunks of burned hardwood)*	Somewhat harder to find than standard briquets. By weight they are usually more expensive, but they burn hotter so you need less. They also ignite more easily and give a slightly different, more wood-smoked flavor to foods.
Flavored wood chips	Chips of mesquite, fruit or nut trees. The chips serve as flavor enhancers for charcoal fires. Most call for soaking the chips before tossing onto the fire, resulting in fragrant smoke.
Seasoned hardwood	Aged (dried) oak and fruitwood logs, either purchased or culled from your own yard. Not practical for use in lightweight metal grills but good for outdoor stone or brick fireplaces. Let the logs burn brightly for a while until the flames die down, leaving glowing hot coals for cooking.

medium-high coals. When the outside is nicely browned, check for desired doneness by cutting into a beef cube and making sure the interior is warm and opaque.

◆ *Boneless pork chops.* Thin boneless chops cook quickly, in 7 to 12 minutes over medium-high coals. Cook the pork until it is no longer pink (or has just a faint tinge of pink in the center) but make sure to remove it from the heat while it is still juicy.

Grilling with Charcoal

◆ For direct-heat cooking (ideal for steaks, burgers, chops, hot dogs), use enough briquets to extend 2 inches beyond the food when it is placed in a single layer.

◆ Use indirect heat for larger pieces of meat (whole or split chickens, chicken parts, leg of lamb) so they retain moisture and develop a smoky flavor. Arrange the hot briquets either on one half of the grill base or in a ring around the edges, leaving the center empty. Set the food on the grill rack over the area with no briquets.

◆ If more briquets are needed after the fire is started, add them to the edges, gradually moving them into the center for even distribution. Rearrange briquets as little as possible after the fire is established.

◆ Light the charcoal about 30 minutes before cooking food. Charcoal is ready for cooking when partially covered with gray ash. If you are partially cooking foods in the microwave oven or on the stove before grilling, have the grill ready when precooking is completed.

◆ The recipes in this book are tested with coals that are medium-high in temperature. To test temperature, hold your hand 4 to 5 inches from coals. If you can hold that position for 3 seconds before the heat forces you to pull away, you are nearing this temperature.

◆ Trim meats before grilling to avoid uneven cooking, curling edges and flare-ups. Avoid grilling high-fat items like bacon.

◆ Baste with care, using small amounts of marinade to avoid flare-ups.

◆ Grill bone-in items bone side down first. This distributes heat throughout the food for slower, more even cooking.

◆ To prevent loss of juices, use tongs rather than a fork to turn meats and other foods.

◆ A band of foil secured around the edge of the grill can serve as a windbreak, and foil loosely tucked over food can serve as a grill cover.

◆ Use a meat thermometer whenever possible to determine doneness. Always pay close attention to food as it cooks to avoid overcooking or unsafe undercooking.

HIGH-ALTITUDE BAKING

Baking at high altitudes, 3,500 feet above sea level or more, can be a challenge. For best results, follow the high-altitude directions when they're included in the recipe. In addition, here are some general guidelines:

◆ Because there is generally lower humidity at high altitudes, flour tends to dry out more quickly and may absorb more liquid in a recipe. Store flour in an airtight container.

◆ At any altitude above sea level, the air pressure is lower. This lower air pressure allows baked foods to rise faster. Leavening agents such as yeast, baking powder and baking soda create larger gas bubbles that expand rapidly. The larger bubbles can weaken the structure of baked goods and cause cakes and breads to collapse unless recipe adjustments are made. In addition, too much sugar can weaken the structure of baked goods.

◆ Water boils at a lower temperature than at sea level (as elevation increases, the boiling point is reduced 2 degrees per 1,000-foot increase) so foods take longer to cook. Liquids evaporate faster at high altitudes so foods such as cooked frostings and candies will become harder more rapidly.

If no high-altitude adjustments are given in a recipe, here are some suggestions to try:

◆ In cakes made with fats or oil, reduce the sugar called for in the recipe by 3 tablespoons per cup. If given a choice, use the largest pan size suggested.

◆ In cake or bar-type cookies, reduce the sugar called for in the recipe by 3 tablespoons per cup. If given a choice, use the largest pan size suggested.

◆ In yeast breads, use slightly less flour since flour is drier at high altitudes. Yeast breads will require a shorter rising time and should rise only until doubled in size to prevent them from collapsing during baking.

◆ Quick breads often need 2 to 4 tablespoons additional flour and a higher baking temperature.

SPICES, HERBS AND BLENDS

By adding flavor and aromas, many herbs and spices make good sodium and sugar substitutes.

Use these seasonings judiciously; the flavors increase during cooking and storage.

◆ Spices are the seeds, buds, fruit or flower parts, bark or roots of plants.
◆ Herbs are aromatic leaves.
◆ Blends are mixtures made commercially or by home cooks.

Buying Seasonings

Purchase both dried and fresh seasonings in small amounts to use while the flavor is at its peak. As a general rule, for 1 tablespoon of a fresh herb, substitute 1 teaspoon dried or ¼ teaspoon of the powdered or ground form.

Storing Seasonings

Store fresh herbs in plastic wrap for up to two weeks in the refrigerator. Dill, parsley and rosemary keep fairly well. Basil is more delicate: Trim the stem ends and stand the basil in a jar or glass with a small amount of water; cover with plastic and store in the refrigerator.

Store dried seasonings in a cool, dark, dry place—not over the stove or in direct sunlight.

1. Allspice
2. Anise
3. Caraway
4. Cardamom
5. Cayenne
   (*ground red pepper*)
6. Chili powder
7. Cinnamon
8. Cloves
9. Cumin
10. Curry
11. Ginger
12. Mace
13. Mustard
14. Nutmeg
15. Paprika
16. Pepper flakes
17. Peppercorns
18. Saffron
19. Turmeric
20. Vanilla

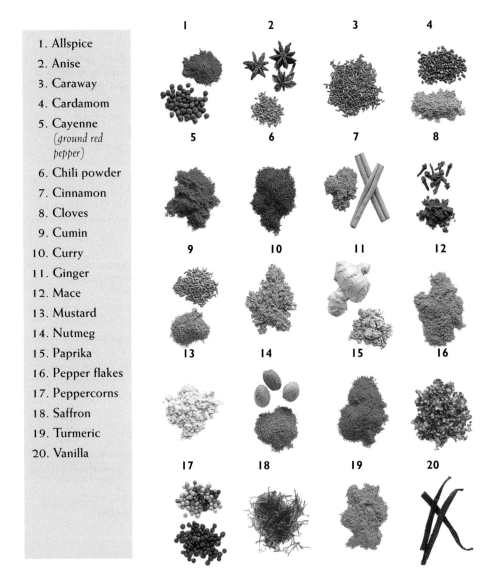

SPICES

SPICE	FLAVOR AND USE
Allspice	Sweet. Compatible with fruits, desserts, breads, duckling, beef, pork, ham, yellow vegetables, tomato sauces and relishes.
Anise	Sweet licorice flavor. Compatible with chicken, duck, shellfish, noodles and rice, fruit desserts, chutneys, marinades and sweet breads.
Caraway	Nutty, delicate anise flavor. Compatible with cheese, breads, cakes, stews, vegetables, beef, pork, goose, noodles and stuffings.
Cardamom	Pungent. Compatible with breads, coffee cakes, rice and meats.
Cayenne (ground red pepper)	Piquant. Compatible with meats, chili, salsas and beans.
Cinnamon	Sweet. Compatible with fruits, desserts, breads, tomato-meat sauces, yellow vegetables, beverages, pork, chicken, some beef and ground beef dishes.
Cloves	Sweet, pungent. Compatible with pickled fruits, desserts, baked goods, beverages, lamb, pork, corned beef, tongue, yellow vegetables, tomato sauces and beets.
Cumin	Earthy, pungent. Compatible with meat, chili, poultry, beans and rice dishes.
Ginger	Sweet. Compatible with fruits, squash, poultry, sauces for fish, pork, some beef dishes, cheese and desserts.
Mace	Pungent version of nutmeg. Compatible with chicken, duck, shellfish, many vegetables, beans, lentils, noodles, polenta, rice, almost any cheese dish, chocolate and fruit desserts, chutneys and marinades.
Mustard	Earthy, pungent. Compatible with meats, poultry, vegetables, soups, beans and rice.
Nutmeg	Sweet. Compatible with fruits, eggnog, cheese, desserts, ground beef, poultry, most vegetables and many sauces.
Paprika	Usually mild, but hot versions are available. Compatible with beef, poultry, soups, salads, stews, eggs and goulash.
Pepper flakes	Hot, pungent. Compatible with barbecue and savory sauces, chili, corn-bread, eggs, fish, meats and vegetables.
Peppercorns	Pungent. Compatible with salads, soups, poultry, fish and shellfish, meats, vegetables, pasta, grains, beans, cheese dishes, egg dishes, sauces, marinades and stuffings.
Saffron	Pungent, aromatic. Compatible with meat, fish, poultry, vegetables, sauces and rice.
Turmeric	Earthy, slightly bitter. Compatible with soups, stews, relishes, rice, beef and pork.
Vanilla	Compatible with cake mixes, chocolate, ice cream, pastry dough, sauces and many sweet dishes.

EMERGENCY SUBSTITUTIONS
Although best results are achieved using the ingredients called for in recipes, emergency substitutions can sometimes be made. Recipe results may vary slightly.

BAKING

INGREDIENT	SUBSTITUTE
1 teaspoon baking powder	½ teaspoon baking soda plus ½ teaspoon cream of tartar
1 pkg. active dry yeast	1 tablespoon dry yeast or 1 cake compressed yeast, crumbled
1 cup honey	1¼ cups sugar plus ¼ cup liquid, or 1 cup molasses
1 cup corn syrup	1 cup sugar plus ¼ cup water
1 cup cake flour	1 cup sifted all-purpose flour minus 2 tablespoons
All-purpose flour	An equal amount of whole wheat flour can be substituted in some breads, cookies and bars; texture will be coarser
¼ cup dry bread crumbs	¼ cup cracker crumbs or 1 slice bread, cubed, or ⅔ cup quick-cooking oats
1 whole egg	For custards and puddings, 2 egg yolks; for cookies and bars, 2 egg yolks plus 1 tablespoon water; liquid egg products may sometimes be used

CHOCOLATE

INGREDIENT	SUBSTITUTE
1 ounce (1 square) unsweetened chocolate	3 tablespoons unsweetened cocoa plus 1 tablespoon shortening or margarine
1 ounce (1 square) semisweet chocolate	1 square unsweetened chocolate plus 1 tablespoon sugar, or 3 tablespoons semisweet chocolate chips
½ cup semisweet chocolate chips for melting	3 ounces (3 squares) semisweet chocolate

DAIRY PRODUCTS

INGREDIENT	SUBSTITUTE
1 cup whole milk	½ cup evaporated milk plus ½ cup water, or 1 cup nonfat milk or reconstituted nonfat dry milk plus 2 teaspoons butter or oil
1 cup buttermilk or sour milk	1 tablespoon cider vinegar or lemon juice plus enough milk to equal 1 cup; let stand 5 minutes
1 cup sour cream	1 cup plain yogurt, or 1 cup evaporated milk plus 1 tablespoon vinegar, or 1 cup cottage cheese mixed in blender with 2 tablespoons milk and 1 tablespoon lemon juice
1 cup half-and-half	¾ cup and 2 tablespoons milk plus 3 tablespoons margarine or butter, or 1 cup evaporated milk
1 cup plain yogurt	1 cup sour milk or 1 cup buttermilk

SEASONINGS

INGREDIENT	SUBSTITUTE
1 tablespoon snipped fresh herbs	1 teaspoon same herb, dried, or ¼ teaspoon powdered or ground
1 teaspoon dry mustard	2 teaspoons prepared mustard
1 teaspoon poultry seasoning	¾ teaspoon sage plus ¼ teaspoon thyme
1 teaspoon pumpkin pie spice	½ teaspoon cinnamon, ½ teaspoon ginger, ⅛ teaspoon ground all-spice and ⅛ teaspoon nutmeg
1 garlic clove, minced or pressed (crushed)	⅛ to ¼ teaspoon instant minced garlic, or ⅛ tea-spoon garlic powder
1 medium onion	2 tablespoons instant chopped or minced onion or onion flakes, or 1½ teaspoons onion powder
1 medium lemon	2 to 3 tablespoons juice (fresh or bottled)
1 medium orange	¼ to ⅓ cup orange juice (fresh or reconstituted frozen)
White wine	Equal amount of apple juice or cider
1 cup chicken or beef broth	1 teaspoon instant bouillon or bouillon cube plus 1 cup hot water

THICKENERS

INGREDIENT	SUBSTITUTE
1 tablespoon cornstarch	2 tablespoons flour or 1 tablespoon plus 1 tea-spoon quick-cooking tapioca
1 tablespoon flour	1½ teaspoons corn-starch or 2 teaspoons quick-cooking tapioca
1 tablespoon tapioca	1 tablespoon plus 1½ teaspoons all-purpose flour

VEGETABLES

INGREDIENT	SUBSTITUTE
1 cup canned tomatoes	1⅓ cups cut-up fresh tomatoes, simmered 10 minutes
1 cup tomato sauce	8-ounce can stewed tomatoes, blended in blender, or 1 cup tomato puree, or ¾ cup tomato paste plus ¼ cup water
1 cup tomato juice	½ cup tomato sauce plus ½ cup water
½ cup ketchup or chili sauce	½ cup tomato sauce plus 2 tablespoons sugar and 1 tablespoon vinegar
½ lb. fresh mushrooms	4-ounce can mushrooms
Legumes	With the exception of lentils, dried beans can be used interchangeably

Fresh Herbs

HERBS	
HERB	**FLAVOR AND USE**
Basil	Sweet, mild. Compatible with cheese, pesto, vegetables, particularly green beans, corn, tomatoes and tomato sauces, poultry, meat, potato salad and sauces. Used in Italian cuisine.
Bay leaves	Sweet, mellow. Compatible with any foods requiring a bouquet garni, court bouillon, soups, stews, vegetables, pickling and other marinades and spaghetti sauce.
Chervil	Delicate, slight anise flavor. Compatible with poultry, veal, lamb, soups, stews, fish and eggs.
Chives	Mild, onion flavor. Compatible with sauces, salad dressing, cream, mild fish, poultry and veal.
Cilantro	Assertive, citrus flavor. Compatible with fish, salsa, chili and dishes inspired by the cuisines of Asia, India or Latin America.
Dill	Mild. Compatible with fish (particularly salmon), pork, cottage cheese, potatoes, sauerkraut and other cabbage dishes, cauliflower, beans, pickles and sauces.
Fennel	Aromatic, sweet, anise flavor. Compatible with breads, eggs, fish, sauces, sausages, soups and sweet pickles. Used in Italian cuisine.
Marjoram	Sweet, mild. Compatible with meat (particularly lamb), poultry, stuffing, cheese, vegetables, tomato-based sauces and soups.
Mint	Strong, aromatic. Compatible with meats, vegetables, fruits, beverages, salads and desserts.
Oregano	Spicy, pungent. Compatible with tomato dishes, fish (especially red snapper), vegetables, stews, chili, beef and pork. Used in Italian cuisine.
Parsley	Mild. Compatible with bouillon, soups, stews, meat, poultry, fish, sauces, cheese, many vegetables and eggs.
Rosemary	Strong pine flavor. Compatible with duckling, poultry, meat (especially pork and lamb), fish, stuffing and some vegetables such as spinach, mushrooms, carrots, tomatoes, potatoes and beans.
Sage	Strong. Compatible with stuffing, pork, poultry, tomatoes, rice dishes and Brussels sprouts.
Savory	Aromatic, slightly pungent. Compatible with poultry, meats, salads, sauces, soups, stuffings and vegetables.
Tarragon	Mild, slight licorice flavor and sweet. Essential for bearnaise sauce; compatible with fish, poultry, lamb, veal, salad dressings, vinegar, potato salad and some vegetables such as beans, mushrooms, carrots and spinach.
Thyme	Pungent, aromatic. Compatible with soups, stews, stuffing, rice dishes, Mediterranean vegetables, dishes with red wine or tomatoes, veal, lamb, fish and poultry.

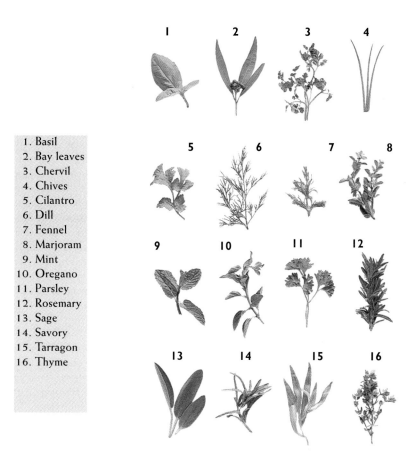

1. Basil
2. Bay leaves
3. Chervil
4. Chives
5. Cilantro
6. Dill
7. Fennel
8. Marjoram
9. Mint
10. Oregano
11. Parsley
12. Rosemary
13. Sage
14. Savory
15. Tarragon
16. Thyme

BLENDS

NAME	FLAVOR AND USE
Bouquet garni	Savory, aromatic, pungent. Traditional components include parsley, thyme and bay leaf. Compatible with meats, fish, poultry, vegetables, soups and stews.
Chili powder	Mild to hot. Made with dried ground chiles plus a variety of spices. Compatible with chili con carne and other ground beef and pork dishes, cocktail and barbecue sauces, eggs, Creole and Mexican recipes and poultry.
Curry powder	Mild to hot. Mixtures vary from brand to brand but may include cumin, coriander, turmeric and more. Compatible with eggs, sauces, salad dressings, lamb, poultry, seafood, veal, rice, cheese and fruit.
Fines herbes	Delicate. Traditional French combination of minced parsley, tarragon, chervil and chives; other herbs are sometimes added. Compatible with eggs, mild fish, salad dressing; cream, white wine and butter sauces; poultry and veal.
Garam masala	Hot. This blend of dry-roasted, ground spices from northern India varies in combination and may contain up to 12 spices. It may include black pepper, cinnamon, cloves, coriander, cumin, cardamom, dried chiles, fennel, mace, nutmeg and other spices. Compatible with Indian cuisine.
Herbes de Provence	Savory, aromatic. Combination of herbs used in southern France including basil, fennel seed, lavender, marjoram, rosemary, sage, summer savory and thyme. Compatible with meat, poultry and vegetables.

FOOD STORAGE

Proper storage in the pantry, refrigerator and freezer is essential for preserving the freshness and quality of food.

Dry Storage

◆ The best shelf and pantry storage areas are dark, dry and within a temperature range of 50 to 70°F. Avoid areas near heat sources and water pipes.

◆ Discourage insects by keeping storage areas free of dust and food particles.

◆ Protect food from air, moisture and insects by using plastic, glass or metal containers with tight-fitting lids. Rewrap packaged foods that have torn or damaged wrappers.

◆ Date foods not already marked by the manufacturer and use older items first.

◆ Dispose of cans with bulges or leaks. Use contents of dented cans promptly.

◆ Store all food items away from household cleaning products and other potentially hazardous substances to avoid any possibility of mix-up or contamination.

Refrigerator Storage

◆ Maintain refrigerator temperature between 34 and 40°F. Check periodically by placing a thermometer inside.

◆ After shopping, refrigerate perishable items promptly.

◆ To allow proper air circulation for even cooling, do not overcrowd shelves.

◆ Store foods wrapped in plastic or in covered containers to prevent the food from drying out and to keep odors from spreading.

◆ Check expiration dates to use products before quality is jeopardized.

◆ Cover and refrigerate leftovers promptly. All high-moisture foods or those with meats, fish, poultry, eggs, custard and cream cheese fillings, cream sauces or cheeses are especially prone to bacteria growth at room temperature.

◆ Use cooked meats and poultry within two days.

Freezer Storage

When preparing foods to freeze, allow them to cool so their warmth does not raise the freezer temperature above 0°F. Then freeze them promptly. Season lightly because flavors can intensify during storage. After wrapping, label each package with contents, date by which it should be used and number of servings or intended use.

In general, food that has thawed should not be refrozen unless it is cooked first. (Baked goods are an exception.) If partially thawed goods still have ice crystals, they can often be refrozen safely; however, the quality may suffer. Thawed dishes containing a mixture of ingredients (stews, soups, pies, casseroles, etc.) cannot safely be refrozen.

◆ Keep your freezer at 0°F. or colder.

◆ Use well-made containers and wraps designed for freezing. Refer to "Fruit Freezing Chart" and "Vegetable Freezing Chart," pages 486 to 488, for more information. To protect foods from cold air deterioration, use only moisture and vaporproof materials such as plastic containers with tight-fitting lids, freezer paper and heavy-duty plastic bags, wraps and foil.

◆ Leave room in containers for expansion. When wrapping foods, press out the air and wrap tightly.

◆ A wide variety of foods freeze well, but some do not: salad greens, bananas, potatoes, custard, mayonnaise and sour cream mixtures, fried meat, hard-cooked egg whites and boiled frosting.

Here are some packaging techniques for freezing various foods:

◆ Liquids such as broth, beverages, uncooked egg whites and puree can be frozen in ice cube trays until firm, then removed and stored in plastic bags to use individual cubes as necessary.

◆ Ground meat can be divided into portions and frozen as is or formed into meatballs or patties.

◆ To freeze small items, such as berries and vegetables, in individual pieces rather than a solid block, spread them on a tray, freeze them until firm and then package them in bags or containers.

◆ Make your own "TV dinners" by arranging cooked foods on divided foil trays. Fill air spaces with gravies and sauces, seal trays tightly with foil and freeze immediately.

Place waxed paper or parchment paper between layers of flat foods such as pancakes, chops, fish fillets, chicken pieces and steaks to allow them to separate easily for thawing. Freeze soups, stews and casseroles in foil-lined dishes. When mixture is solid, remove the dish so you can continue to use it. To thaw and serve the food, unwrap and return it to the dish.

Safely Holding or Transporting Food

◆ Safe temperatures for holding foods are 140°F. or above for hot foods and 40°F. or below for cold foods, according to the U.S. Department of Agriculture.

◆ For safe transport, use proper equipment such as thermal containers, ice chests and insulated coolers so that hot foods will stay hot and cold foods will remain chilled.

◆ Take extra precaution with any foods that are highly susceptible to bacterial growth, such as dairy products, eggs and mayonnaise, creamed and custard mixtures, meats, poultry, seafood and stuffing.

◆ Pack food separately from nonfood items and in the order you will need them. Pack heated and chilled foods in separate containers.

◆ Pack liquids in tightly sealed containers and surround the containers with other items to keep them upright.

◆ Do not leave any food sitting in the hot sun. Even food that might not spoil may deteriorate in quality. At a picnic, store the ice chest in the shade and cover it with a blanket or thick folded towel.

◆ Take only as much food as you think will be eaten. Leftovers are best discarded after sitting out.

◆ Food spoilage happens quickly and with no obvious signs. It takes only 15 to 30 minutes for bacteria to grow in warm, moist conditions. This may not alter the taste, odor or appearance of most foods at the time they are served.

COOK'S NOTE

FREEZING CASSEROLES

Tuck a casserole or two away in your freezer for those inevitable rushed-day dinners. Here's a super-simple way to freeze a one-dish meal in foil so that you don't tie up your baking dishes.

Lightly grease an ovenproof casserole or baking dish. Line the dish with a sheet of foil large enough to bring the edges together to fold and seal. Place the casserole mixture in the foil-lined dish. Bake it according to the recipe directions, or leave it unbaked.

After the casserole or stew has cooled, bring the edges of foil together and seal tightly, making sure the foil touches the top of the mixture to shut out any air. Freeze it until firm.

Lift the frozen casserole from the dish.

For additional protection, wrap the casserole in another layer of foil or place it in a freezer bag. Label the outer wrap with casserole name, date frozen, use-by date, number of servings and reheating or baking instructions. Return the labeled casserole to the freezer.

When ready to use the casserole, place it in the original baking dish. Thaw in refrigerator; reheat or bake. (If baking directly from freezer to oven, add additional baking time; see individual recipes for specific baking time.) (Note: When using a microwave oven to bake or reheat, remove the foil first.)

STORING FOODS IN THE FREEZER

As long as your freezer maintains a steady temperature of 0°F., food can be safely frozen indefinitely. Quality, however, will eventually deteriorate. The "maximum suggested freezing time" below estimates how long frozen foods will retain quality.

FOOD	WHAT CAN I FREEZE?	TIPS FOR FREEZING	MAXIMUM SUGGESTED FREEZING TIME	TO THAW AND SERVE
BREADS	Yeast breads, coffee cakes, muffins and quick breads can be frozen.	Cool completely. Do not frost or decorate. Place coffee cakes on foil-wrapped cardboard before wrapping.	Up to 12 months	Unwrap slightly, thaw at room temperature 2 to 3 hours. Serve at room temperature or reheat, wrapped in foil, at 350°F. for 15 to 20 minutes, or wrap in paper towels and microwave (briefly, to avoid a tough texture) for 5 to 40 seconds.
CAKES	Cakes can be frozen either frosted or unfrosted. Not recommended for freezing are egg-white frostings or custard fillings.	Cool unfrosted cake completely. Place frosted cake in freezer to harden frosting before wrapping. Buttercream frosting freezes best. Place layer cakes in cake containers or bakery boxes to prevent crushing. Over-wrap box. Angel and sponge cakes are best left in pan or place in rigid container to avoid crushing. Cakes can be filled or frosted with whipped cream or whipped topping before freezing.	Unfrosted: 4 to 6 months Frosted: 1 to 3 months	Unfrosted: Thaw at room temperature, covered, 2 to 3 hours. Frost or serve according to recipe. Frosted: Thaw, loosely covered, overnight in refrigerator.
CANDIES	Most kinds freeze well.	Prepare and allow to set. Package and freeze.	12 months	Thaw wrapped at room temperature 1 to 2 hours.
CASSEROLES, CHILIES, SOUPS, SPAGHETTI, STEWS	Most mixtures freeze well.	Those with condensed soup base or low-fat sauce	3 months In sauce or gravy: 6	Thaw in refrigerator before heating or heat unthawed. To thaw and

FOOD	WHAT CAN I FREEZE?	TIPS FOR FREEZING	MAXIMUM SUGGESTED FREEZING TIME	TO THAW AND SERVE
CASSEROLES, CHILIES, SOUPS, SPAGHETTI, STEWS (cont.)		freeze best. If sour cream is to be added, add after thawing and reheating. Cook meats, vegetables and pasta or rice until just tender to avoid over-cooking during reheating. Package in meal-sized amounts and, if possible, in freezer-to-oven dishes; wrap tightly.	months	heat a casserole of 4 to 6 servings, cover and heat at 375°F. for 1 to 1½ hours, stirring occasionally. If mixture cannot be stirred, bake 1½ to 2 hours. For a crisp top, remove cover last 15 minutes. Or thaw in saucepan over low heat about 20 minutes, or in double boiler over simmering water about 45 minutes. For microwave reheating, follow manufacturer's guidelines.
CHEESECAKES	Baked or unbaked.	If baked, cool completely and wrap.	4 to 5 months	Thaw wrapped in refrigerator 4 to 6 hours.
COOKIES	Most baked cookies. Some doughs can be formed into rolls for slicing or dropped and frozen before packaging for baking later.	Package cookies in airtight, moistureproof wrap or containers. If frosted or decorated before freezing, freeze on cookie sheet; then package frozen cookies between layers of waxed paper in rigid container with outer wrap for further freezing.	Unfrosted: up to 12 months Frosted: 1 to 2 months	Thaw in package at room temperature. Remove from container cookies that should be crisp when thawed.
CREPES, WAFFLES, PANCAKES OR FRENCH TOAST	Cooked according to recipe.	Cool completely, separating pieces with waxed paper. Wrap in airtight, moistureproof, resealable wrap.	2 months	Thaw and heat waffles and French toast in toaster. Thaw and heat pancakes and French toast, uncovered, at 350°F. about 15 minutes. Thaw and heat crepes, uncovered, at 350°F. about 20 minutes or microwave one portion 25 seconds or less in a single layer on paper towels or paper plate.

FOOD	WHAT CAN I FREEZE?	TIPS FOR FREEZING	MAXIMUM SUGGESTED FREEZING TIME	TO THAW AND SERVE
MEAT OR POULTRY, COOKED	Most freeze well.	Prepare as for serving. Cool quickly; wrap tightly. Gravies, broths or sauces help prevent drying and retain flavor.	Without broth: 1 to 3 months With broth: 6 months	Leave wrapped and thaw in refrigerator about 8 hours. Meats with sauces can be thawed over low heat in a saucepan or in 350°F. oven in a covered casserole, about 45 minutes. For microwave reheating, follow manufacturer's guidelines.
PIES	Baked pumpkin or pecan pies. Fruit pies either baked or unbaked.	Cool baked pies quickly. For unbaked pies, brush bottom crust with egg whites before filling to prevent sogginess; do not slit top crust. Cover with inverted plate, (foil or paper), then wrap.	Baked: 3 to 4 months Unbaked: 2 to 3 months	Baked: Heat, unwrapped, in oven at 325°F. for 45 minutes or until warm or room temperature. Unbaked: Unwrap, cut slits in top crust and bake at 425°F. for 15 minutes, then at 375°F. for 30 to 45 minutes or until center is bubbly.
PIES	Chiffon pies. Not recommended are custard and cream pies or meringue toppings.	Omit any whipped topping. Refrigerate to set. Wrap as directed for fruit pies.	1 to 2 months	Unwrap, thaw in refrigerator 2 to 3 hours. Top as desired.
SANDWICHES	Use cooked meats, poultry, tuna, salmon, peanut butter or cheese. Use cream cheese, margarine or butter for spread.	Package individually.	Up to 1 month	Thaw wrapped sandwich at room temperature about 3 hours.

FREEZING FRUIT

Almost all fruits are suitable for freezing whole, sliced or pureed. Choose fruits that are thoroughly ripened, yet firm. Prepare only a small amount at a time—2 to 3 quarts is a good amount. Work quickly and freeze fruit immediately after preparation.

There are three ways to pack fruit for freezing. Fruits packed unsweetened or in sugar are best for making pies, fillings or jams. Those packed in syrup are best for desserts. The chart on pages 486 to 487 provides recommended preparations and packaging instructions.

- ✦ Dry pack: Fill freezer containers or plastic freezer bags with prepared, unsweetened fruit; seal tightly, label and freeze. For individually frozen fruit pieces, spread fruit in a single layer on a tray. Place tray in freezer and freeze fruit just until firm; then package, seal and return to freezer.
- ✦ Sugar pack: Sprinkle prepared fruit with sugar. Mix carefully to distribute and allow sugar to dissolve. Fill freezer containers, seal tightly, label and freeze.
- ✦ Syrup pack: Prepare sugar syrup for fruits, according to directions below, allowing 1 to 1½ cups of syrup for each quart of fruit. Fill freezer containers one-third full with syrup. Add fruit, leaving 1 inch of air space at the top. If necessary, add more syrup to cover fruit. Place a small piece of crumpled waxed paper or plastic wrap on top of fruits, pressing to hold fruit under syrup. Seal, label and freeze.

SUGAR SYRUP FOR FRUITS

TYPE OF SYRUP	SUGAR (CUPS)	WATER (CUPS)	YIELD
Thin	1	3	3½
Medium	1	2	2½
Heavy	1	1	1½

In large saucepan, combine sugar and water. Heat to boiling, stirring to dissolve sugar. To freeze fruits, chill before using.

PRESERVING COLOR

Some fruits darken with exposure to air. Ascorbic acid can be used to prevent this discoloration. Purchase ascorbic acid compounds that are intended for home preservation and use them according to directions. For dry-pack and sugar-pack freezing, dissolve the ascorbic acid in water, then sprinkle over fruit just before packing or adding sugar. For syrup-pack freezing, dissolve ascorbic acid in the syrup.

USING FROZEN FRUIT

Thaw fruit at room temperature or submerge the container in cold water. Serve when there are still a few ice crystals remaining. When frozen fruits are used in cooking, allowance should be made for any sugar added before freezing (such as packaged frozen fruit with added sugar).

FREEZING VEGETABLES

Fresh vegetables should be frozen as soon as possible after picking or purchasing. If the freezing process is delayed, refrigerate them to preserve quality and nutrients.

All vegetables should be blanched (cooked briefly in boiling water) before freezing. The heat from blanching stops the action of enzymes that cause loss of color, flavor and vitamins. See "Vegetable Freezing Chart" (page 488) for blanching time.

To blanch, heat a large, deep saucepan two-thirds full of water (about 1 gallon of water for a pound of produce) to a full boil. Place prepared vegetables, about 1 pound at a time, in a wire strainer, basket or cheesecloth; lower vegetables into boiling water to cover. Cover the saucepan.

Follow blanching times carefully. Overcooking causes loss of flavor, color, vitamins and minerals. Undercooking stimulates the destructive action of enzymes.

At the end of the blanching time, lift vegetables from boiling water and immerse them in ice-cold water to stop the cooking process. Change the chilling water until vegetables are completely cooled. Drain vegetables thoroughly before filling freezer containers. For individually frozen vegetables, spread vegetable pieces in a single layer on a tray. Freeze vegetables just until firm, then package and return to the freezer.

Microwave blanching is possible. For best results, use the manufacturer's directions.

FRUIT FREEZING CHART

FRUIT	AMOUNT TO YIELD 1 QUART	PREPARATION	TYPES OF PACK	ADD ASCORBIC ACID
APPLES	2½ lb. or 8 medium	Wash, peel and core; slice.	Syrup pack: Use medium syrup.	Yes
APPLESAUCE	3 lb. or 10 medium	Prepare applesauce (page 454). Cool.	No additional treatment needed.	No
APRICOTS	2 lb. or 24 medium	Wash, halve, and pit. If not peeled, place in boiling water 30 seconds to prevent peel from toughening.	Syrup pack: Use medium syrup. Sugar pack: ½ cup sugar per quart.	Yes
BERRIES *(except blueberries, cranberries and gooseberries)*	1½ quarts	Stem, sort, wash and drain. With strawberries, slice or leave whole.	Syrup pack: Use medium syrup. Sugar pack: ¾ cup sugar per quart. Dry pack.	No
BLUEBERRIES, CRANBERRIES OR GOOSEBERRIES	1 quart	Stem, sort, wash and drain.	Syrup pack: Use medium syrup. Dry pack.	No
CHERRIES	2½ lb. unpitted	Stem, sort, wash and drain. If desired, pit.	Syrup pack: Use medium or heavy syrup. Sugar pack: ½ to ¾ cup sugar per quart. Dry pack.	Yes
GRAPEFRUIT OR ORANGES	4 to 5 medium	Wash, peel, section fruit, removing membrane and seeds.	Syrup pack: Use medium syrup.	No

FRUIT	AMOUNT TO YIELD 1 QUART	PREPARATION	TYPES OF PACK	ADD ASCORBIC ACID
GRAPES	1 quart	Wash and stem. Leave seedless grapes whole. Halve and remove seeds from others.	Syrup pack: Use medium syrup. Dry pack.	No
MELONS (*cantaloupe, honeydew or watermelon*)	4 lb. of melon	Remove seeds and peel. Cut into 1-inch slices, cubes or balls.	Syrup pack: Use light syrup.	No
PEACHES OR NECTARINES	2 lb. or 8 medium	Peel, halve and pit; cut into slices.	Syrup pack: Use medium syrup. Sugar pack: ¾ cup sugar per quart.	Yes
PEARS	2 lb. or 8 medium	Peel, halve or quarter and core. Heat in boiling syrup 1 to 2 minutes. Cool, then pack into containers.	Syrup pack: Use medium syrup.	Yes
PINEAPPLE	1 large	Remove peel, core and eyes.	Syrup pack: Use medium syrup. Sugar pack: ½ cup sugar per quart. Dry pack.	No
PLUMS OR PRUNES	2 lb. or 20 medium	Wash, leave whole, halve or quarter.	Syrup pack: Use medium syrup. Sugar pack: ¾ cup sugar per quart. Dry pack.	Yes
RHUBARB	1½ lb. or 10 stalks	Wash and cut into ½-inch pieces.	Syrup pack: Use medium syrup. Sugar pack: 1 cup sugar per quart. Dry pack.	No

VEGETABLE FREEZING CHART

VEGETABLE	AMOUNT TO YIELD 1 QUART	PREPARATION	BLANCHING TIME
ASPARAGUS	About 32 spears (2 lb.)	Wash and trim; break or cut into desirable length.	3 to 4 minutes
BEANS (*green or wax*)	1½ lb.	Wash and trim; cut or break into pieces or leave whole.	3½ minutes
BEANS (*lima*)	4 lb. (in pod)	Shell and wash.	3 to 4 minutes
BROCCOLI	2 lb.	Wash, remove large leaves and tough stalks; split lengthwise so stalks are no more than 1 inch thick.	4 minutes
BRUSSELS SPROUTS	2 lb.	Remove outer leaves; wash.	4 to 5 minutes
CARROTS	2½ lb.	Remove tops, wash and peel; slice, dice or cut into strips.	3½ minutes
CORN ON THE COB	—	Husk, remove silk and trim.	Medium ears: 8 minutes. Large ears: 11 minutes
CORN, WHOLE KERNEL	12 ears	Husk, remove silk and trim; blanch, then cool and cut kernels from cob.	4½ minutes
OKRA	1½ lb.	Wash and trim; slice or leave whole.	3 to 4 minutes
PEAS, GREEN	4 lb. (in pod)	Shell and wash.	1½ minutes
PEPPERS (*green, red, yellow and chile*)	—	Wash, remove stem and seeds; cut into strips or chop. Package and freeze.	No blanching needed.
PUMPKIN	—	See Winter Squash.	—
SPINACH AND OTHER GREENS	2 to 3 lb.	Sort, trim and wash.	Leafy greens: 2 minutes. Stems of Swiss chard: 3 to 4 minutes
SUMMER SQUASH AND ZUCCHINI	2 lb.	Wash; cut into ½-inch slices.	3 minutes
WINTER SQUASH AND PUMPKIN	3 lb.	Wash, remove seeds and cut into large pieces; steam or bake until tender. Scoop out pulp; put through sieve, ricer or blender. Cool. Package and freeze.	No blanching needed.

High Altitude: Above 2000 feet, add 30 seconds; above 4000 feet, add 1 minute; above 6000 feet, add 2½ minutes to blanching time.

TYPES OF APPLES

TYPE	APPEARANCE	FLAVOR AND TEXTURE	BEST USES
BRAEBURN	Gold-green with red stripes	Sweet but with good acidity, crisp and juicy	Eating, salads, cooking
CORTLAND	Round, red and gold skinned	Milder than a McIntosh; coarse-textured and moderately juicy	A good choice for recipes where a soft texture is desirable
EMPIRE	Bright red	Aromatic, slightly spicy; juicy	Eating, salads, cooking
FUJI	Yellow-green blushed with reddish orange; reddish orange may predominate	Sweet with a hint of tartness; crisp and juicy	Eating, salads
GALA	Red-striped over yellow or red skin	Sweet and crisp	Eating, salads
GOLDEN DELICIOUS	Evenly golden skin, sometimes with an underlying greenish tone	Sweet and mild; juicy	Eating, salads
GRANNY SMITH	Bright green, similar in shape to Delicious	Firm-textured, tart	Equally fine for eating and baking; retains shape and often some crispness when cooked
GREENING	Fat and round; green, somewhat coarse skin	Hard, mealy texture; tart flavor	Cooking brings out sweetness, with enough tartness for contrast
IDARED	Almost red	Tart, tangy; firm-crisp and juicy	Eating, cooking
JONAGOLD	Red over gold	Sweet-tart; firm and juicy	Eating, salads
JONATHAN	Red over gold	Spicy, sweet-tart; crisp and juicy	Eating, salads, cooking
MCINTOSH	Shiny red skin with some green patches	Juicy, crisp flesh	Becomes very tender when cooked and has enough tartness to retain bright flavor
NEWTON PIPPIN	Green with yellow highlights	Tangy and sweet; firm flesh	Cooking
RED DELICIOUS	Dark red; shape tapers to "points" at the bottom	Crisp, sweet flesh	Eating, salads
ROME BEAUTY	Fat, deep red	Firm texture, mild flavor	Eating, salads, cooking
SPENCER	Green and red skin	Cross between Delicious and McIntosh; shape and texture of Delicious, flavor of both varieties	Eating, salads, cooking
WINESAP	Deep red with yellow	Spicy-tart; firm, crisp flesh	Cooking

TYPES OF BERRIES

BERRY/PEAK AVAILABILITY	CHOOSING	HANDLING
STRAWBERRIES: April to June	Choose fragrant berries that are an even, deep red with no white tips. Avoid berries that look mushy or moldy and cartons that are stained, which indicate mushy berries.	Prepare as close to serving time as possible. Rinse and remove hulls just before using.
BLUEBERRIES: June to August	Blueberries should look firm and plump, with an even coating of whitish "bloom" to the skin.	Pick over berries before rinsing to remove any mushy ones and to pinch off any stems.
RASPBERRIES: July to August	These are the most delicate berries, so check packages carefully. Raspberries should look firm and dry with no signs of mush or mold.	Use them the same day if possible. Rinse just before using.
BLACKBERRIES: July to August	Choose plump, firm-looking berries that are glossy black with no whitish or purplish-red patches.	The soft, edible white core remains in the berries, but pick off any bits of leaves or stems before rinsing. Rinse just before using.

TYPES OF PEARS

TYPE	DESCRIPTION
Anjou	Robed in shiny green skin that becomes slightly golden as it ripens, the Anjou pear has a less-pronounced neck than the Bosc or Bartlett. The flesh is mild, sweet and firmer than that of Bartlett and keeps its shape better when cooked.
Asian pear-apples	Fat, golden-brown globes with incredibly crisp-juicy flesh. Sweet flavor is reminiscent of a cross between a pear and an apple.
Bartlett	One of the most popular pears, the Bartlett is large, plump and very juicy and sweet when golden-ripe. Ripen green fruit at room temperature until the skin is yellow and yields to gentle pressure. Good for cooking or eating fresh.
Bosc	The brownish skin becomes only slightly more golden as the fruit ripens, and the texture remains fairly crisp even when fully ripe. If a Bosc pear is as soft as a ripe Bartlett, it will probably be mushy or mealy inside. Bosc pears retain their sweetness and shape when cooked.
Comice	Fat, almost round, with somewhat speckled greenish-gold skin, Comice pears have a smooth, buttery texture and rich, sweet flavor.
Seckel	Miniature pears that are best served raw. They look pretty in a cornucopia or mixed into a bowl of other diminutive fruits such as kumquats, lady apples and mini-bananas.

FRUIT AVAILABILITY

Today, fruits that were once considered seasonal are now available throughout the year. However, you will find the best flavor, texture and price for fruits during their peak season.

FRUIT/PEAK AVAILABILITY	USES	STORING AND HANDLING
APPLES: September to May	Snacks, salads, pies, cakes, tarts, breads, desserts	Refrigerate. Toss with citrus to prevent discoloration of cut surfaces.
APRICOTS: May to September	Snacks, salads, compotes, cakes, pies	Ripen at room temperature, then refrigerate. Bring out the flavor of bland fruit by baking or stewing.
AVOCADOS: April to June	Salads, appetizers, dips	Let ripen at room temperature until the skin becomes soft to the touch. Rub cut surfaces at once with lemon juice or another citrus to avoid discoloration.
BANANAS: Year-round	Snacks, salads, quick breads, cakes	Do not refrigerate. Bananas that are very ripe can be mashed for baked goods or peeled and frozen. The frozen bananas are good for snacking.
BLUEBERRIES: June to July	Snacks, salads, pies, quick breads, coffee cakes, desserts	Refrigerate. Pick over berries before use and discard mushy ones; pinch off any remaining stems. Toss with a little flour before mixing with cake or muffin batter to prevent all from sinking.
CANTALOUPE: June to December	Snacks, salads, uncooked desserts	Ripen at room temperature. Rinse before cutting. Do not cook. If melon is bland, spritz with fresh lime.
CHERRIES: June to July	Snacks, salads, pies, sauces	Refrigerate. Choose red or golden cherries that are darkly colored and firm. For pie and chutney, choose sour cherries.
CRANBERRIES: September to February	Relish, sauces, quick breads, cakes, desserts	Refrigerate. Tart flavor adds bright contrast to many sweet recipes. Combines well with orange and nuts. Freeze extras for later use. Pick over berries and remove mushy ones; pinch off any stems.
GRAPEFRUIT: November to May	Snacks, salads, fruit cups, sorbets	Refrigerate. Can be sectioned or cut in half to serve.
GRAPES: August to October	Snacks, salads, uncooked desserts	Refrigerate. Pick off any moldy or shriveled grapes. Serve them fresh and uncooked.
HONEYDEW MELON: August to October	Snacks, salads, fruit cups	Refrigerate. Serve raw. Choose honeydew with a velvety surface and a sweet smell. Rinse and halve melon and scoop out seeds. Cut flesh into slices or chunks, or scoop out with a melon baller.
KIWI FRUIT: Year-round	Snacks, salads, fruit garnish for cream pie, cheesecake or New Zealand pavlova	Refrigerate unless the fruit feels very hard. Best uncooked. The fuzzy brown skin is edible, but most people pare it away and cut the green fruit into slices or chunks. Or, simply cut the fruit in half across the "equator" and scoop out the flesh with a spoon. Kiwi fruit

FRUIT/PEAK AVAILABILITY	USES	STORING AND HANDLING
KIWI FRUIT (*cont.*)	(meringue and whipped cream dessert)	cannot be used in gelatin salads or desserts because the papain enzyme prevents gelling.
LEMONS: Year-round	Garnishes, condiments, dressings, desserts, cakes, pies	Refrigerate. Both the juice and the peel, or "zest" are used for flavoring. Remove the thin colored part only, not the bitter white pith underneath, with a zester tool, a sharp paring knife or a vegetable peeler. Use a lemon juicer to remove juice.
LIMES: Year-round	Garnishes, condiments, dressings, pies	Refrigerate. Both the juice and the peel or "zest" are used for flavoring. Remove the thin colored part only, not the bitter white pith underneath, with a zester tool, a sharp paring knife or a vegetable peeler. Use a lemon juicer to remove juice.
MANGOES: May to September	Snacks, fresh-fruit desserts	Let green, hard mangoes ripen at room temperature until the skin changes color and the flesh yields to gentle pressure. Serve ripe fruit chilled. To prepare, cut parallel to the large, flat stone that dominates the center of the fruit. Score the flesh in a diamond pattern, then push the skin inside out. The cubes will stand up like porcupine quills and the edible fruit can be sliced off.
NECTARINES: July to August	Snacks, salads, pies, quick breads, cakes, desserts	Ripen at room temperature, then refrigerate. Freestone varieties are best for cooking. Toss cut fruit with citrus to prevent the flesh from turning brown.
ORANGES: Year-round	Snacks, salads, quick breads, cakes, muffins	Refrigerate. Both the juice and the zest are used for flavoring. To remove the membrane, use a small, sharp knife to pare away the skin and expose the flesh. Make V-shaped cuts between the segment membranes to release juicy, membrane-less segments of fruit. Work over a bowl to catch the juice.
PAPAYAS: Year-round	Snacks, salads, fruit cups, desserts	Be patient and let the papaya ripen at room temperature until it is quite tender to the touch, or it will be mouth-puckering. Scoop out the mass of dark seeds in the center. (They are edible, but bitter.) Cut slices of the fruit or spoon away from the skin. Serve raw; spritz with lime juice if desired. Papaya cannot be used in gelatin salads or desserts because the papain enzyme prevents gelling.
PEACHES: July to September	Snacks, salads, cakes, pies, quick breads, desserts	Let ripen at room temperature until tender, then refrigerate, especially if the weather is very hot. Choose freestone varieties for easiest preparation. Toss the cut fruit with citrus juice to prevent discoloration.
PEARS: Nearly year-round	Salads, snacks, pies, desserts Snacks, fresh	Let ripen at room temperature until they yield to gentle pressure, then refrigerate. (Bosc pears are still crisp when ripe.) Toss cut pears with citrus juice to prevent discoloration.

FRUIT/PEAK AVAILABILITY	USES	STORING AND HANDLING
PINEAPPLES: March to July	fruit salads, upside-down cakes, sweet-and-sour main courses	Refrigerate. A sweet aroma is the most reliable clue to sweet flavor. To prepare, cut off the spiky green top. Cut the fruit in half top to bottom. Cut each half into lengthwise wedges; trim away the tough core from the top of each wedge. Run a knife between the flesh and the skin removing the black "eyes," then cut the flesh into pieces. Pineapple cannot be used in gelatin salads or desserts because the papain enzyme prevents gelling.
PLUMS: July to August	Snacks, salads, fruit cups, ice cream	Let ripen at room temperature until the flesh yields to gentle pressure, then refrigerate. Red, green, yellow, black and purple varieties have varied flavor and texture. Most varieties are best for eating fresh.
POMEGRANATES: January	Snacks; sprinkle the fresh seeds into fruit salads or atop rice or poultry dishes	Refrigerate. Cut the fruit in half to reveal a multitude of jewel-like, edible seeds. Pick or pull the seeds from the surrounding white membrane.
RASPBERRIES: July to early August; some varieties have a brief second crop in October.	Fruit cups, pies, garnish for cream pies or cheesecakes, dessert sauces	Refrigerate, preferably in a single layer to avoid bruising. Handle gently and use as soon as possible. Strain sauces to remove the tiny seeds.
RHUBARB: April to May	Compotes, dessert sauces, pies (especially strawberry)	Refrigerate. Discard the dark green leaves, which are poisonous. Trim and scrub stalks. Must be cooked.
STAR FRUIT (*carambola*)**:** September to January	Salads, desserts, garnishes, pies	Refrigerate. Star fruit does not require peeling. Delicious eaten fresh.
STRAWBERRIES: April to June	Fruit cups, salads, short-cakes, pies, cake garnishes, quick breads	Refrigerate. To prevent berries from getting water-logged, rinse berries just before removing the green hulls. Strawberries are most often served raw but sometimes are used in baked desserts or quick breads.
TANGERINES AND CLEMENTINES: December to February	Snacks, salads, fruit cups	Refrigerate. Clementines are generally smaller and sweeter than tangerines. They are best served raw and the skin can be easily peeled for sectioning.
WATERMELON: June to August	Snacks, fresh fruit salads	Refrigerate and serve chilled. There are seedless varieties available but most have seeds that need to be removed before eating.

TYPES OF CHEESE

TYPE	CHARACTER	USES
ASIAGO	Pale yellow and hard, with a buttery, nutty flavor. Similar to Parmesan.	Grate over pasta; serve with fruit.
BLUE	White streaked with bluish veins. Assertive, tangy flavor. Firm and crumbly.	Crumble into salads or onto grilled hamburgers.
BRIE	Rich, creamy and soft pale yellow in a thick white edible skin.	Serve as a spread, at room temperature or warm from the oven.
CHEDDAR	Rich, creamy flavor. Golden, orange or creamy white with smooth, firm texture.	Melts well. Grate for casseroles or slice for sandwiches.
COLBY	Similar to Cheddar but with milder flavor.	Serve on crackers; grate for casseroles.
EDAM	Pale yellow interior; shaped like a flattened ball and coated with inedible red wax. Mild buttery, nutty flavor with smooth, firm texture.	Serve with crackers and fruit.
FETA	Made of sheep's or goat's milk, cured in brine. Tart and salty with crumbly texture.	Crumble into Greek salad; melt over baked dishes.
FONTINA	Semisoft to hard, slightly yellow with mild to medium sharpness.	Grate into baked dishes.
GOUDA	Similar to Edam but with more fat. Red wax covering indicates mild flavor; yellow or clear wax, aged or flavored; black wax, smoked.	Pair with fruit and crackers.
GRUYÈRE	Similar to Swiss. Buttery, nutty, firm texture with small holes. Slices, cubes and shreds well.	Excellent for fondue, omelets and casseroles.
HAVARTI	Creamy, slightly acidic, pale yellow. Smooth, porous texture that slices and cubes well.	Slice for a cheese platter.
MONTEREY JACK	Semisoft and creamy with buttery flavor. Creamy white color. Sometimes flavored.	Melts nicely: Grate for tacos; slice for quesadillas.
MOZZA-RELLA	Moist, almost rubbery texture and mild flavor. Creamy white color.	Grate for pizza or lasagna.
MUENSTER	Semisoft and smooth with orange or white exterior and creamy white interior. Mild flavor. Slices, cubes, shreds and melts nicely.	Slice for a sandwich, grate for omelets and casseroles.
PARMESAN	Very hard grating cheese with pale yellow color and sharp, nutty flavor.	Grate finely to sprinkle over salad, pasta and soup.
PROCESSED AMERICAN	Smooth, elastic in texture. Mild flavor and melts well.	Classic for grilled cheese sandwiches and cheeseburgers.
PROVOLONE	Ivory to pale beige with mild smoky flavor. Has firm texture and melts well.	Good for pizza, gratins and stuffings.
ROMANO	Creamy white, hard, granular cheese with sharp, piquant flavor. Grates and melts well.	Grate onto pasta or soups.
SWISS	Ivory colored with small holes. Firm with mellow, buttery, nutty flavor.	Slice for sandwiches; grate for quiche.

COOKBOOK GLOSSARY

à la king A rich sauce containing mushrooms, pimiento and sherry, usually combined with cooked chicken.

across grain Cooked meat is most tender when cut across the grain rather than with the grain.

active dry yeast Dried yeast granules.

Alfredo A rich, creamy pasta sauce made with cream, butter and grated Parmesan cheese.

almond bark See CANDY COATING.

alternately add A portion of two ingredients such as flour and a liquid are mixed into a batter alternately.

amandine Dishes made or garnished with almonds.

amaretto An Italian liqueur flavored with almonds.

anchovy A small, strong-flavored saltwater fish, usually marketed canned in oil.

anchovy paste Pulverized anchovy fillets, packaged in tubes.

angel food cake A moist, airy cake leavened with stiffly beaten egg whites instead of baking powder, usually baked in a tube pan and white inside.

anglaise See CRÈME ANGLAISE.

antipasto An assortment of savory hot or cold appetizers commonly served as the first course at an Italian meal.

apple pie spice A blend of ground cinnamon, cloves, nutmeg or mace and allspice.

au gratin Cooking food under the broiler or in a hot oven to form a crisp, golden crust. The food often is topped with bread crumbs and/or cheese.

au jus "With juice," referring to the unthickened natural juices served with roasted meat.

baguette A long, thin loaf of chewy, crusty bread, typically only a few inches in diameter.

baking dish A coverless glass dish, for use in the oven. It can be square, round or rectangular and comes in various sizes. Because glass is a good conductor of heat, foods such as breads and cakes should be baked at an oven temperature 25 degrees lower than stated in the recipe.

baking pan A coverless metal pan, of various sizes, for use in the oven. (Note: The terms "baking dish" and "baking pan" apply to recipes in this cookbook. Other recipes may not differentiate between glass and metal utensils.)

baking powder A leavening agent that makes food rise when it bakes, made up of a combination of baking soda, an acid and starch. The acid reacts with the baking soda to produce gas bubbles in the mixture.

baking soda A leavening agent which, combined with moisture and an acid ingredient, releases carbon dioxide and makes the product rise and become light. The soda starts to react as soon as it comes in contact with the liquid, so the product should be baked as soon as it is mixed.

barbecue/barbecued (v.) To cook food over hot coals or other charcoal-like heat, also called grilling.

baste/basting To moisten food by brushing or spooning on a liquid during cooking.

bearnaise sauce A rich, tangy sauce similar to hollandaise sauce, except it includes vinegar instead of lemon juice. It also includes butter and egg yolks, and is flavored with tarragon.

betty A baked fruit dessert topped with soft bread cubes.

biscotti Twice-baked dry cookies, often used for dunking in coffee and sweet dessert wine.

blackened A Cajun method for cooking fish fillets over high heat in a heavy skillet until the fish is charred or blackened.

blend Combining two or more ingredients so they are smooth and uniform in texture, color and flavor.

boil To cook food in liquid in which the bubbles consistently rise to the surface and break.

bone-in Cuts of meat or poultry containing the bone.

boned Meat, fish or poultry from which bones have been removed.

bordelaise sauce A classic French wine-based sauce usually served with broiled or grilled meats.

borscht Beet soup, traditional in Eastern Europe. It can be made with a meat base or contain only vegetables.

bouillabaisse A hearty soup or stew made from a variety of fish and shellfish.

bouillon A seasoned clear broth usually made from beef or chicken. It also is available as commercially prepared cubes, granules or a liquid.

braid (v.) To shape yeast dough by weaving three or more long, narrow strips of dough over and under each other to form a braid.

braise/braised To cook food over low heat in a small amount of liquid in a covered pan. Food may or may not first be browned in a small amount of fat.

bratwurst A spicy link sausage, available either precooked or fresh.

brioche A rich, slightly sweet yeast roll, either bun-shaped with a topknot or as a large loaf, baked in a special pan.

brioche pan A large fluted pan, especially designed for brioche.

broil To cook by direct dry heat in the broiler section of an oven.

broiler pan A pan with a rack positioned below the broiler on which food is cooked.

broth Liquid in which meat, poultry or vegetables have been cooked.

brown/browned To cook food in a hot skillet or an oven or broiler to develop a rich color and flavor and to help seal in natural juices.

bruschetta Grilled slices of bread brushed with olive oil and garlic and served warm.

brush (v.) To use a pastry brush to spread food lightly with a liquid such as oil, milk or beaten egg.

Bundt® pan A specially shaped fluted tube pan.

burrito A sandwich or snack consisting of a large flour tortilla wrapped around a filling of meat, refried beans and/or cheese.

buttered (pan) Butter is spread lightly over a dish or pan to prevent sticking.

butterflied A boneless piece of meat or seafood cut almost in half to form a butterfly shape.

buttermilk A smooth, tangy dairy product made commercially by adding special bacterial cultures to milk, usually skim.

by hand Using a spoon or other utensil to combine ingredients, rather than an electric mixer.

cacciatore "Hunter's style," describing chicken or meat cooked in a sauce that includes tomatoes, onions, mushrooms, wine and herbs.

Cajun seasoning A commercial product that varies from brand to brand. May contain garlic, onions, chiles, black pepper, mustard and celery.

cake pan An 8 or 9-inch round metal pan.

calcium An essential mineral required for healthy bones and teeth, muscle contractions, blood clotting, and normal nerve functioning. Found primarily in milk and milk products such as cheese, yogurt, ice cream and puddings, and in lesser amounts in dark leafy vegetables.

calories A unit for measuring the amount of energy a food will supply the body and the amount of energy the body uses. Carbohydrates, protein, fat and alcohol provide calories but in different amounts per gram weight. Fat supplies 9 calories per gram, alcohol 7 calories per gram, carbohydrate and protein 4 calories per gram.

Canadian bacon Cured and smoked boneless pork loin, which resembles ham more than bacon.

canapé cutter A small cutter used to cut bread as the base for appetizers.

candied fruit Fruit or citrus peel cooked in a sugar syrup, used in desserts and sweet breads.

candy coating Term used for several kinds of products used for candy dipping and candy making. Sometimes called almond bark or confectioner's coating. It comes in vanilla and chocolate flavors. It is made with vegetable fat, not cocoa butter, so differs from white chocolate.

candy-coated chocolate pieces Generic term for M&M's®.

capers The flower bud of the Mediterranean caper bush. Usually available pickled in vinegar or salted and sold in bulk.

cappuccino An Italian version of *café au lait*, made with espresso and frothy hot milk or cream.

caramelize To heat sugar in a skillet over low heat until it melts and browns.

carbohydrate The nutrient that is the leading source of energy for the body. Carbohydrates are classified into two basic groups: simple sugars and complex carbohydrates (starches and fiber), which are chains of simple sugars linked together. All carbohydrates except dietary fiber break down to simple sugars during digestion. Carbohydrates are found primarily in plant-based foods such as bread, cereals, beans, rice, vegetables and fruit.

carob chip A substitute for chocolate chips. Carob is made from the ground, dried seed of the carob tree.

carve To cut or slice cooked meat, poultry, game or fish into serving sizes.

casserole (dish) A round or oval dish, often covered, used for cooking in the oven, made of glass, ceramic or metal. It can also double as a serving dish.

casserole (entrée) Food cooked in a casserole.

cassoulet A rich baked casserole from France consisting of white beans and an assortment of meats.

Catawba grape juice Nonalcoholic sparkling juice of the Catawba grape.

cayenne Ground red pepper; has a hot, pungent flavor.

charcoal grill Cooking equipment consisting of a rack over a heat source. Can be heated by charcoal, gas or electricity.

charlotte russe A dessert made with layers of ladyfingers or sponge cake and a filling.

cheesecloth Loosely woven cotton cloth that has many uses in cooking.

chess pie A one-crust pie with a rich lemon-flavored custard filling containing cornmeal. Nuts and raisins also may be added.

chestnuts Fruit of the chestnut tree. They have a sweet starchy flavor and a moist crumbly texture. Fresh unshelled chestnuts are available during winter months. They can be roasted for eating and to make them easier to shell. Chestnuts also are available dried throughout the year.

chiffon cake Similar to angel food but includes vegetable oil and egg yolks, so is richer; is leavened with baking powder as well as beaten egg whites.

chile The pod of various pepper plants.

  Anaheim: One of the mildest hot peppers; light green with a slender, elongated shape.

  ancho: A dried poblano, mild to medium-hot flavor.

chipotle: A smoked, dried jalapeño; also sold reconstituted in tomato sauce; very hot.

green: A mild chile available whole or chopped in cans.

pepperoncini: Small thin chile that varies from medium to medium-hot. Best known when pickled and used as part of antipasto.

poblano: Long, irregularly shaped dark green; mild to medium-hot.

serrano: Tiny deep green; may ripen to red. Very hot.

chili paste A fiery-hot condiment, used in Oriental cooking.

chili powder A ground mixture of chile peppers, oregano, cumin, garlic and salt. May also include other herbs and spices.

chimichanga A Tex-Mex version of a burrito fried in hot fat (see BURRITO).

Chinese five-spice powder A blend of ground spices used in Asian cooking. Usually contains cinnamon, star anise, fennel, pepper and cloves.

Chinese noodles Three common Chinese noodles are thin, nearly transparent cellophane noodles, the very fine Chinese egg noodles and rice noodles or rice sticks.

Chinese plum sauce A thick piquant sauce used as a table condiment and as an ingredient in sauces for appetizers.

chives A culinary herb belonging to the onion family. The long slender green leaves have a mild onion or garlic flavor.

chocolate Pure chocolate is made from roasted ground cacao beans and contains about 50% cocoa butter.

bittersweet: Must contain at least 35% pure chocolate along with cocoa butter and sugar. It is similar to semisweet chocolate but may be less sweet and have a deeper chocolate flavor.

milk: Used for eating, cooking and baking, it contains extra cocoa butter plus sugar and milk.

premelted unsweetened: Semiliquid, made of cocoa powder and vegetable oil.

semisweet: Used for eating, cooking and baking, it contains at least 35% pure chocolate, extra cocoa butter and sugar.

sweet baking: Generic term for German's Brand Sweet Chocolate Bar.

unsweetened cocoa: Pure chocolate with no sugar or flavoring added, it is used for cooking and baking.

white: Made of sugar, cocoa butter, milk solids, lecithin and flavorings. It does not contain the chocolate liquor that gives other chocolate its color.

chocolate-flavored syrup: Ready-to-use syrup, usually made with unsweetened cocoa, sugar or corn syrup and flavorings.

cholesterol A waxy, fatlike substance present in foods of animal origin and present in body cells. The liver manufactures an adequate supply of cholesterol from saturated fat in food. Overconsumption of saturated fats can lead to increased levels of cholesterol in the bloodstream.

chop (v.) To cut food into small pieces with a knife, blender or food processor.

chorizo sausage A spicy fresh sausage, in links or bulk.

chowder A thick soup, usually milk-based, made from seafood, fish, corn, potatoes or chicken.

chutney A fruit or vegetable relish. Flavor can vary from sweet and mild to very hot. Commercial chutney is often made from mangoes; homemade chutneys are made from a variety of ingredients.

cider The juice pressed from apples.

cioppino A rich fish stew from San Francisco. Similar to the French bouillabaisse, it includes fish, shellfish, tomatoes, onion and wine.

clarify Making cloudy food clear by separating solids from the liquid. Foods commonly clarified include butter, broth for clear soup and fat used for deep fat frying.

coat (v.) To cover a food with a thin layer of crumbs, flour or a batter to add flavor and texture and to help keep the food moist.

cobbler A baked dessert with a fruit filling and biscuit topping.

cocktail bread Specialty bread that has a small diameter and is usually thinly sliced, used as a base for appetizers.

colander A perforated, bowl-shaped utensil used for draining liquids from solids.

conserve (n.) A sweet jamlike spread composed of at least two fruits. Raisins and nuts also may be included.

consommé A flavorful clarified stock from the liquid of simmering meat or poultry and their bones.

cookie press Consists of a hollow tube fitted at one end with a plunger and at the other with templates to make various cookie shapes. The tube is filled with dough and the plunger forces it through the template.

cookie sheet A flat, rigid pan with one or more turned-up sides. Light-colored heavy metal with a dull finish is preferred. Other cookbooks may call this a baking sheet.

coq au vin A classic French dish in which chicken is cooked in red wine along with onions, mushrooms, bacon and herbs.

coquille (n.) A shell-shaped dish in which seafood and other creamed mixtures are baked. Can also mean "scallop."

cordon bleu Boneless meat, especially veal or poultry, pounded and layered with ham and cheese. This is formed into a roll, coated with crumbs and cooked.

cored With core removed; e.g., apples.

corn syrup The liquid form of sugar refined from corn, available as light or dark syrup.

corned beef Beef, usually a brisket, cured in a salt brine with spices.

Cornish game hen A specially bred small chicken.

cornmeal Finely ground dried corn.

cornstarch A white, powdery thickening agent made from corn.

couscous A tiny pasta made from semolina flour.

cream of tartar A white powder from the natural fruit acid in grape juice after it ferments.

crème anglaise A custard made from eggs and milk, used as a dessert sauce and a base for other desserts.

crème caramel A dessert made from a custard baked in a caramel-coated dish. When the custard is inverted, the caramel forms a layer on top. Also called a flan.

crème fraîche A naturally thickened dairy product made from heavy cream and a bacterial culture.

cremini mushroom See MUSHROOMS.

Creole seasoning See CAJUN SEASONING.

crepe A thin, delicate pancake served with sweet or savory fillings.

crepe pan A 6-inch skillet with sloping sides.

crisp (*n.*) A baked fruit dessert with a crumbly topping.

crostata A thin fruit-filled tart or pie.

crostini Toasted bread slices brushed with olive oil and spread with savory toppings.

crumble (*n.*) A dessert, usually fruit, with a crumbly flour and sugar topping.

crumble (*v.*) To break food into irregularly sized pieces.

crumbs Fine particles made from crushing food like crackers and bread.

crushed red pepper flakes Crushed dried cayenne chiles.

cube/cubed To cut food into uniform pieces, so all sides of the piece are equal.

cup For food preparation, a cup for measuring dry ingredients can be filled to the top and leveled off with a knife. One for wet ingredients should have a spout and be made of a see-through material like glass. The l-cup marking is a little below the top. A cup equals 8 oz.

curdled Describes a dairy product that has developed semisolid pieces of coagulated protein. This occurs when it is heated at too high a temperature or combined with acid foods.

custard cup Small glass or ceramic mold for baking custard.

cut in To work a solid fat into dry ingredients with fingers, a pastry blender, fork or two knives.

cutlets Thin boneless slices of meat cut from the sirloin portion of the animal or from poultry breast.

dash $1/16$ teaspoon of a dry or liquid ingredient.

decorating bag A cone-shaped bag with two open ends. The small end is fitted with decorative tips while doughs, fillings, etc., are spooned into the large end. When the bag is squeezed, these are forced through the tips.

deep fryer A deep pot with a strainer, often electric, heavy enough to hold oil at an even temperature.

deli Delicatessen; a store or a section of a food store where prepared and ready-to-eat foods are sold.

devein Removing the black vein from shrimp.

deviled Food highly seasoned with spicy and hot ingredients such as mustard, hot pepper sauce and Worcestershire sauce.

diagonally slice To cut at a 45° angle.

dietary fiber The parts of plant food that cannot be digested or are only partially digested by the body.

Dijon mustard Prepared mustard made with brown or black mustard seeds, white wine and seasonings. It has a very smooth texture and sharp flavor.

dip (*v.*) To immerse food for a short time into a liquid or dry mixture to coat, cool or moisten the food.

dissolve To stir a solid and a liquid food together to form a mixture in which none of the solid remains.

divan A term applied to a main dish made with broccoli and cream sauce. Originally it applied to a dish made with chicken breasts.

divide To separate uncooked or prepared food into two or more parts.

divinity A soft-textured candy made by beating hot cooked sugar syrup into beaten egg whites.

dot To place small amounts of an ingredient over another food (e.g., to dot with butter).

double boiler A two-piece saucepan consisting of an upper pan where the food is heated or cooked over a pan filled with simmering water.

dough A mixture of flour and liquids to which other ingredients such as sweeteners, eggs, fat and flavorings are added.

doughnut cutter A round cutter with a small center cutter for shaping doughnuts.

drain To allow liquid or fat to run off from solid food before adding other ingredients or serving.

dressed To prepare food for cooking by removing internal organs, feathers, scales, etc., from poultry, fish and game.

dried currants Tiny seedless raisins from sun-dried black Corinth grapes.

drippings The fat and browned bits that collect in the pan when meat or poultry has been roasted.

drizzle To slowly pour a fine stream or a thin mixture over food (e.g., to drizzle icing over a coffeecake).

dry measuring cups Containers that come in graduated sizes used to measure ingredients. Usually available in sets that include 1-cup, ½-cup, ⅓-cup, ¼-cup and can include 2-cup, ¾-cup, and/or ⅛-cup (or 2-tablespoon) measurements.

dry mustard A powder made from mustard seed, used as a seasoning.

duckling A young duck, 8 weeks old or younger.

dumpling Savory dumplings are mounds of dough dropped into a hot mixture like soup or stew and cooked. This term also refers to a dessert made by wrapping a fruit, such as an apple or pear, in pastry and baking it.

Dungeness crab A West Coast crab weighing 1½ to 3½ lb., usually sold as a whole cooked crab.

Dutch oven A deep heavy pot with a tight-fitting lid, holding 4½ to 8 quarts.

eggbeater A kitchen tool for beating eggs by hand.

electric mixer Heavy-duty mixer on a stand, equipped with removable bowls and interchangeable mixing equipment like beaters and dough hooks.

electric skillet Usually square or oblong, the heat is controlled by an adjustable thermostat.

enchilada A corn or flour tortilla rolled around a filling and topped with a spicy tomato sauce or cheese and baked.

evaporated milk Canned milk from which 60 percent of the water has been removed, heat sterilized so it doesn't need refrigeration until opened.

extract (*n.*) Flavorings from highly concentrated oils suspended in alcohol to use in cooking and baking.

fajita Marinated strips of beef cooked and wrapped in a flour tortilla and served with assorted accompaniments.

fast-acting yeast A highly active form of yeast that makes dough rise faster than with regular yeast.

fat The most concentrated source of energy for the body with 9 calories per gram.

fat-free A food that contains under ½ gram of fat.

fat-free egg product Egg substitute containing egg white and other ingredients but no egg yolk or fat. It can be used in many of the same ways as eggs in the shell.

fillet (*n.*) A small boneless piece of meat, fish or poultry.

fines herbes A mixture of chopped fresh tarragon, parsley, chervil and chives.

fingers/with fingers Using the tips of the fingers (e.g., to push dents in the surface of pizza dough to prevent bubbling).

firm (*adj.*) Having a solid or compact structure that resists pressure.

firm-ball stage 244 to 248°F. on the candy thermometer. Drops of candy will form a ball firm enough to hold its shape when removed from cold water but will quickly flatten.

flake/flaked (*v.*) To gently break food into small flat pieces.

flan See CRÈME CARAMEL.

flour

 all-purpose: Made from a combination of hard and soft wheat to give a product that works well for home baking. It is available bleached and unbleached.

 bread: Made from hard wheat, which gives it a high gluten strength, which makes it well suited for making yeast breads.

 cake: A soft wheat blend with low protein and gluten content, making it especially suitable for making fine-textured cakes.

 oat: Rolled oats ground until powdery. Available in specialty stores or made at home in a blender or food processor.

 rye: Finely ground rye. Light rye flour is sifted; dark rye contains more bran.

 self-rising: All-purpose flour with salt and leavening added.

 whole wheat: A coarse-textured flour ground from the entire wheat kernel. Sometimes called graham flour.

fluffy Light and airy.

flute (*v.*) A method of making a decorative pattern on food. The term is most often used to describe sealing the pastry edges of a pie.

focaccia An Italian yeast flat bread baked plain or topped with ingredients like herbs, onions and cheese.

foil Aluminum foil.

fold in To combine delicate ingredients such as whipped cream or egg whites with other ingredients by using a gentle circular motion to cut down into the mixture, sliding across the bottom of the bowl and bringing some of the mixture up and over the surface.

fold over To double or to lay one part over another.

fondant A rich, creamy candy often used as the center for dipping chocolates or made into flavored patties.

fondue pot/forks A ceramic or metal pot with its own heat source used for cooking meat, cheese or dessert fondues and the long-handled forks used to hold and remove food.

food color Paste or liquid gel-based edible dyes used to tint food.

fork-tender When a fork can easily pierce the food.

frittata An Italian open-faced omelet.

frost *(v.)* To spread frosting or other kind of topping evenly over the surface of a food.

frothy Mixtures that are foamy, having a formation of tiny, light bubbles.

fry To cook food over hot heat in a small amount of fat.

funnel *(n.)* A hollow bowl-shaped container with a tube extending from the narrow end. Narrow-mouthed and wide-mouthed funnels are available.

ganache Icing made by combining hot whipping cream and chopped chocolate. The mixture thickens as it chills.

garnish *(v.)* To decorate a finished dish with edible foods such as fresh herbs, thinly sliced fresh vegetables or toasted chopped nuts.

gas grill A grill with the fire source from lava rock or ceramic briquets heated by gas.

gazpacho A spicy soup made from finely chopped fresh tomatoes, cucumbers, green bell peppers and onions, usually served cold.

gelatin A commercial product containing powdered natural animal protein that will set or thicken a liquid. It is available unflavored or flavored with sugar and flavorings added.

giblets The heart, liver and gizzard of poultry.

glaze/glazed A sweet thin, glossy coating on a food such as cake, cookies or bread; also a sweet or fruit mixture spread on ham or a sweet mixture used to glaze vegetables.

gnocchi An Italian dumpling made from potatoes, semolina flour or puff pastry.

goblet A stemmed drinking vessel.

granola A cereal made from various grains, one of which is usually oats, plus a sweetener, oil, dried fruit and nuts.

gratinée To create a golden crust by covering the surface of a food with bread crumbs or grated cheese and browning it in the oven or under the broiler. (See AU GRATIN.)

grease *(v.)* To coat a utensil with a thin layer of fat.

grease and flour To sprinkle the greased pan or dish with a small amount of flour, then to tap or rotate the pan until the surface is coated with flour. The pan then is inverted and the excess flour shaken out.

gremolata A mixture of chopped parsley, garlic and lemon peel used to add a piquant flavor to food.

griddle A heavy round or rectangular flat pan used to cook foods with a minimum amount of fat; usually rimless.

grill *(v.)* To cook food by direct or indirect heat on a barbecue grill or a griddle with little or no fat.

grits Ground hominy (dried corn with the hull and germ removed), often cooked and served as a breakfast cereal.

guacamole A dip made of mashed avocados seasoned with onion and lemon juice. Tomatoes, chiles and cilantro are sometimes added.

gumbo A Cajun stew or thick soup made with meat or seafood and served over rice. It usually contains okra and filé powder.

half-and-half A mixture of half milk and half cream. It can be used when light cream is specified.

hand mixer A hand-held electric mixer.

hard-ball stage 250 to 260°F. on the candy thermometer. When drops of candy are shaped in cold water, the ball will hold its shape but will flatten when pressed.

hazelnuts Also called filberts. A sweet, mild-flavored nut, usually roasted before using to develop flavor and help remove the skin.

heat *(v.)* To bring the oven or a utensil to a specific temperature.

heavy saucepan A saucepan made from a heavyweight material with a thick bottom, to prevent food from scorching or burning.

herbs See "Herbs" chart, page 478.

high altitude At altitudes of more than 3,500 feet above sea level, some methods of food preparation must be adjusted because of lower atmospheric pressure.

hoagie bun An oblong roll or small loaf of French bread used for a sandwich.

hoisin sauce A rich, dark, sweet barbecue sauce used in Asian cooking for marinades and basting.

hollandaise sauce A classic rich, lemony sauce made from butter, egg yolks and lemon juice, served warm with eggs, vegetables, poultry and fish.

hot pepper sauce A commercial hot sauce made from hot peppers, vinegar or sherry. Generic term for Tabasco.

hummus Cooked garbanzo beans mashed and seasoned with oil, lemon juice, garlic and parsley, usually served as an appetizer.

husk The green covering on fresh corn on the cob. Corn is husked when the covering is removed.

ignite To set afire.

instant coffee granules or crystals A form of ground coffee that dissolves instantly in hot water.

instant espresso coffee powder Powdered form of a strong, dark-roasted coffee.

instant nonfat dry milk powder A powdered form of skim milk with the water removed.

invert To turn upside down.

iron An essential mineral found in food and a component of hemoglobin, the part of the red blood cells that carries oxygen from the lungs to the body tissues and carbon dioxide from the tissues to the lungs.

Italian plum tomatoes Thick, meaty tomatoes with few seeds, little juice and a rich flavor.

jam A sweet spread made from crushed or mashed fruit cooked with sugar, usually opaque and firm enough to hold its shape.

jelly A sweet spread made from strained fruit juice cooked with sugar. It usually is translucent and firmer than jam.

jelly roll (*n.*) A dessert made from a thin layer of sponge cake spread with filling and rolled up into a log shape.

jelly-roll fashion A technique of rolling something as you would a jelly roll, so it has the same coiled shape.

jelly-roll pan A 15 × 10 × 1-inch baking pan.

jerk Meat or chicken prepared with a spicy dry seasoning blend (called jerk seasoning). The method originated in the Caribbean.

jicama A large tuberous root vegetable with a thin, light brown skin and crisp white interior.

juice (*v.*) To extract the natural juice from fruits and vegetables.

julienne-cut Food cut in thin matchstick-like pieces, a term usually applied to vegetables.

kabob Meat, fish, poultry, seafood and/or vegetables threaded onto a skewer and broiled or grilled over a fire.

Kahlúa A coffee-flavored liqueur.

kaiser roll A large, crusty roll, often used for sandwiches.

kalamata olive A dark purple-black olive from Greece with a slender oval shape, soft texture and rich flavor.

Key lime A small, rather tart lime with a yellow-green skin, considered to be an essential ingredient in Key Lime Pie.

kielbasa sausage A spicy, uncooked smoked sausage, also called Polish sausage.

knead Method of working yeast dough with the heels of the hands in a pressing and folding motion until it becomes smooth and elastic.

knife/knives Some of the more useful knives are a paring knife, a medium-sized utility knife, a chef's knife, a bread knife and a boning knife.

kuchen German for "cake." In America, a breakfast pastry or dessert, usually made from yeast dough and filled with fruit or cheese.

ladle (*n.*) A deep-bowled, long-handled spoon used for dipping up and transferring liquids or food. (*v.*) To dip and transfer food or liquids with a ladle.

lattice The top crust of a pie made from loosely woven strips of pastry instead of a solid piece of pastry.

layer (*v.*) To form or arrange in layers.

lemon-pepper seasoning A commercial seasoning made from black pepper, dried grated lemon peel and salt.

lentil A small disk-shaped seed, commonly brownish green but also red or yellow. A member of the legume family, it is a good source of vegetable protein.

light texture Ingredients beaten until air has been incorporated and the mixture is fluffy and has an appropriate volume.

line (with foil) Arranging foil on the surface of a pan, usually to prevent sticking.

liqueur A sweetened alcoholic beverage made from fruits or plants. Liqueurs come in a variety of flavors.

Liquid Smoke A commercial product made by diffusing smoke in liquid, used to add a hickory-smoked flavor to foods.

liquid measuring cup Glass cup that holds 1 cup and is marked off in smaller measurements, used to measure liquids.

lite A term used in labeling food to indicate a product low in sodium, fat and/or calories.

loaf pan 8 × 4 or 9 × 5-inch metal or glass pans.

long-handled tongs A 12 to 16-inch metal tool with handles for lifting and turning food while cooking and grilling.

low-fat A food with 3 grams of fat or less per serving size.

macadamia nut The sweet, buttery nut from the macadamia tree. Because of its hard shell, it is nearly always sold shelled.

maple syrup Sap from the maple tree, boiled down to a thick sweet syrup.

maple-flavored syrup A blend of pure maple syrup and corn syrup.

maraschino cherry Yellow cherries preserved and dyed with red or green food color.

Marengo A chicken stew made with wine, tomatoes and garlic.

marinade A liquid in which food is allowed to stand to flavor or tenderize it.

marinara sauce A highly seasoned Italian tomato sauce used for pasta and some meats.

marmalade A sweet spread composed of fruit, fruit peel and sugar cooked to a jam-like consistency.

mash To beat or press a food with a fork, potato masher, etc., until the lumps are gone and the mixture is smooth.

mayonnaise A commercial or homemade uncooked dressing made using egg and salad oil and seasonings.

mealy Food that has a crumbly texture and looks like coarsely ground meal.

meat mallet A tool used to pound meat to break up the connective tissue and tenderize it.

Melba Nellie Melba was a famous late-nineteenth-century opera star who had many dishes named for her. The most famous was Peach Melba, ice cream with peaches and a raspberry sauce. "Melba" used in other dessert names usually refers to the sauce.

Melba toast rounds A commercial product; small, thin rounds of crisp toasted bread, used as a base for appetizers and spreads.

melon baller A small tool used to shape melon into round balls.

melt (v.) To heat a solid food such as butter until it becomes liquid or semiliquid.

meringue Egg whites, stiffly beaten and sweetened. Soft meringues are used for topping pies; hard meringues are formed into crisp shells.

mesquite A small hardwood tree growing wild in the U.S. Southwest. Used in barbecuing and smoking foods, the wood or wood chips give a slightly sweet smoky flavor to the food.

microwave (n.) An oven that works by converting electric energy into microwave energy. It cooks food quickly from the outside in, in all directions at once.

microwave (v.) To cook in a microwave oven.

mimosa Finely chopped hard-cooked egg yolk used as a garnish. Also, a drink consisting of champagne and orange juice.

mince/minced To cut into very small pieces using a knife, blender or food processor.

mincemeat A fruit filling for pies and tarts made from apples, raisins and spices. Originally it often contained ground or chopped meat and suet.

minerals Substances found in food that are necessary in relatively small amounts for good health, such as calcium, iron, potassium and phosphorus.

minestrone An Italian soup made with beans, pasta or rice and vegetables.

mix (n.) A commercially prepared combination of ingredients (e.g., cake mix).

mix (v.) To combine two or more foods by stirring or beating.

moisten/moistened To add enough liquid to dry ingredients to dampen them.

mold (n.) A hollow form that holds food until the food sets and can be turned out to serve.

mostaccioli "Little mustaches"; a short tube-shaped pasta.

mousse A light, airy, creamy dessert or main dish. It usually contains whipped egg white and/or whipped cream.

muffin cups A pan with cups for baking muffins. The cups come in various sizes but most commonly hold ½ cup of batter.

muffuletta A hero-style sandwich originating in New Orleans. Meats and cheeses are layered in a round loaf of crusty bread and topped with a flavorful olive salad mixture.

mushrooms Fleshy fungi in various sizes, shapes and colors.

    button: Ordinary white grocery-store mushrooms.

    cremini: Like button mushrooms but are grown outdoors and have light brown caps and richer flavor.

    enoki: Long, thin stems with rounded, snowy-white, thumbtack-sized heads. The wild form has orangy-brown, very shiny caps.

    oyster: The cap color varies from white to gray to brown. The flavor is fairly robust and slightly peppery but becomes milder when cooked.

    porcini: Large wild mushrooms with thick stalks and reddish caps. Also called cèpes.

    portobello: A very large cultivated mushroom. It is a full-grown cremini, with a meaty, robust flavor.

    shiitake: Flat brown cap with chewy texture and distinctive flavor that hints at onion. Readily available fresh and dried; fibrous stems can be discarded or used to flavor soup stock.

mussels A shellfish enclosed in blue-black hinged oblong shell, sold in the shell or shucked.

newburg Usually lobster or shrimp in a rich sauce of cream, egg yolks and sherry.

niçoise "Food cooked in the style of Nice." It may include olives, anchovies, tomatoes, green beans and garlic.

nonaluminum Specified in recipes where aluminum cookware can react chemically with certain foods.

nonfat Food that contains less than ½ gram of fat.

nonstick cooking spray A fat-free spray that can be used to coat baking pans, for frying, grilling and other uses, to prevent sticking.

nutrients Substances in food that are needed by the body for life, to maintain health and for the growth and repair of damaged cells. The six categories of nutrients are carbohydrates, fats, proteins, minerals, vitamins and water. Nutrients provide energy, make up body structures and regulate body processes.

omelet Beaten eggs cooked in a skillet and served either open-faced or folded in half or thirds.

oven-fried Food cooked in a hot oven that has the appearance and flavor of fried food but contains less fat.

overbeat To beat beyond the stage specified in the recipe for best results (e.g., egg whites).

overmix To stir or mix ingredients beyond the stage where they are properly mixed (e.g., brownies).

oyster sauce Dark brown Asian sauce used as an ingredient and a table condiment.

palmier A cookie made of sheets of pastry that are rolled in sugar and folded to resemble palm leaves.

pancake turner A utensil to lift or remove food from a pan or a cookie sheet or for turning food to cook the second side.

panfry To cook food in a skillet using a small amount of fat or oil.

panzanella A salad consisting of toasted bread cubes tossed with vegetables such as tomatoes, peppers, cucumbers and onions and vinaigrette.

paper baking cups Paper liners with fluted sides placed in muffin cups.

papillote "Curled paper." Heavy parchment paper folded to make a packet to enclose food which is cooked and usually served in the packet.

paprikash A Hungarian dish, usually made with chicken and onions that are browned, then braised in chicken broth with paprika and other seasonings.

parchment paper A heavy grease and moisture-resistant paper used to line baking pans and cookie sheets and for a number of other culinary uses.

parfait glass A tall, slender glass dish used to serve chilled or frozen desserts that are often assembled in layers.

parmigiana A dish prepared with Parmesan cheese.

partially baked Not fully baked (e.g., pie shell to be filled and further baked until the filling is cooked.)

pasta See the "Pasta Cooking Reference"

chart, page 315.

pasteurized eggs Whole eggs that have been processed to kill the salmonella bacteria, so can be used in recipes calling for raw eggs.

pasteurized process cheese Natural cheese with other ingredients added for flavor, softer texture and longer shelf life.

pastry blender A small tool made with wire strands that cuts fat into flour; used in making pie crust.

pâté A rich, well-seasoned ground mixture made from meat, liver, fish and/or vegetables, served as an appetizer.

patty shell Puff pastry made into a cup-shaped, crisp shell to hold an individual serving of food.

pectin A natural substance found in some fruit that makes jam or jelly set up. Commercial pectin also is available in powder or liquid forms.

peel (*n.*) The skin or outer covering of a fruit or vegetable.

peel (*v.*) To remove the skin or outer covering of a fruit or vegetable.

penuche A golden-brown fudge with a caramel-like flavor, made with brown sugar.

pepper Commonly used spice from the tiny red berries of a tropical vine. Black pepper comes from ground dried immature berries. White pepper comes from the hulled mature pepper berries.

peppercorns Whole dried pepper berries.

pesto A sauce made from fresh basil, olive oil, garlic and Parmesan cheese. Pine nuts or walnuts also may be added. Served with pasta or used as an ingredient in other dishes.

petits fours Tiny cakes glazed with icing and decorated.

phyllo (filo) A Greek pastry made from a flour and water mixture stretched paper thin and cut into sheets. Frozen phyllo is available commercially.

piccata A recipe with a sauce of dry white wine, lemon juice, butter and seasonings added to pan drippings and simmered to thicken slightly.

pickling salt Finely ground salt without additives, which could cloud pickling liquids.

pie pan Round 8, 9 or 11-inch pan; may be metal or glass. (Other cookbooks may instead refer to pie plate.)

pierce (with fork) To insert the tines of a fork into food.

pilaf A rice dish prepared with broth and seasonings. Vegetables sometimes are added.

pipe To force a semisoft food such as frosting through a pastry tip to form attractive shapes for decorating or garnishing.

pit (*n.*) The single seed inside fruit.

pit (*v.*) To remove the single seed inside fruit.

pita (pocket) bread A round, flat unleavened Middle Eastern bread that typically forms a pocket when cut crosswise.

pizza pan A 12-inch round metal baking pan.

plastic wrap A clear food wrap that has the ability to cling to food and containers. Some is microwave-safe.

poach To cook food by submerging it in simmering water.

polenta Italian-style cornmeal mush, often served with Parmesan cheese or a tomato sauce. Can be molded, sliced and fried.

popover pans A special pan for baking popovers with extra-deep cups, spaced apart so they can "pop over" the top of the cups.

potato masher A kitchen tool with a plastic or wood handle and a heavy wire base for mashing cooked potatoes into a smooth puree.

poultry seasoning A blend of ground dried herbs, usually thyme, sage, marjoram, rosemary and pepper.

pound (*v.*) To strike food with a heavy utensil to crush it or for meat, to tenderize it by breaking up connective tissue.

pound cake A rich, fine-textured cake originally named because the recipe called for a pound of butter, sugar, eggs and flour.

praline A rich, patty-shaped candy made with sugar, cream, butter and pecans.

precook To partially or completely cook a food before using it as an ingredient in a recipe.

preserves A sweet spread made from chopped fruit and sugar. It is similar to jam except the fruit pieces are bigger and more distinct.

protein The nutrient that is composed of amino acids that are essential for building and repairing body cells. Food sources include meat, fish, eggs, legumes, nuts and grains. Quality of protein food is determined by the presence of nine essential amino acids. Plant foods can be combined to make a high-quality protein comparable to meat protein.

Provençal Referring to dishes prepared in the style of Provence, in southeastern France. Tomatoes, garlic, olive oil, olives and eggplant are typical ingredients.

puff pastry A crisp, flaky baked product with numerous layers, used for patty shells, appetizers and desserts. Frozen puff pastry is available commercially.

pumpernickel A heavy, dark rye yeast bread.

punch down To push the fist into the center of risen yeast dough, then to pull the edges to the center.

puree/pureed To change a solid food into a paste or liquid using a blender, food processor or food mill.

quesadilla A tortilla stuffed with cheese, cooked meat, fish or poultry and/or cooked vegetables and baked on a griddle.

queso fresco A white, slightly salty fresh Mexican cheese with a texture like farmer cheese.

quiche A rich baked pie or tart with a pastry crust and a savory custard filling containing cheese, vegetables, meat and/or seafood.

quiche dish A round baking dish, usually ceramic, with fluted edges.

ramen noodles Asian instant-style deep-fried noodles, usually sold in cellophane wrap.

reduce/reduced To partially boil away a liquid such as sauce or stock to thicken the consistency and intensify the flavor.

resealable plastic bag A plastic bag that can be tightly sealed by pressing the top edges together.

Reuben sandwich A sandwich made with corned beef, Swiss cheese and sauerkraut on rye bread, served hot or cold.

riblets Pork ribs cut in half by the butcher to get appetizer-sized ribs.

rice

    Arborio: A medium-grain Italian rice with a higher starch content, often used for risotto because it cooks to a creamy consistency but still has a little "bite."

    basmati: A long-grain rice with a fine texture and a perfumey, nutlike flavor. Basmati rice can be found in Indian and Middle Eastern markets and some supermarkets.

    brown: The entire grain with only the inedible outer husk removed. The barn coating gives it a light tan color, nutlike flavor and chewy texture.

    converted: White rice that has been par-boiled, then dried. When cooked to completion, the kernels are fluffier and more separated than those of regular white rice.

    instant or quick: Rice that has been partially cooked and dehydrated.

    wild: The long, dark brown or black nutty-flavored seed of an annual marsh grass, erroneously called rice because it grows in water.

rise The stage of yeast dough when gas bubbles trapped in the elastic gluten mesh of dough make it increase in size. This sometimes is called proofing.

risotto A creamy Italian rice dish that results when stock is added a little at a time to rice which is stirred continually when cooking, Arborio rice traditionally is used in the preparation.

roasted red bell peppers A commercial product available in jars.

roasting pan A shallow metal or ceramic pan that sometimes includes an inside rack.

rolled oats Oats minus the hull that are steamed and flattened by steel rollers into flakes.

rolling boil The stage where a mixture is boiling so rapidly it can't be stirred down.

rolling pin Usually, a long wooden cylinder with handles for rolling out dough. It also can be tapered or made of marble.

Romanoff Indicates a sour cream and cheese sauce combined with noodles.

room temperature About 70°F.

rounded When used with measuring spoon, not leveled off.

rub (*n.*) A dry mixture or paste of herbs and spices rubbed on food before cooking to marinate.

rumaki A hot appetizer composed of bacon wrapped around a slice of water chestnut and a piece of chicken liver, then broiled.

salad dressing A bottled salad dressing; or a

creamy commercial spread similar to mayonnaise, except made without egg yolks (e.g., Miracle Whip®).

salsa A variety of highly seasoned cooked or uncooked sauces, often made with tomatoes but also can be made with other vegetables or fruit.

salt/coarse salt Common table salt contains additives to keep it from clumping and may be iodized. Kosher salt is coarsely ground and has no additives.

saltimbocca An Italian dish made from thin slices of veal topped with ham and may be rolled up with cheese in the center. It is cooked in a skillet.

sangria A beverage made with red wine, fruit juices, soda water and fruit, served over ice.

saucepan A cooking utensil with one handle, generally holding 1 to 4 quarts.

sautéed (*v.*) Used in recipe titles to describe food cooked quickly in a small amount of oil in a skillet.

scallop (*n.*) A shellfish with a hinged shell similar to the oyster and clam. Sea scallops are the largest; bay scallops are smaller.

scallop (*v.*) To prepare a food by layering it with cream or a cream sauce in a baking dish or casserole.

scalloped (*adj.*) Made with a wavy border (e.g., a cookie cutter with scalloped edges).

scaloppine An Italian dish featuring very thin boneless slices of meat, usually veal, coated with flour, browned and served with a sauce.

scampi The Italian name for the shellfish similar to a large prawn or shrimp.

scant Less than (e.g., a scant teaspoonful).

scone A rich biscuitlike quick bread.

scoop (*v.*) To ladle out.

score (*v.*) To cut narrow slits part way through the outer surface of a food to tenderize it or to form a decorative pattern.

seasoned salt Salt combined with other flavoring ingredients.

section (*n.*) A pulpy section of citrus fruit that has had the membrane removed.

section (*v.*) The process of separating the segments of a citrus fruit from the membrane with a knife.

sesame oil The oil from sesame seeds. One type is light in color and flavor. The dark Asian oil has a much stronger flavor and is used as a seasoning.

shell (*v.*) To remove the shell or outer covering of a food (e.g., eggs, nuts, shrimp).

sherry A fortified wine. The flavor ranges from light and dry to sweet.

shortbread A rich, very tender shaped cookie made from flour, sugar and butter.

shortcake A dessert of layers of rich, flaky biscuit, fruit and whipped cream. The biscuit also is called shortcake.

shortening Commonly, a vegetable oil processed to be solid at room temperature, used for baking and frying.

shred (*v.*) To cut food into narrow strips by hand or with a grater or food processor. Well-done meat can be shredded by pulling it apart with two forks.

simmer To cook food gently in liquid just below boiling so tiny bubbles just begin to break on the surface.

skewer A long, thin pointed rod of various sizes made of bamboo, wood or metal.

skillet A long-handled, usually round, pan with low sloping sides. Sizes range from 7 to 12 inches.

skim (*v.*) To remove unwanted surface fat or residue from food such as soup.

skim milk Milk from which the fat has been removed so that it contains no more than 0.5 percent fat; also called nonfat milk.

slivered Food cut into long, thin pieces.

slotted spoon A long-handled spoon with slits in the bowl.

slow cooker An electric appliance designed to cook food over a long period with low, steady moist heat.

slush A partially frozen, slightly watery mixture.

s'more An informal dessert sandwich made by placing a toasted marshmallow and a thin square of chocolate between two graham crackers and gently squeezing the crackers together.

sodium An element needed to maintain normal body fluid volume. Common sources are table salt, milk, cheese and leavenings. Excessive intake should be avoided.

soft peaks The stage when peaks in whipped cream or egg whites bend over slightly when the beaters are lifted out of the mixture.

soft-ball stage 234 to 240°F. When drops of

candy are put into cold water, the ball will immediately flatten and run between the fingers when removed from the water.

sorbet A frozen dessert similar to sherbet except that it never contains milk and has a softer consistency.

soufflé A light, airy baked main dish or dessert made from a thickened sauce combined with stiffly beaten egg whites and ingredients such as cheese, vegetables or chocolate.

soufflé dish A round, ovenproof dish with straight sides designed to facilitate a soufflé's rising.

sourdough Bread with a tangy, slightly sour flavor leavened with a sourdough starter instead of yeast.

spatula A straight metal utensil used for spreading or for leveling off dry ingredients.

sponge cake A light, airy cake similar to angel food except it includes egg yolks and sometimes, baking powder.

spread (v.) Applying a soft food or mixture to another food (e.g., butter, jelly).

springform pan A round pan with high, straight sides. The bottom of the pan can be removed when a clamp on the side is released. Used for cheesecake and other foods that might be difficult to remove.

starch A digestible carbohydrate of many plants, especially vegetables and grains. Foods that contain starch provide energy, fiber, vitamins and minerals.

steam (v.) To cook food in the vapor given off by boiling water.

steamer basket A utensil that fits inside a pan, holding the food above the boiling water, allowing it to be cooked in the steam.

sterilize To destroy the microorganisms that can cause spoilage and disease in food by applying heat.

stew (n.) A mixture of good-sized pieces of foods such as meat and vegetables, cooked slowly in liquid for a long time.

stiff dough A dough that is firm enough to be rolled out easily (e.g., pie crust).

stiff glossy peaks In meringue, egg whites beaten until the mixture stands straight when the beaters are lifted, but still looks glossy.

stiff peaks Whipping cream or egg whites beaten until the peaks stand straight when the beaters are lifted.

stir-fry (n.) Any dish of food that has been prepared by the stir-fry method.

stir-fry (v.) To cook pieces of food quickly over high heat with constant stirring; the term "cook and stir" is used in recipe directions. Also the name of the dish so prepared.

stockpot A large metal cooking utensil with two side handles, ranging in size from 6 to 16-quart capacity.

strain To filter a food or beverage, usually by using a cloth or fine wire strainer.

strainer A utensil with a perforated or mesh bottom, used to strain liquids or semi-liquids or to sift dry ingredients.

strata A baked casserole made by layering ingredients, usually bread and cheese, with a milk-egg mixture poured over.

streusel A crumbly mixture of flour, sugar, butter and often spices, rolled oats or nuts sprinkled on top of breads and desserts before baking.

stroganoff A meat dish in a thickened sauce made with sour cream and often containing mushrooms and onions.

strudel A dessert made from layers of paper-thin dough, around a fruit or cheese filling.

stuffing A seasoned mixture often based on bread cubes or crumbs, used to stuff poultry, fish, meat or vegetables.

succotash A vegetable side dish combining whole kernel corn and lima beans.

sugar The carbohydrate that is easiest for the body to absorb and digest. Honey, syrup, table sugar and fruit are the chief sources.

sundae A dessert made from scoops of ice cream with a topping, sometimes garnished with whipped cream, nuts or fruit.

sun-dried tomatoes Intensely flavored, chewy tomatoes, sold dry-packed in cellophane or packed in oil.

surimi Processed fish that is flavored and reformed to make restructured seafood products. Imitation crabmeat is the most popular product.

sweetened condensed milk A concentrated milk made from whole milk with sugar added and half the water removed.

tabbouleh A Middle Eastern salad made

with bulgur wheat mixed with chopped fresh vegetables, mint, olive oil and lemon juice.

tablespoon A measuring tablespoon equals 3 teaspoons.

taco A snack or sandwich made with crisp corn tortilla shells or soft flour tortillas filled with seasoned meat or poultry. Refried beans, chopped tomato, shredded lettuce, shredded cheese, etc., are often added.

taffy A chewy candy made by boiling a sugar syrup, then pulling the cooled mixture by hand until it is light and creamy; then cutting the long strands into bite-sized pieces.

tandoori A traditional Indian oven; food such as chicken cooked in this oven is identified as tandoori chicken.

tapioca A starch extracted from the roots of the cassava plant, used to thicken a variety of cooked foods.

tart A single-serving pie or a full-sized pie baked in a special pan with straight sides and a removable bottom.

tea ball A small container with tiny holes that holds the tea leaves and lets the boiling water combine with them.

tequila A nearly colorless liquor made from fermenting and distilling the sweet sap of the agave plant.

teriyaki A Japanese dish consisting usually of beef or chicken marinated in a mixture of soy sauce, sherry, sugar and spices; also referred to as a teriyaki sauce.

tetrazzini A rich baked spaghetti and poultry dish. The creamy sauce is flavored with sherry and includes mushrooms.

thermometer An instrument for measuring cooking temperature. Ones especially useful for cooking are candy/deep fat frying, meat and an instant-read thermometer.

thicken When a food substance such as a sauce or pudding gets a thicker consistency by the addition of an ingredient like flour, cornstarch, egg yolk or tapioca.

thread In making kabobs, piercing the meat and vegetables with the skewer and arranging the pieces for broiling or grilling.

tiramisu A refrigerated Italian dessert composed of spongecake or ladyfingers dipped in a coffee-marsala mixture and layered with creamy mascarpone cheese and grated chocolate.

tofu Soy bean curd made from soybean milk. It is available in soft, firm and extra-firm style.

toothpick A short flat or round wooden stick.

torte A rich dessert made of layers of cake, tender pastry or hard meringue with a filling and/or frosting or whipped cream topping.

tortilla A small, thin, flat round Mexican bread baked, but not browned, in a griddle or skillet. It can be made from corn or wheat flour.

toss To mix ingredients lightly by lifting and dropping them with two utensils such as spoons or forks.

transfer To move food from the cooking utensil to a serving platter.

trifle A layered dessert composed of sponge cake, ladyfingers or macaroons sprinkled with a wine and layers of fruit and pudding or custard. It is topped with whipped cream, garnished and then refrigerated.

trim/trimmed To remove the fat from meat or to cut off the inedible parts of a vegetable.

truffle A rich ball-shaped candy made with melted chocolate, butter, cream and sometimes eggs, often flavored with liquor; also an edible fungus.

tube pan A round pan with deep sides and a hollow center tube used for baking cake, especially angel food or sponge.

turnover (*n.*) Pastry dough circles or squares covered with a sweet or savory filling, then folded in half and baked or deep-fried.

unmold To remove molded food from the container in which it was made.

unwrap To remove wrappers before using (e.g., caramels).

upside-down cake A dessert made by covering the bottom of a cake pan with butter and sugar topped with decoratively arranged fruit, then cake batter. The butter, sugar and fruit juice make a glaze during baking. The cake is inverted before serving, so the glazed fruit becomes the top of the cake.

vegetarian One who does not eat meat or other animal foods.

lacto-ovo vegetarian: One who eats

dairy products (lacto) and eggs (ovo).

lacto vegetarian: One who eats dairy products but no eggs.

vegan vegetarian: One who follows a plant-based diet exclusively and consumes no animal protein, not even milk or eggs.

veggie Vegetable.

vichyssoise A rich, creamy potato and leek soup served cold.

vinaigrette A basic oil and vinegar combination, commonly used as a dressing for salads.

vinegar

balsamic: Dark brown, slightly sweet aged vinegar made from the juice of a sweet white grape.

cider: A rather fruity flavored vinegar made from fermented apple cider.

red wine: A full-bodied vinegar made from red wine.

rice: A mild, slightly sweet vinegar made from fermented rice.

white wine: A pleasantly pungent vinegar made from white wine.

vitamins Complex chemical substances needed in small amounts to keep the body functioning smoothly. Thirteen essential vitamins have been identified and categorized as water soluble or fat soluble.

waffle iron A hinged cooking utensil with two honeycomb-patterned griddles. The waffle batter is poured in the bottom griddle, the top is closed over it and the waffle is cooked until crisp and brown.

wassail A hot, spiced punch, sometimes containing alcohol, usually served at Christmastime.

waxed paper Semitransparent paper with a thin coating of wax on both sides.

wheat germ The embryo of the wheat berry. It has a nutty flavor and is used to add nutrients to a variety of foods.

whip (*v.*) To beat ingredients such as egg whites or whipping cream, thus incorporating air into them and increasing their volume until they are light and fluffy.

whipping cream Contains from 30 to 36 percent milk fat (light whipping cream) or 36 to 40 percent milk fat (heavy whipping cream). Light whipping cream is the most commonly available.

wire rack A network of closely arranged wires set on short legs to raise it above the countertop. The raised surface provides air circulation so baked goods can cool without getting soggy on the bottom.

wire whisk A utensil consisting of a series of looped wires forming a three-dimensional teardrop shape.

wok A large, deep slope-sided pan traditionally used for stir-fry recipes.

wonton A thin square of dough with a small amount of meat, seafood or vegetable filling wrapped inside; then steamed, deep-fried or boiled.

wonton skins Paper-thin sheets of dough made with flour, eggs and salt. They can be purchased prepackaged in supermarkets.

Worcestershire sauce A thin, pungent dark brown sauce used to season meats, gravies and soups.

wrap (*n.*) A sandwich made with a flour tortilla wrapped around a filling.

INDEX

CONVERSION CHART

Equivalent Imperial and Metric Measurements

American cooks use standard containers, the 8-ounce cup and a tablespoon that takes exactly 16 level fillings to fill that cup level. Measuring by cup makes it very difficult to give weight equivalents, as a cup of densely packed butter will weigh considerably more than a cup of flour. The easiest way therefore to deal with cup measurements in recipes is to take the amount by volume rather than by weight. Thus the equation reads:

1 cup = 240 ml = 8 fl. oz.   ½ cup = 120 ml = 4 fl. oz.

It is possible to buy a set of American cup measures in major stores around the world.

In the States, butter is often measured in sticks. One stick is the equivalent of 8 tablespoons. One tablespoon of butter is therefore the equivalent to ½ ounce/15 grams.

Liquid Measures

Fluid Ounces	U.S.	Imperial	Milliliters
	1 teaspoon	1 teaspoon	5
¼	2 teaspoons	1 dessertspoon	10
½	1 tablespoon	1 tablespoon	14
1	2 tablespoons	2 tablespoons	28
2	¼ cup	4 tablespoons	56
4	½ cup		110
5		¼ pint or 1 gill	140
6	¾ cup		170
8	1 cup		225
9			250, ¼ liter
10	1¼ cups	½ pint	280
12	1½ cups		340
15		¾ pint	420
16	2 cups		450
18	2¼ cups		500, ½ liter
20	2½ cups	1 pint	560
24	3 cups		675
25		1¼ pints	700
27	3½ cups		750
30	3¾ cups	1½ pints	840
32	4 cups or 1 quart		900
35		1¾ pints	980
36	4½ cups		1000, 1 liter
40	5 cups	2 pints or 1 quart	1120

Solid Measures

U.S. and Imperial Measures		Metric Measures	
Ounces	Pounds	Grams	Kilos
1		28	
2		56	
3½		100	
4	¼	112	
5		140	
6		168	
8	½	225	
9		250	¼
12	¾	340	
16	1	450	
18		500	½
20	1¼	560	
24	1½	675	
27		750	¾
28	1¾	780	
32	2	900	
36	2¼	1000	1
40	2½	1100	
48	3	1350	
54		1500	1½

Oven Temperature Equivalents

Fahrenheit	Celsius	Gas Mark	Description
225	110	¼	Cool
250	130	½	
275	140	1	Very Slow
300	150	2	
325	170	3	Slow
350	180	4	Moderate
375	190	5	
400	200	6	Moderately Hot
425	220	7	Fairly Hot
450	230	8	Hot
475	240	9	Very Hot
500	250	10	Extremely Hot

Any broiling recipes can be used with the grill of the oven, but beware of high-temperature grills.

Equivalents for Ingredients

all-purpose flour—plain flour
unbleached flour—strong, white flour
cornstarch—cornflour
coarse salt—kitchen salt
half and half—12% fat milk
heavy cream—double cream
light cream—single cream

OTHER TITLES
BY PILLSBURY

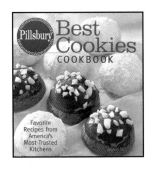

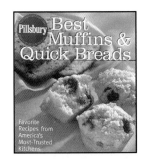

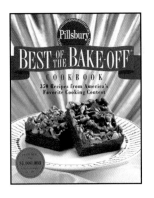

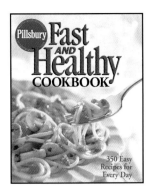

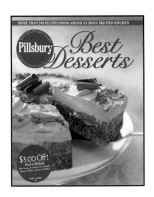

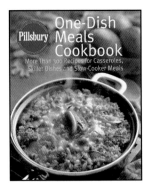